Applied
Management
Science

Modeling, Spreadsheet Analysis, and Communication for Decision Making

SECOND EDITION

JOHN A. LAWRENCE, JR.

California State University—Fullerton

BARRY A. PASTERNACK

California State University—Fullerton

John Wiley & Sons, Inc.

**To our wives Shari and Kathleen
and our children:
Jami and Jonelle Lawrence
and
Jeffrey, Laura, Julia, and Alyssa Pasternack**

Acquisitions Editor	Beth Lang Golub
Editorial Assistant	Jennifer Battista
Assistant Editor	Cynthia Snyder
Marketing Manager	Gitti Lindner
Senior Production Editor	Christine Cervoni
Designer	Kevin Murphy/Nancy Field
Photo Editor	Sara Wight
Illustration Editor	Anna Melhorn
Cover Art	*Quartet* (*Night in Tunisia*) Private Collection/Gil Mayers/SuperStock
Production Management Services	UG / GGS Information Services, Inc.

This book was set in 10/12 Novarese by UG / GGS Information Services, Inc. and printed and bound by Von-Hoffman Press. The cover was printed by Von Hoffman Press.

Recognizing the importance of preserving what has been written, it is a policy of John Wiley & Sons, Inc. to have books of enduring value published in the United States printed on acid-free paper, and we exert our best efforts to that end.

Library of Congress Cataloging in Publication Data:

Lawrence, John A.
    Applied management science : modeling, spreadsheet analysis, and communication for
    decision making / John A. Lawrence, Barry Alan Pasternack.—2nd ed.
        p. cm.
    Includes index.
    ISBN 0-471-39190-5 (cloth : alk. paper)
    1. Management—Mathematical models. 2. Decision support systems. 3. Communication in
management. 4. Management science. I. Pasternack, Barry Alan. II. Title.

HD30.25.L39 2001
658.4′033—dc21

               2001045640

Printed in the United States of America
10 9 8 7 6 5 4 3 2 1

About the Authors

John A. Lawrence, Jr.

John Lawrence is a professor and a past department chairman of the Department of Information Systems and Decision Sciences at California State University, Fullerton, where he has received several awards for his teaching, professional, and service contributions. He has spent over 30 years developing and teaching introductory and advanced upper division and graduate courses in management science and statistics for students majoring in business and economics at the university. He has presented and published several papers on the role and structure of management science courses in business curricula. His current research interest is in the area of distance learning.

Dr. Lawrence received his B.S. in Operations Research from Cornell University and worked at IBM in Endicott, New York, and with NASA at the Kennedy Space Center at Cape Canaveral, Florida. After serving as a communications officer with the U.S. Navy, he received his M.S. and Ph.D. in Industrial Engineering and Operations Research from the University of California, Berkeley, with a research emphasis in linear programming.

Dr. Lawrence has served as a consultant to several companies in the areas of linear programming, inventory, and quality control and has published papers in these areas in professional journals. For over 15 years, he and coauthor Barry Pasternack wrote study guides for the management science texts written by Anderson, Sweeney, and Williams and published by West Publishing Company. He serves as secretary-treasurer of Inform-Ed, the education forum of INFORMS, the Institute for Operations Research and Management Science.

Barry A. Pasternack

Barry Alan Pasternack is a professor and chair of the Information Systems and Decision Sciences Department at California State University, Fullerton. During his 24 years on the faculty, he has been the recipient of numerous awards for teaching, research, and service. For five years he served as the Executive Director of the University's Center for Professional Development. Currently, he is a member of the California State University Statewide Academic Senate and is Chair of the California State University Computer Science and Information Systems Discipline Council. He is a past President of the campus chapter of the California Faculty Association, as well as a former member of the Association's Statewide Board of Directors. He has also served as a University Educational Policy Fellow and a Bautzer Faculty Fellow.

Dr. Pasternack received his B.A. in mathematics from Antioch College, having spent his junior year studying statistics and operations research at the University of Birmingham in England. He earned his M.S. and Ph.D. degrees in Operations Research from the University of California, Berkeley, with a research emphasis in stochastic processes. Upon graduation from Berkeley, Dr. Pasternack worked for three years in the Network Planning Department of Bell Laboratories.

In addition to his teaching experience at Fullerton, Dr. Pasternack has also been a faculty member at Stevens Institute of Technology, Boston University, and California Polytechnic University, Pomona, and an invited guest lecturer at universities in the Czech Republic and Germany. He has served as a consultant to numerous corporations and governments, including the nations of Thailand, Zambia, and Ghana. He has also done work for NASA in the area of avionics and for the Department of Health and Human Services in the area of mental health care utilization.

Dr. Pasternack's research interests include inventory systems, channel coordination, gambling theory, and optimal option strategies. He is the author of some two dozen publications, and his work has appeared in such journals as *Naval Research Logistics, Marketing Science, Interfaces, SIAM Journal on Applied Mathematics, and Journal of the Operational Research Society*. Dr. Pasternack helped develop the Educational Testing Service assessment examination in business and is one of the contributors to the latest edition.

Student to Student

You may be wondering why, as a business major, you are taking this management science course. When I started taking the course at Cal State Fullerton, I was wondering the same thing. After a while, though, my professor, John Lawrence, one of the authors of this text, showed me the importance of management science in my education. In today's information-based, fast-paced society, this course will play a key role in your future, whatever path you may choose. The ideas presented in this course provide reliable solutions to everyday problems that occur in business, whether you work in Marketing, Accounting, Finance, Management, or Economics. At times you may find the information overwhelming and challenging, but it is actually quite applicable. This text was written to help you gain an understanding of how to apply the ideas presented in the many areas of business.

For as many hours as you have spent in the classroom, at some point, you probably have wondered how you would apply what you have learned to your life. As a full-time employee for a swimsuit manufacturer, that was the first question that came to my mind. I wondered, "How can I apply these general ideas to specific day-to-day problems in my career?" As a purchasing manager, using techniques discussed in this text, I have been able to solve quality problems concerning our fabrics. I have used forecasting to aid in my future fabric and trim purchases. And I have benefited from inventory modeling because it guides me in the total quantities I need to order and a time frame in which to reorder. In the near future I will be getting more involved in the production process, where I already see the immediate application of linear programming to assist in determining our product mix.

Management science is applicable to all segments of business. The following are a few more examples:

- Decision analysis is used to evaluate various production scenarios given the likelihood of sales, production shutdowns, and the like.
- Forecasting is useful in making long-term and short-term business decisions. Controllers could use forecasting to make predictions on the future of their companies.
- Quality control is extremely important to a company because its reputation, costs and market shares, and legal responsibilities are at risk. In manufacturing, it is important that a company design and produce a product that conforms to the specification that satisfies the need of the end-user.
- In making any business decision, linear programming, PERT/CPM, inventory modeling, queuing, and simulation assist the individual in making the best decisions with a limited amount of resources available.

The best approach is to keep an open mind while using this text and listening to your instructor. You may not believe it now, but many of the concepts presented here will most likely cross your path in the future as you use them to help you make decisions in your chosen careers.

Dana Linderman
California State University Fullerton
College of Business and Economics

Preface

Management scientists are faced with dynamic, challenging situations that require forethought, analysis, and solutions on a daily basis. How does American Airlines management know how to schedule its flight crews for maximum efficiency? How were the individual tasks necessary to rebuild the Santa Monica Freeway after the 1994 Los Angeles earthquake coordinated to complete the project? How does Citibank management know how many tellers should be working at a particular time during the day? Management science is an intriguing field that combines quantitative procedures, hypothesis formulation, and reasoning to analyze such complex problems with the goal of improving operations. It can be viewed as a process of:

- Developing mathematical models of complex situations
- Using or deriving solution techniques for analyzing these models
- Using spreadsheets or other specialized computer programs to perform the necessary mathematical operations to solve the models
- Analyzing the results of the computer output in order to recommend appropriate courses of action
- Communicating these recommendations to management

New in This Edition

Consistent with our goals of the first edition, in *Applied Management Science, 2nd ed.*, we continue to stress model building, analysis of computer output, and communication of results of management science models. Reflecting current trends, in this edition, we focus on the use of spreadsheets, in particular Microsoft Excel, as our vehicle for solving and generating computer output for the mathematical models developed in each chapter. Although we give considerable coverage to creating attractive and effective spreadsheets to solve the various mathematical models, we have also developed and included Excel templates for solving most models so that we do not deflect attention from the model building, analysis, and communication emphasis.

Besides the exclusive use of Excel, several pedagogical changes have been made in this edition. We have condensed the total number of chapters from 16 in the first edition (including three on CD) to 13 (including three on the CD), without deleting topic coverage. In particular in this edition:

- The first two chapters from the first edition have been combined to form Chapter 1, giving a basic text introduction and overview of the management science process in one continuous, cohesive presentation.
- The three chapters on linear and integer programming models have now been combined into two (Chapters 2 and 3) with new coverage of models for data envelopment analysis and supply chain management.
- Treeplan, a commercial Excel Add-In program for solving decision models, is discussed in the decision analysis chapter (Chapter 6). A student version of Treeplan is included on the CD-ROM.
- An appendix discussing whether to include seasonal variables in forecasting models when some variables cannot be shown to be statistically significant has been added to the forecasting chapter (Chapter 7).

- The two chapters on inventory modeling in the first edition have been reorganized. Material relating to MRP has been shifted to the CD-ROM.
- The analysis of single-period inventory models is now included with the discussion of other inventory models in Chapter 8.
- The discussion of assembly-line balancing and statistical analysis of simulation output has been shifted from the queuing and simulation chapters, respectively, to the CD-ROM.
- Crystal Ball and Extend, two commercial Excel Add-In simulation packages, are discussed in the simulation chapter (Chapter 10). Student versions of Crystal Ball and Extend are also included on the CD-ROM.

Many of the opening vignettes have been updated, and several new modeling situations have been added to the text. In addition, numerous problems have been added. Each chapter in the main text now has 50 varied problems (ten of which are on the CD), while each of the supplementary chapters on the CD-ROM has over 30 problems. Approximately three or four larger, more complex case problems that can be used as the basis for generating business reports are also included in each chapter.

Goals

Our primary objective in writing this text is to provide a balanced approach reflective of our teaching pedagogy and professional and consulting experiences. In meeting this overarching objective, we have identified three goals that exemplify the message of our book. We feel that it is important for students of management science:

- *To be aware of the pitfalls encountered in building mathematical models and to be able to build the most appropriate model possible from the available data*
- *To be cognizant of the solution techniques available to solve the models*
- *To be able to analyze and effectively present results to the appropriate decision maker*

These issues are the primary focus of our text.

Features

The goals we set out to meet are intended to take mathematical modeling a couple of steps further by emphasizing the decision-making process and the communication of results. In the model-building process, great care is taken to emphasize the model's assumptions and limitations. Each chapter is then organized around a clearly defined set of pedagogical features designed to guide the student through the management science process.

RELEVANCE

Every chapter opens with a brief *vignette* describing a scenario reflective of those which managers face every day. Throughout the chapter a number of similar scenarios are introduced in highlighted *applications*. Many of these are revisited throughout the chapter as new concepts are introduced.

STUDENT PEDAGOGY

With the textual narrative, important terminology is introduced that is critical to understanding the concepts applied to solving the problem at hand. These **key concepts** are boldfaced throughout the text and defined in a highlighted box so that the student can easily find the explanation when first learning the concept and when reviewing for exams. *Key equations* and *calculations* are treated similarly, boxed and highlighted for easy recognition. The steps involved in calculating many of the equations are accentuated, helping the student grasp and recall the procedures. The last section of each chapter is a *summary* of the concepts and main points of the chapter material. The summary is written in an approachable, narrative style, providing a review of the key concepts of the chapter.

ANALYSIS OF THE MODELS

Each model introduced in the chapter is solved using Excel and analyzed from a manager's perspective. We demonstrate for each technique how the appropriate Excel spreadsheet can be constructed, and we also provide easy-to-use templates that facilitate the model analysis. The actual algorithms and other solution approaches for solving each model are included on the accompanying CD-ROM (packaged with this text), not because we feel they are any less important, but because including them within the text disrupts the flow of the discussion of the model formulations and analyses.

COMMUNICATION OF RESULTS

The management scientist's job does not end when a solution is found. In fact, the most important responsibility of the management scientist is to communicate the results of the analysis to the organization's management. Therefore, we have devoted an entire section of Chapter 1 to instructing the student in how to communicate the results of a management science study to an organization's management. The student is asked to take the perspective of a member of a consulting group called the Student Consulting Group. All subsequent chapters include additional business *memorandums* developed by the Student Consulting Group to various organizations. These memorandums analyze the situation at hand, evaluate various decision alternatives, and recommend an appropriate course of action. While the use of memoranda is our medium of communication in this text, the principles developed here extend naturally to other communication models such as PowerPoint presentations or web development.

PROBLEM SOLVING

Consistent with our philosophy of problem solving as an integral component of the management science process, the text is replete with numerous *problems and cases*, many based on actual real-world situations (with modified data for illustrative purposes). We have included a wide variety of problems selected from the functional areas of business as well as from the government and public sectors. The cases at the end of each chapter represent more elaborate models that frequently require the use of more than one management science technique. Each can be used as a project requiring a comprehensive written report. Solutions to approximately 40% of the problems are included in the back of the text.

UNIQUE CONTENT FEATURES

The 10 chapters of the parent text include the topics typically covered in an introductory management science course. In addition to these 10 chapters, auxiliary topics that are frequently omitted in the introductory course due to the degree of complexity or lack of time are included on the CD-ROM. Also on the CD-ROM are additional topics that supplement the ten text chapters of the book are included on the CD-ROM.

The following is a list of other topics covered on the CD-ROM:

- In our experience, many management science studies involve issues of quality. Therefore, we have devoted an entire chapter, Chapter 11, "Quality Management Models," to this topic, which bridges the gap between management science, operations management, and statistics.

- Chapter 12 provides a comprehensive overview of "Markov Process Models."

- Nonlinear models are grouped together in Chapter 13, "Nonlinear Models: Dynamic, Goal, and Nonlinear Programming."

- Five supplementary units on the CD-ROM provide coverage of more complicated mathematical concepts and derivations: Duality, The Simplex Method, Branch and Bound Algorithms for Integer Programming Models, Algorithms for Network Models, and Production Inventory Models.

- An additional supplementary unit, Review of Probability and Statistics Concepts, provides a brief review of material covered in a first course in statistics (up through regression). While many topics in the text can be taught without the use of statistics, many cannot, and a course in probability and statistics is assumed to be a prerequisite. This brief statistical review can be used as the basis for a first lecture or review assignment in the course so that all students are "up to speed" with statistics. In some cases, more advanced statistical topics are necessary to solve some problems; these are discussed in the appropriate chapter rather than in the review supplement.

- Beginning with Chapter 3, additional chapter appendices are included on the CD-ROM to provide more extensive mathematical and theoretical coverage of the algorithms, mathematical derivations, heuristics, and calculations used in the models.

- Excel templates as well as Excel files for the problems and applications presented in Chapters 2–13 are included on the CD-ROM.

- The CD-ROM also includes student versions of three software packages, TreePlan, an Excel add-in for solving decision tree problems, Crystal Ball, an Excel supplement for analyzing simulations, and Extend, a software program for conducting simulations.

- The CD-ROM contains Power Point slides paralleling the topics in the 13 chapters. Many slides include motion that allow the reader to view dynamically the concepts discussed in the text.

- To conserve space, ten additional problems per chapter (problems 41–50), additional cases, problem motivations for topics covered in the chapter, and additional topic coverage are included on the CD-ROM.

Computer Integration

As has been mentioned, we use Excel to solve models developed in the text. Although this is not a text on programming mathematical models into spreadsheets we not only include sample spreadsheets that show how a student can program Excel to utilize the technique being studied, but also provide easy-to-use templates that students can use to solve problems without the need to program Excel. Examples of both approaches are included in the text, and the corresponding Excel files are contained on the accompanying CD-ROM. Appendices are included at the end of each chapter, giving detailed explanations on the use of the Excel templates described in the chapter. (We have elected to focus on Excel because there are literally millions of copies of Excel in use worldwide and many problems can be solved fairly easily using a spreadsheet approach.)

Supplements

In addition to the CD-ROM packaged with the text, *Applied Management Science: A Computer-Integrated Approach for Decision Making* is supplemented by a comprehensive ancillary package, which includes the following:

- *Instructor's Manual with Complete Solutions*   This manual contains suggestions for first-time instructors and extensive outlines and objectives for each chapter of the text and CD-ROM. In addition, complete solutions for all end-of-chapter problems and cases are provided in this valuable teaching tool.
- *Test Bank*   This comprehensive test package includes approximately 1000 multiple-choice, computer-based, short answer, true-false, and critical thinking questions. An IBM computerized version of the entire test bank is also available with editing features to help instructors customize exams.
- *Wiley/Nightly Business Report Video Series*   This video collection contains segments from the highly respected *Nightly Business Report* program. Selected for their applicability to management science topics, each of the segments is approximately 3 to 5 minutes long and can be used to introduce topics to the student, enhance lecture material, and provide dynamic real-world business examples directly related to the concepts introduced in the text.
- *Internet Website*   You can access the Wiley home page at www.wiley.com/college. The Lawrence/Pasternack website supports and extends the text presentation with links to companies, internet exercises, and other material.
- *Quantitative Business Custom Publishing Program*   This custom publishing program allows you to choose a subset of chapters from *Applied Management Science: Modeling, Spreadsheet Analysis, and Communication for Decision Making*, and supplement it with selected chapters from other Wiley texts in Operations Management and Business Statistics to create your own custom textbook. Contact your local Wiley sales representative for more details.
- WinQSB is available separately or in a special package with *Applied Management Science*. A new manual, prepared by Kiran Desai, relates Win QSB to each chapter of the second edition.

Flexible Structuring of a Course Around this Text

Applied Management Science: Modeling, Spreadsheet Analysis, and Communication for Decision Making is part of a comprehensive learning program that can be adapted to virtually any emphasis one wishes to place on the course. We envision using this text in either a one- or two-semester course to meet any or all of the following objectives:

- ***Teach modeling and analysis of output***: Utilize the extensive problem set included in the text.
- ***Include a focus on communication/presentation***: Accentuate the study of Chapter 1 and cover one or more of the numerous cases included in the text.

- *Focus on spreadsheet solutions*: Assign the appendices at the end of each chapter, which give ample instructions for using the Excel templates. Data files for all text examples are available on the CD-ROM.
- *Provide more mathematical/theoretical coverage*: Refer to the supplements on the CD-ROM that discuss and illustrate:
  - the simplex model
  - the dual simplex method
  - the branch and bound approach for mixed integer models
  - the branch and bound approach for binary models
  - the transportation simplex algorithm
  - the out of kilter algorithm
  - the Hungarian method for assignment problems
  - the branch and bound approach for traveling salesman problems
  - the Dijkstra shortest path algorithm
  - the Greedy minimal spanning tree algorithm
  - the Ford-Fulkerson maximum flow algorithm
  - the golden search technique for unimodel optimization
  - tests for concavity and convexity
  - the method of steepest ascent
  - the modified simplex approach for quadratic programming
  - Daniel's test for trend
  - tests for autocorrelation
  - forecasting by taking first differences
  - the interpolation method for generating random variable inputs in simulation
  - variance reduction techniques
  - tests for normality of data
  - the Silver-Meal heuristic
  - the Wagner-Whitten algorithm
  - development of formulas for inventory models
  - transition diagrams, balance equations for finding steady-state queuing results
- *Expand beyond the "basic" topics in management science*: Cover additional and/or more advanced topics that are included on the CD-ROM, such as duality, quality management, Markov processes, dynamic programming, goal programming, and nonlinear programming.

Given the organization and variety of materials included in the parent text, the CD-ROM, and the ancillary package, we hope this text can more than fulfill your needs.

Acknowledgments

No book such as this could have been written without the help of many individuals. Among the many people who have assisted us in this endeavor, we would like to thank Robert Miller, Prem Gupta and Nat Sankahavasi for providing us with assistance in the development of problems and cases. We would also like to thank Zvi Goldstein for preparing the PowerPoint slides and Raymond Hill for performing the accuracy check of the solutions manual.

Development of this text was assisted by the invaluable insights provided by the following colleagues who served as reviewers:

Ted Boone	*Pennsylvania State University*
Barbara Downey	*University of Missouri, Columbia*
Zvi Drezner	*California State University, Fullerton*
David Eldredge	*Murray State University*

Jorge Haddock	*Rensselaer Polytechnic Institute*
Mike Hall	*University of Mississippi*
Raymond R. Hill	*Air Force Institute of Technology*
Faizul Huq	*University of Texas, Arlington*
Lucia M. Kimball	*Bentley College*
John F. Kros	*Hawaii Pacific University*
Choong Y. Lee	*Pittsburg State University*
David L. May	*Oklahoma City University*
Zubair M. Mohamed	*Western Kentucky University*
Kenneth E. Murphy	*Florida International University*
Leonard Presby	*William Paterson University*
Ronald D. Schwartz	*Shenandoah University*
Carlton Scott	*University of California, Irvine*
Chwen Sheu	*Kansas State University*
Natalie Simpson	*University at Buffalo*

We also gratefully acknowledge the wonderful staff at John Wiley & Sons who helped transform our manuscript into a finished text. Of particular importance to making this endeavor a success was our acquisitions editor, Beth Lang Golub; the editorial assistance provided by Jennifer Battista; the excellent production staff made up of Christine Cervoni, Sara Wight, Anna Melhorn, and Kevin Murphy; coordination of the supplements package by Cynthia Snyder; and the marketing staff, led by Gitti Lindner. A thank you also to Sandra Gormley of UG / GGS Information Services for her assistance during the production process.

We also thank our secretarial staff Suzanne Tappe, Grace Glazer, and Chalida Tiyasuksawad.

Finally, we would like to thank our families, without whose love and support this book could not have been written.

John A. Lawrence, Jr.
Barry A. Pasternack

California State University, Fullerton

Contents

Chapter 10   Simulation Models   551

Appendices   603

Glossary   618

Answers to Selected Problems   626

Photo Credits   639

Index   641

CD-ROM Contents

FOLDERS ON THE CD-ROM

ADDITIONAL CHAPTERS FOLDER
SUPPLEMENTS FOLDER
APPENDICES FOLDER
PROBLEM MOTIVATIONS FOLDER
ADDITIONAL PROBLEMS/CASES FOLDER

EXCEL TEMPLATES FOLDER
EXCEL FILES FOLDER
EXCEL AD-INS AND SOFTWARE FOLDER
POWERPOINT SLIDES FOLDER

THE ADDITIONAL CHAPTERS FOLDER

THE SUPPLEMENTS FOLDER

THE APPENDICES FOLDER

THE TEMPLATES FOLDER

CPM-Budget.xls

CPM-Deadline.xls

Decision Payoff Table.xls

forecast.xls

inventory.xls

Markov.xls

network.xls

PERT-COST.xls

PERT-CPM.xls

QC.xls

queue.xls

THE EXCEL SOFTWARE ADD-INS FOLDER

Crystal Ball

Extend

Treeplan

THE EXCEL FILES FOLDER

Chapter 1 Subfolder

Delta Hardware.xls
Greeting Card Sales.xls
Test Grades.xls

Chapter 2 Subfolder

Barnes.xls
Boxcar.xls
Galaxy.xls
Galaxy Alt1.xls
Navy Sea Rations.xls
Rinaldo.xls (Case Problem)

Chapter 3 Subfolder

Calgdesk.xls (Case Problem)
Euromerica Liquors Revised.xls
Euromerica Liquors.xls
Galaxy Expansion.xls
Globe Plant Analysis.xls
Globe.xls
Jones Investment.xls
Powers.xls
Saint Joseph (Revised).xls
Saint Joseph.xls
Salem.xls
Sir Loin Composite.xls
Sir Loin.xls
Sunset.xls
United Oil.xls
Vertex Software.xls

Chapter 4 Subfolder

Ballston Electronics.xls
Ballston-net.xls
Carlton.xls
Carlton-net.xls
Depot Max-net.xls
Fairway-net.xls
FEMA.xls
Fema-assignment-net.xls
Metropolitan.xls
Montpelier-net.xls
United-net.xls

Chapter 5 Subfolder

Baja Budget.xls
Baja Deadline.xls
Klonepalm(Revised)-180.xls
Klonepalm(Revised)-200.xls
Klonepalm-180.xls
Klonepalm-200.xls
Klonepalm EXCEL.xls
Klonepalm Gantt.xls
Klonepalm Probabilties.xls
Klonepalm.xls
Larkin PERT-COST.xls

Chapter 6 Subfolder

BGD.xls
IGA.xls
Tom Brown Expected Value.xls
Tom Brown Insufficient Reason.xls
Tom Brown Maximax.xls
Tom Brown Maximin.xls
Tom Brown Minimax Regret Revised.xls
Tom Brown Minimax Regret.xls
Tom Brown.xls

Chapter 7 Subfolder

American Family Forecast (revised).xls
American Family Forecast.xls
American Family Holt's.xls
American Family Regression.xls
CFA Decomposition.xls
Cfa forecast.xls
Four period weighted moving average.xls
Solver exponential smoothing.xls
Troy's Forecast.xls
YoHo exponential smoothing.xls
YoHo Forecast.xls
YoHo four period moving average technique.xls
YoHo four period weighted moving average technique.xls
YoHo last period technique.xls
YoHo Yo-Yo.xls

FOLDER: Chapter 7 Problem Data Files

Amazing.com.xls
Armco.xls
Bee's Candy company.xls

Chapter 12 Subfolder

Dr Bandon—Stovall.xls
Dr Bandon—Tovar.xls
Dr. Bandon—Stovall markov.xls
Dr. Dale Bandon.xls
Fast-Food Revised.xls
Fast-Food steady state probabilities.xls
Fast-Food.xls
Rolley's Rentals.xls

Chapter 13 Subfolder

New England Cycle.xls
Toshi.xls
PBI Industries.xls

Supplement CD1 Subfolder

Mission Viejo.xls

THE POWERPOINT SLIDES FOLDER

Ch-1 Introduction
Ch-2 LP and ILP models
Ch-3-1 LP applications
Ch-3-2 ILP applications
Ch-4 Networks
Ch-5 Project Scheduling
Ch-6 Decision.ppt
Ch-7 Forecasting.ppt

Ch-8 Inventory.ppt
Ch-9 Queuing.ppt
Ch-10 Simulation.ppt
Ch-11 Quality.ppt
Ch-12-1 Markov.ppt
Ch-12-2 Markov.ppt
Ch-13 NLP.ppt

PROBLEM MOTIVATIONS FOLDER

CHAPTERS 2–10

ADDITIONAL PROBLEM/CASES FOLDER

CHAPTERS 1–10

Introduction to Management Science Models

Chapter 1

UNITED AIRLINES (http://www.ual.com) OP-
ERATES a fleet of hundreds of different types of
aircraft and employs thousands of people as pilots,
flight attendants, ticket agents, ground crews, and service personnel in its operations throughout the United
Sates, Canada, Central and South America, Europe,
Asia, and Australia. The complexity of its operations requires United to be highly mechanized and to utilize the
latest mathematical tools, information, and computer
technology so that it can:

- Develop master flight schedules
- Forecast demand for its routes
- Determine an aircraft lease/purchase plan
- Assign planes and crews to the routes
- Set fares
- Purchase fuel
- Schedule airport ticket agents and service personnel
- Schedule maintenance crews
- Maintain service facilities
- Lease airport gates
- Design and monitor its frequent flyer program

Factors impacting these decisions include:

- Budget, equipment, and personnel restrictions
- Union agreements for personnel scheduling
- Federal Aviation Administration guidelines
- Safe distance/turnaround time requirements
- The flexibility to react in real time to complications
  due to weather, congestion, and other causes

These are but a few of the complicated and interrelated
problems and constraints affecting United's bottom-line
profitability. Proper planning and operations require
more sophisticated analyses than merely making educated guesses. Accordingly, United Airlines makes liberal
use of management science models to increase profits
and customer satisfaction in a constrained environment.

1.1 What Is Management Science?

Management science is the discipline that adapts the scientific approach for problem solving to executive decision making in order to accomplish the goal of "doing the best you can with what you've got." It involves:

- Analyzing and building mathematical models of complex business situations
- Solving and refining the mathematical models typically using spreadsheets and/or other software programs to gain insight into the business situation
- Communicating/implementing the resulting insights and recommendations based on these models

BUSINESS AND MANAGEMENT SCIENCE

Every enterprise has an objective it wishes to accomplish. Companies that operate for profit want to provide products or services to customers in order to make money for their owners or stockholders. A nonprofit organization such as a hospital may want to provide services to patients at minimum cost. The stated objective of government entities is to serve their citizens well.

No matter what the enterprise, certain responsibilities and restrictions affect the organization's ability to meet its objectives. For example, a manufacturing company's suppliers demand payment in a reasonable time period; their employees demand a fair wage and good working conditions; their distributors expect good products at reasonable prices so they can make a profit; and their customers expect both quality and prompt efficient service. There are also various government agencies (local, state, and federal) that expect the company to obey laws and regulations, pay taxes, function safely, and operate so as not to endanger the community or national security. The scarcity of needed resources, including capital, personnel, equipment, space, and technology, further limits a company's ability to succeed.

Nonprofit organizations, such as charities, municipal hospitals, public television stations, public universities, and the military, also operate in a restrictive environment. While turning a profit is not the goal of such enterprises, they are responsible to their overseers (donors, subscribers, voters, taxpayers) to provide the best possible service.

In general, the goal of both for-profit and not-for-profit organizations is to optimize the use of available resources, given all the internal and external constraints placed on them. Success is usually measured by how well they do so. Thus, an organization is always looking for ways to run more efficiently, more effectively, and, in the case of profit-motivated businesses, more profitably; in other words, organizations want "to do the best they can with what they've got." This is the realm in which management science operates.

THE MANAGEMENT SCIENCE APPROACH

Modern-day management science grew out of successful applications of the scientific approach to solving military operational problems during World War II. Hence, it was originally dubbed "operational research." After the war, as this approach found its way into all areas of the military, government, and industry, the term was shortened to "operations research (OR)." As *managers* in business began using operations research approaches to aid in decision making, the term "management science (MS)" was coined. Today, there is little distinction between the terms, and they are used interchangeably in the literature.

So what exactly is the MS/OR approach? Philip McCord Morse, who established the pioneer operations research group within the Navy during World War II, and George Kimball, who was head of the Washington research section of this group, defined it in the first book ever published in the field in 1951 as; "A scientific method of providing *executive* departments with a quantitative basis for decisions regarding operations under their control.[1]" They note that, from the beginning, the field supported the executive function but was distinct from it.

Gene Woolsey, a leader in MS/OR consulting, defines MS/OR as; "The use of logic and mathematics in such a way as to not interfere with common sense.[2]" In his definition, Woolsey introduces two important concepts: logic and common sense. Both play a key role in any MS/OR analysis. As we discuss in Sections 1.3 and 1.4 much of management science deals with mathematical modeling and developing or applying quantitative solution techniques. Some of the models can be quite complex, and some of the solution techniques can be quite sophisticated. But when management science is actually used, it should, as Woolsey bluntly puts it, "look, feel, and taste like common sense."

Since MS/OR had its roots in military applications during World War II, it might be useful to examine the military's official definition of MS/OR. According to U.S. Army Pamphlet 600-3, MS/OR involves:

> The use of techniques such as statistical inference and decision theory, mathematical programming, probabilistic models, network and computer science [to solve complex operational and strategic issues].

Although this definition is more specific about the approaches used in MS/OR, it again emphasizes the decision-making purpose of the field.

MANAGEMENT SCIENCE APPLICATIONS

Management science analyses, which have been applied to a wide variety of situations, have had a dramatic impact on the effectiveness of many organizations. A small sampling of the many successful applications of the MS/OR approach include the following.

Producing Hamburgers at Burger King   Burger King, a division of Grand Metropolitan Corporation, uses *linear programming* (see Chapters 2 and 3) to determine how different cuts of meat should be blended together to produce hamburger patties for its restaurants. The objective of this analysis is to produce the patties at minimum cost while still meeting certain specifications such as fat content, texture, freshness, and shrinkage. As the cost of different cuts of meat changes, the company reevaluates its model to determine whether its recipe should be modified.

Scheduling Crews at American Airlines   Scheduling aircraft crews is a complex problem involving such factors as the type of aircraft to be flown, the cities of origination and termination for the flight, the intermediary cities visited by the aircraft, and the length of the flight. Federal and union rules govern the placement of personnel on the aircraft. To address these issues, American Airlines has developed an **integer linear programming** (see Chapters 2 and 3) **model** that allows the company to quickly determine an optimal flight schedule for its personnel.

---

[1] John D. C. Little, "Operations Research in Industry: New Opportunities in a Changing World," *Operations Research*, 39, No. 4 (July–August 1991): 531–542.

[2] Rick Hesse and Gene Wooley, *Applied Management Science: A Quick and Dirty Approach* (Science Research Associates, 1980).

Planning the Sony Advanced Traveler Information System   The marriage of the microprocessor with the Global Positioning Satellite System has enabled Sony Corporation to develop an onboard navigation system capable of giving directions to a car's driver. This information is especially valuable during traffic conditions such as rush hour congestion. The software is based on a management science model known as a **shortest path network**. (See Chapter 4.)

Rebuilding the Interstate 10 Freeway   Following the disastrous California earthquake in January 1994, Interstate 10, a main freeway serving the Los Angeles area, needed to be rebuilt quickly. The project's prime contractor was given a fairly short five-month deadline to reopen the roadway. To encourage the work to be done as quickly as possible, the contractor was offered a bonus of $500,000 for each day by which it was able to beat the deadline. Using a project scheduling technique known as the **critical path method** (see Chapter 5), the contractor was able to schedule work crews so as to be able to complete the repair work a month earlier than the project deadline. As a result, the contractor collected a $15 million bonus.

Planning Environmental Policy in Finland   Political decisions about environmental issues are often complex. To assist in the development of a comprehensive framework for future water policy issues in Finland, that country's National Board of Waters and the Environment used a **decision analysis** (see Chapter 6) approach to analyze a wide range of issues. Among the items studied were standards for allowable water level changes in lakes resulting from energy production and measures to fight acid rain.

Cooking at Mrs. Fields   Mrs. Fields operates a nationwide chain of cookie shops specializing in fresh-baked chocolate chip cookies. The chain has equipped each shop with a PC-based information system to aid personnel in deciding when additional cookies should be baked and the amounts that should be produced. This system relies on management science techniques such as demand **forcasting** (see Chapter 7) and *inventory modeling* (see Chapter 8).

Designing Attractions at Disneyland and Disneyworld   Disneyland and Disneyworld are two of the most visited family resort destinations in the world. The attractions at these theme parks draw a large number of people daily. Lines form as visitors await their turn to ride or view the most popular attractions. Today, "imagineers" at these parks incorporate waiting line or *queuing models* (see Chapter 9) into their overall design plans for the park. These models mirror customer behavior and tolerance for waiting in line. As a result of these models, Disney park planners developed an entirely new "industry" of waiting line entertainment to maintain customer satisfaction levels and enhance the value and excitement of the ride or attraction.

Transporting Trash in New York City   The New York City Department of Sanitation handles over 20,000 tons of garbage per day. To dispose of this trash, the department operates three incinerators. Refuse is also sent by barge from marine transfer stations to the Fresh Kills Landfill. To determine future operational plans for this landfill, the Department of Sanitation undertook a management science analysis. The result of this analysis was the development of the BOSS (barge operation systems simulation) model. This *simulation model* (see Chapter 10) enabled the Department of Sanitation to determine the number of additional barges that should be purchased to handle future demands. It also helped plan the dispatching of these barges.

Establishing Quality Management at Ford Motor Company During the 1970s, U.S. automobile manufacturers saw a steady decline in their market share due to competition from Japanese and European manufacturers. In response, the Ford Motor Company embarked on a "Quality Is Job One" campaign. Suppliers were held to tighter standards, and new quality control procedures were developed. As a result of these *quality management* activities (see Chapter 11 on the accompanying CD-ROM) Ford Motor Company was able to reverse its decline in market share and profitability.

As these examples illustrate, management science techniques have been applied in numerous settings. They have been used to increase profitability and improve performance. In some cases, they have meant the difference between an enterprise's success and failure.

1.2   A Brief History of Management Science

Doing the best you can with the resources at your disposal is an age-old problem. It was not until the late nineteenth and early twentieth centuries, however, that the rudiments of the modern-day quantitative approach for decision making took shape. Figure 1.1 shows a time line denoting some of the significant developments in management science during the twentieth century. Disciplines specific to management science are included in parentheses.

Whereas much of the early research done in management science focused on developing the tools necessary to solve complex decision problems, lately the primary focus of the field has been on developing models and systems for such diverse areas as:

- E-commerce
- Health care services
- Supply chain management
- Global warming
- Telecommunications
- Banking
- Flexible manufacturing
- Neural networks
- International economics
- Transportation systems
- Environmental impact
- Robotics

Today, spreadsheets have become a staple in most organizations. Excel, as well as other spreadsheet packages, now include many management science and statistical tools. Their use has become an essential part of many management science-based models. As a result, many individuals who may not have even heard of the term *management science* now routinely use such models in their businesses.

Management science continues to be a mainstay in large organizations. From General Motors to Bell Laboratories, from American Airlines to Federal Express, from Weyerhauser to Whirlpool, management science has proven successful in improving corporate operations. Municipal, state, and federal agencies routinely

Management Science Time Line

-1890s
- Frederick Taylor develops the field of "scientific management" applying the scientific approach to improving operations in a production setting. (*Industrial Engineering*)

-1900s
- Henry Gantt develops a control chart approach for minimizing machine job completion times. (*Project Scheduling*)
- Andrey A. Markov studies how systems change over time. (*Markov Processes*)
- The general assignment approach is developed. (*Networks*)

-1910s
- F.W. Harris develops approaches to determine the optimal inventory quantity to order. (*Inventory Theory*)
- E.K. Erlang develops a formula for determining the average waiting time for telephone callers. (*Queuing Theory*)

-1920s
- William Shewart introduces the concept of control charts.
- H. Dodge and H. Romig develop the technique of acceptance sampling. (*Quality Control*)

-1930s
- Jon von Neuman and Oscar Morgenstern develop strategies for evaluating competitive situations. (*Game Theory*)

-1940s
- World War II provides the impetus for the application of mathematical modeling for solving military problems.
- George Dantzig develops the simplex method for solving problems with a linear objective and linear constraints. (*Linear Programming*)
- The first electronic computer is developed.

-1950s
- H. Kuhn and A.W. Tucker determine required conditions for optimality for problems with a nonlinear structure. (*Nonlinear Programming*)
- Ralph Gomory develops a solution procedure for problems in which some variables are required to be integer valued. (*Integer Programming*)
- PERT and CPM are developed. (*Project Scheduling*)
- The Operations Research Society of America (ORSA) and The Institute of Management Science (TIMS), two professional societies dealing with management science issues, are established.
- Richard Bellman develops a methodology for solving multistage decision problems. (*Dynamic Programming*)

-1960s
- John D.C. Little proves a theoretical relationship between the average length of a waiting line and the average time a customer spends in line. (*Queuing Theory*)
- Specialized simulation languages such as SIMSCRIPT and GPSS are developed. (*Simulation*)

-1970s
- The microcomputer is developed.

-1980s
- N. Karmarkar develops a new procedure for solving large-scale linear programming problems. (*Linear Programming*)
- The personal computer is developed.
- Specialized management science software packages that can run on microcomputers are developed.

-1990s
- Spreadsheet packages begin to play a major role in modeling and solving management science models.
- TIMS and ORSA merge to form the Institute of Operations Research and Management Science (INFORMS).

FIGURE 1.1 Management Science Time Line

undertake many projects using a management science approach. Although the Cold War may be over, the U.S. Department of Defense still requires and utilizes management science models in its daily operations as well as in emergency or wartime situations, such as Operation Desert Storm in 1991.

Surveys printed in such prestigious periodicals as *Money* magazine and the *Los Angeles Times* have consistently ranked management science as one of today's fastest growing occupations. No less an authority than *Business Week* has recognized and reported on the value of management science to a business education. In its MBA issue of October 2, 2000, the magazine began applying a new standard to judge the top business based on "intellectual capital." *Business Week* then chose 12 top publications, including the *Harvard Business Review* and the *Sloan Management Review*, to aid in its preparation of its evaluations. Two of the other 10 scholarly publications consulted were leading management science publications, *Operations Research* and *Management Science*, clearly pointing out the value this discipline plays in their interpretation of "intellectual capital." Also, in the month of October 2000 alone, three other *Business Week* print and on-line editions featured articles on management science and optimization.

As the twenty-first century begins, there is overwhelming evidence that major organizations are looking for individuals in all disciplines who have strong quantitative, computer, and communications skills. Management science, with its emphasis on all these areas, as well as its direct application to problems of optimization and efficiency, is recognized as an important element in a well-rounded business education.

1.3 Mathematical Modeling

Many problems requiring managerial decisions lend themselves to quantitative or management science analyses. Throughout this text numerous decision problems, each with specific objectives and restrictions, are presented and analyzed from a management science perspective. Here, we examine the *general* management science process by detailing the steps required for a successful analysis. It is important for the analyst and the decision maker alike to be cognizant of the particulars of this process so that management science can be applied correctly and assume its proper role in managerial decision making.

THE MATHEMATICAL MODELING APPROACH

Management science relies on **mathematical modeling**, a process that translates observed or desired phenomena into mathematical expressions. For example, suppose, NewOffice Furniture produces three products—desks, chairs, and molded steel (which it sells to other manufacturers)—and is trying to decide on the number of desks (D), chairs (C), and pounds of molded steel (M) to produce during a particular production run. If NewOffice nets a $50 profit on each desk produced, $30 on each chair produced, and $6 per pound of molded steel produced, the total profit for a production run can be modeled by the expression:

$$50D + 30C + 6M$$

Similarly, if 7 pounds of raw steel are needed to manufacture a desk, 3 pounds to manufacture a chair, and 1.5 pounds to produce a pound of molded steel, the amount of raw steel used during the production run is modeled by the expression:

$$7D + 3C + 1.5M$$

A **constrained mathematical model** is a model with an objective and one or more constraints. **Functional constraints** are "≤", "≥", or "=" restrictions that involve expressions with one or more variables. For example, if NewOffice has only 2000 pounds of raw steel available for the production run, the functional constraint that expresses the fact that it cannot use more than 2000 pounds of raw steel is modeled by the inequality:

$$7D + 3C + 1.5M \leq 2000$$

Variable constraints are constraints involving only one of the variables. Examples of variable constraints that will be discussed in this text include the following:

Variable Constraint	*Mathematical Expression*
Nonnegativity constraint	$X \geq 0$
Lower bound constraint	$X \geq L$ (a number other than 0)
Upper bound constraint	$X \leq U$
Integer constraint	X = integer
Binary constraint	$X = 0$ or 1

In the NewOffice example, no production can be negative; thus, we would require the nonnegativity constraints $D \geq 0$, $C \geq 0$, and $M \geq 0$. If at least 100 desks must be produced to satisfy contract commitments, and due to the availability of seat cushions, no more than 500 chairs can be produced, these can be expressed by the variable constraints $D \geq 100$ and $C \leq 500$, respectively. Finally, if the quantities of desks and chairs produced during the production run must be integer valued (the amount of molded steel need not be integer valued), we have the following constrained mathematical model for this problem:

MAXIMIZE	$50D + 30C + 6M$		(Total profit)
SUBJECT TO	$7D + 3C + 1.5M \leq 2000$		(Raw steel)
	$D \geq 100$		(Contract)
	$C \leq 500$		(Cushions)
	$D, C, M \geq 0$		(Nonnegativity)
	D, C are integers		

Mathematical models translate important business problems into a form suitable for determining a good or, in many cases, a "best" or *optimal* solution by use of spreadsheets or other computer software. For example, using an appropriate solution technique for the above constrained mathematical model, we can show that producing 100 desks, 433 chairs, and two-thirds of a pound of molded steel yields a maximum total profit of $17,994. Any other combination of desks, chairs, and molded steel that satisfies all of the constraints will yield a profit less than $17,994. Solving constrained mathematical models is a primary focus of much of this text.

CLASSIFICATION OF MATHEMATICAL MODELS

There are various ways to classify mathematical models. One way is by the purpose of the model. **Optimization models** seek to maximize a quantity (profit, efficiency, etc.) or minimize a quantity (cost, time, etc.) that may be restricted by a set of constraints (limitations on the availability of capital, personnel, and supplies; requirements to meet contract deadlines; etc.). At times, however, the function of a model is not to maximize or minimize any particular quantity but to describe or predict events (sales forecasts, project completion dates, etc.) given certain conditions. These models are known as **prediction models**.

Prediction models are almost always part of larger optimization models, however. For example, the manager of a fast-food restaurant could use a prediction model to determine the reduction in average customer waiting time and the corresponding increase in sales resulting from hiring an additional clerk. The information gained from the results of this prediction model could then be used as input for an optimization model. This model can help determine whether the benefits from the predicted increase in sales and reduction in customer waiting time more than offsets the costs of hiring the additional clerk.

Another way to classify mathematical models is by the degree of certainty of the data in the model. **Deterministic models** are those in which the profit, cost, and resource data are assumed to be known with certainty, whereas in **probabilistic** or **stochastic models**, one or more of the input parameters' values are determined by probability distributions. For example, in a manufacturing process in which the speed of an assembly line can be controlled by operators, the number of parts per hour arriving at one station on the assembly line from another could be modeled using a deterministic arrival rate. By contrast, the number of customer arrivals per hour at a major supermarket would not be known with certainty; accordingly, a stochastic model would be more appropriate in this case.

SPREADSHEET MODELING

Spreadsheets can provide a convenient way to both display and solve mathematical models. They can range from simple spreadsheets for model solution only to carefully constructed spreadsheets designed to convey both input information and resulting recommendations in a pleasing, easy to read format that might be used by others. Suggestions and examples for creating maximum impact spreadsheets for the end-user are presented in Chapter 3. In this text we utilize both types of spreadsheet models.

1.4 The Management Science Process

Management science is a discipline that adapts the scientific method to provide management with key information for executive decision making. In its simplest form, management science can be thought of as a four-step procedure, as shown in Figure 1.2. Projects rarely proceed smoothly through this sequential process, how-

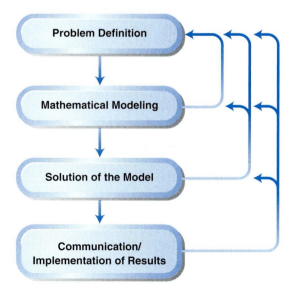

FIGURE 1.2
The Management
Science Process

ever. Usually, models have to be revised, solution approaches altered, or reports rewritten, as historical, simulated, or current data are used to verify and fine tune the original sets of assumptions and data. Hence, parts of the process may need to be repeated until the analyst is comfortable with the results. In this section, the complexities and thought processes involved in each of the four phases of the management science process are discussed in detail.

THE TEAM CONCEPT

Building good mathematical models is an art that is at the heart of the management science process. The greater the knowledge of the project under study, the more reliable the model is in assessing the true situation. While relatively small projects requiring a management science approach are sometimes assigned to a single consultant or specialist, most larger projects utilize a *team approach* that capitalizes on the talents of the management science analyst as well as those from other relevant business or scientific disciplines germane to the project.

The petroleum industry is one that has made liberal use of management science models. One such model involves the purchase of crude oil and the manufacture and distribution of various grades of gasoline. In addition to the management science analyst, the "team" responsible for constructing the model and evaluating its results might consist of some or all of the following:

Team Member	Expertise
Chemical engineer	Petroleum blending requirements
Economist	Forecasts of oil prices
Marketing analyst	Forecasts of market demand for gasoline
Financial officer	Analysis of cash flow
Accountant	Cash flow/tax requirements
Production manager	Analysis of production capabilities
Transportation specialist	Distribution of refined oil products

Each individual member of this team brings to the project his or her own perspective and can make contributions that might otherwise be lost with a more narrow focus.

STEP 1: DEFINING THE PROBLEM

The most important part of the modeling process is identifying the problem under consideration. As noted management consultant Peter Drucker has stressed, the wrong answer to the right question is not fatal, for revisions can be made and different alternatives may be explored; however, the right answer to the wrong question can be disastrous. It is critical that the problem be properly defined before enormous amounts of time and energy are expended on perhaps a worthless (or worse) model and solution.

"PROBLEMS" IN MANAGEMENT SCIENCE

Management science is generally applied in three situations:

1. Designing and implementing new operations or procedures
2. Evaluating an ongoing set of operations or procedures
3. Determining and recommending corrective action for operations and procedures that are producing unsatisfactory results

When contemplating new operations or procedures, the "problem" facing the management scientist is to recommend approaches that will yield profitable and efficient results within a reasonable time period, given limited or no previous historical data. A company contemplating the introduction of a new product, for example, will need to determine the exact production process, the materials and labor required, and the production quantities based on forecasted demand for its product and the availability of required resources. In this case the management science analysis revolves around the question, *"How do we get started?"*

When analyzing an ongoing business venture, a "problem" does not necessarily refer to a department or an operation that is experiencing substandard or unacceptably low results. For example, a small grocery store generating $500,000 a year in gross profits may not seem to have a problem. But could a change in operations yield another $100,000? The management science analysis here is attempting to answer the question, *"Can we do better?"*

Management science is also applied when a company has experienced significant or repetitious failures or shortfalls. Russell Ackoff, a pioneer in the field, refused to characterize such situations as "problems" but rather as "messes." He referred to such cases in management science as "mess management." In this case, the management science analysis is a response to a cry for *"Help!"*

In each of these situations, an analyst is typically faced with some or all of the following factors:

1. "Fuzzy," incomplete, or conflicting data
2. "Soft" constraints (i.e., goals rather than restrictions)
3. Differing opinions among and between workers and management
4. Very limited budgets for analyses
5. Narrow time frames for solutions and recommendations
6. Political "turf wars"
7. No firm idea by management of exactly what is wanted (managers sometimes look to the consultant to tell *them* what *they* want)

PROBLEM DEFINITION

The analyst's success will be determined in large part by how well these factors are dealt with in the problem definition phase of the project. The following box suggests steps to be taken in the problem definition phase.

Problem Definition

1. Observe operations
2. Ease into complexity
3. Recognize political realities
4. Decide what is really wanted
5. Identify constraints
6. Seek continuous feedback

Observe Operations

Those performing a management science analysis should make every effort to observe the problem from various points of view within the organization, with the goal of understanding the problem *at least as well as, if not better than,* those individuals directly involved. In a manufacturing process, the perspectives of managers, foremen, and workers might be solicited. In a service operation, input might come from supervisors, clerks, and support personnel. Frequently, accounting personnel can also provide valuable insights into the true nature of the problem.

In an effort to get a feel for what's really going on, it is important that the management science team "speak the same language" as those supplying input data and those responsible for making the ultimate decisions. Since recommendations will often be based on what many in the firm consider "voodoo mathematics," it is important to establish *credibility* early with these personnel and to reinforce it throughout the entire process. The analyst must realize that decision makers, in particular, take a critical look at recommendations stemming from a management science study since the success of any implemented policy will directly affect the evaluation of their performance.

Ease into Complexity

At the beginning of the study, the team should strive to ask simple, basic questions of individuals, which do not go beyond the realm of each person's expertise. This avoids putting those questioned on the defensive and aids in establishing the trust and respect that are crucial to the success of the analysis.

By initially asking similar questions of workers at all levels on the organization chart, the analysts may find that there are differences in opinion as to the exact nature of the problem. Once the individuals or units who have expertise in each of several key areas have been identified, the team can then probe more deeply into complex issues in a significantly less intimidating manner.

Recognize Political Realities

Analysts should always be cognizant of the politics present in any organization. Natural conflicts may exist between labor and management and between various managers. Operating in this kind of environment, the management science team can expect to receive distorted or incomplete information from each group. A manager is naturally reluctant to provide negative information that would show her division to be inefficient; a foreman most likely will not provide information that might result in significant reductions of his resources or personnel; and a worker will not offer suggestions that might result in the elimination of her job! Thus, all information gathered by the management science team must be scrutinized with these limitations in mind.

Decide What Is *Really* Wanted

Two situations typify the environment that exists before a management science analysis begins:

1. Management has a *fuzzy* idea of what the problem is.
2. Management has a *definite* idea of what (it thinks) the problem is.

There is rarely an in-between. In either case, the management science team should try to decide for itself what is needed.

An example of the first case involves a store that carries a product that has not been selling well. Management might simply indicate that "something is wrong here" and may actually be looking for help in identifying the root causes of the problem. The "problem" could be defined quite differently, and the possible recommendations vary greatly depending on such factors as the age of the items, the amount of advertising done by both the manufacturer and the store, the relationship between the store and the manufacturer, the "seasonality" of the product, and so on. Gathering relevant facts is crucial to accurate problem definition.

The following situation represents the second case. A health products distribution company, which orders products from various manufacturers and distributes them to local stores, was not able to fill over 10% of its orders because of inventory stockouts. The company was convinced that, in order to reduce lost revenues due to excessive stockouts, it should reduce stockouts to less than 4%. To meet this objective, however, the company was concerned that it might have to carry an excessive amount of inventory. Management science consultants were called in to develop an effective ordering policy.

Upon further investigation of the situation, it was determined that while reducing stockouts on high-volume, high-profit items was indeed crucial to company profits, less stringent inventory policies were necessary for lower-volume, lower-profit items. In fact, the resulting model, which was credited with saving the company hundreds of thousands of dollars annually, actually recommended an increase in the probability of stockouts for these items! The moral is simple: *the management science team should make certain that the company is sure of its objective before developing and solving a model.*

Identify Constraints

Businesses operate in a restrictive environment. It is important to seek input from various operational levels to identify these restrictions or constraints. Advertising budgets for a beer company, warehouse space limitations for a department store, the order of task completion in a construction project, and the maximum size of a waiting line at a supermarket checkout stand are all examples of constraints that might be included in mathematical models. Only those restrictions that could possibly affect operations should be included. Those that will obviously be satisfied by any reasonable solution should be omitted.

Seek Continuous Feedback

In order for the management science team to solve the "right" problem, the analysts need to seek *ongoing* feedback from management, both orally and by written communication (or e-mail), in the problem formulation stage. This allows both parties to continuously modify their initial perceptions and remain "in sync" about the problem.

Communications should be concise, articulate, and precise so that there is no misunderstanding on either side of what will be modeled and solved. This consensus allows the modeling phase to proceed more smoothly and gives more credence to the recommendations based on the solution of the model.

PROBLEM IDENTIFICATION FOR DELTA HARDWARE

To help motivate the development and solution of a mathematical model, throughout the remainder of this chapter, we will analyze a situation faced by Delta Hardware Stores. After soliciting input and analyzing the situation, the management at Delta Hardware and the management science team mutually agreed on the following problem statement.

DELTA HARDWARE STORES—PROBLEM STATEMENT

Delta Hardware Stores is a regional retailer with warehouses in three cities in California: San Jose in northern California, Fresno in central California, and Azusa in southern California. Each month, Delta restocks its warehouses with its own brand of paint (among other products). Delta has its own paint manufacturing plant in Phoenix, Arizona. Although the plant's production capacity is sometimes insufficient to meet monthly demand, a recent feasibility study commissioned by Delta found that it was not cost effective to expand production capacity at this time. To meet demand, Delta subcontracts with a national paint manufacturer to produce paint under the Delta label and deliver it (at a higher cost) to any of its three California warehouses.

Given that there is to be no expansion of plant capacity, the problem is to determine a least cost distribution scheme of paint produced at its manufacturing plant and shipments from the subcontractor to meet the demands of its California warehouses.

STEP 2: BUILDING A MATHEMATICAL MODEL

According to David Gray, who has been a senior consultant with American Airlines Decision Technologies, the solution to an applied management science problem may be "the organization of scattered thoughts, ideas, and conflicting objectives and constraints into a more logical coherent decision framework for a client who is too close to the problem to solve it objectively." While simple, common-sense, nonquantitative approaches may solve some problems, in most cases large amounts of quantitative data need to be organized into this "more logical coherent decision framework."

Mathematical modeling is a procedure that recognizes and verbalizes a problem and then quantifies it by turning the words into mathematical expressions. While modeling requires a number of basic skills, in some sense, mathematical modeling is an art that improves with experience. Some of the steps involved in the modeling process include:

Mathematical Modeling

1. Identifying decision variables
2. Quantifying the objective and constraints
3. Constructing a model shell
4. Data gathering—Consider time/cost issues

IDENTIFYING DECISION VARIABLES

A crucial step in building a mathematical model is determining those factors in the decision-making process over which the decision maker has control. These items are known as the **controllable inputs** or **decision variables** for the problem. For example, in a manufacturing process, the quantity of goods produced and the amount of overtime assigned during the week are controllable inputs, or decision variables, for the model. The shift foremen or plant managers (the decision makers) make these determinations. Decision variables usually include a *time frame*. In this case, it is important that the decision variables reflect the production and overtime schedules as *"per week."*

The number of machines in the plant, the amount of resources needed to make one unit of the product, and the overall plant capacity are factors over which the manager has no direct influence. They are the **uncontrollable inputs**, or **parameters**.

In many cases, determining the appropriate decision variables is the hardest part of building a mathematical model. Frequently, the rest of the modeling process follows quite naturally once the decision variables have been properly defined. The following is a quick rule of thumb for determining the decision variables of a mathematical model.

Defining Decision Variables

1. Ask, "What does the decision maker want to learn by solving this problem?" In other words, "Does the decision maker have the authority to decide the numerical value (amount) of the item?" If the answer is "yes," it is a decision variable.

2. Be very precise in the units (and if appropriate, the time frame) of each decision variable.

Variable Definition for Delta Hardware

Let us apply this approach to the Delta Hardware problem.

DELTA HARDWARE STORE PROBLEM—VARIABLE DEFINITION

After analyzing the problem as presented, it is clear that the decision maker has no control over demand, production capacities, or unit costs. The decision maker is simply being asked, "How much paint should be shipped *this month* (note the time frame) from the plant in Phoenix to San Jose, Fresno, and Azusa, and how much extra should be purchased from the subcontractor and sent to each of the three cities to satisfy their orders?"

SOLUTION

There are six decisions to be made, hence six decision variables. These can be expressed as

X_1 = amount of paint shipped this month from Phoenix to San Jose
X_2 = amount of paint shipped this month from Phoenix to Fresno
X_3 = amount of paint shipped this month from Phoenix to Azusa
X_4 = amount of paint subcontracted this month for San Jose
X_5 = amount of paint subcontracted this month for Fresno
X_6 = amount of paint subcontracted this month for Azusa

The choice of the variable names is arbitrary. More descriptive and longer names are possible. However, using subscripted variables, particularly when models are more complex, typically yields a more compact model.

QUANTIFYING THE OBJECTIVE FUNCTION AND CONSTRAINTS

The objective of most management science studies, and of *all* optimization models, is to figure out how to do the best you can with what you've got. "The best you can" implies maximizing something (such as profit or efficiency) or minimizing something (such as costs or time).

Although a company may be satisfied with a substantial improvement over a current situation, the goal usually is to seek an optimal value for some **objective function**. **Total profit maximization** (Total Profit = Total Revenues − Total Costs) is perhaps the most common objective for mathematical models. Note that if costs are constant, maximizing profit is equivalent to maximizing revenue; if revenues are constant, it is equivalent to minimizing cost.

Most management science models are formulated to maximize or minimize a single objective function. Cases in which two or more conflicting objectives exist are called **multicriteria decision problems**. (Multicriteria problems are discussed briefly in Chapter 13 on the accompanying CD-ROM.)

As discussed earlier, when seeking the optimal value for an objective function, one is usually operating under restrictive conditions, or **constraints**. Examples of typical constraints include limits on the amount of resources available (workers, machines, budgets, etc.) and contractual requirements for monthly production.

Constraints can also be definitional in nature. A constraint expressing that the inventory at the end of a month is equal to the inventory at the beginning of the month plus production minus sales during the month is an example of one such definitional constraint. The following is a useful aid for writing constraints.

Writing Constraints

1. Create a limiting condition *in words* in the following manner:

    (The amount of a resource required)
    ⟨Has some relation to⟩
    (The availability of the resource)

2. Make sure the units on the left side of the relation are the same as those on the right side.

3. Translate the words into mathematical notation using known or estimated values for the parameters and the previously defined symbols for the decision variables.

4. Rewrite the constraint, if necessary, so that all terms involving the decision variables are on the left side of the relationship, with only a constant value on the right side.

CONSTRUCTING MODEL SHELL

In the formative stages of model building, generic symbols can be used for the parameters until the actual data are determined. In the NewOffice Furniture example, the symbols A_1, A_2, and A_3 might have been used to represent the amount of steel required to make one desk, one chair, and one pound of molded steel, respectively, and the symbol B could have been used to represent the amount of steel available during the production run. Thus, the functional constraint could be written as the following *shell*:

$$A_1 D + A_2 C + A_3 M \leq B$$

When it was determined that it takes 7 pounds of raw steel to make a desk, 3 pounds of raw steel to make a chair, and 1.5 pounds of raw steel to make a pound of molded steel, and that there were 2000 pounds of steel available weekly, the appropriate substitutions for A_1, A_2, A_3, and B would be made to the shell, giving the constraint: $7D + 3C + 1.5M \leq 2000$. Often these parameter values of 7, 3, 1.5, and 2000 are entries in a structured spreadsheet.

Model Shell for Delta Hardware

By having a model shell, the modeler can focus directly on the exact data required to complete the model. Let us illustrate this procedure for the Delta Hardware problem.

DELTA HARDWARE STORE PROBLEM—FORMULATING THE MODEL SHELL

Although the actual data have not yet been collected, it is certain that there is a finite production capacity at the paint plant in Phoenix as well as an upper bound on the amount of paint available from the subcontractor. There are also different requirements for paint at each of the three Delta warehouses.

Further investigation by the management science team indicates that the delivery trucks that transport the paint from Phoenix to the warehouses carry 1000 gallons of paint at a time. Since Delta requires the warehouses to order in units of 1000, this is equivalent to ordering a certain number of truckloads. The cost of shipping each truckload can then be determined based on the time and distance between Phoenix and each of the warehouse cities.

It has also been determined that the cost of purchasing the paint from the subcontractor is higher than manufacturing the paint in Phoenix, and to obtain the best prices from the subcontractor, orders must be in 1000-gallon increments. The subcontractor charges a fixed fee for each 1000 gallons ordered and a delivery charge to each of the three warehouse cities. This delivery charge varies depending on the city.

The objective is to minimize the total overall monthly costs of manufacturing, transporting, and subcontracting paint, subject to

1. The Phoenix plant cannot operate beyond its capacity.
2. The amount ordered from the subcontractor cannot exceed a maximum limit.
3. The orders for paint at each warehouse will be fulfilled.

The decision variables capture an amount, but we have yet to specify exactly what that amount is. Since truckloads and purchases from the subcontractor are based on *thousands* of gallons of paint, let us assume that the decision variables X_1, $X_2, \ldots, X_6$ are defined in these units. For example, X_1 will represent the number of thousands of gallons of paint (i.e., truckloads) shipped from Phoenix to San Jose, X_6 will represent the number of thousands of gallons of paint subcontracted this month for Azusa, and so on.

To determine the overall costs, one must determine: (1) the manufacturing cost per 1000 gallons of paint at the plant in Phoenix (M); (2) the respective truckload shipping costs from Phoenix to San Jose, Fresno, and Azusa (T_1, T_2, T_3); (3) the fixed purchase cost per 1000 gallons from the subcontractor (C); and (4) the respective shipping charges per 1000 gallons from the subcontractor to San Jose, Fresno, and Azusa (S_1, S_2, S_3). Minimizing total monthly costs can then be written as:

$$\text{MINIMIZE} \quad (M+T_1)X_1 + (M+T_2)X_2 + (M+T_3)X_3 + (C+S_1)X_4 + (C+S_2)X_5 + (C+S_3)X_6$$

To write the constraints, we need to know (in thousands of gallons): (1) the capacity of the Phoenix plant (Q_1); (2) the maximum number of gallons available from the subcontractor (Q_2); and (3) the respective orders for paint at the warehouses in San Jose, Fresno, and Azusa (R_1, R_2, R_3). The constraints can then be written as:

1. The number of truckloads shipped out from Phoenix cannot exceed the plant capacity:

$$X_1 + X_2 + X_3 \leq Q_1$$

2. The number of thousands of gallons ordered from the subcontractor cannot exceed the order limit:

$$X_4 + X_5 + X_6 \leq Q_2$$

3. The number of thousands of gallons received at each warehouse equals the total orders of the warehouse:

$$X_1 \quad\quad + X_4 \quad\quad = R_1$$
$$X_2 \quad\quad + X_5 \quad = R_2$$
$$X_3 \quad\quad\quad + X_6 = R_3$$

4. All shipments must be nonnegative and integer:

$$X_1 \geq 0, X_2 \geq 0, X_3 \geq 0, X_4 \geq 0, X_5 \geq 0, X_6 \geq 0$$
$$X_1, X_2, X_3, X_4, X_5, X_6 \text{ integer}$$

Given this model shell, the modeler can now begin gathering data to determine or approximate values for the parameters M, C, T_1, T_2, T_3, S_1, S_2, S_3, Q_1, Q_2, R_1, R_2, and R_3.

DATA GATHERING—CONSIDER TIME/COST ISSUES

All mathematical models are simply that—models of reality. There are usually numerous ways to model most situations, some quite simplistic, and others very complex. The modeler usually must ask the question, "Is a very sophisticated model that will give relatively accurate results needed, or will a simpler model which will likely yield less accurate, but hopefully, 'ball park' results suffice?" The answer depends on three time/cost considerations:

1. *The time and cost of collecting, organizing, and sorting relevant data*
Data collection can be very time consuming and expensive. Key data may turn out to be unavailable or subject to error for a variety of reasons, including poor recordkeeping, company or union policies, ignorance, or evasiveness of potentially affected personnel. Substantial costs may be incurred to obtain *hard data* (precise values, good forecasts, or exact estimates) to analyze even one factor in the model.

For example, months of continuous recordkeeping may be required to determine an arrival pattern of customers to a grocery store; estimating the typical production time for a single product might require lengthy and involved time and motion studies; sales projections can require hundreds of man-hours to analyze numerous voluminous reports. Even when raw data are readily available, organizing and sorting the data to obtain relevant information can itself be quite costly and time consuming.

As an alternative to hard data, models can use *soft data*, such as short-term studies or even best guesses from experts. In general, the "harder" the data, the more costly and time consuming it is to obtain. Consequently, mathematical models often contain varying amounts of both hard and soft data.

2. *The time and cost of generating a solution approach*
Conventional solution techniques exist for many "traditional" management science models, including all those developed in this text. In "real life," however, mathematical models formulated by a management science team frequently fail to meet the required conditions of these models. In this case, we have two choices:

1. Make some simplifying assumptions so that a standard solution technique may be used.

or

2. Develop a new solution technique, or modify an existing one, to handle this special problem.

Using simplifying assumptions saves the time and cost of developing, testing, programming, and debugging a new technique. However, oversimplification may result in an unrealistic model of the true situation. Thus, care must be taken not to make assumptions that will jeopardize the integrity of the results from the model.

3. *The time and cost of using the model*

Managers and executives must respond rapidly to dynamically changing sets of conditions. For example, changing weather conditions could force an airline to reroute its entire fleet of planes and reassign flight personnel. New arrival and departure schedules, gate requirements, and crew and maintenance schedules must be generated quickly. Optimal solutions that could be generated "overnight," after the solution is required, are worthless.

When selecting an appropriate model, the end-user must also be considered. The sophistication of the model might be quite different, if, for example, it is to be used by executives at General Motors, where a 1% improvement in efficiency would result in savings of tens of millions of dollars, as opposed to a small store where such a small percentage improvement may not even cover the cost of the study. The model could certainly be more complex (and costly) if it were monitored by a management science department within a large organization rather than a single employee with limited training in the field.

Judgments about these time/cost factors play a key role in determining the amount and methods of data collection and selecting the models to utilize. An informal "rule of thumb," known as the 80/20 *rule*, is often used as a guide when selecting an appropriate model. It states that, in general, a business client settles for 80% of the optimal solution at 20% of the cost to obtain it. Thus, simpler, easier to use, less costly (though admittedly less accurate) models are often selected to generate "good" results rather than "optimal" ones.

Determining the Model for Delta Hardware

Let us now consider the data collection and model selection for Delta Hardware.

DELTA HARDWARE STORE PROBLEM—DATA COLLECTION AND MODEL SELECTION

Initial data received by the management science analyst indicate that the warehouses in San Jose, Fresno, and Azusa are to be restocked with 4000, 2000, and 5000 gallons of paint, respectively. The subcontractor has agreed to sell Delta paint for $5 per gallon ($5000 per 1000 gallons) plus shipping fees of $1200 per 1000 gallons to San Jose, $1400 per 1000 gallons to Fresno, and $1100 per 1000 gallons to Azusa.

Delta management has informed the analyst that no more than 50% of the total paint supplied to the warehouses (in this case 5500 gallons) is to be supplied by the subcontractor. Since shipments from the subcontractor are to be in 1000-gallon units, this implies that at most 5000 gallons will be supplied by the subcontractor.

The modeler must now decide which model to use and the appropriate data to analyze in order to determine the values of the other parameters in the model.

SOLUTION

The structure of the model developed earlier is a standard management science model known as the **transportation problem**. But in this model, all factors other than manufacturing, ordering, and transportation costs have been ignored. Many other simplifying assumptions have been made, such as requiring that all trucks carry a full load of 1000 gallons of paint. In reality, partial truckloads or larger trucks might be used. It is also assumed that the cost of sending two trucks is exactly twice the cost of sending one truck, that this cost does not change, and that the cost of driving from Phoenix to a warehouse city is always the same. Also ignored are the facts that production rates and costs vary from month to month; external costs can change at a moment's notice; and additional subcontractor suppliers of paint might be solicited.

Although the model developed for Delta lacks a certain degree of reality, solution modules for transportation models are readily available in management science and spreadsheet packages. Thus, by using this simplified model, at least as a first pass to determine "ballpark" results, Delta can avoid the time and expense of deriving and testing more complex models. If the results from this approach prove suspect, a more sophisticated model can then be developed.

Having elected to use a transportation model, the next step is to determine the value of the parameters of the model shell. Certain hard data have already been ascertained:

- The number of orders (in thousands of gallons) at the San Jose, Fresno, and Azusa warehouses are, respectively, $R_1 = 4$, $R_2 = 2$, and $R_3 = 5$.
- The maximum order limit from the subcontractor (in thousands of gallons) is $Q_2 = 5$.
- The fixed purchase cost per 1000 gallons of paint from the subcontractor is $C = \$5000$.
- The shipping charges per 1000 gallons of paint from the subcontractor to San Jose, Fresno, and Azusa are, respectively, $S_1 = \$1200$, $S_2 = \$1400$, and $S_3 = \$1100$.

Data that are more difficult to obtain and prone to more uncertainty include the production limits at the Phoenix plant and the manufacturing and transportation costs.

Production Limit   Most likely, a theoretical plant production limit exists, which assumes that the plant runs continuously at full capacity with no machine failures, full staffing, and ample resources. Because such ideal conditions rarely exist, monthly production levels vary. One way for the model to account for such unpredictable problems might be to multiply the theoretical production limit by some reduction factor. Another alternative could be simply to ask the plant manager, "What's your best estimate for production capability this month?"

In this case, the modeler decided to forecast plant capacity based on past data. Accordingly, the monthly production data listed in Table 1.1 for the number of gallons produced over the past 24 months were obtained from company records (month 24 being the most recent month).

These data show that, with the exception of month 21, production was relatively constant over the past 12 months. Upon further investigation, it was found that during month 21, one of the production machines was experiencing intermittent breakdowns and management shut down the plant for a week and a half to perform a major overhaul of all machines. It was therefore decided that data for month 21 was an *outlier*—data not representative of normal production levels— and should be discarded.

TABLE 1.1   Delta's Monthly Production

Month	Production	Month	Production	Month	Production
1	7500	9	8000	17	7900
2	7000	10	7200	18	8000
3	6500	11	7700	19	7600
4	7000	12	7500	20	8000
5	7000	13	8100	21	3900
6	6500	14	8000	22	8100
7	7200	15	7600	23	7900
8	5000	16	8000	24	8100

It was also discovered that 12 months ago the plant went from a $37\frac{1}{2}$-hour to a 40-hour work week. As a consequence, although data from months 1 to 12 were available, these data would not be used in the forecast. Thus, it was decided that monthly production would be forecasted based on the average of production for the past year, excluding month 21:

$$(8100 + 8000 + 7600 + \ldots + 8100)/11 = 7936 \text{ gallons}$$

Since, for model simplicity, full truckloads of 1000 gallons are assumed, a rounded amount of $Q_1 = 8$ (thousand) gallons will be used for the production capacity.

Plant Production and Transportation Costs   To determine unit production costs, all direct and indirect costs that go into production, including warehouse and machine leasing, employee wages and benefits, utilities, insurance, and so on must be considered. Transportation costs might include loading in Phoenix and unloading in each of the warehouse cities, mileage, and per diem expenses, among others. The management science team relied on the data supplied by the accounting department in Table 1.2 detailing the manufacturing and shipping costs of paint manufactured at the Phoenix plant.

Using this information, and the assumption that the Phoenix plant expects a production capacity of 8000 gallons per month, the per gallon production cost can be calculated by: (Direct per Gallon Manufacturing Cost) + (Apportioned per Gallon Indirect Cost) = \$2.25 + (\$6000/8000) = \$3.00 per gallon. Thus, the production cost per 1000 gallons is M = \$3000.

Given the fact that each truckload will carry 1000 gallons of paint, the transportation costs to each warehouse can now be determined by (Load Cost in Phoenix) + (Unload Cost at the Warehouse) + (Mileage Cost to the Warehouse):

$$\text{San Jose:} \quad T_1 = \$100 + \$150 + \$800 = \$1050$$
$$\text{Fresno:} \quad T_2 = \$100 + \$100 + \$550 = \$\ 750$$
$$\text{Azusa:} \quad T_3 = \$100 + \$120 + \$430 = \$\ 650$$

TABLE 1.2   Costs Associated with Production of Paint

Direct manufacturing costs	\$2.25/gallon
Indirect costs	\$6,000/month
Loading costs in Phoenix	\$100/truckload
Unloading costs in San Jose	\$150/truckload
Unloading costs in Fresno	\$100/truckload
Unloading costs in Azusa	\$120/truckload
Mileage/other costs to San Jose	\$800/truckload
Mileage/other costs to Fresno	\$550/truckload
Mileage/other costs to Azusa	\$430/truckload

The complete mathematical model for Delta Hardware derived by substituting the parameter values into the model shell is:[3]

$$\text{MINIMIZE} \quad 4050X_1 + 3750X_2 + 3650X_3 + 6200X_4 + 6400X_5 + 6100X_6$$

$$\text{SUBJECT TO}$$

$$
\begin{array}{rcrcrcrcrcrl}
X_1 & + & X_2 & + & X_3 & & & & & & & \leq 8 \\
& & & & & & X_4 & + & X_5 & + & X_6 & \leq 5 \\
X_1 & & & & & + & X_4 & & & & & = 4 \\
& & X_2 & & & & & + & X_5 & & & = 2 \\
& & & & X_3 & & & & & + & X_6 & = 5
\end{array}
$$

$$X_1 \geq 0, X_2 \geq 0, X_3 \geq 0, X_4 \geq 0, X_5 \geq 0, X_6 \geq 0, X_1, X_2, X_3, X_4, X_5, X_6 \text{ integer}$$

STEP 3: SOLVING A MATHEMATICAL MODEL

Mathematical models are formulated so that they can be solved to provide input to a decision maker. Steps in the **model solution** process include:

> ### Model Solution
>
> 1. Choose an appropriate solution technique.
> 2. Generate model solutions.
> 3. Test/validate model results.
> 4. Return to modeling step if results are unacceptable.
> 5. Perform "what-if" analyses.

CHOOSE AN APPROPRIATE SOLUTION TECHNIQUE

We've seen that the choice of the model to be used is linked to the considerations of the time, cost, and accuracy of using models for which solution techniques are known versus those for which solution techniques must be developed. Fortunately, there are large classes of problems for which efficient solution techniques have already been developed, many of which are discussed in this text.

Although some simplifying assumptions may be made so that a standard solution technique may be used, care must be taken to assure that the "meat" of the true problem has not been "assumed away." Oversimplifying models and misapplying management science tools have been primary impediments to the success and acceptance of management science approaches on a more global scale.

Management science teams often use algorithms to solve mathematical models. An **algorithm** is a structured series of steps that must be performed to solve the model. Usually, the individual steps involve simple, but repetitious, mathematical operations, such as adding, subtracting, multiplying, dividing, and comparing numbers.

Most algorithms are intended to provide an optimal solution for a model. Sometimes, however, problems can prove to be too complex, cumbersome, or time consuming to employ optimization algorithms. In such cases, a **heuristic**—a "rule of thumb" or common-sense procedure—may be employed to yield what the analyst feels may be a good, though not necessarily optimal, solution. Heuristic methods may range from simplistic procedures (such as "produce as much of the most profitable item as possible") to far more complex ones. They are sometimes used to generate a good *starting solution* for a model that is then improved upon by

---

[3] The development of this relatively simple model illustrates the fact that, when we use phrases in this text such as "The cost of shipping 1000 gallons of paint from Phoenix to San Jose is $4050," much background work has been done to generate even this single "given" value.

using an optimization algorithm. An alternative to using an algorithm is to use simulation. The simulation approach is discussed in Chapter 10.

Practitioners have emphasized time and time again that the most intuitive and simplest solution techniques are those that have the greatest likelihood of being understood and accepted by the client; hence, they have a higher probability of being implemented and used correctly. As Captain Richard Staats observed during the successful implementation of management science during the Persian Gulf War, "[Complex techniques] have a tendency to break down under the worst possible conditions."[4] Furthermore, complex techniques are usually far more costly.

Based on his vast experience as a management science consultant, Gene Woolsey has made three observations (which he calls *Woolsey's Laws*) that have served as a useful guide to the selection of a solution technique:

1. Managers would rather live with a problem they can't solve than use a technique they don't trust.
2. Managers don't want the best solution; they simply want a better one.
3. If the solution technique will cost you more than you will save, don't use it.

GENERATE MODEL SOLUTIONS

Once a solution procedure has been selected, the model can finally be solved. Since most models involve manipulations of large amounts of data, the sheer volume and sequencing of these operations require the use of computers. Fortunately, all of the standard management science solution procedures have been programmed either as stand-alone products or as parts of comprehensive integrated management science packages. Current versions of most common spreadsheet programs include built-in optimizers that perform many optimization analyses.

TEST/VALIDATE MODEL RESULTS

Because mathematical models are nothing more than simplifications of reality, optimal, heuristically generated or simulated solutions to a model may not be optimal or even good solutions for the true real-life situation. In fact, they may not even be possible. Thus, testing the model to validate its results is a key component of the solution phase. This can be a very time-consuming process. A few questions to ask in evaluating the validity of a model are:

1. Do the results make sense, or are they counterintuitive?
2. Can the solution be integrated successfully under current conditions, or will radical changes be necessary for implementation?
3. Does the solution provide a degree of continuity with present and future plans of the organization?

Both *historical and simulated (hypothetical) data* can be used to test the validity of the model. Each has its benefits and drawbacks.

Historical data can be used to judge directly how the results generated from the model would have performed under actual past conditions. Because the same data may have been used to generate many of the model's parameters, however, caution must be used when validating the model with historical data. Using historical data may tend to overstate the accuracy of the model, yielding biased results. In addition, such data may not reflect current conditions.

---

[4] Richard Staats, "Desert Storm! A Re-examination of the Ground War in the Persian Gulf and the Key Role Played by OR," OR/MS *Today* 18, No. 6 (December 1991): 42–56.

Using hypothetical data will yield hypothetical results, which may be hard to verify. If the results generated using hypothetical data defy common sense, however, this is a clear indication that the model needs to be modified. Using hypothetical data also allows for the input of extreme values of the parameters, which may not yet have occurred but for which the true solution may be obvious. Counterintuitive results for these extreme cases can provide another indication that the model may need modification.

Another approach used to validate a model is for the organization to do a pilot program using the model. This is perhaps the best way to get legitimate feedback of how well the model performs in real (and current) situations. There are drawbacks to this approach, however, including the cost of setting up and operating in real time, the learning curve of workers using and interpreting the model results (skewing initial performance results), and the length of time required for the pilot project to begin generating credible results. In many cases, the time period needed to validate the model's reliability may be so long that using a pilot program would not be feasible.

RETURN TO MODELING STEP IF RESULTS ARE UNACCEPTABLE

No model is 100% accurate, and no validation procedure is foolproof. If results of the validation tests prove unsatisfactory, the model should be reexamined. Assumptions should be reevaluated, data rechecked for accuracy, approximations loosened or tightened, and/or new constraints added. In the extreme, the entire model may have to be scrapped and a new one developed.

After any modifications are made, the new model must then be tested. This process of "model–solve–verify" continues until both the analysts and management feel comfortable about the model's ability to yield relatively valid results.

If, after numerous attempts to model the problem, management still lacks confidence in the results, it may conclude that this group should abandon its modeling attempts. Another group of analysts, taking a fresh approach to modeling the problem, may be able to develop a model that is more acceptable to management. Alternatively, management may conclude that a qualitative rather than a quantitative approach will have to suffice.

PERFORM "WHAT-IF" ANALYSES

The computer solution to a model is usually "an answer" for the model. Typically, however, a manager will want a *range* of options from which to choose. A good management science analyst should anticipate management concerns, potential new opportunities, and possible changes and be ready to discuss their impact. Managers are always impressed when many of their "what-if" questions have been anticipated and answered before they are asked.

All spreadsheet users are familiar with playing the what-if game. Similarly, most management science computer packages allow problems to be easily resolved in light of changes to the input data. In addition, many of these packages provide **sensitivity analysis** reports, which give the user valuable information about the effect of changes to the solution as certain parameters change. Based on such information, the management science team may often recommend additional courses of action that may not have occurred to the decision maker.

Solution to the Delta Hardware Model

Let us now consider the solution of the model developed for Delta Hardware Stores.

DELTAHARDWARE.xls

DELTA HARDWARE STORES PROBLEM—MODEL SOLUTION

Simplifying assumptions and approximations were made in the modeling phase so that the model would have deterministic unit shipping costs, known availabilities of paint at the production plant and from the subcontractor, and known demands by the warehouses. This was done because solution modules for this type of problem are readily available on spreadsheets and comprehensive management science software packages.

The model was solved using the SOLVER[5] module from Excel, and it yielded the screen shown in Figure 1.3. The screen shows the number of truckloads to be shipped from Phoenix and the number of thousands of gallons to be sent by the subcontractor to each of the three cities. For example, we see from cell B13 that one truckload should be shipped from Phoenix to San Jose.

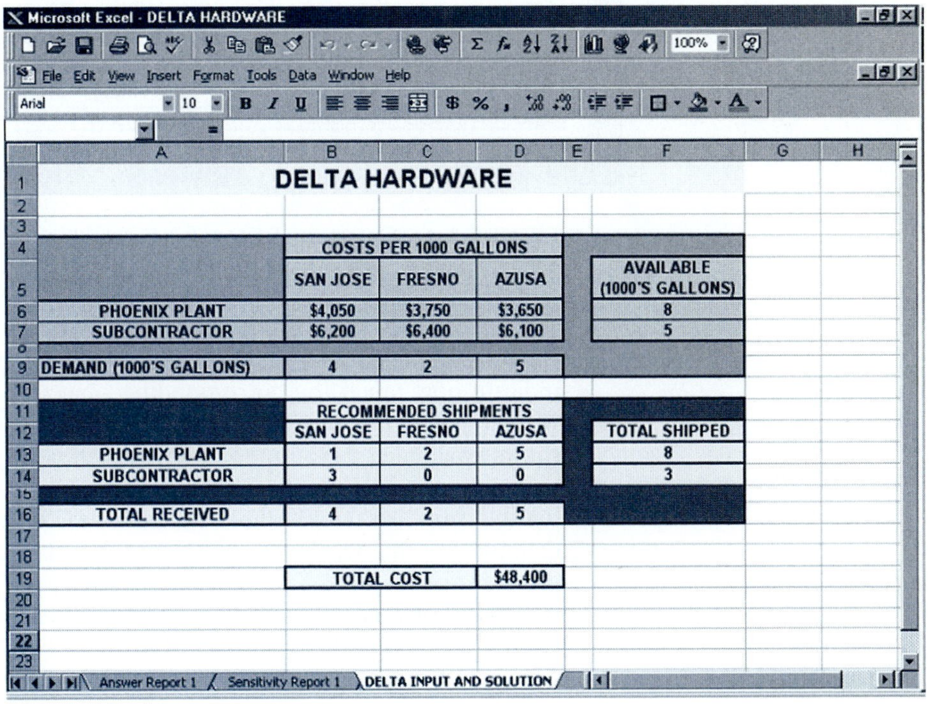

FIGURE 1.3
Optimal Spreadsheet Solution for Delta Hardware

Microsoft Excel - DELTA HARDWARE

DELTA HARDWARE

	COSTS PER 1000 GALLONS			AVAILABLE (1000'S GALLONS)
	SAN JOSE	FRESNO	AZUSA	
PHOENIX PLANT	$4,050	$3,750	$3,650	8
SUBCONTRACTOR	$6,200	$6,400	$6,100	5
DEMAND (1000'S GALLONS)	4	2	5	

	RECOMMENDED SHIPMENTS			TOTAL SHIPPED
	SAN JOSE	FRESNO	AZUSA	
PHOENIX PLANT	1	2	5	8
SUBCONTRACTOR	3	0	0	3
TOTAL RECEIVED	4	2	5	

	TOTAL COST	$48,400

Answer Report 1 / Sensitivity Report 1 \ DELTA INPUT AND SOLUTION /

In addition, Excel generates an Answer Report and a Sensitivity Report that give pertinent "what-if" information for the problem. Figure 1.4 is the Sensitivity Report. Although this report is discussed in detail in Chapter 2, we point out here that entries in the column labeled "Reduced Cost" indicate the amount that the shipping costs would have to be reduced before it would be cost effective to make a shipment between the corresponding "From-To" pairs. For example, the subcontractor would have to reduce its cost by more than $500 per 1000 gallons ($0.50 per gallon) to an amount less than $5900 per 1000 gallons before it would be economically feasible to ship paint from the subcontractor to Fresno. Similarly, it would have to reduce its cost by more than $300 per 1000 gallons ($0.30 per gallon) to an amount less than $5800 before it is cost effective to ship paint from the subcontractor to Azusa.

[5] SOLVER is an Excel Add-In that is discussed in detail in Section 2.5.

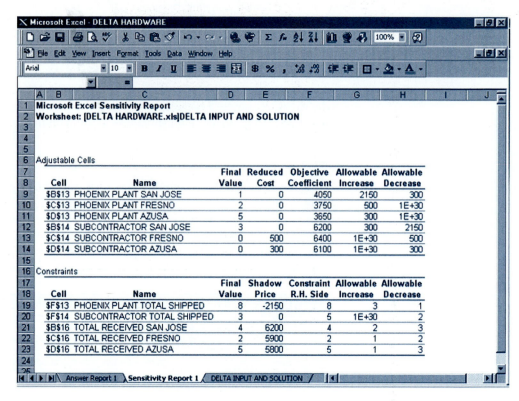

FIGURE 1.4   Sensitivity Report for Delta Hardware

Other what-if information is also provided. The "Allowable Increase" and "Allowable Decrease" columns next to the column labeled "Objective Coefficient" indicate how much the corresponding objective function coefficient can change without changing the optimal solution. The column labeled "Shadow Price" shows how much the optimal total cost will change per thousand gallon change in the corresponding supplies and demands, respectively. The columns labeled "Allowable Increase" and "Allowable Decrease" next to the "Constraint R. H. Side" column give the maximum change to the right-hand side for which these shadow prices remain valid.

To determine the impact of other cost changes on the optimal solution, we can simply modify the original problem to reflect the new price structure (an easy change in Excel and most other packages) and re-solve the problem.

Various questions should be addressed that are not reflected in the output to the above model. Of particular interest is the effect of Delta's production plant's inability to meet the production quantity of 8000 gallons. For instance, suppose that only 7700 rather than 8000 gallons were produced at the Phoenix plant. Would Delta (1) send eight trucks with one only partially loaded? (2) store 700 gallons until the next month, incurring a storage expense? (3) use a common carrier delivery service to ship the 700 gallons in lieu of shipping a partial truckload? or (4) allow warehouse cities to order or receive less than 1000-gallon units? Each of these options leads to a more complicated analysis.

If it is assumed, however, that Delta rigidly adheres to its policy of shipping only full truckloads of paint from Phoenix and ordering only in units of 1000 from the subcontractor, then, if production at the manufacturing plant is indeed 7700 gallons, only seven full truckloads can be sent from Phoenix. The input to the transportation model can then easily be modified to reflect a change to seven truckloads and re-solved to determine a new optimal solution. Any charges for producing the 700 gallons not shipped, including storage charges, would have to be added to the output from the transportation model to reflect the true overall cost.

The model for Delta Hardware was based on past data. With all of its assumptions and approximations, there is no way to verify the validity of the model results without actually putting them into practice. Thus, the "solution" transmitted to the decision maker, including any what-if analyses of costs and factory production, has to be evaluated for viability by company experts.

STEP 4: COMMUNICATING/MONITORING THE RESULTS

The final step in the management science process is the *post-solution phase*. This phase involves two functions:

> ### The Post-Solution Phase
>
> **1.** Prepare a business report or presentation
> **2.** Monitor the progress of the implementation

PREPARE A BUSINESS REPORT OR PRESENTATION

Effective communication of the results of a management science study is essential to its success. An analysis is of little use if those who will be making the decisions and implementing the policies do not fully appreciate its value. The decision maker should completely understand the team's approach to the problem, the assumptions and approximations made, and the logic of any recommendations.

Oral presentations (using slides, videos, or presentation software such as PowerPoint) and business memos or reports are the traditional forms of communication. In Section 1.5 we present guidelines for writing effective business reports.

MONITOR THE PROGRESS OF THE IMPLEMENTATION

After a business presentation or report has been submitted, management will be responsible for implementation of the recommendations. These policies may result in changes that might be resisted by members of the firm. The management science team should be ready to stand side by side with management to share responsibility for the procedures required for implementation.

Once the new policies have been implemented, they should be constantly scrutinized. Given the dynamic nature of most business environments, it is almost inevitable that changes to the model will be required over time. The management science team should be prepared to determine when changes to the model are necessary and make such changes swiftly when called upon.

1.5 Writing Business Reports/Memos

GUIDELINES FOR PREPARING BUSINESS REPORTS/PRESENTATIONS

Whether one is writing a report or preparing a presentation, it is important that the communication be well organized and presented in a clear manner that emphasizes the main recommendations of the study. The following are general guidelines for such presentations.

Be Concise

While not leaving out important details, get to the point. Managers do not like to read lengthy reports or attend lengthy presentations. In general, the fewer words needed to make a point the better, and the more the report is appreciated. Do not fill the report with extraneous material. When choosing which what-if analyses to include, make sure the scenarios are plausible and have a reasonable likelihood of occurring.

Use Common, Everyday Language

The terminology and symbols used to represent decision variables and parameters in management science models may be familiar to the analyst, but avoid the use of technical terms and symbols in a report. For example, while the Delta Hardware problem included both the symbol, X_1, which was used to represent the number of truckloads of paint shipped from Phoenix to San Jose, and the term *reduced cost*, neither should appear in a business report. Know your audience and express the information in terms they can understand.

Whenever possible, let someone else proofread the report carefully for clarity and style. The proofreader should also check the report to ensure that it contains no misspellings and that paragraphs are well constructed and written in complete sentences.

Make Liberal Use of Graphics

The use of properly labeled charts, graphs, and pictures, and the minimization of text, make a report much more readable and appealing to the eye. A business report or presentation is one place where the saying "a picture is worth a thousand words" is actually an underestimation of a picture's worth. Managers prefer visualizing results that allow them to make comparisons easily. No one wants to find results or recommendations buried in lengthy, hard-to-find paragraphs.

The actual presentation of figures is also important. All charts and graphs should be large, easy to read, and properly labeled, including the conditions under which the graph applies. Common sense should always guide a chart's preparation. For example, tables and graphs should not be split over two or more pages, if at all possible.

STRUCTURE OF A BUSINESS REPORT

Although there is no rigid structure for business reports, the following format has served the authors well in their industrial and consulting experiences.

Components of a Business Presentation

1. Introduction—problem statement
2. Assumptions/approximations made
3. Solution approach/computer program used
4. Results—presentation/analysis
5. What-if analyses
6. Overall recommendation
7. Appendices

Introduction—Problem Statement

The introduction should outline the problem that management and the management science team mutually agreed upon, so that there are no misunderstandings of the results discussed in the presentation. The actual length and style of the introduction will vary, depending on the audience for which the report is intended. Since the recipient is interested primarily in the recommendations, however, the introduction should be just long enough to explain the problem fully.

Assumptions/Approximations Made

This section could be included either as part of the introduction or as a separate section. Because the recommendations are based on a mathematical model that is an idealization of real life, the decision maker should be aware of any simplifying assumptions or approximations that are made. This allows the decision maker to make an independent judgment as to the model's usefulness.

Solution Approach/Computer Program Used

This section should be very brief (a sentence or two) and could also be part of a general introduction. In a slide presentation, it would most likely appear on one overhead outlining the procedure used. No details should be presented. A statement indicating that the problem was modeled as a linear program, a transportation model, or a periodic review inventory model may be all that is needed. For an audience not familiar with these terms, a brief one- or two-sentence description of the approach will suffice. Finally, a sentence detailing the computer program used (Excel, specialized software, etc.) lends credence to the validity of the results.

Results—Presentation/Analysis

This is the "meat" of the report and should be written concisely and clearly and include graphics. Charts and graphs should not only present the solution, but should also show *how the solution meets the restrictions of the problem*. Try to analyze the implications of the solution as they affect the business and note any unusual or striking conclusions that can be drawn from the results.

What-If Analyses

In this section, the management science team demonstrates to the decision makers that they have considered contingencies that might result from changes in the assumptions and parameters of the model. Some information can be obtained from sensitivity reports contained in standard computer output; other results may be generated by resolving the model to account for these changes. Although several possibilities may be analyzed, this section may lose some of its appeal if too many contingencies are considered.

Overall Recommendation

This section differs from the Results section in that it gives the best overall recommendations after considering the what-if contingencies. These recommendations may indeed differ from those of the basic model. These recommendations can be prominently displayed through the use of boxes, color, or some other highlighting device. Again, using charts, tables, and pictures were possible is preferable to presenting results in paragraph form.

Appendices

Material in appendices can be much more technical. An appendix is the place to put supporting computer output or hand calculations, or to detail any approaches used. Depending on the recipients of the report, an appendix may include a complete mathematical model formulation, replete with mathematical symbols and notation.

BUSINESS MEMO FOR DELTA HARDWARE

We now present a business memo for Delta management based on the results from the model developed and solved in Section 1.4. As with all memos presented in this text, it will be assumed to be prepared by a team of management science consultants known as the Student Consulting Group.

In the following memo, using a few short paragraphs, the problem is clearly laid out, the assumptions are stated, and the approach is given. The results are then presented and the major findings highlighted.

What-if analyses include a statement of the effect of changes in subcontractor pricing (which can be determined directly form the computer output) and a graph showing how the total cost is affected by the production levels of 6000, 7000, 8000, 9000, and 10,000 gallons at the Phoenix plant. An overall recommendation is then presented in an easy-to-read table. Finally, other factors that could substantially affect costs are recommended for future study.

For space reasons, no appendices are given. In addition to the computer printout of the solution and total cost values for the various possible production levels at the Phoenix plant, such appendices might include (1) the complete mathematical model; (2) an analysis of the forecasted production level at Phoenix for the next month; and (3) calculations of the per gallon costs at the Phoenix plant. These appendices would be based on discussions of these topics developed earlier in this chapter.

·SCG·
STUDENT CONSULTING GROUP

MEMORANDUM

To: Patricia Winters
            Delta Hardware Stores
From: Student Consulting Group
Subj: Shipment Plan for Paint from the Phoenix Plant

Delta Hardware Stores is seeking a shipping policy for paint from its Phoenix plant and an ordering policy of paint from its subcontractor to meet demand at its warehouses in San Jose, Fresno, and Azusa. The objective is to minimize the overall total cost of next month's operations.

The current company policy is to ship only trucks fully loaded with 1000 gallons of paint from the Phoenix plant to the warehouse cities. To obtain the lowest shipping fees and a $5 per gallon price for paint from your subcontractor, Delta's policy requires that shipments from its subcontractor must also be in 1000-gallon batches. You have directed that no more than 5000 gallons of paint be purchased next month from the subcontractor.

Since monthly production at the Phoenix plant has not been constant, production for the upcoming month was forecasted using production data of the past 12 months, excluding the period in which the plant was shut down for machine overhaul. Direct and indirect production and shipping costs attributed to the manufacture and distribution of the paint from the Phoenix plant were supplied by the accounting department.

Using these data, your problem was formulated as a transportation problem and solved using an Excel spreadsheet.

RESULTS
Based on a forecast of an 8000-gallon production level at the Phoenix plant for the coming month and the orders from the warehouse cities, we recommend the shipping pattern shown in Table I.

TABLE I Recommended Shipping Pattern for a Projected Production Capacity of 8000 Gallons

From	To	Gallons	Cost
Phoenix	San Jose	1000	$4,050
	Fresno	2000	$7,500
	Azusa	5000	$18,250
Subcontractor	San Jose	3000	$18,600
	Total Cost		$48,400

Shipments should be at these levels, unless the subcontractor lowers its ordering/shipping costs by more than $0.50 per gallon to Fresno or by more than $0.30 per gallon to Azusa. Below these values, it would be more cost effective for the subcontractor to send paint to Fresno or Azusa, respectively. As a result, Delta would decrease its shipment of paint from the Phoenix plant to those cities and increase its shipment of paint from Phoenix to San Jose by a similar amount.

Because monthly production levels at the Phoenix plant have varied, we have examined the effects of production levels between 6000 and 10,000 gallons. Figure I depicts the reduction in the total cost with increasing production levels from 6000 to 10,000 gallons at the Phoenix plant. These cost levels are attained as follows:

Achieving Minimum Total Cost

1. Fill the Fresno order from the Phoenix plant.
2. Fill as much of the Azusa order as possible from the Phoenix plant.
3. Use any remaining paint at the Phoenix plant to fill as much of the San Jose order as possible.
4. Meet the outstanding demand at any warehouse through shipments from the subcontractor.

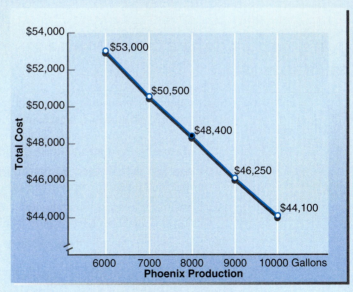

FIGURE I Total Cost vs. Phoenix Production

RECOMMENDATION

Table II summarizes the recommended shipping patterns for the month based on production levels at the Phoenix plant varying between 6000 and 10,000 gallons.

TABLE II   Recommended Shipping Patterns

Plant Production	Shipments From	To San Jose	To Fresno	To Azusa
6000	Phoenix plant		2000	4000
	Subcontractor	4000		1000
7000	Phoenix plant		2000	5000
	Subcontractor	4000		
8000	Phoenix plant	1000	2000	5000
	Subcontractor	3000		
9000	Phoenix plant	2000	2000	5000
	Subcontractor	2000		
10,000	Phoenix plant	3000	2000	5000
	Subcontractor	1000		

PROPOSAL FOR ADDITIONAL STUDY

Production levels at the Phoenix plant may not be in 1000-gallon units. If production falls between 1000-gallon units, it may well be more cost effective to ship a large partial shipment and pay increased per gallon fees to the subcontractor than to pay the storage costs necessary to carry an inventory of a few hundred gallons of paint from this month to the next at the Phoenix plant. An analysis of these storage costs, partial truckload shipment costs from the Phoenix plant, and increased per gallon fees by the subcontractor should be conducted.

The Student Consulting Group is available to assist Delta Hardware in obtaining these data and determining optimal policies under these modified conditions.

1.6   Using Spreadsheets in Management Science Models

Spreadsheets have become a powerful tool in management science modeling. The following are just some of the reasons for their growing importance.

1. Data are often submitted to the modeler in a spreadsheet.
2. Data can easily be turned into information on the spreadsheet using formulas, embedded functions, and statistical or optimization subroutines.
3. Data and information can easily be turned into informative visual displays using spreadsheet charting and graphing functions.
4. Spreadsheets have become the de facto "language of business."

Although many spreadsheets are available on the market (including Quattro Pro, Lotus 1-2-3, and Microsoft Works), Microsoft Excel has emerged as the industry leader. Therefore, Excel is illustrated in every chapter throughout this text.

All versions of Excel have a rich set of instructions, included functions, and subroutines. We assume the reader has access to a version of Excel 97 or Excel 2000 that includes the Data Analysis statistical package and Solver optimization package under the Tools menu. These packages are also available on earlier versions of Excel, although there are very slight differences. If you do not have either or both of these packages visible under the Tools menu:

1.   From the Tools menu and click on Add-Ins.

2.   To add Data Analysis, click on **Analysis ToolPak** and **Analysis ToolPak-VBA** (see Figure 1.5).

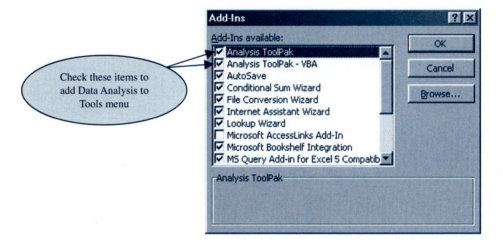

FIGURE 1.5
Add-Ins Required to Add
Data Analysis to the
Tools Menu

3.   To add Solver, click on **Solver Add-In** (see Figure 1.6).

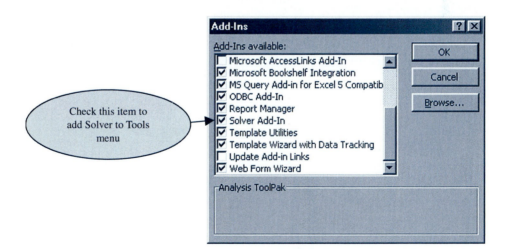

FIGURE 1.6
Add-In Required to Add
Solver to the Tools Menu

If either of these is unavailable, a complete reinstall of Excel may be necessary to include these library functions.

WHAT EXCEL KNOWLEDGE IS ASSUMED

We assume only a basic working knowledge of Excel. The spreadsheets in this text use no macros. In fact, simple arithmetic functions are used most frequently in the spreadsheets. These and other functions and subroutines that are used in the text, together with illustrative examples, are summarized here. Many of them should already be in your repertoire; others you may be seeing for the first time; still others are explained in detail in subsequent chapters. You may wish to use this section for reference when Excel approaches are discussed in subsequent chapters.

ARITHMETIC OPERATIONS

Addition of cells A1 and B1:   = A1 + B1
Subtraction of cell B1 from A1:   = A1 − B1
Multiplication of cell A1 by B1:   = A1 * B1
Division of cell A1 by B1:   = A1 / B1
Cell A1 raised to the power in cell B1: = A1 ∧ B1

RELATIVE AND ABSOLUTE ADDRESSES

All row and column references are relative unless preceded by a "$" sign. When relative addresses are copied, the addresses change relative to the position of the original cell.

COPYING AND PASTING

Example 1: Suppose cell E5 is to be copied and pasted in cell G9.

- Column G is "to the right" two columns from column E. All <u>relative</u> column references will be adjusted two columns "to the right."
- Row 9 is "down" four rows from row 5. All <u>relative</u> row references will be adjusted "down" by four rows.

Consider the following formula in cell E5. Note the formula when it is copied and pasted into cell G9.

Cell E5: =A1 + B$3 + $C4 + $D$6
Cell G9: =C5 + D$3 + $C8 + $D$6

DRAGGING

Dragging occurs when:

- A cell or set of cells is selected by holding down the left mouse key.
- Then the cursor is placed over the lower right corner of the last cell selected until a large "+" sign appears.
- The left mouse key is held down and the cursor is moved to left or right across a row or up or down a column.

The effect is to copy the contents of the selected cell(s) to these adjacent cells. Relative addresses will change as the formula is dragged to adjacent cells.

Example 2: Suppose the contents in cell E5 is: =A1 + B$3 + $C4 + $D$6

Figure 1.7 shows the results in cells E6, E7, and E8 when cell E5 is dragged *DOWN* to cells E6:E8. (This means to cells E6, E7, and E8.)

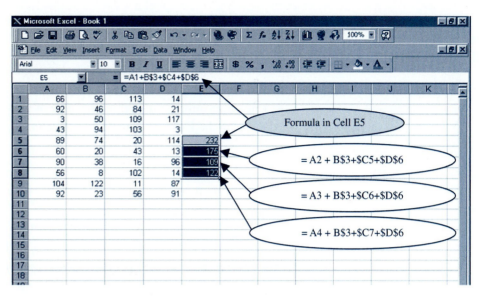

FIGURE 1.7   Dragging Cell E5 Down to Cells E6:E8

Figure 1.8 shows the results in cells F5, G5, and H5 when cell E5 is dragged *ACROSS* to cells F5:H5. (This means to cells F5, G5, and H5.)

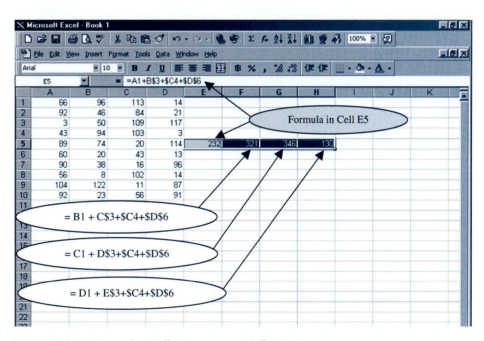

FIGURE 1.8   Dragging Cell E5 across to Cells F5:H5

THE F4 KEY

The F4 key acts like a toggle switch that will automatically put "$" signs in highlighted portions of formulas in the formula bar.

- Highlight the entire formula or a portion of a formula in the formula bar where you wish to insert "$" signs.

- Pressing the F4 key once will put "$" signs in front of all row and column references in the highlighted area of the formula.
- Pressing the F4 key a second time will put "$" signs in front of the row references only in the highlighted area of the formula.
- Pressing the F4 key a third time will put "$" signs in front of the column references only in the highlighted area of the formula.
- Pressing the F4 key a fourth time will eliminate the "$" signs altogether in the highlighted area of the formula.

Example 3: Suppose that = A3 + B5 − C7 is in the formula bar and that only A3 + B5 is highlighted.

- Pressing the F4 key once changes the formula to: $A3 + $B$5 − C7
- Pressing the F4 key a second time changes the formula to: A$3 + B$5 − C7
- Pressing the F4 key a third time changes the formula to: $A3 + $B5 − C7
- Pressing the F4 key a fourth time changes the formula to: A3 + B5 − C7

ARITHMETIC FUNCTIONS

SUM   *Example*: =SUM(A1:A3)
    Sums the entries in cells A1 to A3:
AVERAGE   *Example*: =AVERAGE(A1:A3)
    Average the entries in cells A1 to A3
SUMPRODUCT   *Example*: =SUMPRODUCT(A1:A3,B1:B3)
    Returns the result of A1*B1 + A2*B2 + A3*B3
ABS   *Example*: =ABS(A3)
    Returns the absolute value of the entry in cell A3
SQRT   *Example*: =SQRT(A3)
    Returns the square root of the entry in cell A3
MAX   *Example*: =MAX(A1:A9)
    Returns the maximum of the entries in cells A1:A9
MIN   *Example*: =MIN(A1:A9)
    Returns the minimum of the entries in cells A1:A9

STATISTICAL FUNCTIONS

RAND( )   *Example*: =RAND( )
    Generates a random number between 0 and 1 from a uniform distribution

Normal Distribution Probabilities and Values

NORMDIST   *Example*: =NORMDIST(25,20,3,TRUE)
    Returns $P(X < 25)$ from a normal distribution with mean $\mu = 20$ and standard deviation $\sigma = 3$
    (Note: FALSE returns the probability density)
NORMSDIST   *Example*: =NORMSDIST(1.78)
    Returns $P(Z < 1.78)$
NORMINV   *Example*: =NORMINV(.55,20,3)
    Returns the x value from a normal distribution with mean $\mu = 20$ and standard deviation $\sigma = 3$ such that 55% of the probability lies below x
NORMSINV   *Example*: =NORMSINV(.55)
    Returns the z value so that 55% of the probability lies below z

t-Distribution Probabilities and Values

TDIST   *Example*: =TDIST(1.5,12,1)
   Returns P(t > 1.5) from a t-distribution with 12 degrees of freedom)
   (Note: =TDIST(1.5,12,2) returns P(t < −1.5 or t > 1.5 from a t-distribution
   with 12 degrees on freedom)
TINV   *Example*: =TINV(.05,15)
   Returns the t-value that puts probability .025 in the upper tail above t and
   .025 in the lower tail below −t with 15 degrees of freedom

Other Probability Distributions

POISSON   *Example*: =POISSON(7,5,TRUE)
   Returns P(X ≤ 7) from a Poisson distribution with mean $\lambda = 5$.
   (Note: Poisson (7,5, FALSE) returns P(X = 7).)
EXPONDIST   *Example*: =EXPONDIST(40,1/20,TRUE)
   Returns P(X < 40) from an exponential distribution with mean $1/\mu = 20$.
   (Note: FALSE returns the probability density)

CONDITIONAL FUNCTIONS

IF   *Example*: =IF(A4>4,B1+B2,B1-B2)
   Adds cells B1 and B2 if cell A4 > 4, and subtracts cell B2 from cell B1 if A4 ≤ 4
SUMIF   *Example*: =SUMIF(F1:F12,">60",G1:G12)
   Sums the numbers in cells G1:G12 only if the corresponding numbers in cells
   F1:F12 are greater than 60
VLOOKUP   *Example*: =VLOOKUP(6.6,A1:E6,4)
   (See 5 × 6 table in Figure 1.9)
   If the entries in column A are sorted in ascending order, this returns the
   number in column D (the fourth column of the table defined by entries
   A1:E6) in the same row as the largest number in column A that is ≤6.6."
   (Note: If the entries in column A are in any order, =VLOOKUP(6.6,A1:E6,4,FALSE)
   returns the number in column D (the fourth column of the table) in the same
   row as the number in column A that exactly equals 6.6.)

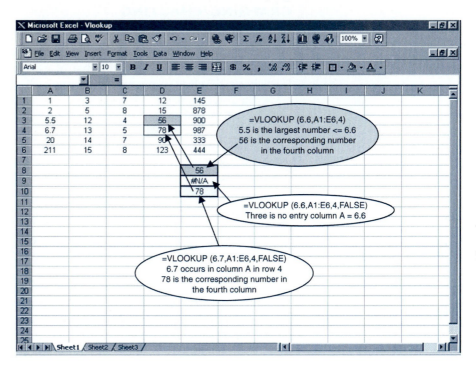

FIGURE 1.9
The VLOOKUP Function

HLOOKUP   *Example*: =HLOOKUP(10,A1:E6,5)

If the entries in row 1 are sorted in ascending order, this returns the number in row 5 in the same column as the largest number in row 1 that is ≤ 10 (Note: If the entries in row 1 are in any order, =HLOOKUP(10,A1:E6,5,FALSE) returns the number in row 5 in the same column as the the number in row 1 that exactly = 10)

STATISTICAL/OPTIMIZATION

Data Analysis

From the Tools menu, select Data Analysis. Among the entries we use in this text are the following:

Descriptive Statistics	Returns sample statistics, including the mean ($\bar{x}$), standard error ($s/\sqrt{n}$), sample standard deviation (s), sample variance (s^2), median, mode, and the $\pm$ part of the corresponding t-interval for a set of numbers.
Regression	Returns regression statistics, including the regression equation, the p-value for the F-test (Significance F), the p-value for the individual t-tests of the independent variables, and r^2.
Exponential Smoothing	Returns the exponentially smoothed values of a time series for a given value of the damping factor. This is discussed in detail in Chapter 7.
Anova	Returns the p-values for tests for differences among treatment means for single factor, randomized block (Two-Factor Without Replication) and two factor (Two-Factor With Replication) tests.

GRAPHING/CHARTING

Excel's chart wizard, located on the standard tool bar, allows us to create various kinds of graphs and charts. Clicking the chart wizard gives the dialogue box shown in Figure 1.10. This screen is the first of a structured series of step-by-step dialogue boxes that lead to a completed graph.

We will use the following charts in this text to represent sets of data:

Column charts
Line charts
Pie charts
Scatterplots
Floating bar charts (discussed in Chapter 5)

Each of these will be created using the Chart Wizard feature of Excel.

Hiding Rows or Columns

Sometimes for aesthetic purposes, certain rows or columns are hidden on the spreadsheet. The cells in these rows or columns usually contain data or formulas that are crucial for generating information displayed on the spreadsheet, but do not themselves contain information that needs to be expressed on the spreadsheet to the user.

FIGURE 1.10 Chart Wizard

To hide a row or set of continuous rows:

- Highlight the rows by clicking on the first numbered row to be hidden in the leftmost column (the column with the row numbers in it) and dragging down to highlight all rows to be hidden.
- Then click the right mouse key and select Hide.

To hide a column or set of continuous columns:

- Highlight the columns by clicking on the top row of the first column to be hidden (the row with the column letters in it) and dragging across to highlight all columns to be hidden.
- Then click the right mouse key and select Hide.

1.7   Summary

Management science adapts the scientific principle to executive decision making. The management science approach consists of four steps: (1) problem definition, (2) mathematical modeling, (3) solution of the model, and (4) communication and monitoring of results.

It is essential that both the decision maker and the management science analysts agree on the exact problem to be solved. Once agreement is reached, time, cost, and complexity issues are considered when choosing an appropriate mathematical model. Solutions to management science models should include examinations of appropriate "what-if" analyses. A report or presentation of results should be carefully prepared in a clear and concise format utilizing tables, charts, and graphs to convey model results effectively. Spreadsheets have become a common vehicle to display, model, and solve many management science problems.

TABLE 1.3 Advantages and Disadvantages of Using the Management Science Approach

Advantages	Disadvantages
1. Helps the decision maker focus on the true goals of the problem	1. Uses idealized models that may be oversimplified
2. Helps deal with a problem in its entirety	2. May not be cost effective
3. Helps sort out data that are relevant to the problem	3. Can be misused by untrained personnel
4. Describes the problem in concise mathematical relationships	4. Requires quantification of all model inputs
5. Helps reveal cause-and-effect relations in the problem	5. May create models requiring excessive computer resources
6. Can be used to solve complex problems with large amounts of data	6. May create models that are difficult to explain to users
7. Yields an optimal (or at least a good) solution	7. Can yield suspect or unsatisfactory results due to a rapidly changing environment

Management science modeling offers the manager the opportunity to develop good solutions to complex problems based on supporting quantitative data. The management science approach has both advantages and disadvantages. Some of these are listed in Table 1.3.

ON THE CD-ROM

- Excel spreadsheet of a mathematical model   **DELTA HARDWARE.xls**

- Review of Probability and Statistics   **Supplement CD1**

- Problems 41–50   **Additional Problems/Cases**

Problems

1. List the four steps in the management science process and give a brief statement about the importance of each step.

2. Ford Motor Company requires thousands of parts to build and assemble cars at its plants. The Villa Park Ford dealership requires parts to service its customers' Ford products. Both are concerned with finding optimal inventory policies.

Ford Motor Company employs a large staff of personnel who use mathematical models to develop optimal inventory policies, whereas Villa Park Ford relies on the input of one service manager, who uses, at best, crude "mathematical models." Discuss why it is important for Ford Motor Company to employ sophisticated mathematical models to determine its inventory policies (with the associated expense of many high-paying analytical jobs), whereas it would probably not be worthwhile for Villa Park Ford to employ a full-time inventory analyst.

3. Crestline Bank would like to minimize its labor costs by hiring as few tellers as possible while still maintaining a stated service level. In particular, it desires the average waiting time for a customer from the time he or she enters a line until the transaction is completed to be at most three minutes. Define:

T = the number of tellers employed by Crestline Bank

$W(T)$ = a function giving the average customer waiting time when there are T tellers

Write a mathematical model for this problem. Is it an optimization or a prediction model?

4. The Dixie Champions tennis tournament will be held in Charlotte, North Carolina, on August 15, and it must be decided whether the event should be scheduled indoors or outdoors. Weather is a factor. For simplicity, assume that on August 15 Charlotte will either (a) be exceedingly hot and muggy, (b) be very pleasant, (c) have mild showers, or (d) have severe rain. Weather will certainly affect attendance (and profits), but much more so if the tournament is held outdoors. The following table relates predicted weather conditions to expected profit:

	Muggy	Pleasant	Showers	Rain
Outdoors	$25,000	$100,000	$30,000	−$25,000
Indoors	$45,000	$ 50,000	$45,000	$35,000

Define:

X_1 = the number of outdoor tournaments held
X_2 = the number of indoor tournaments held

a. Write the functional and variable constraints that express the fact that exactly one tournament will be held.
b. Write the objective function and (easily) solve for the optimal solution if the objective is to maximize the minimum expected profit.

5. Flores File Company makes inexpensive, grey two-drawer, three-drawer, and four-drawer filing cabinets. It estimates that it makes a net profit of $4 for each two-drawer model, $6 for each three-drawer model, and $10 for each four-drawer model produced.
a. Write a mathematical expression for the objective of maximizing total net profit.
b. The filing cabinets are made from $\frac{3}{8}''$-thick sheet metal. Each two-drawer cabinet requires 40 square feet of sheet metal; each three-drawer cabinet requires 55 square feet; and each four-drawer requires 70 square feet. For the current production run, Flores has 25,000 square feet of $\frac{3}{8}''$ sheet metal available. Write a constraint that states the following: "The number of square feet of sheet metal used cannot exceed the amount of sheet metal available."

6. The Institute for Operations Research and Management Science (INFORMS) has contracted with Sentinel Security to provide security service for its upcoming three-day, four-night national meeting in New York at a cost of $B.

During the meeting hours from 8:00 A.M. to 6:00 P.M., Sentinel will pay its security guards $D per hour. In the evening, security guards will be paid a lesser amount of $E per hour. INFORMS requires that at least N guards be on duty during the evening. During the day there should be at least two guards as well as one additional guard for every 1000 people attending the meeting. In addition to paying for its guards, Sentinel Security expects to have fixed expenses of $F (for equipment, communications, etc.) during the meeting.

Net profit to the firm is attained by subtracting its payments to its guards plus the fixed expenses from the contracted amount negotiated with INFORMS.

a. Formulate a model shell for this simplified problem. The objective of which is to maximize the net profit to Sentinel Security for supplying security service for T attendees to the national meeting in New York using the following decision variables:

X_1 = number of guards needed each day
X_2 = number of guards needed each evening

b. Explain why this problem of maximizing net profit is equivalent to minimizing the variable cost of payments to its security guards.
c. INFORMS expects 2000 attendees, and it wishes to have at least two guards on duty each evening. If the contracted price from INFORMS is $10,000, fixed costs are expected to be $1000, and Sentinel pays its guards $15 per hour for day security and $12 per hour for evening security, develop a complete mathematical model for security at the INFORMS meeting.
d. Suppose attendance is expected to be 2200. Now what would be the model? (Did you forget to include in your constraints that the number of guards must be an integer?)

7. Sometimes different managers or executives approach the same data with different objectives. Circuit Guys is a retail computer store that displays the latest computers from COMPAQ and IBM. The store averages a profit of $200 on every COMPAQ system sold and $300 on every IBM system sold. For each COMPAQ system displayed, the estimated probability that Circuit Guys will sell the system on a particular day is .02. Each IBM system displayed has an estimated probability of .01 of sale on that day.
a. One manager at Circuit Guys suggests that, since this is a new store, it should maximize the total number of units on display. Write the expression that models this objective.
b. Another manager feels that the way to impress corporate headquarters is to show a large number of sales at the new store. Write the expression that models this objective.
c. Still another manager maintains that the bottom line is what is important. He feels that, in the long run, maximizing expected profit is what the stockholders want. Write the expression that models this objective.

8. Lawn fertilizer is rated according to three levels: nitrogen, phosphorus, and potassium. The nitrogen content affects the greening; the phosphorus affects the sturdiness of the root structure; and the potassium affects the disease-fighting capabilities of the plants. For example, the rating of one Scotts Turf Builder product is 27–3–4, meaning that it consists of 27% nitrogen, 3% phosphorus, and 4% potassium.

Beauty Grow plans to market two lawn-fertilizing products, which it will call Beauty Green and Beauty Turf. It plans to sell a 20-pound bag of Beauty Green for $G and a 20-pound bag of Beauty Turf for $T. Lawn fertilizer is a mixture of many different compounds, but, for simplicity, let us suppose that it is a mixture of three, each of which has various amounts of nitrogen, phosphorus, and potassium. They sell for C_1, C_2, and C_3 *per pound*, respectively.

During a production run, limited amounts of each of the three compounds are available (L_1, L_2, and L_3, respectively), and demand for bags of each of the two lawn fertilizers (D_1 and D_2) is limited.

a. What are the uncontrollable inputs (i.e., the parameters) for this problem?

b. The controllable inputs (i.e., the decision variables) for this problem are the total amount (pounds) of each of the three compounds that are to be mixed into bags of Beauty Green and the total number of pounds of each of the three compounds that are to be mixed into bags of Beauty Turf. Define six decision variables for this problem. Be sure to include the units for your decision variables. (This is very important!)

9. For the Beauty Grow Fertilizer production problem (problem 8).

a. Use an appropriate sum of the decision variables to write model shells for the total number of: (i) pounds of Compound 1 used; (ii) pounds of Compound 2 used, and (iii) pounds of Compound 3 used.

b. Write model shells for: (i) bags of Beauty Green produced; and (ii) bags of Beauty Turf produced.

c. Using your answers to parts (a) and (b), write a model shell expressing the constraints on the amount of each compound used and the number of bags of each fertilizer produced.

d. Write a model shell for the profit function.

10. For the Beauty Grow Fertilizer production problem (problem 18), the following table represents the percentage of nitrogen, phosphorus, and potassium in each of the three compounds:

	Nitrogen	Phosphorus	Potassium
Compound 1	$N_1\%$	$P_1\%$	$K_1\%$
Compound 2	$N_2\%$	$P_2\%$	$K_2\%$
Compound 3	$N_3\%$	$P_3\%$	$K_3\%$

Beauty Green is to be labeled 25–5–5, while Beauty Turf is to be labeled 10–18–5. These values are the minimum percentages of nitrogen, phosphorus, and potassium, respectively, that must be in each bag.

a. Write a model shell that states that the minimum percentage of nitrogen in Beauty Green is 25%. Do this by expressing the actual percentage of nitrogen as a weighted average of the percentage of nitrogen in each compound. It will take the following form:

(Proportion of Compound 1 in Beauty Green) (N_1)
+ (Proportion of Compound 2 in Beauty Green) (N_2)
+ (Proportion of Compound 3 in Beauty Green) (N_3)
$$\geq 25$$

b. Write a model shell stating that the minimum percentage of nitrogen in Beauty Turf is 10%. Do this by expressing the actual percentage of nitrogen as a weighted average of the percentage of nitrogen in each compound. It will take the following form:

(Proportion of Compound 1 in Beauty Turf) (N_1)
+ (Proportion of Compound 2 in Beauty Turf) (N_2)
+ (Proportion of Compound 3 in Beauty Turf) (N_3)
$$\geq 10$$

c. Constraints for the percentages of phosphorus and potassium in Beauty Green and Beauty Turf have the same form as those in (a) and (b). Develop a complete mathematical model for Beauty Grow Fertilizer using the following values of the parameters:

Selling price of a bag of Beauty Green:	$4.00
Selling price of a bag of Beauty Turf:	$3.50
Cost per pound of Compound 1:	$0.15
Cost per pound of Compound 2:	$0.12
Cost per pound of Compound 3:	$0.10
Demand (bags) of Beauty Green:	1000
Demand (bags) of Beauty Turf:	800
Availability (pounds) of Compound 1:	15,000
Availability (pounds) of Compound 2:	20,000
Availability (pounds) of Compound 3:	30,000

	Nitrogen	Phosphorus	Potassium
Compound 1	30%	20%	10%
Compound 2	10%	30%	10%
Compound 3	40%	10%	0%

Problems 11–40 are designed to illustrate the Excel skills referred to in Section 1.6. Problems 11–25 refer to the on page 43 spreadsheet of greeting card sales made by Ann, Bob, Charles, David, and Ellen. (See file: Greeting Card Sales.xls on the CD-ROM.)

11. In cell G6 write a formula giving Ann's total sales using the SUM function.

12. Drag the formula in G6 to cells G7:G10. Did this give the right values for Bob's, Charles's, David's, and Ellen's total sales?

13. Without using the SUM function, enter a formula in cell B11 giving the total sales of boxes of Christmas cards.

14. Drag the formula in cell B11 to cells C11:F11. Did this give the right values for total sales of boxes of Birthday, All Occasion, Thank You, and Mixed cards?

15. In cell B12, enter a formula for the total profit made by these five persons selling Christmas cards. Do not enter any numbers, only cell references.

16. Drag the formula in cell B12 to cells C12:F12. Did this give you the right values for the total profit on boxes of Birthday, All Occasion, Thank You, and Mixed cards?

17. Using the SUMPRODUCT function, enter a formula in cell H6 giving Ann's total profit from selling all types of cards.

18. Drag the formula in H6 to cells H7:H10. Do not enter any numbers, only cell references. Did this give the right values for Bob's, Charles's, David's, and Ellen's total

Greeting Cards Sales

profit from selling all types of cards? If not, it is because you did not use absolute addresses for the profits per box. If that is the case, go back to cell H6. In the formula bar, highlight each unit profit and use the F4 key to make the reference absolute. After making all the references to unit profits absolute, now drag the formula in H6 to cells H7:H10. Now, did this give the right values for Bob's, Charles's, David's, and Ellen's total profit from selling all types of cards?

19. In cell B13, use the MAX function in order to determine the maximum Christmas card sales.

20. Drag the formula in cell B13 to cells C13:F13. Did this give the maximum values of Birthday, All Occasion, Thank You, and Mixed card sales?

21. In cell I5 enter "Most Christmas Sales." In cell I6, enter an IF statement that will compare Ann's Christmas card sales to the maximum value in cell B13. If it is equal to this value, Ann's name (the entry in cell A6) should be printed in I6; otherwise, nothing should be printed—this is accomplished by entering " ".

22. Make sure the reference to cell B13 is absolute in the formula in the IF statement formula in cell I6. Drag cell I6 formula down to I7:I10. Did it print the person with the most Christmas card sales?

23. Instead of the profit per box values in row 4, assume that Ann's profit is calculated as follows: $0.12(\text{Christmas Cards Sales})^2 + 0.02(\text{Birthday Card Sales})^3 + 3.50\sqrt{(\text{All Occasion Card Sales})} + 0.05(\text{Thank You Card Sales}) * (\text{Mixed Card Sales})$. In cell C15, determine Ann's total profit.

24. In cell C16, use an IF statement that compares Ann's profit using the new method proposed in problem 33 (given in cell C15) with that of the old method proposed in problem 27 (given in cell H6). If the new profit is higher, "NEW" should be printed in cell C16; otherwise, "OLD" should be printed in the cell.

25. Suppose we wish to calculate the sum of all Mixed card sales of those persons who sold less than 20 boxes of Christmas cards. In cell C19, use a SUMIF command to determine this quantity.

Questions 26–29 refer to the following situation: The time it takes a professor to travel from his home to his office is normally distributed with a mean of 47 minutes and a standard deviation of 5.5 minutes. Create a spreadsheet to answer questions 26–29.

26. a. In cell B1 enter a formula to determine the probability that it will take the professor less than one-half hour to travel from his home to his office.
   b. Verify this by hand using the Table of Normal Probabilities in Appendix A.

27. a. In cell B2 enter a formula to determine the probability that it will take the professor more than one hour to travel from his home to his office.
   b. Verify this by hand using the Table of Normal Probabilities in Appendix A.

28. a. In cell B3 enter a formula to determine the probability that it will take the professor between 40 and 50 minutes to travel from his home to his office.
   b. Verify this by hand using the Table of Normal Probabilities in Appendix A.

29. a. In cell B4 enter a formula to determine by what time he is 95% sure of reaching his office if he leaves home at 8:00 A.M.
   b. Verify this by hand using the Table of Normal Probabilities in Appendix A.

	A	B	C	D	E	F	G	H	I	J
1	NAME	# Other Tests	Study Hours	Test Grade						
2	Ann	0	6	75						
3	Bill	1	6	66						
4	Carl	1	7	80						
5	Dave	0	9	90						
6	Ellen	1	3	50						
7										
8										
9										
10										

Test Scores vs. Study Time and Number of Other Tests

Questions 30–38 refer to the spreadsheet above in which the grades of five randomly selected students on a management science test are recorded (column D) along with the amount of time each studied for the test (column C) and the number of other tests the students had on the same day (column B). (See file: Test Grades.xls on the CD-ROM.)

30. Using the Chart Wizard, construct a scatterplot between Test Grade and Study Hours. Add a trendline by right mouse clicking on any data point and selecting Add Trendline.

31. a. Using Descriptive Statistics on column C from the Data Analysis menu, determine the best estimate for the mean and standard deviation of the study time of all students for the test.
    b. Verify these values by solving for $\bar{x}$ and s by hand.

32. a. Using the results from Descriptive Statistics, determine a 95% confidence interval for the average study time of all students for the test.
    b. Verify these values by generating the interval by hand using the t-table in Appendix D.

33. It has been hypothesized that, on the average, students study more than five hours for the test. Calculate the t-value for this test in cell B8 using the values for the mean and standard error from the results of Descriptive Statistics. Compare this t-value to the critical t-value found in Appendix D for $\alpha = .05$. What is your conclusion?

34. Refer to problem 33. In cell B9, use the TDIST command for the t-value found in cell B8 in order to generate the p-value for this test. What is this p-value? Do you reach the same conclusion as that found in problem 33 if you use $\alpha = .05$?

35. Using Regression from the Data Analysis menu, perform a multiple regression analysis on the dependent variable Test Grade and the two independent variables, Study Hours and # of Other Tests. What is the best linear relationship between these variables?

36. Refer to the output from the multiple regression analysis in problem 35.
    a. Why can you conclude that at least one of the independent variables is significant in predicting test scores? (Use $\alpha = .05$.)

    b. Why can you conclude that one of the independent variables is not significant in this model? (Use $\alpha = .05$.)

37. Using Regression from the Data Analysis menu, perform a simple linear regression on Test Grade using Study Hours only as the independent variable.
    a. What is the best linear relationship between these variables?
    b. Verify this by solving for the regression equation by hand.

38. Why can you conclude that a linear relation exists between Test Grade and Study Hours? Use $\alpha = .05$.
    a. Use the results from the Regression output to answer this question.
    b. Verify this by solving for the appropriate t-value by hand and comparing the result to a critical t-value from Appendix D.

Questions 39–40 refer to the following.
Suppose the probability distribution for the number of days of rain in San Antonio, Texas, in November is as follows:

Days With Rain	Probability
2	.45
3	.20
4	.15
5	.12
6	.08

39. In cell B1 type the word "Prob." and enter the probabilities in cells B2:B6. In cell C1 type the word "Rain" and enter the number of days with rain in cells C2:C6. In cell A1 type the word "Cumulative" for cumulative probability. In cell A2 enter 0, meaning the probability of up to *but not including* two days of rain is 0. In cells A2:A6 write formulas using cell values already in column A and in column B to model the cumulative probabilities of rain up to *but not including* the number of days in column C. *Hint:* The value in cell A6 should be .92.

40. Simulate a November month in San Antonio as follows.
    a. In cell A10 enter the formula RAND( ) to generate a random number between 0 and 1.

b. Note that if you make other entries on the spreadsheet the number in cell A10 will change. To fix this value, COPY cell A10. Then with the cursor still in A10, go to Edit—Paste Special and put a bullet in Values and click OK. The number will not change now.

c. In cell A11 use the VLOOKUP command to generate the number of days using the random number in A10 and the table in cells A2:C6. Note that days of rain is the third column of this table. The result is a simulated number of days of rain in San Antonio in November.

PROBLEMS 41–50 ARE ON THE CD

CASE STUDY

CASE 1: Gunther's Appliance Corporation

Gunther's Appliance Corporation is a small manufacturer that produces toasters, microwave ovens, mixers, blenders, food processors, and steamers. A mathematical model was developed to determine the optimal production quantities for the month of July in order to maximize the company's total daily profit. Twenty constraints were included in the model, as outlined below:

Constraints	Relation
1	≤48 hours of production time are available.
2–6	Limits must be placed on five materials used in production.
7–8	Between 5% and 25% of production must be toasters.
9–10	Between 5% and 25% of production must be microwaves.
11–12	Between 5% and 25% of production must be mixers.
13–14	Between 5% and 25% of production must be blenders.
15–16	Between 5% and 25% of production must be food processors.
17–18	Between 5% and 25% of production must be steamers.
19	At least 50% of production must be toasters, mixers, and blenders.
20	At most 150 total items are to be produced daily.

The following figures show the output generated by the Solver option of Microsoft Excel.

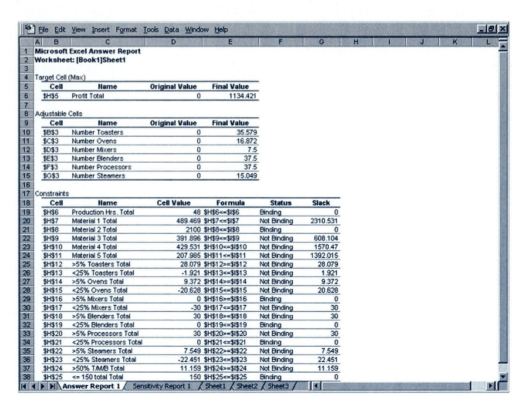

FIGURE CASE 1.1
Answer Report for Gunther's Appliance Corporation

FIGURE CASE 1.2
Sensitivity Report for
Gunther's Appliance
Corporation

Although a complete discussion of this output is presented in Chapter 2, the following is a brief explanation.

1. The optimal daily profit is the Final Value of the target cell on the Answer Report (cell H5).
2. The optimal solution is given as the Final Values of the adjustable cells on both the Answer Report and the Sensitivity Report.
3. The Cell Value in the Constraints Section of the Answer Report gives the total value of the left side of the constraints. The difference between the left side and the right side of the constraints is the Slack. If the Slack is 0, it is called a Binding constraint.
4. If a change is made to a single objective function coefficient, the optimal solution will not change as long as the increase or decrease is within the limits specified by the Allowable Increase and Allowable

Decrease of the Adjustable cells on the Sensitivity Report. (Note 1E + 30 means "Infinity.")

5. A shadow price is the amount the objective function value changes per unit change in the right hand side value of the constraint as long as the change is within the Allowable Increase and Allowable Decrease specified in the Constraints Section of the Sensitivity Report.

Based on the output, write a brief memorandum to communicate relevant information that would be of interest to a potential decision maker at Gunther's. In your report, use appropriate charts, graphs, or tables to convey:

1. Your recommendation for daily production during July
2. How the constraints would be satisfied

Linear and Integer Programming Models

WITH ASSETS TOTALING over $4.4 billion, San Miguel Corporation (http://www.sanmiguel.com.ph), the most diversified company in the Philippines, generates over 4% of that country's gross national product. Beverage production and distribution is a major component of the company's operations. San Miguel produces six brands of beer and bottles three wine and spirit brands at three different sites. It also bottles five brands of soft drinks for Coca-Cola Bottlers Philippines at 18 bottling plants.

Among its other endeavors are the manufacturing of packaging materials, such as glass containers, plastic crates, polybags, and cardboard boxes, and the development and manufacturing of animal feeds for its chicken, hog, and cattle interests. Other sources of profit are the manufacture and distribution of ice cream, butter, cheese, and other dairy and nondairy products, the raising of prawns for export, and the pro-

cessing and trading of coconut oil.

Since 1971, management science, in general, and linear models, in particular, have had a significant impact on the company's bottom line. Projects in which linear models have played a major role include blending problems for determining animal feed mixes and ice cream base composition, distribution problems for determining allocations among its 68 production facilities and 230 sales offices, and marketing problems, such as minimizing the cost of television advertising.

Over the course of several years, use of these models has saved the company millions of dollars, allowing it to expand at a vigorous rate. By 1995, San Miguel had become the first non-Japanese and non-Australian firm to rank in the top 20 Asian food and beverage companies. As it looks to the future, San Miguel will continue to refine and develop integrative linear models in order to enhance its growth and financial strength.

2.1   Introduction to Linear Programming

Mathematical programming is the branch of management science that deals with solving optimization problems, in which we want to maximize a function (such as profit, expected return, or efficiency) or minimize a function (such as cost, time, or distance), usually in a constrained environment. The recommended course of action is known as a *program*; hence, the term **mathematical programming** is used to describe such problems.

As discussed in Chapter 1, a constrained mathematical programming model consists of three components: (1) a set of *decision variables* that can be controlled or determined by the decision maker; (2) an *objective function* that is to be maximized or minimized; and (3) a set of *constraints* that describe the restrictive set of conditions that must be satisfied by any solution to the model. The most widely used mathematical programming models are **linear programming (LP) models**:

> ### Linear Programming Models
>
> A **linear programming model** is a model that seeks to maximize or minimize a *linear* objective function subject to a set of *linear* constraints.

That's a mouthful! But all that means is that the objective function and constraints contain only mathematical terms involving variables (X_1, X_2, X_3, etc.) that are raised to the first power (e.g., $5X_1$, $-2X_2$, or $0X_3$). Models with terms such as X_1^2, X_1X_2, X_1/X_2, e^{X_2} and $\sqrt{X_1}$ are classified as **nonlinear programming (NLP) models**. Linear models in which at least one of the variables is required to be integer-valued are called **integer linear programming (ILP) models**.

Large companies such as the San Miguel Corporation, Texaco, American Airlines, and General Motors have used linear models to affect efficiency and improve the bottom line. But linear models can also be applied in smaller venues. In fact a wide variety of cases lend themselves to linear modeling, including problems from such diverse areas as manufacturing, marketing, investing, advertising, trucking, shipping, agriculture, nutrition, e-commerce, restaurant operations, and the travel industry.

WHY LINEAR PROGRAMMING MODELS ARE IMPORTANT

Linear programming models are important for three basic reasons.

> ### Why Linear Programming Models are Important
>
> 1. Many problems naturally lend themselves to a linear programming formulation, and many other problems can be closely approximated by models with this structure.
> 2. Efficient solution techniques exist for solving models of this type.
> 3. The output generated from linear programming packages provides useful "what-if" information concerning the sensitivity of the optimal solution to changes in the model's coefficients.

ASSUMPTIONS OF LINEAR MODELS

Because linear models are solved so efficiently, linear programming formulations have proven quite valuable for solving numerous problems in business and government. As with all mathematical models, however, certain inherent assumptions must be made in order to use the linear programming approach. The modeler must be keenly aware of the impact of these assumptions on the real-life situation being modeled; if the assumptions are deemed unacceptable, the model must be modified or another model developed.

All linear models satisfy three assumptions.

Assumptions for Linear Programming and Integer Linear Programming Models

1. The parameter values are known with *certainty*.
2. The above function and constraints exhibit *constant returns to scale*.
3. There are *no interactions* between the decision variables.

The **certainty assumption** asserts that all parameters of the problem are known, fixed constants. Although this assumption is crucial for solving a linear model, as we show in Section 2.4, the "optimal solution" to a linear model may be valid within a range of the parameter values. Hence, in some cases, when a model includes a parameter whose value is not known precisely, the model may still successfully be solved by approximating this parameter value and assuming it to be constant.

The **constant returns to scale (proportionality) assumption** implies that, if for instance, one unit of an item adds $4 to profit and requires three hours to produce, then 500 units will contribute $4(500) = $2000 to profit and require $3(500) = 1500$ hours to produce. This assumption is frequently violated in practice. For example, a good deal of time and expense might go into setting up a production run for a given set of products. Thus, if only one item were produced, the unit production cost would be quite high. As more and more of the products are made, however, production costs per unit tend to stabilize, yielding a relatively fixed unit profit. Then, as even more are produced, from a supply and demand perspective, selling prices may have to be reduced, resulting in a decrease in the unit profits. When using a linear model, we must assume the constant returns to scale assumption is reasonable within the range of possible values of the decision variables.

The **additivity assumption** implies that the total value of some function can be found by simply adding the linear terms. Suppose in the model above that X_1, X_2, and X_3 were the amounts of three different but similar items produced during a production run. In this case, it might be argued that since the expertise and materials required to produce all three items are similar, a cost saving would result from producing all three types of items. However, in linear models, the additivity assumption implies no such cost saving would result.

In addition to these three assumptions, *linear programming models* also require the assumption that the variables are continuous. This **continuity assumption** implies that the decision variables can take on *any* value within the limits of the functional constraints. In *integer linear programming models*, for those variables restricted only to integer values, this assumption is replaced by an **integer assumption**.

Although these assumptions might appear to be overly restrictive, they frequently provide "close enough" approximations for many practical problems. As a result, linear programming techniques have been applied successfully in many diverse areas including those in Table 2.1. Several of these applications are illustrated in examples and end-of-chapter exercises in this and ensuing chapters.

TABLE 2.1   Applications of Linear Programming

Application Area	Objective	Constraints
Manufacturing	Determine production quantities that maximize profit	• Labor availability • Resource availability
Finance	Allocate funds to maximize expected return	• Diversification • Acceptable risk levels
Advertising	Select a media mix that maximizes exposure to a target population	• Budget • Length of advertising campaign
Worker Training	Assign workers to production and training activities to maximize profit while building a workforce	• Production quotas • Number of qualified instructors and trainees available
Construction	Plan tasks and assign labor to meet a production schedule	• Ordering of tasks • Project deadline
Oil Refining	Blend raw crude oils into different grades of gasolines	• Supply of raw crude oil and demand for different grades of gasolines • Required characteristics of the different grades of gasolines
Transportation	Assign delivery of resources to minimize transportation costs	• Supply/demand of product • Shipping capacities
Agriculture	Determine a plant rotation plan to maximize long-term profit	• Anticipated demand for crops • Rotation restrictions
Military Operations	Assign troops and material to accomplish a military mission	• Troop availability/ training • Transportation of resources

2.2   A Linear Programming Model— A Prototype Example

In this section we illustrate the procedure used to construct linear programming models by considering the situation faced by Galaxy Industries. Although this prototype model requires only two decision variables, it will be used to develop the concepts that hold true for linear programming models with any number of decision variables.

GALAXY INDUSTRIES

Galaxy Industries is an emerging toy manufacturing company that produces two "space age" water guns that are marketed nationwide, primarily to discount toy stores. Although many parents object to the potentially violent implications of these products, the products have proven very popular and are in such demand that Galaxy has had no problem selling all the items it manufactures.

The two models, the Space Ray and the Zapper, are produced in lots of one-dozen each and are made exclusively from a special plastic compound. Two of the

Barnes.xls
Galaxy.xls

limiting resources are the 1000 pounds of the special plastic compound and the 40 hours of production time that are available each week.

Galaxy's marketing department is more concerned with building a strong customer demand base for the fledgling company's products than with meeting high production quotas. Two of its recommendations, which Galaxy's management has already accepted, are to limit total weekly production to at most 700 dozen units and to prevent weekly production of Space Rays from exceeding that of Zappers by more then 350 dozen. Table 2.2 summarizes the per dozen resource requirements and profit values (calculated by subtracting variable production costs from their wholesale selling prices).

TABLE 2.2   Galaxy's Resource Requirements and Profit Values

Product	Profit per Dozen	Plastic (lb.) per Dozen	Production Time (min.) per Dozen
Space Ray	$8	2 lb convert into dozen	3 min
Zapper	$5	1 lb space ray	4

Figure 2.1 shows a simple Excel spreadsheet which Hal Barnes, Galaxy's production manager, built to calculate the total profit and keep track of the usage of plastic and production time for assigned production quantities. Hal reasoned that since the $8 profit per dozen Space Rays exceeds the $5 profit per dozen Zappers by 60%, the company would maximize its profits by producing as many Space Rays as possible, while still remaining within the marketing guidelines. That is, if the resources were sufficient, Space Ray production should exceed Zapper production by 350 dozen, with the combined total production not exceeding 700 dozen.

Hal entered formulas into cells B5, B6, and B7 as shown to keep track of the total products produced, the total amount of plastic, and the total production minutes, respectively, given the number of dozen Space Rays and Zappers produced (cells B2 and C2). To ensure that Space Ray production (cell B2) exceeded Zapper production (cell C2) by 350 dozen, Hal entered the formula = C2 + 350 into cell B2.

He then used a trial-and-error approach of entering increasingly larger values into cell C2. With each change he observed the values in cells B5, B6, and B7 to ensure that these values did not exceed the weekly limits 700, 1000, and 2400 (in cells C5, C6, and C7), respectively.

In Figure 2.1 we see the result of Hal entering 100 for the weekly production of Zappers (in dozens) in cell C2. At this value, all available plastic would be used. Thus, Hal ordered a production schedule of 450 dozen Space Rays and 100 dozen Zappers weekly, giving Galaxy a profit of $4100 per week or 52($4100) = $213,200 per year.

Although this was considered a good profit, upper management began to question whether a different production schedule might increase company profits.

SOLUTION

We begin our analysis by building a mathematical model of the situation.

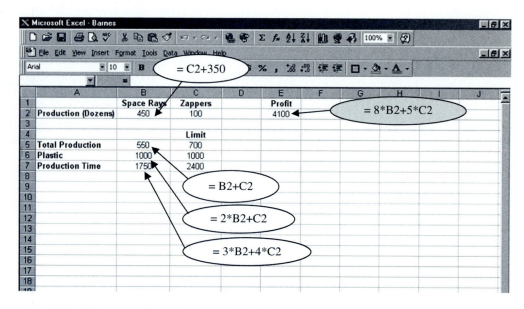

FIGURE 2.1   Hal Barnes's Spread Solution for Galaxy Industries

FORMULATION OF THE GALAXY INDUSTRIES MODEL

Recall that a mathematical model consists of three parts:

1. A well-defined set of decision variables
2. An overall objective to be maximized or minimized
3. A set of constraints

A helpful starting point for determining each of these components is to briefly summarize the details of the problem statement.

From the problem statement for Galaxy Industries we can make a number of observations:

- Production is to be in terms of dozens and scheduled on a weekly basis.
- The overall objective is to maximize weekly profit.
- Production must be scheduled so that the weekly supply of plastic and the availability of production time are not exceeded.
- The two marketing department guidelines concerning maximum total production and the product mix must be met.

Using this brief overview, we can now construct a mathematical model which management at Galaxy Industries can use to determine the most profitable product mix.

DECISION VARIABLES

The decision maker can control the production levels of Space Rays and Zappers. Noting that the production units are in terms of *dozens* and production is done on a *weekly* basis, we observe that the appropriate decision variables are:

$$X_1 = \text{number of dozen Space Rays produced weekly}$$
$$X_2 = \text{number of dozen Zappers produced weekly}$$

OBJECTIVE FUNCTION

The objective of maximizing total weekly profit is obtained by summing the weekly profits of each of the two types of items produced. For each product the weekly profit is:

(Profit per Dozen Units Produced) ×
(Number of Dozen Units Produced Weekly)

Thus, the objective is to:

$$\text{MAXIMIZE } 8X_1 + 5X_2$$

CONSTRAINTS

In addition to the nonnegativity constraints for the decision variables, there are four functional constraints:

1. The availability of plastic
2. The weekly limit for production time
3. The maximum production limit of total units
4. The mix of Space Rays and Zappers

Our approach to formulating these constraints is first to express, in words, a restriction of the form:

(Some quantity) ⟨has some relation to⟩ (Another quantity)

We can then substitute mathematical functions or constants for the appropriate "quantities." Finally, if necessary, we can rewrite the expression so that all terms involving the decision variables are on the left side of the constraint and the constant term is on the right side.

Plastic

(The total amount of plastic used weekly) cannot exceed
(The amount of plastic available weekly)

Since each dozen Space Rays requires two pounds of plastic and each dozen Zappers requires one pound, the total amount of plastic used in a week is $2X_1 + 1X_2$. Because this amount cannot exceed the limit of 1000 pounds weekly, the constraint is:

$$2X_1 + 1X_2 \leq 1000$$

Production Time

(The amount of production minutes used weekly) cannot exceed
(The total number of production minutes available weekly)

Because each dozen Space Rays requires three minutes of labor and each dozen Zappers requires four minutes of labor, the total number of labor minutes used weekly is $3X_1 + 4X_2$. This number cannot exceed the number of labor *minutes* available weekly. Since 40 *hours* are available, the number of available minutes is $(40)(60) = 2400$. Thus, the production time constraint is:

$$3X_1 + 4X_2 \leq 2400$$

Total Production Limit

(The total number of dozen units produced weekly) cannot exceed
(The marketing limit)

The total number of dozens of units produced is simply the sum of the number of dozen Space Rays produced and the number of dozen Zappers produced. Since this is not to exceed 700 dozen, the constraint is:

$$X_1 + X_2 \leq 700$$

Balanced Product Mix

(The number of dozen Space Rays produced weekly) cannot exceed
(The number of dozen Zappers) plus 350

The number of dozen Space Rays produced weekly is X_1, and the number of dozen Zappers produced weekly is X_2. So the appropriate constraint is:

$$X_1 \leq X_2 + 350$$

Rewriting the equation so that X_2 is on the left side yields:

$$X_1 - X_2 \leq 350$$

Nonnegativity of Decision Variables   Negative production of Space Rays and Zappers is impossible. Thus,

$$X_1, X_2 \geq 0$$

THE MATHEMATICAL MODEL

The complete mathematical model for Galaxy Industries is:

$$
\begin{array}{lll}
\text{MAX} & 8X_1 + 5X_2 & \text{(Total weekly profit)} \\
\text{ST} & 2X_1 + \ X_2 \leq 1000 & \text{(Plastic)} \\
& 3X_1 + 4X_2 \leq 2400 & \text{(Production time)} \\
& X_1 + \ X_2 \leq \ 700 & \text{(Total production)} \\
& X_1 - \ X_2 \leq \ 350 & \text{(Mix)} \\
& X_1, X_2 \geq \ \ \ 0 & \text{(Nonnegativity)}
\end{array}
$$

This model is expressed using the standard mathematical programming conventions of grouping all the nonnegativity constraints together and putting them at the end of the model and using the abbreviations "MAX" for "Maximize" and "ST" for "subject to" or "such that." Note that the objective function and the expressions on the left side of the constraints are all linear functions. Hence this mathematical model is a linear program.

In Section 2.5 we discuss how we can use the Solver function in Excel to obtain an optimal solution to this model. First, however, we shall use a graphical approach to illustrate many of the important properties of linear programming models.

2.3 A Graphical Analysis of Linear Programming

Exactly what production combinations of Space Rays and Zappers are possible for Galaxy Industries? And, of these possible production values, which maximizes the objective function? A graphical representation of the model will help answer both questions.

To determine the set of possible production combinations, we graph one constraint and determine all the points that satisfy that constraint. Then we add a second constraint. Some points that satisfy this second constraint also satisfy the first; others do not, and we eliminate them from consideration. We repeat this process until all the constraints, including the nonnegativity constraints, have been considered. The reader may wish to refer to the PowerPoint slides for an animated presentation of this process.

Here, we begin with the nonnegativity constraints. Because both variables must be nonnegative, we consider points in the first quadrant. This is illustrated in Figure 2.2a. Next, we graph the plastic constraint: $2X_1 + 1X_2 \leq 1000$.[1] The shaded region in Figure 2.2b shows all the points satisfying the nonnegativity constraints and the plastic constraint.

Repeating this process for the production time constraint, $3X_1 + 4X_2 \leq 2400$, yields Figure 2.2c. The shaded region now contains all the points satisfying the nonnegativity constraints, the plastic constraint, and the production time constraint. Note that some of the points that satisfied only the plastic constraint and the nonnegativity constraints have been eliminated.

Figure 2.2d illustrates what happens when we add the constraint on total production, $X_1 + X_2 \leq 700$. As you can see, adding this constraint does not eliminate any additional points from consideration. Constraints with this characteristic are called **redundant constraints**.

Redundant Constraints

A redundant constraint is one that, if removed, will not affect the feasible region.

Figure 2.3 shows the completed graph for this problem, which is formed by adding the mix constraint, $X_1 - X_2 \leq 350$, to the previously graphed constraints.[2] The shaded region of Figure 2.3, which consists of all the "possible" or "feasible" points satisfying all of the model's functional and variable constraints, is known as the **feasible region**.

Feasible Region

The set of all points that satisfy all the constraints of the model is called the **feasible region**.

---

[1] In cases in which both the coefficients of X_1 and X_2 are positive, first set $X_1 = 0$ and solve for X_2 (in this case $X_2 = 1000$), yielding one point on the line. Then set $X_2 = 0$ and solve for X_1 (in this case $X_1 = 500$). We can now draw $2X_1 + X_2 = 1000$ by connecting these two points. The "$<$" part consists of all points below the line.

[2] The line $X_1 - X_2 = 350$ is generated differently since the coefficient of X_2 is negative. One point $(350,0)$ is determined as usual by setting X_2 to zero and solving for X_1. To find a second point on the line that is in the first quadrant, we set X_1 to any number greater than 350 (say 750) and solve for X_2. This yields $X_2 = 400$. Connecting the point $(350,0)$ with the point $(750,400)$ gives the required line segment. Note that the point $(0,0)$ is on the "$<$" side of the line. Hence, values to the left of the line represent the points with $X_1 - X_2 < 350$.

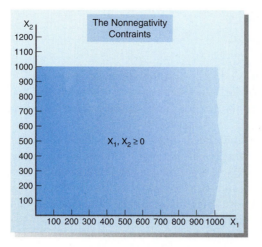

FIGURE 2.2a Nonnegativity Constraints

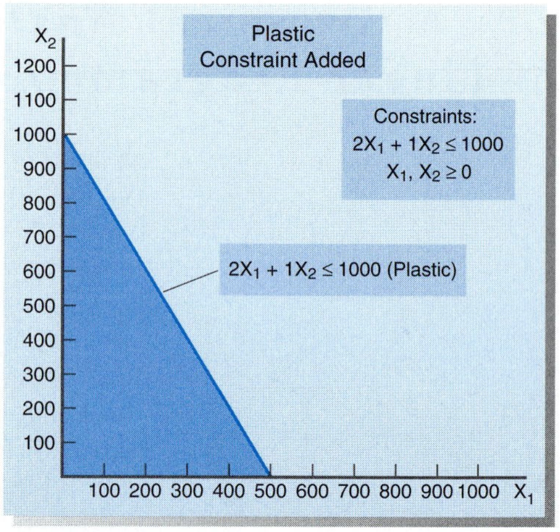

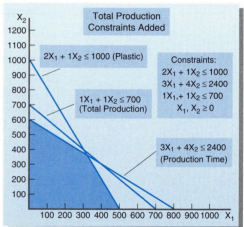

FIGURE 2.2b Plastic Constraint Added

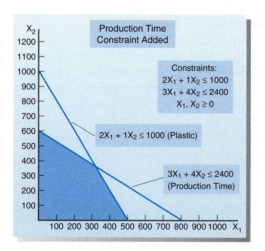

FIGURE 2.2c Production Time Constraint Added

Total Production Constraints Added figure

FIGURE 2.2d Total Production Constraint Added

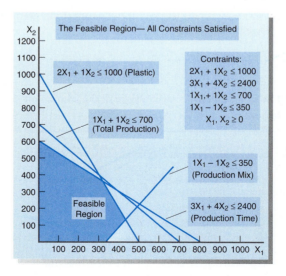

FIGURE 2.3
Mix Constraint Added—The Result Is the Feasible Region

INFEASIBLE AND FEASIBLE POINTS

Infeasible points—those lying outside the feasible region—violate one or more of the function or variable constraints. In Figure 2.4, you can see that the infeasible point (300,500) violates both the plastic constraint and the mix constraint. Figure 2.4 also illustrates three types of **feasible points** that satisfy all the constraints of the model, as defined in Table 2.3.

The characterization of these points is quite important. As we will show in the next section, an optimal solution to a linear programming model *must* occur at an extreme point, *may* occur at a boundary point, but can *never* occur at an interior point.

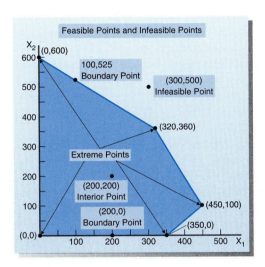

FIGURE 2.4

Feasible Region—Interior Points, Boundary Points, Extreme Points, and Infeasible Points

TABLE 2.3   Types of Feasible/Infeasible Points

Point	Characteristic	Example(s)
Feasible Points		
Interior point	Satisfies all constraints, but none with equality	(200,200)
Boundary point	Satisfies all constraints, at least one with equality	(100,525), (200,0)
Extreme point	Satisfies all constraints, two with equality	(0,0), (350,0), (450,100), (320,360) (0,600)
Infeasible Point	Violates at least one constraint	(300,500)

EXTREME POINTS

Because extreme points play a crucial role in determining the optimal solution to linear programming models, we should discuss them in a little more detail. Extreme points are the "corner points" of the feasible region, occurring at the intersection of two of the boundary constraints. The X_1 and X_2 values for extreme points can be found by solving the two equations in two unknowns that determine the point.

For example, to find the point at the intersection of boundaries of the plastic and the mix constraint, in Figure 2.4 we solve the following two equations in two unknowns:

$$2X_1 + X_2 = 1000$$
$$X_1 - X_2 = 350$$

Adding these two equations gives us $3X_1 = 1350$, or $X_1 = 450$. Substituting $X_1 = 450$ into the second equation gives $450 - X_2 = 350$, or $X_2 = 100$. Thus, this extreme point is $X_1 = 450$, $X_2 = 100$. Similarly, the extreme point at the intersection of the production time constraint and the X_2 axis is $(0,600)$, which is found by solving the equations $3X_1 + 4X_2 = 2400$ and $X_1 = 0$ (the equation of the X_2 axis).

For models requiring three dimensions, an extreme point is a feasible point that lies at the intersection of three boundary constraints. Thus, we would have to solve *three* equations in *three* unknowns to determine these extreme points. This notion extends naturally to problems with any number of dimensions.

SOLVING GRAPHICALLY FOR AN OPTIMAL SOLUTION

All but the simplest linear programming models (those with only a few variables and constraints) make use of computer software such as Microsoft Excel to perform the voluminous (though straightforward) mathematical operations required in the solution process. Here, however, we present a graphical solution approach that can be used to solve problems with two variables, such as the Galaxy Industries model.

In Figure 2.4, we see that there are an *infinite number of points* in the feasible region. The question is, "Which one gives the maximum profit?" That is, "Which one maximizes the objective function $8X_1 + 5X_2$?" If there were only five or ten feasible points; we could substitute simply the X_1 and X_2 values for each of these points into the objective function, and the point with the largest value would be the optimal solution. However, since the feasible region consists of an infinite number of points, we must take a different approach.

Suppose we ask, "Are there any solutions that would yield a $5000 weekly profit?" This is equivalent to saying, "Are there any feasible points that satisfy the following equation $8X_1 + 5X_2 = 5000$?" When this line is graphed, as illustrated in Figure 2.5*a*, we see that it lies entirely above the feasible region. Thus, to our dismay, we find that no point in the feasible region gives a value of the objective function as large as $5000.

So let's set our sights lower. Let's see whether any solutions yield a $2000 weekly profit. Figure 2.5*b* shows us that when we draw the line, $8X_1 + 5X_2 = 2000$, many solutions (the points on the line, $8X_1 + 5X_2 = 2000$, that are in the feasible region) give us a $2000 weekly profit. Thus, Galaxy can do no worse than a $2000 weekly profit.

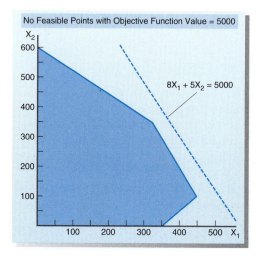

FIGURE 2.5*a*   No Feasible Points with Objective Function Value of 5000

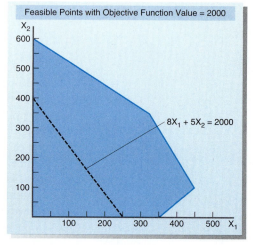

FIGURE 2.5*b*   There Are Feasible Points with Objective Function Value of 2000

If a \$2000 profit can be made, perhaps even larger profits are possible. Are there any combinations of the decision variables that could yield, say, a \$3000 profit or even a \$4000 profit? To determine whether Galaxy could attain such profits, we add the lines $8X_1 + 5X_2 = 3000$ and $8X_1 + 5X_2 = 4000$ to the graph. As shown in Figure 2.6, both lines intersect the feasible region.

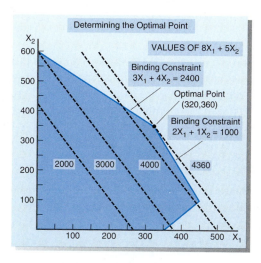

FIGURE 2.6
Determining the Optimal Point

Because the profit lines have the same slope, they are parallel; the lines yielding higher profits lie above those with lower profits. Therefore, if the objective function line is moved parallel to itself upward through the feasible region, the optimal feasible point is found when the objective function line touches the last point of the feasible region.

The last point of the feasible region that is touched by the objective function is the **extreme point** at the intersection of the limit for the availability of plastic ($2X_1 + 1X_2 = 1000$) and the limit on production time ($3X_1 + 4X_2 = 2400$). These constraints, known as the **binding constraints** of the model because they are satisfied with equality. The two other functional constraints and the nonnegativity constraints are the *nonbinding constraints*, which are not satisfied with equality at the optimal point.

To determine the values for X_1 and X_2 at the optimal point, the two *equations* of the binding constraints that must be solved are:

$$2X_1 + 1X_2 = 1000$$
$$3X_1 + 4X_2 = 2400$$

Multiplying the first equation by 4 gives us:

$$8X_1 + 4X_2 = 4000$$
$$3X_1 + 4X_2 = 2400$$

Subtracting the bottom equation from the top equation gives us $5X_1 = 1600$, or $X_1 = 320$. Substituting $X_1 = 320$ into the original first equation gives us $2(320) + 1X_2 = 1000$, or $X_2 = 360$. Thus, the optimal solution is:

$$X_1 = 320$$
$$X_2 = 360$$

To determine the optimal profit, we substitute these values into the objective function:

$$8X_1 + 5X_2 = 8(320) + 5(360) = \$4360$$

Thus, Hal Barnes should recommend to management at Galaxy Industries a weekly production of 320 dozen Space Rays and 360 dozen Zappers. This would give the company an increase of $260 (=$4360 − $4100), or over a 6.3% increase in weekly profit over Hal's "intuitive" weekly policy of producing 450 dozen Space Rays and 100 dozen Zappers. On a yearly basis, this will net the company 52(260) = $13,520 in increased profits.

SLACK

This solution utilizes all the plastic and production time (there is no **slack** for these constraints). There is, however, slack on both of the other functional constraints. Since $X_1 + X_2 = 320 + 360 = 680$, there is a slack of $700 − 680 = 20$ for the total production limit constraint. And since $X_1 − X_2 = 320 − 360 = −40$, there is a slack of $350 − (−40) = 390$ for the product mix constraint.

SUMMARY OF THE GRAPHICAL SOLUTION APPROACH

To summarize, the following steps are used to find the optimal solution to a two-variable linear programming model graphically.

Graphical Solution Procedure for Two-Variable Linear Programs

1. Graph the constraints to find the feasible region.
2. Set the objective function equal to an arbitrary value so that the line passes through the feasible region.
3. Move the objective function line parallel to itself in the direction of improvement until it touches the last point of the feasible region.
4. Solve for X_1 and X_2 by solving the two equations that intersect to determine this point.
5. Substitute these values into the objective function to determine its optimal value.

EXTREME POINTS AND OPTIMAL SOLUTIONS

It is useful to recognize where the optimal solution for a linear program can occur. Consider problems that have the same feasible region as Galaxy Industries but different objective functions, as shown in Figures 2.7a–d. Table 2.4 presents the optimal solution for various objective functions,[3] including the original objective function for Galaxy Industries (MAXIMIZE $8X_1 + 5X_2$).

TABLE 2.4 Optimal Solutions

Figure	Objective Function	Optimal Extreme Point
2.6	MAXIMIZE $8X_1 + 5X_2$	(320,360)
2.7(a)	MINIMIZE $8X_1 + 5X_2$	(0,0)
2.7(b)	MAXIMIZE $8X_1 + 1X_2$	(450,100)
2.7(c)	MAXIMIZE $8X_1 + 20X_2$	(0,600)
2.7(d)	MINIMIZE $8X_1 − 20X_2$	(350,0)

[3] For minimization problems, the objective function line is moved in the direction opposite to that for a maximization problem.

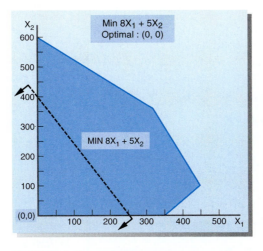

FIGURE 2.7a Objective Function: MIN $8X_1 + 5X_2$ OPTIMAL: (0,0)

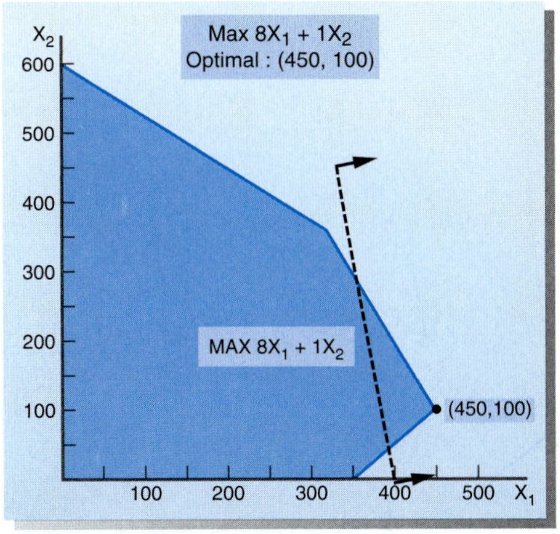

FIGURE 2.7b Objective Function: MAX $8X_1 + 1X_2$ OPTIMAL: (450,100)

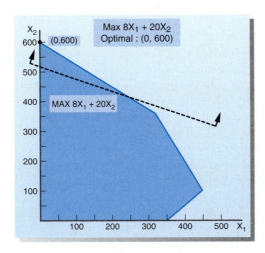

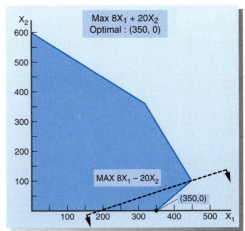

FIGURE 2.7c Objective Function: MAX $8X_1 + 20X_2$ OPTIMAL: (0,600)

FIGURE 2.7d Objective Function: MAX $8X_1 - 20X_2$ OPTIMAL: (350,0)

It is not coincidental that, in each case, the optimal solution occurs at an extreme point; rather, it is a fundamental property of linear programming.

> ### Extreme Point Property of Optimality
>
> If a linear programming problem has an optimal solution, an extreme point is optimal.

ALTERNATE OPTIMAL SOLUTIONS

In some cases, a linear programming model may have more than one optimal solution, as when the objective function line is parallel to one of the constraints; that is, the slope of the objective function line is the same as the slope of one of the constraints. Recall that the slope of a line = $-(X_1$ coefficient$)/(X_2$ coefficient$)$.

For example, suppose, as shown in Figure 2.8, that the objective function is:

MAXIMIZE $8X_1 + 4X_2$

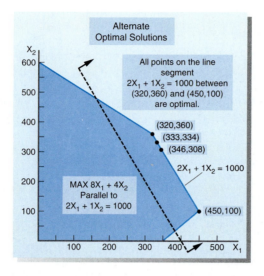

FIGURE 2.8

Multiple Optimal Solutions: Objective Function: MAX $8X_1 + 4X_2$ Is Parallel to Plastic Constraint: $2X_1 + 1X_2 = 1000$

In this case, when we move the objective function line parallel through the feasible region, the slope of the objective function line ($-8/4 = -2$) is the same as the slope of the boundary of the plastic constraint ($-2/1 = -2$), and the last "point" that is touched is actually a *set* of points, namely, all those on the line $2X_1 + X_2 = 1000$ between the extreme points (320,360) and (450,100). Since at least one optimal solution is an extreme point, the fact that some optimal points are not extreme points does not violate the extreme point property of optimality.

Note, however, that if the objective function would have been MINIMIZE $8X_1 + 4X_2$, even though the slope is still parallel to the boundary of the plastic constraint, there is now a unique optimal solution, $X_1 = 0$, $X_2 = 0$. Thus, the slope of the objective function line being parallel to a boundary constraint is a *necessary* but not a *sufficient* condition for a model to have multiple optimal solutions.

As Figure 2.8 illustrates, there will never be just two optimal solutions. Any point on the line segment connecting two optimal points is also optimal. The co-ordinates of points on this line segment can be found by taking any weighted average of the two optimal points.

For example, $X_1 = 320$, $X_2 = 360$ is one optimal solution in Figure 2.8, and $X_1 = 450$, $X_2 = 100$ is another. Each gives an optimal objective function value of $8(320) + 4(360) = 8(450) + 4(100) = 3800$. Then another optimal solution on the line segment $2X_1 + 1X_2 = 1000$ that puts a weight of .8 on the first point and .2 on the second is:

$$X_1 = .8(320) + .2(450) = 346$$
$$X_2 = .8(360) + .2(100) = 308$$

Note that the objective function value is still 3800 ($=8(346) + 4(308)$).

Similarly, we can show that using weights of .9 and .1 gives $X_1 = 333$, $X_2 = 334$ and using weights of .5 and .5 gives $X_1 = 385$, $X_2 = 230$. You can verify that each of these also gives an objective function value equal to \$3800. In fact, any combination of weights of the form w, $(1 - w)$ with $0 \le w \le 1$, will also give an optimal solution.

Alternate Optimal Solutions

1. For alternate optimal solutions to exist, the objective function must be parallel to a part of the boundary of the feasible region.

2. Any weighted average of optimal solutions is also an optimal solution.

Having more than one optimal solution allows the decision maker to consider secondary criteria in selecting an optimal strategy. For example, one optimal solution may have more of the decision variables equal to 0. In some cases, management might consider this a plus—fewer product types may mean more attention and better quality for the products that are produced. In other cases, this may be a minus—the greater the variety of products produced, perhaps the greater the likelihood of attracting more customers. Another optimal solution may have a more equal product mix than another, which, under some conditions, might be more appealing. In any event, having multiple optimal solutions affords management the luxury of being able to select that solution most to its liking from the set of optimal solutions.

WHY "< CONSTRAINTS" AND "> CONSTRAINTS" ARE NOT PART OF A LINEAR PROGRAMMING MODEL

The constraints of a linear programming model must consist of "$\leq$" constraints, "$\geq$" constraints, and "$=$" constraints. The "$<$" and "$>$" constraints are not allowed because, using them, there would be no "last" point touched by moving the objective function line parallel to itself through the feasible region.

For example, if both the plastic and production time constraints were the strict inequalities $2X_1 + X_2 < 1000$ and $3X_1 + 4X_2 < 2400$, respectively, the point (320,360) would not be feasible. The point (319.99,359.99) would be feasible, but the feasible point (319.999,359.999) gives a higher objective function value and the point (319.9999,359.9999) an even higher value. Thus, there would be no "best value" because, no matter what solution was proposed, adding a "9" in the next decimal place would yield another feasible solution with an even better objective function value.

If a strict inequality is part of a formulation, the constraint should be approximated using a nonstrict inequality. For example, if Galaxy Industries required that less than 1000 pounds of plastic be used weekly ($2X_1 + X_2 < 1000$), in order to use linear programming solution methods, the mathematical modeler might approximate the constraint by $2X_1 + X_2 \leq 999.99999$.

2.4   The Role of Sensitivity Analysis of the Optimal Solution

Inevitably, once an optimal solution has been determined, questions arise about how sensitive the optimal solution is to changes in one or more of the input parameters or to other changes, such as the addition or elimination of constraints or variables. The effect of these changes is known as **sensitivity** or **post-optimality analysis**. Decision makers at Galaxy Industries might be interested in sensitivity analyses for the following reasons.

1. *Some of the input parameters may not have been known with certainty but are approximations or best estimates.*

   - The profit coefficients might have been based solely on estimates of the production costs for Space Rays and Zappers.
   - The 40 production hours might have assumed no vacations, illnesses, power failures, and so on.
   - The production times to produce Space Rays and Zappers may have been approximations or averages.

2. *The model may have been formulated in a dynamic environment in which some of the parameters are subject to change.*

- The availability of specially treated plastic might be disrupted by, among other factors, weather or manufacturer stockouts.
- The price of labor and materials could change.
- Higher or lower interest rates could change the profitability of each product.

3. *The manager may simply wish to perform a "what-if" analysis resulting from changes to some of the input parameters.*

- "What-if" overtime is scheduled?
- "What-if" the marketing department modifies its recommendations?
- "What-if" another item is added to the product line?

Of course, if a change is made to a linear programming model, the problem can simply be re-solved. This can be a time-consuming process, however, that in many cases may not even be necessary. Rather, sensitivity reports generated by linear programming software packages can tell us at a glance the ramifications of certain changes to the objective function and the right-hand side coefficients of the model.

SENSITIVITY ANALYSIS OF OBJECTIVE FUNCTION COEFFICIENTS

Once the optimal solution to a linear programming model has been found, the decision maker may be concerned about how changes to any one of the objective function coefficients affect the optimal solution. As shown in Section 2.3, the optimal solution may change depending on the values of the objective function coefficients.

RANGE OF OPTIMALITY

Sensitivity analysis of an objective function coefficient focuses on answering the following question: "Keeping *all* other factors the same, how much can an objective function coefficient change without changing the optimal solution?"

Let us see what happens when the objective function coefficient per dozen Space Rays (which we designate as C_1) changes from the current value of $8. Figure 2.9 illustrates the effect of increasing and decreasing this coefficient. As C_1 is decreased from $8, the objective function line, $C_1X_1 + 5X_2$, becomes more horizontal. The optimal point, however, remains (320,360) until the line becomes parallel to (has the same slope as) the production time constraint, $3X_1 + 4X_2 = 2400$. Recall that the slope of a straight line is expressed by ($-$Coefficient of X_1/Coefficient of X_2). Thus, the slope of the production time constraint is $-3/4$, and the slope of the objective function line is $-C_1/5$. These slopes are equal when $C_1/5 = -3/4$ or $C_1 = 3.75$.

As C_1 is increased from $8, the objective function line, $C_1X_1 + 5X_2$ becomes more vertical, but the optimal point remains (320,360) until the line becomes parallel to (has the same slope as) the plastic constraint, $2X_1 + 1X_2 = 1000$. Since the slope of the plastic constraint is $-2/1$ and the slope of the objective function line is $-C_1/5$, the slopes are equal when $C_1/5 = -2/1$ or $C_1 = 10$.

This range of values for C_1 from $3.75 to $10.00 is called the **range of optimality** for C_1, the objective function coefficient of Space Rays. This is an *Allowable Increase* of $10 − $8 = $2 and an *Allowable Decrease* of $8 − $3.75 = $4.25

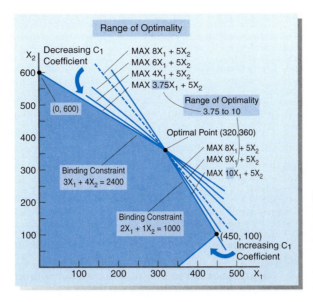

FIGURE 2.9

Range of Optimality—Obtained by Rotating the Objective Function Line Through the Optimal Point Until It Becomes Parallel to a Binding Constraint

from the original objective function coefficient value of $C_1 = \$8$. (We shall see in the next section that Excel expresses the range of optimality in terms of an Allowable Increase and an Allowable Decrease.) We further observe in Figure 2.9 that if C_1 falls below $3.75, the point $(0,600)$ becomes the new optimal solution, whereas if C_1 is increased above $10.00, the point $(450,100)$ becomes optimal.

Note that in this range of optimality, although the optimal solution remains $X_1 = 320$, $X_2 = 360$, the value of the objective function will change with changes to C_1. For example, if the profit per dozen Space Rays were decreased from $8 to $6, the optimal profit would now be $\$6(320) + \$5(360) = \$3720$. It is important to note that this analysis is predicated on the assumption that no other changes occur, other than that to C_1.

Range of Optimality

Assuming that there are no other changes to the input parameters:

1. The **range of optimality** is the range of values for an objective function coefficient in which the optimal solution remains unchanged.
2. The value of the objective function will change if this coefficient multiplies a variable whose value is positive.

The range of optimality for C_2, the objective function coefficient of Zappers, is similarly calculated. This time the equation of the objective function line is $8X_1 + C_2X_2$, whose slope is $-8/C_2$. The range of optimality for C_2 is again bounded by the slopes of the binding constraints of $-3/4$ for the production time constraint and -2 for the plastic constraint. Thus, we get the limits for its range of optimality by: $-8/C_2 = -3/4$ or $C_2 = 10.67$ and $-8/C_2 = -2/1$ or $C_2 = 4$.

Thus the range of optimality for C_2, the objective function coefficient of Zappers, is then between $4.00 and $10.67 (an Allowable Increase of $5.67 and an Allowable Decrease of $1.00).

REDUCED COSTS

The optimal solution to the Galaxy Industries model has positive values for both of the decision variables. But as we just argued from Figure 2.9, if the profit coefficient for Space Rays is below $3.75, the optimal solution is $X_1 = 0$, $X_2 = 600$. So let us suppose that the objective function had been MAX $2X_1 + 5X_2$. Since the optimal solution will be $X_1 = 0$, $X_2 = 600$, the optimal objective function value is $2(0) + \$5(600) = \$3000$.

In this case, $X_1 = 0$ (no Space Rays are produced) because the $2 profit for the coefficient of X_1 is not large enough to justify the production of Space Rays. It is then reasonable to ask, "How much will the profit coefficient for X_1 have to increase before X_1 can be positive (i.e., to justify the production of some Space Rays) in the optimal solution?" The answer is expressed by the **reduced cost** for this profit coefficient.

We see from Figure 2.9, that the point $(0,600)$ is the optimal solution until the profit per dozen Space Rays increases to more than $C_1 = \$3.75$. Beyond this value, the optimal solution changes to $(320,360)$. Thus, C_1 must increase by $1.75 from $2 to $3.75 before it becomes economically feasible to produce Space Rays. Increasing the profit by $1.75 is equivalent to reducing the cost component of the coefficient by $1.75; hence, we say that the reduced cost of this coefficient is -1.75.

Another question that might arise is, "Although it is not economically feasible to produce Space Rays at this value of $2 per dozen ($X_1 = 0$), how much would the optimal profit decrease if we were forced to produce at least one dozen Space Rays ($X_1 \geq 1$)?" Again the answer is expressed by the reduced cost. As shown in Figure 2.10, with the addition of the constraint $X_1 \geq 1$, the optimal solution is now $X_1 = 1$, $X_2 = 599.25$, giving an objective function value of $2998.25. This represents a $1.75 reduction in profit from $3000.

Reduced Cost

Assuming that there are no other changes to the input parameters:

1. The **reduced cost** for a variable that has a solution value of 0 is the negative of the objective function coefficient increase necessary for the variable to be positive in the optimal solution.

2. The **reduced cost** is also the amount the objective function will change per unit increase in this variable.

Note that if a variable is already positive, its reduced cost is 0. Thus, either the value of a variable is 0 or its reduced cost is 0. This property is known as the **complementary slackness** property for objective function coefficients.

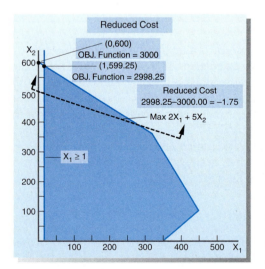

FIGURE 2.10
Reduced Cost for X_1 When Objective Function is $2X_1 + 5X_2$. Add $X_1 \geq 1$ and compare optimal objective function values. Reduced Cost = Value after Constraint Is Added—Original Value

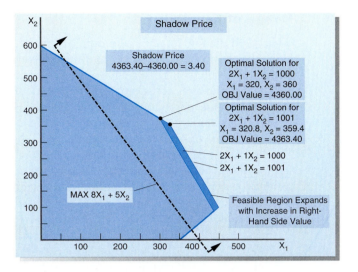

FIGURE 2.11
Shadow Price: Calculated by the Difference in Objective Function Values When the Right-Hand Side of a Constraint Is Increased by 1

SENSITIVITY ANALYSIS OF RIGHT-HAND SIDE COEFFICIENTS

Any change to a right-hand side value of a binding constraint will change the optimal solution. For example, as shown in Figure 2.11, if the amount of available plastic is increased from 1000 to 1001 pounds, the new optimal solution is found by solving:

$$2X_1 + 1X_2 = 1001$$
$$3X_1 + 4X_2 = 2400$$

You can verify that the solution to this pair of equations is $X_1 = 320.8$, $X_2 = 359.4$.

Shadow Prices

When the optimal solution changes to $X_1 = 320.8$, $X_2 = 359.4$, the optimal objective function value also changes to $\$8(320.8) + \$5(359.4) = \$4363.40$. This is a difference of $\$4363.40 - \$4360.00 = \$3.40$.

If 1002 pounds (two additional pounds) of plastic are available, the optimal solution is found by solving:

$$2X_1 + 1X_2 = 1002$$
$$3X_1 + 4X_2 = 2400$$

The solution to this pair of equations, $X_1 = 321.6$, $X_2 = 358.8$, gives an optimal objective function value of $\$8(321.6) + \$5(358.8) = \$4366.80$. This is a $\$6.80$ increase, or a $\$6.80/2 = \$3.40$ per pound increase, over the original objective function value. Similarly, it can be shown that if there are only 999 pounds of plastic available (one less pound), the resulting optimal solution of $X_1 = 319.2$, $X_2 = 360.6$, gives an optimal objective function value of $\$8(319.2) + \$5(360.6) = \$4356.60$, a decrease of $\$3.40$ per pound! It is this $\$3.40$ change to the optimal value per unit change in the amount of plastic that is called the **shadow price** for a pound of plastic.

Shadow Price

Assuming that there are no other changes to the input parameters, the **shadow price** for a constraint is the change to the objective function value per unit increase to its right-hand side coefficient.

Range of Feasibility

This $3.40 shadow price is valid only over a certain range of values for the availability of plastic, however. If we continued to change the right-hand side value for plastic, we would still get changes of $3.40 per unit in the objective function value as long as the plastic constraint and the production time constraint determine the optimal extreme point. But if the change to the amount of plastic is too great, whether it is too large an increase or too large a decrease, there can come a point when different constraints determine the optimal point.

The **range of feasibility** for plastic gives the limits on the right-hand side values for plastic between which these two constraints, the plastic constraint and the production time constraint, continue to determine the optimal point. It is given this name because, over its range of values, the solution to the current set of binding constraint equations is a *feasible* solution.

Figures 2.12*a* and 2.12*b* illustrate how the range of feasibility for plastic can be determined. Notice that increasing the right-hand side value for plastic from 1000 expands the feasible region, while the feasible region contracts when its value is decreased. In each case, the slope of the plastic constraint remains the same; however, its X_2-intercept changes. Thus, changing its right-hand side value creates a new constraint line that is *parallel* to the original constraint line for plastic.

Figure 2.12*a* shows what happens as the availability of plastic increases. The plastic and the production constraints continue to determine the optimal point until the plastic constraint line passes through the intersection of the production time and the total production constraints at (400,300). This point is determined by solving $3X_1 + 4X_2 = 2400$ and $X_1 + X_2 = 700$. At (400,300), the right-hand side of the plastic constraint is $2(400) + 1(300) = 1100$. For values above 1100 the production time constraint and the total mix constraint will now determine the optimal point, while the intersection of the plastic and production time lines yields an *infeasible* point outside the new feasible region. Thus, the upper limit of the range of feasibility for plastic is 1100. This is an **Allowable Increase** of $1100 - 1000 = 100$ pounds.

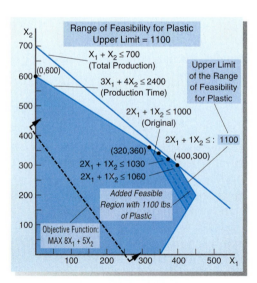

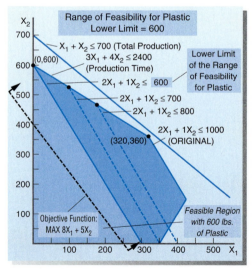

FIGURE 2.12*a* Upper Limit of the Range of Feasibility for Plastic. The plastic constraint *and* the production time constraint continue to determine the optimal solution until the RHS exceeds 1100.

FIGURE 2.12*b* Lower Limit of the Range of Feasibility for Plastic. The plastic constraint *and* the production time constraint continue to determine the optimal solution until the RHS is less than 600.

Similarly, Figure 2.12*b*, shows that as the availability of plastic decreases, the plastic and the production time constraints continue to determine the optimal point until the plastic constraint passes through the intersection of the production time boundary and the X_2 axis at (0,600). At (0,600) the right-hand side of the plastic constraint is $2(0) + 1(600) = 600$. For values of plastic below 600, the optimal solution is determined by the plastic constraint and X_2 axis, while the intersection of the plastic and production time lines yields an *infeasible* point outside the new feasible region. Thus, the lower limit of the range of feasibility for plastic is 600, an **Allowable Decrease** of $1000 - 600 = 400$ pounds.

The range of feasibility of plastic, that is, the range of values for which the $3.40 shadow price for plastic is valid, is between 600 and 1100 pounds. In this range, the value of the objective function will change by $3.40 for each unit change to the availability of plastic.

Range of Feasibility

Assuming that there are no other changes to the input parameters:

1. The **range of feasibility** is the range of values for a right-hand side value in which the shadow prices for the constraints remain unchanged.

2. In the range of feasibility, the value of the objective function will change by the amount of the shadow price times the change to the right-hand side value.

Shadow Prices and Ranges of Feasibility for the Other Constraints

The shadow price for production minutes can be found in a similar fashion by solving:

$$2X_1 + \ X_2 = 1000$$
$$3X_1 + 4X_2 = 2401$$

The solution to this set of equations is: $X_1 = 319.8$, $X_2 = 360.4$. This solution gives a profit of $4360.40, a $0.40 increase over the original optimal value of the objective function. Thus, the shadow price for production minutes is $0.40 or $60($0.40) = $24 per hour.

You can verify that, as the availability of the production minutes increases, the plastic and production time constraints continue to determine the optimal point until the production time constraint passes through the intersection of the plastic constraint and the total production constraint at $X_1 = 300$, $X_2 = 400$. At that point, the value of the right-hand side of the production time constraint is $3(300) + 4(400) = 2500$, an allowable increase of $2500 - 2400 = 100$.

As the availability of the production minutes decreases, the plastic and production time constraints continue to determine the optimal point until the production time constraint passes through the intersection of the plastic constraint and the product mix constraint at $X_1 = 450$, $X_2 = 100$. At that point, the value of the right-hand side of the production time constraint is $3(450) + 4(100) = 1750$, an Allowable Decrease of $2400 - 1750 = 650$.

Since the constraints $X_1 + X_2 \le 700$ and $X_1 - X_2 \le 350$ do not determine the optimal point (i.e., there is slack on each of these constraints), these are said to be **nonbinding constraints**. Their shadow prices will both be 0, since for at least small changes in these coefficients, all that changes in the optimal solution is the amount of slack on these constraints; the optimal point remains the same at $X_1 = 320$, $X_2 = 360$. Increasing the right-hand side values of either of these two constraints will not change the optimal solution.

The optimal point will not change until the right-hand side coefficient of a nonbinding constraint is decreased sufficiently so that it passes through the optimal point! Thus, the lower bound of the range of feasibility for the total production constraint is 1(320) + 1(360) = 680 (an Allowable Decrease of 700 − 680 = 20), and the lower bound for the product mix constraint is 1(320) − 1(360) = −40 (an Allowable Decrease of 350 −(−40) = 390.) This leads to the **complementary slackness** property for right-hand side values: The shadow price for a resource is 0 if there is slack on the constraint; if the shadow price is not 0, there is no slack.

The Correct Interpretation of Shadow Prices

Since the shadow price for plastic is $3.40 per pound, it would seem, then, that management should be willing to pay up to, but no more than, $3.40 for each additional pound of plastic. However, as we show below, this would be true *only if the cost of plastic were not included in the calculation of the profit coefficients of the decision variables*. Let us now consider two cases.

Case 1: Sunk Costs   Suppose the 1000 pounds of plastic were automatically delivered to Galaxy each week at a cost of $3 per pound or $3000 per week, and that production time is scheduled for 40 hours per week at $20 per hour ($0.3333 per minute), for a total cost of $800. Because the $3000 for plastic and the $800 for production time must be paid regardless of the amount of plastic and production time actually used during the week, they are **sunk costs**. Thus, we would not include the cost of plastic or production time in determining the objective function coefficients for Space Rays and Zappers.

The net profit for the problem can be obtained by subtracting the total sunk costs of $3000 + $800 = $3800 from the optimal objective function value of the model. Because additional pounds of plastic add $3.40, and additional minutes of production time add $0.40 to the optimal objective function value, these shadow prices do, in fact, represent an upper limit that management would be willing to pay for additional pounds of plastic and additional minutes of production time, respectively.

Case 2: Included Costs   Suppose, instead, that management could order any amount of plastic it wanted to, up to 1000 pounds per week at $3 per pound, and it could schedule any amount of production time, up to 2400 minutes. Management would then order only enough plastic and schedule only enough production time needed for the optimal solution.

In this case, the costs of the required plastic and production time (and perhaps other resources) should be *included* in the derivation of the profit coefficients of Space Rays and Zappers. For instance, suppose that the selling price was $17 per dozen Space Rays and $11 per dozen Zappers and that other production costs amounted to $2 per dozen Space Rays and $1.67 per dozen Zappers. Table 2.5

TABLE 2.5   Objective Function Coefficients

	Space Rays (per dozen)	Zappers (per dozen)
Revenue		
Selling price	$17.00	$11.00
Costs		
Plastic (@ $3/lb.)	$ 6.00 (2 lbs.)	$ 3.00 (1 lb.)
Production time (@ $20/hr.)	$ 1.00 (3 min.)	$ 1.33 (4 min.)
Other	$ 2.00	$ 1.67
Total Costs	$ 9.00	$ 6.00
Unit Profit	$ 8.00	$ 5.00

shows the calculations required to determine the respective $8 and $5 objective function coefficients per dozen Space Rays and Zappers.

The optimal solution of 320 dozen Space Rays and 360 dozen Zappers uses all 1000 pounds of plastic and all 2400 minutes of production time. The objective function value of $4360 is the *net* profit, which includes $3000 (=$3/lb. × (1000 lbs.)) spent for plastic and $800 (=$20/hr. × (40 hours), or $0.3333/min. × (2400 min.)) spent for production time.

If 1001 pounds of plastic are available, the optimal objective function value will increase by $3.40 to $4363.40; this includes $3003 (=$3/lb. × (1001 lbs.)) spent for plastic. Thus, the shadow price of $3.40 represents a *premium* above $3.00 which management should be willing to pay for extra pounds of plastic; that is, Galaxy should be willing to pay up to $6.40 (=$3.40 + $3.00) for an extra pound of plastic. Similarly, Galaxy would be willing to pay up to $0.7333 (=$0.40 + $0.3333) for an extra minute of production.

Sunk and Included Costs

Sunk costs—the cost of the resource is not included in the calculation of objective function coefficients—the shadow price is the value of an extra unit of the resource.
Included costs—the cost of the resource is included in the calculation of objective function coefficients—the shadow price is the premium value above the existing unit value for the resource.

OTHER POST-OPTIMALITY CHANGES

The addition or deletion of constraints, the addition or deletion of variables, and changes to the left-hand side coefficients of a linear programming model are additional post-optimality analyses that may be of interest to the decision maker. Typically, such changes are made directly to the model formulation, and the problem is simply resolved. However, there are some observations worth considering in these cases.

ADDITION OF A CONSTRAINT

When a constraint is added to a linear programming model, the first step is to determine whether this constraint is satisfied by the current optimal solution. If it is, it is not necessary to re-solve the problem; the current solution will remain optimal.

If the new constraint is violated, however, the problem must be re-solved. Of course, the optimal objective function value will not be better than the original optimal value (smaller for maximization problems; larger for minimization problems) because the problem is now more constrained.

DELETION OF A CONSTRAINT

If the constraint to be deleted from the model is nonbinding, the current optimal solution will not change. If it is binding, however, the problem must be re-solved. Since the problem is less restrictive, the new optimal solution will generate optimal objective function at least as good as that to the original model.

DELETION OF A VARIABLE

If the variable to be deleted is zero in the optimal solution, deleting it will not affect the optimal solution. If the value of the variable is not zero in the optimal solution, the problem must be re-solved. Deleting a variable that was nonzero in the original optimal solution will result in a worse objective function value or one that is at best no better than the original objective function value.

ADDITION OF A VARIABLE

When a variable is added, in most cases, the problem must be re-solved. There is, however, a **net marginal profit** procedure that can determine whether the addition of the new variable will have any effect on the optimal solution. Net marginal profit is the difference between the objective function coefficient and the total marginal cost of the resources (calculated using the current values of the shadow prices).

To illustrate, suppose that a new product, Big Squirts, requiring three pounds of plastic and five minutes of production time, can be produced, yielding a profit of $10 per dozen. The new model is:

$$
\begin{array}{lll}
\text{MAXIMIZE} & 8X_1 + 5X_2 + 10X_3 & \\
\text{ST} & 2X_1 + X_2 + 3X_3 \leq 1000 & \text{(Plastic)} \\
& 3X_1 + 4X_2 + 5X_3 \leq 2400 & \text{(Production time)} \\
& X_1 + X_2 + X_3 \leq 700 & \text{(Total units)} \\
& X_1 - X_2 + \leq 350 & \text{(Space Ray/Zapper mix)} \\
& X_1, X_2, X_3 \geq 0 &
\end{array}
$$

The shadow prices for the constraints turn out to be $3.40, $0.40, $0, and $0, respectively. Thus, the net marginal profit for the production of a dozen Big Squirts is:

$$\$10 - ((\$3.40)(3) + (\$0.40)(5) + (\$0)(1) + (\$0)(0)) = -\$2.20$$

Hence, it would not be profitable to produce Big Squirts, and the current solution of producing 320 dozen Space Rays and 360 dozen Zappers remains optimal. If the profit per dozen Big Squirts had been $15, however, the net marginal profit would have been $2.80. This would indicate that there is a new optimal solution, which includes the production of Big Squirts, yielding a higher optimal profit.

CHANGES IN THE LEFT-HAND SIDE COEFFICIENTS

When a left-hand side coefficient is changed, the entire feasible region is reshaped. If the change is made to a coefficient in a nonbinding constraint, the first step is to ascertain whether the current optimal solution satisfies the modified constraint. If it does, it remains the optimal solution to the revised model; if it does not, or if the change is made in a coefficient of a binding constraint, both the optimal solution and the shadow prices change in ways that are more complex to calculate than changes resulting from modifications to objective function coefficients or right-hand side values. In this case, the model must be re-solved.

2.5   Using Excel Solver to Find an Optimal Solution and Analyze Results

In this section, we illustrate the use of Excel's Solver to determine an optimal solution for the Galaxy Industries model and discuss the information generated by its sensitivity reports. The step-by-step procedure outlined here is very valuable, for it can be used to solve any linear model with any number of decision variables.

Solver is an option found in the Tools menu. If you do not see Solver listed, you must check the Solver Add-In box of the Add-Ins option under the Tools menu. If you do not see this option listed, you may have to re-install part or all of Excel using the disks that include the Solver option.

To use Solver, designate cells to contain:

- The values of the decision variables (known as **changing** or **adjustable cells**)
- The value of the objective function (known as the **target cell**)
- The total value of the left-hand side of the constraints

The cells for the objective function value and the left hand side values contain formulas that can be written as the sum of several terms. While the complete formulas can be entered explicitly, using Excel's SUM and SUMPRODUCT functions usually simplifies the input.

We shall use the spreadsheet developed in Figure 2.13 to solve the Galaxy Industries model. Although color coding and boxing cells can have an impact on the effect of the presentation of the spreadsheet (we discuss this in more detail in Chapter 3), here we concentrate on the basics of Solver.

Galaxy.xls

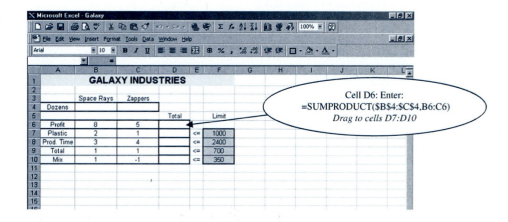

FIGURE 2.13
Excel Spreadsheet for
Galaxy Industries

Begin by entering the data for the model as shown. Designate cells B4 and C4 as the adjustable cells that will contain the values of the decision variables for Space Rays and Zappers. Cell D6 will be "programmed" to contain the value of the objective function, and cells D7 to D10 (written as D7:D10) will be programmed to contain the left-hand side of the constraints.

ENTERING FORMULAS FOR THE OBJECTIVE FUNCTION AND LEFT-HAND SIDE VALUES

The formula for the total profit in cell D6 could be written as B4*B6 + C4*C6. This is fine when there are only two variables. But when there are many variables, this is more easily done using the SUMPRODUCT function of Excel. This function has the form =SUMPRODUCT(*array1, array2*). Here array 1 and array 2 are rows or columns of equal length.[4] The arrays can be entered by highlighting

---

[4] If one of the arrays is a row and the other is a column, the equivalent formula is =MMULT(array1, array2), where array 1 is the *row* and array 2 is the *column*.

the appropriate cells (cells B4 and C4 and cells B6 and C6 in this case) using the left mouse key. Thus, as shown in Figure 2.13, for cell D6, we enter:

$$=SUMPRODUCT(B4:C4,B6:C6)$$

Cells D7, D8, D9, and D10 will contain the total on the left side for the plastic, production time, total production, and mix constraints, respectively, resulting from a given solution. Each has a formula similar to that in cell D6 with the same first array (B4:C4) and a second array that is relative to the row. To easily enter these formulas, return to cell D6. Highlight only the first array (B4:C4) of the formula in the formula bar and press the F4 function key at the top of the keyboard. This makes these cell references absolute by inserting $ signs. After pressing Enter, the formula in cell D6 is now:

$$=SUMPRODUCT(\$B\$4:\$C\$4,B6:C6)$$

When we drag this formula to cells D7, D8, D9, and D10, the resulting respective formulas in those cells give the total left-hand side for each of the constraints. The formulas in these cells are shown in Table 2.6.[5]

TABLE 2.6 Cell Formulas in Figure 2.13

Cell	Quantity	Formula	Excel Formula
D6	Total Weekly Profit	$8X_1 + 5X_2$	=SUMPRODUCT($B$4:$C$4,B6:C6)
D7	Total Plastic Used Weekly	$2X_1 + 1X_2$	=SUMPRODUCT($B$4:$C$4,B7:C7)
D8	Total Production Minutes Used Weekly	$3X_1 + 4X_2$	=SUMPRODUCT($B$4:$C$4,B8:C8)
D9	Total Weekly Production	$1X_1 + 1X_2$	=SUMPRODUCT($B$4:$C$4,B9:C9)
D10	Amount Space Ray Production Exceeds Zapper Production Each Week	$1X_1 - 1X_2$	=SUMPRODUCT($B$4:$C$4,B10:C10)

We now call Solver from the Tools menu. This gives the dialogue box shown in Figure 2.14.

FIGURE 2.14
Solver Dialogue Box

[5] Alternatively, we could have *defined* the word **Dozens** to be cells B4:C4 by highlighting these cells and then going to **Insert** menu and selecting **Name**, then **Define** and click OK. The formula in cell D6 would now be programmed as =SUMPRODUCT(Dozens,B6:C6) which would be dragged to cells D7, D8, D9, and D10.

FILLING IN THE SOLVER DIALOGUE BOX

Step 1: Set Target Cell

The target cell is the cell containing the value of the objective function. This cell must have a formula in it. For this model, this is cell D6 since it will contain the total weekly profit.

> **With the cursor in the Set Target Cell box: Click on Cell D6.**

Step 2: Equal To

This tells Solver whether you want to find a solution that maximizes or minimizes the value of the objective function or find a solution that gives a particular value for the objective function. In linear programming we are always seeking to maximize or minimize the objective function value. For this model, we wish to maximize cell D6.

> **Leave the button for Max highlighted.**

Step 3: By Changing Cells

Changing cells are the cells that contain the decision variables. Solver will return values to these cells that optimize the objective function subject to the constraints entered below.[6] For this model the decision variables are in cells B4 and C4.

> **With the cursor in the By Changing Cells box: Highlight Cells B4 and C4.**

Step 4: Subject to the Constraints

To enter constraints we click the Add button. This brings up the Add Constraint dialogue box shown in Figure 2.15.

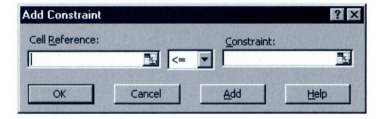

FIGURE 2.15
The Add Constraint Dialogue Box

Note that the default direction for a constraint is "≤," but this can be changed by clicking on the arrow of the drop down box. Options include "≤," "=," "≥," "int," and "bin." The last two options allow us to restrict a Cell Reference to be integer-valued or binary (0 or 1), respectively.

In the Cell Reference box, designate the cell containing the value for the left side of the constraint. In the Constraint box, input a number, a formula, or a cell containing the right side of the constraint. Several constraints can be entered at one time as long as they have the same direction. For our model, all the constraints are "≤," and thus we input them all at once.

[6] Note that if formulas are entered in any of the cells designated as Changing Cells, Solver will simply ignore these formulas.

> **With the cursor in the Cell Reference box: Highlight cells D7 through D10. Leave the direction as "≤." With the cursor in the Constraint box: Highlight cells F7 through F10.**

If more constraints were to be added, we would click **Add** and follow the same procedure. When we are done entering constraints in the Add Constraint dialogue box and click   OK   .

Step 5: Options

Clicking Options brings up the dialogue box shown in Figure 2.16.

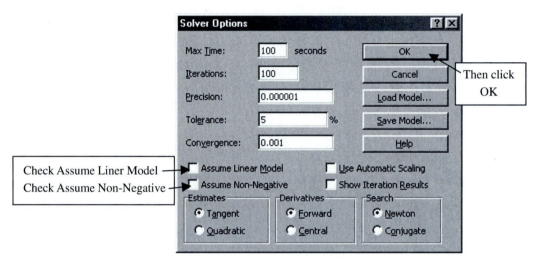

FIGURE 2.16   The Solver Options Dialogue Box

This dialogue box allows us to reset several parameters of a technical nature that are beyond the scope of our discussion here. However, it is important that we designate that the variables are restricted to be "≥0" (Assume Non-Negative) and that the problem be solved specifically as a linear program rather than a general mathematical programming model (Assume Linear). Doing these two things allows relevant "what-if" sensitivity analyses to be generated. Check these boxes and click   OK   .

Step 6: Solve

Figure 2.17 shows the completed Solver dialogue box for the Galaxy Industries model.

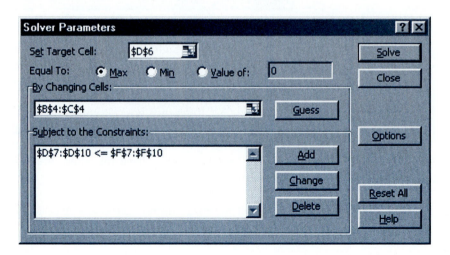

FIGURE 2.17
Completed Solver Dialogue Box for Galaxy Industries

To solve for the optimal solution, click [Solve].

The values in the spreadsheet are changed to reflect the optimal solution, the optimal value of the objective function, and the total left-hand side values in their respective cells.

Step 7: Reports

On top of the spreadsheet is the Solver Results dialogue box shown in Figure 2.18.

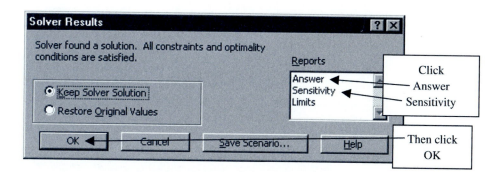

FIGURE 2.18
Solver Results Dialogue Box

This indicates that an optimal solution was found, it also asks which reports we wish to have generated. The two reports that are of interest to us are the Answer Report and the Sensitivity Report. Highlight them and click [OK].

We are finally done! Now let us analyze the results.

Analyzing the Excel Spreadsheet

Figure 2.19 shows the optimal Excel spreadsheet for the Galaxy Industries model.

	Space Rays	Zappers	Total		Limit
GALAXY INDUSTRIES					
Dozens	320	360			
Profit	8	5	4360		
Plastic	2	1	1000	<=	1000
Prod. Time	3	4	2400	<=	2400
Total	1	1	680	<=	700
Mix	1	-1	-40	<=	350

FIGURE 2.19   Optimal Excel Spreadsheet for Galaxy Industries

From this spreadsheet we can see that the optimal solution for this model is:

- Produce 320 dozen Space Rays (cell B4) and 360 dozen Zappers (cell C4) weekly
- Total weekly profit = $4360 (cell D6)

From column D, we see that this solution uses all 1000 pounds of plastic (cell D7) and all 2400 production minutes (cell D8). Since these two constraints hold as *equalities* at the optimal solution, they are said to have *no slack* and they are the *binding constraints*. The left side of the total production constraint is 680 (cell D9), and it indicates that there is a *slack* of 20 for the total production constraint (calculated by subtracting the left-side value (680) from right-side limit for the constraint (700)). Similarly, the slack for the mix constraint is 350 −(−40) = 390.

The Answer Report

The above information is summarized in the Answer Report. Clicking on the Answer Report tab at the bottom of the spreadsheet gives the window shown in Figure 2.20.

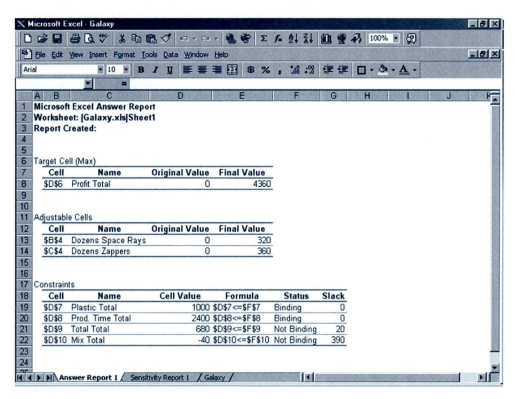

FIGURE 2.20   Galaxy Industries Answer Report

The Answer Report is divided into three sections: the Target Cell section, the Adjustable Cells section, and the Constraints section. What appears in the **Name** column of each of these sections is a combination of the last nonnumeric cell to the left and the last nonnumeric cell above the corresponding cell entry.

In the **Target Cell** Section, the optimal value of the objective function is given in the column labeled **Final Value**. Similarly, the optimal values for the decision variables are found in the **Final Value** column of the **Adjustable Cells** section.

In the **Constraints** section, the **Cell Value** column gives the total values of the left side of the constraints (i.e., the values in cells D7, D8, D9, and D10). The information entered in the Constraint Dialogue Box of Solver is given in the **Formula** column. The **Slack** column shows the amount of slack for each constraint.

Note that if the slack is 0, the word "Binding" is printed in the **Status** column; "Not Binding" is printed when the slack is positive.

The Sensitivity Report

The Sensitivity Report shown in Figure 2.21 contains the relevant information concerning the effects of changes to either an objective function coefficient or a right-hand side value as discussed in Section 2.4. The Adjustable Cells section includes the reduced costs and ranges of optimality for objective function coefficients (expressed in terms of Allowable Increases and Allowable Decreases). The Constraints section details the shadow prices and ranges of feasibility for right-hand side values (again expressed in terms of Allowable Increases and Allowable Decreases). This report can be thought of as the linear programming equivalent of a *marginal analysis* in economics, as the results deal with the effects of making *one and only one parameter value change* to the model.

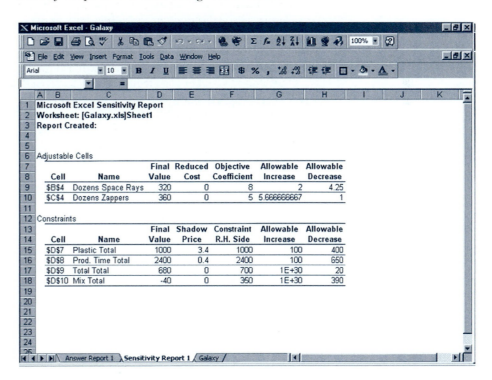

FIGURE 2.21
Galaxy Industries
Sensitivity Report

Note that in Figure 2.21 there is a value of "1E+30" for the Allowable Increase for the total production and mix constraints. "1E+30" is Excel's way of saying "infinity." That is, the range of feasibility for the total production is from $700 - 20 = 680$ to infinity, and the range of feasibility for the mix constraint is from $350 - 390 = -40$ to infinity.

2.6 Using Computer Output to Generate a Management Report

Given the computer solution to the problem faced by Galaxy Industries, the following report can be prepared for Hal Barnes, Galaxy's production manager. This report compares the results of the recommended policy to those of the current policy at Galaxy Industries. It not only summarizes the results but also details the distribution of the resources as well as sensitivity issues that might be of interest to management. The statements made about the shadow price for plastic and production hours outside their ranges of feasibility are based on completely re-solving the problem.

·SCG·
STUDENT CONSULTING GROUP

MEMORANDUM

To: Hal Barnes, Production Manager
         Galaxy Industries

From: Student Consulting Group

Subj: Optimal Production Quantities for Space Rays and Zappers

Galaxy Industries wishes to determine production levels for its Space Ray and Zapper water guns, which will maximize the company's weekly profit. It is our understanding that production of these products occurs in batches of one dozen each; however, any batch not completed in a given week is considered "work in progress" and will be finished at the beginning of the following week.

Physical production limitations include the amount of plastic (1000 pounds) and available production time (40 hours) to the company on a weekly basis. In addition, the company wishes to adhere to marketing recommendations that limit total production to 700 dozen units weekly and restrict weekly production of Space Rays to a maximum of 350 dozen more than the number of Zappers produced. Current weekly production levels of 450 dozen Space Rays and 100 dozen Zappers result in a $4100 weekly profit for Galaxy.

We have had the opportunity to determine the plastic and production time requirements for these products and to analyze Galaxy's situation. By assuming profit and production requirements are fixed and constant, we were able to solve this as a linear programming model using Excel.

ANALYSIS AND RECOMMENDATION

Based on the results of our model, we recommend that Galaxy change its production levels to the following:

Space Rays	320 dozen
Zappers	360
Weekly profit	$4360

The current and proposed policies are compared in Table I.

TABLE I. Current vs. Proposed Policies—Galaxy Industries

Current Policy (Weekly basis)				
	Production (doz.)	Plastic (lb.)	Production Time (hr.)	Profit ($)
Space Rays	450	900	22.50	$3,600
Zappers	100	100	6.67	$ 500
Total	550	1000	29.17	$4,100
Unused		0	10.83	

Proposed Policy (Weekly basis)				
	Production (doz.)	Plastic (lb.)	Production Time (hr.)	Profit ($)
Space Rays	320	640	16.00	$2,560
Zappers	360	360	24.00	$1,800
Total	680	1000	40.00	$4,360
Unused		0	0	

As this table indicates, both policies produce less than the limit of 700 dozen suggested by the marketing department. The proposed policy has a more balanced production of Space Rays and Zappers than the present production policy. Under the current policy, weekly production of Space Rays exceeds that of Zappers by the maximum limit of 350 dozen. Under the proposed plan, production of Zappers actually exceeds that of Space Rays by 40 dozen per week.

The $4360 weekly profit corresponding to the recommended production schedule represents a 6.34% (or $260) increase in weekly profit, or $13,520 annually. This amount could be used to increase marketing of the current products, fund production of the new Big Squirt model under development, or lease more efficient machines to improve product profit contributions.

Although this model is based on profit projections of $8 per dozen Space Ray units and $5 per dozen Zapper units, our analysis reveals that our recommendation would remain unchanged unless the Space Ray profit is higher than $10.00 or lower than $3.75 (a 25% underestimation or a 59% overestimation), or the Zapper profit is higher than $10.67 or lower than $4.00 (a 113% underestimation or a 20% overestimation). We are confident that our profit projections fall well within this margin of error.

If Galaxy has the opportunity to purchase additional plastic from its vendor, our analysis shows that it will prove profitable to purchase up to 100 additional pounds of plastic, as long as the cost does not exceed $3.40 per pound over its normal cost. If the additional 100 pounds of plastic are purchased, giving a total of 1100 pounds of plastic, our recommendation is to produce 400 dozen Space Rays and 300 dozen Zappers.

If more than 1100 pounds of plastic were available, it would be profitable to purchase up to an additional 125 pounds of plastic (for a total of 1225 pounds) as long as the cost of these additional 125 pounds does not exceed $3.00 per pound. If a total of 1225 pounds of plastic were available, we recommend a production schedule of 525 dozen Space Rays and 175 dozen Zappers.

There is insufficient production time to use more than 1225 pounds of plastic while still adhering to the marketing department recommendation that Space Ray production not exceed Zapper production by more than 350 dozen.

In lieu of purchasing plastic, if Galaxy considers scheduling overtime, we recommend that scheduling up to $1\frac{2}{3}$ hours of overtime weekly will be profitable if total overtime costs do not exceed $24 over the normal hourly wage rate. Using this overtime, the company should produce 300 dozen Space Rays and 400 Zappers weekly.

Production Recommendations with Additional Resources

Additional Resource	Space Rays (doz.)	Zappers (doz.)	Weekly Profit
150 pounds of plastic	400	300	$4700
225 pounds of plastic	525	175	$5075
$1\frac{2}{3}$ overtime hours	300	400	$4400

These recommendations are based on changes in only one resource—plastic or overtime. The Student Consulting Group is available to analyze any combination of changes in plastic availability and overtime, changes in the marketing department's restrictions, or any other changes in the company's position. Please do not hesitate to call on us again for such analyses.

2.7 Models Without Unique Optimal Solutions—Infeasibility, Unboundedness, and Alternate Optimal Solutions

Not every linear programming model possesses a unique optimal solution. We already saw in Section 2.3 that when the objective function is parallel to a constraint, the problem can have more than one optimal solution. Under certain conditions, linear programming models may also have no feasible solutions at all, or they may have unbounded feasible regions giving the possibility of theoretically generating infinite profits. We now examine such situations.

INFEASIBILITY

In some cases, a linear program possesses no feasible solutions whatsoever. For example, suppose that, in addition to the other constraints, management at Galaxy Industries wishes to produce at least 500 dozen Space Rays per week. This constraint is expressed as $X_1 \geq 500$ and is illustrated in Figure 2.22. As you can see, there are no feasible points satisfying all the constraints.

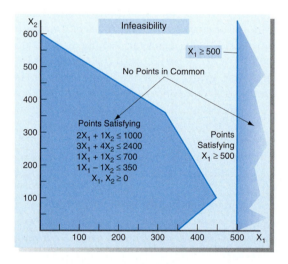

FIGURE 2.22
Infeasibility—No Points Satisfy All Constraints

When infeasible models are detected by Excel Solver, the dialogue box shown in Figure 2.23 appears on the spreadsheet stating a feasible solution could not be found.

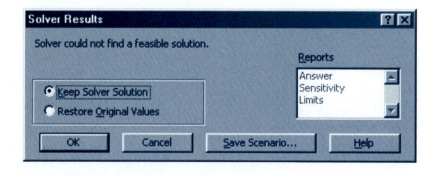

FIGURE 2.23
Infeasible Solution Dialogue Box

On the one hand, **infeasibility** can occur because the problem has been misformulated at either the modeling or the data input stage, or, as was the case above, the problem may be modeled correctly but is overconstrained; management has simply given the modeler a situation to which there is no solution. If infeasibility is detected, some of the constraints must be relaxed in order to obtain a feasible solution. Note that changing the objective function will never make an infeasible problem feasible.

Infeasibility

A model that has no feasible points is an *infeasible* model.

UNBOUNDEDNESS

Consider the model for Galaxy Industries depicted in Figure 2.24. The model is constrained only by the nonnegativity constraints and the marketing constraint that Space Ray production should not exceed Zapper production by more than 350 dozen per week ($X_1 - X_2 \leq 350$). In this situation, the feasible region extends indefinitely, bounded only by the X_1 axis, the X_2 axis, and the functional constraint $X_1 - X_2 \leq 350$. Such a feasible region, which extends "forever" in a particular direction, is called an **unbounded feasible region**.

Problems with unbounded feasible regions may or may not possess optimal solutions. In Figure 2.24, we see that when the objective function line, MAXIMIZE $8X_1 + 5X_2$, is moved parallel outwardly through the feasible region, this gives ever-increasing objective function values. This is an example of a linear program with an **unbounded solution**.

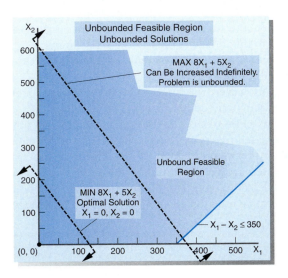

FIGURE 2.24
Unbounded Feasible Region for $X_1 - X_2 \leq 350$, $X_1 \geq 0$, $X_2 \geq 0$. Problem is unbounded if objective function is MAX $8X_1 + 5X_2$; problem has an optimal solution (0,0) if objective function is MIN $8X_1 + 5X_2$

When Excel's Solver detects that the model has an unbounded solution, the dialogue box shown in Figure 2.25 appears on the spreadsheet.

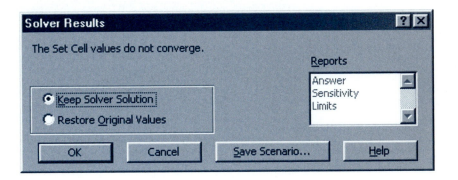

FIGURE 2.25
Unbounded Solution Dialogue Box

"The Set Cell values do not converge" is Excel's way of stating that the problem has an unbounded solution.

Unbounded Solutions

A linear program with an **unbounded solution** is one in which feasible solutions exist but there is no bound for the value of the objective function.

For a linear program to have an unbounded solution, the feasible region must be unbounded. But the fact that the feasible region is unbounded does not necessarily imply that the linear program has an unbounded solution. We see in Figure 2.24 that if the objective function were MINIMIZE $8X_1 + 5X_2$, although the feasible region is unbounded, (0,0) is the optimal point.

Linear programs with unbounded solutions are theoretically possible, but they do not occur in business situations. A business cannot make an infinite profit, or, in the case of a minimization problem, have an infinitely negative cost. If we determine that a linear programming formulation of a "real" business problem has an unbounded solution, a data entry error must have occurred or some constraint has been omitted from the formulation.

Alternate Optimal Solutions

In Section 2.3 we pointed out that alternate optimal solutions to a linear programming model can exist when the objective function line is parallel to a constraint. When alternate optimal solutions exist, many software packages alert the user to this event and assist the user in determining some, if not all, additional optimal extreme points. Unfortunately, Solver does not explicitly indicate when alternate optimal solutions exist.

However, when the Allowable Increase (or Allowable Decrease) for an objective function coefficient is 0, this usually indicates the existence of alternative optima.[7] This condition indicates that if the objective function coefficient were increased (decreased) even slightly, Excel would generate a new optimal solution. Because of the change to the objective function coefficient, this new solution would have a slightly higher (lower) value of the objective function. The trick is to get Excel to generate this solution without increasing (decreasing) the value of an objective function coefficient. This can be done as follows.

Generating Alternate Optimal Solutions with Excel

1. Observe that an Allowable Increase or Allowable Decrease for the objective function coefficient of some variable X_j is 0.

2. Add a constraint that sets the value of the objective function cell to the printed optimal value in that cell.

3. If the Allowable Increase = 0, change the objective to MAXIMIZE X_j by changing the target cell to the cell containing the value of X_j and setting the Equal To bullet to Max.

   If the Allowable Decrease = 0, change the objective to MINIMIZE X_j by changing the target cell to the cell containing the value of X_j and setting the Equal To bullet to Min.

---

[7] There are special cases in which these conditions hold, but there are no alternate optimal solutions.

We illustrate the procedure for the Galaxy Industries model in which the objective function has been changed to MAXIMIZE $8X_1 + 4X_2$. Using this objective function, Solver generates the worksheet shown in Figure 2.26. Note that these show an optimal solution of 450 dozen Space Rays and 100 dozen Zappers, yielding an optimal profit of $4000.

Galaxy Alt1.xls

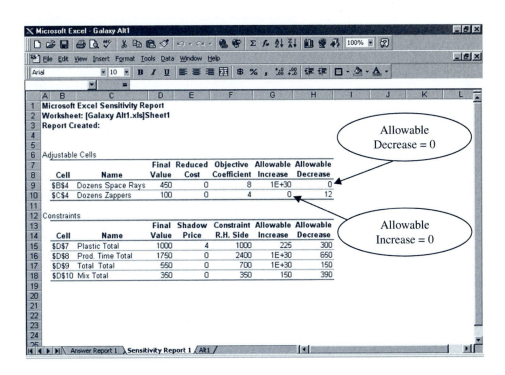

FIGURE 2.26
An Optimal Solution
with Objective Function:
MAX $8X_1 + 4X_2$

Step 1: We note in the Sensitivity Report in Figure 2.27, that there is an Allowable Decrease of 0 for the profit coefficient of Space Rays and an Allowable Increase of 0 for the profit coefficient for Zappers. Thus, we could choose MIN X_1 or MAX X_2 to generate an alternate optimal solution. We shall use the latter.

FIGURE 2.27
Sensitivity Report for Model
with Objective Function:
MAX $8X_1 + 4X_2$

Step 2: Add the constraint that the value of the objective function (in cell D6) must equal 4000 to the Solver dialogue box. Go to Solver: Click ADD, enter the constraint as in Figure 2.28, and click OK.

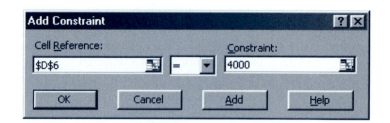

FIGURE 2.28
Adding the Constraint That
the Objective Function Value
Must Remain 4000

Step 3:   Change the objective function to MAX X_2. Since X_2 is in cell C4, position the cursor in Set Target Cell and click on cell C4 as shown in Figure 2.29.

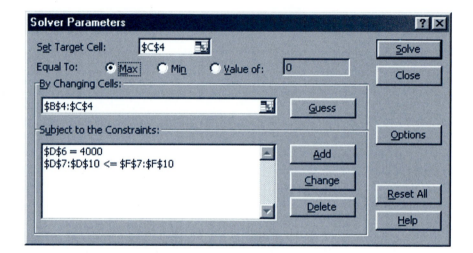

FIGURE 2.29
Resetting the Target Cell
to MAX X_2

Clicking Solve gives the spreadsheet shown in Figure 2.30, reflecting a second optimal solution. This alternate optimal solution requires the production of 320 dozen Space Rays and 360 dozen Zappers. Notice that the solution has the same objective function value of $4000.

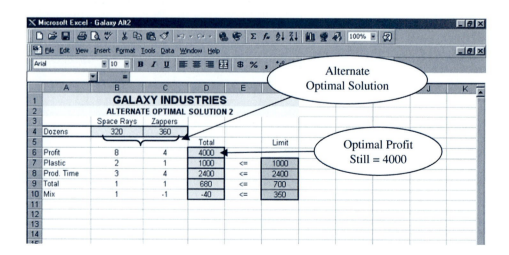

FIGURE 2.30
An Alternate Optimal
Solution with Objective
Function MAX $8X_1 + 4X_2$

2.8 A Minimization Problem

The Galaxy Industries problem is a typical example of a common linear programming model known as a **product mix problem**. In its simplest form, this type of problem has a maximization objective function and all "≤" functional constraints. That is, management is trying to maximize something, but limited amounts of resources are restricting it or holding it back.

The inverse of this type of problem is one in which the objective function is to be *minimized* and the constraints are of the "≥" variety. Problems with this structure have come to be known as **diet problems**. This is because finding a least cost diet that meets minimum nutritional standards was one of the earliest applications of linear programming, dating back to the World War II era. The following Navy sea ration problem is a simplified version of a diet problem.

NAVY SEA RATIONS

The Department of the Navy has been downsizing and is looking for cost savings opportunities to meet mandated congressional budget cuts. One suggestion under consideration is to change the makeup of the content of Navy sea rations, the canned food supplies containing certain minimum daily requirement (MDR) of Vitamin A, Vitamin D, iron, and other nutrients, which combat troops carry into battle.

Navy Sea Rations.xls

According to Texfoods, the current supplier of sea rations for the Navy, each two-ounce portion of its product supplies 20% of the required amount of Vitamin A, 25% of the MDR of Vitamin D, and 50% of the required amount of iron. Each portion costs the Navy $0.60. Because all minimum standards must be met in each serving, the current sea ration container must contain 10 ounces of the Texfoods product (to meet the MDR of Vitamin A). This costs the Navy $3.00 (=5 × $0.60) per serving.

The Navy is considering switching to another product from a different supplier, Calration. A two-ounce portion of Calration costs $0.50 and provides 50% of the MDR of Vitamin A and 25% of the requirement of Vitamin D, but only 10% of the MDR for iron. Substituting the Calration product, the sea ration container would have to contain 20 ounces in order to meet the MDR for iron, costing the Navy $5.00 (=10 × $0.50) per serving.

One bright Navy lieutenant has suggested that a mixture of the two products might meet the overall standards at a lower cost than the current $3 per serving. The Navy has never worried about the taste of sea rations; hence, mixing them, either by combining them or by packing a portion of each, is an acceptable alternative. The lieutenant has been given permission to evaluate the data.

SOLUTION

The following is a brief synopsis of the problem posed by the lieutenant:

- Determine the amount of 2-ounce portions of each sea ration product in the mix.
- Minimize the total cost of the sea rations.
- Meet the MDR for Vitamin A, Vitamin D, and iron.

DECISION VARIABLES

The following decision variables must be included in the problem:

X_1 = number of 2-ounce portions of Texfoods product used in a serving of sea rations

X_2 = number of 2-ounce portions of Calration product used in a serving of sea rations

OBJECTIVE FUNCTION

The objective is to minimize the total cost of a serving of sea rations. Since each 2-ounce serving of Texfoods costs \$0.60 and each 2-ounce serving of Calration costs \$0.50, the objective function is:

MINIMIZE $.60X_1 + .50X_2$

CONSTRAINTS

Each 2-ounce portion of Texfoods product provides 20% of the MDR for Vitamin A; each 2-ounce portion of the Calration product provides 50%. If X_1 2-ounce portions of Texfoods and X_2 2-ounce portions of Calration are included in the sea rations, this would give $20X_1 + 50X_2$ percent of the MDR for Vitamin A. The constraint that at least 100% of the MDR of Vitamin A must be met can then be written as

(The total percent of Vitamin A) $\geq$ (100%)
$$20X_1 + 50X_2 \geq 100$$

Similar constraints for Vitamin D and iron, respectively, are:

$$25X_1 + 25X_2 \geq 100$$

and

$$50X_1 + 10X_2 \geq 100$$

Together with the nonnegativity constraints, this gives us the following linear programming model:

MINIMIZE $.60X_1 + .50X_2$
ST

$$20X_1 + 50X_2 \geq 100$$
$$25X_1 + 25X_2 \geq 100$$
$$50X_1 + 10X_2 \geq 100$$
$$X_1, X_2 \geq 0$$

This problem is illustrated in Figure 2.31. Note that the feasible region is unbounded. Since the objective is to minimize the objective function, however, the objective function line is moved downward toward the origin, and the optimal point is (1.5, 2.5).

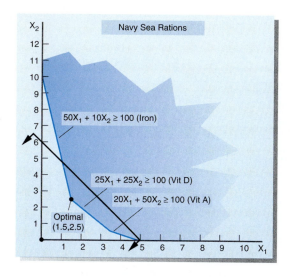

FIGURE 2.31
Navy Sea Rations—
Graphical Solution

THE EXCEL SPREADSHEET

Figure 2.32 shows the Excel Spreadsheet and Solver Dialogue box for this model.

Navy Sea Rations.xls

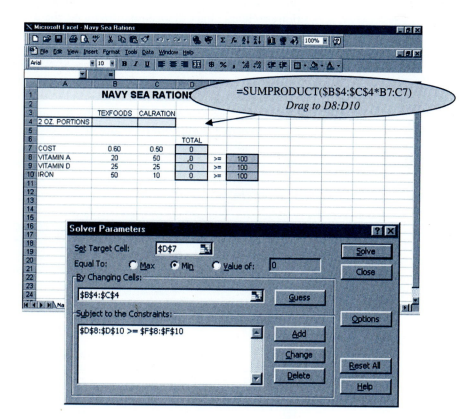

FIGURE 2.32
Spreadsheet for Navy
Sea Rations

The only cell programmed is the target cell D7 giving the total cost. Its formula is dragged to cells D8, D9, and D10 to give the total Vitamin A, Vitamin D, and iron, respectively, in a serving.

In the Solver dialogue box we highlighted the MIN button, and in the Options box we checked, Assume Linear Model and Assume Non-Negative. Figure 2.33 gives the optimal spreadsheet for the model.

	A	B	C	D	E	F
1		NAVY SEA RATIONS				
2						
3		TEXFOODS	CALRATION			
4	2 OZ. PORTIONS	1.5	2.5			
5						
6				TOTAL		
7	COST	0.60	0.50	2.15		
8	VITAMIN A	20	50	155	>=	100
9	VITAMIN D	25	25	100	>=	100
10	IRON	50	10	100	>=	100

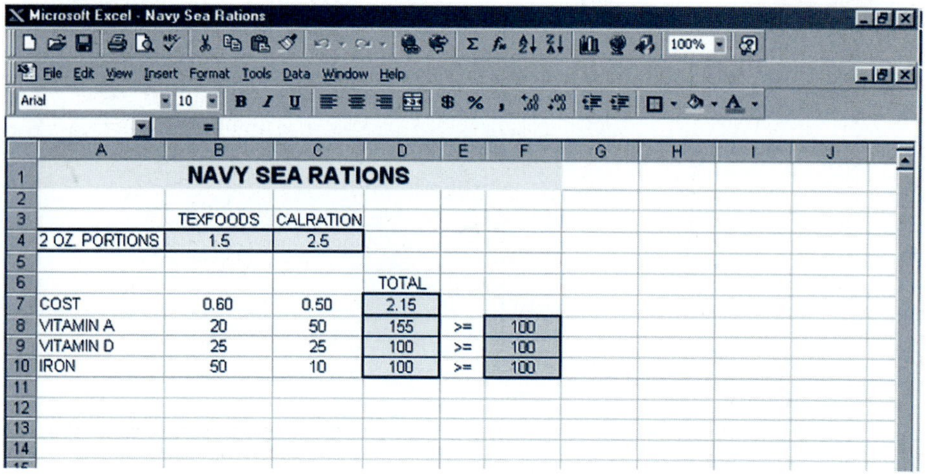

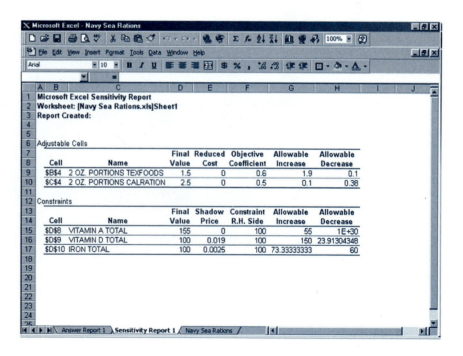

FIGURE 2.33
Optimal Spreadsheet for Navy Sea Rations

ANALYSIS OF EXCEL OUTPUT

The Optimal Solution

From the spreadsheet in Figure 2.33 we see that the optimal solution is to mix 1.5 portions (=3 ounces) of Texfoods product with 2.5 portions (=5 ounces) of Calration product. This 8-ounce mixture meets the MDR's for Vitamin D and iron (the binding constraints). The percentage of Vitamin A in the mixture is 20(1.5) + 50(2.5) = 155%, a *surplus* of 155% − 100% = 55% above the MDR for Vitamin A. The total cost per serving is \$2.15, an \$0.85, or 28.33% (=\$0.85/\$3.00), reduction in the cost of sea rations from the current \$3 level.

An additional benefit of this solution is the reduced quantity of sea rations a sailor must carry—from 10 ounces to 8 ounces per serving. This reduction in weight means a significant reduction in the fuel consumption required to transport the sea rations to the sailors. Given the large supply of sea rations purchased by the Navy, this adds up to a considerable cost savings.

Let us now analyze the output given on the Sensitivity Report shown in Figure 2.34.

Microsoft Excel Sensitivity Report
Worksheet: [Navy Sea Rations.xls]Sheet1
Report Created:

Adjustable Cells

Cell	Name	Final Value	Reduced Cost	Objective Coefficient	Allowable Increase	Allowable Decrease
\$B\$4	2 OZ. PORTIONS TEXFOODS	1.5	0	0.6	1.9	0.1
\$C\$4	2 OZ. PORTIONS CALRATION	2.5	0	0.5	0.1	0.38

Constraints

Cell	Name	Final Value	Shadow Price	Constraint R.H. Side	Allowable Increase	Allowable Decrease
\$D\$8	VITAMIN A TOTAL	155	0	100	55	1E+30
\$D\$9	VITAMIN D TOTAL	100	0.019	100	150	23.91304348
\$D\$10	IRON TOTAL	100	0.0025	100	73.33333333	60

FIGURE 2.34
Sensitivity Report for Navy Sea Rations

Reduced Costs

Because both decision variables are positive in the optimal solution, the reduced costs are zero. If one of the variables had been zero, then, for a minimization problem, increasing its value by one unit would increase the minimized value of the objective function; that is, the reduced cost for a minimization problem would be positive.

Ranges of Optimality

From Figure 2.34, we can make the following observations regarding the ranges of optimality for 2-ounce portions of the Texfoods and Calrations products. These are summarized in Table 2.7.

TABLE 2.7   Ranges of Optimality

Unit Cost for 2 oz. of	Current Value	Allowable Increase	Allowable Decrease	Range of Optimality	Interpretation (if no other changes are made)
Texfoods	$0.60	$1.90	$0.10	$0.50 ↔ $2.50	If the cost of 2 oz. of Texfoods is between $0.50 and $2.50, it is optimal to blend 1.5 portions (3 oz.) of Texfoods with 2.5 portions (5 oz.) of Calrations.
Calration	$0.50	$0.10	$0.38	$0.12 ↔ $0.60	If the cost of 2 oz. of Calration is between $0.12 and $0.60, it is optimal to blend 1.5 portions (3 oz.) of Texfoods with 2.5 portions (5 oz.) of Calrations.

Shadow Prices and Ranges of Feasibility

Figure 2.34 also gives us information about the effect of the required percentages of Vitamin A, Vitamin D, and iron on the total cost of the mixture. These are summarized in Table 2.8.

TABLE 2.8   Shadow Prices and Ranges of Feasibility

Nutrient	Shadow Price	Current Requirement	Allowable Increase	Allowable Decrease	Range of Feasibility	Interpretation (if no other changes are made)
Vitamin A	$0.000	100%	55%	Infinite	$-\infty$ ↔ 155%	As long as the mixture must contain less than 155% of the MDR for Vitamin A, the optimal total cost will remain $2.15.
Vitamin D	$0.019	100%	150%	23.91%	76.09% ↔ 250%	As long as the mixture must contain between 76.09% and 250% of the MDR for Vitamin D, the total cost of $2.15 will increase (decrease) by $0.019 for each 1% increase (decrease) in the required percent of MDR for Vitamin D from 100%.
Iron	$0.0025	100%	73.33%	60%	40% ↔ 173.33%	As long as the mixture must contain between 60% and 173.33% of the MDR for Iron, the total cost of $2.15 will increase (decrease) by $0.0025 for each 1% increase (decrease) in the required percent of MDR for Iron from 100%.

2.9   Integer Linear Programming (ILP) Models

Thus far we have focused on the formulation and analysis of linear programming problems that allow decision variables to take on a continuous range of values within the confines of the other constraints. For many models, however, some or all of the decision variables make sense only if they are restricted to integer values. These are known as **integer linear programming (ILP)** models. The number of aircraft United Airlines will purchase this year from McDonnell-Douglas; the number of machines needed for production at Galaxy Industries; the number of trips a company president will take to potential new markets in the Pacific Rim; the number of police personnel to be assigned to the night shift in Portland, Oregon—these are all examples of integer decision variables.

WHEN ARE INTEGER VARIABLES REQUIRED?

It is easy to reason that decision variables expressed in pounds, inches, hours, acres, and the like, need not be restricted to integers. But even if a decision variable represents airplanes, televisions, or desks, depending on the context of the problem, it still may not be necessary to require that these variables take on integer values.

For example, an integer requirement would be essential for the number of MD-11 aircraft McDonnell-Douglas sells to United Airlines. However, the number of MD-11s McDonnell-Douglas produces in a year need not necessarily be an integer. If McDonnell-Douglas's optimal annual production of MD-11s were 24.37, the .37 or an aircraft would be considered work in progress to be completed at a later date. Thus, when determining whether or not a variable should be integer-valued, we should ask, "Does the model represent a one-time decision or an ongoing operation?"

Designating Integer Variables in Excel

It is easy to designate variables as "Integer" when using Excel Solver by using the Add Constraint dialogue box. In the Cell Reference section we denote the cells containing the variables that must be integer. Then we use the pull down menu in the middle input area and select "int." Solver will then print "integer" in the Constraint side of the box (see Figure 2.35).

FIGURE 2.35
Defining Variables to Be Integer

The integer constraints will appear in the Subject to the Constraints section of the Solver dialogue box. To generate the optimal integer solution we click
Solve .

You may notice, particularly for larger problems, that it takes Solver longer to generate the optimal solution when there are integer variables than it would if no integer variables were present. More computation time is required when integer variables are present because the solution procedure Solver uses actually solves many linear programming models just to generate the one optimal integer solution. Furthermore, when we select the Sensitivity Report option, once Solver has determined the optimal solution the box shown in Figure 2.36 appears.

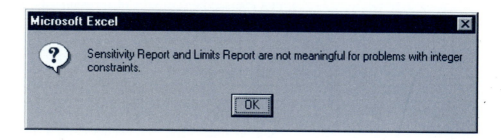

FIGURE 2.36
Dialogue Box Indicating No Sensitivity Information for Integer Models

Rounding

Because of the longer computation times and the lack of sensitivity analyses, it may be worthwhile to solve the model as a linear programming model and round the noninteger solution. However, the rounded solution may be infeasible. Even if the rounded solution is feasible, there is no way of telling whether it is the optimal integer solution.

DIFFICULTIES WITH MODELS REQUIRING INTEGER VARIABLES

Why is it important to designate whether or not a variable is required to be integer-valued? It might seem that restricting variables to integers would actually simplify the solution process, since a finite[8] number of integer points exist, compared to an infinite number for linear programming models.

But, alas, much is lost when integer requirements are imposed. Compared to linear programming solution methods, unless the problem has some special structure (such as the network problems we will discuss in Chapter 4), algorithms for solving models with integer-valued decision variables are more complex, require *much* more computation time, and as we have seen, do not yield valuable sensitivity analysis information. Hence, if an integer programming formulation is not essential, it may be worthwhile to keep a linear programming structure. Thus when rounding is done, one of three situations will occur.

> **Possible Outcomes from Rounding to Integer Values**
>
> 1. The rounded point may be infeasible.
> 2. The rounded point may be feasible but not optimal.
> 3. The rounded point may be the optimal point.

So is rounding ever done? The answer to this question is an emphatic, "*yes,*" particularly if the values of the positive decision variables are relatively large and the values of the objective function coefficients are relatively small. For example, suppose a producer of multiple vitamins used linear programming to determine the production quantities of 50-tablet, 100-tablet, and 500-tablet bottles to be

---

[8] If the feasible region is unbounded, at least the number of feasible solutions is countably infinite, as opposed to continuously infinite.

produced during a production run. If the unit profits for these items are $1.20, $1.75, and $4.80, respectively, and the linear program indicates that 12,253.43, 34,876.90, and 22,623.47 bottles, respectively, should be produced, then rounding these quantities will have little effect on either the value of the objective function or the viability of the constraints.

Of course, the feasibility of any rounded solution should be checked. If the rounded solution does, in fact, violate some constraints, we need to determine whether the violations are significant. For instance, in the vitamin example, suppose one constraint is a marketing restriction requiring that no product is to account for more than 50% of production. If the above solution were rounded to 12,253 50-tablet bottles, 34,877 100-tablet bottles, and 22,623 500-tablet bottles, the proportion of 100-tablet bottles would now be 50.001%—is this so terrible?

On the other hand, if rounding yields a solution that is simply not possible (there is just not enough of a particular resource to achieve this solution), the rounded solution would have to be altered. In this case, a trial-and-error approach might be used.

Although rounding and using trial and error is not guaranteed to produce the true optimal integer solution, it frequently yields a "pretty good" solution. It is important to check the difference between the objective function values of the optimal LP solution and the result of rounding using trial and error. If the difference is small, it may not be worthwhile to use an integer programming optimization procedure that could tie up computer resources for long periods with no guarantee that the optimal result would be better or even different.

AN ILP MODEL

To illustrate these concepts, consider the problem faced by Boxcar Burger Restaurants.

Boxcar.xls

BOXCAR BURGER RESTAURANTS

Boxcar Burger is a new chain of fast-food establishments planning to expand to locations in and around the Washington, D.C., area. Although the food is of high quality and geared to today's health concerns, the main attraction is the boxcar motif. In downtown locations, the interiors of former office buildings are decorated to resemble the inside of a boxcar, while at suburban locations, fast-food sites are remodeled into Boxcar Burger restaurants by using actual boxcars.

The company has $27 million available for the expansion. Each suburban location requires a $2 million investment, and each downtown location a $6 million investment. It is projected that, after expenses, the net weekly profit generated by suburban locations open 24 hours per day will average $12,000. The downtown locations will be open only 12 hours per day, but because of the extremely high customer volume during the workweek, projections indicate that net weekly profits will average $20,000. The company wishes to open at least two restaurants downtown.

Boxcar Burger currently employs 19 managers to run the restaurants. Each suburban location will require three managers for its 24-hour per day operation, whereas the company feels it can get by with just one manager for each downtown location.

Boxcar Burger would like to determine how many restaurants it should open in suburban and downtown Washington, D.C., locations in order to maximize its total net weekly profit.

SOLUTION

The following is a brief synopsis of the problem facing Boxcar Burger:

- Boxcar Burger must decide how many suburban and downtown locations to open in the Washington, D.C., area.
- It wishes to maximize its total average net weekly profits.
- Boxcar Burger's total investment cannot exceed $27 million.
- At least two downtown restaurants are to be opened.
- No more than the current 19 managers can be assigned.

DECISION VARIABLES

Let,

X_1 = number of suburban Boxcar Burger restaurants to be opened
X_2 = number of downtown Boxcar Burger restaurants to be opened

OBJECTIVE FUNCTION

The objective is to maximize total average net weekly profits:

MAX $12,000X_1 + 20,000X_2$

CONSTRAINTS

The following constraints apply:

1. The total investment cannot exceed $27 million. In $1,000,000's this can be written as

$$2X_1 + 6X_2 \leq 27$$

2. The number of downtown restaurants is at least 2:

$$X_2 \geq 2$$

3. The number of managers needed cannot exceed 19:

$$3X_1 + X_2 \leq 19$$

THE MATHEMATICAL MODEL

Clearly, the number of restaurants opened must be an integer. Thus, the complete mathematical programming formulation for the Boxcar Burger problem is:

MAX $12,000X_1 + 20,000X_2$
ST
$$2X_1 + 6X_2 \leq 27$$
$$X_2 \geq 2$$
$$3X_1 + X_2 \leq 19$$
$$X_1, X_2 \geq 0 \text{ and integer}$$

To solve this model we shall use the spreadsheet shown in Figure 2.37.

Boxcar.xls

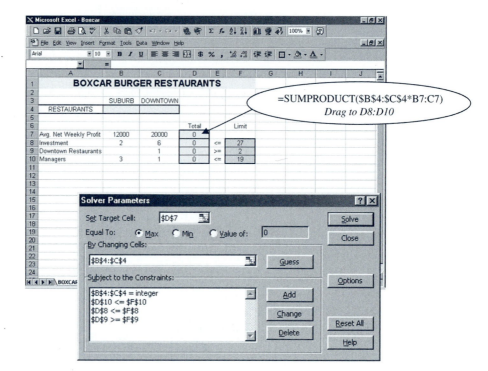

FIGURE 2.37
Spreadsheet for
Boxcar Burger

The target cell (D7), is programmed to give the total average net weekly profit as shown in Figure 2.37. We then drag this formula to cells D8, D9, and D10 to give the total investment (in $1,000,000's), the total number of downtown restaurants, and the total number of managers required, respectively. Note that since the constraints are not ordered by type (i.e., the two "≤" do not follow one another), we add them one at a time, each time clicking the Add button in the Solver dialogue box.

We also click in the Options box and check, Assume Linear Model and Assume Non-Negative.

Clicking Solve in the Solver dialogue box results in the spreadsheet in Figure 2.38, showing that it is optimal to open four suburban restaurants and three downtown restaurants, netting the company a total average weekly profit of $108,000.

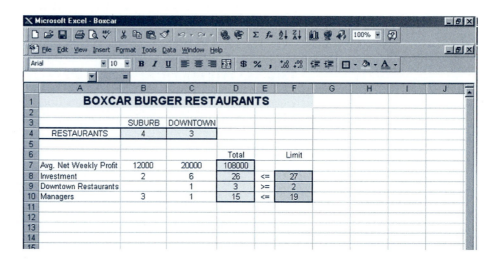

FIGURE 2.38
Solution to Boxcar
Burger Model

A Graphical Analysis

Figure 2.39 shows that the feasible region for the integer model is the set of 13 integer points that fall within the linear programming feasible region. Thus, the objective is to determine which of these 13 feasible points gives the highest value for the objective function. For a small problem like this one, we could simply enumerate all 13 points shown on the graph, substitute their values into the objective function, and select the one giving the highest value. However, for larger problems, the number of feasible points can be in the thousands, millions, or even billions, and simply identifying all feasible points is itself quite a task. Thus, a total enumeration approach is impractical.

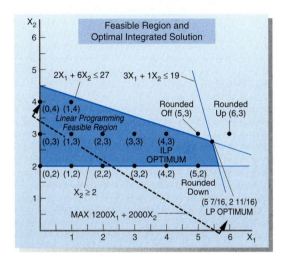

FIGURE 2.39

Integer Points in the Linear Programming Feasible Region. The optimal ILP solution is *not* one of the rounded solutions.

Let us consider the rounding approach. If the model is solved as a linear programming model, ignoring the integer constraints, the optimal solution is $X_1 = 5\ 7/16$, $X_2 = 2\ 11/16$, giving an optimal weekly profit of $12,000(5\ 7/16) + 20,000(2\ 11/16) = \$119,000$. If both fractions are *rounded up*, the integer solution attained is $X_1 = 6$, $X_2 = 3$. If the solution is *rounded off* to the nearest whole number, the integer solution generated is $X_1 = 5$, $X_2 = 3$. From Figure 2.39, we see that neither of these points is in the linear programming feasible region; that is, each violates at least one of the functional constraints. If, however, both fractions are *rounded down*, the resulting integer solution is $X_1 = 5$, $X_2 = 2$. While this solution gives a "relatively good" objective function value of $12,000(5) + 20,000(2) = \$100,000$, this falls $8000 short of the \$108,000 generated by the optimal integer point of $X_1 = 4$, $X_2 = 3$.

We note two things from this discussion. First, in this case, no form of rounding gave the optimal integer solution. Second, the profit generated by the optimal integer solution is less than that of the optimal solution to the linear model. This is because although the integer linear program (ILP) model has the same functional constraints as the LP, it is more constrained by the addition of the two integer constraints: X_1 = integer and X_2 = integer.

Lack of Sensitivity Analysis

As we have mentioned, one of the ILP's biggest drawbacks is its lack of sensitivity analyses. For example, suppose we wished to find the range of values for the profit of suburban restaurants (currently $12,000) which keeps the optimal ILP solution the same ($X_1 = 4$, and $X_2 = 3$). If we connect the feasible integer points that are "farthest out" in all possible directions,[9] we can then attempt to apply the graphical techniques discussed in Section 2.5 to find the ranges of optimality for the objective function coefficients.

From Figure 2.40, we can reason that the point (4,3) will remain the optimal point as long as the objective function coefficients yield a slope between $-1/3$ (the slope of the line between (1,4) and (4,3)) and -1 (the slope of the line between (4,3) and (5,2)). You can verify that this implies that the range of optimality for the average weekly profit for suburban restaurants is between $6333.33 and $20,000 and that for downtown restaurants it is between $12,000 and $36,000.

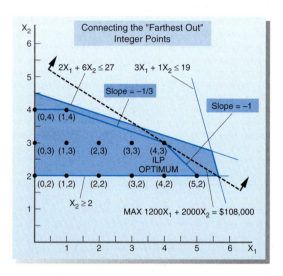

FIGURE 2.40
Boxcar Burger—Connecting the "Farthest Out" Points

The difficulty with this analysis is that we would have to know the "farthest-out" integer points, which itself is a computationally complex problem. Furthermore, the slope of the lines connecting these points usually has no relationship to the slopes of the lines formed by the functional constraints. In this model, for example, the slope of one of the lines restraining the objective function is -1. No functional constraint has this slope. The other restraining line has a slope of $-1/3$, which is only coincidentally the slope of the first functional constraint line.

Integer linear programming offers no parallel to shadow price analysis. In *linear programming*, a shadow price of $10 for a resource implies that the marginal improvement for *each* extra unit of the resource is $10, as long as the change occurs within the resource's range of feasibility. Two extra units of the resource would improve the objective function $20, and half an extra unit would improve it by $5. This is not the case for integer models, however. For example, in the Boxcar Burger model, consider the constraint for investment:

$$2X_1 + 6X_2 \leq 27 \text{ (\$1,000,000's)}$$

Figure 2.41 shows that increasing the amount of investment will have no effect on the optimal solution until the investment equals $28 (million), an increase of $1 (million). Thus, if an extra $999,999.99 is invested, the optimal solution is still $X_1 = 4$, $X_2 = 3$, with a total average weekly profit of $108,000. Then with the next penny, the right-hand side of the investment constraint increases to $28 (million) and the optimal ILP solution becomes $X_1 = 5$, $X_2 = 3$. This results in a total average weekly profit of $12,000(5) + 20,000(3) = $120,000. Thus, for the first

---

[9] This is called forming the "convex hull" of the feasible region. If the feasible region is unbounded, it cannot be done.

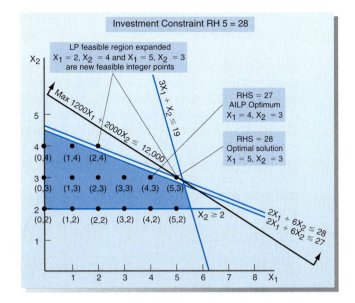

FIGURE 2.41
Boxcar Burger Investment
Constraint Changed to:
$2X_1 + 6X_2 \leq 28$

$999,999.99 of additional investment, no additional profit is made; then with the next penny, there is an increase in profit of $12,000 per week!

This example points out that there is no pattern to the disjoint effects of changes to the objective function and right-hand side coefficients. When do changes occur, they occur in big "steps," rather than the smooth, marginal changes experienced in linear programming. Thus, unfortunately, when we contemplate changes in either objective function coefficients or right-hand side values, re-solving the problem is usually the only viable means for determining the resulting effect.

2.10   Algebraic Solution Approaches for Solving Linear Models

In this chapter we have presented examples with only two decision variables so that we could motivate the discussion of linear and integer programming concepts graphically. However, Excel, as well as all other linear programming packages, can be used to solve problems with any number of variables and constraints, limited only by the capacity of the program and your computer.

But, of course, these packages do not solve the problems by drawing graphs and moving objective function lines until the last point of the feasible region is touched. Instead, these problems are solved algebraically. The most common solution procedure for linear programming models is the simplex method, first proposed by Dr. George Dantzig, circa 1947. In this approach, an extreme point is generated and evaluated for optimality. If it is found not to be optimal, using a simple but tedious procedure of adding multiples of one constraint equation to the others, an *adjacent* extreme point is generated with an improved value of the objective function. This process is repeated until it is determined that the last extreme point generated is optimal. The simplex method is the one used by Excel Solver to solve linear programming models. The details of this approach are outlined in Supplement CD3 on the accompanying CD-ROM.

Another method, proposed by Narendra Karmarkar circa 1985, first generates an interior point and then makes a series of movements to other interior points closer to the boundary. Ultimately, it approaches the optimal extreme point of the feasible region. This method is far more complex than the simplex method, but for many larger models, it has been shown to generate optimal solutions in a fraction of the time of the simplex method.

Various approaches may also be used to solve linear models with integer variables. Virtually all involve adding more and more linear constraints to the original set of functional constraints. Each time a new constraint is added, the problem is re-solved as a linear program and the optimal solution is checked for integrality. If it is not integer-valued, more constraints are added.

In one method, known as the cutting plane approach, each added constraint is guaranteed to be satisfied by all integer points in the original feasible region. A more popular solution method, however, is the branch and bound approach which is discussed in detail in Supplement CD4 on the accompanying CD-ROM. In this approach, when an optimal solution to a linear programming model has one or more noninteger variables, two new "branches" of the model are explored. In each branch a new constraint dealing with one of the noninteger variables is added, making the last optimal solution infeasible.

For example, in the Boxcar Burger model, the optimal solution to the linear model without integer constraints was $X_1 = 5\ 7/16$, $X_2 = 2\ 11/16$. We could now concentrate on X_1 and generate two new linear programming models. One would add $X_1 \geq 6$ to the current set of constraints, and the other would add $X_1 \leq 5$ to the current set of constraints. Both of these new models would then be solved as linear programs with their optimal solutions checked for integer values. If the optimal solution to either or both still had noninteger values, the process would then be repeated.

2.11   Summary

In this chapter we have introduced the concepts of building simple linear models (both with and without integer restrictions for the decision variables) and have shown how to solve linear models using the Solver feature from the Tools menu of Excel. We have pointed out that the linear approach can be used to model a variety of business situations. Additional examples having greater complexity are discussed in detail in Chapter 3.

For models without integer restrictions we have discussed the value of the information generated from Solver's Sensitivity Report, including:

Reduced Cost	The amount a variable's objective function coefficient must change in order for it to become positive in the optimal solution. It is also the amount the objective function value will be affected by increasing this variable by one unit.
Range of Optimality	The range of values for an objective function coefficient such that the optimal solution does not change.
Shadow Price	The per unit change to the optimal objective function value when a right-hand side value changes within its range of feasibility. If the resource's cost is included in the calculation of the objective function coefficients, the shadow price will represent a "premium" value beyond the current price of the resource.
Range of Feasibility	The range of values for a right-hand side coefficient within which the shadow prices are valid.

No sensitivity information is generated from the solution to integer models.

An important theoretical concept in linear programming is that of complementary slackness. For objective function coefficients, this principle states that, at optimality, either the value of a variable is 0 or its reduced cost is 0. For right-hand side coefficients, the complementary slackness principle states that, at optimality, either there is no slack (or surplus) on a given constraint or the value of the shadow price is 0.

For linear models with integer variables, the optimal integer solution is not always the one generated by rounding the optimal solution to the linear programming model. In fact, the rounded solution may not even be feasible. Instead, methods for solving integer models usually involve repeatedly solving linear models. Because of the time and complexity involved to solve integer models, it is often advantageous to solve the models as linear programming models absent the integer restrictions. Rounding and using trial error usually leads to a good, if not optimal, integer solution.

ON THE **CD-ROM**

- Excel spreadsheet for a trial-and-error approach to solving linear programming models — **Barnes.xls**

- Excel spreadsheets for solving basic linear programming models — **Galaxy.xls** / **Navy Sea Rations.xls**

- Excel spreadsheet for determining alternate optimal solutions — **Galaxy Alt1.xls**

- Excel spreadsheet for solving integer linear programming models — **Boxcar.xls**

- Duality — **Supplement CD2**

- The Simplex Method — **Supplement CD3**

- Branch and Bound Algorithms for Integer Linear Programming Models — **Supplement CD4**

- Problem Motivations — **Problem Motivations**

- Problems 41–50 — **Addition Problems/Cases**

Problems

Problems 1–30 can be formulated as linear programming models.

Problems 31–40 require the use of integer variables.

Most problems in these exercises require only two decision variables so that they may be solved graphically or using Excel. In Chapter 3 we focus on more complex problems requiring more than two decision variables.

1. PRODUCT PRODUCTION. Kite 'N String manufactures old-fashioned diagonal and box kites from high-strength paper and wood. Each diagonal kite, which nets the company a $3 profit, requires 8 square feet of paper and 5 linear feet of wood (including waste). Box kites net a $5 profit and, including waste, require 6 square feet of paper and 10 linear feet of wood. Each is packaged in similar boxes. This week Kite 'N String has 1500 boxes and capacity to tailor 10,000 square feet of paper and 12,000 linear feet of wood for kite production. How many of each type of kite do you recommend Kite 'N String produce this week?

2. MANUFACTURING. Golden Electronics manufactures several products, including 45-inch GE45 and 60-inch GE60 televisions. It makes a profit of $50 on each GE45 and $75 on each GE60 television produced. During each shift, Golden allocates up to 300 man-hours in its production area and 240 man-hours in its assembly area to manufacture the televisions. Each GE45 requires two man-hours in the production area

and one man-hour in the assembly area, whereas each GE60 requires two man-hours in the production area and three man-hours in the assembly area.

   a. What production levels of GE45 and GE60 television sets optimize the expected profit per shift? What is the optimal expected profit per shift?

   b. What is the shadow price for extra assembly hours? Interpret.

   c. Would the optimal solution change if the unit profit for GE60 televisions were increased to (i) $135? (ii) $300?

3. MANUFACTURING. Suppose that management at Golden Electronics (see problem 2) has decided to do extensive testing on every television manufactured to ensure its quality standards. Each GE45 television will require inspection time of 30 minutes and each GE60 television 45 minutes.

   a. Reformulate the linear program for television production for Golden Electronics if management made available 80 hours for quality control inspections during each production run.

   b. Give an optimal solution that manufactures as many GE60 television sets as possible.

   c. Give an optimal solution that manufactures exactly three times as many GE45 television sets as GE60 television sets during a shift.

4. MANUFACTURING. Compaids, Inc. manufactures two types of slide-out keyboard trays for use with personal computers. Model C15 is designed for desktop use. It can stand alone, or it can fit under a desktop CPU or monitor. Model UN8 is designed to be mounted underneath a desk with screws. Both units are manufactured from laminated particle board supplied by SSS Industries and use two slide assemblies purchased from Corrigation, Inc. The following table summarizes the wholesale selling price and requirements for each keyboard tray.

Model	Selling Price	Cost of Screws	Particle Board	Production Time
C15	$11.10	$0.40	8 sq. ft.	4 min.
UN8	$12.40	$0.90	5 sq. ft.	6 min.

Each week, SSS can sell Compaids up to 15,000 square feet of laminated particle at $0.40 per square foot, and Compaids can purchase up to 4500 slide assemblies from Corrigation at $0.75 each. Screws are in abundant supply and do not restrict production. Up to five Compaids workers, working eight hours a day, five days a week, can be assigned to the production of the keyboard trays; however, their labor costs are considered sunk costs.

   a. Show that the net unit profit for the model C15 and UN8, excluding the sunk labor costs, are $6 and $8, respectively.

   b. Solve for the optimal weekly production quantities, given the limits on laminated particle board, slide assemblies, and production time.

   c. If 200 additional slide assemblies were made available each week, what is the most Compaids should consider paying for the 200 slide assemblies?

   d. If one additional worker were made available, explain why the shadow prices would change.

   e. What is the maximum selling price for the model C15 units for which the optimal weekly production schedule, found in part (b), remains unchanged?

5. MANUFACTURING. Anderson & Blount (A&B) Woodworks makes tables and chairs from 30-inch wide mahogany sheets that it purchases by the linear foot. It can purchase whatever mahogany it desires for $10 per linear foot up to 2250 linear feet per week. Each table requires 9 linear feet and each chair 3 linear feet (including waste). Each chair also utilizes a soft cushion. Up to 500 cushions can be purchased each week for $25 each. Other required hardware (supports, braces, nuts, bolts, etc.) averages $45 for each table and $25 for each chair. A&B sells the tables to retailers for $300 each and each chair for $150 each.

The 10 craftsmen employed by A&B are salaried workers. Their wages of $800 each per week as well as the $5000 per week in rent, insurance and utility costs are all considered fixed costs. To produce a table requires 1 hour of a craftsmen's time, whereas each chair requires only 36 minutes. Each craftsman averages 37.5 productive work-hours per week. Company policy mandates that the ratio of chairs to tables must be between 4 to 1 and 6 to 1.

   a. Develop a linear programming model for A&B. The objective function should maximize its gross weekly profit (gross revenue less the variable costs of wood, cushions and other materials). Express the feasible region by the nonnegativity constraints and a set of five functional constraints (wood and cushion availability, the minimum and maximum chair to table ratios, and the maximum weekly production time).

   b. Solve for A&B's optimal weekly production schedule of tables and chairs. What is the optimal gross weekly profit? What is the optimal net weekly profit (gross weekly profit less the fixed labor, rent, insurance and utility costs)?

   c. Determine and interpret the shadow prices for:
     i. linear feet of mahogany
     ii. cushions
     iii. production hours

6. ADVERTISING. Print Media Advertising (PMA) has been given a contract to market Buzz Cola via newspaper ads in a major Southern newspaper. Full-page ads in the weekday editions (Monday through Saturday) cost $2000, whereas on Sunday a full-page ad costs $8000. Daily circulation of the newspaper is 30,000 on weekdays and 80,000 on Sunday.

PMA has been given a $40,000 advertising budget for the month of August. The experienced advertising executives at PMA feel that both weekday and Sunday newspaper ads are important; hence, they wish to run the equivalent of at least eight weekday and at least two Sunday ads during August. (Assume that a fractional ad would simply mean that a smaller ad is placed on one of the days; that is, 3.5 ads would mean three full-page ads and one one-half page ad. Also assume that smaller ads reduce exposure and costs proportionately.) This August has 26 weekdays and 5 Sundays.

a. If the objective is to maximize cumulative total exposure (as measured by circulation) for the month of August, formulate and solve a linear program to determine the optimal placement of ads by PMA in the newspaper during August. Comment on the validity of the "no interaction" assumption of linear programming for this model.

b. Explain why the constraints on the maximum number of weekday ads and the maximum number of Sunday ads are both redundant.

c. Suppose the minimum restriction for Sunday ads were eliminated. What would be the new optimal solution? What would be the reduced cost for Sunday ads?

7. PRODUCTION. Wilson Manufacturing produces both baseballs and softballs, which it wholesales to vendors around the country. Its facilities permit the manufacture of a maximum of 500 dozen baseballs and a maximum of 500 dozen softballs each day. The cowhide covers for each ball are cut from the same processed cowhide sheets. Each dozen baseballs require 5 square feet of cowhide, including waste, whereas each dozen softballs require 6 square feet. Wilson has 3600 square feet of cowhide sheets available each day.

Production of baseballs and softballs includes making the inside core, cutting and sewing the cover, and packaging. It takes about one minute to manufacture a dozen baseballs and two minutes to manufacture a dozen softballs. A total of 960 minutes is available for production daily.

a. Formulate a set of linear constraints that characterize the production process at Wilson Manufacturing and draw a graph of the feasible region.

b. Wilson is considering manufacturing either 300 dozen baseballs and 300 dozen softballs or 350 dozen baseballs and 350 dozen softballs. Characterize each of these solutions as an interior point, extreme point, or infeasible point and explain why, regardless of Wilson Manufacturing's objective, neither could be an optimal solution.

c. If Wilson estimates that its profit is $7 per dozen baseballs and $10 per dozen softballs, determine a production schedule that maximizes Wilson's daily profit.

8. MATERIAL BLENDING. Missouri Mineral Products (MMP) purchases two unprocessed ores from Bolivia Mining, which it uses in the production of various compounds. Its current needs are for 800 pounds of copper, 600 pounds of zinc, and 500 pounds of iron. The amount of each mineral found in *each* 100 *pounds* of the unprocessed ores and MMP's cost *per* 100 *pounds* are given in the following table.

Ore	Copper	Zinc	Iron	Waste	Cost
La Paz ore	20	20	20	40	$100
Sucre ore	40	25	10	25	$140

a. Formulate and solve a linear program to determine the amount of each ore that should be purchased in order to minimize total purchasing costs.

b. Calculate and interpret the range of optimality for the cost of 100 pounds of each unprocessed ore.

c. Suppose the cost of Sucre ore was $250 per 100 pounds. Why would the solution in part (a) not be optimal? What is the reduced cost for Sucre ore in this case? Explain.

d. Calculate and interpret the shadow prices and the range of feasibility for the requirements for copper, zinc, and iron.

e. Suppose a constraint were added that required that waste be limited to a maximum of 1000 pounds. Characterize this revised problem.

9. BLENDING. Ocean Juice produces both a cranberry juice cocktail and a raspberry-cranberry blend. Each day Ocean Juice can receive up to 1000 gallons of a raspberry concentrate that costs $2.00 per gallon and up to 4000 gallons of a cranberry concentrate that costs $1.20 per gallon. Purified water, which is in unlimited supply, costs Ocean Juice $0.08 per gallon. The cranberry juice cocktail is 25% cranberry concentrate and 75% water. The raspberry-cranberry blend is 20% raspberry concentrate, 15% cranberry concentrate, and 65% water.

The juices are bottled in glass quart containers costing $0.05 each. Other costs including labor and packaging amount to $0.15 per quart for the cranberry juice cocktail and $0.18 per quart for the raspberry-cranberry blend. The minimum daily required production is 10,000 quarts of cranberry juice cocktail and 8000 quarts of the raspberry-cranberry blend. The total daily production capacity is 50,000 quarts. Ocean Juice sells the cranberry juice cocktail to stores for $0.75 per quart and the raspberry cranberry blend for $0.95 per quart.

a. What is its optimal daily production schedule and daily profit?

b. How much should Ocean Juice be willing to pay for:
   i. An extra quart of production capacity?
   ii. Extra gallons of raspberry concentrate?
   iii. Extra gallons of cranberry concentrate?

10. DIET PROBLEM. Charley Judd is a salesman for Futura Farm Foods, which is currently marketing a feed for dairy cattle called Moo Town Buffet. On a recent visit to Norfolk, Nebraska, Charley called on Dan Preston, a successful dairy farmer with a herd of 100 dairy cattle.

Dan's success is due in part to a rigid diet he feeds his cattle. In particular, each cow receives a daily minimum of 100 units of calcium, 20,000 calories, and 1500 units of protein. To accomplish this regimen, Dan has been giving his cattle Cow Chow Feed. Each ounce costs

$0.015 and supplies 1 unit of calcium, 400 calories, and 20 units of protein. In contrast, each ounce of the Moo Town Buffet Feed would cost Dan $0.020 and supply 2 units of calcium, 250 calories, and 20 units of protein.

a. How much is Dan Preston currently spending to feed a dairy cow each day using Cow Chow?

b. Why would Charley Judd not be successful in persuading Dan Preston to abandon his use of Cow Chow and switch exclusively to Moo Town Buffet?

c. Charley is a resourceful salesman, and he has offered Dan a plan to mix Cow Chow and Moo Town Buffet. The result would be a lower overall cost to Dan for a feed mixture that meets the minimum calcium, calorie, and protein requirements, and a sale for Charley. What overall mix should Charley recommend to minimize Dan's overall feeding cost per cow? How much would Dan Preston save daily by feeding his 100 cattle the mixture recommended by Charley Judd?

11. TOY PRODUCTION. J&J Toy Company produces two dolls that are popular with young girls, the male Jack doll and the female Jill doll. Both dolls are made from plastic and come with a variety of outfits in standard packages. The Jack doll is slightly larger requiring 4 ounces of plastic as compared to 3.5 ounces for the Jill doll. Because the Jill doll is packaged with more clothes, it uses 2 linear feet of cloth as compared to only 1 linear foot of cloth for the clothes packaged with the Jack doll. Due to the popularity of the Jill doll, it is priced to net a unit profit of $7 on each doll while each Jack doll only nets a profit of $5. In a typical week J&J will have the following resources:

- 4200 square feet of cloth for clothes
- 600 pounds of plastic
- production time to make at most 3000 dolls

What production quantities do you recommend for weekly production of Jack and Jill dolls? What is the expected weekly profit?

12. AGRICULTURE. Frank Hurley is a farmer with 250 acres on which he wishes to plant wheat and corn to maximize his expected return for the season. For crop rotation purposes he must plant at least 50 acres of each crop. He can participate in a federal program that will require him to produce at least as much wheat as corn. Under this program, he is guaranteed to earn $150 per acre of wheat planted and $200 per acre of corn planted. Alternatively, he can opt not to participate in the program, in which case he projects he would make only $125 per acre of wheat planted and $184 per acre of corn planted. What would you recommend to Frank?

13. RECYCLING. Alpine Attic is the charity sponsored by local Episcopal churches in Denver, Colorado. Literally thousands of items, including televisions and stereos, are donated each year, most in need of repair. When Alpine Attic receives either a television or a stereo, it determines whether it can be sold "as is" or should be scrapped for parts. Those not sold "as is" are sent directly to JKL Electronics, whose owner, John K.

Lucas, is a deacon at St. Paul's Episcopal Church. In addition to his primary business, each month John donates 45 hours of an electrician's time and 30 hours of a technician's time to rebuild and test televisions and stereos for Alpine Attic. In addition to a tax write-off, he feels rewarded by helping out his church.

The recycled televisions and stereos typically sell for $50 and $30 each at the Alpine Attic Thrift Store. Each recycled television averages 90 minutes of an electrician's time to rebuild and 30 minutes of a technician's time to test, whereas each stereo averages 30 minutes of an electrician's time to rebuild and 60 minutes of a technician's time to test. What is the best use of the electrician's and technician's time to help Alpine Attic realize its optimal profit each month?

14. POLITICAL CAMPAIGNING. Bob Gray is running for a seat in the House of Representatives from a very competitive district in Atlanta, Georgia. With six days to go in the campaign, he has 250 volunteers who can be assigned to either phone banks or door-to-door canvassing. The average time he expects a volunteer to spend on the campaign is 25 hours.

The campaign manager can staff 20 telephones from 8:00 A.M. to 10:00 P.M. each day. On the average, 30 voters can be reached by phone contact each hour, whereas only 18 voters can be reached each hour by door-to-door canvassing. However, Bob wants at least one-third of the remaining volunteer hours to be used for personal door-to-door contacts and at least 15 phones to be used on a continuous basis during the remaining days of the campaign.

a. How many volunteer hours should be allocated to phone contacts and how many to door-to-door canvassing if Bob wishes the maximum number of voters to be contacted during the final six days of the campaign?

b. Suppose Bob's campaign manager feels that door-to-door contacts are twice as valuable in terms of swaying voter opinion as phone contacts. How many volunteer hours should be allocated to phone contacts and how many to door-to-door canvassing if Bob wishes to maximize the "value" of the contacts during the final six days of the campaign?

15. ADVERTISING. Intronix uses copy editors, computer graphics specialists, and Java programmers to produce ads for magazines and the Internet. The average new ad for magazines typically requires 180 hours of a copy editor's time and 135 hours of a computer graphics specialist's time, whereas ads produced for the Internet require 35 hours of copy editor time, 195 hours of computer graphics time, and 60 hours of a Java programmer's time.

Lassie Foods, a dog food manufacturer, has hired Intronix to produce ads in the next four weeks. Although currently it considers magazine ads 3 times more valuable than Internet ads, it still wishes to have at least 2 of each produced within the next four weeks. Intronix has assigned up to 3 copy editors, 4 computer graphics specialists, and 1 Java programmer, each committed to work up to 70 hours per week on the project. How many of each type of ad should be produced to maximize the overall value to Lassie Foods?

16. MERCHANDISE DISPLAYS. The upscale toy store August Kids has a picture window with 100 linear feet of display space. The theme this month is bicycles and tricycles. At least ten tricycles and eight bicycles are to be displayed. Each tricycle needs three linear feet of space in the window display, and each bicycle requires five linear feet. August Kids makes a profit of $40 on each tricycle and $80 on each bicycle it sells. The probability that, on a given day, a displayed tricycle will be sold is .10 and that a displayed bicycle will be sold is .12. Solve for the optimal number of tricycles and bicycles August Kids should display in its picture window daily under each of the following objectives:
a. Maximize total expected daily profit.
b. Maximize the total expected number of daily sales of tricycles and bicycles.
c. Minimize the total number of tricycles and bicycles displayed.

17. PERSONAL INVESTMENTS. George Rifkin is considering investing some or all of a $60,000 inheritance in a one-year certificate of deposit paying a fixed 6% or a venture capital group project with a guaranteed 3% return but the potential of earning 10%. George would like to invest the minimum amount of month necessary to achieve a potential return of at least $4000 and a guaranteed return of at least $2000.

Formulate a mathematical model and recommend an investment strategy for George. How much of his $60,000 can he keep for his personal use during the year and still meet his investment criteria?

18. PERSONAL INVESTMENTS. Consider the situation faced by George Rifkin in problem 17. He has decided to invest the entire $60,000 inheritance. Besides the certificate of deposit paying 6% and the venture capital group paying a minimum of 3% (but with a potential maximum return of 10%), he is considering investing in an oil exploration company. Although this investment could yield a 100% one-year return, George could also lose his entire investment in the company. (*Note:* This is not a 0% return but a loss of 100%.)
a. Formulate and solve a three-variable mathematical model for George that will maximize the potential value of his inheritance after one year, given the following investment criteria:
   • At most $30,000 is to be invested in the oil exploration company.
   • At least $20,000 is to be invested in the certificate of deposit.
   • The value of the portfolio must be at least $40,000 at the start of next year.
   • All $60,000 is to be invested.
b. What is the maximum potential return? Thus what is the maximum potential value of the portfolio at the beginning of next year? What is the minimum value of the portfolio at the beginning of next year?

19. AGRICULTURE. Gilroy Farms of California owns 200 acres of land on which it plants garlic (for which the region is famous) and onions. It estimates that it makes $550 per acre of garlic and $400 per acre of onions planted. During the growing season each acre of garlic requires the use of 4 tons of fertilizer and 2 acre feet of water, whereas each acre of onions requires 3 tons of fertilizer and 1.5 acre-feet of water. Gilroy has contracted for at most 750 tons of fertilizer and 400 acre-feet of water.
a. How many acres of land should be devoted to each crop to maximize its profit for the season? Is there any land left unfarmed?
b. What is the minimum profit per acre for onions that would make it economically feasible for Gilroy Farms to grow onions.
c. If the profit per acre of onion were $450, how many acres of land should Gilroy plant of each crop to maximize its profit for the season?
d. Gilroy Farms is considering leasing another 200-acre parcel adjoining its current property on which it would expand its planting of garlic and onions. If Gilroy can lease this site for $1000, how much additional profit would it make during the growing season if it could not increase its fertilizer and water allocation?

20. BLENDING. Corless Chemical Company can purchase up to 1000 gallons of each of three pesticide compounds, which it blends to make two different commercial products: Bugoff, a plant pesticide, and Weedaway, a lawn pesticide. Bugoff sells for $5 per *quart* and Weedaway for $4 per *quart*. The number of gallons of each of the pesticides required to make a gallon of each commercial product and the cost per gallon are summarized in the following table.

| | Requirements per Gallon | | |
Pesticide	Xylothon	Diazon	Sulferious
Bugoff	.25	.50	.25
Weedaway	.60	.10	.30
Cost per gallon	$12.00	$8.00	$9.00

Corless wants to produce at least 1000 quarts of each product. The cost of the quart bottle container for Bugoff is $0.20; for Weedaway it is $0.30.
a. How many gallons of each commercial product should be blended to yield the maximum net profit to Corless?
b. How much of the 1000 gallons of each of the pesticides will be used? How much of each will Corless *not* purchase?

21. LEASE/BUY. Schick Industries needs to replace some of its aging equipment that produces molded frames for its best-selling Schick racing cycle. Schick can lease machines with a rated capacity of 2000 frames per month for $3000 monthly. Alternatively, it can purchase smaller machines with a rated capacity of 800 frames per month for $10,000 down and $1000 monthly.

Schick only has $50,000 available to purchase machines now, which limits the number of machines that it could purchase to five. Schick must produce at least 10,000 frames per month to keep up with customer demand.

a. Formulate and solve a linear program for Schick to minimize its total monthly payments for machines.

b. Suppose that instead of minimizing total monthly payments, Schick wished to maximize total production capacity. Solve the problem with this objective and comment.

c. Comment on the validity of the linear programming assumptions for this model.

22. INTERNATIONAL SHIPPING. The Takahashi Transport Company (TTC) leases excess space on commercial vessels to the United States at a reduced rate of $10 per square foot. The only condition is that goods must be packaged in standard 30-inch-high crates.

TTC ships items in two standard 30-inch-high crates, one 8-square-foot crate (2 feet by 4 feet) and one 4-square-foot (2 feet by 2 feet) specially insulated crate. It charges customers $160 to ship an 8-square-foot crate and $100 to ship the insulated 4-square-foot crate. Thus, allowing for the $10 per square foot cost, TTC makes a profit of $80 per standard 8-foot crate and $60 on the 4-foot crate.

TTC stores the crates until space becomes available on a cargo ship, at which time TTC receives payment from its customers.

TTC has been able to lease 1200 square feet of cargo space on the *Formosa Frigate* cargo ship, which leaves for the United States in two days. As of this date, TTC has 140 8-square-foot crates and 100 insulated 4-square-foot crates awaiting shipment to the United States. It has 48 hours to finish loading the crates, and it estimates the average loading time to be 12 minutes (0.2 hour) per 8-square-foot crate and 24 minutes (0.4 hour) per 4-square-foot crate (owing to the special handling of the insulated crates).

a. Formulate and solve a *linear* program for TTC to optimize its profit on the upcoming sailing of the *Formosa Frigate*. What are the optimal values of the slack on each constraint in the optimal solution? Express this result in words.

b. Determine the shadow price and the range of feasibility for the number of square feet available. What problem would you have interpreting the shadow prices and the range of feasibility? (*Hint:* Consider what would happen if there were one more square foot of space available. What would be the new optimal solution? Would this make sense?)

c. Suppose that, at the last second, the *Formosa Frigate* decided to raise its charge per square foot from $10 to $12. Note how this change would affect the objective function coefficients. Show that the optimal solution would not change. How does this $2 per square foot increase in leasing charges to TTC affect the shadow price for a square foot of space? Does this make sense?

23. STOCK INVESTMENTS. Idaho investments is a small, newly formed investment group that will invest exclusively in local stocks. The group is planning its initial investment of $100,000, which it will allocate between two stocks—Tater, Inc. and Lakeside Resorts. If the group is successful with these investments, it plans to expand its portfolio further into other Idaho-based stocks. For each of the stocks, the group has estimated three numbers:

• The projected annual return per share with reinvested dividends
• A "potential" index—a number between 0 and 1 that measures the likelihood of high returns in a one-year period
• A "risk" index—a number between 0 and 1 that measures the likelihood of a substantial loss in a one-year period.

The portfolio potential factor is obtained by summing the products of the potential factor for an investment times the fraction of the total investment *dollars* in that investment. For example, if X_1 is the amount invested in Tater and X_2 is the amount invested in Lakeside Resorts, the portfolio potential would be:

$$(X_1/100000)(\text{potential index for Tater}) + (X_2/100000)(\text{potential index for Lakeside})$$

The portfolio risk factor is obtained in a similar manner. The current share price and the group estimates for these factors are summarized in the following table.

Stock	Share Price	Estimated Annual Return	Potential Index	Risk Index
Tater, Inc.	$40	10%	.20	.30
Lakeside Resorts	$50	12%	.40	.80

Formulate and solve for the optimal investment strategy in order to maximize overall expected annual return for Idaho investments if it wishes to:

• Invest all $100,000.
• Keep the portfolio potential at .25 or higher.
• Restrict the portfolio risk to .5 or lower.

24. MANUFACTURING. Lawn Master produces 19-inch and 21-inch lawn mowers, which it sells to membership warehouses and discount stores nationwide. Each lawn mower is powered by a Briggs and Stratton 3.5-horsepower engine. The 19-inch model is a "side-bagger" and requires 40 minutes (2/3 hour) to assemble, test, and package. The 21-inch model is a "rear-bagger" with a variable speed assembly and requires one hour to perform the same operations.

Each week Lawn Master can receive up to 200 Briggs and Stratton engines and has production facilities to manufacture up to 100 variable-speed assemblies. There are four production lines, each working eight hours a day, five days a week, for assembly, testing, and packaging. Each 19-inch model nets Lawn Master a $50 profit, whereas each 21-inch model nets a $60 profit.

a. Formulate and solve a linear programming problem for Lawn Master to determine an optimal weekly production schedule of 19-inch and 21-inch lawn mowers. What is the optimal weekly profit?

b. Determine and interpret the range of feasibility for (i) engines; (ii) variable speed assemblies; (iii) production hours.

c. If an emergency developed so that the amount of production time fell just below the lower limit determined in part (b), what would be the new optimal production schedule?

25. **TRUCKING.** Bay City Movers is a local company that specializes in intercity moves. In the business plan submitted to its backers, Bay City has committed itself to a total trucking capacity of at least 42 tons.

The company is in the process of replacing its entire fleet of trucks with 1-ton pickup trucks and $2\frac{1}{2}$-ton moving van-type trucks. The 1-ton pickup trucks will be manned by one worker, whereas the large vans will utilize a total of four workers for larger moves.

Bay City Movers currently employs 63 workers and has facilities for at most 50 trucks. Pickup trucks cost the company $24,000 each; the moving vans cost $60,000 each. The company wishes to make a minimum investment of capital that will provide a trucking capacity of at least 42 tons while not requiring any additional workers or trucking facilities.

a. Use a linear programming model to determine the optimal number of pickup trucks and moving vans Bay City Movers should purchase.

b. There are alternate optimal solutions to this model. Determine the one that:
    i. Purchases only one type of truck
    ii. Purchases the same number of pickup trucks as moving vans
    iii. Purchases the minimum number of trucks

26. **BAKERY.** Mary Custard's is a pie shop that specializes in custard and fruit pies. It makes delicious pies and sells them at reasonable prices so that it can sell all the pies it makes in a day. Every *dozen* custard pies nets Mary Custard's $15 and requires 12 pounds of flour, 50 eggs, 5 pounds of sugar and no fruit mixture. Every dozen fruit pies nets a $25 profit and uses 10 pounds of flour, 40 eggs, 10 pounds of sugar, and 15 pounds of fruit mixture.

On a given day, the bakers at Mary Custard's found that they had 150 pounds of flour, 500 eggs, 90 pounds of sugar, and 120 pounds of fruit mixture with which to make pies.

a. Formulate and solve a linear program that will give the optimal production schedule of pies for the day.

b. If Mary Custard's could double its profit on custard pies, should more custard pies be produced? Explain.

c. If Mary Custard's raised the price (and hence the profit) on all pies by $0.25 ($3.00 per dozen), would the optimal production schedule for the day change? Would the profit change?

d. Suppose Mary Custard's found that 10% of its fruit mixture had been stored in containers that were not air-tight. For quality and health reasons, it decided that it would be unwise to use any of this portion of the fruit mixture. How would this affect the optimal production schedule? Explain.

e. Mary Custard's currently pays $2.50 for a five-pound bag of sugar from its bakery supply vendor. (The $0.50 per pound price of sugar is included in the unit profits given earlier.) Its vendor has already made its deliveries for the day. If Mary Custard's wishes to purchase additional sugar, it must buy it from Donatelli's Market, a small, local independent grocery store that sells sugar in one-pound boxes for $2.25 a box. Should Mary Custard's purchase any boxes of sugar from Donatelli's Market? Explain.

27. **BAKERY.** For the problem faced by Mary Custard's in problem 26:
    a. Each pie is baked and sold in an aluminum pie tin. Suppose at the start of the day Mary Custard's had 200 pie tins available. Would the production schedule change from that determined in part (a) of problem 29?
    b. Answer part (a) assuming that there were only 100 pie tins.
    c. Mary Custard's has, in the past, made a third type of pie—a chocolate pie. Given the current prices of ingredients, Mary Custard's estimates that it would net a profit of $27 per dozen chocolate pies. Each dozen chocolate pies requires 15 pounds of flour, 30 eggs, 12 pounds of sugar and no fruit mixture. Show that it would not be profitable to bake any chocolate pies this day even if Mary Custard's had an abundant supply of chocolate. What is the minimum profit for a dozen chocolate pies which would justify their production?

28. **MANUFACTURING.** Klone Computers manufactures two models of its current line of personal computers: the KCU and the KCP. The KCU, which is purchased primarily by universities and other businesses that network their computers, is equipped with two floppy drives and no hard disk drive. The KCP is designed for home and personal use and is equipped with one floppy drive and one hard disk drive. Each model is housed in a tower case. During the current production run, Klone must manufacture at least 300 KCU computers to satisfy a contract to Texas State University. The following table summarizes the resource requirements and unit profits for each computer model and the resources available for the current production run.

Model	Floppy Drives	Hard Drives	Tower Cases	Production Hours	Unit Profit
KCU	2	0	1	0.4	$100
KCP	1	1	1	0.6	$250
Available	1800	700	1000	480	

Formulate and solve a linear program for Klone to determine its optimal production schedule for this production cycle. How many of the current inventory of floppy drives, hard disk drives, and tower cases will be used in the production cycle? How many are unused? Is all the available production time utilized?

29. MANUFACTURING. For the Klone Computer problem (problem 28):
    a. Suppose the unit profit for the KCU model were increased to $150 per unit. Does the optimal solution change? Does the total profit change? Suppose the profit for the KCU model could be increased to $200 per unit. Does the optimal solution change? Does the total profit change?
    b. The unit profit coefficients took into account the $50 per unit cost to Klone of the floppy disk drives. Klone has negotiated a deal with another company to purchase floppy disk drives at $35 each. Will the optimal solution change? If so, what will be the new optimal profit?
    c. Suppose the constraint requiring the production of at least 300 KCU models were eliminated. Determine the new optimal solution.

30. PRODUCTION. Klone Computer (see problems 28, 29) is making one last production run of its KCU and KCP computers before introducing its new line of models, which includes CD-ROM drives, utilizes faster CPUs and floppy disk drives, and has larger hard disk drives. Because this is the last run of "old technology" machines, Klone's net profit per computer has been reduced from $100 and $250 to $75 and $105 for KCU and KCP models, respectively. The following table summarizes the resource requirements and unit profits for each computer model and the resources available for this *final* production run of these models.

Model	Floppy Drives	Hard Drives	Tower Cases	Production Hours	Unit Profit
KCU	2	0	1	.4	$ 75
KCP	1	1	1	.6	$105
Available	2800	1400	2000	960	

Formulate this problem and solve it as a *linear* program. Note that the optimal solution to the linear program gives integer values. Why is this also the optimal solution to the ILP model?

31. ROUNDING PRODUCTION. Suppose in problem 30 there were 970 production hours available.
    a. Solve the model as a *linear* programming model, ignoring the integer restrictions, and show that the optimal solution is attained with fractional values for the decision variables.
    b. Round your solution in part (a) by (i) rounding off, (ii) rounding up, and (iii) rounding down. In each instance state whether or not the solution is feasible. Determine the profit for any feasible results.
    c. Solve for the optimal integer solution. Did you get any of the rounded answers in part (b)? What is the difference in the optimal profit between the true optimal integer solution and the best feasible rounded linear programming solution? *Note:* This illustrates that when large quantities are involved, rounding the

optimal linear programming solution usually gives a "good enough answer."

32. PHYSICAL FITNESS. Sarah Stone measures her performance in the gym as follows: 10 points for every Nautilus machine used, and 1 point for every minute on the treadmill. Including preparation time and transition time between machines, Sarah spends an average of 6.5 minutes on each Nautilus machine. Formulate a model with both an integer and a continuous variable to determine the optimal number of Nautilus machines she should use and the number of minutes she should spend on the treadmill if:

    • The total time of the workout is not to exceed 1 hour.
    • At least 20 minutes must be spent on the treadmill.
    • At least 5 different Nautilus machines should be used.

33. MANUFACTURING. Plant Equipment Corporation (PEC) manufactures two large industrial machines—a metal compactor and a drill press. Next month PEC will convert its production facilities to produce new machine designs and will cease producing the current models. PEC must determine its production schedule for this month, however.

    PEC could sell up to three compactors and two drill presses to customers who are not anxious to pay the increased price PEC will charge for the new models. Current models net PEC a $24,000 profit for metal compactors and $30,000 for drill presses. Each metal compactor requires 50 hours to produce, whereas each drill press requires 60 hours to produce; 160 production hours are available during the current month.
    a. Formulate and solve this problem as an integer linear programming problem.
    b. Solve the problem as a linear program and note that when the optimal solution is rounded (up, down, or off), the result is *not* the optimal integer solution.
    c. Why would a linear programming model be a correct model if the production process were to continue indefinitely?

34. RESTAURANT OPERATION. Jackson's Sports Bar and Grill would like to minimize the cost of installing television sets throughout the restaurant so that it can accommodate a potential viewership of at least 750 patrons. It is considering purchasing two models of Sony televisions. The large-screen 60-inch model costs $3500 and, with proper placement, could be viewed by 150 customers. The 27-inch models cost $800 each and can be seen by 35 customers. Jackson's wishes to have at least one 60-inch television and no more than 20 27-inch models.
    a. Formulate the model for the problem faced by Jackson's.
    b. Solve for the optimal linear programming solution. Round the solution to integer values. What is the total cost of the rounded solution?
    c. Solve for the optimal solution for the integer programming model. Did you get the rounded solution of part (b)? What is the total cost of the optimal integer solution?

35. AIRCRAFT LEASING. Des Moines Airlines (DMA) is a small new commuter airline that will locate its hub in Des Moines, Iowa. DMA plans to have 11 mechanics, 15 pilots, and 21 flight attendants available daily.

DMA will be leasing two types of aircraft—the DM4 and the B77. The Federal Aviation Association's (FAA's) mandatory requirements for these aircraft are summarized in the following table. DMA's objective is to maximize its total passenger capacity.

	Mechanics Required	Pilots Required	Flight Attendants Required
DM4	1	1	1
B77	1	2	3

a. Formulate and graph a feasible region for this problem. Without knowing the seat capacity on each aircraft, why can we say for certain that the optimal solution to the linear programming model would also be the optimal solution to the integer linear programming model? (*Hint:* What are the possible optimal points for a linear programming model?)
b. The seat capacity is 25 for the DM4 and 70 for the B77. What is the optimal leasing plan for DMA?
c. If DMA must make do with one less worker to operate its fleet, should it be a mechanic, a pilot, or a flight attendant?
d. Excluding certain fixed costs (including pilot costs), each seat of fleet capacity gives DMA a net yearly profit of $25,000. If DMA plans to pay its pilots $110,000 per year, including benefits, should it hire an additional pilot?
e. DMA is considering redesigning the interior of the B77 to increase its seat capacity beyond 70. What is the maximum seating capacity for which the leasing plan found in part (a) remains optimal?
f. Suppose DMA could squeeze one more row of three seats into each of the two types of aircraft, increasing the seating capacity of the DM4 to 28 and the B77 to 73. Given no other changes in the assumptions of the problem, would the optimal leasing decision change? What practical considerations might you consider before implementing such a change?

36. AIRCRAFT LEASING. Consider the problem faced by Des Moines Airlines (DMA) in problem 35. Now suppose that the B77 aircraft actually requires 4 flight attendants rather than three.
a. Solve for the optimal solution to the (i) linear programming model and (ii) integer programming model.
b. Explain why the optimal solution in (ii) gives a smaller total seat capacity than that in (i).

37. AIRCRAFT LEASING (*continued*). Consider the Des Moines Airlines (DMA) problem referred to in problem 35. Now suppose DMA is considering leasing a third aircraft, the L-200. The L-200, as currently configured, has a seating capacity of 110 and requires two mechanics, three pilots, and five flight attendants.

a. Solve the DMA problem as a *linear* program and show that the solution found in 35(b) remains optimal; that is, no L-200 aircraft should be leased.
b. According to the sensitivity analysis for the linear program in part (a), what is the minimum seating capacity for the L-200 that would justify DMA leasing them?
c. Suppose the seating arrangement of the L-200 could be reconfigured so that the capacity is increased to 120. Solve for the optimal leasing plan for DMA.

38. HELICOPTER SERVICE. Wolfe Helicopters is to begin flying passengers from a helicopter pad in Berkeley, California, to the two large airports in the area, Oakland and San Francisco. Wolfe will operate two models—the HG30 and the WH10. The characteristics for each aircraft are given in the following table.

	Estimated Monthly Profit	Purchase Cost	Required Monthly Maintenance (Hours)	Capacity
HG30	$3000	$600,000	20	20
WH10	$2000	$200,000	60	8

Wolfe has $1,800,000 available to purchase helicopters, and it wishes to have a total fleet capacity of at least 25. It also has a service contract with HMC, a helicopter maintenance company, for up to 140 hours of maintenance per month. (Additional hours would require a complete renegotiation of the service contract at a much higher cost; thus, Wolfe wishes not to exceed the 140 hours of the contract.)
a. Formulate and solve for the mix of helicopters that would bring Wolfe its maximum monthly profit.
b. Show graphically that there are only five feasible integer solutions. Evaluate the profit of each and verify that the answer to part (a) is correct.
c. What would be Wolfe's optimal mix of helicopters if it had only $1,799,999 available to purchase helicopters? If Wolfe had only $1,799,999 for the purchase of helicopters, would you "invest" a dollar with Wolfe for a small percentage of the increased profits?

39. INVESTMENTS. Carol Klein has $10,000 she wishes to invest in a particular stock and a bond. The stock has the potential to earn a 15% annual return whereas the bond will yield only a 6% annual return. However, due to the volatility in the stock market, she wishes to invest no more than $5000 in the stock.
a. Determine Carol's optimal allocation of the $10,000 between the stock and the bond and her maximum potential return if:
  i. There are no other restrictions on her investment decisions
  ii. Carol must purchase whole shares of the stock at $165 per share. *Note:* Solver *may* incorrectly state that this problem is infeasible; but the solution it generates is feasible and optimal.

iii. Carol must purchase whole shares of the stock at $165 per share and the bond must be purchased in multiples of $100 each.

b. Discuss why each of the above scenarios yielded a different optimal solution and why the maximum potential return was lower in case (ii) than in case (i) and lower still in case (iii).

40. e-COMMERCE. Designdotcom.com is a company that designs websites for clients. Much of the work is done in-house, but it finds that it must subcontract some work to graduate students at a local university when the demand is great. It charges clients $2500 to build a typical website. Designdotcom pays the graduate students $1500 for their services in building a website, thus reducing its profit to $1000. In March, it would like to design at least 200 websites, with no more than 100 subcontracted to graduate students.

PROBLEMS 41–50 ARE ON THE CD

Designdotcom would like to determine how many websites it should design in-house and how many should be subcontracted in the month of March.

a. Formulate this problem as a linear problem and solve. Explain the result.

b. Designdotcom failed to mention that it takes approximately 40 man-hours to design a website in-house and approximately 20 man-hours to supervise and monitor a website design by the graduate students. Workers at Designdotcom average 12-hour workdays. During March there are 26 workdays. Formulate, solve, and explain the revised model if Designdotcom has:
   i. 15 employees
   ii. 20 employees

CASE STUDIES

Case 1: Franklin Furniture

This case can be solved by splitting it into three small cases, two of which can be analyzed using only two decision variables.

Franklin Furniture produces tables and chairs at its Eastside plant for use in university classrooms. The unit profit for tables is $70, while that for chairs is $30.

Tables and chairs are manufactured using finished pressed wood and polished aluminum fittings. Including scrap, each table uses 20 square feet of pressed wood, whereas each chair uses 12.5 square feet of the pressed wood. Franklin has 6000 square feet of the pressed wood available for the Eastside plant weekly. The aluminum fittings that reinforce the legs of both the tables and chairs are purchased from an outside supplier. Franklin can purchase up to 400 boxes of fittings weekly; one box is required for each table or chair manufactured.

Production time is 72 minutes (1.2 hours) per table and 18 minutes (.3 hour) per chair. Franklin has eight employees, each of whom works an average of 7.5 hours per day. Thus, in an average five-day work week, the company has available 8(7.5)(5) = 300 production hours.

Franklin Furniture also produces desks and computer workstations at its Westside plant. Each desk nets the company a profit of $100, while each computer workstation nets $125. These products are also produced from finished pressed wood and aluminum. The amount of each, as well as the labor time needed to produce a desk or computer workstation, is given in the following table.

	Pressed Wood	Aluminum Fittings	Labor
Desks	20 sq. ft.	1 box	1.5 hours
Workstations	30 sq. ft.	1 box	2.0 hours
Available	6000 sq. ft.	400 boxes	300 hours

Franklin is considering combining operations of both plants into a single plant. This consolidation will combine the weekly available resources so that 12,000 square feet of pressed wood, 800 boxes of aluminum fittings, and 600 production hours will be available weekly. However, the accounting department estimates the cost of renovating the plant will be $5000 per week, on an amortized basis.

Prepare a business report for Franklin Furniture giving optimal weekly production schedules for each of its plants operating separately. Then include an analysis and a recommendation to Franklin for combining operations at both plants into a single plant.

CASE 2:   Rinaldo's Hatch 'N Ax

Rinaldo's Hatch 'N Ax is the manufacturer of the store brand of hatchets and axes sold by Home Supply Hardware (HSH) Stores. Each item consists of a hickory handle produced in Rinaldo's processing facility and a steel blade forged and polished in its machine shop. These items are then transported to an assembly area where the blade is attached to the handle and the item is packaged for shipment. Because of its exclusive contract with HSH, Rinaldo's can sell all the hatchets and axes it produces. The accompanying spreadsheet is an Excel spreadsheet giving the following details for each item. (This information is also available in file RINALDO.xls in the Excel files folder on the accompanying CD-ROM.)

- The contract selling price to HSH
- The amount of hickory required for its handle
- The amount of steel required for its blade
- The number of minutes required to produce the handle in its processing facility
- The number of minutes required to produce the blade in the machine shop
- The number of minutes required for assembly and packaging

The file also gives the current hourly cost and availability for the skilled and unskilled labor of Rinaldo's workforce. Skilled laborers produce the handles and blades, whereas unskilled laborers assemble and package the items. Also given is the information on contracts negotiated with HSH for minimum shipments for the next three months of each item as well as details of contracts Rinaldo's has made for the purchase price and availability of the hickory and steel for the same time period.

Given this data, program the following cells and use Excel Solver three times (once for each month) to determine the production schedule for the quarter:

Cells	Quantities
E9-G10	Hickory/Steel Used Each Month
E13-G14	Handle/Blade Production Time Used Each Month
C15-D15	Total Skilled Labor per Unit
E15-G15	Total Skilled Labor Used Each Month
E18-G19	Assembly/Packaging Time Used Each Month
C20-D20	Total Unskilled Labor per Unit
E20-G20	Total Unskilled Labor Used Each Month
Column H	Quarter Totals
K16-M17	Unit Profits for Hatchets/Axes Each Month
E24-E26	Total Profit Each Month
C27-E27	Total Production/Profit for the Quarter

Prepare a report detailing your production recommendations for the quarter. Include quarter totals of relevant quantities of interest to management at Rinaldo's. Discuss the following in the report:

- An interpretation of the shadow prices and the range of feasibility for the binding constraints of this model for each month
- How the accuracy in the estimates of the profit coefficients affects your analyses

		Hatchets	Axes	April	May	June	Quarter Totals		April	May	June
1	Rinaldo's Hatch 'N Ax Production Schedule										
2	Quarter II										
4		Hatchets	Axes						April	May	June
5								Contracted Minimum Production			
6	Selling Price to HSH	$16.00	$29.50					Hatchets -- Min. Production	400	300	200
7				Resources Used		Quarter		Axes -- Min. Production	175	300	350
8				April	May	June	Totals	Costs			
9	Hickory Required (Ft./Unit)	1.6	3.1					Costs			
10	Steel Required (Lbs./Unit)	1.8	4.2					Skilled Labor Costs ($/hr.)	$12.00	$12.00	$12.84
11								Unskilled Labor Costs ($/hr.)	$7.00	$7.00	$7.35
12	Skilled Labor Required Per Unit							Hickory ($/ft.)	$1.00	$1.20	$1.05
13	Handle Production (Min/Unit)	5.0	2.6					Steel ($/lb.)	$1.18	$1.06	$0.98
14	Blade Production (Min/Unit)	11.0	9.4								
15	Total Skilled Labor (Min/Unit)							Unit Profits			
16								Hatchets			
17	Unskilled Labor Required Per Unit							Axes			
18	Assembly (Min/Unit)	4.0	5.5								
19	Packaging (Min/Unit)	2.0	2.5					Resource Availability			
20	Total Unskilled Labor (Min/Unit)							Skilled Labor (Hours)	220	250	200
21								Unskilled Labor (Hours)	120	100	140
22								Hickory (Feet)	2000	2200	1500
23	Production Schedule			Total Profit				Steel (Pounds)	2000	2000	2000
24	April										
25	May										
26	June										
27	Quarter Totals										

| CASE 3:   Kootenay Straw Broom Company

The Kootenay Straw Broom Company, located in British Columbia, Canada, is a small, family-run business that handmakes two models of straw brooms, the Pioneer and the Heritage models, which are sold in "country stores" throughout Canada and the northwestern United States. Given its current production capacity and selling price, Kootenay is able to sell all the brooms it produces.

The Pioneer model is the company's basic model. It consists of a plain wooden handle, utilizes one pound of straw, and takes an average of 15 minutes (.25 hour) to make. Kootenay sells them for $12.75 each. The Heritage model is the company's deluxe model. Although the same wooden handles are used, they are run through a decorative lathe and attached to a larger base consisting of 1.5 pounds of straw. These two factors increase the production time of the Heritage broom to 24 minutes (.40 hour), and Kootenay sells them for $18 each.

Kootenay receives daily deliveries of straw that is specially treated for their brooms from Tyler Farms. Tyler can supply Kootenay with up to 350 pounds daily of the specially treated straw. This straw costs Kootenay $1.50 per pound.

Kootenay purchases its handles from Adhor Mills, which manufactures the handles according to Kootenay's specifications. Adhor Mills is a two-hour drive from Kootenay. It currently makes only one daily delivery to Kootenay in a truck capable of hauling 30 boxes of 10 handles each (or 300 handles). Adhor charges Kootenay $7.50 per box of 10 for manufacture and delivery of the handles.

Adhor also makes a major delivery of products to a town 45 miles from Kootenay and has offered to swing by Kootenay with one additional box of 10 handles. However, the added expense for making this detour means that

Kootenay would have to pay Adhor $25 for this extra box of 10 handles.

Kootenay averages 80 production hours per day. Since Kootenay is a family-run business, it considers the daily cost of $2800 for its overhead and "family labor" of its 10 members as sunk costs required for the business. Kootenay is ready to consider several options that could increase the daily profit:

1. Seeking additional sources for treated straw
2. Taking Adhor Mills up on its offer to deliver an extra box of handles (for $25)
3. Adding a half-time worker (four hours per day) for $50 per day

Prepare a report for the Kootenay Straw Broom Company that evaluates the option or set of options it should implement. The report should:

1. Recommend an optimal production under current conditions.
2. Include a summary of the determination of unit profits of $10.50 and $15.00, respectively, for the Pioneer and Heritage broom models, showing that the costs of both treated straw and broom handles are included in these calculations.
3. Show that after subtracting fixed costs, the business nets $500 per day.
4. Give a brief analysis of the sensitivity of the objective function coefficients.
5. Analyze the options using the correct interpretation of the shadow prices considering which costs are included and which costs are sunk. (*Remember:* Do not call them shadow prices in the report.)

Applications of Linear and Integer Programming Models

WITH APPROXIMATELY **$20 BILLION** in revenues, FedEx Corporation (http://www.fedex.com) has become a world leader in providing integrated transportation, information, and logistics solutions. As the company has expanded, it has created a high-level management science group to provide senior management with recommendations on a wide variety of issues. This group uses state-of-the-art computer-based mathematical models to analyze a broad range of complex corporate problems with an overall goal of maintaining and increasing company profits while continuing to provide a consistently high level of service to its customers.

One of the models developed by this group is its Global Supply Chain Model, built to redesign its supply chain for revenue packaging. The model has helped management answer the following questions:

- Should FedEx pursue offshore production of packaging? If so, which items and where?
- Should FedEx consolidate nearby warehouses and pick centers into a new form of distribution center?
- Should FedEx pursue expansion of distribution center locations?
- What transportation modes on each link would most reliably get packaging from suppliers to stations while reducing costs?
- What should the service area boundaries be for each distribution center?

The Global Supply Chain Model uses, among other techniques, a large-scale **mixed integer programming** approach. This model has already resulted in a cost savings to FedEx of over $10 million.

3.1 The Evolution of Linear Programming Models in Business and Government

Following World War II, the U.S. Air Force sponsored research for solving military planning and distribution models. In 1947, the simplex algorithm was developed for solving these types of linear models. Not long after, the first commercial uses of linear programming were reported in "large" businesses that had access to digital computers. Seemingly unrelated industries, such as agriculture, petroleum, steel, transportation, and communications, saved millions of dollars by successfully developing and solving linear models for complex problems.

As computing power has become more accessible, the realm of businesses and government entities using linear models has expanded exponentially. In this chapter we present numerous "small" examples selected from a wide variety of applications areas, designed to accomplish four goals:

1. To examine potential applications areas where linear models may be useful
2. To develop good modeling skills
3. To demonstrate how to develop use of the power of spreadsheets to effectively represent the model in unambiguous terms and generate results
4. To gain confidence in interpreting and analyzing results from spreadsheet reports

Although the examples illustrated in this chapter represent "scaled-down" versions of potential real-life situations, today linear and integer programming models proliferate in a wide variety of actual business and government applications. Banking models, large economic/financial models, marketing strategy models, production scheduling and labor force planning models, computer design and networking models, and health care and medical models are but a few notable examples of successful linear programming applications. Below is just a sampling of the thousands of actual documented uses of linear programming models.

- Aircraft fleet assignments
- Telecommunications network expansion
- Air pollution control
- Health care
- Bank portfolio selection
- Agriculture
- Fire protection
- Defense/aerospace contracting
- Land use planning
- Dairy production
- Military deployment

An example of each of the above is detailed in Appendix 3.1 on the accompanying CD-ROM. The reader is encouraged to reference this subfolder for details.

These are but a few of the numerous applications areas of linear optimization models. Additional applications include traffic analysis, fast-food operations, transportation, assignment of medical personnel, coal, steel, gas, chemical, and paper production, recycling, educational assignments, worker evaluations, awarding of contracts, manufacturing, railroads, forestry, school desegregation, government planning, tourism, and sports scheduling. Each year hundreds of new applications appear in the professional literature. Add to that the numerous unreported models that are regularly utilized in business and government, and you can see that linear programming continues to play a significant role in today's world.

3.2 Building Good Linear and Integer Programming Models

Given the widespread use of linear models today, it has become increasingly important for practitioners to be able to develop good, efficient models to aid the manager in the decision-making process. Three factors—familiarity, simplification, and clarity—are important considerations when developing such models.

The greater the modeler's *familiarity* with the relationships between competing activities, the limitations of the resources, and the overall objective, the greater the likelihood of generating a usable model. Viewing the problem from as many perspectives as possible (e.g., those of various management levels, front-line workers, and accounting) helps in this regard.

Linear models are always *simplifications* of real-life situations. Usually, some or all of the required linear programming assumptions discussed in Chapter 2 are violated by an actual situation. Because of the efficiency with which they are solved and the associated sensitivity analysis reports generated, however, linear models are generally preferable to more complicated forms of mathematical models.

When developing a model, it is important to address the following question: "Is a very sophisticated model needed, or will a less sophisticated model that gives fairly good results suffice?" The answer, of course, will guide the level of detail required in the model.

Although a model should reflect the real-life situation, one should not try to model every aspect or contingency of the situation. This could get us bogged down in minutiae, adding little, if any, real value to the model while unnecessarily complicating the solution procedure, delaying solution time, and compromising the usefulness of the model. As George Dantzig, the developer of the simplex algorithm for solving linear programming models, points out, however, "What constitutes the proper simplification, is subject to individual judgment and experience. People often disagree on the adequacy of a certain model to describe the situation."[1] In other words, although experience is the best teacher, you should be aware that even experienced management scientists may disagree as to what level of simplification is realistic or warranted in a model.

Finally, a linear programming model should be *clear*; that is, it should be easy to follow and as transparent as possible to the layperson. From a practitioner's point of view, the model should also be easy to input and yield accurate results in a timely manner.

SUMMATION VARIABLES AND CONSTRAINTS

In an effort to make the model easier to understand and debug, we can introduce **summation variables** and corresponding **summation constraints** into the formulation. A summation variable is the sum of two or more of the decision variables. It is particularly useful when there are constraints involving maximum or minimum percentages for the value of one or more of the decision variables.

To illustrate the use of a summation variable, consider the situation in which X_1, X_2, and X_3 represent the production quantities of three television models to be produced during a production run in which 7000 pounds of plastic are available.

---

[1] George B. Dantzig, *Linear Programming and Extensions* (Princeton, NJ: Princeton University Press, 1963).

The unit profits are \$23, \$34, and \$45, and the amount of plastic required to produce each is 2 pounds, 3 pounds, and 4 pounds, respectively. In addition, management does not want any model to exceed 40% of total production ($X_1 + X_2 + X_3$).

First, we note that although the proportion of model 1 televisions produced during the production run is $X_1/(X_1 + X_2 + X_3)$. However a constraint of the form: $X_1/(X_1 + X_2 + X_3) \le .4$ is not a linear constraint. But, because we know that the total production, $X_1 + X_2 + X_3$ is positive, we could multiply both sides of this constraint by the denominator to obtain the equivalent linear constraint: $X_1 \le .4(X_1 + X_2 + X_3)$. The constraints $X_2 \le .4(X_1 + X_2 + X_3)$ and $X_3 \le .4(X_1 + X_2 + X_3)$ require that models 2 and 3 represent no more than 40% of the total production. Thus, the model could be written as:

$$
\begin{aligned}
\text{MAX} \quad & 23X_1 + 34X_2 + 45X_3 \\
\text{ST} \quad & 2X_1 + 3X_2 + 4X_3 \le 7000 \\
& X_1 \le .4(X_1 + X_2 + X_3) \\
& X_2 \le .4(X_1 + X_2 + X_3) \\
& X_3 \le .4(X_1 + X_2 + X_3) \\
& X_1, X_2, X_3 \ge 0
\end{aligned}
$$

or,

$$
\begin{aligned}
\text{MAX} \quad & 23X_1 + 34X_2 + 45X_3 \\
\text{ST} \quad & 2X_1 + 3X_2 + 4X_3 \le 7000 \\
& .6X_1 - .4X_2 - .4X_3 \le 0 \\
& -.4X_1 + .6X_2 - .4X_3 \le 0 \\
& -.4X_1 - .4X_2 + .6X_3 \le 0 \\
& X_1, X_2, X_3 \ge 0
\end{aligned}
$$

Written in this form, not only are the coefficients cumbersome to input into a spreadsheet, but the last three constraints do not immediately convey the fact that each television model is not to exceed 40% of the total production.

To clarify the above formulation, a *summation variable* representing the total production and a *summation constraint* expressing this relationship may be introduced into the model as follows:

- Define the summation variable:
  X_4 = the total production of televisions during a production run.
- Add the following summation constraint:
  $X_1 + X_2 + X_3 = X_4$ or equivalently $X_1 + X_2 + X_3 - X_4 = 0$ to the model formulation.
- The 40% production limit constraints can now be written as:
  $X_1 \le .4X_4$, $X_2 \le .4X_4$, and $X_3 \le .4X_4$ respectively.

By subtracting $.4X_4$ from both sides of each of the above production limit constraints, the complete set of constraints can now be written as:

$$
\begin{aligned}
\text{MAX} \quad & 23X_1 + 34X_2 + 45X_3 \\
\text{ST} \quad & 2X_1 + 3X_2 + 4X_3 \le 7000 \\
& X_1 + X_2 + X_3 - X_4 = 0 \text{ (Summation Constraint)} \\
& X_1 - .4X_4 \le 0 \\
& X_2 - .4X_4 \le 0 \\
& X_3 - .4X_4 \le 0 \\
& \text{All X's} \ge 0
\end{aligned}
$$

Although by adding the summation variable and the summation constraint we have increased the number of constraints and number of variables each by one, the new set of constraints is easier to input and easier to read and interpret when checking the model.[2]

When using spreadsheets, a convenient way of modeling this situation without listing all the percentage constraints explicitly is shown in Figure 3.1. In this figure, cells B2, C2, and D2 are used for the decision variables, while another cell (H2) is set aside to represent total production. The formula in cell H2 is =SUM(B2:D2). Note that summation variable cell H2 is not considered a "Changing Cell." As shown in the accompanying Solver dialogue box, the percentage constraints can be included by $B$2:$D$2 <= .4*$H$2.

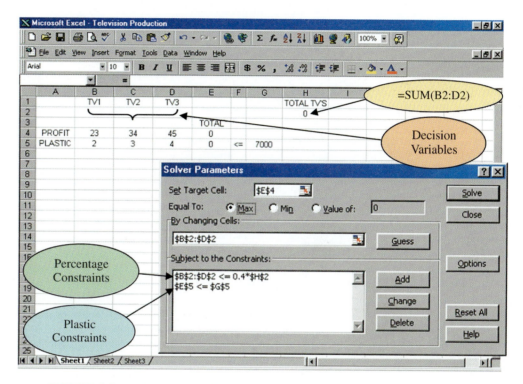

FIGURE 3.1   Solver Spreadsheet for Television Production Model

BINARY VARIABLES

In Chapter 2 we saw that sometimes one or more of the decision variables in a linear model are required to be integer-valued. Some models may also contain **binary variables**, variables that can only assume values of 0 or 1. Any situation that can be modeled by "yes/no," "good/bad," "right/wrong," and so on, can be considered a binary variable. Such situations include whether or not a plant is built, whether or not a particular highway is used when traveling between two cities, and whether or not a worker is assigned to perform a job. (The latter two examples are discussed in Chapter 4.)

A MODELING CHECKLIST

Mathematical modeling is an art that improves with experience. To this point we have suggested several modeling tips that can aid your development of mathematical models. For your convenience we offer a summary of many of these tips in the form of a checklist.

---

[2] The time needed to solve a linear programming problem typically depends on: (1) the number of constraints; and (2) the percentage of nonzero coefficients in the constraints. Although adding a definitional variable adds one more constraint to the formulation, the efficiency gained in this case by having fewer nonzero coefficients could offset this factor.

A Checklist for Building Linear Models

1. Begin by listing the details of the problem in short expressions. (We have done this in Chapter 2 using "bullets.")

2. Determine the objective in general terms and then determine what is within the control of the decision maker to accomplish this goal. These controllable inputs are *decision variables*.

3. If, during the course of the formulation, you find that another decision variable is needed, add it to the list at that time and include it in the formulation.

4. Define the decision variables precisely using an appropriate time frame (i.e., cars per month, tons of steel per production run, etc.).

5. When writing a constraint or a function, first formulate it in words in the form: (some expression) ⟨has some relation to⟩ (another expression or constant); then convert the words to the appropriate mathematical symbols.

6. Keep the units in the expressions on both sides of the relation consistent (e.g., one side should not be in hours, the other in minutes).

7. If the right-hand side is an expression rather than a constant, do the appropriate algebra so that the end result is of the form:
   (mathematical function) ⟨has a relation to⟩ (a constant)

8. Use *summation variables* when appropriate, particularly when many constraints involve percentages.

9. Indicate which variables are restricted to be nonnegative, which are restricted to be integer valued, and which are binary.

3.3   Building Good Spreadsheet Models

When we employed spreadsheets to solve linear programming models in Chapter 2, the models were written in a rectangular fashion with columns used for the variables and rows used for constraints. This approach, which is used in many nonspreadsheet software packages, presents a structured approach for inputting the coefficients of the model. Any linear or integer programming model can be represented and solved in this manner.

But with spreadsheets, you are not burdened with such a restrictive format. You can present the data and results in such a way that they do not even look like a linear programming model. This can be very valuable, particularly when information is shared with nonquantitative end-users. With spreadsheets you can:

- Embed formulas that represent required values or subsets of values into individual cells
- Express coefficients as mathematical expressions rather than specific numbers
- Designate various cells scattered throughout the spreadsheet to contain left-hand side and right-hand side values of the constraints without confining them to be in a single column or row

Solver even allows the right-hand side of constraints to be mathematical expressions instead of constants or cell references. Add to this the use of color, various border designs, and other formatting techniques, and this flexibility allows the user to present a spreadsheet in a way that conveys the requisite information in a visually pleasing manner. For instance, the modeler can:

- Group certain types of constraints together
- Designate certain cells for the left sides and right sides of these constraints at positions on the spreadsheet disjoint from the left-hand coefficients

- Highlight the information by using a thick or colored border
- Use a different color background for cells containing the left-hand side values as opposed to the cells that contain the right-hand side restrictions
- Create entries on the spreadsheet that give other relevant information such as subtotals or proportions
- Use various formulas in cells representing the total left-hand side values. This can simply be a cell representing the value of a decision variable, a formula, or the result of a function such as SUMPRODUCT, SUM, and SUMIF

Another option that one might take advantage of is Excel's ability to name cells or sets of cells. Cells can be named by following these steps:

- Highlight the cell(s) to be named.
- Click on the Name box (the far left box immediately above column A) and type in what you wish to call the cells. (The name must start with a letter, and no spaces are allowed.)
- Press Enter.

Then when these cells are referenced in a Solver dialogue box, for instance, the name appears rather than the cell references. This can make it easier to follow the logic of the model. For instance, in the television production model in Section 3.2 which was illustrated in Figure 3.1, we could have assigned the following names:

Cells	NAME
B2:D2	SetsProduced
H2	TotalSets
E4	TotalProfit
E5	PlasticUsed
G5	AvailablePlastic

Then by highlighting the same cells as before, the dialogue box would appear as in Figure 3.2. Note that when we input a formula (such as .4*$H$2) for the right side of a constraint, the name does not appear.

FIGURE 3.2
Dialogue Box Using Named Cells

Although we could do this throughout our illustrations of linear models, we leave cell references as they are so that they can be easily referenced on the spreadsheet itself. But for large models, naming cells certainly has its advantages. In short, a spreadsheet offers a variety of ways other than a matrix format to convey the input coefficients. Solver is still used, but the results will be placed on spreadsheets that make them ripe for discussion or inclusion into business reports or PowerPoint presentations.

In Sections 3.4 and 3.5, the mathematical and spreadsheet modeling tips discussed in the last two sections are illustrated in various formulations of linear and integer models from the private and public sectors. In these models we shall:

- Show how linear models can be applied to different situations arising from the functional areas of business and government
- Illustrate the modeling approach, including some of the problems that might arise in the modeling process
- Employ effective spreadsheet modeling techniques
- Interpret, analyze, and extend the output generated from Excel Solver

In the process we shall illustrate a number of concepts, including how to:

- Choose an appropriate objective function
- Define an inclusive set of decision variables
- Write accurate expressions to model the constraints
- Interpret sensitivity outputs for both maximization and minimization models
- Recognize and address unboundedness
- Recognize and address infeasibility
- Recognize and address alternate optimal solutions

To simplify matters, we identify the applications area and the concepts illustrated for each model introduced in this chapter.

3.4 Applications of Linear Programming Models

In Chapter 2, we introduced the basic concepts of linear programming through the use of two-variable models. These concepts included modeling, using Excel's Solver to generate an optimal solution (or determine that the model is unbounded or infeasible), and interpretation of the output on the Answer and Sensitivity Reports. In this section we illustrate how to model more realistic problems requiring more than two decision variables. However, the concepts developed for two-variable models apply equally as well to these more complex ones.

The models in this section represent small versions of problems one might find in such diverse areas as production, purchasing, finance, and cash flow accounting. Besides spanning a range of applications areas, each model was constructed to illustrate at least one new linear programming concept. Thus, for each model take note of its application area, the model development, the spreadsheet design, and the analysis and interpretation of the output.

3.4.1 PRODUCTION SCHEDULING MODELS

Assisting manufacturing managers in making production decisions that efficiently utilize scarce resources is an area in which a variety of linear programming models have been applied. Determining production levels, scheduling shift workers and overtime, and determining the cost effectiveness of purchasing additional resources for the manufacturing process are just some of the key decisions that these managers must make. The Galaxy Industries model introduced in Chapter 2 is a simplified version of a production scheduling situation. Here, in a slightly larger version of that model, we illustrate how linear programming can help make some of these management decisions.

Galaxy Expansion.xls

GALAXY INDUSTRIES—AN EXPANSION PLAN

Concepts: Maximization
Sensitivity Analysis (All constraint types)
Both Signs in Objective Function
Unit Conversion
Summation Variables, Percentage Constraints

Galaxy Industries has been very successful during its first six months of operation and is already looking toward product expansion and possible relocation within the year to a facility in Juarez, Mexico, where both labor and material costs are considerably lower. The availability of the cheaper labor and a contract with a local distributor to supply up to 3000 pounds of plastic at a substantially reduced cost will effectively double the profit for Space Rays to $16 per dozen and triple the profit for Zappers to $15 per dozen.

The new facility will be equipped with machinery and staffed with workers to facilitate a 40-hour regular time work schedule. In addition, up to 32 hours of overtime can be scheduled. Accounting for wages, benefits, and additional plant operating expenses, each scheduled overtime hour will cost the company $180 more than regular time hours.

Galaxy has been test marketing two additional products, tentatively named the Big Squirt and the Soaker, which appear to be as popular as the Space Ray and Zapper. Table 3.1 summarizes the profit and requirements for each product line.

Galaxy has a signed contract with Jaycee Toys, Inc. to supply it with 200 dozen Zappers weekly once the relocation has taken place. The marketing department has revised its strategy for the post-relocation period. It has concluded that, to keep total demand at its peak, Galaxy's most popular model, the Space Ray, should account for exactly 50% of total production, while no other product line should account for more than 40%. But now, instead of limiting production to at most 700 dozen weekly, the department wishes to ensure that production will total at least 1000 dozen units weekly.

Management would like to determine the weekly production schedule (including any overtime hours, if necessary) that will maximize its net weekly profit.

TABLE 3.1   Profit and Requirements Per Dozen

Product	Profit	Plastic (lb.)	Production Time (min.)
Space Rays	$16	2	3
Zappers	$15	1	4
Big Squirts	$20	3	5
Soakers	$22	4	6
Available		3000	40 hrs. (Reg.) 32 hrs. (O/T)

SOLUTION

The following is a brief synopsis of the problem.

- Galaxy wants to maximize its Net Weekly Profit = (Weekly Profit from Sales) − (Extra Cost of Overtime).
- A weekly production schedule, including the amount of overtime to schedule, must be determined.
- The following restrictions exist:
  1. Plastic availability (3000 pounds)
  2. Regular time labor (2400 minutes)
  3. Overtime availability (32 hours)
  4. Minimum production of Zappers (200 dozen)
  5. Appropriate product mix
     (Space Rays = 50% of total production)
     (Zappers, Big Squirts, Soakers ≤ 40% of total production)
  6. Minimum total production (1000 dozen)

DECISION VARIABLES

Galaxy must not only decide on the weekly production rates but also determine the number of overtime hours to utilize each week. Thus, we define five decision variables:

X_1 = number of *dozen* Space Rays to be produced each week
X_2 = number of *dozen* Zappers to be produced each week
X_3 = number of *dozen* Big Squirts to be produced each week
X_4 = number of *dozen* Soakers to be produced each week
X_5 = number of *hours* of overtime to be scheduled each week

OBJECTIVE FUNCTION

The total net weekly profit will be the profit from the sale of each product less the cost of overtime. Since each overtime hour costs the company an extra $180, the objective function is:

$$\text{MAXIMIZE } 16X_1 + 15X_2 + 20X_3 + 22X_4 - 180X_5$$

CONSTRAINTS

The following constraints exist in the Galaxy problem:

- *Plastic*: (Amount of plastic used weekly) ≤ 3000 lbs.

$$2X_1 + X_2 + 3X_3 + 4X_4 \quad \le 3000$$

- *Production Time*: (Number of production *minutes* used weekly) ≤ (Number of regular *minutes* available) + (Overtime *minutes* used)

Here,

Number of regular time *minutes* available = 60(40) = 2400
Number of overtime *minutes* used is 60(O/T hours used) = $60X_5$

Thus, the production time constraint is:

$$3X_1 + 4X_2 + 5X_3 + 6X_4 \le 2400 + 60X_5, \text{ or}$$
$$3X_1 + 4X_2 + 5X_3 + 6X_4 - 60X_5 \le 2400$$

- *Overtime Hours*: (Number of overtime *hours* used) ≤ 32

$$X_5 \le 32$$

- *Zapper Contract*: (Number of zappers produced weekly) ≥ 200 doz.

$$X_2 \ge 200$$

- *Product Mix*: Since each of the product mix restrictions is expressed as a percentage of the total production, to clarify the model we introduce the following summation *variable*:

$$X_6 = \text{Total weekly production (in dozens of units)}$$

- *Summation Constraint*: Before expressing the product mix constraints, we introduce the *summation constraint* showing that the total weekly production, X_6, is the sum of the weekly production of Space Rays, Zappers, Big Squirts, and Soakers: $X_6 = X_1 + X_2 + X_3 + X_4$, or

$$X_1 + X_2 + X_3 + X_4 - X_6 = 0$$

Now the product mix constraints can be written as

(Weekly production of Space Rays) = (50% of total production)
$$X_1 \qquad\qquad = .5X_6$$
(Weekly production of Zappers) ≤ (40% of total production)
$$X_2 \qquad\qquad \le .4X_6$$
(Weekly production of Big Squirts) ≤ (40% of total production)
$$X_3 \qquad\qquad \le .4X_6$$
(Weekly production of Soakers) ≤ (40% of total production)
$$X_4 \qquad\qquad \le .4X_6$$

or

$$
\begin{aligned}
X_1 && - .5X_6 &= 0\\
X_2 && - .4X_6 &\le 0\\
X_3 && - .4X_6 &\le 0\\
X_4 && - .4X_6 &\le 0
\end{aligned}
$$

- *Total Production*: (Total weekly production) ≥ 1000 dozen.

$$X_6 \ge 1000$$

- *Nonnegativity*: All decision variables ≥ 0

$$X_1, X_2, X_3, X_4, X_5, X_6 \ge 0$$

THE MATHEMATICAL MODEL

Thus, the complete mathematical model for the Galaxy Industries expansion problem is:

MAXIMIZE $16X_1 + 15X_2 + 20X_3 + 22X_4 - 180X_5$ (Weekly profit)
ST

$2X_1 + X_2 + 3X_3 + 4X_4$	≤ 3000	(Plastic)
$3X_1 + 4X_2 + 5X_3 + 6X_4 - 60X_5$	≤ 2400	(Production time)
X_5	≤ 32	(Overtime)
X_2	≥ 200	(Contract)
$X_1 + X_2 + X_3 + X_4 \qquad - X_6$	$= 0$	(Definition)
$X_1 \qquad\qquad - .5X_6$	$= 0$	(Space Rays)
$X_2 \qquad\qquad - .4X_6$	≤ 0	(Zappers)
$X_3 \qquad\qquad - .4X_6$	≤ 0	(Big Squirts)
$X_4 - .4X_6$	≤ 0	(Soakers)
X_6	≥ 1000	(Total)
All X's ≥ 0		(Nonnegativity)

EXCEL SOLVER INPUT/OUTPUT

There are many ways we could set up a spreadsheet to represent the model. Although we use more sophisticated spreadsheets that generate a great deal of additional information in later models in this chapter, at this point, the one we show in Figure 3.3*a* is only a slight extension of that in Chapter 2. Note that the numbers in row 4 giving the production quantities and scheduled overtime and the numbers in column G giving the total production, the total profit, and the resources used, are the results of executing Solver. The model is constructed as follows:

- Row 4 is set aside for the values of the decision variables.
- Input data for the profit and the first four functional constraints are entered into rows 6 through 10. The SUMPRODUCT function is used to get the total left-hand side values.
- Cell G4 is programmed to be the sum of the other variables. This represents the summation constraint, and since it will be determined by the other variables, it is NOT a changing cell.
- The percentage constraints of exactly 50% for Space Rays and at most 40% for the other models and the restriction of a minimum production of 1000 dozen units are reflected in the Solver dialogue box. Note that the right-hand side of these constraints is not a cell. For the percentage constraints, it is an expression, and for the minimum production constraint, it is a constant.

Clicking Solve gives the result shown in Figure 3.3*a*. Figure 3.3*b* is the corresponding Sensitivity Report.

Galaxy Expansion.xls

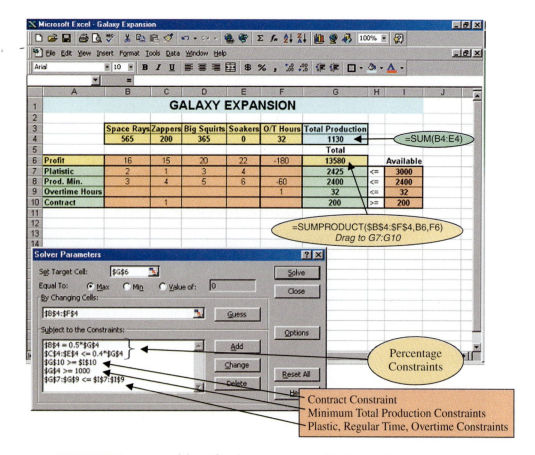

FIGURE 3.3*a* Spreadsheet for the Expansion of Galaxy Industries

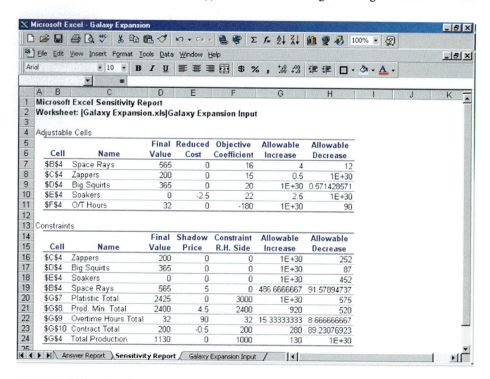

FIGURE 3.3*b* Sensitivity Report for the Expansion of Galaxy Industries

Analysis

From Figure 3.3*a* we can determine the gross profit for each model by multiplying the unit profit per dozen times the number of dozens produced. The cost of overtime is 32($180) = $5760. This gives the following results.[3]

Model	Dozens Produced	Total Gross Profit	Percent of Total
Space Rays	565	$ 9,040	50.0%
Zappers	200	$ 3,000	17.7%
Big Squirts	365	$ 7,300	32.3%
Soakers	0	$ 0	0%
Total	1130	$19,340	
	Cost of Overtime	$ 5,760	
	NET PROFIT	$13,580	

Furthermore, we note that:

- The total production of 1130 dozen exceeds the minimum requirement by 130 dozen.
- All 2400 minutes of regular time and all 32 hours of overtime will be used.
- Only 2425 of the 3000 pounds of available plastic will be used.

From the Sensitivity Report information shown in Figure 3.3*b*, we subtract the Allowable Decrease from and add the Allowable Increase to the profit coefficients to determine the following ranges of optimality for which the above solution will remain

---

[3] In a more elaborate spreadsheet design, such as several of those given in the remainder of this chapter, we could have programmed various cells to generate this information automatically.

optimal. Recall that the range of optimality is the range of values for an objective function coefficient within which the optimal solution remains valid, as long as no other changes are made.

Model	Profit Per Dozen	Minimum Profit Per Dozen	Maximum Profit Per Dozen
Space Rays	$16.00	$ 4.00	$20.00
Zappers	$15.00	No Minimum	$15.50
Big Squirts	$20.00	$19.43	No Maximum
Soakers	$22.00	No Minimum	$24.50

We further note from Figure 3.3*b* that:

- The above solution will remain optimal as long as the cost of overtime hours is less than $270 (Allowable Decrease from -180 is 90 (cell H11)).
- The profit per dozen Soakers must increase by $2.50 (cell E10) to $24.50 before they will be profitable to produce.
- Additional regular time minutes will add $4.50 per minute or $270 per hour to the total profit (cell E21). This holds true for up to an additional 920 minutes or $15\frac{1}{3}$ hours (cell G21).
- Additional (or fewer) overtime hours above or below the 32 scheduled overtime hours will add (or subtract) $90 to the total profit (cell E22). This holds true as long as the total number of overtime hours is between $23\frac{1}{3}$ hours and $47\frac{1}{3}$ hours (obtained from $32 - 8\frac{2}{3}$ (cell H22) and $32 + 15\frac{1}{3}$ (cell G22)).
- Each additional dozen Zappers added to the contract with Jaycee Toys will subtract $0.50 (cell E23) from the total profit (up to an additional 280 dozen (cell G23)). A reduction in the contract amount will save $0.50 per dozen for a reduction not to exceed 89.23 dozen (cell H23). If the contract requirement was outside this range, we would have to re-solve the problem to determine a new shadow price.
- Each dozen Space Rays that are allowed to be produced *above 50% of the total* will add $5.00 (cell E19) to the total profit (up to $486\frac{2}{3}$ dozen more than 50% (cell G19)). Again the problem must be re-solved if the change is outside this range.

Based on this information, the manager might ask for permission to schedule additional overtime hours, increase the percentage of Space Rays produced, reduce the contract with Jaycee Toys, or find ways to increase the profit for Soakers. However, if any changes are made, before proceeding management should first determine if the changes would affect any of the other parameters or basic assumptions underlying the model.

3.4.2 PORTFOLIO MODELS

Numerous mathematical models have been developed for a variety of financial/portfolio models. These models take into account return projections, measures of risk and volatility, liquidity, and long- and short-term investment goals. Some of these models are nonlinear in nature. However, here we present a situation that could be modeled as a linear program.

JONES INVESTMENT SERVICE

Concepts: Minimization
                 Sensitivity Analysis (All constraint types)

Charles Jones is a financial advisor who specializes in making recommendations to investors who have recently come into unexpected sums of money from inheritances, lottery winnings, and the like. He discusses investment goals with his clients, taking into account each client's attitude toward risk and liquidity.

After an initial consultation with a client, Charles selects a group of stocks, bonds, mutual funds, savings plans, and other investments that he feels may be appropriate for consideration in the portfolio. He then secures information on each investment and determines his own rating. With this information he develops a chart giving the risk factors (numbers between 0 and 100, based on his evaluation), expected returns based on current and projected company operations, and liquidity information. At the second meeting Charles defines the client's goals more specifically. The responses are entered into a linear programming model, and a recommendation is made to the client based on the results of the model.

Frank Baklarz has just inherited $100,000. Based on their initial meeting, Charles has found Frank to be quite risk-averse. Charles, therefore, suggests the following potential investments that can offer good returns with small risk.

Potential Investment	*Expected Return*	*Jones's Rating*	*Liquidity Analysis*	*Risk Factor*
Savings account	4.0%	A	Immediate	0
Certificate of deposit	5.2%	A	5-year	0
Atlantic Lighting	7.1%	B+	Immediate	25
Arkansas REIT	10.0%	B	Immediate	30
Bedrock Insurance annuity	8.2%	A	1-year	20
Nocal Mining bond	6.5%	B+	1-year	15
Minicomp Systems	20.0%	A	Immediate	65
Antony Hotels	12.5%	C	Immediate	40

Based on their second meeting, Charles has been able to help Frank develop the following portfolio goals.

1. An expected annual return of at least 7.5%

2. At least 50% of the inheritance in A-rated investments

3. At least 40% of the inheritance in immediately liquid investments

4. No more than $30,000 in savings accounts and certificates of deposit

Given that Frank is risk-averse, Charles would like to make a final recommendation that will minimize total risk while meeting these goals. As part of his service, Charles would also like to inform Frank of potential what-if scenarios associated with this recommendation.

SOLUTION

The following is a brief summary of the problem.

- Determine the amount to be placed in each investment.
- Minimize total overall risk.
- Invest all $100,000.
- Meet the goals developed with Frank Baklarz.

THE MATHEMATICAL MODEL

Defining the X's as the amount Frank should allot to each investment, the following linear model represents the situation:

$$\text{MINIMIZE} \qquad 25X_3 + 30X_4 + 20X_5 + 15X_6 + 65X_7 + 40X_8 \qquad \text{(Risk)}$$

ST

$$
\begin{aligned}
X_1 + X_2 + X_3 + X_4 + X_5 + X_6 + X_7 + X_8 &= 100{,}000 \text{ (Total)}\\
.04X_1 + .052X_2 + .071X_3 + .1X_4 + .082X_5 + .065X_6 + .2X_7 + .125X_8 &\geq 7500 \text{ (Return)}\\
X_1 + X_2 \qquad\qquad + X_5 \qquad + X_7 &\geq 50{,}000 \text{ (A-Rated)}\\
X_1 \qquad + X_3 + X_4 \qquad\qquad + X_7 + X_8 &\geq 40{,}000 \text{ (Liquid)}\\
X_1 + X_2 &\leq 30{,}000 \text{ (Savings/CD)}
\end{aligned}
$$

$$\text{All X's} \geq 0$$

Since Jones Investment Service shares its findings directly with its clients, Charles wants to have a spreadsheet designed with his client in mind. Thus, the spreadsheet should convey all the requisite information without looking like a linear programming model. Accordingly, Charles used the "user-friendly" spreadsheet shown in Figure 3.4a. Here the right-hand sides of the constraints are in cells C2, F16, F17, F18, and F19, respectively, and cells C14, B13, D16, D17, D18, and D19 have been programmed as shown to give the quantity designated in the cells to their left. Note that SUMIF formulas in cells D17 and D18 sum only the values that meet the criteria of "A" rating and "Immediate" liquidity, respectively. Cells B5:B12 are reserved for the values of the decision variables.

Jones Investment.xls

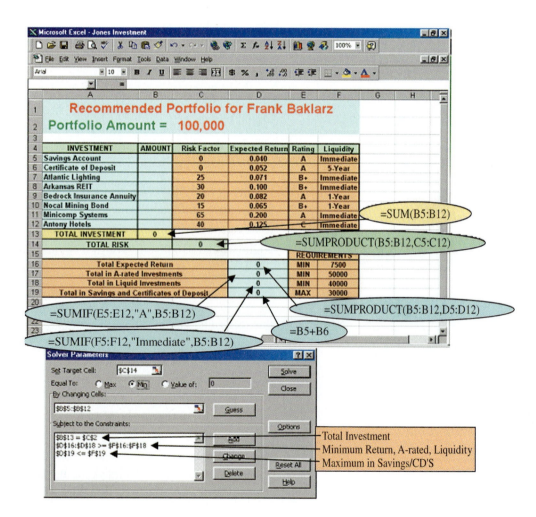

FIGURE 3.4a
Excel Spreadsheet and Dialogue Box for Frank Baklarz

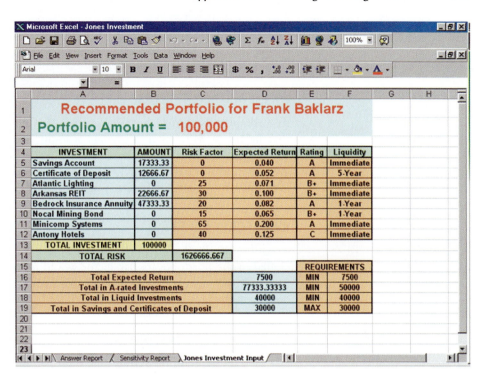

FIGURE 3.4b
Optimal Portfolio for
Frank Baklarz

After verifying all requirements with Frank Baklarz, Charles clicked on Excel
Solver giving the results and Sensitivity Report in Figures 3.4b and 3.4c, respectively.

Microsoft Excel Sensitivity Report
Worksheet: [Jones.xls]Jones Investment Input

Adjustable Cells

Cell	Name	Final Value	Reduced Cost	Objective Coefficient	Allowable Increase	Allowable Decrease
$B$5	Savings Account AMOUNT	17333.33333	0	0	1.176470588	0.5
$B$6	Certificate of Deposit AMOUNT	12666.66667	0	0	0.5	1.176470588
$B$7	Atlantic Lighting AMOUNT	0	4.666666667	25	1E+30	4.666666667
$B$8	Arkansas REIT AMOUNT	22666.66667	0	30	0.384615385	1.176470588
$B$9	Bedrock Insurance Annuity AMOUNT	47333.33333	0	20	0.425531915	0.5
$B$10	Nocal Mining Bond AMOUNT	0	0.666666667	15	1E+30	0.666666667
$B$11	Minicomp Systems AMOUNT	0	1.666666667	65	1E+30	1.666666667
$B$12	Antony Hotels AMOUNT	0	1.666666667	40	1E+30	1.666666667

Constraints

Cell	Name	Final Value	Shadow Price	Constraint R.H. Side	Allowable Increase	Allowable Decrease
$B$13	TOTAL INVESTMENT AMOUNT	100000	-7.333333333	100000	4634.146341	6341.463415
$D$16	Total Expected Return Expected Return	7500	333.3333333	7500	520	380
$D$17	Total in A-rated Investments Expected Ret	77333.33333	0	50000	27333.33333	1E+30
$D$18	Total in Liquid Investments Expected Retur	40000	4	40000	21111.11111	28888.88889
$D$19	Total in Savings and Certificates of Deposit	30000	-10	30000	17333.33333	6333.333333

FIGURE 3.4c
Sensitivity Report for
Frank Baklarz

Analysis

The spreadsheet is designed for easy reading and interpretation. In addition to
the optimal solution, it is easy to see that the binding constraints are those requiring an expected annual return of at least $7500, a minimum amount of $40,000 in

immediately liquid investments, and a maximum amount of $30,000 in the savings account and the certificate of deposit. This portfolio exceeds Frank's minimum requirement of at least $50,000 in A-rated investments by $27,333.

RECOMMENDATION

According to the spreadsheet in Figure 3.4b, Charles should recommend to Frank that he invest $17,333 in a savings account, $12,667 in a certificate of deposit, $22,667 in Arkansas REIT, and $47,333 in the Bedrock Insurance Annuity. This gives an overall risk value of 1,626,667 (an average risk factor of 16.27 per dollar invested). Any other combination of investments will give a higher risk value.

REDUCED COSTS

According to the Sensitivity Report in Figure 3.4c, for Atlantic Lighting to be included in the portfolio, its risk factor would have to be lowered by 4.67 to 20.33. Similarly, to include Nocal Mining, Minicomp Systems, or Antony Hotels requires a reduction in their risk factors of 0.67, 1.67, and 1.67, respectively.

RANGE OF OPTIMALITY

For each investment, the "Allowable Increase" and "Allowable Decrease" columns in the Sensitivity Report give the minimum and maximum amounts that the risk factors can change without altering Charles's recommendation. For example, the range of optimality of the risk factor for the Bedrock Insurance annuity is between $19.5(=20 - 0.5)$ and $20.43(=20 + 0.43)$. Recall that the range of optimality applies to changing one investment at a time. Since negative risk factors do not make sense, the minimum risk factors for the savings account and certificate of deposit would be 0.

SHADOW PRICES

The shadow prices in the Sensitivity Report give us the following information:

- If an extra dollar were invested above the $100,000, the risk value would improve (decrease) by 7.33.
- For every extra dollar increase to the minimum expected annual return, the overall risk value would increase by 333.33.
- For every extra dollar that must be made immediately liquid, the overall risk value would increase by 4.
- For every extra dollar that is allowed to be invested in a savings account or a certificate of deposit, the risk value would decrease by 10.
- No change in total risk value would result from requiring that additional dollars be invested in A-rated investments.

RANGE OF FEASIBILITY

The Allowable Increase and Allowable Decrease to the original right-hand side coefficients give the range of feasibility of individual changes to the right-hand side within which the shadow prices remain constant. For example, the range of feasibility corresponding to the $7500 minimum return is ($7500 − $380) to ($7500 + $520) or from $7120 to $8020. An Allowable Decrease of 1E+30 is effectively infinity; thus, −∞ is the minimum right-hand side value in the range of feasibility for the amount invested in A-rated investments.

3.4.3 PUBLIC SECTOR MODELS

National, state, and local governments and agencies are charged with distributing resources for the public good. Frequently, political pressures and conflicts cause these entities to try to do more than the available resources will allow. When that happens, several remedies are possible. One is to try to meet a subset, but not all, of a perceived set of constraints, as is the case of one of the homework exercises in this chapter. A second approach is to treat several of the constraints as "goals" and to prioritize and weight these goals. This is called a "goal programming" approach, which is discussed in Chapter 13 on the accompanying CD-ROM. A third approach, and the one illustrated here, is simply to scale back and try to "live within one's means."

Saint Joseph.xls
Saint Joseph (Revised).xls

ST. JOSEPH PUBLIC UTILITY COMMISSION

Concepts: Ignoring Integer Restrictions
Summation Variable
Infeasibility
Multiple Optimal Solutions

The St. Joseph Public Utilities Commission has been charged with inspecting and reporting utility problems that have resulted from recent floods in the area. Concerns have been raised about the damage done to electrical wiring, gas lines, and insulation. The Commission has one week to carry out its inspections. It has been assigned three electrical inspectors and two gas inspectors, each available for 40 hours, to analyze structures in their respective areas of expertise. In addition, the Commission has allocated $10,000 for up to 100 hours (at $100 per hour) of consulting time from Weathertight Insulation, a local expert in home and industrial insulation.

These experts are assigned to inspect private homes, businesses (office complexes), and industrial plants in the area. The goal is to thoroughly inspect as many structures as possible during the allotted time in order to gather the requisite information. However, the minimum requirements are to inspect at least eight office buildings and eight industrial plants, and to make sure that at least 60% of the inspections are of private homes.

Once the total number of each type of structure to be inspected has been determined, the actual inspections will be done by choosing a random sample from those that are served by the St. Joseph Public Utility Commission. The Commission has mandated the following approximate inspection hours for each type of inspection:

	Electrical	*Gas*	*Insulation*
Homes	2	1	3
Offices	4	3	2
Plants	6	3	1

A team of management science consultants has been hired to suggest how many homes, office buildings, and plants should be inspected.

SOLUTION

The following is a brief summary of the problem faced by the St. Joseph Public Utilities Commission.

- St. Joseph must determine the number of homes, office complexes, and plants to be inspected.
- It wishes to maximize the total number of structures inspected.
- At least eight offices and eight plants are to be inspected.
- At least 60% of the inspections should involve private homes.
- At most, 120 hours (3×40) can be allocated for electrical inspections, 80 hours (2×40) for gas inspections, and 100 consulting hours for insulation inspection

The management science team has decided to formulate the problem as a linear program, although the results should be integer-valued. If the linear program does not generate an integer solution, another method such as integer programming or dynamic programming (which is discussed in Chapter 13 on the accompanying CD-ROM) must be used, or St. Joseph could accept a feasible rounded solution.

DECISION VARIABLES

The team defined the following variables:

$$X_1 = \text{number of homes to be inspected}$$
$$X_2 = \text{number of office complexes to be inspected}$$
$$X_3 = \text{number of industrial plants to be inspected}$$

and they used the following summation variable

$$X_4 = \text{total number of structures to be inspected}$$

OBJECTIVE FUNCTION

The problem is to determine the maximum number of structures that can be inspected, subject to the constraints. Thus, the objective function of the model is simply:

$$\text{MAXIMIZE } X_4$$

CONSTRAINTS

The summation constraint for X_4 is:

$$X_1 + X_2 + X_3 - X_4 = 0$$

The minimum number of office complexes and plants to be inspected are simply modeled as

$$X_2 \geq 8$$
$$X_3 \geq 8$$

The fact that at least 60% of the inspections must be of homes is modeled as

$$X_1 \geq 0.6X_4$$

or

$$X_1 - 0.6X_4 \geq 0$$

Finally, the constraints on the time limits for electrical, gas, and insulation inspections are:

$$2X_1 + 4X_2 + 6X_3 \leq 120 \text{ (Electrical)}$$
$$1X_1 + 3X_2 + 3X_3 \leq 80 \text{ (Gas)}$$
$$3X_1 + 2X_2 + 1X_3 \leq 100 \text{ (Insulation)}$$

THE LINEAR PROGRAMMING MODEL

The complete linear programming model for the St. Joseph Public Utility Commission is:

$$
\begin{aligned}
\text{MAXIMIZE} \quad & X_4 && \text{(Total structures)} \\
\text{ST} \quad & \\
X_1 + X_2 + X_3 - X_4 &= 0 && \text{(Summation)} \\
X_2 &\geq 8 && \text{(Minimum offices)} \\
X_3 &\geq 8 && \text{(Minimum plants)} \\
X_1 - 0.6X_4 &\geq 0 && (\geq 60\% \text{ Homes}) \\
2X_1 + 4X_2 + 6X_3 &\leq 120 && \text{(Electrical)} \\
X_1 + 3X_2 + 3X_3 &\leq 80 && \text{(Gas)} \\
3X_1 + 2X_2 + 1X_3 &\leq 100 && \text{(Insulation)} \\
\text{All X's} &\geq 0
\end{aligned}
$$

EXCEL SOLVER INPUT/OUTPUT AND ANALYSIS

Figure 3.5*a* shows the Excel spreadsheet and Solver dialogue box used by management science consultants. Note that the summation constraint is included in cell B9. The constraint requiring a minimum limit of 60% of the inspections to be houses can be expressed as $X_1 \geq .6X_4$. By entering the formula =.6*B9 into cell C5, this constraint requires (cell B5) $\geq$ (cell C5), which is part of the first set of constraints in the dialogue box.

Saint Joseph.xls

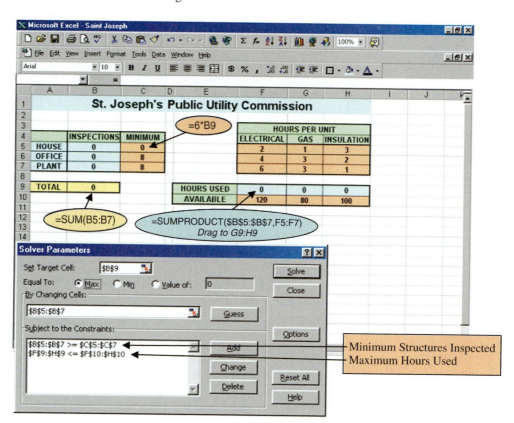

FIGURE 3.5*a*   Input for the St. Joseph Public Utility Commission

But when Solve was clicked, instead of an optimal solution, Solver returned the dialogue box shown in Figure 3.5*b*.

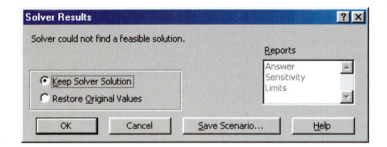

FIGURE 3.5*b*
Solver Found the St. Joseph Utility Model to Be Infeasible

Needless to say, the Commission was not too pleased with this analysis. In fact, it was beginning to conclude that the management science consultants (and perhaps management science itself) could not be trusted to give the desired results.

When the consultants were asked to explain this result, they pointed out the reason for infeasibility. Even if only the minimum eight offices and eight plants were inspected, 80 of the 120 electrical hours [4(8) + 6(8)] would be used, leaving only 40 hours to inspect homes. At two hours per home, a maximum of 20 homes could be inspected. Thus, a total of 36 structures would be inspected, only 20 of which would be homes. This represents only 55.56% of the total homes (=20/36), not the minimum 60% the Commission desired.

In other words, the problem had been formulated correctly by the management science team, but the Commission had simply given them a set of constraints that were impossible to meet. Given this situation, after much debate the Commission decided that it could get by with inspecting a minimum of six office buildings and six plants. This would use up 60 electrical hours, leaving 60 electrical hours to inspect 30 homes, which far exceeds the 60% minimum limit on homes.

The Commission was about to initiate this action when it was pointed out that inspecting 30 homes, six office buildings, and six plants would use up 108 hours for insulation inspection [3(30) + 2(6) + 1(6)], exceeding the 100 available inspection hours. What to do?

The Commission asked the management science consultants to reconsider their problem in light of these relaxed constraints and offer a recommendation. The consultants changed the values in cells C6 and C7 of their spreadsheet from 8 to 6 and again called Solver to determine an optimal solution. The resulting spreadsheet and the Sensitivity Report are shown in Figures 3.6*a* and 3.6*b*, respectively.

The optimal solution turned out to have integer values, and thus the consultants could now report that a maximum of 40 structures (27 houses, 6 office buildings, and 7 plants) could be inspected; 67.5% (=27/40) of the inspected structures would be houses. All 120 electrical inspection hours and all 100 insulation inspection hours would be used. A total of 12 hours of gas inspection time would remain unused.

An Alternate Optimal Solution

But the consultants noted from the Sensitivity Report in Figure 3.6*b* that the Allowable Increase of Office Inspections and the Allowable Decrease for both House Inspections and Plant Inspections were all 0. From our discussion in Chapter 2, recall that this is an indication that there may be alternate optimal solutions. Fol-

Saint Joseph (Revised).xls

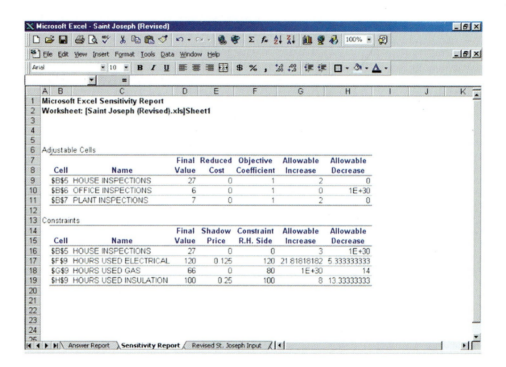

FIGURE 3.6a Optimal Solution for the St. Joseph Public Utility Commission

FIGURE 3.6b Sensitivity Report for the St. Joseph Public Utility Commission

lowing the procedure for generating alternate optimal solutions outlined in Chapter 2, the consultants:

- Added a constraint requiring the total number of inspections to be 40
- Changed the objective function to MAX X_2 (cell B6), since the Allowable *Increase* for office building inspections is 0. (Alternatively, they could have chosen to *minimize* either cell B5 or B7 since the Allowable *Decrease* for house inspections or plant inspections is also 0.)

Figure 3.7 shows the dialogue box and the resulting spreadsheet.

This spreadsheet shows that inspecting 26 houses, 8 office buildings, and 6 plants would be an alternative way of inspecting 40 structures while staying within the constraints of the model. In this solution, 65% (=26/40) of the structures inspected would be houses.

Saint Joseph (Revised).xls
(Alternative Solution
Worksheet)

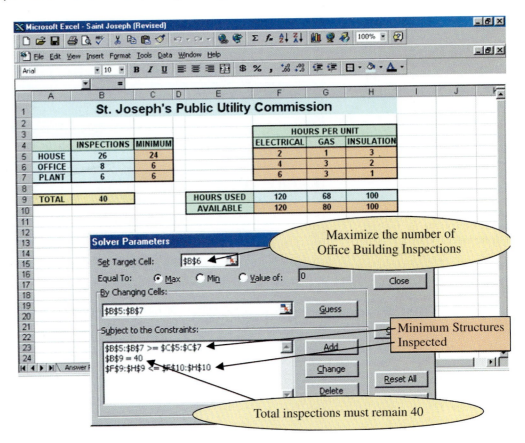

FIGURE 3.7 Alternate Optimal Solution for St. Joseph's Public Utility Commission

Although any weighted average of these two solutions would also be optimal, since the first solution calls for inspecting 26 homes and the second 27 homes, any weighted average of the two solutions would yield a *fractional* solution of between 26 and 27 homes to be inspected. Thus, the consultants reported that these two solutions are the only optimal solutions that yield integers for the number of homes, office complexes, and plants to be inspected.

Faced with two feasible alternatives, the Commission had the opportunity to inject some political preferences into the decision process while still inspecting 40 structures.

3.4.4 PURCHASING MODELS

Purchasing models can take into account customer demand, budgets, cash flow, advertising, and inventory restrictions. In today's global economy, purchasing models play a key role in balancing customer satisfaction levels within the limited resources of the business enterprise. In the following application we present a very simplified model that takes only a few of these factors into account. We have purposely presented this problem in such a way as to illustrate another situation that can arise when building mathematical models—that of failing to consider all (or at least not enough) of the limiting factors in the original formulation.

EUROMERICA LIQUORS

Concepts: Choosing an Objective
Lower Bound Constraints
Unboundedness
"Slightly" Violated Constraints
Interpretation of Reduced Costs for Bounded Variables

Euromerica Liquors of Jersey City, New Jersey purchases and distributes a number of wines to retailers. See Table 3.2. Purchasing manager Maria Arias has been asked to order at least 800 bottles of each wine during the next purchase cycle. The only other direction Maria has been given is that, in accordance with a long-standing company policy, she is to order at least twice as many domestic (U.S.) bottles as imported bottles in any cycle. Management believes that this policy promotes a steady sales flow that keeps inventory costs at a minimum. Maria must decide exactly how many bottles of each type of wine the company is to purchase during this ordering cycle.

TABLE 3.2   Euromerica Liquors' Wine Purchases and Distribution

Wine	Country	Cost	Selling Price
Napa Gold	U.S.	$2.50	$4.25
Cayuga Lake	U.S.	$3.00	$4.50
Seine Soir	France	$5.00	$8.00
Bella Bella	Italy	$4.00	$6.00

SOLUTION

To summarize, Maria must:

- determine the number of bottles of each type of wine to purchase
- order at least 800 of each type
- order at least twice as many domestic bottles as imported bottles
- select an appropriate objective function

DECISION VARIABLES

The four decision variables can be defined as:

X_1 = bottles of Napa Gold purchased in this purchase cycle
X_2 = bottles of Cayuga Lake purchased in this purchase cycle
X_3 = bottles of Seine Soir purchased in this purchase cycle
X_4 = bottles of Bella Bella purchased in this purchase cycle

OBJECTIVE FUNCTION

At first, Maria reasoned that since Euromerica Liquors' goal is to make good profits, her objective should be to maximize the profit from the purchases made during this purchase cycle. Because inventory costs are assumed to be small due to the company's ordering policy, she defined the profit coefficients in terms of the selling price minus the purchase cost per bottle. Thus, the unit profits for the respective decision variables are $1.75, $1.50, $3, and $2, and the objective function is:

$$\text{MAX } 1.75X_1 + 1.50X_2 + 3X_3 + 2X_4$$

CONSTRAINTS

The following constraints must be considered

Minimum Production: At least 800 bottles of each of the wines are to be purchased:

$$X_1 \geq 800$$
$$X_2 \geq 800$$
$$X_3 \geq 800$$
$$X_4 \geq 800$$

These constraints could be entered in linear programming software either as functional constraints or as lower bound constraints that would replace the nonnegativity constraints for the variables.

Mix Constraint: (The number of bottles of domestic wine purchased) should be at least (twice the number of bottles of imported wine purchased):

$$X_1 + X_2 \geq 2(X_3 + X_4)$$

or

$$X_1 + X_2 - 2X_3 - 2X_4 \geq 0$$

THE MATHEMATICAL MODEL

The complete model can now be formulated as

$$
\begin{aligned}
\text{MAXIMIZE} \quad & 1.75X_1 + 1.50X_2 + 3X_3 + 2X_4 \\
\text{ST} \qquad\quad & X_1 \qquad\qquad\qquad\qquad \geq 800 \\
& \qquad X_2 \qquad\qquad\qquad \geq 800 \\
& \qquad\qquad X_3 \qquad\qquad \geq 800 \\
& \qquad\qquad\qquad X_4 \geq 800 \\
& X_1 + X_2 - 2X_3 - 2X_4 \geq \quad 0
\end{aligned}
$$

EXCEL INPUT/OUTPUT AND ANALYSIS

Maria created the Excel spreadsheet and Solver dialogue box shown in Figure 3.8*a*, with cells C4:C7 set aside for the number of bottles to order.

When she clicked Solve, however, she got the result shown in Figure 3.8*b*. Recall that the message "The Set Cell values do not converge" is Excel's way of stating that the problem is unbounded.

But Euromerica cannot make an infinite profit! When Maria examined the model, she realized that she had ignored the following considerations when building the model:

- Euromerica has a finite budget for the procurement of bottles of wine during the purchase cycle.
- The suppliers have a finite amount of product available.
- There is a limit on demand from the wine-buying public.

Undaunted, Maria discussed the situation with management and discovered that they wished to commit no more than $28,000 to purchase wine during this cycle. She then contacted the wine producers and found that there were ample supplies of Cayuga Lake and Bella Bella, but that only 300 cases of Napa Gold and

Euromerica Liquors.xls

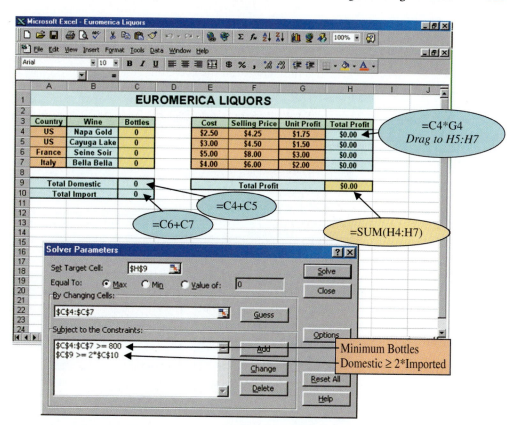

FIGURE 3.8a Spreadsheet and Dialogue Box for Euromerica Liquors

FIGURE 3.8b Solver Result for Euromerica Liquors—Unbounded Solution

200 cases of Seine Soir were available (each case contains 12 bottles). Finally, she performed a market survey and, based on the results, concluded that no more than 10,000 total bottles should be purchased. Thus, the revised model is:

$$
\begin{array}{lll}
\text{MAXIMIZE} & 1.75X_1 + 1.50X_2 + 3X_3 + 2X_4 & \\
\text{ST} & X_1 & \geq 800 \\
& X_2 & \geq 800 \\
& X_3 & \geq 800 \\
& X_4 & \geq 800 \\
& X_1 + X_2 - 2X_3 - 2X_4 & \geq 0 \\
& 2.50X_1 + 3.00X_2 + 5X_3 + 4X_4 & \leq 28{,}000 \ (\text{Budget}) \\
& X_1 & \leq 3600 \ (\text{Napa}) \\
& X_3 & \leq 2400 \ (\text{Seine}) \\
& X_1 + X_2 + X_3 + X_4 & \leq 10{,}000 \ (\text{Total})
\end{array}
$$

Maria revised her spreadsheet to reflect these changes by adding cells C11 and C13 to reflect the total number of bottles purchased and the amount of budget spent and cells G11 and G13 to reflect the limits on the maximum number of bottles purchased and the cycle budget. When the constraints for the maximum number of bottles purchased and the maximum budget expenditure along with limits on the availability of Napa Gold and Seine Soire were added to the Solver dialogue box, clicking Solve generated the optimal spreadsheet and Sensitivity Report shown in Figures 3.9*a* and 3.9*b*.

Euromerica Revised.xls

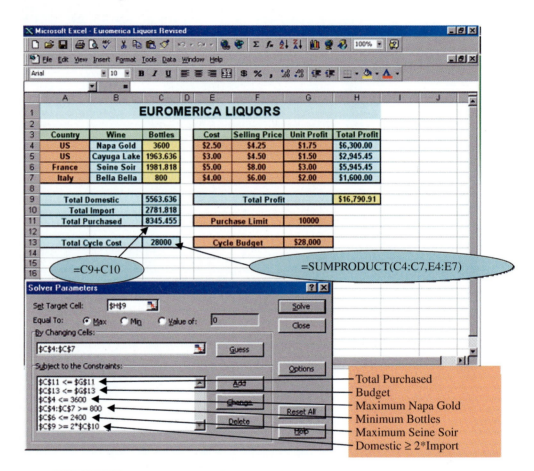

FIGURE 3.9*a*   Revised Spreadsheet for Euromerica Liquors

Maria rounded off the solution to *full cases* and placed them in the order shown in Table 3.3. Note that this proposal is $20 over the budget limit of $28,000. Although the $28,000 limit was a restriction, it was probably a strong guideline rather than a hard and fast value. Hence, Maria had no qualms about recommending this solution.

TABLE 3.3   Euromerica Liquors' Solution

Wine	Bottles	Cases	Cost	Profit
Napa Gold	3600	300	$ 9,000	$ 6,300
Cayuga Lake	1968	164	$ 5,904	$ 2,952
Seine Soir	1980	165	$ 9,900	$ 5,940
Bella Bella	804	67	$ 3,216	$ 1,608
Total	8352	696	$28,020	$16,800

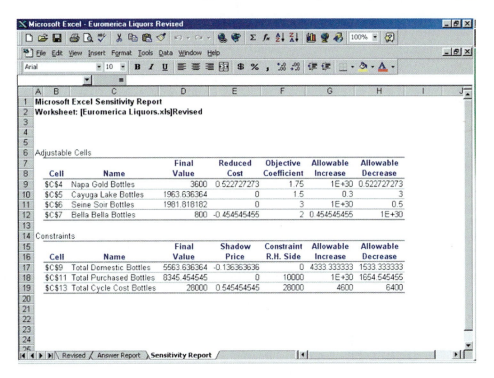

FIGURE 3.9b Sensitivity Report for Revised Euromerica Liquors

Reduced Cost for Bounded Variables

In Chapter 2 we defined the reduced cost for a variable as the amount the objective function would change if the value of that variable were increased from 0 to 1. There we implicitly assumed that the lower bound for the variable was 0 and that there was no upper bound. When a variable is defined to be a **bounded variable** by restricting its cell value in the spreadsheet to be at least or at most some nonzero constant, the reduced cost indicates the change in the objective function value if that bound were changed by 1.

In Figure 3.9b Maria noticed that the number of Napa Gold bottles purchased would be its upper bound of 3600. She also noticed that the number of Bella Bella bottles purchased would be at its lower bound of 800. Thus, she reported to management that if she were allowed to *increase* the number of bottles of Napa Gold (above 3600), overall profit would increase by slightly more than $0.52 per bottle, whereas if she were allowed to *decrease* the number of bottles of Bella Bella ordered (below 800), profit would increase by slightly more than $0.45 per bottle.

3.4.5 BLENDING MODELS

One of the early successful applications of linear programming models was that of aiding executives in the oil industry in determining how much raw crude oil to purchase from various sources and how to blend these oils into useful gasoline and other byproducts. Each of these products has certain specifications that must be met such as a minimum octane rating or a maximum vapor pressure level. The United Oil Company model presented here is a simplified version of such a model. Other industries where similar blending models are useful include the garment and food industries, which blend several raw materials from various sources into finished products.

United Oil.xls

UNITED OIL COMPANY

Concepts: Variable Definitions for Blending Models
Calculation of Objective Coefficients
Ratio Constraints
Summation Variables
Alternate Optimal Solutions
Hidden Cells on Spreadsheet

United Oil blends two input streams of crude oil products—alkylate and catalytic cracked (c.c.)—to meet demand for weekly contracts for regular (12,000 barrels), mid-grade (7500 barrels), and premium (4500 barrels) gasolines. Each week United can purchase up to 15,000 barrels of alkylate and up to 15,000 barrels of catalytic cracked. Because of demand, it can sell all blended gasolines, including any production that exceeds its contracts.

To be classified as regular, mid-grade, or premium, gasolines must meet minimum octane and maximum vapor pressure requirements. The octane rating and vapor pressure of a blended gasoline is assumed to be the weighted average of the crude oil products in the blend. Relevant cost/pricing, octane, and vapor pressure data are given in Tables 3.4 and 3.5.

United must decide how to blend the crude oil products into commercial gasolines in order to maximize its weekly profit.

TABLE 3.4   Cost/pricing, Octane, and Vapor Pressure Data—United Oil

	Crude Oil Product Data		
Product	Octane Rating	Vapor Pressure (lb./sq. in.)	Cost per Barrel
Alkylate	98	5	$19
Catalytic cracked	86	9	$16

TABLE 3.5   Gasoline Octane Rating, Vapor Pressure, and Barrel Profit

	Blended Gasoline Requirements		
Gasoline	Minimum Octane Rating	Maximum Vapor Pressure	Selling Price per Barrel
Regular	87	9	$18
Mid-grade	89	7	$20
Premium	92	6	$23

SOLUTION

The problem for United Oil is to:

- determine how many barrels of alkylate to blend into regular, mid-grade, and premium and how many barrels of catalytic cracked to blend into regular, mid-grade, and premium each week
- maximize total weekly profit

- remain within raw gas availabilities
- meet contract requirements
- produce gasoline blends that meet the octane and vapor pressure requirements

DECISION VARIABLES (FIRST PASS)

The pending decision is to determine how much of each crude oil (X, Y) to blend into each of the three grades (1, 2, 3) each week:

X_1 = number of barrels of alkylate blended into regular weekly
X_2 = number of barrels of alkylate blended into mid-grade weekly
X_3 = number of barrels of alkylate blended into premium weekly
Y_1 = number of barrels of catalytic cracked blended into regular weekly
Y_2 = number of barrels of catalytic cracked blended into mid-grade weekly
Y_3 = number of barrels of catalytic cracked blended into premium weekly

OBJECTIVE FUNCTION

The profit made on a barrel of crude product blended into a commercial gasoline is the difference between the selling price of the blended gasoline and the cost of the crude product. Table 3.6 gives the profit coefficients. The objective function is:

$$\text{MAX} - 1X_1 + 1X_2 + 4X_3 + 2Y_1 + 4Y_2 + 7Y_3$$

TABLE 3.6   Profit Coefficients for Oil

Variable	Crude Product Cost	Gasoline Selling Price	Barrel Profit
X_1	$19	$18	−$1
X_2	$19	$20	$1
X_3	$19	$23	$4
Y_1	$16	$18	$2
Y_2	$16	$20	$4
Y_3	$16	$23	$7

CONSTRAINTS

United must consider the following constraints in its analysis:

Crude Availability: United cannot blend more than the product available from either input source. The total amount blended from a source is simply the sum of the amounts blended into regular, mid-grade, and premium gasoline:

$$X_1 + X_2 + X_3 \leq 15,000$$
$$Y_1 + Y_2 + Y_3 \leq 15,000$$

Contract Requirements: Although the contract requirements must be met, they may be exceeded; thus, although at least 12,000 barrels of regular must be produced, the actual amount produced will be the sum of the amounts of alkylate and catalytic cracked blended into regular: $X_1 + Y_1$. Similarly, the amount of mid-grade gas produced will be $X_2 + Y_2$, and the amount of premium gas produced will be $X_3 + Y_3$. Since these quantities are of interest to United Oil (and will figure into the remaining constraints), to simplify the formulation, summation variables can be used.

DECISION VARIABLES (SECOND PASS)

Define the following summation variables

$$R = \text{barrels of regular gasoline produced weekly}$$
$$M = \text{barrels of mid-grade gasoline produced weekly}$$
$$P = \text{barrels of premium gasoline produced weekly}$$

Doing so requires adding the following summation constraints:

$$X_1 + Y_1 - R = 0$$
$$X_2 + Y_2 - M = 0$$
$$X_3 + Y_3 - P = 0$$

Now the contract constraints can then be written as

$$R \geq 12{,}000$$
$$M \geq 7500$$
$$P \geq 4500$$

Octane and Vapor Constraints: The octane rating for regular gasoline is the weighted average of the octane ratings for alkylate and catalytic cracked blended into regular. The appropriate weights are the ratios of the amount of alkylate to the amount of regular and the amount of catalytic cracked to the amount of regular, respectively:

98 (Amount of alkylate in regular/Total amount of regular) +
86 (Amount of catalytic cracked in regular/Total amount of regular) =
$$98(X_1/R) + 86(Y_1/R)$$

Since this must be at least 87, the constraint is:

$$98(X_1/R) + 86(Y_1/R) \geq 87$$

The terms (X_1/R) and (Y_1/R) make this a *nonlinear* constraint. Since R will be positive in the optimal solution, however, multiplying both sides by R gives the following linear constraint:

$$98X_1 + 86Y_1 \geq 87R$$

or

$$98X_1 + 86Y_1 - 87R \geq 0$$

The remaining octane and vapor pressure constraints are constructed similarly; thus, the complete set of octane and vapor pressure restrictions is:

$$98X_1 + 86Y_1 - 87R \geq 0$$
$$98X_2 + 86Y_2 - 89M \geq 0$$
$$98X_3 + 86Y_3 - 92P \geq 0$$
$$5X_1 + 9Y_1 - 9R \leq 0$$
$$5X_2 + 9Y_2 - 7M \leq 0$$
$$5X_3 + 9Y_3 - 6P \leq 0$$

THE MATHEMATICAL MODEL

The complete model is as follows:

$$\text{MAXIMIZE} \quad -1X_1 + 1X_2 + 4X_3 + 2Y_1 + 4Y_2 + 7Y_3$$

$$\begin{aligned}
\text{ST} \quad X_1 + X_2 + X_3 && &&&& &\leq 15{,}000 \\
&& Y_1 + Y_2 + Y_3 && &&&& \leq 15{,}000 \\
X_1 && + Y_1 && - R && &= 0 \\
X_2 && + Y_2 && - M && &= 0 \\
X_3 && + Y_3 && - P &= 0 \\
&& && R && &\geq 12{,}000 \\
&& && M && &\geq 7500 \\
&& && P &\geq 4500 \\
98X_1 && - 86Y_1 && - 87R && &\geq 0 \\
98X_2 && + 86Y_2 && - 89M && &\geq 0 \\
98X_3 && + 86Y_3 && - 92P &\geq 0 \\
5X_1 && + 9Y_1 && - 9R && &\leq 0 \\
5X_2 && + 9Y_2 && - 7M && &\leq 0 \\
5X_3 && + 9Y_3 && - 6P &\leq 0
\end{aligned}$$

$$\text{All variables} \geq 0$$

EXCEL INPUT/OUTPUT AND ANALYSIS

Figure 3.10*a* shows the completed worksheet for United Oil. On the left side in columns A:E are the parameter inputs. On the right side, columns H:K give output values generated when Solver solves the model. The values of the decision variables are given in cells H7:J8. Cell formulas used in the spreadsheet are described in Table 3.7.

United Oil.xls

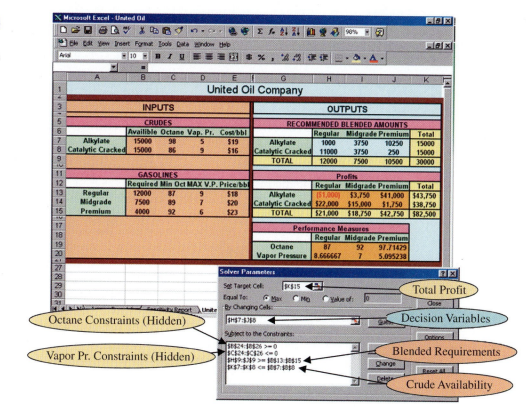

FIGURE 3.10*a*   Optimal Spreadsheet for United Oil Company

TABLE 3.7   Cell Formulas and Analysis of Spreadsheet in Figure 3.10*a*

		Spreadsheet Formulas/Analysis	
Cell	Quantity	Formula	Observations
K7	Alkylate Used	=SUM(H7:J7)	All 15,000 barrels of each are used.
K8	Catalytic Cracked Used	=SUM(H8:J8)	
H9	Regular Produced	=SUM(H7:H8)	Regular and mid-grade are produced at the minimum required
I9	Midgrade Produced	=SUM(I7:I8)	levels. The 10,500 barrels of premium exceed the minimum
J9	Premium Produced	=SUM(J7:J8)	requirement of 4,000 barrels by 6,500 barrels.
K9	Total Gasoline Produced	=SUM(H9:J9)	30,000 barrels are produced.
H13	Profit from Alk. in Reg.	=(E13-E7)*H7	There is actually a loss for blending alkylate into regular.
H14	Profit from Alk. in Mid.	=(E14-E7)*I7	
H15	Profit from Alk. in Prem.	=(E15-E7)*J7	
I13	Profit from C.C. in Reg.	=(E13-E8)*H8	
I14	Profit from C.C. in Mid.	=(E14-E8)*I8	
I15	Profit from C.C. in Prem.	=(E15-E8)*J8	
K13	Total Profit from Alk.	=SUM(H13:J13)	Profit from alkylate = $43,750
K14	Total Profit from C.C.	=SUM(H14:J14)	Profit from c.c. = $38,750
H15	Total Profit from Reg.	=SUM(H13:H14)	Profit from Reg. = $21,000
I15	Total Profit from Mid.	=SUM(I13:I14)	Profit from Mid. = $18,750
J15	Total Profit from Prem.	=SUM(J13:J14)	Profit from Prem. = $42,750
K15	Total Profit (Maximized)	=SUM(H15:J15)	Max. Total Profit = $82,500
H19	Octane Rating Regular	=C7*(H7/H9)+C8*(H8/H9)	Octane ratings are found by weighting the octane ratings of
I19	Octane Rating Midgrade	=C7*(I7/I9)+C8*(I8/I9)	alkylate and cc by the proportion in each blended gasoline.
J19	Octane Rating Premium	=C7*(J7/J9)+C8*(J8/J9)	Regular and mid-grade meet minimum octane ratings; the premium rating of 97.5 exceeds its minimum rating of 92.
H20	Vapor Pressure Regular	=D7*(H7/H9)+D8*(H8/H9)	Vapor pressure of a blended gasoline is found by weighting the
I20	Vapor Pressure Midgrade	=D7*(I7/I9)+D8*(I8/I9)	vapor pressures of alkylate and cc by the proportion in each
J20	Vapor Pressure Premium	=D7*(J7/J9)+D8*(J8/J9)	blended gasoline. Mid-grade is produced at its highest possible vapor pressure level. Regular and premium vapor pressures are less than their maximum allowable limits.

Construction and Analysis of the Spreadsheet Hidden Cells

The octane ratings and vapor pressures of the blended gasolines in cells H19:J20 were found by taking the weighted averages of the octane ratings and vapor pressures of alkylate and catalytic cracked blended into each grade. For example, as seen in Table 3.7, the formula in cell H19 is: =C7*(H7/H9)+C8*(H8/H9). But the denominator, cell H9, is the sum of the six decision variables in H7:J8, making the expression in cell H19 nonlinear in terms of the decision variables. There are similar formulas in cells H20, I19, I20, J19, and J20. Thus, if this nonlinear term were included in the left side of a constraint, a linear programming approach could not be used. That is why we wrote the mathematical model the way we did—to obtain a linear programming formulation!

Accordingly, the formulas for the left side of the last six functional constraints of the model for the octane and vapor pressure constraints are entered into cells B24:B26 and C24:C26, respectively, as shown in Table 3.8. Although these values are required to be nonnegative for octane and nonpositive for vapor pressure, their precise values are meaningless and add nothing to the manager's analysis of the results. Thus, the corresponding rows were hidden in Figure 3.10*a* by holding down the left mouse key over the selected row numbers in the left margin and then clicking "Hide" with the right mouse key.

TABLE 3.8   Hidden Cells—Left-Hand Sides of the Last Six Functional Constraints

	Left-Hand Side Values of the Last Six Functional Constraints (Hidden in Rows 24–26)		
Cell	Left Side Quantity	Left-Hand Side	Spreadsheet Formula
B24	Reg. Octane Rating	$98X_1+86Y_1-87R$	=SUMPRODUCT(C7:C8,H7:H8)-C13*H9
B25	Mid. Octane Rating	$98X_2+86Y_2-89M$	=SUMPRODUCT(C7:C8,I7:I8)-C14*I9
B26	Prem. Octane Rating	$98X_3+86Y_3-92P$	=SUMPRODUCT(C7:C8,J7:J8)-C15*J9
C24	Reg. Vapor Pressure	$5X_1+9Y_1-9R$	=SUMPRODUCT(D7:D8,H7:H8)-D13*H9
C25	Mid. Vapor Pressure	$5X_2+9Y_2-7M$	=SUMPRODUCT(D7:D8,I7:I8)-D14*I9
C26	Prem. Vapor Pressure	$5X_3+9Y_3-6P$	=SUMPRODUCT(D7:D8,J7:J8)-D15*J9

Analysis of the Sensitivity Report

Figure 3.10*b* shows the corresponding Sensitivity Report for this model.

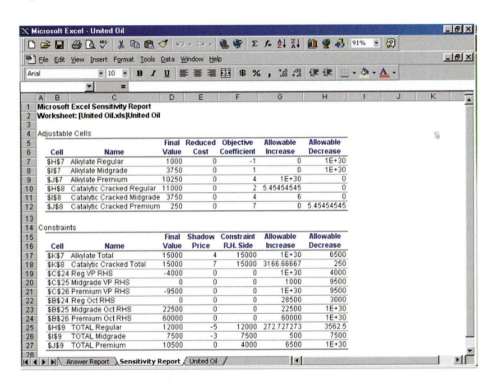

FIGURE 3.10*b*
Sensitivity Report for
United Oil

From this Sensitivity Report we observe the following.

Effects of Extra Crude   All additional barrels of alkylate will add $4 each to the total profit. Additional barrels of catalytic cracked will add $7 each for each of the next 3166.67 barrels. That is, United should be willing to pay up to $19 + $4 = $23 for an additional barrel of alkylate and up to $16 + $7 = $23 for additional barrels of catalytic cracked.

Effects of Changing Grade Requirements   Decreasing the requirement for regular from 12,000 barrels will increase profits by $5 per barrel up to a maximum decrease of 3562.5 barrels (to 8437.5 barrels); increasing this minimum requirement will decrease profits $5 per barrel, up to a maximum increase of 272.73 barrels (to 12,272.73 barrels). Changing the requirement for mid-grade will have a $3 effect for a maximum decrease of 7500 barrels (down to 0) or a maximum increase of 500 barrels (up to 8000). Changing the minimum requirement for premium would have no effect unless the increase puts the requirement above the proposed production level of 10,500 barrels.

Alternative Optimal Solutions   There are Allowable Increases and Allowable Decreases of 0 for the profit coefficients of the various blends, indicating the existence of alternate optimal solutions. Thus, the crudes can be blended in other ways to make a profit of $82,500 while meeting the octane and vapor pressure requirements.

Other Linear Models

Sections 3.4.1–3.4.5 described just a few possibilities which might be solved using linear programming models. Space considerations have precluded us from presenting even more examples of linear models in this text. However, two other slightly more complex, but very important applications are presented on the accompanying CD-ROM. These models illustrate a multiperiod cash flow scheduling model (Appendix 3.2) and a model for evaluating the efficiency operations using a process known as data envelopment analysis (Appendix 3.3). Since these models illustrate new ideas and spreadsheet approaches, you are encouraged to access them from the Appendix folder on the CD-ROM.

3.5   Applications of Integer Linear Programming Models

In many real-life models, at least one of the decision variables is required to be integer-valued. If all the variables are required to be integer, the model is called an **all-integer linear programming model (AILP)** and if all are required to be binary (values of 0 or 1), the model is called a **binary integer linear programming model (BILP)**. If some of the variables are required to be either integer or binary whereas others have no such restriction, the model is called a **mixed integer linear programming model (MILP)**. In this section we present several such models including a personnel scheduling (AILP), a project selection model (BILP), a supply chain model (MILP), and an advertising model (AILP) on the accompanying CD-ROM.

We observed in Chapter 2 that to convert a linear programming model to an integer programming model in an Excel spreadsheet only involves a mouse click in the Add Constraint dialogue box of Solver. We also stated, however, that when integer variables are present, the solution time can increase dramatically and no sensitivity output is generated. Thus, rounding a linear programming solution is sometimes a preferred option.

Using Binary Variables

Appropriate use of binary variables can aid the modeler in expressing comparative relationships. To illustrate, suppose Y_1, Y_2, and Y_3 are binary variables representing whether each of three plants should be built ($Y_i = 1$) or not built ($Y_i = 0$). The following relationships can then be expressed by these variables. (You can verify these relationships by substituting all combinations of 0's and 1's into the given constraints.)

- At least two plants must be built. $Y_1 + Y_2 + Y_3 \geq 2$
- If plant 1 is built, Plant 2 must not be built. $Y_1 + Y_2 \leq 1$
- If plant 1 is built, Plant 2 must be built. $Y_1 - Y_2 \leq 0$
- One but not both of Plants 1 and 2 must be built. $Y_1 + Y_2 = 1$
- Both or neither of Plants 1 and 2 must be built. $Y_1 - Y_2 = 0$
- Plant construction cannot exceed $17 million, and the costs to build Plants 1, 2, and 3 are $5 million, $8 million, and $10 million, respectively. $5Y_1 + 8Y_2 + 10Y_3 \leq 17$

Binary variables can also be used to indicate restrictions in certain conditional situations. For example, suppose X_1 denotes the amount of a product that will be produced at Plant 1. (Note that $X_1 \geq 0$.) If Plant 1 is built, there is no other restriction on the value of X_1, but if it is not built, X_1 must be 0. This relation can be expressed by:

$$X_1 \leq MY_1$$

In this expression, M denotes an extremely large number that does not restrict the value of X_1 if $Y_1 = 1$. For example we might use 10^{20} (or $1E + 20$) for M. If Plant 1 is not built ($Y_1 = 0$), the constraint becomes $X_1 \leq 0$; however, since $X_1 \geq 0$, this implies $X_1 = 0$; that is, no product will be produced at Plant 1. If Plant 1 is built ($Y_1 = 1$), then $X_1 \leq M$, which, because of the extremely large value assigned to M, effectively does restrict the value of X_1.

Now suppose that we are considering building a new plant in Chicago to produce two products, bicycles and tricycles. Suppose each bicycle requires 3 pounds of steel and each tricycle 4 pounds of steel. If the plant is built, it should have 2000 pounds of steel available per week. Thus, there will be at most 2000 pounds of steel if the plant is built but 0 pounds of steel available if it is not built. Define:

X_1 = the number of bicycles produced each week at the Chicago plant
X_2 = the number of tricycles produced each week at the Chicago plant

Now let Y_1 represent whether or not the Chicago plant is built. This situation can then be modeled as: $3X_1 + 4X_2 \leq 2000Y_1$ or, $3X_1 + 4X_2 - 2000Y_1 \leq 0$. We see that if the plant is built ($Y_1 = 1$), then the constraint is $3X_1 + 4X_2 \leq 2000$. If it is not built ($Y_1 = 0$), the constraint reduces to $3X_1 + 4X_2 \leq 0$ (which will hold only if both X_1 and X_2 are 0). That is, if the plant is not built, there is no production.

These are just some of the ideas that are modeled in the examples in this section.

3.5.1 PERSONNEL SCHEDULING MODELS

One problem that requires an integer solution is the assignment of personnel or machines to meet some minimum coverage requirements. Typically, these models have constraints that link the resources available during one period with those available for subsequent periods. The situation faced by the City of Sunset Beach is an example of one such problem.

SUNSET BEACH LIFEGUARD ASSIGNMENTS

Concepts: Integer Variables
Linking Constraints
Hidden Cells

Sunset.xls

In the summer, the City of Sunset Beach staffs lifeguard stations seven days a week. Regulations require that city employees (including lifeguards) work five days a week and be given two consecutive days off. For most city employees, these days are Saturday and Sunday, but for lifeguards, these are the two busiest days of the week.

Insurance requirements mandate that Sunset Beach provide at least one lifeguard per 8000 average daily attendance on any given day. Table 3.9 gives the average daily attendance figures and the minimum number of lifeguards required during the summer months, at Sunset Beach.

Given the current budget situation, Sunset Beach would like to determine a schedule that will employ as few lifeguards as possible.

TABLE 3.9   Average Daily Attendance and Lifeguard Requirements

Day	Average Attendance	Lifeguards Required
Sunday	58.000	8
Monday	42,000	6
Tuesday	35,000	5
Wednesday	25,000	4
Thursday	44,000	6
Friday	51,000	7
Saturday	68,000	9

SOLUTION

Sunset Beach's problem is to:

- Schedule lifeguards over five consecutive days
- Minimize the total number of lifeguards required
- Meet the minimum daily lifeguard requirements

DECISION VARIABLES

Sunset Beach must decide how many lifeguards to schedule beginning Sunday and working for five consecutive days, the number to schedule beginning Monday and working for five consecutive days, and so on:

$$X_1 = \text{number of lifeguards scheduled to begin on Sunday}$$
$$X_2 = \text{number of lifeguards scheduled to begin on Monday}$$
$$X_3 = \text{number of lifeguards scheduled to begin on Tuesday}$$
$$X_4 = \text{number of lifeguards scheduled to begin on Wednesday}$$
$$X_5 = \text{number of lifeguards scheduled to begin on Thursday}$$
$$X_6 = \text{number of lifeguards scheduled to begin on Friday}$$
$$X_7 = \text{number of lifeguards scheduled to begin on Saturday}$$

OBJECTIVE FUNCTION

The goal is to minimize the total number of lifeguards scheduled:

$$\text{MIN } X_1 + X_2 + X_3 + X_4 + X_5 + X_6 + X_7$$

CONSTRAINTS

For each day, at least the minimum required number of lifeguards must be on duty. Those on duty on Sunday begin their shift either on Sunday, Wednesday, Thursday, Friday, or Saturday; those on duty on Monday begin their shift either on Monday, Thursday, Friday, Saturday, or Sunday; and so on. Thus,

$$(\text{The number of lifeguards on duty Sunday}) \geq 8$$

or

$$X_1 \qquad + X_4 + X_5 + X_6 + X_7 \geq 8$$

For Monday the constraint would be:

$$X_1 + X_2 \qquad + X_5 + X_6 + X_7 \geq 6$$

THE MATHEMATICAL MODEL

The constraints for the other days are similarly derived, yielding the following model:

$$
\begin{array}{llllllllll}
\text{MIN} & X_1 & + X_2 & + X_3 & + X_4 & + X_5 & + X_6 & + X_7 \\
\text{ST} \\
& X_1 & & & + X_4 & + X_5 & + X_6 & + X_7 & \geq 8 & \text{(Sunday)} \\
& X_1 & + X_2 & & & + X_5 & + X_6 & + X_7 & \geq 6 & \text{(Monday)} \\
& X_1 & + X_2 & + X_3 & & & + X_6 & + X_7 & \geq 5 & \text{(Tuesday)} \\
& X_1 & + X_2 & + X_3 & + X_4 & & & + X_7 & \geq 4 & \text{(Wednesday)} \\
& X_1 & + X_2 & + X_3 & + X_4 & + X_5 & & & \geq 6 & \text{(Thursday)} \\
& & X_2 & + X_3 & + X_4 & + X_5 & + X_6 & & \geq 7 & \text{(Friday)} \\
& & & X_3 & + X_4 & + X_5 & + X_6 & + X_7 & \geq 9 & \text{(Saturday)}
\end{array}
$$

$$\text{All variables} \geq 0 \text{ AND Integer}$$

EXCEL INPUT/OUTPUT AND ANALYSIS

Figure 3.11 shows a spreadsheet for this model. The formula in cell B5 (=ROUNDUP(B4/8000,0) gives the number of required lifeguards on Sunday by dividing the projected attendance (B4) by the 8000 lifeguard to attendance ratio and rounding this number up. The 0 means include 0 decimal places. This formula is dragged to cells C5:H5 to obtain the daily requirements.

Sunset.xls

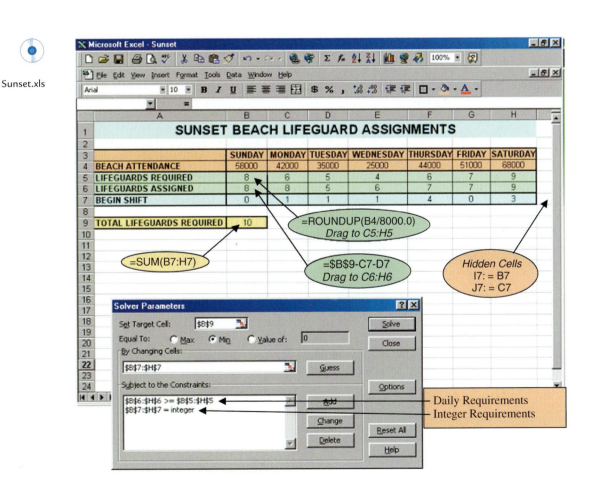

FIGURE 3.11   Optimal Spreadsheet for Sunset Beach Lifeguard Assignments

The formula in cell B6 (=$B$9-C7-D7) states that the number of lifeguards on duty on Sunday includes all lifeguards ($B$9) except those who begin their shift on Monday (C7) or Tuesday (D7). Those who begin their shift on Monday or Tuesday will finish their shifts on Friday and Saturday, respectively. So that we can drag this formula across to cells C6:H6, formulas have been assigned to (hidden) cells I7 and J7; they also give the number of lifeguards who begin their shift on Sunday and Monday.

We see that the city can get by with a total of 10 lifeguards, 1 of whom starts his shift on Monday, 1 on Tuesday, 1 on Wednesday, 4 on Thursday, and 3 on Saturday.[4] The minimum requirement for lifeguards is met on each day, with Monday and Wednesday having two extra lifeguards and Thursday one extra lifeguard assigned.

3.5.2 PROJECT SELECTION MODELS

Project selection models involve a set of "go/no-go" decisions, represented by binary decision variables, for various projects under consideration. Such models typically involve budget, space, or other restrictions, as well as a set of priorities among certain projects. For example, one might specify that project 1 may be done (or will be done) only if project 2 is done, or only if project 3 is not done, or that at least two of projects 1, 2, 3, 4, and 5 be accomplished. The situation faced by the Salem City Council is a simplified version of one such model.

SALEM CITY COUNCIL

Concepts: Binary Decision Variables
                Priority Relationships

Salem.xls

At its final meeting of the fiscal year, the Salem City Council will be making plans to allocate funds remaining in this year's budget. Nine projects have been under consideration throughout the entire year.

To gauge community support for the various projects, questionnaires were randomly mailed to voters throughout the city asking them to rank the projects (9 = highest priority, 1 = lowest priority). The council tallied the scores from the 500 usable responses it received. Although the council has repeatedly maintained that it will not be bound by the results of the questionnaire, it plans to use this information while taking into account other concerns when making the budget allocations.

The estimated cost of each project, the estimated number of permanent new jobs each would create, and the questionnaire point tallies are summarized in Table 3.10.

The council's goal is to maximize the total perceived voter support (as evidenced through the questionnaires), given other constraints and concerns of the council, including the following:

- $900,000 remains in the budget.
- The council wants to create at least 10 new jobs.
- Although crime deterrence is a high priority with the public, the council feels that it must also be fair to other sectors of public service (fire and education). Accordingly, it wishes to fund at most three of the police-related projects.
- The council would like to increase the number of city emergency vehicles but feels that, in the face of other pressing issues, only one of the two emergency vehicle projects should be funded at this time. Thus, *either* the two police cars *or* the fire truck should be purchased.

---

[4] It turns out that there are several optimal solutions to this model, each of which requires a total of 10 lifeguards.

- The council believes that if it decides to restore funds cut from the sports programs at the schools, it should also restore funds cut from their music programs, and vice versa.
- By union contract, any additional school funding must go toward restoring previous cuts before any new school projects are undertaken. Consequently, both sports funds and music funds must be restored before new computer equipment can be purchased. Restoring sports and music funds, however, does not imply that new computers *will* be purchased, only that they *can* be.

TABLE 3.10   Project Costs, New Jobs, and Point Tallies

	Project	Cost ($1000)	New Jobs	Points
X_1	Hire seven new police officers	$400	7	4176
X_2	Modernize police headquarters	$350	0	1774
X_3	Buy two new police cars	$ 50	1	2513
X_4	Give bonuses to foot patrol officers	$100	0	1928
X_5	Buy new fire truck/support equipment	$500	2	3607
X_6	Hire assistant fire chief	$ 90	1	962
X_7	Restore cuts to sports programs	$220	8	2829
X_8	Restore cuts to school music	$150	3	1708
X_9	Buy new computers for high school	$140	2	3003

SOLUTION

The Salem City Council must choose which projects to fund. Its objective is to determine, within the constraints and concerns listed earlier, the set of projects that maximizes public support for its decisions as evidenced through the returned questionnaires.

DECISION VARIABLES

The variables, $X_1, X_2, \ldots, X_9$, are binary decision variables: $X_j = 1$ if project j is funded, and $X_j = 0$ if project j is not funded.

OBJECTIVE FUNCTION

The council's objective is to maximize the overall point score of the funded projects:

$$\text{MAXIMIZE} \quad 4176X_1 + 1774X_2 + 2513X_3 + 1928X_4 + 3607X_5 + 962X_6 + 2829X_7 + 1708X_8 + 3003X_9$$

CONSTRAINTS

Budget Constraint   The maximum amount of funds to be allocated cannot exceed $900,000. Using coefficients to represent the number of thousands of dollars, this constraint can be written as:

$$400X_1 + 350X_2 + 50X_3 + 100X_4 + 500X_5 + 90X_6 + 220X_7 + 150X_8 + 140X_9 \leq 900$$

Job Creation Constraint   The number of new jobs created must be at least 10:

$$7X_1 + X_3 + 2X_5 + X_6 + 8X_7 + 3X_8 + 2X_9 \geq 10$$

Maximum of Three Out of Four Police Projects Constraint   The number of police-related activities to be funded is at most 3:

$$X_1 + X_2 + X_3 + X_4 \leq 3$$

Mutually Exclusive Projects Constraint (Two Police Cars or a Fire Truck)   Either the two police cars should be purchased or the fire truck should be purchased. This is equivalent to saying that the number of police car purchase projects plus the number of fire truck purchase projects to be funded is exactly 1:

$$X_3 + X_5 = 1$$

Corequisite Projects Constraint—Sports Funding/Music Funding   If sports funds are restored music funds will be restored, and if sports funds are not restored music funds will not be restored. This constraint implies that the number of restored music fund projects funded must equal the number of sports fund projects funded; that is $X_7 = X_8$, or:

$$X_7 - X_8 = 0$$

Prerequisite Projects Constraint—Equipment vs. Sports and Music Funding   Sports funding and music funding must be restored before new computer equipment can be purchased. This relationship can be expressed as two prerequisite constraints: the number of sports projects funded must be at least as great as the number of computer equipment projects funded ($X_7 \geq X_9$) AND the number of music projects funded must be at least as great as the number of computer equipment projects funded ($X_8 \geq X_9$), or:

$$X_7 - X_9 \geq 0$$
$$X_8 - X_9 \geq 0$$

Note that, taken together, these constraints mean that if $X_9 = 1$, then both X_7 and X_8 must be 1, but if either or both X_7 and $X_8 = 1$, X_9 is not required to be 1.

MATHEMATICAL MODEL FOR THE SALEM CITY COUNCIL

The complete model for the Salem City Council, which includes the objective function, the functional and conditional constraints, and the binary restrictions, can now be stated as follows:

MAXIMIZE

$4176X_1 + 1774X_2 + 2513X_3 + 1928X_4 + 3607X_5 + 962X_6 + 2829X_7 + 1708X_8 + 3003X_9$
ST

$400X_1 +$	$350X_2 +$	$50X_3 +$	$100X_4 +$	$500X_5 +$	$90X_6 +$	$220X_7 +$	$150X_8 +$	$140X_9$	$\leq$	900
$7X_1 +$		$X_3 +$		$2X_5 +$	$X_6 +$	$8X_7 +$	$3X_8 +$	$2X_9$	$\geq$	10
$X_1 +$	$X_2 +$	$X_3 +$	X_4						$\leq$	3
		$X_3 +$		X_5					$=$	1
						$X_7 -$	X_8		$=$	0
						$X_7 -$		X_9	$\geq$	0
							$X_8 -$	X_9	$\geq$	0

All X's = 0 or 1

Excel Input/Output and Analysis

Figure 3.12 shows an optimal spreadsheet for the decisions faced by the Salem City Council. The binary decision variables are in cells B4:B12, and we present the formulas for the left side of the constraints shown in cells B17:B23.

Salem.xls

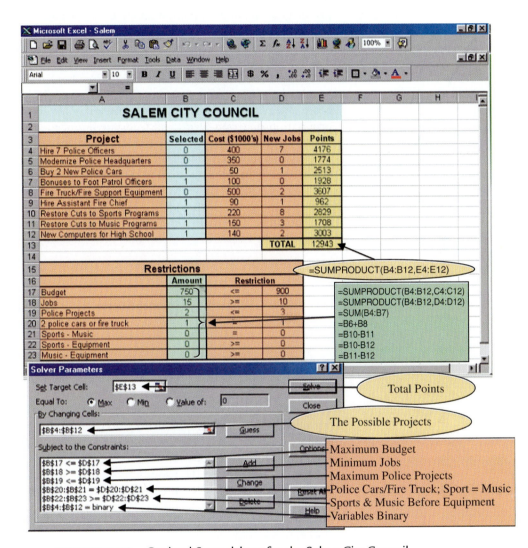

FIGURE 3.12 Optimal Spreadsheet for the Salem City Council

Much to the council's surprise, the optimal solution does not fund the two items the people most wanted—hiring seven new police officers and purchasing a new fire truck and fire support equipment! Upon further observation, the council noted that these items were also the most costly, but they were still amazed that neither would be funded given the extremely high public support for them. The solution also does not recommend funding renovations to police headquarters; instead it recommends funding all six other projects. If this recommendation is followed, the council will create five more jobs than its goal of 10 and will have a budget surplus of $1,500,000 that it can apply to next year's projects or return to the people as a tax rebate (a very popular political idea!)

3.5.3 SUPPLY CHAIN MANAGEMENT MODELS

One of the most significant managerial developments in recent years has been the emergence of supply chain management models that integrate the process of manufacturing goods and getting them to the consumer. A typical supply chain can be thought of as a decision support system that treats the acquisition of materials to produce products as well as the manufacturing, storing, and shipping of finished products as an integrated system of events rather than as stand-alone separate components of the process.

Numerous management science models discussed in this text, including manufacturing models, network models, scheduling models, forecasting models, inventory models, and queuing models, are now embraced under the ever growing set of supply chain management techniques. The overall objective of these models has been, and continues to be, to minimize total system costs while maintaining appropriate production levels and transporting needed quantities to the right locations in a timely and efficient manner. While just a few short years ago, employing efficient supply chain models gave many firms an edge in the market, today their use has nearly become essential to even compete in the marketplace.

One link in the supply chain can involve determining which plants should be made operational, which should produce specified items, and what shipping pattern should be used to distribute the finished products to retailers. Such is the situation faced by Globe Electronics, Inc.

GLOBE ELECTRONICS, INC.

Concepts: Supply Chain Management
Mixed Integer Modeling of Fixed Charges
Rounding Noninteger Solutions

Globe.xls
Globe Plant Analysis.xls

Globe Electronics, Inc. manufactures two styles of remote control cable boxes (the G50 and the H90) that various cable companies supply to their customers when cable service is established. Different companies require different models. During the late 1980s and early 1990s, due to an explosion in the demand for cable services, Globe expanded rapidly to four production facilities located in Philadelphia (the original plant), St. Louis, New Orleans, and Denver. The manufactured items are shipped from the plants to regional distribution centers located in Cincinnati, Kansas City, and San Francisco; from these locations they are distributed nationwide.

Because of a decrease in demand for cable services and technological changes in the cable industry, demand for Globe's products is currently far less than the total of the capacities at its four plants. As a result, management is contemplating closing one or more of its facilities.

Each plant has a fixed operating cost, and, because of the unique conditions at each facility, the production costs, production time per unit, and total monthly production time available vary from plant to plant, as summarized in Table 3.11.

The cable boxes are sold nationwide at the same prices: $22 for the G50, and $28 for the H90.

Current monthly demand projections at each distribution center for both products are given in Table 3.12.

To remain viable in each market, Globe must meet at least 70% of the demand for each product at each distribution center. The transportation costs between each plant and each distribution center, which are the same for either product, are shown in Table 3.13.

Globe management wants to develop an optimal distribution policy utilizing all four of its operational plants. It also wants to determine whether closing any of the production facilities will result in higher company profits.

TABLE 3.11   Production Costs, Times, Availability

Plant	Fixed Cost/ Month ($1000)	Production Cost Per Unit		Production Time (Hr./Unit)		Available Hours per Month
		G50	H90	G50	H90	
Philadelphia	40	10	14	.06	.06	640
St. Louis	35	12	12	.07	.08	960
New Orleans	20	8	10	.09	.07	480
Denver	30	13	15	.05	.09	640

TABLE 3.12   Monthly Demand Projections

	Demand		
	Cincinnati	Kansas City	San Francisco
G50	2000	3000	5000
H90	5000	6000	7000

TABLE 3.13   Transportation Costs per 100 Units

	To		
	Cincinnati	Kansas City	San Francisco
From			
Philadelphia	$200	$300	$500
St. Louis	$100	$100	$400
New Orleans	$200	$200	$300
Denver	$300	$100	$100

SOLUTION

The situation facing Globe Electronics is the portion of the supply chain that involves the manufacture and delivery of finished products to various distribution centers. Prior to this, Globe would be involved with ordering raw materials and scheduling personnel in the production process. Subsequent links would involve the storage process at the distribution centers and the sale and dissemination of the completed goods to retail establishments. Specifically for this portion of the model, Globe is seeking to:

- Determine the number of G50 and H90 cable boxes to be produced at each plant
- Determine a shipping pattern from the plants to the distribution centers
- Maximize net total monthly profit
- Not exceed the production capacities at any plant
- Ensure that each distribution center receives between 70% and 100% of its monthly demand projections

The model Globe uses to solve for the optimal solution with all four plants operating is developed in the following section.

DECISION VARIABLES

Management must decide the total number of G50 and H90 cable boxes to produce monthly at each plant, the total number to be shipped to each distribution center, and the shipping pattern of product from the plants to the distribution centers. The entries in the following two matrices designate the decision variables for this model.

Shipment of G50 Cable Boxes:

	Cincinnati	Kansas City	San Francisco	Total Produced
Philadelphia	G_{11}	G_{12}	G_{13}	G_P
St. Louis	G_{21}	G_{22}	G_{23}	G_{SL}
New Orleans	G_{31}	G_{32}	G_{33}	G_{NO}
Denver	G_{41}	G_{42}	G_{43}	G_D
Total Received	G_C	G_{KC}	G_{SF}	G

Shipment of H90 Cable Boxes:

	Cincinnati	Kansas City	San Francisco	Total Produced
Philadelphia	H_{11}	H_{12}	H_{13}	H_P
St. Louis	H_{21}	H_{22}	H_{23}	H_{SL}
New Orleans	H_{31}	H_{32}	H_{33}	H_{NO}
Denver	H_{41}	H_{42}	H_{43}	H_D
Total Received	H_C	H_{KC}	H_{SF}	H

OBJECTIVE FUNCTION

The *gross profit* (exclusive of fixed plant costs) is given by \$22 (Total G50's Produced) + \$28 (Total H90's Produced) − (Total Production Cost) − (Total Transportation Costs). Thus, the objective function is:

$$\text{MAX } 22G + 28H - 10G_P - 12G_{SL} - 8G_{NO} - 13G_D - 14H_P - 12H_{SL} -$$
$$10H_{NO} - 15H_D - 2G_{11} - 3G_{12} - 5G_{13} - 1G_{21} - 1G_{22} - 4G_{23} - 2G_{31} -$$
$$2G_{32} - 3G_{33} - 3G_{41} - 1G_{42} - 1G_{43} - 2H_{11} - 3H_{12} - 5H_{13} - 1H_{21} -$$
$$1H_{22} - 4H_{23} - 2H_{31} - 2H_{32} - 3H_{33} - 3H_{41} - 1H_{42} - 1H_{43}$$

From this quantity we would subtract the total monthly fixed costs for the four plants of \$125,000.

CONSTRAINTS

This model contains summation constraints for the total amounts of G50 and H90 cable boxes produced at each plant and the total number shipped to each distribution center, production time limits at the plants, and shipping limits to the distribution plants.

1. *Summation Constraints for Total Production*

	Total G50's Produced	**Total H90's Produced**
Philadelphia:	$G_{11} + G_{12} + G_{13} = G_P$	$H_{11} + H_{12} + H_{13} = H_P$
St. Louis:	$G_{21} + G_{22} + G_{23} = G_{SL}$	$H_{21} + H_{22} + H_{23} = H_{SL}$
New Orleans:	$G_{31} + G_{32} + G_{33} = G_{NO}$	$H_{31} + H_{32} + H_{33} = H_{NO}$
Denver:	$G_{41} + G_{42} + G_{43} = G_D$	$H_{41} + H_{42} + H_{43} = H_D$
TOTAL:	$G_P + G_{SL} + G_{NO} + G_D = G$	$H_P + H_{SL} + H_{NO} + H_D = H$

2. *Summation Constraints for Total Shipments*

	Total G50's Shipped	**Total H90's Shipped**
Cincinnati:	$G_{11} + G_{21} + G_{31} + G_{41} = G_C$	$H_{11} + H_{21} + H_{31} + H_{41} = H_C$
Kansas City:	$G_{12} + G_{22} + G_{32} + G_{42} = G_{KC}$	$H_{12} + H_{22} + H_{32} + H_{42} = H_{KC}$
San Francisco:	$G_{13} + G_{23} + G_{33} + G_{43} = G_{SF}$	$H_{13} + H_{23} + H_{33} + H_{43} = H_{SF}$

3. *Production Time Limits at Each Plant*

Philadelphia:	$.06G_P + .06H_P \leq 640$
St. Louis:	$.07G_{SL} + .08H_{SL} \leq 960$
New Orleans:	$.09G_{NO} + .07H_{NO} \leq 480$
Denver:	$.05G_D + .09H_D \leq 640$

4. *Minimum Amount Shipped to Each Distribution Center $\geq 70\%$ (Total Demand);*
Maximum Amount Shipped to Each Distribution Center $\leq$ (Total Demand)

	Minimum Shipment	**Maximum Shipment**
Cincinnati:	$G_C \geq 1400$	$G_C \leq 2000$
	$H_C \geq 3500$	$H_C \leq 5000$
Kansas City:	$G_{KC} \geq 2100$	$G_{KC} \leq 3000$
	$H_{KC} \geq 4200$	$H_{KC} \leq 6000$
San Francisco:	$G_{SF} \geq 3500$	$G_{SF} \leq 5000$
	$H_{SF} \geq 4900$	$H_{SF} \leq 7000$

5. *Nonnegativity*

$$\text{All G's and H's} \geq 0$$

Theoretically, we should also require that the variables be integers, but we will ignore this restriction and round if necessary. This will substantially reduce the solution time. The rounding could result in a slightly less than optimal result, or it might slightly violate one of the constraints. But in the context of this problem, such minor violations would probably be acceptable.

EXCEL INPUT/OUTPUT AND ANALYSIS

Figure 3.13 shows a spreadsheet and the resulting solution for this model. In this figure cells F5:F9 and F14:F18 contain the row sums giving the total G50 and H90 production at the plants. Cells C9:E9 and C18:E18 contain the column sums giving the total shipments to the distribution centers. Hidden cells C29:E29 and C30:E30 contain formulas giving 70% of the G50 and H90 demand at the distribution centers respectively. The objective function formula in cell K19 is the total revenue of G50's + the total revenue of H90's less the total production costs of G50's, the total production costs of H90's, the total shipping costs of G50's, the total shipping costs of H90's, and the fixed costs of operating each plant.

Globe.xls

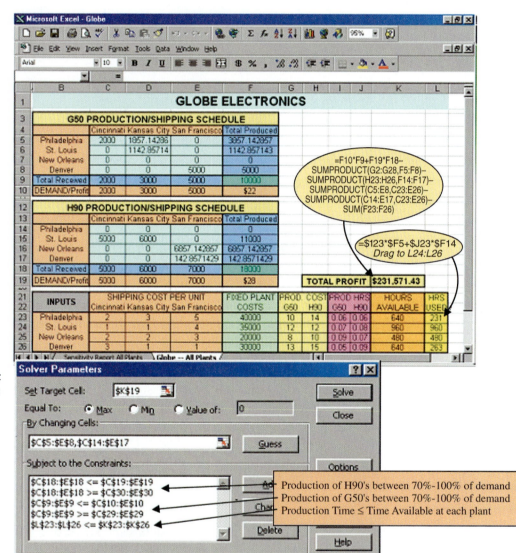

FIGURE 3.13
Optimal Spreadsheet for Globe Electronics with All Plants Operational

When the model is solved, we see that the optimal solution contains noninteger values in cells D5, D6, E16, and E17. But if these values are simply rounded down, the result is a feasible solution with a net monthly profit reduced to $231,550. Because this is so close to the optimal value for the linear programming model of $231,571.43 shown in cell K19, while it may not be the exact optimal integer solution, it is at least very close to it!

The preceding solution assumes that all plants are operational. However, because of the large fixed cost component at each plant, this may not be the best overall solution. As part of the supply chain model, Globe should consider which plants it wishes to keep operational.

Using Binary Variables to Model Fixed Charge Components

Whether or not each plant remains operational can be expressed by using the following binary variables.

$$Y_P = \text{number of operational Philadelphia plants}$$
$$Y_{SL} = \text{number of operational St. Louis plants}$$
$$Y_{NO} = \text{number of operational New Orleans plants}$$
$$Y_D = \text{number of operational Denver plants}$$

The fixed operating costs can be accounted for in the objective function by subtracting from the previous objective function the expression: $40,000Y_P + 35,000Y_{SL} + 20,000Y_{NO} + 30,000Y_D$.

The production constraints are modified as follows:

$$.06G_P + .06H_P \leq 640Y_P$$
$$.07G_{SL} + .08H_{SL} \leq 960Y_{SL}$$
$$.09G_{NO} + .07H_{NO} \leq 480Y_{NO}$$
$$.05G_D + .09H_D \leq 640Y_D$$

Thus if, for instance, the Philadelphia plant is closed ($Y_P = 0$), the first constraint will force total production at the Philadelphia plant to be 0. This in turn implies that all shipments from the Philadelphia plant would also be 0.

The revised spreadsheet model is shown in Figure 3.14. Note that the binary decision variables are in cells A5:A8. These values are copied to cells A14:A17 and to cells A23:A26. Hidden cell N23 contains the formula K23*A5, which is dragged to N24:N26. These cells give the actual production hour availability depending on whether or not the corresponding plant is operational. This allows for easy modification of the last entry in the Solver dialogue box.

Although we require binary variables, we will not require that the shipping variables be integers. If you try it, you will see that this would increase the solution time from a couple of seconds to many minutes, if not hours!

From Figure 3.17 we see that this supply chain model is optimized by closing the Philadelphia plant, running the other three plants at capacity, and scheduling monthly production according to quantities (rounded down) shown in the spreadsheet.[5] The rounded down solution gives a net monthly profit of $266,083 (again very close to the linear programming value of $266,114.91). This is $266,083 − $231,550 = $34,533 per month greater than the optimal monthly profit with all four plants operational, resulting in an annual increase in profit of 12($34,533) = $414,396!

A MANAGEMENT REPORT

The results from this supply chain model and the one used to solve the problem with no plant closures can form the basis for a management report. One item of interest to management may be a breakdown of the distribution of costs and production time under each plan so that Globe can determine where the major costs lie. In addition, management may wish to explore further options. These issues are addressed in the memorandum to Globe Electronics on the following page.

OTHER INTEGER MODELS

Numerous other situations lend themselves to integer programming formulations. One such application, dealing with the selection of advertising media, is discussed in Appendix 3.4 in the Appendix folder on the accompanying CD-ROM. Since several formulation and spreadsheet concepts are illustrated by this example, the reader is encouraged to read and study this model.

---

[5] Note that the entry in cell C5 is 9.6E-09 = .0000000096. This is roundoff error; it should be 0.

Globe Plant Analysis.xls

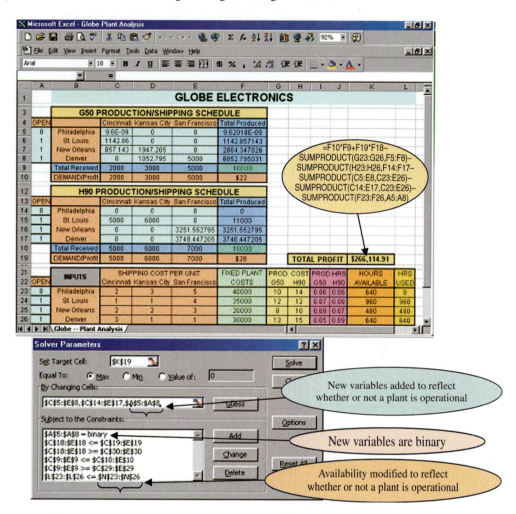

FIGURE 3.14 Optimal Spreadsheet for Globe Electronics Allowing for Closure of Plants

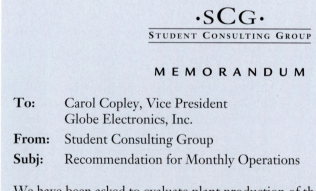

·SCG·
STUDENT CONSULTING GROUP

MEMORANDUM

To: Carol Copley, Vice President
Globe Electronics, Inc.

From: Student Consulting Group

Subj: Recommendation for Monthly Operations

We have been asked to evaluate plant production of the G50 and H90 cable boxes manufactured at the Philadelphia, St. Louis, New Orleans, and Denver plants. Recent product demand projections for the coming year from the Cincinnati, Kansas City, and San Francisco distribution centers have dropped to such a point that a substantial amount of unused production time is available at the plants. Given the large fixed plant operating costs, we have been asked to evaluate the feasibility and the potential cost savings of closing one or more of the plants.

In our analysis we assumed that the demand forecast for the upcoming year, as shown in Table I, is an accurate reflection of future sales.

TABLE I Monthly Demand Forecasts for the Next Fiscal Year

	Cincinnati	Kansas City	San Francisco
G50	2000	3000	5000
H90	5000	6000	7000

Based on production time data and the information in Table I, we developed profit maximization models for your situation. These models assume a $22 and $28 selling price for G50 and H90 models, respectively, and take into account the following:

1. The fixed operating cost at each plant
2. The variable production costs associated with each product at each plant
3. The unit transportation costs of shipping cable boxes from the plants to the distribution centers
4. Production not exceeding demand

Management's imposed condition that at least 70% of the demand for each product be supplied to each distribution center did not turn out to be a limiting factor in the analysis.

OPTIMAL PRODUCTION SCHEDULES

Given the current situation at the four plants in operation, Table II gives a production schedule that should maximize Globe's total net monthly profit.

TABLE II Production/Transportation Schedule: All Plants Operational

Plant	Product	Amount	Cincinnati	Kansas City	San Francisco
Philadelphia	G50	3857	2000	1857	
	H90	0			
St. Louis	G50	1143		1143	
	H90	11000	5000	6000	
New Orleans	G50	0			
	H90	6857			6857
Denver	G50	5000			5000
	H90	143			143
Total	G50	10000	2000	3000	5000
	H90	18000	5000	6000	7000

Notice that, although this production plan meets the full demand at the distribution centers, no G50 models are produced in New Orleans, no G90 models are produced in Philadelphia, and only 143 H90 models are produced monthly at the Denver plant. As a result, there is considerable excess capacity at both the Philadelphia and Denver plants.

Under this plan, as shown in Table III, Globe will be utilizing only 1934 production hours, or 71% of available production capacity. Observe from Table IV that the Philadelphia plant will be *un*profitable, while the Denver plant will be only marginally profitable.

TABLE III Distribution of Production Time (Hours) All Plants Operational

Plant	G50	H90	Total	Total Capacity	Excess Capacity
Philadelphia	231	0	231	640	409
St. Louis	80	880	960	960	0
New Orleans	0	480	480	480	0
Denver	250	13	263	640	377
Total	561	1373	1934	2720	786

TABLE IV Distribution of Monthly Revenues and Costs (All Plants Operational)

Plant	Revenue Sales	Production	Costs Trans-portation	Operations	Total Cost	Net Profit
Philadelphia	$ 84,854	$ 38,570	$ 9,571	$ 40,000	$ 88,141	($ 3,287)
St. Louis	$333,146	$145,716	$12,143	$ 35,000	$192.859	$140,287
New Orleans	$191,996	$ 68,570	$20,571	$ 20,000	$109,141	$ 82,855
Denver	$114,004	$ 67,145	$ 5,143	$ 30,000	$102,288	$ 11,716
Total	$724,000	$320,001	$47,428	$125,000	$492,429	$231,571

Plant Closings Tables V, VI, and VII give a production and distribution schedule that would result from closing the Philadelphia plant. We estimate that, by closing the Philadelphia plant, Globe can achieve an approximate 15% increase in profit, from $231,571 to $266,115 per month. This is an annual increase in profit of $414,528.

TABLE V Production/Transportation Schedule (Philadelphia Plant Closed)

Plant	Product	Amount	Cincinnati	Kansas City	San Francisco
St. Louis	G50	1143		1143	
	H90	11000	5000	6000	
New Orleans	G50	2804	2000	804	
	H90	3252			3252
Denver	G50	6053		1053	5000
	H90	3748			3748
Total	G50	10000	2000	3000	5000
	H90	18000	5000	6000	7000

TABLE VI Distribution of Production Time (Hours) (Philadelphia Plant Closed)

Plant	G50	H90	Total	Total Capacity	Excess Capacity
St. Louis	80	880	960	960	0
New Orleans	252	228	480	480	0
Denver	303	337	640	640	0
Total	635	1445	2080	2080	0

TABLE VII Distribution of Monthly Revenues and Costs (Philadelphia Plant Closed)

Plant	Revenue Sales	Production	Costs Trans-portation	Operations	Total Cost	Net Profit
St. Louis	$333,146	$145,716	$12,143	$35,000	$192,859	$140,287
New Orleans	$152,744	$ 54,952	$15,364	$20,000	$ 90,316	$ 62,428
Denver	$238,110	$134,909	$ 9,801	$30,000	$174,710	$ 63,400
Total	$724,000	$335,577	$37,308	$85,000	$457,885	$266,115

Based on this analysis, it would seem prudent to close the Philadelphia plant. The remaining three plants will then be fully utilized, and all projected demand will be met.

Because Globe Electronics has its roots in the Philadelphia area, however, the company may wish to examine additional alternatives. We conducted another analysis to determine the most profitable production schedule while keeping the Philadelphia plant operational.

The best production plan in this case is to close the Denver plant and execute the manufacturing and distribution plan detailed in Table VIII. Net profit under this plan would be $256,667 per month, approximately 4% less than if the Philadelphia plant were closed. Although this amounts to annual profit that is approximately $113,000 less than if the firm closes the Philadelphia plant, it is still approximately an 11% (or about a $300,000) annual increase over the best schedule with all plants operational.

Note that under this plan:

- The Philadelphia plant produces only G50 models.
- The St. Louis plant produces only H90 models.
- The New Orleans plant ships only to San Francisco.

TABLE VIII Production/Transportation Schedule (Denver Plant Closed)

Plant	Product	Amount	Cincinnati	Kansas City	San Francisco
Philadelphia	G50	9333	2000	3000	4333
	H90	0			
St. Louis	G50	0			
	H90	12000	5000	6000	1000
New Orleans	G50	667			667
	H90	6000			6000
Total	G50	10000	2000	3000	5000
	H90	18000	5000	6000	7000

Such a pattern may have additional benefits or detractions of which we are unaware and which were not considered in our analysis. Barring such additional costs or cost savings, Tables IX and X detail the production time and cost distribution for this schedule. Note that this schedule also has the benefit of the availability of some excess capacity (at the Philadelphia plant) to cover any unanticipated surges in demand.

TABLE IX Distribution of Production Time (Hours)
(Denver Plant Closed)

Plant	G50	H90	Total	Total Capacity	Excess Capacity
Philadelphia	560	0	560	640	80
St. Louis	0	960	960	960	0
New Orleans	60	420	480	480	0
Total	620	1380	2000	2080	80

TABLE X Distribution of Monthly Revenues and Costs
(Denver Plant Closed)

Plant	Revenue Sales	Costs Production	Costs Transportation	Costs Operations	Total Cost	Net Profit
Philadelphia	$205,326	$ 93,330	$34,665	$40,000	$167,995	$ 37,331
St. Louis	$336,000	$144,000	$15,000	$35,000	$194,000	$142,000
New Orleans	$182,674	$ 65,336	$20,000	$20,000	$105,336	$ 77,338
Total	$724,000	$302,666	$69,665	$95,000	$467,331	$256,669

SUMMARY AND RECOMMENDATION The results of our analysis are as follows:

Options for Globe Electronics, Inc.

Option	Annual Profit
Close the Philadelphia plant	$3,193,380
Close the Denver plant	$3,080,028
All plants operational	$2,778,852

Although we have detailed the cost and transportation distribution of each plan, management must decide whether extenuating circumstances would make one of the less profitable plans more acceptable. Factors such as the impact on the community of plant closings, the costs (not included in this report) of actually closing a facility, and the benefits of a structured distribution pattern or available excess capacity to meet demand fluctuations should all be considered before a final decision is made.

Should management require further study on any of these points, we would be happy to assist in the analysis.

3.6 Summary

Linear and integer programming models have been applied successfully in a wide variety of business and government applications, some of which are cited in the first section of this chapter. We have given an outline and numerous hints on how to build successful mathematical models and how to convert these models into good, easy to understand spreadsheet models. We have applied these concepts to simplified applications taken from a variety of business and government sectors. In the process, we offered a thorough analysis of output results and illustrated many of the pitfalls and anomalies that can occur in both the modeling and solution phases. These include how to detect and resolve situations involving unboundedness, infeasibility, and multiple optimal solutions; when and how to use summation variables and constraints; and how to use integer and binary variables to appropriately model particular situations. We have also introduced the concepts of data envelopment analysis (on the CD-ROM) and supply chain management, both of which are important topics in today's business climate.

Not all mathematical models can be modeled by a linear objective function and linear constraints. Chapter 13 on the accompanying CD-ROM discusses the topics of goal programming (which can involve repeated solving of linear programs), dynamic programming (which involves making a sequence of interrelated decisions), and the general nonlinear model.

ON THE CD-ROM

● Excel spreadsheets for linear programming models	**Galaxy Expansion.xls**
	Jones Investment.xls
Infeasibility→	**St. Joseph.xls**
Alternate Optimal Solutions→	**St. Joseph (Revised).xls**
Unbounded Solution→	**Euromerica Liquors.xls**
	Euromerica Liquors (Revised).xls
	United Oil.xls
	Powers.xls
	Sir Loin.xls
	Sir Loin Composite.xls
● Excel spreadsheets for integer linear programming models	**Sunset.xls**
	Vertex Software.xls
	Salem.xls
	Globe.xls
	Globe Plant Expansion.xls
● Duality	**Supplement CD2**
● The Simplex Method	**Supplement CD3**
● Algorithms for Solving Integer Models	**Supplement CD4**
● Problem Motivations	**Problem Motivations**
● Additional "Real Life" Applications	**Appendix 3.1**
● A Multiperiod Cash Flow Scheduling Model	**Appendix 3.2**
● Data Envelopment Analysis	**Appendix 3.3**
● An Integer Programming Advertising Model	**Appendix 3.4**
● Problems 41–50	**Additional Problems/Cases**
● Cases 4–6	**Additional Problems/Cases**

Problems

Problems 1–27 can be formulated as linear programming models.

Problems 28–40 can be formulated as integer linear programming models.

1. PRODUCTION SCHEDULING. Coolbike Industries manufactures boys and girls bicycles in both 20-inch and 26-inch models. Each week it must produce at least 200 girl models and 200 boys models. The following table gives the unit profit and the number of minutes required for production and assembly for each model.

Bicycle	Unit Profit	Production Minutes	Assembly Minutes
20-inch girls	$27	12	6
20-inch boys	$32	12	9
26-inch girls	$38	9	12
26-inch boys	$51	9	18

The production and assembly areas run two (eight-hour) shifts per day, five days per week. This week there are 500 tires available for 20-inch models and 800 tires available for 26-inch models. Determine Coolbike's optimal schedule for the week. What profit will it realize for the week?

2. APPLIANCE PRODUCTION. Kemper Manufacturing can produce five major appliances—stoves, washers, electric dryers, gas dryers, and refrigerators. All products go through three processes—molding/pressing, assembly, and packaging. Each week there are 4800 minutes available for molding/pressing, 3000 available for packaging, 1200 for stove assembly, 1200 for refrigerator assembly, and 2400 that can be used for assembling washers and dryers. The following table gives the unit molding/pressing, assembly, and packing times (in minutes) as well as the unit profits.

	Molding/ Pressing	Assembly	Packaging	Unit Profit
Stove	5.5	4.5	4.0	$110
Washer	5.2	4.5	3.0	$ 90
Electric Dryer	5.0	4.0	2.5	$ 75
Gas Dryer	5.1	3.0	2.0	$ 80
Refrigerators	7.5	9.0	4.0	$130

a. What weekly production schedule do you recommend? What is the significance of the fractional values?
b. Suppose the following additional conditions applied:
   • The number of washers should equal the combined number of dryers.
   • The number of electric dryers should not exceed the number of gas dryers by more than 100 per week.

• The number of gas dryers should not exceed the number of electric dryers by more than 100 per week.

Now what weekly production schedule do you recommend?

3. MANUFACTURING. Kelly Industries manufactures two different structural support products used in the construction of large boats and ships. The two products, the Z345 and the W250, are produced from specially treated zinc and iron and are produced in both standard and industrial grades. Kelly nets a profit of $400 on each standard Z345 and $500 on each standard W250. Industrial models net a 40% premium.

Each week, up to 2500 pounds of zinc and 2800 pounds of iron can be treated and made available for production. The following table gives the per unit requirements (in pounds) for each model.

	Z345		W250	
	Standard	Industrial	Standard	Industrial
Zinc	25	46	16	34
Iron	50	30	28	12

Kelly has a contract to supply a combined total of at least 20 standard or industrial Z345 supports to Calton Shipbuilders each week. Company policy mandates that at least 50% of the production must be industrial models and that neither Z345 models nor W250 models can account for more than 75% of weekly production. By adhering to this policy, Kelly feels, it can sell all the product it manufactures.

a. Determine a weekly production plan for Kelly Industries. What interpretation can you give to the fractional values that are part of the optimal production quantities?
b. What proportion of the production are W250 models? What does that tell you about how the profit will be affected if the 75% limit is loosened or eliminated?
c. State whether you should buy *additional* shipments of zinc, should they become available at the following premiums above zinc's normal cost.
   i. 100 pounds for $1500
   ii. 100 pounds for $2600
   iii. 800 pounds for $10,000

4. FINANCIAL INVESTMENT. The Investment Club at Bell Labs has solicited and obtained $50,000 from its members. Collectively, the members have selected the three stocks, two bond funds, and a tax-deferred annuity shown in the following table as possible investments.

Investment	Risk	Projected Annual Return
Stock—EAL	High	15%
Stock—BRU	Moderate	12%
Stock—TAT	Low	9%
Bonds—long term		11%
Bonds—short term		8%
Tax-deferred annuity		6%

The club members have decided on the following strategies for investment:

- All $50,000 is to be invested.
- At least $10,000 is to be invested in the tax-deferred annuity.
- At least 25% of the funds invested in stocks are to be in the low-risk stock (TAT).
- At least as much is to be invested in bonds as stocks.
- No more than $12,500 of the total investment is to be placed in investments with projected annual returns of less than 10%.

a. Formulate and solve a linear program that will maximize the total projected annual return subject to the conditions set forth by the Investment Club members.

b. What is the projected rate of return of this portfolio? What rate of return should investors expect on any additional funds received, given the restrictions of the club? Explain why this rate would hold for all additional investment dollars.

c. For which investment possibilities are the estimates for the projected annual return most sensitive in determining the optimal solution?

d. Give an interpretation of the shadow prices for the right-hand side of each constraint.

5. PRODUCTION. Minnesota Fabrics produces three sizes of comforters (full, queen, and king size) that it markets to major retail establishments throughout the country. Due to contracts with these establishments, Minnesota Fabrics must produce at least 120 of each size comforter daily. It pays $0.50 per pound for stuffing and $0.20 per square foot for quilted fabric used in the production of the comforters. It can obtain up to 2700 pounds of stuffing and 48,000 square feet of quilted fabric from its suppliers.

Labor is considered a fixed cost for Minnesota Fabrics. It has enough labor to provide 50 hours of cutting time and 200 hours of sewing time daily. The following table gives the unit material and labor required as well as the selling price to the retail stores for each size comforter.

	Stuffing (pounds)	Quilted Fabric (sq. ft.)	Cutting Time (minutes)	Sewing Time (minutes)	Selling Price
Full	3	55	3	5	$19
Queen	4	75	5	6	$26
King	6	95	6	8	$32

a. Determine the daily production schedule that maximizes total daily gross profit (= selling price − material costs.). How much of the available daily material and labor resources would be used by this production schedule?

b. What is the lowest *selling price* for queen size comforters that Minnesota Fabrics could charge while maintaining the optimal production schedule recommended in part a?

c. Suppose Minnesota Fabrics could obtain additional stuffing *or* quilted fabric from supplementary suppliers. What is the most it should be willing to pay for:
    i. An extra pound of stuffing? Within what limits is this valid?
    ii. An extra square foot of quilted fabric? Within what limits is this valid?
    iii. An extra *minute* of cutting time? Within what limits is this valid?
    iv. An extra minute of sewing time? Within what limits is this valid?

d. Suppose the requirement to produce at least 120 king size comforters were relaxed. How would this affect the optimal daily profit?

6. HIGH PROTEIN/LOW CARBOHYDRATE DIET. One of the current diets that seems to produce substantial weight loss in some persons is the high protein/low carbohydrate diet advocated by such authors as Atkins in his book, *Diet Revolution*, and Eades and Eades in their book, *Protein Power*. Although many nutritionists are concerned about the side effects of these diets, others feel the potential risks are outweighed (no pun intended) by the weight loss.

The following table gives the grams of fat, carbohydrates, and protein as well as the calorie count in four potential foods: steak (8 oz. portion), cheese (1 oz.), apples (1 medium), and whole milk (8 oz.). Jim Blount, a 45-year-old male, has done the calculations suggested in these books and has determined that he should have a calorie intake of between 1800 and 2000 calories and protein intake of at least 100 grams, but he should not consume more than 45 grams of carbohydrates daily. For breakfast Jim had two eggs and three strips of bacon, one piece of buttered high protein toast, and water. This breakfast contained 390 calories, 15 grams of carbohydrates, 20 grams of protein, and 29 grams of fat. Although these diets do not limit fat intake, Jim wishes to minimize his total fat consumed by constructing a diet for lunch and dinner consisting of only the four foods listed in the table. What do you recommend?

	Calories	Fat (grams)	Protein (grams)	Carbohydrates (grams)
Steak (8 oz.)	692	51	57	0
Cheese (1 oz.)	110	9	6	1
Apple	81	1	1	22
Milk	150	8	8	12

7. COMPUTER PRODUCTION. MVC Enterprises can manufacture four different computer models; the Student, Plus, Net, and Pro models. The following gives the configurations of each model:

	Student	Plus	Net	Pro
Processor	Celeron	Pentium	Celeron	Pentium
Hard Drive	20 gb	20 gb	20 gb	30 gb
Floppy Drives	1	1	2	1
Zip Drive	YES	YES	NO	YES
Audio/Video	CD R/W	DVD	DVD + CD R/W	DVD + CD R/W
Monitor	15″	15″	17″	17″
Case	Tower	Mini-Tower	Mini-Tower	Tower
Production Time (hrs.)	.4	.5	.6	.8
Unit Profit	$70	$80	$130	$150

- MVC must satisfy a contract that produces a minimum of 100 Net models per week.
- MVC employs 25 workers, each of whom averages 30 production hours each per week.
- The following resources are available weekly:

Processors	*Hard Drives*	*Other Drives*
Celeron—700	20 gb—800	Floppy—1600
Pentium—550	30 gb—950	Zip—1000

Audiovisual	*Monitors*	*Cases*
CD R/W—1600	15″—850	Mini-Tower—1250
DVD—900	17″—800	Tower—750

a. Determine the optimal weekly production schedule for MVC. What is the optimal weekly profit?
b. What is the minimum price that would justify producing the Plus model? Explain.
c. If MVC could purchase additional 17″ monitors for $15 more than what they are currently paying for them, should they do this? Explain.
d. Suppose an additional worker could be hired for $1000 per week over the existing weekly worker salary. (*Recall that workers average 30 hours per week.*) Should MVC do this? Explain.

8. PRODUCTION. Pacific Aerospace is one of four subcontractors producing computer-controlled electrical switching assemblies for the proposed NASA space station. Pacific has the capability to produce three types of systems in-house: the Pacific Aerospace Delta, Omega, and Theta. NASA needs hundreds of all three systems and will purchase whatever Pacific chooses to produce.

All assemblies contain the tiny modified X70686 computer chip that cost Pacific $500 to manufacture. Seven such chips are available daily. Other materials needed for the manufacture of the assembly cost $200 for the Delta, $400 for the Omega, and $300 for the Theta, but they are not considered in short enough supply to restrict production.

Each assembly must pass through a production center; it is then subjected to rigorous testing and quality control checks. The following table gives the relevant data for each assembly.

	Delta	Omega	Theta	Daily Availability
Contract price	$1500	$1800	$1400	
X70686 Chip	$ 500	$ 500	$ 500	7
Other material/labor	$ 200	$ 400	$ 300	—
Net profit	$ 800	$ 900	$ 600	
Production (hrs.)	2	1	1	8
Quality checks (hrs.)	$1\frac{1}{3}$	$2\frac{2}{3}$	$1\frac{1}{3}$	8

a. Formulate and solve for the optimal daily production schedule. Note that no Omega systems would be produced. Why not?
b. What is the minimum contract price that would initiate production of the Omega systems?
c. What is the minimum X70686 availability for which the solution in (a) remains optimal?
d. Suppose you have the option of improving the profit by instituting one of the following options. Which would be of most value to Pacific Aerospace?
   i. Receiving, on a daily basis, six additional X70686 chips for $3100.
   ii. Utilizing three extra production hours daily at a cost of $525 ($175/hr.)
   iii. Utilizing one additional quality check hour daily at a cost of $200 ($200/hr.)

9. SURVEY SAMPLING. Gladstone and Associates is conducting a survey of 2000 investors for the financial advising firm of William and Ryde to determine satisfaction with their services. The investors are to be divided into four groups:

Group I: Large investors with William and Ryde
Group II: Small investors with William and Ryde
Group III: Large investors with other firms
Group IV: Small investors with other firms

The groups are further subdivided into those that will be contacted by telephone and those that will be visited in person. Due to the different times involved in soliciting information from the various groups, the estimated cost of taking a survey depends on the group and method of survey collection. These are detailed in the following table.

Group	Survey Costs	
	Telephone	Personal
I	$15	$35
II	$12	$30
III	$20	$50
IV	$18	$40

Determine the number of investors that should be surveyed from each group by telephone and in person to minimize Gladstone and Associates' overall total estimated cost if:

- At least half of those surveyed invest with William and Ryde.
- At least one-fourth are surveyed in person.
- At least one-half of the large William and Ryde investors surveyed are contacted in person.
- At most 40% of those surveyed are small investors.
- At least 10% and no more than 50% of the investors surveyed are from each group.
- At most 25% of the small investors surveyed are contacted in person.

10. DIET PROBLEM. Grant Winfield is a 71-year-old grandfather who likes to mix breakfast cereals together for taste and as a means of getting at least 50% of the recommended daily allowances (RDA) of five different vitamins and minerals. Concerned about his sugar intake, he wishes his mixture to yield the lowest possible amount of sugar. For taste, each of the cereals listed in the following table must make up at least 10% of the total mixture. The table shows the amounts of the vitamins, minerals, and sugar contained in one ounce together with 1/2 cup of skim milk.

Percentage of RDA per Ounce with 1/2 Cup Skim Milk

| | Vitamins | | | | | Sugars (Grams) |
	A	C	D	B6	Iron	
Multigrain Cheerios	30	25	25	25	45	12
Grape Nuts	30	2	25	25	45	9
Product 19	20	100	25	100	100	9
Frosted Bran	20	25	25	25	25	15

a. Formulate and solve for the number of ounces in each cereal that should be mixed together in order to minimize total sugar intake while providing at least 50% of the RDA for each of Vitamins A, C, D, B6, and iron. How much sugar would be consumed in the process?

b. How much total cereal does Grant need to eat to achieve the minimum 50% RDA in all five categories? How much milk does he consume in doing this?

c. Determine the shadow prices for this problem. Interpret the shadow prices and the corresponding ranges of feasibility.

d. If Grant eliminates the restriction that each cereal must account for at least 10% of the mixture, then, by inspection, why wouldn't any Frosted Bran be included in the mix? Verify this conclusion by deleting these constraints from the original formulation and re-solving.

11. VENTURE CAPITAL. Delta Venture Capital Group is considering whether to invest in Maytime Products, a new company that is planning to compete in the small kitchen appliance market. Maytime has three products in the design and test phase: (1) a unique refrigerator/oven that can be programmed in the morning to cook foods (like chicken) but keeps the food refrigerated until the cooking process begins; (2) a French fry maker that can make long thick French fries or small thin shoestring fries; and (3) a French toast maker that cooks French toast of any size evenly on the top and bottom simultaneously.

Delta's primary concern is how much money it must invest with Maytime before it will show a profit. The company will need an immediate initial investment of $2,000,000 to secure a plant and cover overhead costs. This investment must be paid back with initial profits. The following table gives the anticipated selling price, the variable cost per unit manufactured, and the initial demand for each product obtained through market research. Delta would have to commit to the $2,000,000 and then would like to minimize its total variable cost outlay until Maytime turns a profit (i.e., until Maytime can cover the initial $2,000,000 investment with profits (=selling price − variable cost) from its sales.)

Product	Selling Price	Variable Cost	Initial Demand
Refrigerator/Oven	$240	$140	5000
French Fry Maker	$ 85	$ 50	4000
French Toast Maker	$ 63	$ 36	2300

Maytime will initially produce no more than 15,000 units of any of the items but will meet anticipated initial demand. What production quantities for the products will minimize the total variable cost of the items produced while attaining a "profit" of $2,000,000?

12. MANUFACTURING. Bard's Pewter Company (BPC) manufactures pewter plates, mugs, and steins that include the campus name and logo for sale in campus book stores. The time required for each item to go through the two stages of production (molding and finishing) and the corresponding unit profits are given in the following table.

	Molding Time (min.)	Finishing Time (min.)	Unit Profit
Plates	2	8	$2.50
Mugs	3	12	$3.25
Steins	6	14	$3.90

BPC employs 12 workers, each of whom works 8 hours per day; 4 are assigned to the molding operation, the others to the finishing operation. BPC's marketing department has recommended the following:

- At least 150 mugs should be produced daily.
- The number of steins produced can be at most twice the combined total number of plates and mugs produced.
- Plates can account for no more than 30% of the total daily unit production.

a. If management accepts the marketing department's recommendations in full, determine an optimal daily production schedule for BPC.

b. Suppose the 12 workers could be reassigned optimally to the two operations. By how much would the daily profit change?

13. MORTGAGE INVESTMENT. Tritech Mortgage specializes in making first, second, and even third trust deed loans on residential properties and first trust deeds on commercial properties. Any funds not invested in mortgages are invested in an interest-bearing savings account. The following table gives the rate of return and the company's risk level for each possible type of loan.

Loan Type	Rate of Return	Risk
First Trust Deeds	7.75%	4
Second Trust Deeds	11.25%	6
Third Trust Deeds	14.25%	9
Commercial Trust Deeds	8.75%	3
Savings Account	4.45%	0

Tritech wishes to invest $68,000,000 in available funding so that:

- Yearly return is maximized.
- At least $5,000,000 is to be available in a savings account for emergencies.
- At least 80% of the money invested in trust deeds should be in residential properties.
- At least 60% of the money invested in residential properties should be in first trust deeds.
- The average risk should not exceed 5.

a. What distribution of funding do you recommend? What is the rate of return on this distribution of funds?

b. Suppose the rate of return on first trust deeds increases. What is the maximum rate of return so that your recommendation in part (a) remains optimal? What would be the overall rate of return on the investment if this rate were increased to its maximum limit?

14. PRODUCTION INVENTORY. The Mobile Cabinet Company produces cabinets used in mobile and motor homes. Cabinets produced for motor homes are smaller and made from less expensive materials than are those for mobile homes. The home office in Ames, Iowa, has just distributed to its individual manufacturing centers the production quotas required during the upcoming summer quarter. The scheduled production requirements for the Lexington, Kentucky, plant are given in the following table.

Production Requirements—Mobile Cabinet Company

	July	August	September
Motor home	250	250	150
Mobile home	100	300	400

Each motor home cabinet requires three man-hours to produce, whereas each mobile home cabinet requires five man-hours. Labor rates normally average $18 per hour. During July and August, however, when Mobile employs many part-time workers, labor rates average only $14 and $16 per hour, respectively. A total of 2100 man-hours are available in July, 1500 in August, and 1200 in September. During any given month, management at the Lexington plant can schedule up to 50% additional man-hours, using overtime at the standard rate of time and a half. Material costs for motor home cabinets are $146; for mobile home cabinets they are $210.

The Lexington plant expects to have 25 motor home and 20 mobile home assembled cabinets in stock at the beginning of July. The home office wants the Lexington plant to have at least 10 motor home and 25 mobile cabinet assemblies in stock at the beginning of October to cover possible shortages in production from other plants.

The Lexington plant has storage facilities capable of holding up to 300 cabinets in any one month. The costs for storing motor home and mobile home cabinets from one month to the next are estimated at $6 and $9 per cabinet, respectively. Devise a monthly production schedule that will minimize the costs at the Lexington plant over the quarter.

Hint: Define variables so that you can fill in the following charts.

Quarterly Production Schedule of Motor Home Cabinets

	Regular Time	Overtime
July		
August		
September		

Quarterly Production Schedule of Mobile Home Cabinets

	Regular Time	Overtime
July		
August		
September		

Quarterly Storage Schedule

	Motor Home	Mobile Home
July		
August		
September		

15. AGRICULTURE. BP Farms is a 300-acre farm located near Lawrence, Kansas, owned and operated exclusively by Bill Pashley. For the upcoming growing season, Bill will grow wheat, corn, oats, and soybeans. The following table gives relevant data concerning expected crop yields, labor required, expected preharvested expenses, and water required (in addition to the forecasted rain). Also included is the price per bushel Bill expects to receive when the crops are harvested.

Crop	Yield (bu./acre)	Labor (hr./acre)	Expenses ($/acre)	Water (acre-ft./acre)	Price ($/bu.)
Wheat	210	4	$50	2	$3.20
Corn	300	5	$75	6	$2.55
Oats	180	3	$30	1	$1.45
Soybeans	240	10	$60	4	$3.10

Bill wishes to produce at least 30,000 bushels of wheat and 30,000 bushels of corn, but no more than 25,000 bushels of oats. He has $25,000 to invest in his crops, and he plans to work up to 12 hours per day during the 150-day season. He also does not wish to exceed the base water supply of 1200 acre-feet allocated to him by the Kansas Agriculture Authority.

a. Formulate the problem for BP Farms as a linear program and solve for the optimal number of acres of each crop Bill should plant in order to maximize his total expected return from the harvested crops.

b. If the selling price of oats remains $1.45 a bushel, to what level must the yield increase before oats should be planted? If the yield for oats remains 180 bushels per acre, to what level would the price of oats have to rise before oats should be planted?

c. If there were no constraint on the minimum production of corn, would corn be planted? How much would the profit decrease if corn were not grown?

d. La Mancha Realty owns an adjacent 40-acre parcel, which it is willing to lease to Bill for the season for $2000. Should Bill lease this property? Why or why not?

16. SUPPLY CHAIN MANAGEMENT. Lion Golf Supplies operates three production plants in Sarasota, Florida; Louisville, Kentucky; and Carson, California. The plant in Sarasota can produce the high-end "professional" line of golf clubs and the more moderate "deluxe" line. The plant in Louisville can produce the deluxe line and basic "weekender" line, while the one in Carson can produce all three models. The amount of steel, aluminum, and wood required to make a set of each line of clubs (including waste), the monthly availability of these resources at each of three plants, and the gross profit per set are given in the following table.

	Steel	Aluminum	Wood	Gross Profit
Professional	3.2 lbs.	5.0 lbs.	5.2 lbs.	$250
Deluxe	3.6 lbs.	4.0 lbs.	4.8 lbs.	$175
Weekender	2.8 lbs.	4.5 lbs.	4.4 lbs.	$200
Available Monthly— Sarasota	5000 lbs.	7000 lbs.	10000 lbs.	
Available Monthly— Louisville	9000 lbs.	13000 lbs.	18000 lbs.	
Available Monthly— Carson	14000 lbs.	18000 lbs.	20000 lbs.	

Lion has three major distribution centers in Anaheim, California, Dallas, Texas, and Toledo, Ohio. The projected monthly demand and the unit transportation costs for each line between the manufacturing centers and distribution centers are given in the following table. Lion must ship between 80% and 100% of the demand for each line to each distribution center.

Professional	Sarasota	Louisville	Carson	Total Demand
Anaheim	$45		$9	600
Dallas	$32		$40	400
Toledo	$30		$50	200

Deluxe	Sarasota	Louisville	Carson	Total Demand
Anaheim	$40	$34	$6	800
Dallas	$28	$18	$35	1000
Toledo	$25	$10	$40	1100

Weekender	Sarasota	Louisville	Carson	Total Demand
Anaheim		$30	$5	800
Dallas		$15	$30	1500
Toledo		$9	$36	1000

Determine an optimal production/shipping pattern for Lion Golf Supplies.

17. SUPPLY CHAIN MANAGEMENT. Consider the Lion Golf Supplies model of problem 16.

a. Suppose that the following table gives the fixed monthly operating cost of each of the production plants.

Plant	Cost
Sarasota	$250,000
Louisville	$350,000
Carson	$500,000

Assuming that between 80% and 100% of the demand for each line must be filled at each distribution center, what recommendation would you now make concerning which plants should be operational and the production and shipping distribution pattern at each operational plant?

b. Suppose that *in addition to the fixed plant operating expenses*, each distribution center has fixed monthly operating expenses as shown in the following table.

Distribution Center	Cost
Anaheim	$ 50,000
Dallas	$100,000
Toledo	$ 90,000

Assuming that between 80% and 100% of the demand for each line must be met at each distribution center that is operational, what recommendation would you now make concerning which plants should be operational and the production and shipping distribution pattern at each operational plant?

18. PORTFOLIO ANALYSIS. Sarah Williams has $100,000 to allocate to the investments listed in the following table. Bill Wallace, her investment counselor, has prepared the following estimates for the potential annual return on each investment.

Investment	Expected Return	Minimum Return	Maximum Return
Bonanza Gold (high-risk stock)	15%	−50%	100%
Cascade Telephone (low-risk stock)	9%	3%	12%
Money market account	7%	6%	9%
Two-year Treasury bonds	8%	8%	8%

Sarah wishes to invest her money in such a way as to maximize her expected annual return based on Bill Wallace's projections, with the following restrictions:

- At most $50,000 of her investment should be in stocks.
- At least $60,000 of her investment should have the potential of earning a 9% or greater annual return.
- At least $70,000 should be liquid during the year; this implies that at most $30,000 can be in two-year Treasury bonds.
- The minimum overall annual return should be at least 4%.
- All $100,000 is to be invested.

Assume that the investments will perform independently of one another so that the returns on the investment opportunities are uncorrelated. Formulate and solve a linear program for Sarah.

19. BLENDING—OIL REFINING. California Oil Company (Caloco) produces two grades of unleaded gasoline (regular and premium) from three raw crudes (Pacific, Gulf, and Middle East). The current octane rating, the availability (in barrels), and the cost per barrel for a given production period are given in the following table.

Crude	Octane	Availability	Cost
Pacific	85	3000 barrels	$14.28/barrel
Gulf	87	2000 barrels	$15.12/barrel
Middle East	95	8000 barrels	$19.74/barrel

For this period, Caloco has contracts calling for a minimum of 200,000 gallons of regular and 100,000 gallons of premium gasoline, and it has a refining capacity of 400,000 total gallons. (A barrel is 42 gallons.) Caloco sells regular gasoline to retailers for $0.52 and premium gasoline for $0.60 per gallon.

To be classified as "regular," the refined gas must have an octane rating of 87 or more; premium must have an octane rating of 91 or more. Assume that the octane rating of any mixture is the weighted octane rating of its components.

a. Solve for the optimal amount of each crude to blend into each gasoline during this production period.

b. Suppose Caloco could obtain an additional 50,000 gallons in refining capacity for the period by putting other projects on hold. Putting these projects on hold is estimated to cost Caloco $5000 in contract penalties. Should the company absorb these fees and secure this extra 50,000-gallon refining capacity?

c. Given your answer to part (a), calculate the amount Caloco would spend purchasing Middle East oil for the period. Suppose Middle East distributors currently have a glut of crude and are in need of some hard currency. They are willing to enter into a contract with Caloco to sell it all 8000 barrels at $16.80 a barrel. Would the Middle East distributors receive more cash from Caloco under this arrangement? Would it be profitable to Caloco to accept this offer? Discuss the ramifications of this action for domestic oil producers.

20. PERSONNEL EVALUATION. At Nevada State University, the process for determining whether or not a professor receives tenure is based on a combination of qualitative evaluations and a quantitative formula derived by using linear programming. The process works as follows.

In an Annual Personnel File (APF), the professor submits evidence of his or her (1) teaching effectiveness, (2) research performance, (3) other professional activities, and (4) on-campus professional service. A personnel committee of three evaluators (who are full professors) independently evaluate the professor's file and assign a numerical rating between 0 and 100 to each of the four categories. For each category, the scores from the three evaluators are averaged together to give a single score for that category.

To determine the maximum overall score for the professor, a linear program is used for selecting the best weights (percentages) to assign to each category, satisfying the following university criteria.

- Teaching must be weighted at least as heavily as any other category.
- Research must be weighted at least 25%.
- Teaching plus research must be weighted at least 75%.
- Teaching plus research must be weighted no more than 90%.
- Service is to be weighted at least as heavily as professional activities.
- Professional activities must be weighted at least 5%.
- The total of the weights must be 100%.

Professor Anna Sung is up for tenure. To receive tenure, she must receive a weighted total score of at least 85. The three personnel committee members evaluated Anna as follows:

Committee	Teaching	Research	Professional	Service
Ron	90	60	90	80
Mabel	75	60	95	95
Nick	90	75	85	95

Will Professor Sung be awarded tenure?

21. BOAT BUILDERS/DISTRIBUTION. California Catamarans builds the Matey-20 catamaran boat in three locations: San Diego, Santa Ana, and San Jose. It ships the boats to its company-owned dealerships in Newport Beach (NB), Long Beach (LB), Ventura (VEN), San Luis Obispo (SLO), and San Francisco (SF). Production costs and capacities vary from plant to plant, as do shipping costs from the manufacturing plants to the dealerships. The following tables give costs, capacities, and demands for August.

Costs

Plant	Production Cost	Shipping Cost to				
		NB	LB	VEN	SLO	SF
San Diego	$1065	$200	$220	$280	$325	$500
Santa Ana	$1005	$125	$125	$280	$350	$400
San Jose	$ 975	$390	$365	$300	$250	$100

Plant Capacities and August Demand

Plant Capacity		August Demand	
San Diego	38	Newport Beach	42
Santa Ana	45	Long Beach	33
San Jose	58	Ventura	14
		San Luis Obispo	10
		San Francisco	22

Develop a production and shipping schedule for the Matey-20 catamaran for this period that minimizes the total production and shipping costs.

22. TRIM LOSS. The Cleveland Sprinkler Company buys 3/4-inch Schedule 40 PVC pipes, which come in 10-foot lengths, and cuts them into the 30-inch, 42-inch, and 56-inch lengths it requires for its projects. The following table gives the number of pieces of each on hand and the current requirements for each of the three lengths. Any cut of less than 30 inches is considered waste (trim loss) and is discarded. The company would like to purchase enough pipe to satisfy its requirements while minimizing its total trim losses.

	30″	42″	56″
Current inventory	0	400	150
Required	1500	900	750

Hint: The 10-foot (120 inches) pipes can be cut into several variations (e.g., four 30-inch lengths, two 30-inch lengths, and one 42-inch length with 18 inches of trim loss; one 30-inch length and two 42-inch lengths with 6 inches of trim loss; etc). The decision variables are the number of pipes cut into each of these configurations.

23. MARKETING. DAQ Electronics sells nearly 200 consumer electronics products to the general public under its own brand name, including computers, stereos, CD-ROMs, and radar detectors. DAQ's annual budget for advertising in television, radio, newspapers, and its own circulars is $700,000. This year DAQ wishes to spend at least half of its budget in television and radio, and it does not wish to spend more than $300,000 in any one advertising medium.

The company measures its success in exposure units, which are estimates of the audience reached per advertising dollar spent. The following table gives the relevant exposure unit estimates for the total public in general and for the various target populations DAQ wishes to reach.

Exposure Units

Medium	Total	Yuppie	College	Audiophile
Television	28	10	5	5
Radio	18	7	2	8
Newspapers	20	8	3	6
Circular	15	4	1	9
Minimum exposure		2,500,000	1,200,000	1,800,000

a. Comment on the fact that a person may fit into more than one category. Does this violate any linear programming assumption?

b. Ignore the possible conflict in part (a) and formulate and solve a linear program that seeks to maximize the total overall exposure given the $700,000 budget and the restrictions imposed.

c. How would deleting the constraint that a total of at least $350,000 must be spent on television and radio affect the results?

24. RETAILING. Bullox Department Store is ordering suits for its spring season. It orders four styles of suits. Three are "off-the-rack suits": (1) polyester blend suits, (2) pure wool suits, and (3) pure cotton suits. The fourth style is an imported line of fine suits of various fabrics. Studies have given Bullox a good estimate of the amount of hours required of its sales staff to sell each suit. In addition, the suits require differing amounts of advertising dollars and floor space during the season. The following table gives the unit profit per suit as well as the estimates for salesperson-hours, advertising dollars, and floor space required for their sale.

Suit	Unit Profit	Salesperson Hours	Advertising Dollars	Display Space (sq. ft.)
Polyester	$35	0.4	$2	1.00
Wool	$47	0.5	$4	1.50
Cotton	$30	0.3	$3	1.25
Import	$90	1.0	$9	3.00

Bullox expects its spring season to last 90 days. The store is open an average of 10 hours a day, 7 days a week; an average of two salespersons will be in the suit department. The floor space allocated to the suit department is a rectangular area of 300 feet by 60 feet. The total advertising budget for the suits is $15,000.

a. Formulate the problem to determine how many of each type of suit to purchase for the season in order to maximize profits and solve as a linear program.

b. For polyester suits, what would be the effect on the optimal solution of
   i. overestimating their unit profit by $1; by $2?
   ii. underestimating their unit profit by $1; by $2?
c. Show whether each of the following strategies, individually, would be profitable for Bullox:
   i. utilizing 400 adjacent square feet of space that had been used by women's sportswear. This space has been projected to net Bullox only $750 over the next 90 days.
   ii. spending an additional $400 on advertising.
   iii. hiring an additional salesperson for the 26 total Saturdays and Sundays of the season. This will cost Bullox $3600 in salaries, commissions, and benefits but will add 260 salesperson-hours to the suit department for the 90-day season.
d. Suppose we added a constraint restricting the total number of suits purchased to no more than 5000 for the season. How would the optimal solution be affected?

25. ZOO DESIGN. The San Diego Wild Animal Park has won countless awards for its design and concepts and its record of successfully breeding many endangered species. Now an investment group wishes to bring a similar attraction to the Orlando, Florida, area. The group has secured and plans to develop a 350-acre parcel of land not too far from Disneyworld, Universal Studios, and other central Florida attractions.

The animal park can be thought of as being divided into seven general areas:

- Zoo habitat attractions
- Show areas where animal shows will be seen throughout the day
- Restaurant areas
- Retail establishments
- Maintenance areas
- "Green" areas—consisting of parks and other required green spaces
- Walkways and service roads that intermingle throughout the park

The following is a list of zoning agency and other conditions that must be met by zoo planners:

- Each acre devoted to habitat areas is expected to generate $1000 per hour in gross profit to the park and is to be surrounded by .03 acre of green area. At least 40% of the park will consist of habitat areas (not including the required green areas).
- Each acre devoted to show areas is expected to generate $900 per hour in gross profit to the park and is to be surrounded by .40 acre of green areas. At least 5% of the park will consist of show areas (not including the required green areas).
- Combined, the habitat and show areas (excluding corresponding green areas) should not account for more than 70% of the park. Also, the show areas (including corresponding green areas) should not represent more than 20% of the combined acreage for habitat and show areas (including their corresponding green areas).
- At least 25% of the park that is not dedicated to habitat and show areas (not including their required green areas) should be green areas.
- Maintenance facility space is required as follows: .01 acre for each acre of habitat, .10 acre for every acre of shows, .08 acre for every acre of restaurants, .06 acre for every acre of retail establishments, .02 acre for every acre of green space, and .04 acre for every acre of walkways/roads.
- Restaurants will average .25 acre. Each must be surrounded by .15 acre of green space. It is estimated that each restaurant will generate $800 per hour in gross profit. The park should contain between 20 and 30 restaurants.
- Retail stores will average .20 acre and will be surrounded by .10 acre of green areas. Each store will generate approximately $750 per hour in gross profit. The park should contain between 15 and 25 stores, but there should be at least as many restaurants as retail stores.
- At least 10 acres of the park should be walkways and service roads. Adjoining each walkway and service road must be green areas equal to 25% of the corresponding walkway/service area.
- At least 100 acres of the animal park should be park areas, which are green areas not required by the habitat and show areas, restaurant and retail establishments, and walkways/pathways.
- The park will be open 10 hours per day 365 days per year. It has fixed daily operating expenses of $2,000,000.

Create an optimal design for the park that will maximize total hourly gross profit. The design should indicate the number of acres devoted to zoo habitat, show attractions, maintenance, walkways, and park areas. It should also detail the number and acreage required for restaurant and retail store areas and summarize the total green space in the animal park. What would be the annual *net* profit of this design?

26. HEALTH FOODS. Health Valley Foods produces three types of health food bars in two-ounce sizes: the Go Bar, the Power Bar, and the Energy Bar. The Energy Bar also comes in an 8-ounce size. The three main ingredients in each bar are a protein concentrate, a sugar substitute, and carob. The recipes for each bar in terms of percentage of ingredients (by weight) and the daily availabilities of each of the ingredients are as follows.

Bar	% Protein Concentrate	% Sugar Substitute	% Carob
Go	20	60	20
Power	50	30	20
Energy	30	40	30
Daily availability	600 lbs.	1000 lbs.	800 lbs.

The following costs are incurred in the production of the health food bars:

	Costs
Labor and packaging (2-oz. bars)	$0.03/bar
Labor and packaging (8-oz. bars)	$0.05/bar
Protein concentrate	$3.20/lb.
Sugar substitute	$1.40/lb.
Carob	$2.60/lb.

Health Valley's wholesale selling prices to health food stores are $0.68, $0.84, and $0.76, respectively, for 2-ounce sizes of the Go Bar, the Power Bar, and the Energy Bar, and $3.00 for the 8-ounce Energy Bar. The company has facilities for producing up to 25,000 2-ounce bars and 2000 8-ounce bars daily. It manufactures at least 2500 of each of the 2-ounce bars daily. No 2-ounce bar is to account for more than 50% of the total production of 2-ounce bars, and the total production (by weight) of Energy Bars is not to exceed more than 50% of the total production (by weight).

Determine an optimal daily production schedule of health food bars for Health Valley Foods.

27. **ADVERTISING.** JL Foods is planning to increase its advertising campaign from $1.4 million to $2 million based, in part, on the introduction of a new product. JL Taco Sauce, to accompany its traditional products, JL Ketchup and JL Spaghetti Sauce. In the past, JL Foods promoted its two products individually, splitting its advertising budget equally between ketchup and spaghetti sauce.

From past experience, the marketing department estimates that each dollar spent advertising *only* ketchup increases ketchup sales by four bottles and each dollar spent advertising *only* spaghetti sauce increases its sales by 3.2 bottles. Since JL makes $0.30 per bottle of ketchup and $0.35 per bottle of spaghetti sauce sold (excluding the sunk cost of the given advertising budget), this amounts to a return of $1.20 ($=4 \times$ $0.30) per advertising dollar on ketchup and $1.12 ($=3.2 \times$ $0.35) per advertising dollar on spaghetti sauce. Because taco sauce is a new product, its initial return is projected to be only $0.10 per bottle, but each advertising dollar spent solely on taco sauce is estimated to increase sales by 11 bottles. The company also projects that sales of each product would increase by another 1.4 bottles for each dollar spent on joint advertising of the three products.

JL wishes to maximize its increase in profits this year from advertising while also "building for the future" by adhering to the following guidelines for this year's advertising spending:

- A maximum of $2 million total advertising
- At most $400,000 on joint advertising
- At least $100,000 on joint advertising
- At least $1 million promoting taco sauce, either individually or through joint advertising
- At least $250,000 promoting ketchup only

- At least $250,000 promoting spaghetti sauce only
- At least $750,000 promoting taco sauce only
- At least as much spent this year as last year promoting ketchup, either individually or by joint advertising
- At least as much spent this year as last year promoting spaghetti sauce, either individually or by joint advertising
- At least 7.5 million total bottles of product sold

a. Determine the optimal allocation of advertising dollars among the four advertising possibilities (advertising for each product individually and joint advertising). Give the total return per advertising dollar of this solution and express this as a percentage of the $2 million advertising budget.

b. What is the return on additional advertising dollars?

c. Suppose the constraint requiring that at least $750,000 be spent promoting only taco sauce were lowered to $700,000. How much would the profit increase?

28. **RESTAURANT CREW ASSIGNMENT.** Burger Boy Restaurant is open from 8:00 A.M. to 10:00 P.M. daily. In addition to the hours of business, a crew of workers must arrive one hour early to help set up the restaurant for the day's operations, and another crew of workers must stay one hour after 10:00 P.M. to clean up after closing.

Burger Boy operates with nine different shifts:

Shift		Type	Daily Salary
1.	7AM–9AM	Part-time	$15
2.	7AM–11AM	Part-time	$25
3.	7AM–3PM	Full-time	$52
4.	11AM–3PM	Part-time	$22

Shift		Type	Daily Salary
5.	11AM–7PM	Full-time	$54
6.	3PM–7PM	Part-time	$24
7.	3PM–11PM	Full-time	$55
8.	7PM–11PM	Part-time	$23
9.	9PM–11PM	Part-time	$16

A needs assessment study has been completed, which divided the workday at Burger Boy into eight 2-hour blocks. The number of employees needed for each block is as follows:

Time Block	Employees Needed
7AM–9AM	8
9AM–11AM	10
11AM–1PM	22
1PM–3PM	15
3PM–5PM	10
5PM–7PM	20
7PM–9PM	16
9PM–11PM	8

Burger Boy wants at least 40% of all employees at the peak time periods of 11:00 A.M. to 1:00 P.M. and 5:00 P.M. to 7:00 P.M. to be full-time employees. At least two full-time employees must be on duty when the restaurant opens at 7:00 A.M. and when it closes at 11:00 P.M.

- Formulate and solve a model Burger Boy can use to determine how many employees it should hire for each of its nine shifts to minimize its overall daily employee costs.

29. **LAW ENFORCEMENT.** The police department of the city of Flint, Michigan, has divided the city into 15 patrol sectors, such that the response time of a patrol unit (squad car) will be less than three minutes between any two points within the sector.

Until recently, 15 units, one located in each sector, patrolled the streets of Flint from 7:00 P.M. to 3:00 A.M. However, severe budget cuts have forced the city to eliminate some patrols. The chief of police has mandated that each sector be covered by at least one unit located either within the sector or in an adjacent sector.

The accompanying figure depicts the 15 patrol sectors of Flint, Michigan. Formulate and solve a binary model that will determine the minimum number of units required to implement the chief's policy.

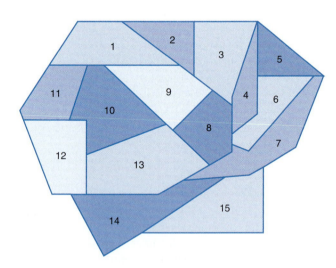

Police Patrol Sectors Flint, Michigan

30. **POLLUTION CONTROL.** General Motors has received orders from the City of Los Angeles for 30 experimental cars, 20 experimental vans, and 10 experimental buses that meet clean air standards due to take effect in three years. The vehicles can be manufactured in any of four plants located in Michigan, Tennessee, Texas, and California. Due to differences in wage rates, availability of resources, and transportation costs, the unit cost of production of each of these vehicles varies from location to location. In addition, there is a fixed cost for producing any experimental

vehicles at each location. These costs (in $1000's) are summarized in the following table.

	Cars	Vans	Buses	Fixed Cost
Michigan	15	20	40	150
Tennessee	15	28	29	170
Texas	10	24	50	125
California	14	15	25	500

Using an integer model with 12 integer variables (representing the number of each model produced at each plant) and four binary variables (indicating whether or not a particular plant is to be used for production of the experimental vehicles), determine how many experimental vehicles should be produced at each plant? What are the total production costs and fixed costs of this plan?

31. **REAL ESTATE.** Atlantic Standard Homes is developing 20 acres in a new community in the Florida Keys. There are four models it can build on each lot, and Atlantic Standard must satisfy three requirements: at least 40 are to be one story; at least 50 are to have three or more bedrooms; and there are to be at least 10 of each model. Atlantic Standard estimates the following gross profits:

Model	Lot Size (acre)	Stories	Bedrooms	Profit
Tropic	.20	1	2	$40,000
Sea Breeze	.27	1	3	$50,000
Orleans	.22	2	3	$60,000
Grand Key	.35	2	4	$80,000

a. Formulate the problem as an integer linear programming model and solve for Atlantic Standard's optimal production of homes in this community.
b. If the variables had not been restricted to be integers, the optimal linear programming solution gives $X_1 = 30$, $X_2 = 10$, $X_3 = 35.45$, $X_4 = 10$. Round this solution to an integer point. Is is feasible? How much lower is the optimal profit of the rounded solution than the optimal integer solution found in part (a)?
c. Assume that a minimum of 12 homes must be built for at least three of the four models. Using four additional binary variables and five additional constraints, modify the model to reflect this new condition and solve for the new optimal distribution of homes for the Atlantic Standard project.

32. **VANPOOLING.** Logitech, a rapidly growing high-tech company located in suburban Boston, Massachusetts, has been encouraging its employees to carpool. These efforts have met with only moderate success, and now the company is setting aside up to $250,000 to purchase small- and medium-size vans and minibuses to establish a van-pool program that will transport employees between various pickup points and company headquarters. Four models of vans and two models of

minibuses are under consideration, as detailed in the following table.

	Maker	Cost	Passenger Capacity	Annual Maintenance
Vans				
Nissan	Japan	$26,000	7	$ 5000
Toyota	Japan	$30,000	8	$ 3500
Plymouth	U.S.	$24,000	9	$ 6000
Ford (Stretch)	U.S.	$32,000	11	$ 8000
Minibuses				
Mitsubishi	Japan	$50,000	20	$ 7000
General Motors	U.S.	$60,000	24	$11,000

a. Formulate and solve a vehicle purchase model for Logitech that will maximize the total passenger capacity of the fleet given that:
- Up to $250,000 will be spent on vehicles.
- Annual maintenance cost should not exceed $50,000.
- Total number of vehicles purchased should not exceed eight.
- At least one minibus should be purchased.
- At least three vans should be purchased.
- At least half the vehicles should be made in the United States.

b. Determine the optimal solution if the amount Logitech committed for vehicle purchase were: (i) $253,900; (ii) $254,000; (iii) $249,900; (iv) $259,900; (v) $260,000. Comment.

c. Characterize the problem if the amount Logitech committed to the program were $100,000.

33. **MERCHANDISING.** Office Warehouse has been downsizing its operations. It is in the process of moving to a much smaller location and reducing the number of different computer products it carries. Coming under scrutiny are 10 products Office Warehouse has carried for the past year. For each of these products, Office Warehouse has estimated the floor space required for effective display, the capital required to restock if the product line is retained, and the short-term loss that Office Warehouse will incur if the corresponding product is eliminated (through liquidation sales, etc.).

Product Line	Manufacturer	Cost of Liquidation	Capital to Restock	Floor Space (ft²)
Notebook computer	Toshiba	$10,000	$15,000	50
Notebook computer	Compaq	$ 8,000	$12,000	60
PC	Compaq	$20,000	$25,000	200
PC	Packard Bell	$12,000	$22,000	200
MacIntosh computer	Apple	$25,000	$20,000	145
Monitor	Packard Bell	$ 4,000	$12,000	85
Monitor	Sony	$15,000	$13,000	50
Printer	Apple	$ 5,000	$14,000	100
Printer	HP	$18,000	$25,000	150
Printer	Epson	$ 6,000	$10,000	125

Office Warehouse wishes to minimize the loss due to liquidation of product lines subject to the following conditions:

- At least four of these product lines will be eliminated.
- The remaining products will occupy no more than 600 square feet of floor space.
- If one product line from a particular manufacturer is eliminated, all products from that manufacturer will be eliminated. (This affects Compaq, Packard Bell, and Apple.)
- At least two computer models (notebook, PC, or MacIntosh), at least one monitor model, and at least one printer model will continue to be carried by Office Warehouse.
- At most $75,000 is to be spent on restocking product lines.
- If the Toshiba notebook computer is retained, the Epson line of printers will also be retained.

Solve for the optimal policy for Office Warehouse.

34. **SOFTWARE DEVELOPMENT.** The Korvex Corporation is a company concerned with developing CD-ROM software applications that it sells to major computer manufacturers to include as "packaged items" when consumers purchase systems with CD-ROM drives. The company is currently evaluating the feasibility of developing six new applications. Specific information concerning each of these applications is summarized in the following table.

Application	Projected Development Cost	Programmers Required	Projected Present Worth Net Profit
1	$ 400,000	6	$2,000,000
2	$1,100,000	18	$3,600,000
3	$ 940,000	20	$4,000,000
4	$ 760,000	16	$3,000,000
5	$1,260,000	28	$4,400,000
6	$1,800,000	34	$6,200,000

Korvex has a staff of 60 programmers and has allocated $3.5 million for development of new applications.

a. Formulate and solve a binary integer linear programming model for the situation faced by the Korvex Corporation.

b. Assume also that the following additional conditions hold:
- It is anticipated that those interested in application 4 will also be interested in application 5, and vice versa. Thus, if either application 4 or application 5 is developed, the other must also be developed.
- The underlying concepts of application 2 make sense only if application 1 is included in the package. Thus, application 2 will be developed only if application 1 is developed.
- Applications 3 and 6 have similar themes; thus, if application 3 is developed, application 6 will not be developed, and vice versa.

- To ensure quality products, Korvex does not wish to expand its product line too rapidly. Accordingly, it wishes to develop at most three of the potential application products at this time.

Incorporate these constraints into the model developed for part (a), and determine the optimal choice of applications Korvex should develop.

35. ACCOUNTING/PERSONNEL HIRING. Jones, Jimenez, and Sihota (JJS) is expanding its tax service business into the San Antonio area. The company wishes to be able to service at least 100 personal and 25 corporate accounts per week.

    JJS plans to hire three levels of employees: CPAs, experienced accountants without a CPA, and junior accountants. The following table gives the weekly salary level as well as the projection of the expected number of accounts that can be serviced weekly by each level of employee.

Employee	Total Number of Accounts	Maximum Number of Corporate Accounts	Weekly Salary
CPAs	6	3	$1200
Experienced accountant	6	1	$ 900
Junior accountant	4	0	$ 600

JJS wishes to staff its San Antonio office so that at least two-thirds of all its employees will be either CPAs or experienced accountants. Determine the number of employees from each experience level the firm should hire for its San Antonio office to minimize its total weekly payroll.

36. ADVERTISING. Century Productions is in the process of promotion planning for its new comedy motion picture. *Three Is a Crowd*, through television, radio, and newspaper advertisements. The following table details the marketing department's estimate of the cost and the total audience reached per exposure in each medium.

	TV	Radio	Newspaper
Cost per exposure	$4,000	$500	$1,000
Audience reached per exposure	500,000	50,000	200,000

The marketing department does not wish to place more than 250 ads in any one medium.

a. What media mix should Century use if it wishes to reach the maximum total audience with an advertising budget of $500,000?

b. What media mix should Century use if it wishes to reach an audience of 30 million at minimum total cost?

c. The cost of producing the television advertisement is $500,000; the radio spot costs $50,000 to write and produce; and the newspaper ad costs $100,000 for design, graphics, and copy. If the total promotional budget is not to exceed $1 million (including the cost of producing the television or radio spot or the newspaper advertisement), use a mixed integer model to determine the production and media mix Century Productions should use.

37. MANUFACTURING. Floyd's Fabrication has just received an order from Gimbal Plumbing Fixtures for 100,000 specially designed three-inch-diameter casings to be delivered in one week. The contract price was negotiated up front; hence, Floyd's maximum profit will be obtained when its costs are minimized.

    Floyd's has three production facilities capable of producing the casings. Production costs do not vary between locations, but the changeover (setup) costs do vary, as does the cost of transporting the finished items to Gimbal. The following table details these costs.

Location	Changeover Cost	Transportation Cost (per 1000)	Maximum Weekly Production
Springfield	$1200	$224	65,000
Oak Ridge	$1100	$280	50,000
Westchester	$1000	$245	55,000

Formulate and solve this problem as a mixed integer linear programming model.

38. PERSONAL FINANCE. After many years of earning extremely low bank interest rates, Shelley Mednick has decided to give the stock market a try. This is her first time investing, and she wants to be extra cautious. She has heard that a new stock offering from TCS, a telecommunication company, is being sold at $55 per share (including commissions) and is projected to sell at $68 per share in a year. She is also considering a mutual fund, MFI, which one financial newsletter predicts will yield a 9% return over the next year.

    For this first venture into the market, Shelley has set extremely modest goals. She wants to invest just enough so that the expected return on her investment will be $250. Furthermore, since she has more confidence in the performance of the mutual fund than the stock, she has set the restriction that the maximum amount invested in TCS is not to exceed 40% of her total investment, or $750, whichever is smaller.

    What combination of shares of TCS and investment in MFI is necessary for Shelley to meet her goal of a projected $250 gain for the year? (*Note*: The number of shares of TCS must be integer-valued.)

39. TRUCKING. The We-Haul Company is about to lease 5000 new trucks for its California operations. The specifications of each truck under consideration are as follows.

Truck	Country	Capacity	Capital Outlay	Monthly Lease
Ford	U.S.	1 ton	$2000	$500
Chevrolet	U.S.	1 ton	$1000	$600
Dodge	U.S.	3/4 ton	$5000	$300
Mack	U.S.	5 tons	$9000	$900
Nissan	Japan	1/2 ton	$2000	$200
Toyota	Japan	3/4 ton	$ 0	$400

We-Haul has decided that, for public relations reasons, given the current "Buy American" atmosphere, it will lease at least 60% or 3000 of the trucks from American manufacturers. Each truck requires an initial capital outlay as well as monthly lease payments. We-Haul feels that it can support a total monthly lease payment of at most $2,750,000. Its fleet requirements mandate at least a 10,000-ton total payload capacity for the 5000 trucks leased. Determine the number of each truck We-Haul should lease to minimize its total initial capital outlay.

40. K OUT OF N CONSTRAINTS PUBLIC POLICY. You can model the situation in which only K out of N constraints must hold, by doing the following. First, choose a cell to hold M, a very, very high value—usually 1E10 which is 10,000,000,000 will do, but you may wish to make it larger. Then do the following

1. For *each* of the N constraints, define a binary variable Y_i to be 0 if constraint i *does* hold and 1 if constraint i *does not* hold.

2. Modify the right-hand sides of each N constraint as follows:
   • If constraint i is a "≤" constraint:
       Add the term $M*Y_i$ to the right-hand side.
   • If constraint i is a "≥" constraint:
       Subtract the term $M*Y_i$ from the right-hand side.
   • If constraint i is an "=" constraint:
       • Change the constraint to two constraints, one with a "≤" sign, the other with a "≥" sign.
       • Add the term $M*Y_i$ to the right-hand side of the new "≤" constraint.
       • Subtract the term $M*Y_i$ from the right-hand side of the new "≥" constraint.

3. Add the constraint $Y_1 + Y_2 + \ldots + Y_N \leq K - N$.

Now apply this technique to the Salem City Council

PROBLEMS 41–50 ARE ON THE CD

model in Section 3.5.3, suppose that the council would like to convey to the public that it is fiscally responsible, concerned about safety, interested in job growth, and sensitive to Salem's educational needs.

To show it is fiscally responsible, the council would like to:

• Carry over at least $250,000 to next year's budget. That is, it would like year-end spending to be at most $900,000 − $250,000 = $650,000.

To show concern for public safety, the council would like to:

• Fund at least 3 of the 6 police and fire projects.
• Add the 7 new police officers.

To show interest in job growth, the council would like to:

• Create at least 15 new full-time jobs, not just 10.

To demonstrate sensitivity to education, the council would like to:

• Fund all three educational projects.

The council members realize that there are not enough resources to meet all five of these objectives, but they feel the voters would look favorably upon them if at least three of these 5 objectives are met, in addition to meeting the other constraints in the model.

Which projects do you recommend that the Salem City Council accomplish so that:

• The original set of conditions discussed in Section 3.5.3 is still met.
• At least 3 of the 5 new objectives are met.
• The total overall point score of funded projects is maximized.

CASE STUDIES

CASE 1: Calgary Desk Company

It is August and the Calgary Desk Company (CALDESCO) of Calgary, Alberta, is about to plan the production schedule for its entire line of desks for September. CALDESCO is a well-established manufacturer. Due to an internal policy of production quotas (which will be detailed later), it has been able to sell all desks manufactured in a particular month. This, in turn, has given the company reliable estimates of the unit profit contributed by each desk model and style.

The Desks

CALDESCO manufactures a student size desk (24 in. × 42 in.), a standard size desk (30 in. × 60 in.), and an executive size desk (42 in. × 72 in.) in each of the three lines: (1) economy, (2) basic pine, and (3) hand-crafted pine.

The economy line uses aluminum for the drawers and base and a simulated pine-laminated 1-inch particle board top. Although the basic pine desk use $1\frac{1}{2}$-inch pine sheets instead of particle board, they are manufactured on the same production line as the tops of the economy line models. Because its drawers and base are made of wood, however, a different production line is required for this process.

Hand-crafted desks have solid pine tops that are constructed by craftsmen independent of any production line. This desk line uses the same drawers and base (and hence the same production line for this process) as the basic pine desk line. Hand-crafted desks are assembled and finished by hand.

Production

Production Line 1 is used to manufacture the aluminum drawers and base for the economy models; production line 2 is used to manufacture the tops for the economy and basic models. There are two production lines 3, which are used to manufacture drawers and bases for the basic and hand-crafted lines. (Two lines are necessary to meet production targets.)

The production times available on the three production lines are summarized on the Excel spreadsheet below. The time requirements (in minutes) per desk for the three different types of production lines, the finishing and assembly times, and the time required to hand-craft certain models are also summarized on the spreadsheet.

Labor

CALDESCO currently employs a workforce of 30 craftsmen, but due to vacations, illnesses, etc., CALDESCO expects to have only an average of 80% of its craftsmen available throughout the month. Each available craftsman works 160 hours per month. The expected total labor availability, which is also given on the spreadsheet, is:

$$(.80) * (30 \text{ craftsmen}) * (160 \text{ hours/craftsmen})$$
$$* (60 \text{ minutes/hour}) = 230,400 \text{ worker-minutes.}$$

Each craftsman in CALDESCO's shop is capable of doing all the tasks required to make any model desk; including running of the manufacturing lines, assembling the product, or performing the detailed operations necessary to produce the hand-crafted models.

Two craftsmen are required for each production line, but only a single craftsman is needed for hand crafting and a single craftsman is needed for assembly and finishing. Thus, the total amount of man-minutes required to produce a desk = 2 × (the total production line time) + (hand-crafting time) + (assembly/finishing time).

Materials Requirements

As detailed earlier, the economy desks use aluminum and laminated particle board, whereas the basic and hand-

CALDESCO--SEPTEMBER

PROFIT, ORDERS, MATERIALS (SQ.FT.), PRODUCTION TIME (MIN) PER DESK

LINE	SIZE	PROFIT	SEPT. ORDERS	ALUMINUM	PARTICLE BOARD	PINE SHEETS	LINE 1 TIME	LINE 2 TIME	LINE 3 TIME	ASSEM./FINISHING	HAND-CRAFTING
ECONOMY	STUDENT	25	750	14	8		1.5	1		10	
	STANDARD	30	900	24	15		2.0	1		11	
	EXECUTIVE	40	100	30	24		2.5	1		12	
BASIC	STUDENT	50	400			22		1	3	15	
	STANDARD	80	800			40		1	4	18	
	EXECUTIVE	125	100			55		1	5	20	
HAND-	STUDENT	100	25			25			3	20	50
CRAFTED	STANDARD	250	150			45			4	25	60
	EXECUTIVE	350	50			60			5	30	70

RESOURCE AVAILABILITY FOR SEPTEMBER

LABOR(MAN-MINUTES)	230400
ALUMINUM (SQ.FT.)	50000
PARTICLE BOARD(SQ.FT.)	30000
PINE SHEETS(SQ.FT.)	200000
PRODUCTION LINE 1 (MIN.)	9600
PRODUCTION LINE 2 (MIN.)	9600
PRODUCTION LINE 3 (MIN.)	19200

PRODUCTION QUOTAS (OF TOTAL PRODUCTION)

	MIN %	MAX %
ECONOMY	25	50
BASIC	35	55
HAND-CR.	15	25
STUDENT	20	40
STANDARD	40	65
EXECUTIVE	10	25

Production Process

crafted models use real pine. The amounts of aluminum, particle board, and $1\frac{1}{2}$-inch thick pine sheets (in square feet) required to produce each style of desk are summarized on the spreadsheet along with the September availability of aluminum, particle board, and pine sheets.

Company Policy/Quotas

CALDESCO has been able to sell all the desks it produces and to maintain its profit margins in part by adhering to a set of in-house quotas. These maximum and minimum quotas for desk production are given on the spreadsheet.

CALDESCO will meet all outstanding orders for September. These are also summarized on the spreadsheet.

Profit Contribution

The unit profits, which have been determined for each style of desk, are also summarized on the spreadsheet.

The Report

Prepare a report recommending a production schedule to CALDESCO for September. In your report, analyze your results, detail the amount of each resource needed if your recommendation is implemented, and discuss any real-life factors that might be considered that have not been addressed in this problem summary nor listed on the spreadsheet. Discuss some appropriate "what-if" analyses including

- An analysis of the viability of instituting a bonus plan costing about $35,000 per month that is anticipated to reduce absenteeism from 20% to 15%.
- An analysis of the possibility of purchasing a new production line 2 for $400,000 and hiring 10 new workers at $30,000 each per year (assume the 20% absentee rate). Assume that September is a typical month and that the resulting increased production per month would be matched each month. Specifically determine:
  - How long it would be before these changes became profitable (i.e., until these fixed costs were paid off).
  - After the purchase of the line was paid off, how much additional profit you would expect to earn each month. (Don't forget the added cost of new workers.)
- Other observations and scenarios you feel might be reasonable.

Your report should give a complete description/analysis of your final recommendation complete with tables, charts, graphs, and so on. The complete model and the computer printouts are to be included in appendices.

Note: The Excel file giving the spreadsheet is CALGDESK.XLS in the Excel files folder on the CD-ROM.

CASE 2: Lake Saddleback Development Corporation

Lake Saddleback Development Corporation (LSDC) is developing a planned community of homes and condominiums around a section of Lake Saddleback, Texas. The idea is to develop 300 acres of land it owns on and near the lake in such a way that it maximizes its profits from the development while offering an appropriate variety of different home plans in different products. In addition, the corporation wishes to analyze the feasibility of developing a 10-acre sports/recreational complex.

LSDC is building four products: (1) the Grand Estate Series; (2) the Glen Wood Collection; (3) the Lakeview Patio Homes; and (4) the Country Condominiums. Within each product are three to four floor plans of various styles, as described in the following list.

Lot Sizes

Lots for all models include the land on which the house resides, the garage (which is not considered part of the advertised square footage of the house), and yard space. It excludes outside parking and space for parks, roads, undeveloped landscape, and so on.

All models in the Grand Estate series are built on one-half acre lots, and 50 half-acre lots on the lake are to be used exclusively by the Grand Estate Series homes. The selling price of these exclusive homes will be an additional

30% plus $50,000 more than the models not on the lake. (For example, the $700,000 Trump model would sell for $960,000 if on the lake.) Each of the Grand Estate series plans must have at least eight units on the lake.

Some Grand Cypress models (in the Glen Wood Homes series) may be built on "premium" quarter-acre lots. In addition, some Bayview models (in the Lakeview Patio Homes series) may be built on "premium" one-sixth acre lots. No more than 25% of the total Grand Cypress models and 25% of the total Bayview models may be built on the premium lots.

Lot sizes for the Country Condominiums are fixed at 1500 square feet.

The minimum standard lot for homes in the Glen Wood and Lakeview series homes (except for the premium models) is $\frac{1}{10}$ of an acre. Lot sizes for certain models can be higher if the following calculation exceeds $\frac{1}{10}$ acre.

$$\text{Lot Size} = (\text{Ground Area of House}) + (\text{Yard Size}) + (\text{Garage Size})$$

Ground Area   The ground area of any single-story house is the advertised square footage of the house. The ground area for two-story homes is 75% of the advertised square footage.

Plan	Selling Price	Size (sq. ft.)	Bedrooms	Bathrooms	Stories	Garage Size
Grand Estates						
The Trump*	$700,000	4000	5 + den	4	2	3 car
The Vanderbilt*	$680,000	3600	4 + den	3	2	3 car
The Hughes*	$650,000	3000	4	3	1	3 car
The Jackson*	$590,000	2600	3	3	1	3 car
Glen Wood Collection						
Grand Cypress*	$420,000	2800	4 + den	3	2	3 car
Lazy Oak	$380,000	2400	4	3	2	2 car
Wind Row	$320,000	2200	3	3	2	2 car
Orangewood	$280,000	1800	3	$2\frac{1}{2}$	1	2 car
Lakeview Patio Homes						
Bayview*	$300,000	2000	4	$2\frac{1}{2}$	2	2 car
Shoreline	$270,000	1800	3 + den	$2\frac{1}{2}$	2	2 car
Docks Edge	$240,000	1500	3	$2\frac{1}{2}$	1	2 car
Golden Pier	$200,000	1200	2	2	1	2 car
Country Condominiums						
Country Stream	$220,000	1600	3	2	2	—
Weeping Willow	$160,000	1200	2	2	1	—
Picket Fence	$140,000	1000	2	$1\frac{1}{2}$	1	—

*Some of these models may occupy larger premium or lakeside lots with higher selling prices.

Yard Size   For homes in the Glen Wood series, yard sizes are 1200 square feet for single-story homes, and the same as the ground area of the house for two-story homes. For homes in the Lakeview Patio Home series, yard sizes are 900 square feet for single-story homes. For two-story homes in this series, the yard size is 600 square feet + 50% of the ground area of the house.

Garage Size   Two-car garages occupy 500 square feet of ground space, and three-car garages occupy 750 square feet of ground space. Note that there are no garages for the Country Condominium models.

Parking

Current code requires one parking space per bedroom for each unit built. For example, outside parking space for two cars would be required for a four-bedroom house with a two-car garage. Each outside parking space will occupy 200 square feet of space. No more than 15 acres of the project may be used for *outside* parking. All parking for the Country Condominiums is outside.

Roads/Greenbelts, Etc.

A total of 1000 square feet per house is to be set aside for the building of roads, greenbelts, and small parks to add both to the aesthetics and necessities of the project.

Variety

Throughout the entire project, the following maximum and minimum percentages have been established by the marketing department (*Note*: Condominiums are included in the following figures.)

	Maximum	Minimum
Two-bedroom homes	25%	15%
Three-bedroom homes	40%	25%
Four-bedroom homes	40%	25%
Five-bedroom homes	15%	5%

In addition, none of the four products (Grand Estate, Glen Wood, Lakeview, and Country) is to make up more than 35% or less than 15% of the units built in the development. Furthermore, within each product, each plan must occupy between 20% and 35% of the total units of that product. For appearances' sake, no more than 70% of the single-family homes (all homes except the Country Condominiums) may be two-story homes.

Affordable Housing

In the affluent Lake Saddleback area, any house priced at $200,000 or below is considered "affordable" housing. The federal government requires at least 15% of the project to be designated affordable housing.

Profit

LSDC has determined the following percentages of the sales prices to be net profits:

Grand Estates	22%
Glen Wood*	18%
Lakeview*	20%
Country Condominiums	25%

*There is a 20% premium added to the selling price for the premium Grand Cypress and the premium Bayview models. Two-thirds of this premium can be considered additional profit on these models.

Objectives

1. LSDC needs to determine the number of units of each plan of each product to build in order to maximize its profit.
2. If LSDC builds a 10-acre sports/recreation complex on the property, this would:
   - Decrease the usable area to build houses by 10 acres—all other constraints still apply.
   - Cost LSDC $8,000,000 to build.
   - Enhance the value of all houses so that LSDC would raise the selling prices of the homes by the following amounts:
     —Grand Estates (not on lake)—add 5% (e.g., add $35,000 to profit for Trumps, etc.)
     —Grand Estates (on lake)—add another $40,000 (e.g., profits increase by $40,000)
     —Glen Wood and Lakeview Patio Homes (nonpremium except Golden Pier)
       —Add 3% (e.g., add $12,600 to profit of Grand Cypress)

—Premium Models—add a flat $16,000
—Golden Pier—$0 (no change, so that it can still qualify as affordable housing)
—Country Condominiums—add a flat $10,000

All of the selling price increases would be added to the original gross profits to determine the new gross profit (prior to subtracting the $8,000,000 for the complex).

The Report

Prepare a detailed report analyzing this project and make suggestions for the number of each type of each unit to be built. Give and support your recommendations on whether or not to build the sports/recreation complex. Do appropriate "what-if" analyses and give a summary of your final recommendations. (*Hint*: You may wish to solve as a linear program and round.)

CASE 3:   Pentagonal Pictures, Inc.

Pentagonal Pictures produces motion pictures in Hollywood and distributes them nationwide. Currently, it is considering 10 possible films; these include dramas, comedies, and action adventures. The success of each film depends somewhat on both the strength of the subject matter and the appeal of the cast. Estimating the cost of a film and its potential box office draw is inexact at best; still, the studio must rely on its experts' opinions to help it evaluate which projects to undertake.

The following table lists the films currently under consideration by Pentagonal Pictures, including the projected cost and box office gross receipts.

Film	Rating	Type	No-Name Cast		Big Star Cast	
			Cost	Box Office Gross	Cost	Box Office Gross
Two-Edged Sword	PG-13	Action	$ 5M	$ 8M	$10M	$15M
Lady in Waiting	R	Drama	$12M	$20M	$25M	$35M
Yesterday	PG	Drama	$ 8M	$10M	$12M	$26M
Golly Gee	PG	Comedy	$ 7M	$12M	$15M	$26M
Why I Cry	PG-13	Drama	$15M	$30M	$30M	$45M
Captain Kid	PG	Comedy	$10M	$20M	$17M	$28M
Oh Yes!	R	Comedy	$ 4M	$ 7M	$ 8M	$12M
Nitty Gritty	PG	Comedy	$11M	$15M	$14M	$20M
The Crash	R	Action	$20M	$28M	$40M	$65M
Bombs Away	R	Action	$25M	$37M	$50M	$80M

In addition to these production costs, each movie will have a $1 million advertising budget, which will increase to $3 million if the movie is to have a "big star" cast. Assume that the studio receives 80% of a film's gross receipts. The company would like to maximize its net profit (gross profit − production costs − advertising costs) for the year.

Pentagonal has a production budget of $100 million and an advertising budget of $15 million. In addition, it would like to adhere to the following restrictions:

1. At least half the films produced should have a rating of PG or PG-13.

2. At least two comedies are to be produced.
3. If *The Crash* is produced, *Bombs Away* will not be.
4. At least one drama is to be produced.
5. At least two films should have big-name casts.
6. At least two PG films should be produced.
7. At least one action movie with a big-name cast should be produced.

Prepare a report for Pentagonal Pictures that recommends which films should be produced and with which casts. Detail how the budgets will be spent. Include in your report a sensitivity analysis that considers how varying budgets for both production costs and advertising (while spending at most a total of $115 million) would affect your recommendation. Finally, discuss the effects of Pentagonal's seven restrictions and report the effect of requiring only six of the seven, five of the seven, and four of the seven to hold.

CASES 4–6 ARE ON THE CD

Network Models

Chapter 4

NATURE'S BEST, http://www.naturesbest.net, is the leading full–line distributor of health and natural food products in the western United States, supplying over 18,000 products. Many manufacturers deliver their products directly to Nature's Best's warehouse, but for some products, Nature's Best must make the pickup itself. One of its weekly challenges is to schedule its big rig trucks for pickups from various manufacturers around the state. The locations of the pickups vary from week to week, but each truck must begin at the warehouse location in southern California, stop at several destinations to fill its trailer with products, and return.

Another situation the company faces involves the transportation of goods to its customers. In most instances, after Nature's Best receives a purchase order, the goods are taken from the company's inventory, loaded on small pickup trucks, and transported to the customer. In other cases, the company delivers the product directly from the manufacturer to the customer, leaving only a paper trail indicating that the item was in its inventory.

To determine how much product to order from manufacturers, Nature's Best employs several buyers, who review customer orders and the inventory position of the products within the company's warehouse. The buyers possess different skills and expertise, and Nature's Best must decide which buyers to assign to which group of manufacturers.

Each of these situations is typical of a problem that can be described using a *network model*. One network consists of the highways and cities the trucks must visit before returning to the warehouse. The company would like the trucks to make these trips at minimum cost. Another network is comprised of local streets that must be traversed in order to reach an ultimate destination in minimal time. Finally, there is a network of buyers and manufacturers that should be paired to maximize the efficiency of the purchasing operations.

The use of network models provides both a convenient way of expressing the situation pictorially and an efficient mechanism for finding optimal solutions with minimal input.

187

4.1   Introduction to Networks

Our mental image of a network may be a series of wires that make up an electrical network, a system of roads that make up a transportation network, or perhaps a group of affiliated stations that make up a television network. Whatever the image, our concept involves some entities (microchips, cities, local television stations) that are somehow linked together (by wires, roads, satellite transmissions). The entity can have or use some resource (electrical current, delivery trucks, television programming) that is "delivered" over the links at some cost. This intuitive description does, in fact, provide the basis for what management scientists call **networks**.

In management science models, the "entities" are represented by *nodes* in the network, some of which are linked together by *arcs* connecting one node with another. At each of the nodes, there may be some quantity of a resource, such as current generated or required, trucks available or needed, or television shows sent or received. To "travel" on each of the arcs one must pay a cost in units, such as dollars, miles, or time, and the amount that can be "transported" over each of the arcs may be limited. These quantities are known as the *functions* defined on the nodes and arcs.

Network

A **network** problem is one that can be represented by

1. A set of nodes
2. A set of arcs
3. Functions defined on the nodes and/or arcs

Network models can be divided into two basic groups: network flow models and network connectivity models. **Flow models** involve the delivery of goods or resources from one or more supply nodes, perhaps through one or more intermediate nodes, to one or more demand nodes. In **connectivity models**, the primary concern is to link all the nodes together in a certain manner.

Many business situations can be modeled as networks. *Network flow models* discussed in this chapter include:

- **Transportation Models** that seek to minimize the total cost of directly shipping supplies from source nodes to meet demand at demand nodes.
- **Capacitated Transshipment Models** that seek to minimize the total cost of shipping supplies from source nodes, possibly through some intermediate nodes before satisfying demand at demand nodes while not exceeding arc flow capacities.
- **Assignment Models** that seek to assign workers to jobs at minimum total cost.
- **Shortest Path Models** that seek to find the minimum total distance between two designated nodes.
- **Maximum Flow Models** that seek to find the maximum possible flow between two designated nodes.

Network connectivity models discussed in the chapter include:

- **Traveling Salesman Models** that seek to find a minimum cost cycle that includes all nodes in the network.
- **Minimal Spanning Tree Models** that simply seek to connect all nodes in the network using the minimum total arc lengths.

SOLUTION ALGORITHMS AND SPREADSHEET SOLUTIONS FOR NETWORK MODELS

Management scientists have developed compact and generally simple algorithms for solving each of the above network models. Many of these are detailed in Supplement CD5 on the accompanying CD-ROM. These algorithms are typically easy enough to do by hand for small models, but many do not lend themselves to spreadsheet implementation without using macros.

Each of the network flow models we have described, however, does have a simple linear programming formulation. Technically, network flow models are integer linear programming models, but because of the special form of the constraints[1] in these models, if the parameters of the model are integers, the linear programming model is guaranteed to have an optimal solution with integer values. Using a linear rather than an integer model allows us to use the linear programming sensitivity reports to evaluate the effects of changes to the input parameters. In this chapter we show how Solver can be used to generate optimal solutions for each of the network flow models (transportation, capacitated transshipment, assignment, shortest path, and maximal flow models). In addition we exhibit the results of using the network.xls template that is included on the accompanying CD-ROM. The instructions for using this template are given in Appendix 4.1.

Connectivity models (traveling salesman and minimal spanning tree) are different. Although a traveling salesman model can be formulated and solved using linear programming, the number of functional constraints required to accurately depict such models is extremely large, even when there are only five or six nodes. Hence, a straightforward linear programming approach is not recommended for such models. The solution to large traveling salesman problems has, in fact, been the subject of research for many years. On the accompanying CD-ROM, we discuss a branch and bound approach that is relatively efficient for solving problems with up to 20 nodes.

Minimal spanning tree models, on the other hand, do not have a linear programming formulation, and hence Solver cannot be used to determine optimal solutions for this model. However, we will show how to use an extremely simple solution algorithm for solving minimal spanning tree models that is easy to implement even without using a computer!

NETWORK TERMINOLOGY

Most of the terms used in conjunction with network models have common-sense meanings. Here are some of the basic concepts.

Flow

When two nodes are connected by an arc as shown in Figure 4.1, a **flow** of some kind (current, traffic, microwaves, time, etc.) can occur directly between them. The amount of flow the decision maker will choose to send between the two nodes is typically a decision variable, X_{ij}. This flow can sometimes be restricted by a *maximum capacity* that is permitted along the arc.

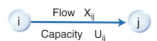

FIGURE 4.1 Flow

---

[1] The constraints form what is called a *totally unimodular* matrix. This is a matrix of 1's, 0's, and -1's arranged in a particular format. An optimal solution to models with totally unimodular constraint matrices and integer right-hand sides will be integer-valued.

Directed/Undirected Arcs

Flow is sometimes allowed in only one direction. This is indicated by putting an arrow at the end of the arc into the terminal node as shown in Figure 4.2(*a*). In this case the arc is said to be a **directed arc**. In the absence of this restriction, no arrow is placed on the arc as in Figure 4.2(b), and it is called an **undirected arc**.

FIGURE 4.2
Directed/Undirected Arcs

(a) Directed Arc flow may only be from i to j

(b) Undirected Arc flow may be in either direction

In network flow models, we assume that all arcs are directed arcs. If we wish to allow flow in both directions between two nodes, two directed arcs will be drawn, one from the first node to the second and one from the second node to the first. In connectivity models, we assume that all arcs are undirected.

Paths/Connected Nodes

The collection of arcs formed by a series of adjacent nodes, such as nodes 1, 3, 4, 5 in Figure 4.3, is a *path* between node 1 and node 5. When a path exists between two nodes, these nodes are said to be *connected*. Since there is no path between nodes 1 and 7 (in Figure 4.3), these nodes are not connected.

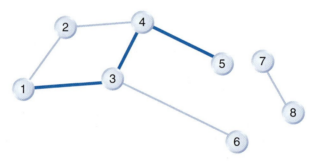

The selected arcs from node 1 to node 3, node 3 to node 4, and node 4 to node 5 form a **path** from node 1 to node 5; node 1 is **connected** to node 5.

FIGURE 4.3
Paths/Connected Nodes

There is **no path** between node 1 and node 7; node 1 is **not connected** to node 7.

CYCLES

In Figure 4.4, we see that a path can be traced from a node that returns to the same node without including any arc more than once. This circuitous path is called a **cycle**.

CYCLES

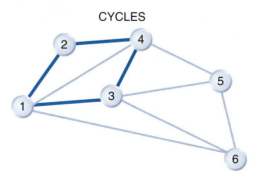

The selected arcs form a **cycle**. A path can be traced from node 1 to node 1 via nodes 2, 4, and 3, respectively.

FIGURE 4.4   A Cycle

TREES/SPANNING TREES

If the arcs of a series of connected nodes do not contain any cycles, as in Figure 4.5a, the resulting figure is called a **tree**. A tree that connects *all* the nodes in a network, as in Figure 4.5b, is a **spanning tree**. It can easily be shown that a tree that connects n nodes of a network consists of n − 1 connected arcs. Hence, the number of arcs in a spanning tree is one less than the number of nodes in the entire network.

TREES

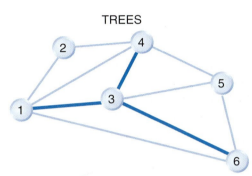

SPANNING TREES

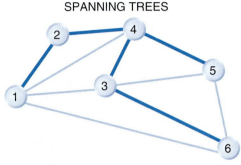

(a) The selected arcs shown form a **tree** connecting four nodes (nodes 1,3,4, and 6). They contain no cycles.

(b) The selected arcs from node 1 to node 2, node 2 to node 4, node 4 to node 5, node 3 to node 4, and node 3 to node 6 form a **spanning tree** for the network. All nodes are connected, and there are no cycles.

FIGURE 4.5a A Tree

FIGURE 4.5b Spanning Tree

4.2 Transportation Networks

A **transportation network** arises when a cost-effective pattern is needed to ship items from origins that have limited supply to destinations that have demand for the goods. In its basic form, a transportation model assumes that the cost of shipping items from a source to a destination is proportional to the number of units shipped between the two points. Thus, the basic transportation model can be summarized as follows.

Transportation Model

1. There are m sources.
   The supply of a resource at source i is S_i.
2. There are n destinations.
   The demand for the resource at destination j is D_j.
3. The unit shipping cost between nodes i and j is C_{ij}.

Goal: Minimize the total shipping cost of supplying the destinations with the required demand from the available supplies at the sources.

To illustrate, consider the problem Carlton Pharmaceuticals is facing in "transporting" cases of vaccine from its production plants to its distribution warehouses.

Carlton.xls
Carlton-net.xls

CARLTON PHARMACEUTICALS

Carlton Pharmaceuticals supplies drugs and other medical supplies to hospitals and pharmacies throughout the southern and midwestern United States. Carlton has three production plants (located in Cleveland, Ohio; Detroit, Michigan;

and Greensboro, North Carolina) and four distribution warehouses (located in Boston, Massachusetts; Richmond, Virginia; Atlanta, Georgia; and St. Louis, Missouri).

Carlton routinely stocks its warehouses with drugs and medical supplies on an as-needed basis. Because the Hong Kong A flu virus has begun sweeping the nation, however, supplies of Carlton's flu vaccine are running short at its distribution warehouses, and there is a critical need to resupply all four warehouses within the week.

At full production, Carlton will be able to produce and make available for shipment 1200 cases of the vaccine in Cleveland, 1000 in Detroit, and 800 in Greensboro by the end of the week. Taking into account the population, the number of hospitals and doctors, and the likelihood of a flu epidemic in the service area of each warehouse, the company has decided to allocate the 3000 cases as follows: 1100 to Boston, 400 to Richmond, 750 to Atlanta, and 750 to St. Louis.

Because the shipping department will be unable to deliver the vaccine in time using its normal trucking/rail operations, the company has contacted a number of express freight delivery services in order to determine the lowest shipping price per case between each plant–warehouse pair of cities. These costs are given in Table 4.1.

Management at Carlton would like to ship the cases to the warehouses as economically as possible.

TABLE 4.1   Shipping Cost per Case of Vaccine

	To			
	Boston	Richmond	Atlanta	St. Louis
From				
Cleveland	$35	$30	$40	$32
Detroit	$37	$40	$42	$25
Greensboro	$40	$15	$20	$28

SOLUTION

The Carlton Pharmaceuticals problem is an example of a transportation model, with the following characteristics: $m = 3$ sources, with supplies $S_1 = 1200$, $S_2 = 1000$, and $S_3 = 800$, respectively; and $n = 4$ destinations, with demands $D_1 = 1100$, $D_2 = 400$, $D_3 = 750$, and $D_4 = 750$, respectively. The unit shipping costs from city i to city j (the C_{ij}'s) are the costs given in the problem statement (for example $C_{23} = 42$). Carlton's goal is to minimize the total cost of shipping the cases from the production plants to the warehouse sites.

THE NETWORK

Figure 4.6 shows the network representation for the transportation problem faced by Carlton Pharmaceuticals. The nodes on the left side represent the sources; the function defined on these nodes is the supply of vaccine. The nodes on the right side represent the destinations; the function defined on these nodes is the demand for the vaccine. The arcs represent the transportation routes between each source and each destination; the function defined on the arcs is the unit shipping cost.

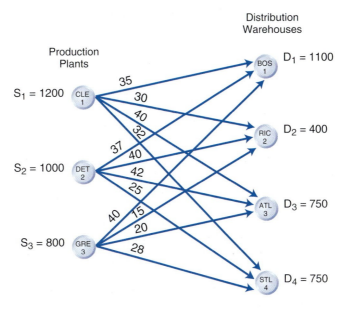

FIGURE 4.6 Carlton Pharmaceuticals Transportation Network Representation

ASSUMPTIONS

In order to solve for the optimal shipping pattern, we make several simplifying assumptions so that it meets the criteria of a basic transportation model.

1. ***The per item shipping cost remains constant, regardless of the number of units shipped.***

Although this assumption may be valid for the Carlton Pharmaceuticals problem, it would be violated if the express freight services offered discounts based on the quantities shipped or if there had been transportation expenses with a high fixed cost component. For example, suppose Carlton used its own trucks, each of which can hold up to 3000 cases, to transport the vaccine between the plants and the warehouses. If a truck transported only the vaccine, the cost of shipping 1000 cases would *not* be ten times the cost of shipping 100 cases because the fixed cost of operating the trucks (i.e., driver time, fuel, tolls, etc.) is independent of the quantities shipped. In such cases, using this basic transportation model would not be valid.

2. ***All the shipping from the sources to the destinations occurs simultaneously (or within some fixed time frame).***

If time is not a factor—that is, if Carlton does not have to resupply its warehouses within a week—Carlton could wait for more vaccine to be produced at plants with less expensive delivery charges.

3. ***The vaccine can be shipped only between sources and destinations.***

The vaccine is not shipped between one source and another source, or between one destination and another destination. There are also no shipments to intermediate destinations.

MATHEMATICAL PROGRAMMING FORMULATION

Given these assumptions, the Carlton Pharmaceuticals problem has the following structure:

MINIMIZE ⟨Total Shipping Cost⟩
ST
    ⟨Amount shipped from each source⟩ ≤ ⟨Supply at that source⟩
  ⟨Amount received at each destination⟩ = ⟨Demand at that destination⟩
                  ⟨No negative shipments⟩

For the Carlton Pharmaceutical model, we define:

$$X_{ij} = \text{the number of cases shipped from plant i to warehouse j}$$

where: i = 1 (Cleveland), 2 (Detroit), 3 (Greensboro)
   and j = 1 (Boston), 2 (Richmond), 3 (Atlanta), 4 (St. Louis)

Thus, there are 12 decision variables: $X_{11}, X_{12}, X_{13}, \ldots, X_{34}$. The amount shipped (the flow) from Cleveland (source 1) is: $X_{11} + X_{12} + X_{13} + X_{14}$. Since this cannot exceed the supply at the Cleveland plant of 1200 cases, we have the constraint:

$$X_{11} + X_{12} + X_{13} + X_{14} \leq 1200$$

Similarly, for Detroit and Greensboro we have, respectively,

$$X_{21} + X_{22} + X_{23} + X_{24} \leq 1000$$
$$X_{31} + X_{32} + X_{33} + X_{34} \leq 800$$

The amount shipped into Boston (destination 1) is: $X_{11} + X_{21} + X_{31}$. This must equal the demand in Boston for 1100 cases. This can then be expressed as:

$$X_{11} + X_{21} + X_{31} = 1100$$

Similarly, for Richmond, Atlanta, and St. Louis we have, respectively,

$$X_{12} + X_{22} + X_{32} = 400$$
$$X_{13} + X_{23} + X_{33} = 750$$
$$X_{14} + X_{24} + X_{34} = 750$$

Thus the complete mathematical model for the Carlton Pharmaceutical problem is:

MINIMIZE $\quad 35X_{11} + 30X_{12} + 40X_{13} + 32X_{14} + 37X_{21} + 40X_{22} + 42X_{23} + 25X_{24} + 40X_{31} + 15X_{32} + 20X_{33} + 28X_{34}$

ST
$$
\begin{array}{rrrrrrrrrrrrl}
X_{11} + & X_{12} + & X_{13} + & X_{14} & & & & & & & & & \leq 1200 \\
& & & & X_{21} + & X_{22} + & X_{23} + & X_{24} & & & & & \leq 1000 \\
& & & & & & & & X_{31} + & X_{32} + & X_{33} + & X_{34} & \leq 800 \\
X_{11} & & & & + X_{21} & & & & + X_{31} & & & & = 1100 \\
& X_{12} & & & & + X_{22} & & & & + X_{32} & & & = 400 \\
& & X_{13} & & & & + X_{23} & & & & + X_{33} & & = 750 \\
& & & X_{14} & & & & + X_{24} & & & & + X_{34} & = 750
\end{array}
$$
$$X_{ij} \geq 0, \text{ for all i and j}$$

Note that there is one constraint for each of the m = 3 sources and one constraint for each of the n = 4 destinations, or a total of m + n = 3 + 4 = 7 constraints.

USING SOLVER TO SOLVE TRANSPORTATION MODELS

Because the transportation model is a linear program, we shall use Excel Solver to determine a minimum cost solution.[2]

We now construct the spreadsheet shown in Figure 4.7 by setting aside cells for:

- The value of the objective function (B4)
- The optimal solution (B7:E9)
- The total amount shipped from each plant (G7:G9)
- The total amount received at each warehouse (B11:E11)

Carlton.xls

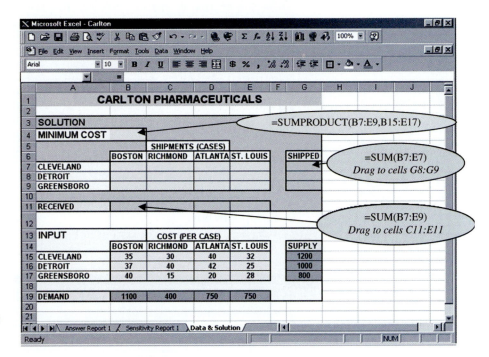

FIGURE 4.7
Input Spreadsheet for Carlton Pharmaceuticals

Using Copy and Paste, we copy the names of the origins and destinations, and we set aside cells and enter data for:

- The supplies at each plant (G15:G17)
- The demands at each warehouse (B19:E19)
- The unit shipping costs (B15:E17)

We now enter the formulas shown on the spreadsheet in Figure 4.7 into cells B4, G7:G9, and B11:E11. These will calculate the values for the total cost, the amounts shipped from each plant, and the amounts received at each warehouse, respectively. We also color some of the unused cells in order to clearly delineate the input and output.

[2] Before we begin setting up the appropriate spreadsheet, we will go to the Tools menu and select Options and go to the View tab. There we will make sure the box labeled "Zero values" is NOT checked so that zero values will not appear on the spreadsheet. This will make the spreadsheet easier to read.

Solver is now used to determine the optimal solution. Figure 4.8 shows the Solver dialogue box. Note that the problem is a minimization. The constraints state:

- The total shipment received at a destination node must equal the demand at that node.
- The total shipment out of a supply node cannot exceed the supply at the node.

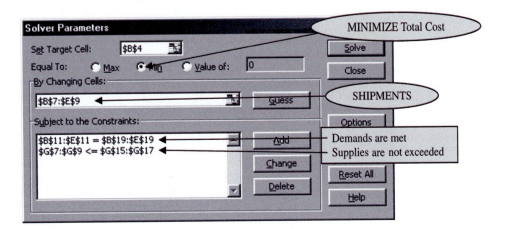

FIGURE 4.8
Solver Dialogue Box for Carlton Pharmaceuticals

As usual, the Assume Linear Model and Assume Non-Negative boxes are checked in the Options box.

Clicking Solve gives the output in Figure 4.9.

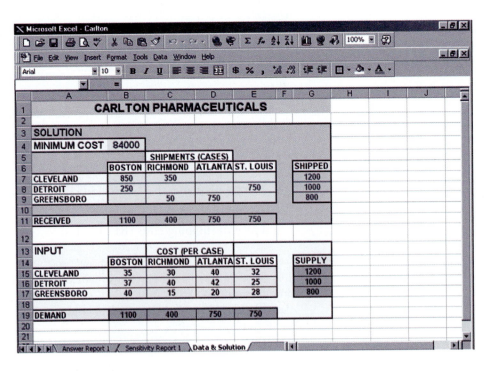

FIGURE 4.9
Optimal Spreadsheet Solution for Carlton Pharmaceuticals

Note that Answer and Sensitivity Reports have been generated so that further analyses can be made. As can be seen from the output, the minimum total shipping cost of $84,000 is obtained by the following shipping pattern:

From	To	Cases
Cleveland	Boston	850
Cleveland	Richmond	350
Detroit	Boston	250
Detroit	St. Louis	750
Greensboro	Richmond	50
Greensboro	Atlanta	750

Any other shipping pattern from the plants to the warehouses will result in a cost higher than $84,000. It is interesting to note that only 6 of the 12 possible transportation routes are used in the optimal solution.[3]

SENSITIVITY ANALYSIS

The Sensitivity Report shown in Figure 4.10 provides the typical information regarding changes to the objective function and right-hand side coefficients.

Microsoft Excel Sensitivity Report
Worksheet: [Carlton.xls]Data & Solution

Adjustable Cells

Cell	Name	Final Value	Reduced Cost	Objective Coefficient	Allowable Increase	Allowable Decrease
$B$7	CLEVELAND BOSTON	850	0	35	2	5
$C$7	CLEVELAND RICHMOND	350	0	30	5	17
$D$7	CLEVELAND ATLANTA	0	5	40	1E+30	5
$E$7	CLEVELAND ST. LOUIS	0	9	32	1E+30	9
$B$8	DETROIT BOSTON	250	0	37	5	2
$C$8	DETROIT RICHMOND	0	8	40	1E+30	8
$D$8	DETROIT ATLANTA	0	5	42	1E+30	5
$E$8	DETROIT ST. LOUIS	750	0	25	9	1E+30
$B$9	GREENSBORO BOSTON	0	20	40	1E+30	20
$C$9	GREENSBORO RICHMOND	50	0	15	17	5
$D$9	GREENSBORO ATLANTA	750	0	20	5	1E+30
$E$9	GREENSBORO ST. LOUIS	0	20	28	1E+30	20

Constraints

Cell	Name	Final Value	Shadow Price	Constraint R.H. Side	Allowable Increase	Allowable Decrease
$G$7	CLEVELAND SHIPPED	1200	-2	1200	250	0
$G$8	DETROIT SHIPPED	1000	0	1000	1E+30	0
$G$9	GREENSBORO SHIPPED	800	-17	800	250	0
$B$11	RECEIVED BOSTON	1100	37	1100	0	250
$C$11	RECEIVED RICHMOND	400	32	400	0	250
$D$11	RECEIVED ATLANTA	750	37	750	0	250
$E$11	RECEIVED ST. LOUIS	750	25	750	0	750

FIGURE 4.10
Sensitivity Report for Carlton Pharmaceuticals

Analysis of the Adjustable Cells Portion of the Sensitivity Report
The reduced costs have the conventional meaning for minimization models. For example, since the reduced cost for shipment of cases from Cleveland to Atlanta is $5 this means that: (1) the cost for shipments between these two cities must be *reduced* by at least $5 per case (to at most $35) before it is economically feasible to utilize this route; and (2) if this route is used under the current cost structure, then the total cost will increase by $5 for each case shipped between these two cities.

[3] In general, as discussed in Supplement CD5 on the accompanying CD-ROM, unless alternative optimal solutions exist, the number of routes used will be at most k, where k is the total number of all supply and demand nodes; it will be at most k − 1 if total supply equals total demand.

The Allowable Increase and Allowable Decrease portion of the report allows us to construct typical ranges of optimality for the cost coefficients. For example, the current cost of shipping cases between Cleveland and Boston is $35. Given an Allowable Increase of $2 and an Allowable Decrease of $5, this implies that the optimal solution will not change as long as this shipping cost is between $30 and $37 per case.

Analysis of the Constraints Portion of the Sensitivity Report   This portion of the Sensitivity Report allows us to analyze the sensitivity of the supplies and demands (the right-hand sides of the constraints). The shadow prices for the plants convey the cost savings realized for extra cases of vaccine produced, whereas the shadow prices for the warehouse demands represent cost savings for *fewer* cases being demanded. For example, the shadow price of −$2 associated with cases produced at Cleveland indicates that if additional cases of vaccine were available at Cleveland, the total shipping cost could be reduced by $2 per case. The $37 shadow price associated with demand at Boston indicates that if *fewer* cases were demanded at Boston, the total shipping cost would be reduced by $37 each. This is indicated by the range of feasibility for Boston, which shows that the cost savings of $37 per unit would be valid for a decrease in demand of up to 250 fewer units (down to 850) but would not be valid for any increase in demand.

Normally, this reduced cost would also mean that if *additional* cases were demanded at Boston, the total shipping cost would increase by $37 per case. But in this model, since total supply equals total demand, the problem would actually become infeasible if any additional cases were demanded at *any* demand node.

MODIFICATIONS TO THE TRANSPORTATION MODEL

Cases may arise in transportation models that require slight modifications to the basic model. Among these are blocked routes or a minimum or maximum shipping requirement from a source to a destination.

Blocked Routes

Sometimes a particular shipping route from a source to a destination may be blocked or unusable for some reason. For example, suppose that because of road conditions due to a hurricane no shipments can be made from Greensboro to Richmond. There are numerous ways to modify the transportation model to reflect this situation, including any *one* of the following:

1. Assign an objective function coefficient to this route (say 1,000,000) that is several magnitudes larger than the largest cost coefficient in the model.

2. Add a constraint to Excel Solver stating that the shipment from Greensboro to Richmond (cell C9) must be 0, as shown in Figure 4.11.

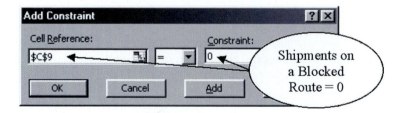

FIGURE 4.11   Using a Constraint to Indicate a Blocked Route

3. Do not include Cell C9 in the Changing Cells. The designation of Changing Cells need not be a continuous range but can be sets of ranges or individual cells separated by commas as shown in Figure 4.12.

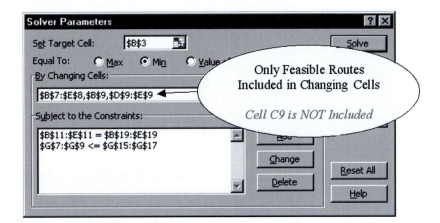

FIGURE 4.12
Eliminating a Blocked Route from Changing Cells

Minimum/Maximum Shipments

Sometimes a minimum shipment for one or more of the routes is required. For example, suppose management at Carlton Pharmaceuticals required that at least 400 cases be shipped from Greensboro to Boston. Because the management scientist has no control over this constraint, he or she can simply set aside 400 cases for this route at the unit cost of $40 per case, or $16,000, reducing the supply at Greensboro to 400 and the demand at Boston to 700. The transportation problem is then solved using these modified quantities, and the $16,000 is simply added to the minimum cost of the revised problem. Alternatively, a constraint could have been added to the original formulation stating that the number of cases shipped from Greensboro to Boston (cell B9) must be at least 400 (see Figure 4.13).

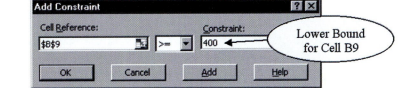

FIGURE 4.13
Adding a Constraint to Indicate a Lower Bound

Likewise, if the number of trucks available to ship product from Detroit to St. Louis (cell E8) limits the total shipment along this route to 500 cases, we simply add the constraint that $E$8 ≤ 500. When many such constraints are to be added, it may be advisable to create another matrix for the maximum shipments and to include all the adjustable cells in the Cell Reference portion of the Add Constraint dialogue box, and the cells containing the maximum shipments in the Constraint portion. In the next section we discuss capacitated transshipment models that include problems of this sort. Such problems can be further complicated by allowing shipments between sources, between destinations, and through intermediate points.

USING THE NETWORK.XLS TEMPLATE TO SOLVE TRANSPORTATION MODELS

If you do not wish to create your own spreadsheet, you may use the network.xls template that is included on the accompanying CD-ROM. This template can be used to solve all types of flow models in this chapter, including transportation models. Using the template requires only that the required problem parameters be entered. For the transportation model, these are the supplies, demand, and unit costs. The requisite entries are resident in the Solver dialogue box for the module, so one merely needs to select Solver and click Solve to generate the results. A complete discussion of how to use the template is presented in Appendix 4.1.

Figure 4.14 shows the results of using the Transportation worksheet on the network.xls template for solving the Carlton Pharmaceutical model. We see that the template yields the same results as we obtained in Figure 4.9.

Carlton-net.xls

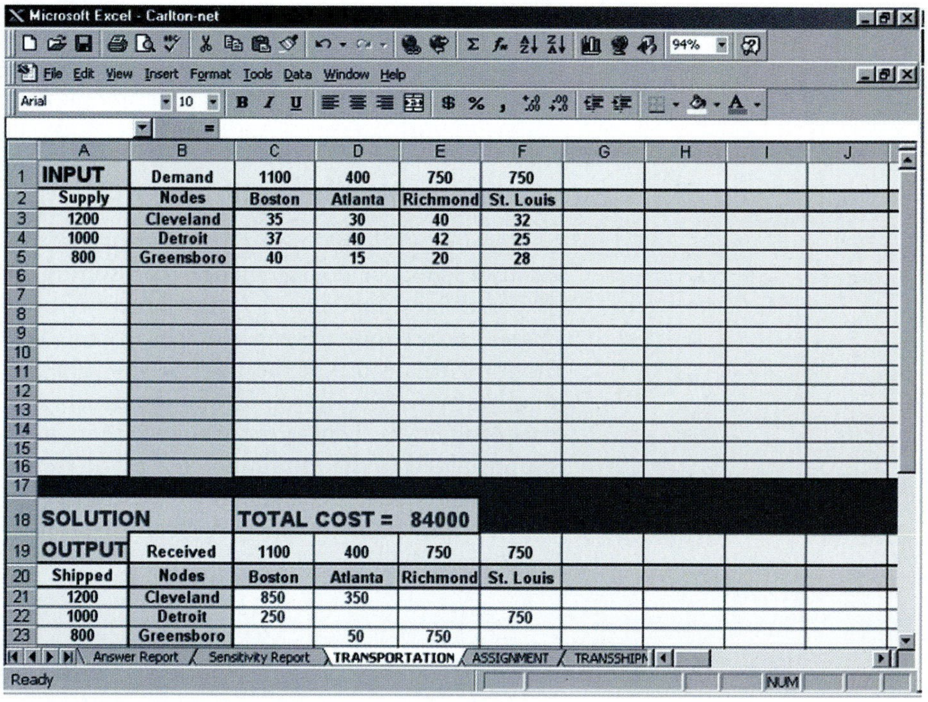

	A	B	C	D	E	F
1	INPUT	Demand	1100	400	750	750
2	Supply	Nodes	Boston	Atlanta	Richmond	St. Louis
3	1200	Cleveland	35	30	40	32
4	1000	Detroit	37	40	42	25
5	800	Greensboro	40	15	20	28
18	SOLUTION		TOTAL COST =	84000		
19	OUTPUT	Received	1100	400	750	750
20	Shipped	Nodes	Boston	Atlanta	Richmond	St. Louis
21	1200	Cleveland	850	350		
22	1000	Detroit	250			750
23	800	Greensboro		50	750	

FIGURE 4.14
Carlton Pharmaceutical Output Using the network.xls Template

USING A TRANSPORTATION MODEL FOR PRODUCTION SCHEDULING

Although transportation models are usually regarded as a way to optimize the transportation of goods, numerous other management science applications have been found to have the same model structure. The problem faced by the Montpelier Ski Company is an example of how a production planning situation can be expressed as a transportation model.

MONTPELIER SKI COMPANY

Montpelier-net.xls

The Montpelier Ski Company is planning its third-quarter production schedule of Glide-Rite snow skis. During the month of July, the company's plant employs a substantial number of college students. This number decreases in August as the students begin preparing to return to school; by September, the company employs no college students. Because the company pays lower wages and benefits to college students than it does to its full-time staff, the number of college students it employs affects both the production capacity and the unit production costs during these months.

Montpelier is expected to have 200 pairs of Glide-Rite skis in inventory as it begins production in July. Forecasted demand and production capacities for the months of July, August, and September are given in Table 4.2.

In addition to this demand from retail customers, Montpelier must have 1200 pairs of Glide-Rite skis available to ship to its company-owned Ski Chalet outlets around the country on September 30. It plans to start October with no inventory and to operate at full-production capacity of 400 pairs of skis in regular time and 200 pairs of skis in overtime throughout the fourth quarter. The production costs of a pair of Glide-Rite skis based on normal wage rates are estimated at $25 for skis produced in July, $26 for those produced in August, and $29 for those produced in September. Although skis produced using overtime have the same material costs, extra labor and overhead costs add $5 to the production cost for a pair of skis produced in July, $6 in August, and $8 in September. The holding cost to store a pair of skis from one month to the next is figured at 3% of their production cost.

Montpelier's management would like to schedule production to minimize its costs for the quarter while meeting the monthly demand forecasts and the September 30 inventory requirement.

TABLE 4.2   Montpelier Ski Company: Pairs of Skis

Month	Forecasted Demand	Production* Capacity
July	400	1000
August	600	800
September	1000	400

*These capacities can be increased up to 50% by scheduling overtime.

SOLUTION

Analysis of Demand

Since Montpelier already has 200 pairs of skis in inventory at the start of the quarter, the net demand to satisfy for the month of July is $400 - 200 = 200$ additional pairs. The demand for August is 600 pairs of skis. In September, Montpelier must have enough supply to meet its forecasted demand of 1000 pairs as well as the desired in-house inventory of 1200 pairs at the end of the month. Hence, the total requirement for September is for $1000 + 1200 = 2200$ pairs of skis.

Analysis of Supplies

For this problem, the production capacities can be thought of as the "supplies." There are two sets of production capacities for the quarter: the set of given capacities of 1000 (July), 800 (August), and 400 (September) for regular time production, and the set of capacities of 500 (July), 400 (August), and 200 (September) for overtime production. Thus, six "sources" of supply (July regular time, July overtime, August regular time, August overtime, September regular time, and September overtime) supply three "destinations" (end of July, end of August, and end of September.) Since total production capacity for the quarter is $1000 + 800 + 400 + 500 + 400 + 200 = 3300$, and total demand is $200 + 600 + 2200 = 3000$, an optimal production schedule that satisfies the demand may be possible.

Analysis of Unit Costs In addition to the unit production costs associated with manufacturing skis in regular time and overtime, Montpelier also incurs inventory storage costs. Skis manufactured in July incur no inventory costs if they are sold in July. If they are sold in August, however, a storage cost of 3% of the production cost will increase the cost of skis manufactured in regular time by $0.75 to $25.75 and for those manufactured overtime by $0.90 to $30.90. If they are sold in September, the total inventory costs are $1.50 and $1.80, respectively, bringing total unit costs to $26.50 per pair for skis produced during regular time and $31.80 per pair for skis produced during overtime.

Skis produced in August and sold in August incur no storage costs. Those sold in September, however, incur a storage cost of 3%, adding $0.78 to the $26 cost of skis produced in regular time and $0.96 to the $32 cost of skis produced in overtime. This brings the total unit costs to $26.78 and $32.96, respectively. Obviously, skis produced in August could not be sold in July, and skis manufactured in September could not be sold in either July or August.

Figure 4.15 shows the transportation network for the Montpelier problem.

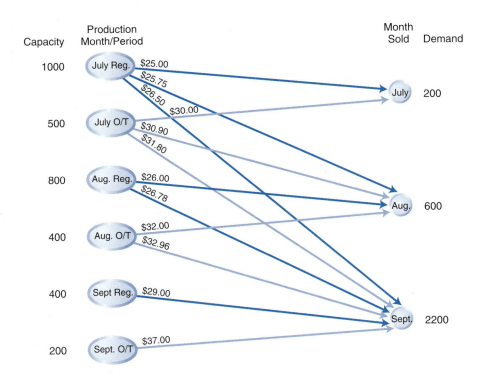

FIGURE 4.15
Montpelier Ski Company
Transportation Network
Representation

COMPUTER SOLUTION

As you see, this is a transportation network model, except that there are no arcs for some supply node to demand node combinations (such as from September Regular Production to July Sales). In order to use the transportation worksheet of the network.xls template, we will block flows on these nonexistent arcs by assigning a very high cost ($100,000) to these arcs. The results from the network.xls template are given in Figure 4.16.

From Figure 4.16 we see that the plant should run at capacity in July, producing 1000 pairs of skis in regular time and 500 pairs in overtime. This would necessitate storing 1500 − 200 = 1300 pairs of skis at the end of July.

Montpelier-net.xls

	A	B	C	D	E
1	INPUT	Demand	200	600	2200
2	Supply	Nodes	July	August	September
3	1000	July Reg	25.00	25.75	26.50
4	500	July O/T	30.00	30.90	31.80
5	800	Aug. Reg.	100000	26.00	26.78
6	400	Aug O/T	100000	32.00	32.96
7	400	Sept. Reg.	100000	100000	29.00
8	200	Sept. O/T	100000	100000	37.00
18	SOLUTION		TOTAL COST =		84394
19	OUTPUT	Received	200	600	2200
20	Shipped	Nodes	July	August	September
21	1000	July Reg			1000
22	500	July O/T	200	300	
23	800	Aug. Reg.			800
24	300	Aug O/T		300	
25	400	Sept. Reg.			400
26		Sept. O/T			

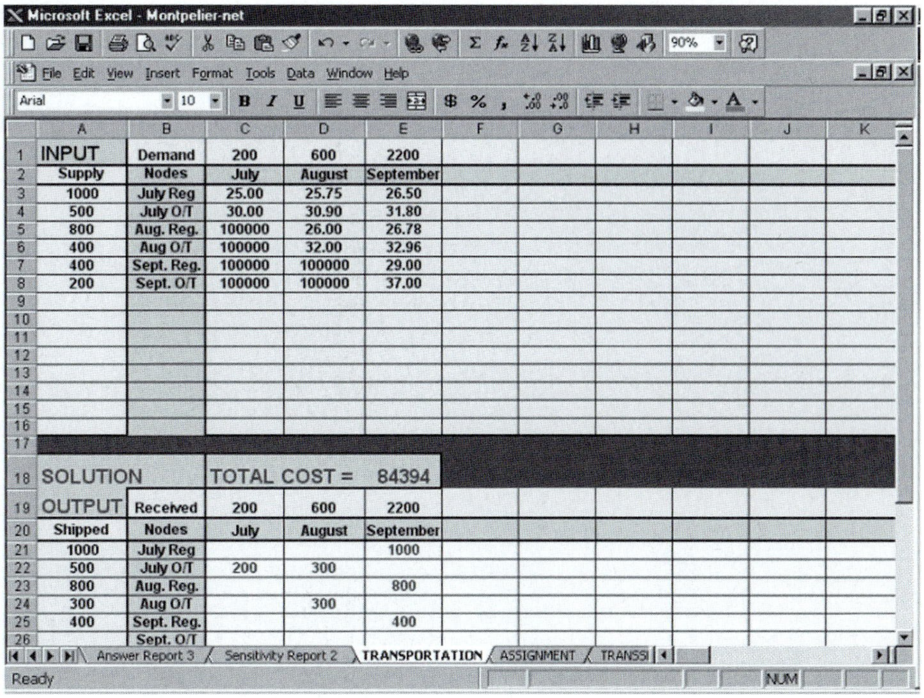

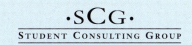

FIGURE 4.16
network.xls Template Solution to Montpelier Ski Model

In August, 800 pairs of skis should be produced in regular time and 300 in overtime. Because demand for August is only 600, this will add another 800 + 300 − 600 = 500 skis to inventory. Hence, 1300 + 500 = 1800 pairs of skis would be stored from August to September. In September only 400 skis should be produced. With retail demand for 1000 pairs in September, the desired 1200 pairs of skis will be available for shipment to the Ski Chalet stores at the end of the month.

The following memo to the production manager of the Montpelier Ski Company documents these results. The memo includes a sensitivity analysis for smoothing overtime production in the quarter motivated by an interpretation of the reduced costs.

·SCG·

STUDENT CONSULTING GROUP

MEMORANDUM

To: Gunter Klaus, Production Manager
Montpelier Ski Company

From: Student Consulting Group

Subj: Third-Quarter Production Planning for Glide-Rite Skis

We have prepared an analysis for Montpelier's production of Glide-Rite skis during the upcoming third quarter (July–September). This analysis considered:

1. The current inventory position of Glide-Rite skis
2. The projected changing demand for skis during the third quarter

3. The company's desire to have an inventory position of 1200 pairs of skis at the end of September for shipment to its Ski Chalet stores

4. The anticipated regular time and overtime production capacities

5. The varying monthly production costs due to the mix of part-time college students and full-time experienced employees

Table I details the forecasts for monthly demand, production costs, and production capacity per pair of skis for the three-month period. The capacity and cost estimates are based, in part, on the number of college students employed by the company during the quarter. The monthly demand estimates are based on historical analysis, orders received to date, and a forecast of the trend in demand.

TABLE I   Third-Quarter Estimates per Pair of Glide-Rite Skis

Month	Forecasted Demand	Production Capacity		Production Costs	
		Regular	Overtime	Regular	Overtime
July	400*	1000	500	$25	$30
August	600	800	400	$26	$32
September	1000	400	200	$29	$37

*Montpelier's projected inventory position at the beginning of July is 200 pairs of Glide-Rite skis.

As per discussion with the Accounting Department, we used a 3% monthly holding cost rate in the analysis.

ANALYSIS

Using the information given, we developed a specially structured model in keeping with the objective of minimizing total third-quarter costs. The resulting production schedule is shown in Table II.

TABLE II   Third-Quarter Recommended Production Schedule, Glide-Rite Skis

Month	Beginning Inventory	Production		Ending Inventory	Monthly Costs			
		Regular	Over-time		Regular	Over-time	Inven-tory	Total
July	200	1000	500	1300	$25,000	$15,000	$1,020	$41,020
August	1300	800	300	1800	$20,800	$ 9,600	$1,374	$31,774
September	1800	400	0	1200	$11,600	$ 0	$ 0	$11,600
							Total	$84,394

Figure I compares the regular time and overtime production on a monthly basis.

Following the assumption that demand and production rates will be relatively constant within each month of the third quarter, Figure II shows the company's inventory position for the quarter. Note that inventory of 1200 pairs of skis at the end of September will be immediately shipped to Ski Chalet incurring no additional inventory costs.

As can be seen from Table II and Figures I and II, the production quantities and the company's inventory position vary substantially from month to month owing to differing monthly production costs.

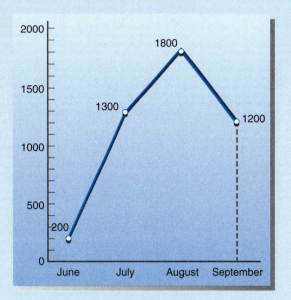

FIGURE I Recommended Third-Quarter Production Schedule— Glide-Rite Skis

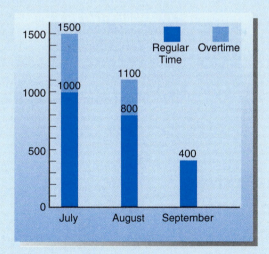

FIGURE II Monthly Inventory Levels—Glide-Rite Skis

September and Fourth-Quarter Production The recommended schedule utilizes overtime heavily in July and August, and not at all in September. Because Montpelier will rely on full-time workers working overtime during the fourth quarter, it may wish to smooth the transition by scheduling some overtime production in September. A minimum cost schedule that meets the company's third-quarter objectives while operating at full overtime capacity during the month of September is presented in Table III.

TABLE III   Third-Quarter Recommended Production Schedule, Glide-Rite Skis (Revised for full overtime production in September)

Month	Beginning Inventory	Production		Ending Inventory	Monthly Costs			
		Regular	Over-time		Regular	Over-time	Inven-tory	Total
July	200	1000	500	1300	$25,000	$15,000	$1,020	$41,020
August	1300	800	100	1600	$20,800	$ 3,200	$1,218	$25,218
September	1600	400	200	1200	$11,600	$ 7,400	$ 0	$19,000
							Total	$85,238

If all full-time workers desire the opportunity to earn extra wages by working overtime, this revised policy, which shifts overtime production of 200 pairs of skis from August to September, would certainly increase goodwill between management and labor while increasing company costs in the third quarter by only $844 (approximately 1%). This relatively small increase might be more than offset by other factors not addressed in this study, such as start-up and shut-down costs for overtime production.

If some workers do not wish to work overtime during September, the total cost for the quarter only increases by approximately $4.10 for each pair of skis produced during September overtime rather than in August. Any such shift will reduce the maximum inventory level during the third quarter as well as the variation in total monthly costs during the last two months of the quarter. We feel that such factors merit consideration when making final decisions for third-quarter production. Thus, unless there is some overriding rationale of which we are unaware, we recommend that management solicit full-time worker input and honor all requests for overtime in September.

If there are any other modifications or scenarios that Montpelier Ski Company desires to investigate, please feel free to contact us.

4.3 Capacitated Transshipment Networks

Sometimes shipments take place by first transporting goods through one or more *transshipment* nodes before reaching their final destination. The transshipment nodes may be independent intermediate nodes (with no supply or demands of their own) or other supply or destination points. Such problems are known as **transshipment problems**. If, in addition, an upper limit is placed on the amount of flow along one or more arcs in the network, the problem is called a **capacitated transshipment** or a **general network model**.

The capacitated transshipment model can be modeled as a linear program and hence can be solved using Excel Solver.[4] The constraints of the model restrict the

---

[4] A more efficient approach, known as the *out of kilter* algorithm, is used in some computer packages to solve capacitated transshipment models. This technique is illustrated in Supplement CD5 on the accompanying CD-ROM.

net flow out of a node (FLOW OUT–FLOW IN) and the maximum flow along any arc. Specifically, the constraints require that:

1. For each *supply node*: The net flow out must not exceed its supply.
2. For each *intermediate node*: The net flow out must be 0.
3. For each *demand node*: The net flow out must equal the negative of the demand (since the net flow *into* the node must equal the demand).
4. For each *arc*: The flow cannot exceed its capacity.

To illustrate the use of the general network model, consider the situation faced by Depot Max, an office supply superstore.

Depot Max-net.xls

DEPOT MAX

Depot Max has six stores located in the Washington, D.C. area. It is Saturday night, and stores in Falls Church and Bethesda have found themselves running low on the Model 65A Arcadia workstation that will be advertised in the Sunday *Washington Post*. They request that 12 and 13 workstations, respectively, be shipped to them to cover the anticipated increase in demand from the ad.

Management has identified stores in Alexandria and Chevy Chase as being able to supply 10 and 17 workstations, respectively. However, the stores can only utilize the space available on delivery trucks currently scheduled to transport other supplies between the stores. The unit shipping costs and the maximum number of workstations that can be shipped between stores is shown in Figure 4.17. Depot Max wishes to transport the available workstations from Alexandria and Chevy Chase to Falls Church and Bethesda, at minimum total cost.

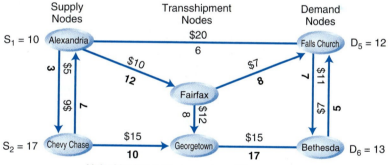

FIGURE 4.17
Capacitated Transshipment Model Network Representation for Depot Max

Unit shipping costs are on top of the arcs. Capacities are in **color** on the bottom of the arcs.

SOLUTION

In this problem, the stores in Alexandria and Chevy Chase have supplies, the stores in Falls Church and Bethesda have demand for supplies, and other stores in Fairfax and Georgetown are transshipment points that have no supply and demand of their own. There are also maximum limits that can be shipped on available trucks. These are the conditions required for using a general network model.

The flows (X_{ij}) must then satisfy the following conditions:

1. Supply nodes: The *net flow out* of the node [(flow out) – (flow in)] cannot exceed the supply at the node.

$$X_{12} + X_{13} + X_{15} - X_{21} \leq 10 \text{ (node 1 Alexandria)}$$
$$X_{21} + X_{24} \qquad - X_{12} \leq 17 \text{ (node 2 Chevy Chase)}$$

2. Intermediate transshipment nodes: The total flow out of the node must equal the total flow into the node, that is, the difference is 0.

$$\begin{aligned} X_{34} + X_{35} - X_{13} &= 0 \text{ (node 3 Fairfax)} \\ X_{46} - X_{24} - X_{34} &= 0 \text{ (node 4 Georgetown)} \end{aligned}$$

3. Demand nodes: The *net flow out* of a demand node [(flow out) − (flow in)] must equal the negative of the demand for the node.

$$\begin{aligned} X_{56} - X_{15} - X_{35} - X_{65} &= -12 \text{ (node 5 Falls Church)} \\ X_{65} - X_{46} - X_{56} &= -13 \text{ (node 6 Bethesda)} \end{aligned}$$

4. Arcs: The flow along each arc must not exceed its upper bound capacity (U_{ij}) or be less than its minimum flow requirements (L_{ij}, which we assume here to be 0).

$$0 \leq X_{ij} \leq U_{ij}$$

Thus the complete mathematical model for the problem depicted in Figure 4.17 is:

$$\begin{array}{ll} \text{MIN} & 5X_{12} + 10X_{13} + 20X_{15} + 6X_{21} + 15X_{24} + 12X_{34} + 7X_{35} + 15X_{46} + 11X_{56} + 7X_{65} \\ \text{ST} & X_{12} + X_{13} + X_{15} - X_{21} \leq 10 \\ & -X_{12} + X_{21} + X_{24} \leq 17 \\ & -X_{13} + X_{34} + X_{35} = 0 \\ & -X_{24} - X_{34} + X_{46} = 0 \\ & -X_{15} - X_{35} + X_{56} - X_{65} = -12 \\ & -X_{46} - X_{56} + X_{65} = -13 \\ & X_{12} \leq 3; X_{13} \leq 12; X_{15} \leq 6; X_{21} \leq 7; X_{24} \leq 10; X_{34} \leq 8; X_{35} \leq 8; X_{46} \leq 17; X_{56} \leq 7; X_{65} \leq 5 \\ & \text{All } X_{ij}\text{'s} \geq 0 \end{array}$$

We can develop a spreadsheet and solve this linear programming model directly. However, in Figure 4.18 we show the results from using the TRANSSHIPMENT worksheet of the network.xls template. The input instructions are given in Appendix 4.1.

Depot Max-net.xls

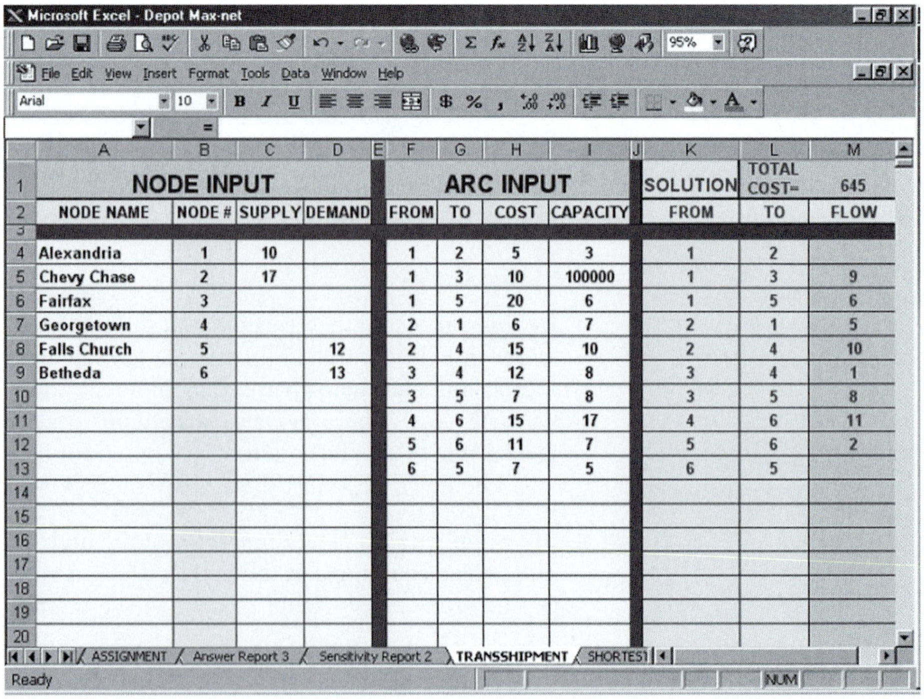

Microsoft Excel - Depot Max-net

NODE INPUT				ARC INPUT				SOLUTION	TOTAL COST=	645
NODE NAME	NODE #	SUPPLY	DEMAND	FROM	TO	COST	CAPACITY	FROM	TO	FLOW
Alexandria	1	10		1	2	5	3	1	2	
Chevy Chase	2	17		1	3	10	100000	1	3	9
Fairfax	3			1	5	20	6	1	5	6
Georgetown	4			2	1	6	7	2	1	5
Falls Church	5		12	2	4	15	10	2	4	10
Betheda	6		13	3	4	12	8	3	4	1
				3	5	7	8	3	5	8
				4	6	15	17	4	6	11
				5	6	11	7	5	6	2
				6	5	7	5	6	5	

FIGURE 4.18 Optimal Solution for Depot Max

As we see from the right side of this screen, the optimal solution is to follow the shipping pattern below to achieve a minimum total shipping cost of $645.

Alexandria–Fairfax	(1–3)	9 workstations
Alexandria–Falls Church	(1–5)	6 workstations
Chevy Chase–Alexandria	(2–1)	5 workstations
Chevy Chase–Georgetown	(2–4)	10 workstations
Fairfax–Georgetown	(3–4)	1 workstation
Fairfax–Falls Church	(3–5)	8 workstations
Georgetown–Bethesda	(4–6)	11 workstations
Falls Church–Bethesda	(5–6)	2 workstations

4.4   Assignment Networks

In many business situations, management finds it necessary to assign personnel to jobs, jobs to machines, machines to job locations within a plant, or salespersons to territories within the distribution area of the business. In each of these cases, management would like to make the most effective or cost-efficient assignment of a set of *workers* (or *objects*) to a set of *jobs* (or *assignments*). The criteria used to measure the effectiveness of a particular set of assignments may be total cost, total profit, or total time to perform a set of operations. Such **assignment models** are characterized as follows:

Assignment Model

1. m workers are to be assigned to m jobs.
2. A unit cost (or profit) C_{ij} is associated with worker i performing job j.

Goal: Minimize the total cost (or maximize the total profit) of assigning workers to jobs so that each worker is assigned one job and each job is performed.

Which set is considered objects and which set assignments is irrelevant. For example, assigning four machines to four projects is equivalent to assigning four projects to four machines, as long as each project is completed and each machine is assigned.

The assignment model has been studied extensively since the early part of the twentieth century, and many solution algorithms have been proposed, including: (1) total enumeration of all possibilities; (2) linear programming; (3) a transportation approach (we will show that the problem is indeed a special case of the transportation problem); (4) dynamic programming (see Chapter 13); (5) a binary branch and bound approach (see Supplement CD4); and (6) an efficient approach developed specifically for this problem, known as the Hungarian algorithm (see Supplement CD5).[5]

The problem faced by Ballston Electronics is typical of problems for which the assignment model is appropriate.

Ballston.xls
Ballston-net.xls

BALLSTON ELECTRONICS

Ballston Electronics, a manufacturer of small electrical devices, has purchased an old warehouse and converted it into a primary production facility. The physical dimensions of the existing building left the architect little leeway for designing locations for the company's five assembly lines and five inspection and storage areas, but these have now been constructed and exist in fixed areas within the building.

[5] Named for two Hungarian mathematicians who proved the underlying theorems on which the algorithm is based. This approach is illustrated in Supplement CD5 on the accompanying CD-ROM.

The following is a simplified view of Ballston's manufacturing process. Products are manufactured simultaneously on each assembly line. As items are taken off the assembly lines, they are temporarily stored in containers (moderately large bins) at the end of each line. At approximately 30-minute intervals, the bins are physically transported from the temporary storage area near the end of the assembly line to one of the five inspection areas within the plant. Those products that pass inspection are stored in a space directly behind the inspection area, while those that do not pass are put into the inspection station's recycling bin.

Because different volumes of product are manufactured at each assembly line and different distances must be traversed from each assembly line to each inspection station, transporting items between each assembly line and inspection area location requires different times. The company must designate a separate inspection area for each assembly line.

An industrial engineer at Ballston has performed a study showing the times needed to transport finished products from each assembly line to each inspection area in minutes (see Table 4.3).

Under the current arrangement, which has been operational since Ballston moved into the building, work performed on assembly lines 1, 2, 3, 4, and 5 is transported to inspection areas A, B, C, D, and E, respectively. This arrangement of 1-A, 2-B, 3-C, 4-D, and 5-E requires $10 + 7 + 12 + 17 + 19 = 65$ man-minutes of labor each half hour. Given that the average worker costs Ballston $12 per hour, Ballston incurs a labor cost of $(\$12)(65/60) = \$13$ during each half-hour period.

Since Ballston runs two eight-hour shifts a day, 250 days per year, it operates $(250)(16) = 4000$ hours a year, or $(4000)(2) = 8000$ half-hour periods annually. Thus, the total annual cost of moving items from the assembly lines to the inspection areas is $(\$13)(8000) = \$104,000$.

Ballston is under severe pressure to cut costs. One possible cost savings would result from a more efficient arrangement for this process. Accordingly, management would like to determine whether some other designation of production lines to inspection areas may require less total time, and, if so, what the annual savings would be.

TABLE 4.3   Minutes to Transport from Assembly Lines to Inspection Areas

		Inspection Area				
		A	B	C	D	E
	1	10	4	6	10	12
	2	11	7	7	9	14
Assembly Line	3	13	8	12	14	15
	4	14	16	13	17	17
	5	19	11	17	20	19

SOLUTION

The problem Ballston Electronics faces is an example of the classic assignment problem consisting of m = 5 workers (the assembly lines) and m = 5 jobs (the inspection areas). Management can use the assignment model to determine how items will be transported from the assembly lines to the inspection areas in order to minimize the "total cost" (expressed in minutes). Each assembly line is assigned to *one* inspection area, and each inspection area services *one* line. Ballston can determine the actual dollar costs of a policy by multiplying the total time required to transport the products by the labor cost of $12 per hour.

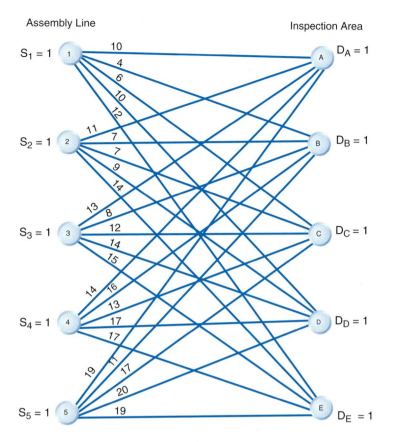

FIGURE 4.19
Ballston Electronics
Assignment Network
Representation

Figure 4.19 shows the network representation for the Ballston assignment model. As you can see, an assignment model can be viewed as a transportation model in which all the supplies and all the demands equal 1. Thus, techniques that solve the transportation model can also be used to solve the assignment model.

The mathematical programming formulation of the assignment model parallels that of the transportation model discussed in Section 4.2, except that the right-hand side for each constraint is 1. The Ballston problem contains 25 variables, X_{ij} (i and j both range from 1 to 5), defined as the number of assembly lines of type i assigned to inspection area j. Obviously, each X_{ij} can only be 1 (if assembly line i is assigned to inspection area j) or 0 (if it is not). But, again, because of the special structure of this problem, these restrictions can be ignored in the problem formulation.

The complete linear programming model for Ballston Electronics is:

X_{ij} = the number of assignments of assembly line i to inspection area j

MIN $10X_{11} + 4X_{12} + \cdots + 20X_{54} + 19X_{55}$
ST
$X_{11} + X_{12} + X_{13} + X_{14} + X_{15} = 1$ (Assembly Line 1 is assigned)
$X_{21} + X_{22} + X_{23} + X_{24} + X_{25} = 1$ (Assembly Line 2 is assigned)
$X_{31} + X_{32} + X_{33} + X_{34} + X_{35} = 1$ (Assembly Line 3 is assigned)
$X_{41} + X_{42} + X_{43} + X_{44} + X_{45} = 1$ (Assembly Line 4 is assigned)
$X_{51} + X_{52} + X_{53} + X_{54} + X_{55} = 1$ (Assembly Line 5 is assigned)
$X_{11} + X_{21} + X_{31} + X_{41} + X_{51} = 1$ (Inspection Area 1 is assigned)
$X_{12} + X_{22} + X_{32} + X_{42} + X_{52} = 1$ (Inspection Area 2 is assigned)
$X_{13} + X_{23} + X_{33} + X_{43} + X_{53} = 1$ (Inspection Area 3 is assigned)
$X_{14} + X_{24} + X_{34} + X_{44} + X_{54} = 1$ (Inspection Area 4 is assigned)
$X_{15} + X_{25} + X_{35} + X_{45} + X_{55} = 1$ (Inspection Area 5 is assigned)
All X_{ij}'s ≥ 0

COMPUTER SOLUTION OF ASSIGNMENT MODELS

One approach used to solve assignment models is to list all worker–job possibilities and choose the one with the lowest cost. For small problems that have only two or three workers and jobs, this may, in fact, be the most efficient method. We can easily show, however, that the number of such possibilities is m!. The problem faced by Ballston Electronics involves m = 5 workers and jobs; thus, 5! = 120 such combinations exist. For problems requiring m = 8 assignments, over 40,000 assignment combinations are possible; for m = 11, almost 40,000,000; and for m = 20, almost 250,000,000,000,000,000.

Thus, we must employ a technique other than direct enumeration for problems of any practical size. Since an assignment model is simply a special case of a transportation model, we can develop a spreadsheet similar to that developed in Section 4.2. Figure 4.20 gives the spreadsheet for the Ballston Electronics model. This spreadsheet is equivalent to the one in Figure 4.9 for the Carlton Pharmaceutical model except that there is no supply column or demand row. Since we know that the "supplies" and "demands" are all equal to 1, we simply enter the number "1" in the right side of the Add Constraint dialogue box, giving the resulting Solver Parameters dialogue box shown in Figure 4.20.

Ballston Electronics.xls

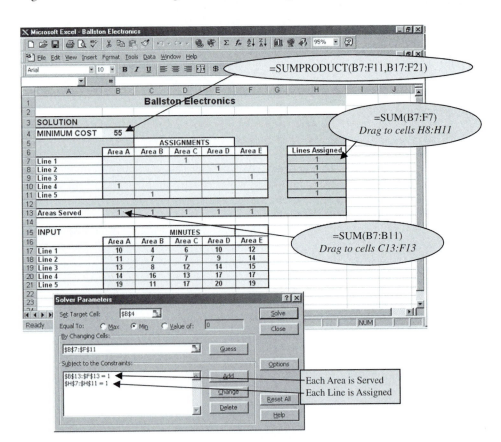

FIGURE 4.20
Spreadsheet Solution for Ballston Electronics

This same result can also be generated using the ASSIGNMENT worksheet of the network.xls template as shown in Figure 4.21.

Using either approach, we see that only 55 man-minutes are required to transport products from the assembly lines to the inspection areas each half-hour. This is accomplished by reassigning line 1 to area C, line 2 to area D, line 3 to area E, line 4 to area A, and line 5 to area B. The labor savings is 10 man-minutes per half hour, or 32(10) = 320 man-minutes per day over the current arrangement, an av-

Ballston-net.xls

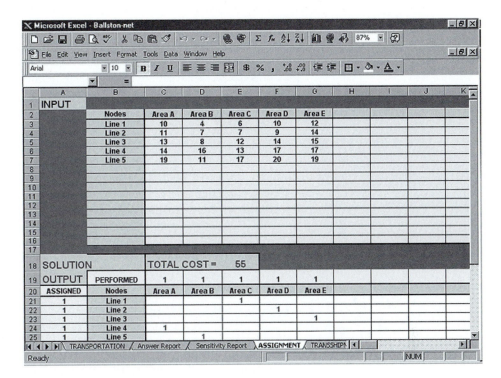

FIGURE 4.21
Solution for Ballston
Electronics Using the
network.xls Template

erage savings of 10/65 = 15.4%. The company will save (0.154)($104,000) =
$16,000 annually.

ASSUMPTIONS AND MODIFICATIONS

In the model for Ballston Electronics, the number of assembly lines to be assigned
exactly equals the number of inspection areas. In a general assignment model in
which workers are assigned to jobs, in order for each job to be completed, the
number of possible workers must be *at least* equal to the number of jobs to be performed. This model parallels a transportation model in which the workers represent supply nodes, each with a supply of 1, and the jobs represent demand nodes,
each with a demand of 1, and the total supply (workers) must be at least equal to
the total demand (jobs). In this case, the constraint for each worker would be
changed from a "=" constraint to a "≤" constraint.

A second modification to the general assignment model is that workers may be
able to perform more than one job. Another is that the objective criterion could be
a maximization. These are easily handled in the Excel spreadsheet by changing the
right-hand side of the corresponding worker constraint to the number of jobs the
worker can perform and by placing the dot in the Max option, of the Solver dialogue box respectively.

4.5 Shortest Path Networks

We have all had occasion to look at a road map and try to plan the best route to
our destination. This may mean finding the route of shortest distance or time, or,
considering the costs of gasoline, maintenance, and tolls, the route of least cost.
Our objective is to choose a path of minimum distance, time, or cost from a starting point, the *start node*, to a destination, the *terminal node*. Such problems are
called **shortest path** models.

Shortest Path Model

1. There are n nodes, beginning with start node 1 and ending with terminal node n.

2. Arcs connect adjacent nodes i and j with nonnegative distances, d_{ij}.

Goal: Find the path of minimum total distance that connects node 1 to node n.

There are several specialized algorithms for shortest path models that greatly reduce the computational time and effort required to determine an optimal solution. The **Dijkstra algorithm** (named for its developer, Dutch researcher E. W. Dijkstra) is particularly efficient for solving the traditional shortest path problem. The details of this algorithm are provided in Supplement CD5 on the accompanying CD-ROM. However, a shortest path model is also a network flow problem that can be solved as a linear program with binary variables.

The situation faced by Fairway Van Lines is a typical shortest path model.

FAIRWAY VAN LINES

Fairway-net.xls

Fairway Van Lines is a nationwide household mover with franchisees located in every state of the continental United States. One of its current jobs is to move goods from a household in Seattle, Washington, to El Paso, Texas.

Fairway trucks travel interstate highways almost exclusively, since average driving speeds are reasonable and driving difficulty is minimal. The move will take place in the summer, so weather conditions should not be a factor.

Figure 4.22 shows the set of interstate highways Fairway trucks can travel to transport the goods. Management would like to determine the route of minimum distance from Seattle to El Paso.

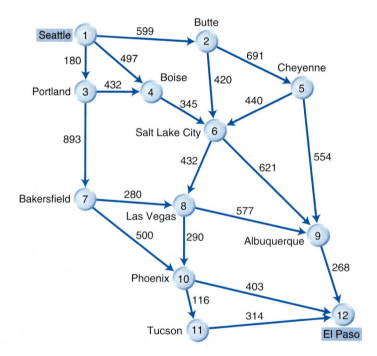

FIGURE 4.22   Fairway Van Lines Shortest Route Network Representation

SOLUTION

The Linear Programming Approach

This problem can be formulated and solved using linear programming with decision variables, X_{ij}, representing utilization of the highway *from* City i *to* City j. X_{ij} is 1 if a truck travels on the highway from City i to City j; it is 0 if it does not. Thus, $X_{12} = 1$ implies that a truck uses the highway *from* Seattle *to* Butte, while $X_{56} = 0$ implies that the truck does not travel the highway *from* Cheyenne *to* Salt Lake City.

The objective is to minimize the total distance traveled from Seattle to El Paso, which is found by summing all the distances (d_{ij}) of the highways traveled. Since $X_{ij} = 1$ for the highways traveled, and $X_{ij} = 0$ for those not traveled, the objective can be expressed as: MINIMIZE $\sum d_{ij}X_{ij}$.

The constraints for the shortest path model require that for each intermediate city:

(The number of highways used to travel into the city) −
(The number of highways traveled leaving the city) = 0

For example, the constraint for Boise (City 4) is:

$$X_{14} + X_{34} - X_{46} = 0$$

This implies that if Boise were on the route, the number of highways traveled into Boise would be 1, and the number of highways traveled leaving Boise would also be 1. Similarly, if Bosie were *not* used on the route, the number of highways traveled into Boise would be 0, as would the number of highways traveled leaving Boise.

In addition, we must ensure that the number of highways traveled out of Seattle is 1 and that the number of highways traveled into El Paso is 1. This is accomplished by adding the constraints

$$X_{12} + X_{13} + X_{14} = 1$$

and

$$X_{9,12} + X_{10,12} + X_{11,12} = 1$$

Since our model is expressed in terms of the net flow *out* of each node, we rewrite this last expression as:

$$-X_{9,12} - X_{10,12} - X_{11,12} = -1$$

Thus the complete linear programming model is:

MIN $599X_{12} + 180X_{13} + \ldots + 314X_{11,12}$

ST
$$
\begin{aligned}
X_{12} + X_{13} + X_{14} &= 1 \quad \text{(Seattle: Flow Out = 1)} \\
X_{25} + X_{26} - X_{12} &= 0 \quad \text{(Butte: Flow out = Flow in)} \\
X_{34} + X_{37} - X_{13} &= 0 \quad \text{(Portland: Flow out = Flow in)} \\
X_{46} - X_{14} - X_{34} &= 0 \quad \text{(Boise: Flow out = Flow in)} \\
X_{56} + X_{59} - X_{25} &= 0 \quad \text{(Cheyenne: Flow out = Flow in)} \\
X_{68} + X_{69} - X_{26} - X_{46} - X_{56} &= 0 \quad \text{(Salt Lake City: Flow out = Flow in)} \\
X_{78} + X_{7,10} - X_{37} &= 0 \quad \text{(Bakersfield: Flow out = Flow in)} \\
X_{89} + X_{8,10} - X_{68} - X_{78} &= 0 \quad \text{(Las Vegas: Flow out = Flow in)} \\
X_{9,12} - X_{59} - X_{69} - X_{89} &= 0 \quad \text{(Albuquerque: Flow out = Flow in)} \\
X_{10,11} + X_{10,12} - X_{7,10} - X_{8,10} &= 0 \quad \text{(Phoenix: Flow out = Flow in)} \\
X_{11,12} - X_{10,11} &= 0 \quad \text{(Tucson: Flow out = Flow in)} \\
-X_{9,12} - X_{10,12} - X_{11,12} &= -1 \quad \text{(El Paso: Flow In = 1 (Flow Out = -1))}
\end{aligned}
$$

All X_{ij}'s = 0 or 1

Solution Using the network.xls Template

We could solve this model straightforwardly by creating a spreadsheet with one column for each decision variable (corresponding to each arc) and one row for each functional constraint (corresponding to each node). In Figure 4.23 we show the results generated from using the SHORTEST PATH worksheet of the network.xls template. Input instructions for this worksheet are given in Appendix 4.1.

Fairway-net.xls

NODE INPUT		ARC INPUT			SOLUTION	TOTAL DISTANCE=	1731
NODE NAME	NODE #	FROM	TO	DISTANCE	FROM	TO	FLOW
Seattle	1	1	2	599	1	2	
Butte	2	1	3	180	1	3	
Portland	3	1	4	497	1	4	1
Boise	4	2	5	691	2	5	
Cheyenne	5	2	6	420	2	6	
Salt Lake City	6	3	4	432	3	4	
Bakersfield	7	3	7	893	3	7	
Las Vegas	8	4	6	345	4	6	1
Albuquerque	9	5	6	440	5	6	
Phoenix	10	5	9	554	5	9	
Tucson	11	6	8	432	6	8	
El Paso	12	6	9	621	6	9	1
		7	8	280	7	8	
		7	10	500	7	10	
		8	9	577	8	9	
		8	10	290	8	10	
		9	12	268	9	12	1
		10	11	116	10	11	
		10	12	403	10	12	
		11	12	314	11	12	

TRANSSHIPMENT / Answer Report / Sensitivity Report / SHORTEST PATH / MAX FLOW

FIGURE 4.23
Solution for Fairway Van Lines Using the network.xls Template

In Figure 4.23 the arcs with a flow value of 1 in column J are the ones that make up the shortest path. Thus the shortest path is: node 1 (Seattle) to node 4 (Boise) to node 6 (Salt Lake City) to node 9 (Albuquerque) to node 12 (El Paso). The minimum distance of 1731 (shown in cell J1) is the sum of the arc lengths along this path.

The Effects of Bidirectional Arcs

Sometimes flow is allowed in both directions along an arc between node i and node j. In addition, the distance from node i to node j may not be the same as the distance from node j back to node i. In cases where flow is allowed in either direction, one would simply treat this situation as if there were two arcs, one from i to j and one from j to i.

4.6   Maximal Flow Networks

Have you ever been stuck in traffic and wondered why you weren't moving? Or have you ever attempted to call your mother on Mother's Day only to get the message, "We're sorry! All circuits are busy at this time. Please try again later." Both problems arise because the system is bottlenecked somewhere between you and your ultimate destination. Designing systems that eliminate or reduce such bottlenecks is a task that can be modeled as a maximal flow problem.

Maximal flow models consist of a single start node, called the *source*, from which all flow emanates, and a terminal node, called the *sink*, into which the flow is deposited. Along the way, the flow travels on arcs connecting intermediate nodes. Each arc has a capacity that cannot be exceeded; the arc capacities need not be the same in each direction. For example, an arc corresponding to a "one-way street" may have a capacity of 400 cars per hour in one direction but a capacity of 0 cars per hour in the other.

The Maximal Flow Model

1. There is a source node (labeled 1), from which the network flow emanates, and a terminal node (labeled n), into which all network flow is eventually deposited.

2. There are $n - 2$ intermediate nodes (labeled $2, 3, \ldots, n - 1$). At each of these nodes, the flow into the node must equal the flow out of the node.

3. There are capacities C_{ij} for flow on the arc *from* node i to node j.

Goal: Find the maximum total flow possible out of node 1 that can flow into node n without exceeding the capacities on any arc.

The situation faced by United Chemical Company can be represented using a maximal flow model.

United-net.xls

UNITED CHEMICAL COMPANY

The United Chemical Company is a small producer of pesticides and lawn care products. One production area contains a huge drum that holds up to 100,000 gallons of a poisonous chemical used in making various insecticides. The drum is routinely filled to a level somewhere between 80,000 and 90,000 gallons. The flow of the chemical is then regulated through a series of pipes to production areas, where the chemical is mixed with other ingredients and blended into finished products.

In Figure 4.24, the drum is denoted by node 1, and the production areas are labeled nodes 2, 3, 4, 5, and 6. Node 7 is the disposal area, where waste is deposited into a large "safe tub." It is then collected from the tub and disposed of in a manner consistent with federal regulations.

The flows during the production process occur at relatively low speeds that do not begin to approach the flow capacities of any of the pipes. But, as part of the company's Emergency Preparedness Plan, the Safety Division of the company

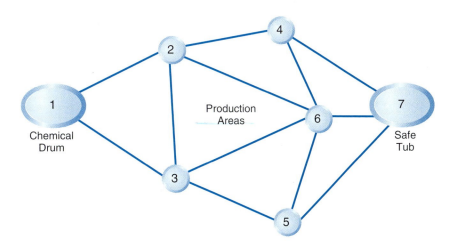

FIGURE 4.24
United Chemical Company
Piping System

must have a procedure to empty the tank completely into the safe tub in the event of an unforeseen emergency. In such an emergency, the company must shut the valves correctly at the production sites to regulate the flow so that the drum containing the poisonous chemicals can empty in the minimum amount of time.

Table 4.4 gives the volume that can flow through each pipe expressed in terms of thousands of gallons per minute.

The plan must determine which valves to open and shut, as well as provide an estimated time for total discharge of the poisonous chemicals into the secure waste area.

TABLE 4.4 Capacity of Pipes (in 1000 gallons/minute)

| | | To | | | | | |
		1	2	3	4	5	6	7
F	1		10	10				
r	2			1	8		6	
o	3		1			12	4	
m	4						3	7
	5						2	8
	6			4	3	2		2
	7							

SOLUTION

Figure 4.25 gives a network representation for this problem. The numbers closest to each node indicate the capacity on the corresponding arc for flow *from* that node. Note that flow is possible in either direction between nodes 2 and 3, 3 and 6, 4 and 6, and 5 and 6. Flow is restricted to one direction for all other arcs.

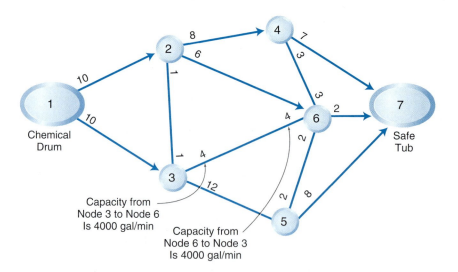

FIGURE 4.25
United Chemical Company
Maximum Flow Network
Representation

A LINEAR PROGRAMMING APPROACH

This problem can easily be formulated as a linear program and solved using a standard linear programming module. Again, because of the network structure, the solution will be integer-valued. Using X_{ij} to represent the flow (in thousands of gallons per hour from node i to node j), we can set out the linear programming formulation for the United Chemical problem as follows:

Objective

Maximize the flow out of source node 1:

$$\text{MAX} \quad X_{12} + X_{13}$$

Constraints

There are no restrictions concerning the net flow out of node 1 or the net flow into node 7. For the intermediate nodes 2, 3, 4, 5, and 6, the total flow out of the node must equal the total flow into the node, that is (flow out) − (flow in) = 0:

$$
\begin{aligned}
X_{23} + X_{24} + X_{26} &\quad - X_{12} - X_{32} &&= 0 \text{ (node 2)} \\
X_{32} + X_{35} + X_{36} &\quad - X_{13} - X_{23} - X_{63} &&= 0 \text{ (node 3)} \\
X_{46} + X_{47} &\quad - X_{24} - X_{64} &&= 0 \text{ (node 4)} \\
X_{56} + X_{57} &\quad - X_{35} - X_{65} &&= 0 \text{ (node 5)} \\
X_{63} + X_{64} + X_{65} + X_{67} &- X_{26} - X_{36} - X_{46} - X_{46} - X_{56} &&= 0 \text{ (node 6)}
\end{aligned}
$$

The flows cannot exceed the arc capacities:

$$
\begin{aligned}
&X_{12} \leq 10; X_{13} \leq 10; X_{23} \leq 1; X_{24} \leq 8; X_{26} \leq 6; X_{32} \leq 1; \\
&X_{35} \leq 12; X_{36} \leq 4; X_{46} \leq 3; X_{47} \leq 7; X_{56} \leq 2; X_{57} \leq 8; \\
&X_{63} \leq 4; X_{64} \leq 3; X_{65} \leq 2; X_{67} \leq 2
\end{aligned}
$$

The flows cannot be negative:

$$\text{All } X_{ij}\text{'s} \geq 0$$

COMPUTER SOLUTION OF THE MAXIMAL FLOW MODEL

Since this model is a linear programming network flow model, we can use the MAX FLOW worksheet of the network.xls template to solve for the maximal flow.[6] Input instructions are given in Appendix 4.1.

Using this worksheet generates the output shown in Figure 4.26. (Flows and capacities are in thousands of gallons.) We see that a maximum flow of 17,000 gallons per minute can be attained by sending flows along the arcs as indicated in the figure. If the drum is full with 100,000 gallons, it will take about 100,000/17,000 = 5.88 minutes to empty the entire contents into the safe tub.

THE ROLE OF CUTS IN MAXIMAL FLOW NETWORKS

Consider drawing any straight line through the network which puts the source node 1 on one side of the line and the terminal node 7 on the other. In Figure 4.27 the line "cuts" the network in two, putting node 1 on one side of the cut and nodes 2, 3, 4, 5, 6, and 7 on the other. Since all flow that runs from node 1 to node 7 must cross this line, the sum of the arc capacities of 20 on the cut (10 from 1–2 and 10 from 1–3) provides one *upper bound* for the maximum flow from node 1 to node 7. The maximal flow would *equal* 20 if, in the optimal solution, the arcs from both 1–2 and 1–3 are saturated.

---

[6] An alternative way to solve this model is to employ a specialized network flow algorithm known as the Ford/Fulkerson method. The basic idea behind this algorithm is to find a path from the source to the sink, with remaining capacity along each of its arcs. Flow is then augmented by the minimum of these remaining capacities, and then all the remaining capacities on this path are adjusted to reflect this increased flow. This process is repeated until there is no path from the source to the sink that has capacity remaining on all of its arcs. This network approach for solving the maximal flow models is detailed in Supplement CD5 on the accompanying CD-ROM.

United-net.xls

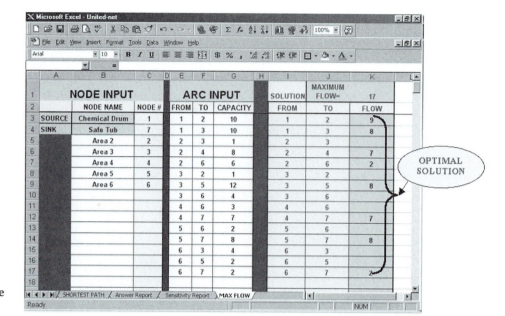

FIGURE 4.26
Optimal Solution for United
Chemical Company Using the
network.xls Template

FIGURE 4.27
Cut Between Nodes (1) and
(2, 3, 4, 5, 6, 7)

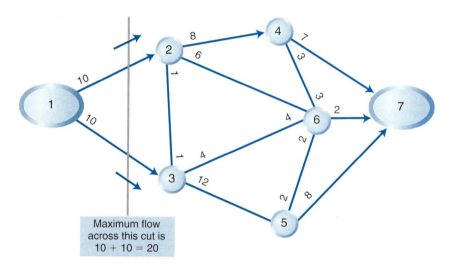

The sum of the arc capacities of *any* cut that puts node 1 on one side and node 7 on the other similarly provides an additional upper bound for the value of the maximum flow. Figures 4.28 and 4.29 illustrate two additional cuts. In Figure 4.28, another upper bound is 27, found by summing the capacities on the arcs from 1–3, 2–3, 2–6, 4–6, and 4–7 (= 10 + 1 + 6 + 3 + 7). The upper bound of 20 from Figure 4.27 is a tighter upper bound, however.

In Figure 4.29 we find still another upper bound by summing the capacities on the arcs from 4–7, 6–7, and 5–7. This gives us an upper bound of 7 + 2 + 8 = 17, which is less than our previously observed upper bound of 20. Because the capacities of any cut in the network place an upper bound on the maximum flow, the cut with the minimum capacity is the tightest upper bound for the total flow in the network. This lowest upper bound is actually met and is the value of the maximal flow. This condition is known as the **Max Flow/Min Cut** result.

The Max Flow/Min Cut Theorem
1. The value of the maximum flow = the sum of the capacities of the minimum cut.
2. The flow of all arcs on the minimum cut will be at their upper bounds.

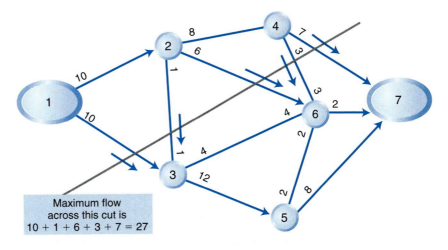

FIGURE 4.28
Cut Between Nodes (1, 2, 4)
and (3, 5, 6, 7)

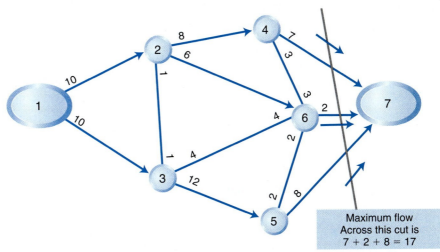

FIGURE 4.29
Cut Between Nodes (1, 2, 3,
4, 5, 6) and (7)

For example, from the template we see that the maximum flow is indeed 17 and that all arcs on the cut of Figure 4.29 are saturated. That is, the flow on each of the arcs on the cut equals the capacity of that arc: the flow on the arc 4–7 is its capacity of 7; the flow on arc 6–7 is its capacity of 2; and the flow on arc 5–7 is its capacity of 8.

4.7 Traveling Salesman Network

We now discuss the first of two models we designate as network connectivity models. The **traveling salesman model** (which some now designate as the "traveling salesperson" model) has been the subject of intense study for over half a century. In its simplest form, the traveling salesman problem can be expressed as follows:

The Traveling Salesman Problem

1. There are m nodes.
2. Unit costs C_{ij} are associated with utilizing the arc from node i to node j.

Goal: Find the cycle that minimizes the total distance required to visit all nodes without visiting any node twice.

The problem gets its name from the situation faced by the traveling salesman who begins at his home city (City m) and visits each of m − 1 other cities (in no particular order) before returning to the home city. He wishes to make this *tour* at minimum total cost, without making a return visit to any city.

The traveling salesman problem, which can be expressed so easily in words, is cumbersome to express mathematically. A problem that involves 20 cities requires over 500,000 linear constraints; 50 cities requires over 500 trillion constraints; 120 cities,[7] well, . . . Efficient algorithms, especially for large problems, have been elusive.

The traveling salesman problem has a variety of scheduling applications, including determining a salesperson's route, ordering drill positions on a drill press, school bus routings, and military bombing sorties. Such problems are also of theoretical importance to mathematicians because they represent a large class of difficult problems known as *NP-hard problems*. If an efficient solution scheme can be found for the traveling salesman problem, the same type of approach could be applied to solving any other NP-hard problem.[8]

A traveling salesman model can be used to solve the problem faced by officials at the Federal Emergency Management Agency (FEMA) after a recent earthquake in southern California.

Fema-assignment-net.xls
Femalp.xls

THE FEDERAL EMERGENCY MANAGEMENT AGENCY

FEMA, the Federal Emergency Management Agency, has responded to a recent earthquake in southern California by setting up a home office in Northridge, near the quake's epicenter. The director in charge is responsible for visiting each of four local offices and returning to the home office in Northridge to file his reports and manage the operations. Given the blockage of certain major transportation arteries, Table 4.5 gives the estimated travel time between each pair of offices.

The director wishes to visit each local office and return to the home office in the shortest time possible.

TABLE 4.5   Travel Time in Minutes Between Offices

	To			
	Office 2	Office 3	Office 4	Home
From				
Office 1	25	50	50	30
Office 2		40	40	45
Office 3			35	65
Office 4				80

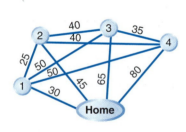

FIGURE 4.30
Federal Emergency Management Agency (FEMA) Traveling Salesman Network Representation

SOLUTION

The FEMA situation is an example of a *symmetric* traveling salesman problem; that is, the travel time between a pair of offices is the same in each direction. For example, the travel time from office 1 to office 2 or from office 2 to office 1 is 25 minutes.[9] Figure 4.30 shows the network representation for this model.

[7] Around 6,000,000,000,000,000,000,000,000,000,000,000,000 linear constraints are required to express a traveling salesman problem of 120 cities.

[8] One example of an NP-hard problem is breaking a code used to encrypt a message.

[9] In some traveling salesman models, the times are asymmetric. For example, if the northbound lanes between office 1 and office 2 were partially blocked, while the southbound lanes were clear, the time going north could be greater than the time going south.

SOLUTION APPROACHES FOR THE TRAVELING SALESMAN PROBLEM

One approach to solving a traveling salesman problem is to list every possible cycle, sum the values on the arcs for each cycle, and select the one yielding the lowest total. A problem with m nodes has (m − 1)! possible cycles. For symmetric problems, since the total cost of a cycle is the same as the total cost of that cycle listing the nodes in reverse order, there are actually only (m − 1)!/2 cycles. The (5 − 1)!/2 = 4!/2 = 12 different cycles for the FEMA problem are listed in Table 4.6.

TABLE 4.6 Possible Cycles for FEMA

Cycle	Total Cost
1. H-O1-O2-O3-O4-H	210
2. H-O1-O2-O4-O3-H	195 ← Minimum
3. H-O1-O3-O2-O4-H	240
4. H-O1-O3-O4-O2-H	200
5. H-O1-O4-O2-O3-H	225
6. H-O1-O4-O3-O2-H	200
7. H-O2-O3-O1-O4-H	265
8. H-O2-O1-O3-O4-H	235
9. H-O2-O4-O1-O3-H	250
10. H-O2-O1-O4-O3-H	220
11. H-O3-O1-O2-O4-H	260
12. H-O3-O2-O1-O4-H	260

Here, H stands for the home office, while O1, O2, O3, and O4 stand for offices 1, 2, 3, and 4, respectively. As this table indicates, the optimal cycle is H-O1-O2-O4-O3-H (or H-O3-O4-O2-O1-H), with a minimum time of 195 minutes.

This method can only be used on the smallest of problems, however. The number of cycles for just 10 nodes is 181,440; for 15 nodes, the number swells to over 840 trillion. Obviously, for most practical problems, direct enumeration is unrealistic, even using the fastest computer and the best computer code.

You might think that this problem is akin to a typical assignment problem; here the workers are the "From" nodes, the jobs the "To" nodes, and the costs the times on the arcs between the nodes. This interpretation results in the symmetric matrix shown in Table 4.7.

TABLE 4.7 Matrix of Times Between Offices

	To				
	Office 1	Office 2	Office 3	Office 4	Home
From					
Office 1	—	25	50	50	30
Office 2	25	—	40	40	45
Office 3	50	40	—	35	65
Office 4	50	40	35	—	80
Home	30	45	65	80	—

When this approach is taken, however, the network.xls template provides the output shown in Figure 4.31. (Note that we have entered a large distance—100,000—for distances from one office to itself to ensure that these impossibilities do not occur.) As you can see, instead of one cycle covering all the nodes, the result is two cycles: O1-O2-H-O1 and O3-O4-O3. These two cycles are called *subtours*.[10]

Fema-assignment-net.xls

	A	B	C	D	E	F	G	H	I	J	K
1	INPUT										
2		Nodes	Office 1	Office 2	Office 3	Office 4	Home				
3		Office 1	100000	25	50	50	30				
4		Office 2	25	100000	40	40	45				
5		Office 3	50	40	100000	35	65				
6		Office 4	50	40	35	100000	80				
7		Home	30	45	65	80	100000				
18	SOLUTION		TOTAL COST =		170						
19	OUTPUT	PERFORMED	1	1	1	1	1				
20	ASSIGNED	Nodes	Office 1	Office 2	Office 3	Office 4	Home				
21	1	Office 1		1							
22	1	Office 2					1				
23	1	Office 3				1					
24	1	Office 4			1						
25	1	Home	1								

FIGURE 4.31
Solving a the FEMA Traveling Salesman Model As an Assignment Model

LINEAR PROGRAMMING FORMULATION FOR THE TRAVELING SALESMAN PROBLEM

In order to build a mathematical model for the traveling salesman problem, we define the variables X_{ij} as the number of arcs used from i to j in the cycle. X_{ij} is 1 if the arc is on the tour, and 0 if it is not. Thus two constraints are as follows.

1. The sum of the arcs used out of each node is 1.
2. The sum of the arcs used into each node is 1.

These are precisely the constraints of an assignment problem. As we discussed earlier, however, using the assignment approach may result in a series of subtours. To prevent subtours from occurring, additional constraints, known as *subtour constraints*, must be added to the model. Unfortunately, there is no compact way to express mathematically the requirement, "No subtours." Instead, an inequality constraint must be created for each possible subtour.

For example, to state that the subtour H-O2-O1-H is not permissible, it must be true that all three arcs (H-O2, O2-O1, and O1-H) are *not* utilized at the same time. Referring to the home office as node 5, we find that this constraint is:

$$X_{52} + X_{21} + X_{15} \leq 2$$

[10] Although using an assignment model to solve a traveling salesman model did not work in this case, another approach for solving relatively small problems with m = 20 or fewer nodes is based on a combination of the assignment model and the branch and bound technique used for solving integer linear programs. This method is illustrated in Supplement CD5 on the accompanying CD-ROM.

To state that the subtour O1-O2-O3-O4-O1 is not permissible, the constraint is:

$$X_{12} + X_{23} + X_{34} + X_{41} \leq 3$$

The traveling salesman problem then has all the constraints of the assignment model (e.g., $X_{11} + X_{12} + X_{13} + X_{14} + X_{15} = 1$, etc., and $X_{11} + X_{21} + X_{31} + X_{41} + X_{51} = 1$, etc.). Also, all possible subtours must be identified and a constraint written forbidding each such subtour possibility. The FEMA problem has five 1-node subtour constraints, ten 2-node subtour constraints, ten 3-node subtour constraints, and five 4-node subtour constraints. These are as follows.

One-Node Subtour Constraints

$$X_{11} \leq 0, X_{22} \leq 0, X_{33} \leq 0, X_{44} \leq 0, X_{55} \leq 0$$

Two-Node Subtour Constraints

$$
\begin{array}{ll}
X_{12} + X_{21} \leq 1 & X_{13} + X_{31} \leq 1 \\
X_{14} + X_{41} \leq 1 & X_{15} + X_{51} \leq 1 \\
X_{23} + X_{32} \leq 1 & X_{24} + X_{42} \leq 1 \\
X_{25} + X_{52} \leq 1 & X_{34} + X_{43} \leq 1 \\
X_{35} + X_{53} \leq 1 & X_{45} + X_{54} \leq 1
\end{array}
$$

Three-Node Subtour Constraints

$$
\begin{array}{ll}
X_{12} + X_{23} + X_{31} \leq 2 & X_{12} + X_{24} + X_{41} \leq 2 \\
X_{12} + X_{25} + X_{51} \leq 2 & X_{13} + X_{34} + X_{41} \leq 2 \\
X_{13} + X_{35} + X_{51} \leq 2 & X_{14} + X_{45} + X_{51} \leq 2 \\
X_{23} + X_{34} + X_{42} \leq 2 & X_{23} + X_{35} + X_{52} \leq 2 \\
X_{24} + X_{45} + X_{52} \leq 2 & X_{34} + X_{45} + X_{53} \leq 2
\end{array}
$$

Four-Node Subtour Constraints

$$
\begin{array}{l}
X_{12} + X_{23} + X_{34} + X_{41} \leq 3 \\
X_{12} + X_{23} + X_{35} + X_{51} \leq 3 \\
X_{12} + X_{24} + X_{45} + X_{51} \leq 3 \\
X_{13} + X_{34} + X_{45} + X_{51} \leq 3 \\
X_{23} + X_{34} + X_{45} + X_{52} \leq 3
\end{array}
$$

Although certain of these constraints are redundant (an even greater number are redundant when the matrix is symmetric), as we have noted, the number of such constraints grows astronomically as the number of nodes in the problem increases. Solving a traveling salesman problem with even a modest number of nodes by linear programming can involve billions of constraints (or more). Even the fastest supercomputers cannot solve such problems in our lifetime.

SOLVING TRAVELING SALESMEN MODELS USING SOLVER

Traveling salesmen models with a modest number of nodes can be solved using Solver by writing the model in the manner we used in Chapters 2 and 3, with one column used to represent each X_{ij} variable and one row required for each constraint. Given the 10 constraints of the assignment model as well as the 30 subtour constraints developed earlier, Figure 4.32 shows the output from using Solver.

As can be seen from the output, the minimal total traveling distance is 195 miles. Since X_{53}, X_{34}, X_{42}, X_{21}, and $X_{15} = 1$, the optimal circuitous route is the one that goes from Home Office (node 5) to Office 3 to Office 4 to Office 2 to Office 1 back to the Home Office.

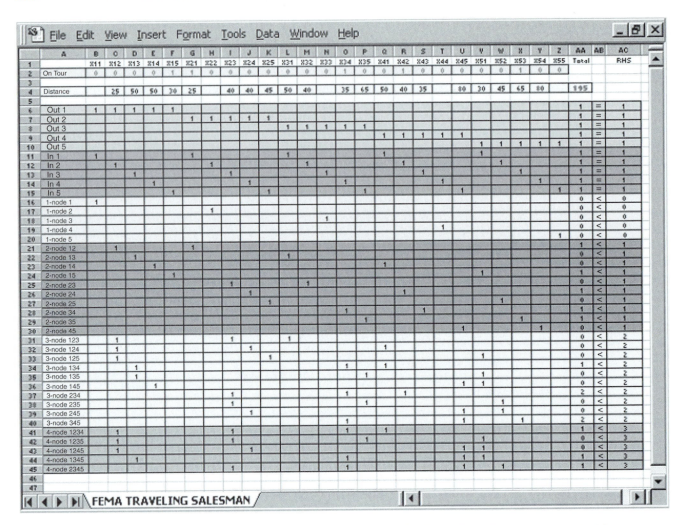

FIGURE 4.32   Optimal Solution to the FEMA Traveling Salesman Model

Fema.xls

SPECIAL CASES

The following "special cases" may arise in applying the traveling salesman problem.

Revisiting Nodes

One special case of the traveling salesman problem occurs when the salesman *is* allowed to return to a city before returning home. For example, suppose a salesman is on the last leg of a trip, returning home to Boston from Los Angeles after already stopping in New York, Chicago, and Dallas. As frequent fliers know, airlines often give better fares to travelers who accept a change of plane rather than a nonstop flight. Thus, although the salesman may have already visited Chicago, it may be worthwhile to go there again on the return flight to obtain the cheaper air fare.

This situation can easily be converted to a traveling salesman problem by first finding the cheapest or shortest path from each city to each other city and substituting this value for the "direct distance" value. Although such prescreening requires additional work, algorithms for finding shortest distances are very efficient (see Section 4.5) and can be found quickly using a computer.

n-Person Traveling Salesman Problem

Consider a school bus routing problem in which n = 15 school buses must pick up students at 80 stops. Each school bus travels to several pickup points, but no two school buses visit the same point. The goal might be to minimize (1) the overall miles traveled, (2) the longest distance traveled by any bus, or (3) the total costs incurred. Such problems are known as *n-person traveling salesman problems*. Solutions to these problems are beyond the scope of this text.

4.8   Minimal Spanning Tree Networks

In Section 4.1, we defined a *tree* as a set of connected arcs that contains no cycles, and we showed that a *spanning tree* that connects all n nodes of a network consists of n − 1 arcs. Although there can be a large number of spanning trees in a network, the **minimal spanning tree** is the one that connects all the nodes in minimal total distance.

Minimal Spanning Tree Model

1. There are n nodes.

2. There are distances d_{ij} between nodes i and j. The arcs are bidirectional.

Goal: Find the set of arcs that connects all the nodes in minimum total distance. (The result is a spanning tree.)

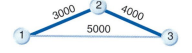

FIGURE 4.33
A Minimal Spanning Tree

A minimal spanning tree approach typically is appropriate for problems for which redundancy is expensive (such as building trails between campsites in a national park) or the flow along the arcs is considered instantaneous (such as electrical current). To illustrate the concept of a minimal spanning tree, consider the simple three-node problem depicted in Figure 4.33.

Suppose the arcs represent the cost (in $1000s) to connect three campsites. If the arcs between location 1 and location 2 and between location 2 and location 3 are selected, it will cost $3000 + $4000 = $7000 to connect all three locations. While the cost from location 1 to location 3 is $7000, compared to $5000 for a direct route between the two, the optimal strategy is to give up this convenience to minimize the overall total construction cost.

To further illustrate the use of a minimal spanning tree model, consider the situation faced by the Metropolitan Transit District.

Metropolitan.xls

THE METROPOLITAN TRANSIT DISTRICT

The Metropolitan Transit District has held public hearings concerning the development of a new light rail transportation system for the city of Vancouver. As a result of these hearings, the district has decided to build a system linking eight residential and commercial centers at minimum cost to taxpayers.

The district's engineers have drafted a series of feasible lines, as illustrated in Figure 4.34. The district has solicited sealed bids from contractors interested in building some or all of the system, and determined the lowest feasible bid for each possible link. These costs may be further reduced on certain routes due to private funding pledges made by local businesses that have a stake in the design of the system.

The numbers on the arcs in Figure 4.34 represent the lowest bid less any amount pledged by local businesses (in $1 million). The district must decide which set of routes to select in order to minimize the total cost to taxpayers, while still providing a way to travel from any one of the centers to any of the other seven centers served by the system.

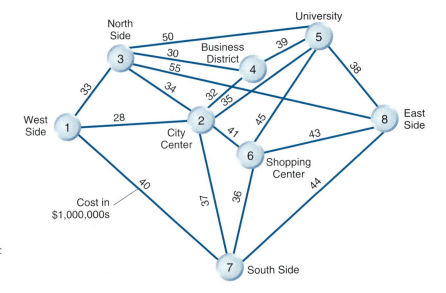

FIGURE 4.34
Metropolitan Transit District
Spanning Tree Network
Representation

SOLUTION

The problem is to find the most cost-effective way to connect all eight centers. This is precisely the situation that can be modeled using a minimal spanning tree approach.

A NETWORK APPROACH

Minimal spanning tree models do not lend themselves to linear programming formulations. Fortunately, very easy (some might even say trivial) algorithms can be applied to the network to solve the minimal spanning tree problem. These algorithms, which we illustrate here and in Supplement CD5 on the accompanying CD-ROM, are from a class of techniques known as **Greedy algorithms**.

One Greedy algorithm that is perhaps the easiest to implement visually is to simply be "greedy" and start by including the two smallest arcs as a "selected set" for the tree. Then the next smallest arc will be added unless it forms a cycle with the arcs already in the selected set. This process of selecting the next smallest arc unless it forms a cycle with those already in the selected set is repeated until all nodes are connected. For a network with n nodes, the spanning tree will require exactly n − 1 arcs.

For the Metropolitan Transit District model in Figure 4.34, the process is shown in the following list. Note that (1,2) means the node from node 1 to node 2 or from node 2 to node 1.

Arc Distance	Arc	Added to Selected Set?
28	(1,2)	YES—smallest
30	(3,4)	YES—second smallest
32	(2,4)	YES—does not form a cycle
33	(1,3)	NO—forms a cycle with (1,2), (2,4), (3,4)
34	(2,3)	NO—forms a cycle with (2,4), (3,4)
35	(2,5)	YES—does not form a cycle
36	(6,7)	YES—does not form a cycle
37	(2,7)	YES—does not form a cycle
38	(5,8)	YES—does not form a cycle

At this point, 7 arcs (n − 1) have been selected and all 8 nodes are connected. Thus, the minimum taxpayer cost of building the light rail transit system is $236 million, using routes from the City Center to West Side, Business District, University, and South Side, and routes from Business District to North Side, from East Side to University, and from South Side to Shopping Center. The minimal spanning tree giving the recommended transit links is shown in Figure 4.35.

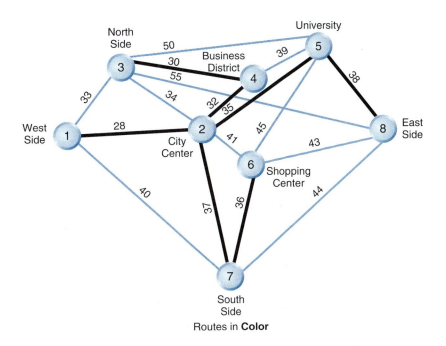

FIGURE 4.35
Metropolitan Transit District Minimum Cost Light Rail System

A second form of the greedy algorithm begins by selecting the arc with the smallest arc length. This time, at each subsequent iteration, arcs are added *only if the arc connects to an already selected arc* and it does not form a cycle. In this approach, the selected arcs at any iteration form a tree and exactly one new node is connected to the tree at each iteration. Arcs can be skipped at one iteration because they do not connect to arcs in the selected set, but could be added in a subsequent iteration as more nodes are added to the tree. At the end of n − 1 iterations, the tree will be a minimal *spanning* tree.

This added condition, that an arc is added only if it connects to the selected set, is easier to program and monitor on a spreadsheet. Although standard spreadsheet operations do not allow these operations to be performed without programming a macro, Figure 4.36 shows how we can use a spreadsheet to perform the process manually. Initially, all arc lengths and their starting and ending nodes are listed in columns A, B, and C. Then by highlighting all three columns and using the sort ascending feature on the standard toolbar (AZ↓), the arcs will be arranged in order from the smallest to the largest.

By having the arcs in ascending order, the selected arcs of the tree can be manually selected from the smallest arc that adds *exactly one* more node to the selected set. In Figure 4.36 we show which of these arcs are selected at each iteration in column E, and we keep track of the selected nodes after the arc is selected in columns F through M. The formulas in column N print the distance of the arc if it is added at a particular iteration. The formula in cell Q5 keeps a running total of the selected arc distances.

Metropolitan.xls

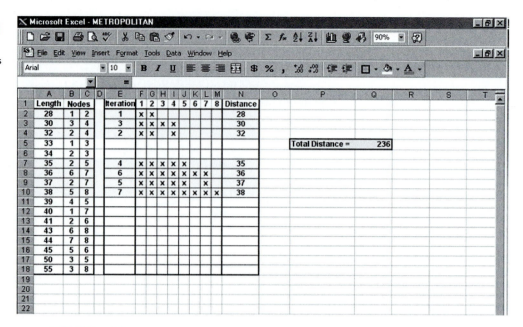

FIGURE 4.36   Optimal Solution for Metropolitan Transit

Let us illustrate how this procedure was implemented to determine the minimal spanning tree for the Metropolitan Transit District in Figure 4.36.

Iteration 1:   We begin the algorithm by selecting the arc of minimum distance (28) which is from node 1 to node 2. We enter a 1 in cell E2 and "x's" into cells F2 and G2 to denote the selected set after this iteration. Its distance (28) will appear in cell N2 because of the formula entered in that cell.

Iteration 2:   The next shortest arc (30) from node 3 to node 4 is not selected at this iteration since neither node 3 nor node 4 is in the connected set. Thus we drop down to the next shortest arc (32) from node 2 to node 4. Since *one* of these nodes (node 2) is in the selected set and one is not (node 4), this arc is added to the spanning tree. We put a 2 in cell E4 (to indicate that it was selected at the second iteration) and x's in cells F2, G2, and I2 to denote that the selected set now consists of nodes 1, 2, and 4.

Iteration 3:   The unselected arc of minimum distance (30) is again the one from node 3 to node 4. Since now one node is in the selected set (node 4) and one is not (node 3), the arc is added this time. The selected set now consists of nodes 1, 2, 3, and 4.

Iteration 4:   The unselected arc of minimum distance (33) is from node 1 to node 3. Since both of these nodes are in the selected set, this arc will never be added to the tree and can be dismissed from further consideration. The same is true for the next unselected arc (34) from nodes 2 to 3. Continuing down the list, the next shortest arc (35) is from a node in the selected set (node 2) and one in the unselected set (node 5). Thus it is added to the spanning tree, and the connecting set consists of nodes 1, 2, 3, 4, and 5.

Iteration 5:   Given that the arcs from 1 to 3 and 2 to 3 will not be selected, the unselected arc of minimum distance (36) is the one from node 6 to node 7. However since neither of these are in the selected set, it is skipped at this iteration. Rather, the next shortest arc (37), having one node in the connected set (node 2) and one from the unselected set, is added to the spanning tree. The connected set now consists of nodes 1, 2, 3, 4, 5, and 7.

Iteration 6: Now the arc from the unselected node 6 to the selected node 7 (36) is added, and the selected set consists of nodes 1, 2, 3, 4, 5, 6, and 7.

Iteration 7: The next shortest arc (38) is from the connected node 5 to the unselected node. Since the selected set now consists of all 8 nodes, this completes the minimal spanning tree.

4.9 Summary

Many typical managerial situations can best be expressed using network models. Network models—problems expressed in terms of nodes and arcs and functions defined on the nodes and/or arcs—are easy to work with. Because of their special structure, many network problems provide efficient solution techniques that are streamlined versions of linear programming algorithms or that do not rely on linear programming solution techniques at all to obtain an optimal solution.

Network models fall into two basic groups: (1) network flow models and (2) network connectivity models. Network flow models can be formulated as linear programs that can be easily solved using spreadsheets or specialized software or spreadsheet templates such as network.xls.

Network connectivity models include the traveling salesman model and the minimal spanning tree model. Minimal spanning tree models cannot be expressed as a linear program, while the number of constraints required to define a traveling salesman model of any real size prohibits the use of linear programming in general, and spreadsheets in particular, as useful solution strategies.

The following table summarizes the characteristics of each of the network models introduced in this chapter and lists some potential applications.

Network Model	Description	Applications
Transportation/Transshipment Capacitated Transshipment	Find the total minimum cost of shipping goods from supply points to destination points.	• Department store branch shipments • Monthly production scheduling • Marketing strategy approaches • Emergency supply allocation
Assignment	Find the minimum cost assignment of objects to tasks.	• Salesmen to territories • Pilots to aircraft • Programming tasks to programmers • Machines to locations
Shortest Path	Find a path through *some* of the nodes of the network which minimizes the total distance from a source node to a destination node.	• Highway travel between cities • New road construction • Facility location • Equipment replacement
Maximal Flow	Find the maximum total flow possible from a source node to a sink mode without violating arc capacities.	• Traffic flow systems • Production line flows • Shipping
Traveling Salesman	Find the minimum cost of visiting *all* nodes of a network, returning to a starting node without repeating any node.	• Scheduling service crews • Designing robotics manufacturing equipment • Scheduling security patrols
Minimal Spanning Tree	Find the minimum total distance that connects *all* nodes in the network.	• Sewer system design • Computer system layout • Cable television connections • Mass transit design

ON THE CD-ROM

- Template for solving network flow models — **network.xls**
- Excel spreadsheet for a transportation model — **Carlton.xls**
- Excel spreadsheet for an assignment model — **Ballston.xls**
- Excel spreadsheet of a linear programming model for a traveling salesman model — **Fema.xls**
- Excel template spreadsheet for a transportation model — **Carlton-net.xls**
- Excel template spreadsheet for a transshipment model — **Office Depot-net.xls**
- Excel template spreadsheet for an assignment model — **Ballston-net.xls**
- Excel template spreadsheet for a shortest path model — **Fairway-net.xls**
- Excel template spreadsheet for a maximum flow model — **United-net.xls**
- Excel spreadsheet for a minimal spanning tree model — **Metropolitan.xls**
- Algorithms for Solving Network Models — **Supplement CD5**
- Problem Motivations — **Problem Motivations**
- Problems 41–50 — **Additional Problems**

APPENDIX 4.1

Using the network.xls Template

A4.1.1 General Information

- The network.xls template can be used to solve the following network flow models: (1) transportation; (2) transshipment; (3) assignment; (4) shortest path; and (5) maximum flow.

- Each model has its own worksheet on the template and has a Solver dialogue box preprogrammed so that the user only has to call Solver and click:

- The size of the model that can be solved is limited. Model sizes are given in the discussion of each worksheet. Some of this limitation is due to the fact that the standard version of Solver allows for a maximum of 200 decision variables.

- Solver is preprogrammed to solve the maximum size problem. Hence the solution time may be a couple of seconds rather than virtually instantaneously.

- When saving a particular model, Excel will save the entire workbook, including the worksheets for the four modules you did not use. This can utilize a lot of space on your disk or hard drive. The following is recommended:

  1. Open network.xls and select the appropriate worksheet for your module.
  2. From the Edit menu select Move or Copy Sheet.
  3. As shown in Figure A4.1, in the Move or Copy dialogue box, select (new book) from the pull down menu under "To book:". Also check "Create a copy." You can rename the worksheet by using "Save As" from the File menu.
  4. Click OK.

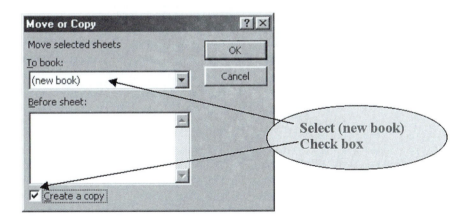

FIGURE A4.1
Move or Copy Dialogue Box

- You can add to or modify the entries in the default Solver dialogue box. Although this is not recommended, eliminating some of the default rows and columns can speed up the solution time and eliminate meaningless entries in the Answer and Sensitivity Reports. Note that some of the entries refer to hidden columns that you may not wish to modify.

A4.1.2   The Transportation Worksheet

Default Size Limitations: 14 sources and 14 destinations
Default objective criterion: Minimization
    If objective criterion is maximization, change bullet in Solver dialogue box in MAX (Figure A4.2).

1. Enter source names in column B and destination names in row 3
   Note: These will automatically be copied to the source and destination names for the solution, further down in column B and in row 20 respectively.

2. Enter supplies in column A and demands in row 2
   Requirement: (Total Supply) $\geq$ (Total Demand), or else the problem will be infeasible. If (Total Demand) $>$ (Total Supply), add a supply node having a supply equal to the excess demand and unit shipping costs to all demand nodes of 0.

3. Enter unit Shipping Costs in cells C3:P16.

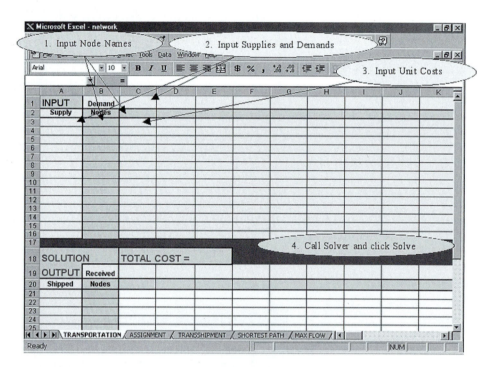

FIGURE A4.2   Input for the Transportation Worksheet

A4.1.3   The Assignment Worksheet

Default Size Limitations: 14 workers and 14 tasks
Default objective criterion: Minimization
    If objective criterion is maximization, change bullet in Solver dialogue box to MAX (Figure A4.3).

1. Enter worker names in column B and task names in row 2
    Note: These will automatically be copied to the worker and task names for the solution further down in column B and in row 20 respectively. The number of workers (rows) must be at least as great as the number of tasks (columns) or the problem will be infeasible. If the number of workers is less than the number of tasks, add the required number of workers with 0 costs for all tasks.

2. Enter Worker-Task Costs in cells C3:P16

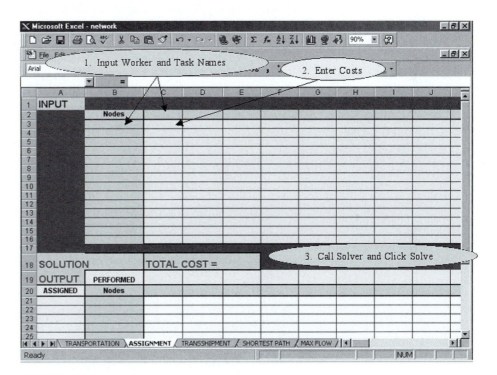

FIGURE A4.3   Input for the Assignment Worksheet

A4.1.4 The Transshipment Worksheet

Default Size Limitations: 30 total nodes and 60 total arcs
Default objective criterion: Minimization
    If objective criterion is maximization, change bullet in Solver dialogue box to MAX (Figure A4.4).

1. In the Node Input Section enter:
- Node names in column A
- The corresponding supply in column B (if the node is a supply node)
- The corresponding demand in column C (if the node is a demand node)

Notes:
(1) Node numbers will automatically be assigned in column B when the node name is entered.
(2) Rows 1, 2, and 3 will always be on the screen.
(3) The total supply must be at least as great as the total demand or the problem will be infeasible. If the total supply is less than the total demand, add a node with supply equal to the excess demand and add arcs having 0 shipping costs from this node to all nodes with demand.

2. In the Arc Input Section, for each arc enter:
- Its beginning node, ending node, unit shipping cost, and capacity in columns F, G, H, and I, respectively

Notes:
(1) If there is no capacity,
do not leave the entry in column I blank; enter a large number.
(2) The beginning and ending node numbers will automatically be copied to the Solution section in columns K and L.
(3) Rows 1, 2, and 3 will always be on the screen.

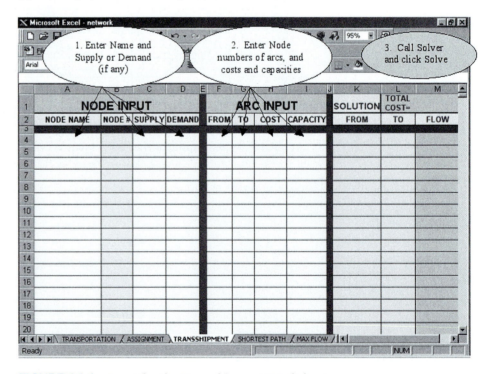

FIGURE A4.4   Input for the Transshipment Worksheet

A4.1.5   The Shortest Path Worksheet

Default Size Limitations: 50 total nodes and 100 total arcs (Figure A4.5)

1. In the Node Input Section enter node names in column A

Notes:
(1) Node numbers will automatically be assigned in column B when the node name is entered.
(2) Rows 1 and 2 will always be on the screen.

2. In the Arc Input Section for each arc, enter its beginning node, ending node, and corresponding arc distance in columns D, E, and F, respectively

Notes:
(1) The beginning and ending node numbers for each arc will automatically be copied to the Solution section in columns H and I respectively.
(2) Rows 1 and 2 will always be on the screen.

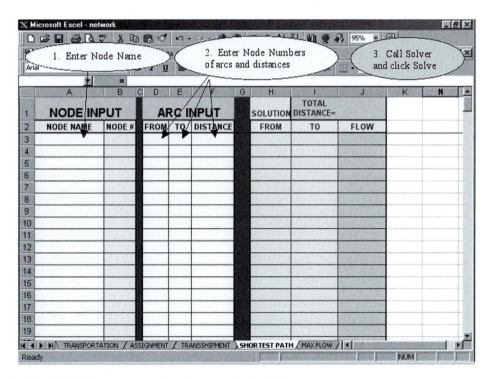

FIGURE A4.5   Input for the Shortest Path Worksheet

A4.1.6 The MAX FLOW Worksheet

Default Size Limitations: 50 total nodes and 100 total arcs (Figure A4.6)

1. In the Node Input Section enter node names. The source node must be entered in cell B3 and the sink node must be entered in cell B4. Then the other nodes are entered in column B beginning with row 5.

Notes:
(1) Node numbers will automatically be assigned when the node name is entered, and the Sink node will be assigned the highest number.
(2) Rows 1 and 2 will always be on the screen.

2. In the Arc Input Section for each arc, enter its beginning node, ending node, and corresponding arc capacity in columns E, F, and G, respectively.

Notes:
(1) The beginning and ending node numbers for each arc will automatically be copied to the Solution section in columns I and J.
(2) Rows 1 and 2 will always be on the screen.

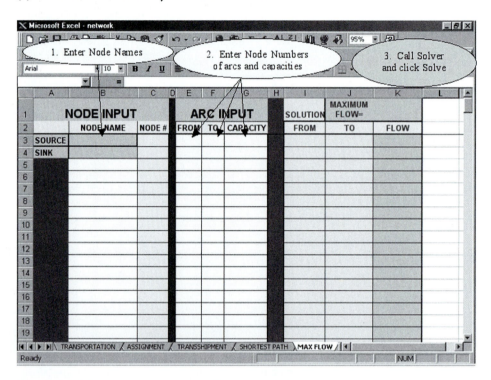

FIGURE A4.6 Input for the MAX FLOW Worksheet

Problems

1. NW Lumber is a logging and lumber processor located in northern California, Oregon, and Washington. NW is currently logging in an area near Garberville, California, as well as Grant's Pass, Oregon, and Willard, Washington. It owns and operates processing plants in Eureka, California, Crescent City, California, and Coos Bay, Oregon. For the upcoming month, processing capacities are 2000 tons at Eureka, 1400 tons at Crescent City, and 1500 tons at Coos Bay. It is forecasted that NW could harvest 1600 tons of timber during the month at each of the three logging locations.

   The following table gives the transportation costs per ton. How should the 4800 tons of timber be shipped to the processing plants in the coming month in order to minimize total transportation costs for NW Lumber?

   Transportation Cost per Ton

	To		
	Eureka	Crescent City	Coos Bay
From			
Garberville	$175	$225	$250
Grant's Pass	$150	$100	$100
Willard	$300	$275	$200

2. The city of Beckley, West Virginia, has solicited bids from interested construction firms for five projects it wishes to complete during this fiscal year. Six firms have submitted bids on the projects, as indicated in the table for problem 2. (An "X" means that the firm did not submit a bid for that project.)

   Since the projects will be ongoing simultaneously, no firm will be able to complete more than one project.
   a. How should the contracts be awarded?
   b. If the total amount budgeted this year for these capital projects is $2 million, can all the projects be funded? If not, list some options the city of Beckley may wish to consider.

3. Calimex International is an agricultural company that has two primary regions for growing tomatoes, one in the Coachella Valley of California, the other in northern Mexico. During the peak season, tomatoes are picked daily and sent to one of three inspection stations in southern California. After the tomatoes have been inspected, they are transported to one of four packing houses.

   Each day 4500 pounds of tomatoes are picked in California, and 4000 pounds are picked in Mexico. Each inspection station can process over 10,000 pounds per day. Since total daily supplies amount to only 8500 pounds, capacity at the inspection stations imposes no constraints on the shipments. That is, all tomatoes that arrive at any of the three inspection stations can be processed and sent on to the packaging plants. The packaging plants can handle 1500, 2500, 2000, and 2500 pounds per day, respectively.

   The table for problem 3 gives the shipping cost per truck from each growing region to each inspection station and from each inspection station to each packaging plant; 500 pounds of tomatoes are shipped in each truck.
   a. Find the shipping pattern that minimizes transportation costs from the growing area to the packaging plants.
   b. Suppose a maximum of three trucks are available to travel each route. Which shipping pattern minimizes transportation costs from the growing areas to the packaging plants?
   c. The situation modeled here consists of picking and loading tomatoes in the growing region, inspecting them at the inspection stations, and packing them at the packaging plants. Why might the assumption that the flow into the transshipment points (inspection stations) equals the flow out of the transshipment points be violated?

Problem 2

	Refurbish Courthouse	Build New Library	Modernize Playground	Build Parking Structure	Improve City Park
Millard Associates	$800,000	$750,000	$300,000	$450,000	$200,000
QM Construction	$950,000	$725,000	X	$500,000	$275,000
Latham Brothers	X	X	$200,000	X	$225,000
Beckley Engineering	$650,000	$700,000	$250,000	$400,000	$225,000
WRT, Inc.	$700,000	$800,000	$175,000	$300,000	$300,000
B&P Enterprises	$850,000	$900,000	$270,000	$475,000	X

Problem 3

	Inspection Station				Packaging Plant			
	1	2	3		1	2	3	4
Region				Inspection Station				
California	$200	$400	$900	1	$1000	$1400	$1800	$2000
Mexico	$600	$200	$400	2	$1800	$1200	$1400	$2000
				3	$2800	$1600	$1400	$ 800

4. A recent tragic fire in Carbonville, Illinois, has prompted the City Council to draft a new ordinance requiring all buildings to have fully operational sprinkler systems installed by the end of the year. The Talcon Building is affected by this ordinance. From the original blueprints, engineers have designed positions for the location of eight powerful sprinkler heads that are to be connected to the sprinkler controller. The feasible connections between these eight sprinkler heads and the controller with distance shown in feet are depicted in the figure for problem 4.
   a. What design of the sprinkler system will minimize the total amount of pipe required (and hence give the maximal water pressure throughout the system)?
   b. Suppose the engineers discovered that the connection between Office #1 and the Storage Room could not be made because of a recently installed air conditioning duct. What design of the sprinkler system would now minimize the total amount of pipe required?

Problem 4

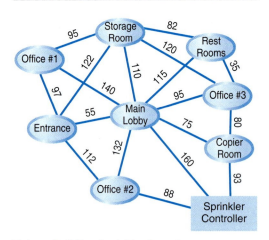

Talcon Building Sprinkler Location

5. Clare Walker sells hospital supplies throughout the Midwest and Plains states. She depends on small, local commuter airlines for transport between cities. The following table gives the current air fares between the cities she must visit this week, as well as between these cities and her home in Kansas City. In which order should Clare visit the cities to minimize her total air fare cost for the week?

	To			
	Lincoln	Daven-port	St. Louis	Tulsa
From				
Kansas City	$200	$260	$ 75	$125
Lincoln		$330	$145	$180
Davenport			$100	$300
St. Louis				$110

6. Jo Yu, vice president of Broadtech, Inc., a distributor of PC clone computers located in San Bernardino, California, must travel to the port of Los Angeles, located in San Pedro, California, to pick up a shipment of computers from Taiwan. A freeway map of southern California with distances in miles shown on the arcs is given.
   a. What route should Jo take to minimize the distance between his office and San Pedro?
   b. Suppose Jo is traveling during the morning rush hour. Jo's average speed on east-west routes during rush hour is only 25 miles per hour, whereas he averages 40 miles per hour on north-south routes. (The routes considered east-west routes are in black; the north-south routes are in blue.) What route should Jo take to minimize the travel time between his office and San Pedro?

Problem 6

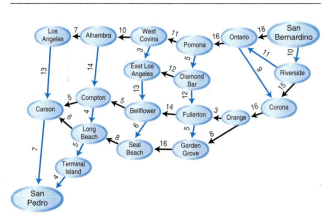

Southern California Freeway System

7. Silverton is the latest planned community to be proposed for central Florida. The community will have two exits onto Interstate 4 and will consist of 11 small roads. The traffic capacities of each road (in terms of hundreds of vehicles per hour) are provided on the following map of the project. What is the maximal hourly flow of vehicles that can travel from the north exit of Interstate 4 through Silverton to the south exit of Interstate 4?

Problem 7

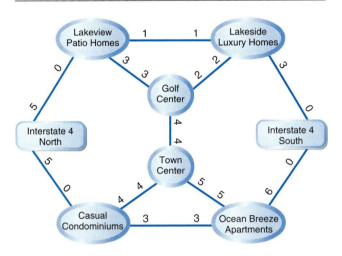

Silverton Road System

8. Pauline's, the Queen of Big Screen, is a chain of electronics stores specializing in big-screen televisions. In late January, the week before the Super Bowl, Pauline's always has a big sale. This January, two of its seven stores have excess supply of Mitsubishi 50-inch televisions, and the other five are requesting additional shipments. The word from Mitsubishi is that the orders will not arrive until after the Super Bowl. Hence, Pauline's has decided to redistribute some of its current inventory among its seven stores.
   a. What assumption about the individual transportation costs in the standard transportation model will most likely be violated in this situation?
   b. The network shown in the figure for problem 8 shows the stores with excess demand (the Downtown store and Harbor Boulevard store), the stores requesting additional televisions (stores at Taylor Mall, Ocean View Center, Edison Heights, Cypress Hill, and Regents Street), and the mileages between them. The network also shows the amount of excess supply, the demands, and the *distances* between those stores with supply and those with demand.
      Transportation costs are figured at $0.50 per mile per television. This cost must be added to the fixed labor charges for loading and unloading, given in the following table.

Store	Labor Charges per Television
Downtown	$5.50
Harbor Boulevard	$4.50
Taylor Mall	$3.00
Ocean View Center	$3.25
Edison Heights	$3.75
Cypress Hill	$4.00
Regents Street	$5.00

How should the stock of 50-inch Mitsubishi television sets be redistributed prior to Super Bowl Sunday?
   c. If each store requesting additional stock must receive at least 50% of its request, how should the stock of 50-inch Mitsubishi television sets be redistributed prior to Super Bowl Sunday?
   d. What would happen if Pauline's insisted that every store requesting additional stock receive at least 75% of its request?

Problem 8

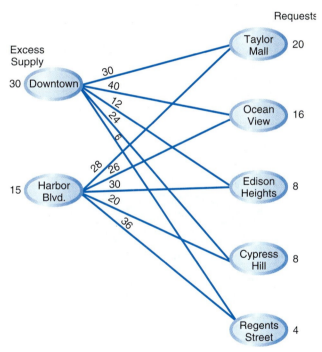

Pauline's: the Queen of Big Screen

9. Lisa Alvarez has just been hired by Fox Television to help the station compete more successfully against the other commercial networks and cable television. Management has given her free rein to keep or bring in whomever she feels necessary to run the various operations: News, Sports, Features, Marketing, and Development. Lisa is considering seven people for the five positions. They have submitted resumes listing the following years of experience in each field.

Problem 9   Years of Experience

	News	Sports	Features	Marketing	Development
Tony Hernandez	8	7	0	0	2
Jim Lampsy	2	12	4	1	3
Monica Fish	7	2	7	2	4
Connie Chu	2	0	7	8	6
Scott Young	0	10	0	0	5
Linda Harlan	10	0	10	5	2
Ann Chambers	5	0	5	11	9

a. If years of experience is a measure of success, whom should Lisa choose to head each department?

b. Suppose Lisa is considering consolidating Features and Development into one unit. In this case, whom should she choose to head each department?

10. Ponderosa Homes has just made a commitment to build the new gated community of Windstream. This community will consist of 110 homes in an undeveloped area off Hicks Canyon Boulevard. The gate for the community will be placed on a 150-foot-long street (tentatively called Venida Street) that will lead from Hicks Canyon Boulevard into the Windstream community. Venida Street as well as any other street constructed in the community, will be 35 feet wide.

Roads inside the community must be built so that every house has access to Venida and, hence, to all the other houses. Given the geography and other cost factors, the figure for problem 10 shows the possible set of streets that can be built between the 10 clusters (of 11 homes each) and Venida Street. (Distances are in feet.)

Problem 10

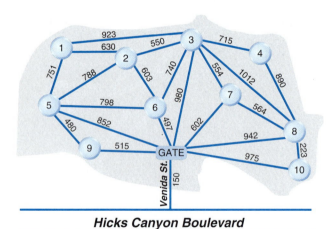

Hicks Canyon Boulevard

The Windstream Community

Since Ponderosa Homes, and not the city, must pay for constructing the streets, and costs are proportional to the total area of streets built, what set of streets do you recommend Ponderosa build? Including Venida Street, what is the total square footage of streets required for the Windstream community?

11. Elders Tax Service employs tax specialists in four different regional offices who will be assigned to four separate accounts in various parts of the country. The costs (transportation, lodging, per diem, etc.) are given in the following table.

	Phoenix	Fresno	Austin	Miami
Ann Byers	$2,300	$3,210	$1,850	$4,000
Bill Cole	$2,850	$2,980	$3,320	$3,450
Ko Nguyen	$2,500	$2,500	$1,900	$3,200
Dave King	$3,000	$2,950	$2,875	$3,350

a. Determine the minimum cost assignment of tax specialists to cities.

b. Suppose Elders' client list has grown to 20 accounts in Phoenix, 15 in Fresno, 22 in Austin, and 36 in Miami and that Elders now employs 25 specialists in each of Ann's, Bill's, Ko's, and Dave's offices. If the assignment cost per specialist has not changed, determine the optimal number of specialists Elders should send from each office to each city.

12. Harris Rent-A-Truck operates exclusively in California and rents large-capacity vehicles designed primarily for household moves. One reason Harris fares well against its competitors in California is that it offers attractive one-way rates between the various cities it serves.

Although Harris has 250 trucks, at any point in time many of these trucks are rented and are not available for new customers. Every two weeks the company analyzes the location of the trucks it has available and attempts to balance its inventory by keeping at least 12 trucks at each of its seven locations. Thus trucks are relocated to cities having fewer than 12 trucks from cities that have an excess. Transportation is to take no more than one day, however; hence trucks in the northernmost areas of the state (Eureka and Redding) are unavailable to those in the southernmost areas (Los Angeles and Needles), and vice versa.

On March 15, Harris found that 160 of its trucks were out on rentals. The remaining 90 trucks were at the following locations:

Eureka—11
Redding—7
San Francisco—6
Fresno—25
Bakersfield—18
Los Angeles—7
Needles—16

The table for problem 12 gives the cost of relocating a truck between cities. These costs include driver time, gasoline, and driver return air/bus trip cost.

What should Harris's relocation strategy be on March 15?

Problem 12   Cost of Relocating a Truck*

	To					
	Redding	San Francisco	Fresno	Bakersfield	Los Angeles	Needles
Eureka	$175	$250	$400	$480	N/A	N/A
Redding		$220	$380	$420	N/A	N/A
San Francisco			$300	$300	$350	$650
Fresno				$110	$200	$300
Bakersfield					$150	$275
Los Angeles						$350

(*Costs are the same in either direction.)

13. In designing a new digital circuit module for a component of the space shuttle, engineers must connect the six pins in the figure for problem 13 with small strands of copper. Distances are in millimeters. In order to give maximum clarity to the signal, the total length of the wiring should be minimized.

   If any number of wires can be attached to a single pin, find the minimum amount of wire required for the circuit design.

Problem 13

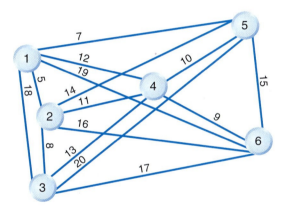

Digital Circuit Module

14. Thirteen Savage Beasts is a popular rock group that has toured all over North America. It is now beginning its Japanese tour and will be playing to a sold-out house in a major sports stadium in Osaka.

   After strategically positioning 12 banks of loudspeakers, the manager for the group has found that the local government requires all cables and wires be housed in specially insulated rigid casings. (In the United States, the group simply lays the cables along the ground or across rafters, but this is unacceptable to the Japanese authorities.)

   A diagram of the stage area and the 12 banks of loudspeakers with distances in meters is shown in the figure for problem 14. What is the minimum amount of the insulated casings the group must purchase before the rock concert can proceed? (*Note: Loudspeakers may be connected to one another or directly to the stage.*)

Problem 14

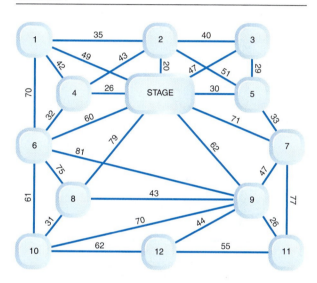

Distances are in meters

15. The accounting firm of Barnes, Fernandez, and Chou has just hired six new junior accountants, who are to be placed into six specialty areas within the firm: auditing, corporate tax, personal tax, financial analysis, information systems, and general accounting. Each applicant has been given an overall skills test in the specialty areas; the results are presented in the table for problem 15.

   a. If test scores are judged to be a measure of potential success, which junior accountant should be assigned to which specialty?

   b. In addition to the primary specialty area, each new junior accountant will be trained in a second specialty so that the company has two junior accountants with training in each specialty area. Eliminating the original assignments found in part a, what assignments now give the maximal potential for the second specialty?

Problem 15   Barnes, Fernandez, and Chou Test Scores

	Auditing	Corporate Tax	Personal Tax	Financial Analysis	Information Systems	General Accounting
Amy Cheng	62	75	80	93	95	97
Bob Szary	75	80	82	85	71	97
Sue Crane	80	75	81	98	90	97
Maya Pena	78	82	84	80	50	98
Koo Thanh	90	85	85	80	85	99
Lyn Ortiz	65	75	80	75	68	96

16. Pisa Pizza makes home deliveries of pizzas. Pisa usually waits until four pizzas need to be delivered, but it will deliver any pizza that has been out of the oven for 12 minutes. During peak hours, the former condition usually applies.

Vince Petralia is one of several college students working as a delivery person for Pisa Pizza. The following network depicts the time between the destinations of the four pizzas he is to deliver at 6:00 P.M. Note that, because of traffic patterns, delivery times between points could depend on the direction traveled.

Problem 16

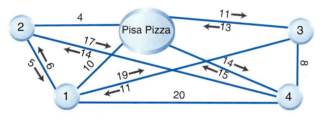

*Times are the same in each direction unless noted.

Pisa Pizza Delivery Times*

a. Suppose the time spent at each delivery point (walking to the door and collecting the money) is about three minutes. What is the minimum time it will take Vince to deliver the four pizzas and return to Pisa Pizza?

b. Suppose the situation in part (a) is representative of a "typical" pizza run for Vince during his shift from 5:00 P.M. to 11:00 P.M. Assume that, on the average, once Vince returns to Pisa Pizza he spends 15 minutes at the store (depositing the money collected from the previous run, waiting for and picking up the pizzas, and studying the map to determine the locations of the next set of deliveries). If he is paid $5 per hour by Pisa Pizza and averages a $1 tip from each pizza delivery, how much can Vince expect to earn in a typical night?

17. Build and Grow is a chain of five hardware stores serving southern Alabama and Mississippi. Each morning at

6:00, five large trucks are loaded at the warehouse with orders from each store. Given loading times at the warehouses and unloading time at the stores, the shipments are received at the stores by 1:00 P.M. and the trucks return to the warehouse by 5:00 P.M., where they are prepared for the next day's operations.

Each truck usually goes out full, but, on occasion, there may be some excess capacity. Around 2:30 each afternoon, large vans travel between stores transferring goods that are needed by one and in excess supply at another.

On April 23, the store at location 5 in the following network requested 500 50-pound bags of Topper Mulch from the warehouse after the delivery trucks from the warehouse to locations 4 and 5 had already left. No other store could spare any Topper Mulch for location 5. However, there was spare capacity in the trucks that had not yet left from the warehouse to stores 1, 2, and 3 of 200, 200, and 150 bags, respectively. This situation is depicted in the network for problem 17, along with the corresponding capacities left in the vans traveling between stores.

Will location 5 be able to receive the 500 bags of Topper Mulch by the end of the day? If not, how many bags will it receive? How will the bags be transported?

Problem 17

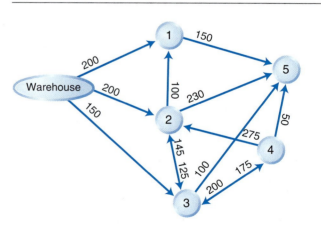

Build and Grow Distribution Network

18. Eastern Europe is interested in building a highway system similar to the Interstate Highway System of the United States. Currently, few such highways exist—none between Budapest, Hungary, and the Polish Baltic port of Gdansk. This route is of particular interest to Hungary, the Czech Republic, Slovakia, and Poland.

   Funds for such construction in Eastern Europe are still scarce; thus, the governments have decided to build a superhighway between the two cities by expanding certain existing smaller highways and secondary roads, as shown in the figure for problem 18. Distances are in kilometers. What series of roads minimizes the highway distance between Budapest and Gdansk?

Problem 18

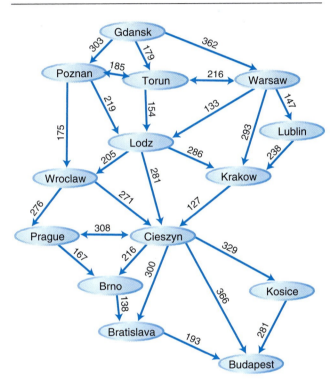

Eastern European Highway System

19. The Police Department in Fargo, North Dakota, begins the morning shift by informing all first-shift patrol persons of the previous evening's activities and giving assignments to the various team members. On a particular day, the following three activities must be accomplished: (1) delivery of a DARE (Drug Abuse Resistance Education) lecture at a local elementary school; (2) instruction of the rookie police class in using the baton; and (3) preparation of a report for the evening's City Council meeting on drug activities over the past three months.

   To help fulfill the mayor's promise of "keeping more police on the street," only three officers will be assigned to these activities. The goal is to minimize the total time these officers will be absent from street patrol. Given the expertise of each officer, the table for problem 19 gives each officer's time estimates for each activity, including any preparation time that may be needed. Because the assignments will be occurring simultaneously, each officer will be assigned to only one of the activities.

	Expected Times (Hours)		
	DARE Lecture	Baton Training	Drug Analysis
Officer Borel	4	2	8
Officer Frank	4	3	7
Officer Klaus	3	1	6

a. Determine the minimal time assignment by direct enumeration of all possible combinations.
b. Draw the network representation of this problem.
c. Give the linear programming formulation for this problem and solve using a linear programming module.
d. Interpret this problem as a special case of the transportation problem and solve using the transportation approach.
e. Use the assignment approach to solve the problem.

20. Consider the police allocation problem for Fargo, North Dakota (problem 19). Suppose that two additional officers are available for assignment to one of the three activities:

	Expected Times (hours)		
	DARE Lecture	Baton Training	Drug Analysis
Officer Muntz	5	4	5
Officer Clark	3	3	6

a. If you were to consider all possible assignments by direct enumeration, how many combinations would have to be considered? How many combinations would there be if there were *also* one additional activity? two additional activities?
b. Solve the five-officer, three-activity problem using the assignment approach to the model.
c. Suppose Officer Clark could perform two of the activities. Give the linear programming formulation for this problem and solve using a linear programming module.
d. Develop an assignment matrix for the problem in part c and solve.

21. Heavenly Flower Shop contracts with Floral Transportation Service (FTS) to deliver phone orders to the four cemeteries in town. FTS charges Heavenly a flat $2.50 per order plus $0.15 per mile for delivery per arrangement from one of Heavenly's two locations to the appropriate cemetery. The distances from

Heavenly's two stores to the four cemeteries are given in the table for problem 21.

Problem 21

Heavenly Store Locations	Cemetery			
	Lilac Hills	Forest Glen	St. Mary's	Chelsea Pines
City Center	26	17	20	15
North Central	18	5	35	24

It is Memorial Day, and Heavenly has received telephone orders for 20 arrangements to be delivered to Lilac Hills, 16 to Forest Glen, 18 to St. Mary's, and 22 to Chelsea Pines. Heavenly has enough flowers in its City Center location to make 45 arrangements, and enough in its North Central location to make 40 arrangements. Heavenly adds a flat $10 fee for delivery charges to all telephone orders.

How many of the orders for each cemetery should be filled at each location so that Heavenly maximizes its profit from delivery charges? What is the optimal profit?

22. Gerald Morris, president of Queen's County National Bank, makes periodic trips from the bank's home office to each of its seven branch offices in the Queen's County area. The map for problem 22 shows the driving times (in minutes) between the home office and the branches. Since some of the routes are major highways, and others are surface streets with many stop lights, driving times are not directly proportional to the distance traveled.

What are the minimum driving times and the routes that should be taken from the home office to each of the branches?

23. Next Tuesday, Gerald Morris, president of Queen's County National Bank (problem 22), will make a surprise inspection of each branch office. He plans to leave the home office at 9:00 A.M., have a one-hour lunch break during the day, and return at 5:00 P.M.
   a. In which order should Gerald Morris visit the branches to minimize his total driving time for the day if he wishes to visit or drive by any branch only once?
   b. What is the minimum total driving time?

c. If Gerald is to spend the same amount of time inspecting each of the four branch offices, how much time will he be able to spend at each branch?

24. For the Queen's County National Bank problem (problems 22 and 23), Gerald Morris has decided that although he will not revisit any branch, he is willing to drive by a previously visited branch if doing so will decrease his overall driving time.
   a. Find the minimum driving time between each branch pair.
   b. Use your result for part a to determine the minimum driving time to visit each branch if Gerald can drive by a previously visited branch.
   c. Assume that Gerald will spend the same amount of time at each branch. Give a minute-by-minute schedule that begins with his leaving the home office at 9:00 A.M. and ends with his return to the home office at 5:00 P.M. Schedule Gerald's one-hour lunch break to be as close to 12:00 as possible.

25. Federal Electric produces compressors for air conditioning units. Labor and production costs average $60 per unit when they are produced during regular time and $66 per unit when they are produced in overtime. The average carrying (holding) cost for a unit from one quarter to the next is $15 per compressor. Thus a unit produced in the first quarter during regular time but not sold until the third quarter would cost the company $60 to produce plus $30 in carrying costs ($15 for each of the two quarters stored). Each quarter, 750 hours of regular time and 500 hours of overtime are available for production. The average time it takes to produce a compressor is 30 minutes.

Given the following quarterly demand projections for compressors, what production plan minimizes total yearly costs for Federal Electric?

Quarter	Projected Demand
1	1250
2	625
3	3750
4	2500

Problem 22

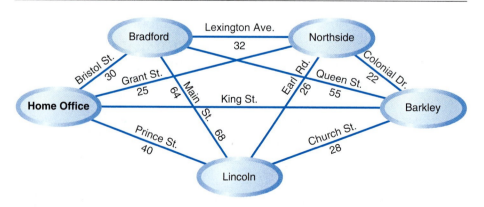

Queen's County National Bank Distances Between Branches

26. The Orange County Transportation Commission is planning to develop a road system linking Mission Viejo (City 1) and Fullerton (City 10). Two proposals are under serious consideration:

a. A series of six-lane "superstreets" linking all 10 Orange County cities between Mission Viejo and Fullerton.

b. A 10-lane freeway extension connecting Mission Viejo with Fullerton (which does not necessarily pass through all 10 cities).

Forecasts indicate that either proposal will improve north-south traffic flow through the county and ease traffic congestion on other secondary streets. The proposed transportation corridors are depicted in the following network, including mileages between various Orange County cities.

Superstreets are estimated to cost taxpayers $500,000 per mile to build, whereas each mile of freeway will cost $700,000. Although many factors should be considered, if total cost is the primary consideration, which system would Orange County taxpayers prefer?

Problem 26

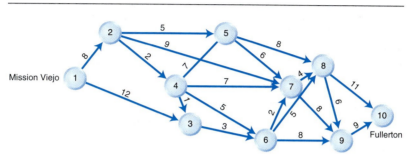

Orange County Transportation Corridors

27. AlaCom, a manufacturer of motherboards for personal computers, is opening a new manufacturing plant in Birmingham, Alabama. Once the boards have been manufactured at various areas in the plant, they will be transported to a packaging area, using an overhead conveyor belt system. A line in the system will be installed from each of the four production areas to a central switching station. From the switching station, the products will be rerouted along the main conveyor belt to the packaging area. Given the location of air conditioning, ventilation, and lighting systems in the plant, there are many possible configurations for the design of the conveyor belt system from the switching station to the packaging area as shown in the figure for problem 27. Distances are in feet.

Each leg of the system will consist of two conveyor belts, one going in each direction. It will cost AlaCom $100 per linear foot to install the conveyor belt in each direction. Additional costs include $18,000 for each start station at the production area, $20,000 for the finish station at the packaging area, and $52,000 for the switching station. Given the possible choices for constructing the conveyor belt system, what is the minimum-cost conveyor belt system AlaCom can install?

Problem 27

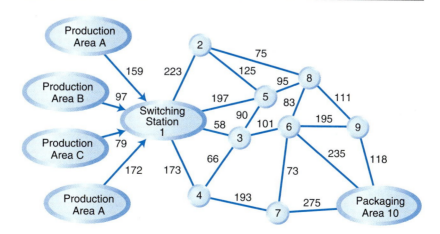

28. Ithaca Delivery of Ithaca, New York, makes daily pickup/deliveries to four locations in the city and is interested in finding a route that will begin at its headquarters, make deliveries to all four locations, and return to its headquarters in the minimum amount of time. The network for problem 28 depicts the situation, giving the average driving times between each point.

What routing do you recommend if Cornell University is to be visited at the: (i) earliest time on the route; (ii) the latest time on the route. *Hint: The problem is symmetric. An optimal solution in one direction is optimal in the reverse direction.*

Problem 28

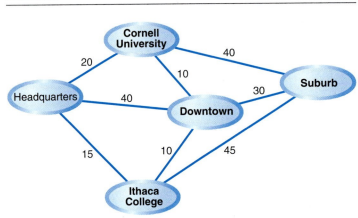

29. The College of Business and Economics at Minnesota State University is designing a local area network of computers that connect to the file server on the third floor of Langford Hall. This network will link together computers in smart classrooms, the dean's office, and two computer support labs. The network for problem 29

shows the costs of laying cable between possible computer connections.
a. How should the local area network be designed to minimize the total cost for Minnesota State University?
b. What will be its total cost?

Problem 29

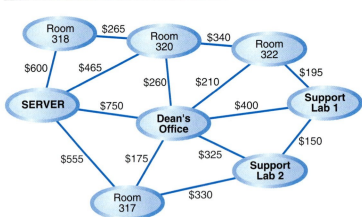

30. PrimeBeef.com supplies four major restaurant chains (Ponderosa, Ranchero, Bar H, and TexMex) in the Oklahoma City area with top grade steaks prepared and stored in three warehouses located in the northern, southern, and western parts of the city. It receives orders over the Internet daily, and every morning at 6:30 A.M. deliveries are made to the restaurant locations. On July

23, PrimeBeef.com received orders of 2400 pounds from Ponderosa, 2000 pounds from Ranchero, 1600 pounds from Bar H, and 2800 pounds from TexMex. The following table gives the transportation costs per truckload from each PrimeBeef.com warehouse to each restaurant distribution location. Each truckload consists of 400 pounds. If PrimeBeef.com has 3200 pounds of beef at each warehouse, how should it ship the beef from its warehouses to the restaurant distribution locations to minimize its total shipping cost?

	Ponderosa	Ranchero	Bar H	Tex Mex
North	$90	$55	$75	$75
South	$65	$90	$50	$65
West	$45	$45	$60	$35

31. In an effort to increase sales, Wilbury Press has experimented with rotating its sales staff of business college textbooks among its six sales regions. Based on past performance, the table for problem 31 gives a computer model of projected revenues of sales (in $1000s) for the fall semester, based on assigning each book representative to each sales region. Using these projections, which book representatives should it send to each region to *maximize* its projected fall semester sales?

Problem 31

	North-east	South-east	Mid-west	South-west	West Coast	Foreign
Annie	235	135	85	115	200	35
Barbara	285	155	50	123	201	75
Curt	335	238	99	146	253	85
Marla	250	149	104	130	192	18
Gerri	171	154	45	105	210	66
Noreen	290	132	85	115	222	56
Phil	288	187	77	134	185	27
Steve	212	101	111	100	225	44

32. Riosplash Sportswear is gearing up for the summer season. Its manufacturing season for bikinis is January through June, for sales to retail outlets from March through August. Because of the availability of temporary workers and fabric, manufacturing costs differ from month to month. The table for problem 32 gives the average production cost, the storage costs, the monthly production capacities, and the demands during each of the months from January to August *per 1000 bikinis*.

Problem 32

	Average Prod. Cost	Storage Cost (first month)	Storage Cost (each additional month)	Prod. Capacity	Demand
Jan.	$8200	$125	$75	12	3
Feb.	$8800	$125	$75	15	7
Mar.	$8700	$135	$75	18	14
Apr.	$8900	$150	$75	30	20
May	$9000	$165	$75	32	28
June	$8500	$170	$75	40	31
July					30
Aug.					8

Use a transportation model to determine an optimal production/storage/sales plan for bikinis at Riosplash Sportswear.

33. Tiffany Thair is an independent salesperson of medical supplies. On a particular day Tiffany must visit Children's Hospital, Dr. Rashid, Lakeview Pharmacy, and the County Medical Center. Tiffany, who has a dinner date at 7:00 P.M. and would like to be home by 5:00 P.M. to get ready, will leave her house at 9:00 A.M. She estimates she will have to spend one hour each at Children's Hospital and the County Medical Center, 30 minutes at Dr. Rashid's office, 45 minutes at the Lakeview Pharmacy, and she plans to take a one-hour lunch break. Given the table for problem 33 of estimated travel times (in minutes) between locations, will Tiffany be able to take a one-hour lunch break if she wants to be home by 5:00 P.M.?

Problem 33

	Children's Hospital	Dr. Rashid	Lakeview Pharmacy	County Med. Center
Home	33	69	57	75
Children's Hospital		85	78	99
Dr. Rashid			45	25
Lakeview Pharmacy				80

34. CompLounge Industries produces three different models of recliners. All three have a computer and keyboard installed in the left arm. Installed in the right arm, Model 234 has a telephone, Model 450 has a small refrigerator (for drinks), and Model 815 has a smaller refrigerator and a keypad that can be used as both a telephone and a remote control. The models are sold to retailers for $1500, $2000, and $2200, respectively.

CompLounge produces some recliners itself but also contracts with independent manufacturers (Lazyman, Relaxer, and SeatComp) to fill its orders. The following table gives the cost to CompLounge for each model. For the upcoming month CompLounge has orders for 300 Model 234s, 250 Model 450s, and 500 Model 815s.

	CompLounge	Lazyman	Relaxer	SeatComp
Model 234	$770	$850	$800	$900
Model 450	$900	$1250	$1125	$1050
Model 815	$1150	$1350	$1400	$1500

a. If it takes roughly the same amount of time to produce each type of chair, and production capacities at the four plants are 400, 375, 275, and 125 per month, respectively, how should production be scheduled at the plants this month? What is the minimum total cost to CompLounge? What will be its total profit?

b. Suppose that resources at the independent manufacturers (LazyMan, Relaxer, and SeatComp) are such that the maximum number of Model 450s that can be produced are 75, 100, and 50, respectively, and the maximum number of Model 815s that can be produced are 125, 150, and 25, respectively. Now, how should production be scheduled at the plants this month? What is the minimum total cost to CompLounge? What will be its total profit?

35. Socker Shoes manufactures "Made in the USA" sneakers at plants in Tallahassee, Florida, and Tucson, Arizona. The shoes are shipped weekly in truckloads from each of the two plants to four regional distribution warehouses located in Allentown, Pennsylvania, Gary, Indiana, Houston, Texas, and Riverside, California. Inventory at each warehouse is evaluated on a weekly basis, and forecasts of demands for additional shoes are faxed to Socker Shoe's management. This information determines the weekly production schedule for each plant and the shipping pattern between the plants and warehouses.

During the week of February 14, the following requests were received from the individual warehouses:

Warehouse	Request
Allentown	6000
Gary	8000
Houston	9000
Riverside	15,000

Each plant can produce up to 19,000 pairs of shoes for the week, and production costs for a pair of shoes are the same at each plant. The shoes are shipped via truck in lots of 1000 pairs. The forecasted shipping cost per truckload from each plant to each warehouse is given in the table for problem 35.

Problem 35   Shipping Cost per Truckload

From	To			
	Allentown	Gary	Houston	Riverside
Tallahassee	$2500	$2800	$2200	$3500
Tucson	$3000	$2900	$2200	$1800

a. For the week of February 14, how many pairs of shoes should be produced in Tallahassee? in Tucson?

b. What is Socker Shoes' minimum cost shipping pattern for the week of February 14? What will be the total shipping cost?

36. Consider the Socker Shoe situation in problem 35.

a. What is the largest value for the shipping cost from Tucson to Riverside for which this solution remains optimal?

b. Suppose that the maximum weekly production capacity at each plant was 15,000 instead of 19,000. What is the new minimum cost shipping pattern? What are the ramifications of this situation? Do you think this minimum cost solution is tolerable? Explain.

c. Suppose that weekly production capacity is 25,000 at Tallahassee and 25,000 at Tucson. What is the new optimal shipping pattern? How should production be scheduled between the two plants? Does this seem practical and sensible from a management point of view?

37. Consider the Socker Shoe situation in problem 35. Suppose Socker decided to locate a plant in Juarez, Mexico, which is also capable of producing 19,000 pairs of shoes per week. (It will therefore change the "Made in the USA" slogan to "Made in North America.")

Mexican drivers' wages and benefits are lower, a factor that has been taken into account in the following estimates of the shipping cost (per truckload) from Juarez to the warehouse distribution centers:

From	To			
	Allentown	Gary	Houston	Riverside
Juarez	$2800	$2400	$2000	$1500

a. Suppose a tariff of $2 per pair of shoes from Mexico exists. If this plant were in operation, what is the effect on the production schedule for the week of February 14 given that production costs per shoe are the same for the Juarez plant as for the Tallahassee and Tucson plants?

b. Mexican production costs are substantially lower than U.S. costs, for both labor and material. Estimates indicate that overall production costs in Mexico are only 40% of U.S. costs. Currently, it costs roughly $5.00 to produce each pair of sneakers in the United States. Considering both the tariff costs and the savings in production costs, what would be the effect on the production schedule for the week of February 14?

c. Suppose that under union contract, Socker Shoe has agreed to produce at least 30,000 pairs of sneakers each week in the United States. Modify your formulation of part b and express the results in a transportation format. Solve for the optimal production and shipping schedule for the week of February 14.

d. Under the North American Free Trade Agreement (NAFTA), all tariffs between Mexico and the United States will be eliminated. At the same time, Mexican wages should rise. Assume that the increase in driver wages would add $400 per truckload to the figures given above. To what level (in terms of the percentage of U.S. production costs) would Mexican production costs have to rise for there to be no difference between producing all the units in the United States and producing some units in Mexico?

38. Red Tag Maintenance Corporation runs a "fixed fee" repair operation using seven independent repair people. Its motto is: "We do it right for less!" Red Tag's policy is to quote, over the phone, a fixed fee for the service, plus parts and taxes. Thus it is in their best interest to assign repair people to services so that the total cost is minimized. Because of the various skill levels of the individual repair persons and the locations of the service calls, different costs will be accrued by Red Tag for the various service/repair person assignments.

On Thursday morning six service calls were waiting when the company opened for business. Given the location of the job and the type of repair, the computer generated the job cost estimates in the table for problem 38. (An "X" means the repair person is not capable of doing this repair.)

a. Which repairman should be assigned to each service call? What will be the total cost to Red Tag?

b. If Red Tag wants to make a 30% profit on each service, how much should it quote for each individual repair? What will be Red Tag's profit on these six service calls?

Problem 38

	Washer	Dishwasher	Air Conditioner	Toilet	Refrigerator	Stove
Alice	$40	$45	$250	X	$125	$ 80
Bob	$50	$50	$275	$95	$150	$125
Chuck	$35	$35	X	X	X	X
Darren	$25	$60	$190	$75	$100	$100
Ellen	$20	$30	$200	$50	$180	$145
Francisco	$40	$40	$180	$80	$140	$130
George	$50	$25	X	X	$130	$115

39. TransGlobal Airlines (TGA), based in New York City, is a charter airline with seven pilots. In assigning routes, the most senior pilot chooses first, then the next most senior, and so on. TGA discovered, however, that some pilots had very little preference, while others cared a great deal about which route they were assigned. Hence, a senior pilot sometimes selected a route that a more junior pilot would have preferred, even though the senior pilot was ambivalent about his or her choice.

As a result of complaints from some of the junior pilots, TGA is considering implementing a new policy. Each pilot, regardless of seniority, would rate in numerical order his or her five most preferred cities as well as standby and vacation preference. (Each period, one pilot is on standby and another pilot is on vacation.) TGA would then create a schedule that maximizes overall pilot satisfaction (giving the lowest total overall preference value).

a. Given the rankings in the table for problem 39 submitted by the pilots for the current scheduling period, what schedule should be assigned?

b. The pilots are listed in order of seniority. Explain why Captain Smith and Captain Jones, the two most senior pilots, are particularly upset with this period's schedule.

Problem 39

	Route						
	London	Paris	Moscow	Hawaii	Tokyo	Standby	Vacation
Captain Smith	1	2	5	3	4	6	7
Captain Jones	2	1	7	3	6	4	5
Captain Heinz	7	2	6	3	4	5	1
Captain Chang	2	1	6	4	7	5	3
Captain Wells	1	3	7	2	4	6	5
Captain Blinn	2	3	7	1	6	5	4
Captain Klein	5	4	7	3	2	6	1

40. Consider the TGA situation in problem 39. When TGA attempted to schedule pilots using the new policy, it found that there can be many options for the total minimal ranked schedule. Furthermore, sometimes the most senior pilots are relegated to routes they truly do not prefer, while more junior pilots receive their first choice. Another problem is that such a ranking procedure does not show the depth of displeasure between one route and the next. For example, Captain Smith may be relatively indifferent to the London and Paris routes but certainly prefers either to Hawaii (his third choice).

In an effort to take seniority into account, a young management consultant has suggested another method. Each pilot would receive 10 points for each year of service to distribute in any manner among the five routes, standby, and vacation. Suppose this method yielded the point scores for this period shown in the table for problem 40.

a. Construct a lost opportunity matrix from these points by replacing the numbers in each column by the difference between the numbers and the maximum number in the column.

b. Solve the optimal assignment using this approach.

c. Why is Captain Smith still unhappy? How could Captain Smith be assured of always getting his first preference using this approach?

d. List some other potential pitfalls that might occur using this approach. Suggest other approaches that might be fairer.

Problem 40

	Route						
	London	Paris	Moscow	Hawaii	Tokyo	Standby	Vacation
Captain Smith	115	115	0	0	0	0	0
Captain Jones	50	150	0	10	0	0	0
Captain Heinz	0	50	0	50	50	0	50
Captain Chang	75	100	0	0	0	0	15
Captain Wells	160	0	0	0	0	0	0
Captain Blinn	0	0	0	80	0	0	0
Captain Klein	20	10	10	1	4	3	2

PROBLEMS 41–50 ARE ON THE CD

CASE STUDIES

CASE 1:   Kaybee Amusements, Inc.

Kaybee Amusements, Inc. is developing a theme park for the city of Baton Rouge, Louisiana. It is tentatively titled Heritageland; the concept is to build theme areas based on heritages common to six of the cultures that have influenced the Southern and Midwestern regions of the United States: (1) English; (2) French; (3) Spanish; (4) African; (5) German; and (6) Native American. Each of the six theme areas will have a theme restaurant, a cultural center with a 360° theater, a stage show pavilion, and amusement attractions. In addition, the park will include a main plaza area with a multicultural atmosphere and a parking lot.

The following map of the park includes all pedestrian corridors between the theme areas, the plaza, and the parking lot. Distances are in feet.

One of the proposed attractions is the Far West Streetcar Line, which, for a fee, will transport visitors in street-

cars powered by underground cables. Because of costs, the park will only run seven streetcars, each starting in one theme area, traversing to a second area, and then returning to the original one through the same corridor. Each streetcar ride will move directly down the center of the pedestrian corridor running between the two theme areas. Kaybee would like to use the minimal distance of underground cable while enabling patrons to travel to any theme area, the plaza, and the parking lot via street cars.

For those who prefer a more modern form of transportation, a monorail system will be constructed to provide transportation among all areas. The system will consist of two circuitous routes. One will include the parking lot, the Main Plaza, and the Spanish, French and Native American pavilions. The other will link the parking lot, the Main Plaza, and the English, German, and African pavilions. The links for the monorail system among areas will be constructed directly above pedestrian corridors. To conserve costs, the monorail lines should be constructed to minimize distance.

Finally, for those who prefer walking (or do not wish to pay for the other modes of transportation within the park), the park will provide every visitor with a welcome brochure. One page in the brochure will be a map, including directions showing the visitor how to get "From Here to There" in the shortest walking distance.

Prepare a report for Kaybee Amusements suggesting the design of the most cost-effective streetcar and monorail routes. Also provide the copy for the page entitled "From Here to There" in the welcoming brochure that gives visitors the routes of shortest distance between any two theme areas, the plaza, and the parking lot.

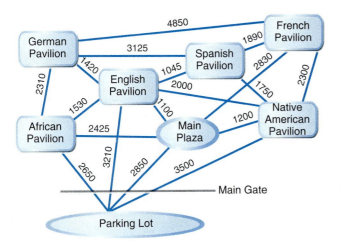

CASE 2:   GSA Industries

GSA Industries produces four models of prefabricated housing units in each of two locations: one in El Cajon, California, the other in Elkhart, Indiana. The manufactured houses are transported to regional distribution centers in Phoenix, Nashville, and Miami. Because of current economic conditions, GSA is able to sell all the units it manufactures during the year. The following table gives the outstanding orders for the year as well as the production plan GSA has approved for the Elkhart, Indiana, plant.

Orders and Production Quantities at Elkhart, Indiana

	Model			
	Picket Fence	Town House	Gentle Stream	El Presidente
Phoenix	50	60	60	90
Nashville	80	60	30	20
Miami	75	90	85	90
Production at Elkhart Plant	100	75	75	120

The El Cajon plant is being reconfigured for this year's models. The plant consists of four separate buildings, each of which will produce a different model. The number of prefabricated houses that can be produced in a building depends on many factors, including the size and shape of the building and the existing production facilities. The accompanying table gives the estimated production quantities of each model.

For example, if Building 1 is used to produce the Picket Fence Model, 30 such models can be produced; if it is used to produce the Town House model, 25 such models can be produced, and so on. Because of the design of Building 3, no El Presidente models can be produced in Building 3.

Production Levels

	Model			
	Picket Fence	Town House	Gentle Stream	El Presidente
Building 1	30	25	20	10
Building 2	60	55	50	45
Building 3	40	35	30	N/A
Building 4	95	85	See text	65

These production quantities were determined by analyzing the rate at which various subassemblies can be manufactured and passed along to the next operation. The production of the subassemblies has constraining capacities. A network representation for the Gentle Stream model in Building 4 is shown below.

The gross profit per unit (excluding transportation costs and fixed labor and overhead cost) for GSA is given in the following table.

Gross Profit per Unit

Model	Gross Profit
Picket Fence	$ 9,600
Town House	$11,520
Gentle Stream	$15,360
El Presidente	$19,200

Unit transportation charges from either the Elkhart, Indiana, plant or the El Cajon plant are independent of the model shipped. Thus, each model has exactly the same transportation cost between a particular pair of cities. The following unit transportation costs have been determined for the Elkhart, Indiana, plant.

Unit Transportation Costs from Elkhart, Indiana

To	Cost
Phoenix	$1,450
Nashville	$ 725
Miami	$2,500

The unit transportation costs from El Cajon depend on the mode and time of transportation. Various truck, rail, and boat routes are available under contract to GSA. These are summarized in the table at the top of the next page. The cost of changing modes of transportation at a city (rail to truck, truck to rail, or truck to ship) is $250 per vehicle.

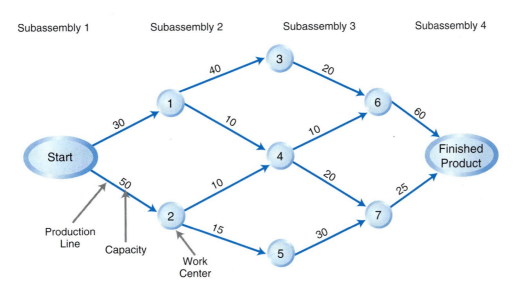

Building 4 Subassembly Capacities for Gentle Stream Model

Shipping Routes

From	To	No. of Days	Cost/Day
Truck Routes			
El Cajon	Phoenix	1	$375
El Cajon	Dallas	3	$300
Phoenix	Rapid City	2	$250
Phoenix	Oklahoma City	2	$175
Dallas	New Orleans	1	$300
Rapid City	Chicago	3	$325
Rapid City	Oklahoma City	2	$250
Rapid City	Nashville	4	$200
Chicago	Nashville	2	$300
Chicago	Raleigh	3	$375
Oklahoma City	New Orleans	3	$225
Oklahoma City	Nashville	4	$300
Oklahoma City	Raleigh	5	$200
Nashville	Miami	3	$350
Raleigh	Miami	4	$250
Rail Routes			
El Cajon	Phoenix	2	$250
El Cajon	Dallas	4	$350
Phoenix	Rapid City	3	$175
Chicago	Nashville	3	$200
Chicago	Raleigh	4	$225
Oklahoma City	Raleigh	3	$250
Raleigh	Miami	3	$300
Boat Routes			
New Orleans	Miami	4	$400

Fixed labor costs at both plants combined are expected to be $3 million; other overhead is estimated to be $2 million.

Prepare a report for GSA that analyzes the El Cajon operation in light of previous commitments at the Elkhart, Indiana, plant. Analyze:

1. The maximum production capacity of the Gentle Stream model at Building 4 in El Cajon.
2. Which building should produce which model at the El Cajon plant in order to maximize gross profit. (Ignore transportation costs in this analysis and discuss why this is probably valid with this particular set of data. Discuss how the model would change if it were not valid.)
3. The minimal total transportation costs from El Cajon to each of the distribution cities. (Discuss any *time* implications of your recommendation.)
4. The allocation of each housing model from each production city to each distribution city.
5. The net profit for the company for the year.

CASE 3: The Sandy Company[1]

The Sandy Company is an excavation company located in southwestern Colorado. In recent months, the company has expanded its activities, purchased several new bulldozers, and sought out new contracts. This past week it successfully obtained a contract for a new project to begin on July 15. The contract involves excavation at four separate sites in the area: (1) Los Bungalos, (2) Buffalo Valley, (3) Parker Falls, and (4) Upper Lufferton.

A major cost faced by the Sandy Company is the transportation of bulldozers from their sites at the three storage locations of Groveton, High Point, and Grand River along some very narrow construction roads to the excavation sites. The bulldozers will be transported by the Emmons Company using commercial trailers specifically designed for this purpose. The transportation cost per

[1] This case is based on a problem developed by Dr. Zvi Goldstein, California State University, Fullerton.

bulldozer is $200 plus $6 per mile from any storage location to any excavation site.

The four sites require a total of 21 bulldozers: five at Los Bungalos; six at Buffalo Valley; six at Parker Falls; and four at Upper Lufferton. Thus the fixed cost, over which the Sandy Company has no control, is $4200 *each way* (= 21 × $200). The company must determine the most efficient routes to travel from each of the storage sites to the excavation sites and how many bulldozers to transport from each storage site to each excavation site.

The Sandy Company has 24 bulldozers: eight at Groveton; nine at High Point; and seven at Grand River. The bulldozers must be returned to their original sites. A map detailing the distances between junction points of the construction roads and between the storage sites and the excavation sites follows. Complicating the process is the possibility that the project will not be completed until late October. By that time snow could make certain roads

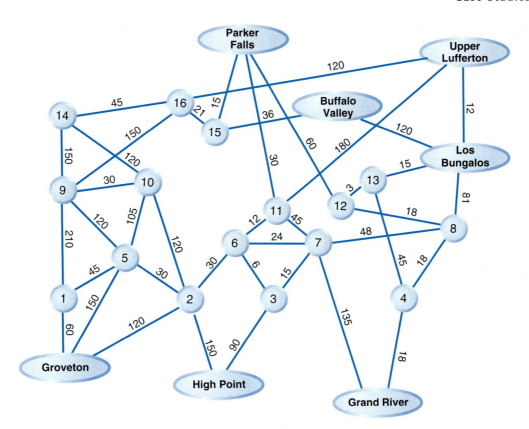

impassable. In particular, the roads between Grand River and Junction 4, and between Junction 13 and Los Bungalos are very susceptible to closure. In addition, a new 70-mile construction road between Junction 2 and Junction 15 may be open.

Prepare a report that includes the following.

1. The minimum cost distribution and transportation plan to the excavation sites under current conditions
2. Given that the bulldozers have been allocated as in (1), a minimum cost return transportation plan under each of the eight possible sets of conditions:

	Grand River–Junction 4	Junction 13–Los Bungalos	Junction 2–Junction 15	
1.	Open	Open	Closed	(Current)
2.	Open	Open	Open	
3.	Open	Closed	Closed	

	Grand River–Junction 4	Junction 13–Los Bungalos	Junction 2–Junction 15
4.	Open	Closed	Open
5.	Closed	Open	Closed
6.	Closed	Open	Open
7.	Closed	Closed	Closed
8.	Closed	Closed	Open

3. An analysis of the situation in which Sandy knows in advance that both the Grand River–Junction 4 road and the Junction 13–Los Bungalos road will be closed on the return trip (i.e., suppose the roads automatically close on October 1). Recommend a minimum cost distribution and transportation plan for both the case in which the Junction 2–Junction 15 road is open and the case in which it is closed (cases 7 and 8).

(*Hint:* Since the bulldozers must be returned to their original sites, round-trip mileages must now be considered.)

Project Scheduling Models

DURING THE LAST week of April 1992, the worst riots in recent U.S. history occurred in south central Los Angeles. Within a three-day period, hundreds of businesses were damaged or destroyed. Among them was a local Taco Bell restaurant.

To demonstrate its commitment to the people of the community, Taco Bell (http://www.tacobell.com) pledged to rebuild and reopen the restaurant in record time. On Tuesday, June 9, 1992, Taco Bell began a crash project to construct a new restaurant on the same site as the one devastated by the riots. At 10:00 A.M. on Thursday, June 11, just 48 hours later, construction of the restaurant was completed, and the first taco was sold.

Less than two years later, in January 1994, another disaster struck the Los Angeles area. An earthquake measuring 6.7 on the Richter scale devastated homes, businesses, and property. Several freeways, including the Santa Monica Freeway, the most heavily traveled in the world, were severely damaged, as concrete cracked and bridges tumbled.

Roadways had to be repaired, and bridges and overpasses retrofitted to meet earthquake standards. In only three months, more than two months ahead of what many had considered to be an overly optimistic schedule, the repair work was completed and the freeway was reopened. Because the project was completed well ahead of schedule, the federal government covered all costs, and contractors were awarded $15 million in bonuses for their efforts.

The positive outcomes in both of these cases were accomplished with considerable coordination and management of the numerous individual tasks that had to be performed. Response to a disaster, of course, is only one area in which project planning plays a crucial role. New product development, manufacture of existing products, conference planning, audit design, and development of marketing campaigns are just some of the many areas in which careful project planning is essential.

5.1   Introduction to Project Scheduling

We can think of a *project* as a collection of tasks a person or firm desires to complete in minimum time or at minimal cost. For example, in painting the outside of a house a contractor must: (1) select color(s); (2) purchase paint; (3) clean existing siding; (4) mask windows; (5) spray paint large areas; (6) hand paint trim; and (7) clean up. Factors affecting the completion time might include the number of painters the contractor employs, the availability of the individual paint colors, and the square footage and special details of the house. The painting contractor's primary objective might be to finish painting the outside of the house in minimal time so that he can move on to another project, or at minimal total cost so that he will earn the maximum profit from his work.

The tasks of a project are called *activities*. Estimated completion times (and sometimes costs) are associated with each activity of a project. Activities can be defined broadly or narrowly, depending on the situation. For example, an activity involved in bringing a new play to Broadway might be "Hire Cast." Although this description is appropriate for some models, in other cases it might be beneficial to subdivide this part of the project into much narrower sets of activities, such as:

> "Hold Auditions for Principal Characters"
> "Arrange for Call-Back Auditions of Principal Characters"
> "Cast Principal Characters"
> "Hold Auditions for Extras"
> "Cast Extras"
> "Hold Preliminary Run-Through"
> "Make Final Cast Selections"

The degree of detail depends on both the application and the level of specificity in the available time and cost data.

In any project, certain activities must be completed before others are started, whereas others may be completed simultaneously. For a Broadway play, "Hire Cast" certainly must precede "Dress Rehearsal," but "Dress Rehearsal" need not precede "Advance Ticket Sales," or vice versa. Determining an accurate set of *precedence relations* among the activities—that is, detailing which activities must precede others—is crucial to developing an optimal schedule for the individual activities.

The completion time for each activity, and, thus, the overall project completion time, is generally related to the amount of resources committed to it. In the opening vignette, the completion time of the Taco Bell restaurant could not have been reduced from its *normal completion time* of almost two months to its *crash completion time* of two days without spending extra money (on overtime wages and talented crews willing to work at night). And even though Taco Bell was committed to meeting a prepublicized deadline of 48 hours, it wished to do so at minimum total cost. Similarly, in the freeway repair problem, since contractors were offered a bonus of $15 million for completing the repairs before a specified date, additional resources were committed to critical activities in the successful effort to meet this deadline. In both cases, the positive results did not just happen. Rather, each success was the result of careful and comprehensive project planning, scheduling, and monitoring.

OBJECTIVES OF PROJECT SCHEDULING

Project scheduling is used to plan and control a project efficiently. Some of the objectives of project scheduling include:

- Determining a schedule of earliest and latest start and finish times for each activity that leads to the earliest completion time for the entire project

- Calculating the likelihood that a project will be completed within a certain time period
- Finding the minimum cost schedule that will complete a project by a certain date
- Investigating how delays to certain activities affect the overall completion time of a project
- Monitoring a project to determine whether it is proceeding on time and within budget
- Finding a schedule of activities that will smooth out the allocation of resources over the duration of the project

The above objectives can be accomplished using project scheduling approaches, such as PERT (Program Evaluation and Review Technique) and CPM (Critical Path Method). These methods, which were both developed in the mid-1950s, use project networks to help schedule a project's activities. Although the distinction between the two techniques has blurred in recent years, PERT is generally regarded as a method that treats the completion time of the activities as random variables with specific probability distributions, whereas CPM assumes that the completion time of an activity is solely dependent on the amount of money spent to complete the activity.

Both PERT and CPM require the modeler to identify the activities of the project and the *precedence relations* between them. This involves determining a set of *immediate predecessors* for each activity. An activity's immediate predecessors are those jobs that must be completed just prior to the activity's commencement. A **precedence relations chart** identifies the separate activities of the project and their precedence relations. From this chart a PERT/CPM network representation of the project can then be constructed.

5.2   Identifying the Activities of a Project

To illustrate the concepts of project scheduling, consider the situation faced by Klone Computer, Inc.

Klonel.cpm

KLONE COMPUTERS, INC.

Klone Computers is a small manufacturer of personal computers which is about to design, manufacture, and market the Klonepalm 2000 palmbook computer. The company faces three major tasks in introducing a new computer: (1) manufacturing the new computer; (2) training staff and vendor representatives to operate the new computer; and (3) advertising the new computer.

When the proposed specifications for the new computer have been reviewed, the manufacturing phase begins with the design of a prototype computer. Once the design is determined, the required materials are purchased and prototypes manufactured. Prototype models are then tested and analyzed by staff personnel who have completed a staff training course. Based on their input, refinements are made to the prototype and an initial production run of computers is scheduled.

Staff training of company personnel begins once the computer is designed, allowing the staff to test the prototypes once they have been manufactured. After the computer design has been revised based on staff input, the sales force undergoes full-scale training.

Advertising is a two-phase procedure. First, a small group works closely with the design team so that once a product design has been chosen, the marketing team can begin an initial preproduction advertising campaign. Following this initial campaign and completion of the final design revisions, a larger advertising team is introduced to the special features of the computer, and a full-scale advertising program is launched.

The entire project is concluded when the initial production run is completed, the salespersons are trained, and the advertising campaign is underway. As a first step in generating a project schedule, Klone needs to develop a precedence relations chart that gives a concise set of individual tasks for the project and shows which other tasks must be completed prior to the commencement of each task.

SOLUTION

The entire project can be represented by the ten activities—five manufacturing, three training, and two advertising—given in Table 5.1. For easy reference, each activity is designated by a letter symbol.[1] After identifying the activities, we determine the immediate predecessors for each one using the reasoning in Table 5.2.

TABLE 5.1   Klonepalm 2000 Activity Description

	Activity	Description
Manufacturing activities	A	Prototype model design
	B	Purchase of materials
	C	Manufacture of prototype models
	D	Revision of design
	E	Initial production run
Training activities	F	Staff training
	G	Staff input on prototype models
	H	Sales training
Advertising activities	I	Preproduction advertising campaign
	J	Post-redesign advertising campaign

These relations, along with Klone's estimates of the expected completion time for each activity (based on its past experiences manufacturing similar products), are summarized in the *precedence relations chart* shown in Table 5.3. We will use this chart to construct graphical representations of the project.

If each activity of the Klonepalm 2000 project were performed sequentially, ignoring the possibility that some of the activities of the project could be completed simultaneously, the estimated completion time of the project would be $90 + 15 + 5 + 20 + 21 + 25 + 14 + 28 + 30 + 45 = 293$ days. Since work on several of the activities *can* be underway at the same time, however, the time required to complete the project will be less than 293 days. The goal of the management science team is to schedule activities so that the entire project is completed in the minimal number of days.

---

[1] Instead of letters, we could have used abbreviations or some other identifier. Which letter will designate which activity is a purely arbitrary decision and has no implications for which activity must be completed first.

TABLE 5.2   Immediate Predecessors for Klonepalm 2000 Activities

Activity	Requirements	Immediate Predecessors
A Prototype design	No requirements	—
B Purchase of materials	Materials can be purchased only after the prototypes have been designed (A).	A
C Manufacture of prototypes	Materials must be purchased (B) before the prototypes can be manufactured.	B
D Revision of design	Both prototype manufacturing (C) and staff input (G) must precede the design revision. However, since prototype manufacturing precedes staff input, it is not an *immediate* predecessor.	G
E Initial production run	The production run can begin after the design has been revised (D).	D
F Staff training	Staff training begins after the prototype is designed (A).	A
G Staff input on prototype	For staff input on prototypes, the prototype must be built (C) and the staff trained (F).	C,F
H Sales training	Salespersons can be trained immediately after the design revision (D).	D
I Preproduction advertising campaign	The initial preproduction advertising campaign can begin as soon as the prototypes have been designed (A).	A
J Post-redesign advertising campaign	The large-scale postproduction advertising campaign begins when the initial ad campaign has been completed (I) and the design has been revised (D).	D,I

TABLE 5.3   Klonepalm 2000 Precedence Relations Chart

Activity	Immediate Predecessors	Estimated Completion Time (days)
A	—	90
B	A	15
C	B	5
D	G	20
E	D	21
F	A	25
G	C,F	14
H	D	28
I	A	30
J	D,I	45

THE PERT/CPM NETWORK

PERT/CPM is one popular approach used in project scheduling. The PERT/CPM approach is based on a network representation that reflects activity precedence relations. As shown in the network in Figure 5.1, the nodes designate activities and their time duration, and the arcs define the precedence relations between the activities. When an activity immediately precedes one or more other activities, a directed arc is drawn from its node to each node representing one of the subsequent activities. Note that there is one arc for each distinct entry in the immediate predecessor column in Table 5.2.

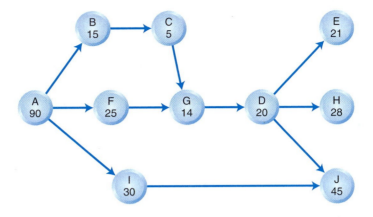

FIGURE 5.1
PERT/CPM Network for the
Klonepalm 2000 Project

5.3   The PERT/CPM Approach
for Project Scheduling

Two primary objectives of PERT/CPM analyses are (1) to determine the minimal possible completion time for the project; and (2) to determine a range of start and finish times for each activity so that the project can be completed in minimal time. To illustrate how the above network can be used to achieve these objectives, let us return to the planning process faced by Klone Computers.

Klonel.cpm

KLONE COMPUTERS, INC. (CONTINUED)

Management at Klone Computers would like to schedule the activities of the Klonepalm 2000 project so that it is completed in minimal time. In particular, management wishes to know:

1. The earliest completion date for the project
2. The earliest and latest start times for each activity which will not alter this date
3. The earliest and latest finish times for each activity which will not alter this date
4. The activities that must adhere to a rigid fixed schedule and the activities that can possibly be delayed without affecting the project completion time.

SOLUTION

The PERT/CPM approach for the Klonepalm 2000 computer project is illustrated by referring to the network developed for this problem in Figure 5.1. This is dynamically displayed on the PowerPoint slides on the accompanying CD-ROM.

EARLIEST START/FINISH TIMES—
EARLIEST COMPLETION DATE

To determine the **earliest start time (ES)** and the **earliest finish time (EF)** for the activities, a *forward pass* is made through the network. We begin by evaluating all activities that have no immediate predecessors—in this case, only activity A. The ES for an activity with no predecessors is 0; its EF is simply the activity's completion time. Thus, for activity A, ES(A) = 0, EF(A) = 90.

We then proceed by selecting any node for which the EF of all its immediate predecessors has been determined—in this case B, F, and I. Since *all* of an activity's immediate predecessors must be completed before the activity can begin, the

ES for this activity is the *maximum* of the EFs of its immediate predecessors. Its EF then equals its ES plus the time to complete the activity. Since activities B, F, and I require only the completion of activity A, and since the activity completion times for activities B, F, and I are 15, 25, and 30, respectively, we conclude:

$$ES(B) = 90 \qquad EF(B) = 90 + 15 = 105$$
$$ES(F) = 90 \qquad EF(F) = 90 + 25 = 115$$
$$ES(I) = 90 \qquad EF(I) = 90 + 30 = 120$$

Since activity B is the immediate predecessor for activity C and EF(B) = 105, we now can conclude:

$$ES(C) = 105 \qquad EF(C) = 105 + 5 = 110$$

Now consider activity G. Both activity C (with earliest finish time of 110) and activity F (with earliest finish time of 115) are immediate predecessors of activity G. Since both must be completed before activity G can commence, the earliest start time for activity G is the maximum of the earliest finish times for activities C and F:

$$ES(G) = MAX(EF(C), EF(F)) = MAX(110, 115) = 115$$

and,

$$EF(G) = 115 + 14 = 129$$

Hence we see that the following relationships exist when calculating ES and EF times.

Earliest Start/Finish Time for an Activity

ES = MAXIMUM EF of all its immediate predecessors

EF = ES + (Activity Completion Time)

We now repeat this process until all nodes have been evaluated. This gives us a schedule of earliest start and finish times for each activity. The maximum of the EF times of all nodes is the earliest completion time for the project. The sequence of calculations that determine these times is given in Table 5.4. **The maximum of EF times, 194, is the estimated completion time of the entire project.**

TABLE 5.4   Sequence of ES and EF Calculations

Activity	Immediate Predecessors (EF)	ES	EF
A	—	0	0 + 90 = 90
B	A (90)	90	90 + 15 = 105
F	A (90)	90	90 + 25 = 115
I	A (90)	90	90 + 30 = 120
C	B (105)	105	105 + 5 = 110
G	C (110), F (115)	115	115 + 14 = 129
D	G (129)	129	129 + 20 = 149
E	D (149)	149	149 + 21 = 170
H	D (149)	149	149 + 28 = 177
J	D (149), I (120)	149	149 + 45 = 194

The ES and EF for each activity are represented on the PERT/CPM network by a pair of numbers above the node representing the activity, as shown in Figure 5.2.

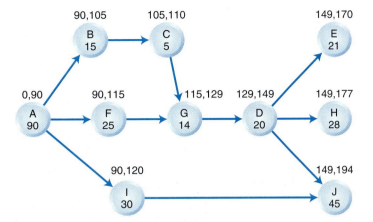

FIGURE 5.2
Earliest Start and Finish Times for the Klonepalm 2000 Project

LATEST START/FINISH TIMES

To determine the **latest start time (LS)** and **latest finish time (LF)** for each activity which allows the project to be completed by its minimal completion date of 194 days, a *backwards pass* is made through the network. We begin by evaluating all activities that have no successor activities. These are activities E, H, and J, which have completion times of 21, 28, and 45, respectively. The LF for each of these activities is the minimal project completion time (194 days). The LS for each of these activities is determined by subtracting the corresponding activity's duration from its LF value. Thus,

$$LF(E) = 194 \quad LS(E) = 194 - 21 = 173$$
$$LF(H) = 194 \quad LS(H) = 194 - 28 = 166$$
$$LF(J) = 194 \quad LS(J) = 194 - 45 = 149$$

Continuing the backwards pass through the network, we see that activity J is the only successor activity to activity I. Activity I must therefore be finished in time to start activity by activity J's latest start time:

$$LF(I) = LS(J) = 149$$

Thus,

$$LS(I) = 149 - 30 = 119$$

Activity D, however, is the predecessor to three activities (E, H, and J). Hence it must be finished in time to start each of these activities by their LS times. That is, activity D must be finished in time to start activity E by day 173, in time to start activity H by day 166, and in time to start activity J by day 149. For all three of these conditions to be met, activity D must be finished by day 149, that is,

$$LF(D) = MIN(LS(E), LS(H), LS(J)) = MIN(173, 166, 149) = 149$$

Thus,

$$LS(D) = 149 - 20 = 129$$

From this discussion we see that the following relationships exist for calculating LF and LS times for any activity.

> **Latest Start/Finish Times for an Activity**
>
> LF = MINIMUM LS of all immediate successor activities
>
> LS = LF − (Activity Completion Time)

We repeat this process until all nodes have been evaluated, as shown in Table 5.5.

TABLE 5.5   Sequence of LF and LS Calculations

Activity	Immediate Successors (LS)	LF	LS
J	—	194	194 − 45 = 149
H	—	194	194 − 28 = 166
E	—	194	194 − 21 = 173
I	J (149)	149	149 − 30 = 119
D	E (173), H (166), J (149)	149	149 − 20 = 129
G	D (129)	129	129 − 14 = 115
C	G (115)	115	115 − 5 = 110
F	G (115)	115	115 − 25 = 90
B	C (110)	110	110 − 15 = 95
A	B (95), F (90), I (119)	90	90 − 90 = 0

We denote the LS and LF for each activity on the PERT/CPM network by placing these numbers below the corresponding node representing it. Figure 5.3 is a complete network representation showing both the earliest and latest start and finish times for the Klonepalm 2000 project.

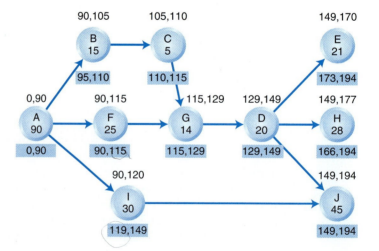

FIGURE 5.3
Earliest/Latest Start and Finish Times for the Klonepalm 2000 Project

THE CRITICAL PATH AND SLACK TIMES

In the course of completing a project, both planned and unforeseen delays can affect activity start or completion times. For example, revising the design of the computer (activity D), which is scheduled to take 20 days, may actually require 30 days. Or management may have to delay the start of sales training (activity H) by five days because the firm's training classroom might have been previously booked for another function. Some of these delays affect the overall completion date of the project; others may not.

To analyze the impact of such delays on the project, we determine the **slack time** for each activity. Slack time is the amount of time an activity can be delayed from its ES without delaying the project's estimated completion time. It is calculated by subtracting an activity's ES from its LS (or its EF from its LF). This value for an activity's slack time assumes that *only the completion time of this single activity has been changed* and that there are *no other delays to activities in the project*. Table 5.6 details the slack time calculations for each activity in the Klonepalm 2000 project.

TABLE 5.6 Slack Times

Activity A:	Slack (A)	= LS(A) − ES(A) =	0 − 0 =	0
Activity B:	Slack (B)	= LS(B) − ES(B) =	95 − 90 =	5
Activity C:	Slack (C)	= LS(C) − ES(C) =	110 − 105 =	5
Activity D:	Slack (D)	= LS(D) − ES(D) =	119 − 119 =	0
Activity E:	Slack (E)	= LS(E) − ES(E) =	173 − 149 =	24
Activity F:	Slack (F)	= LS(F) − ES(F) =	90 − 90 =	0
Activity G:	Slack (G)	= LS(G) − ES(G) =	115 − 115 =	0
Activity H:	Slack (H)	= LS(H) − ES(H) =	166 − 149 =	17
Activity I:	Slack (I)	= LS(I) − ES(I) =	119 − 90 =	29
Activity J:	Slack (J)	= LS(J) − ES(J) =	149 − 149 =	0

When an activity has slack time, the manager has some flexibility in scheduling and may be able to distribute the workload more evenly throughout the project's duration without affecting its overall completion date. This is especially important in projects with limited staff or resources. The concept of **resource leveling** is discussed in more detail in Section 5.7.

Activities that have *no* slack time (activities A, D, F, G, and J) are called **critical activities**. These activities must be rigidly scheduled to start and finish at their specific ES and EF times, respectively. Any delay in completing a critical activity will delay completion time of the entire project beyond 194 days by the corresponding amount.

Slack Time/Critical Activities

Slack time for an activity = LS − ES or LF − EF.

Critical activities are those with slack time = 0.

As Figure 5.4 illustrates, these critical activities form a path, called a **critical path**, through the network. The sum of the completion times of the activities on the critical path is the minimal completion time for the project (90 + 25 + 14 + 20 + 45 = 194). Because it consists of the sequence of activities that cannot be delayed without affecting the earliest project completion date, the critical path is actually the *longest path in the directed network*. Summarizing, for the Klonepalm 2000 project, we have:

EXPECTED PROJECT COMPLETION TIME: 194 days
CRITICAL PATH: A–F–G–D–J

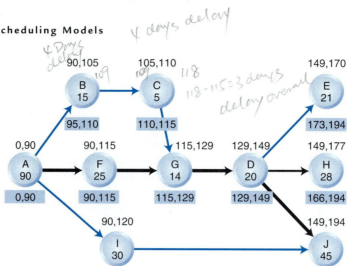

FIGURE 5.4
Critical Path for the
Klonepalm 2000 Project:
A–F–G–D–J

It is possible to have more than one critical path in a PERT/CPM network. For example, if the completion time of activity I had been 59 days rather than 30 days, both its earliest and latest start times would be 149. Thus, a second critical path giving a total completion time of 194 days would have consisted of activities A, I, and J.

Critical Path

1. The critical activities (activities with 0 slack) form *at least one* critical path in the network.
2. A critical path is the longest path in the network.
3. The sum of the completion times for the activities on the critical path gives the minimal completion time of the project.

ANALYSIS OF POSSIBLE DELAYS

The ES, EF, LS, LF, and slack for each activity are frequently condensed into a single chart, known as an *activity schedule chart* (see Table 5.7).

TABLE 5.7   Activity Schedule Chart: Klonepalm 2000 Project

Activity	ES	EF	LS	LF	Slack
A	0	90	0	90	0
B	90	105	95	110	5
C	105	110	110	115	5
D	129	149	129	149	0
E	149	170	173	194	24
F	90	115	90	115	0
G	115	129	115	129	0
H	149	177	166	194	17
I	90	120	119	149	29
J	149	194	149	194	0

Using this chart and the PERT/CPM network, we can analyze the effect of possible delays in individual activities on the completion time of the entire project.

SINGLE DELAYS

A delay in a single critical activity will result in an equivalent delay in the entire project. For example, if activity D, a critical activity with no slack, were delayed six days, the entire project would be delayed six days.

A delay in a noncritical activity will only delay the project by the amount the delay exceeds the activity's slack; a delay less than the slack time of the activity will not affect the project completion time. For example, since activity B has a slack of five days (as shown in the activity chart), delaying it by four days will not delay the entire project, while delaying it by seven will delay the project by $7 - 5 = 2$ days.

MULTIPLE DELAYS

When there is a delay in starting or finishing more than one activity, the activity chart must be complemented by the PERT/CPM network representation to carry out the analysis. Let us consider three cases in which completion of two noncritical activities is delayed.

CASE 1: Activities E and I are each delayed 15 days.   From the activity chart we see that activity E has a slack time of 24 days and activity I has a slack time of 29 days. Thus, if either were delayed 15 days individually, the overall project completion date would be unaffected. But we must determine whether the delay in one of these activities will result in the added delay in the start of the other. From the PERT/CPM network (Figure 5.3) we see that there is no path from activity E to activity I. Hence, the completion time of activity E will have no effect on the completion time of activity I, and vice versa.
PROJECT DELAY: 0 *days.*

CASE 2: Activity B is delayed 4 days and activity E is delayed 15 days.
Again, if either of these delays occurred individually, the project would not be delayed. From the PERT/CPM network we see that since activity B has five days of slack, this delay does not affect the start and finish dates of activities G and D on the critical path. Thus, activities G and D can be completed on time, and, since activity E has 24 days of slack time, a delay of 15 days will not affect the minimum completion time of the project.
PROJECT DELAY: 0 *days.*

CASE 3: Activity B is delayed 4 days and activity C is delayed 4 days.
Once again, if only one of these delays occurs, the completion time of the entire project is not affected. However, as we see in Figure 5.5, if activity B is delayed 4 days, its EF is now 109 instead of 105. Thus the ES for activity C is now 109. Adding the normal completion time of five days plus the four-day delay for activity C, we see that its EF is now 118. Since the original LF for activity C is 115, there is a delay in the overall project completion time.
PROJECT DELAY: $118 - 115 = 3$ days.

In each of these three cases, two noncritical activities are simultaneously delayed but by less than their slack times. How do these cases differ? In Case 1, there is no path linking the two activities; hence, delaying one does not affect the other. In Case 2, the noncritical activities are on the same path but are separated

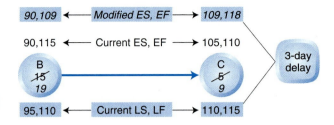

FIGURE 5.5
Case 3: Multiple Delays along the Critical Path

by a critical activity. In both cases, the overall project completion date does not change.

In Case 3, however, the two noncritical activities are on the same path and are not separated by a critical activity. Here, a delay in one of the activities reduces the slack time available for the others on the path because activities along a noncritical path "share" the available slack time. In this case, further investigative analyses are required to accurately determine the total effect on the entire project.

Most projects of any size are solved using software specifically designed for project scheduling. When multiple delays are incurred, the easiest way to determine the effect to the project completion time and the critical path is simply to reenter the updated information and re-solve the model.

5.4   A Linear Programming Approach to PERT/CPM

Given the estimated completion times for each activity and the immediate predecessor relationships, PERT/CPM networks can actually be modeled and solved as linear programs. One way to do this is to define variables X_A, X_B, X_C, and so on, to represent the start times for each of the corresponding activities. The constraint set consists of the nonnegativity constraints and one constraint for each immediate predecessor relationship in the project. These immediate predecessor constraints state that:

Activity Start Time ≥ Immediate Predecessor Finish Time

Since the finish time for any activity equals its start time plus its completion time, we can restate the relationship above as:

> **Linear Programming Constraints for PERT/CPM**
>
> Start Time for an Activity ≥
>
> Start Time for the Immediate Predecessor Activity +
>
> Immediate Predecessor's Activity Completion Time

For example, in the Klonepalm 2000 network developed in the last section, both activities C (completion time = 5) and F (completion time = 25) are immediate predecessors for activity G. Thus two constraints of this model are:

$$X_G \geq X_C + 5$$
$$X_G \geq X_F + 25$$

Applying this approach to the entire Klonepalm 2000 network, we find that the complete constraint set for this model is:

$$X_E \geq X_D + 20$$
$$X_H \geq X_D + 20$$
$$X_J \geq X_D + 20$$
$$X_J \geq X_I + 30$$
$$X_D \geq X_G + 14$$
$$X_G \geq X_C + 5$$
$$X_G \geq X_F + 25$$
$$X_C \geq X_B + 15$$
$$X_I \geq X_A + 90$$
$$X_F \geq X_A + 90$$
$$X_B \geq X_A + 90$$
$$\text{All X's} \geq 0$$

CALCULATING THE EARLIEST START AND FINISH TIMES

It can be shown that if we make the objective function: MIN ΣX's (in this model, MIN $X_A + X_B + X_C + X_D + X_E + X_F + X_G + X_H + X_I + X_J$), although the actual value of the objective function is meaningless, the resulting set of X's will give the *earliest* start (ES) times for each of the activities. The earliest finish (EF) times can then be calculated by adding the activity completion times to these earliest start times. *The overall project completion time is then the maximum of these earliest finish times.*

CALCULATING THE LATEST START AND FINISH TIMES

After solving this linear program and determining that 194 is the expected project completion time, we solve a second linear program. This time we assume that the precedence relations are reversed (the arrows on the activity on the PERT/CPM network now point in the opposite direction), and the problem is solved again with constraints now representing this set of reversed directions. The *latest finish* (LF) times are then found by subtracting the X values generated by this second linear program from 194. Then the *latest start* (LS) times are found by subtracting the activity completion times from the LS times.

5.5   Obtaining Results Using Excel

The Klonepalm model is small enough so that a hand solution is neither tedious nor difficult. To solve this problem using an Excel spreadsheet, one could program each cell's ES and LF times individually as shown in columns D and G of Figure 5.6. The formulas for the cells in columns D and G are given in columns I and J respectively. These formulas show that the ES times must equal the maximum of the corresponding EF times of its immediate predecessor activities listed in column B and the LF times must equal the minimum of the LS for which the corresponding activity is an immediate predecessor. As you can imagine, doing this can take much longer than solving the problem by hand. In fact, you are actually solving the problem by inputting the formulas; all Excel is doing is performing the simple arithmetic operations.

Another approach is to solve the model as a linear program as discussed in the last section. But again, the constraints are problem specific, and entering each constraint into the Solver dialogue box would require about as much work as solving the model by hand.

Klonepalm Excel.xls

KLONEPALM 2000

Activity	Immediate Predecessors	Completion Time	ES	EF	LS	LF	SLACK	Column D Formulas	Column G Formulas
A		90	0	90	0	90	0	0	=MIN(F5,F9,F12)
B	A	15	90	105	95	110	5	=E4	=F6
C	B	5	105	110	110	115	5	=E5	=F10
D	G	20	129	149	129	149	0	=E10	=MIN(F11,F13)
E	D	21	149	170	173	194	24	=E7	=E15
F	A	25	90	115	90	115	0	=E4	=F10
G	C,F	14	115	129	115	129	0	=MAX(E6,E9)	=F7
H	D	28	149	177	166	194	17	=E7	=E15
I	A	30	90	120	119	149	29	=E4	=F13
J	D,I	45	149	194	149	194	0	=MAX(E7,E12)	=E15

PROJECT COMPLETION TIME = 194

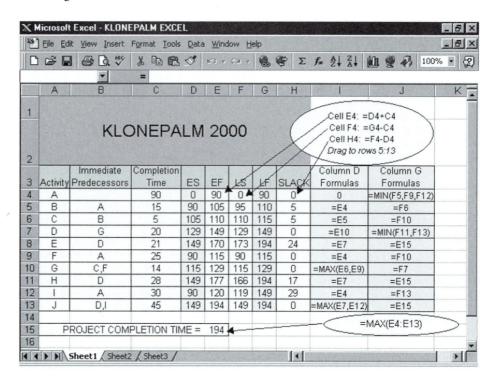

FIGURE 5.6
Excel Spreadsheet for the Klonepalm 2000 Project

In this text we include four Excel templates on the accompanying CD-ROM for solving each of the project scheduling models introduced in this chapter: (1) PERT-CPM; (2) CPM-Deadline; (3) CPM-Budget; and, (4) PERT-COST. Each template is based on the linear programming approach but requires no programming on the user's part. After entering the required input for the specific model, Solver is called and one only needs to click "Solve" to obtain the results. Solver is preprogrammed to perform the necessary operations and generate usable output. Each project template operates slightly differently. Instructions for using each template are given in Appendix 5.1.

The output from the PERT-CPM template for the Klonepalm 2000 model is shown in Figure 5.7. At this point ignore the references to standard deviation,

Klonepalm.xls

CRITICAL PATH ANALYSIS

MEAN	194
STANDARD DEVIATION*	0
VARIANCE*	0
PROBABILITY COMPLETE BEFORE	=

*Assumes all critical activities are on one critical path
If not, enter in gold box, the variance on one critical path of interest.

Acitivty	Node	Critical	μ	σ	σ^2	ES	EF	LS	LF	Slack
Design	A	*	90			0	90	0	90	0
Materials	B		15			90	105	95	110	5
Manufacture	C		5			105	110	110	115	5
Design Revision	D	*	20			129	149	129	149	0
Production Run	E		21			149	170	173	194	24
Staff Training	F	*	25			90	115	90	115	0
Staff Input	G	*	14			115	129	115	129	0
Sales Training	H		28			149	177	166	194	17
Preprod. Advertise	I		30			90	120	119	149	29
Post. Advertise	J	*	45			149	194	149	194	0

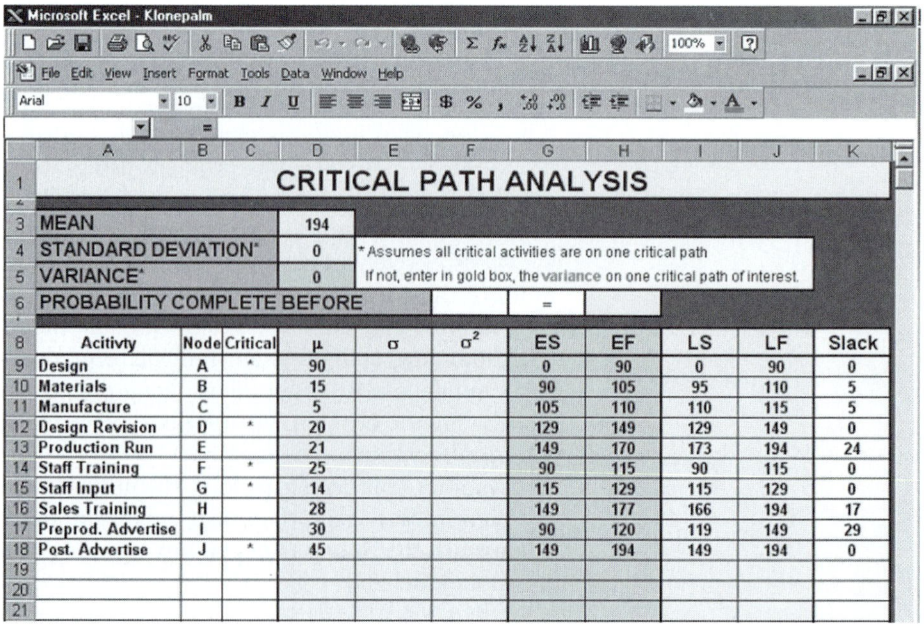

FIGURE 5.7
PERT-CPM Template Output for the Klonepalm 2000 Model

variance, and probability; these will be discussed in Section 5.8. You can see that this output contains the estimated activity times in column D labeled "μ", identifies the activities on the critical path in column C by an "*", and gives the ES, EF, LS, LF, and slack times in columns G, H, I, J, and K respectively. The estimated project completion time is given in cell D3 (labeled "MEAN").

5.6   Gantt Charts

One responsibility of project managers is to track the progress of the project. A popular device used to display activities and monitor their progress is the **Gantt chart**.[2] In a Gantt chart, time is measured on the horizontal axis, each activity is listed on the vertical axis, and a bar is drawn corresponding to its expected completion time. In an *earliest time Gantt chart*, the bar begins at the earliest moment the activity can be started (which is when all the activity's immediate predecessors are expected to be completed). The end of the bar represents the earliest completion time for the activity.

Figure 5.8 shows the earliest time Gantt chart for the Klonepalm 2000 project. In Appendix 5.2 we give instructions for how to construct this chart from the PERT OUTPUT worksheet of the PERT-CPM template.

Klonepalm Gantt.xls

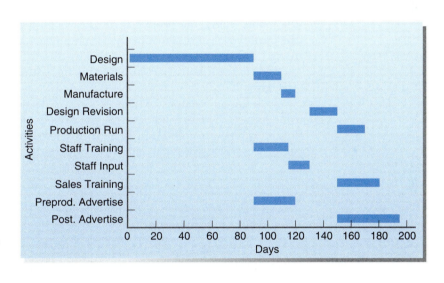

FIGURE 5.8
Earliest Time Gantt Chart for the Klonepalm 2000 Project

Latest time Gantt charts can be similarly constructed as shown in the file Klonepalm Gantt.xls on the accompanying CD-ROM.

MONITORING PROJECT PROGRESS ON A GANTT CHART

A crucial step in meeting a target completion date and containing costs is management's ability to monitor a project's progress. We can use a Gantt chart as a visual aid for tracking the progress of project activities by shading an appropriate percentage of the corresponding bar to document the completed work. A manager then need only glance at the chart on a given date to see if the project is being completed on schedule with respect to the earliest possible completion times of the activities.

For example, suppose the chart in Figure 5.9 indicates the progress of the Klonepalm 2000 project after 135 days. At this point, the following activities have been completed: prototype design (A), purchase material (B), manufacture prototype (C), staff training (F), and the staff input (G). The design revision activity (D) is about 40% complete, and the preproduction advertising activity (I) is about 50% complete.

---

[2] Named for Henry Gantt, who developed the first such chart in 1918.

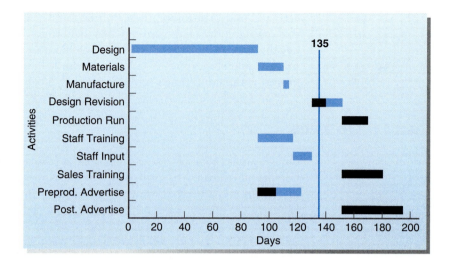

FIGURE 5.9
Klonepalm 2000 Project: Monitoring the Project after 135 Days

It is important not to misinterpret the meaning of such a chart, however. We might be tempted to say that because activity I is only about one-half completed at day 135 (instead of being totally completed by day 120 as indicated by the bar on the Gantt chart), the project is running behind schedule. *This is not true.* In fact, the overall project might actually be running *ahead* of schedule! This is because activity I does *not* have to be completed by the earliest possible completion time indicated on the Gantt chart in order for the entire project to be completed within 194 days.

We saw in Section 5.3 that as long as delays do not extend the completion time for activity I beyond day 149, the project will not be delayed. This potential misinterpretation points out one of the deficiencies of Gantt charts. Table 5.8 summarizes other pros and cons of Gantt charts.

TABLE 5.8   Advantages and Disadvantages of the Earliest Time Gantt Chart Approach

Advantages	Disadvantages
1. The Gantt chart is easy to construct.	1. The Gantt chart gives only one possible schedule (the earliest) for the activities.
2. An earliest possible completion date can be determined.	2. It may not be possible to tell whether the project is behind schedule.
3. A schedule of earliest possible start and finish times for the activities is given that will meet the earliest possible project completion date.	3. Because precedence relations are not revealed on a Gantt chart, it is not obvious from the chart alone how a delay in one activity will affect the start date of another.

5.7 Resource Leveling

The concept of controlling daily resource requirements and smoothing out their use over the course of the project is known as **resource leveling**. Because of the mathematical complexities of resource leveling models, heuristics are typically used to generate good, if not optimal, resource leveling plans. For example, suppose it can be assumed that (1) once an activity has been started it is worked on continuously until it is completed; and (2) that costs accrue at a constant rate over the activity's duration. Then we can determine the cost per day of the critical activities, whose schedule is fixed, and attempt to schedule the noncritical activities in such a way that:

1. The noncritical activities begin within their ES and LS times.
2. They are performed during periods in which there is less required spending on critical and previously scheduled noncritical activities.

To illustrate such an approach, let us revisit the situation at Klone Computer, Inc.

KLONE COMPUTER INC. (REVISITED)

Management at Klone Computers wishes to design a schedule that will complete the Klonepalm 2000 project in minimal time (194 days), while keeping daily expenditures as constant as possible. Analysts have supplied management with the cost estimates for the activities shown in Table 5.9.

TABLE 5.9   Cost Estimates for Klonepalm 2000 Activities

Activity	Description	Total Cost ($1000)	Total Time (Days)	Cost Per Day ($1000)
A	Prototype model design	2250	90	25
B	Purchase of materials	180	15	12
C	Manufacture of prototype models	90	5	18
D	Revision of design	300	20	15
E	Initial production run	231	21	11
F	Staff training	250	25	10
G	Staff input on prototype models	70	14	5
H	Sales training	392	28	14
I	Preproduction advertising campaign	510	30	17
J	Postproduction advertising campaign	1350	45	30
	Total Cost =	5623		

SOLUTION

As we saw in the last section, the Klonepalm 2000 project can be completed in 194 days as long as each activity is scheduled between its ES, EF, LS, and LF times. In Figure 5.10 we plot the cumulative daily expenditures using an earliest time assignment (the top solid line) and a latest time assignment (the bottom solid line) of the activities. For example, referring to Table 5.8, using an earliest time assignment, we estimate the total cost at day 118 to be $3,261,000 since activities A, B, C, and F should be finished costing $2,770,000, three days of work on activity G should be complete costing 3($5000) = $15,000, and 28 days of activity I should be complete costing 28($17,000) = $476,000. The total cost using a latest time assignment of activities is estimated to be $2,785,000, since again, activities A, B, C, and F should be finished, three days of work on activity G should be complete, but activity I has not been started.

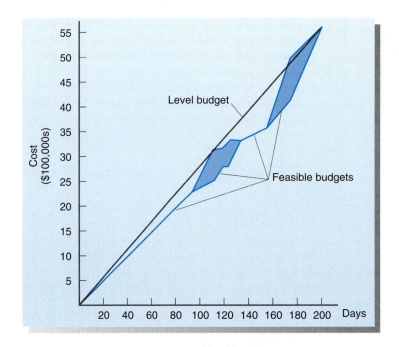

FIGURE 5.10
Cumulative Daily
Expenditures—Klonepalm
2000 Project Using Earliest
Time Assignments

We see from Figure 5.10 that the two lines coincide between days 0 to 90 when, in both schedules, only activity A is being completed, and from days 129 to 149 when, again in both schedules, activities A, B, C, F, G, and I have been finished and only activity D is being completed. These two lines and the two shaded regions on either side of days 129 and 149 represent *feasible budgets*. The straight line represents a "level budget" of $28,985 (=$5,623,000/194) per day.

Although we cannot construct a feasible budget that is level throughout the duration of the project, our goal is to smooth the costs as evenly as possible while still completing the project within 194 days. Figure 5.11 is a plot of the average daily expenditures of the critical activities A, F, G, D, and J.

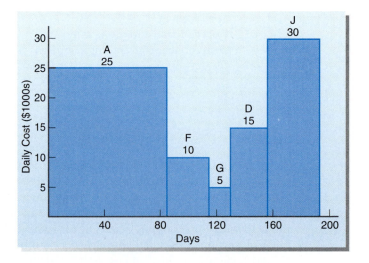

FIGURE 5.11
Average Daily Cost of
Critical Activities

Noncritical activities B and I must be scheduled to begin after day 90 (when activity A is completed), and activities C and I must be completed before day 149 (when activity J is started. It would seem reasonable to schedule these activities in such a way as to take advantage of the lower cost periods from day 90 to day 115

(10 per day) and from day 115 to day 129 (5 per day). This can be done by scheduling activities B and C at their earliest start times of 90 and 105, respectively, and then scheduling activity I to start immediately upon completion of activity C (from day 110 to day 140).

We also note that activities E and H must be scheduled during the completion of activity J (from day 149 to 194). To try to get as little overlap as possible, we can schedule activity E to begin at its earliest start time (149) and schedule activity H to conclude at its latest finish time (194). The result of all these schedule modifications is shown in Figure 5.12.

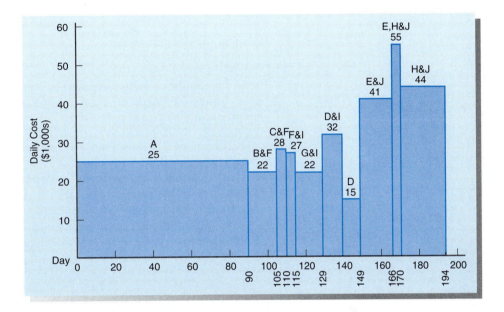

FIGURE 5.12
Resource Scheduling Chart

MANAGEMENT MEMO

Based on this analysis, the following memo to management summarizes the project and resource leveling results. Tables and graphs highlight the main points of the analysis.

·SCG·
STUDENT CONSULTING GROUP

M E M O R A N D U M

To: Stephen Chores
             Klone Computers, Inc.

From: Student Consulting Group

Subj: Project Scheduling for the Development of the Klonepalm 2000
             Palmbook Computer

We have conducted an analysis of the work assignments required to develop, produce, and market the Klonepalm 2000 computer. Based on interviews with management and staff, we have divided the project into ten broad tasks, consisting of five manufacturing, three training, and two advertising activities.

Manufacturing

1. Design the Klonepalm 2000 model
2. Purchase materials required to manufacture the product
3. Manufacture the first batch of prototype models
4. Design revision based on staff input
5. Produce initial production run for public distribution

Training

1. Staff training
2. Solicitation of staff input for product modifications
3. Training of sales personnel

Advertising

1. Preproduction advertising campaign to prepare the public (in general terms) for the introduction of the new model
2. Final advertising campaign

Proper scheduling of these tasks is crucial to ensure that the product will be ready for distribution at the earliest possible date. Accordingly, we have collected cost and time estimates from the departments involved in the project development. Although these data are only forecasts and best estimates, we feel that, because Klone has had experience developing other computer models in the past, these estimates should provide a reasonable foundation on which to base our recommendations.

RECOMMENDATIONS

Given a February 1 start date, we have developed a schedule for the individual tasks of the Klonepalm 2000 project using a standard project planning technique known as PERT (Programmed Evaluation and Review Technique). The schedule assumes a five-day work week and takes into account holidays such as Presidents Day, Memorial Day, Independence Day, and Labor Day. It also keeps daily expenditures as level as possible throughout the project while completing the project in a minimal time of 194 workdays. The project should be completed by November 3, in time to meet the anticipated demand generated by the Christmas season.

THE SCHEDULE

The schedule we have developed is shown in Table I.

TABLE I   Klonepalm 2000 Schedule

Project Activity	Activity Cost	Work-days	Begin Date	Finish Date
Prototype design	$2,250,000	90	Feb. 1	June 8
Purchase of materials	$ 180,000	15	June 9	June 29
Manufacture of prototypes	$ 90,000	5	June 30	July 7
Revision of design	$ 300,000	20	Aug. 4	Aug. 31
Initial production run	$ 231,000	21	Sept. 1	Sept. 30
Staff training	$ 250,000	25	June 9	July 14
Staff recommendations	$ 70,000	14	July 15	Aug. 3
Sales training	$ 392,000	28	Sept. 26	Nov. 3
Preproduction advertising	$ 510,000	30	July 8	Aug. 18
Final advertising campaign	$1,350,000	45	Sept. 1	Nov. 3

We recommend using the time chart depicted in Figure I to schedule project tasks. Figure II shows the anticipated daily cost requirements of this schedule throughout the lifetime of the project.

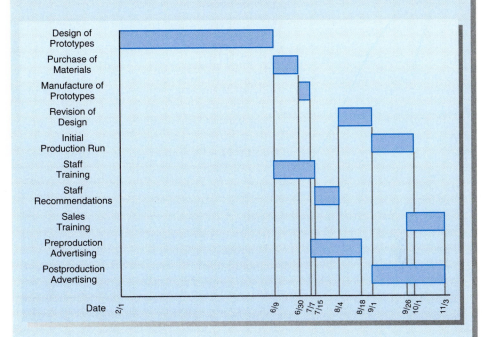

FIGURE I Klone Computers, Inc.—Klonepalm 2000 Project

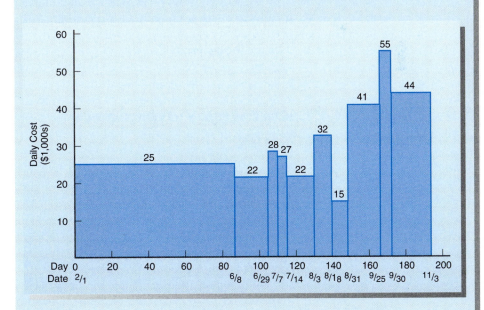

FIGURE II Klonepalm 2000 Project: Daily Cost Requirements

The average daily cost of the project is $28,985 and ranges from a low of $15,000 during the period from August 19 to August 31 to a high of $55,000 during the period from September 26 to September 30. Management should plan its financing accordingly.

In order to meet the target completion date of November 3, the following components must be completed on schedule:

1. Design of the prototype models
2. Staff training
3. Staff recommendations
4. Revised product design
5. Final advertising campaign

A delay in any one of these will extend the project beyond November 3. There is some flexibility in the scheduling of other activities which will still allow completion by the November 3 target date, as summarized in Table II.

TABLE II Flexibility in Klonepalm 2000 Scheduling

Activity	May Start By	Must Finish By	Total Flexibility	Recommended Start Date
Purchase of materials	June 9	July 7	5 days*	June 9
Manufacture of prototypes	June 30	July 14	5 days*	June 30
Initial production run	Sept. 1	Nov. 3	24 days	Sept. 1
Sales training	Sept. 1	Nov. 3	17 days	Sept. 26
Preproduction advertising	June 9	Aug. 31	29 days	July 8

*The total flexibility in scheduling both the purchase of materials and the manufacturing of the prototypes is a *combined* total of five days.

Any change to the recommended start and finish times can result in additional project expenses, however, and will definitely affect the distribution of the daily expenditures required for the project. Should scheduling changes be required, we can supply you with revised time and expenditure distribution charts for the project.

5.8 PERT—A Probabilistic Approach to Project Scheduling

Activity completion times are seldom known with 100% accuracy. When it comes to projects that have never been done before, subjective estimates for activity completion times must be made. Even in projects that are repeatedly performed, variability in the activity completion times occurs from one repetition to another. Given this uncertainty, PERT, a technique that treats activity completion times as random variables, can be used to determine the likelihood that a project will be completed within a certain time period.

One method used in PERT to convey activity variability without the undue burden of trying to make forecasts under a potentially limitless set of circumstances is the *three time estimate approach*. This approach, which is particularly useful for new projects, solicits three time estimates for each activity's completion time:

a = an optimistic time to perform the activity
m = the most likely time to perform the activity
b = a pessimistic time to perform the activity

Estimates a and b are reasonable "best case" and "worst case" scenarios that take into account normal fluctuations in performing the activity and any unforeseen events that may accelerate or deter its completion. The most likely time estimate, m, is an estimate of a usual or typical time to complete an activity; it corresponds to the statistical mode of the probability distribution for completion time.

In reality, we can never be certain that an activity will be completed even within the time period from a to b. There is always some (small) probability that the activity will require less time than the optimistic time, a, or more time than the pessimistic time, b. However, the time estimates selected for a and b should allow for only a relatively small chance, say less than 1%, of this occurring.

With only these three points to work with (a, m, and b), it is difficult to give a true estimate of this underlying probability distribution. It is important, however, to have *some* estimate so that we can approximate the mean and standard deviation of the activity's completion time. Statisticians have found that a **Beta distribution** is useful in approximating distributions with limited data and fixed end points.

The Beta distribution (which many statisticians affectionately term the "chameleon" of the statistical world) can assume a wide variety of shapes, depending on the judicious choice of its defining parameters. Figures 5.13a, b, and c show a few forms of *unimodal Beta* distributions that can arise in a PERT analysis. In each case, all the probability lies within the extreme values a and b, and the highest probability density occurs at the modal value, m.

In actuality, the assumption that activity times follow a Beta distribution has only a modest effect on the analysis of the completion time of the entire project. Of more concern are approximations for the average, or mean, activity completion time, μ, and its standard deviation, σ, which are based on the time estimates a, m, and b. These estimates are:

$$\mu = \frac{a + 4m + b}{6}$$

$$\sigma = \frac{b - a}{6}$$

The approximation for the mean, μ, is a weighted average of the three data points; $\frac{1}{6}$ of the weight is assigned to each of the extreme values a and b, and $\frac{4}{6}$ of the weight is assigned to the mode, m. The expression for the standard deviation, σ, is derived from the fact that, for many distributions (particularly smooth unimodal distributions), the range of values from the highest to the lowest ($b - a$) covers roughly six standard deviations.

It has been shown that if the mode is within roughly the middle 75% of the range between a and b, theses approximations for μ and σ are very good estimates. For example, if a given activity has an optimistic completion time, $a = 10$ days, and a pessimistic completion time, $b = 30$ days, the range is $b - a = 20$ days. Thus, if the mode lies in the middle 15 days (=.75 × 20), from 12.5 to 27.5 days, the above formulas do indeed provide good approximations for the mean and standard deviation. For modal values *outside* this interval, correction factors have been derived for these approximations.

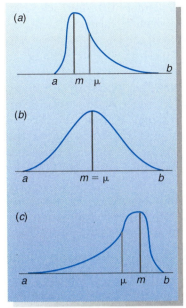

FIGURE 5.13
(a) Unimodal Beta Distribution Skewed Left; (b) Symmetric Unimodal Beta Distribution; (c) Unimodal Beta Distribution Skewed Right

---

Assumptions for Distribution of Activity Times in PERT

For each activity in a PERT/CPM network:

1. The probability density function for the activity's completion time is a unimodal Beta distribution.

2. Average (Mean) Completion Time: $\mu = \dfrac{a + 4m + b}{6}$

3. Standard Deviation of Completion Time: $\sigma = \dfrac{b - a}{6}$

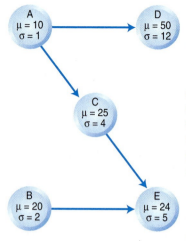

FIGURE 5.14
Mean and Standard Deviation of Activity Completion Times

The probabilistic approach to project scheduling assumes that, for each activity, j, its mean, μ_j, and its standard deviation, σ_j, have been calculated. The procedure for determining the mean and standard deviation of the *project completion time* is then based on several simplifying assumptions.

ASSUMPTION 1: A critical path can be determined by using the mean completion times for the activities as if they were fixed completion times. The <u>mean</u> completion time for the <u>project</u> is the sum of the mean completion times of the <u>activities along this critical path</u>; the <u>variance</u> of the completion time of the <u>project</u> is the sum of the variances of the completion times of the <u>activities along this critical path</u>.

This assumption implies that the critical path will not change even though the actual completion time of an activity on the critical path might be less than its average time, and/or the actual completion time of an activity off the critical path might be longer than its average time.

This assumption is often questionable, as we see in Figure 5.14. Using the mean activity completion times, we find that the critical path is A–D, with an expected completion time of $10 + 50 = 60$ days. But the large standard deviations for activities C, D, and E make it likely that activity C could take 30 days instead of 25, activity E could take 28 days instead of 24, and activity D could take 40 days instead of 50. In this case, if the other activity times were equal to their mean time, the new critical path would be A–C–E, and the completion time would actually be 68 days rather than the 50 days of the revised A–D path. *Such a change in the critical path is expressly ruled out by assumption 1.*

ASSUMPTION 2: The time to complete one activity is independent of the time to complete any other activity.

This assumption implies that a hastening or a delay in the completion of one activity will have no effect on the completion time of the other activities in the project. This assumption should be checked for validity.

For example, in a project to build furnished apartments, one activity might be "install refrigerators in the apartments," and another might be "install washer/dryer units." If the same contractor were in charge of installing both the refrigerators and the washer/dryers, should labor problems with the contractor delay the installation of the refrigerators, installation of the washer/dryer units would also likely be delayed. If these installations were performed by different contractors, however, a delay by one subcontractor most likely would not affect the installation time of the other. *Assumption 2 reflects this latter situation.*

ASSUMPTION 3: There are enough activities on the critical path so that the distribution of the project completion time can be approximated by a normal distribution.

Recall that one form of the central limit theorem of statistics states that the sum of a large number of independently distributed random variables is approximately normally distributed, with a mean equal to the sum of the random variable means and a variance equal to the sum of the random variable variances. In this case, the random variables are the activity completion times of the activities *on the critical path*.

Assumptions 1 and 2 state that the project completion time is determined by the activities on the critical path and that these variables are independent. As a general rule, we typically want to have 30 or more independent random variables in the sum to employ the central limit theorem. But since we assume that each of these independent random variables has a distribution close to the shape of a normal distribution (as is the case for unimodal Beta distribution), far fewer than 30 independent random variables are necessary for the normal distribution to provide a good approximation. Since most real-life PERT problems have a significant number of activities on the critical path (each with a Beta distribution), assumption 3 usually does not present a problem.

Taken together, these three assumptions imply that the overall project completion time has an approximately normal distribution, with mean equal to the sum of the mean completion times along the critical path, and variance equal to the sum of the variances of the activities along the critical path. Note that *variances are summed, not standard deviations*. (Recall that a variance is simply the square of the standard deviation.)

If any one of these assumptions does not hold, simulation methods (discussed in Chapter 10) should be used rather than the method discussed in this section. But if these assumptions are accepted, then the following summarizes the sequence of steps required to describe the overall project completion time.

Determining the Distribution of the Overall Project Completion Time

1. For each activity j, calculate:

$$\mu_j = \frac{a + 4m + b}{6}, \qquad \sigma_j = \frac{b - a}{6}$$

2. Determine the critical path using the μ_j's as fixed times.

3. The overall project completion time has a *normal distribution* with

$$\text{Mean: } \mu = \sum_{j \text{ on Critical Path}} \mu_j$$

$$\text{Variance: } \sigma^2 = \sum_{j \text{ on Critical Path}} \sigma_j^2$$

$$\text{Standard deviation: } \sigma = \sqrt{\sigma^2}$$

To illustrate how we can use probabilities in PERT analyses, consider a revision of the model for the Klonepalm 2000 project.

Klonepalm.xls
Klonepalm Probabilities.xls

KLONE COMPUTERS, INC. (REVISED)

Rather than giving precise estimates for the activities of the Klonepalm 2000 project, the company has supplied the three time estimates for the completion of the activities shown in Table 5.10.

Management at Klone is interested in the following:

1. The probability that the project will be completed within 194 days

2. A reasonable interval estimate of the number of days to complete the project

3. The probability that the project will be completed within 180 days

4. The probability that the project will take longer than 210 days

5. An upper limit for the number of days within which it can be virtually sure the project will be completed.

TABLE 5.10   Time Estimates for Completion of Klonepalm 2000 Activities

Activity	Optimistic	Most Likely	Pessimistic
A	76	86	120
B	12	15	18
C	4	5	6
D	15	18	33
E	18	21	24
F	16	26	30
G	10	13	22
H	24	28	32
I	22	27	50
J	38	43	60

SOLUTION

The mean, variance, and standard deviation for activity A can be found by

$$\mu_A = \frac{76 + 4(86) + 120}{6} = 90$$

$$\sigma_A = \frac{120 - 76}{6} = 7.33$$

$$\sigma_A^2 = (7.33)^2 = 53.78$$

Similar calculations for the other activities give the results shown in Table 5.11.

TABLE 5.11   Mean, Variance, and Standard Deviation of Klonepalm 2000 Activities

Activity	μ	σ	σ^2
A	90	7.33	53.78
B	15	1.00	1.00
C	5	.33	.11
D	20	3.00	9.00
E	21	1.00	1.00
F	25	2.33	5.44
G	14	2.00	4.00
H	28	1.33	1.78
I	30	4.67	21.78
J	45	3.67	13.44

Note that the means for the activities are the same as those used in the previous PERT/CPM analysis. Thus the critical path is A–F–G–D–J, and the expected completion time of the project, μ, is:

$$\mu = \mu_A + \mu_F + \mu_G + \mu_D + \mu_J$$
$$= 90 + 25 + 14 + 20 + 45 = 194$$

The project variance, σ^2, is:

$$\sigma^2 = \sigma_A^2 + \sigma_F^2 + \sigma_G^2 + \sigma_D^2 + \sigma_J^2$$
$$= 53.78 + 5.44 + 4.00 + 9.00 + 13.44$$
$$= 85.66$$

Thus the standard deviation for the project, σ, is:

$$\sigma = \sqrt{\sigma^2} = 9.255$$

If management is willing to accept the three assumptions underlying PERT, the completion time for the Klonepalm computer project can be modeled by a normal random variable with mean, $\mu = 194$ days and standard deviation, $\sigma = 9.255$ days. We can then use this model to answer the questions posed by management. In these analyses, we define the following random variable:

$$X = \text{completion time of the project}$$

We can then convert the normally distributed random variable, X, into the standard normal random variable, Z, by

$$Z = \frac{X - \mu}{\sigma}$$

Here, Z represents *the number of standard deviations X is from the mean, μ*. A table for the standard normal random variable (Appendix A) can then be used to determine the probability of completing the project within any given time period, including those of concern to management.

1. The first concern—the probability that the project will be completed within 194 days—can be expressed as $P(X \le 194)$. Since 194 is the mean, μ, of the distribution,

$$P(X \le 194) = P(Z \le 0) = .5000$$

2. An interval in which we are reasonably sure the completion date lies depends on our interpretation of the words "reasonably sure." Here, we assume that "reasonably sure" means 95% sure. This includes the middle 95% of the probability from a normal distribution with $\mu = 194$ and $\sigma = 9.255$. This interval is:

$$\mu \pm z_{.025}\sigma$$

where $z_{.025}$ is the z-value that puts a probability of .025 in each tail of the normal distribution. $z_{.025} = 1.96$; hence, the interval is

$$194 \pm 1.96(9.255) = 194 \pm 18.14 \text{ days}$$

Because management would most likely prefer the interval in whole days, we round 18.14 up to 19 days, and the interval is from 175 to 213 days.

3. The probability that the project will be completed within 180 days can be expressed as $P(X \le 180)$. Referring to Figure 5.15, we see that when x = 180, z = $(180 - 194)/9.255 = -1.51$. Then, $P(X \le 180) = P(Z \le -1.51) = .5000 - .4345 = .0655$.

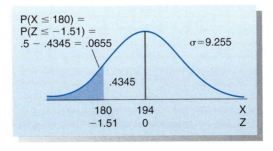

FIGURE 5.15
Probability of Completing the Klonepalm 2000 Project in 180 Days

4. The probability that the project will take longer than 210 days can be expressed as P(X ≥ 210). Referring to Figure 5.16, when x = 210, z = (210 − 194)/9.255 = 1.73. Then, P(X ≥ 210) = P(Z ≥ 1.73) = .5000 − .4582 = .0418.

5. "Virtually sure" can mean different things to different people, so let us assume that management will accept a date by which it is 99% certain of completing the project. This situation is depicted in Figure 5.17.

The z-value such that P(Z ≤ z) = .9900 is the value such that P(0 ≤ Z ≤ z) = .4900. From Appendix A, we see that this z-value is approximately 2.33. Since z = (x − μ)/σ, then x = μ + zσ. Thus,

$$x = \mu + z\sigma = 194 + 2.33(9.255) = 215.56 \text{ days}$$

As a result, we can report to management that we are virtually sure that the project will be completed within 216 days.

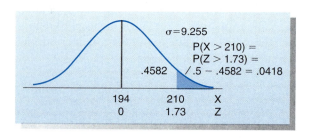

FIGURE 5.16 Probability That the Klonepalm 2000 Project Will Take Longer Than 210 Days

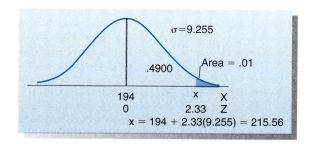

FIGURE 5.17 (99%) Certainty of Completing the Klonepalm 2000 Project

These results can be generated using the NORMINV and NORMDIST functions discussed in Chapter 1, as shown in Figure 5.18. They differ from the hand calculations due to roundoff error.

Klonepalm Probabilities.xls

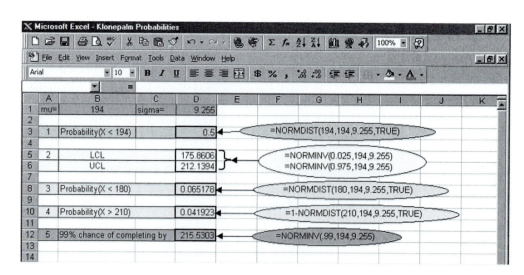

FIGURE 5.18 Klonepalm Results for Management Inquiries

USING THE PERT-CPM.xls TEMPLATE TO SOLVE FOR PROBABILITIES

We can use the PERT.xls template for solving models in which the activity completion times are random variables. The input instructions are given in Appendix 5.1. Figure 5.19 shows the resulting output screen. Note that on this screen we found that the probability of completing the project within 180 days is .065192. The slight difference in probability from that shown in Figure 5.18 is due to the fact that in Figure 5.18, the standard deviation was rounded to 9.255. Here we see the standard deviation is actually 9.255629.

Klonepalm-180.xls

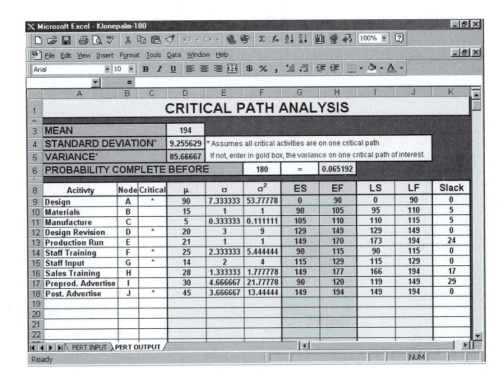

FIGURE 5.19
PERT-CPM.xls Template
Output for the Klonepalm
3-Time Estimate Model

CRITICAL PATH ANALYSIS

MEAN			194								
STANDARD DEVIATION*			9.255629	* Assumes all critical activities are on one critical path							
VARIANCE*			85.66667	If not, enter in gold box, the variance on one critical path of interest.							
PROBABILITY COMPLETE BEFORE			180	=	0.065192						

Acitivty	Node	Critical	μ	σ	σ²	ES	EF	LS	LF	Slack
Design	A	*	90	7.333333	53.77778	0	90	0	90	0
Materials	B		15	1	1	90	105	95	110	5
Manufacture	C		5	0.333333	0.111111	105	110	110	115	5
Design Revision	D	*	20	3	9	129	149	129	149	0
Production Run	E		21	1	1	149	170	173	194	24
Staff Training	F	*	25	2.333333	5.444444	90	115	90	115	0
Staff Input	G	*	14	2	4	115	129	115	129	0
Sales Training	H		28	1.333333	1.777778	149	177	166	194	17
Preprod. Advertise	I		30	4.666667	21.77778	90	120	119	149	29
Post. Advertise	J	*	45	3.666667	13.44444	149	194	149	194	0

MULTIPLE CRITICAL PATHS

Sometimes there exists more than one critical path in the PERT/CPM network. Usually, the critical paths are not independent. That is, one or more activities might be part of several critical paths. As a result, even though calculating the probability that the activities along any one critical path will be completed by a certain date is straightforward, calculating the probability that the entire project will be completed before a specific deadline date is a very complex calculation. As mentioned earlier, a simulation approach based on the concepts discussed in Chapter 10 can give a more reliable estimate.

5.9 Cost Analyses Using the Expected Value Approach

We have seen that, under a certain set of assumptions, the completion time of a project can be approximated by a normally distributed random variable. This condition can be quite useful when evaluating whether or not to spend extra money in an attempt to shorten a project. In general, spending extra money should decrease the project completion time, but we must evaluate whether this potential decrease in project completion time is cost effective.

One analytical approach to this problem is to use the **expected value criterion** to evaluate possible alternatives. Although a more complete discussion of the expected value approach is detailed in Chapter 6, here we will give a brief example of how it can be applied to project scheduling.

The main idea behind the expected value approach is to compare the mean or expected profits (or costs) for each possible alternative. Recall that the expected value of any discrete random variable, Y, denoted E(Y), is the weighted average of possible outcomes for Y, the weights being the probabilities for each possible outcome of Y; that is, $E(Y) = \Sigma P(y_i)y_i$.

The following example illustrates the use of the expected value approach in a situation faced by Klone Computers, Inc.

Klonepalm-180.xls
Klonepalm-200.xls
Klonepalm(Revised)-180.xls
Klonepalm(Revised)-200.xls

KLONE COMPUTERS: COST ANALYSIS USING PROBABILITIES

Klone has conducted an analysis of its two major competitors, which are known to be developing computers similar to its proposed Klonepalm 2000 models. According to this analysis, one competitor will have its model ready for market in 180 days, the other in about 200 days. Speedy completion of the Klonepalm 2000 project is therefore essential.

The analysis also indicated that if Klone can get the jump on both competitors and have its model ready for sale within 180 days, it should garner an additional profit of $1 million. If the Klonepalm 2000 is ready for sale after the first competitor's model is introduced, but before the second (i.e., between 180 and 200 days from now), Klone will gain an additional profit of $400,000.

In order to advance the anticipated completion date of the Klonepalm 2000 project, management is considering spending additional funds on training either the staff or the sales personnel. This training will involve extensive overtime and some travel, lodging, and meal expenses for both the trainers and the trainees.

Klone has estimated that by spending an additional $200,000 on sales training, it can reduce the optimistic, most likely, and pessimistic times for this training from 24, 28, and 32 days to 19, 21, and 23 days, respectively. It has also estimated that spending an additional $250,000 on training the technical staff can reduce the time estimates for staff training from 16, 26, and 30 days to 12, 14, and 16 days, respectively. Management would like to decide which, if either, of these options to pursue.

SOLUTION

EVALUATION OF SPENDING AN ADDITIONAL $200,000 FOR SALES TRAINING

The training of sales personnel, activity H, is not on the critical path for the project. Given the assumption that the overall completion time is determined solely by the activities on the critical path, a reduction in the expected completion time for activity H will not affect the overall completion time of the project. Thus management should not spend the additional $200,000 for sales training.

EVALUATION OF SPENDING AN ADDITIONAL $250,000 FOR STAFF TRAINING

Staff training, activity F, *is* on the critical path. Hence, a reduction in its expected completion time will reduce the overall completion time of the project. But will the time savings justify the $250,000 expenditure? Using the expected value approach, we can evaluate both spending and not spending the additional $250,000.

In this analysis, the gross additional profit earned by Klone is $1 million if the project is completed in less than 180 days, $400,000 if the project is completed within 180 to 200 days, and $0 if the project takes longer than 200 days to complete.

Klonepalm-180.xls
Klonepalm-200.xls

Case 1: The $250,000 is *not* spent on additional staff training.   This case represents the current situation in which the project, with the critical path of A–F–G–D–J, has an expected completion time of 194 days and a standard deviation of 9.255 days. We shall let the random variable X denote the completion time of the project.

We saw in Klonepalm-180.xls file shown in Figure 5.19 that:

$$P(X \leq 180) = .065192$$

When we enter 200 into cell F6 of that spreadsheet (see file Klonepalm-200.xls on the accompanying CD-ROM), we find that:

$$P(X \leq 200) = .741590$$

Therefore

$$P(180 \leq X \leq 200) = .741590 - .065192 = .676398$$

and

$$P(X \geq 200) = 1 - .741590 = .258410$$

Thus the expected gross additional profit, if the $250,000 is not spent is:

$$E(GP) = .065192(\$1,000,000) + .676398(\$400,000) + .258410(\$0) = \$335,751.20$$

Because no additional funds were spent, this is also the net additional expected profit, E(NP).

Klonepalm(Revised)-180.xls
Klonepalm(Revised)-200.xls

Case 2: The $250,000 is spent on additional staff training.   If the additional $250,000 is spent on activity F, its revised time estimates are $a = 12$, $m = 14$, and $b = 16$. Solving by using the PERT-CPM.xls template, we now find that the project has a new critical path of A–B–C–G–D–J with mean completion time of 189 days and a standard deviation of 9.0185 days. Using the probability calculator on the PERT OUTPUT worksheets, we now find (see files Klonepalm (Revised)-200.xls and Klonepalm(Revised)-180.xls, respectively):

$$P(X \leq 200) = .888713$$
$$P(X \leq 180) = .159152$$

Therefore

$$P(180 \leq X \leq 200) = .888713 - .159152 = .729561$$

and

$$P(X \geq 200) = 1 - .888713 = .111287$$

Thus the expected gross additional profit, if the $250,000 is spent is:

$$E(GP) = .159152(\$1,000,000) + .729561(\$400,000) + .111287(\$0) = \$450,976.40$$

Hence, if the additional $250,000 were spent, the net additional expected profit, E(NP), would be:

$$E(NP) = \$450,976.40 - \$250,000.00 = \$200,976.40$$

Because this is less than the net expected profit of $335,751.20 if the $250,000 is not spent, the additional staff training should not be undertaken. Thus management should not pursue either of the two extra spending options for sales or staff training.

IS IT APPROPRIATE TO USE THE EXPECTED VALUE APPROACH?

A word of caution must be offered about using the expected value approach. An expected value is a "long-run average" value, which means that if the project were repeated over and over again, in the long run it would not pay to spend the additional $250,000 each time for staff training. However, many projects, including this one, are performed only once. Hence, while the results from an expected value analysis can be used as a guide, the decision maker should also consider other data, hunches, and judgments before making a final decision about whether or not to spend the $250,000 on additional staff training.

5.10 The Critical Path Method (CPM)

The **critical path method (CPM)** is a deterministic approach to project planning, based on the assumption that an activity's completion time can be determined with certainty. This time depends only on the amount of money allocated to the activity. The process of reducing an activity's completion time by committing additional monetary resources is known as *crashing*.

CPM assumes that there are two crucial time points for each activity: (1) its *normal completion time* (T_N), achieved when the usual or *normal cost* (C_N) is spent to complete the activity; and (2) its *crash completion time* (T_C), the minimum possible completion time for the activity; the T_C is attained when a maximum *crash cost* (T_C) is spent. The assumption is that spending an amount greater than C_C on an activity will not significantly reduce the completion time any further.

To illustrate this CPM assumption, think of a building project that includes the construction of a large brick wall. The wall will be completed in a normal time if the normal cost is paid to one bricklayer. If extra funds are available to hire two bricklayers, the completion time should be less; a third bricklayer could reduce the completion time even more. But there comes a point when the addition of another bricklayer will not significantly reduce the time further. Plaster between the bricks takes a certain time to dry, regardless of the number of bricklayers. Carried to the extreme, if there are more bricklayers than the number of bricks required for the wall, the completion time cannot be reduced further. Hence, an activity's maximum crash cost is the cost at which most of its significant time reduction has been achieved. CPM analyses are based on the following **linearity assumption**:

CPM Linearity Assumption

If any amount between C_N and C_C is spent to complete an activity, the *percentage decrease* in the activity's completion time from its normal time T_N to its crash time T_C equals the *percentage increase* in cost from its normal cost to its crash cost.

Figure 5.20 illustrates the linearity concept of crashing. Here:

$$R = T_N - T_C = \text{the maximum possible time reduction (crashing)}$$
of an activity

$$E = C_C - C_N = \text{the maximum } \textit{additional} \text{ (crash) costs required to achieve the}$$
maximum time reduction

$$M = E/R \quad = \text{the } \textit{marginal} \text{ cost of reducing an activity's completion time}$$
by one unit

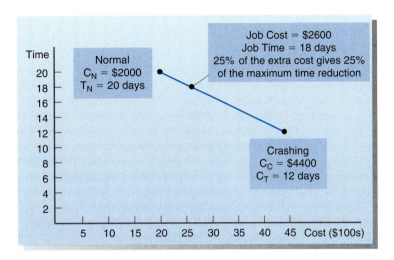

FIGURE 5.20   CPM Linearity Assumption

Figure 5.20 shows that as costs are increased from the normal cost, $C_N = \$2000$, to the maximum crash cost, $C_C = \$4400$, the activity's completion time is reduced proportionately from the normal time of $T_N = 20$ days to the crash time of $T_C = 12$ days. The maximum time reduction is $R = 20 - 12 = 8$ days, and the maximum additional cost is $E = \$4400 - \$2000 = \$2400$. Thus the cost per day reduction is $M = E/R = \$2400/8 = \$300/\text{day}$.

If management allocates $2600 to complete the activity ($600 more than its normal cost of $2000), the time reduction from this increase is $600/$300 = 2 days. That is, the activity is now expected to take $20 - 2 = 18$ days to complete.

MEETING A DEADLINE AT MINIMUM COST

Suppose management is willing to commit additional monetary resources in an attempt to meet a deadline date, D. It would first check to see whether this can be accomplished by spending the normal costs for the activities. In other words, a deterministic PERT/CPM approach (discussed in Section 7.5.3) can be applied to a network using the normal activity times. If this analysis determined that the project could, indeed, be accomplished by time D, no additional funds would have to be spent on the project.

If, however, the completion time of the project using normal times exceeds the target completion date, management will need to spend additional resources to "crash" some of the activities to meet the target deadline. Its objective is to meet the target date at minimal additional cost. To illustrate this concept, consider the problem faced by management at Baja Burrito Restaurants.

BAJA BURRITO RESTAURANTS

Baja Burrito Restaurants, commonly called BB's, is a chain of fast-food Mexican-style restaurants with over 100 locations throughout the Southwest and Great Plains states. It features such items as the Taco Loco Grande, the Quesadilla Quatro (a quesadilla made with four different cheeses), and specialty burritos named after many of the states BB's services (such as the Arizona burrito, the Texas burrito, and the Oklahoma burrito). Like most fast-food restaurants, the basic style and décor of the individual restaurants do not vary greatly from restaurant to restaurant, although the basic design must be modified somewhat to adjust to size constraints and to conform to local codes and ordinances.

BB's is planning to open a new restaurant in Lubbock, Texas, near the site where Texas Tech University plays its football games. It wishes to have the restaurant built and operational prior to the first Texas Tech home football game on September 11, which is 19 weeks away. Table 5.12 details the activities and the immediate predecessor relations in the first two columns and the approximate normal times (in weeks) and costs (in $1000s) for building a restaurant in the third and fourth columns. Thus, under normal conditions, it costs BB's about $200,000 to construct a new restaurant.

Based on the normal time estimates, using the PERT-CPM.xls template, we can show that it will take 29 weeks for BB's to complete the construction project. Since this does not meet the 19-week deadline, management at BB's has requested department heads and project engineers look for ways to speed up the individual activities. These are reflected in the last two columns in Table 5.12. Therefore, if all activities are crashed to their minimum times, the restaurant could be built in 17 weeks at a cost of $300,000.

Management is willing to assume that spending additional funds up to the crash amounts submitted by the department heads and engineers will reduce the activity completion times proportionately. They are seeking a minimum cost activity schedule for building the new Lubbock Baja Burrito restaurant that will meet the 19-week deadline.

TABLE 5.12 Activity Chart for Baja Burrito Restaurants

Activity	Immediate Predecessors	Normal Time	Normal Cost	Crash Time	Crash Cost
A. Plan revisions/approvals	—	5	25	3	36
B. Grade land	A	1	10	0.5	15
C. Purchase materials	A	3	18	1.5	22
D. Order/receive equipment	A	2	8	1	12
E. Order/receive furniture	A	4	8	1.5	15
F. Pour concrete floor	B,C	1	12	0.5	15
G. Erect frame	F	4	20	2.5	30
H. Install electrical	G	2	12	1.5	17
I. Install plumbing	G	4	13	2.5	21
J. Install drywall/roof	H,I	2	10	1.5	16
K. Construct bathrooms	I	2	8	1	12
L. Install equipment	D,J	3	14	1.5	22
M. Finish/paint inside	K,L	3	10	1.5	18
N. Tile floors	M	3	6	1	9
O. Install furniture	E,M	4	8	2.5	14
P. Finish/paint outside	J	4	18	2.5	26
TOTAL		29*	$200	17*	$300

*As determined by the PERT.xls template.

SOLUTION

Figure 5.21 shows the PERT/CPM network for this model. If this model were solved by hand, the first step would be to determine whether construction of the restaurant would meet the 19-week deadline using the normal time/cost data. As mentioned earlier, using normal times/costs would give a 29-week completion time determined by a critical path consisting of activities A, C, F, G, I, J, L, M, and O.

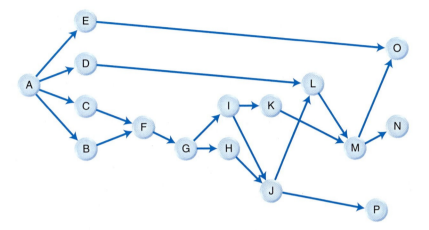

FIGURE 5.21
PERT/CPM Network for Baja Burrito Restaurants

Thus to meet the 19-week deadline, some of the activities must be crashed. Table 5.13 details the maximum time reductions, R ($=T_N - T_C$), the extra costs for these reductions, E, and the marginal cost per week reductions, M ($=E/R$).

In order to reduce the project time, the completion time of one or more of the critical activities must be crashed. When the completion time for a critical activity is reduced by a large enough amount, however, other paths will also become critical. To achieve further time reductions, activities on *all* critical paths must be crashed.

TABLE 5.13   R, E, and M Values for Baja Burrito

Activity	Maximum Reduction R	Extra Cost E	Cost Per Week Reduction M = E/R
A	2.0	11	5.50
B	0.5	5	10.00
C	1.5	4	2.67
D	1.0	4	4.00
E	2.5	7	2.80
F	0.5	3	6.00
G	1.5	10	6.67
H	0.5	5	10.00
I	1.5	8	5.33
J	0.5	6	12.00
K	1.0	4	4.00
L	1.5	8	5.33
M	1.5	8	5.33
N	2.0	3	1.50
O	1.5	6	4.00
P	1.5	8	5.33

A heuristic approach to determine the amount of time each activity should be crashed can be developed by taking into account the following: (1) the project time is reduced only when activities on the critical path are reduced; (2) the maximum time reduction for each activity is limited; and (3) the amount of time an activity on the critical path can be reduced before another path also becomes a critical path is limited. For *very* small problems, an approach based on these observations can work rather well, but as the number of critical paths increases, the procedure becomes cumbersome rather rapidly.

LINEAR PROGRAMMING APPROACH TO CRASHING

Fortunately, the use of such a heuristic approach is unnecessary. A simple modification to the linear program given in Section 5.4 is all that is required. For this model, we now define two variables for each activity, j.

$$X_j = \text{start time for the activity}$$
$$Y_j = \text{the amount by which the activity is to be crashed}$$

Since the normal cost must always be paid, the objective is to minimize the sum of the *additional* funds spent to reduce the completion times of activities. The cost per unit reduction for an activity is M_j, and the amount of time the activity is reduced is the decision variable, Y_j. Therefore, the total extra amount spent crashing the activity is M_jY_j. Because we want to minimize the total additional funds spent to crash the project, the objective function is the sum of all such costs:

$$\text{MIN} \sum_j M_jY_j$$

For Baja Burrito Restaurants the objective function is:

$$\text{MIN } 5.5Y_A + 10Y_B + 2.67Y_C + 4Y_D + 2.8Y_E + 6Y_F + 6.67Y_G + 10Y_H + $$
$$5.33Y_I + 12Y_J + 4Y_K + 5.33Y_L + 5.33Y_M + 1.5Y_N + 4Y_O + 5.33Y_P$$

Constraints

There are three types of constraints in this approach:

1. *No activity can be reduced more than its maximum time reduction.*
For each activity, there is a constraint of the form:

$$Y_j \leq R_j$$

2. *The start time for an activity must be at least as great as the finish time of all immediate predecessor activities.*
This represents a series of constraints similar to those described in Section 5.4, of the form:

(Start Time for an Activity) ≥
(Finish Time for an Immediate Predecessor of the Activity)

Now, however, since the activity finish times are reduced by the amount of time each activity is crashed, these constraints have the form:

(Start Time for an Activity) ≥
(Start Time for a Predecessor Activity) +
(Normal Completion Time of the Predecessor Activity) −
(Time the Predecessor Activity is Crashed)

There is one such constraint for each immediate predecessor relationship. (This is equivalent to saying that there is one constraint for each arc in the PERT/CPM network.) In this project, for example, activity I (which has a normal completion time of four weeks) is one of the immediate predecessors for activity J. Thus one of the constraints in the linear programming formulation would be:

$$X_J \geq X_I + (4 - Y_I)$$

3.   *The project must be completed by its deadline, D.*
Since the project completion time is determined by the maximum of the finish times of the terminal activities[3] in the project (the ones that are not predecessors for any other activities), we add constraints of the form:

$$(\text{Finish Time for a Terminal Activity}) \leq D$$

or for each *terminal* activity,

$$(\text{Activity Start Time}) + (\text{Activity's Normal Completion Time}) - (\text{Time Activity is Crashed}) \leq D$$

In this model, activities N, O, and P, having normal completion times of 3, 4, and 4, respectively, are not predecessors for any other activities. Thus the following constraints would be added:

$$X_N + 3 - Y_N \leq 19$$
$$X_O + 4 - Y_O \leq 19$$
$$X_P + 4 - Y_P \leq 19$$

The complete linear programming model for Baja Burrito Restaurants is then:

$$\text{MIN } 5.5Y_A + 10Y_B + 2.67Y_C + 4Y_D + 2.8Y_E + 6Y_F + 6.67Y_G + 10Y_H$$
$$+ 5.33Y_I + 12Y_J + 4Y_K + 5.33Y_L + 5.33Y_M + 1.5Y_N + 4Y_O + 5.33Y_P$$

ST

$$
\begin{aligned}
Y_A &\leq 2.0 \\
Y_B &\leq 0.5 \\
Y_C &\leq 1.5 \\
Y_D &\leq 1.0 \\
Y_E &\leq 2.5 \\
Y_F &\leq 0.5 \\
Y_G &\leq 1.5 \\
Y_H &\leq 0.5 \\
Y_I &\leq 1.5 \\
Y_J &\leq 0.5 \\
Y_K &\leq 1.0 \\
Y_L &\leq 1.5 \\
Y_M &\leq 1.5 \\
Y_N &\leq 2.0 \\
Y_O &\leq 1.5 \\
Y_P &\leq 1.5
\end{aligned}
\qquad (1)
$$

[3] If you do not wish to identify the terminal activities, you can simply require *all* finish times not to exceed D. This will add several redundant constraints, but for small problems these will not significantly impact the solution time of the linear program.

$$
\left.\begin{aligned}
X_B &\geq X_A + (5 - Y_A) \\
X_C &\geq X_A + (5 - Y_A) \\
X_D &\geq X_A + (5 - Y_A) \\
X_E &\geq X_A + (5 - Y_A) \\
X_F &\geq X_B + (1 - Y_B) \\
X_F &\geq X_C + (3 - Y_C) \\
X_G &\geq X_F + (1 - Y_F) \\
X_H &\geq X_G + (4 - Y_G) \\
X_I &\geq X_G + (4 - Y_G) \\
X_J &\geq X_H + (2 - Y_H) \\
X_J &\geq X_I + (4 - Y_I) \\
X_K &\geq X_I + (4 - Y_I) \\
X_L &\geq X_D + (2 - Y_D) \\
X_L &\geq X_J + (2 - Y_J) \\
X_M &\geq X_K + (2 - Y_K) \\
X_M &\geq X_L + (3 - Y_L) \\
X_N &\geq X_M + (3 - Y_M) \\
X_O &\geq X_E + (4 - Y_E) \\
X_O &\geq X_M + (3 - Y_M) \\
X_P &\geq X_J + (2 - Y_J)
\end{aligned}\right\} \quad (2)
$$

$$
\left.\begin{aligned}
X_N + 3 - Y_N &\leq 19 \\
X_O + 4 - Y_O &\leq 19 \\
X_P + 4 - Y_P &\leq 19
\end{aligned}\right\} \quad (3)
$$

All X's and Y's ≥ 0

The constraints could be rewritten so that they resemble our usual linear programming form of having the variables on the left side of the constraints and only constants on the right. Regardless, we see that even for this relatively small problem, the linear program consists of 32 variables and 39 functional constraints.

USING CPM-DEADLINE.xls TEMPLATE

Fortunately, one does not actually have to write the linear program for CPM; many computer packages do this automatically. We have included the CPM-Deadline.xls template on the accompanying CD-ROM to do just that. Figure 5.22 shows the results from the CPM DEADLINE OUTPUT worksheet for the Baja Burrito Restaurant model. We see that the project can be completed in 19 weeks at a cost of $248,750 by crashing activities A, C, F, I, L, M, N, and O by certain amounts. A scheduling of the activities that meets this deadline is shown in columns C and D. (*Incidentally, the 7.87637×10^{-11} entry for the cost of crashing for activity G is simply a roundoff error generated internally from solving the linear program. This number is actually 0.*)

OPERATING OPTIMALLY WITHIN A FIXED BUDGET

The CPM approach presented for the Baja Burrito Restaurants model sought to find the minimum cost of constructing the restaurant within 19 weeks. Many projects, however, including construction projects, marketing campaigns, and research and development studies, must operate within a given fixed budget. In such cases, the objective is to complete the project in minimum time, subject to the budget restrictions. The CPM approach can be modified for these models.

Baja Deadline.xls

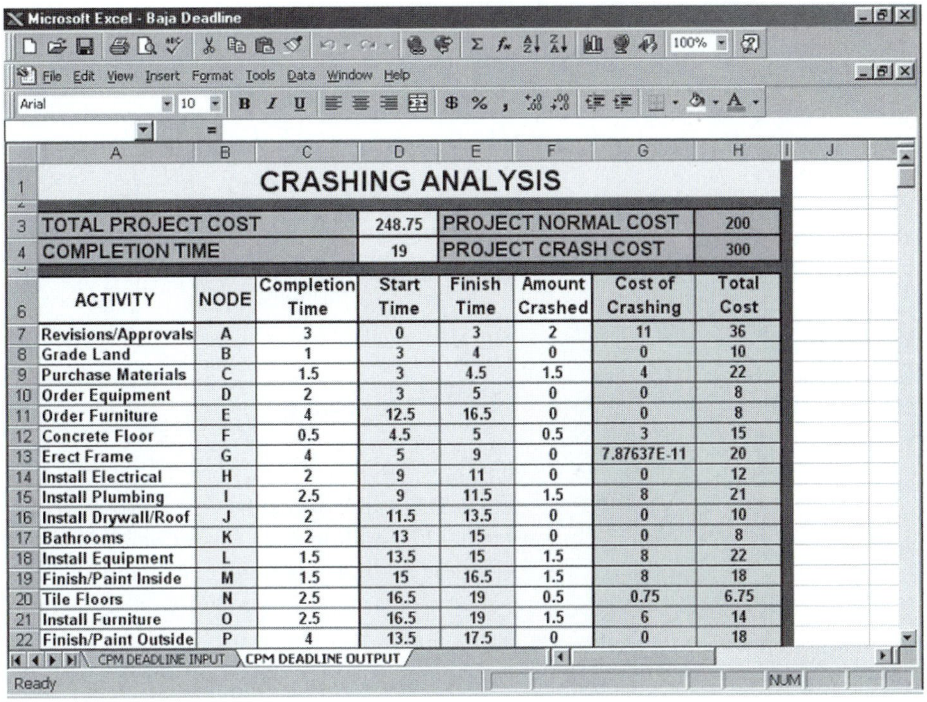

Baja Budget.xls

FIGURE 5.22
CPM DEADLINE OUTPUT
Worksheet for
Baja Restaurants

				CRASHING ANALYSIS				
TOTAL PROJECT COST			248.75	**PROJECT NORMAL COST**			200	
COMPLETION TIME			19	**PROJECT CRASH COST**			300	
ACTIVITY	**NODE**	**Completion Time**	**Start Time**	**Finish Time**	**Amount Crashed**	**Cost of Crashing**	**Total Cost**	
Revisions/Approvals	A	3	0	3	2	11	36	
Grade Land	B	1	3	4	0	0	10	
Purchase Materials	C	1.5	3	4.5	1.5	4	22	
Order Equipment	D	2	3	5	0	0	8	
Order Furniture	E	4	12.5	16.5	0	0	8	
Concrete Floor	F	0.5	4.5	5	0.5	3	15	
Erect Frame	G	4	5	9	0	7.87637E-11	20	
Install Electrical	H	2	9	11	0	0	12	
Install Plumbing	I	2.5	9	11.5	1.5	8	21	
Install Drywall/Roof	J	2	11.5	13.5	0	0	10	
Bathrooms	K	2	13	15	0	0	8	
Install Equipment	L	1.5	13.5	15	1.5	8	22	
Finish/Paint Inside	M	1.5	15	16.5	1.5	8	18	
Tile Floors	N	2.5	16.5	19	0.5	0.75	6.75	
Install Furniture	O	2.5	16.5	19	1.5	6	14	
Finish/Paint Outside	P	4	13.5	17.5	0	0	18	

BAJA BURRITO RESTAURANTS (CONTINUED)

Suppose Baja Burrito has a policy of not funding a project for more than $12\frac{1}{2}\%$ above "normal cost" forecasts. In this case, $12\frac{1}{2}\% = \$25,000$, meaning that the maximum spending limit for the project would be $225,000. Given this spending limit, management is interested in the earliest it can expect the Lubbock BB's construction project to be completed.

SOLUTION

The problem is basically the same as that for the previous model, with the following exceptions:

1. The constraints, labeled (3), which state that the project must be completed within 19 weeks, are eliminated.

2. A new constraint is added stating that the maximum "extra spending" cannot exceed $25,000:

$$5.5Y_A + 10Y_B + 2.67Y_C + 4Y_D + 2.8Y_E + 6Y_F + 6.67Y_G + 10Y_H$$
$$+ 5.33Y_I + 12Y_J + 4Y_K + 5.33Y_L + 5.33Y_M + 1.5Y_N + 4Y_O + 5.33Y_P \le 25$$

3. The objective is changed to $\text{Min}(\text{Max}(EF))$.

This objective function, however, is not a linear function. In addition, imposing a constraint similar to MIN ΣX's that we used in Section 5.4, this time does not guarantee an optimal solution.

To convert this to a linear program, we can imagine creating a dummy node called "END," signifying the end of the project. All termination activities, activities that are not predecessors for other activities, are then immediate predecessors of this END node. In this case, activities N, O, and P are not predecessors for any other activities and thus would be predecessors for this END node. The end of the PERT/CPM network for this model is shown in Figure 5.23.

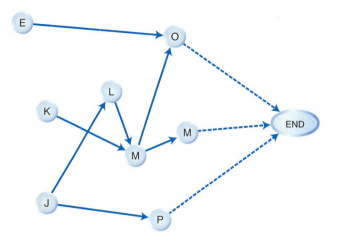

FIGURE 5.23
Termination Nodes
(N, O, P) of the Baja
Restaurant Network

The constraints of the previous model would then be amended by deleting the constraints (3), adding the constraint above restricting extra spending to at most $25,000, and adding three more precedence relation constraints:

$$X_{END} \geq X_N + (3 - Y_N)$$
$$X_{END} \geq X_O + (4 - Y_O)$$
$$X_{END} \geq X_P + (4 - Y_P)$$

The *linear* objective now is:

$$MIN \; X_{END}$$

USING THE CPM-BUDGET.xls TEMPLATE

The above is precisely the approach used in the CPM-Budget.xls template. This template is designed specifically to solve project scheduling models with limited budgets. Input instructions are given in Appendix 5.1. Figure 5.24 shows the CPM BUDGET OUTPUT worksheet for the Baja Burrito model.

Baja Budget.xls

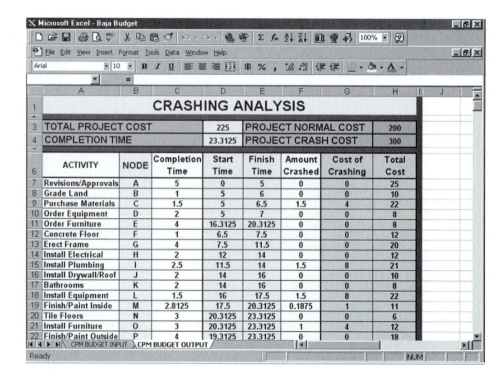

FIGURE 5.24
CPM BUDGET OUTPUT
Worksheet for Baja
Burrito Restaurants

CRASHING ANALYSIS

TOTAL PROJECT COST			225	PROJECT NORMAL COST		200	
COMPLETION TIME			23.3125	PROJECT CRASH COST		300	

ACTIVITY	NODE	Completion Time	Start Time	Finish Time	Amount Crashed	Cost of Crashing	Total Cost
Revisions/Approvals	A	5	0	5	0	0	25
Grade Land	B	1	5	6	0	0	10
Purchase Materials	C	1.5	5	6.5	1.5	4	22
Order Equipment	D	2	5	7	0	0	8
Order Furniture	E	4	16.3125	20.3125	0	0	8
Concrete Floor	F	1	6.5	7.5	0	0	12
Erect Frame	G	4	7.5	11.5	0	0	20
Install Electrical	H	2	12	14	0	0	12
Install Plumbing	I	2.5	11.5	14	1.5	8	21
Install Drywall/Roof	J	2	14	16	0	0	10
Bathrooms	K	2	14	16	0	0	8
Install Equipment	L	1.5	16	17.5	1.5	8	22
Finish/Paint Inside	M	2.8125	17.5	20.3125	0.1875	1	11
Tile Floors	N	3	20.3125	23.3125	0	0	6
Install Furniture	O	3	20.3125	23.3125	1	4	12
Finish/Paint Outside	P	4	19.3125	23.3125	0	0	18

We see that activities C, I, L, M, and O would all require some crashing and that the minimum completion time for the construction of the restaurant in Lubbock with a $225,000 budget is 23.3125 weeks.

5.11 PERT/Cost

Prior to the start of a project, management determines cost and time estimates and a set of precedence relations for the activities of the project. PERT/CPM analyses can then be used to calculate the expected project completion time and a set of earliest and latest start and finish times for each activity. Management can then use this information to set an appropriate schedule.

Once a schedule is in place, however, what *should* happen according to the schedule may differ greatly from what *actually does* happen. Unexpected expenses can send a project way over budget, while unexpected delays in the completion of some activities can cause a project to fall behind schedule. Because management is interested in completing the project on time and within budget, it is important to be able to gauge a project's progress against scheduled time and cost estimates so that it can take corrective actions if necessary.

Accounting information systems can serve as a mechanism for monitoring the progress of a project, providing management with "snapshot" progress reports that summarize the allocation of total project expenses and activity completion status at any given instant. **PERT/Cost**,[4] is one such accounting information system that helps management determine whether the project is coming in under or over budget.

Unlike typical cost accounting systems, which are cost-center based (by location, function, or department), PERT/Cost is a project-oriented system that is based on analyzing a project that has been segmented into a collection of work packages. **Work packages** are sets of related activities within a project which share common costs or are under the control of one contractor, department, or individual. PERT/Cost utilizes work packages rather than individual activities because, for most projects, the large number and narrow detail of activities make it difficult, if not impossible, to determine how to allocate and measure costs (such as indirect and overhead costs).

Two assumptions are made concerning work packages in PERT/Cost systems:

> ### Work Package Assumptions for a PERT/Cost System
>
> 1. Once a work package has begun, it is performed continuously until it has been completed.
> 2. The costs associated with a work package are spread evenly throughout its duration.

The first assumption implies that once a work package has commenced, it will not be interrupted for a period of time, begun again, interrupted again, and so on. The second assumption implies that there are no huge costs at any single point of time during the duration of the work package; hence, costs are relatively constant from day to day and week to week. Given these assumptions, a forecasted (weekly)[5] cost for each work package can be calculated as follows:

$$\text{Work Package Forecasted Weekly Cost} = \frac{\text{Budgeted Total Cost for Work Package}}{\text{Expected Completion Time for Work Package}}$$

---

[4] Originally developed by the U.S. government as a way of controlling the costs of defense and NASA (National Aeronautics and Space Administration) projects.

[5] Any time unit is acceptable.

Once a schedule is in place, a PERT/Cost system monitors the progress of a project as it is performed to see whether it is being completed on schedule and within budget. This is done by obtaining current completion and cost data for each work package, including the actual expenditures to date for the work package and an estimate of the percent of the work package completed, p. Using these data, we can calculate the value of the work done to date (expressed in terms of budgeted cost) and the expected time remaining to complete the work package as follows.

Current Status of a Work Package

Value of Work to date = p*(Budgeted Total Cost for the Work Package)

Expected Remaining Completion Time = (1 − p)*
(Original Expected Completion Time)

COMPLETION TIME ANALYSIS

Using the estimates for the expected remaining completion times for each incomplete work package, we can use a standard PERT analysis to calculate a revised estimate for the project completion time. This estimate is compared to the project's original completion time estimate to discern whether the project is ahead or behind schedule.

COST OVERRUN/UNDERRUN ANALYSIS

For each work package that is either completed or in progress, a **cost overrun** can be determined as follows.

Cost Overrun = (Actual Expenditures to Date) − (Value of Work to Date)

A negative cost overrun is a **cost underrun**. The cost overrun for a work package that has not yet been started is 0. The cost overruns and underruns for all work packages are then summed to determine a cost overrun or underrun for the entire project.

CORRECTIVE ACTION

What happens if a project is found to be behind schedule or experiencing a cost overrun? The obvious answer is for the manager to seek out the causes for the delay or cost overrun and determine whether corrective action needs to be taken. Perhaps an incorrect estimate was made of a project's completion time or cost. Unforeseen problems can also warrant a reassessment of work package completion times and costs. However, some delays or cost overruns may be the result of problems with one activity within the work package or with one department or contractor, which affect the costs and times of several activities.

In some cases, a moderate delay in the overall completion date of the project may be acceptable and no corrective action need be taken if the project is coming in as budgeted. In other cases, meeting a target completion date is imperative.

Completed work packages that experienced cost overruns or delays are lost causes in terms of meeting project deadlines or budgets. Hence, attention must focus on work yet to be performed. If the project is behind schedule, the manager is interested in determining whether expediting some activities at additional cost is possible or desirable. For projects experiencing a cost underrun, additional resources may be channeled to problem activities. Even if there is no cost underrun, possible funding may be found within the budget by reducing allocations to some of the noncritical activities of the project.

If the project is coming in over budget, noncritical activities or work packages are evaluated first for cost savings. If reduced funding would cause a delay in a critical activity or work package, however, the estimated project completion date will have to be extended. This may be the price the manager has to pay to correct such cost overruns. Of course, the accumulated delay may be so great or the cost overrun so high that no amount of corrective action will facilitate either an "on-time" or "within budget" project.

The PERT/Cost technique is illustrated by the situation faced by Tom Larkin.

Larkin PERT-COST.xls

TOM LARKIN'S POLITICAL CAMPAIGN

With nine months (39 weeks) to go before the mayoral election, the incumbent mayor of Springfield, Missouri, has decided not to run for reelection. Tom Larkin, a supporter of the incumbent and a political activist in southern Missouri politics for almost 10 years, has been considering running for mayor himself.

Tom, his family, and a few close friends met and decided on a set of campaign activities necessary to run a competitive campaign. Based on their years of political experience, they were able to determine a set of time and cost estimates for each of these activities as shown in Table 5.14. Bob Stanford, a confidant of Tom Larkin and a graduate of the University of Missouri in Management Science, ran a PERT/CPM analysis and was able to determine that with a $40,000 budget, the campaign would take 36 weeks.

Given these estimates, Tom took three weeks to make his decision and, to no one's surprise, chose to enter the mayoral race.

Following Tom's directions, 20 weeks into the campaign, Bob prepared an assessment of the progress to date and the financial outlook for the campaign, as shown in Table 5.15. Tom wants to know if the campaign is on target for completion in 36 weeks and if it is progressing within budget. If it is not, he wants staff recommendations for corrective action.

TABLE 5.14 Mayoral Campaign Activities

Activity		Immediate Predecessors	Expected Time (Weeks)	Expected Cost	Forecasted Weekly Cost
A.	Hire campaign staff	—	4	$ 2,000	$ 500
B.	Prepare position papers	—	6	$ 3,000	$ 500
C.	Recruit volunteers	A	4	$ 4,500	$1,125
D.	Raise funds	A,B	6	$ 2,500	$ 417
E.	File candidacy papers	D	2	$ 500	$ 250
F.	Prepare campaign material	E	13	$13,000	$1,000
G.	Locate/staff headquarters	E	1	$ 1,500	$1,500
H.	Run personal campaign	C,G	20	$ 6,000	$ 300
I.	Run media campaign	F	9	$ 7,000	$ 778
	TOTAL			$40,000	

TABLE 5.15   Mayoral Campaign Status Report: End of Week 20

Work Package	Expenditures	Status	Forecasted Weekly Cost
A. Hire campaign staff	$ 2,600	Finished	$ 500
B. Prepare position papers	$ 5,000	Finished	$ 500
C. Recruit volunteers	$ 3,000	Finished	$1,125
D. Raise funds	$ 5,000	Finished	$ 417
E. File candidacy papers	$ 700	Finished	$ 250
F. Prepare campaign material	$ 5,600	40% Complete	$1,000
G. Locate/staff headquarters	$ 700	Finished	$1,500
H. Run personal campaign	$ 2,000	25% Complete	$ 300
I. Run Media campaign	$ 0	0% Complete	$ 778
Expenditures to Date	$24,600		

SOLUTION

Because the number of activities in the campaign is so small and broadly defined, we shall treat each as a work package. Figure 5.25 shows the PERT/CPM network for this model.

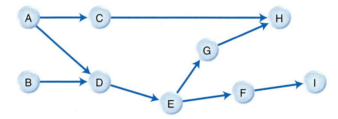

FIGURE 5.25
PERT/CPM Network for the Tom Larkin Political Campaign

TIME ANALYSIS

Figure 5.26 shows the network remaining at the end of week 20. Only work packages (F, H, and I) remain to be completed. We use a start week of 20 (reflecting the current week) for completing "the rest of the work package." Since, at the end of week 20, work package F is only 40% complete and its anticipated completion time is 13 weeks, it is expected to take another $(1 - .40)(13) = 7.8$ weeks to complete. Similarly, work package H is expected to require another $(1 - .25)(.20) = 15$ weeks to complete.

Carrying out the remainder of the forward pass, we see that the current expected project completion date is now 36.8 weeks from inception. Thus the staff must find a way of saving 0.8 week from the remaining schedule. This savings must come from work packages F or I.

FIGURE 5.26
Remaining Status As of Week 20

COST ANALYSIS

Table 5.16 is one version of a *project cost control report*, which details the cost overruns and underruns for each work package by listing its total budgeted cost, the "to date" status of the percentage of completed work, the estimated value of its completed work to date, and its actual expenditures. The estimated value of the completed work is calculated by multiplying the percentage complete by its budgeted value. The cost overrun is the difference between this value and the actual cost to date.

TABLE 5.16 Project Cost Control Report

Week = 20

Work Package	Budgeted Values		To Date Values			Cost Overrun
	Total Time	Total Cost	Percent Complete	Estimated Work Value	Actual Expenditure	
A	4	$ 2,000	100%	$ 2,000	$ 2,600	$ 600
B	6	$ 3,000	100%	$ 3,000	$ 5,000	$2,000
C	4	$ 4,500	100%	$ 4,500	$ 3,000	($1,500)
D	6	$ 2,500	100%	$ 2,500	$ 5,000	$2,500
E	2	$ 500	100%	$ 500	$ 700	$ 200
F	13	$13,000	40%	$ 5,200	$ 5,600	$ 400
G	1	$ 1,500	100%	$ 1,500	$ 700	($ 800)
H	20	$ 6,000	25%	$ 1,500	$ 2,000	$ 500
I	9	$ 7,000	0%	$ 0	$ 0	$ 0
Total		$40,000		$20,700	$24,600	$3,900

For instance, the entries for work package F, which was budgeted for $13,000 and is currently 40% complete with expenditures of $5600, are calculated as follows.

$$\text{Estimated Work Value to Date} = .40(\$13{,}000) = \$5200$$
$$\text{Cost Overrun} = \$5600 - \$5200 = \$400$$

USING THE PERT-COST.xls TEMPLATE

The PERT-COST.xls template provided on the accompanying CD-ROM can be used to solve the Tom Larkin political campaign model. Input instructions are given in Appendix 5.1. The PERT-COST OUTPUT worksheet shown in Figure 5.27 analyzes the status of the project given the expenditures and work completed as of Week 20.

As we can observe, the PERT/COST OUTPUT worksheet gives a table similar to Table 5.16. We see from Figure 5.27 that currently:

- The project is .8 week behind schedule.
- There is a cost overrun of $3900.
- The remaining uncompleted work packages, F, H, and I, have remaining expected completion times of 7.8, 15, and 9 weeks, respectively.
- Work package F is already experiencing a $400 cost overrun, and work package H is currently experiencing a $500 cost overrun.

CORRECTIVE ACTION

Since the PERT/Cost analysis indicates that the campaign is experiencing both a cost overrun of $3900 and a project delay of .8 week, Tom may wish to divert funds from personal campaigning (work package H, which is not on the critical path) to preparing campaign material (F) and the media campaign (I). This diversion may involve less travel and personal appearances and save on security expenses.

A relatively minor shift in funds away from work package H could bring the campaign in within 36 weeks. Although the original target date of this work package is not met, the overall project deadline of 36 weeks is. Tom has only $6000

Larkin PERT-COST.xls

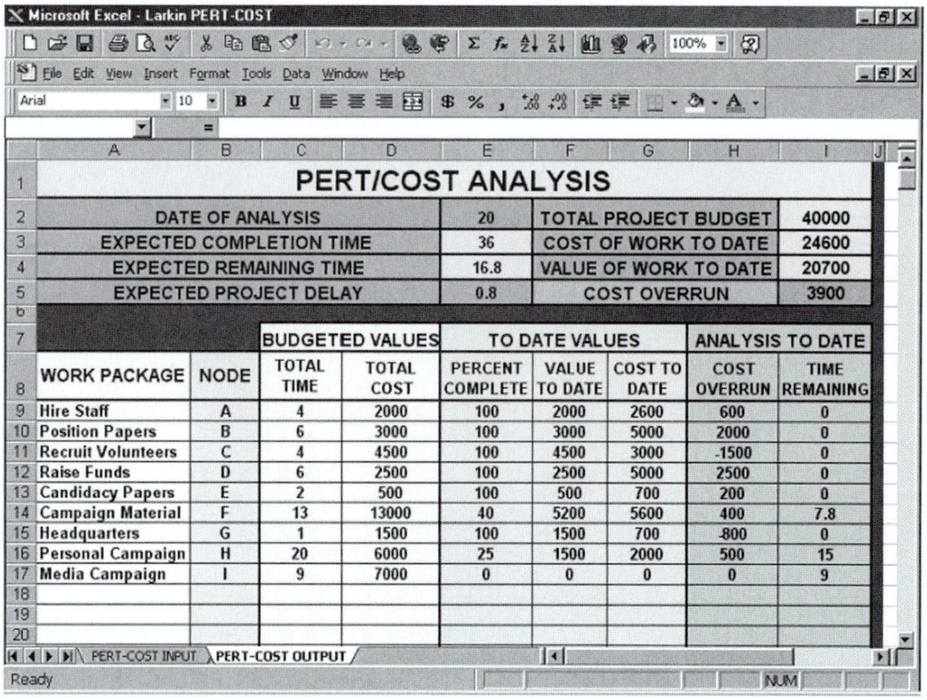

FIGURE 5.27
PERT-COST OUTPUT
Worksheet for the Tom
Larkin Political Campaign

X Microsoft Excel - Larkin PERT-COST

PERT/COST ANALYSIS

DATE OF ANALYSIS				20	TOTAL PROJECT BUDGET			40000
EXPECTED COMPLETION TIME				36	COST OF WORK TO DATE			24600
EXPECTED REMAINING TIME				16.8	VALUE OF WORK TO DATE			20700
EXPECTED PROJECT DELAY				0.8	COST OVERRUN			3900

WORK PACKAGE	NODE	BUDGETED VALUES		TO DATE VALUES			ANALYSIS TO DATE	
		TOTAL TIME	TOTAL COST	PERCENT COMPLETE	VALUE TO DATE	COST TO DATE	COST OVERRUN	TIME REMAINING
Hire Staff	A	4	2000	100	2000	2600	600	0
Position Papers	B	6	3000	100	3000	5000	2000	0
Recruit Volunteers	C	4	4500	100	4500	3000	-1500	0
Raise Funds	D	6	2500	100	2500	5000	2500	0
Candidacy Papers	E	2	500	100	500	700	200	0
Campaign Material	F	13	13000	40	5200	5600	400	7.8
Headquarters	G	1	1500	100	1500	700	-800	0
Personal Campaign	H	20	6000	25	1500	2000	500	15
Media Campaign	I	9	7000	0	0	0	0	9

PERT-COST INPUT PERT-COST OUTPUT

budgeted for work package H, however, and work package H itself is currently experiencing a $500 cost overrun. Although some of the resources might be shifted from H to meet the deadline, large shifts may increase the completion time of this work package so much that it would become a critical work package. In fact, there is not enough money left in the budget to both complete activity H in a reasonable amount of time and cover the current $3900 cost overrun.

Hence, an overall project cost overrun appears inevitable unless Tom can find ways to complete work packages F and I within their expected times at much lower projected costs. If the goal is not to come in too far above the targeted budget, Tom should try to make some cost savings in these work packages.

Another option might be for Tom to hold another fund raiser. This would be an added activity in the project, however, and could affect the completion time for the campaign.

5.12 Summary

Two basic approaches to project management, PERT and CPM, can help establish efficient scheduling of project activities. PERT assumes that activity completion times are not known with certainty but vary according to a probability distribution with known mean and standard deviation. One method used to estimate an activity's mean time and standard deviation is the three-time estimate approach, which assumes a Beta distribution for an activity's completion time.

Given the time estimates for the mean and standard deviation for each activity, we assume: (1) only the completion times for the activities on the critical path will determine the mean and standard deviation of the entire project; (2) activity completion times are independent; and, (3) there are enough activities on the critical path so that the normal distribution provides a reasonable approximation for the completion time of the project. Thus a project's mean completion time is the sum of the mean completion times of the activities on the critical

path, and its *variance* is the sum of the *variances* of the
cal path. The standard deviation of the project com
root of its variance.

The CPM approach, which assumes that activity
the monetary amount spent to complete the activity,
ther the minimal amount of funding needed to compl
fied time period or the minimal completion time of
budget.

Managers typically prefer a fairly consistent expenditur
tic resource leveling approaches are commonly used to smooth the disc
the necessary resources over the duration of a project.

PERT/Cost, an accounting system used for monitoring the progress of a project
during its completion, can determine whether a project is on schedule and within
budget. It can indicate areas where corrective action may be taken to bring the
project closer in line with targets.

ON THE CD-ROM

- Template for solving PERT/CPM models — **PERT-CPM.xls**
- Template for solving CPM deadline models — **CPM-Deadline.xls**
- Template for solving CPM budget models — **CPM-Budget.xls**
- Template for solving PERT/Cost models — **PERT-COST.xls**
- Spreadsheet for a PERT/CPM model that does not use a template — **Klonepalm EXCEL.xls**
- Spreadsheet for calculating PERT/CPM probabilities that does not use a template — **Klonepalm Probabilities.xls**
- Excel template spreadsheet for a PERT/CPM model without probabilities — **Klonepalm.xls**
- Excel template spreadsheets for PERT/CPM models that require calculating probabilities — **Klonepalm-180.xls** **Klonepalm-200.xls** **Klonepalm(Revised)-180.xls** **Klonepalm(Revised)-200.xls**
- Excel template spreadsheet for constructing a Gantt chart — **Klonepalm Gantt.xls**
- Excel template spreadsheet for a CPM model with a time deadline — **Baja Deadline.xls**
- Excel template spreadsheet for a CPM model with a budget restriction — **Baja Budget.xls**
- Excel template spreadsheet for a PERT/Cost Model — **Larkin PERT-COST.xls**
- Problem Motivations — **Problem Motivations**
- Problems 41–50 — **Additional Problems/Cases**
- Case 4 — **Additional Problems/Cases**

APPENDIX 5.1

Using the Project Scheduling Templates

A5.1.1   General Information

- Project scheduling templates are included for solving the following: (1) PERT/CPM models (with or without probabilities); (2) CPM models with project completion deadlines; (3) CPM models with budget restrictions; and (4) PERT/COST models.

- If a dialogue box appears that begins, "The workbook you are opening contains macros," then, at the bottom, click "Enable Macros."

- The templates are limited to models that have at most 26 nodes and at most 50 arcs.

- Each model has its own template and has Solver dialogue box(es) preprogrammed so that the user only has to call Solver and click Solve.

- The following procedure is recommended:
  1. Open the appropriate template.
  2. Before entering any data, do a "SAVE AS" to a file with an appropriate name to a floppy disk or your hard drive.
  3. Enter the required data and follow the instructions for the template as outlined below.

A5.1.2   The PERT-CPM.xls Template

On the PERT INPUT worksheet (see Figure A5.1):

1. Enter activity names beginning in cell A4.
   Note: These will automatically assign node labels (letter designations) in column B.

2. Enter values for a, m, and b (optimistic, most likely, and pessimistic times) in columns C, D, and E if using the three-time estimate approach **OR** values for μ and σ (the mean and standard deviation of the activity completion times) in columns F and G.
   Notes: (1) For problems that do not involve using standard deviations, leave column G blank. (2) If for some activities μ and σ are given, while for others μ and σ must be calculated using the three-time estimate approach, you can mix input methods on the template.

3. Enter the precedence relations one by one. The ending node label of a predecessor relationship is entered in column I, while its immediate predecessor node label is entered in column J.
   Note: If a node has more than one immediate predecessor, the ending node label must be listed in column I each time with a corresponding immediate predecessor label in column J.

4. After entering the input data, call Solver and click SOLVE. When Solver is done, click OK.
   Note: Nothing will have changed on the PERT INPUT worksheet!

5. Select the PERT OUTPUT worksheet (see Figure A5.2). Call Solver again and click SOLVE. When Solver is done, click OK.
   Note: At this point, the ES, EF, LS, LF, Slack times, the designation of the critical path, the values of μ and σ, the overall project completion time, and the variance and standard deviation of the project completion time (assuming one critical path) are displayed.

6. If you wish to calculate the probability of completing the project by a certain time, enter this value in cell F6 of the PERT OUTPUT worksheet. The probability will be given in cell H6.

Note: Before doing this check to see that the critical activities form just one critical path. If more than one critical path exists, you can select one critical path and enter in cell D5 a value or a formula that sums the variances along one of the critical paths. The result in cell H6 will be the probability that the activities along this one critical path are completed by the time period entered into cell F6.

Figures A5.1 and A5.2 show the input and output for the Klonepalm probability model discussed in Section 5.9.

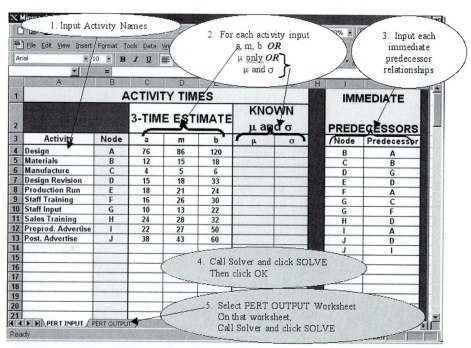

FIGURE A5.1
PERT INPUT Worksheet for the Klonepalm Model with Probabilities

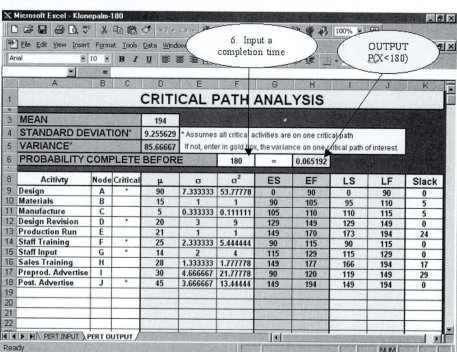

FIGURE A5.2
PERT OUTPUT Worksheet for the Klonepalm Model with Probabilities

A5.1.3 The CPM-Deadline.xls Template

On the CPM DEADLINE INPUT worksheet (see Figure A5.3):

1. Enter activity names beginning in cell A4.
   Note: These will automatically assign node labels (letter designations) in column B.

2. Enter the normal time, normal cost, crash time, and crash costs in columns C, D, E, and F, respectively.

3. Enter the precedence relations one by one. The ending node label of a predecessor relationship is entered in column H, while its immediate predecessor node label is entered in column I.
   Note: If a node has more than one immediate predecessor, the ending node label must be listed in column H each time with a corresponding immediate predecessor label in column I.

4. Enter the deadline date in cell E1.

5. After entering the input data, call Solver and click SOLVE. When Solver is done, click OK.
   Note: Nothing will have changed on the CPM DEADLINE INPUT worksheet! The results will be given on the CPM DEADLINE OUTPUT worksheet.

Figure A5.3 shows the input for the Baja Burrito Restaurants Deadline model discussed in Section 5.10. The output is that in Figure 5.22 in that section.

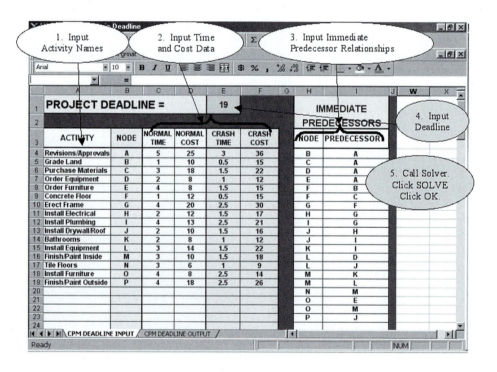

FIGURE A5.3
CPM DEADLINE INPUT
Worksheet for Baja
Burrito Restaurants

A5.1.4 The CPM-Budget.xls Template

On the CPM BUDGET INPUT worksheet (see Figure A5.4):

1. Enter activity names beginning in cell A4.
    Notes: (1) These will automatically assign node labels (letter designations) in column B. (2) After all the activities have been entered, *enter END in the cell after the last entry in column A*.

2. Enter the normal time, normal cost, crash time, and crash costs in columns C, D, E, and F, respectively.

3. Enter the precedence relations one by one. The ending node label of a predecessor relationship is entered in column H, while its immediate predecessor node label is entered in column I.
    Notes: (1) If a node has more than one immediate predecessor, the ending node label must be listed in column H each time with a corresponding immediate predecessor label in column I. (2) *For all nodes that are not immediate predecessors for any other activity, enter these nodes as immediate predecessors for END*.

4. Enter the available budget in cell E1.

5. After entering the input data, call Solver and click SOLVE. When Solver is done, click OK.
    Note: Nothing will have changed on the CPM BUDGET INPUT worksheet! The results will be given on the CPM BUDGET OUTPUT worksheet.

Figure A5.4 shows the input for the Baja Burrito Restaurants Budget model discussed in Section 5.10. The output is that in Figure 5.24 in that section.

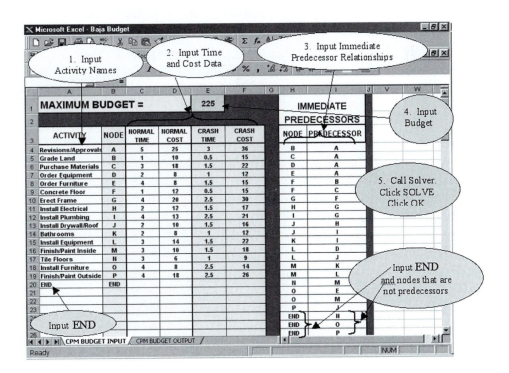

FIGURE A5.4
CPM BUDGET INPUT Worksheet for Baja Burrito Restaurants

A5.1.5 The PERT-COST.xls Template

On the PERT-COST INPUT worksheet (see Figure A5.5):

1. Enter work package names beginning in cell A4.
   Note: These will automatically assign node labels (letter designations) in column B.

2. Enter the budgeted time, budgeted cost, percent complete, and cost to date data in columns C, D, E, and F, respectively.

3. Enter the precedence relations one by one. The ending node label of a predecessor relationship is entered in column H, while its immediate predecessor node label is entered in column I.
   Note: If a node has more than one immediate predecessor, the ending node label must be listed in column H each time with a corresponding immediate predecessor label in column I.

4. Enter the current date in cell D1.

5. After entering the input data, call Solver and click SOLVE. When Solver is done, click OK.
   Note: Nothing will have changed on the PERT-COST INPUT worksheet!

6. Select the PERT-COST OUTPUT Worksheet, call Solver, and click SOLVE.

Figure A5.5 shows the input for the Tom Larkin political campaign model discussed in Section 5.11. The output is that given in Figure 5.27 of that section.

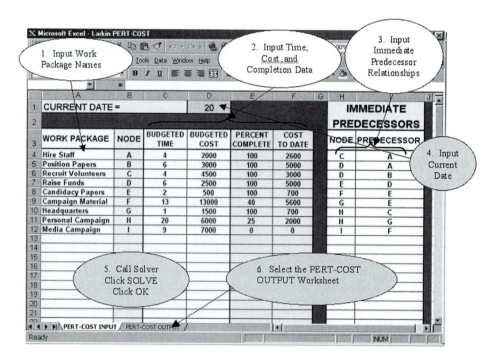

FIGURE A5.5
PERT-COST INPUT Worksheet for the Tom Larkin Political Campaign

APPENDIX 5.2

Using the PERT-CPM Template to Create Gantt Charts

Creation of a Gantt chart using the Chart Wizard function in Excel requires four columns in this order:

1. Node Labels
2. Activity Names
3. ES times (if creating an Earliest Time Gantt Chart) or LS times (if creating a Latest Time Gantt Chart)
4. Expected Completion Times (μ)

These are all entries on the PERT OUTPUT worksheet.
 Begin by creating a new worksheet (Gantt Data) with these entries.

1. Select worksheet from the INSERT menu.
2. Select the PERT OUTPUT worksheet and highlight the entries in column B beginning with cell B8 and select Copy from the Edit menu.
3. Select the new Gantt Data worksheet and click on cell A1. From the Edit menu select Paste Special and check Values in the dialogue box (Figure A5.6). The node labels will now be in column A of the Gantt Data worksheet.

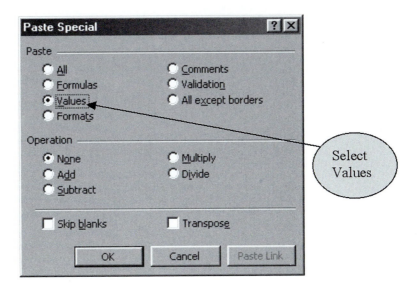

FIGURE A5.6
Paste Special Dialogue Box

4. In a like manner, copy the activity names in column A, the ES in column G (or LS in column H), and the expected times (μ) in column D from the PERT OUTPUT worksheet and, using the Paste Special-Values function, paste these values into columns B, C, and D, respectively, of the new Gantt Data worksheet.

5. Reverse the order of the activities by highlighting all the data in columns A, B, C, and D beginning with row 2 by using the Sort Descending function as shown in Figure A5.7.

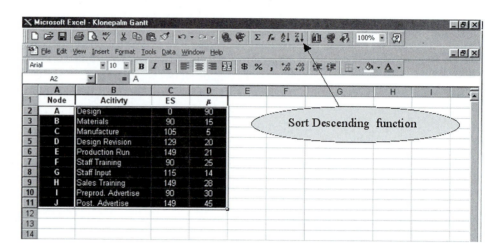

FIGURE A5.7
Use of Sort Descending
Function

The data in columns A through D of the Gantt Data worksheet will be those in Figure A5.8.

6. From the Chart Wizard, select the **Custom Types** tab; then select the **Floating Bars** option as shown in Figure A5.8.

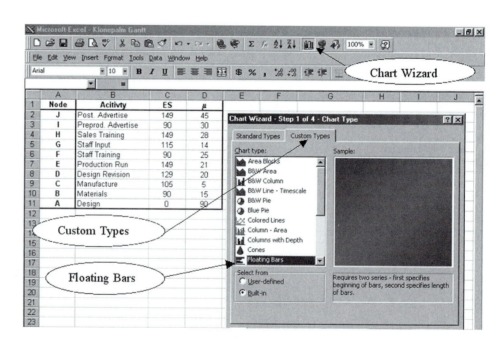

FIGURE A5.8
Selecting Floating Bars from
the Chart Wizard

7. In Step 2 of the Chart Wizard, in the Data Range enter all data beginning with cell B2 as shown in Figure A5.9.

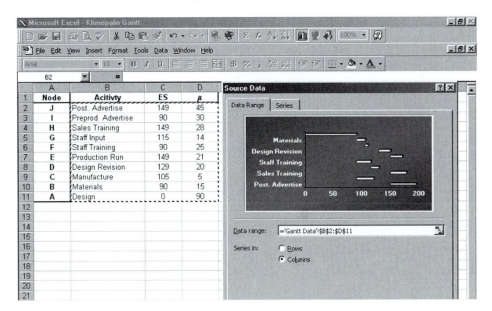

FIGURE A5.9
Entry for Data Range in Step 2

8. In Step 3, fill in a chart title and labels for the Category X-axis and Value Z-axis. Note that the entry for the Category X-axis is actually the Y-axis label and the entry for the Value Z-axis is actually the X-axis label. We entered "Klonepalm 2000," "ACTIVITIES," and "DAYS" respectively, for these values. In Step 4, enter a new worksheet name and click Finish.

The result is the Gantt chart shown in Figure A5.10. We can now make it more attractive by changing the background colors, changing bar colors, and so on. This can be done by right mouse clicking on the item, selecting Format Data Series, and then experimenting with the options until we have an attractive Gantt chart such as that in Figure 5.8 in Section 5.6.

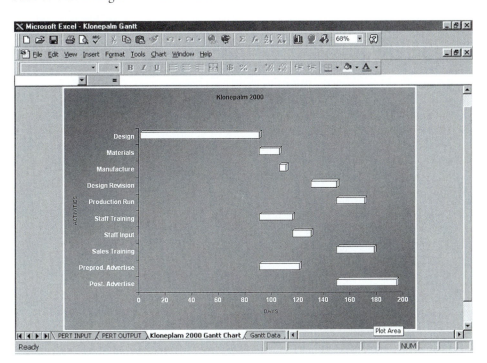

FIGURE A5.10
Resulting Gantt Chart Created from Chart Wizard

Problems

1. Paul Nguyen is designing a new safety cap for medicine bottles to replace the cumbersome child safety caps used by manufacturers today. Construct a PERT/CPM network of the project, given the activities Paul has listed in the following table.

Safety Cap Project

Activity	Immediate Predecessors
A. Complete design	—
B. Manufacture prototype	A
C. Test and redesign cap	B
D. Determine interest in product	B
E. Apply for patent	C
F. Manufacture limited quantities	C
G. Design packaging	C
H. Negotiate with manufacturers	D,E,F
I. Sign contract	H
J. Ship initial supplies	G,I

2. St. Paul's Episcopal Church has a parking lot in need of repair. It has determined that these repairs will cost around $150,000, although formal bids have not yet been solicited from construction companies. The clergy has determined that the following set of activities make up the project.

Activity	Immediate Predecessors
A. Inform congregation of upcoming project	—
B. Solicit funds in church and newsletter	A
C. Obtain bids	A
D. Do volunteer parking lot preparation work	C
E. Solicit by telephone	C
F. Borrow remaining funds	B, D, E
G. Choose company and have work performed	F

Draw a PERT/CPM network for this project.

3. The library at Kaufman Products has just received authorization to spend up to $40,000 on new journal subscriptions and book purchases. Accordingly, the librarian has developed the following small project.

	Immediate Predecessors	Time (weeks)
A. Solicit input from employees	—	4
B. Identify obsolete material in library	—	3
C. Clear out space for new purchases	B	2
D. Hold sale/discard obsolete material	B	3
E. Review input from employees given budget and space requirements	A,C	2
F. Order/receive new materials	E	5

Draw a PERT/CPM network for the Kaufman Products librarian and use this representation to determine the expected number of weeks it will take

before the new materials are in the library. What is the critical path? Explain its significance.

4. Ponderosa Construction has budgeted $350,000 to build a new clubhouse at the Sun Lakes Golf Course outside Tampa, Florida. Ponderosa uses a mixture of union and nonunion personnel. Grading of the land, electrical, and plumbing work is subcontracted out to union shops. The actual construction of the project, though supervised by union carpenters, is performed mainly by nonunion laborers to conserve costs. Project planning has produced the following chart.

	Immediate Predecessors	Expected Completion Time (Days)
A. Grade land	—	3
B. Order building supplies	—	4
C. Hire nonunion labor	—	7
D. Pour concrete slab	A	8
E. Receive/organize supplies	B	8
F. Build clubhouse frame	C,D,E	30
G. Electrical installation	F	15
H. Plumbing installation	F	11
I. Stucco/paint outside	H	20
J. Dry wall/paint/tile inside	G,H	18
K. Finish/cleanup	I,J	6
L. Landscaping	K	8

a. Draw a PERT/CPM network for this problem.
b. Prepare a chart showing the earliest/latest start and finish times and the slack for each activity. What is the expected completion time for the project?

5. Consider the Sun Lakes Golf clubhouse project in problem 4. The $350,000 allocated for the project was budgeted as per the second column below. The last two columns show the progress and costs incurred as of day 12.

Day 12

Activity	Budgeted Cost	Percent Complete	Cost to Date
A	$ 10,000	100%	$ 9,100
B	$ 1,000	100%	$ 1,100
C	$ 10,000	100%	$15,100
D	$ 8,000	90%	$ 7,100
E	$ 1,000	50%	$ 700
F	$210,000	0%	$ 0
G	$ 10,000	0%	$ 0
H	$ 30,000	0%	$ 0
I	$ 25,000	0%	$ 0
J	$ 35,000	0%	$ 0
K	$ 1,000	0%	$ 0
L	$ 9,000	0%	$ 0
TOTAL BUDGET = $350,000			

Is the project coming in on time and within budget? If not, can you suggest some corrective action?

6. When buyers purchase new houses, they are frequently responsible for installing their own landscaping. The PERT/CPM network shown in the accompanying figure represents a landscaping project for a new home in Jackson, Mississippi. The times are in days.

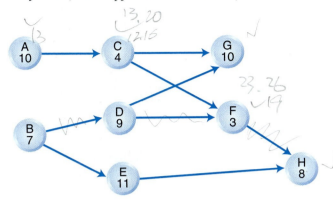

a. What are the expected completion time and the critical path for the landscaping project?
b. What are the earliest and latest start and finish times for activity C?
c. How long can activity A be delayed without delaying the minimum completion time of the project?
d. If activities A, C, and F are *each* delayed three days, how long will the landscaping project be delayed?

7. George Washington High School is planning a reunion for the graduating class of 1975. The D'Onofrio twins, who are in charge of planning the entire event, have determined the following tasks.

	Immediate Predecessors	Time Estimates (Days)		
Tasks		Best	Probable	Worse
A. Determine current addresses of graduates	—	20	25	50
B. Determine a budget	—	3	5	12
C. Choose a site	B	10	14	21
D. Hire a band	B	5	14	18
E. Design commemorative sweatshirts	—	10	10	14
F. Write/mail announcements	A, C	8	14	25
G. Hire a photographer	B	3	4	7
H. Determine excess funds	D, F, G	32	40	50
I. Buy door prizes	E, H	2	5	8

What is the probability that the D'Onofrio twins will have to commit more than 90 days to this project?

8. Keith Littlefield is a racecar driver on the NASCAR circuit. He has promised to participate in the Pocono 300, to be held 15 weeks from now. In order to be competitive, Keith feels he must completely modify his racecar. The following activity chart summarizes the normal crash costs and completion times of the rebuilding project activities

Activity	Immediate Predecessors	Normal Time (Weeks)	Crash Time (Weeks)	Normal Cost	Crash Cost
A	—	8	4	$4800	$5400
B	C, E	7	4	$3900	$4800
C	A	7	2	$5100	$6600
D	G	4	2	$1200	$2400
E	A	9	3	$3600	$4800
F	C, D	9	3	$3300	$6000
G	A	7	3	$2700	$3900

a. Determine the minimal time it will take to modify the racecar if no activities are crashed.
b. Which activities should be crashed and by what amount to meet the 15-week target date? What are the total costs of the modifications if the deadline is met?

9. In problem 8, the figures in the table come from Eurogem Bodyworks, a company that has previously modified two of Keith Littlefield's racecars. Activity F is the modification of the aerodynamics of the car. An associate of Keith's has informed him of a company known as Glidestone, Inc. that can also do the required modifications. Glidestone's normal cost is $4200, but the modification will only take eight weeks. Its crash time of only one week can be met with a crash cost of $5250. Should Keith switch to Glidestone? If so, which activities should now be crashed and by what amount? Also give the total overall project completion cost.

10. Carter, Fine, and Groetche (CF&G) is an advertising firm specializing in marketing cosmetics. A typical project begins with a meeting between executives from the cosmetics firm and senior CF&G representatives to get a general feel for the product. This usually takes about two weeks. CF&G then takes about a week to review the current assignments and strengths of its personnel and assemble an advertising group it feels can most effectively develop the ad campaign.

After the group has been formed, several of its members meet with both senior and line personnel at the cosmetics firm for a general assessment of the strengths and any unusual features of the product. This typically takes about four weeks. After meeting with senior and line personnel, these members conduct a test sampling of consumer reactions to the product, which also takes about four weeks.

At the same time that some of the group is meeting with company representatives and test marketing, other members of the group are researching competitive products and developing charts of market shares, prices, perceived consumer feelings about the products, and the like. This work usually takes about six weeks. Based on the results from sample testing and the research on competitive products, CF&G puts together a full-scale ad campaign lasting about eight weeks.

a. Determine the minimum completion time for this project.
b. What is the critical path?
c. Draw a Gantt chart for the advertising process at CF&G.

11. L&P Janitorial Service provides cleaning services to many clients, including the Johnson Tower complex. L&P personnel begin their operations at 10:00 P.M. and must leave before 6:00 A.M. the following morning. Certain cleaning operations must be completed before others are started, as illustrated by the following network. The times are in minutes.

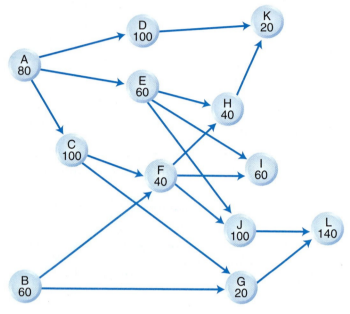

a. Prepare a chart giving the earliest and latest start and finish times and the slack times for each cleaning activity. Express the earliest and latest start and finish times as actual clock times (i.e., 10:00 P.M., etc.).
b. L&P Janitorial wants to conserve costs and will send the minimum number of workers required to complete a cleaning project. Employees work eight-hour shifts, and any worker can perform any of the cleaning operations. Show how the Johnson Tower complex project can be completed using only two workers. Give a schedule for each worker.

12. The following table is a plan for a major freeway renovation project at the intersection of Interstate Highway 5 and Highway 55, a major north-south freeway in Santa Ana, California.

Activity	Expected Time (months)	Immediate Predecessors
A. Obtain federal funding	16	—
B. Obtain state funding	28	—
C. Design/subcontract freeway lanes	14	A
D. Design/subcontract bridges/exits	22	A
E. Build new freeway sound walls	12	B,C
F. Rebuild southbound lanes	26	B,C
G. Rebuild transition roads/exits	18	D,E
H. Build new bridges/overpasses	50	D,E
I. Rebuild northbound lanes	44	F,G

a. Determine an overall estimated project completion time.
b. What is the effect of: (i) a delay in federal funding of five months? (ii) a delay in state funding of five months?
c. Suppose *each* activity has a standard deviation of four months. What is the probability that the freeway construction will be completed in: (i) six years; (ii) seven years; (iii) eight years; (iv) nine years?

13. *Mustang and Me* is a new movie from Nickledime Studios about a 12-year-old boy and a talking 1965 Ford Mustang convertible. The film is due out in 16 weeks. Originally, the studio was simply going to promote this as a "feel good" movie. However, further research has shown that merchandising of the modified Mustang used in the movie could be quite lucrative if the products are available no later than the release date of the movie.

The following table details the activities of this project. Because of the studio's long experience with product design and distribution, it has been able to determine normal and crash times and costs for each of the activities. Times are in weeks, and costs are in $100,000s.

Activity	Normal Time	Normal Cost	Crash Time	Crash Cost
A. Design/test product	6	12	4	22
B. Hire workers	3	4	2	5
C. Train workers	3	5	3	5
D. Order/receive materials	2	10	1.5	12
E. Reconfigure machinery/setup	7	10	4	19
F. Advertise product	8	20	5	32
G. Production	8	12	4.5	26
H. Pay purchase orders	3	1	2	2

The following is the PERT/CPM network representation of the project.

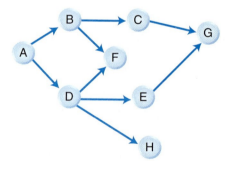

a. Write the linear program that models this situation.
b. Determine a minimum cost schedule to complete the project within 16 weeks.

14. Consider the merchandising problem faced by Nickledime Studios in problem 13. At present, the studio can only allocate $8 million to the merchandising project.
    a. Write the linear program that models this situation.
    b. What is the minimal completion time of the project, given this budgetary constraint?

15. Consider the Nickledime model in problems 13 and 14.
    a. Draw a Gantt chart using the suggested times for the minimum cost deadline model in problem 13.
    b. Draw a Gantt chart using the suggested times for the minimum time budget model in problem 14.

16. The Platters, a rock-and-roll group that had many hits in the late 1950s, has undergone many personnel changes since that era. However, a group performing under that name is still touring the country giving concerts. The group would like to stop in Detroit, Michigan, on its current tour. An "oldies" radio station, WDMI, is in charge of making the arrangements.

    The station has listed activities that must be completed prior to the concert in the table for problem 16. Times are in weeks.

Problem 16

Activity	Immediate Predecessors	Optimistic	Most Likely	Pessimistic
A. Negotiate lease terms	—	3	4	5
B. Hire opening acts	A	2	4	12
C. Hire security	B	1	2	3
D. Hire technicians	B	2	3	10
E. Ticket outlets	B	2	3	4
F. Initial promotion	E	2	3	4
G. Lodging/ transportation	A	.5	1	1.5
H. Final promotion	F	4	5	12
I. Rehearsals	C,D,G	2	5	8
J. Concession sales	A	5	13	15

    a. Give an estimated completion time for this project.
    b. Which activities have the most slack?
    c. What is the probability that the project will be completed in 12 weeks?
    d. Give a time within which the station can be 99% sure of completing the project.

17. One of the primary proponents of PERT/CPM analyses has been the Department of Defense (DOD). Suppose that Congress has allocated funds to build the new F-21A attack fighter aircraft. The Secretary of Defense must make a recommendation to the President concerning which of two companies, Boeing and McDonnell-Douglas, should be given the contract. Each company has submitted verified DOD time estimates for the major activities of the building process shown in the table for problem 17. Times are in months.

Problem 17

	Boeing Estimates			McDonnell-Douglas Estimates		
Activity	a	m	b	a	m	b
A. Design engine	7	10	24	10	12	16
B. Manufacture engine	1	2	3	2	3	4
C. Plan aircraft	11	15	28	10	16	24
D. Manufacture fuselage	7	14	17	12	15	18
E. Engine to fuselage	1	2	3	1	2	3
F. Manufacture wings	6	8	11	8	9	10
G. Manufacture tail	5	7	10	4	5	6
H. Contract for equipment	9	10	11	5	9	13
I. Equipment installed	2	3	4	1	2	5
J. Final assembly	5	7	9	6	7	8
K. Co. testing/modifications	8	12	17	8	13	14

The project can be represented by the following PERT/CPM network.

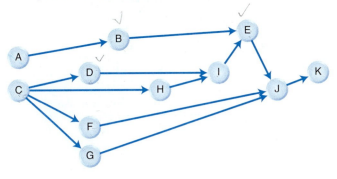

    a. Based solely on the probability of having the aircraft ready for test flights within 60 months and the company time estimates, which contractor, Boeing or McDonnell-Douglas, should the Secretary of Defense recommend?
    b. Based solely on the expected completion time of the project, which contractor, Boeing or McDonnell-Douglas, should the Secretary of Defense recommend?

18. Tamako Landscaping designs and installs landscaping for large office complexes. The activities for one such installation project are shown in the network for problem 18. Note that each node gives both budgeted time (in days) and cost data.
    a. Determine the estimated completion time and total cost of the project.
    b. What is the effect on the completion time of the entire project for each of the following activity delays?
        i. H delayed 2 days
        ii. C delayed 2 days
        iii. F delayed 11 days
        iv. F delayed 14 days
        v. G delayed 2 days
        vi. C delayed 2 days and F delayed 11 days
        vii. C delayed 2 days and G delayed 2 days

Problem 18

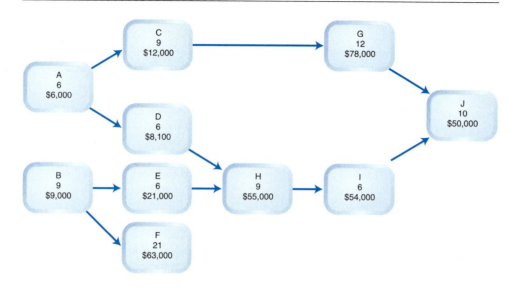

19. In the project initiated by Tamako Landscaping (problem 18), suppose that after 18 days Tamako observes the following status.

Work Package	Expenses Incurred	Percent Complete
A	$ 7,000	100%
B	$12,000	100%
C	$15,000	90%
D	$ 8,500	100%
E	$20,000	95%
F*	$25,000	40%

*The other activities (G–J) have not been started.

a. Is the project coming in on time?
b. Is the project coming in within budget?
c. Comment on a strategy to complete this project.

20. It is June 1, and popular recording star Chocolate Cube is planning to add a separate recording studio to his palatial complex in rural Connecticut. The blueprints have been completed, and the table for problem 20 lists the time estimates of the activities in the construction project.
a. Determine the expected completion time and the critical path for this project. Also determine the expected earliest and latest start and finish dates for each of the separate activities. (Assume the workers work seven days per week, including July Fourth and Labor Day.)
b. Chocolate Cube has committed himself to a recording session beginning September 8 (99 days from now). What is the probability that he will be able to begin recording in his own personal studio on that date?

c. If his studio is not ready in 99 days, Chocolate Cube will be forced to lease his record company's studio, which will cost $120,000. For $3500 extra, Eagle Electric, the company hired for the electrical installation (activity G), will work double time; each of the time estimates for this activity will therefore be reduced by 50%. Using an expected cost approach, determine if the $3500 should be spent.

Problem 20   Chocolate Cube Recording Studio

Activity	Immediate Predecessors	Optimistic Time (days)	Most Likely Time (days)	Pessimistic Time (days)
A. Order materials	—	1.0	2.0	9.0
B. Clear land	—	2.5	4.5	9.5
C. Obtain permits	—	2.0	5.0	14.0
D. Hire subcontractors	C	4.0	6.5	18.0
E. Store materials	A	2.0	4.0	18.0
F. Primary structure	B,D,E	22.0	30.0	50.0
G. Electrical work	F	15.0	20.0	37.0
H. Plumbing	F	4.5	10.0	21.5
I. Finish/paint	G,H	12.0	15.0	24.0
J. Complete studio	H	14.0	14.5	48.0
K. Cleanup	I,J	5.0	5.0	5.0

21. TV and radio stations in Birmingham, Alabama, are planning their annual "Mike Awards" banquet, which is 15 weeks away. The following is a list of the activities with projected costs and expedited costs (in $1000s), that must take place. Times are in weeks. Determine a schedule of events that will meet the 15-week deadline at minimum total cost.

Problem 21 Mike Awards

Activity	Immediate Predecessors	Projected Cost	Projected Time	Expedited Cost	Expedited Time
A. Secure facility	—	9	4	15	2
B. Prepare guest list	—	2	2	3	1
C. Hire band	A	7	3	10	2
D. Design stage	A	6	4	11	3
E. Choreograph program	C,D	8	4	18	2
F. Hire caterer	B	9	2	20	1
G. Build stage	D	8	4	12	2
H. Hold program rehearsal	E,G	7	3	17	2
I. Make final preparations	B,H	8	5	22	3

Extra Sources. apply source on the critical activities [handwritten]

22. Consider the planning of the "Mike Awards" banquet in problem 21. Suppose the planning committee adopted your recommendation for the scheduling of events. After 10 weeks it finds the following situation. Is the project on time and within budget? If not, can you suggest some corrective actions that might be taken.

Progress Report at the end of Week 10:

Activity	Percent Complete	Cost to Date
A	100	$12,000
B	100	$ 2,500
C	100	$ 6,500
D	100	$ 8,000
E	100	$12,500
F	15	$ 5,000
G	80	$ 7,500
H	0	$ 0
I	0	$ 0

23. Virtual Golf, Inc. (VGI) is contemplating introducing a new virtual reality golf experience that would, if successful, be located in many amusement parks and entertainment centers throughout the country. If the project gets the "go-ahead," it must be completed within 20 weeks (140 days) to be installed in the Mall of America in Bloomington, Minnesota, for test marketing. The table for problem 23 gives cost and time estimates (in days) for the activities of the project.

Activity	Immediate Predecessors
A. Feasibility study	—
B. Input from golf professionals	A
C. Conceptual design	B
D. Professional feedback	C
E. Final design	D
F. Manufacture of unit	E
G. Software development	E
H. Equipment/software coordination	F,G
I. In-house unit testing	H
J. Operator training	H
K. Construct unit in mall store	I,J
L. Testing of unit in mall store	K

Activity	Normal Days	Crash Days	Normal Cost	Crash Cost
A. Feasibility study	14	12	$15,000	$17,500
B. Input from golf professionals	14	11	$55,000	$64,000
C. Conceptual design	8	8	$50,000	$50,000
D. Professional feedback	12	9	$40,000	$50,000
E. Final design	18	16	$50,000	$65,000
F. Manufacture of unit	20	16	$40,000	$55,000
G. Software development	14	10	$55,000	$70,000
H. Equipment/software coordination	21	19	$25,000	$65,000
I. In-house unit testing	10	8	$25,000	$32,000
J. Operator training	21	21	$50,000	$50,000
K. Construct unit in mall store	9	6	$25,000	$40,000
L. Testing of unit in mall store	15	10	$10,000	$40,000

a. What is the minimum project cost that will allow the project to be completed within 20 weeks? How would you schedule the individual activities? *CPM-Budget* [handwritten]

b. What would be your recommendation if the project had to be completed within 18 weeks? *not poss* [handwritten]

24. Consider the project facing VGI in problem 23. If the company allocated a maximum of $500,000 to this project, what is the minimum time it would take to complete the project?

25. The Ohio Preservation Society (OPS) has discovered a house once occupied by Rutherford B. Hayes, the nineteenth president of the United States (1877–1881). OPS plans to restore the building to reflect the period during which the former president lived there and eventually open it for public tours. Contractors for the restoration project will have to do the following:

Wall/Ceiling Activities
A. Strip the existing wallpaper
B. Clean and repair the walls/ceilings
C. Paint the walls/ceilings

Flooring Activities
D. Remove old carpeting
E. Lay a floor foundation
F. Install, stain, and seal hardwood flooring
G. Install rugs and carpet runners (for tourists)

Exterior Activities
H. Sand and repair outside wood surfaces
I. Paint exterior to reflect the period.

a. Construct a PERT/CPM network for the renovation project faced by OPS, assuming:
   i. The wall/ceiling activities, the flooring activities, and the exterior activities are listed in the order in which they are to be performed.
   ii. Cleaning and repairing the walls/ceilings, removing the old carpeting, and sanding and repairing the exterior must precede any painting activity (interior or exterior).
   iii. The walls/ceilings must be painted before hardwood flooring is installed, stained, and sealed.
   iv. All painting (interior and exterior) must be completed before new rugs and carpet runners are installed.
   v. Stripping the wallpaper, removing the old carpeting, and sanding and repairing the exterior may all commence at the same time.
b. If the estimated time of each wall/ceiling activity is two weeks, the estimated time of each flooring activity is one week, and the estimated time of each exterior activity is three weeks, prepare a Gantt chart for the restoration project.
c. What is OPS's estimated completion time for the restoration project?

26. Hanover Toys, Inc. is interested in developing and marketing Lover's Baskets as a specialty gift product. The preliminary idea is that the baskets would have a teddy bear centerpiece on a bed of wrapped gourmet chocolates, cakes, and petite fours. The basket would be wrapped in colored cellophane and tied with a fancy bow that includes a fresh rose. The table for problem 26 is a simplified analysis of the project components.

Problem 26

	Immediate Predecessors	Optimistic Time	Most Likely Time	Pessimistic Time
A. Focus group of likely buyers	—	1	2	2
B. Market analysis	A	3	5	7
C. Designs developed	A	3	6	8
D. Marketing blitz	B,C	2	3	4
E. Production run	C	3	5	9
F. Analysis of buyer response	D,E	2	4	5

a. What is the expected completion time of the project? What is the critical path?
b. Which activities have the most flexibility in scheduling?
c. The company would like to complete the entire project within three months (13 weeks). What is the probability it will be able to meet this target date?

27. Universal Travel is planning to move its headquarters from Cincinnati to Columbus, Ohio. The table for problem 27 details the steps that must be taken. Times are in weeks.

Problem 27

	Immediate Predecessors	Optimistic Time	Most Likely Time	Pessimistic Time
A. Select a site	—	8	12	20
B. Refurbish building	A	9	10	12
C. Determine which staff will transfer	—	2	2	3
D. Hire staff replacements in Columbus	C	3	6	8
E. Pack boxes in Cincinnati	A,C	1	2	5
F. Move equipment	B	2	3	4
G. Move files	B,E	1	2	5
H. Set up equipment/ files in Columbus	F,G	3	4	5
I. Occupancy	D,H	5	6	10

a. What is the expected completion time of the project? What is the critical path?
b. What is the probability the project will be completed within 36 weeks?
c. Suppose Universal will be charged for both sites if it is not completely moved in within 36 weeks. This will cost the company $5000. The company is considering two options to improve its chances to meet this deadline.
   • For $1000, additional movers can be hired to move the files. This would cut each of the three time estimates for that activity in half.
   • Additional movers can be hired for $1000 to assist in moving the equipment. This would cut the three time estimates for that activity by one week each.
   The company can pursue either OR BOTH of these options. What is your recommendation?

28. Whitehead Construction is building the new Crumpet Towers high-rise complex using the PERT/CPM network for problem 28.

Problem 28

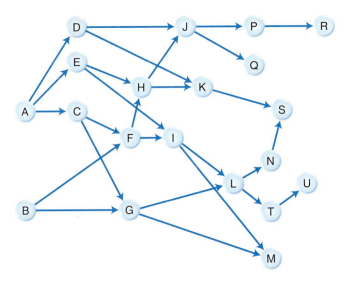

Several of the project's activities have been designated as plumbing or electrical activities that Whitehead will subcontract out. Two electrical subcontractors (Wizard Electric and Coast Electric) and two plumbing subcontractors (Reliable Plumbing and County Plumbing) are being considered for the project. The bids submitted by the subcontractors are as follows:

Wizard Electric	$228,000
Coast Electric	$312,000
Reliable Plumbing	$196,000
County Plumbing	$282,000

The following table, based on Whitehead's years of experience with similar projects, gives the three time estimates (in months) for each activity.

Activity	Optimistic Time	Most Likely Time	Pessimistic Time
A	1.0	2.2	3.1
B	2.1	3.0	4.1
E	0.9	2.2	5.1
G	3.5	4.0	6.0
I	1.1	1.2	1.8
J	2.1	2.8	4.4
K	4.1	6.2	9.9
N	2.7	3.7	4.5
P	0.8	1.5	3.1
R	3.3	4.4	5.5
T	1.0	2.0	2.8
U	1.3	3.0	7.5

Electrical Activities

Activity	Optimistic Time	Most Likely Time	Pessimistic Time
Wizard Electric			
C	1.0	2.6	4.7
H	1.3	3.0	8.0
L	0.5	0.8	2.0
S	2.7	3.0	5.5
Coast Electric			
C	0.8	1.6	2.0
H	1.3	2.8	6.6
L	0.4	0.6	1.4
S	2.5	3.5	4.8

Plumbing Activities

Activity	Optimistic Time	Most Likely Time	Pessimistic Time
Reliable Plumbing			
D	0.7	1.6	2.0
F	2.2	4.4	6.6
M	6.0	7.0	9.9
Q	3.3	5.1	8.9
County Plumbing			
D	0.5	1.5	2.5
F	1.5	3.5	5.5
M	4.5	5.5	6.5
Q	4.5	5.5	6.5

a. Determine the expected completion time of the project for each of the four electric/plumbing combinations.
b. Discuss the validity of the PERT assumptions for this approach.

29. Consider the Crumpet Towers project in problem 28.
   a. A penalty of $500,000 will be invoked if the project is not finished within two years (24 months). Use the expected value approach to recommend which combination of subcontractors should be used.
   b. Using your recommendation from part (a), determine a date by which Whitehead can be 99% sure of completing the project.

30. The California Medical Association (CMA) is holding a meeting at the Anaheim Hilton Hotel on September 8. On that day, the CMA will host a theme party reception for the over 2000 members and spouses who are expected to attend. Stacey Geyer is the Hilton's convention services manager in charge of arranging the reception.

   Planning the meeting consists of the activities detailed in the table for problem 30:

Problem 30   Time Requirements for CMA Reception

Task	Immediate Predecessors	Expected Days	Standard Deviation
A. Plan meeting with Howard Klein	—		
B. Secure reception room	A	3	1
C. Plan theme	A	8	2
D. Plan menu	C		
E. Hire musicians	C	7	2
F. Plan space layout of reception room	B,D	4	1
G. Review plans/charges	E,F		

Stacey has been able to estimate the mean and standard deviation of activities B, C, E, and F, based on her past experience. Her estimates for activities A, D, and G, however, depend somewhat on Howard Klein, the arrangements chairperson for the CMA.

At this point, Stacey has estimated that the initial planning meeting with Howard Klein will take at least two days and as many as ten days, but most likely about three days. She feels that menu planning will take between one and three days, most likely two days. In order to review the plans and charges completely, Howard Klein must check with his arrangements committee. This will most likely take about 10 days but could take anywhere from 4 to 22 days.

   a. Determine the critical path, the expected completion time, and the standard deviation of the completion time of the project.
   b. Analyze the effect on the expected project completion time of each of the following.
      i. Activity A is delayed five days.
      ii. Activity B is delayed five days.
      iii. Activity D is delayed five days.
      iv. Activity F is delayed five days.
      v. Activities B and D are each delayed five days.
      vi. Activities D and F are each delayed five days.

31. Consider the CMA scheduling situation in problem 30. Suppose Stacey would like to be relatively sure (99% sure) that the project is completed by September 1, a week before the actual reception. To meet Stacey's goal, by what date should she begin her first meeting with Howard Klein? *Be sure to take into account the variability in completion times and do not count Saturdays and Sundays (or July 4, if relevant). Count August 31 as day 1; that is, if the project took only one day it would have to start on August 31. Round up any fraction of a day to a whole day.*

32. Consider the CMA scheduling problem (problem 30). There is a possibility that another group may also be scheduling a meeting at the same time at the Anaheim Hilton, so that securing an appropriate reception room (activity B) *may* present more of a problem for Stacey Geyer. Accordingly, she has raised her pessimistic estimate of its completion time; the expected time is now 10 days (instead of three), and its standard deviation is 6 (instead of 1).

Show that, given the basic assumptions of PERT, the expected time of the project does not change from that derived in problem 30. What basic PERT assumption *could* be violated under this scenario, however?

33. Consider the CMA scheduling problem (problem 30). Howard Klein's schedule does not allow him to meet with Stacey for their initial planning session until 35 workdays before the meeting on September 8; that is, the entire project must be completed in 35 days. If it is not completed within 35 days, the CMA will use an alternative backup site for the reception, and the Hilton will forego the $100,000 profit from the reception.

The agent for Billy and the Goats, the musicians the CMA wants to book for the reception (activity E), has indicated to the Hilton that, for an additional $3000, he can wrap up contract negotiations with the group in only two days (with no variance), instead of the projected seven days with a standard deviation of two days. Is it worth it for Stacey to spend the extra $3000?

34. Berryesa Cabin Company builds vacation cabins for customers from prepackaged cabin "kits." Although the kits are designed so that the novice can build his or her own cabin, most do not and contract Berryesa to complete the cabin. The network for problem 34 shows the PERT/CPM network for cabin construction by Berryesa.

Problem 34

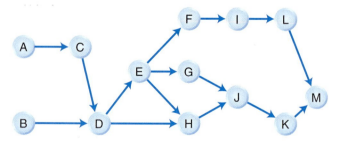

The following table lists the activities, and the expected completion time (in days) required to complete each task.

Activity	Expected Completion Time
A. Secure land permits	10
B. Pick up/modify prepackaged kit	5
C. Clear area for cabin	4
D. Lay foundation/floor	4
E. Erect frame	2
F. Install outside walls	3
G. Install electrical	3
H. Install plumbing	6
I. Install roof	2
J. Install inside walls/floors	4
K. Finish/paint inside	5
L. Finish/paint outside	3
M. Final cleanup	2

Determine the minimum project completion date.

35. Vertical software is software written using specific packages but designed especially for one company (or type of company). VSI (Vertical Software, Inc.) specializes in writing database programs for various industries. Recently, it signed a contract with the Rhode Island Basketball Officials Association to write an assigning and database system. The software takes the rankings of the officials (Levels 1, 2, 3, 4, and 5), each official's availability, and the level of the official required for each game, and randomly assigns the appropriate officials to each game. The database of assignments must be accessible by date, level, school, and official.

Although the association is paying VSI for the program, VSI retains the right to market the product nationwide after development. The table for problem 35 is a simplified budget for the project.

Problem 35

Work Package	Immediate Predecessors	Expected Time (days)	Budget
A. Meet with association	—	2	$ 800
B. Write software	A	20	$9000
C. Debug software	B	6	$1500
D. Prepare brief manual	B	3	$1000
E. Meet with RI assignors	D	2	$ 900
F. Test in RI for season	C,E	40	$2500
G. Make final changes	F	10	$4000
H. Write complete manual	G	15	$5000
I. Advertise	C,E	45	$9500

After 50 days, VSI finds itself in the following position:

Day 50

Work Package	Percent Complete	Expenditures to Date
A. Meet with association	100%	$1000
B. Write software	100%	$8000
C. Debug software	100%	$2500
D. Prepare brief manual	100%	$1000
E. Meet with RI assignors	100%	$1000
F. Test in RI for season	50%	$1000
G. Make final changes	0%	$ 0
H. Write complete manual	0%	$ 0
I. Advertise	10%	$2000

Is this project currently experiencing a cost overrun or underrun? Is it on target to be completed in its expected completion time? Should any corrective action be taken?

36. Consider the VSI model in problem 35.
    a. Draw an earliest time Gantt chart for this model.
    b. Draw a latest time Gantt chart for this model.
    c. Fill in the bars to show the percent complete as of day 50. Does either Gantt chart indicate that the project is behind schedule?

37. The PERT/CPM network for problem 37 details the construction of a new Senior Center in York, Pennsylvania. The times for the activities are in weeks.
    a. Determine the earliest and latest start and finish times and slack times for each activity in the project.
    b. What is the critical path and the expected completion time for this project?
    c. Activity H is the fencing activity. Because of other commitments, Kelly Fencing, the subcontractor in charge of building the fences for the project, will be delayed 10 weeks. Each week of delay in the construction of the Senior Center costs the investors in the project $5000 due to lack of occupancy. Which of the following alternatives would you recommend to the investors in light of this information?
        i. Keep Kelly Fencing and its $6000 contract.
        ii. Hire Colonial Landscapers, even though Colonial will take six weeks to complete activity H (instead of two) and will charge $17,500.
        iii. Have its own landscaping crew (currently doing landscaping activity E) design and build the fencing. The design and purchase of the materials for the fencing will cost $4000 and will add five weeks to activity E. The actual construction of the fencing, activity H, will take six weeks and cost $5500.

Problem 37

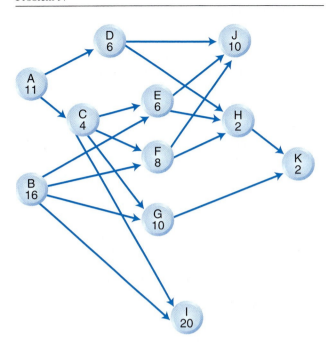

38. Campusgrocer.com is a start-up website that will allow college students at Southern Oregon University in Ashland, Oregon, to order grocery items over the Internet and have them delivered to campus dorm rooms. The idea is the brainchild of a young entrepreneurial student, Alan Roney, who has listed the activities for his project in the table for problem 38.

Problem 38   Campusgrocer.com

	Expected # Weeks	Immediate Predecessors
A. Survey a random sample of students to determine the items should be included	4	—
B. Determine the items/suppliers to be included on the website	4	A
C. Secure a list of e-mail addresses of all students in the college dorms	3	—
D. Design web page to appeal to the students and convey products offered in a pleasing format	4	B
E. Secure banking needs—financing/ checking accounts/establishment of credit card services	5	B
F. Purchase initial supply of items before commencing service	2	E
G. Advertise to students of upcoming operations through campus fliers posted on university kiosks	2	B
H. Advertise to students of upcoming operations by targeting student e-mail accounts	1	C,D
I. Final preparations/commence initial campusgrocer.com operations	2	F,G,H

a. Based on these time estimates, can Alan expect to start operations prior to the end of this 16-week semester?

b. If Alan revises his estimate of the time it will take to advertise by e-mail from 1 week to 4 weeks, how will this affect the overall estimate of the project's completion time?

c. If Alan revises his estimate of the time it will take to design the web page from 4 weeks to 7 weeks, how will this affect the overall estimate of the project's completion time?

d. Suppose that Alan feels that a reasonable estimate for each activity's standard deviation is 30% of its completion time. What is the probability he will be able to start operations prior to the end of this 16-week semester?

39. One aspect of what is called *PERTING a project* is to decide which activities are immediate predecessors of others. There may be a difference of opinion as to what these relationships might be. For example, suppose management at the very successful South Coast Repertory Theater (SCR) in Costa Mesa, California, held a brainstorming session to try to identify the steps to putting on a play. In no particular order, the management team came up with the following 11 activities:

Script Activities

    A-Commission the writing of the play
    B-Completed script
    C-Script changes to author's work

Cast Activities

    D-Auditions
    E-Cast changes
    F-First rehearsals
    G-Final dress rehearsal

Set Activities

    H-Set design
    I-Set construction

PROBLEMS 41–50 ARE ON THE CD

Marketing Activities

    J-Advertising strategy
    K-Advance ticket sales

a. Construct a list of immediate predecessors you feel is appropriate for each of the activities. *Note*: Different managers at SCR probably would come up with different sets of predecessors.

b. Construct a PERT/CPM network of your result in part a.

Questions 48–50 are designed so that you can construct your own PERT/CPM network.

40. Writing a book (particularly with a coauthor) can be a rewarding, yet tedious, process for both the authors and the publisher. Suppose you and your coauthor have an idea for a new management science text with features that are not found in any other current text and with a point of view that you feel is more in tune with current systems thinking than traditional texts. Develop an activity chart for writing such a text.

Some of the activities include: (1) writing a prospectus; (2) creating a few sample chapters; (3) mailing the chapters to various publishers; (4) having discussions with publishers; (5) choosing a publisher from those who are interested; (6) researching current trends; (7) researching current applications; (8) writing chapters; (9) correcting chapters based on coauthor suggestions; (10) writing problems; (11) responding to feedback from the publisher; (12) sending out parts of the manuscript for review; (13) revising chapters based on reviews; (14) selecting art work; (15) producing galley proofs; (16) proofreading and correcting galleys. (Believe us, this is just a sampling of the activities necessary to develop a text.)

Add some activities of your own and try to estimate reasonable times for each activity. (They will probably be optimistic!) Based on your activity chart, develop a Gantt chart for a text-writing project. (*Note: Many publishers do use a simplified Gantt chart for this process.*)

CASE STUDIES

CASE 1: Saratoga Mountain National Park

The Department of the Interior has named the Saratoga Mountain area a national park. It is in the planning stages of developing a campsite area over 500 acres of currently undeveloped land. This campsite will span the extremities of the park, from the proposed Mission Creek Campsite area in the west to the Wild Coyote Campsite area in the east.

At this time, all the contracts for this project have been

awarded, with the exception of selecting the company that will develop the management information system (MIS) for Saratoga National Park. The three bidders for this contract are: (1) QM Associates, (2) MS Infostructures, and (3) the SBAE Company.

The project has been subdivided into 10 individual activities, as depicted in the PERT/CPM network on the next page. Activity J is the MIS task.

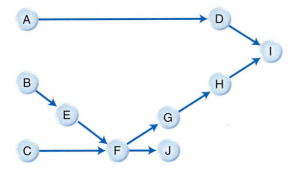

PERT/CPM Network for Saratoga National Park

Based on similar projects, it has been possible to determine a cost/time correspondence between the various activities of the project. The normal and crash costs and times (in weeks) are given in the following table.

Activity	Normal		Crash	
	Time	Cost	Time	Cost
A	15	$ 85,000	5	$165,000
B	12	$ 40,000	6	$100,000
C	20	$ 90,000	10	$250,000
D	24	$145,000	16	$315,000
E	10	$100,000	4	$220,000
F (Ellis Electric)				
G	10	$200,000	2	$600,000
H	12	$175,000	6	$475,000
I (Harriman Construction)				
J MIS PROJECT				

Activity F, which will be performed by Ellis Electric, involves laying the electrical cable for the project. To minimize its cost, Ellis Electric will design the system to use the least amount of electrical cable.

Ellis Electric will charge the government an amount between $100,000 and $200,000. For $100,000, Ellis Electric can assign enough workers to lay 300 feet of cable per week. For $200,000, Ellis will assign additional workers to lay 500 feet of cable each week.

Activity I involves constructing one (narrow) paved two-lane road from Mission Creek in the west to Wild Coyote in the east. This work will be done by Harriman Construction. To minimize the costs, the department will pay Harriman to build the road of minimum distance between the two campsites. At a cost to the government of $25,000 per week, 200 feet of roadway can be completed in a week. If the cost is increased to $36,000 per week, the completion rate will increase to 250 feet per week.

Due to the heavy brush and mountainous nature of the area, 13 possible dirt paths exist between the campsites. Neither Ellis Electric nor Harriman Construction is permitted to clear out additional areas for constructing either underground cable or the paved road. Thus the electrical cable must be laid, and the road must be built along areas of the dirt paths. Below is a map of the possible dirt paths between campsites showing distances in feet.

Each of three companies competing for the MIS task has been asked to submit a minimal cost and a minimal time (in weeks) bid. The bids are summarized in the following table.

Company	Minimum Cost Bid		Minimum Time Bid	
	Bid	Time	Time	Bid
QM	$150,000	40	20	$350,000
MS	$250,000	39	12	$450,000
SBAE	$300,000	28	8	$600,000

Possible Dirt Paths Between Campsites at Saratoga National Park

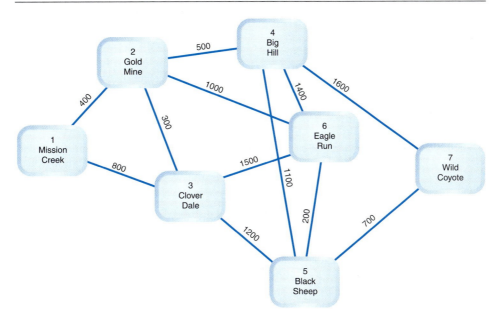

The "grand opening" of Saratoga National Park has been scheduled for exactly 52 weeks from now. It is imperative that the project be completed within the 52-week period because a delay of even one day in the opening of the park would result in revised travel costs for the dignitaries, lost income to the park, and other expenses.

Based on the given time and cost estimates, prepare a report giving the costs and scheduling for each activity so that the project will be completed within 52 weeks at min-imum total cost to the Department of the Interior. Be sure to emphasize the assumptions you made to perform your analysis. Include in your report:

- A recommendation for which firm should be awarded the MIS contract and its funding level
- A recommendation for the layout and funding for the Ellis Electric cable-laying activity
- A recommendation for the design and funding for the Harriman Construction paved road activity

CASE 2: Oak Glen Country Club Villas

Calico Construction is building the new Oak Glen Country Club Villas project, consisting of 18 buildings, each housing 12 condominiums. Each building will border the Oak Glen Golf Course designed by Jack Nicklaus. The minimum price for a condominium unit is $275,000, and buyers expect a high-quality project.

Response to the initial promotion was so great that Calico Construction presold all 216 units based solely on an artist's conception and schematic plans of the project. One reason for the quick sellout may have been the "YOU CAN MOVE IN BY SUMMER" campaign. As part of this campaign, Calico promised rebates of $10,000 cash to all 216 buyers if all the facilities, buildings, and other amenities were not completed by June 15 of next year.

As of September 15, the project is well underway. The PERT/CPM network for the Oak Glen Country Club Villas project details the precedence activities of the tasks remaining to be completed in the project.

All tasks except for activity R, the underground sewer activity, and activity T, the stream building activity, have been assigned to the appropriate subcontractors. Three time estimates (in days) for each of the other activities have been determined and are given in the following table.

	Opti-mistic	Most Likely	Pessi-mistic
A. Land measurements	5	8	15
B. Layout of measurement stakes	7	12	20
C. Environmental analysis	10	17	31
D. Building of foundation	12	22	38
E. Construction approval	6	13	21
F. Layout of building framework	11	15	27
G. Gas line installment	9	18	22
H. Electrical wiring	25	27	31
I. Interior plumbing	18	20	35
J. Wall construction	12	25	32
K. Insulation	10	23	33
L. Drywall	15	20	25
M. Roofing	3	10	20
N. Restaurant construction	25	40	55
O. Swimming pool	9	20	40
P. Fencing	6	10	21
Q. Telephone lines	12	22	40
R. Underground sewers			

	Opti-mistic	Most Likely	Pessi-mistic
S. Snack bar	10	20	30
T. Stream building			
U. Outside lighting	8	12	15
V. Parking lots	3	5	7
W. Drainage construction	5	10	18
X. Safety inspection	9	15	25
Y. Landscaping	6	24	40
Z. Final permits/releases	10	15	25

Activity R, the underground sewer activity, consists of installing pipes and connections to join all 18 buildings to the main city sewer system. Calico Construction has two alternatives for this activity.

1. Reedy Brothers has submitted a bid of $300,000 for the design and construction of the required sewer project. It estimates a most likely completion time of 25 days, with a difference of plus or minus two days for the optimistic and pessimistic time estimates.
2. Calico can design the sewer project itself and hire another company, Paramount Construction, to build the system according to Calico's specifications. Paramount will charge Calico $20 per foot of sewer built. Paramount estimates that it can build between 200 and 360 feet of sewers per day; its most likely estimate is 300 feet per day. To minimize disruption to the aesthetic beauty of the project, sewers will run underneath the paths between condominium buildings.

Activity T, the stream-building activity, involves building a stream that runs throughout the project and connects the western and eastern boundaries. Again Calico has two alternatives.

1. Calico has received a bid of $400,000 from Lakepro, Inc. to design and build a meandering stream that will most likely be finished in 30 days, give or take five days.
2. Calico can design and direct the stream construction. The actual work will be performed by the Oberlin Company, at a price of $50 per foot. Oberlin estimates that it will take a full day to complete 60 feet on the stream project. Since Calico would like to conserve costs,

Case 2

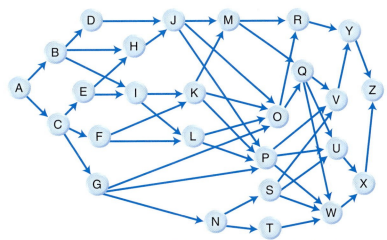

PERT/CPM Network for the Oak Glen Country Club Villas Project

if it designs the stream, it will have the minimal distance and will parallel paths between the condominium buildings. Calico estimates that overall completion time for this activity will be no more than 10 days longer or less than 10 days shorter than the Oberlin estimate.

Below is a map of the feasible pathways between the condominium buildings which may be used for sewer construction or stream construction.

Assume that today is Monday, September 15, and that all work is to be done on a five-day-per-week basis that includes holiday periods. Prepare a report for Calico Construction that will

1. Develop tentative target start and completion dates for each activity
2. Recommend which alternative to select for the sewer activity

3. Recommend which alternative to select for the stream activity
4. Estimate the total expected cost for the two contractors selected for the sewer and stream activities
5. Give a date by which you are 99% sure that the entire project will be completed.
6. Recommend whether to spend $25,000 for additional legal assistance that would reduce the most likely time to attain the final permits and releases (activity Z) from 15 to 12 days and its pessimistic time from 25 to 18 days

To answer (6), compare the $25,000 expenditure to the expected savings from the increased probability of completing the project by June 15. Your report should also include any assumptions you made to apply your solution technique and some appropriate "what-if" analyses.

Map of Feasible Pathways Between Condominium Buildings

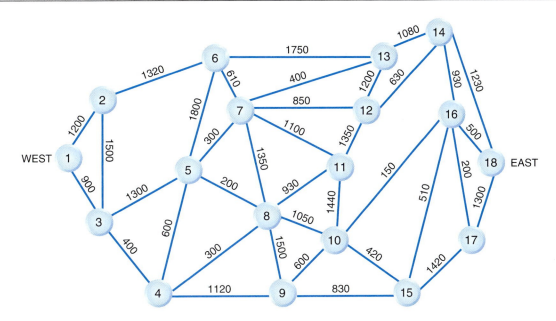

CASE 3:   Igloo Frozen Yogurt

Fifty-eight days ago a nervous Board of Directors of Igloo Foods, owners of the Igloo Frozen Yogurt chain, watched as the company began a program to test market its product in London, England. The target opening date for the first store was four months (122 days) from the inception of the project. If the store proves successful, Igloo plans to open up at least two dozen Igloo Frozen Yogurt stores across Great Britain and the European continent. This is the first such venture for Igloo Foods outside of the United States.

The project consists of the 18 work packages summarized in the table for Case 3, together with budget information and time estimates.

Case 3

Work Package	Immediate Predecessor	Optimistic Time	Estimates Likely	Pessimistic (days)	Budget
A. Select vice president for Europe	—	5	9	13	$ 0
B. Select menu consultant	—	6	14	34	$ 2,000
C. Choose district for shop	A	8	13	30	$ 0
D. Make exact site selection	C	4	11	18	$ 15,000
E. Negotiate lease	D	9	10	11	$ 4,000
F. Design store layout	A	19	38	63	$ 40,000
G. Construct store	E,F	46	75	80	$260,000
H. Develop recipes	B	10	30	50	$ 15,000
I. Test recipes	H	9	16	17	$ 10,000
J. Purchase equipment	F,I	10	17	30	$150,000
K. Design accessories	F,I	16	22	28	$ 15,000
L. Purchase supplies	K	8	22	24	$100,000
M. Develop training program	J,K	15	23	43	$ 18,000
N. Train employees	M	8	10	18	$ 7,000
O. Select advertising agency	A	30	36	60	$ 12,000
P. Develop marketing program	D,O	41	47	77	$ 90,000
Q. Purchase advertising space	P	4	5	6	$ 80,000
R. Install signs	G,Q	3	6	21	$ 26,000

A timetable based on the three time estimate approach was used to generate a schedule of work packages for the project. Now, 58 days into the project, the Board of Directors has received the following project status report.

LONDON, ENGLAND PROJECT
Date: Day 58
Expenditures to Date: $195,000
Progress Report

Work Package	Percent Complete
A. Select vice president for Europe	100%
B. Select menu consultant	100%
C. Choose district for shop	100%
D. Make exact site selection	100%
E. Negotiate lease	50%
F. Design store layout	100%
G. Construct store	0%
H. Develop recipes	100%
I. Test recipes	100%
J. Purchase equipment	75%
K. Design accessories	25%
L. Purchase supplies	0%
M. Develop training program	0%

Work Package	Percent Complete
N. Train employees	0%
O. Select advertising agency	50%
P. Develop marketing program	0%
Q. Purchase advertising space	0%
R. Install signs	0%

Prepare a report for the Board of Directors of Igloo Foods which analyzes the progress of the project from both a budget and time point of view. Compare the initial probability of finishing the project in 122 days with the probability that the project will now be finished by the end of day 122. (Assume that the *standard deviation* for each unfinished work package is reduced by an amount proportional to the completion percentage of the work package.)

Igloo has planned a big gala "grand opening" for the morning of day 123 with visiting dignitaries and a popular rock band. If the project is not completed in time (by the end of day 122), the event will have to be canceled, and Igloo will suffer a $100,000 loss. Three suggestions have been proposed for reducing the times of certain of the remaining work packages:

Suggestion	Extra Expenditure	Projected Effect
1	$ 8000	Reduce the most likely and pessimistic times to purchase supplies (activity L) by 50%
2	$10,000	Reduce the expected training time of employees (activity N) by three days
3	$ 3000	Reduce the pessimistic time to install signs (activity R) to nine days

Include in your report a recommendation of which suggestion or combination of suggestions (if any) Igloo should consider adopting. Base your analysis on an expected value approach, and discuss the validity of such an approach in these circumstances.

CASE 4 IS ON THE CD

Decision Models

LINDAL CEDAR HOMES, Inc. (http://www.lindal.com/) is engaged primarily in the manufacture and distribution of customer cedar homes, windows, and sunrooms. The Company also remanufactures standard dimensional cedar lumber. Founded in 1945, the company is the world's oldest and largest manufacturer of top-of-the-line, year-round cedar homes.

Lindal Cedar Homes' management makes numerous decisions throughout the year. Among these, the company must decide which new product lines to introduce, what promotional materials to develop, what forms of financing to obtain, what advertising media to select, which material hedging strategies to adopt, and what prices to charge for its products.

A recent decision that has had a major impact on the company's operations was the introduction of the Select product line of housing. This product line, which utilizes conventional design and construction techniques, costs approximately 30% less than the company's cedar frame specification and is aimed at the middle of the custom housing market. In determining whether to introduce this line, the company had to estimate the potential product market, analyze its manufacturing capabilities and forecast the product's impact on the sales of existing product lines.

Another recent company decision was to close and subsequently sell a Canadian sawmill. In this decision, the company had to forecast future lumber needs, the cost of relocating and/or laying off employees, and the immediate costs versus long-term savings of taking this action. Complicating this decision was the fact that closing the sawmill could jeopardize a timber award made by the Province of British Columbia to the company.

To address these issues, Lindal management uses decision analysis techniques.

6.1 Introduction to Decision Analysis

Throughout our day we are faced with numerous decisions, many of which require careful thought and analysis. In such cases, large sums of money might be lost or other severe consequences can result from the wrong choice. For example, you probably would do a careful analysis of the car you are going to purchase, the house you are going to buy, or the college you will attend.

Businesses continuously make many crucial decisions, such as whether or not to introduce a new product or where to locate a new plant. The outcome of these decisions can severely affect the firm's future profitability. The field of **decision analysis** provides the necessary framework for making these types of important decisions.

Decision analysis allows an individual or organization to *select a decision* from a set of possible *decision alternatives* when *uncertainties regarding the future* exist. The goal is to optimize the resulting return or *payoff* in terms of some *decision criterion*.

Consider an investor interested in purchasing an apartment building. Possible decisions include the type of financing to use and the building's rehabilitation plan. Unknown to the investor are the future occupancy rate of the building, the amount of rent that can be charged for each unit, and possible modifications in the tax laws associated with real estate ownership. Depending on the investor's decisions and their consequences, the investor will receive some payoff.

Although the criterion used in making a decision could be noneconomic, most business decisions are based on economic considerations. When probabilities can be assessed for likelihoods of the uncertain future events, one common economic criterion is maximizing expected profit. If probabilities for the likelihoods of the uncertain future events cannot be assessed, the economic criterion is typically based on the decision maker's attitude toward life.

Often, elements of risk need to be factored into the decision-making process. This is especially true if there is a possibility of incurring extremely large losses or achieving exceptional gains. **Utility theory** can provide a mechanism for analyzing decisions in light of these risks, as well as evaluating situations in which the criterion is noneconomic.

While decision analysis typically focuses on situations in which the uncertain future events are due to chance, there are business situations in which competition shapes these events. **Game theory** is a useful tool for analyzing decision making in light of competitive action.

6.2 Payoff Table Analysis

We begin our discussion of decision analysis by focusing on the basic elements of decision making: (1) decision alternatives, (2) states of nature, and (3) payoffs.

PAYOFF TABLES

When a decision maker faces a finite set of discrete *decision alternatives* whose outcome is a function of a single future event, a **payoff table** analysis is the simplest way of formulating the decision problem. In a payoff table, the rows correspond to the possible decision alternatives and the columns correspond to the possible future events (known as **states of nature**). The states of nature of a payoff table are defined so that they are mutually exclusive (at most one possible state of nature will occur) and collectively exhaustive (at least one state of nature will occur). This way we know that exactly one state of nature must occur. The body of the table contains the *payoffs* resulting from a particular decision alternative when the corresponding state of nature occurs. Although the decision maker can determine which decision alternative to select, he or she has no control over which state of nature will occur.

Figure 6.1 shows the general form of a payoff table. In this figure a payoff table with three states of nature and four possible decision alternatives is shown. To illustrate payoff table analysis, consider the following example.

Possible States of Nature

		S1	S2	S3
	D1	P_{11}	P_{12}	P_{13}
Possible	D2	P_{21}	P_{22}	P_{23}
Decisions	D3	P_{31}	P_{32}	P_{33}
	D4	P_{41}	P_{42}	P_{43}

"Payoff" if decision D1 and state of nature S2 occur

FIGURE 6.1

A Payoff Table with Four Decisions and Three States of Nature

PUBLISHERS CLEARING HOUSE

Publishers Clearing House is a nationwide firm that markets magazine subscriptions. The primary vehicle it uses to contact customers is a series of mailings known collectively as the Publishers Clearing House Sweepstakes. Individuals who receive these mailings can enter the sweepstakes even if they do not order any magazine subscriptions. Various prizes are available, the top prize being $10 million. Suppose you are one of the many individuals who are not interested in ordering magazines. You must decide whether or not to enter the contest.

SOLUTION

To help evaluate this problem, you can construct a payoff table. In this model, you have two possible *decision alternatives*.

D1: Spend the time filling out the contest application and pay the postage.
D2: Toss the letter in the recycling bin.

Obviously, if you knew the outcome in advance, your decision would be quite simple: Enter the contest if you are going to win something valuable; do not enter the contest if you are not. Unfortunately, winners are not known in advance, and you cannot win unless you enter. The act of winning or losing is something over which you have no control.

A number of different prizes are available. In a recent contest, these ranged from a flag to $10 million. The possible outcomes, or *states of nature*, for this model are:

S1: The entry would be a losing one.
S2: The entry would win a flag.
S3: The entry would win $100.
S4: The entry would win $500.
S5: The entry would win $10,000.
S6: The entry would win $1 million.
S7: The entry would win $10 million.

Note that these states of nature are mutually exclusive and collectively exhaustive.

For each decision alternative and state of nature combination there is a resulting payoff. For example, if you enter the contest and do not win, the loss is equivalent to the opportunity cost of the time spent completing the contest application plus the cost of the postage. Let's assume that these costs total $1.

If, on the other hand, you enter the contest and win $100, this results in a net payoff of $99 ($100 minus the $1 cost). Similarly, if the flag is worth $5, winning a flag will result in a net payoff of $4 ($5 − $1).

The $1 million and $10 million prizes are paid out over several years. To get the present value of these prizes you must calculate their discounted future cash flows. If you assume that the discounted present value of these prizes amounts to approximately 35% of their face amount, then the net payoff values for the $1 million and $10 million winners would be $349,999 and $3,499,999, respectively.

The resulting payoff table is shown in Table 6.1. Once this payoff table is constructed, you can utilize it to determine which decision alternative you should pursue.

TABLE 6.1   Payoff Table for Publishers Clearing House

| | States of Nature | | | | | | |
Decision Alternatives	Do Not Win	Win Flag	Win $100	Win $500	Win $10,000	Win $1 Million	Win $10 Million
Enter contest	−$1	$4	$99	$499	$9,999	$349,999	$3,499,999
Do not enter contest	$0	$0	$0	$0	$0	$0	$0

CHOOSING THE STATES OF NATURE

Although determining the states of nature for the Publishers Clearing House example was rather straightforward, often the decision maker has a great deal of flexibility in defining them. Selecting the appropriate definition for the states of nature can require careful thought about the situation being modeled. To illustrate, consider the situation faced by Tom Brown.

TOM BROWN INVESTMENT DECISION

Tom Brown Maximin.xls
Tom Brown Minimax Regret.xls
Tom Brown Minimax Regret Revised.xls
Tom Brown Maximax.xls
Tom Brown Insufficient Reason.xls
Tom Brown Expected Value.xls
Tom Brown.xls

Tom Brown has inherited $1000 from a distant relative. Since he still has another year of studies before graduation from Iowa State University, Tom has decided to invest the $1000 for a year. Literally tens of thousands of different investment possibilities are available to him, including growth stocks, income stocks, corporate bonds, municipal bonds, government bonds, futures, limited partnerships, annuities, and bank accounts.

Given the limited amount of money he has to invest, Tom has decided that it is not worthwhile to spend the countless hours required to fully understand these various investments. Therefore, he has turned to a broker for investment guidance.

The broker has selected five potential investments she believes would be appropriate for Tom: gold, a junk bond, a growth stock, a certificate of deposit, and a stock option hedge. Tom would like to set up a payoff table to help him choose the appropriate investment.

SOLUTION

The first step in constructing a payoff table is to determine the set of possible decision alternatives. For Tom, this is simply the set of five investment opportunities recommended by the broker.

The second step is to define the states of nature. One choice might be the percentage change in the gross national product (GNP) over the next year (rounded to the nearest percent). A principal drawback of this approach, however, is the difficulty most people would have in determining the payoff for a given investment from the percentage change in the GNP. Even if Tom had a doctorate in economics, he might find it extremely difficult to assess how a 2% rise in GNP would affect the value of a particular investment.

Another possibility is to define the states of nature in terms of general stock market performance as measured by the Standard & Poor's 500 or Dow Jones Industrial Average. But even if he were to spend the time doing this, it is doubtful whether Tom or anyone else could correctly differentiate the return on an investment if, say, the Dow Jones Industrial Average went up 800 points as opposed to 810 points. Even if Tom used 100-*point* intervals, modeling a possible 3000-point increase or decrease in the Dow Jones Industrial Average would still require 61 states of nature for each of the five investments.

Instead Tom decided to define the states of nature qualitatively as follows:

S1: A large rise in the stock market over the next year
S2: A small rise in the stock market over the next year
S3: No change in the stock market over the next year
S4: A small fall in the stock market over the next year
S5: A large fall in the stock market over the next year

Since these states must be mutually exclusive and collectively exhaustive, there should be a clear understanding as to exactly what each of these terms means. In terms of the Dow Jones Industrial Average, for example, Tom might use the following correspondence:

State of Nature	*Change in Dow Jones Industrial Average*
S1: large rise	an increase of over 1500 points
S2: small rise	an increase of between 500 and 1500 points
S3: no change	a decrease or increase of less than 500 points
S4: small fall	a decrease of between 500 and 1200 points
S5: large fall	a decrease of more than 1200 points

Although the intervals corresponding to these states of nature are not of the same size, the states of nature are mutually exclusive and collectively exhaustive.

Based on these definitions for the states of nature, the final step in constructing the payoff table is to determine the payoffs resulting from each decision alternative (investment) and state of nature. In doing so, Tom's broker reasoned that stocks and bonds generally move in the same direction as the general market, whereas gold is an investment hedge that tends to move in the opposite direction from the market. The C/D account always pays 6% ($60 profit). The specific payoffs for the five different investments, based on the broker's analysis, are given in Table 6.2.

TABLE 6.2   Payoff Table for Tom Brown

Decision Alternatives	States of Nature				
	Large Rise	Small Rise	No Change	Small Fall	Large Fall
Gold	−$100	$100	$200	$300	$ 0
Bond	$250	$200	$150	−$100	−$150
Stock	$500	$250	$100	−$200	−$600
C/D account	$ 60	$ 60	$ 60	$ 60	$ 60
Stock option hedge	$200	$150	$150	−$200	−$150

DOMINATED DECISIONS

It is worth comparing the payoffs associated with the stock option hedge investment to those associated with the bond investment. For each state of nature, Tom would do at least as well with the bond investment as with the stock option hedge, and for several of the states of nature, the bond actually offers a higher return. In this case, the decision alternative to invest in the bond is said to *dominate* the stock option hedge decision alternative. A decision alternative that is dominated by another can never be optimal and thus, it can be dropped from further consideration. Eliminating the dominated decision alternative of "stock option hedge" gives a payoff table with the remaining four decision alternatives.

Now that a payoff table has been created, an optimization criterion can be applied to determine the best decision for Tom.

6.3 Decision-Making Criteria

In this section, we consider approaches for selecting an "optimal" decision based on some decision-making criterion. One way of categorizing such criteria involves the decision maker's knowledge of which state of nature will occur. The decision maker who knows "for sure" which state of nature will occur is said to be **decision making under certainty**.

Knowing which state of nature will occur makes choosing the appropriate decision alternative quite easy. For example, in the Publishers Clearing House Model, if you knew for certain that you were going to win the $10 million grand prize, you would definitely enter the contest. Because few things in life are certain, however, you might wonder whether decision making under certainty is really ever done. The answer is an emphatic "yes!" Many management science models assume that the future is known with certainty.

For example, the linear programming model for Galaxy Industries discussed in Chapter 2 assumed that the unit profit and production time required per dozen Space Rays and Zappers, as well as the amount of plastic and available production time, were all known with certainty. Although we investigated relaxing these assumptions through sensitivity analysis, solving the problem as a linear program was, in effect, making a decision under certainty.

If the decision maker does not know with certainty which state of nature will occur, the model is classified as either decision making under uncertainty or decision making under risk. **Decision making under risk** assumes that the decision maker has at least some knowledge of the probabilities for the states of nature occurring; no such knowledge is assumed in **decision making under uncertainty**.

One method for making decisions under risk is to select the decision with the best expected payoff, which is calculated using the probability estimates for the states of nature. However, since decision making under uncertainty assumes no knowledge of the probabilities for the states of nature, expected values cannot be calculated, and decisions must be made based on other criteria. Because probability information regarding the states of nature is not always available, many decision problems are analyzed using decision making under uncertainty.

To contrast decision making under uncertainty and risk, let us return to the Publishers Clearing House situation. In this model, the values of the prizes in the contest are known to participants. Because the chance of winning a prize depends on the number of entries received, the exact probabilities of winning a given prize are unknown; thus, decision making under uncertainty should be used to analyze this problem.

On the other hand, if you called Publishers Clearing House and learned that it receives an average of 1.75 million entries a day for its contest, you would be able to estimate the probability of winning each of the prizes offered. In this case, decision making under risk would be possible.

DECISION MAKING UNDER UNCERTAINTY

When using decision making under uncertainty to analyze a situation, the decision criteria are based on the decision maker's attitudes toward life. These include an individual being pessimistic or optimistic, conservative or aggressive.

Pessimistic or Conservative Approach—Maximin Criterion

A *pessimistic* decision maker believes that, no matter what decision is made, the worst possible result will occur. A *conservative* decision maker wishes to ensure a guaranteed minimum possible payoff, regardless of which state of nature occurs.

For either individual, the **maximin criterion** may be used to make decisions. Since this criterion is based on a worst-case scenario, the decision maker first finds the minimum payoff for each decision alternative. The optimal decision alternative is the one that *maxi*mizes the *min*imum payoff.

To illustrate, let us return to the Tom Brown investment model. (Recall that the dominated stock option hedge decision was eliminated.) From Table 6.2 we see that if Tom chooses to buy gold, the worst possible outcome occurs if there is a large rise in the stock market, resulting in a $100 loss. If he buys the bond or stock, the worst possible outcome occurs if the stock market has a large fall; in this case, his loss would be $150 for the bond and $600 for the stock. If Tom chooses the C/D account, he will earn $60 no matter which state of nature occurs. Hence, if Tom is a conservative decision maker, he will try to maximize his returns under this worst-case scenario. Accordingly, he will select the decision that results in the best of these minimum payoffs—in this case, the C/D account.

Figure 6.2 shows an Excel spreadsheet for the Tom Brown investment problem. Column H is added to identify the minimum payoff for each decision. The optimal decision for the maximum criterion is identified in cell B11 using the VLOOKUP command shown, and the maximin payoff is given in cell B10.

Tom Brown Maximin.xls

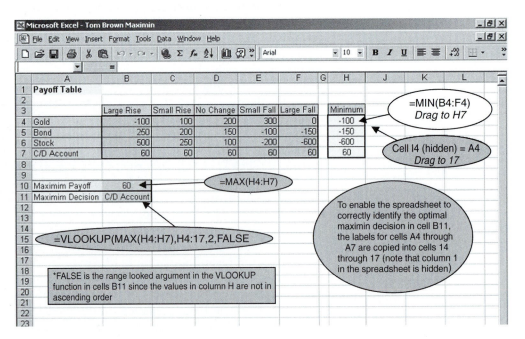

FIGURE 6.2   Excel Spreadsheet Showing Maximin Decision

MINIMIZATION MODELS

In the Tom Brown investment model, the numbers in the payoff table represented returns or profits. If the numbers in the payoff table represented costs rather than profits, however, the worst outcome for each decision alternative would be the one with the maximum cost. A pessimistic or conservative decision maker would then select the decision alternative with the *min*imum of these *max*imum costs; that is, use a **minimax criterion**.

Maximin Approach for Profit Payoffs

1. Determine the minimum payoff for each decision alternative.
2. Select the decision alternative with the maximum minimum payoff.

Minimax Approach for Cost Payoffs

1. Determine the maximum cost for each decision alternative.
2. Select the decision alternative with the minimum maximum cost.

Minimax Regret Criterion

Another criterion that pessimistic or conservative decision makers frequently use is the **minimax regret criterion**. This approach is identical to the minimax approach for cost data except that the optimal decision is based on "lost opportunity," or "regret" rather than costs. It involves calculating the regret or lost opportunity corresponding to each payoff and then using the minimax criterion on the calculated regret values.

In decision analysis, the decision maker incurs regret by failing to choose the "best" decision (the one with the highest profit or lowest cost). Of course, this best decision depends on the state of nature. For this model, if there is a small rise in the stock market, the best decision is to buy the stock (yielding a return of $250). Tom will have no regret if this is his decision. If, instead, Tom purchases gold, his return will be only $100, resulting in a regret of $150 (=$250 − $100). Similarly, the regret associated with buying the bond for this state of nature is $50 (=$250 − $200), and from investing in the C/D it is $190 (=$250 − $60).

Calculation of Regret Values for a State of Nature

1. Determine the best value (maximum payoff or minimum cost) for the state of nature.
2. Calculate the regret for each decision alternative as the difference between its payoff value and this best value.

When this process is repeated for each state of nature, the result is the regret table shown in Table 6.3

TABLE 6.3 Regret Table for Tom Brown

Decision Alternatives	States of Nature				
	Large Rise	Small Rise	No Change	Small Fall	Large Fall
Gold	$600	$150	$ 0	$ 0	$ 60
Bond	$250	$ 50	$ 50	$400	$210
Stock	$ 0	$ 0	$100	$500	$660
C/D account	$440	$190	$140	$240	$ 0

The decision maker using the minimax regret criterion also assumes that the worst state of nature (the one with the maximum regret) will occur no matter what decision is made. He therefore chooses the decision that has the minimum of the maximum regrets.

> ### Minimax Regret Approach
>
> 1. Determine the best value (maximum payoff or minimum cost) for each state of nature.
> 2. For each state of nature, calculate the regret corresponding to a decision alternative as the difference between its payoff value and this best value.
> 3. Find the maximum regret for each decision alternative.
> 4. Select the decision alternative that has the minimum maximum regret.

Figure 6.3 is an Excel spreadsheet showing the original payoff table as well as the regret table for the Tom Brown investment problem. The optimal decision using the minimax regret criterion is identified in this spreadsheet in cell B19, and the corresponding payoff is given in cell B18. We see from the Excel spreadsheet that if Tom uses the minimax regret criterion, he should decide to buy the bond.

Tom Brown Minimax Regret.xls

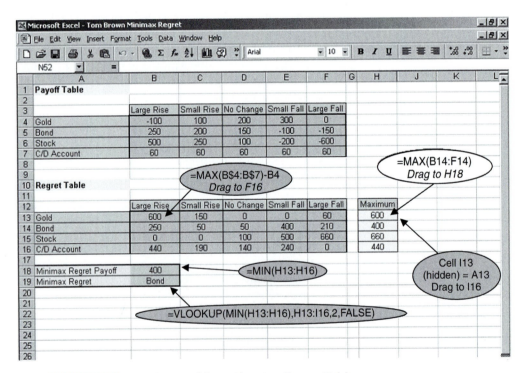

FIGURE 6.3   Excel Spreadsheet Showing Regret Table

The difference between the maximin and minimax regret criteria is as follows. When using the maximin criterion, the decision maker wishes to select the decision with the best possible assured payoff. Under the minimax regret criterion, the decision maker wishes to select the decision that minimizes the maximum deviation from the best return possible for each state of nature. In this case, it is not the return itself that is important, but rather how well a *given* return compares to the *best possible* return for that state of nature.

EFFECTS OF NONOPTIMAL ALTERNATIVES

When using the minimax regret criterion, the optimal decision can be influenced by introducing a nonoptimal decision alternative. For example, suppose the broker had suggested that Tom consider the purchase of a put option instead of the stock option hedge, resulting in the payoff and regret table shown in Figure 6.4.

Tom Brown Minimax
Regret Revised.xls

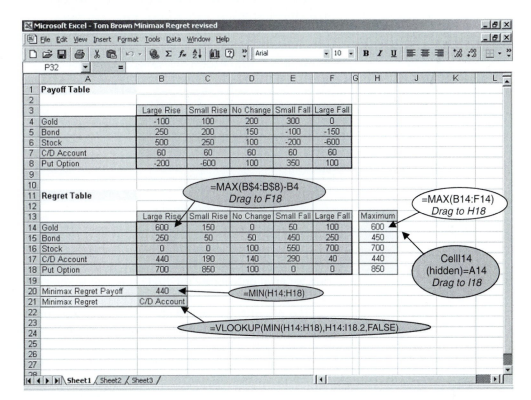

FIGURE 6.4 Excel Spreadsheet Showing Minimax Regret Decision with Put Option Included

We see that now Tom's optimal decision using the minimax regret criterion would be to invest his $1000 in the C/D account instead of his earlier decision to invest in the bond. This is because the addition of the put option investment increases the maximum regret for the bond from $400 to $450 which is now higher than that for the C/D.

Some may argue that it should be no surprise Tom's optimal decision could change since the introduction of the put option as a decision alternative changes his attitude toward the different investments. Others, however, feel that because a decision model frequently does not consider every possible alternative, changing the decision selection due to the introduction of additional nonoptimal decision alternatives is a major shortcoming of the minimax regret approach.

Optimistic or Aggressive Approach—Maximax Criterion

In contrast to a pessimistic decision maker, an optimistic decision maker feels that luck is always shining and whatever decision is made, the best possible outcome (state of nature) corresponding to that decision will occur.

Given a payoff table representing profits, an optimistic decision maker would use a **maximax criterion** that determines the maximum payoff for each decision alternative and selects the one that has the *maxi*mum "*max*imum payoff." The maximax criterion also applies to an aggressive decision maker looking for the decision with the best payoff.

Based on the data in Table 6.2 (with the stock option hedge eliminated), the maximum payoffs for each decision alternative in the Tom Brown investment problem are as shown in Table 6.4. If Tom were an optimistic or aggressive decision maker, he would choose the stock investment since it is the alternative with the maximum of the maximum payoffs. The file Tom Brown Maximax.xls on the accompanying CD-ROM illustrates how one can construct an Excel spreadsheet to do this analysis.

TABLE 6.4   Tom Brown Investment Decision—Maximum Payoff

Decision Alternatives	Maximum Payoff	
Gold	$300	
Bond	$250	
Stock	$500	← maximum
C/D account	$ 60	

Note that the alternative chosen using the maximax decision criterion is the one associated with the highest value in the payoff table. Hence to use this criterion we need only locate the highest payoff in the table and select the corresponding decision.

If a payoff table represents costs rather than profits, an optimistic or aggressive decision maker would use the **minimin criterion** and select the alternative with the lowest possible, or *mini*mum *mini*mum, cost. In this case, the optimal decision would be the one corresponding to the lowest entry in the payoff table.

Maximax Approach for Profit Payoffs

1. Determine the maximum payoff for each decision alternative.
2. Select the decision alternative that has the maximum maximum payoff.

Minimin Approach for Cost Payoffs

1. Determine the minimum cost for each decision alternative.
2. Select the decision alternative that has the minimum minimum cost.

Principle of Insufficient Reason

Another decision criterion that can be used is the **principle of insufficient reason**. In this approach each state of nature is assumed to be equally likely. The optimal decision alternative can be found by adding up the payoffs for each decision alternative and selecting the alternative with the highest sum. (If the payoff table represents costs, we select the decision alternative with the lowest sum of costs.)

The principle of insufficient reason might appeal to a decision maker who is neither pessimistic nor optimistic. Table 6.5 gives the sum of the payoffs for each decision alternative for the Tom Brown investment problem. Thus, if Tom uses the principle of insufficient reason, he should invest in gold.

TABLE 6.5   Tom Brown Investment Decision—
Sum of Payoffs

Decision Alternatives	Sum of Payoffs	
Gold	$500	← maximum
Bond	$350	
Stock	$ 50	
C/D account	$300	

The file Tom Brown Insufficient Reason.xls on the accompanying CD-ROM illustrates how one can construct an Excel spreadsheet to do this analysis.

While it is not difficult to determine the optimal decision for the different criteria used in decision making under uncertainty either by hand or using Excel, we have developed a spreadsheet template, Decision Payoff Table.xls (contained on the accompanying CD-ROM), to solve payoff table problems with up to eight decisions and eight states of nature. Complete details on using this spreadsheet are given in Appendix 6.1 at the conclusion of the chapter. The worksheet labeled Payoff Table can be used for analyzing a payoff table when doing decision making under uncertainty.

Figure 6.5 gives the results of using this template for the Tom Brown investment problem. The default names for the decision alternatives (d1, d2, etc.) and states of nature (s1, s2, etc.) were changed to the actual decisions and states of nature for this problem. Note that we have hidden the rows and columns in this spreadsheet that are not needed for analysis of this problem.

Tom Brown.xls

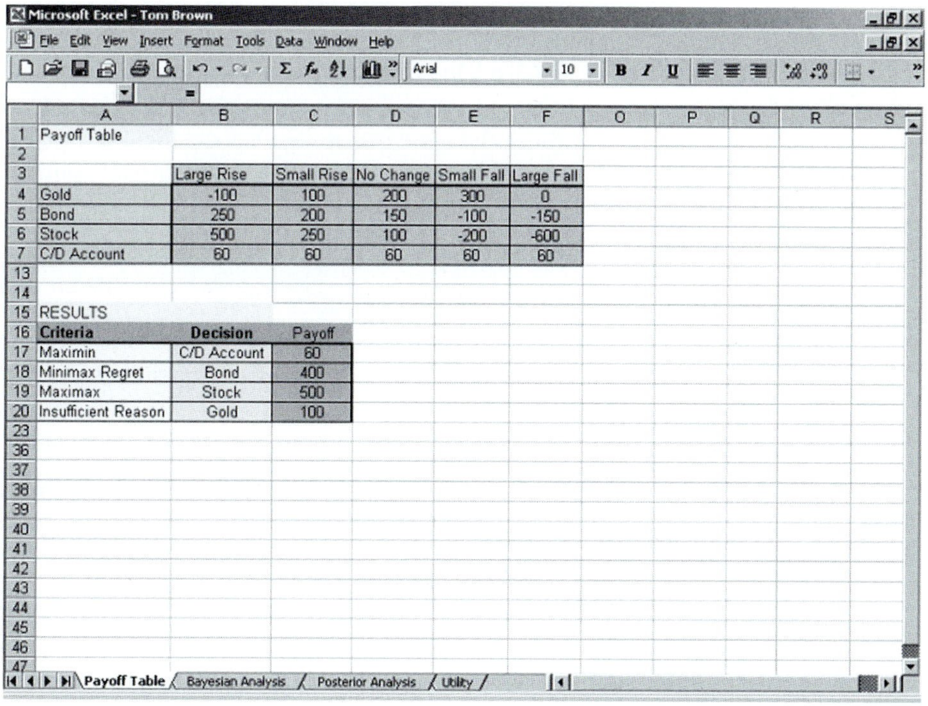

	Large Rise	Small Rise	No Change	Small Fall	Large Fall
1 Payoff Table					
3	Large Rise	Small Rise	No Change	Small Fall	Large Fall
4 Gold	-100	100	200	300	0
5 Bond	250	200	150	-100	-150
6 Stock	500	250	100	-200	-600
7 C/D Account	60	60	60	60	60

15 RESULTS		
16 Criteria	**Decision**	**Payoff**
17 Maximin	C/D Account	60
18 Minimax Regret	Bond	400
19 Maximax	Stock	500
20 Insufficient Reason	Gold	100

FIGURE 6.5
Excel Spreadsheet Showing
Payoff Table Template
for Tom Brown
Investment Problem

The optimal decisions and payoffs for the different criteria are given in cells B17 through B20 and cells C17 through C20 respectively. We observe that each decision is optimal for some decision criterion.

Since the criterion depends on the decision maker's attitude toward life (optimistic, pessimistic, or somewhere in between), utilizing decision making under uncertainty can present a problem if these attitudes change rapidly. One way to avoid the difficulty of using subjective criteria is to obtain probability estimates for the states of nature and implement decision making under risk.

DECISION MAKING UNDER RISK

Expected Value Criterion

If a probability estimate for the occurrence of each state of nature is available, it is possible to calculate an expected value associated with each decision alternative. This is done by multiplying the probability for each state of nature by the associated return and then summing these products. Using the **expected value criterion**, the decision maker would then select the decision alternative with the best expected value.

For the Tom Brown investment problem, suppose Tom's broker offered the following projections based on past stock market performance:

$$P(\text{large rise in market}) = .2$$
$$P(\text{small rise in market}) = .3$$
$$P(\text{no change in market}) = .3$$
$$P(\text{small fall in market}) = .1$$
$$P(\text{large fall in market}) = .1$$

Using these probabilities, we can calculate the expected value (EV) of each decision alternative as follows:

$$EV(\text{gold}) = .2(-100) + .3(100) + .3(200) + .1(300) + .1(0) = \$100$$
$$EV(\text{bond}) = .2(250) + .3(200) + .3(150) + .1(-100) + .1(-150) = \$130$$
$$EV(\text{stock}) = .2(500) + .3(250) + .3(100) + .1(-200) + .1(-600) = \$125$$
$$EV(\text{C/D}) = .2(60) + .3(60) + .3(60) + .1(60) + .1(60) = \$60$$

Since the bond investment has the highest expected value, it is the optimal decision.

Figure 6.6 gives an Excel spreadsheet containing the calculation of the optimal decision using the expected value (EV) criterion.

Tom Brown Expected
Value.xls

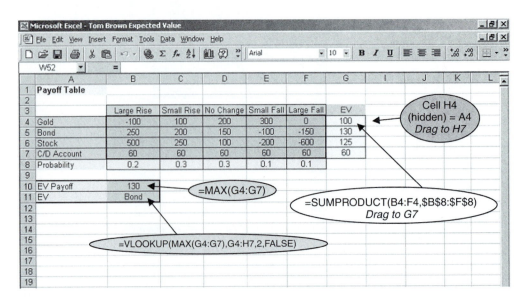

FIGURE 6.6   Excel Spreadsheet Showing Expected Value Criterion

The Payoff Table Worksheet on the Decision Payoff Table.xls template determines the optimal decision using the expected value approach in row 21.

Expected Value Approach

1. Determine the expected payoff for each decision alternative.
2. Select the decision alternative that has the best expected payoff.

Expected Regret Criterion

The approach used in the expected value criterion can also be applied to a regret table. Because the decision maker wishes to minimize regret, under the **expected regret criterion**, he or she calculates the expected regret (ER) for each decision and chooses the decision with the smallest expected regret.

By applying this approach to the regret table for the Tom Brown investment problem, the expected regrets for the decision alternatives are calculated as

$$ER(gold) = .2(600) + .3(150) + .3(0) + .1(0) + .1(60) = \$171$$
$$ER(bond) = .2(250) + .3(50) + .3(50) + .1(400) + .1(210) = \$141$$
$$ER(stock) = .2(0) + .3(0) + .3(100) + .1(500) + .1(660) = \$146$$
$$ER(C/D) = .2(440) + .3(190) + 3(140) + .1(240) + .1(0) = \$211$$

Using this approach, Tom would again select the bond investment since it is the decision alternative with the smallest expected regret.

Expected Regret Approach

1. Determine the best value (maximum payoff or minimum cost) for each state of nature.
2. For each state of nature, the regret corresponding to a decision alternative is the difference between its payoff value and this best value.
3. Find the expected regret for each decision alternative.
4. Select the decision alternative that has the minimum expected regret.

Note that the same optimal decision was found using the expected regret criterion and the expected value criterion. This is true for any decision problem because, for pairs of decision alternatives, the differences in expected regret values are the same as the differences in expected return values. Because the two approaches yield the same results, the expected value approach is generally used since it does not require the calculation of a regret table.

When to Use the Expected Value Approach

Because the expected value and expected regret criteria base the optimal decision on the relative likelihoods that the states of nature will occur, they have a certain advantage over the criteria used in decision making under uncertainty. It is worth noting, however, that basing a criterion on expected value assures us only that that the decision will be optimal in the long run when the same problem is faced over and over again. In many situations, however, such as the Tom Brown investment problem, the decision maker faces the problem a single time; in this case, basing an optimal decision solely on expected value may not be optimal.

Another drawback to the expected value criterion is that it does not take into account the decision maker's attitude toward possible losses. Suppose, for example, you had a chance to play a game in which you could win $1000 with probability .51

but could also lose $1000 with probability .49. While the expected value of this game is .51($1000) + .49(−$1000) = $20, many people (perhaps even yourself) would decline the opportunity to play due to the possibility of losing $1000. As we will see in Section 6.7, utility theory offers an alternative to the expected value approach.

6.4 Expected Value of Perfect Information

Suppose it were possible to know with certainty the state of nature that was going to occur prior to choosing the decision alternative. The **expected value of perfect information (EVPI)** represents the *gain* in expected return resulting from this knowledge.

To illustrate this concept, recall that using the expected value criterion, Tom Brown's optimal decision was to purchase the bond. However, Tom can't be sure if this will be one of the 20% of the times that the market will experience a large rise, or one of the 10% of the times that the market will experience a large fall, or if some other state of nature will occur. If Tom repeatedly invested $1000 in the bond, under similar economic conditions (and assuming the same probabilities for the states of nature), we showed that in the long run he should earn an average of $130 per investment. The $130 is known as the **expected return using the expected value criterion (EREV)**.

But suppose Tom could find out in advance which state of nature were going to occur. Each time Tom made an investment decision, he would be practicing decision making under certainty (see Section 6.3).

For example, if Tom knew the stock market were going to show a large rise, naturally he would choose the stock investment because it gives the highest payoff ($500) for this state of nature. Similarly, if he knew a small rise would occur, he would again choose the stock investment because it gives the highest payoff ($250) for this state of nature, and so on. These results are summarized as follows.

If Tom Knew in Advance the Stock Market Would Undergo	His Optimal Decision Would Be	With a Payoff of
a large rise	stock	$500
a small rise	stock	$250
no change	gold	$200
a small fall	gold	$300
a large fall	C/D	$ 60

(Interestingly, Tom would never choose the bond investment, the expected value decision, if he knew in advance which state of nature would occur.)

Under these conditions, since 20% of the time the stock market would experience a large rise, 20% of the time Tom would earn a profit of $500. Similarly, 30% of the time the market would experience a small rise and Tom would earn $250, 30% of the time the market would experience no change and he would earn $200; and so on.

The expected return from knowing for sure which state of nature will occur prior to making the investment decision is called the **expected return with perfect information (ERPI)**. For Tom Brown

$$ERPI = .2(500) + .3(250) + .3(200) + .1(300) + .1(60) = 271.$$

This is a gain of $271 − $130 = $141 over the EREV. The difference ($141) is the *expected value of perfect information (EVPI)*.

Another way to determine EVPI for the investment problem is to reason as follows: If Tom knows the stock market will show a large rise, he should definitely buy the stock, giving him $500, or *a gain of $250 over what he would earn from the bond investment* (the optimal decision without the additional information as to which state of nature would occur). Similarly, if he knows the stock market will show a small rise, he should again buy the stock, earning him $250, or *a gain of $50 over the return from buying the bond*, and so on. These results are summarized as follows.

If Tom Knew in Advance the Stock Market Would Undergo	His Optimal Decision Would Be	With a Gain in Payoff of
a large rise	stock	$250
a small rise	stock	$ 50
no change	gold	$ 50
a small fall	gold	$400
a large fall	C/D	$210

Hence, to find the expected gain over always investing in the bond (i.e., the EVPI), we simply take the possible gains from knowing which state of nature will occur and weight them by the likelihood of that state of nature actually occurring:

$$EVPI = .2(250) + .3(50) + .3(50) + .1(400) + .1(210) = 141$$

This calculation of EVPI might look somewhat familiar since it is the same one we performed in order to calculate the expected regret for the bond investment.

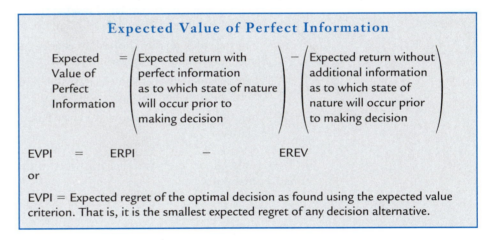

Expected Value of Perfect Information

$$\begin{pmatrix} \text{Expected} \\ \text{Value of} \\ \text{Perfect} \\ \text{Information} \end{pmatrix} = \begin{pmatrix} \text{Expected return with} \\ \text{perfect information} \\ \text{as to which state of nature} \\ \text{will occur prior to} \\ \text{making decision} \end{pmatrix} - \begin{pmatrix} \text{Expected return without} \\ \text{additional information} \\ \text{as to which state of} \\ \text{nature will occur prior} \\ \text{to making decision} \end{pmatrix}$$

EVPI   =   ERPI   —   EREV

or

EVPI = Expected regret of the optimal decision as found using the expected value criterion. That is, it is the smallest expected regret of any decision alternative.

The Payoff Table worksheet on the Decision Payoff Table.xls template determines the expected value of perfect information (EVPI) in row 22 (see Figure A6.1 of Appendix 6.1).

Having perfect information regarding the future for any situation is virtually impossible. However, often it is possible to procure imperfect, or *sample*, information regarding the states of nature. We calculate EVPI because it gives an upper limit on the expected value of any such sample information.

6.5 Bayesian Analyses—Decision Making with Imperfect Information

In Section 6.3 we contrasted decision making under uncertainty with decision making under risk. Some statisticians argue that it is unnecessary to practice decision making under uncertainty because one always has at least *some* probabilistic information that can be used to assess the likelihoods of the states of nature. Such individuals adhere to what is called **Bayesian statistics**.[1]

---

[1] Named for Thomas Bayes, an eighteenth-century British clergyman and mathematician.

USING SAMPLE INFORMATION TO AID IN DECISION MAKING

Bayesian statistics play a vital role in assessing the value of additional *sample information* obtained from such sources as marketing surveys or experiments, which can assist in the decision-making process. The decision maker can use this input to revise or fine tune the original probability estimates and possibly improve decision making.

Making Decisions Using Sample Information

To illustrate decision making using sample information, again consider the Tom Brown investment problem.

Toma.xls
Tomb.xls

TOM BROWN INVESTMENT DECISION (CONTINUED)

Tom has learned that, for only $50, he can receive the results of noted economist Milton Samuelman's multimillion dollar econometric forecast, which predicts either "positive" or "negative" economic growth for the upcoming year. Samuelman has offered the following verifiable statistics regarding the results of his model:

1. When the stock market showed a large rise, the forecast predicted "positive" 80% of the time and "negative" 20% of the time.

2. When the stock market showed a small rise, the forecast predicted "positive" 70% of the time and "negative" 30% of the time.

3. When the stock market showed no change, the forecast was equally likely to predict "positive" or "negative."

4. When the stock market showed a small fall, the forecast predicted "positive" 40% of the time and "negative" 60% of the time.

5. When the stock market showed a large fall, the forecast always predicted "negative."

Tom would like to know whether it is worthwhile to pay $50 for the results of the Samuelman forecast.

SOLUTION

Tom must first determine what his optimal decision should be if the forecast predicts positive economic growth and what it should be if it predicts negative economic growth. If Tom's investment decision changes based on the results of the forecast, he must determine whether knowing the results of Samuelman's forecast would increase his expected profit by more than the $50 cost of obtaining the information.

Using the relative frequency method, we have the following conditional probabilities based on the forecast's historical performance:

$$P(\text{forecast predicts "positive"}|\text{large rise in market}) = .80$$
$$P(\text{forecast predicts "negative"}|\text{large rise in market}) = .20$$

$$P(\text{forecast predicts "positive"}|\text{small rise in market}) = .70$$
$$P(\text{forecast predicts "negative"}|\text{small rise in market}) = .30$$

$$P(\text{forecast predicts "positive"}|\text{no change in market}) = .50$$
$$P(\text{forecast predicts "negative"}|\text{no change in market}) = .50$$

$$P(\text{forecast predicts "positive"}|\text{small fall in market}) = .40$$
$$P(\text{forecast predicts "negative"}|\text{small fall in market}) = .60$$

P(forecast predicts "positive"|large fall in market)   =   0
P(forecast predicts "negative"|large fall in market)   = 1.00

What Tom really needs to know, however, is how the results of Samuelman's economic forecast affect the probability estimates of the stock market's performance. That is, he needs probabilities such as P(large rise in market|forecast predicts "positive"). Unfortunately, in general, P(A|B) ≠ P(B|A), so it is incorrect to assume P(large rise in market|forecast predicts "positive") = .80.

One way to obtain probabilities of this form from the above probabilities is to use a Bayesian approach, which enables the decision maker to revise initial probability estimates in light of additional information. The original probability estimates are known as the set of *prior* or *a priori* probabilities. A set of revised or *posterior probabilities* is obtained based on knowing the results of *sample* or *indicator* information.

Bayesian Analysis

| Prior Probability | → | Additional Information | → | Posterior Probability |

BAYES' THEOREM

The Bayesian approach utilizes *Bayes' Theorem* to revise the prior probabilities.[2] This theorem states:

Given events B and $A_1, A_2, A_3, \ldots, A_n$, where $A_1, A_2, A_3, \ldots, A_n$ are mutually exclusive and collectively exhaustive, posterior probabilities, $P(A_i|B)$ can be found by:

$$P(A_i|B) = \frac{P(B|A_i)\,P(A_i)}{P(B|A_1)\,P(A_1) + P(B|A_2)\,P(A_2) + \ldots + P(B|A_n)\,P(A_n)}$$

Although the notation of Bayes' Theorem may appear intimidating, a convenient way of calculating the posterior probabilities is to use a tabular approach. This approach utilizes five columns:

Column 1—States of Nature   A listing of the states of nature for the problem (the A_i's).
Column 2—Prior Probabilities   The prior probability estimates (before obtaining sample information) for the states of nature, $P(A_i)$.
Column 3—Conditional Probabilities   The known conditional probabilities of obtaining sample information given a particular state of nature, $P(B|A_i)$.
Column 4—Joint Probabilities   The joint probabilities of a particular state of nature and sample information occurring simultaneously, $P(B \cap A_i) = P(A_i)*P(B|A_i)$. These numbers are calculated for each row by multiplying the number in the second column by the number in the third column. The sum of this column is the marginal probability, $P(B)$.
Column 5—Posterior Probabilities   The posterior probabilities found by Bayes' Theorem, $P(A_i|B)$. Since $P(A_i|B) = P(B \cap A_i)/P(B)$, these numbers are calculated for each row by dividing the number in the fourth column by the sum of the numbers in the fourth column.

---

[2] Bayes' Theorem is a restatement of the conditional law of probability $[P(A|B) = P(A \cap B)/P(B)]$. In the parlance of decision theory, the A's correspond to the states of nature, and B is the sample or indicator information. We give a discussion of Bayes' Theorem in Supplement CD1 on the accompanying CD-ROM.

TABLE 6.6   Indicator Information–"Positive" Economic Forecast for Tom Brown

States of Nature S_i	Prior Probabilities $P(S_i)$	Conditional Probabilities $P(\text{positive}|S_i)$	Joint Probabilities $P(\text{positive} \cap S_i)$	Posterior Probabilities $P(S_i|\text{positive})$
Large rise	.20	.80	.16	.16/.56 = .286
Small rise	.30	.70	.21	.21/.56 = .375
No change	.30	.50	.15	.15/.56 = .268
Small fall	.10	.40	.04	.04/.56 = .071
Large fall	.10	0	0	0/.56 = 0
			P(positive) = .56	

Table 6.6 gives the tabular approach for calculating posterior probabilities assuming that Tom responds to Milton Samuelman's offer and learns that Samuelman's economic forecast for next year is "positive."

As you can see, although the initial probability estimate of the stock market's showing a large rise was .20, after Samuelman's "positive" economic forecast Tom has revised this probability upward to .286. Similarly, based on this forecast Tom has revised his probability estimates for a small rise, no change, small fall, or large fall in the market from .30, .30, .10, and .10 to .375, .268, .071, and 0, respectively. We also see that the probability that Samuelman's forecast will be "positive" is .56 (the sum of the values in Column 4). A similar procedure is used to obtain the posterior probabilities corresponding to a "negative" economic forecast, as shown in Table 6.7.

TABLE 6.7   Indicator Information—"Negative" Economic Forecast for Tom Brown

States of Nature S_i	Prior Probabilities $P(S_i)$	Conditional Probabilities $P(\text{negative}|S_i)$	Joint Probabilities $P(\text{negative} \cap S_i)$	Posterior Probabilities $P(S_i|\text{negative})$
Large rise	.20	.20	.04	.04/.44 = .091
Small rise	.30	.30	.09	.09/.44 = .205
No change	.30	.50	.15	.15/.44 = .341
Small fall	.10	.60	.06	.06/.44 = .136
Large fall	.10	1.00	.10	.10/.44 = .227
			P(negative) = .44	

As you can see, for a "negative" economic forecast the respective probability estimates for the states of nature have been revised to .091, .205, .341, .136, and .227. Also note that the probability that Samuelman's forecast will give a "negative" forecast is .44 (the sum of the values in Column 4).

The Bayesian Analysis worksheet on the Decision Payoff Table.xls template calculates posterior probabilities and is linked to the Payoff Table worksheet in the template. Figure 6.7 shows the worksheet for the Tom Brown investment problem. To use this worksheet, conditional probabilities are entered for the four indicators in the appropriate cells in columns C and I. (Note that the rows associated with the unused states of nature are hidden.) The worksheet then calaculates the posterior probabilities in columns E and K.

Tom Brown.xls

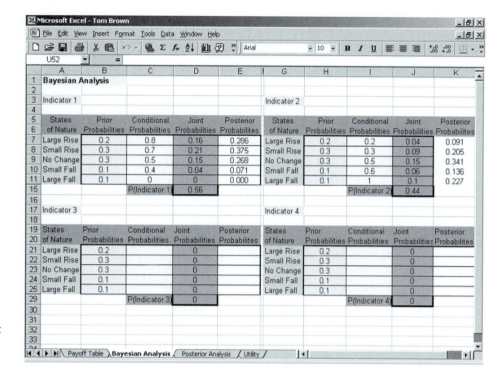

FIGURE 6.7
Bayesian Analysis Worksheet
for the Tom Brown
Investment Problem

Expected Value of Sample Information

The Samuelman forecast generates two sets of probabilities for the states of nature, one based on a positive economic forecast and the other on a negative economic forecast. We can now determine the optimal investment for each forecast using the expected value criterion.

If Samuelman forecasts positive economic growth, the revised expected values for the decision alternatives (rounded to the nearest dollar) are:

$$\text{EV(gold|``positive")} = .286(-100) + .375(100) + .268(200) + .071(300) + 0(0) = \$84$$
$$\text{EV(bond|``positive")} = .286(250) + .375(200) + .268(150) + .071(-100) + 0(-150) = \$180$$
$$\text{EV(stock|``positive")} = .286(500) + .375(250) + .268(100) + .071(-200) + 0(-600) = \$249$$
$$\text{EV(C/D|``positive")} = .286(60) + .375(60) + .268(60) + .071(60) + 0(60) = \$60$$

If Samuelman's forecast is negative, the expected returns are:

$$\text{EV(gold|``negative")} = .091(-100) + .205(100) + .341(200) + .136(300) + .227(0) = \$120$$
$$\text{EV(bond|``negative")} = .091(250) + .205(200) + .341(150) + .136(-100) + .227(-150) = \$67$$
$$\text{EV(stock|``negative")} = .091(500) + .205(250) + .341(100) + .136(-200) + .227(-600) = -\$33$$
$$\text{EV(C/D|``negative")} = .091(60) + .205(60) + .341(60) + .136(60) + .227(60) = \$60$$

Thus, if Samuelman's forecast is positive, buying the stock would be optimal since it yields Tom the highest expected value ($249); if the forecast is negative, buying gold would be optimal since it yields the highest expected value ($120).

We see that information regarding Samuelman's forecast dramatically changes the probability estimates for the states of nature and, therefore, the optimal decision. But is knowing the results of the Samuelman forecast worth $50? To answer this question, Tom must calculate his expected gain from making decisions based on the forecast results. This expected gain is known as the **expected value of sample information (EVSI)**.

To determine the EVSI, we compare the expected return available *with* the sample information (ERSI) to the expected return available *without* the additional sample information (EREV). The difference is the EVSI.

Expected Value of Sample Information

$$\begin{array}{ccccc} \text{Expected Value} & = & \left(\begin{array}{c}\text{Expected Return with}\\ \text{Sample Information}\end{array}\right) & - & \left(\begin{array}{c}\text{Expected Return Without}\\ \text{Additional Information}\end{array}\right)\\ \text{of Sample}\\ \text{Information}\\ \\ \text{EVSI} & = & \text{ERSI} & - & \text{EREV}\end{array}$$

The investment with the largest expected return for a positive forecast is the stock (expected return = \$249.11); for a negative forecast, it is the gold (expected return = \$120.45). The probability Samuelman's forecast will be positive is .56; the probability his forecast will be negative is .44. Hence,

$$\text{ERSI} = .56(249.11) + .44(120.45) = \$192.50$$

Since the expected return without Samuelman's forecast, EREV, is the \$130 obtained from buying the bond, the expected value of sample information is:

$$\text{EVSI} = \$192.50 - \$130 = \$62.50$$

Because the expected gain from the Samuelman forecast is greater than its \$50 cost, Tom should acquire it.

Figure 6.8 shows the worksheet Posterior Analysis contained in the Decision Table.xls template for the Tom Brown investment problem. The prior probabilities and payoff values are linked to those inputted in the Payoff Table worksheet, while the posterior probabilities used in the analysis are linked to the ones calculated in the Bayesian Analysis worksheet.

Tom Brown.xls

	A	B	C	D	E	F	J	K	L	P	Q
1	Payoff Table										
2											
3		Large Rise	Small Rise	No Change	Small Fall	Large Fall	EV(prior)	EV(ind. 1)	EV(ind. 2)		
4	Gold	-100	100	200	300	0	100	83.93	120.45		
5	Bond	250	200	150	-100	-150	130	179.46	67.05		
6	Stock	500	250	100	-200	-600	125	249.11	-32.95		
7	C/D Account	60	60	60	60	60	60	60.00	60.00		
12	Prior Prob.	0.2	0.3	0.3	0.1	0.1					
13	Ind. 1 Prob.	0.286	0.375	0.268	0.071	0.000		0.56			
14	Ind 2. Prob.	0.091	0.205	0.341	0.136	0.227			0.44		
17											
18											
19	RESULTS										
20		Prior	Ind. 1	Ind. 2	Ind. 3	Ind. 4					
21	optimal payoff	130.00	249.11	120.45	0.00	0.00					
22	optimal decision	Bond	Stock	Gold							
23											
24	EVSI =	62.5									
25	EVPI =	141									
26	Efficiency=	0.44									

FIGURE 6.8
Posterior Analysis Worksheet for the Tom Brown Investment Problem

The optimal decisions for the different indicators are given in row 22, and the expected values corresponding to these indicators are given in row 21. The EVSI is given in cell B24, while the EVPI is given in cell B25.

It is important to note that the Samuelman forecast gives additional, but not perfect, information. If the forecast could perfectly predict the future, the gain from the information would be the expected value of perfect information (EVPI) discussed earlier. If the same decision would be made regardless of the results of the indicator information, the value of the information would be 0. Thus,

$$0 \leq \text{EVSI} \leq \text{EVPI}$$

Efficiency

A measure of the relative value of sample information is its **efficiency**, defined as the ratio of its EVSI to its EVPI.

> **Efficiency**
>
> $$\text{Efficiency} = \frac{\text{EVSI}}{\text{EVPI}}$$

Since $0 \leq \text{EVSI} \leq \text{EVPI}$, efficiency is a number between 0 and 1. For Tom Brown's problem, the efficiency of the Samuelman information is:

$$\text{Efficiency} = \text{EVSI/EVPI} = 62.50/141 = .44$$

Efficiency provides a convenient method for comparing different forms of sample information. Given that two different types of sample information could be obtained at the same cost, the one with the higher efficiency is preferred. Note that the efficiency for the sample information is calculated on the Posterior Analysis worksheet in cell B26.

6.6 Decision Trees

Although the payoff table approach is quite handy for some problems, its applicability is limited to situations in which the decision maker needs to make a single decision. Many real-world decision problems consist of a sequence of dependent decisions. For these, a **decision tree** can prove useful.

A decision tree is a chronological representation of the decision process. The root of the tree is a node that corresponds to the present time. The tree is constructed outward from this node into the future using a network of **nodes**, representing points in time where decisions must be made or states of nature occur, and **arcs (branches)**, representing the possible decisions or states of nature, respectively. The following table summarizes the elements of decision trees.

Decision Tree Construction		
Node Type	**Branches**	**Data on Branches**
Decision (Square Nodes)	Possible decisions that can be made at this time	Cost or benefit associated with the decision
States of Nature (Circle Nodes)	Possible states of nature that can occur at this time	Probability the state of nature will occur given all previous decisions and states of nature

To illustrate how a decision tree can be a useful tool, let us consider the following situation faced by the Bill Galen Development Company.

BILL GALEN DEVELOPMENT COMPANY

The Bill Galen Development Company (BGD) needs a variance from the city of Kingston, New York, in order to do commercial development on a property whose asking price is a firm $300,000. BGD estimates that it can construct a shopping center for an additional $500,000 and sell the completed center for approximately $950,000.

A variance application costs $30,000 in fees and expenses, and there is only a 40% chance that the variance will be approved. Regardless of the outcome, the variance process takes two months. If BGD purchases the property and the variance is denied, the company will sell the property and receive net proceeds of $260,000. BGD can also purchase a three-month option on the property for $20,000, which would allow it to apply for a variance. Finally, for $5000 an urban planning consultant can be hired to study the situation and render an opinion as to whether the variance will be approved or denied. BGD estimates the following conditional probabilities for the consultant's opinion:

$$P(\text{consultant predicts approval} \mid \text{approval granted}) = .70$$
$$P(\text{consultant predicts denial} \mid \text{approval denied}) = .80$$

BGD wishes to determine the optimal strategy regarding this parcel of property.

SOLUTION

Initially, the company faces two decision alternatives: (1) hire the consultant and (2) do not hire the consultant. Figure 6.9 shows the initial tree construction corresponding to this decision. Note that the root of the tree is a decision node, two branches lead out from that node. The value on the "do not hire consultant" branch is 0 (there is no cost to this decision), while the −$5000 value on the "hire consultant" branch is the cash flow associated with hiring the consultant.

Consider the decision branch corresponding to "do not hire consultant." If the consultant is not hired, BGD faces three possible decisions: (1) do nothing; (2) buy the land; or (3) purchase the option. Thus we find a decision node at the end of this branch and three branches (corresponding to the three decision alternatives) leaving the node. As shown in Figure 6.10, the values on the three decision branches—0, −$300,000, and −$20,000—correspond to the cash flows associated with each action.

If BGD does not hire the consultant and decides to do nothing, the total return to the company is 0. If, on the other hand, it decides to buy the land, it must then decide whether or not to apply for a variance. Clearly, if BGD were not

FIGURE 6.9 Bill Galen Development Company

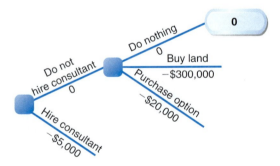

FIGURE 6.10 Bill Galen Development Company

going to apply for a variance, it would not have bought the land in the first place. Therefore, there is only one logical decision following "buy land," and that is to "apply for variance."

Extrapolating this path further into the future, BGD will next learn whether the variance will be approved or denied. This is a chance or state of nature event, signified by a round node at the end of the "apply for variance" branch. This node leads to two branches—"variance approved" or "variance denied"—on which the values, .4 and .6, respectively, are the corresponding state of nature probabilities.

At the end of each path through the tree is the total profit or loss connected with that particular set of decisions and outcomes. These values are calculated by adding the cash flows on the decision branches making up the path. This is shown in Figure 6.11.

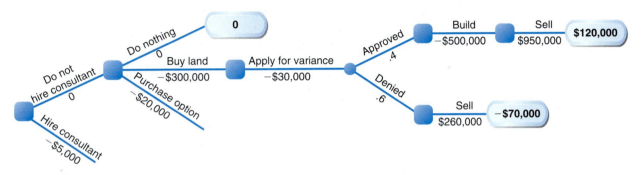

FIGURE 6.11   Bill Galen Development Company

For example, if BGD does not hire the consultant, buys the land, gets the variance approved, builds the shopping center, and sells it, the profit will be 0 − $300,000 − $30,000 − $500,000 + $950,000 = $120,000. If, after buying the land, the variance is denied, BGD will sell the property for $260,000, and the total profit will be 0 − $300,000 − $30,000 + $260,000 = −$70,000, i.e., a net loss of $70,000.

Now if BGD decides to purchase the option, it would apply for the variance, which would then be either approved or denied. If the variance is approved, BGD will exercise the option and buy the property for $300,000, construct the shopping center for $500,000, and sell it for $950,000. If the variance is denied, BGD will simply let the option expire. Figure 6.12 shows the complete decision tree emanating from the decision not to hire the consultant.

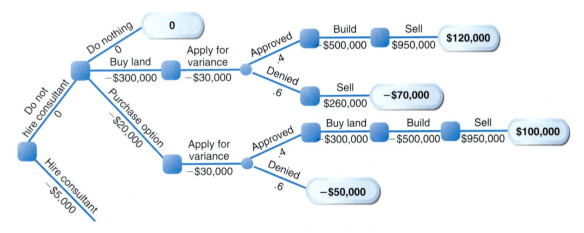

FIGURE 6.12   Bill Galen Development Company

Now consider the decision process if BGD does hire the consultant. The consultant will predict that the variance will either be approved or denied. This chance event is represented by a round state of nature node. The probability that the consultant will predict approval or denial is not readily apparent but can be calculated using Bayes' Theorem.

Let us first determine the posterior probabilities for approval and denial assuming that the consultant predicts that the variance will be *approved*.

Since:

$$P(\text{consultant predicts approval}|\text{approval granted}) = .70$$

then

$$P(\text{consultant predicts denial}|\text{approval granted}) = 1 - .70 = .30$$

Similarly, since

$$P(\text{consultant predicts denial}|\text{approval denied}) = .80$$

then

$$P(\text{consultant predicts approval}|\text{approval denied}) = 1 - .80 = .20$$

Tables 6.8 and 6.9 detail the Bayesian approach. Table 6.8 corresponds to the consultant's prediction of approval, and Table 6.9 corresponds to the consultant's prediction of denial.

TABLE 6.8   Indicator Information—Consultant Predicts Approval of Variance

States of Nature	Prior Probabilities	Conditional Probabilities	Joint Probabilities	Posterior Probabilities
Variance approved	.40	.70	.28	.28/.40 = .70
Variance denied	.60	.20	.12	.12/.40 = .30
	P(consultant predicts approval)		.40	

TABLE 6.9   Indicator Information—Consultant Predicts Denial of Variance

States of Nature	Prior Probabilities	Conditional Probabilities	Joint Probabilities	Posterior Probabilities
Variance approved	.40	.30	.12	.12/.60 = .20
Variance denied	.60	.80	.48	.48/.60 = .80
	P(consultant predicts denial)		.60	

Once the consultant's prediction is known, BGD faces the same decision choices it did when the consultant was not hired: (1) do nothing; (2) buy the land; or (3) purchase the option. The differences here are the probabilities for the states of nature and the fact that the firm has spent $5000 for the consultant. Using this information, we can complete the decision tree as shown in Figure 6.13.

To determine the optimal strategy, we work backward from the ends of each branch until we come to either a state of nature node or a decision node.

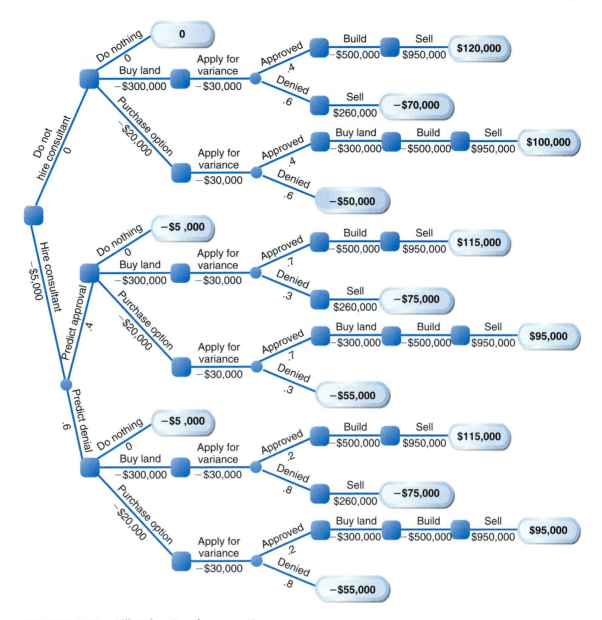

FIGURE 6.13   Bill Galen Development Company

At a state of nature node, we calculate the expected value of the node using the ending node values for each branch leading out of the node and the probability associated with that branch. The expected value is the sum of the products of the branch probabilities and corresponding ending node values. This sum becomes the value for the state of nature node.

At a decision node, the branch that has the highest ending node value is the optimal decision. This highest ending node value, in turn, becomes the value for the decision node. Nonoptimal decisions are indicated by a pair of lines across their branches.

To illustrate, consider in Figure 6.13 the possible paths reached if BGD does not hire the consultant. If BGD decides to buy the property and applies for the variance, two outcomes (branches) are possible: (1) the variance is approved and BGD earns $120,000; or (2) the variance is denied and BGD loses $70,000. The expected return at this state of nature node is found by (Probability Variance Is Approved)*(Expected Return If Variance Is Approved) + (Probability

Variance Is Denied)*(Expected Return If Variance Is Denied) = .4($120,000) + .6(−$70,000) = $6000. This is the expected value associated with buying the land. The expected value associated with buying the option is .40($100,000) + .60(−$50,000) = $10,000.

Thus, if BGD decides not to hire the consultant, the corresponding expected values that result if it does nothing, buys the land, or purchases the option are $0, $6000, and $10,000, respectively; thus purchasing the option is the optimal decision. The expected return corresponding to the purchase option decision ($10,000) then becomes the expected return corresponding to the decision node not to hire the consultant.

The remaining portion of the tree, in which BGD *does* hire the consultant, is calculated by working backwards in a similar fashion. The completed decision tree is given in Figure 6.14. As you can see, the optimal decision is to hire the consultant. Then if the consultant predicts approval, BGD should buy the property, but if the consultant predicts denial, BGD should do nothing.

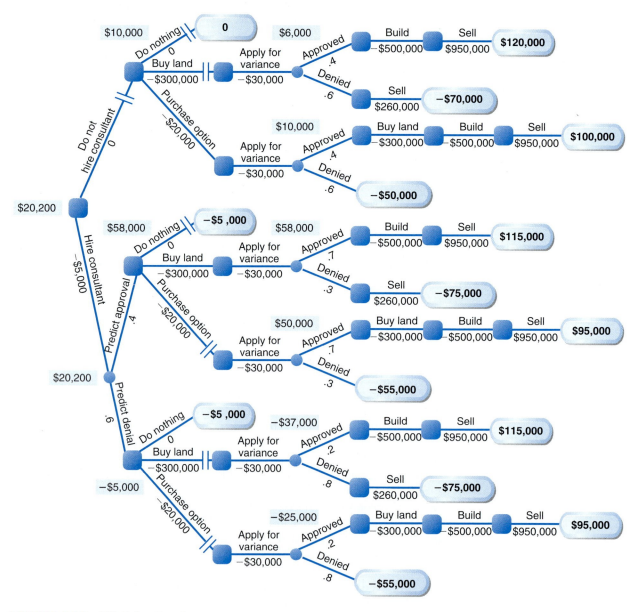

FIGURE 6.14   Bill Galen Development Company

This problem illustrates that the calculations required to analyze a problem using a decision tree can be lengthy and cumbersome. Fortunately, specialized computer programs and Excel add-ins exist to help the analyst set up and analyze decision trees. One such Excel add-in is TreePlan which is available on the CD-ROM accompanying this textbook.

Let us use TreePlan to construct the decision tree for the Bill Galen Development problem. To simplify the tree, we will combine actions where appropriate. For example, since BGD will always apply for a variance if it buys the land or purchases the option, we will combine these activities into one branch. Similarly, if the variance is approved, BGD will always Build and then Sell and we will combine these activities into one branch.

After installing the TreePlan software open up the add-in by selecting Decision Tree under Tools on the menu bar. You will see the opening tree as shown in Figure 6.15.

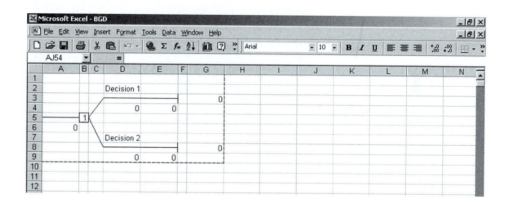

FIGURE 6.15
Opening Spreadsheet When Using TreePlan

The default decision tree has two decision arcs leading from the root node. One can rename the arc names by putting the cursor in the appropriate cell and retyping the desired name. For the BGD problem, we would rename Decision 1 in Cell D2 to "Do not hire consultant" and Decision 2 in Cell D7 to "Hire Consultant." Below each arc are two 0 values. The value on the left is where you enter the cash flow associated with the particular decision. The value on the right is the cumulative cash flow along the branches of the tree and is determined by the program.

For example, the cash flow associated with not hiring the consultant is 0, but the cash flow of hiring the consultant is −$5,000. Expressing the values in the tree in $1000's, −5 is entered under the "Hire Consultant" branch. Note that the cash flow at the end of the path also changes to −5 and the decision tree looks as shown in Figure 6.16.

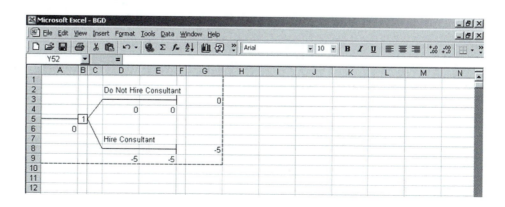

FIGURE 6.16
Initial TreePlan Tree as Modified for Bill Galen Development

We also note the number 1 in the node box. This indicates that for the problem, as currently formulated, the optimal decision is decision 1. This is because it is better to gain nothing than to lose $5000.

The principal way of modifying the tree is to put the cursor in the appropriate cell and hold down the Control and t keys (control + t). For example, for the BGD model to add a decision node at the end of the "Do not hire" consultant branch, put the cursor in cell F3 (the end of the branch) and press the Control and t keys. Since cell F3 is currently a terminal node, this brings up the dialogue box shown in Figure 6.17.

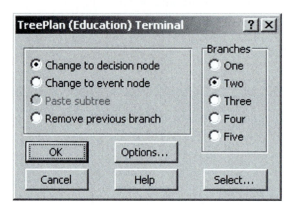

FIGURE 6.17
Dialogue Box for
Terminal Node

Because this node is to be a decision node with three decisions emanating from it, we would leave the "Change to decision node" button highlighted but change the number of branches from "Two" to "Three."

The names for Decisions 3, 4, and 5 would then be changed to "Do nothing," "Buy land/Apply for variance," and "Purchase option/Apply for variance" by entering these names in cells H2, H7, and H12, respectively. Since the "Buy land/Apply for variance" decision results in a $330,000 cash outflow and the "Purchase option/Apply for variance" decision results in a $50,000 outflow, we enter a −330 in cell H9 and −50 in cell H14. This gives the tree shown in Figure 6.18.

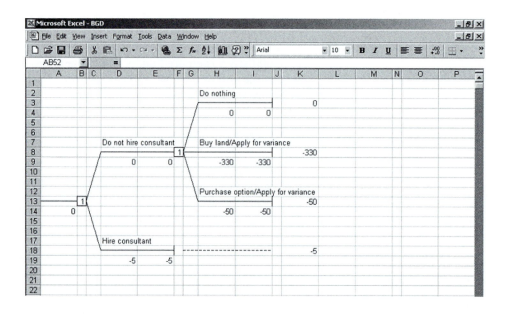

FIGURE 6.18
Modified TreePlan Tree
Showing Decisions If
Consultant Is Not Hired

To complete the section of the tree corresponding to "Buy land/Apply for variance," we now add a state of nature node at the end of the "Buy land/Apply for variance" branch to allow the possibility of the variance either being approved or denied. This is done by positioning the cursor in cell J10, typing Control + t, highlighting the button corresponding to "Change to event node," and indicating that the number of branches should be "Two." This gives the tree as shown in Figure 6.19.

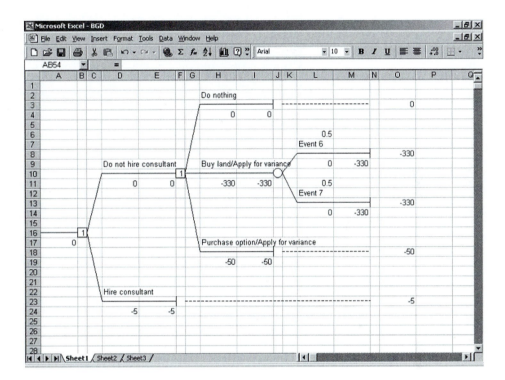

FIGURE 6.19
Modified TreePlan Tree Showing States of Nature Following Buy Land/Apply for Variance

Notice that cell J10 is a round node as it corresponds to a chance event. Since there are two possible events the default probabilities inserted by TreePlan are .5 and .5. Modify the default names "Event 7" and "Event 8" in cells L7 and L12 to "Variance approved/Build/Sell" and "Variance denied/Sell," respectively. Also change the probability of .5 in cell L6 and L11 to .4 and .6, respectively, since these are the probabilities of the variance being approved or denied. Since the cash flow associated with the Variance approved/Build/Sell is −$500,000 + $950,000 = $450,000, put +450 in cell L9. Similarly, since the cash flow associated with Variance denied/Sell is +$260,000, put +260 in cell L14. The completed section of this tree looks as shown in Figure 6.20.

Note that TreePlan automatically calculates the ending values for each node as well as the expected value at the chance node (the value of 6 in cell I11).

To finish the tree for the "Purchase option/Apply for variance" branch, use the same procedure as for adding the branches following the "Buy land/Apply for Variance" branch. Specifically, the cursor is positioned at cell J18 to add two branches. The branches are then renamed, and the relevant probability and cash flow information is added to the appropriate cells. Note that the cash flow for the branch "Variance approved/Buy land/Build/Sell" is 300 less than the branch "Variance approved/Build/Sell" since the cost of the land is $300,000. This results in the decision tree shown in Figure 6.21.

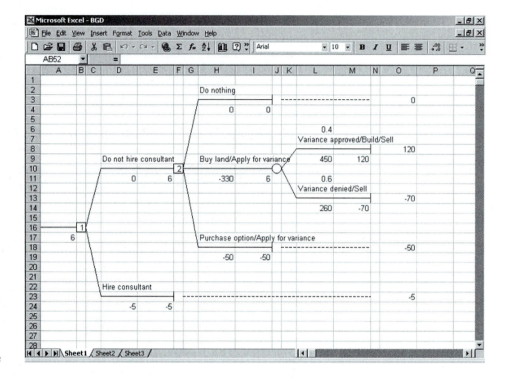

FIGURE 6.20
TreePlan Tree Showing Ending Branches Following Buy Land/Apply for Variance

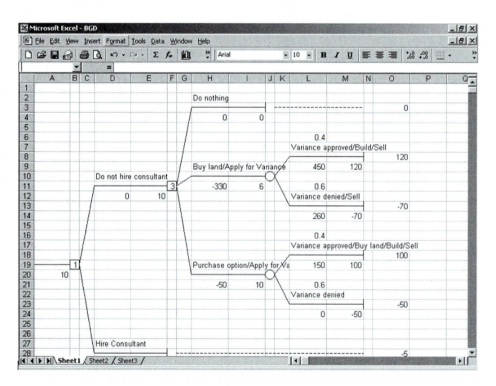

FIGURE 6.21
Decision Tree If Consultant Is Not Hired

We see from this tree that the best decision if the consultant is not hired is to Purchase the option and Apply for the variance since there is a 3 (third decision) in cell F11. The expected value corresponding to this action is 10 (the value given in cell E12).

Now consider the subtree dealing with hiring the consultant. The consultant will predict either approval or denial. These branches are added by clicking on cell

F28 (the end of the "Hire consultant" branch), typing Control + t, highlighting the "Change to event node" button, and indicating that there are two branches. Inserting the appropriate event names and probabilities gives rise to the tree shown in Figure 6.22.

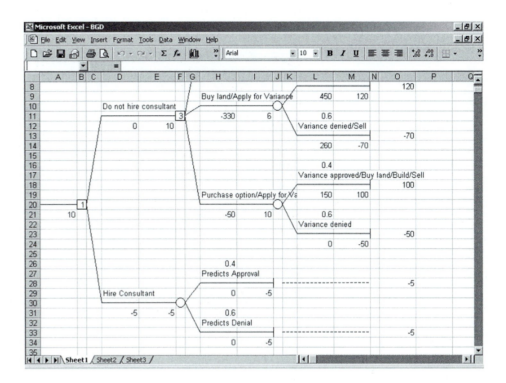

FIGURE 6.22
Portion of Decision Tree Corresponding to Hiring Consultant

The easiest way to complete the decision tree following the consultant "Predicts approval" is to copy the portion of the tree following the branch "Do not hire consultant." This is done by positioning the cursor at cell F11, the end of the branch, and typing Control + t. This results in the dialogue box shown in Figure 6.23.

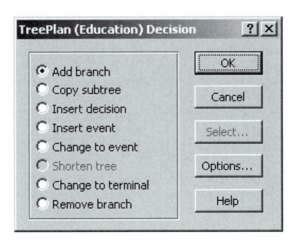

FIGURE 6.23
Dialogue Box for Existing Node

Since we wish to copy the subtree following cell F11, highlight the radio button next to "Copy subtree" and click on OK. The cursor is then positioned at cell J28, the end of the "Predicts approval" branch. Pressing Control + t again gives rise to the same dialogue box shown in Figure 6.17, but now with "Paste subtree" as an active option. Pasting the subtree and changing the probabilities for the variance being approved and denied to the correct posterior values gives the tree shown in Figure 6.24.

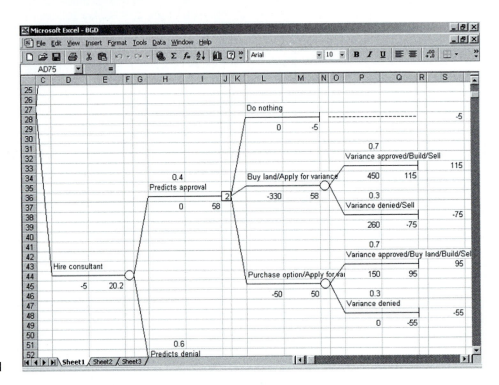

FIGURE 6.24
Portion of Decision Tree If Consultant Predicts Approval

Note that in Figure 6.24 there is a value of 2 in cell J36. Hence we see that, if the consultant predicts approval, the best course of action is to buy the land and apply for the variance. The expected value of this decision is 58 (the value in cell I37).

To complete the tree, again paste the subtree into the node following the consultant "Predicts denial" branch. Changing the probabilities to reflect the correct posterior probabilities results in the completed decision tree. This is contained in the Excel file *BGD.xls* on the accompanying CD-ROM.

TreePlan has several options that one may use in analyzing the decision tree. One of these options enables the analyst to use the expected utility criterion (discussed in the next section) instead of the expected value criterion. If this option is selected, TreePlan assumes that the utility function is exponential. To consider different criteria when using TreePlan, one selects Options in the appropriate TreePlan dialogue box.

A BUSINESS REPORT

Using the information obtained from the decision tree analysis, we can prepare the following business report to assist BGD in determining an optimal decision strategy. This memorandum cogently identifies the critical factors BGD should consider and highlights the possible risks the company may encounter.

·SCG·

STUDENT CONSULTING GROUP

MEMORANDUM

To: Bill Galen, President, Bill Galen Development Company
From: Student Consulting Group
Subj: 5th and Main Street Property

We have analyzed the situation regarding the parcel of property located at 5th and Main Streets in Kingston, New York, which your firm is interested in developing for a strip shopping center. The property is currently zoned residential and would require a variance in order to complete construction. Our analysis was completed assuming that BGD wishes to maximize the expected profit this project could potentially generate.

Based on cost and revenue estimates supplied by management, the following table gives the returns available from different strategies the firm might pursue.

TABLE I Expected Return Available from Different Possible Strategies

Strategy	Expected Return
Consultant not hired	
Do nothing	$0
Buy land	$6000
Buy option	$10,000
Consultant hired and predicts variance will be approved	
Do nothing	−$5000
Buy land	$58,000
Buy option	$50,000
Consultant hired and predicts variance will be denied	
Do nothing	−$5000
Buy land	−$37,000
Buy option	−$25,000

We analyzed this information using standard decision-making techniques and recommend the following strategy:

Hire the consultant for $5000. If the consultant predicts that the variance will be approved, BGD should purchase the property for $300,000. If the consultant predicts that the variance will be denied, BGD should not proceed with this project. *Your expected return from this strategy is $20,200.*

Table II summarizes the potential maximum loss from each strategy and the probability that the firm will incur such a loss.

If the consultant predicts that the variance will be approved and it is, in fact, *not* approved, BGD potentially will suffer a loss of $75,000. The likelihood of the consultant predicting approval is estimated to be 40%, and the possibility that the variance will be denied in this case is estimated to be 30%. Hence, there is approximately a 12% chance that BGD will incur a loss of $75,000 if this recommendation is followed.

TABLE II Maximum Potential Loss and Likelihood of Such Loss from Different Possible Strategies

Strategy	Maximum Loss	Probability
Consultant not hired		
Do nothing	0	100%
Buy land	$70,000	40%
Buy option	$50,000	40%
Consultant hired and predicts variance will be approved		
Do nothing	$5000	40%
Buy land	$75,000	12%
Buy option	$55,000	12%
Consultant hired and predicts variance will be denied		
Do nothing	$5000	60%
Buy land	$75,000	48%
Buy option	$55,000	48%

If BGD feels that the potential loss from the recommended strategy is greater than the company can afford, instead of purchasing the property if the consultant predicts the variance will be approved, the company can buy the option. This lowers the expected return to $17,000 but will only expose BGD to a maximum potential loss of $55,000. Should this potential loss still be too large, we would be happy to meet with management to discuss alternative strategies.

6.7 Decision Making and Utility

The underlying basis for using the expected value criterion is that the decision maker wishes to choose the decision alternative that maximizes the expected return (or minimizes the expected cost). This criterion may not be appropriate, however, if the decision is a one-time opportunity with substantial risks.

For example, as pointed out in the BGD management memo, following the recommended strategy carries a potential loss of $75,000 for the company. If the maximum the company could currently afford to lose is $55,000, it may prefer to buy the option and not hire the consultant, even though this strategy has a lower expected return. The concept of utility has been developed to explain such behavior in a rational format.

Social scientists have long observed that individuals do not always choose decisions based on the expected value criterion, even when the payoffs and probabilities for the states of nature are known. For example, suppose you could play a coin toss game in which you will win $1 if the coin is heads and lose $1 if the coin is tails. If the coin is bent so that the probability of the coin landing heads is 55% and tails is 45%, your expected return from playing the game would be .55($1) + .45(−$1) = $.10. Given this expected return, you probably would wish to play this game.

Consider what happens, however, when the stakes increase so that you win $100,000 if the coin comes up heads and lose $100,000 if the coin comes up tails. Even though this game has an expected return of $10,000 = .55($100,000) +

.45(−$100,000), you might be reluctant to play due to the potential of losing $100,000.

Playing state lottery games is an example of a case in which people do not base a decision on expected value. In most state lottery games, the expected return to the purchaser of a $1.00 lottery ticket is only about $0.50. Thus, if people decided whether or not to buy a lottery ticket based on expected value alone, lottery sales would be nonexistent.

Purchasing insurance is another such example. Insurance industry profits are predicated on the fact that, on the average, people will pay more for a policy than the expected present value of the loss for which they are insured. Again, if people's decisions were based solely on the expected value criterion, no one would buy insurance.

UTILITY APPROACH

In the utility approach to decision making, **utility values**, U(V)s, reflective of the decision maker's perspective are determined for each possible payoff. The utility of the least preferred outcome is given the lowest utility value (usually 0), whereas the most preferred outcome is given the highest utility value (usually 1). Utility values for the other possible payoffs are set between these values, with higher payoffs receiving higher utility values, although not necessarily proportionally higher. The optimal decision is then chosen by an **expected utility criterion**, which uses these values rather than the payoff values in the calculations.

DETERMINING UTILITY VALUES, U(V)

Although the following technique for finding utility values corresponding to payoffs may seem contrived, it does provide an insightful look into the amount of risk the decision maker is willing to take. The concept is based on the decision maker's preference to taking a sure thing (a particular payoff) versus risking receiving only the highest or lowest payoff.

Indifference Approach For Assigning Utility Values

1. List every possible payoff in ascending order.
2. Assign a utility of 0 to the lowest payoff and a utility of 1 to the highest payoff.
3. For all other possible payoff values ask the decision maker, "Suppose you could receive this payoff for sure, or, alternatively, you could receive either the highest payoff with probability p and the lowest payoff with probability (1−p). What value of p would make you *indifferent* between the two situations?" These *indifference probabilities* for the payoffs are the utility values.

To illustrate the utility approach, let us consider once again the Tom Brown investment problem.

Tom Brown.xls

TOM BROWN INVESTMENT PROBLEM (CONTINUED)

We observed that the highest possible return for Tom in the payoff table calculated based on the broker's analysis was $500. Tom would achieve this payoff if he invested in the stock and there were a large rise in the market. The lowest possible payoff was a loss of $600, which Tom would incur if he invested in the stock and there were a large fall in the market.

The second highest possible return was $300. Tom would receive this sum if he invested in gold and there were a small fall in the market. We asked Tom, "If you could receive $300 for sure or you could receive $500 with probability p and lose $600 with probability $(1-p)$, what value of p would make you indifferent between these two choices?"

Tom thought for a moment and replied, "I'd have to be pretty certain of receiving the $500 payoff to pass up a certain payoff of $300; say about 90%." We repeated this question for all possible outcomes from the payoff table, and Tom's responses were as follows:

Certain Payoff	Probability
-600	0
-200	.25
-150	.30
-100	.36
0	.50
60	.60
100	.65
150	.70
200	.75
250	.85
300	.90
500	1.00

In light of these preferences, Tom wishes to determine his optimal investment decision.

SOLUTION

The indifference preferences Tom gave in response to our questions are his utility values for the payoffs. To determine the optimal decision under the expected utility criterion, we substitute the corresponding utility values for the nondominated payoffs given in Table 6.2 and calculate the expected utility for each decision.

Figure 6.25 shows the Utility worksheet contained in the Decision Payoff Table.xls template for the Tom Brown investment problem with unused columns hidden.

In this spreadsheet, the certain payoffs and corresponding utility values are entered in columns M and N. The optimal decision and corresponding expected utility are given in cells B17 and C17. Since the decision with the highest expected utility is the stock investment, it would be selected using the expected utility criterion. Comparing the expected utility of the stock investment to the bond investment, however, we note there is little difference in the two values. In fact, had the utility values been slightly different, the bond investment could have had the *higher* expected utility.

It is therefore important not to dismiss the bond investment from consideration. (Remember that in management science we are modeling in order to obtain insights into the optimal decision.) Tom may, in fact, wish to do some further investigation before making a final choice between the stock and the bond.

Tom Brown.xls

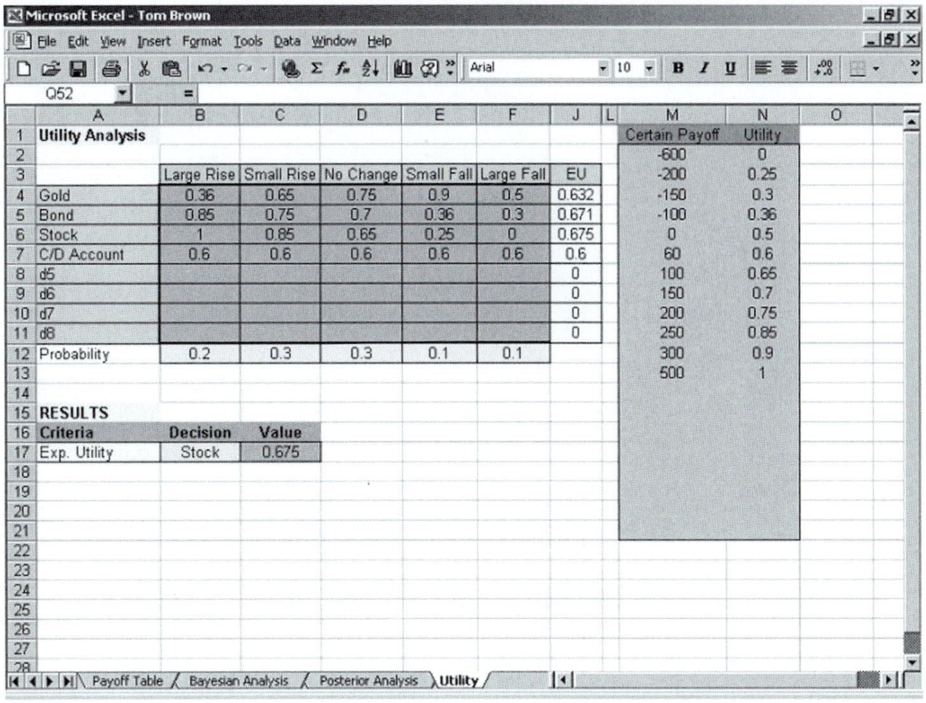

	A	B	C	D	E	F	J	L	M	N	O
1	**Utility Analysis**								Certain Payoff	Utility	
2									-600	0	
3		Large Rise	Small Rise	No Change	Small Fall	Large Fall	EU		-200	0.25	
4	Gold	0.36	0.65	0.75	0.9	0.5	0.632		-150	0.3	
5	Bond	0.85	0.75	0.7	0.36	0.3	0.671		-100	0.36	
6	Stock	1	0.85	0.65	0.25	0	0.675		0	0.5	
7	C/D Account	0.6	0.6	0.6	0.6	0.6	0.6		60	0.6	
8	d5						0		100	0.65	
9	d6						0		150	0.7	
10	d7						0		200	0.75	
11	d8						0		250	0.85	
12	Probability	0.2	0.3	0.3	0.1	0.1			300	0.9	
13									500	1	
14											
15	**RESULTS**										
16	**Criteria**	**Decision**	**Value**								
17	Exp. Utility	Stock	0.675								

FIGURE 6.25
Utility Analysis Spreadsheet for the Tom Brown Investment Problem

FIGURE 6.26 Risk-Averse Utility Curve

FIGURE 6.27 Risk-Taking Utility Curve

RISK-AVERSE, RISK-NEUTRAL, AND RISK-TAKING DECISION MAKERS

Within the context of utility theory, behavior can be classified as risk averse, risk taking, or risk neutral. A *risk-averse* decision maker prefers a certain outcome to a chance outcome having the same expected value. For example, suppose you have the choice of receiving $10,000 with probability .20 and $0 with probability .80. The expected value of this outcome is $2000 (=.20*$10,000 + .80*0). If you preferred receiving $2000 with certainty to the random outcome, you would be exhibiting risk-averse behavior. An example of risk-averse behavior is the purchase of an insurance policy. The concave utility curve depicted in Figure 6.26 is that of a risk-averse decision maker.

A *risk-taking* decision maker prefers a chance outcome to a certain outcome having the same expected value. Returning to the above example, if you were a risk-taking decision maker, you would prefer the chance outcome to receiving $2000. An example of risk-taking behavior is the purchase of a lottery ticket. The convex utility curve depicted in Figure 6.27 is that of a risk-taking decision maker.

A *risk-neutral* decision maker is indifferent between a chance outcome and a certain outcome having the same expected value. Using the above example once again, if you were a risk-neutral decision maker, you would be indifferent between the two outcomes. Typically, large corporations are assumed to be risk neutral because they do not have a preference for or an aversion to risk with regard to the amounts of money involved in normal business situations. The linear utility curve depicted in Figure 6.28 is that of a risk-neutral decision maker.

The optimal decision for a risk-neutral decision maker can be determined using the expected value criterion on the payoff values. Therefore, the expected value criterion is generally used in decision making at large corporations.

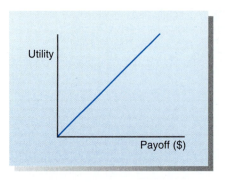

FIGURE 6.28   Risk-Neutral Utility Curve

Most individuals are not entirely risk averse, risk taking, or risk neutral. Social scientists have shown that, in general, people tend to be risk taking when dealing with small amounts of money while they tend to be risk averse when it comes to large amounts. Between large and small amounts of money, people are generally risk neutral. This explains why the same individual might purchase a lottery ticket as well as fire insurance. Figure 6.29 depicts Tom Brown's utility values. As you can see, Tom appears to exhibit such typical behavior.

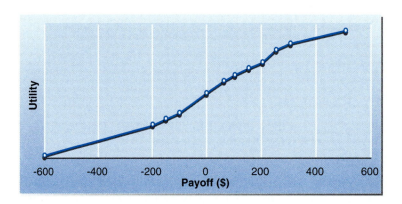

FIGURE 6.29
Tom Brown's Utility Curve

6.8   Game Theory

Playing games is a popular form of amusement. People typically play games such as poker, bridge, and chess, for the challenge and enjoyment they afford (and, if betting is allowed, for financial gain).

Similarly, the business environment provides numerous decision-making situations in which one firm or individual is "playing" against another. For example, an oil company bidding for exploration rights to a tract of land is, in a sense, playing a game against other oil companies bidding for the tract. When an airline lowers its fare on a particular route in order to capture a greater market share, it is playing a game against the other carriers serving that route.

Game theory can be used to determine the optimal decision in the face of other decision-making players. In game theory, the payoff is based on the action taken by competing individuals who are also seeking to maximize their return. In decision theory, however, an individual (player) makes a decision and receives a payoff based on the outcome of a noncompetitive random event (the state of nature). You can therefore view decision theory as a special case of game theory in which the decision maker is playing against a single disinterested party (nature).

As shown in Table 6.10, games can be classified in a number of ways—by the number of players, the total return to all players, or the sequence of moves, to name a few.

TABLE 6.10 Classification of Games

Classification	Description	Example
Number of Players		
Two player	Two competitors	Chess
Mutliplayer	More than two competitors	Poker
Total Return		
Zero sum	The amount won by all players equals the amount lost by all players.	Poker among friends
Nonzero sum	The amount won by all players does not equal the amount lost by all players.	Poker in a casino; the "house" takes a percentage of each pot
Sequence of Moves		
Sequential	Each player gets a turn in a given sequence.	*Monopoly*
Simultaneous	All players make their decisions simultaneously.	Paper, rock, scissors

While game theory is an extensive topic, here we focus solely on two-person, zero-sum games in which all decisions are made simultaneously. The situation faced by IGA Supermarket can be modeled by such a game.

IGA.xls

IGA SUPERMARKET

The town of Gold Beach, Oregon, is served by two supermarkets—IGA and Sentry. In a given week, the market share of the two supermarkets can be influenced by their advertising policies. In particular, the manager of each supermarket must decide weekly which area of operations to discount heavily and emphasize in the store's newspaper flyer. Both supermarkets have three areas of operation in common: meat, produce, and groceries. Sentry, however, has a fourth—an in-store bakery.

The weekly percentage gain to IGA in market share as a function of the advertising emphasis of each store is indicated by the following payoff table (Table 6.11). Here it is assumed that a gain in market share to IGA will result in the equivalent loss in market share to Sentry, and vice versa.

Since the IGA manager does not know which operation Sentry will emphasize each week, she wishes to determine an optimal advertising strategy that will maximize IGA's expected change in market share *regardless* of Sentry's action.

TABLE 6.11 Percentage Change in IGA's Market Share as a Function of Advertising Emphasis

		Sentry's Emphasis			
		Meat	Produce	Groceries	Bakery
IGA's *Emphasis*	Meat	2	2	−8	6
	Produce	−2	0	6	−4
	Groceries	2	−7	1	−3

SOLUTION

The IGA manager should vary the weekly advertising emphasis; otherwise the Sentry manager will always be able to select an advertising emphasis that ensures a loss of market share for IGA. Hence, the optimal strategy for the IGA manager is to change her advertising emphasis randomly. But what proportion of the time should the emphasis be on meat or produce or groceries?

Let us define:

X_1 = the probability IGA's advertising focus is on meat
X_2 = the probability IGA's advertising focus is on produce
X_3 = the probability IGA's advertising focus is on groceries

The manager at IGA wants to maximize the store's expected change in market share, regardless of Sentry's advertising focus. This expected change, which we denote by V, is known as the *value* of the game.

Let us see what restrictions are placed on V. If Sentry's advertising focus is on meat, then the expected change in IGA's market share is expressed as $2X_1 - 2X_2 + 2X_3$. This expected change must be at least V, since V represents IGA's change in market share regardless of Sentry's action. Thus, $2X_1 - 2X_2 + 2X_3 \geq V$.

By using similar reasoning for Sentry's advertising emphasis on produce, groceries, and bakery, we arrive at the following conditional relationships:

Sentry's Advertising Emphasis	Relationship
Meat	$2X_1 - 2X_2 + 2X_3 \geq V$
Produce	$2X_1 - 7X_3 \geq V$
Groceries	$-8X_1 + 6X_2 + X_3 \geq V$
Bakery	$6X_1 - 4X_2 - 3X_3 \geq V$

Because the sum of the probabilities of IGA's advertising focus must equal 1, we also know that $X_1 + X_2 + X_3 = 1$. These conditions result in the following linear programming model, which IGA can use to determine its optimal advertising strategy:

$$\text{MAX} \quad V$$
$$\text{ST}$$
$$2X_1 - 2X_2 + 2X_3 - V \geq 0$$
$$2X_1 - 7X_3 - V \geq 0$$
$$-8X_1 + 6X_2 + X_3 - V \geq 0$$
$$6X_1 - 4X_2 - 3X_3 - V \geq 0$$
$$X_1 + X_2 + X_3 = 1$$
$$X_1, X_2, X_3 \geq 0, \text{ V unrestricted}$$

Solver can be used to determine the oprtimal solution.[3] Figure 6.30 shows the resulting Sensitivity Report for this model. Thus IGA should focus its advertising on meat about 39% of the time, on produce 50% of the time, and on groceries about 11% of the time.

The average change in IGA's market share using this strategy is 0%, implying that, in the long run, the market shares of the two supermarkets will not change. When the value of a game is 0, it is known as a *fair game*.

[3] Since V is an unrestricted variable the "Assume Non-Negative" box would not be checked. Rather the constraints $X_1 \geq 0$, $X_2 \geq 0$, and $X_3 \geq 0$ are entered in the constraints section of the solver dialogue box.

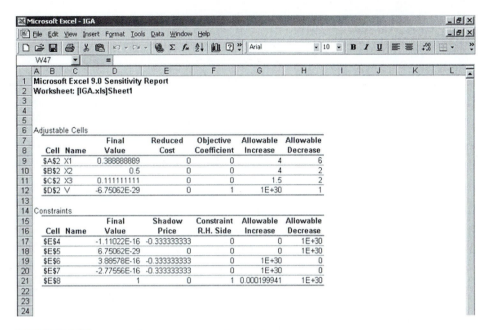

FIGURE 6.30 Partial Output for IGA Problem

Had the value of the game not been zero, then, on the average, each week the market share would change by that value. If this trend continued, at some point, the estimated percentage changes given in Table 6.11 would cease to be valid.

THE OPTIMAL STRATEGY FOR SENTRY MARKET

From Sentry's perspective, the model can be formulated by letting

Y_1 = the probability Sentry's advertising focus is on meat
Y_2 = the probability Sentry's advertising focus is on produce
Y_3 = the probability Sentry's advertising focus is on groceries
Y_4 = the probability Sentry's advertising focus is on bakery

Sentry also wishes to maximize its expected change in market share regardless of IGA's advertising focus. Since IGA's "gain" is Sentry's loss, this is equivalent to maximizing $-V$. Because the numbers in Table 6.11 are expressed as "gains" in market share to IGA, negatives of these numbers are the "gains" in market share for Sentry. Thus, $-2Y_1 - 2Y_2 + 8Y_3 - 6Y_4$ represents the expected gain in market share to Sentry if IGA focuses its advertising on meat.

Using the reasoning developed for the IGA model, we see that the following conditional relationships hold for the Sentry model:

IGA's Advertising Emphasis	Relationship
Meat	$-2Y_1 - 2Y_2 + 8Y_3 - 6Y_4 \geq -V$
Produce	$2Y_1 - 6Y_3 + 4Y_4 \geq -V$
Groceries	$-2Y_1 + 7Y_2 - Y_3 + 3Y_4 \geq -V$

Note that maximizing $-V$ is equivalent to minimizing V. Multiplying the above expressions by -1 (allowing us to use the original numbers in Table 6.11), we can use the following linear programming model[4] to solve for Sentry's optimal advertising strategy:

MIN $\qquad\qquad\qquad\qquad\qquad\qquad\qquad\qquad\qquad\qquad$ V
ST

$$2Y_1 + 2Y_2 - 8Y_3 + 6Y_4 - V \le 0$$
$$-2Y_1 \qquad\quad + 6Y_3 - 4Y_4 - V \le 0$$
$$2Y_1 - 7Y_2 + Y_3 - 3Y_4 - V \le 0$$
$$Y_1 + Y_2 + Y_3 + Y_4 \qquad = 1$$
$$Y_1, Y_2, Y_3, Y_4 \ge 0, \text{ V unrestricted}$$

Solving this model using Excel will indicate that Sentry's advertising focus should be on meat $\frac{1}{3}$ of the time, groceries $\frac{1}{3}$ of the time, and the bakery $\frac{1}{3}$ of the time.[5] However, these values are the negative of the corresponding shadow prices in the Sensitivity Report shown in Figure 6.30.

We would be remiss if we did not point out that using changes to market share as the decision criterion may not be appropriate. A business typically wishes to maximize its long-term weekly profit rather than its market share. If the cost structures for the two supermarkets are similar, however, it is probably not unreasonable to assume that a change in a store's market share is directly proportional to a change in its profitability.

6.9 Summary

Decision analysis is useful for making decisions that have major profit or cost implications. Payoff tables, in which rows correspond to the decision alternatives and columns correspond to states of nature, are useful for analyzing problems that concern a single decision.

When probability information regarding the states of nature is not available, maximax, maximin, minimax regret, and principle of insufficient reason criteria can be used. The choice of criterion is a function of the decision maker's attitude. When probability information for the states of nature are available, the decision can be determined using an expected payoff or expected regret approach.

Bayes' Theorem can be used to revise the probabilities for the states of nature based on additional experimentation. Using this information, the decision maker can determine the expected value of sample or indicator information. The expected value of perfect information provides an upper limit on the expected value of sample information.

For problems that are too complex to fit into the form of a payoff table, a decision tree approach can be utilized. Utility theory provides a rational basis for human behavior and to make optimal decisions incorporating risk attitudes. Game theory is an approach used for decision situations involving competitive play. The optimal strategy for a two-person zero-sum game can be determined using a linear programming approach.

[4] This problem is known as the *dual* of the problem faced by IGA. Duality in linear programming is discussed in Supplement CD2 on the accompanying CD-ROM.

[5] This problem actually has alternative optimal solutions. Another possible solution is to have Sentry focus on meat 60% of the time, produce 20% of the time, and groceries 20% of the time.

ON THE CD-ROM

- Excel spreadsheet for determining maximin decision for Tom Brown investment problem — **Tom Brown Maximin.xls**
- Excel spreadsheet for determining minimax regret decision for Tom Brown investment problem — **Tom Brown Minimax Regret.xls**
- Excel spreadsheet for determining minimax regret decision for Tom Brown investment problem — **Tom Brown Minimax Regret Revised.xls**
- Excel spreadsheet for determining maximax decision for Tom Brown investment problem — **Tom Brown Maximax.xls**
- Excel spreadsheet for determining insufficient reason decision for Tom Brown investment problem — **Tom Brown Insufficient Reason.xls**
- Excel spreadsheet for determining expected value payoff decision for Tom Brown investment problem — **Tom Brown Expected Value.xls**
- Excel template for solving decision payoff table problems — **Decision Payoff Table.xls**
- Excel template for Tom Brown investment problem — **Tom Brown.xls**
- Decision tree for BGD model — **BGD.xls**
- Linear programming output for IGA model — **IGA.xls**
- Problem Motivations — **Problem Motivations**
- Problems 41–50 — **Additional Problems/Cases**
- Case 4 — **Additional Problems/Cases**

APPENDIX 6.1

Using the Decision Payoff Table.xls Template

The Excel Spreadsheet Decision Payoff Table.xls allows one to solve payoff table problems with up to eight decision alternatives and eight states of nature. The template contains four worksheets: Payoff Table, Bayesian Analysis, Posterior Analysis, and Utility. These worksheets are linked so that the information you input into the Payoff Table worksheet appears in the Bayesian Analysis, Posterior Analysis, and Utility worksheets and the results of the Bayesian Analysis worksheet appear in the Posterior Analysis worksheet.

THE PAYOFF TABLE WORKSHEET

Figure A6.1 shows the Payoff Table worksheet on the template. The worksheet can handle up to eight decision alternatives and eight states of nature. The names of the decision alternatives are entered in cells A4 through A11. The names of the states of nature are entered in cells B3 through I3. The payoff values corresponding to a particular decision alternative and state of nature are entered into the appropriate cell in the range from cells B4 through I11. If probability information is known for the states of nature, these values are entered into cells B12 through I12. Note that columns J through N are used for determining the outputs and are hidden.

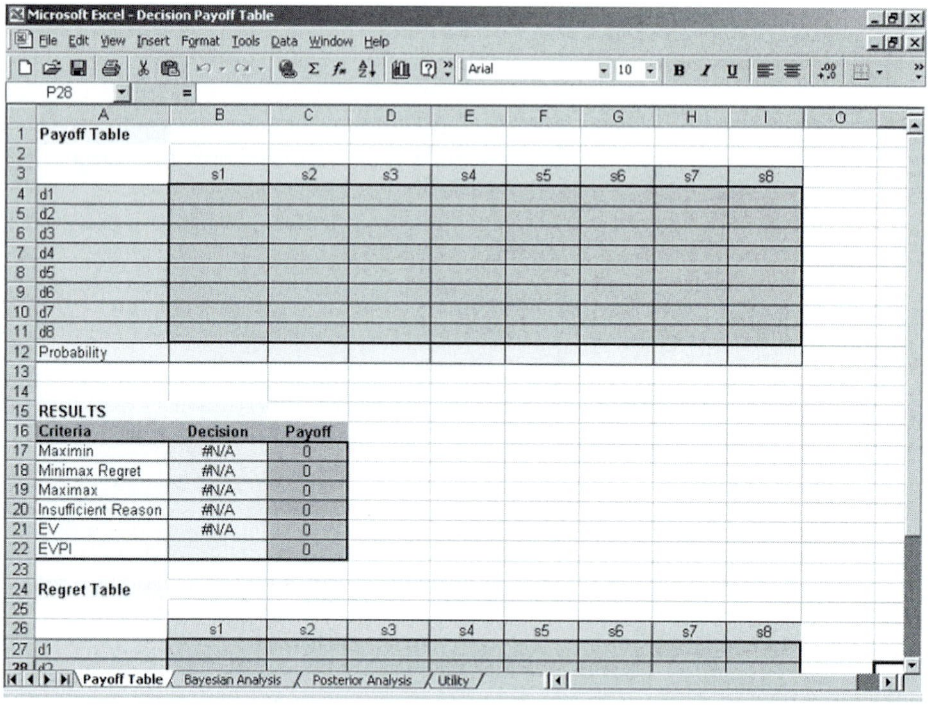

FIGURE A6.1
Payoff Table Worksheet in Decision Payoff Table.xls Template

For the four criteria for decision making under uncertainty, the optimal decisions and corresponding payoffs are given in rows 17 through 20. The regret table values are given in rows 27 through 34. If probability information is provided, the spreadsheet will calculate the optimal decision and expected payoff under the expected value (EV) criterion in row 21 and the EVPI value in cell C22.

Figure A6.2 gives the payoff table for the Tom Brown investment problem.

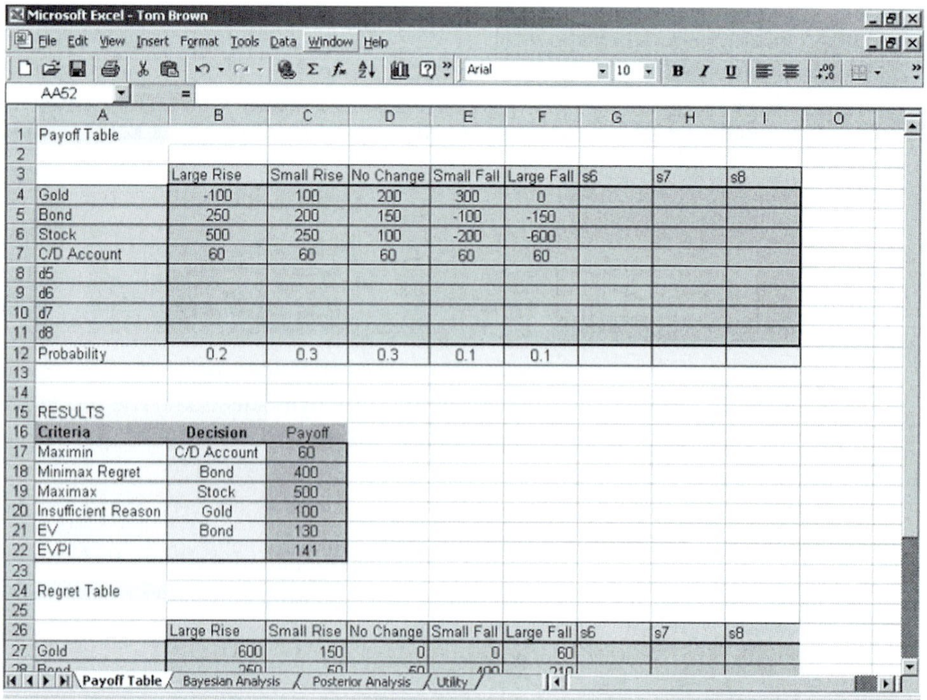

FIGURE A6.2
Payoff Table for the Tom Brown Investment Problem

THE BAYESIAN ANALYSIS WORKSHEET

The Bayesian Analysis worksheet can solve models having up to eight states of nature and four indicators. Figure A6.3 shows the Bayesian Analysis worksheet on the template.

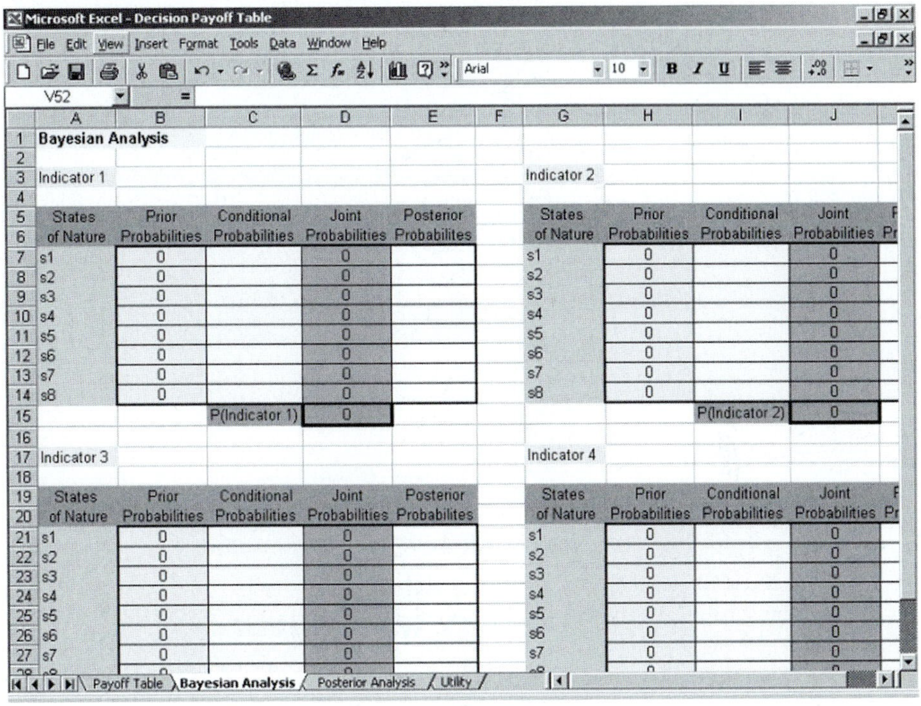

FIGURE A6.3
Bayesian Analysis Worksheet

If probabilities are entered in the Payoff Table worksheet, these are carried forward in the Bayesian Analysis worksheets in the cells in columns B and H. If these values are not entered on the Payoff Table worksheet, the appropriate values can be entered in columns B and H of the worksheet. Similarly, if the names of the state of nature are entered in the Payoff Table worksheet, they are carried forward in columns A and G of the Bayesian Analysis worksheet.

The conditional probabilities are entered in columns C and I corresponding to the appropriate indicator. The joint and posterior probabilities are then calculated, and the posterior probabilities are carried forward to the Posterior Analysis worksheet.

Figure 6.7 in Section 6.5 gives the Bayesian Analysis worksheet for the Tom Brown investment problem.

POSTERIOR ANALYSIS WORKSHEET

The Posterior Analysis worksheet will solve models with up to eight decision alternatives, eight states of nature, and four indicators. Figure A6.4 gives the Posterior Analysis worksheet on the template.

If information has been entered in the Payoff Table and Bayesian Analysis worksheets, no additional information need be entered in this worksheet. The optimal payoff and decision based on the prior probabilities as well as for each indicator is given in rows 20 and 21. The EVSI, EVPI, and Efficiency are determined in cells B23 through B25. If data has not been entered in either the Payoff Table or Bayesian Analysis worksheets, it may be entered directly on the Posterior Analysis worksheet. Figure 6.8 in Section 6.5 shows the Posterior Analysis worksheet for the Tom Brown investment problem.

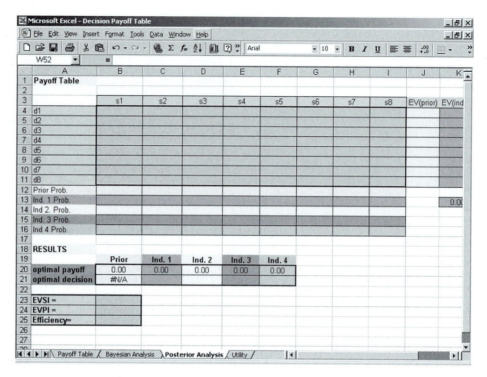

FIGURE A6.4   Posterior Analysis Worksheet

UTILITY WORKSHEET

The utility worksheet will solve models having up to eight decision alternatives, eight states of nature, and twenty different certainty equivalent (utility) values. Figure A6.5 gives the utility worksheet on the template.

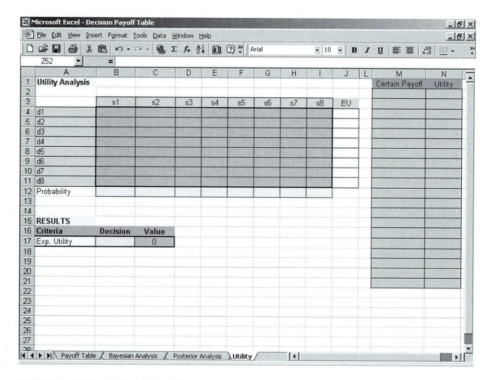

FIGURE A6.5   Utility Worksheet

If payoff table information has been entered on the Payoff Table worksheet, this information is carried over to the Utility Worksheet. If this information has not been entered on the Payoff Table worksheet, the payoff table data should be entered in cells B4 through I11 and the relevant probability information should be entered in cells B12 through I12. The certain payoffs and corresponding utilities are entered in columns M and N in ascending order. They should be entered in ascending order. The spreadsheet will calculate expected utility values for each decision in column J and identify the optimal decision under the expected utility criterion in cell B17 and the corresponding expected utility in cell C17.

Figure 6.25 in Section 6.7 shows the Utility Worksheet for the Tom Brown investment problem.

|Problems

1. The Campus Bookstore at East Tennessee State University must decide how many economics textbooks to order for the next semester's class. The bookstore believes that either seven eight, nine, or ten sections of the course will be offered next semester; each section contains 40 students. The publisher is offering bookstores a discount if they place their orders early. If the bookstore orders too few texts and runs out, the publisher will air express additional books at the bookstore's expense. If it orders too many texts, the store can return unsold texts to the publisher for a partial credit. The bookstore is considering ordering either 280, 320, 360, or 400 texts in order to get the discount. Taking into account the discounts, air express expenses, and credits for returned texts, the bookstore manager estimates the following resulting profits.

Number of Textbooks to Order	Number of Introductory Economics Classes Offered			
	7	8	9	10
280	$2800	$2720	$2640	$2480
320	$2600	$3200	$3040	$2880
360	$2400	$3000	$3600	$3440
400	$2200	$2800	$3400	$4000

a. What is the optimal decision if the bookstore manager uses the maximax criterion?
b. What is the optimal decision if the bookstore manager uses the maximin criterion?
c. What is the optimal decision if the bookstore manager uses the minimax regret criterion?

2. Consider the data given in problem 1 for the Campus Bookstore at East Tennessee State University. Based on conversations held with the chair of the economics department, suppose the bookstore manager believes that the following probabilities hold:

$$P(7 \text{ classes offered}) = .10$$
$$P(8 \text{ classes offered}) = .30$$
$$P(9 \text{ classes offered}) = .40$$
$$P(10 \text{ classes offered}) = .20$$

a. Using the expected value criterion, determine how many economics books the bookstore manager should purchase in order to maximize the store's expected profit. Do you think the expected value criterion is appropriate for this problem?
b. Based on the probabilities given in part a, determine the expected value of perfect information. Interpret its meaning.

3. National Foods has developed a new sports beverage it would like to advertise on Super Bowl Sunday. National's advertising agency can purchase either one, two, or three 30-second commercials advertising the drink. It estimates that the return will be based on Super Bowl viewership, which in turn, is based on fans' perception of whether the game is "dull," "average," "above average," or "exciting."

National Foods' ad agency has constructed the following payoff table giving its estimate of the expected profit (in $100,000's) resulting from purchasing one, two, or three advertising spots. (Another possible decision is for national Foods not to advertise at all during the Super Bowl.) The states of nature correspond to the game being "dull," "average," "above average," or "exciting."

Number of 30-Second Commercials Purchased	Perceived Game Excitement			
	Dull	Average	Above Average	Exciting
One	−2	3	7	13
Two	−5	6	12	18
Three	−9	5	13	22

a. What is the optimal decision if the National Foods advertising manager is optimistic?
b. What is the optimal decision if the National Foods advertising manager is pessimistic?
c. What is the optimal decision if the National Foods advertising manager wishes to minimize the firm's maximum regret?

4. Consider the data given in problem 3 for National Foods. Based on past Super Bowl games, suppose the decision maker believes that the following probabilities hold for the states of nature:

P(Dull Game) = .20
P(Average Game) = .40
P(Above-Average Game) = .30
P(Exciting Game) = .10

a. Using the expected value criterion, determine how many commercials National Foods should purchase.
b. Based on the probabilities given here, determine the expected value of perfect information.

5. Consider the data given in problems 3 and 4 for National Foods. The firm can hire the noted sport's pundit Jim Worden to give his opinion as to whether or not the Super Bowl game will be interesting. Suppose the following probabilities hold for Jim's predictions:

P(Jim predicts game will be interesting|game is dull) = .15
P(Jim predicts game will be interesting|game is average) = .25
P(Jim predicts game will be interesting|game is above average) = .50
P(Jim predicts game will be interesting|game is exciting) = .80
P(Jim predicts game will not be interesting|game is dull) = .85
P(Jim predicts game will not be interesting|game is average) = .75
P(Jim predicts game will not be interesting|game is above average) = .50
P(Jim predicts game will not be interesting|game is exciting) = .20

a. If Jim predicts the game will be interesting, what is the probability the game will be dull?
b. What is national's optimal strategy if Jim predicts the game will be (i) interesting or (ii) not interesting?
c. What is the expected value of Jim's information?

6. Wednesday Afternoon is a chain of stores that specialize in selling close-out merchandise. The firm has the opportunity to acquire either three, six, nine, or twelve store leases from the bankrupt In Focus chain. Each lease runs five years, and the profitability of these leases depends on the economy over this time period. The economists at Wednesday Afternoon believe that the average growth rate in GNP will be either 2, 3, 4, 5, or 6% per annum during the five-year period, with probabilities .1, .2, .2, .4, and .1, respectively. The following tables give the expected return to Wednesday Afternoon over the next five years (in $100,000s) as well as the utility values for these amounts.

Number of	Average Annual Growth in GNP				
Leases Acquired	2%	3%	4%	5%	6%
3	7	6	6	5	3
6	2	6	8	7	4
9	1	5	7	8	6
12	1	4	7	8	9

	Payoff (in $100,000s)								
	1	2	3	4	5	6	7	8	9
Utility	0	.05	.15	.30	.50	.65	.75	.90	1.0

Determine the number of leases the company should acquire if its objective is to:
a. Maximize expected profit over the next five years.
b. Maximize expected utility over the next five years.

7. EIEIO.com is a new website devoted to providing news to farmers. The company plans to make money by selling banner ads and providing links to companies that wish to sell items to this market. To run its website, the server the company is considering purchasing is from one of four manufacturers, IBM, H-P, Compaq, or Dell. Since the company has limited funding, this server will have to meet its needs for the next six months.

The company estimates that its profits over the six-month period will be a function of the server purchased and the average number of "hits" per hour that the website generates. The following payoff table (showing total estimated profits over the six-month period in $10,000s) has been developed to assist management in determining which model of server to purchase.

	Average Number of "Hits" Per Hour				
Server Model	10	25	50	100	300
IBM	−20	−10	5	15	10
H-P	−30	−15	8	22	45
Compaq	−45	−25	2	30	75
Dell	−40	−20	6	18	50

Management wishes to use a utility function of the form

$$U(x) = 1 - \left(\frac{x - 75}{120}\right)^2 \text{ (where } x \text{ is the estimated profit in } \$10,000s).$$

a. Would you characterize management as risk averse, risk loving, or risk neutral?
b. Suppose management believes the following probabilities hold for the states of nature: P(10) = .05, P(25) = .15, P(50) = .40, P(100) = .30, and P(300) = .10. Which server should the firm purchase if it uses the expected utility criterion for decision making?

8. Steve Johnson believes that this winter is going to be extremely rainy, and he is trying to decide whether he should repair or replace his roof. Steve can install a new roof for $7000 or have it repaired for $1000. While the repair work will probably mean that the house will not have any leaks during the upcoming year, Steve believes that he will definitely need a new roof next year and would have to pay $7000 at that time if he does not get the roof replaced this year.

There is a 60% chance that Steve will be transferred during the upcoming year and will have to put his house on the market. Steve feels that a new roof will enable him to get $4000 more if he sells his house. If he does not repair or replace the roof Steve believes there is a 70% chance that there will be rain damage to his home.

He estimates the likelihood that the damage will be $500 is .10, $1000 is .20, $1500 is .30 and $2000 is .40. Using a decision tree analysis, determine Steve's optimal strategy for dealing with his roof.

9. Brenton Software Publishing Company (BSP) offers its sales representatives a choice of three compensation plans based on how many universities adopt Brenton's new statistical software package. The three plans are as follows:

   Plan 1: A fixed salary of $2000 per month.
   Plan 2: A fixed salary of $1000 per month plus a commission of $300 for each university that adopts the statistical package.
   Plan 3: A commission of $700 for each university that adopts the statistical package.

   Ted Benson is a new sales representative for BSP and must decide which compensation plan to accept. Experienced sales representatives have told him that he can expect that up to six universities per month will adopt the software. Ted is free to change his compensation plan at the beginning of any month.

   a. Construct a payoff table showing Ted's monthly compensation as a function of the compensation plan he chooses and the monthly adoptions.
   b. Which plan should Ted choose if he uses the minimax regret criterion?
   c. Suppose Ted believes that the following probabilities hold regarding monthly adoptions for his first month with the firm:

   $$P(0 \text{ adoptions}) = .10$$
   $$P(1 \text{ adoption}) = .15$$
   $$P(2 \text{ adoptions}) = .25$$
   $$P(3 \text{ adoptions}) = .20$$
   $$P(4 \text{ adoptions}) = .15$$
   $$P(5 \text{ adoptions}) = .10$$
   $$P(6 \text{ adoptions}) = .05$$

   On the basis of these data, which compensation plan should Ted select for the upcoming month?

10. The town of Boswell, British Columbia, has two bed and breakfast resorts: Kootenay Rose and Kootenay Lake Lodge. Currently, the Kootenay Rose gets 35% of the town's bookings, and the Kootenay Lake Lodge gets 65% of the town's bookings. Each season the two resorts prepare a brochure stressing different aspects of the resort. These include room price, recreational facilities, breakfast quality, and room décor. The following table gives the change in the expected market share of the Kootenay Rose based on its and the Kootenay Lake Lodge's brochure's principal focus.

		Kootenay Lake Lodge			
		Room Price	Recreational Facilities	Breakfast Quality	Room Décor
Kootenay Rose	Room Price	−2	−4	+6	+1
	Recreational Facilities	+2	−2	+3	−1
	Breakfast Quality	−4	+1	+2	−3
	Room Decor	+1	−3	−6	+3

a. Determine the optimal strategy for the Kootenay Rose to use in preparing the principal focus of their advertising brochure.
b. What will be the expected change in the market share for the Kootenay Rose?

11. Southern Homes is a home builder located in a suburb of Atlanta. The company must decide whether to leave its model homes unfurnished, furnish them with minimal accessories, or completely furnish them using a custom decorator. The new-home market is generally quite profitable, but Southern is suffering cash flow problems. The following table gives the expected profit per lot for Southern Homes based on how Southern furnishes its model homes and the overall demand for housing in the Atlanta market:

Model Furnishing	Housing Market in Atlanta			
	Weak	Moderate	Strong	Very Strong
Unfurnished	−$1,500	$1,000	$2,000	$3,000
Minimal Accessories	−$4,000	$ 500	$3,500	$6,000
Custom Decorated	−$7,000	$1,500	$2,500	$9,500

a. If Southern management is conservative, how should it decorate the model homes?
b. If Southern believes that each state of nature is equally likely, how should it decorate the model homes? What approach did you use?

12. Consider the data given in problem 11 for Southern Homes. Although Southern management believes that each state of nature is equally likely, it is also considering hiring an economic forecaster to improve the probability estimates for the states of nature. The forecaster will predict whether there will be an above-average, average, or below-average rise in the GNP for the upcoming year. Based on past experience, the following conditional probabilities are believed to hold for the forecaster's predictions:

P(above average rise|Weak Housing Market) = .1
P(above average rise|Moderate Housing Market) = .3
P(above average rise|Strong Housing Market) = .6
P(above average rise|Very Strong Housing Market) = .9
P(average rise|Weak Housing Market) = .3
P(average rise|Moderate Housing Market) = .4
P(average rise|Strong Housing Market) = .2
P(average rise|Very Strong Housing Market) = .1
P(below average rise|Weak Housing Market) = .6
P(below average rise|Moderate Housing Market) = .3
P(below average rise|Strong Housing Market) = .2
P(below average rise|Very Strong Housing Market) = 0

a. How should Southern decorate the homes if the forecaster predicts: (i) an above-average rise in GNP? (ii) an average rise in GNP? (iii) a below-average rise in GNP?
b. What is the expected value of the forecaster's information?
c. What is the efficiency of the forecaster's information?

d. The data for this problem were constructed to illustrate the concept of the Bayesian decision process. Realistically, do you feel that GNP is a good indicator for housing sales in Atlanta? List some other indicators that might yield a higher efficiency.

13. Ken Golden has just purchased a franchise from Paper Warehouse to open a party goods store in a newly developed suburb of Orlando, Florida. Paper Warehouse offers three sizes of stores that franchisees can develop: Standard Store—4000 square feet, Super Store—6500 square feet, or MegaStore—8500 square feet. Ken estimates the present worth profitability of this store will be based on the size of the store he selects to build as well as the number of competing party goods stores that will open in the suburb. He feels that between one and four stores will open to compete with his. Ken has developed the following payoff table (showing estimated present worth profits in $10,000s) to help him in his decision making.

	Number of Competing Stores That Will Open			
Type of Store	1	2	3	4
Standard	30	25	10	5
Super	60	40	30	20
Mega	100	65	15	−100

a. If Ken is an optimistic decision maker, what size store should he open?
b. If Ken wishes to minimize his maximum regret, what size store should he open?
c. Ken believes that there is a 50% chance that two competing stores will open and that the likelihood that four competing stores will open is half the likelihood that three competing stores will open and three times the likelihood that one competing store will open. If Ken uses the expected value criterion, which size store should he open?

14. BMW is planning to launch a new sport utility vehicle (SUV). Initially it will have limited production for this model, with a total of only 20,000 units being produced for the year. King's BMW has been offered up to four of the SUV's for sale. King's estimates that the profit it earns from purchasing these SUV's will be based on the review it receives from *Road and Track* magazine. The review will give the SUV one of five ratings: poor, good, very good, excellent, or outstanding. The following table gives the profitability Jan King estimates the dealership will earn from ordering the SUV's based on the rating the vehicle receives.

	Review in *Road and Track*				
SUV's Ordered	Poor	Good	Very Good	Excellent	Out-standing
0	$2,000	$5,000	$3,000	−$1,000	−$4,000
1	−$1,000	$3,000	$6,000	$4,000	$1,000
2	−$5,000	−$1,000	$4,000	$8,000	$9,000
3	−$9,000	−$4,000	$3,000	$12,000	$15,000
4	−$14,000	−$7,000	$2,000	$12,000	$20,000

How many SUV's should the firm order if
a. It uses the maximin criterion.
b. It uses the minimax regret criterion.
c. It uses the principle of insufficient reason criterion.

15. Consider the data given in problem 14. Based on some preliminary information provided by BMW, Jan King estimates that the following probabilities hold for the states of nature: P(Poor review) = .10, P(Good review) = .15, P(Very Good review) = .25, and P(Excellent review) = .35.
a. Calculate the probability of an Outstanding review and use the expected value criterion to determine how many SUV's King's should order.
b. What is the most amount of money King's should pay for advance information regarding the review the SUV will get from *Road and Track*.

16. The dean of the School of Business at Northern Connecticut State University has been approached by a government agency in Hunan Province, China, to provide MBA training to a group of 30 midlevel officials. The dean is considering submitting a bid of $225,000, $250,000, or $300,000 for providing this program. If the bid is $225,000, the dean estimates there is a 90% chance that the school will get the contract. This probability decreases to .60 if the bid is $250,000 and .20 if the bid is $300,000.

Materials are expected to cost an average of $1000 per participant. The dean estimates that she will have to pay total faculty salaries of either $180,000 or $220,000. There is a 40% chance that the faculty union will accept $180,000 and a 60% chance that the union will hold out for $220,000.

Using a decision tree approach, determine the dean's optimal strategy.

17. The Jeffrey William Company is considering introducing a new line of Christmas tree ornaments that glow in the dark and play melodies. If it introduces the product, it will back it up with a $100,000 advertising campaign using the slogan "let your tree sing out in joy." The company estimates that sales will be a function of the economy and demand will be for 10,000, 50,000, or 100,000 cases. Each case nets the company $24 and costs $18 to produce (not including the expense of the advertising campaign). Because the ornaments will be produced in a factory in Asia, the firm must order in multiples of 40,000 cases. Any unsold cases can be sold to a liquidator for $15 per case. If the company introduces the product and demand for the ornaments exceeds availability, management estimates it will suffer a goodwill loss of $1 for each case the company is short.
a. Determine the payoff table for this problem.
b. If the company president wishes to minimize the firm's maximum regret, what decision will she make regarding the ornaments?
c. Suppose demand for 100,000 ornaments is twice as likely as demand for 10,000 ornaments, and demand for 50,000 ornaments is three times as likely as demand for 100,000 ornaments. What decision should the company make using the expected value criterion?

d. Suppose the company can conduct a marketing survey to get a better idea of the demand for the ornaments. What is the most the company should pay for any such survey?

18. Consider the data given in problem 17 for the Jeffrey William Company. Suppose the firm uses a utility function of the form $U(x) = \left(\dfrac{x + 37}{81}\right)^2$ (where x is the firm's expected profit in $10,000s).

    a. Would you characterize the firm as risk averse, risk loving, or risk neutral?
    b. Using the expected utility criterion, determine the firm's optimal strategy.

19. Mildred Smith has a friend who claims she can tell whether cream is added to coffee before or after the coffee is poured. Mildred's prior belief of her friend's claim is 20%. That is, she believes that the probability her friend's claim is true is .20. Mildred decides to test her friend's claim by making 10 cups of coffee and not showing her friend how the coffee was prepared. To prepare the coffee, she flips a coin. If the coin comes up heads she adds cream to the coffee, and if the coin comes up tails she adds coffee to the cream. Mildred's friend correctly identifies how the coffee was made in each of the 10 cases. What should Mildred's posterior belief be regarding her friend's claim?

20. Marriott Hotels is planning to build a new hotel property in a suburb of Portland, Oregon. The company is considering one of four sizes of hotels to construct: 120 rooms, 200 rooms, 260 rooms, or 320 rooms. Construction will take one year to complete. Profitability of the property will, to a great extent, depend on whether an industrial park or a university is developed in the area. The following table gives the long-term present worth profit (in $100,000s) based on the size of hotel constructed and the development that could take place in the area.

	Type of Development to Occur			
Room Size	None	Industrial Park Only	University Only	Industrial Park and University
120	12	22	18	30
200	8	28	25	40
260	3	34	28	48
320	−10	30	22	65

Marriott management estimates that there is a 60% chance that an industrial park will be developed and a 30% chance that the university will be developed. The two developments are believed to be independent of each other. Determine the optimal size hotel Marriott should construct based on the expected value criterion.

21. Bill Peterson has been offered the opportunity to invest $15,000 in a start-up company that intends to supply personal digital assistants (PDAs) to physicians in order to enable them to determine the approved medication for each HMO patient they treat. The business plan for this start-up calls for raising a total of between $10 million and $40 million in financing and then taking the company public.

To be successful in raising these funds, the firm must first be able to hire a respected professional in the medical industry to be the firm's CEO. Bill believes that there is a 60% chance of the firm accomplishing this requirement. Following the hiring of the CEO, the firm will also need to get backing from at least two of the leading four HMOs. Bill believes that there is a 30% chance that each of the leading four HMOs will want to be involved in this project. If two HMOs sign on to the project, Bill believes the firm can raise $10 million. Bill believes that the firm can raise an additional $5 million for each additional HMO that signs on to the project.

Once the HMOs have signed on, the firm must then recruit physicians to adopt the system. If fewer than 5000 physicians agree to sign on to test the system, the project will fail. Bill believes that there is only a 35% chance that the firm will be able to recruit 5000 or more physicians. Finally, if the firm is successful in getting HMO and physician support, it will try to get two major drug chains to each invest $10 million. The likelihood of one drug chain investing is 30%, and the likelihood of two drug chains investing is 10%.

If the project fails to hire a CEO, recruit at least 5000 physicians, or to raise at least $10 million, Bill feels he will lose his entire investment. Bill estimates the following profits on his investment if the firm is successful in raising the required funds.

Amount Firm Raises (in $millions)	Bill's Profit
10	$60,000
15	$100,000
20	$130,000
25	$180,000
30	$250,000
35	$350,000
40	$500,000

On the basis of this data, determine whether Bill should invest the $15,000.

22. TV Town must decide how many, if any, new Panasony 50-inch television sets to order for next month. The sets cost TV Town $1850 each and sell for $2450 each. Because Panasony is coming out with a new line of big-screen television sets in a month, any sets not sold during the month will have to be marked down to 50% of the normal retail price to be sold at the TV Town Clearance Center. TV Town estimates that if it does not have enough television sets on hand to satisfy demand, it will suffer a goodwill loss of $150 for each customer who cannot get a set. TV Town management feels that the maximum customer demand over the next month will be for three big-screen sets. Defining the states of nature to correspond to the number of sets demanded by customers and the decision alternatives to the number of sets ordered, determine the payoff table for TV Town.

23. Consider the data given in problem 22 for TV Town. Suppose the manager of TV Town estimates customer demand for next month as follows:

$$P(\text{demand} = 0 \text{ sets}) = .20$$
$$P(\text{demand} = 1 \text{ set}) = .30$$
$$P(\text{demand} = 2 \text{ sets}) = .30$$
$$P(\text{demand} = 3 \text{ sets}) = .20$$

   a. How many Panasony big-screen television sets should TV Town order?
   b. The manager of TV Town is considering conducting a telephone survey of 30 randomly selected customers. The survey will determine whether at least one of the 30 is likely to buy a big-screen set within the next month. What is the maximum amount TV Town should pay for the telephone survey?

24. Consider the data given in problems 22 and 23 for TV Town. Suppose the manager of TV Town believes that the following conditional probabilities hold for the telephone survey being conducted on 30 randomly selected customers:

$$P(\text{At Least One Survey Customer Likely to}$$
$$\text{Buy}|\text{Demand} = 0) = .1$$
$$P(\text{At Least One Survey Customer Likely to}$$
$$\text{Buy}|\text{Demand} = 1) = .2$$
$$P(\text{At Least One Survey Customer Likely to}$$
$$\text{Buy}|\text{Demand} = 2) = .4$$
$$P(\text{At Least One Survey Customer Likely to}$$
$$\text{Buy}|\text{Demand} = 3) = .7$$

   a. If TV Town conducts the survey, what is the optimal strategy for ordering the Panasony big-screen television sets?
   b. What is the most amount of money TV Town should pay for this telephone survey?
   c. What is the efficiency of the telephone survey?
   d. Discuss in general terms how the results of the survey could be modified to result in improved efficiency.

25. The AMC 24-plex cinema is trying to decide how many screens it should have showing the new action comedy movie *Lost Wages in Las Vegas*. The theater must sign a contract with the movie's distributor indicating how many screens it will play the movie on before reviews of the movie are public. The manager has decided, based on the actors involved in the movie, to devote between one and five screens to this movie during its two-week summer run. The profit the manager expects to earn on the movie is based on the consensus review of the movie (one to four stars). The payoff table showing these estimated profits is as follows.

# of Screens	Consensus Rating			
	*	**	***	****
One	−200	600	400	−100
Two	−800	100	1200	600
Three	−1800	−500	1100	1200
Four	−2500	−1500	700	1900
Five	−4000	−2000	300	3500

   a. If the theater manager wishes to minimize his maximum regret, how many screens should the movie be booked in?
   b. If the theater manager is risk averse and wishes to use the maximin criterion, how many screens should the movie be booked in?
   c. Suppose the theater manager believes, based on the director's previous releases, that the probability the movie will be rated one star is .10, two stars .20, three stars .40, and four stars .30. If the manager wishes to use the expected value criterion, how many screens should the movie be booked in?

26. Consider the situation faced by the theater manager in problem 25. Suppose the probabilities given in part c hold.
   a. What is the most amount of money the theater manager should pay for advance information regarding the review the movie will receive?
   b. The theater manager can subscribe to "Advance Screening," a rating service that purports to predict the review a movie will receive. The rating service either gives the movie a "thumbs up" or a "thumbs down." Based on previous predictions made by this service, the manager believes the following conditional probabilities hold.

$$P(\text{Thumbs Up}|\text{One Star}) = .20$$
$$P(\text{Thumbs Up}|\text{Two Stars}) = .40$$
$$P(\text{Thumbs Up}|\text{Three Stars}) = .60$$
$$P(\text{Thumbs Up}|\text{Four Stars}) = .90$$

   If "Advance Screenings" wants a fee of $50 for giving its prediction, should the theater manager purchase the information?
   c. What is the efficiency of "Advance Screenings" information?

27. Bees Candy Company must decide whether or not to introduce a new lower-calorie candy assortment for Christmas. Management feels that if it introduces the candy, it will earn a profit of $150,000 if sales are 70,000 pounds and a profit of $50,000 if sales are 40,000 pounds. It will lose $100,000 if sales are only 10,000 pounds. If Bees does not introduce the lower-calorie candy assortment, it believes it will lose $20,000 due to lost sales.
   a. Construct a payoff table for this problem.
   b. Should Bees introduce the candy if management is conservative?
   c. Construct a regret table for this problem.
   d. If Bees management uses the minimax regret criterion, should the new candy be introduced?

28. Consider the information given in problem 27 for Bees Candy. Suppose Bees management believes that the following probabilities hold:

$$P(\text{Sales} = 70,000 \text{ pounds}) = .2$$
$$P(\text{Sales} = 40,000 \text{ pounds}) = .5$$
$$P(\text{Sales} = 10,000 \text{ pounds}) = .3$$

   a. Using the expected value criterion, determine whether the company should introduce the lower-calorie candy assortment.

Bees is considering hiring a market consulting firm to analyze people's attitudes toward lower-calorie candy. The market research firm will report back to Bees management whether attitudes are favorable or unfavorable. Management believes that the following conditional probabilities hold:

P(favorable attitude|Sales = 70,000 pounds) = .90
P(favorable attitude|Sales = 40,000 pounds) = .60
P(favorable attitude|Sales = 10,000 pounds) = .20

b. If the survey is performed and results in a favorable attitude toward lower-calorie candy, would you recommend that the candy be produced?

c. Determine the expected value and efficiency of this sample information.

29. Craig Computer Company (CCC) manufactures supercomputers based on parallel processing technology. Next month the firm has scheduled demonstrations for its new Model 4365 with four potential customers. This model sells for $725,000 and CCC believes that the probability of each customer purchasing a computer is 30%. The company cannot completely shut down its assembly line over the next month and plans to manufacture at least one computer; it could manufacture as many as four. Production costs for the month are as follows:

Number of Computers Built	Total Production Costs
1	$ 800,000
2	$1,400,000
3	$1,800,000
4	$2,400,000

Any computers Craig manufactures during a given month but does not sell are exported overseas. Craig receives $500,000 for these computers and can sell as many as it is willing to export. If Craig sells more computers than it manufactures in a month, the customer must wait for delivery. In this case, Craig estimates it loses a total of $30,000 on the sale.

a. Determine the payoff table for this problem.
b. What decision alternatives are undominated?
c. Determine the optimal strategy using the expected value criterion. (*Hint: The binomial distribution can be used to determine the probabilities for the states of nature.*)

30. Stefan Chirac has a cabana rental business in the exclusive resort of St. Tropez. Stefan can handle up to four cabanas daily. These must be assembled in the morning and taken down in the evening. Stefan pays the company he gets the cabanas from a rental fee of $50 per cabana per day, and he rents the cabanas to tourists for either $80 or $100 per day.

The weather in St. Tropez is either rainy, cloudy, or sunny. Each day there is a 10% chance of rainy weather, a 20% chance of cloudy weather, and a 70% chance of sunny weather. While Stefan must decide how many cabanas to rent before knowing what the weather will be, he can set the rental price after determining the day's weather.

If the weather is rainy, there will be no rental demand. If the weather is cloudy, demand will follow a Poisson distribution with a mean of 2 if Stefan charges $80 for the rental and a mean of 1.5 if Stefan charges $100. If the weather is sunny, demand will follow a Poisson distribution with a mean of 4 if Stefan charges $80 and a mean of 3 if Stefan charges $100. Using a decision tree analysis, determine how many cabanas Stefan should rent and what price he should charge if the weather is cloudy or sunny.

31. Zeus Athletic Wear is in the process of lining up potential Olympic athletes to endorse its planned line of sports apparel in company advertisements. Zeus is quite interested in signing Dan Miller, an athlete who will be vying for a medal in the decathlon. The firm has been negotiating with Dan's agent for a two-year contract (six months before the upcoming games and a year and a half afterward). The parties have discussed one of three arrangements.

I. Dan will work exclusively for Zeus and be paid $1 million.
II. Dan will work for Zeus on a semi-exclusive basis (he can also work for at most one other noncompeting firm) and be paid $400,000.
III. Dan will be a Zeus-sponsored athlete. This means that Zeus will supply Dan's garments but Dan will not appear in advertisements for Zeus. Dan will be paid $100,000 for this arrangement.

Zeus's management estimates that the gain in profitability it will achieve from its association with Dan will be a function of the type of medal, if any, Dan wins at the Olympics. Based on the results of previous advertising campaigns involving Olympic medal winners, management has prepared the following payoff table. (The figures are profits or losses in $100,000s.)

Compensation Arrangement	Medal Won by Dan at the Olympics			
	Gold	Silver	Bronze	None
Plan I	100	20	10	−20
Plan II	60	40	20	−5
Plan III	15	10	5	0

According to sports pundits, Dan has a 20% chance of wining a gold medal, a 30% chance of winning a silver medal, and a 10% chance of wining a bronze medal. Which endorsement plan should Zeus management select?

32. In the game of rock, scissors, paper, each of two players simultaneously puts out either a fist (for rock), two fingers (for scissors), or an open hand (for paper). If player 1 puts out rock and player 2 puts out scissors, then player 1 wins (rock breaks scissors). Alternatively, if player 1 puts out rock and player 2 puts out paper, then player 2 wins (paper covers rock). If player 1 puts out scissors and player 2 puts out paper, then player 1 wins (scissors cuts paper). If both players put out the same

symbol, the game is a draw. The following is the payoff table from player 1's point of view:

		PLAYER 2		
		Rock	Scissors	Paper
	Rock	0	1	−1
PLAYER 1	Scissors	−1	0	1
	Paper	1	−1	0

Determine the optimal strategies for players 1 and 2 for this game.

33. Roney Construction Company is considering purchasing a home in the historic district of Lexington, Massachusetts, for restoration. The cost of the home is $150,000, and Roney believes that, after restoration, the home can be sold for $290,000. Roney will pay $2000 per month in finance charges until the project is completed.

    The company's architect has developed two sets of plans for the restoration. Plan A does not require changes to the front facade. Under this plan, the renovation will cost $120,000 and take three months to complete. Plan B does involve changes in the front facade of the building. Under this plan, Roney believes that it can do the restoration work in four months, at a cost of $80,000.

    Because Plan B changes the exterior of the house, it must be approved by the town's Historic Commission. The approval process takes two months and will cost $10,000. If Roney decides on Plan B, it can play it safe and wait to begin construction until after the plan has been approved by the Historic Commission. Alternatively, it can take a chance and begin construction immediately in the hopes that the commission will approve the plan.

    If the Historic Commission denies Plan B, Roney will have to resort to Plan A for the renovation work. If Roney begins construction under Plan B and the Historic Commission denies the plan, the company estimates that doing the construction work under Plan A will cost $140,000 and the project will take five additional months to complete.

    Roney estimates that there is a 40% chance that the Historic Commission will approve Plan B. However, if the firm were to contribute $6000 to the mayor's reelection campaign, Roney believes the chances for approval would increase to 50%. Determine an optimal strategy for the Roney Construction Company.

34. Steve Greene is considering purchasing fire insurance for his home. According to statistics for Steve's county, Steve estimates the damage from fire to his home in a given year is as follows:

Amount of Damage	Probability
0	.975
$10,000	.010
$20,000	.008
$30,000	.004
$50,000	.002
$100,000	.001

a. If Steve is risk neutral, how much should he be willing to pay for the fire insurance?
b. Suppose Steve's utility values are as follows:

	Amount of Loss ($1000s)						
	100	50	30	20	10	1	0
Utility	0	.65	.75	.8	.95	.995	1

What is the expected utility corresponding to fire damage?
c. Determine approximately how much Steve would be willing to pay for the fire insurance.

35. Rolley's Rentals of Lahaina, Hawaii, rents bicycles and roller skates. Mr. Rolley is considering expanding his line of bicycle rentals to include tandem bicycles. He estimates that he will need a maximum of three tandem bicycles to handle estimated demand for the upcoming year.

    Profitability from the tandem bicycles in the upcoming year will be a function of the number of tandem bicycles purchased and the number of sunny days during the year in Lahaina. To help him determine how many tandem bicycles to purchase, Mr. Rolley has developed the following payoff table representing expected profits.

Number of Tandem Bicycles to Purchase	Number of Sunny Days in Lahaina During Upcoming Year			
	250	275	300	325
0	0	0	0	0
1	−140	80	130	220
2	−130	120	180	280
3	−160	−10	250	400

a. What decision alternatives, if any, are dominated?
b. If Rolley's wishes to minimize its maximum regret, how many tandem bicycles should it purchase?
c. Suppose that Rolley's believes that the likelihood of 250 sunny days in Lahaina over the upcoming year is equal to the probability of 325 sunny days. In addition, the probability of 300 sunny days is twice as great as the probability of 325 sunny days and three times as great as the probability of 275 sunny days. Using the expected monetary criterion, determine how many tandem bicycles Rolley's should purchase.

36. The Post Office uses two freight carriers, Federal Parcel and Emery Express, to carry mail between New York and Boston. Federal Parcel has 30% of this business, and Emery Express has 70%. The Post Office is interested in signing an exclusive contract with one of the carriers to handle the mail between the cities. Federal Parcel is considering bidding either $0.02, $0.04, or $0.06 per ounce as the fee charged the Post Office. Emery Express is considering bidding either $0.02, $0.05, or $0.06 per ounce as the fee charged the Post Office. The carrier who submits the lower bid will get the contract; if both bids are the same, the Post Office will use the carriers to carry an equal amount of mail.

The following table describes the change in market share that Federal Parcel will experience as a function of the amount that the two carriers bid.

		Emery Express's Bid		
		$.02	$.05	$.06
Federal Parcel's Bid	$.02	+20%	+70%	+70%
	$.04	−30%	+70%	+70%
	$.06	−30%	−30%	+20%

a. What is Federal Parcel's optimal strategy if it wishes to maximize its expected change in market share?

b. Suppose that Federal Parcel estimates that the total weight the Post Office will be sending between the two cities this year will be 1.5 million pounds. Federal Parcel estimates that serving this route will cost it a fixed amount of $20,000 plus $0.01 per ounce. If Emery Express is believed to be equally likely to bid $0.02, $0.05, or $0.06 per pound, what should Federal Parcel's bid be in order to maximize its expected profit?

37. Consider the following two-player game played in a particular office lunch room. Player 1 picks an integer between 1 and 4, and player 2 picks an integer between 3 and 6. If the sum of the two numbers equals 7, player 2 wins $8 from player 1. If the sum of the two numbers equals 6, player 1 wins $6 from player 2. If the sum of the two numbers equals 9, player 1 wins $9 from player 2. If the sum of the numbers is anything other than 6, 7, or 9, the game is a tie and neither player wins or loses.

Determine the expected strategy for player 1 and the expected value of this game to player 1.

38. Two oil brokerage firms, Murphy Company and Sardon Brothers, supply heating oil to 10 oil delivery companies in northern New Jersey. Each day the two brokerage firms fax their offering prices to these delivery companies, and the delivery companies purchase their daily needs from the firm that has the cheapest offering price. (If both brokerage firms have the same offering price, Murphy Company tends to get 40% of the business, while Sardon Brothers gets 60%.)

The two oil brokers' offering price is pegged at $0.01, $0.02, or $0.03 above the New York spot price of Number 2 fuel oil. The management science analyst working for Sardon Brothers believes that the following payoff table holds regarding the expected daily profit earned by Sardon Brothers based on its and Murphy Company's offering price.

The management scientist also believes that Murphy Company will use an offering price of Spot + $.0.01 with probability 30% and an offering price of Spot + $0.02 with probability 50%.

a. If the company's objective is to maximize its expected daily profit, what should Sardon Brothers use as an offering price?

b. What is the most that Sardon Brothers should pay for information that would improve its probability estimates for Murphy Company's pricing strategy?

c. Suppose Sardon Brothers uses the following utility function: $U(x) = 2^{(x+600)/1600} - 1$. (For example, the utility of a $200 profit to the company equals $2^{(200+600)/1600} - 1 = 2^{(1/2)} - 1 = 1.41 - 1 = .41$.) Would you characterize Sardon Brothers as risk averse, risk neutral, or risk loving?

d. Using the utility function given in part (c), what offering price should Sardon Brothers use for the oil if its objective is to maximize its expected utility?

39. United Aerospace has been invited to bid on doing the development work for a new U.S. Air Force bomber. United estimates that the cost of doing the development work will depend on potential technical difficulties but will be either $150 million or $200 million. United estimates that it is three times more likely that the cost will be $150 million than $200 million.

United is planning to bid $125 million, $175 million, $200 million, or $225 million for this project. If it bids $125 million, it feels that there is a 85% chance it will win the contract, whereas if it bids $175 million it feels that there is a 70% chance it will get the contract. If the firm bids $200 million it feels that the chance of winning the contract decreases to 40%, and if the firm bids $225 million it feels that there is only a 15% chance that it will win the contract.

Following the development work, the Air Force will want to hire a firm to build 100 of these bombers. If United Aerospace wins the development contract, it feels that it will have the inside track for winning the contract to build the 100 bombers. Specifically, United Aerospace believes that there is a 70% chance that it will win this contract, whereas if it does not do the development work, the chance of the firm getting the contract to build the bombers is only 15%. On the building project, United Aerospace estimates that there is a 30% chance it would earn $300 million, a 40% chance that it would earn $100 million, a 20% chance that it would earn $50 million, and a 10% chance that it would lose $75 million.

Determine United Aerospace's optimal strategy for bidding on the development project.

Table for Problem 38

		Murphy Company Offering Price		
		Spot + $0.01	Spot + $0.02	Spot + $0.03
Sardon Brothers	Spot + $0.01	$160	$420	$420
Offering Price	Spot + $0.02	−$600	$300	$1000
	Spot + $.0.03	−$600	−$600	$500

40. Little Trykes is considering offering a toy scooter that it will sell for $20 each. The company has two production options:

(i) Manufacture the scooters in their existing facilities.

(ii) Import the scooters from overseas

Little Trykes believes that the demand for the scooters will be between 100 and 300 units per day and has decided to model the situation as a decision analysis problem with three states of nature: demand = 100 units per day; demand = 200 units per day; and demand = 300 units per day. This was done because the company will either manufacture or import the units in lot sizes that are multiples of 100. The following table gives the per unit costs for the two production options.

	Amount Supplied Per Day		
Option	100	200	300
Use Existing Facilities	$18	$14	$10
Import	$15	$13	$ 9

PROBLEMS 41–50 ARE ON THE CD

If the company decides to import the scooters, there is a 30% chance that a tariff of $2 per unit will be imposed on the scooters. The company will learn whether there is a tariff only after it has made its decision on the source of its scooter production. The amount produced or imported will correspond to daily demand. The probability distribution for daily demand with no advertising versus spending $1000 a day on advertising is as follows:

Daily Demand	Probability with No Advertising	Probability with Spending $1000 a Day for Advertising
100	.3	.1
200	.5	.2
300	.2	.7

Determine Little Trykes's optimal course of action regarding manufacturing, importing, and advertising the scooters.

CASE STUDIES

CASE 1: Swan Valley Farms

Swan Valley Farms produces dried apricots, which it sells to two cereal producers—Kellogg's and General Foods. Swan Valley forecasts that for the upcoming year Kellogg's will want to purchase either 10, 20, or 30 tons of dried apricots, and General Foods will want to purchase either 10, 20, 30, or 40 tons. Kellogg's and General Foods order independently of each other. The following probability distributions are believed to hold:

Kellogg's Demand	Probability	General Food's Demand	Probability
10 tons	.20	10 tons	.20
20 tons	.50	20 tons	.30
30 tons	.30	30 tons	.30
		40 tons	.20

Swan Valley is currently contracting with local farmers for delivery of apricots for drying. It takes approximately four pounds of apricots to produce one pound of dried apricots. Swan Valley can purchase apricots at $0.15 per pound; it costs an additional $0.02 to produce one pound of dried apricots.

Swan Valley's contract with Kellogg's and General Foods calls for purchase in units of 10 tons at a price of $1500 per ton plus delivery costs.

The process of drying apricots takes several weeks; therefore, Swan Valley must sign its contract with growers before it knows the exact amount that Kellogg's and Gen-

eral Foods will be ordering. If Swan Valley dries more apricots than its two customers demand, it will sell the surplus dried apricots to a food wholesaler at a price of $1100 per ton, plus delivery. If Swan Valley produces fewer dried apricots than the two cereal manufacturers demand, it can purchase additional dried apricots from a competitor at a price of $1400 per ton.

Swan Valley is considering offering one of two new pricing plans. Under the first plan, Swan Valley will lower its selling price to $1400 a ton if the cereal company agrees to order four months in advance of delivery. This will enable Swan Valley to know how many apricots will be demanded by a customer prior to its having to contract with growers. The company believes that there is a 30% chance that Kellogg's will accept this offer and a 40% chance that General Foods will accept this offer.

Under the second plan, Swan Valley will lower the selling price to $1375 a ton if the cereal company agrees to order four months in advance of delivery. Swan Valley believes there is a 60% chance that Kellogg's will accept this plan and an 80% chance that General Foods will accept.

Prepare a business report to Henry Swan, owner of Swan Valley Farms, giving your recommendation as to which of the two pricing plans, if any, the firm should adopt. Include in your report a recommendation for the number of pounds of apricots Swan Valley should purchase from farmers and the expected profit the company will earn.

CASE 2: Pharmgen Corporation

Pharmgen Corporation has developed a new medication for the treatment of high blood pressure. Tests on laboratory animals have been promising, and the firm is ready to embark on human trials in order to gain approval from the Food and Drug Administration (FDA). The firm estimates that it will cost an additional $4 million to do the required testing. Although the firm has this amount of money available, if the product turns out to be unsuccessful, the company will be virtually wiped out.

If the tests prove successful, the firm believes that the amount it will earn on the drug will be a function of the number of competing drugs of this type that also gain approval. If no other drugs gain approval, the firm estimates it will earn $50 million in present worth profits on the drug. For every other drug that gains approval, Pharmgen believes the expected present worth profit will

drop by $10 million. Based on industry publications, four other firms are working on similar drugs. Pharmgen's management estimates that the probability that its drug will gain FDA approval is 40% but that each of its four competitors' drugs only has a 20% chance of FDA approval.

Wyler Laboratories, a larger drug firm, has approached Pharmgen about acquiring the rights to the drug. Wyler is willing to pay Pharmgen $5 million for a half interest in the drug (and split any costs or profits from the drug with Pharmgen) or $8 million for the full rights to the drug. Pharmgen's management has used the indifference approach to determine the utility values shown below.

Prepare a business report to Dr. Joseph Wolf, president of Pharmgen, detailing your recommendation regarding the development of this drug.

Expected Present Worth Profit or Loss (in Millions)	−4	3	8	10	15	20	25	30	40	50
Utility	0	.30	.40	.45	.50	.55	.65	.75	.85	1.0

CASE 3: Pickens Exploration Company

Pickens Exploration Company has been offered a lease to drill for oil on a particular piece of property. While oil has been found on nearby land, there are no assurances that Pickens will be successful in finding oil. The company feels that it will strike either a major find, an average find, or a dry hole. A major find can be sold to an oil company for $6 million, while an average find will only bring in $2 million. A dry hole will cost the company $80,000 to cap.

The cost of the lease is $400,000 plus 20% of the revenue if the oil well is sold to an oil company. Pickens estimates that it can drill a well at a cost of $160,000. Without further testing, Pickens' geologist estimates that there is a 5% chance that the well will be a major find, a 35% chance that it will be an average find, and a 60% chance that it will be a dry hole.

In order to get a better estimate of the probability of finding oil in the well, the geologist is contemplating performing either a geologic or a seismic test. A geologic test will cost $20,000. If the test predicts oil, the geologist believes that the following probabilities hold:

P(test predicts oil|major find) = .70
P(test predicts oil|average find) = .50
P(test predicts oil|dry hole) = .30

Instead of the geologic test, the firm can perform the more detailed seismic test, which costs $50,000. If this test predicts oil, the geologist believes that the following probabilities hold:

P(test predicts oil|major find) = .90
P(test predicts oil|average find) = .70
P(test predicts oil|dry hole) = .10

Pickens can do the testing prior to deciding whether or not to procure the lease. If Pickens gets a prediction of oil from either the geologic or seismic tests, it can sell a half-interest in the well to a Dallas investor for $800,000. In this case Pickens will be responsible for any and all losses on the well should it lose money, but will split profits on the well equally with the investor.

Prepare a business report that recommends Pickens' optimal strategy. Include in your report an analysis of the change in probability estimates due to the outcomes of the geologic and seismic tests.

CASE 4 IS ON THE CD

Forecasting

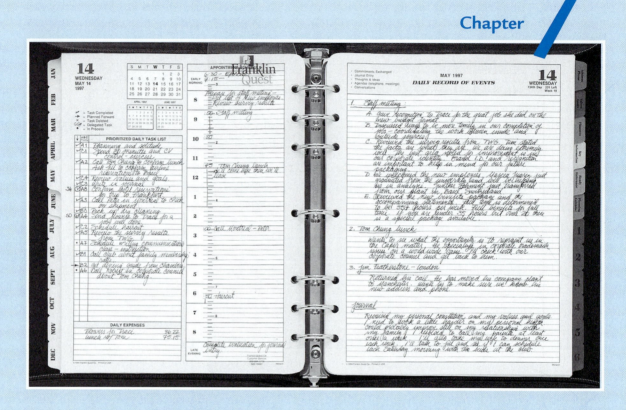

F**RANKLIN**C**OVEY** **(http://www.franklincovey. com)** **IS** the leading learning and performance services firm assisting professionals and organizations in measurably increasing their effectiveness in leadership, productivity, communication, and sales. It is a manufacturer of pocket calendars and executive organizing systems. Since these systems are printed for a specific year, much of the firm's production has a limited shelf life. More than 60% of the retail sales of the company's products occur from the middle of October through the middle of the following January. As a re- sult, the firm's sales to distributors and national retail accounts are concentrated between August through November.

While FranklinCovey has been a leading manufacturer of such high-end products, due to an increased use of Personal Digital Assistants (PDA's), recently the firm has found itself left with a substantial amount of unsold inventory. In order to plan production properly for the future calendar years, company management has proposed developing a system for forecasting retail demand for its products.

7.1 Introduction to Time Series Forecasting

Forecasting is the process of predicting the future. It is an integral part of almost all business enterprises. Manufacturing firms forecast demand for their products in order to have the necessary manpower and raw materials to support production. Companies specializing in service operations forecast customer arrival patterns in an effort to maintain adequate staffing to serve customer needs. Security analysts forecast company revenues, profits, and debt ratios, as well as general trends in financial markets, in order to make investment recommendations. Numerous firms consider economic forecasts of indicators, such as housing starts and changes in the gross national profit, before deciding on capital investments.

Forecasting Time Series with Trend, Seasonal, and Cyclical Variation

A college is trying to forecast its upcoming annual expenditures. The forecasting model used accounts for variations in expenditures due to the differing number of classes offered each quarter. (See problem 34.)

Proper forecasting can result in reduced inventory costs, lower overall personnel costs, and increased customer satisfaction. By contrast, poor forecasting can result in decreased profitability or even outright collapse of the firm.

One way to perform a forecast is simply to venture an educated guess. An improvement upon guessing is to gather expert opinions from various sources and come to an overall consensus based on these opinions. Often, a past history of data values, known as a **time series**, is available and can be helpful in developing the forecast. For example, we may be able to predict future sales for a product by examining historic demands for that product, or we could forecast the customer arrival rate at a bank by examining how many customers actually arrived during similar time periods in prior weeks. In this chapter, we examine the use of such time series in performing forecasts.

COMPONENTS OF A TIME SERIES

A time series is comprised of one or more of the following four components: (1) long-term trend, (2) seasonal variation, (3) cyclical variation, and (4) random effects.

> ### Components of a Time Series
>
> - Long-term trend
> - Seasonal variation
> - Cyclical variation
> - Random effects

Long-Term Trend

A time series may be relatively stationary, or it may exhibit *trend* over time. Such trend may indicate that the time series is increasing or decreasing. A relatively new product might experience increasing demand over time, while demand for a mature product might be reasonably stationary or could even show a declining trend. Long-term trend in a time series is typically modeled as linear, quadratic, or exponential, but it can have some other functional form.

Seasonal Variation

A time series experiences *seasonal variation* if it is expected that, during certain time intervals, the time series increases or decreases due to calendar or climatic changes. For example, toy sales at Toys R Us typically are higher during the Christmas and Hanukkah season in December than in June; demand for bathing suits is higher during spring and summer than in fall or winter; and consumption of heating fuel is high in the winter and low in the summer months.

Seasonal variation is frequently tied to yearly cycles, but this need not be the case. A company that pays its bills at the beginning of each month shows seasonal variation in its bank balance; in this case, one "season" is the early part of each monthly cycle. At many grocery stores, shopping is typically higher on the weekends than during the middle of the week. In this case, one "season" is the weekend of a weekly cycle.

Cyclical Variation

In contrast to seasonal variation, a time series may experience *cyclical variation*, a temporary upturn or downturn that seems to follow no discernible pattern. Cyclical variation usually results from changes in economic conditions. The time series of demand for new cars typically has a cyclical component since such demand is linked to overall changes in the economy; sales of new cars are lower in recessionary periods than in nonrecessionary periods. But predicting when a recessionary period will occur is challenging, if not impossible.

Random Effects

Even if we were able to identify the trend, seasonal, and cyclical components of a time series correctly, it is still impossible to predict the exact value for some future time period because of the presence of a *random* component. For example, we might be able to measure fairly accurately the long-term trend, the seasonal variation, and the effects of cyclical components for sales of ice cream at a Baskin Robbins ice cream store. However, sales also differ simply because a few customers more or less choose to purchase ice cream on a day-to-day basis.

STEPS IN THE TIME SERIES FORECASTING PROCESS

The goal of a time series forecast is to identify those factors that *can* be predicted so that the forecast is as accurate as possible. This analysis can be thought of as a systematic approach involving the following steps:

> ### Steps in the Time Series Forecasting Process
>
> 1. Hypothesize a form for the time series model
> 2. Select a forecasting technique
> 3. Prepare a forecast

Step 1: *Collect historic data, graph the data versus time to aid in hypothesizing a form for the time series model, and verify this hypothesis statistically.*

In this first step, we attempt to identify which of the time series components should be included in the model. One way to determine whether a time series exhibits trend, seasonal, or cyclical components is to plot a graph of data values over time. Based on this graph, a model for the time series can be hypothesized. Figures 7.1*a*–7.1*d* depict four situations of time series data plotted over time: (1) linear trend, (b) nonlinear trend, (c) trend and seasonality, and (d) a stationary pattern.

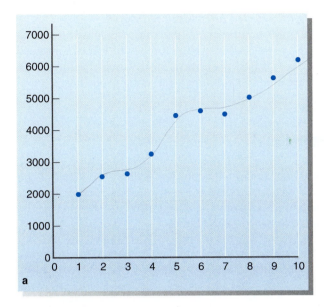

FIGURE 7.1a Time Series with Linear Trend

Linear regression ; Holt's

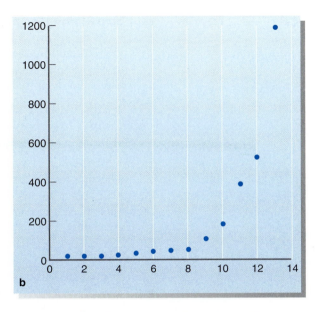

FIGURE 7.1b Time Series with Nonlinear Trend

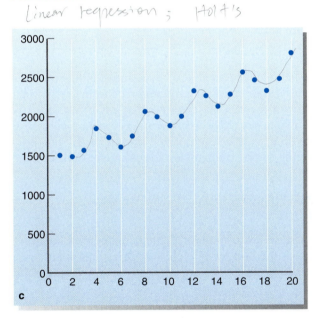

FIGURE 7.1c Time Series with Trend and Seasonality

Classical decomposition
Additive model

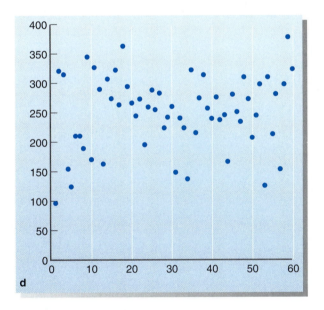

FIGURE 7.1d Stationary Time Series

Simple moving Average
Weight moving Average
Exp Smooth

Once a time series model has been hypothesized, it is important to test its validity statistically. In this chapter, we present several statistical tests that can be used to determine whether particular components of a time series are present.

Step 2: *Select an appropriate forecasting technique for the time series model and determine the values of its parameters.*

For each hypothesized model, several techniques can be chosen to predict the future values for the time series. These techniques can differ in the steps taken to perform the forecast or in the values of certain parameters that can be assigned at the decision maker's discretion. Performance measures such as those discussed in Section 7.3 can be used to assess the relative effectiveness of each technique.

Step 3: *Prepare a forecast using the selected forecasting technique.*

To perform a forecast, the appropriate data values must be substituted into the selected forecasting model. Key issues affecting the forecasted values addressed in this chapter include the number of past observations on which the forecast is based and the initial forecast value used to begin the forecasting procedure.

7.2 Stationary Forecasting Models

The simplest time series forecasting model is one in which the mean value of the item being examined is assumed to be relatively constant, or *stationary*, over time. Since these time series do not exhibit any trend, seasonal, or cyclical components, the general form of such models can be expressed by:

Stationary Forecasting Model

$$y_t = \beta_0 + \epsilon_t$$

where: y_t = the value of the time series at time period t

β_0 = the unchanging mean value of the time series

ϵ_t = a random error term at time period t

The values of ϵ_t are assumed to be independent and to have a mean of 0. The independence assumption means that the value of the random error term at one time period has no effect on the value of the random error term at any other time period. In stationary models we assume that the error term has a mean value of 0 since the expected value of the time series at each period should be β_0. The purpose of the forecast is to determine a good estimate for the unknown value of β_0.

CHECKING THE ASSUMPTIONS—IS A STATIONARY MODEL APPROPRIATE?

We can use several forecasting methods to estimate β_0 in a stationary forecasting model. But before employing such methods, we should first determine whether or not a stationary model is, in fact, appropriate for our data. Obviously, if we get the results shown in Figures 7.1a–c when we plot the data, we should not expect a stationary model to reflect the true situation accurately.

Checking for Trend

One statistical technique commonly used to detect trend is to perform a regression analysis of the historical values of the time series versus the time period t. If linear trend exists over time, the time series can be represented by the following model:

$$y_t = \beta_0 + \beta_1 t + \epsilon_t$$

where β_1, the coefficient multiplying the time period t, is nonzero. If there were no linear trend, then $\beta_1 = 0$ and the model would be that of a stationary time series. Thus we can perform the following hypothesis test:

$$H_0: \beta_1 = 0 \text{ (no linear trend is present)}$$
$$H_A: \beta_1 \neq 0 \text{ (linear trend is present)}$$

This test can be performed in Excel by selecting Data Analysis from the Tools menu and clicking on Regression. Figure 7.2 shows the Excel dialogue box for doing regression analysis. The Y Range is the column of time series values, and the X Range is the column listing the time period (1, 2, 3, . . .). Check the Labels box if a label name is included as the first cell entry in the Y Range and X Range, respectively.

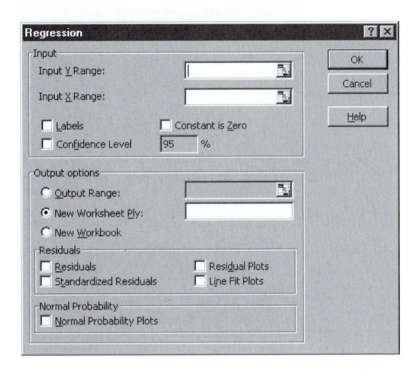

FIGURE 7.2
Excel Dialogue Box for
Regression Analysis

The p-value for the above hypothesis test is found next to the t-value for the dependent variable (the time period) in the bottom row of the Excel output as shown later in Figure 7.4. If the p-value is greater than the preselected significance level, α, we will not reject H_0 and we conclude that a stationary model is acceptable.[1] Here, α represents the probability of concluding that linear trend is present when it is not.

 An alternative to using Excel Regression analysis is to use the Trendline feature of Excel. Use of this feature is explained in Appendix 7.6 on the CD-ROM.

Checking for Seasonality Components

Autocorrelation is the measure of how the value at one time period affects the value at some subsequent time period. The correlation between time series values that are k periods apart is called autocorrelation of *lag k*. Generally, we check for autocorrelation between successive time periods (lag 1) and between time periods that correspond to possible seasonality (e.g., lag 7 for daily data; lag 12 for monthly data; lag 4 for quarterly data). Autocorrelation between successive periods is another indication that trend may be present in a time series; autocorrelation between time periods corresponding to seasons is a good indication of seasonality. In Appendix 7.3 on the accompanying CD-ROM, we present statistical procedures for determining whether or not autocorrelation exists for a given time series.

---

[1] The regression test for trend assumes that the random error terms, ε_t, are independent and normally distributed with a constant variance over the time series. If it is felt that these assumptions are not valid, one can use a nonparametric procedure, such as Daniel's test (outlined in Appendix 7.2 on the accompanying CD-ROM). A nonparametric test is generally a less powerful test, and hence, in some cases, it may not detect linear trend even if linear trend is present.

Checking for Cyclical Components

As mentioned earlier, because cyclical components have no discernible pattern, they are often difficult to detect. Typically, cyclical components are identified solely by examining the graph of the time series.

MOVING AVERAGE METHODS FOR FORECASTING STATIONARY MODELS

If we conclude that a stationary model accurately reflects the time series data, we must choose a forecasting method appropriate for this model. Three of the simplest forecasting approaches for stationary models are the last period technique, the moving average method, and the weighted moving average method.

The Last Period Technique

Using the **last period technique**, the forecast for the next period is simply the last observed value of the stationary time series. Thus, given observed values for t time periods, $y_1, y_2, \ldots, y_t$, using the last period technique, our forecasted value for time period $t + 1$, F_{t+1}, is:

$$F_{t+1} = y_t$$

The Moving Average Method

In the **moving average method**, the forecast for any time period is the average of the values for the immediately preceding n periods, when n is a value chosen by the modeler. For example, using an $n = 4$ period moving average, the forecasted value for time period $t + 1$ is calculated by

$$F_{t+1} = (y_t + y_{t-1} + y_{t-2} + y_{t-3})/4$$

By averaging over n periods, unusually high or low observed values will have a less radical effect on future predictions. Note that the last period technique is a special case of the moving average method, with $n = 1$.

The Weighted Moving Average Method

In the last period technique, all the weight of the forecast is placed on the most recent observed value of the time series. In the moving average method, the most recent observation is weighted equally with the previous $n - 1$ values. One might expect, however, that, although not all of the weight should be placed on the most recent observation, a forecast should reflect more heavily on more recent values.

One way to do this is by using a **weighted moving average technique**. In this procedure, the sum of the weights used must equal 1, and the weights given to observation values are nonincreasing with their age.[2] Thus, if w_i is the weight given to the ith previous observation, the w_i values should satisfy the following properties:

> ### Properties of Weights Used in Developing n Period Weighted Moving Average Forecasts
>
> 1. $\sum w_i = 1$
> 2. $w_1 \geq w_2 \geq w_3 \geq \ldots \geq w_n$

---

[2] The simple moving average technique can be viewed as a special case of the weighted moving average technique, in which all weights equal $1/n$.

For example, a four-period weighted moving average technique might place a weight of .4 on the most recent value of the time series, .3 on the value at the previous time period, .2 on the value from two periods ago, and .1 on the value from three periods ago. Then, the forecast for time period t + 1 using this four-period weighted moving average is determined by

$$F_{t+1} = .4y_t + .3y_{t-1} + .2y_{t-2} + .1y_{t-3}$$

In the weighted moving average technique, both the number of periods, n, and the weights assigned to each period are chosen by the modeler.

FORECASTS FOR FUTURE TIME PERIODS

When a stationary model is used, the forecast for time period t + 1 is the forecast for all future time periods. *The forecasts for these future periods are revised only when data from additional periods have been obtained.*

To illustrate the concepts developed thus far for stationary models, consider the sales of YoHo brand of yo-yos at Galaxy Industries.

YoHo Yo-Yo.xls
exponential smoothing.xls
YoHo last period technique.xls
YoHo four-period moving average technique.xls
YoHo four-period weighted moving average technique.xls
YoHo exponential smoothing.xls
Yoho Forecast.xls
four-period weighted moving average.xls
solver exponential smoothing.xls

YOHO BRAND YO-YOS

Galaxy Industries is interested in forecasting weekly demand for its YoHo brand yo-yos over the coming year so that it can properly allocate a budget for this division. Because YoHo yo-yos are a reasonably mature product, Galaxy believes that next year's demand for the yo-yos will be quite similar to the demand encountered this year; hence the firm has decided to base its forecast on the past 52 weeks of demand. Weekly yo-yo demand (in boxes of 12) during the past 52 weeks is given in Table 7.1, with week 52 representing the most recent week.

If, in fact, a stationary model proves to be appropriate, one member of the Galaxy Industries management science team, Amy Chang, has suggested using the last period forecasting technique, while another member of the team, Bob Gunther, has suggested using a four-period moving average technique. A third member, Carlos Gonzalez, feels that a four-period weighted moving average technique using weights of .4, .3, .2, and .1 would better forecast demand.

Management wants to determine if it can use a stationary model to forecast demand, and, if so, what Amy's, Bob's and Carlos's forecast for demand would be for the next three weeks.

TABLE 7.1 Weekly YoHo Yo-yo Demand

Week	Demand	Week	Demand	Week	Demand	Week	Demand
1	415	14	365	27	351	40	282
2	236	15	471	28	388	41	399
3	348	16	402	29	336	42	309
4	272	17	429	30	414	43	435
5	280	18	376	31	346	44	299
6	395	19	363	32	252	45	522
7	438	20	513	33	256	46	376
8	431	21	197	34	378	47	483
9	446	22	438	35	391	48	416
10	354	23	557	36	217	49	245
11	529	24	625	37	427	50	393
12	241	25	266	38	293	51	482
13	262	26	551	39	288	52	484

SOLUTION

To determine whether a stationary model is appropriate, the first step is to plot the time series of demand over the past 52 weeks. As is seen in Figure 7.3, no apparent trend, seasonal, or cyclical effects can be observed.

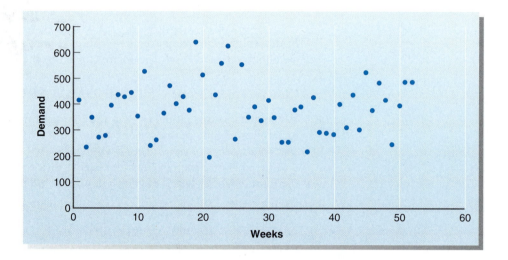

FIGURE 7.3
YoHo Yo-yo Demand

Checking the Assumptions

To test the assumption that no trend is present in this time series, we can perform a regression analysis of these values versus the time period (labeled Week). The regression module in Excel generated the output shown in Figure 7.4.

YoHo Yo-Yo.xls

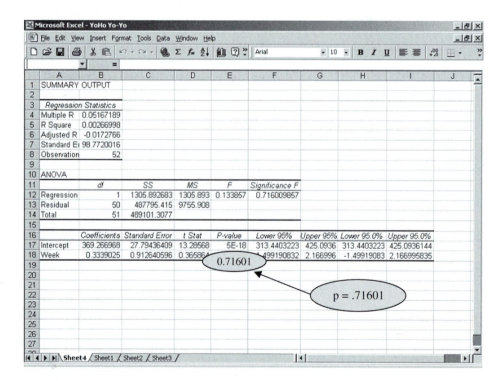

FIGURE 7.4
Excel Regression Analysis

The high p-value for Week of .71601 (much higher than a typical value for α, such as .05) indicates there is little evidence that linear trend exists in the time series. We therefore conclude that a stationary model may be appropriate.

Visually checking for autocorrelation, we do not find any apparent seasonality by week, month, or quarter, nor does it appear that the time series exhibits cyclical variation. These assumptions can also be verified using the techniques described in Appendix 7.3 on the accompanying CD-ROM.

Forecasts for Week 53

Amy's forecast using the *last period forecasting technique* is:

$$F_{53} = y_{52} = 484 \text{ boxes}$$

Bob's forecast using a *four-period moving average method* is:

$$F_{53} = (y_{52} + y_{51} + y_{50} + y_{49})/4$$
$$= (484 + 482 + 393 + 245)/4 = 401 \text{ boxes}$$

Carlos's forecast using the *four-period weighted moving average method* with weights of .4, .3, .2, and .1 is:

$$F_{53} = .4y_{52} + .3y_{51} + .2y_{50} + .1y_{49}$$
$$= .4(484) + .3(482) + .2(393) + .1(245)$$
$$= 441.3 \text{ boxes}$$

Because demand must be for full boxes, Carlos reports a demand forecast of 441 to management.

Forecasts for Weeks 54, 55, and Beyond

Since a stationary model is used in each case, the forecast demand for weeks 54, 55, and beyond is the same as the forecast demand for week 53. Therefore, for weeks 54 and 55, Amy forecasts demand of 484 boxes, Bob of 401 boxes, and Carlos of 441 boxes. Based on these estimates Amy would forecast yearly demand of $52(484) = 25,168$, whereas Bob's forecast would be for $52(401) = 20,852$ and Carlos's would be for $52(441.3) = 22,948$. These forecasts will be revised upon observation of the actual demand in week 53.

THE EXPONENTIAL SMOOTHING METHOD FOR FORECASTING STATIONARY MODELS

While the n-period weighted moving average technique can be used to put greater weight on the more recent observations, it uses only the last n periods and ignores the history of the time series prior to that time. This prior history should not affect the prediction nearly as much as the more recent n data values, but many modelers feel that it is wrong to totally exclude their values in the analysis.

A problem that arises from using all prior historical data in forecasting, however, is that many companies must forecast demand for thousands or even hundreds of thousands of items on a regular basis. This could require them to keep huge databases dating back many years and involve lengthy calculations each time a new forecast is warranted. Such difficulties can be overcome by using **exponential smoothing**. This forecasting technique requires only two data values to forecast a value for the next time period: (1) the current value of the time series, y_i, and (2) the forecast value for the current period, F_t.

The idea behind exponential smoothing is to reduce the random effects associated with an individual point of the time series by calculating a "smoothed" value that in some sense is more representative of the period. This smoothed value, L_t, is generated using a weighted average of the actual value for the time period y_t, and the forecast value for the period, F_t. This smoothed value, L_t, becomes the forecast for the next time period, $t + 1$, that is, $F_{t+1} = L_t$.

The weight given to the current period's *actual value*, y_t, denoted by α, is called the *smoothing constant*. Thus the weight given to the current period's *forecast value*, F_t, is $(1 - \alpha)$, which Excel calls the **damping factor**. The forecast for period $t + 1$ is then given by the recursive relationship,

$$F_{t+1} = L_t = \alpha y_t + (1 - \alpha)F_t \qquad (7.1)$$

We need a starting point, however, to begin the recursive relationship in Equation 7.1. There is no forecast for time period 1, F_1, since there are no previous data values. At time period 2, we would have only the one observation of the time series from time period 1, y_1. Thus, based on this one time series value, y_1, we would forecast the value for the second period F_2 to be equal to this value. That is, our "first" forecasted value would be for time period 2 and would be $F_2 = y_1$. All future forecasts can now be generated using Equation 7.1.[3]

For a time series with n periods of data, the forecast for period $n + 1$ would then be: $F_{n+1} = L_n = \alpha y_n + (1 - \alpha)F_n$. Since the time series is assumed to be stationary, the forecasted value F_{n+1} would be the forecast for all subsequent periods until additional periods are observed.

Summarizing, the exponential smoothing procedure begins by selecting a value for the smoothing constant α for the level of the time series. Higher values for α place more weight on the recent values. Once this smoothing constant has been selected, the following are the steps of the forecasting process.

Exponential Smoothing Forecasting Technique

INITIALIZATION

Forecast for period 2: $\qquad F_2 = y_1$

RECURSIVE FORMULA

Forecast for period t: $\qquad F_{t+1} = \alpha y_t + (1 - \alpha)F_t$

FORECASTS FOR PERIODS n + 1, n + 2, n + 3, ETC.

Forecast for period $n + 1$: $F_{n+1} = \alpha y_n + (1 - \alpha)F_n$
Forecast for period $n + 2$: $F_{n+2} = F_{n+1}$

.

.

Forecast for period $n + k$: $F_{n+k} = F_{n+1}$

(where n is the number of periods for which one has time series data)

We indicated that the exponential smoothing approach considers all previous values of the historical time series. To illustrate, consider the equation for deriving the forecast value:

$$F_{t+1} = \alpha y_t + (1 - \alpha)F_t$$

---

[3] Another approach that can be used to find a "first" forecast when a large number of historical values exist is to average the first n periods to get a value, $\bar{y}_n$, and use $F_{n+1} = \bar{y}_n$ as the "first" forecast. Subsequent forecasts would be generated using Equation 7.1. The total weight given to early forecasts is very small and thus virtually any reasonable technique can be used to generate a "first" forecast.

Since the forecast at time period t, F_t, is found using $F_t = \alpha y_{t-1} + (1 - \alpha)F_{t-1}$, we have:

$$F_{t+1} = \alpha y_t + (1 - \alpha)(\alpha y_{t-1} + (1 - \alpha)F_{t-1})$$
$$= \alpha y_t + \alpha(1 - \alpha)y_{t-1} + (1 - \alpha)^2 F_{t-1}$$

And since the forecast at time period $t - 1$, F_{t-1}, is found using $F_{t-1} = \alpha y_{t-2} + (1 - \alpha)F_{t-2}$, we have:

$$F_{t+1} = \alpha y_t + \alpha(1 - \alpha)y_{t-1} + (1 - \alpha)^2(\alpha y_{t-2} + (1 - \alpha)F_{t-2})$$
$$= \alpha y_t + \alpha(1 - \alpha)y_{t-1} + \alpha(1 - \alpha)^2 y_{t-2} + (1 - \alpha)^3 F_{t-2}$$

Continuing in this fashion, we can express F_{t+1} by:

$$F_{t+1} = \alpha y_t + \alpha(1 - \alpha)y_{t-1} + \alpha(1 - \alpha)^2 y_{t-2} + \alpha(1 - \alpha)^3 y_{t-3}$$
$$+ \ldots + \alpha(1 - \alpha)^k y_{t-k} + (1 - \alpha)^{k+1}F_{t-k}$$

Since $(1 - \alpha)$ is a fraction, the weights given to past terms decrease as they become more distant from the present. Also, the last term of this equation, $(1 - \alpha)^{k+1}$ (which represents the weight given to the forecast k periods in the past) approaches 0 as the value of k is increased.[4]

The forecasts generated from exponential smoothing depend on the modeler's choice for the smoothing constant, α. When α is large, greater weight is given to the current period's actual value, so the forecast tracks changes in the time series quite rapidly. When α is small, less weight is given to the current period's actual value, resulting in relatively small changes in the forecast; hence the forecast tracks time series changes quite slowly.

To illustrate the concepts involved in exponential smoothing, let us return to the problem of forecasting demand of YoHo yo-yos at Galaxy Industries.

YOHO BRAND YO-YOS (CONTINUED)

Dick Gates, a recent hire at Galaxy Industries with a degree in both management science and statistics, has suggested forecasting sales using an exponential smoothing technique that puts a weight of .1 on the most recent observation. Management has asked Dick to forecast demand for weeks 53, 54, and 55.

SOLUTION

To perform the exponential smoothing analysis, Dick begins with the forecast in week 2 being the value of the time series in week 1, $F_2 = y_1 = 415$. His forecast for week 3 is therefore:

$$F_3 = .1y_2 + .9F_2 = .1(236) + .9(415) = 397.10$$

Similarly, for week 4 the forecast is:

$$F_4 = .1y_3 + .9F_3 = .1(348) + .9(397.10) = 392.19$$

Dick can easily use Excel to generate the values for the exponential forecast for this model. Figure 7.5 shows an Excel spreadsheet that calculates these values.

---

[4] The term *exponential smoothing* is derived from the fact that the exponent of the damping term, $(1 - \alpha)$, increases for more distant data values of the time series.

exponential smoothing.xls

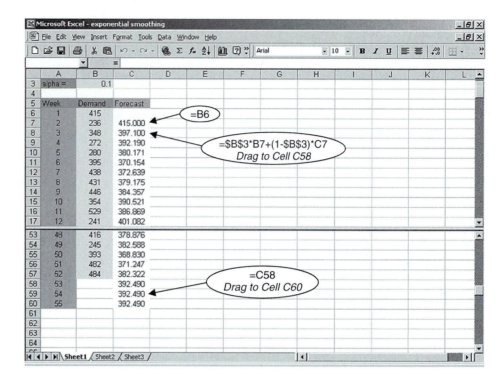

FIGURE 7.5
Excel Spreadsheet for
Exponential Smoothing
Forecasting

We see from this spreadsheet that the forecast for week 53 is for 392.49 yo-yos, which we would round off to 392. Since this forecast is based on a stationary model, this becomes the forecast for periods 54 and 55 and beyond.

The numbers in column C can also be generated by choosing Exponential Smoothing from Data Analysis in the Tools menu. To generate the same sequence of numbers in the same cells as Figures 7.5, choose column B from B5 to B57 as the input range. Then Excel uses the value of $1 - \alpha$ as its "damping factor." Figure 7.6 shows the Excel dialogue box for exponential smoothing.

FIGURE 7.6
Excel Dialogue Box for
Exponential Smoothing

The Output Range should start at cell C6 corresponding to the forecast for time period 1. Excel will print #N/A in cell C6 (indicating that a forecast for time period 1 is "not applicable" and then print the values from Figure 7.5 in cells C7:C57. To get the forecast for time period 53 in cell C58, the formula for cell C57 can be dragged down to cell C58.

RELATIONSHIP BETWEEN EXPONENTIAL SMOOTHING AND MOVING AVERAGES

As we have seen, both exponential smoothing and simple moving averages are special cases of the weighted moving average approach. We can, in a sense, equate simple moving averages with exponential smoothing by calculating the average age of the observations used in developing the two forecasts. For simple moving averages of length k, the average age of the data is $(1 + 2 + 3 + \ldots + k)/k = (k + 1)/2$ periods. For exponential smoothing, the average age of the data used in the forecast is $(1)\alpha + (2)\alpha(1 - \alpha) + (3)\alpha(1 - \alpha)^2 + (4)\alpha(1 - \alpha)^3 \ldots = 1/\alpha$.

Equating the two average ages, $(k + 1)/2$ and $1/\alpha$, gives us the following relationship:

$$k = (2 - \alpha)/\alpha \qquad (7.2)$$

Equation 7.2 can prove a useful guide to the appropriate value of the smoothing constant, α. For example, exponential smoothing with $\alpha = .10$ can be thought of as being, in a sense, equivalent to a moving average based on 19 periods of data ($k = (2 - .1)/.1) = 19$), while exponential smoothing with $\alpha = 1.0$ is equivalent to a moving average based on only one period of data. Therefore, if we want the forecast to be based on a larger number of past data values, a smaller value of α is appropriate.

7.3 Evaluating the Performance of Forecasting Techniques

Thus far, we have presented four different techniques for generating forecasts for stationary models; each has arrived at a different forecast for week 53 in the Galaxy Industries YoHo yo-yo problem. The obvious question is, "Which of these methods gives the *best* forecast?"

To answer this question, we must be able to evaluate forecasting techniques. One commonly used approach is to select a forecasting technique for which historic forecast errors are small. The *forecast error* for time period t, denoted as Δ_t, is the difference between the actual value of the time series for the period, y_t, and the value that would have been forecasted for the period using a particular forecasting approach, F_t. That is, $\Delta_t = y_t - F_t$.

Four of the most popular measures used to evaluate forecast errors are the mean squared error (MSE), the mean absolute deviation (MAD), the mean absolute percent error (MAPE), and the largest absolute deviation (LAD). In the **mean squared error approach**, the squares of the Δ_t values are averaged, while in the **mean absolute deviation approach** the absolute values for Δ_t are averaged.

In the **mean absolute percent error approach**, the absolute values for Δ_t are divided by the corresponding actual values, y_t; these values are then multiplied by 100% to give the absolute percentage the forecast varies from the actual value. Averaging these percentages gives the MAPE. To find the **largest absolute deviation**, we simply find the largest of the absolute values for Δ_t. These four measures are summarized in Table 7.2.

TABLE 7.2   Measures for Evaluating Forecast Errors

Measure	Description	Formula
Mean Squared Error (MSE)	Averages the squared differences of the forecasted values from the actual values	$\sum \Delta_t^2/n = \sum(y_t - F_t)^2/n$
Mean Absolute Deviation (MAD)	Averages the absolute values of the differences of the forecasted values from the actual values	$\sum |\Delta_t|/n = \sum |y_t - F_t|/n$
Mean Absolute Percent Error (MAPE)	Averages the absolute percentage differences of the forecasted values from the actual values	$\sum((|\Delta_t|/y_t) * 100\%)/n = \sum((|yt - Ft|/yt) * 100\%)/n$
Largest Absolute Deviation (LAD)	Finds the largest absolute difference between the forecasted and actual values	$MAX|\Delta_t| = MAX|y_t - F_t|$

Which Performance Measure Should Be Used?

The forecasting approach with the lowest MSE, MAD, MAPE, or LAD is the best one for that corresponding measure of performance. If one forecasting approach is superior to the others *using all four of these measures*, clearly this approach is the most reliable for forecasting future values. It is possible, however, that one forecasting approach may have the lowest value using one performance measure and that another approach may have the lowest value using another criterion. Therefore, it is important to know which performance measure to use to evaluate the forecasting approach.

Both the MSE and the MAD performance measures look at the total magnitude of the forecast error. The MSE approach gives greater weight to larger deviations, however, since the forecast errors are squared in calculating this total. Thus the MSE is preferred over the MAD when the modeler wishes to give larger forecast errors proportionately more weight than smaller errors.

In contrast to the MSE and MAD, the MAPE considers the forecast errors relative to the corresponding values of the time series. Hence a large error corresponding to a large time series value may count less than a small error based on a small time series value. The MAPE performance measure is generally used when the values of the time series show wide variations.

While the MSE, MAD, and MAPE performance measures consider all forecast errors in their calculations, the LAD performance measure is determined by the single largest absolute deviation. Therefore it is used when we are interested in selecting a technique for which all forecast errors fall below some threshold value.

To illustrate these performance measures, we return to the situation for forecasting demand for YoHo yo-yos at Galaxy Industries.

YOHO BRAND YO-YOS (CONTINUED)

Management at Galaxy Industries is uncertain about which demand forecast it should accept for YoHo yo-yos for the next three weeks. They have asked the management science team to analyze the four forecast approaches suggested by Amy, Bob, Carlos, and Dick and to recommend which to use to forecast demand for yo-yos.

SOLUTION

The management science team has decided to evaluate each forecasting approach using the MSE, MAD, MAPE, and LAD approaches.

Amy's Forecast

Amy's forecast is based on the last period technique. Figure 7.7 shows an Excel spreadsheet giving the actual values, the squared differences, the absolute differences, and the absolute percent differences.

YoHo last period technique.xls

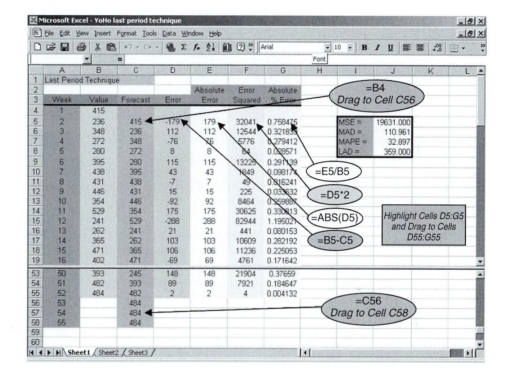

FIGURE 7.7
Excel Spreadsheet for Last Period Technique Forecast

The cells in column J for this spreadsheet are calculated as follows:

Cell	Value	Formula
J5	MSE	=AVERAGE(F5:F55)
J6	MAD	=AVERAGE(E5:E55)
J7	MAPE	=100*AVERAGE(G5:G55)
J8	LAD	=MAX(E5:E55)

Thus we see that for the last period forecasting technique the MSE = 19,631, the MAD = 110.961, the MAPE = 32.897, and the LAD = 359.

Bob's Forecast

Figure 7.8 shows an Excel spreadsheet based on Bob's four-period moving average approach.

YoHo four-period moving average technique.xls

FIGURE 7.8
Excel Spreadsheet for Four-Period Moving Average Forecast

Note that the forecasting begins in period 5 since four periods are necessary to construct the forecast. With the exception of the forecast cells, the cells in this spreadsheet are calculated in an analogous fashion to those in the spreadsheet used to evaluate the last period technique. The cells in column J are calculated in a similar fashion to the spreadsheet shown in Figure 7.7.

Thus we see that for the four-period moving average technique the MSE = 11,037.164, the MAD = 88.75, the MAPE = 25.608, and the LAD = 223.25.

We can graph the forecast versus the original time series data using the Chart feature in Excel. Selecting the line option and using the data in columns B and C from row 3 through row 56 of Figure 7.8 gives the chart shown in Figure 7.9. As

YoHo four-period moving average technique.xls

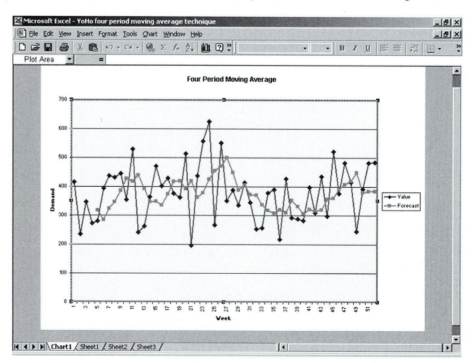

FIGURE 7.9
Excel Plot of Forecast Versus Original Time Series Values

we see from this figure, the forecast follows the original data values but with less variability.

Carlos's Forecast

Recall that Carlos is using a weighted moving average with weights $w_1 = .4$, $w_2 = .3$, $w_3 = .2$, and $w_4 = .1$ to forecast demand for YoHo yo-yos. Figure 7.10 shows an Excel spreadsheet that can be used to forecast the weighted moving average proposed by Carlos.

YoHo four-period weighted moving average technique.xls

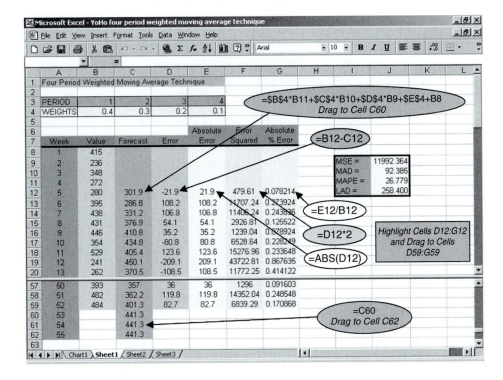

FIGURE 7.10
Excel Spreadsheet for Weighted Moving Average Forecast

In this spreadsheet the weightings are entered in row 4. The weighting for the previous period is given in cell B4, the next previous period in cell C4, and so on. The formulas for this spreadsheet are the same as those for the four-period simple moving average except for the formulas in cells C12 through C60.

For these weights, the MSE = 11,992.364, the MAD = 92.385, the MAPE = 26.779, and the LAD = 258.40. A different weighting would, of course, yield a different forecast and performance measure results.

Dick's Forecast

Figure 7.11 gives an Excel spreadsheet for the exponential smoothing model proposed by Dick.

Here we see that for the exponential smoothing technique, the MSE = 10,441.844, the MAD = 85.127, the MAPE = 25.442, and the LAD = 224.089.

Table 7.3 summarizes the results for the four forecasting techniques. As we see from this table, Dick's exponential smoothing forecast has lower forecasting errors than Amy and Carlos's approaches and has lower forecast errors than Bob's approach except for the LAD measure. For that measure Bob's technique has a slightly smaller error than Dick's; however, on balance, Dick's approach seems to be the superior one in terms of minimizing forecast error.

YoHo exponential smoothing.xls

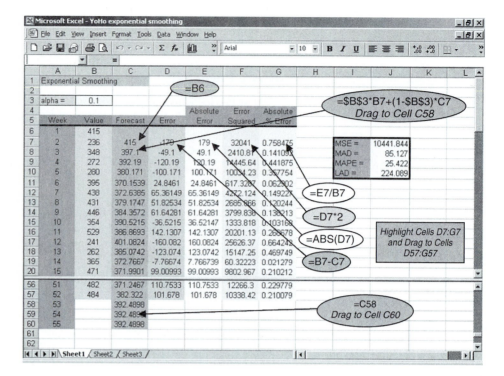

FIGURE 7.11
Excel Spreadsheet for Exponential Smoothing Forecast

TABLE 7.3 Comparison of the Four Performance Measures

Forecast	MSE	MAD	MAPE	LAD
Amy	19,631.00	110.96	32.90	359.00
Bob	11,037.16	88.75	25.61	223.25
Carlos	11,992.36	92.39	26.78	258.40
Dick	10,441.84	85.13	25.42	224.09

THE FORECAST.XLS TEMPLATE

As an alternative to constructing your own Excel spreadsheet for forecasting the stationary models we have discussed, a template, forecast.xls, is contained on the accompanying CD-ROM. This template has worksheets that can be used to perform forecasts for each of the methods discussed in this chapter. For stationary models the worksheets are Simple MA (simple moving average), Weighted MA (weighted moving average), and Exp. Smooth (exponential smoothing). Details on using the template are contained in Appendix 7.1 at the end of the chapter.

SELECTING MODEL PARAMETERS

Often the modeler must select different parameters for a chosen technique. In the moving average technique, the modeler must select the number of periods to include in the moving average. In the weighted moving average technique, the modeler must select the number of periods and the weights to be given for each past period making up the average. In the exponential smoothing technique, the modeler must select the smoothing constant to use as well as the initial forecast value.

DETERMINING THE OPTIMAL NUMBER OF PERIODS FOR A SIMPLE MOVING AVERAGE

Using the Simple MA worksheet in the forecast.xls template, it is easy to determine the effect of using differing numbers of periods in the moving average. For example, Figure 7.12 shows the Simple MA worksheet for a five-period simple moving average.

Yoho Forecast.xls

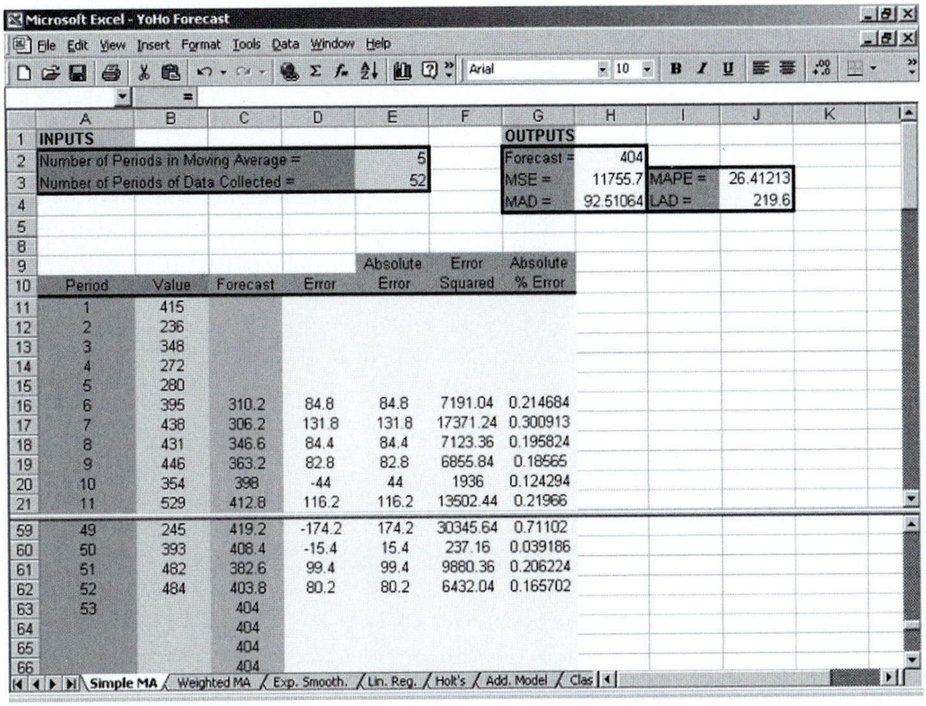

FIGURE 7.12

Excel Spreadsheet for a Five-Period Moving Average Forecast

By changing the number of periods in the moving average (cell E2), we can observe the corresponding effect on the performance measure.

Table 7.4 shows the value of mean squared forecast error of an n period moving average for values of n between 1 and 10.

TABLE 7.4   Mean Squared Forecast Errors Using *n* Period Moving Averages

n	Mean Squared Forecast Error	n	Mean Squared Forecast Error
1	19,631	6	11,332
2	12,996	7	11,104
3	12,467	8	10,737
4	11,037	9	10,791
5	11,756	10	11,400

While it can be seen from this table that the eight-week moving average gives a slightly smaller mean squared forecast error than does the four-week moving average, the four-week moving average may still be preferred. This is because when the moving average is based on too many historical values, the forecast is not as responsive to recent changes in the time series.

USING SOLVER TO DETERMINE PARAMETERS

Excel Solver can be used to determine an appropriate set of weights to use in a weighted moving average as well as the smoothing constant to use in exponential smoothing. While Solver will select values that do a good job in forecasting according to the selected criterion, unfortunately, there is no guarantee that Solver will find the best parameters to use. This is because the function we wish to minimize is not necessarily convex. Hence Solver can get "stuck" at a local minimum and may never find the global minimum.

SELECTING THE WEIGHTED MOVING AVERAGE WEIGHTS USING SOLVER

We use the spreadsheet shown in Figure 7.10 without the explanatory bubbles (renamed the four-period weighted moving average technique.xls) to illustrate how Solver can be used to find weightings that minimize the MSE for a four-period weighted moving average.

- In cell F4 enter =SUM(B4:E4); this gives the sum of the weights.
- Call Solver and enter the data as shown in Figure 7.13.

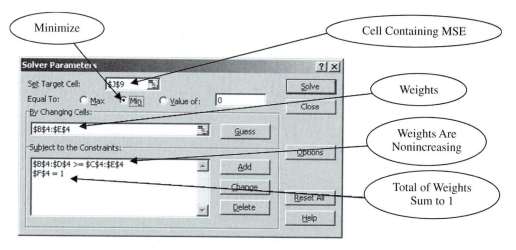

FIGURE 7.13 Solver Dialogue Box

Before running Solver, be sure to check Assume Non-Negative in the Options dialogue box. Clicking on Solve then gives the result shown in Figure 7.14.

We see from this output that in this particular case for the four-period weighted moving average each period should have an equal weighting. Interestingly, this is equivalent to the four-period simple moving average.

SELECTING THE EXPONENTIAL SMOOTHING CONSTANT USING SOLVER

The method we use to find the smoothing coefficient closely parallels the method used to find the weightings in a weighted moving average. We use the spreadsheet shown in Figure 7.11 without the explanatory bubbles (renamed solver exponential smoothing.xls) to illustrate how Solver can be used to find the smoothing constant that minimizes the MAD. Figure 7.15 shows the Solver dialogue box for this

four-period weighted moving
average.xls

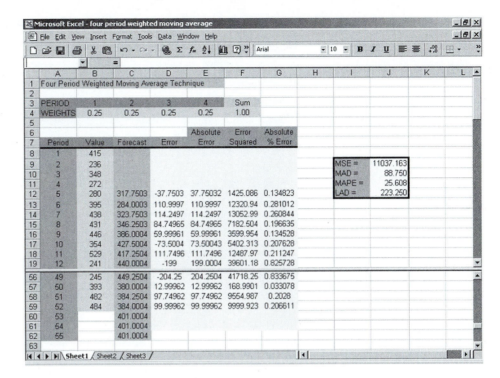

FIGURE 7.14   Excel Spreadsheet for Weighted Moving Average Forecast

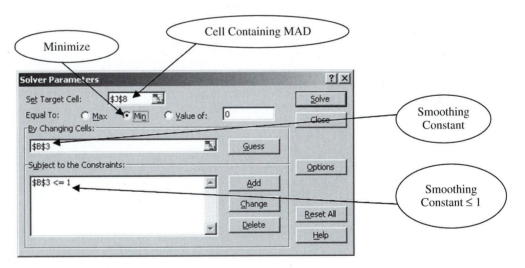

FIGURE 7.15   Solver Dialogue Box

problem. Again, make sure Assume Non-Negative is checked in the Option dialogue box before running Solver. Figure 7.16 shows the results.

We see from this figure that the best smoothing constant (in terms of minimizing MAD) is $\alpha = .02$. This gives a MAD of 82.874, a 2.65% lower value for the MAD than when a value of $\alpha = .10$ is used.

It is interesting to note that for this set of data, the best smoothing constant is a value of α close to 0. This means that the time series forecast will change very slowly over time and will be reasonably insensitive to dramatic shifts in the time series values. For this reason a smoothing constant of $\alpha = .10$ may still be preferred.

solver exponential smoothing.xls

	A	B	C	D	E	F	G	H	I	J	K	L

Microsoft Excel - solver exponential smoothing

	Week	Demand	Forecast	Error	Absolute Error	Error Squared	Absolute % Error
1	Exponential Smoothing						
3	alpha =	0.020993					
6	1	415					
7	2	236	415.000	-179	179	32041	0.758475
8	3	348	411.242	-63.2422	63.24221	3999.577	0.18173
9	4	272	409.915	-137.915	137.9145	19020.42	0.507039
10	5	280	407.019	-127.019	127.0193	16133.89	0.45364
11	6	395	404.353	-9.35272	9.35272	87.47336	0.023678
12	7	438	404.156	33.84362	33.84362	1145.391	0.077269
13	8	431	404.867	26.13314	26.13314	682.9408	0.060634
14	9	446	405.415	40.58452	40.58452	1647.103	0.090997
15	10	354	406.267	-52.2675	52.26749	2731.89	0.147648
16	11	529	405.170	123.8298	123.8298	15333.81	0.234083
17	12	241	407.770	-166.77	166.7698	27812.17	0.691991
18	13	262	404.269	-142.269	142.2688	20240.4	0.543011
54	49	245	390.434	-145.434	145.4342	21151.1	0.593609
55	50	393	387.381	5.618963	5.618963	31.57275	0.014298
56	51	482	387.499	94.501	94.501	8930.44	0.19606
57	52	484	389.483	94.51712	94.51712	8933.486	0.195283
58	53		391.467				
59	53		391.467				
60	53		391.467				

MSE = 10372.338
MAD = 82.874
MAPE = 25.768
LAD = 221.688

FIGURE 7.16
Excel Spreadsheet for Exponential Smoothing Forecast

Quick response time is especially critical when there is evidence that positive autocorrelation exists or when the mean of the series is anticipated to shift at a future point in time. In general, if the time series does not exhibit significant autocorrelation, a low value of α (such as .10) is appropriate. If the time series shows significant autocorrelation, however, it is more desirable to track changes in the observation values quickly. In this case, a higher value of α should be set.

To summarize, the following are the key issues in determining which approach and parameters to use for forecasting a stationary time series.

> ### Key Issues in Determining Which Forecasting Technique to Use for a Stationary Time Series
>
> 1. The degree of autocorrelation suspected in the data
> 2. The possibility of future shifts in time series values
> 3. The desired responsiveness of the forecasting technique
> 4. The amount of data that is required to calculate the forecast

7.4 Forecasting Time Series that Exhibit Linear Trend

In Section 7.2 we showed how to detect linear trend in a time series. If we suspect trend, we should assess whether the trend is linear or nonlinear (curvilinear). This determination is frequently based on the modeler's knowledge of the means by which the time series is generated. For example, an epidemiologist may know from theoretical analyses that the number of cases of a particular disease will grow initially at an exponential rate; an economist may believe that certain economic measures change logarithmically; or historical data may suggest that home use of natural gas has a quadratic relationship with daily low temperature readings.

Here, however, we restrict our attention to forecasting a time series that demonstrates linear trend. The model for such a time series is:

$$y_t = \beta_0 + \beta_1 t + \epsilon_t \tag{7.3}$$

In this model, β_0 represents the y-intercept and β_1 the slope of the time series. ϵ_t is the random error term at time t. As discussed in Section 7.2, we can use linear regression to test for trend. If the p value is small (less than α) we can conclude that a linear trend model is appropriate.

REGRESSION APPROACH

If we determine that a linear trend is present, the next step is to select a forecasting method. One technique is to use the regression equation based on the historical time series data to forecast future time series values. Although theoretically the regression equation should only be used within the range of observed values of t (from 1 to n), as long as the period we wish to forecast is not too far into the future, using the regression equation should give reasonable forecasts. The forecast for a time period t is obtained by substituting t into the regression equation.

HOLT'S APPROACH

Suppose there are n values of the time series and we wish to forecast values for periods n + 1, n + 2, n + 3, and so on. One potential drawback of the regression approach is that the formulas used to determine the values for the y-intercept (β_0) and slope (β_1) of the regression line treat all time series points equally. Consequently, earlier observations of the time series from periods 1 and 2 have as much influence on these estimates as later values from periods n − 1 and n.

Holt's linear exponential smoothing technique is one approach used in forecasting models with trend that makes adjustments for the slope at each time period so that more weight is placed on the more recent observations. Holt's technique uses an exponential smoothing approach to obtain a smoothed value for the level of the time series (L_t) at time t, that is,

$$L_t = \alpha y_t + (1 - \alpha)F_t \tag{7.4}$$

Because the model exhibits trend, however, the forecast for the next period, F_{t+1}, will not simply be the level, L_t, as it is for stationary models. It must be adjusted by the trend of the time series at time t, T_t, which is the estimate of how the time series is changing from one period to the next at time t.

To obtain an estimate for the trend at time period t, T_t, Holt's method uses a second exponential smoothing calculation with a different smoothing constant, γ. Consistent with the exponential smoothing approach for the level, Holt's method generates T_t values as follows: $T_t = \gamma*$(most recent observation for the trend) + $(1 - \gamma)*$(last estimate for the trend). The most recent observation for the trend is most accurately expressed as the difference in the last two smoothed values for the time series level, $L_t - L_{t-1}$, and the last estimate for the trend is T_{t-1}. Thus

$$T_t = \gamma(L_t - L_{t-1}) + (1 - \gamma)T_{t-1} \tag{7.5}$$

The forecast for time period t + 1 is then:

$$F_{t+1} = L_t + T_t \tag{7.6}$$

Recall that to start the recursive exponential smoothing process, initial values must be assigned. Since two periods are needed to forecast trend, Holt's method begins at time period 2 by assigning the level at period 2 to the actual time series value at time period 2, ($L_2 = y_2$), and the trend at time period 2 to be the difference between first two time series values, ($T_2 = y_2 - y_1$). The first forecasted value would then be $F_3 = L_2 + T_2$.

The process then continues for each period by first calculating the level, L_t, then the trend, T_t and from these, the forecast for the next period, F_{t+1}. For a time series having n periods, the forecast for period n + 1 is $F_{n+1} = L_n + T_n$. Because this is a trend model, until additional values for the time series are observed, the forecasts for periods n + 2, n + 3, and so on will differ from each other by the last estimated value for the trend T_n. Thus $F_{n+2} = L_n + 2*T_n$, $F_{n+3} = L_n + 3*T_n$, etc.

Summarizing, Holt's procedure begins by selecting values for a smoothing constant α for the level and a smoothing constant γ for the trend. Higher values for these constants place more weight on the recent values. Once these smoothing constants have been selected, the following are the steps of the forecasting process.

INITIALIZATION

1.	Initial Level:	$L_2 = y_2$
2.	Initial Trend:	$T_2 = y_2 - y_1$
3.	Initial Forecast:	$F_3 = L_2 + T_2$

RECURSIVE FORMULAS

1.	Level at period t:	$L_t = \alpha y_t + (1 - \alpha)F_t$
2.	Trend at period t:	$T_t = \gamma(L_t - L_{t-1}) + (1 - \gamma)T_{t-1}$
3.	Forecast for period t + 1:	$F_{t+1} = L_t + T_t$

FORECASTS FOR PERIODS n + 1, n + 2, n + 3, ETC.

1.	Forecast for period n + 1:	$F_{n+1} = L_n + T_n$
2.	Forecast for period n + 2:	$F_{n+2} = L_n + 2*T_n$
3.	Forecast for period n + 3:	$F_{n+3} = L_n + 3*T_n$
	·	·
	·	·
k	Forecast for period n + k:	$F_{n+k} = L_n + k*T_n$

(where n is the number of periods for which one has time series data)

To illustrate both the regression and Holt's exponential smoothing approaches for models with linear trend, consider the year-end current asset data for American Family Products.

American Family Regression.xls
American Family Forecast.xls
American Family Holt's.xls
American Family Forecast
(revised).xls

AMERICAN FAMILY PRODUCTS CORPORATION

Hank Richards and Juanita Garcia, financial analysts with the bond rating firm of Standard and Poor's (S&P), are currently conducting an analysis of American Family Products Corporation (AFP) to determine whether the bond rating of the firm should be modified. One important factor in making this assessment is the projected year-end current assets of the firm. Table 7.5 provides information regarding American Family Products' year-end current assets (in millions of dollars) for the previous 10-year period (year 10 corresponds to the most recent year).

Hank and Juanita wish to forecast year-end current assets for American Family Products for years 11 and 12. Both feel that the company's assets have been increasing at a relatively constant rate over time. If this can be verified, Hank has decided to forecast year-end current assets for future years using a linear regression approach, whereas Juanita will use Holt's method to determine this forecast. S&P would like to determine a forecast for year-end current assets for AFP based on both approaches.

TABLE 7.5   American Family Products' Year-End Current Assets

Year	Current Assets (in million $)	Year	Current Assets (in million $)
1	1990	6	3310
2	2280	7	3256
3	2328	8	3533
4	2635	9	3826
5	3249	10	4119

SOLUTION

Figure 7.17 is a graph generated by Excel showing the year-end current assets of American Family Products over the past 10 years. While the time series appears to exhibit a linear trend, we verify this statistically by regressing the year-end current assets against time. Figure 7.18 shows the Excel output for this analysis.

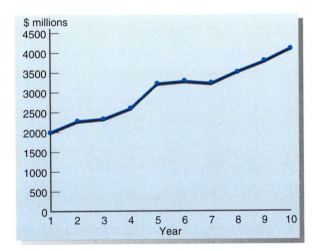

FIGURE 7.17
Year-end Current Assets of American Family Products

The p-value associated with the slope is 6.53E-07 $= 6.53 \times 10^{-7} =$ 0.000000653. Since this figure is far less than $\alpha = .05$, we conclude that the data show significant linear trend, and a linear forecasting model is appropriate.

Hank's Forecasts Using Linear Regression

From the Excel output, Hank observes that the following regression equation can be used to forecast future values of the time series:

$$F_t = 1788.2 + 229.89t \qquad (7.7)$$

American Family Regression.xls

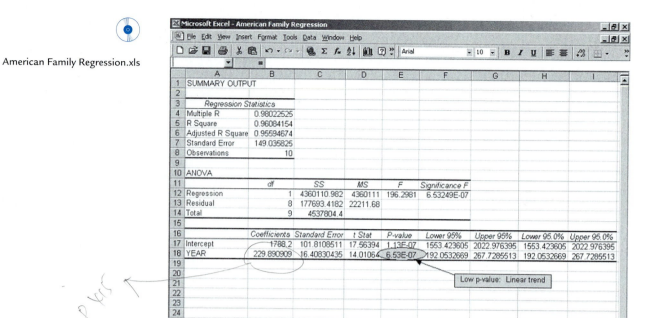

FIGURE 7.18   Excel Regression Output for American Family Time Series

Figure 7.19 shows the results of using Excel to generate the forecasts for the time series. The regression formula =$B$31 + $B$32*A2 is entered into cell C2, and the formula is dragged down to cells C3:C13. We see that Hank would forecast assets of $4317 million for year 11 and $4546.89091 million for year 12.

American Family Regression.xls

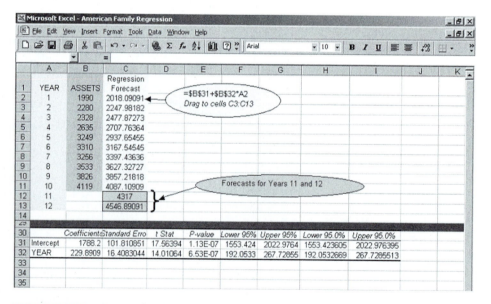

FIGURE 7.19   Regression Forecasts for Years 11 and 12

Alternatively, one could use the linear regression worksheet contained in the forecast.xls template. Figure 7.20 shows this worksheet for the American Family time series data.

By using the charting feature of Excel, Hank generated Figure 7.21, which shows the fit of this line to the time series.

American Family Forecast.xls

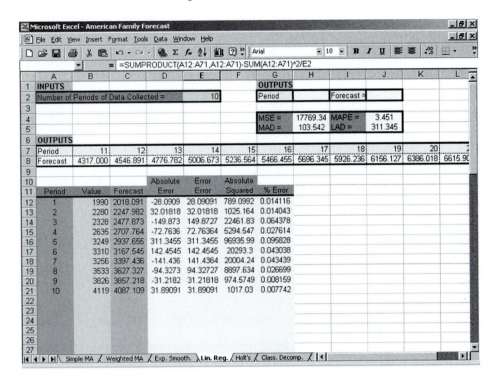

FIGURE 7.20   Excel Spreadsheet for American Family Time Series

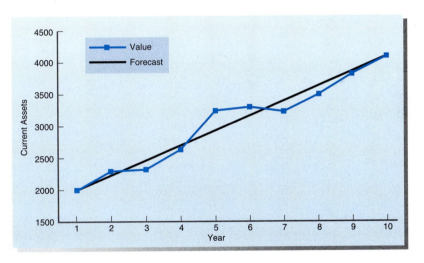

FIGURE 7.21   Hank's Forecast Using Linear Regression

JUANITA'S FORECAST USING HOLT'S TECHNIQUE

Juanita has decided that she wants to track the time series level and trend slowly; hence she has selected smoothing constants of $\alpha = .1$ for the level and $\gamma = .2$ for the trend. To begin the Holt process, the first step is to set the initial values for the level and trend and first forecast based on the data for years 1 and 2. Here,

$$L_2 = y_2 \qquad\qquad = 2280$$
$$T_2 = y_2 - y_1 = 2280 - 1990 = 290$$
$$F_3 = L_2 + T_2 = 2280 + 290 = 2570$$

Then the recursive formulas can be applied to years 3 through 10. For years 3 and 4, for example, Holt's method proceeds as follows.

Year 3:

$$L_3 = .1y_3 + (1 - .1)F_3 \qquad = .1(2328) + .9(2570) \qquad = 2545.80$$
$$T_3 = .2(L_3 - L_2) + (1 - .2)T_2 = .2(2545.80 - 2280) + .8(290) = \quad 285.16$$
$$F_4 = L_3 + T_3 \qquad = 2545.80 + 285.16 \qquad = 2830.96$$

Year 4:

$$L_4 = .1y_4 + (1 - .1)F_4 \qquad = .1(2635) + .9(2830.96) \qquad = 2811.36$$
$$T_4 = .2(L_4 - L_3) + (1 - .2)T_3 = .2(2811.36 - 2545.80) + .8(285.16) = \quad 281.24$$
$$F_5 = L_4 + T_4 \qquad = 2811.36 + 281.24 \qquad = 3092.60$$

This process is repeated for years 5, 6, 7, 8, 9, and 10. The results calculated using Excel are shown in Figure 7.22. The forecast for year 11 is:

$$F_{11} = L_{10} + T_{10} = 4337.17 + 256.20 = 4593.38$$

American Family Holt's.xls

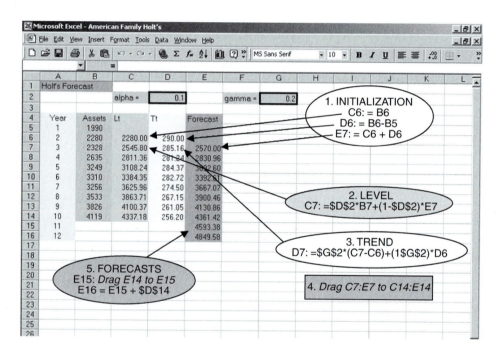

FIGURE 7.22

Holt's Forecast for American Family Products

Using the last estimate for the trend, $T_{10} = 256.20$, Juanita will have a forecast for each future year that will be 256.20 higher than that of the previous year's forecast. Thus her forecast for year 12 is:

$$F_{12} = F_{11} + T_{10} = 4593.38 + 256.20 = 4849.58$$

The formulas and steps required to complete the spreadsheet in Figure 7.22 are straightforward based on the previously outlined Holt approach and are shown on the figure. We see that indeed the forecasts for the next two years are $F_{11} = 4593.38$ and $F_{12} = 4849.58$, respectively.

As an alternative to having to program Excel to do Holt's technique, one can use the Holt's worksheet contained in the forecasting.xls template. Figure 7.23 shows the spreadsheet for Juanita's forecast. The results are identical to those shown in Figure 7.22.

American Family Forecast.xls

Microsoft Excel - American Family Forecast

INPUTS	
Number of Periods of Data Collected =	10
Smoothing Constant (alpha) =	0.1
Smoothing Constant (gamma) =	0.2
Initial Forecast Value (Level) =	2280
Initial Forecast Value (Trend) =	290

OUTPUTS			
Period		Forecast =	
MSE =	72994.37	MAPE =	7.752572
MAD =	250.3462	LAD =	411.0682

OUTPUTS											
Period	11	12	13	14	15	16	17	18	19	20	2
Forecast	4593.378	4849.579	5105.779	5361.98	5618.18	5874.38	6130.581	6386.781	6642.982	6899.182	7155.38

Period	Value	Forecast Level	Forecast Trend	Forecast	Error	Absolute Error	Error Squared	Absolute % Error
1	1990							
2	2280	2280	290					
3	2328	2545.8	285.16	2570	-242	242	58564	0.103952
4	2635	2811.364	281.2408	2830.96	-195.96	195.96	38400.32	0.074368
5	3249	3108.244	284.3687	3092.605	156.3952	156.3952	24459.46	0.048136
6	3310	3384.352	282.7164	3392.613	-82.613	82.61302	6824.912	0.024959
7	3256	3625.961	274.4951	3667.068	-411.068	411.0682	168977	0.126249
8	3533	3863.711	267.146	3900.456	-367.456	367.4564	135024.2	0.104007
9	3826	4100.371	261.0488	4130.857	-304.857	304.8567	92937.63	0.07968
10	4119	4337.178	256.2004	4361.42	-242.42	242.4199	58767.4	0.058854
11		4134.04	164.3329	4593.378				

Simple MA / Weighted MA / Exp. Smooth. / Lin. Reg. / Holt's / Class. Decomp.

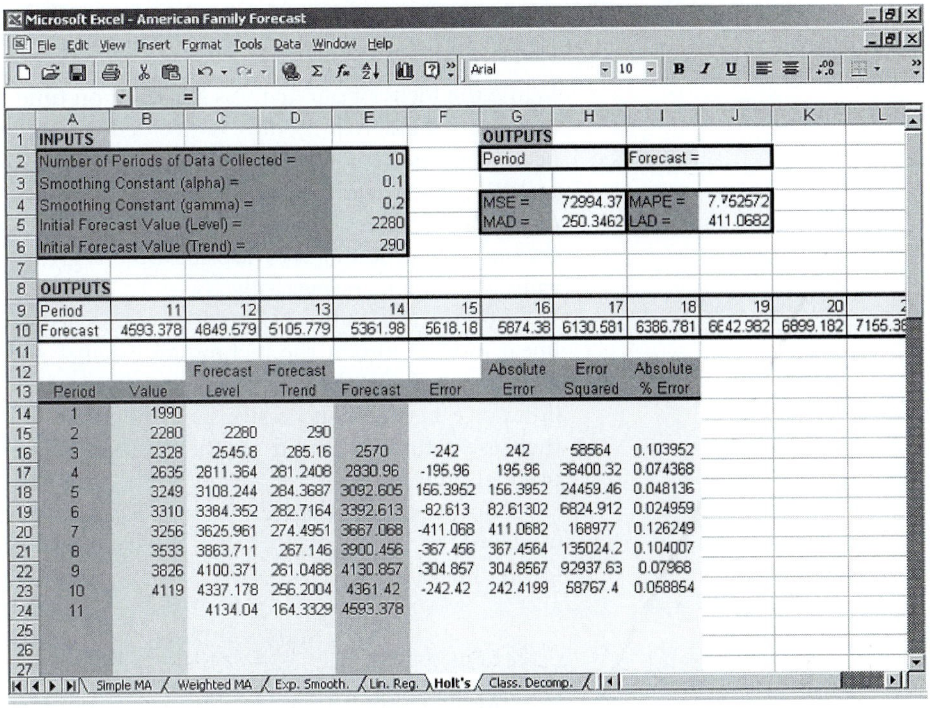

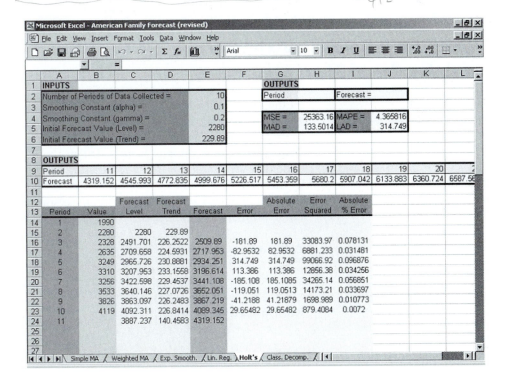

FIGURE 7.23
Excel Spreadsheet Showing Holt's Method Forecast

We observe from Figure 7.23 that in all but one year (year 5) the forecast error was negative. This indicates that the technique regularly forecasts values higher than the actual data values. The principal reason for this is that the initial value selected for the trend, 290, is too high. (Recall from the linear regression analysis that the slope of the regression line is only 229.89.) For example, using the template with an initial trend value of 229.89 results in the spreadsheet shown in Figure 7.24. We now see a more even distribution of the error terms and a reduction in the MSE from 72,994.37 to 25,363.16.

American Family Forecast (revised).xls

Microsoft Excel - American Family Forecast (revised)

INPUTS	
Number of Periods of Data Collected =	10
Smoothing Constant (alpha) =	0.1
Smoothing Constant (gamma) =	0.2
Initial Forecast Value (Level) =	2280
Initial Forecast Value (Trend) =	229.89

OUTPUTS			
Period		Forecast =	
MSE =	25363.16	MAPE =	4.365816
MAD =	133.5014	LAD =	314.749

OUTPUTS											
Period	11	12	13	14	15	16	17	18	19	20	2
Forecast	4319.152	4545.993	4772.835	4999.676	5226.517	5453.359	5680.2	5907.042	6133.883	6360.724	6587.56

Period	Value	Forecast Level	Forecast Trend	Forecast	Error	Absolute Error	Error Squared	Absolute % Error
1	1990							
2	2280	2280	229.89					
3	2328	2491.701	226.2522	2509.89	-181.89	181.89	33083.97	0.078131
4	2635	2709.658	224.5931	2717.953	-82.9532	82.9532	6881.233	0.031481
5	3249	2965.726	230.8881	2934.251	314.749	314.749	99066.92	0.096876
6	3310	3207.953	233.1558	3196.614	113.386	113.386	12856.38	0.034256
7	3256	3422.598	229.4537	3441.108	-185.108	185.1085	34265.14	0.056851
8	3533	3640.146	227.0726	3652.051	-119.051	119.0513	14173.21	0.033697
9	3826	3863.097	226.2483	3867.219	-41.2188	41.21879	1698.989	0.010773
10	4119	4092.311	226.8414	4089.345	29.65482	29.65482	879.4084	0.0072
11		3887.237	140.4583	4319.152				

Simple MA / Weighted MA / Exp. Smooth. / Lin. Reg. / Holt's / Class. Decomp.

FIGURE 7.24
Excel Spreadsheet Showing Holt's Method Forecast

TRANSFORMING MODELS WITH NONLINEAR TREND INTO MODELS WITH LINEAR TREND

While the focus of our analysis has been on time series with linear trend, the trend in some time series models is decidedly nonlinear. Numerous techniques have been developed for solving these models as well. For instance, if the plot of a time series seems to indicate quadratic trend, one could hypothesize the model: $y_t = \beta_0 + \beta_1 t + \beta_2 t^2 + \epsilon$. One approach to determining the best fitting parabola through these points is to use multiple regression, with the "x-values" being the values of t and t^2, respectively.

By appropriate transformations, some nonlinear models can be converted into linear models so that the techniques discussed in this chapter can be used to perform forecasts. In the case of the quadratic model, $y_t = \beta_0 + \beta_1 t + \beta_2 t^2 + \epsilon_t$, the difference between successive pairs of data values yields a linear model. We can then use a forecast based on these differences to determine the forecast for the original time series.

Another model that can be transformed into a linear model is an exponential model of the form $y_t = \beta_0 \beta_1^t \gamma_t$. If we take logarithms of both sides, we get the following linear model:

$$\log(y_t) = \log(\beta_0) + t \log(\beta_1) + \log(\epsilon_t) \tag{7.8}$$

We can then obtain a forecast for $\log(y_t)$ and transform it back into a forecast for y_t using the relationship $y_t = e^{\log(yt)}$.

OTHER FORECASTING TECHNIQUES FOR MODELS WITH LINEAR TREND

In addition to linear regression and Holt's method, a number of other techniques exist for forecasting time series with linear trend. Like Holt's technique, some of these methods are based on exponential smoothing. One method *not* based on exponential smoothing but on the difference between successive time series values is described in Appendix 7.4 on the accompanying CD-ROM.

7.5 Time Series with Trend, Seasonal, and Cyclical Variation

In the previous section, we considered how to develop forecasting models that account for trend in the time series. Many time series, however, exhibit seasonal and cyclical variations along with trend. Such variation principally arises due to calendar, climatic, or economic factors. When these patterns can be anticipated, they should be accounted for in the forecasting model in order to improve the accuracy of the forecasts.

Two models that account for trend, seasonal, and cyclical variation are the *additive model* and the *multiplicative model*:

Additive Model

$$y_t = T_t + S_t + C_t + \epsilon_t \tag{7.9}$$

Multiplicative Model

$$y_t = T_t S_t C_t \epsilon_t \tag{7.10}$$

In these models,

y_t = the time series value at time t

T_t = the trend component of the time series at time t

S_t = the seasonal component of the time series at time t

C_t = the cyclical component of the time series at time t

ϵ_t = the random error component of the time series at time t

The major difference between the two models is how one views the effects of the cyclical and seasonal variations on trend. An additive model is more appropriate when the seasonal and cyclical variations do not change in proportion to the time series values; whereas a multiplicative model is more appropriate if they do.

To illustrate this difference, consider a forecast of electricity consumption for a household that has electric baseboard heating and electric air conditioning. We would expect a seasonal variation in electricity usage due to heating in the winter and cooling in the summer. As measured in *kilowatt hours*, we expect seasonal effects to be additive because, while the overall electrical usage may increase over time (due to the family's purchase of more electrical appliances), the change in kilowatt usage during the winter and summer due to climatic variations does not vary in proportion to overall usage. In this case, an additive forecasting model may be appropriate.

On the other hand, if the *cost* of electricity is being forecast and the household is in a region in which the cost per kilowatt hour has been rising rapidly, the trend in cost data may be due primarily to the higher cost per kilowatt hour rather than the increase in the number of kilowatt hours used. If this is the case, the variation in utility cost in the summer and winter is proportional to the overall cost, and a multiplicative model is more appropriate.

In an additive model, the magnitude of the seasonal variations is reasonably constant over time, while in a multiplicative model the magnitude of the seasonal variations grows in proportion to the trend of the series. Because the effects of seasonality can usually be more appropriately modeled as a percentage of the trend (such as in the case of a time series dealing with the *cost* of electricity), multiplicative time series models are more frequently used to handle seasonal variation.

One technique often used to develop an additive or multiplicative forecasting model is **classical decomposition**. In this technique, the trend, cyclical, and seasonal components are isolated and forecast separately. The random error component is assumed to have a mean of 0 for additive models and a mean of 1 for multiplicative models. Once the trend, seasonal, and cyclical component forecasts have been determined, in additive models they are added together to obtain forecasts for the time series, while in multiplicative models they are multiplied together to obtain forecasts.

The classical decomposition approach is somewhat complicated, although the work can be done quite easily using Excel. The idea is the following.

1. *Smooth the data so that the seasonal and random effects are removed from the data.*
   We will use a centered moving average approach by assigning the average over all n seasons to its centered value. For example, with daily data we would average seven days of data. That is, the average from Sunday (period 1) to Saturday (period 7) would be assigned to the "middle" period Wednesday (period 4), the average from Monday (period 2) to the next Sunday (period 8) would be assigned to period 5 (Thursday), and so on.

When there are an even number of seasons, like quarters, the average of the first four quarters (beginning with period 1) will be assigned to period 2.5, the average of the four quarters beginning with period 2 to period 3.5, and so on. Since there is no period 2.5 or 3.5, the average of these two values will provide the *centered moving average* for period 3. You can verify that this is equivalent to assigning weights of $\frac{1}{8}$ to periods 1 and 5 and weights of $\frac{1}{4}$ to periods 2, 3, and 4.

2. Determine the *period factors* by dividing the actual data value by its centered moving average.

3. Determine *unadjusted seasonal factors* by averaging all the period factors corresponding to the same season.

4. Determine *adjusted seasonal factors* by dividing each seasonal factor by the average of all seasonal factors. This ensures that the average adjusted seasonal factor is 1.

5. Determine *deseasonalized data values* for all values of the time series by dividing the actual values of the time series by their corresponding adjusted seasonal factor. This will allow us to determine the overall trend component, absent the seasonality effects.

6. Determine a *trend forecast of the deseasonalized values*. We will use linear regression on the deseasonalized time series to do this.

7. Determine an *adjusted seasonal forecast* by multiplying each unadjusted forecast value by its appropriate seasonal factor.

USING CLASSICAL DECOMPOSITION FOR MULTIPLICATIVE MODELS

The following example illustrates the classical decomposition approach for a multiplicative model. A similar approach can be used for an additive model.

CFA Decomposition.xls
CFA Forecast.xls

CANADIAN FACULTY ASSOCIATION (CFA)

The Canadian Faculty Association (CFA) is the exclusive bargaining agent for the approximately 21,000 faculty members who teach in state-supported Canadian colleges and universities. Under Canadian law, membership in the organization is voluntary, but CFA is required to represent the interests of all full-time and part-time faculty, as well as librarians and coaches. Membership in the organization has grown gradually over the years. However, because approximately half the teaching faculty are lecturers who are hired on a year-to-year basis, membership in the organization tends to decline in the summer months and increase during the academic year.

While some 210 members pay dues to the organization directly, the vast majority pay through payroll deduction. Table 7.6 shows average CFA membership based on payroll deduction each quarter during the four-year period 1997–2000.

To prepare the budget for the 2001 fiscal year, the CFA treasurer requires a forecast of average quarterly membership during 2001.

TABLE 7.6   Average Dues-Paying CFA Members Through Payroll Deduction

Period	Year	Quarter	Average Membership
1	1997	1	7130
2		2	6940
3		3	7354
4		4	7556
5	1998	1	7673
6		2	7332
7		3	7662
8		4	7809
9	1999	1	7872
10		2	7551
11		3	7989
12		4	8143
13	2000	1	8167
14		2	7902
15		3	8268
16		4	8436

SOLUTION

The first step is to graph this data over time to get an idea of the enrollment pattern. Using the Chart feature in Excel, we obtain the graph shown in Figure 7.25 of the average membership paid through payroll deduction over the 16 periods.

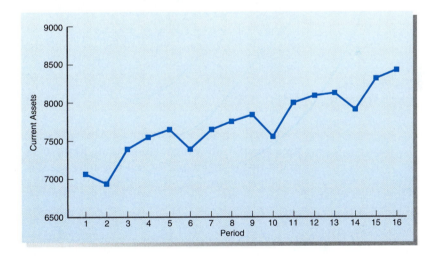

FIGURE 7.25
Excel Graph of Average Membership by Payroll Deduction

As we see from Figure 7.25, membership is gradually increasing over time and exhibits a pattern of seasonal variation within each calendar year. Since it is believed that changes in average quarterly membership will increase as the general level of membership increases, we will use the following multiplicative model for the forecast:

$$y_t = T_t\, S_t\, C_t\, \epsilon_t$$

Appendix 7.7 on the accompanying CD-ROM details the steps of performing classical decomposition for this problem using Excel. As an alternative to developing an Excel spreadsheet to perform the forecast however, one may simply use the worksheet Class.Decomp. on the forecast.xls template. Figure 7.26 shows the template results for the CFA problem. Forecasts for next twelve periods are given in row 8. To forecast a specific future period one can input the period number in cell H2 and the forecast will be displayed in cell J2.

Thus we forecast that the average number of members who elect payroll deduction during the first quarter of the next year will be 8523. We predict 8186 during the second quarter, 8600 during the third quarter, and 8773 during the fourth quarter. Adding the 210 who pay dues directly each quarter gives a forecast for total average membership of 8733, 8396, 8810, and 8983 during each of the four quarters, respectively.

CFA Forecast.xls

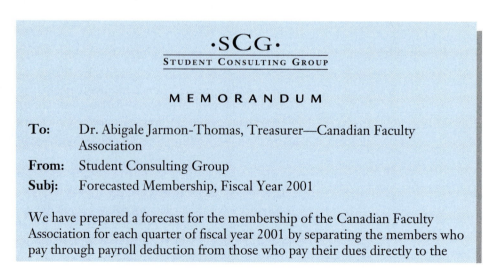

FIGURE 7.26
Output for CFA Problem
Using Forecast.xls Template

Based on this analysis for CFA membership, the Student Consulting Group prepared the following memorandum to the treasurer of the CFA. In this memo, a graph of the membership over the four years is presented, and the forecasts are summarized in an easy-to-read table.

·S C G·

STUDENT CONSULTING GROUP

M E M O R A N D U M

To: Dr. Abigale Jarmon-Thomas, Treasurer—Canadian Faculty
         Association

From: Student Consulting Group

Subj: Forecasted Membership, Fiscal Year 2001

We have prepared a forecast for the membership of the Canadian Faculty Association for each quarter of fiscal year 2001 by separating the members who pay through payroll deduction from those who pay their dues directly to the organization. The reason for this distinction is that, while the membership paying dues directly has remained fairly constant at approximately 210 members over the past four years, the number paying by payroll deduction has varied significantly from month to month. Hence our approach is to add a constant 210 members to the forecasted number of members paying by payroll deduction in order to obtain a forecast of total membership.

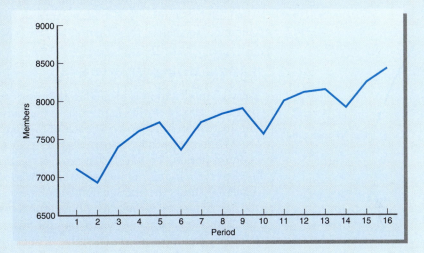

FIGURE 1 Average Payroll Deduction for Members over Four-Year Period

In developing this forecast, we have analyzed a historical pattern of membership to gain insight into its trend and variability. Figure 1 shows the membership pattern of average payroll deduction members over the past four-year period.

Based on this pattern, we have determined a forecasting model for members paying dues through payroll deduction. This model accounts for both the upward trend and periodic variation in membership, and it gives the following quarterly forecast of total membership (including those who pay directly to the organization).

Quarter	Membership Forecast
1. 2001	8733
2. 2001	8396
3. 2001	8810
4. 2001	8983

It is important to realize that these forecasts implicitly assume that the historic trend in the past years' data will continue into the upcoming year. It is our understanding that the current fiscal difficulties experienced by a number of Canadian provinces may result in a decrease in the number of faculty employed by state-supported universities, which in turn, would be expected to have a negative impact on CFA membership.

If this situation does arise, it would be necessary to revise our forecast of membership downward. Hence we recommend close monitoring of provincial budgets, and, if there is a decrease in employment, we can modify the forecast appropriately.

We hope that this information has been of value to you. Should you have any questions, please do not hesitate to contact us.

THE ADDITIVE MODEL

We conclude this section by considering an additive forecasting model for time series that exhibit trend, seasonal, and cyclical components. If we believe that an additive model is appropriate for forecasting, we can use a decomposition approach similar to that described earlier for the multiplicative model. However, another technique, based on multiple regression, is often used for such models.

In the multiple regression approach to forecasting models with trend and seasonal effects, dummy variables are introduced to denote the seasons. We use this technique to analyze the situation at Troy's Mobil Station.

Troy's Forecast.xls

TROY'S MOBIL STATION

Troy's Mobil station is located in the resort town of Liberty, New York. Over the past five years, Troy has kept track of his daily gasoline sales and noticed an apparent fluctuation in sales during each of the four seasons.

While the town has experienced a steady increase in the year-round population over this period, Troy feels that most of the seasonal variation in sales can be attributed to the varying number of tourists who visit the region throughout the year. Table 7.7 shows the average number of gallons of gasoline Troy has sold daily over the past five years during each of the four seasons. (Year 5 is the most recent year.)

Troy is interested in forecasting the average daily gasoline sales during each of the four seasons over the upcoming year in order to determine his inventory and personnel needs.

TABLE 7.7 Average Gallons of Gasoline Sold Daily at Troy's Mobil Station

Season	Year				
	1	2	3	4	5
Fall	3497	3726	3989	4248	4443
Winter	3484	3589	3870	4105	4307
Spring	3553	3742	3996	4263	4466
Summer	3837	4050	4327	4544	4795

SOLUTION

Figure 7.27 shows the pattern of average gasoline sales over the five-year period. Because the change in the number of tourists each season has been fairly constant

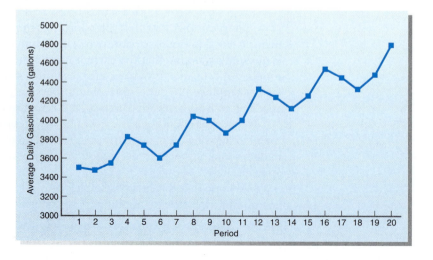

FIGURE 7.27
Troy's Average Daily Gasoline Sales over Five-year Period

over the past five years, an additive seasonality model may be appropriate. Multiple regression can be used to generate these forecasts.

In this approach, the item being forecasted (gasoline sales) is the dependent (y) variable. The independent variables are the period number and dummy variables that indicate the period's season. The dummy indicator variable for a season is 1 if the period corresponds to that season; otherwise, it is 0. Since there are four seasons, only three dummy variables are used; season 4 is indicated by assigning 0's to the other three.[5] Thus, the model (neglecting the cyclical component) is:

$$y_t = \beta_0 + \beta_1 t + \beta_2 F + \beta_3 W + \beta_4 S + \epsilon_t \tag{7.11}$$

where: t = period number
  β_0 = level of the time series
  β_1 = slope (trend) of the time series
  β_2 = seasonal factor for fall
  β_3 = seasonal factor for winter
  β_4 = seasonal factor for spring
   F = indicator for fall
  W = indicator for winter
   S = indicator for spring
   ϵ_t = random term in period t

That is, F, W, and S are binary variables denoting the appropriate season (i.e., 1, if the period corresponds to that season and 0, if it does not. Summer is indicated by $F = 0$, $W = 0$, and $S = 0$). The data for this problem are summarized in Table 7.8. Our objective is to obtain estimates for the parameters, β_0, β_1, β_2, β_3, and β_4, of the multiple regression model.

TABLE 7.8   Quarterly Input Data for Troy's Mobil Station Problem

Year	Season	y_t	t	F	W	S
1	Fall	3497	1	1	0	0
	Winter	3484	2	0	1	0
	Spring	3553	3	0	0	1
	Summer	3837	4	0	0	0
2	Fall	3726	5	1	0	0
	Winter	3589	6	0	1	0
	Spring	3742	7	0	0	1
	Summer	4050	8	0	0	0
3	Fall	3989	9	1	0	0
	Winter	3870	10	0	1	0
	Spring	3996	11	0	0	1
	Summer	4327	12	0	0	0
4	Fall	4248	13	1	0	0
	Winter	4105	14	0	1	0
	Spring	4263	15	0	0	1
	Summer	4544	16	0	0	0
5	Fall	4443	17	1	0	0
	Winter	4307	18	0	1	0
	Spring	4466	19	0	0	1
	Summer	4795	20	0	0	0

[5] In general, if there are N seasons, only N − 1 dummy variables are needed in the model.

We avoid building a specific worksheet by using the forecast.xls template. It contains a worksheet titled Add. Model. This worksheet automatically adds the necessary independent variables to the spreadsheet. All one must do is specify the number of periods of data collected in cell E2, the number of seasons in cell E3, and the time series values in column A beginning in row 7. Figure 7.28 gives the spreadsheet for Troy's Mobil station using the Add. Model worksheet.

Troy's Forecast.xls

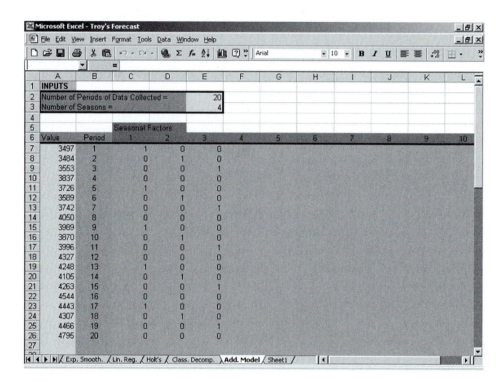

FIGURE 7.28   Excel Spreadsheet for Troy's Mobil Station Data

We can use the regression analysis option under data analysis to determine the appropriate multiple regression equation. The dependent variable is in column A, and the independent variables are in columns B through E in this example. The rows 1 through 21 in Figure 7.29 show this output.

We note that all the p-values for the period and the seasons are well below any typical value of α such as .05. Hence we can conclude that all factors in this seasonal model are significant. If only some of the p-values proved significant, one would have to decide whether a model that included all the seasonal variables was more useful than one that did not. One test that can be used to determine this is the reduced F-test. The details of this approach are included on the accompanying CD-ROM in Appendix 7.5.

Since all the factors in this model are significant, we can program Excel to generate the forecasted values. We put the periods of interest in A24:A27. The unadjusted forecasts are then given using the simple linear regression equation. This is done in cells B24:B27. These numbers are then adjusted for the season in cells C24:C27. This is done by adding the seasonal components given in cells B19:B22 (note that B22 is a blank cell since the summer quarter has no seasonal adjustment) to the unadjusted forecasts in cells B24:B27. Thus we forecast average daily sales for next year to be 4680.575 gallons in the fall, 4570.975 in the winter, 4703.975 in the spring, and 5010.575 in the summer.

Troy's Forecast.xls

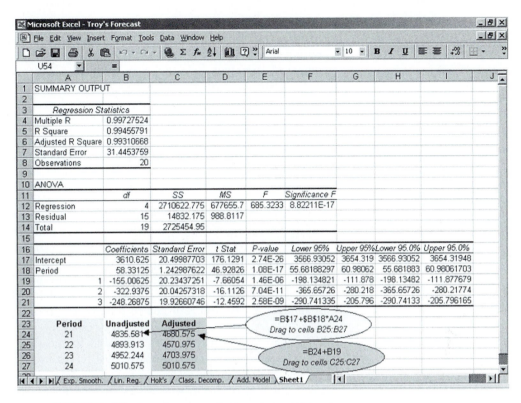

FIGURE 7.29   Excel Output for Troy's Mobil Station

7.6 Other Forecasting Techniques

BOX–JENKINS METHOD

Often, the analyst may not know which model is the most appropriate for describing a time series. Ideally, we would like a technique that can help us select the appropriate underlying forecasting model. A popular advanced forecasting technique, known as the **Box–Jenkins method**, does just that. While the use of this method is beyond the scope of this text, a brief overview of how it works is worthwhile.

The Box–Jenkins method makes use of the autocorrelation function and a related function, known as the partial autocorrelation function, to identify the appropriate forecasting model. The technique bases its forecasts on a combined autoregressive and moving average model. It is called autoregressive because the forecast is based on historic time series values. In addition, n period differences between time series values are used in this forecasting model. These are known as ARIMA, or **autoregressive-integrated-moving average**, forecasting models.

FORECASTING USING MULTIPLE TIME SERIES

While we have focused on forecasting a single time series in this chapter, frequently, several time series are used to derive a forecast. For example, a video rental store may be able to forecast rental demand for a particular movie title based not only on past rental demand, but also on box office receipts during the movie's theatrical release. Similarly, a nationwide retailer selling replacement tires for automobiles could base its forecast of future tire demand not only on the time series of past sales of the tire brand, but also on the time series of past sales of new automobiles. Typically, a technique such as multiple regression is used for models in which more than one time series is used to derive the forecast.

Forecasting an item of interest may require the performance of several different forecasts. For example, a security analyst who wants to forecast a firm's upcoming quarterly profit typically forecasts not only revenues for each of the company's principal divisions or product lines, but also costs for major expense items, such as advertising, labor, and materials. In turn, forecasting revenue for a company's product line may require separate forecasts for both the total market for the product and the company's market share.

QUALITATIVE APPROACHES TO FORECASTING

Time series data may not always be available. For example, a new product has no past history on which to base sales forecasts. When historic time series data are not available (or when they are considered nonrepresentative of future values), we normally gather "expert" opinions on which to base a forecast.

One way to coalesce these opinions into a consensus is through a method known as the **Delphi Technique**. In this method, each member of a panel of experts is asked individually to give his or her forecast. The makeup of the expert panel is typically kept secret from the panel members. Forecasts are compiled into an anonymous list and returned to the experts so that panel members can revise their forecasts if necessary in light of the responses given by other panel members. After revision, the list is again circulated for possible additional revisions. The process continues until a reasonably consistent consensus is reached.

Another qualitative technique for generating forecasts is **scenario writing**. In this technique, we begin with a well-defined set of assumptions and build a scenario regarding the future based on these assumptions. Usually, several scenarios are developed based on different sets of assumptions. The decision maker then selects the scenario that corresponds to the set of assumptions believed most likely to occur.

7.7 Summary

In this chapter, we have examined the process of generating a forecast. In particular, we have focused on how, based on time series data, we determine the appropriate forecasting model to use, and we have discussed techniques that can be applied to these various models in order to obtain forecasts.

Time series that exhibit a stationary pattern can be forecast using techniques such as simple or weighted moving averages or exponential smoothing. Of special concern when selecting the appropriate technique is the ability of the forecast model to respond quickly to changes so that future forecast errors are not too severe.

Some time series exhibit linear trend without seasonal or cyclical factors. Linear regression and Holt's exponential smoothing approach are two techniques for forecasting such models. Other time series exhibit trend, seasonality, and cyclical factors. A multiplicative or an additive model may be appropriate for forecasting such time series. The multiplicative model relies on the classical decomposition technique, whereas a technique based on multiple regression is frequently used for forecasting an additive model.

Other forecasting methods include advanced time series techniques and qualitative approaches that can be used when time series data are not available. Table 7.9 summarizes the principal time series forecasting techniques discussed in this chapter.

It is important to realize that forecasting is not an exact science. No matter which technique is selected, the goal is the same: to develop a prediction regarding the future that is more accurate than simply guessing.

TABLE 7.9 Principal Forecasting Techniques

Time Series Model	Technique	Comments
Stationary	Last Period	*Pros*: Forecast is extremely easy to calculate; requires only one data value to perform forecast; tracks changes in the time series quickly.
		Cons: Past time series data are ignored; forecast errors may be large.
	Moving Average	*Pros*: Easy to calculate forecast; uses past series values.
		Cons: Each historic period is given the same weight; data beyond a certain age are ignored; may be difficult to determine how many periods should be used; data for n periods must be stored in the system; tracks changes in the time series gradually.
	Weighted Moving Average	*Pros*: Uses past time series values but gives greater weight to more recent observations; useful for stationary time series that exhibit autocorrelation; can track changes in the time series quickly.
		Cons: May be difficult to determine how many periods to use and the weights to assign to each period; data beyond a certain age are ignored; data for n periods must be stored in the system.
	Exponential Smoothing	*Pros*: Fairly easy to calculate forecast; uses past time series values indirectly; only two data values must be stored in the system to perform the forecast; can track changes in the time series quickly; useful for stationary time series which exhibit autocorrelation.
		Cons: May be difficult to determine the appropriate smoothing constant and initial forecast value to use; the relative weights given to past observations are fixed by the choice of the smoothing constant.
Trend	Linear Regression	*Pros*: Determines the forecasting model that gives the smallest mean squared forecast error; uses as much historic data in developing the forecast as desired.
		Cons: May not be appropriate if the random error terms are not independent or if they do not have constant variance; data for n periods must be stored in the system; assumes linear trend will continue forever into the future; forecast will track changes quite slowly.
	Holt's Linear Exponential Smoothing	*Pros*: Forecast can respond rapidly to changes in the time series values; a small number of historical values must be stored in the system in order to perform the forecast.
		Cons: It may be difficult to determine the appropriate values for the smoothing constants as well as the initial forecast values; forecast calculations are somewhat difficult to perform.
Trend, Seasonal and Cyclical Component Models	Classical Decomposition for Multiplicative Models	*Pros*: The effects of the various factors on the forecast are clear; calculations are fairly straightforward.
		Cons: May be difficult to determine the cyclical factors; calculations may be time consuming; tracks changes in the time series components slowly.
	Multiple Regression for Additive Models	*Pros*: Easy to perform; the effects of seasonal and trend components on the time series are clear.
		Cons: May be difficult to incorporate cyclical variation; tracks changes in the time series components slowly.

ON THE CD-ROM

● Excel regression analysis	**YoHo Yo-Yo.xls**
● Last period technique spreadsheet	**YoHo last-period technique.xls**
● Moving average technique spreadsheets	**YoHo four-period moving average technique.xls**
	YoHo Forecast.xls
● Four-period weighted moving average technique spreadsheets	**YoHo four-period weighted moving average technique.xls**
	four-period weighted moving average.xls
● Exponential smoothing technique spreadsheets	**exponential smoothing.xls**
	YoHo exponential smoothing.xls
	Solver exponential smoothing.xls
● Regression technique spreadsheets	**American Family Regression.xls**
	American Family Forecast.xls
● Holt's method spreadsheets	**American Family Holt's.xls**
	American Family Forecast.xls
	American Family Forecast (revised).xls
● Classical decomposition spreadsheets	**CFA Decomposition.xls**
	CFA Forecast.xls
● Additive model spreadsheet	**Troy's Forecast.xls**
● Excel template for solving forecasting problems	**forecast.xls**
● Test for Trend	**Appendix 7.2**
● Test for Autocorrelation	**Appendix 7.3**
● Forecasting Based on Taking First Differences	**Appendix 7.4**
● Determining Whether to Include Dummy Seasonal Variables in Regression Models	**Appendix 7.5**
● Use of Excel Trendline Feature	**Appendix 7.6**
● Developing an Excel Spreadsheet for Performing Classical Decomposition	**Appendix 7.7**
● Problem Motivations	**Problem Motivations**
● Problems 41–50	**Additional Problems/Cases**

APPENDIX 7.1

Using the forecast.xls Template

FORECASTING STATIONARY MODELS

For stationary models, the worksheets are Simple MA (simple moving average), Weighted MA (weighted moving average), and Exp. Smooth. (exponential smoothing). For each of these worksheets, the required input includes the number of periods in the time series and the values for the parameters of the model. Note that the last period technique can be performed using the Simple MA worksheet by entering 1 for the number of periods for the Moving Average. Each worksheet can handle forecasting problems with up to 60 periods of data.

For example, the Moving Average worksheet requires the number of periods to be used to calculate the moving average, the Weighted Moving Average worksheet requires the desired weights to be used, and the Exponential Smoothing worksheet requires the value of the smoothing constant, α.

When the number of periods of data collected is entered, the period numbers automatically appear in column A of the worksheet. The user must then input the corresponding values of the time series in column B. The resulting output includes the stationary forecasted value for the next and all succeeding time periods as well as the values of the four performances measures (the MAD, MSE, MAPE, LAD).

Figure A7.1 shows the Weighted MA worksheet on the forecast.xls template.

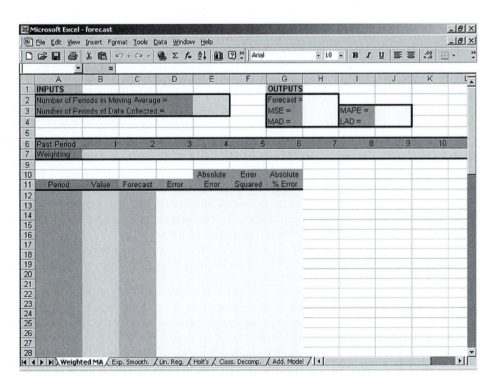

FIGURE A7.1
Weighted MA Worksheet on forecast.xls Template

MODELS WITH TREND

The Lin. Reg. worksheet will determine a forecast using linear regression. To use this worksheet, one enters the number of periods of data that have been collected in cell E2 and the appropriate data values in column B beginning in row 12. The template will give the forecast values for the next 12 periods in row 8. To obtain a forecast beyond that time horizon, one simply enters the desired period number in cell H2. Then the forecast value appears in cell J2. Figure A7.2 shows the Lin. Reg. worksheet.

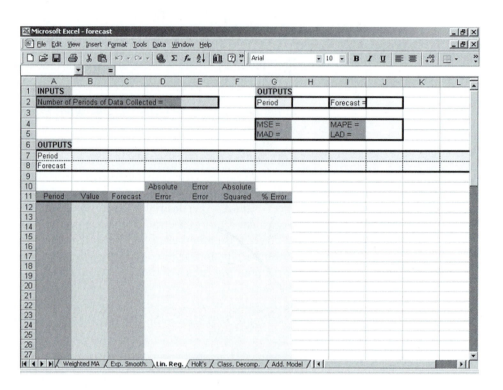

FIGURE A7.2
Lin. Reg. Worksheet

The Holt's worksheet will determine a forecast using Holt's method. In the template, the number of periods of data collected is entered in cell E2, the smoothing constant α is entered in cell E3, and the smoothing constant γ is entered in cell E4. The template will automatically enter the initial level value in cell E5 using the formula $L_2 = y_2$. If you wish to use a different initial level, you may override this value and put a different number in cell E5. Similarly, in cell E6 the template will automatically enter the initial trend value using the formula $T_2 = y_2 - y_1$. Again, one is free to override this value and enter a different estimate in cell E6 for the initial trend.

After entering the data, the forecast for the next 12 periods is given in row 10 of the template. For periods beyond this time horizon, the period value can be entered in cell H2 and the forecast corresponding to that period will be shown in cell J2. Figure A7.3 shows the Holt's worksheet.

MODELS WITH SEASONALITY

The Class. Decomp. worksheet will forecast using the classical decomposition method. In order to use this worksheet, one must specify the number of data points collected in cell E2, the number of seasons in cell E3, and the data values in column B beginning in row 12. The spreadsheet then calculates the forecast for the next 12 periods and displays these values in row 8. If one wishes to determine the forecast for a specific period, the period number can be entered into cell H2 and the forecast will be displayed in cell J2. Figure A7.4 shows the Class. Decomp. worksheet.

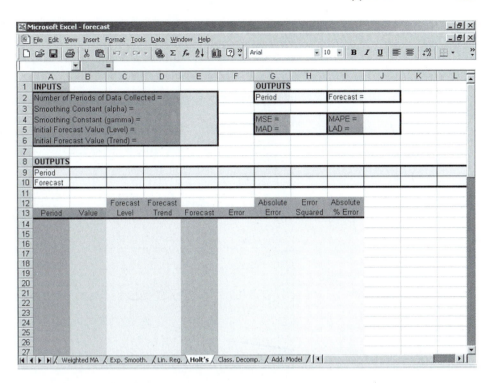

FIGURE A7.3
Holt's Worksheet

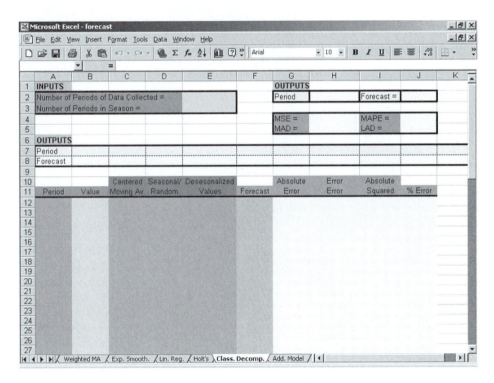

FIGURE A7.4
Class. Decomp. Worksheet

The Add. Model worksheet can be used to set up the necessary format to do a multiple regression, with the period and seasons being the independent variables. It can handle problems with up to 12 seasons and for which 60 periods of data have been collected. The number of periods of data collected is entered in cell E2, and the number of seasons is entered in cell E3. The template will automatically add the period numbers in column B and the dummy seasonal values in columns C through M. The time series values are entered in column B beginning in row 7.

Once the data have been entered into the Add. Model worksheet, one can use Regression (found under Tools/Data Analysis) in order to determine the parameters for the model. Figure A7.5 shows the Add. Model worksheet.

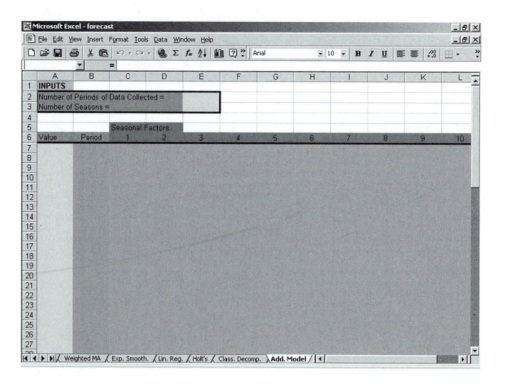

FIGURE A7.5
Add. Model Worksheet

Problems *

* Data files for the problems in this chapter are contained on the accompanying CD-ROM in the Excel file folder for Chapter 7. The file names correspond to the company names.

1. Monthly water usage at the Smith Insurance Agency for the past year, as measured in 100s of cubic feet, has been as follows:

Period	Month	Usage
1	January	17
2	February	24
3	March	21
4	April	20
5	May	17
6	June	21
7	July	21
8	August	19
9	September	17
10	October	18
11	November	20
12	December	21

   a. Graph this time series. Does a stationary model seem appropriate?
   b. Using regression, show that a stationary model is reasonable.

   c. Using a four-month moving average, forecast water usage for the Smith Agency for both the upcoming month of January and the entire upcoming year.
   d. What is the forecast for the upcoming month of January if a three-month weighted moving average with weights, $w_1 = .6$, $w_2 = .3$, and $w_3 = .1$ is used?
   e. Which of the above two forecasting methods would you recommend based on the mean absolute deviation error criterion?

2. Consider the data given for the Smith Agency water usage in problem 1.
   a. Determine the forecast for the upcoming January if exponential smoothing is used with a smoothing constant of $\alpha = .1$.
   b. Repeat part a using $\alpha = .6$
   c. Using the criterion of minimizing the mean squared forecast error, which smoothing constant, $\alpha = .1$ or $\alpha = .6$, appears to give better results?

3. Curaid Company wishes to forecast monthly sales for the upcoming year of its line of designer bandages, introduced two years ago and advertised using the slogan

"What the best-dressed cuts are wearing." Monthly sales (in gross) are as follows:

Month	Sales	Month	Sales
1	424	13	546
2	418	14	557
3	435	15	559
4	449	16	554
5	446	17	573
6	469	18	574
7	500	19	604
8	481	20	611
9	489	21	626
10	506	22	636
11	530	23	649
12	532	24	643

a. Graph this time series.
b. Show statistically that a linear trend forecasting model is appropriate.
c. Using a linear regression technique, forecast monthly sales for the next 12-month period (i.e., months 25–36).

4. Consider the data in problem 3.
   a. Use Holt's Technique with $\alpha = .2$ and $\gamma = .3$ to perform a forecast for the next 12 months.
   b. Repeat part a using $\alpha = .5$ and $\gamma = .7$.
   c. Which set of smoothing constants places more emphasis on more recent observations?
   d. Using the MAD performance measure, for this data, which of the two sets of smoothing constants appears to give better forecasts?

5. Daily donut sales (in dollars) at Watson's Donuts for the past four weeks are as follows:

Day	Week 1	Week 2	Week 3	Week 4
Sunday	291.59	310.57	285.28	307.43
Monday	346.86	336.89	358.67	361.30
Tuesday	319.47	335.68	331.77	342.59
Wednesday	375.34	365.19	369.82	381.43
Thursday	356.73	371.82	395.44	402.56
Friday	298.93	343.96	363.45	357.17
Saturday	327.05	338.05	352.02	354.63

Assume that Watson's wishes to forecast daily sales for weeks 5 and 6 and wants to use a multiplicative model to account for seasonal (daily) variations. Using classical decomposition, determine the forecast of daily demand for weeks 5 and 6.

6. Weekly sales (in hundreds) of Pert shampoo at the SaveMor drug chain for the past 16 weeks are as follows:

Week	Sales	Week	Sales
1	65	9	72
2	61	10	78
3	68	11	73
4	67	12	75
5	74	13	68
6	82	14	64
7	75	15	73
8	63	16	79

Management wishes to forecast the annual demand for Pert shampoo in order to determine an optimal order policy.
   a. Graph this time series.
   b. Verify statistically that a stationary model is appropriate for forecasting this time series.
   c. Using a four-period moving average, forecast the annual demand for Pert shampoo. (Assume sales = demand.)

7. Consider the data given in problem 6. Use exponential smoothing with $\alpha = .10$ to forecast the annual demand for Pert shampoo.

8. Dixon Glass manufactures mason jars for use in home canning. Quarterly sales for this division (in millions of dollars) over the past five years are as follows (year 5 is the most recent year):

Quarter	Year 1	2	3	4	5
1	7.8	7.2	6.8	6.6	6.3
2	12.1	10.7	11.4	10.3	10.2
3	9.4	8.5	8.2	7.4	8.6
4	5.3	4.9	4.3	5.2	4.2

Dixon management believes that an additive model incorporating seasonality is appropriate for forecasting upcoming quarterly sales. Using the multiple regression approach, forecast quarterly sales for year 6.

9. The Hillel Sandwich Shop is trying to estimate its profit for the upcoming month. In order to do this, it must forecast future sandwich sales. Below are the number of sandwiches sold each day of the five-day work week for the past four weeks (week 4 is the most recent week).

Day	Week 1	2	3	4
Monday	140	162	172	159
Tuesday	156	135	163	132
Wednesday	172	158	141	135
Thursday	144	174	162	151
Friday	112	146	138	142

a. Graph this time series.
b. Determine whether the time series exhibits any linear trend.
c. Using a five-day moving average, forecast the number of sandwiches that will be sold daily during the upcoming week.
d. What is the forecast of the number of sandwiches sold daily during the upcoming week if the firm uses exponential smoothing? (Assume that the smoothing constant is $\alpha = .10$.)

10. Consider the data in problem 9.
    a. If the firm wishes to use exponential smoothing to forecast the number of sandwiches sold daily, use Solver to determine the smoothing constant that minimizes the mean squared forecast error.

b. If the firm wishes to use a five-period weighted moving average for performing its forecast, use Solver to determine the weightings. Assume the criterion is to minimize the mean squared forecast error.

c. On the basis of your answers to parts (a) and (b), which forecasting method would you recommend for the company? Assume the criterion is to minimize the mean squared forecast error.

11. Net sales (in millions of dollars) for Armco Plastics over the past five years (year 5 is the most recent year) are as follows:

Year	Sales
1	107,742
2	112,346
3	122,168
4	125,598
5	126,610

Using the linear regression technique, forecast net sales of Armco Plastics for years 6 through 8.

12. Quarterly revenues (in $1000s) of the Gray Rabbit Hotel chain over the past five years have been as follows.

			Year		
Quarter	1	2	3	4	5
1	5108	4871	5248	5365	5423
2	6121	5907	6214	6323	6408
3	6394	6485	6582	6647	6586
4	4593	4798	4893	5021	5134

On the basis of these data, use a multiplicative forecasting model based on classical decomposition to forecast quarterly revenues for year 6.

13. Student enrollments in the management science core class offered at a major university have been as follows: (See file management science.xls.)

Period	Enrollment
Year 1	
Fall	756
Spring	723
Summer	143
Year 2	
Fall	823
Spring	745
Summer	157
Year 3	
Fall	834
Spring	752
Summer	158
Year 4	
Fall	836
Spring	765
Summer	164

Using an additive model based on linear regression to account for seasonality, determine the enrollment forecast for fall, spring, and summer of year 5.

14. Susan Wilson is considering purchasing an eight-unit apartment building as an investment. In order to determine her projected annual return, Susan must estimate the cost of natural gas used to provide hot water and heat to the building. The current owner has provided Susan with copies of the monthly gas bill over the past three years. These data are as follows (year 3 is the most recent year).

	Year		
	1	2	3
January	$396.87	$406.58	$429.04
February	$345.92	$429.56	$405.62
March	$287.56	$319.87	$347.29
April	$265.34	$306.45	$325.70
May	$194.13	$208.56	$254.55
June	$185.39	$196.49	$214.86
July	$156.43	$147.37	$187.72
August	$148.92	$174.63	$166.28
September	$239.58	$227.91	$245.18
October	$275.29	$269.02	$286.04
November	$295.06	$314.38	$337.91
December	$349.73	$319.34	$378.48

Using a multiplicative model based on classical decomposition, forecast the gas utility cost of the apartment building for the upcoming year.

15. The production manager for Bee's Candy Company is trying to decide whether he should purchase cocoa futures to satisfy the firm's cocoa requirements for the upcoming six-month period. The average cost of purchasing cocoa in this fashion is $0.46 per pound. The firm requires 140,000 pounds of cocoa in order to support production over this period.

The manager feels that purchasing futures contracts is worthwhile only if it costs an average of no more than $0.01 per pound over purchasing the cocoa on the spot market. Average spot market prices per pound over the past 20 weeks are given in the following table (week 20 is the most recent week):

Week	Cost/Pound	Week	Cost/Pound
1	$.42	11	$.48
2	.45	12	.49
3	.45	13	.48
4	.43	14	.47
5	.44	15	.47
6	.45	16	.46
7	.44	17	.46
8	.46	18	.45
9	.45	19	.44
10	.47	20	.45

a. Graph this time series.
b. Show statistically that a stationary forecasting model is appropriate. (Test at $\alpha = .05$.)
c. Suppose that the manager uses exponential smoothing with a smoothing constant, $\alpha = .2$. If this procedure begins with an initial cost/pound forecast

of $0.42, forecast the firm's cost of buying its cocoa requirements for the next six months on the spot market.

d. On the basis of your answer to part c, determine whether the firm should purchase futures contracts for the cocoa.

16. Consider the data given in problem 15. Suppose the manager uses a four-period weighted moving average with weights, $w_1 = .4$, $w_2 = .3$, $w_3 = .2$, and $w_4 = .1$. On the basis of this forecasting procedure, would you recommend that the firm purchase the future contract? Explain your reasoning.

17. Year-end book value per share of Kerf Group was as follows:

Year	Book Value per Share
1997	$11.40
1998	11.29
1999	10.91
2000	10.43
2001	9.92

On the basis of these data, Matt Wallace, a security analyst, wishes to forecast the book value per share of Kerf in 2006. Using the linear regression technique determine the book value per share for Kerf stock in:
a. 2006.
b. 2035. Comment.

18. The manager of a recently opened branch of Home Fed Bank wishes to forecast the number of customers who will arrive at the bank between 10 A.M. and 11 A.M. so that he can determine how many tellers should be working during this time period. The number of customers who arrived at the bank during this period was recorded for the past four weeks, and the following data were obtained. (Week 4 is the most recent week.)

Day	Week			
	1	2	3	4
Monday	45	47	46	45
Tuesday	36	35	39	43
Wednesday	42	44	46	50
Thursday	34	38	44	44
Friday	46	49	51	53

a. Graph this time series.
b. Forecast the number of customer arrivals in week 5 using an additive model to account for seasonality.

19. McCoy Motors offers customers a choice of several lease plans. The plan that will be least expensive for a customer depends on the expected number of miles the customer will drive over the first 12 months of the lease. Stan Bender is trying to decide which lease plan to choose and therefore wishes to forecast the number of miles he will drive the car over the lease period. He has reviewed his income tax records over the past two years and found that his monthly mileage is as follows (year 2 is the more recent year).

	Year	
	1	2
January	1051	1398
February	1145	1366
March	1076	1425
April	1344	1286
May	1276	1342
June	1286	1451
July	1157	1486
August	1398	1385
September	1339	1468
October	1291	1536
November	1365	1422
December	1528	1449

a. Graph this time series.
b. Verify statistically that this time series exhibits linear trend.
c. Using a linear regression approach, forecast Stan's mileage over the one-year lease period.

20. Consider the data in problem 19. If Stan uses Holt's method for forecasting mileage over the one-year period, with $\alpha = .1$ and $\gamma = .2$, what is the forecast for his mileage over the one-year lease period?

21. Pat Young, manager of the Burger Barn restaurant in Logan, Utah, is interested in determining an optimal inventory policy for frozen french fries. The number of pounds of french fries used by the restaurant over the past 15 weeks is as follows:

Week	Pounds	Week	Pounds	Week	Pounds
1	16,400	6	14,800	11	17,300
2	15,500	7	16,100	12	16,800
3	18,200	8	15,600	13	17,200
4	17,400	9	16,900	14	15,700
5	16,100	10	17,700	15	16,200

a. Graph this time series.
b. Verify statistically that the time series is stationary.
c. Using a three-week moving average, calculate the forecasted weekly demand for frozen french fries at the restaurant for weeks 16 through 20.
d. Using a four-week moving average, calculate the forecasted weekly demand for frozen french fries at the restaurant for weeks 16 through 20.
e. Which moving average method gives the lower mean squared forecast error?

22. Consider the data in problem 21. Suppose exponential smoothing is used to forecast weekly french fry demand.
a. What is the forecast of the weekly french fry demand for weeks 16 through 20 using a smoothing constant of $\alpha = .10$?
b. What is the forecast of the weekly french fry demand for weeks 16 through 20 using a smoothing constant of $\alpha = .20$?
c. Which of the two smoothing constants gives the lower mean squared forecast error?

d. Which of the two smoothing constants gives the lower mean absolute value of the forecast error?

e. Which of the two smoothing constants gives the lower mean absolute percent of the forecast error?

f. Which of the two smoothing constants gives the lower largest absolute deviation of the forecast error?

23. Consider the data in problem 21. Suppose that exponential smoothing is used to forecast weekly french fry demand; for weeks 16 through 20. Use Solver to:

a. Determine the value of α that minimizes the mean squared forecast error.

b. Determine the value of α that minimizes the mean absolute value of the forecast error.

c. Determine the value of α that minimizes the mean absolute percent of the forecast errors.

24. Carol Wright, Inc. specializes in direct mail coupon advertising for major food manufacturers. One client, Quaker Brands, has run 10 advertising campaigns using this medium. The response rate for coupons for the 10 campaigns is as follows:

Campaign	Response
1	4.6%
2	5.2%
3	4.8%
4	5.3%
5	4.5%
6	5.9%
7	5.2%
8	5.4%
9	4.7%
10	4.9%

a. Graph this time series.

b. Determine statistically whether a stationary forecasting model is appropriate.

c. Forecast the response rate for future advertising campaigns using exponential smoothing with a smoothing constant, $\alpha = .10$ and an initial forecast of 4.6%.

d. Using Solver, determine the value for the smoothing constant that minimizes the mean squared forecast error.

25. Consider the data given in problem 24. Suppose the forecast for the future response rate is based on an n period moving average. Determine the forecast and mean squared forecasting error for:

a. n = 1

b. n = 2

c. n = 3

d. n = 4

Which of the above four values of n would you recommend for use in forecasting the response rate? Explain your reasoning.

26. One Saturday each month Dreyfus Department Stores has a one-day sale. For the past 10 months, the percent increases in sales over the previous Saturday's receipts have been as follows:

Month	% Increase
1	12
2	18
3	18
4	16
5	20
6	18
7	15
8	16
9	15
10	19

a. Using an exponential smoothing model with a smoothing constant of .4, forecast the percent increase in sales for month 11.

b. Does exponential smoothing assume a long-term trend? Does exponential smoothing assume any seasonal effects?

27. Sam's Seafoods is a small new restaurant that has opened in the Georgetown area of Washington, D.C., located less than a mile from the White House. Sales have been steadily increasing as "word of mouth" has spread through the capital. In its first 12 weeks, sales at Sam's Seafoods (in $1000s) have been:

Week	Sales
1	18
2	22
3	26
4	24
5	28
6	32
7	32
8	40
9	38
10	42
11	40
12	46

a. Use Holt's method with a level smoothing constant of .5 and a trend smoothing constant of .2 to forecast sales for weeks 13, 14, and 15.

b. Use a regression approach to forecast sales for weeks 13, 14, and 15.

c. Using the MAD performance measure, which of the methods in parts a and b appears to forecast sales more accurately?

28. Nature's Health is a distributor of health food products in Norman, Oklahoma. Recent weekly demand (in cases) for its NH Vitamin E (100 I.U.) tablets has been as follows:

Week	Demand	Week	Demand
1	40	7	56
2	36	8	40
3	32	9	36
4	22	10	44
5	36	11	40
6	28	12	28

Until last year, forecasts were made using an eight-period moving average approach. Then, beginning in January, the company switched to a forecasting method, which it called AV8, that weights the last eight weeks of demand by .20, .20, .15, .15, .10, .10, .05, and .05, respectively.

a. Based on the data for the past 12 weeks, for each method, forecast demand for weeks 13, 14, and 15.

b. Use the mean absolute deviation performance measure to determine which of these two policies gives the more accurate forecasts.

29. Consider the data for NH Vitamin E given in problem 28. After using the AV8 forecasting measure for about six months, management at Nature's Health was still not convinced that it was a good forecasting method; thus it hired a management science consulting team to develop a universal forecasting policy that it could apply to all its products. After analyzing hundreds of its products, the consultants recommended dividing the company's products into two groups and using exponential smoothing. They recommended that for Group A products, the company should use a smoothing constant of .2, whereas for Group B products a smoothing constant of .7 should be used.

a. Based only on the data given in problem 28, use the mean square error performance measure to determine whether NH Vitamin E should be classified as a Group A or a Group B item.

b. Given the classification you determined for NH Vitamin E in part a, estimate demand for weeks 13, 14, and 15.

30. Sales in thousands of dollars at GetawayComputer.com over the past 40 weeks have been as follows:

Week	Sales	Week	Sales	Week	Sales	Week	Sales
1	238	11	311	21	362	31	396
2	251	12	308	22	360	32	410
3	251	13	314	23	369	33	423
4	263	14	323	24	373	34	424
5	270	15	337	25	373	35	438
6	267	16	340	26	380	36	444
7	278	17	342	27	380	37	443
8	289	18	344	28	393	38	456
9	294	19	342	29	399	39	460
10	302	20	358	30	400	40	459

a. If the firm uses linear regression to forecast future sales, determine total sales over the upcoming 13-week quarter.

b. Suppose the firm uses Holt's method with $\alpha = .10$ and $\gamma = .10$. Determine the forecast of total sales over the upcoming 13-week quarter.

31. Weekly egg sales (in cases) at Saveway Supermarket over the past 52 weeks are as follows:

Week	Sales	Week	Sales	Week	Sales	Week	Sales
1	556	14	510	27	579	40	553
2	517	15	477	28	618	41	531
3	530	16	475	29	598	42	531
4	513	17	502	30	631	43	497
5	488	18	516	31	651	44	519
6	463	19	504	32	625	45	528
7	476	20	540	33	603	46	492
8	453	21	558	34	591	47	470
9	451	22	575	35	560	48	446
10	468	23	599	36	556	49	423
11	468	24	618	37	561	50	436
12	492	25	599	38	544	51	454
13	500	26	608	39	538	52	478

The company would like to forecast future weekly egg sales using exponential smoothing.

a. If a smoothing constant of $\alpha = .2$ is used, what will be the forecast for week 53?

b. If a smoothing constant of $\alpha = .4$ is used, what will be the forecast for week 53?

c. Which smoothing constant (.2 or .4) should the company select? Why?

32. Consider the data given in problem 31 for weekly egg sales at Saveway Supermarket. What smoothing constant (it does not have to be .2 or .4) would you recommend if the company wishes to minimize the mean squared forecast error?

33. Consider the data given in problem 31 for weekly egg sales at Saveway Supermarket.

a. Suppose the company wishes to use a five-period weighted moving average with weights .40, .30, .25, .10, and .05 to forecast weekly demand. What would be the forecast of sales for week 53.

b. Would you recommend using a five-period weighted moving average over a five-period simple moving average if the firm wishes to select a forecasting technique based on the MAPE criterion?

34. Calvert College operates on a July–June fiscal year. The travel expenses (in $100s) for each quarter during the past four years are as follows:

	Time Period (t)	Quarter/ Quarter	Travel Expenditures (Y_t)
	1	Summer	117
Three Years Ago	2	Fall	111
	3	Winter	183
	4	Spring	174
	5	Summer	54
Two Years Ago	6	Fall	168
	7	Winter	246
	8	Spring	81

	Time Period (t)	Quarter/ Quarter	Travel Expenditures (Y_t)
Last Year	9	Summer	123
	10	Fall	207
	11	Winter	147
	12	Spring	198
This Year	13	Summer	162
	14	Fall	126
	15	Winter	270
	16	Spring	198

a. Use an additive regression model to forecast travel expenditures at Calvert College in each quarter for the next two years.

b. Using *annual data* only (by summing the quarterly results for each year), forecast annual travel expenditures at Calvert College for the next two years.

c. Statistically justify whether there is enough evidence to support using a model with quarterly seasonal factors by determining the autocorrelation of lag 4.

35. Quarterly sales at Lindal Cedar Homes for the four-year period from third quarter 1996 through second quarter 2000 were as follows:

	1st Quarter	2nd Quarter	3rd Quarter	4th Quarter
2000	8,452	12,850		
1999	8,105	10,136	10,570	10,694
1998	5,645	11,477	10,793	9,804
1997	7,540	14,913	14,298	12,097
1996			14,632	11,243

Using classical decomposition, forecast Lindal's sales for fiscal year 2001.

36. StayCalm.com is an e-business that sells equipment to help people with hypertension. The weekly sales of the company over the past 52 weeks have been as follows:

Week	Sales	Week	Sales	Week	Sales	Week	Sales
1	8,193	14	12,898	27	16,220	40	33,352
2	7,665	15	13,744	28	16,897	41	31,622
3	8,419	16	15,046	29	19,684	42	34,861
4	7,805	17	13,795	30	22,428	43	37,713
5	8,542	18	12,790	31	23,117	44	38,615
6	8,901	19	12,555	32	24,046	45	39,010
7	10,077	20	11,800	33	22,124	46	43,379
8	9,408	21	11,024	34	23,564	47	40,181
9	9,339	22	11,435	35	23,294	48	41,164
10	10,208	23	13,581	36	24,330	49	43,105
11	11,781	24	15,548	37	28,898	50	40,823
12	13,680	25	18,118	38	30,365	51	48,127
13	12,650	26	17,639	39	34,607	52	43,940

The company would like to forecast sales over the upcoming quarter. As sales seem to be growing at an exponential rate, the company has decided to perform the forecast by first taking the logarithm of weekly sales, next forecasting the log of weekly sales over the next 13 weeks using linear regression, and then transforming the log of future sales back to actual sales forecasts. Following this technique, what will be the forecast of total sales over the upcoming quarter?

37. The number of customers who arrived each month at the HanaBanana Dress Shop over the past 12 months has been as follows:

Month	Number of Customers
1	836
2	849
3	845
4	849
5	845
6	845
7	849
8	855
9	854
10	854
11	854
12	851

The average amount spent per customer each month over the past 12 months has been as follows:

Month	Average Amount Spent per Customer
1	$56.72
2	$70.13
3	$67.95
4	$69.06
5	$61.21
6	$71.93
7	$80.62
8	$93.70
9	$88.65
10	$86.98
11	$92.09
12	$95.24

The company would like to forecast revenue for the upcoming month. To do so, it plans to use exponential smoothing with $\alpha = .10$ to forecast the number of customers arriving during the month and Holt's method with $\alpha = .10$ and $\gamma = .30$ to forecast the average amount spent per customer. It then plans to multiply the two quantities together to get the forecast. What will be the forecast for the upcoming month's revenue?

38. The average daily revenue at the Dilly's Bakery for the past 48 months has been as follows:

Month	Revenue	Month	Revenue	Month	Revenue
1	2446	17	2434	33	2676
2	2389	18	2542	34	2712
3	2365	19	2546	35	2740
4	2278	20	2615	36	2746
5	2312	21	2590	37	2749
6	2401	22	2596	38	2772
7	2456	23	2645	39	2685
8	2470	24	2613	40	2606
9	2497	25	2663	41	2611
10	2508	26	2656	42	2723
11	2560	27	2614	43	2765
12	2571	28	2493	44	2793
13	2608	29	2487	45	2782
14	2597	30	2623	46	2813
15	2559	31	2679	47	2817
16	2410	32	2696	48	2859

a. If the firm uses an additive model with 12 seasons for forecasting, determine the average daily revenue for the upcoming 12-month period.

b. What is the MAD for this technique?

39. Consider the problem faced by Dilly's Bakery (see problem 38). Suppose the firm decides to use classical decomposition for forecasting.

PROBLEMS 41–50 ARE ON THE CD

a. Determine the average daily revenue for the upcoming 12-month period.

b. What is the MAD for this technique?

c. Based on the MAD criterion, which method, the additive model or classical decomposition, gives better results?

40. The average customer check at the Burger Boy Restaurant over the past 20 days has been as follows:

Day	Average Customer Check	Day	Average Customer Check
1	3.68	11	3.68
2	3.59	12	3.62
3	3.59	13	3.62
4	3.68	14	3.62
5	3.62	15	3.68
6	3.56	16	3.56
7	3.56	17	3.62
8	3.62	18	3.56
9	3.75	19	3.59
10	3.62	20	3.62

a. Verify statistically that a stationary model is appropriate.

b. If the company uses exponential smoothing with $\alpha = .10$, determine the forecast for the average customer check for the upcoming week.

CASE STUDIES

CASE 1: Bubble Up Bottling Company

The Bubble Up Bottling Company of Budapest, Hungary, is interested in forecasting sales of Bubble Up over the next two years. The company has analyzed Bubble Up's market share for its service area over the past 20 quarters. Market share has generally been growing as indicated in the table in the next column.

During this same five-year period, total soft drink sales in the region (as measured in 100,000s of cases) have been as follows:

Season	Year 1	2	3	4	5
Winter	114	114	124	132	134
Spring	130	146	151	160	166
Summer	158	177	175	184	205
Fall	131	142	146	144	148

The company would like to forecast Bubble Up soft drink sales for years 6 and 7. To do so, use a linear trend model to forecast market share for each quarter of years 6 and 7 and classical decomposition to forecast total soft drink sales in these periods. Then multiply the forecast of total soft drink sales by Bubble Up's estimated market share in order to get a forecast of Bubble Up's sales during this pe-

riod. Prepare a business report to Bubble Up management containing your forecast and explaining your approach.

Year	Season	Bubble Up's Market Share (in Percent)
1	Winter	6.42
1	Spring	6.58
1	Summer	6.99
1	Fall	6.82
2	Winter	6.64
2	Spring	6.46
2	Summer	6.70
2	Fall	7.00
3	Winter	6.70
3	Spring	6.84
3	Summer	6.78
3	Fall	6.48
4	Winter	6.93
4	Spring	6.79
4	Summer	6.83
4	Fall	7.21
5	Winter	7.73
5	Spring	8.16
5	Summer	8.36
5	Fall	8.23

CASE 2: Oregon Chain Saw

Oregon Chain Saw produces electric and gas-powered chain saws for the professional and do-it-yourself markets. The company purchases the engines from outside suppliers but produces all other components going into the chain saws at its factory in Portland, Oregon. Lee Spencer, manager of the Portland factory, is interested in scheduling next year's production of the chains used in these saws and would therefore like to have a forecast of chain demands over this period.

The two sizes of chains produced by the company at the Portland plant are 17 and 21 inch. Chains produced at the factory are packaged for the replacement parts market as well as used in producing new chain saws.

Monthly data over the past three years reveal the following chain demand:

17-Inch Chains

Total Chain Demand

Year	January	February	March	April	May	June	July	August	September	October	November	December
1	10059	10783	12865	12103	11892	11236	11621	12206	12708	12102	11615	11407
2	10789	12164	13958	13567	12960	12347	13174	13984	13991	13340	12924	12885
3	11991	13307	15219	15309	14752	13586	14725	15514	15705	15193	14578	14128

Chain Demand for Replacement Market

Year	January	February	March	April	May	June	July	August	September	October	November	December
1	3309	3345	3378	3480	3565	3654	3686	3720	3763	3860	3926	4045
2	4045	4159	4257	4320	4451	4593	4713	4802	4837	4873	5045	5099
3	5098	5215	5387	5558	5738	5818	5855	5943	6046	6095	6149	6353

Chain Demand for Production of New Products

Year	January	February	March	April	May	June	July	August	September	October	November	December
1	6750	7438	9487	8623	8327	7582	7935	8486	8945	8242	7689	7362
2	6744	8005	9701	9247	8509	7754	8461	9182	9154	8467	7879	7786
3	6893	8092	9832	9751	9014	7768	8870	9571	9659	9098	8429	7775

21-Inch Chains

Total Chain Demand

Year	January	February	March	April	May	June	July	August	September	October	November	December
1	4090	4168	4107	4118	4098	4085	3963	4031	4025	4110	4216	4381
2	4432	4380	4443	4445	4411	4466	4496	4586	4518	4579	4686	4798
3	4819	4738	4879	4771	4600	4556	4560	4599	4771	4720	4837	4879

Chain Demand for Replacement Market

Year	January	February	March	April	May	June	July	August	September	October	November	December
1	1215	1219	1226	1257	1262	1233	1226	1242	1226	1256	1235	1255
2	1254	1230	1217	1205	1211	1232	1214	1240	1247	1260	1245	1226
3	1226	1253	1226	1201	1195	1220	1216	1188	1208	1216	1216	1235

Chain Demand for Production of New Products

Year	January	February	March	April	May	June	July	August	September	October	November	December
1	2875	2949	2881	2861	2836	2852	2737	2789	2799	2854	2981	3126
2	3178	3150	3226	3240	3200	3234	3282	3346	3271	3319	3441	3572
3	3593	3485	3653	3570	3405	3336	3344	3411	3563	3504	3621	3644

It takes a worker approximately six minutes to produce a 17-inch chain and seven and a half minutes to produce a 21-inch chain.

On the basis of these data, prepare a business memorandum to Lee Spencer that gives a forecast for the total demand of 17- and 21-inch chains over the upcoming year (year 4). Include a forecast for the number of workers that will be needed in each month to produce these chains (assume that each worker is available for 12,000 minutes per month). As part of the report appendix, explain what techniques you used to perform these forecasts and your reasoning for selecting these techniques.

CASE 3:   Coast High School

The boosters at Coast High School hold three fund raisers a year for its sports programs: one during football season (September–November); one during basketball season (December–February); and one during baseball season (March–June). The results over the last three years are as follows:

	Season	Funds Raised
Three Years Ago	Football	$3000
	Basketball	$2500
	Baseball	$1400
Two Years Ago	Football	$3300
	Basketball	$2200
	Baseball	$1700
Last Year	Football	$3900
	Basketball	$3100
	Baseball	$2000

The money raised through fund raisers goes to support not only football, basketball, and baseball, but also the school's other sports programs—track, soccer, and swimming. Coast currently has $5400 left from last year and wishes to carry at least $5000 forward to the next school year.

Lee Hamilton, Coast's athletic director, asked the coaches of each of the programs to submit their top three requests for money that will be paid out of booster funds. No request can exceed $1500, and each coach must state when the request is needed (i.e., prior to the start of the football season, the basketball season, or the baseball sea-

son). Lee then gave an overall ranking to the 18 requests (18 being the highest ranking). His objective in allocating the forecasted funds is to maximize the total ranking of the funded projects while satisfying the following criteria:

1. Funds are to be allocated at three periods: prior to the football season (before this year's fundraising has begun), prior to the basketball season (after the football season fundraiser), and prior to the baseball season (after the basketball season fundraiser).
2. The total funds allocated at any period cannot exceed the forecasted cash on hand for that period; this includes any projected leftover funds from the previous season after requests for that period have been funded.
3. On a yearly basis, the requests funded for both the boy's and girl's sports programs should be between 40% and 60% of the funds allocated.
4. At least one request from each of the six coaches should be funded.
5. At least $5000 should be available prior to next football season.

Below are the funding requests from the coaches and include Lee's rankings:

Prepare a report for Lee Hamilton detailing a forecast of the results he can expect from the fundraising activities during each of the three seasons using a classical decomposition approach. Recommend which requests should be funded and when, based on the results you obtain by solving an appropriate binary integer linear programming model. Perform some what-if-analyses and suggest how much extra would be needed during a fundraising period to fund some additional requests.

Sport	Boys/Girls	Request	Needed Prior To	Cost	Lee's Ranking
Football	B	New Practice Dummies	Football	$1200	3
	B	Videotape Equipment	Football	$1300	11
	B	Kicking Net	Football	$ 100	16
Basketball	B	New 35 sec. Shot Clocks	Basketball	$ 900	1
	G	New 30 sec. Shot Clocks	Basketball	$ 900	6
	G	2 doz. New Girls' Balls	Basketball	$ 576	14
Baseball/	B	New Pitching Machine	Baseball	$1100	13
Softball	G	New Scoreboard	Baseball	$1200	5
	G	New Catcher's Equipment	Baseball	$ 350	9
Track	B	New High Hurdles	Baseball	$ 675	10
	B	Upgrade Pole Vault Area	Football	$1000	2
	G	New Timing Equipment	Baseball	$ 380	8
Soccer	B	1 doz. New Balls	Basketball	$ 360	17
	G	1 doz. New Balls	Football	$ 360	18
	G	Practice Nets	Baseball	$ 400	12
Swimming	B	Part-time Coach	Baseball	$1500	15
	G	Part-time Coach	Baseball	$1500	4
	G	Upgrade Locker Room	Basketball	$1200	7

Inventory Models

R ALPHS GROCERY COMPANY (http://www. ralphs.com), a subsidiary of The Kroger Company, operates over 300 supermarkets in southern California. Typically, such stores occupy 45,000 square feet and carry approximately 30,000 different items. Due to the large number of different goods carried by a typical supermarket, proper inventory control is essential to the profitability of the company.

Although some of the items sold in the supermarkets, such as Ralphs' brand baked goods and dairy products are produced by the company in-house, the majority of the items sold in each supermarket, are goods purchased from other manufacturers. In some cases, manufacturers offer Ralphs discounts if it purchases over certain limits. Certain items have sufficiently long shelf lives that spoilage is typically not a factor. For other items, however (e.g., meat, produce, dairy products, periodicals), items not sold by a particular date must be either discounted or pulled from the shelves and disposed of.

Because the company has its own manufacturing facilities, it must also maintain adequate inventory to operate its machinery. While some of the maintenance is scheduled (and therefore necessary parts inventories can be anticipated), unplanned machine breakdowns requiring spare parts cannot be predicted.

Many of the items sold in the supermarket are stocked by Ralphs' own employees. However, for some items (e.g., soft drinks, snack foods, and baked goods), the company relies on manufacturer's representatives for stocking. In the former case, Ralphs frequently utilizes its automated checkouts system to determine when and how much to order of each item. In the latter case, deliveries of items are scheduled on a regular basis, and the manufacturer's representatives determine the order quantities.

8.1   Overview of Inventory Issues

Proper control of inventory is crucial to the success of an enterprise. Profitability can suffer if a firm has either too much or too little inventory. Companies that have excess inventory are frequently forced to offer substantial mark-downs in order to dispose of this merchandise. This situation is especially prevalent in industries affected by periodic style changes, such as the automobile industry. New-car dealerships are much more willing to deal on price at the end of the model year than at the beginning.

Not having enough inventory can also lead to problems. A retail store that is frequently out of stock of popular items will soon lose its customers to the competition. A manufacturing firm that runs out of a crucial component may have to shut down its production lines, resulting in great expense and lost opportunities.

Managers often use inventory models to develop an optimal **inventory policy**, consisting of an *order quantity* denoted Q and an inventory *reorder point* denoted R. Firms frequently have many thousands of different items known as **stock-keeping units (SKUs)** in their inventories. Ideally, a firm would like to determine the inventory policy for each SKU which minimizes its total variable costs over a given (possibly infinite) time horizon.

> ## Components of an Inventory Policy
>
> Q = Inventory Order Quantity
>
> R = Inventory Reorder Point

In inventory modeling, the costs associated with a particular inventory policy are assessed. If a firm orders in small amounts or produces in small batches, although the size (and cost) of the inventory may be relatively low, orders or production setups are more frequent, resulting in annual costs of ordering inventory or setting up production runs that are higher than those associated with larger quantities. If order or production sizes are larger, the number of orders or production runs and their associated fixed costs are less, but the costs associated with maintaining higher inventory levels are greater. Thus inventory analyses can be thought of as cost-control techniques that strike a balance between having too much and too little inventory.

TYPES OF COSTS IN INVENTORY MODELS

The various costs in inventory models can be categorized into four broad areas: holding or carrying costs; order or setup costs; customer satisfaction costs, and procurement costs.

Holding Costs

Holding, or **carrying**, **costs** are those costs incurred by a firm to maintain its inventory position. The typical annual holding cost of a firm's inventory is between 10% and 40% of the average inventory value. Given the high value of many firms' inventories, this rate can result in large annual expenditures. For example, the annual expense of a medium-sized lumberyard that has an inventory with an average value of a million dollars and a 30% annual holding cost rate is $300,000. If the lumberyard could cut this expense without affecting service, it could experience considerable savings.

Many factors affect a company's *holding cost rate*, not the least of which is the cost of capital. Firms typically must borrow money in order to finance their inventory, and few firms are able to borrow at the prime rate. For small businesses, the cost of capital is typically prime plus 1 to 3%. These costs may be even higher if the firm has financed its expansion through the issuance of "junk" bonds or if it lacks the creditworthiness necessary for standard banking relationships. Even if a firm has not had to borrow money to finance its inventory, it has foregone other investments that could have been made with available capital. Management must account for such *opportunity costs* when determining its holding cost rate.

Several other costs are associated with holding inventory. Since the product must be stored somewhere, the company must pay for rent, utilities, labor, insurance, and security of its inventory. In some localities, taxes must be paid based on the inventory's value. Other costs include theft and breakage of inventory (which are classified under the more polite term **shrinkage**).

Another factor affecting inventory holding costs is deterioration or obsolescence. After a certain period of time, an item may lose some or all of its value. A car dealership stuck with last year's models will have to reduce its prices. A supermarket left with sour milk on its shelves may have to pay to dispose of it.

All these costs are difficult, if not impossible, to measure. Thus the holding cost rate represents management's best judgment of their total net effect. An important factor in determining the optimal inventory policy for an item is the cost of holding one unit of the item in inventory for a full year. When the holding cost rate of an item is known, its annual holding cost per unit, C_h, can be calculated by multiplying the annual holding cost rate, H, of an item by its unit cost, C.

Holding Costs

C_h = Annual Holding Cost per Unit in Inventory (in \$ per unit in inventory per year)

H = Annual Holding Cost Rate (in % per year)

C = Unit Cost of an Item (in \$ per item)

Thus,

$$C_h = H * C$$

Order/Setup Costs

Order costs are incurred when a firm purchases goods from a supplier. These can include postage, telephone charges, the expense to write up or phone in an order, the cost to check the order when it is received, and other fixed labor and transportation expenses that do not depend on the order size.

If the firm produces goods for sale to others, a production **setup cost** is normally incurred. This is the expense associated with beginning production of a particular item. For example, an ice cream manufacturer making a variety of flavors must clean out the machinery before it can begin producing a new flavor; machines producing ball bearings may need to be recalibrated when a new size is produced; and the staff at an aircraft manufacturer may need some refresher training prior to beginning a new production run.

The cost of placing an order or arranging a production setup, C_o, is *independent* of the order or production quantity. Because this cost is principally labor related, it can usually be readily measured.

Order or Setup Costs

C_o = Order or Production Setup Cost (in \$ per order or \$ per setup)

Customer Satisfaction Costs

One possible inventory policy is to stock *no* inventory. Customers desiring the product simply place an order and wait for its arrival. In this case, customer satisfaction is likely to be lower than it would be if the item were readily available. Low customer satisfaction may result in declining revenue and profitability. **Customer satisfaction costs** measure the degree to which a customer is satisfied with the firm's inventory policy and the impact this has on long-term profitability.

In some cases, customer satisfaction costs are relatively easy to quantify. For example, if a retailer is out of stock of an item, the customer may be offered a more expensive substitute at the same price or a discount on the item if the customer is willing to wait. But what about a customer who is unwilling to wait, goes elsewhere for the item, and decides to stick with the competition for future purchases? It is extremely difficult to estimate the satisfaction cost in these cases.

For a customer who encounters an out-of-stock inventory situation and is willing to wait for the item, customer satisfaction costs can have both a fixed and a variable component. The fixed component, C_b, consists of costs that are independent of the length of time a customer must wait for an item, such as the administrative costs of issuing a "rain check," recording the order, and contacting the customer when the merchandise arrives. The variable component, C_s, is a function of the length of time the customer must wait for goods to become available. Typically, the longer a customer waits for the item to arrive, the less satisfied the customer will be. The calculation of the variable component may be straightforward (such as when a firm offers a discount for each week a customer must wait for the item). More often, however, the variable component represents a goodwill cost that may be difficult to estimate. In such instances, focus groups can be used to obtain an estimate of this cost.

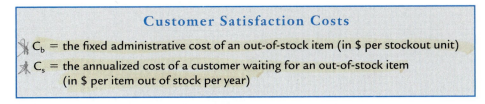

Customer Satisfaction Costs

C_b = the fixed administrative cost of an out-of-stock item (in $ per stockout unit)

C_s = the annualized cost of a customer waiting for an out-of-stock item (in $ per item out of stock per year)

Procurement/Manufacturing Costs

Procurement or **manufacturing costs** represent the cost of the items placed in inventory. If the item is obtained from an outside supplier, the procurement cost is the purchase cost per unit together with any shipping costs paid on a per unit basis. In some cases, a vendor may offer quantity discounts that enable the buyer to pay a reduced cost per unit if the amount purchased is above certain thresholds. In these instances, the order quantity plays an important role in determining the procurement cost. If the item is manufactured in-house, the procurement cost represents the incremental production cost per unit. Note that the procurement cost in this case does not include the production setup cost.

Table 8.1 summarizes these various inventory costs.

TABLE 8.1 Inventory Costs

Holding Costs (C_h)	Order/Setup Costs (C_o)	Satisfaction Costs (C_b, C_s)	Procurement Costs (C)
Cost of capital	Labor	Goodwill	Purchase cost
Rent	Communication	Loss in future sales	Quantity discounts
Utilities	Transportation (fixed)	Labor	Transportation (incremental)
Insurance		Communication	Manufacturing
Labor			
Taxes			
Shrinkage			
Spoilage			
Obsolescence			

DEMAND IN INVENTORY MODELS

A key component affecting an inventory policy is the demand rate for a stock-keeping unit. Although future demand is generally not known with certainty, forecasting techniques (see Chapter 7) can generally provide good estimates for these values. Demand can be estimated for any future period; however, we will typically utilize the *annual demand* in developing our inventory models.

Perhaps the strongest factor influencing how we model a particular inventory situation is the demand pattern for the SKU in question. Demand that is projected to be reasonably constant over time must be modeled differently than demand that is highly variable. In this chapter, we limit our investigation to situations in which demand occurs at a known annual constant rate, D.

Demand in Inventory Models

D = Estimate of the Annual Demand for the Stock-Keeping Unit

INVENTORY CLASSIFICATIONS

Inventory can be classified in various ways, depending on the issues that concern management. Table 8.2 summarizes different inventory classifications.

TABLE 8.2   Inventory Classifications

By Process	By Importance	By Life
Raw materials	A,B,C	Perishable
Work in progress		Nonperishable
Finished goods		

Process Classification

Accountants at manufacturing firms typically classify inventory into three categories as defined by the production process: raw materials, work in progress, and finished goods. This categorization enables management to track the production process and determine whether it has adequate inventory levels to support the projected demand. Financial analysts use such information to detect any changes in a firm's operations that might distort its profitability.

A,B,C Classification

A second way of classifying inventory is by the relative importance of the stock-keeping unit in terms of the firm's capital needs. For example, the annual inventory value for each stock-keeping unit is determined by multiplying its unit cost by its annual demand. Normally, only 5% to 10% of the SKUs account for about 50% of a company's total inventory value. These SKUs are classified as A units. Another 40% to 50% of the SKUs account for all but a small percentage of the firm's total inventory value. These are classified as B units. The remaining nearly 50% of the SKUs usually account for a small percentage (less than 5%) of the firm's total inventory value. These are classified as C units.

This A,B,C classification is useful in determining how much attention should be given to each stock-keeping unit in determining an inventory policy. A items are more carefully analyzed than B items. Because of the cost of inventory control, little, if any, analysis is done for C items.

Shelf Life Classification

Inventory models can also be classified by the shelf life of the inventory units. Certain perishable items, such as dairy products, baked goods, and periodicals, have a very short shelf life (no one wants to buy yesterday's news). Management of these inventory items is quite different than for items that can remain in inventory for long periods of time with no noticeable deterioration of quality.

REVIEW SYSTEMS

Two types of review systems are widely used in business and industry for controlling stock-keeping units. In a **continuous review system**, the inventory is constantly monitored, and a new order is placed when the inventory level reaches a certain critical point. In a **periodic review system**, the inventory position is investigated on a regular basis (once a day, twice a week, etc.), and orders are placed only at these times. Both systems are discussed in this chapter.

8.2 Economic Order Quantity Model

ASSUMPTIONS OF THE EOQ MODEL

One of the most commonly used techniques for inventory optimization is the **economic order quantity (EOQ) model**. This model is useful for analyzing stock-keeping units that meet the following criteria:

- Demand for the item occurs at a known and reasonably constant rate.
- The item has a sufficiently long shelf life (i.e., there is little or no spoilage).
- The item is monitored using a continuous review system.

The EOQ model assumes that all parameters, including demand, remain constant forever—that is, over an *infinite time horizon*. Although no business will carry a stock-keeping unit indefinitely, using an infinite time horizon avoids the need to specify just how long the item will be stocked.

The **lead time**, L, for an order represents the time that elapses between placement of an order and its actual arrival. In a basic EOQ model, we initially make the (unrealistic) assumption that L = 0. (This assumption is modified later.) Under these circumstances, it does not pay to order additional items until the exact instant we run out of stock. Furthermore, because demand is assumed to be constant over an infinite time horizon, whenever the firm runs out of inventory, it faces exactly the same future demand pattern as the previous time it ran out of inventory. For this model, a stationary inventory policy that orders the same amount each time must be optimal.

COST EQUATION FOR THE EOQ MODEL

Figure 8.1 illustrates the inventory profile of ordering Q units each time. In this figure, the horizontal axis represents time, and the vertical axis represents the inventory level. The time between orders, T, is the *cycle time*. To build an EOQ model, we need to know the demand forecast, D, for a given period (typically one year), the unit holding cost, C_h, over the same period, and the ordering cost, C_o. We can then construct an equation for the total annual inventory cost consisting of annual holding costs, ordering costs, and procurement costs, expressed in terms of the order quantity, Q.

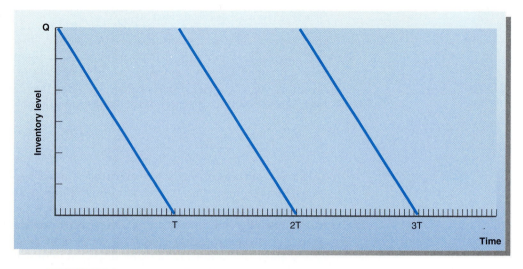

FIGURE 8.1 Inventory Profile—Ordering Q Units Each Time

Total Annual Holding Costs

As Figure 8.1 illustrates, the inventory level for each cycle begins at level Q when the order arrives and is depleted at a constant rate to 0 just prior to the next order's arrival. Due to this constant demand rate, the average inventory level over time is Q/2. Thus the annual holding cost associated with the policy of ordering Q units can be modeled as follows:

Total Annual Holding Cost for the EOQ Model

Total Annual Holding Cost

= (Average Inventory Level) ∗ (Annual Holding Cost per Unit)

$= (Q/2)C_h$

Total Annual Ordering Costs

If the annual demand is D and the order quantity is Q, the number of orders placed during the year is D/Q. Since the cost of placing each order is C_o, the total annual ordering cost is as follows:

Total Annual Ordering Cost for the EOQ Model

Total Annual Order Cost

= (Average Number of Orders Per Year) ∗ (Cost to Place an Order)

$= (D/Q)C_o$

Total Annual Procurement Costs

Since we seek to satisfy demand, we will purchase D items during the year at a cost of $C each. Thus the total annual item costs can be expressed as follows:

> **Total Annual Procurement Costs for an EOQ Model**
>
> Total Annual Procurement Cost
>
> = (Number of Items Purchased Per Year) * (Purchase Price per Item)
>
> = DC

Total Annual Inventory Costs and the EOQ Formula

Because the lead time for delivery of an order is assumed to be 0, there will never be any shortage costs. Thus the total annual inventory costs, TC(Q), can be expressed by:

$$\left(\begin{array}{c}\text{Total Annual}\\\text{Inventory Costs}\end{array}\right) = \left(\begin{array}{c}\text{Total Annual}\\\text{Holding Cost}\end{array}\right) + \left(\begin{array}{c}\text{Total Annual}\\\text{Ordering Cost}\end{array}\right) + \left(\begin{array}{c}\text{Total Annual}\\\text{Procurement Cost}\end{array}\right)$$

or

> $$TC(Q) = \left(\frac{Q}{2}\right)C_h + \left(\frac{D}{Q}\right)C_o + DC \quad * \tag{8.1}$$
>
> Here, since DC is a constant, we can represent the *total annual variable costs* dependent on Q; by
>
> $$TV(Q) = \left(\frac{Q}{2}\right)C_h + \left(\frac{D}{Q}\right)C_o \tag{8.2}$$
>
> * This equation is modified in Equation 8.6 to account for costs related to carrying safety stock.

We can find Q^*, the value of Q that minimizes TV(Q) in Eq. (8.2) (and hence TC(Q) in Equation 8.1) using calculus (see Appendix 8.2 on the accompanying CD-ROM). The following relationship, known as the EOQ *formula*, gives the value for Q^*.

> $$Q^* = \sqrt{\frac{2DC_o}{C_h}} \tag{8.3}$$

SENSITIVITY ANALYSIS IN EOQ MODELS

Figure 8.2 shows a typical graph of TV(Q) versus Q. As you can see, at the point Q^* where TV(Q) is minimized, the total annual holding and ordering costs are equal. The cost curve is also reasonably flat around Q^*. Thus small variations in Q^* will not greatly affect total annual variable inventory costs. This is important because the optimal order quantity Q^* is generally rounded off to an integer value or further modified owing to shipping restrictions. As long as these differences are not too large, the total annual variable cost will not be greatly affected.

Another factor that might affect the calculation of Q^* is the variability in actual demand. If demand varies from the estimated forecast by a modest amount, however, the error in Q^* is small and there is only a minor increase over the optimal cost. Accordingly, demand variability when calculating Q^* for an EOQ model is disregarded and it is assumed that the annual demand is constant and known with certainty.

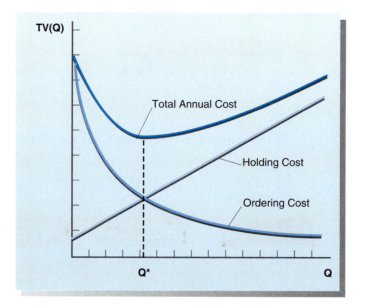

FIGURE 8.2 Total Annual Inventory Holding and Ordering Cost

CYCLE TIME/NUMBER OF ORDERS PER YEAR

The cycle time, T, represents the time that elapses between the placement of orders. It can be calculated by dividing the order quantity by the annual demand, that is, $T = Q/D$. Since the cycle time corresponds to the age of the last item sold from inventory, it can be compared to the shelf life to determine if items will go bad while in inventory. If the cycle time is greater than the shelf life, the model must be modified. The reciprocal of this quantity, D/Q, gives the average number of orders per year, N.

> ### Cycle Time/Number of Orders per Year
> Cycle Time: $T = Q/D$ (in years)
> Number of Orders per Year: $N = D/Q = 1/T$ (in orders per year)

LEAD TIME AND THE REORDER POINT

In the preceding analysis, it was assumed that the lead time, $L = 0$. In reality, lead time is always positive and must be accounted for when deciding when to place an order. The *reorder point*, R, is the inventory position of the item when an order is placed.

To determine the reorder point, we note that, since demand is constant at rate D, the total demand during lead time, L, is simply $L*D$, where L and D are expressed in the same time units (years, weeks, days, etc.). Hence, if an order is placed when the inventory level is at $L*D$, the order will arrive precisely when the inventory level is at 0. This gives the inventory profile shown in Figure 8.1.

$$R = L*D \tag{8.4}$$

In some instances, the lead time may be of sufficient length that it exceeds the cycle time. In such cases, since $L > Q/D$, $L*D$ will exceed Q, and it will be impossible to order the item for delivery during its current inventory cycle. Hence, this order would have to be placed during a previous cycle, and, as shown in Figure 8.3, there will be times when more than one order is outstanding. A company's stock on hand plus the size of any outstanding orders not yet delivered is known as its **inventory position**. At the reorder point, its inventory position is $L*D$.

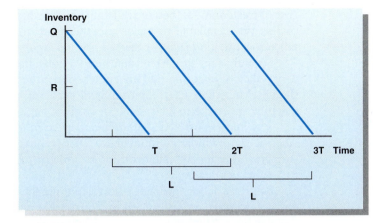

FIGURE 8.3   Lead Time Exceeding Cycle Time

Safety Stock

This calculation of the reorder point assumed that there is constant demand for the SKU and that there is a fixed lead time. In reality, demand usually fluctuates, and lead time varies. To account for these variations, most firms build a **safety stock (SS)** into their inventory policy. The safety stock acts as a buffer to handle higher than average lead time demand or longer than expected lead time. Including the safety stock, the reorder point is expressed by the following formula:

Reorder Point

$$R = (\text{Lead Time}) * (\text{Demand Rate}) + \text{Safety Stock}$$

$$R = L*D + SS \tag{8.5}$$

L and D must be expressed in the same time units.

Carrying safety stock, however, increases the annual holding costs and hence the total annual cost, TC(Q), by an amount equal to C_h times SS.

Total Annual Inventory Costs Including Safety Stock

$$TC(Q) = \left(\frac{Q}{2}\right)C_h + \left(\frac{D}{Q}\right)C_o + DC + C_hSS = TV(Q) + DC + C_hSS \tag{8.6}$$

The determination of the amount of safety stock that a firm should carry is often based on a desired service level approach. In Section 8.3 we show how one can determine the appropriate amount of safety stock based on the desired likelihood of encountering an out-of-stock situation.

To illustrate the concepts, consider the case of the Allen Appliance Company.

Allen Appliance.xls
Allen Appliance Cycle Service
Level.xls
Allen Inventory.xls

ALLEN APPLIANCE COMPANY

Allen Appliance Company (AAC) wholesales small appliances—toasters, mixers, blenders, and so on—to 90 retailers throughout Texas. One of its products, the Citron brand juicer, has shown a gradual decline in sales over the past several years. While this decline may be attributed to several factors, such as increased cost of fresh oranges, better availability of "fresh-squeezed" juice at grocery stores, or less time available to make juice by hand, the bottom line is that sales have fallen to a rate that is lower than in previous years.

Several years ago, Mr. Allen hired a consultant who recommended an inventory policy of ordering 600 juicers whenever the inventory level reached 205. Although Mr. Allen has religiously followed this policy in the past, he wonders whether, given the reduction in sales, this policy is still optimal.

The juicers cost AAC $10 each and are sold to customers for $11.85 each. Mr. Allen is able to borrow money at a 10% annual interest rate. He estimates that storage and other miscellaneous costs amount to about 4% of the average inventory value per year.

Based on labor, postage, and telephone charges, Mr. Allen estimates that it costs $8 to place an order with the Citron Company. It takes a worker who earns $12 per hour 20 minutes to check the shipment when it arrives. AAC is open five days a week, 52 weeks a year. Lead time is approximately eight working days, and AAC monitors its inventory using a continuous review system. Over the past 10 weeks, demand for the juicers has been as shown in Table 8.3. Given this information, Mr. Allen wishes to know if he should revise his current inventory policy.

TABLE 8.3   Sales of Juicers Over Previous 10 Weeks

Week Sales		Sales	Week
1	105	6	120
2	115	7	135
3	125	8	115
4	120	9	110
5	125	10	130

SOLUTION

In order to select the appropriate inventory model to analyze this situation, we must first investigate the demand pattern for the juicers. Weekly sales, though not exactly constant, do not vary greatly. Hence, we will analyze this situation using the economic order quantity model.[1]

To determine a representative value for weekly demand, we can use one of the various time series techniques appropriate for stationary models discussed in Chapter 7. After consulting with other members of the management science team, suppose we select a 10-week simple moving average approach to forecast future weekly demand. By averaging demand over the most recent 10 weeks, we forecast a weekly demand of $(105 + 115 + \ldots + 130)/10 = 120$.

In an EOQ analysis, it is important to express all data values in the same time units. Mr. Allen collects data on an *annual* basis; therefore he needs a forecast of *annual* demand for the juicer. Because he feels reasonably confident that demand for the juicers has bottomed out, our forecast for the annual demand is $(120)(52) = 6240$ units.

The annual holding cost rate for the juicers consists of the sum of the annual interest rate (10%) and the annual storage and miscellaneous costs (4%). Hence, using a holding cost rate of $10\% + 4\% = 14\%$, the annual holding cost of a juicer left in inventory for an entire year, C_h, is $(\$10)(.14) = \$1.40$. Note that we use AAC's *cost, not its selling price*, to determine the annual holding cost per unit.

---

[1] In some situations, the only historic data a firm has are sales data. If sales patterns exhibit erratic behavior, underlying demand could be constant but the item might be frequently out of stock.

Mr. Allen's ordering cost consists of the $8 cost of placing the order and the cost involved in checking the order upon its arrival. Since checking the shipment requires 20 minutes, and checkers make $12 per hour, the checking costs are $(20/60)(\$12) = \$4$ per order. Hence, the total ordering cost, C_o, is $\$8 + \$4 = \$12$. In summary, the following data exist for this problem:

$$D = 6240$$
$$C = \$10$$
$$H = 14\%$$
$$C_h = \$1.40$$
$$C_o = \$12$$

Analysis of Current Policy

Mr. Allen's current policy is to order 600 juicers at a time, yielding an annual holding cost of $(600/2)(\$1.40) = \$420$ and an annual order cost of $(6240/600)(\$12.00) = \$124.80$. Thus the total annual variable cost of this policy is:

$$TV(600) = \left(\frac{600}{2}\right)(\$1.40) + \left(\frac{6240}{600}\right)(\$12) = \$544.80$$

Since AAC is open five days a week, the average weekly demand of 120 juicers translates into an average demand of $120/5 = 24$ juicers per working day. Given a lead time of eight working days, the reorder point[2] without safety stock should be equal to $L*D = 8*24 = 192$. Since AAC is using a reorder point of 205, we can infer that it desires to have $205 - 192 = 13$ units of safety stock. Thus from Equation 8.6 we see that AAC's total annual cost based on its current inventory policy is:

$$TC(600) = \$544.80 + 6240(\$10) + 13(\$1.40) = \$62,963.00$$

Analysis of Optimal Policy with Safety Stock = 13

If we use the EOQ formula to determine the order quantity, we get:

$$Q^* = \sqrt{\frac{(2)(6240)(12)}{1.40}} = 327.065$$

Since Mr. Allen cannot order .065 of a juicer, we round this answer to an order quantity of 327.

Substituting $Q^* = 327$ and $SS = 13$ into Equations 8.2 and 8.6 gives:

$$TV(327) = \left(\frac{327}{2}\right)(\$1.40) + \left(\frac{6240}{327}\right)(\$12) = \$457.89$$

and

$$TC(327) = \$457.89 + 6240(\$10) + 13(\$1.40) = \$62,876.09$$

Thus adopting this policy will result in an annual savings of $\$544.80 - \$457.89 = \$86.91$ in variable costs. This savings might seem small in absolute dollars, but on a percentage basis, it amounts to approximately 16% of the current annual variable costs for this one SKU. To put this in perspective, if AAC carries 2000 different SKUs in inventory and has total annual variable inventory costs of a quarter of a million dollars, a 16% savings in inventory holding and ordering costs for each SKU translates into approximately a $40,000 annual savings!

[2] This calculation is based on L and D expressed in days. Expressed in years, $L = 8/260 = .03077$ and $R = (.03077)(6240) = 192$.

CYCLE TIME

If AAC uses an order quantity of $Q^* = 327$, the cycle time is:

$$T = \frac{Q^*}{D} = \frac{327}{6240} = .0524 \text{ year}$$
$$= (.0524 \text{ year})(52 \text{ weeks/year})(5 \text{ days/week}) \approx 14 \text{ working days}$$

These calculations indicate that the juicers will be sold in a reasonably short period of time after they enter AAC's inventory. Thus shelf life is not a factor. Since $T \approx 14$ working days, AAC will place orders for the juicers approximately every two and three-quarter weeks. This information can be useful if Mr. Allen decides to coordinate orders for other items from Citron along with the juicers.

SENSITIVITY OF THE EOQ RESULTS—LOTS OF 100

Suppose Citron's policy requires AAC to purchase juicers in units of 100. In this case, AAC could not order 327 juicers and would modify its order quantity to, say, 300. The total annual inventory holding and ordering cost of a policy based on orders of 300 juicers at a time amounts to $459.60, an increase of only $1.71 (or less than one-half of 1% of the total variable costs) per year over the cost of ordering 327 juicers at a time. This cost increase is so slight that an order quantity of 300 might even be preferable just for the sake of operational convenience.

EFFECT OF CHANGES IN INPUT PARAMETERS

One of the properties of the EOQ model is that the optimal total cost is relatively insensitive to small or even moderate changes to one of the input parameters of the model. To illustrate, suppose that, due to a "back to nature" craze, the actual annual demand for juicers turns out to be 7500 instead of the forecasted 6240 (an increase of over 20%). Using the EOQ formula, we find that AAC *should have* ordered $Q^* = 359$ juicers at a time rather than the 327 we calculated. The annual holding and ordering cost (excluding safety stock costs) associated with an annual demand of 7500 juicers and an order quantity of 359 is:

$$TV(359) = \left(\frac{359}{2}\right)(\$1.40) + \left(\frac{7500}{359}\right)(\$12) = \$502.00$$

If instead of ordering 359 juicers we used the order quantity of 327, the annual ordering and holding cost would be

$$TV(327) = \left(\frac{327}{2}\right)(\$1.40) + \left(\frac{7500}{327}\right)(\$12) = \$504.13$$

This is an increase of only $2.13, or 0.4% per year! Thus a "mistake" of more than 20% in estimating demand has less than a 0.4% effect on the total annual variable cost.

Software Results

Figure 8.4 gives an Excel spreadsheet that can be used to determine the optimal order quantity and reorder point as well as the inventory costs associated with any specified order quantity.

The input parameters are entered in column B. (Note that the value for Ch in cell B13 can be determined by multiplying the value in cell B11, the cost per

Allen Appliance.xls

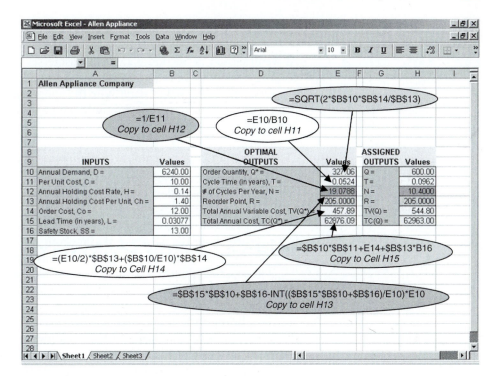

FIGURE 8.4 Excel Spreadsheet for Allen Appliance Company

unit, by the value in cell B12, the annual holding cost rate.) The outputs in column E correspond to the optimal order quantity, Q^*, whereas the outputs in column H are for a predetermined order quantity that is put in cell H10 (in this case $Q = 600$).

While the formulas shown in Figure 8.4 are generally straightforward and follow the algebraic formulas presented above, the formula for the reorder point, R, in cell E13 is somewhat complex. This is because the formula must allow for the possibility that the lead time is so long that multiple orders may be outstanding. The portion of the formula, -INT(($B$15*$B$10+$B$16)/E10)*E10, accounts for this possibility.

USING SOLVER TO DETERMINE Q*

It is also possible to get the value of Q^* by using the Solver option in Excel. To do this with the spreadsheet shown in Figure 8.4, click on Solver and in the "Set Target Cell" box put $H$14, in the "Equal To" section, highlight the Min button, and in the "By Changing Cells" box put $H$10. Then, click Solve. The EOQ solution will appear in cell H10 and the values in column H will be identical to those in column E.

USING THE INVENTORY.XLS TEMPLATE FOR SOLVING THE EOQ MODEL

As an alternative to constructing an Excel spreadsheet to solve EOQ problems, we have included the template **inventory.xls** on the accompanying CD-ROM. This template will enable you to quickly solve all of the inventory models discussed in this chapter without having to construct spreadsheets from scratch. The worksheet **EOQ** contained in the template (which is similar in form to the spreadsheet shown in Figure 8.4), can be used to solve EOQ problems. Details on using the template are contained in Appendix 8.1.

8.3 Determining Safety Stock Levels

As we discussed in Section 8.2, when businesses want to avoid stockouts, they incorporate safety stock requirements to determine the reorder point.

One approach used to determine the appropriate safety stock level for an item is for management to specify a desired *service level*. This can represent one of two quantities:

1. the likelihood or probability of not incurring a stockout during an inventory cycle, or
2. the percentage of demands that are filled without incurring any delay.

The first approach, known as the *cycle service level*, is appropriate when the firm is concerned about the *likelihood* of a stockout and not its magnitude. It is used, for example, in manufacturing settings in which *any* stockout affects production.

The second approach, known as the *unit service level*, is appropriate when the firm is interested in controlling the *percentage* of unsatisfied demands. It corresponds to the term *fill rate* and is what managers commonly mean when they state a service level.

To illustrate the difference between these two service levels, consider again the Allen Appliance Company (AAC) example described in Section 8.2. Table 8.4 shows the juicer demand and number of units on backorder during the last five inventory cycles at AAC when the policy was to order 600 units whenever the inventory level reached 205 units. We see that, during this time period, the cycle service level is 80% since four out of five cycles experienced no stockouts. At the same time, the unit service level is 99.5% since only 15 of 3000 units were backordered.

TABLE 8.4   Juicer Demand and Units on Backorder

Cycle Number	Demand	Number of Units on Backorder
1	585	0
2	610	0
3	628	15
4	572	0
5	605	0

THE CYCLE SERVICE LEVEL APPROACH

Stockouts occur only if demand during the lead time exceeds the reorder point. For example, if AAC uses a reorder point of 205, a stockout occurs only when demand during the lead time exceeds 205 units. Hence, if the lead time demand distribution is known, a statistical analysis can be used to determine the service level corresponding to a given reorder point or the safety stock required to maintain a given cycle service level.

In many cases, long-run demand can be assumed to be relatively constant, even when for shorter intervals, demand can be more appropriately modeled by a normal distribution. Thus demand during the lead time would be modeled by a normal distribution with estimated mean, $\mu_L = L * D$, and standard deviation, σ_L. From basic statistics we know that in this case the demand level that has a probability of α of being exceeded is given by the formula: $\mu_L + z_\alpha \sigma_L$. Here z_α corresponds to the z value that puts probability α in the upper tail of the normal distribution. (The values of z are found in Appendix A.) Hence, since a $(1 - \alpha)$ service level corresponds to a probability of stockout equal to α, is the reorder point is $\mu_L + z_\alpha \sigma_L$. The safety stock, SS, is therefore equal to $z_\alpha \sigma_L$.

> ### Reorder Point Corresponding to a Cycle Service Level of $(1 - \alpha)$
>
> $$R = \mu_L = z_\alpha \sigma_L$$
> $$= \mu_L + SS$$

For example, recall that the lead time for delivery of juicers at AAC is eight working days and that demand over the past 10 weeks is that given in Table 8.3. From these data, the sample mean and variance, which can be used as estimates for the population mean and variance for *weekly* demand is calculated by:

$$\mu \approx \bar{x} = \frac{(105 + 115 + \ldots + 130)}{10} = 120$$

$$\sigma^2 \approx s^2 = \frac{(105^2 + 115^2 + \ldots + 130^2) - 10(120^2)}{9} = 83.33$$

The estimates of the mean, μ_L, and variance, σ_L^2 of the lead time demand are then found by multiplying the weekly demand estimates by the length of the lead time (expressed in weeks). Since the lead time is eight days, or $8/5 = 1.6$ weeks, these values are:

Thus

$$\mu_L \approx 1.6(120) = 192$$
$$\sigma_L^2 \approx 1.6(83.33) = 133.33$$

$$\sigma_L \approx \sqrt{133.33} = 11.55$$

Analysis of Current Policy

If it can be assumed that lead time demand follows a normal distribution,[3] a reorder point of $R = 205$ implies:

$$205 = 192 + z(11.55)$$

Solving for z gives:

$$z = (205 - 192)/11.55 = 1.13$$

We see from Appendix A that the area in the tail above z is $\alpha = 1.13$ is $.5 - .3708 = .1292 \approx .13$. Thus, as shown in Figure 8.5, this policy corresponds approximately to an 87% cycle service level.

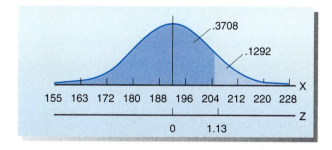

FIGURE 8.5 Determining a Cycle Service Level for AAC

---

[3] This can be verified by performing a standard goodness-of-fit test as described in Appendix 9.2 on the accompanying CD-ROM.

Determining the Reorder Point for a Given Cycle Service Level

Now suppose that AAC management wants to improve its cycle service level from 87% to 99%. In this case, $\alpha = .01$ and $z_{.01} = 2.33$. As illustrated in Figure 8.6, the reorder point is R = 192 + 2.33*11.55) = 219 units. The corresponding safety stock is then $2.33 * 11.55 \approx 27$ units.

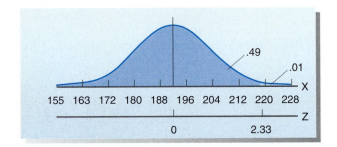

FIGURE 8.6 Reorder Point for AAC Corresponding to a 99% Cycle Service Level

Determining the Reorder Point for a Given Acceptable Number of Stockouts per Year

Another way of expressing a cycle service level is to specify an acceptable value for the likelihood of being out of stock for a given average number of cycles per year. For example, suppose AAC is willing to run out of juicers an average of at most one cycle per year. If the firm uses an order quantity of 327 units, the average number of cycles per year is N = 6240/327 = 19.08. Thus the acceptable probability of a stockout during a lead time is $\alpha = 1/19.08 = .0524$, which corresponds to a 94.76% service level. Referring to Appendix A, this gives us $z_{.0524} \approx 1.62$. In this case, the safety stock, $z_\alpha \sigma_L \approx 1.62(11.55) \approx 19$ and the reorder point would be R = 192 + 19 = 211 units.

Software Results

Figure 8.7 shows an Excel spreadsheet that determines the reorder point for a given cycle service level or the cycle service level for a given reorder point. The appropriate values are entered in column B. (Normally one would specify either the desired service level in cell B7 or the reorder point in cell B8.) The assumption made for lead time demand in this spreadsheet is that it follows a normal distribution.

Allen Appliance Cycle Service Level.xls

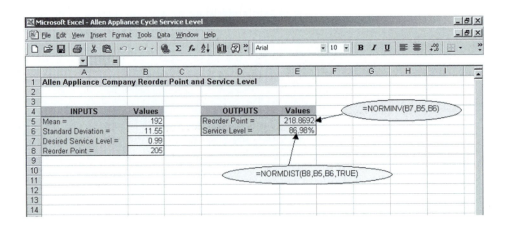

FIGURE 8.7 Excel Spreadsheet for Allen Appliance Company Reorder Point

From this spreadsheet we see that if the desired service level is 99% (.99 in cell B7), the reorder point should be approximately 219 (the value in cell E5). Alternatively, if the reorder point is 205 (the value in cell B8), the corresponding cycle service level is approximately 87% (the value in cell E6).

The Excel template **inventory.xls** on the accompanying CD-ROM contains a worksheet **Cycle Service** that can be used for determining the reorder point using a cycle service level approach. The format for the worksheet is similar to the spreadsheet shown in Figure 8.7.

THE UNIT SERVICE LEVEL APPROACH

Finding the reorder point corresponding to a desired *unit* service level is a bit more complicated than finding the reorder point corresponding to a desired *cycle* service level. Appendix 8.3 on the accompanying CD-ROM contains the general formula used to find this value. When lead time demand follows a normal distribution with estimated mean μ and standard deviation σ, the reorder point, R, can be detemined as follows:

1. Determine the value of z that satisfies the relationship:

$$L(z) = \frac{(1 - \text{service level})Q^*}{\sigma_L} = \frac{\alpha Q^*}{\sigma_L}$$

(Here L(z) represents the partial expected value for the standard normal random variable between some value z and infinity. Values of the L(z) function are given in Appendix B.)

2. Solve for R using the formula $R = \mu_L + z\sigma_L$.

For example, suppose AAC desires a 99% unit service level. Based on values $\mu_L = 192$, $\sigma_L = 11.55$, and $Q^* = 327$, for a 99% unit service level, $L(z) = (.01)(327/11.55) = .2831$. Referring to Appendix B, we see that a value of $L(z) = .2831$ corresponds to $z \approx .26$. Therefore, $R = 192 + .26(11.55) = 195$ and the safety stock = $.26(11.55) \approx 3$ units.

It is interesting to compare the safety stock requirements between a cycle and a unit service level. For the Allen Appliance example, the safety stock equals only three units for a 99% unit service level, compared to 27 units for a 99% cycle service level. The safety stock requirements are lower for the unit service level because the calculations include the nonlead time portions of the inventory cycle. Since it is impossible to be in an out-of-stock situation during these times, fewer safety stock units are necessary. Another way to view this is to recognize that, when we select a reorder point based on a desired unit service level, the corresponding cycle service level will be lower.

Worksheet **Unit Service** contained in the Excel spreadsheet **inventory.xls** on the accompanying CD-ROM is a template for determining the reorder point using a unit service level approach.

MANAGEMENT REPORT

On the basis of the analysis of the last two sections, the following memorandum was prepared. In this report, we outline an optimal inventory policy for AAC and examine the sensitivity of these recommendations to changes in the annual demand and holding cost.

·SCG·

STUDENT CONSULTING GROUP

MEMORANDUM

To: Mr. James P. Allen, President—Allen Appliance Company

From: Student Consulting Group

Subj: Inventory Policy for Citron Juicers

Due to a gradual erosion in demand over the past several years, we have been asked to analyze the current inventory policy for Citron juicers and make policy recommendations that might help Allen Appliance Company lower its inventory costs. We have analyzed the inventory situation for these juicers and are pleased to report our findings.

Our analysis indicates that demand for the juicers is fairly constant and that the products have a shelf life in excess of three months. Based on the past 10 weeks of sales, we forecast the annual demand for juicers to be 6240 units. We assume that AAC will continue to operate five days a week, that lead time for delivery is estimated to be eight working days, and that the juicers must be ordered in multiples of 100 units from Citron.

The following cost data have been provided by Allen management and used in our analysis:

Unit cost per juicer:	$10
Ordering cost:	$12
Annual holding cost rate:	14%

Based on our analysis of this data we recommend the following:

1. Lower the order quantity for Citron juicers from 600 to 300 units. This should result in a reduction in the annual holding and ordering costs from $544.80 to $459.60 (a savings of $85.20, or 15.6% per year).

2. Set the reorder point for the juicers at 219, including a safety stock of 27 units. Although changing the reorder point from 205 to 219 increases the annual safety stock holding costs by $20, this additional cost should be more than offset by the greater customer satisfaction generated from having fewer customers finding an out-of-stock situation.

Figure 1 compares the current and proposed policies.

While we are confident of the ordering cost data, management has indicated some uncertainty regarding both the value of $1.40 used for the annual holding cost per juicer and our forecast of 6240 for the annual juicer demand. We have therefore considered different annual holding cost and demand amounts and examined the savings in total annual variable inventory costs of using our recommended policy versus AAC's current policy. Table I gives these percentage savings.

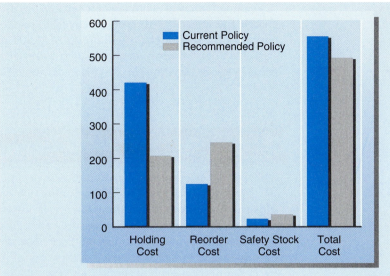

FIGURE 1

TABLE I Percentage Improvement in Annual Variable Inventory Holding and Ordering Costs by Ordering 300 Versus 600 Juicers Per Order

| | | Annual Holding Cost per Unit | | | |
		1.20	**1.40**	**1.60**	**1.80**
	5800	13.4	17.5	20.8	23.5
Annual	6000	12.5	16.7	20.0	22.7
Demand	6200	11.6	15.8	19.2	22.0
	6400	10.7	15.0	18.4	21.3

You can observe from this table that the recommended policy results in annual variable inventory cost savings of between 10.7% and 23.5%. If more precise information regarding the annual demand and annual holding cost per unit were available, we might be able to find a policy that gives even greater cost savings.

Should you have any further questions, please do not hesitate to contact us.

8.4 EOQ Models with Quantity Discounts

Quantity discounts are a common practice in business. By offering such discounts, sellers encourage buyers to order in amounts greater than they would ordinarily purchase, thereby shifting the inventory holding cost from the seller to the buyer. Quantity discounts also reflect the savings inherent in large orders. For example, when the Citron Company receives an order from AAC, a certain amount of work is required to process the order, independent of its size. By selling a larger quantity of juicers, Citron is able to amortize this fixed cost over a larger quantity and charge a lower price for the merchandise.

Perhaps the most important reason firms offer quantity discounts is federal legislation known as the Robinson-Patman Act, which states that a seller cannot discriminate among buyers when setting prices. This means that Citron cannot charge one price to AAC (which sells 6240 juicers a year) and a different price to a nationwide discount chain selling, say, 624,000 juicers a year. A quantity discount schedule does, however, enable a seller to reward its biggest customers with lower prices without violating the Robinson-Patman Act.

QUANTITY DISCOUNT SCHEDULES

A **quantity discount schedule** lists the discounted cost per unit, C_i, corresponding to different purchase volumes. The quantities at which these prices change are called **breakpoints**, B_i. Each breakpoint corresponds to a particular **pricing level**. Normally, the price customers pay for the item declines as the order quantity increases.

Quantity discount schedules fall into two broad categories: **all units schedules** and **incremental schedules**. In an all units schedule, the price the buyer pays for *all the units purchased* is based on the total purchase volume. For example, suppose Citron uses an *all units* discount schedule and offers a discount price of $9.75 corresponding to a breakpoint of 300 juicers. If AAC orders 327 juicers, it will pay $9.75 per unit for each of the 327 juicers.

In an incremental discount schedule, the price discount applies only to the *additional units ordered beyond each breakpoint*. Thus if Citron uses an *incremental* discount schedule and offers a discount price of $9.75 corresponding to a breakpoint of 300 juicers, then if AAC orders 327 juicers, it will pay $10.00 per unit for the first 299 juicers and $9.75 per unit for the remaining 28 juicers. While some firms use incremental discount schedules, the all units discount schedule is more common.

ALL UNITS DISCOUNT SCHEDULE

Because the inventory unit cost is dependent on the quantity purchased, the all units discount inventory model must include the total cost of the goods purchased. The formula for TC(Q), therefore, is as follows:

$$TC(Q) = \left(\frac{Q}{2}\right)C_h + \left(\frac{D}{Q}\right)C_o + DC_i + C_hSS \qquad (8.7)$$

where C_i represents the unit cost at the ith pricing level corresponding to the order quantity, Q.

Since financing costs typically make up a major portion of the holding costs, it is reasonable to assume that the holding cost, C_h, will change proportionally to the unit cost. This assumption may not be totally accurate, however, because changes in the unit cost do not affect nonfinancing holding costs, such as storage costs. One way around this dilemma is to modify the holding cost by some fraction of the change in the unit cost reflecting the percentage of the holding cost represented by the inventory financing cost. Since the EOQ model is quite insensitive to minor changes in the parameters, however, the simplifying assumption that holding costs change proportionately to changes in the unit cost will have a minor effect on the optimal order quantity, Q^*.

Determining the Optimal Order Quantity

To illustrate how to determine the optimal order quantity under all units discount schedule, consider again the Allen Appliance Company example.

Allen inventory.xls

ALLEN APPLIANCE COMPANY (CONTINUED)

Mr. Allen was quite impressed with our analysis. After reading the memorandum, however, he realized that we had not been given complete information concerning the Citron juicers. In particular, while the base price for the Citron juicers is $10 per unit, Citron offers its customers quantity discounts. The all units quantity discount schedule is given in Table 8.5.

Mr. Allen wishes to determine whether he should order more than 300 units to take advantage of the discounts offered by Citron.

TABLE 8.5   All Units Quantity Discount Schedule

Amount Ordered	Price per Unit
1–299	$10.00
300–599	$ 9.75
600–999	$ 9.50
1000–4999	$ 9.40
5000 or more	$ 9.00

SOLUTION

There are four discount pricing levels for Citron juicers beyond the base price of $C = \$10$ per unit. These are $C_1 = \$9.75$, $B_1 = 300$; $C_2 = \$9.50$, $B_2 = 600$; $C_3 = \$9.40$, $B_3 = 1000$; and $C_4 = \$9.00$, $B_4 = 5000$. Figure 8.8 shows five inventory cost curves for the juicer problem. Each represents the total cost $TC(Q)$ as a function of the corresponding unit price, C_i, assuming that C_i is valid for all values of Q. The true total cost function, $TC(Q)$, contains the pieces of each curve corresponding to the range of values for Q over which the corresponding discount price is valid, as highlighted in the figure.

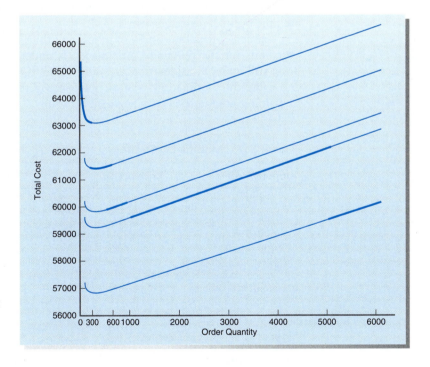

FIGURE 8.8   Inventory Cost Curves for AAC Juicer Problem—All Units Discount Policy

Determining the optimal order quantity for an all units discount schedule is a straightforward process. For the original unit cost, as well as each discount pricing level, we use the EOQ formula

$$Q^* = \sqrt{\frac{2DC_o}{C_h}}$$

to determine the lowest total cost on each curve. Table 8.6 provides this information for the juicer problem. The Q* values change slightly for each pricing level because C_h declines in proportion to the decrease in the price per unit for each pricing level. (If we had assumed a constant holding cost, Q* would have been the same for each pricing level.)

TABLE 8.6   Lowest Total Cost on Each Inventory Cost Curve

Level	Amount Ordered	Price per Unit	Q*
0	1–299	$10.00	327
1	300–599	$ 9.75	331
2	600–999	$ 9.50	336
3	1000–4999	$ 9.40	337
4	5000 or more	$ 9.00	345

It can be seen from Figure 8.8 that, for each pricing level, the cost curves increase as the order quantity increases beyond the Q* value. Hence, when the EOQ value for a curve is below the pricing level's breakpoint, the least expensive way to obtain the discount is to increase the order quantity only up to that breakpoint.

When the Q* value is greater than the next pricing level's breakpoint, as it is for pricing level 0, the pricing level can be dropped from further consideration (since we would be ordering at the next pricing level anyway). Obviously it does not make sense for Allen Appliance to order at pricing level 0 since its optimal order quantity, 327, falls within pricing level 1. But at level 1 the unit cost is $9.75, and the optimal order quantity is 331.

Table 8.7 lists the results of modifying the Q* values to take advantage of the discounts for the remaining pricing levels under consideration. For each pricing level still under consideration the value of TC(Q*) is then calculated by Equation 8.7 using the modified Q* values. Table 8.8 gives the values of TC(Q*) for each remaining pricing level (it is assumed SS = 13).

TABLE 8.7   Modified Q* Values

Amount Ordered	Price per Unit	Modified Q*
1–299	$10.00	*
300–599	$ 9.75	331
600–999	$ 9.50	600
1000–4999	$ 9.40	1000
5000 or more	$ 9.00	5000

Q above breakpoint.

TABLE 8.8   TC(Q*) Values

Amount Ordered	Price per Unit	Modified Q*	TC(Q*)
1–299	$10.00	—	—
300–599	$ 9.75	331	$61,309.88
600–999	$ 9.50	600	$59,821.09
1000–4999	$ 9.40	1000	$59,405.99
5000 or more	$ 9.00	5000	$59,341.36

Thus AAC should order 5000 juicers at a time, since this value minimizes TC(Q*). The process is summarized as follows:

Determining the Optimal Order Quantity for an All Units Pricing Schedule

1. Calculate Q* for each discount level.
2. If Q* is less than the lower quantity limit for the discount level, increase Q* to this lower limit. If Q* is greater than the upper quantity limit for the discount level, eliminate this level from further consideration.
3. Substitute the modified Q* values into the formula:

$$TC(Q) = \left(\frac{Q}{2}\right)C_h + \frac{D}{Q}C_o + DC_1 + C_n\,SS$$

4. Select the Q* value that minimizes TC(Q*).

Although quantity discounts may influence the order quantity, they do not affect the reorder point; this is determined in exactly the same way as for the nondiscounted EOQ problem.

Software Results

Figure 8.9 shows the results of using the **All Units Discount** worksheet on the **inventory.xls** template to determine the optimal order quantity and reorder point for the Allen Appliance Company.

Allen inventory.xls

Calculation of Optimal Inventory Policy Under All-Units Quantity Discounts

	INPUTS	Values			OPTIMAL OUTPUTS	Values
5	Annual Demand, D =	6240.00		Order quantity, Q* =		5000
6	Per Unit Cost, C =	10.00		Cycle Time (in years), T =		0.801282051
7	Annual Holding Cost Rate, H =	0.14		# of Cycles Per Year, N =		1.248
8	Annual Holding Cost Per Unit, Ch =	1.40		Reorder Point, R =		205.0000
9	Order Cost, Co =	12.00		Total Annual Cost, TC(Q*) =		59341.36
10	Lead Time (in years), L =	0.03077				
11	Safety Stock, SS =	13.00				

DISCOUNTS

Level	Breakpoint	Discount Price	Q*	TC(Q*)	Modified Q*
0	1	10.00	327	62876.09	327
1	300	9.75	331	61309.88	331
2	600	9.50	336	59821.09	600
3	1000	9.40	337	59405.99	1000
4	5000	9.00	345	59341.36	5000
5					
6					
7					
8					

EOQ \ **All-Units Discount** / Incremental Discount / Production Lot Size / Planned Shortage / Single Period (unit

FIGURE 8.9 Excel Spreadsheet for Allen Appliance Company Problem with Discounts

The parameters are entered in rows 5 through 11 of column B. (Note that the default value for Ch in cell B8 is determined by multiplying the value in cell B6, the cost per unit, by the value in cell B7, the annual holding cost rate.) The template can handle problems with up to eight breakpoints. The breakpoints and discount prices are entered in rows 17 through 24 of columns B and C. (No entry is made for row 16 as the default value for cell C16 is the unit cost entered in cell B6.)

Other Considerations

These results are based on a mathematical model that made certain simplifying assumptions, such as constant demand and a fixed holding cost rate. However the results should be checked to make sure they are consistent with these assumptions. For example, according to the above analysis, the lowest total annual inventory cost is achieved when AAC orders 5000 juicers at a time. This quantity represents more than a nine-month supply of juicers and could raise some concerns among AAC management.

First, if AAC orders 5000 juicers, it must have some place to store them. This could result in major additional expenses for new warehouse space. These additional costs would violate the fixed holding cost rate assumption.

Second, suppose Mr. Allen has heard rumors that Citron may be introducing a new improved juicer within the next three to four months. This plan could violate the constant demand assumption. AAC would rightfully be concerned about getting stuck with juicers that have been discontinued and need to be sold at drastically reduced prices.

Suppose, in fact, that AAC's policy is to never order more than a three-month supply of any product in order to guard against such possibilities. Consequently, it would never order more than 6240/4 = 1560 juicers at a time. In this case, only the first three discount levels would be available, and, as seen in Figure 8.9, AAC should order 1000 juicers at a time.

INCREMENTAL DISCOUNT SCHEDULES

Figure 8.10 shows a graph of AAC's total annual juicer inventory cost as a function of the order quantity, assuming that Citron offers an incremental discount schedule. The procedure for determining the optimal order quantity for an incremental discount schedule is somewhat more complex than that used for the all units schedule. Details of this procedure are given in Appendix 8.4 on the accompanying CD-ROM. The worksheet **Incremental Discount** in the Excel template **inventory.xls** can be used to obtain results for the discounted EOQ model if the discounting scheme is an incremental one.

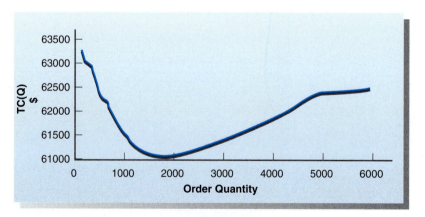

FIGURE 8.10   Total Annual Juicer Inventory Cost as a Function of Order Quantity—Incremental Discount Policy

8.5 Production Lot Size Model

Although the EOQ model is useful for determining an optimal inventory policy for goods obtained from other sources, in many instances the firm itself produces the items it sells. If demand for the item occurs at a constant rate, a **production lot size model** can be used to determine the item's optimal inventory policy.

A production lot size model is useful for manufacturers such as pharmaceutical companies, soft drink bottlers, cosmetics companies, ice cream manufacturers, furniture makers, and household goods producers. In all of these enterprises, a production line is not continuously used to manufacture the same product; rather, production of an item occurs in batches, or lots, that are added to the firm's inventory. Production does not resume until the item's inventory is nearly depleted, at which point another batch is produced. An ice cream producer, for example, does not continuously produce Heavenly Hash ice cream. It makes a batch of this flavor, cleans out its equipment, and moves on to produce another flavor.

Production lot size models assume that the production facility operates at a rate greater than the demand rate for the item. Clearly, if the production rate is less than the demand rate, the firm will not have any inventory problem since it will simply ship out all items as they are produced. This situation sometimes occurs with the introduction of an extremely popular children's toy or musical recording. Normally, this degree of popularity does not last long enough to warrant the firm expanding its production lines. Once demand declines below the production rate, a production lot size model may prove useful.

The discussion here focuses on determining the optimal production quantity for a single product. In the real world, where several products must share the same production line, it may be impossible to follow the resulting schedule for each product. Multiple scheduling problems are quite difficult to solve and are beyond the scope of this text.

The approach parallels that of the EOQ model by developing a general expression for the annual inventory costs associated with producing and storing the stock-keeping unit. In a production process, however, a firm does not actually place an order; instead, it incurs a cost to begin production, known as the **setup cost**. We use the following notation in production lot size models:

D = Estimate of the Annual Demand for the Stock−Keeping Unit
C_h = Annual Holding Cost per Unit in Inventory
C_o = Production Setup Cost
P = Annual Production Rate Assuming Full and Continuous Operation

The goal of the optimal policy is to minimize total annual inventory costs. Because the production lot size model assumes that demand occurs at a constant rate, as with the EOQ model, we can show that, over an infinite time horizon, a stationary policy that produces the same quantity during each production run is optimal. Given a production lot size of Q, an equation for the total annual variable cost, $TV(Q)$, can be developed to represent the sum of the total annual holding cost plus production setup cost. Q^* denotes the value of Q, which minimizes $TV(Q)$.

DETERMINING THE AVERAGE INVENTORY LEVEL

The total annual holding cost is the product of the average inventory level and the annual holding cost per unit. To determine the average inventory level, the *maximum inventory position*, M, must first be calculated. Unlike the EOQ model, in a production lot size model, the maximum inventory position is less than the production lot size, Q. This is because units are demanded and sold while they are being produced. To determine the value of M, refer to Figure 8.11, which profiles the inventory position over time. Here, it is assumed that the production process operates at a constant rate and that production resumes only when the inventory is depleted.

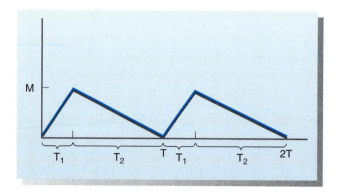

FIGURE 8.11 Production Lot Size Model—Inventory Position over Time

The production cycle time, T, consists of two time periods: (1) the time during which the product is being produced and inventory is increasing, T_1; and (2) the time during which the production line is being used for other purposes and the good is not being produced, T_2.

Since production of Q units takes place in time period T_1, then (assuming T and T_1 are expressed on a yearly basis),

$$Q = PT_1$$

or

$$T_1 = Q/P$$

As Figure 8.11 indicates, the inventory position reaches its highest point during a production cycle at time T_1. At this point, production ceases and the inventory accumulated during the production phase of the cycle begins to be depleted. Because Q units have been produced and DT_1 units have been demanded during time T_1, the inventory position at this point is:

$$M = Q - DT_1 = Q - D(Q/P) = Q(1 - D/P)$$

Total Annual Holding Costs

The average inventory level is, therefore:

$$\frac{M}{2} = \left(\frac{Q}{2}\right)(1 - D/P)$$

and annual inventory holding cost is:

$$\left(\frac{Q}{2}\right)(1 - D/P)C_h$$

Total Annual Setup Costs

The annual production setup cost is found by multiplying the average number of production setups per year, D/Q, by the setup cost incurred for each production run, C_o:

$$\left(\frac{D}{Q}\right)C_o$$

Total Annual Variable Costs

Adding the annual holding cost to the production setup cost gives the following formula for TV(Q):

$$TV(Q) = \frac{Q}{2}(1 - D/P)C_h + \left(\frac{D}{Q}\right)C_o \tag{8.8}$$

In Appendix 8.2 on the accompanying CD-ROM, it is shown that the optimal production quantity is given by the formula:

$$Q^* = \sqrt{\frac{2DC_o}{(1 - D/P)C_h}} \tag{8.9}$$

As in the EOQ model, at Q^* the annual holding costs equal the annual production setup costs.

Comparing Equations 8.2 and 8.3 for the EOQ model to Equations 8.8 and 8.9 for the production lot size model, it can be seen that, if P equals infinity, D/P equals zero and the two sets of equations are identical. Hence the EOQ model can be considered a special case of the production lot size model, in which goods can be supplied infinitely quickly.

To illustrate use of the production lot size model, consider the problem faced by the Farah Cosmetics Company.

FARAH COSMETICS COMPANY

Farah inventory.xls

Management of the Farah Cosmetics Company is interested in determining the optimal production lot size for its most popular shade of lipstick, Autumn Moon. The factory operates seven days a week, 24 hours a day. The lipstick production line can produce 1000 tubes of lipstick per hour when operating at full capacity. Whenever the company changes production to a new shade of lipstick, it costs an estimated $150 to clean out the machinery and do any necessary calibrations.

Demand for Autumn Moon lipstick has been reasonably constant, averaging 980 dozen tubes per week. Farah sells the lipstick to distributors for $.80 per tube, and the firm calculates its variable production cost at approximately $.50 per tube. Because lipsticks must be stored in an air-conditioned warehouse, the firm uses a relatively high annual holding cost rate of 40%.

Farah is currently producing Autumn Moon in batch sizes of 84,000 tubes and would like to determine if this policy is optimal.

SOLUTION

Weekly demand of 980 dozen units is equivalent to a daily demand of 140 dozen, or 1680, units. Thus $D = (1680)(365) = 613{,}200$ per year. The annual holding cost, C_h, for a tube of Autumn Moon lipstick is $(.40)(\$.50) = \$.20$, and the production setup cost, C_o, is \$150. For Autumn Moon, the maximum production rate, P, is $(1000)(24)(365) = 8{,}760{,}000$ units. The unit selling price of the lipstick, \$.80, does not enter into the analysis, since revenue is unaffected by the production lot size decision. In summary:

$$D = 613{,}200$$
$$P = 8{,}760{,}000$$
$$C = \$.50$$
$$C_o = \$150$$
$$C_h = \$.20$$

Analysis of Current Policy

Farah currently schedules production runs of 84,000 tubes of Autumn Moon lipstick so that the time between production runs, T, is:

$$T = \frac{84{,}000 \text{ tubes/run}}{613{,}200 \text{ tubes/year}} = .1370 \text{ years } (\approx 50 \text{ days})$$

Since the production line can manufacture 8,760,000 tubes per year, the length of each production run is:

$$T_1 = \frac{84{,}000 \text{ tubes/run}}{8{,}760{,}000 \text{ tubes/year}} = .0096 \text{ years } (\approx 3.5 \text{ days})$$

Thus the time during each production cycle for which the machine is not used to produce Autumn Moon lipstick is:

$$T_2 = T - T_1 = .1370 - .0096 = .1274 \text{ years } (\approx 46.5 \text{ days})$$

The total annual variable inventory cost for this policy is:

$$TV(84{,}000) = \left(\frac{84{,}000}{2}\right)\left(1 - \frac{613{,}200}{8{,}760{,}000}\right)(\$.20) + \left(\frac{613{,}200}{84{,}000}\right)(\$150) = \$8{,}907$$

Analysis of Optimal Policy

Using Equation 8.9 the optimal production lot size is:

$$Q^* = \sqrt{\frac{2(613{,}200)(150)}{\left(1 - \dfrac{613{,}200}{8{,}760{,}000}\right)(.20)}} \approx 31{,}449$$

This quantity results in a total annual variable inventory cost of

$$TV(31{,}449) = \left(\frac{31{,}449}{2}\right)\left(1 - \frac{613{,}200}{8{,}760{,}000}\right)(\$.20) + \left(\frac{613{,}200}{31{,}449}\right)(\$150) = \$5{,}850$$

This represents a variable inventory cost savings of \$3057, or approximately 34%, over the policy of producing in batches of 84,000.

From a practical standpoint, the firm probably would not wish to schedule a production run of exactly 31,449 tubes of lipstick. A more realistic approach is to round off Q* and recommend a production quantity of 31,000 or 32,000, or even 30,000, tubes of lipstick. As with the EOQ model, small variations in Q* have a minimal effect on the total annual inventory costs.

Software Results

Figure 8.12 shows the results of using the worksheet **Production Lot Size** on the **inventory.xls** template for determining the inventory policy for the Farah Cosmetics Company. The parameters are entered in column B, and the optimal policy outputs are given in column E. One can also assign an order quantity in cell H5 (in this case Q = 84,000), and the resulting inventory values will be given in cells H6 through H10.

Farah inventory.xls

	A	B	C	D	E	F	G	H
1	Determination of Inventory Policy for Production Lot Size Model							
2								
3				OPTIMAL OUTPUTS			ASSIGNED OUTPUTS	
4	INPUTS	Values		OUTPUTS	Values		OUTPUTS	Values
5	Annual Demand, D =	613200.00		Order Quantity, Q* =	31448.88		Q =	84000.00
6	Per Unit Cost, C =	0.50		Cycle Time (in years), T =	0.0513		T =	0.1370
7	Annual Holding Cost Rate, H =	0.40		# of Cycles Per Year, N =	19.4983		N =	7.3000
8	Annual Holding Cost Per Unit, Ch =	0.20		Reorder Point, R =			R =	
9	Set Up Cost, Co =	150.00		Total Annual Variable Cost, TV(Q*) =	5849.49		TV(Q) =	8907.00
10	Annual Production Rate, P =	8760000.00		Total Annual Cost, TC(Q*) =	312449.49		TC(Q) =	315507.00
11	Lead Time (in years), L =							
12	Safety Stock, SS =							

Incremental Discount | **Production Lot Size** | Single Period (normal) | Single Period (uniform) | Planned Short

FIGURE 8.12 Excel Spreadsheet for Farah Cosmetics Company

As with the EOQ model, one can use the Solver option to also determine the optimal production lot size. To do this, click on Solver and in the "Set Target Cell" box put $H$9, in the "Equal To" section highlight the Min button, and in the "By Changing Cells" box put $H$5. Next click Solve. The EOQ solution will appear in cell H5 and the values in column H will be identical to those in column E.

OTHER PRODUCTION SYSTEMS

Many other inventory systems exist for controlling the production of inventory. Supplement CD 6 on the accompanying CD-ROM discusses a number of these systems, including material requirements planning (MRP), just-in-time systems, kanban systems, and flexible manufacturing systems. Also discussed in this supplement are the Wagner-Whitin algorithm and the Silver-Meal heuristic.

8.6 Planned Shortage Model

BACKORDERING

When we go to our local supermarket, we expect to find items like eggs, coffee, spaghetti, and ketchup readily available. If they aren't, we will probably begin shopping elsewhere. In Section 8.3 we discussed a safety stock approach that businesses can use to reduce the likelihood of running out of stock of such items. In other situations, however, we have become accustomed to waiting several days or even weeks or months to get the merchandise we want.

For example, if we wish to purchase a new car complete with a detailed list of specific options, and the car is not currently available at our local new car dealership, it may take the factory six or more weeks to produce and deliver the car. Other products we are typically willing to wait for include quality furniture, some major appliances, and specialty parts. What these items have in common are relatively high holding costs, due to either the high cost of the item or its low demand.

The phenomenon of waiting for merchandise to be delivered is known as **backordering**. If an item desired by a customer is not available, the customer either goes elsewhere for the good (a lost sale) or places a backorder for the item. When the next shipment of the item arrives, all backorders are filled immediately and the remainder of the order is placed into inventory. One approach used to represent such situations is the planned shortage model.

MODEL ASSUMPTIONS

In a **planned shortage model**, it is assumed that no customers will be lost due to an out-of-stock situation; all such customers will backorder. Although this assumption may not necessarily be true if the item or an appropriate substitute is readily available from another source, it might be appropriate if there is no alternative to waiting. Like the EOQ and production lot size models, this model deals with an item with a sufficiently long shelf life, whose demand occurs at a known constant rate over an infinite time horizon. In addition to holding and ordering costs, this model allows us to incorporate both a time-dependent and a time-independent shortage cost component.

Naturally, customers prefer not to have to wait for their merchandise. To incorporate this preference, the planned shortage model includes a cost, C_s, of keeping a customer on backorder for an entire year. (The cost for waiting less than a year is simply prorated.) For example, if a store offers a $10 per week discount for each week, a customer waits for merchandise, then $C_s = \$10(52) = \$520$. Hence, if a customer has to wait only four weeks for the item, the backorder cost for that customer is $(4/52)(\$520) = \$40$.

In general, C_s does not represent a customer discount, but, rather, an estimate of customer dissatisfaction known as a **goodwill cost**. This cost translates into the future reduction in the firm's profitability associated with keeping a customer waiting. Goodwill costs are, at best, difficult to measure, but firms can sometimes get reasonable estimates of such costs from marketing surveys and focus groups.

In addition to the goodwill cost of keeping a customer waiting for the item, an administrative cost, C_b, may also be associated with writing up a backorder and contacting the customer whose item was on backorder when the order arrives. This cost differs from C_s because it is a fixed cost per backorder, independent of how long a customer waits for the item to arrive.

In the planned shortage model, the decision maker can control two quantities: Q, the order quantity, and S, the number of units on backorder at the time the next order arrives. Hence, the total variable inventory cost equation, TV(Q, S), is a function of both of these quantities:

TV(Q, S) = (Total Annual Holding Costs)
+ (Total Annual Ordering Costs)
+ (Total Annual Time-Dependent Shortage Costs)
+ (Total Annual Time-Independent Shortage Costs)

Figure 8.13 is useful in developing expressions for these terms. In this figure:

T_1 = the period in the inventory cycle during which inventory is available
T_2 = the period in the inventory cycle during which items are on backorder
T = the time of the complete inventory cycle = $T_1 + T_2$

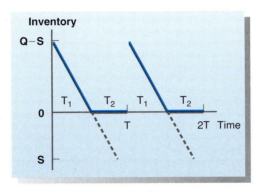

FIGURE 8.13 Planned Shortage Model—Inventory Profile over Time

An inventory cycle begins when S units are on backorder and an order of size Q is received. Since the S backorders are filled immediately, the inventory position at the beginning of the cycle is brought to its maximum inventory position M = Q − S. The model assumes that items are demanded (thus, inventory is depleted) at a constant rate until the inventory level reaches 0 at time T_1. Then, during period T_2, backorders accumulate at the same constant demand rate until, at the end of the cycle, S units are on backorder. At that point the next cycle begins, and the process is repeated. The individual components of TV(Q, S) can now be determined.

ANNUAL HOLDING COST

The average inventory level during the entire cycle, T, is the average inventory level during the in-stock period, (Q − S)/2, times the proportion of time that there is inventory in stock (T_1/T). The demand during period T_1 is D * T_1 = Q − S, while the demand during the entire cycle T is D * T = Q. Dividing Q − S by Q therefore gives the value of T_1/T. Hence we have that:

$$\text{Average Inventory Level} = \left(\frac{(Q - S)}{2}\right)\left(\frac{(Q - S)}{Q}\right) = \frac{(Q - S)^2}{2Q}$$

As in the previous models, the annual holding cost is the average inventory level times C_h. Thus

$$\text{Annual Inventory Holding Costs} = \frac{(Q - S)^2}{2Q} C_h$$

ANNUAL ORDERING COST

The annual ordering cost is found by multiplying the average number of orders per year, $N = D/Q$, by the fixed ordering cost, C_o. Thus the total annual ordering cost is:

$$\left(\frac{D}{Q}\right) C_o$$

ANNUAL TIME-DEPENDENT SHORTAGE COST

The average backorder level during the cycle is the average number of stockouts during the out-of-stock period, $S/2$, times the proportion of time inventory is on backorder, (T_2/T). Since $\dfrac{T_1}{T} = \dfrac{Q - S}{Q}$, and $\dfrac{T_1}{T} + \dfrac{T_2}{T} = 1$, it follows that $\dfrac{T_2}{T} = \dfrac{S}{Q}$ and thus

$$\text{Average Backorder Level} = \left(\frac{S}{2}\right)\left(\frac{S}{Q}\right) = \frac{S^2}{2Q}$$

The annual time-dependent shortage cost equals the average backorder level times C_s. Thus

$$\text{Annual Time-Dependent Backorder Cost} = \left(\frac{S^2}{2Q}\right) C_s$$

ANNUAL TIME-INDEPENDENT SHORTAGE COST

During each inventory cycle there are S backorders, and there are D/Q cycles per year, so that

$$\text{Total Number of Backorders During a Year} = \left(\frac{D}{Q}\right) S$$

The annual shortage cost that is incurred independent of the length of time customers are on backorder is C_b times the total number of backorders during the year. Thus

$$\text{Annual Time-Independent Backorder Cost} = \left(\frac{D}{Q}\right) SC_b$$

TOTAL ANNUAL COSTS

Combining these terms gives the following formula for $TV(Q, S)$:

$$TV(Q, S) = \frac{(Q - S)^2}{2Q} C_h + \frac{D}{Q} (C_o + SC_b) + \frac{S^2}{2Q} C_s \qquad (8.10)$$

OPTIMAL INVENTORY POLICY

Let Q^* and S^* represent the pair of values for Q and S that minimize $TV(Q, S)$. Although it is not always possible to obtain closed-form solutions for a pair of values such as Q^* and S^*, they can be obtained for this model provided that $C_s > 0$ and

$$C_b < \sqrt{2C_o C_h/D}$$

(See Appendices 8.2 and 8.5 on the accompanying CD-ROM.) These values are given below.

Optimal Inventory Policy for the Planned Shortage Model

$$Q^* = \sqrt{\left(\frac{2DC_o}{C_h}\right)\left(\frac{C_h + C_s}{C_s}\right) - \frac{(DC_b)^2}{C_h C_s}} \qquad (8.11)$$

and

$$S^* = \frac{Q^* C_h - DC_b}{C_h + C_s} \qquad (8.12)$$

REORDER POINT

To find the reorder point when there is a lead time of L years, we note that S^* represents the number of orders on backorder when the new shipment arrives. If the annual demand is for D units, the lead time demand equals $L*D$. Hence the reorder point, R, for this model is given by the following formula:

$$R = L*D - S^* \qquad (8.13)$$

The value of R can be negative, implying that the reorder point occurs when several units are already on backorder. If $R = -5$, for example, the order should be placed when five units are on backorder.

To illustrate the planned shortage model, consider the situation faced by the Scanlon Plumbing Corporation.

Scanlon inventory.xls

SCANLON PLUMBING CORPORATION

Scanlon Plumbing Corporation is the exclusive North American distributor of a portable sauna manufactured in Sweden. The saunas cost Scanlon $2400 each, and the company estimates the annual holding cost per unit for this product is $525. Because the saunas must be shipped in a containerized vessel, the fixed ordering cost is fairly high, at $1250. Lead time for delivery is four weeks.

Scanlon receives orders for an average of 15 saunas per week. Customers are willing to place orders for the saunas when Scanlon is out of stock. However, the company estimates the goodwill cost of keeping a customer's sauna on backorder is $20 per week. There is also an administrative cost of $10 for each sauna placed on backorder.

Management wishes to determine an optimal inventory policy for ordering the saunas.

SOLUTION

For the Scanlon Plumbing model the parameters are:

$$D = 15(52) = 780$$
$$C_o = \$1250$$
$$C_h = \$525$$
$$C_s = \$20(52) = \$1040$$
$$C_b = \$10$$

Substituting these quantities into Equations 8.11 and 8.12 gives:

$$Q^* = \sqrt{\left(\frac{2(780)(1250)}{525}\right)\left(\frac{525 + 1040}{1040}\right) - \frac{((780)(10))^2}{(525)(1040)}} \approx 74$$

and

$$S^* = \frac{(74)(525) - (780)(10)}{525 + 1040} \approx 20$$

Since lead time is four weeks, $L = 4/52 = .07692$ years. Orders should therefore be placed when the inventory level reaches:

$$R = .07692(780) - 20 = 40 \text{ units}$$

PRACTICAL CONSIDERATIONS

Again, the validity of the assumptions we used to generate Q^* and S^* should be evaluated. For example, the planned shortage model assumes that goodwill costs are linear; that is, the cost of keeping a customer on backorder for four months is assumed to be four times the cost of keeping a customer on backorder for one month. This is probably not the case in most real-world situations. Customers may be reasonably tolerant of short delays, but long delays can result in a tremendous loss in customer goodwill. Hence the decision maker should analyze the model results to see whether the assumed backorder cost is realistic.

In this case, it was assumed that the backorder cost for saunas is $20 per week. Although management feels that this cost is realistic for delays of a week or less, it believes that delays greater than a week are actually more costly. The maximum delay experienced by any customer can be found by dividing S^* by D. For Scanlon Plumbing, the maximum backorder delay encountered by a customer (in weeks) is $S^*/D = 20/15 = 1\frac{1}{3}$ weeks.

As a result of this analysis, management might feel that a $25 per week backorder cost is more realistic. This variation changes C_s from $1040 to $1300 and, using Equations 8.11 and 8.12, suggests a revised inventory policy of ordering 72 units when the inventory level reaches 44 units. In this case, the maximum number of customers on backorder is approximately 16, and the longest time a customer will spend on backorder is just slightly more than one week.

ECONOMIC IMPLICATIONS

It is worth examining the implications of the formulas for Q^* and S^* on inventory control. (To simplify, assume C_b equals 0.) If C_h is quite large relative to C_s (as it is for custom or big-ticket items for which the buyer expects delays), the ratio $C_h/(C_h + C_s)$ is close to 1 and S^* is approximately Q^*. That is, whenever an inventory order arrives, nearly all units have already been presold and the firm carries virtually no inventory. The optimal order quantity in this case is given approximately by the formula

$$Q^* \approx \sqrt{\frac{2DC_o}{C_s}}$$

In this case, the holding cost plays no role in determining Q^*.

On the other hand, now suppose that C_s is quite large relative to C_h, as it is for products for which customer goodwill costs are quite high if the item is not available for purchase (such as daily staples like bread, milk, and eggs). In this case, $C_h/(C_h + C_s)$ is close to 0, and the firm almost always wants the good to be in stock. Therefore, customers are never intentionally placed on backorder. Furthermore, because $(C_h + C_s)/C_s$ is effectively 1, the formula for Q^* reduces to the EOQ formula (Equation 8.3). Hence we can view the EOQ model as a special case of the planned shortage model for which C_s equals infinity and C_b equals 0.

Thus, if an item has a high holding cost relative to its backorder cost, the firm will carry little, if any, inventory, while if its backorder cost is high relative to its holding cost, the firm generally tries to keep the item in inventory and avoid running out of stock.

SPECIAL CASES

A special case of the planned shortage model occurs when the value of C_b is high relative to the value of C_s. In particular, when $C_b > \sqrt{2C_oC_h/D}$, the optimal solution is to allow no shortages ($S^* = 0$), and Q^* equals the EOQ value.

To understand why this is the case, note that, for the EOQ solution, $Q^* = \sqrt{2DC_o/C_h}$. Substituting this value into the total annual variable cost formula (Equation 8.1) gives:

$$TV(Q^*) = \sqrt{2DC_oC_h} \tag{8.14}$$

Dividing $TV(Q^*)$ by the annual demand, D, results in the variable inventory cost per unit under the EOQ policy, $\sqrt{2C_oC_h/D}$. Hence, if the administrative backorder cost, C_b, is greater than this amount, it must be more expensive to allow backorders than not to allow them.

Another special case of the model occurs when $C_s = 0$. If the value of C_s is 0 and $C_b \leq \sqrt{2C_oC_h/D}$, the model does not make any sense because the optimal policy is to keep all customers on backorder for an infinitely long period of time.

Software Results

Figure 8.14 gives results of using the **Planned Shortage** worksheet on the **inventory.xls** template to determine the optimal order quantity and reorder point for the Scanlon Plumbing Corporation problem.

Scanlon inventory.xls

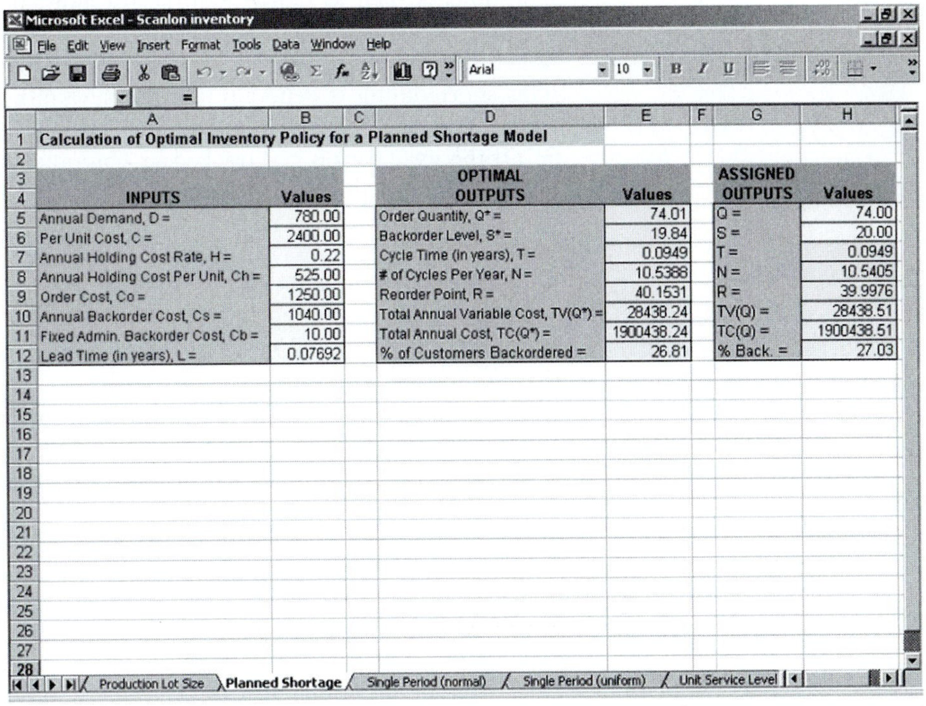

FIGURE 8.14 Excel Spreadsheet for Scanlon Plumbing Corporation

Microsoft Excel - Scanlon inventory		

Calculation of Optimal Inventory Policy for a Planned Shortage Model

INPUTS	Values	OPTIMAL OUTPUTS	Values	ASSIGNED OUTPUTS	Values
Annual Demand, D =	780.00	Order Quantity, Q* =	74.01	Q =	74.00
Per Unit Cost, C =	2400.00	Backorder Level, S* =	19.84	S =	20.00
Annual Holding Cost Rate, H =	0.22	Cycle Time (in years), T =	0.0949	T =	0.0949
Annual Holding Cost Per Unit, Ch =	525.00	# of Cycles Per Year, N =	10.5388	N =	10.5405
Order Cost, Co =	1250.00	Reorder Point, R =	40.1531	R =	39.9976
Annual Backorder Cost, Cs =	1040.00	Total Annual Variable Cost, TV(Q*) =	28438.24	TV(Q) =	28438.51
Fixed Admin. Backorder Cost, Cb =	10.00	Total Annual Cost, TC(Q*) =	1900438.24	TC(Q) =	1900438.51
Lead Time (in years), L =	0.07692	% of Customers Backordered =	26.81	% Back. =	27.03

Production Lot Size ⟩ **Planned Shortage** ⟨ Single Period (normal) ⟨ Single Period (uniform) ⟨ Unit Service Level

In this spreadsheet the parameters are entered in column B. Note that there are entries for C_s, the cost of keeping a unit on backorder for one year, and C_b, the fixed administrative cost of putting a unit on backorder.

The values in cells E5 and E6 give the optimal values for the order quantity, Q^*, and the number of units on backorder when the order arrives, S^*. Cells H5 and H6 allow the user to input specified values for Q and S (in this case 74 for Q and 20 for S).

As with the EOQ model, one can use the Solver option to also determine the optimal values for Q and S. To do this, click on Solver and in the "Set Target Cell" box put $H$10, in the "Equal To" section, highlight the Min button, and in the "By Changing Cells" box enter $H$5:$H$6. For this model, however, we must make sure that Q and S are > 0. Since these are strict inequalities, adding Q ≥ .00001 and S ≥ .00001 in the "Add Constraints" dialogue box roughly approximates these constraints. When Solve is clicked the optimal values for Q and S will appear in cells H5 and H6 respectively and the values in column H will be identical to those in column E.

8.7 Review Systems

CONTINUOUS REVIEW SYSTEMS

The EOQ model, the production lot size model, and the planned shortage model are all examples of continuous review systems because we implicitly assume that the inventory position is *continuously* monitored and an order is placed at the instant the inventory level reaches the reorder point.

(R,Q) Policies

For the EOQ, production lot size, and planned shortage models, an order of size Q is placed whenever the inventory level reaches the reorder point, R. Hence these models are sometimes known as *order point*, *order quantity*, or (R,Q) *policies*.

There are several ways to implement such policies. If inventory is tracked by a point-of-sale (POS) computerized cash register system, as it is in many retail establishments such as department stores and supermarkets, the computer can be programmed to carry out the recommended policy. Because the computer does not record shrinkage (theft and breakage), however, this method is not foolproof. This shortcoming is generally not too severe, however, and can be overcome by introducing a shrinkage factor into the computer program.

If the inventory is not tracked by computer, it may appear impossible, from a practical standpoint, to continuously review the firm's inventory position. Fortunately, there is a fairly easy way of implementing an (R,Q) policy, known as the *two-bin system*. This system, which is used in a number of factories and supply houses, operates as follows.

For a given product, a small bin holds R units and a larger bin holds up to Q units. When a new order arrives, the small bin is filled and tagged, and the remaining inventory from the order is placed in the large bin. Employees are instructed to remove units from the large bin until that bin is depleted. Once the large bin is empty, the small bin is opened up and items are supplied from that bin. At the time the small bin is opened, the order tag is removed and given to the inventory foreman. The order tag alerts the foreman that it is time to place an order for an additional Q units.

(R,M) Policies

Implicit in the development of our previous models is the fact that the firm sells stock-keeping units one at a time. In many businesses, however, the typical customer order may consist of multiple units of the same item. When such an order triggers the reorder point, problems can arise in an (R,Q) system.

For example, suppose that Citron did not offer quantity discounts and AAC adopted the policy recommendation to order Q = 327 units when the inventory level reaches R = 219. If the inventory level is 224 and one of AAC's customers purchases 60 juicers, this purchase triggers a new order. If AAC only orders 327 juicers, it may find itself out of stock again faster than anticipated because the inventory position when the order is placed, I, will only be I = 224 − 60 = 164 juicers. This will be R − I = 219 − 164 = 55 units below the reorder point.

One way to avoid the potential problem caused by exceptionally large orders is to use an *order point, order up to level*, or (R, M) *policy*. Under this system, while a new order is placed whenever the inventory level falls to R or below, the order size is adjusted to Q + (R − I) to bring the inventory level back up to an anticipated level of M, (M = Q + SS). This system effectively amends the (R,Q) policy to account for situations in which the inventory level may be substantially below the reorder point when the order is placed.

Adjusted Order Quantity for (R,M) Model

Order Quantity = Q + (R − I) = (M − SS) + (R − I)

For example, suppose AAC uses an (R, M) policy with reorder point R = 219, and anticipated maximum inventory level M = 354 (the order quantity of 327 plus the safety stock of 27). If a customer orders 60 juicers when the inventory level is at 224, a reorder is triggered when the inventory position, I, equals 224 − 60 = 164. Hence the reorder amount should be equal to 354 − 27 + 219 − 164 = 382 instead of 327 juicers. The difference between 382 and 327, 55, reflects the fact that when the order is placed, the inventory level is 55 units below the desired reorder point of 219.

In the long run, an (R, M) policy typically has a lower average cost than a comparable (R, Q) policy. (R, M) systems are more complicated to monitor than (R, Q) systems, however. For example, implementing an (R, M) policy in a two-bin system requires the employee who removes the tag from the smaller bin to record how many units are being removed from that bin at the time it is opened. This extra control cost is not always worth the savings achieved by the (R, M) system.

PERIODIC REVIEW SYSTEMS

Continuous review systems are not practical for many businesses. Some establishments may not have the resources available to purchase computerized cash register systems or the space available to adopt a two-bin system. Others may order many different items from the same vendor and find it impractical to place separate purchase orders at different time periods for the numerous SKUs. In such instances, many firms use a *periodic review inventory system*. In this system the inventory position for each SKU is observed at fixed periods at which time order decisions are made.

(T, M) Policies

In *replenishment cycle* or (T, M) *policies*, the inventory position is reviewed every T time units (days, weeks, etc.), and an order is placed to bring the inventory level for the stock-keeping unit back up to an anticipated maximum inventory level, M. This anticipated maximum level is determined by forecasting the number of units demanded during the review period and adding the desired safety stock to this amount. Replenishment cycle policies are typically used by rack jobbers who have a scheduled plan for servicing customers. The following formulas can then be used to find the order quantity, Q, and the value of M, for a (T, M) policy:

Optimal Policy for (T,M) Models

Maximum Anticipated Demand Plus Safety Stock During the Review Period:
$$M = T * D + SS$$

Optimal Order Quantity: $Q = M + L * D - I$

where: T = Review Period

L = Lead Time

D = Demand

SS = Safety Stock

I = Inventory Position

To illustrate this technique, let us return to the situation at the Allen Appliance Company.

ALLEN APPLIANCE COMPANY (CONTINUED)

Allen Appliance Company has begun selling several different products from Citron in addition to its juicers and has decided to implement a periodic review system for controlling inventory. Citron makes regular deliveries to AAC every three weeks, based on orders it has received eight days before shipment. Thus AAC reviews its inventory every three weeks, eight days before it expects a shipment, and faxes an order to Citron. It is now time for AAC to place an order, and it finds that 210 juicers are in stock. AAC wants to know how many juicers to order if it now desires a safety stock of 30 units. Recall that Allen operates 260 days per year.

SOLUTION

For this model we will express T, L, and D in years. Hence T = 3 weeks or 3/52 = .05769 years, L = 8 days or 8/260 = .03077 years, D = 6240 units per year, SS = 30 units, and I = 210 units. Thus the anticipated maximum inventory, M, is:

$$M = 360 + 30 = 390 \text{ juicers}$$

and the order quantity should be:

$$Q = 390 + (.03077)(6240) - 210 = 372 \text{ juicers.}$$

(T, R, M) Policies

One shortcoming of a (T, M) policy arises when there has been little demand for the stock-keeping unit during the previous review period. Under these circumstances, it may not even pay to place a new order. We can modify the (T, M) policy by introducing a threshold inventory level R, meaning that orders for the stock-keeping unit are placed only if the current inventory level is R or less. This policy, known as a (T, R, M) *policy*, has a lower long-run cost than a simple (T, M) policy. How the optimal values for T and R are determined is beyond the scope of this text, however, this problem can be analyzed using the simulation approach detailed in Chapter 10.

8.8 Single-period Inventory Model

The inventory models developed thus far assumed that demand occurs at a known and reasonably constant rate and that the shelf life of the stock-keeping units is long enough that the goods will not spoil or deteriorate in value while in inventory. In many situations, however, demand is stochastic, and the inventory shelf life or selling season is quite short. Consequently, the stock-keeping unit cannot be carried in inventory beyond a certain time period. In such cases, we can use the **single-period inventory model** to determine the optimal order quantity. This model assumes that demand varies according to a specified probability distribution and deals with a stock-keeping unit that has a limited shelf life of one period. Hence no inventory is stored from period to period.

A common example is a newsstand where newspapers that are unsold at the end of a day are not kept in inventory but are disposed of to make room for delivery of the next day's papers. For this reason, the single-period inventory model is frequently referred to as the **newsboy problem**. Other commodities that have a limited shelf life include magazines, Christmas trees, Valentine's Day candy, Halloween costumes, baked goods, concert tickets, chemicals, seasonal clothing, and dairy products. The basic assumptions of the single-period inventory model are as follows.

Assumptions of the Single-period Inventory Model

1. Inventory is saleable only within a single time period.
2. During each time period, inventory is delivered only once.
3. Customer demand during each period is stochastic (random) but follows a known probability distribution.
4. At the end of each period, unsold inventory is disposed of for some salvage value (which may be positive, negative, or zero).
5. The salvage value is less than the cost of the good.
6. If customer demand exceeds available supply, the firm may encounter a goodwill or shortage cost for each unsatisfied customer demand.

To determine the optimal order quantity in a single-period inventory model, a balance must be struck between overordering, which would create excess inventory left at the end of the period, and underordering, which would result in unsatisfied customer demand. The following notation is used for single-period inventory models:

$$p = \text{per unit selling price of the good}$$
$$c = \text{per unit cost of the good}$$
$$s = \text{per unit salvage value of unsold goods}$$
$$g = \text{goodwill or shortage cost for each unsatisfied customer}$$
$$K = \text{fixed purchasing costs}$$
$$Q = \text{order quantity}$$
$$EP(Q) = \text{expected profit if Q units are ordered}$$

DEVELOPMENT OF THE SINGLE-PERIOD MODEL

Our analysis begins by developing an expression for $EP(Q)$. Two scenarios are possible depending on whether the actual demand, x, is (1) less than the order quantity, Q: or (2) greater than or equal to the order quantity, Q. Each leads to a different expression for the profit.

Case 1: Demand, x, Is Less Than the Number of Units Stocked, Q In this case, x units are sold at a price of p each, and the remaining (Q − x) units will have to be disposed of for a salvage value of s each. Hence, total revenue is px + s(Q − x). Since demand is less than the available inventory, no goodwill costs are incurred. The cost of stocking the Q units is cQ + K. Accordingly, profit is given by the following expression:

$$\text{Profit} = px + s(Q - x) - cQ - K$$

Case 2: Demand, x, Is Greater Than or Equal to the Number of Units Stocked, Q In this case, all Q units are sold at a price of p each, and no inventory is left to dispose of for salvage value. Hence the total revenue is pQ. As demand exceeds the available inventory, (x − Q) customer demands are unsatisfied at a goodwill cost of g each. The cost of supplying the Q units is cQ + K, bringing total costs to g(x − Q) + cQ + K. Hence the profit is:

$$\text{Profit} = pQ - g(x - Q) - cQ - K$$

Note that, in either case, the profit varies according to the actual demand, x. The expected profit, EP(Q), given an order quantity of Q, is determined by finding the weighted average profit over all possible values of x. When demand follows a discrete probability distribution, p(x), this is done by multiplying the profit corresponding to a demand of x by the probability that x units are demanded and then summing these products over all possible values of x:

> **Expected Profit for the Discrete Demand Distribution**
>
> $$EP(Q) = \sum_x (\text{profit given demand} = x) * p(x)$$

Substituting the formulas for the profit in the two demand cases yields a straightforward, but rather messy, formula for EP(Q).

If demand is assumed to follow a continuous probability distribution with density function f(x), the expected profit function can be determined as follows:

> **Expected Profit for the Continuous Demand Distribution**
>
> $$EP(Q) = \int (\text{profit given demand} = x) * f(x)dx$$

 The objective is to determine the value, Q*, that maximizes this expected profit function. Appendix 8.6 on the accompanying CD-ROM contains detailed formulas for EP(Q) as well as the derivation of Q* for both discrete and continuous probability demand distributions. There it is shown that when demand follows a discrete probability distribution with cumulative probability P(x), Q* is the smallest value of Q, such that:

$$P(D \le Q^*) \ge \frac{p - c + g}{p - s + g} \qquad (8.15)$$

When demand follows a continuous probability distribution with cumulative distribution $F(x)$, Q^* satisfies the following relationship:

$$F(Q^*) = \frac{p - c + g}{p - s + g}$$

(8.16)

Note that the fixed cost, K, plays no role in determining the optimal order quantity. The ratio $(p - c + g)/(p - s + g)$ is known as the **optimal service level**. It represents the long-run percentage of periods in which inventory is sufficient to satisfy all customer demands. This does *not* imply that in any given period the proportion of customer demands that will be satisfied is $(p - c + g)/(p - s + g)$.

A SINGLE-PERIOD MODEL WITH A DISCRETE DEMAND DISTRIBUTION

To help motivate the single-period inventory model when demand can be modeled by a discrete distribution, consider the situation faced by the *Sentinel* newspaper.

Sentinel Newspaper.xls

THE *SENTINEL* NEWSPAPER

Company management at the *Sentinel* newspaper wishes to determine how many papers should be placed in each of several vending machine locations. The newspapers sell for $.30 each. Although they cost the company $.38 each to produce, *Sentinel* receives approximately $.18 in advertising revenue for each paper printed. Hence the net production cost per paper is $.20.

Any unsold papers are delivered to a newspaper recycling firm and net the *Sentinel* $.01 per copy. The company estimates that if a vending machine runs short of papers, it will suffer a goodwill loss of $.10 for each unsatisfied customer. The cost of filling a vending machine averages $1.20.

Based on many prior weeks of sales data, the circulation manager for the *Sentinel* estimates that demand for the Tuesday paper at the Sixth and Main vending machine location approximately follows a discrete uniform distribution with demand between 30 and 49 papers. Management would like to know the optimal number of papers to stock at this location.

SOLUTION

In this model

$$p = \text{selling price per paper} = \$.30$$
$$c = \text{cost per paper} = \$.20$$
$$s = \text{salvage value per paper} = \$.01$$
$$g = \text{goodwill cost per paper} = \$.10$$
$$K = \text{fixed cost} = \$1.20$$

To illustrate the two profit expressions, suppose the *Sentinel* puts 40 newspapers in a vending machine. If demand is only 32 newspapers, this is Case 1 since $32 < 40$. Hence, the profit would be $\$.30(32) + \$.01(40 - 32) - \$.20(40) - \$1.20 = \$.48$. On the other hand, if demand is 45 newspapers, this is Case 2 since $45 \geq 40$. Now the profit would be $\$.30(40) - \$.10(45 - 40) - \$.20(40) - \$1.20 = \$2.30$.

The objective is to determine the optimal number of newspapers, Q*, to stock at the Sixth and Main location. Substituting the values of the parameters for the *Sentinel* newspaper into the right side of Equation 8.15 gives the following optimal service level:

$$\frac{p + g - c}{p + g - s} = \frac{.30 + .10 - .20}{.30 + .10 - .01} = \frac{.20}{.39} = .513$$

Hence Q* is the smallest value for Q such that P(D ≤ Q*) ≥ .513. Because demand is uniformly distributed between 30 and 49 papers, demand will equally likely be 30, 31, 32, . . . , 48, or 49. For these 20 possible values, p(x = 30) = p(x = 31) = p(x = 32) = . . . = p(x = 49) = 1/20 = .05; therefore, P(x ≤ 30) = .05, P(x ≤ 31) = .10, P(x ≤ 32) = .15, and so on. Proceeding in this fashion, P(x ≤ 39) = .50 and P(x ≤ 40) = .55.

Since P(x ≤ 39) = .50 is less than .513, and P(x ≤ 40) = .55 is greater than .513, the *Sentinel* should put 40 newspapers in the vending machine. Note that, given the discrete nature of the probability distribution, stocking the vending machine with 40 papers actually results in a 55% service level.

Software Results

Figure 8.15 shows an Excel spreadsheet that can be used to determine the order quantity for a single-period inventory model in which demand follows a uniform distribution.

Sentinel Newspaper.xls

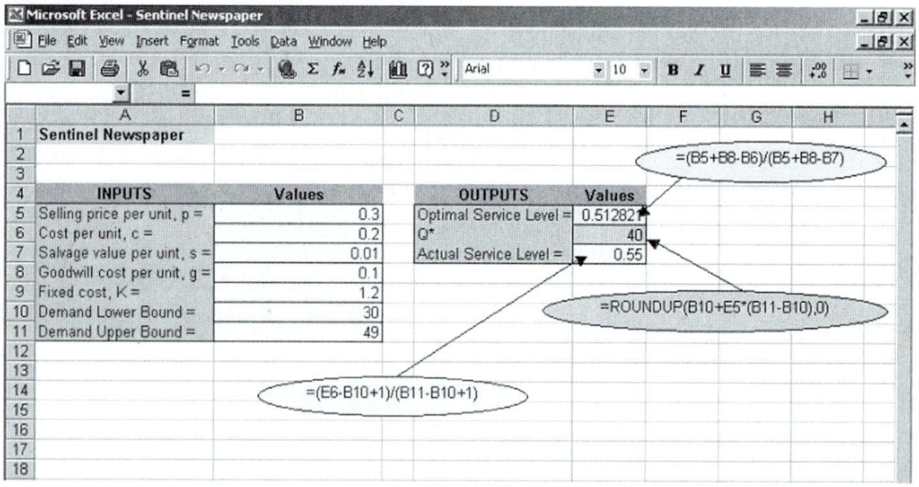

FIGURE 8.15   Excel Spreadsheet for the Sentinel Newspaper

In this spreadsheet the parameters are entered in column B. The outputs for the problem, the optimal service level, the optimal order quantity, and the resulting service level are calculated in cells E5, E6, and E7, respectively.

The worksheet **Single-Period (Uniform)** on the **inventory.xls** template can be used to determine the optimal inventory policy for single-inventory models in which demand follows a uniform distribution. The format for the worksheet is similar to that used in Figure 8.15.

A SINGLE-PERIOD MODEL WITH A CONTINUOUS DEMAND DISTRIBUTION

To illustrate these concepts when there is a continuous probability distribution for demand, consider the case of Wendell's Bakery.

Wendell's Bakery.xls

WENDELL'S BAKERY

Vermont State University has given Wendell's Bakery the concession to sell glazed donuts in the School of Business during evening classes. It costs the bakery $.15 to produce each donut, and Wendell's sells the donuts to students for $.35 each. Any donuts that are unsold at the end of the evening are donated to a local charity, and the bakery obtains a tax credit equal to $.05 per donut. If Wendell's produces too few donuts and does not have enough to satisfy all its customers, it incurs a customer goodwill cost of $.25 per donut demanded. The bakery hires a student to operate the concession and pays the student $15 per evening.

After several months of operations, the bakery has determined that demand for glazed donuts on weekday evenings approximately follows a normal distribution with a mean of 120 and a standard deviation of 20. Wendell's wishes to determine the optimal number of donuts to prepare for weekday evenings.

SOLUTION

For this problem,

$$p = \text{selling price per donut} = \$ \ .35$$
$$c = \text{cost per donut} = \$ \ .15$$
$$s = \text{salvage value per donut} = \$ \ .05$$
$$g = \text{goodwill cost per donut} = \$ \ .25$$
$$K = \text{fixed operating cost} = \$15.00$$

Hence Q^* should be chosen so that: $F(Q^*) = (.35 + .25 - .15)/(.35 + .25 - .05) = .8182$. That is, the bakery should produce enough donuts so that the probability of satisfying all demands during the evening is .8182.

To determine values for the normal distribution, the standard normal random variable, z is used. Recall that z represents the number of standard deviations that a variable, x, is from its mean; z is related to x by the formula $z = (x - \mu)/\sigma$, or $x = \mu + z\sigma$.

In Figure 8.16 it is shown that a cumulative probability of .8182 corresponds to the shaded area of .3182 between 0 and the appropriate z value. Referring to Appendix A, the closest entry in the table to .3182 is .3186, corresponding to a z value of .91. Thus, using z = .91, the number of donuts the bakery should deliver to the School of Business is:

$$Q^* = \mu + z\sigma = 120 + .91 * 20 \approx 138$$

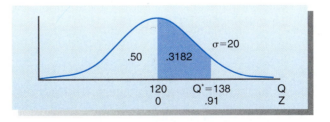

FIGURE 8.16 Optimal Order Quantity for Wendell's Bakery

If demand follows a normal distribution with a mean of μ and a standard deviation of σ, it can be shown that the equation for the expected per period profit, assuming that Q^* units are ordered, is:

$$EP(Q^*) = (p - s)\mu - (c - s)Q^* - (p + g - s)\sigma L\left(\frac{Q^* - \mu}{\sigma}\right) - K \quad (8.17)$$

In this expression, L(z) represents the partial expected value for the standard normal random variable between some value z and infinity. Values for L(z) are given in Appendix B.

For Wendell's Bakery the expected profit per period is:

$$EP(138) = (.35 - .05)(120) - (.15 - .05)(138)$$

$$- (.35 + .25 - .05)(20)L\left(\frac{138 - 120}{20}\right) - 15$$

$$= .30(120) - .10(138) - .55(20)L(.9) - 15$$

$$= 36 - 13.8 - 11(.1004) - 15 = \$6.10$$

Software Results

Figure 8.17 gives an Excel spreadsheet that can be used to determine the order quantity for a single-period inventory model in which demand follows a normal distribution.

Wendell's Bakery.xls

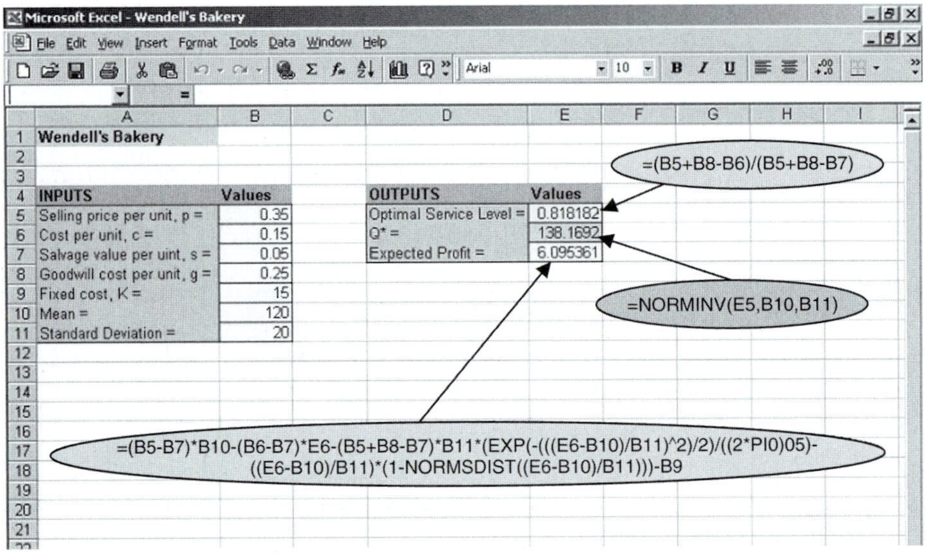

FIGURE 8.17 Excel Spreadsheet for Wendell's Bakery

In this spreadsheet the parameters are entered in column B. The outputs for the problem, including the optimal service level, order quantity, and expected profit, are calculated in cells E5 through E7, respectively.

The worksheet **Single-Period (Normal)** on the **inventory.xls** template can be used to determine the optimal inventory policy for single-inventory models in which demand follows a normal distribution. The format for the worksheet is similar to that used in Figure 8.17.

WENDELL'S BAKERY (CONTINUED)

As an alternative strategy, suppose the bakery is considering paying the student a commission of $.13 for each donut sold rather than a fixed wage of $15 per evening. Wendell's wishes to determine how this compensation will affect its inventory decision and whether its daily profits will increase.

SOLUTION

In this case, the analysis must be done in a slightly different fashion. In particular, the unit selling price from the bakery's standpoint is not the full $.35, but the difference between the $.35 selling price and the $.13 commission. Hence,

$p = \$.35 - \$.22 = \$.13$. For $p = \$.22$, the optimal inventory quantity, Q^*, is chosen so that

$$F(Q^*) = \frac{.22 + .25 - .15}{.22 + .25 - .05} = \frac{.32}{.42} = .7619$$

This corresponds to a z value of approximately .71 and results in an optimal production quantity of

$$x = \mu + z\sigma = 120 + .71 * 20 \approx 134 \text{ donuts}$$

To see whether this quantity will increase the bakery's expected profits, the modified values are substituted into the expected profit equation, giving the following expected per period profit:

$$EP(134) = (.22 - .05)(120) - (.15 - .05)(134)$$
$$- (.22 + .25 - .05)(20)L\left(\frac{134 - 120}{20}\right)$$
$$= .17(120) - .10(134) - .42(20)L(.7) = 20.4 = 13.4 - 8.4(.1429)$$
$$= \$5.80$$

Under this plan, the student's expected compensation can be found by using Equation 8.17, recognizing that from the student's perspective $p = .13$, $c = s = g = K = 0$, $Q^* = 134$, $\mu = 120$, and $\sigma = 20$. Making the appropriate substitutions gives an expected compensation of $15.23. It is worth noting that the increase in the student's expected compensation is less than the decrease in the bakery's expected profit.

This analysis does not account for the possibility that the student's sales motivation may be greater if compensation is based on commission. If this is the case, the increase in mean donut demand should somehow be estimated and incorporated into the analysis.

PRACTICAL CONSIDERATIONS OF USING THE SINGLE-PERIOD INVENTORY MODEL

Whereas the single-period inventory model is easy to solve given the required data inputs, determining the appropriate values for the parameters of a problem is frequently quite difficult. Many businesses do not have any idea what the goodwill cost for an unsatisfied customer might be. Determining the appropriate probability distribution for demand can also be daunting because usually only sales data, which are limited by the amount of inventory available, are observed.

Advanced techniques exist for dealing with these difficulties, but one simplified approach is to solve the problem for a number of different scenarios and determine a "range" of optimal solutions. Once this range has been established, management can select the policy with which it feels most comfortable.

8.9 Summary

In this chapter, we have examined a class of inventory models useful for analyzing goods for which either demand occurs at a known and reasonably constant rate or is random but inventory has a short shelf life. In situations in which a firm purchases goods from a supplier, the economic order quantity (EOQ) model can be used to determine the amount to order. The EOQ solution is quite robust; small errors in estimating parameter values have only minor effects on the EOQ solution.

Firms often offer their customers quantity discounts. Two frequently used discount schedules are the all units schedule and the incremental schedule. For the all units discount schedule, simple modifications to the EOQ analysis help determine the optimal order quantity.

In many manufacturing settings, the production lot size model can be used to determine the optimal production quantity for a good. The EOQ model can be considered a special case of the production lot size model, in which goods are supplied at an infinitely rapid rate.

The planned shortage model incorporates a backorder cost into the EOQ model. Items that have a relatively high shortage cost are most likely carried in stock, while items with a relatively high holding cost are most likely to be on backorder.

While some backorders are planned, many are not. In order to determine the necessary safety stock to accommodate a desired service level, a firm can undertake a statistical analysis. The appropriate safety stock is based on whether a cycle service level or a unit service level is desired.

There are several methods firms can use to control their inventories. Review of inventory may be done on a continuous or periodic basis. Order quantities may be fixed or adjusted to bring the inventory up to a specified level.

The single-period inventory (newsboy) model is used in a wide variety of applications in which demand has an exceedingly short shelf life and orders can only be placed once for the goods.

Finally, the control cost associated with an inventory policy should not be overlooked. Although the inventory techniques discussed in this chapter may reduce a firm's annual inventory expense, there are costs associated with determining inventory policies and controlling the inventory to conform with such policies. Consequently, the methods discussed here generally apply only to A and B type inventory items. For C items, the expense of inventory control generally exceeds the cost savings such control carries.

ON THE CD-ROM

● Excel spreadsheet for EOQ model	**Allen Appliance.xls**
	Allen inventory.xls
● Excel spreadsheet for determining reorder Point and service level using the cycle Service level approach	**Allen Appliance Cycle Service Level.xls**
● Excel spreadsheet for quantity discount models	**Allen inventory.xls**
● Excel spreadsheet for production lot size model	**Farah inventory.xls**
● Excel spreadsheet for planned shortage model	**Scanlon inventory.xls**
● Excel spreadsheets for single-period Inventory models	**Sentinel Newspaper.xls**
	Wendell's Bakery.xls
● Excel template for solving inventory problems	**Inventory.xls**
● Mathematical Formulas for Inventory Models	**Appendix 8.2**
● Determining the Reorder Point, R, Corresponding to a Unit Service Level	**Appendix 8.3**
● Determining the Optimal Order Quantity under an Incremental Discount Schedule	**Appendix 8.4**
● Derivation of the Planned Shortage Model	**Appendix 8.5**
● Single-Period Inventory Model	**Appendix 8.6**
● Production Oriented Inventory Models	**Supplement CD6**
● Problem Motivations	**Problem Motivations**
● Problems 41–50	**Additional Problems/Cases**

APPENDIX 8.1

Using the inventory.xls Template

The template **inventory.xls** contains nine worksheets. These are:

- **EOQ**
- **All Units Discount**
- **Incremental Discount**
- **Production Lot Size**
- **Planned Shortage**
- **Single-Period (uniform)**
- **Single-Period (normal)**
- **Unit Service Level**
- **Cycle Service Level**

For all worksheets, input data are entered in the yellow colored cells. Outputs are calculated and presented in the light blue cells.

EOQ WORKSHEET

Figure A8.1 shows the **EOQ** worksheet.

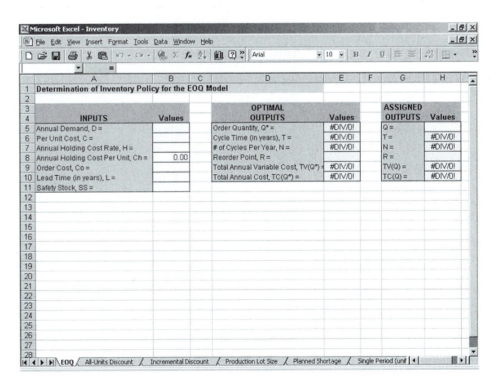

FIGURE A8.1   EOQ Worksheet

The parameters are entered into cells B5 through B10. Inputs include the annual demand in cell B5, the per unit cost in cell B6, the holding cost rate in cell B7, the annual holding cost per unit in cell B8, the ordering cost in cell B9, the lead time (expressed in years) in cell B10, and the desired safety stock in cell B11. We note that in cell B8 the holding cost is automatically calculated as C ∗ H. Should a different value be desired, this value may be entered in the cell.

Outputs for the EOQ model are given in column E. Cell H5 allows one to calculate a specified value of Q. The resulting outputs are given in cells H6 through H10. This information may be useful, for example, if one wishes to round off the value of Q* determined in cell E5 and see the impact of such rounding.

DISCOUNT MODELS

The **All Units Discount** worksheet is shown in Figure 8.9. Figure A8.2 shows the **Incremental Discount** worksheet.

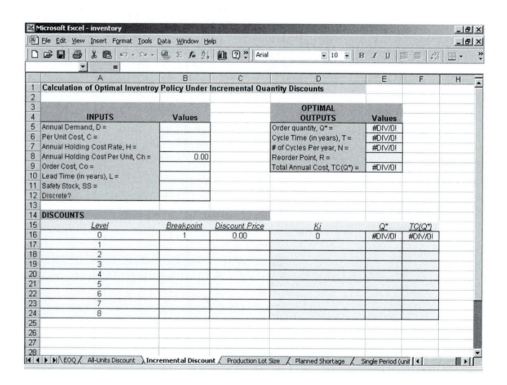

FIGURE A8.2 Incremental Discount Worksheet

This worksheet will solve problems with up to eight levels of quantity discounts. Basic data is entered into cells B5 through B12, while the discount data is entered into cells B17 through C24. Inputs for the Incremental Quantity Discount worksheet in cells B5 through B11 are similar to those for the EOQ worksheet. In cell B12, a 1 is entered if the inventory is in discrete units; otherwise a 0 is entered (or the cell is left empty). For example, if the inventory is cars, we would insert a 1 in cell B12 since one cannot order half a car. Alternatively, if the inventory is flour, we would put a 0 in cell B12 since it is possible to order half a pound of flour.

Breakpoints are entered in ascending order in cells B17 through B24 for up to as many levels as there are discounts offered, and the corresponding discounts are entered in cells C17 through C24. For the 0 discount level (row 16), cell B16 is preset to a value of 1, while cell C16 is set equal to the original unit cost entered in cell B6.

Outputs are given in cells E5 through E9. The cost and quantity information for each level is given in columns D through F beginning in row 16. Note that column G is hidden as it is used to determine the optimal quantity in cell E5.

Data entry and outputs for the **All Units Discounts** worksheet are similar to those presented for the **Incremental Discount** worksheet. However, for the **All Units Discount** worksheet, since it is not necessary to specify whether the units are discrete, there is no data entry in row 12.

PRODUCTION LOT SIZE WORKSHEET

The **Production Lot Size** worksheet is illustrated in Figure 8.12. Inputs and outputs are similar to those for the **EOQ** worksheet, but for this worksheet, the annual production rate must be specified in cell B10.

PLANNED SHORTAGE WORKSHEET

The **Planned Shortage** worksheet is illustrated in Figure 8.14. Inputs and outputs are similar to those for the **EOQ** worksheet; however, for this model one must also enter the annual backorder cost in cell B10 and the fixed administrative cost of putting a customer on backorder in cell B11. Note that safety stock is not entered for this model.

The planned shortage model calculates both an optimal order quantity and a backorder level in cells E5 and E6, respectively. The percentage of customers placed on backorder is calculated in cell E12. One can specify values for the order quantity and backorder level in cells H5 and H6, and the resulting inventory information will be determined in the remaining cells in column H.

SINGLE-PERIOD MODELS

The formats of the worksheets **Single-Period (uniform)** and **Single-Period (normal)** are similar to those shown in Figures 8.15 and 8.17 respectively. For both worksheets, cost and revenue data are entered in cells B5 through B9. For the **Single-Period (uniform)** worksheet the demand lower bound is entered in cell B10, while the upper bound is entered in cell B11. For the **Single-Period (normal)** worksheet the mean of the demand distribution is entered in cell B10, while the standard deviation is entered in cell B11.

For the **Single-Period (uniform)** worksheet the optimal service level is determined in cell E5, the optimal order quantity is determined in cell E6, and the actual service level (since the order quantity is rounded up) is determined in cell E8. The outputs are the same for the **Single-Period (normal)** worksheet except that cell E8 of this worksheet gives the expected profit.

SERVICE LEVELS

The worksheet **Cycle Service Level** is similar to that shown in Figure 8.7. In this worksheet, the inputs are placed in column B. In particular, the mean and standard deviation for lead time demand are inputted in cells B5 and B6, respectively. If one has a desired service level, this information is entered in cell B7 and the corresponding reorder point is calculated in cell E5. If one has a given reorder point, this information is entered in cell B8 and the corresponding cycle service level is calculated in cell E6.

Figure A8.3 shows the worksheet **Unit Service Level**. In this worksheet the mean and standard deviation for lead time demand are inputted in cells B5 and B6, respectively, the order quantity is entered in cell B7, and the desired service level is entered in cell B8. The resulting reorder point and safety stock values are calculated in cells E5 and E6.

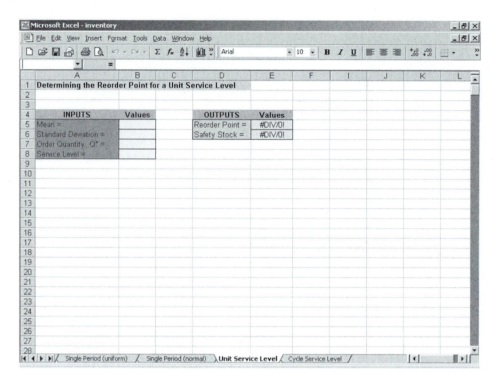

FIGURE A8.3   Unit Service
Level Worksheet

Problems

1. Culton Hair Salon sells an average of 20 bottles of hair conditioner weekly. There is a $25 cost to place an order with the distributor of the conditioner, and the conditioner costs the salon $2.50 per bottle. The annual holding cost rate is 18%, and the lead-time for delivery is one week. The salon desires a safety stock of five bottles and wishes to determine when an order should be placed and how many bottles it should order.

2. Price-Mart.com stores sells an average of two thousand pairs of the Excite brand of jeans per week. While the jeans normally cost retailers $16.00 per pair, Excite offers customers discounts on all pairs ordered if the order exceeds certain threshold amounts. In particular, the discount pricing schedule is as follows:

Order Quantity	Price per Unit
1–1000 pairs	$16.00
1001–5000 pairs	$15.20
5,001–10,000 pairs	$14.40
Over 10,000 pairs	$13.60

Price-Mart.com wishes to determine how many pairs of jeans it should order if the cost of placing an order is $200 and the annual holding cost rate for jeans is 15%.

3. ADM, Inc., a manufacturer of filing cabinets, has an average monthly demand of 500 units for its four-drawer model, ADM-4B. The company's production facility is capable of producing 2000 filing cabinets per month. Because production of each different model of filing cabinet made by the firm requires different stamping tools, the production setup cost to begin producing the four-drawer models is $2000. The firm estimates that the incremental production cost for the four-drawer model is $40 and that its annual holding cost rate is 20%. ADM wishes to determine how many of the four-drawer models it should manufacture during each production run and the number of production runs for this model that it should schedule over the upcoming year.

4. Playhouse World is distributor for a Victorian-style playhouse manufactured in Thailand. If the firm is out of stock of this playhouse, it offers customers a discount of $50 for each week they must wait for delivery. The administrative cost of processing a backorder is estimated to be $10. The playhouses cost the firm $3500 each and sell for $6000 each. Demand averages two units per month. Due to the fairly high cost of preparing customs documents, the cost of placing an order is estimated to be $1500 and an order takes approximately one month to arrive. Playhouse World estimates that the annual holding cost for the Victorian style playhouse is

$450. The company wishes to determine how many Victorian playhouses it should order and the approximate percentage of customers who will have to wait for delivery.

5. SportWorld.com places orders for Wilson golf balls every other week. Weekly demand for these golf balls averages 50 dozen, and the lead time for delivery of the balls is one week. SportWorld.com wishes to have a safety stock of 10 dozen golf balls to allow for variation in weekly demand. If the inventory at the time an order is placed is 15 dozen golf balls, determine how many dozen golf balls the firm should order.

6. Raul's Bakery bakes sourdough bread each day. Demand on past days has followed approximately a normal distribution, with an average of 60 loaves and a standard deviation of 12 loaves. The bread sells for $2.50 per loaf and costs $1.00 to produce. Loaves of bread unsold at the end of the day are donated to a food bank and result in the bakery getting an income tax credit of $.35. If the bakery runs out of sourdough bread, it believes it will suffer a goodwill cost of $5.00 for each loaf that is demanded and is not available. How many loaves of the sourdough bread should Raul's Bakery make each day?

7. Food Town wishes to determine an optimal order policy for Marino brand pasta. The store sells an average of 320 one-pound packages per week. The cost of placing an order is $30, and the annual holding cost rate is estimated to be 14%. The pasta costs the store $.60 per package. Lead time is estimated to be one week, and the store desires a safety stock of 100 packages.
   a. How many packages of pasta should Food Town order?
   b. At what inventory level should the order be placed?

8. Mother Smith's Pies produces frozen fruit pies for sale to local restaurants. Demand for one of its best sellers, apple, averages 150 pies per day. The company's production facility is capable of producing 50 pies per hour and operates eight hours a day, seven days a week. The pies cost $2.25 to produce, and Mother Smith's estimates that its annual holding cost rate is 20%. Because whenever a new type of pie is produced the machinery must be thoroughly cleaned, the cost of a production setup is estimated to be $90. Determine the optimal production quantity of apple pies.

9. Appliance Alley is a retailer of brand-name major appliances. One of its best sellers is the Poseidon brand washing machine. Demand for this machine averages 8 units per week. The machines cost Appliance Alley $625 each and sell for $999 each. Appliance Alley estimates that its annual holding cost rate for the washing machines is 18%. The cost of placing an order is $150, and the lead time is three weeks. If Appliance Alley is out of stock of the washing machines, it offers customers a discount of $5 for each day they must wait for their washing machine. The administrative cost of placing a customer on backorder is estimated to be $10.

   a. What is Appliance Alley's optimal inventory policy for the Poseidon brand of washing machines?
   b. If Appliance Alley follows an optimal inventory policy, what percentage of customers will have to wait for their washing machines?

10. Zeigler's Lumber Supply sells an average of 15,200 board feet of 2 by 4 lumber weekly. Zeigler's purchases its 2 by 4 lumber from Western Cascade Wood Products. Western Cascade offers its customers the following all units quantity discount schedule:

Order Quantity (in Board Feet)	Cost per Board Foot
1–24,999	$.26
25,000–49,999	$.245
50,000–99,999	$.23
100,000–249,999	$.22
250,000–999,999	$.21
1,000,000 or more	$.19

The annual holding cost rate for the lumber is 16%, and the cost of placing an order for the lumber is estimated to be $250. Lead time is three weeks, and Zeigler's desires a safety stock of 8000 board feet. Determine the optimal inventory policy of 2 by 4's for Zeigler's Lumber Supply.

11. Bank Drugs wishes to determine how many tablets of a new arthritis medication it should order. Its policy is to order from the manufacturer every other week and maintain a safety stock of 120 tablets. Based on past weeks' sales, Bank estimates that it sells 800 tablets of the medication each week. The lead time for delivery of the medication is three days. If its current inventory is 350 tablets, determine how many tablets of the medication it should order. Assume Bank is open seven days a week.

12. It is October 15, and Furr's Stationary must decide how many calendars it should order from the World Wildlife Federation. The calendars cost the company $4.25, and Furr's sells them for $9.50. The calendars will arrive on November 1, and demand during the period between November 1 and Christmas is estimated to follow a normal distribution with a mean of 250 units and a standard deviation of 40 units. Any calendars that remain after Christmas will be marked down to $2.00 and sold at Furr's annual after Christmas sale. If Furr's runs out of calendars before Christmas, it estimates it suffers a goodwill cost of $1.50 for each calendar demanded when it is out of stock. If Furr's can only place one order for the calendars and there is a $20 cost of placing an order, determine:
   a. How many calendars it should order.
   b. The expected profit it will earn on the calendars.

13. Demand for Stick disposable razors at Buyright Drugs averages seven packages per day. The razors cost Buyright $0.80 per package and sell for $1.49. Buyright uses a 20% annual holding cost rate and estimates the cost to place an order for additional razors at $25. Buyright is open 365 days a year and desires a safety

stock of 15 packages. The lead time for delivery is five days. Determine the following:

a. The optimal inventory policy (order quantity and reorder point) for Stick razors.

b. The number of days between orders (cycle time).

c. The total annual inventory cost (holding, ordering, and procurement) and the projected annual net profit of this policy.

What assumptions did you make regarding demand in solving this problem?

14. How would your answers to problem 13 change if Stick requires its customers to purchase razors in gross units (multiples of 144) and Buyright desires a safety stock of 20 razors?

15. OfficeHQ is a discount retailer of office goods. One of its most popular products is the Stick brand pen, packaged six to a box and retailing for $1.29. Each box costs OfficeHQ $0.95. OfficeHQ is open five days a week, 52 weeks a year.

Daily demand for Stick pens is reasonably constant, averaging 65 boxes. The cost for OfficeHQ to place an order is $30, and the firm uses an annual inventory holding cost rate of 22%. Lead time for delivery is one week, and OfficeHQ desires a safety stock of 100 boxes of pens. If OfficeHQ must order in increments of 100 boxes, determine the following:

a. The optimal inventory policy (order quantity and reorder point) for Stick pens.

b. The number of calendar days between orders (cycle time).

c. The total annual inventory cost (holding, ordering, safety stock, and procurement) and the projected annual net profit of this policy.

16. Suppose that in problem 15 the daily demand for Stick pens averages 75 boxes (instead of 65).

a. What is the optimal order quantity for Stick pens?

b. If OfficeHQ uses the order policy determined in problem 15, determine the difference in total annual variable inventory costs between this policy and the optimal policy found in part (a).

17. OfficeHQ carries boxes of Disco floppy diskettes. Because the diskettes come in different formats, OfficeHQ has decided to use a periodic review policy, in which it places an order with Disco once every three weeks.

Weekly demand for Disco $3\frac{1}{2}''$ diskettes at OfficeHQ averages 45 boxes. The lead time for delivery is approximately one week, and OfficeHQ desires a safety stock of 30 boxes. OfficeHQ uses an annual holding cost rate of 20% for the diskettes. If the inventory level at the time OfficeHQ places its next order with Disco is 55 boxes, determine its optimal order quantity.

18. Scanlon Plumbing Corporation distributes American Consolidated lavatories. Demand for the basic China White Oval Model 2634 averages 19 units a week. The lavatories cost Scanlon $22.50 each and sell for $35.75. Unfortunately, approximately 5% of the lavatories ordered by Scanlon are either defective or damaged during shipment. Therefore, Scanlon needs 20 (= 19/.95) units a week to meet its demand.

The company uses a periodic review policy with American Consolidated and orders once every four weeks. Lead time for delivery is two weeks, and Scanlon desires a safety stock of 50 units. If the inventory level of the lavatories at the time of the next order is 35 units, determine the optimal inventory policy.

19. GROW Garden Center sells Raincloud automatic sprinkler valves. The valves cost GROW $8.75 each, and GROW uses an annual holding cost rate of 24%. The cost to place an order with Raincloud is approximately $30. Demand over the past eight weeks has been as follows:

Week	Demand	Week	Demand
1	24	5	18
2	20	6	22
3	16	7	28
4	22	8	18

GROW uses a simple eight-week moving average to forecast average annual demand and average lead time demand. Lead time for delivery is two weeks, and GROW desires a cycle service level of 96%. GROW estimates that lead time demand follows a normal distribution with a standard deviation of 5.45 units. On the basis of this information, determine:

a. The optimal inventory policy (order quantity and reorder point) for the sprinkler valves.

b. The number of calendar days between orders (cycle time).

c. The total annual inventory cost (holding, ordering, procurement) for this policy.

20. Bryan's Office Supply sells the Harrington 2000 automatic stapler. Demand for the staplers averages 24 units per week. The staplers cost Bryan's $17.25 each, and Bryan's uses a 22% annual holding cost rate. The cost to place an order with Harrington is $45, and the lead time for delivery is two weeks. Bryan's desires a safety stock of 15 staplers.

Harrington offers its customers the following all unit quantity discount pricing schedule:

Number Ordered	Discount
1–199	none
200–399	4%
400–699	6%
700–999	8%
1000–4999	11%
5000+	15%

Bryan's never orders an amount greater than a 35-week supply for any product. Assuming that holding costs are discounted, determine the following:

a. The optimal inventory policy (order quantity and reorder point) for Harrington staplers.

b. The number of calendar days between orders (cycle time).

c. The total annual inventory cost (holding, ordering, procurement, and safety stock) for this policy.

What assumptions did you make to solve this problem?

21. Archer Pharmaceuticals manufactures Tranquility brand sleeping pills, which have an average weekly demand of 25,000 bottles. The Archer factory operates 10 hours a

day, six days a week. The production line at Archer Pharmaceuticals can produce 10,000 bottles of Tranquility daily. Archer's policy is to make a batch of Tranquility and, after building up sufficient inventory, use the production line to produce other products.

The company estimates that setup for producing Tranquility pills takes about two hours and costs $325. It also estimates that the annual holding cost for a bottle of Tranquility is $0.55.

a. What is the optimal production batch size and the resulting total annual inventory holding and production setup cost of this policy?

b. What is the length of a production run in hours (including setup time)?

c. What is the number of calendar days between the start times of successive production runs?

What assumptions did you make in solving this problem?

22. Bee's Candy manufactures a variety of candy bars in a number of different sizes. One of its more popular products is the three-ounce Smirk bar. Bee's forecasts that demand for this product should be fairly constant over the next year, totaling 21 million bars.

The candy production line, which operates 24 hours a day, 365 days a year, is capable of producing two candy bars per second. A production setup for the three-ounce Smirk bar takes 50 minutes and costs approximately $450. The annual holding cost of a three-ounce Smirk bar is estimated as $0.12.

a. What is the optimal production batch size and the length of a production run in hours (including setup time)?

b. What is the total annual inventory holding and production setup cost for this policy?

c. What is the number of days between the start times of successive production runs?

d. How would your answers to part (a) change if the annual holding cost decreased to $0.10 per bar?

23. Click Pix, a large discount camera shop in New York City is open six days a week, 52 weeks a year. The store has recently begun carrying Sonic model PS58 camcorders which cost $520.00 each and retail for $649.99. Sales average 60 units per week.

The cost of placing an order with Sonic is $90, and the lead time is seven working days. The store estimates that the lead time demand follows a normal distribution with a mean of 70 units and a standard deviation of 15 units. Click Pix uses an annual holding cost rate of 18% for the camcorders. Ideally, it would like to run out of the camcorders during at most one inventory cycle per year. Given this goal, determine the following:

a. The optimal inventory policy (order quantity and reorder point) for Sonic camcorders.

b. The number of working days between orders (cycle time).

c. The total annual inventory cost (holding, ordering, procurement, and safety stock) for this policy and the projected annual profit for this policy.

24. How would your answers to problem 23 change if Sonic offered Click the following all units discount schedule?

Order Quantity	Discount
200–599	5.0%
600–999	7.5%
1000 or more	9.0%

25. Masks-R-Us sells Halloween masks at a kiosk in the local mall. The store is open only during the month of October. Masks are imported from Asia and cost the store $3.45 each; they retail for $9.95 each. Any masks left in inventory after Halloween are sold to a merchandise closeout specialist at a price of $1.80 each. Masks-R-Us estimates that if it runs out of Halloween masks, it will suffer a customer goodwill loss of $15. The company further estimates the cost of rent, utilities, labor, insurance, and so on, to operate the kiosk is approximately $4000 for the month.

Based on past sales, Masks-R-Us estimates that demand for its masks during the month of October will be approximately normally distributed with a mean of 900 masks and a standard deviation of 100 masks. Because the masks are imported from Asia, Masks-R-Us must place its order with the mask manufacturer in May.

Determine the number of masks Masks-R-Us should order and the expected profit or loss it can expect to earn if it follows this policy.

26. Jackson Mint produces collectible plates. It has recently contracted with the estate of well-known artist, Skip Gunther, to produce a series of five commemorative plates bearing copies of the artist's most famous pictures. The plates will be sold by subscription at a cost of $275 plus shipping and handling for the entire five-plate series. Jackson estimates the cost of producing each plate in the series at $12.50 plus a $9.75 royalty that Jackson has agreed to pay the Gunther estate.

Jackson intends to mount a $175,000 nationwide advertising campaign promoting these plates as a "limited edition"; that is, Jackson will specify the number of plates it will produce and limit production to that amount. Any unsold plates will be destroyed. Based on its previous experience with such products, Jackson estimates that customer demand for the series will be approximately normally distributed, with a mean of 1800 and a standard deviation of 250.

If Jackson has more subscribers than plate series, it will refund subscribers' money with a note explaining that the series has been oversubscribed. Reasoning that the unsatisfied customers will be more willing to subscribe to Jackson's future offerings, it estimates that each unsatisfied customer will earn the company an average of $40 in discounted future profits.

a. What is the optimal number of Skip Gunther plate series Jackson should produce?

b. What expected profit or loss will Jackson earn if it follows the production policy found in part (a)?

c. Comment on any assumptions you made to solve this problem.

27. Scott Stereo sells personal tape players. One of its more popular sellers is the Sonic Walkperson. These units cost Scott $18.55 each and retail for $32.95. Weekly demand averages 12 units. The cost of placing an order with Sonic is $25, and lead time is two weeks. Scott uses a 26% annual inventory holding cost rate.

    If Scott is out of stock of the Walkperson, it estimates that it will suffer a customer goodwill cost of $2 for each week a customer must wait for the Walkperson to arrive. A fixed administrative cost of $0.50 is associated with each backordered customer. Determine the following:
    a. The optimal inventory policy (order quantity and reorder point) for the Walkpersons.
    b. The number of calendar days between orders (cycle time).
    c. The percentage of customers who will be placed on backorder.
    d. The total annual inventory cost (holding, ordering, shortage, and procurement) for this policy and the projected total annual profit for this policy.

28. Scott Stereo orders Dutch brand cassette tapes once every three weeks. Weekly demand for the T-60 format is approximately normal with a mean of 200 units and a standard deviation of 30 units. The tapes cost Scott $0.65 each and sell for $1.25. Lead time for delivery is one week. Scott desires a safety stock that will give the store a cycle service level of 98%. If Scott's inventory level for the Dutch T-60 tapes is at 230 units when it places an order, determine:
    a. The order quantity for the tapes.
    b. The desired safety stock.

29. Pete's Coffee is a local shop that roasts and packages its own coffee. The store purchases its Colombian coffee beans from Valdez Importing Company (VIC). VIC offers its customers the following discount pricing schedule for Colombian coffee:

Order Quantity	Price per Pound
under 1000 lbs.	$3.25
1000–3000 lbs.	$3.12
3000–6000 lbs.	$3.055
6000–9000 lbs.	$2.99
over 9000 lbs.	$2.925

    Pete's estimates its annual demand for Colombian coffee beans at 62,000 pounds. The annual holding cost rate for a pound of unroasted coffee beans is estimated at 30%. The cost to place an order with VIC is $125, and the lead time is four weeks. Pete's desires a safety stock of 1000 pounds.
    a. What is the optimal order quantity if the discount pricing schedule is an all units schedule?
    b. What is the optimal order quantity if the discount pricing schedule is an incremental schedule?
    c. What is the reorder point for Colombian coffee? What assumptions did you make in solving this problem?

30. The coffee roaster at Pete's Coffee can roast 600 pounds of coffee per day. Pete's is open 310 days per year, and, because of freshness requirements, the store never roasts more than a 10-day supply of any type of coffee it sells.

    Daily demand for French Roast coffee averages 75 pounds, while daily demand for Amaretto Cream averages 20 pounds. The annual holding cost for a pound of roasted coffee is $1.28, and the production setup cost for roasting a new variety of coffee is $25. Determine the optimal production batch sizes for French Roast and Amaretto Cream coffees.

31. Pete's Coffee is planning to stock the Melvitta brand espresso maker. Pete's estimates the annual demand for this coffee maker to be 180 units. The machines, which retail for $189 each, are imported from Italy and cost Pete's $95 each. The cost to place an order with Melvitta is $150, and the lead time is an estimated five weeks. Pete's uses a 30% annual holding cost rate for the coffee makers.

    Pete's is considering using one of two customer satisfaction plans to deal with the possibility of stockouts of the espresso maker. Under the first plan, Pete's will offer backordered customers one free pound of coffee. This will cost $4.25, and Pete's estimates an additional customer goodwill loss of $15 for each week a customer must wait for the espresso maker.

    Under the second plan, Pete's will offer backordered customers three free pounds of coffee. This will cost $12.75 but will reduce the additional goodwill loss to $3 for each week a customer must wait for the espresso maker.
    a. Which customer satisfaction plan should Pete's adopt?
    b. What is the optimal order quantity and reorder point under this plan?
    c. Using this policy, what is Pete's expected annual profit on the espresso machines?

32. Business Supply Company, Inc. (BSC) is a local distributor of the NCQ electronic cash register. The cash registers cost BSC $320 each, and (neglecting inventory costs) BSC estimates it earns a profit of $80 on each cash register sold. The cost of ordering the cash registers from NCQ is $100, and BSC uses an annual inventory holding cost rate of 20%.

    If BSC runs out of the cash registers, it estimates it will suffer a customer goodwill cost of $50 for each week a customer must wait. There is also a fixed administrative cost of $1.50 to process a backorder. Weekly demand averages 75 units, and the delivery lead time is two weeks. Determine the following:
    a. The optimal inventory policy (order quantity and reorder point) for NCQ cash registers.
    b. The number of weeks between cash register orders.
    c. The percentage of customers who will be placed on backorder.
    d. BSC's annual profit on the cash registers.

33. Clothesline, Inc. is a retailer of moderately priced women's clothing. Clothesline's policy is to give customers a $5 gift certificate if they request an out-of-stock advertised item. This certificate is estimated to cost the company only $3, but it avoids a loss in customer goodwill.

Clothesline is considering selling a line of scarves produced by a noted fashion designer. Because of long lead times, Clothesline can only place one order for the scarves. The scarves cost Clothesline $6.25, and it plans to retail them for $10.95. Clothesline estimates that total demand at its 55 stores during the selling season will follow approximately a normal distribution, with a mean of 8000 units and a standard deviation of 1500 units. Any scarves left in inventory at the end of the selling season will be marked down to a clearance price of $4.95 and sold quickly.

On the basis of this information, determine how many scarves Clothesline should order. Comment on any assumptions you made to solve this problem.

34. Stefani Foods produces fresh pasta products for sale through local supermarkets. One product that is quite popular is fresh linguini and clam sauce. This item has a shelf life of two weeks and costs Stefani $1.19 per unit to produce. The product retails at a suggested price of $1.99 and is sold to supermarkets at a wholesale price of $1.46.

Many supermarkets receive only one delivery per week of Stefani products. In these instances, the delivery route agent is instructed to pick up any unsold linguini to return to the company. The supermarkets receive full credit on these returns, and the returned merchandise is sold in the Stefani owned Thrift Store at a retail price of $1.05. Such sales are estimated to net the company $0.83 per unit.

Van's Supermarket estimates that weekly demand for the linguini follows a uniform distribution between 160 and 239 units. Stefani delivers to Van's once a week. Determine the optimal stocking quantity for the linguini if the goodwill cost to Stefani associated with the supermarket's running out of inventory is:
a. $0.10
b. $0.50
c. $1.00
d. $5.00

35. The Circle 7 convenience store has been receiving deliveries of Royal Cola once a week. Weekly demand for the cola averages 60 cases and follows a normal distribution with a standard deviation of 12 cases. When the delivery truck arrives, the store orders enough cola so that the cycle service level is 99%. Because the orders arrive on a regular basis, there is no ordering cost to Circle 7. The annual holding cost rate for a case of cola is estimated at 25%.

Royal Cola has just instituted a quantity discount schedule. Instead of charging stores like Circle 7 the normal price of $4.25 per case, Royal is offering the following all units discount schedule:

Number of Cases Ordered	Price per Case
under 100	$4.25
100–199	$4.00
200–499	$3.80
500–899	$3.70
900 or more	$3.60

If Circle 7 wants to take advantage of the quantity discounts being offered by Royal Cola, it will have to cancel its regular delivery schedule. In this case, it estimates that the cost to place an order with Royal Cola will be $35 and lead time will be one week. Circle 7 will continue to desire a cycle service level of 99%.
a. If Circle 7 continues with the regular delivery schedule and has 22 cases in inventory when the next delivery arrives, how many cases will be delivered to the store?
b. What is the annual inventory cost (holding, safety stock, and procurement) of the regular delivery schedule?
c. If Circle 7 decides to take advantage of the quantity discount schedule, how many cases should it order each time?
d. What is the reorder point for the answer in part (c)?
e. What is the annual inventory cost (holding, ordering, safety stock, and procurement) associated with the firm using the quantity discount schedule?
f. Do you recommend that Circle 7 take advantage of the quantity discount schedule? Why or why not?
g. How would your answers to parts (c), (d), (e), and (f) change if Circle 7 had enough room to store only 250 cases of Royal Cola?

36. Clark Equipment distributes the Clanton Model 406 bread slicer used in bakeries. The slicers cost $250 each, and Clark sells them to net $306 after marketing and related expenses. The company estimates that the annual demand for this product is 450 units.

The policy at Clark has been never to allow stockouts intentionally, and the company has carried a safety stock of 30 units in order to protect against such occurrences. Because of mounting fiscal pressure, however, Clark is considering eliminating the safety stock for the bread slicers and adopting a policy that allows for stockouts.

Clark estimates that it will suffer a customer goodwill loss of $25 per week for each week a customer must wait for a backordered bread slicer. Clark also believes that there is an administrative cost of $30 in handling a backorder and that adopting such a policy would result in a 4% decrease in annual sales of the bread slicer.

Clark uses a 15% annual inventory holding cost rate, and the cost of ordering slicers from Clanton is $90. Delivery lead time is 10 working days, and Clark is open 250 days a year.
a. Determine the optimal order quantity, reorder point, and annual profit under the current policy of not intentionally allowing backorders.
b. Determine the optimal order quantity, reorder point, and annual profit if Clark intentionally allows for backorders.
c. What is your recommendation to management as to whether Clark should intentionally allow for backorders? Justify this recommendation.

37. Microvision currently purchases a particular computer chip from IMTEL for $12.42 each, for use in its PC computers. Microvision's annual demand for the chip is estimated at 140,000 units, and it has a safety stock requirement of 600 chips. Because of high security expense, the cost to place an order with IMTEL is estimated at $1300 and lead time is 20 working days. The company operates 310 days per year.

Instead of purchasing from IMTEL, Microvision can sign a licensing agreement to manufacture the chips itself. The licensing agreement will cost Microvision $5000 per year. If Microvision signs the agreement, it estimates it can produce the chips on its own assembly line at a cost of $11.60 per chip (not including the licensing or inventory costs). Setup time will take two days.

The production setup cost for making these chips is $15,000, and the production line is capable of manufacturing 2000 chips a day, 310 days a year. If the company produces the chips in-house, it will no longer require any safety stock. Microvision uses a 24% annual holding cost rate.

a. What are the optimal order quantity, reorder point, number of days between orders (cycle time), and total annual inventory cost (holding, ordering, safety stock, and procurement) if Microvision purchases the chips from IMTEL?
b. What are the optimal batch size, length of a production run in days (including production setup time), number of days between the start of successive production runs, and total annual inventory cost (holding, setup, licensing, and production) if Microvision begins producing the chips in-house?
c. What is your recommendation to management as to whether Micrivision should begin in-house production of the chips? Justify this recommendation.

38. Consider the data from problem 37. Suppose IMTEL has decided to offer incremental price discounts on chips sold to Microvision. In particular, the new pricing schedule is as follows:

Order Quantity	Discount
1–4,999	none
5,000–24,999	5%
25,000–49,999	8%
50,000–99,999	10%
100,000 or more	13%

PROBLEMS 41–50 ARE ON THE CD

a. What is Microvision's optimal order quantity for chips under this pricing policy if it continues to purchase chips from IMTEL?
b. Determine the total annual cost of this policy to Microvision.

39. Johansen's Ice Cream Shoppe purchases fresh-baked waffle cones from the Myra Cone Company. The cones cost Johansen $0.28 each and are delivered once each day. Johansen's charges customers who want their ice cream in a waffle cone an extra $0.40. If Johansen's runs out of waffle cones, it estimates that it suffers a customer goodwill loss of $0.75 for each additional customer request for a waffle cone. Unsold waffle cones are ground up and used as toppings on the frozen yogurt sold by the company. Johansen's therefore estimates the salvage value of unsold cones at $.06. Johansen's also estimates that daily demand for the waffle cones follows approximately a normal distribution with a mean of 70 units and a standard deviation of 16 units. Determine how many waffle cones Johansen's should purchase each day from Myra Cone.

40. Frank's Garden Center sells McMurray riding mowers. McMurray has found itself with an excess inventory of Model 412 mowers and is temporarily offering dealers a discount of $75 off its normal wholesale price of $725. Frank's sells the Model 412 at a retail price of $895 and estimates that its demand during the upcoming selling season will be between one and five units, with the following probabilities:

P(Demand = 1 unit) = .25
P(Demand = 2 units) = .20
P(Demand = 3 units) = .10
P(Demand = 4 units) = .30
P(Demand = 5 units) = .15

Unfortunately, Frank's must decide how many mowers to purchase at the temporary price discount before the selling season begins. Once the selling season starts, if demand for the McMurray mower at Frank's exceeds the number ordered at the discounted price, Frank's must pay the normal wholesale price of $725 per unit. Any purchased mowers that Frank's is not able to sell during the normal selling season can be sold for $595 at the annual clearance sale. How many mowers should Frank's purchase from McMurray at the temporary price discount?

CASE STUDIES

CASE 1: TexMex Foods

TexMex Foods operates a plant in Irving, Texas, for manufacturing taco sauce used in fast-food restaurants. The sauce, which is packaged in plastic containers, is made from a special recipe that includes tomato concen-trate, onions, and chile peppers that TexMex purchases from various suppliers. The plant operates 365 days a year, and TexMex uses an annual holding cost rate of 18%.

Tomato Concentrate

TexMex Foods purchases its tomato concentrate from Hunt Farms. The company requires 2500 gallons of concentrate per day to manufacture this sauce. Hunt Farms offers customers the following all units price discount schedule:

Number of Gallons Ordered	Price per Gallon
1–9999	$3.12
10,000–49,999	$3.08
50,000–124,999	$3.02
125,000–249,999	$3.01
250,000 or more	$2.96

The shelf life of the concentrate is 80 days, and the ordering cost is $750. Orders must be placed in 1000-gallon increments. The company desires a safety stock of 10,000 gallons, and the lead time for delivery is 10 days. Management wishes to determine the optimal order quantity for the concentrate as well as the reorder point.

Onions

In the cooking process, TexMex requires 6000 pounds of onions daily. Onions cost the company $0.15 per pound, and the ordering cost is $180. Lead time for delivery is three days, and the company desires a safety stock equal to one day's usage. Management wants to determine the optimal order quantity for onions as well as the reorder point.

Chile Peppers

TexMex also needs an estimated 2000 pounds of chile peppers daily. The peppers cost TexMex $0.37 per pound. Order cost, including transportation, is $1500. Lead time is normally two weeks but may vary somewhat. Because of this variability, the company estimates that the lead time demand for chile peppers follows approximately a normal distribution, with a mean of 28,000 pounds and a standard deviation of 4000 pounds. Management wants to determine the optimal order quantity, reorder point, and safety stock for chile peppers to meet a desired cycle service level of 99.5%.

Plastic Containers

TexMex packages the sauce in one-ounce plastic containers it buys from Union Chemical at $0.003 per unit. The ordering cost is $120. TexMex is contemplating leasing a machine to make the containers. The yearly lease cost of the machine is $45,000, and the production setup cost is $260. The machine can produce 1 million containers per day at a per unit cost of $0.0027 (excluding leasing, inventory holding, and production setup costs). The company estimates that it requires 450,000 containers per day. Management wants to determine whether it should continue purchasing containers from Union Chemical or begin in-house production and what the optimal order quantity or production lot size should be.

Prepare a detailed management report addressing each of the concerns facing TexMex Foods. Include in your report supporting graphs and charts as well as appropriate "what-if" analyses.

CASE 2:   Rodman Industries

Rodman Industries of Barstow, California, sells among other items, specialized tires for off-road vehicles (ORV). A new ORV model requiring tires slightly larger than normal is being developed by Pacific Star Enterprises in nearby Apple Valley. Pacific Star and Rodman have done business together for years, and Rodman has contracted with Pacific Star to supply tires for the new vehicle.

Rodman's staff analyst has estimated that Pacific Star's *weekly* demand will follow approximately a normal distribution, with a mean of 2000 tires and a standard deviation of 100 tires. Rodman charges Pacific Star $25 per tire, and Rodman's holding costs are figured at 20% per year.

Manufacturing/Purchasing Options

Rodman has three choices available to it for supplying tires to Pacific Star:

1. Rodman can convert production line 3 to manufacture the tires. The equipment on this line can be converted at a cost of $150,000 to produce the new tire. This production line will have a maximum production rate of 4000 tires per week. It takes roughly one week to set up between production runs, and each setup costs approximately $4000. Unit production costs (raw materials and labor) are $12 per tire.

2. Rodman can convert production line 5 to manufacture the tires. This line is capable of producing only 1800 tires per week. It is very reliable, however, and, after a conversion cost of $75,000, the line is expected to run without failure. Although this option means that Rodman could supply Pacific Star with only 1800 tires per week, Pacific Star has indicated that it would accept this quantity, if necessary. Again, unit production costs (raw materials and labor) are $12 per tire.

3. Rodman can purchase tires from Hiro Inc., a Japanese firm, and import them to its San Pedro warehouse for distribution directly to Pacific Star. Reorder costs, which include some substantial shipping fees, are estimated at $10,000 per order, and shipping time is consistently two weeks from the time an order is

placed. Hiro charges $14 per tire but offers the following all units discount pricing schedule:

Order Quantity	Discount
under 5000	none
5000–9999	7.5%
10,000 or more	15.0%

Safety Stock

While selecting option 2 allows Rodman to maintain no safety stock, for options 1 and 3 Rodman should have enough safety stock to maintain at least a 90% cycle service level.

CASE 3: Mr. Pretzel

Mr. Pretzel sells soft pretzels to movie theaters, skating rinks, and snack bars. The company bakes the pretzels in its factory and delivers them fresh daily to its various accounts. Mr. Pretzel has recently signed a contract to purchase 50 pretzel vending machines. Management feels that these machines will enable the company to sell its pretzels in new locations, thus expanding company revenue.

Mr. Pretzel's marketing department is busy trying to determine suitable locations for the vending machines. It has decided that, at a minimum, pretzel demand at a vending machine location must average at least 25 units per day. Each vending machine is capable of holding 140 pretzels. The marketing department is interested in determining what compensation it should offer the owners of the sites at which the vending machines will be placed.

According to the company's accounting department, the cost of producing a soft pretzel (fixed and variable) is approximately $.32. The pretzels to be sold in the vending machines are sealed in plastic, adding $.005 to their cost. They are delivered daily and sell for $.75. Any pretzels left in the vending machine from the previous day are removed and returned to the factory. There they are ground up and sold for use in cattle feed, for which the company receives approximately $.02 in net revenue from each returned pretzel. The cost of delivering new pretzels and removing old ones is estimated to be $4.20 per vending machine per day. An additional capital cost of $2.50 per day is associated with each vending machine.

The Report

On the basis of the given information, prepare a business report for Rodman suggesting a policy that will optimize total weekly profit for the company. Assume that this is a three-year project (156 weeks) and that conversion costs can be amortized at a constant rate over this time period. Include in your report any assumptions you made (or model assumptions you violated) in doing your analysis. The report should contain a table giving, for each option, the optimal order or production quantity, the reorder or setup point, and the total weekly revenue, costs, and profit.

If the vending machine runs out of pretzels, there is some likelihood that a dissatisfied customer may kick the machine, causing some damage. Since the company has not had any operating history regarding these machines, it is uncertain of the goodwill and potential damage cost of not having enough pretzels in the machine to satisfy all customers.

The company has three different compensation schemes for site owners:

1. Pay the site owner a fixed revenue of $3 per day.
2. Pay the site owner a commission of $.08 per pretzel sold.
3. Lease the vending machine to the site owner with the stipulation that Mr. Pretzel will service the machine. Mr. Pretzel will charge the site owner $3.25 per day for leasing the machine and $.45 apiece for the pretzels. Mr. Pretzel will give no credit for unsold pretzels, and the pretzels have no salvage value to the site owner.

Prepare a management report indicating the expected daily profit to Mr. Pretzel for each compensation plan, assuming daily demand follows a Poisson distribution with means, λ, of either 25, 50, 75, or 100 units. Use the normal distribution approximation to the Poisson distribution ($\mu = \lambda$ and $\sigma = \sqrt{\lambda}$). Assume that if Mr. Pretzel leases the vending machine to the site owner, the site owner will order the optimal number of pretzels from the company. Do the analysis for at least three possible goodwill costs, including $.05, $.25, and $.75.

Queuing Models

CARL'S JR. (http://www.carlsjr.com) IS planning to open a new restaurant in Logan, Utah. The company has narrowed down its location choices to three potential sites. A principal concern is that the restaurant must be designed to adequately handle the drive-thru business during lunch hour.

One of the sites is quite small and can only accommodate a single drive-thru window with space for up to six cars to wait in line. The second site is somewhat larger and can handle a single drive-thru line with space for up to nine cars to wait. If the site is built with two windows (the customer pays at the first and the food is delivered at the second), the waiting line will accommodate a maximum of only eight cars. The third site is quite large and

has enough room for two separate drive-thru lines. Each line can handle a maximum of either nine cars (when there is a single service window) or eight cars (when there are separate windows for the cashier and food delivery).

The asking prices for the three sites differ, and construction costs will vary, depending on the configuration selected. Labor costs will be higher if there are separate windows for the cashier and food server; at the same time, using two windows will speed up service.

To choose a site and configuration, Carl's Jr. management proposes conducting an analysis of the drive-thru waiting lines, known as a *queuing analysis*. Of principal importance is the effect the lines will have on the potential profitability of each site.

9.1 Introduction to Queuing Models

Every day it seems we spend some amount of time waiting in lines. When we shop at the supermarket we wait in line to check out; when we go to the bank, we wait in line to see a teller; and when we call a business, we are sometimes put on hold for several minutes until a real person answers the phone. Even when we have a confirmed appointment with a doctor, a lawyer, or an accountant, we frequently wait for service. **Queuing theory** is the study of waiting lines, or *queues*.

The objective of a queuing analysis is to design systems that enable an organization to perform optimally according to some criterion. One possible criterion is to maximize profit. Care must be taken to include all relevant factors in this criterion, however. For example, a store may be able to lower staffing costs by reducing the number of clerks. But this action may also increase the time customers must wait in line. If the waiting time becomes too long, customers may take their business elsewhere, which could result in lower revenues and potentially lower profits for the store. Thus, when determining staffing requirements, the store must also account for the loss in customer goodwill attributed to longer waiting lines.

In other cases, an organization's objective is to meet a certain desired level of service at minimum cost. For example, a municipal hospital may wish to determine the minimum number of ambulances it should have on call so that an ambulance will be immediately available for dispatch at least 99% of the time.

The effects of poorly designed queuing systems can range from inconvenience (waiting too long in a bank teller line) to death (needing an ambulance and not having one available). In order to analyze queuing systems properly, it is necessary to have a clear understanding of how service is to be measured. The average time a customer spends in line, the average length of the line, and the probability that an arriving customer must wait for service are some of the measures of queuing performance considered in this chapter.

9.2 Elements of the Queuing Process

A queuing system consists of three basic components:

> ### Components of a Queuing System
>
> 1. *Arrivals*: Customers arrive at a system according to some arrival pattern.
> 2. *Waiting in a Queue*: Arriving customers may have to wait in one or more queues for service.
> 3. *Service*: Customers receive service and leave the system.

This is illustrated in Figure 9.1. Let us briefly examine each component of the queuing system.

THE ARRIVAL PROCESS

In certain situations, customers arrive according to a set schedule. For example, medical patients scheduled for nonemergency treatment may not arrive at the precise moment for which their appointments have been made, but the facility will have a pretty good idea of the number of patients who need to be treated and approximately when each will arrive. Therefore this system can be modeled using a *deterministic arrival process*.

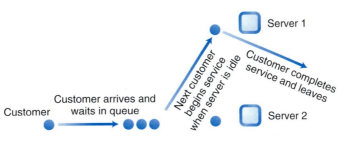

FIGURE 9.1 Three Server Queuing System

By contrast, when you need a loaf of bread or a gallon of milk, you don't call ahead to the supermarket to schedule an appointment to come in. Similarly, customers generally show up at a bank or post office or call an airline when they have a particular need, not according to a set schedule. Since for these businesses a manager does not know when the next customer will arrive, the arrival of customers is a *random process*. Although deterministic arrivals exist for certain situations, a random customer arrival process is more common for most businesses.

In order to analyze a random process, a probability distribution for the arrivals must be determined. One way to estimate an arrival distribution might be to station ourselves outside the business and record the time between customer arrivals or the number of customers who arrive in a given time interval. Then, using statistical analysis, a probability distribution can be "fit" to the data.

THE POISSON DISTRIBUTION

Such a laborious analysis is not always necessary, however. For instance, if a customer arrival process satisfies conditions known as orderliness, stationarity, and independence, it can be modeled by a **Poisson distribution**.[1] Fortunately, these conditions are quite unrestrictive and are approximately satisfied in a great many situations.

The *orderliness* condition states that, during any split second of time, at most one customer will arrive at the service facility. This condition is violated in certain circumstances (such as the instant the doors open for a department store's after-Christmas clearance sale), but, for most business situations, customers do arrive in an orderly fashion—namely, one at a time.

The *stationarity* condition requires that, within some time frame, the probability of customer arrivals remains the same for each incremental time epoch. This does not mean that the probability of an arrival is constant for *all* time periods. For example, the arrival rate of customers at a bank typically is higher on Friday afternoons than on Tuesday mornings. But if the probability of an arrival at the bank on Friday afternoon in the time period between 3:38 P.M. and 3:39 P.M. is the same as the probability of an arrival in the time period between 3:39 P.M. and 3:40 P.M., then the stationarity assumption is satisfied for the time frame between 3:38 P.M. and 3:40 P.M. The stationarity assumption generally holds if the time frame under consideration is small enough.

The *independence* condition is satisfied if the arrival of one customer has no influence on the arrival of another. For example, if Mary Smith decides to go to the

[1] Named for the nineteenth-century French mathematician Simeon Denis Poisson.

local supermarket at 4:45 P.M., her action will not affect when, if ever, Paul Robinson will go to the same supermarket. Although the independence condition is not highly restrictive, it is violated if customers arrive in groups (such as tour groups arriving on a bus to a restaurant)[2] or if the population of potential customers is small (such as the arrival of squad cars from a 10-car police department to the department's repair garage).

Conditions for a Poisson Arrival Process

1. *Orderliness*—In any time instant, at most one customer will arrive at the service facility.
2. *Stationarity*—For a given time frame, the probability that a customer will arrive within a certain time interval is the same for all time intervals of equal length.
3. *Independence*—Customers arrive independently of one another; that is, an arrival during a given time interval does not affect the probability of an arrival during other time intervals.

If one can verify or is willing to accept these conditions, then the probability of k arrivals during any time period of length t can be expressed by the random variable X having the following Poisson distribution:

Poisson Arrival Distribution

Probability of k Arrivals Within Time t

$$P(X = k) = \frac{(\lambda t)^k e^{-\lambda t}}{k!}$$

Here,

$$\lambda = \text{the mean arrival rate per time unit}$$

$$t = \text{the length of the time interval}$$

$$e = 2.7182818 \text{ (the base of the natural logarithm)}$$

$$k! = k(k - 1)(k - 2)(k - 3) \ldots (3)(2)(1)$$

In this expression, λ and t must be expressed in the same time units; that is, if λ is expressed in customers *per hour*, t must be expressed in *hours*.

Fortunately, these probabilities do not have to be calculated by hand. The Excel function POISSON can be used to determine either the point probability, $P(X = k)$, or the cumulative probability, $P(X \leq k)$, by supplying values for k and λt as follows:

Point Probability $P(X = k) = \text{Poisson}(k, \lambda t, \text{FALSE})$
Cumulative Probability $P(X \leq k) = \text{Poisson}(k, \lambda t, \text{TRUE})$

The Poisson arrival distribution is illustrated in the following situation faced by Hank's Hardware.

---

[2] Although the buses may arrive independently, the number of customers on the bus can vary. This is an example of a *compound Poisson process*.

HANK'S HARDWARE

Poisson distribution.xls

Customers arrive at Hank's Hardware according to a Poisson distribution. The store opens at 8:00 A.M., and on Tuesday mornings between 8:00 and 9:00, an average of six customers arrive at the store. Hank was out late partying on Monday evening and would like to sleep an extra half hour on Tuesday. He is concerned, however, that if he opens the store a half hour late, he might lose too much business. Hence Hank would like to know the probability that 0, 1, 2, 3, etc., customers will arrive between 8:00 and 8:30 on Tuesday morning.

SOLUTION

To find the probability that a specific number of customers will arrive during the half-hour interval in question, we use the Poisson distribution with $\lambda = 6$ per hour and $t = .5$ hour (30 minutes). This gives a value for $\lambda t = 6(.5) = 3$. The spreadsheet in Figure 9.2 shows how we generate the Poisson probabilities for $\lambda t = 3$.

In this spreadsheet the value of λt is entered into cell B3, and the calculated probabilities are shown in column B beginning with row 6. The histogram was created from the Chart Wizard using a column chart on cells B6:B16.

Although, theoretically, 100, 1000, or even 1 million customers could arrive during this half-hour period, as can be seen from the histogram, the probability of the number of customer arrivals in the half-hour period decreases rapidly after reaching its peak at three. As shown in cell B18, the probability that more than 10 customers arrive during this period is only .000292.

Poisson distribution.xls

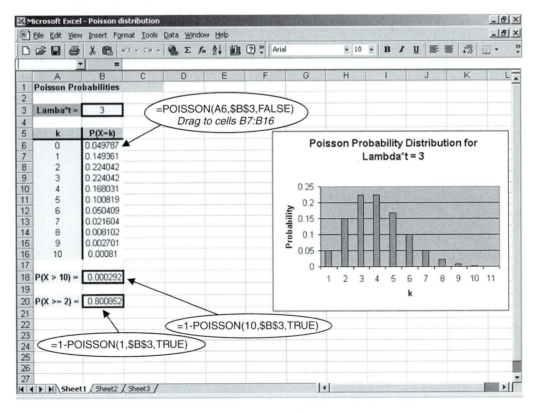

FIGURE 9.2 Spreadsheet for Poisson Probabilities with $\lambda t = 3$

Hank was particularly concerned about missing two or more customers. As we see from cell B20, this probability is .800852. Hence Hank decided it would be best to open on time. (He also resolved not to stay out so late partying in the future!)

THE WAITING LINE

Many factors influence how the actual waiting lines, or queues, are modeled, including:

1. Line configuration (one long line or several smaller ones)
2. Jockeying (line switching among customers)
3. Balking (not joining the queue if it is too long)
4. Priority (the service order of customers)
5. Tandem queues (if additional services are required)
6. Homogeneity (all customers require the same service)

Line Configuration

Figure 9.3 illustrates a number of commonly used queuing system *line configurations*. For example, the line configuration illustrated in (c) is a queuing system found at a typical supermarket, where a separate line forms at each checkstand[3] whereas the line configuration in (b) is that found at most banks or post offices, where one line forms and the next person designated to be served goes to a server when one becomes available.

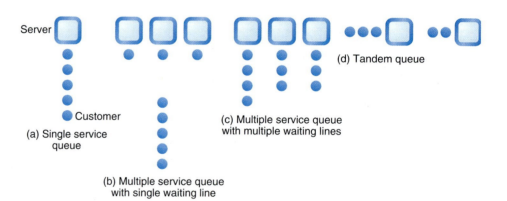

FIGURE 9.3 Commonly Used Queuing System Configurations

Jockeying

Jockeying occurs when customers switch between lines when they perceive that another line is moving faster. Another example of jockeying is when lines are long and a new server begins working. In this case customers in line typically make a mad dash to reach that server first. If customer do, in fact, jockey, there will never be an idle server while customers are in line waiting to begin service.

You might think that a single waiting line is more efficient than multiple lines. In some sense this is true because using a single line reduces the variance of the amount of time customers wait in line. If customers are smart enough to jockey, however, either line configuration results in the same average performance mea-

---

[3] Many supermarkets have designated "express" checkstands for customers purchasing fewer than a given number of items (say, 10 or less) or for cash purchases. In this chapter, we focus on developing queuing models only for the case where all servers work at the same average rate.

sures. Because this is typically how multiple line queuing systems behave, the performance measure results presented in this chapter for systems with a single waiting line will normally hold true for systems with multiple waiting lines.

Balking

Although a single waiting line reduces the variance of waiting time over a multiple line configuration, it does have its disadvantages. For example, if a bank has only three tellers working on a Friday afternoon and 30 customers are present in the bank, 27 people are waiting in a single waiting line. Customers perceiving the waiting line as too long may *balk* (not join the queue) and decide to take their business elsewhere. If too many customers balk, the long-term profitability of the business will suffer. On the other hand, if there were an individual line for each teller, the average number of customers waiting in each line for service would be nine. While a line length of nine is certainly long, it is not as intimidating as 27, and customers may be less likely to balk.

Priority Rules

When a server becomes available, a customer from the waiting line goes to that server to being service. The *priority rule* most commonly used to select the next customer for service is *first come, first served* (FCFS). This means that the first person in the waiting line will be the next one to be served. Other priority rules also exist, however. A clerk processing orders from the top of her "in basket" is using a *last-come, first-served* (LCFS) priority rule. Computer centers often prioritize jobs for processing based on the estimated length of the job run and the resources required for the job. At airports, flight controllers use sophisticated rules for determining the order in which planes should land, including the type of plane requesting landing clearance. The priority rule might even be random, as in the case of a telephone operator selecting which of eight incoming lines to answer when all are ringing simultaneously. Although the priority rule used to choose the next customer affects the waiting time variance, it has no effect on the average customer waiting time.

Tandem Queues

Customers usually need to see only one server in order to complete their necessary business. In some systems, however, multiple servers must be visited, typically in a distinct order. Such systems are known as **tandem queues**. For example, an airline may have separate agents for ticket sales and baggage check-in. If you need to purchase a ticket and check baggage, you will visit two servers; however, you cannot check bags for a flight until you first purchase a ticket.

Homogeneity

Although many queuing models assume a *homogeneous* population of arriving customers, each requiring essentially the same type of service, some queuing models categorize customers according to different arrival patterns or different service treatments. For example, patients needing emergency treatment at a doctor's office are treated differently from those needing routine physical examinations. Such differences, which can influence performance of the system, must be accounted for when developing the queuing model.

THE SERVICE PROCESS

Since it always takes about the same fixed amount of time to dispense a cup of coffee from a vending machine, its service time can be modeled by a constant, or deterministic, service time distribution. In most business situations, however, service times vary widely and are best modeled by a random variable.

Given its mathematical simplicity, the *exponential probability distribution* is sometimes used to model customer service time. This distribution has the following probability density function.

Exponential Service Time Distribution

$$f(t) = \mu e^{-\mu t}$$

Here,

μ = the average number of customers who can be served per time period

---

In this expression, μ is the *mean service rate* for the server and is expressed in terms of customers per hour, per day, etc. $1/\mu$ is the *average service time*. If we know the average service time, then 1/(average service time) is the average service rate. Thus, if the average service time is 10 minutes, the average service rate is 1/10 customers per minute, or 6 customers per hour.

For the exponential distribution, the average customer service time and the standard deviation of the customer service time are both equal to $1/\mu$. Using the exponential distribution, the probability that the service time, X, is less than some value t is as follows.

Probability Service Will Be Completed Within Time t

$$P(X \le t) = 1 - e^{-\mu t}$$

In this expression, μ and t must be expressed in the same time units; that is, if t is in *hours*, μ must be in customers *per hour*. Furthermore, the service rate, μ, should be expressed in the same time units as the arrival rate, λ.

Excel provides a function that generates the probability density function f(t) or the cumulative probability $P(X \le t)$ for an exponential distribution. To use this function you must provide values for t and μ. The time units for μ and t must be consistent; that is, if t is *hours*, μ must be the average number of customers per *hour*, and so on. The density function and the cumulative probabilities are generated by:

Probability Density $f(t)$ = EXPONDIST(t, μ, FALSE)
Cumulative Probability $P(X \le t)$ = EXPONDIST(t, μ, TRUE)

To illustrate the exponential distribution, let us return to the situation at Hank's Hardware.

exponential distribution.xls

HANK'S HARDWARE (CONTINUED)

Hank estimates that it takes an average of four minutes to serve a customer at his store, and service times follow an exponential distribution. Hank has an important luncheon date, so he wishes to find the probability that it will take less than three minutes to serve the next customer.

SOLUTION

Since the average service time, $1/\mu$, is 4 minutes, the average service rate μ equals 1/4 customer per minute, or $60(1/4) = 15$ customers per hour. Because service times follow an exponential distribution, we can use Excel's EXPONDIST function to determine the probability that a service will take less than 3 minutes ($= 3/60 = .05$ hour). Figure 9.4 shows a spreadsheet that determines density function values for an exponential distribution. In this spreadsheet the value of μ is entered in cell B3, and the time, t, for which a cumulative probability is desired is entered in cell B4. The output for the cumulative probability, $P(X \le t)$, is given in cell B6, and the density function values are given in column B beginning in row 10.

exponential distribution.xls

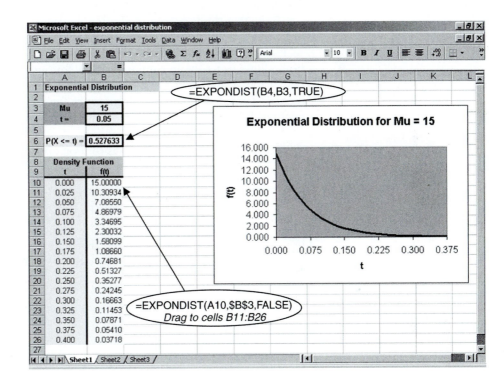

FIGURE 9.4 Exponential Distribution for $\mu = 15$

From cell B6 of Figure 9.4, $P(X \le .05) = .527633$. Hence, there is approximately a .53 probability that it will take Hank less than 3 minutes to serve the next customer.

In Figure 9.4 the density function was generated for values of t in increments of .025 from 0 to .4 and then the XY (Scatter) graph from the Chart Wizard was used to generate the graph of the exponential distribution function. The area under the curve between 0 and any time t represents the probability that the service is completed by time t. As you can see, this distribution is skewed to the right; that is, the mean of the distribution $(1/\mu)$ exceeds its median value (which happens to be $(\ln 2/\mu)$). For Hank's Hardware, the mean service time $1/\mu = \frac{1}{15}$ hour or 4 minutes, whereas the median service time is $\ln 2/15 = .04621$ hour or approximately 2.77 minutes. Therefore, while the average service time is 4 minutes, 50% of all customers will be serviced in less than 2.77 minutes.

Memoryless Property of the Exponential Distribution

The exponential distribution is a *memoryless* distribution. This means that no additional information regarding the probability distribution is gained from observing the service time already expended. In the Hank's Hardware example, this implies that if a customer has already had two minutes of service but the service is not yet completed, the probability that the customer's remaining *additional* service time will be less than 3 minutes is .52763, the same probability as if we had just started observing the customer. Such memoryless distributions are sometimes referred to as *Markovian distributions*.[4]

The Relationship Between the Poisson and Exponential Distributions

The exponential distribution is the "flip side" of the Poisson distribution. That is, if customer arrivals follow a Poisson distribution with arrival rate λ, the time between such arrivals, known as the *interarrival time*, follows an exponential distribution with average interarrival time $1/\lambda$. (Hence, the Poisson distribution also possesses the memoryless property.)

Note that the Poisson distribution describes the probability of a specific number of events, whereas the exponential distribution describes the time between such events. This interrelationship between the Poisson and exponential distributions allows us to obtain simple formulas for queuing performance measures when the customer arrival process is Poisson and the service time distribution is exponential. Table 9.1 summarizes properties for arrivals and services in a Markovian queuing process in which the time units are hours.

TABLE 9.1 Summary of Formulas for Poisson and Exponential Processes

Arrivals		Services	
Arrival Rate = Average number of arrivals per hour	λ customers/ hour	Service Rate = Average number of services[a] per hour	μ customers/ hour
Probability of k arrivals in t hours	$\dfrac{(\lambda t)^k e^{-\lambda t}}{k!}$	Probability of k services[a] in t hours	$\dfrac{(\mu t)^k e^{-\mu t}}{k!}$
Average time between arrivals	$1/\lambda$ hours	Average service time	$1/\mu$ hours
Probability that an arrival will occur within t hours	$1 - e^{-\lambda t}$	Probability that service will be completed within t hours	$1 - e^{-\mu t}$
Probability that the next arrival will not occur within t hours	$e^{-\lambda t}$	Probability that service time will be greater than t hours	$e^{-\mu t}$

[a] This assumes that customers are there to be served. Thus μ is actually the average number of *potential services per hour*.

In this chapter, "closed-form" performance measure results are presented for a number of systems, including those with arrival patterns that can be modeled by a Poisson process and exponential service times. Appendix 9.2 on the accompanying CD-ROM discusses how statistical goodness-of-fit tests can be used to determine whether or not these assumptions are reasonable.

ERLANGIAN DISTRIBUTION

If an exponential distribution is not appropriate for modeling service times (due to the failure of the memoryless property), an alternative is the *Erlangian distribution*. Formulas for the probability density function and cumulative probability distribution, as well as the mean and standard deviation for the Erlangian distribution, are given in Appendix 9.3 on the accompanying CD-ROM.

---

[4] Named for A. A. Markov, a Russian mathematician who introduced this concept in 1907.

9.3 Measures of Queuing System Performance

In a queuing model, performance can be measured by focusing on customers in the *queue* or customers in the entire *system*. (The system includes both those in the queue and those being served.) Which measure is more relevant is a function of the decision criterion.

To illustrate, suppose you are a supermarket customer with a choice of two checkout lines. One has an extremely fast checker, who takes an average of two minutes to check out each customer, and you estimate that you will have to spend four minutes waiting in line before being served by this checker. The other has a slower checker who takes an average of three minutes to wait on each customer, but you estimate you will spend only three minutes waiting in line before service begins. In either case, you figure you will spend six minutes in the *system*, so does it make a difference which line you select?

The answer depends on how you feel about waiting in line, since you expect to wait four minutes in the first line but only three minutes in the second. You might welcome the additional time in the first line (perhaps to catch up with the latest sighting of Elvis in the *National Enquirer* or *Star*), or you might appreciate the extra service time of the second line (perhaps to hear the checker give the latest neighborhood gossip). To account for possible preferences, queuing system performance measures are expressed both in terms of the waiting line and the system.

TRANSIENT AND STEADY-STATE PERIODS

One complicating factor that arises when assessing queuing performance is that most queuing systems experience *start-up bias* at the beginning of the observation period. In this *transient period*, initial system behavior is not representative of long-run performance. This transient period can last minutes, hours, or even days (depending on the service operation).

Following this transient period, the system settles down to what is known as steady-state behavior. In **steady state**, the long-run probabilities of there being 0, 1, 2, 3, or, in general, n customers in the system remain constant over time. Steady state assumes that the queuing system operates over a theoretically infinite time horizon. While no real-life system operates forever, concentrating on steady-state results avoids start-up bias. In practice, most real-life queuing systems quickly approach steady-state performance.

In order to achieve steady state, the effective arrival rate of customers must be less than the sum of the effective service rates of all servers.[5] This condition is stated for various queuing systems as follows:

Requirement to Achieve Steady State	
System	**Requirement**
1 server	$\lambda < \mu$
k servers, possible with different service rates	$\lambda < \mu_1 + \mu_2 + \ldots + \mu_k$
k servers, each with service rate μ	$\lambda < k\mu$

If this condition is violated, the queue will ultimately become infinitely large and steady state will never be achieved. For example, suppose customers arrive at

---

[5] If there are k servers and the arrival rate λ exactly equals $\mu_1 + \mu_2 + \ldots + \mu_k$, this queue will not reach steady state. The combined service rate must be strictly greater than the arrival rate in order to achieve steady state.

the rate of $\lambda = 20$ per hour and there are $k = 3$ servers, each serving an average of 4 customers per hour. On the average, only $3(4) = 12$ customers can be served per hour; therefore, an average of $20 - 12 = 8$ customers will be added to the waiting line each hour. Hence, steady state will never be reached as, over time, the waiting line will continue to lengthen.

In this chapter, steady-state performance measures for queuing systems with one or more servers are presented. For systems with more than one server, our attention is restricted to models in which all servers work at the same rate, μ. If this is not an appropriate assumption, simulation methods can be employed to approximate steady-state queuing performance measures (see Chapter 10).

STEADY-STATE PERFORMANCE MEASURES

The following steady-state performance measures can be calculated directly for many queuing systems:

P_0 = Probability that there are no customers in the system
P_n = Probability that there are n customers in the system
L = Average number of customers in the system
L_q = Average number of customers in the queue
W = Average time a customer spends in the system
W_q = Average time a customer spends in the queue
P_w = Probability that all servers are busy
ρ = Utilization rate of each server (the percentage of time that each server is busy)

The value of P_w has two interpretations. In cases in which a waiting line is permitted to form, P_w is equivalent to the probability an arriving customer must wait to begin service. In cases in which no waiting line is permitted to form, P_w is equivalent to the probability an arriving customer is blocked from service.

LITTLE'S FORMULAS

Two important relationships, known as **Little's Formulas,**[6] exist that relate the average number of customers in the system, L, and the average customer waiting time in the system, W, as well as between the average number of customers waiting for service, L_q, and the average time a customer spends waiting for service, W_q. These formulas state that if a queuing system has a single waiting line, customers arrive at some finite mean rate, λ, and the necessary condition for steady-state exists, then the following relationships hold:

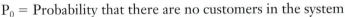

Little's Formulas

$$L = \lambda W$$

$$L_q = \lambda W_q$$

For steady-state models that involve a potentially infinite customer population, if all servers perform at the same rate, μ, then λ/μ represents the average number of customers being served. Hence, $L = L_q + \lambda/\mu$. Therefore, knowing one of the values for L, L_q, W, or W_q allows us to calculate the other three.

---

[6] Named for John D. C. Little, the first to rigorously prove the results in 1961.

QUEUING SYSTEM NOTATION

Different assumptions about arrival and service processes and the number of servers give rise to different queuing system configurations. So that we can easily refer to a particular queuing situation, we use the following shorthand notation to identify the model:[7]

> ### Classification of Queues
>
> Arrival Process/Service Process/Number of Servers

Commonly used notations for the arrival and service distributions include:

M *Markovian*—For arrivals, customers arrive according to a Poisson process at a mean rate of λ or have an interarrival time that follows an exponential distribution with mean $1/\lambda$. For services, service times are exponential, with a mean rate of μ or an average service time of $1/\mu$.

D *Deterministic*—For arrivals, customers arrive at a constant rate of λ. For service, service times are constant at $1/\mu$.

G *General*—For arrivals or departures, G signifies a general probability distribution for arrivals or services having a known mean and variance.

For example, a G/D/5 queue refers to a system in which the arrival process follows a general probability distribution, the service time is constant, and there are five servers.

Sometimes two additional designations are added to the notation to indicate situations in which there is a maximum limit for the number of customers in the system and/or a maximum number of customers in the population. Thus an M/G/6/10/20 model refers to a queuing system for which the interarrival time of customers is exponential, the service time follows a general distribution, there are 6 servers, the maximum number of customers who can be in the system at any one time is 10, and the population of potential customers is 20. An M/G/6//20 model would refer to the same system but with no limit for the maximum number of customers who can be present.

9.4 M/M/1 Queuing Systems

As stated earlier, the arrival process in many business situations follows a Poisson distribution. If, in addition, the service times can be appropriately modeled using the exponential distribution and there is a single server, we have an **M/M/1 queuing system**. Examples of queues modeled as M/M/1 systems include some small banks, rural post offices, and convenience stores.

The following formulas give the steady-state performance measures for the M/M/1 queuing system. Recall that the requirement for steady state to exist is $\lambda < \mu$, λ being the average arrival rate and μ the average service rate. These results are derived using a technique known as *balance equations* (see Appendix 9.4 on the accompanying CD-ROM).

---

[7] The notation used to identify queuing models was first proposed by D. G. Kendall in 1951 and has come to be called **Kendall's notation**.

$$P_0 = 1 - (\lambda/\mu)$$

Performance Measures for the M/M/1 Queue

$$P_0 = 1 - (\lambda/\mu)$$
$$P_n = (1 - (\lambda/\mu))(\lambda/\mu)^n$$
$$L = \lambda/(\mu - \lambda)$$
$$L_q = \lambda^2/(\mu(\mu - \lambda))$$
$$W = 1/(\mu - \lambda)$$
$$W_q = \lambda/(\mu(\mu - \lambda))$$
$$P_w = \lambda/\mu$$
$$\rho = \lambda/\mu$$

DISTRIBUTION OF TIME IN SYSTEMS

For the M/M/1 queue it can also be shown that the distribution of the time a customer spends in the system follows an exponential distribution with mean $1/(\mu - \lambda)$. This implies that the probability that a customer will spend more than t hours in the system is $e^{-(\mu-\lambda)t}$ and less than t hours, $1 - e^{-(\mu-\lambda)t}$.

M/M/1—Time in System

Average Time in System $= 1/(\mu - \lambda)$

P(Time in System $< t$) $= 1 - e^{-(\mu-\lambda)t}$

To illustrate these formulas, consider the situation faced by Mary's Shoes.

MARY'S SHOES

Mary's Shoes.xls

Customers arrive at Mary's Shoes on the average of once every 12 minutes, according to a Poisson process. The store is staffed by Dale Bandy who estimates that he can serve a customer in an average of eight minutes and that his service times follow an exponential distribution. Dale always finishes serving one customer before waiting on the next one.

Mary's management has received an anonymous letter of complaint regarding service at the store and is interested in determining the performance measures for this system.

SOLUTION

Based on the data provided, the average arrival rate is $\lambda = 1/12$ per minute, or $60/12 = 5$ per hour. Since it takes Dale an average of eight minutes to serve a customer, he can serve an average $\mu = 1/8$ per minute, or $60/8 = 7.5$ customers per hour. Substituting these values into the steady-state formulas for the M/M/1 queue yields the following performance measures:

Probability

$$P_0 = 1 - (\lambda/\mu) = 1 - 5/7.5 = 1 - .66667 = .33333$$
$$P_n = (1 - (\lambda/\mu))(\lambda/\mu)^n = (.33333)(.66667)^n$$
$$L = \lambda/(\mu - \lambda) = 5/(7.5 - 5) = 2$$
$$L_q = \lambda^2/(\mu(\mu - \lambda)) = 5^2/(7.5(7.5 - 5)) = 1.33333$$
$$W = 1/(\mu - \lambda) = 1/(7.5 - 5) = 1/2.5 = .4 \text{ hour} = 24 \text{ minutes}$$
$$W_q = \lambda/(\mu(\mu - \lambda)) = 5/(7.5(7.5 - 5)) = .26667 \text{ hour} = 16 \text{ minutes}$$
$$P_w = \lambda/\mu = 5/7.5 = .66667$$
$$\rho = \lambda/\mu = 5/7.5 = .66667$$

Note that the difference between W, the average time a customer spends in the store (24 minutes), and W_q, the average time a customer spends waiting before being served by Dale Bandy (16 minutes), is the average service time of 8 minutes. The difference between L, the average number of customers in the store (2), and L_q, the average number of customers waiting to be served by Dale Bandy (1.3333), is .66667. This is the average number of customers being served, ρ.

You may wonder why the difference between L and L_q is .66667 rather than 1. The reason is because one-third of the time (.33333) no customers are present and Dale is serving 0 customers, whereas two-thirds of the time (.66667) one or more customers are present and Dale is serving one customer. Thus the weighted average number of customers being served is .33333(0) + .66667(1) = .66667. These observations give rise to the following relationships:

Relationship Between System and Queue Performance Measures

Average waiting time in system =

Average waiting time in queue + Average service time

$$W = W_q + 1/\mu$$

Average number of customers in system =

Average number of customers in queue + Average number of customers being served

$$L = L_q + \lambda/\mu$$

Customer waiting time in the system for Mary's Shoes follows an exponential distribution with an average rate of $(\mu - \lambda) = 7.5 - 5 = 2.5$ per hour. Hence, the probability that a customer will wait less than 10 minutes (10/60 hours) is $1 - e^{-2.5(10/60)} = 1 - e^{-.417} = .341$. The probability that a customer will wait less than 20 minutes (20/60 hours) is $1 - e^{2.5(20/60)} = 1 - e^{-.833} = .565$, and the probability that a customer will wait less than 30 minutes (30/60 hours) is $1 - e^{-2.5(30/60)} = 1 - e^{-1.25} = .713$.

If Dale's average service time could be reduced to 6 minutes and 40 seconds, μ would be 9 per hour. Hence, the distribution of customer waiting time in the system would now be exponential with an average rate $(\mu - \lambda) = 9 - 5 = 4$. In this case, the probability that a customer will wait less than 10 minutes (10/60 hours) is $1 - e^{-4(10/60)} = 1 - e^{-.667} = .487$; less than 20 minutes (20/60 hours) is $1 - e^{-4(20/60)} = 1 - e^{-1.333} = .736$; and less than 30 minutes (30/60 hours) is $1 - e^{-4(30/60)} = 1 - e^{-2} = .865$.

Software Results

Figure 9.5 shows an Excel spreadsheet that can be used to determine the steady-state results for the M/M/1 queuing model. Here the arrival rate, λ, is entered in cell B4 and the service rate, μ, in cell B5. The calculated values for L, L_q, W, W_q, P_w, and ρ are given in cells A11 through F11, respectively. The calculated values for P_n for values of n between 0 and 30 are then given in cells H11 through AL11. The values in the spreadsheet correspond to those for the Mary's Shoes problem.

Using the Template queue.xls

As an alternative to programming Excel cells to calculate the performance measures for the M/M/1 queue, an Excel template, queue.xls, is included on the accompanying CD-ROM. Details on using this spreadsheet are included in Appendix 9.1 at the conclusion of the chapter. The template will enable you to

Mary's Shoes.xls

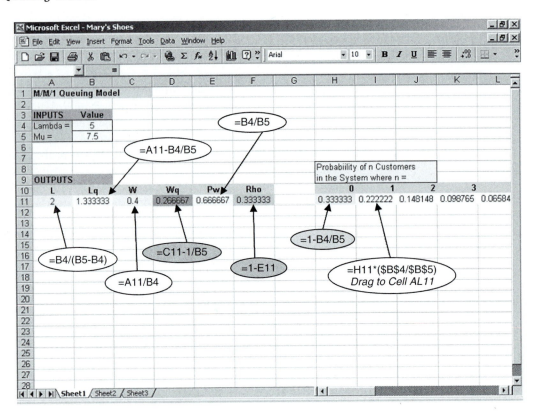

FIGURE 9.5   Excel Spreadsheet for M/M/1 Queue

easily determine performance measures and, where possible, state probabilities for all of the queuing models covered in this chapter. For example, to obtain the results for Mary's Shoes, one could use the MMk worksheet (described in the next section).

Using the above information, the following business report was prepared for Mary Hanes, president of Mary's Shoes. The memo focuses on current performance measures. A graphical breakdown showing customer waiting time as a percentage of total customers clearly indicates that a large proportion of customers are spending too much time in the store under the present systems. The report also analyzes the impact of increases in the arrival rate and suggests improvements to service.

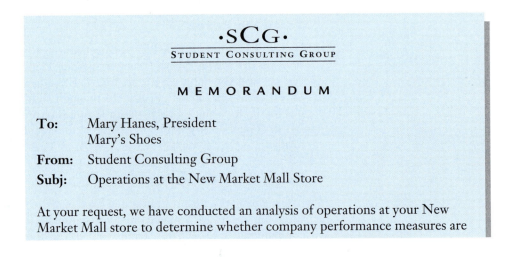

·SCG·
STUDENT CONSULTING GROUP

M E M O R A N D U M

To: Mary Hanes, President
            Mary's Shoes

From: Student Consulting Group

Subj: Operations at the New Market Mall Store

At your request, we have conducted an analysis of operations at your New Market Mall store to determine whether company performance measures are being met. While, at one time, the store had sales volume to support a staff of three shoe salespersons, since the recent construction of a nearby mall, sales have declined dramatically. Currently, only one shoe salesperson is employed at the store, Mr. Dale Bandy. Two issues in particular seem to be of concern:

1. Many customers are encountering a long wait before service begins. This may exacerbate the sales decline that has been prevalent since the competing mall opened.

2. Mr. Bandy appears to be idle for excessive periods of time.

To evaluate these potential problems, we have conducted a queuing analysis. We collected data on customer arrival times and Mr. Bandy's service times over 40 days. A study of these arrival and service patterns indicates that the average time between customer arrivals is approximately 12 minutes and that Mr. Bandy spends an average of about 8 minutes with each customer.

Statistical analyses of the data indicate that distributions based on the following assumptions closely approximate the observed data; (1) no two arrivals or departures occur simultaneously; (2) the arrival and service patterns do not vary significantly throughout the day; (3) the arrival of a customer has no effect on the time to the next customer arrival; and (4) the remaining time for Mr. Bandy to complete a service is not affected by the amount of time he has already spent with the customer. Although this last assumption may appear counterintuitive, the statistical analysis verifies that the observed service times mirror those generated by such an assumption.

GENERAL CONCLUSIONS

Based on these data, we developed a queuing model for operations at your New Market Mall store and derived the following estimates of its current operation.

Waiting Time   The average customer waiting time is 16 minutes. With an average service time of 8 minutes, a customer spends an average total of 24 minutes in the store. Figure I shows customer waiting time as a percentage of total customers. As you can see, 43% of customers spend longer than 20 minutes in the store; 29% spend over 30 minutes; and 8% spend more than an hour.

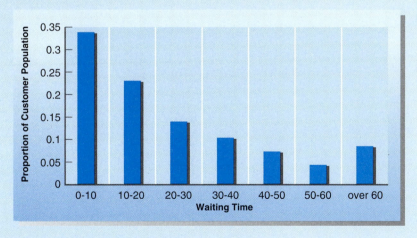

FIGURE I   Customer Waiting Time Assuming an Average Service Time of 8 Minutes

Dale Bandy's Idle Time　The model indicates that Dale Bandy averages 20 minutes of idle time per hour. Furthermore, if Mr. Bandy's average service time does not change, any decrease in his idle time will result in a simultaneous increase in the average time a customer waits for service. For example, if store traffic increases by 20%, although Mr. Bandy's idle time will decrease from 20 minutes to 12 minutes per hour, the average customer waiting time will double from 16 to 32 minutes.

RECOMMENDATIONS

To improve customer satisfaction, Mr. Bandy's service time must decrease. While conducting the study, we observed that much of Mr. Bandy's service time is spent trying to locate the correct shoe size from the store's inventory. We believe that a reorganization of the shoe inventory can reduce Mr. Bandy's average service time by one-sixth, from 8 minutes to about 6 minutes 40 seconds.

Table I summarizes the effect of such a reorganization on various factors that may be of concern to you. As you can see, performance will greatly improve under this plan. Also, Mr. Bandy's idle time should increase from about 20 to $26\frac{2}{3}$ minutes per hour, and hence, we do not expect him to voice any opposition to implementing this policy.

TABLE I　Impact on Performance of Proposed Inventory Reorganization

	Current Operations	Operations After Inventory Reorganization
Average service time	8 minutes	$6\frac{2}{3}$ minutes
Average customer time in store	24 minutes	15 minutes
Average time waiting for service	16 minutes	$8\frac{1}{3}$ minutes
Average number of customers in store	2	1.25
Average number of customers waiting for service	1.53	.69
Average time Mr. Bandy will be idle per hour	20 minutes	$26\frac{2}{3}$ minutes

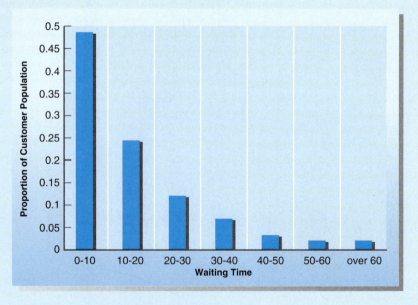

FIGURE II　Customer Waiting Time Assuming an Average Service Time of $6\frac{2}{3}$ Minutes

Figure II shows the revised percentages for customer time in the store for the inventory reorganization plan. In this case, fewer than 15% of the customers will spend more than 30 minutes in the store, and the percentage of customers spending longer than an hour in the store will decrease to about 2%.

Based on the preceding projections, we recommend that you consider such an inventory reorganization. If performance still does not meet your expectations, we regretfully suggest that you consider replacing Mr. Bandy.

9.5 M/M/k Queuing Systems

An **M/M/k queuing system** assumes that

1. Customers arrive according to a Poisson process at mean rate λ.
2. Service times follow an exponential distribution.
3. Each of the k servers works at an average rate μ (with $k\mu > \lambda$).

Typical examples of M/M/k queuing systems include banks with several tellers, post offices with several service windows, and fast-food restaurants with several cashiers.

 Appendix 9.5 on the accompanying CD-ROM contains a derivation of the performance measure formulas for the M/M/k queuing system found using the balance equation approach. The appropriate formulas are as follows:

Performance Measures for an M/M/k Queuing System

$$P_0 = \frac{1}{\left[\sum_{n=0}^{k-1} \frac{1}{n!}\left(\frac{\lambda}{\mu}\right)^n\right] + \frac{1}{k!}\left(\frac{\lambda}{\mu}\right)^k\left(\frac{k\mu}{k\mu - \lambda}\right)}$$

$$P_n = \frac{(\lambda/\mu)^n}{n!} P_0 \qquad \text{for } n \leq k$$

$$P_n = \frac{(\lambda/\mu)^n}{k!k^{(n-k)}} P_0 \qquad \text{for } n > k$$

$$L = \frac{(\lambda/\mu)^k \lambda\mu}{(k-1)!(k\mu - \lambda)^2} P_0 + \frac{\lambda}{\mu}$$

$$W = \frac{(\lambda/\mu)^k \mu}{(k-1)!(k\mu - \lambda)^2} P_0 + \frac{1}{\mu}$$

$$L_q = \frac{(\lambda/\mu)^k \lambda\mu}{(k-1)!(k\mu - \lambda)^2} P_0$$

$$W_q = \frac{(\lambda/\mu)^k \mu}{(k-1)!(k\mu - \lambda)^2} P_0$$

$$P_w = \frac{1}{k!}\left(\frac{\lambda}{\mu}\right)^k\left(\frac{k\mu}{k\mu - \lambda}\right) P_0$$

$$\rho = \frac{\lambda}{k\mu}$$

To illustrate the use of an M/M/k queuing system, consider Saturday operations at the Littletown Post Office.

Littletown Post Office queue.xls

LITTLETOWN POST OFFICE

The Littletown Post Office is open on Saturdays from 9:00 A.M. to 1:00 P.M. On the average, 100 customers per hour visit the post office during this period. Three postal clerks are on duty, and the mean time to serve each customer is 1.5 minutes. Previous studies have shown that a Poisson arrival distribution and an exponential service time distribution provide relatively good approximations of the post office's arrival and service operations.

The Littletown Postmaster has received a number of complaints concerning the length of time required for customers to receive service on Saturdays. In addition, the three postal clerks have filed a grievance alleging excessive workloads during this period. The Postmaster is interested in determining the relevant service measures for the post office on Saturdays in order to respond to these issues. There has also been talk about the need for a budget cut, and the Postmaster would like to know whether reducing the number of clerks on Saturday morning duty to two is feasible.

SOLUTION

The Littletown Post Office is an M/M/3 queuing system with $\lambda = 100$ customers per hour and an average hourly service rate, μ, equal to $60/1.5 = 40$ customers per hour. Since $\lambda < k\mu$ (i.e., $100 < 3(40) = 120$), the steady-state formulas for an M/M/3 model can be used. P_0 is calculated by:

$$P_0 = \frac{1}{\left[\sum_{n=0}^{k-1} \frac{1}{n!}\left(\frac{\lambda}{\mu}\right)^n\right] + \frac{1}{k!}\left(\frac{\lambda}{\mu}\right)^k\left(\frac{k\mu}{k\mu - \lambda}\right)}$$

$$= \frac{1}{\left[\sum_{n=0}^{2} \frac{1}{n!}\left(\frac{100}{40}\right)^n\right] + \frac{1}{3!}\left(\frac{100}{40}\right)^3\left(\frac{3(40)}{3(40) - 100}\right)}$$

$$= \frac{1}{\left[\sum_{n=0}^{2} \frac{1}{n!}(2.5)^n\right] + \frac{1}{6}(15.625)\left(\frac{120}{20}\right)}$$

$$= \frac{1}{\left[1 + 2.5 + \frac{6.25}{2} + 15.625\right]} = \frac{1}{22.25} = .045$$

The values for P_0, λ, and μ are then substituted into the formulas for the other performance measures to obtain the steady-state results. Rather than calculate these service measures by hand, however, we will utilize the Excel template queue.xls.

Software Results

Figure 9.6 shows the results of using the MMk worksheet on the Excel template queue.xls for the Littletown Post Office problem. In this worksheet the arrival rate, λ, is entered in cell B4, and the service rate, μ, is entered in cell B5. Performance measures and probabilities, P_n, for values of n from 0 to 30 are calculated beginning in row 11 for k servers, where k is the value in column A.

Littletown Post Office
queue.xls

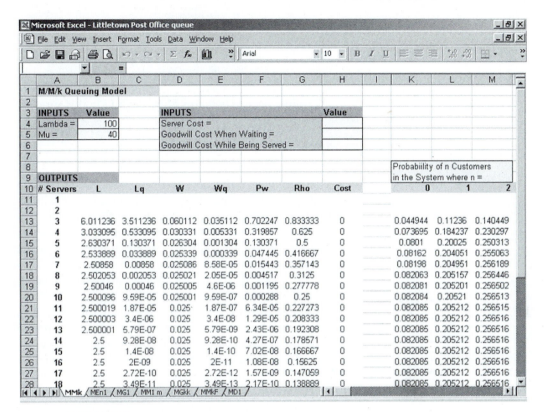

FIGURE 9.6 Excel Spreadsheet for an M/M/k Queue

If $k\mu > \lambda$ steady-state will not be reached and the spreadsheet does not return any output for that specific value of k. Hence, we see in Figure 9.6 that rows 11 and 12 are blank since if there are fewer than three servers, the arrival rate exceeds $k\mu$.

The MMk worksheet can also determine the system cost for differing numbers of servers. This will allow us to easily perform economic analyses (discussed in Section 9.9) to determine the optimal number of servers to utilize. Since for the Littletown Post Office problem we do not have any cost parameters, the values in cells H4 through H6 are left blank. As a result, the cost data in column H of the spreadsheet is 0 for all numbers of servers.

Note that in the template column J, which is used to calculate an intermediate term used in determining P_0, is hidden.[8]

Thus, from Figure 9.6 it can be seen that for k = 3 servers the model has determined the following service measures:

- The average number of customers present in the post office, L, is 6.01.

- The average number of customers who are waiting on line to begin service, L_q, is 3.51.

- The average time a customer waits in the system, W, is .06 hour or 3.6 minutes.

- The average time a customer spends waiting in line, W_q, is .035 hour or 2.1 minutes.

- The probability an arriving customer must wait for service, P_w, is .702.

- The proportion of time a clerk is busy, ρ, is .833.

Based on the values of L, L_q, W, W_q, and P_w, the Postmaster feels that the post office is providing adequate customer service.

---

[8] Specifically, the values in column J correspond to the first term in the denominator of P_0, $\sum_{n=0}^{k-1} \frac{1}{n!}\left(\frac{\lambda}{\mu}\right)^n$.

Figure 9.6 also shows that the probabilities of n customers being in the system (to three decimal places) are:

$$P_0 = .045 \quad P_1 = .112 \quad P_2 = .140$$

Scrolling over to columns N through U in this spreadsheet one would see that:

$$P_3 = .117 \quad P_4 = .098 \quad P_5 = .081 \quad P_6 = .068 \quad P_7 = .056$$
$$P_8 = .047 \quad P_9 = .039 \quad P_{10} = .033$$

For example, if the Postmaster wants to know the probability that *exactly two* people are waiting in line to be served, the solution will be equivalent to the probability of five people in the system (since three people are being served while two are waiting in line), $P_5 = .081$. If the Postmaster wants to determine the probability that *three* or *fewer* people are waiting in line, we will need to calculate the probability that six or fewer people are in the system: $P_0 + P_1 + P_2 + P_3 + P_4 + P_5 + P_6 = .661$. In the Excel spreadsheet given in Figure 9.6, this is attained by = Sum(K13:Q13).

With regard to the workload grievance, the analysis indicates that each postal clerk is serving customers only 83.33% of the time ($\rho = .8333$), or about 50 minutes out of each hour. In addition, approximately 4.5% of the time all three clerks are idle ($P_0 = .044944$); approximately 11.2% of the time two of the clerks are idle ($P_1 = .112$); and approximately 14.0% of the time one of the clerks is idle ($P_2 = .140$). After discussing the grievance with representatives from the Postal Union, the postal clerks agreed that their workload was reasonable and the grievance was withdrawn.

In terms of the budget-cutting issue, note that reducing the number of postal clerks on Saturday mornings to two would result in $\lambda > k\mu$ ($100 > 2(40)$). Hence, the queue would not achieve steady state, and the two remaining postal clerks would eventually never have a spare moment. Thus the Postmaster should consider cost savings measures other than laying off a clerk.

9.6 M/G/1 Queuing Systems

Although the assumption of a Poisson arrival process is appropriate for a large number of studies, frequently, the exponential distribution does not adequately model the service time. When there is a single server, although $P_0 = 1 - \lambda/\mu$ and $\rho = \lambda/\mu$, we cannot use the results based on balance equations to analyze formulas for the P_n values. Instead, a different approach based on Markov Chains (see Chapter 12 on the accompanying CD-ROM) gives rise to the following expression, known as the *Pollaczek-Khintchine formula*, for L:

$$L = \frac{(\lambda\sigma)^2 + (\lambda/\mu)^2}{2(1 - \lambda/\mu)} + \frac{\lambda}{\mu}$$

Here, λ, the mean arrival rate, $1/\mu$, the mean service time, and σ, the standard deviation of the service time, must all be expressed in the same time units. For an **M/G/1 queue**, only the mean and standard deviation for the service time need to be known to calculate the performance measures; it is not necessary to identify the particular service time distribution.

L_q can still be calculated by $L_q = L - \lambda/\mu$, and, using Little's formulas, we can determine $W = L/\lambda$ and $W_q = L_q/\lambda$. The formulas for the performance measures for the M/G/1 queue are given in Table 9.6 in Section 9.11. As we stated above, we cannot obtain formulas for the P_n values for this model.

When comparing the formula for L in an M/G/1 queuing system to the formula for L in an M/M/1 queuing system, it can be seen that the value for L is larger for an M/G/1 system if $\sigma > 1/\mu$. (Recall that $1/\mu$ is the standard deviation for an exponential service time distribution. If $\sigma = 1/\mu$ the performance measure formulas for the M/G/1 system are identical to those derived for the M/M/1 system.

M/D/1 SYSTEMS

One special case of M/G/1 queues occurs when the service time is deterministic (M/D/1). In an **M/D/1 system**, customers are served at a constant (deterministic) rate. This system is equivalent to an M/G/1 system with $\sigma = 0$. Substituting $\sigma = 0$ into the M/G/1 steady-state formulas yields the performance measure formulas listed in Table 9.6 in Section 9.11. Examples of M/D/1 queuing systems include vending machines and automated information systems that have constant service times.

M/E$_n$/1 SYSTEMS

Another special case occurs when customer service is made up of several independent tasks. In this case, service time can often be modeled using an **Erlangian distribution**. An Erlangian random variable is made up of the sum of n independent exponentially distributed random variables, each with a mean equal to $1/n\mu$. Thus an M/E$_n$/1 system is equivalent to an M/G/1 system, having a mean service time $1/\mu$ and service time standard deviation equal to $1/\mu\sqrt{n}$. Performance measure formulas for the M/E$_n$/1 system are listed in Table 9.6. Examples of businesses for which service is frequently modeled using an Erlangian distribution include retail establishments such as grocery stores, service stations, and restaurants. To illustrate the use of an M/G/1 queuing system, let us consider the situation faced by Ted's TV Repair Shop.

Ted's TV Repair Shop queue.xls
Ted's TV Repair Shop New
queue.xls

TED'S TV REPAIR SHOP

Ted's TV Repair is a sole proprietorship that repairs television sets and VCRs. Ted typically takes an average of 2.25 hours to repair a set, with a standard deviation of about 45 minutes. Customers arrive at the shop according to a Poisson process on the average of once every 2.5 hours.

Ted works nine hours a day and has no other employees. He is considering purchasing a new piece of testing equipment that he believes will reduce the average time required to repair a set to two hours, with a standard deviation of 40 minutes.

Ted wants to know how using this equipment will affect the average number of sets in the shop needing repair work, as well as the average length of time a customer will have to wait to have a set repaired.

SOLUTION

Since service times do not exhibit the memoryless property of an exponential distribution, we use an M/G/1 queuing model to calculate the service measures. Currently, for Ted's TV Repair, $\lambda = 1/2.5 = .4$ per hour, $\mu = 1/2.25 = .444444$ per hour, and the standard deviation of the service time, σ, is 45 minutes, $= .75$ hours. If Ted invests in the new testing equipment, μ will be $1/2 = .5$ per hour, and σ will be $40/60 = .666667$ hours.

The MG1 worksheet on the queue.xls template can be used to derive the performance measures for both the current and the new testing equipment. These are summarized in Table 9.2. As you can see, currently the average time a customer

TABLE 9.2   Performance Measures for Ted's TV Repair Shop

Performance Measure	Current Testing Equipment	New Testing Equipment
Average number of customers in the system (L)	5.40	2.58
Average number of customers in the queue (L_q)	4.50	1.78
Average time (in hours) a customer is in the system (W)	13.50	6.44
Average time (in hours) a customer is in the queue (W_q)	11.25	4.44
The probability an arriving customer waits (P_w)	.9	.8
Overall system effective utilization factor (ρ)	.9	.8
The probability that all servers are idle (P_o)	.1	.2

has a set in the repair shop is 13.5 hours, or 1.5 working days, and, while an average of 5.4 sets are in the shop needing repair, 10% of the time Ted will have no sets to work on.

The new testing equipment will reduce the average number of sets in the shop to 2.58. It will also reduce the average time required to repair a customer's set by more than 50% to 6.44 hours, resulting in greater customer satisfaction and potentially more business. At the same time, the probability that Ted will not have any sets in his shop to work on doubles to 20%. This may be desirable if Ted has other activities. If he does not, the increased probability that he is idle may be highly undesirable. Ted should consider this information, together with the cost of the testing equipment, before making his purchase decision.

9.7   M/M/k/F Queuing Systems (Finite Queue Length)

Almost all queuing systems have design or physical characteristics that limit their size. For example, the fire code may limit a fast-food restaurant to a maximum of 150 people at any one time. A telephone switchboard that has three incoming lines will only be able to handle a maximum of three customer calls at any one time.

Often, as in the case of the fast-food restaurant that can hold 150 people, the potential queue size is large enough so that models assuming an infinite queue length give accurate performance measures. When the number of customers who can be accommodated in the system is small, however (like the telephone switchboard with three lines), such models do not give accurate results. In addition to telephone switchboards, finite queuing models are also appropriate in retail establishments that have a limited capacity for customers, such as drive-thru windows at fast-food restaurants and hospital emergency rooms. In such cases, the limitation on the potential number of customers who can be present in the system at any given time must be explicitly accounted for in the model.

An **M/M/k/F model** assumes a Poisson arrival process at mean rate λ, k servers, each having an exponential service time distribution with mean rate μ; and an upper limit of F customers who can be present *in the system* at any one time. Customers attempting to enter when F people are already present (when the system is full) are denied entry, or *blocked*. The model assumes that blocked customers will leave the system forever.[9]

---

[9] In reality, some customers will probably try to reenter the system at a later time. This can be accounted for in the model by increasing the arrival rate of customers by the proportion estimated to return after being blocked.

The implication of blocking arriving customers is that, although an average of λ customers per hour may *attempt to join* the system, some will be turned away. Hence, only a fraction of these λ potential arrivals make it through to the system. This *effective arrival rate* is denoted by λ_e. It is λ_e that must be used in Little's formulas for the M/M/k/F case.

Arriving customers are blocked only if F customers are already in the system. Since the probability of F customers in the system is P_F, the following relationship exists between λ_e and λ:

Effective Arrival Rate for Finite Queues

$$\lambda_e = \lambda(1 - P_F)$$

For finite queues with Markovian arrival and service processes, balance equations can be used to determine formulas for the steady-state performance measures. Because the queue is finite, the restriction that $\lambda < k\mu$ does not have to hold in order to achieve steady-state results. Appendix 9.6 on the accompanying CD-ROM contains a network representation for this queuing system.

Table 9.6 gives performance measure formulas for the M/M/k/F system. When there are multiple servers, the performance measure formulas are quite complex. In two special cases, however, the formulas are reasonably easy to evaluate: (1) when there is a single server (an M/M/1/F queuing system), and (2) when the maximum number of customers permitted in the system equals the number of servers (an M/M/*k*/k queuing system). Interestingly, the performance measure formulas for the M/M/k/k queuing system are identical to those for the M/G/k/k queuing system. Performance measure formulas for the M/M/1/F, and M/G/k/k queuing systems are also given in Table 9.6.

Spreadsheets for the M/M/1/F, M/G/k/k, and M/M/k/F queues are contained in the template queue.xls on the accompanying CD-ROM. The M/M/1/F spreadsheet is on worksheet MM1F, the M/G/k/k spreadsheet is on worksheet MGKK, and the M/M/k/F spreadsheet is on worksheet MMkF. Birthing stations in a hospital maternity ward provide one example of a situation that can be modeled by an M/G/k/k system. An example of an M/M/1/F system is that faced by the Ryan Roofing Company.

RYAN ROOFING COMPANY

Ryan Roofing queue.xls

Ryan Roofing Company is a full-service residential roofer. Although some of its business comes from referrals, the vast majority of business is derived from customers who see Ryan's advertisement in the Yellow Pages. The roofing business is quite competitive, and most customers who need a roofer need one as soon as possible. Hence, management believes that if a customer calls Ryan and gets a busy signal, the customer will select another firm.

Ryan has three telephone lines and one appointments secretary who answers the phone. Because the appointments secretary must get all the relevant details on the potential job, the average length of each phone call is three minutes.

Ryan estimates that an average of 10 customers per hour call the company. The phone system has a music-on-hold feature, and if a customer calls while the appointments secretary is busy with another call, it is assumed that the customer will hold until the appointments secretary becomes available. It is further believed that the arrival process follows a Poisson distribution and that service time follows an exponential distribution.

Ryan's management is concerned that it may be losing too much potential business as a result of customers getting a busy signal. It would like to design a system that has the fewest lines necessary so that, at most, 2% of all callers will get a busy signal. In selecting this system, management would like to know the percentage of time the appointments secretary is speaking to customers, the average number of customers who are on hold, the average time a customer spends on hold, and the actual percentage of callers who encounter a busy signal.

SOLUTION

Based on these data, this queuing system can be modeled as an M/M/1/3 system with $\lambda = 10$ per hour and $\mu = 1/3$ per minute $= 60/3 = 20$ per hour. Using the worksheet MMkF on the queue.xls template gives the following probabilities for this M/M/1/3 queuing system:

$$P_0 = .533 \quad P_1 = .267 \quad P_2 = .133 \quad P_3 = .067$$

Thus, with three telephone lines, 6.7% of the time three customers are in the system and any additional customers calling Ryan Roofing will encounter a busy signal. Because this probability is greater than the stated goal of 2%, Ryan should consider increasing the number of telephone lines to four. The following are the probabilities for such an M/M/1/4 queuing system:

$$P_0 = .516 \quad P_1 = .258 \quad P_2 = .129 \quad P_3 = .065 \quad P_4 = .032$$

For this system there is still a 3.2% chance (P(4)) that a customer will get a busy signal. Increasing the number of telephone lines to five as shown in Figure 9.7 yields the following probabilities:

$$P_0 = .508 \quad P_1 = .254 \quad P_2 = .127 \quad P_3 = .063 \quad P_4 = .032 \quad P_5 = .016$$

Ryan Roofing queue.xls

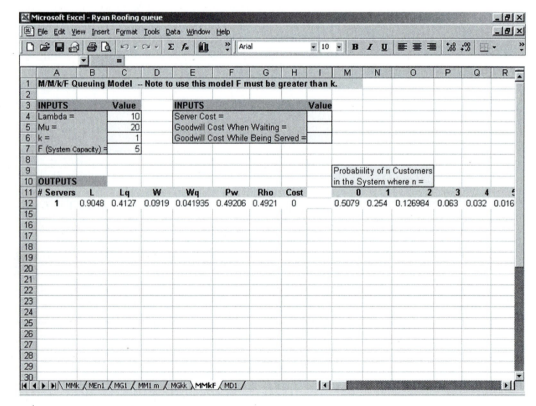

FIGURE 9.7   Excel Template Results for Ryan Roofing Problem

In this case, the stated service goal is met, since only 1.6% of customers will encounter a busy signal. Thus a minimum of five lines should be used.

Figure 9.7 shows that the performance measures for a system with five lines are as follows:

- Average number of customers in the system (L) = .905
- Average number of customers in the queue (L_q) = .413
- Average time a customer is in the system (W) = .092 hour
- Average time a customer is in the queue (W_q) = .042 hour
- The probability that an arriving customer will wait (P_w) = .492
- Overall system effective utilization factor (ρ) = .492
- The probability that the server is idle (P_0) = .508

From these data, the following can be determined:

1. The appointments secretary is on the telephone 49.2% of the time.
2. The average number of customers on hold is .413.
3. The average time a customer spends on hold is .042 hour, or 2.52 minutes.

9.8 M/M/1//m Queuing Systems (Finite Customer Population)

All the models discussed thus far have assumed that the number of potential customers is large enough that the queuing system can be modeled assuming an infinite customer population. If there is a small number of potential customers, however, the number of customers present in the system will affect the rate at which new customers arrive. This situation is frequently referred to as the *machine repair problem*.

An **M/M/1//m system** assumes that there is a single server; that the service time for each customer follows an exponential distribution with mean $1/\mu$; and that there are a total of *m* potential customers. If n of the m customers are already in the system, the interarrival time of the next customer follows an exponential distribution with mean $1/((m-n)\lambda)$.

Appendix 9.7 on the accompanying CD-ROM shows the queuing network used to determine the balance equations for finding P_n, L, and L_q. The values for W and W_q are calculated with Little's formulas using the effective arrival rate of $\lambda_e = \lambda(m - L)$. L being the average number of customers in the system. Table 9.6 gives these performance measure formulas.

To illustrate a finite population system, consider the problem faced by Keith Cooke, vice president for construction at Pacesetter Homes.

Pacesetter Homes queue.xls
Pacesetter Homes New Car
queue.xls

PACESETTER HOMES

Pacesetter Homes is developing four housing tracts in the greater Las Vegas area. While each tract has a construction supervisor situated on site, company policy dictates that any work stoppages arising from labor disputes, governmental regulations, or problems with suppliers must be handled personally by the firm's vice president for construction, Keith Cooke.

Keith believes that each of the four projects will average one work stoppage every 20 working days and that it will take him an average of 16 hours (two days) to solve each problem (including the travel time between sites). The time between work stoppages occurring at a particular construction site, as well as the time required to handle such a stoppage, are expected to follow exponential distributions. Keith handles work stoppages one at a time, and work remains halted until he can personally resolve the problem.

Keith would like the company to purchase him a new Jaguar automobile to drive among the job sites. He claims that having this car will enable him to travel faster, reducing the average time to handle a dispute to 15 hours (1.875 days). The company president feels that a new car is worthwhile only if it reduces the average time a job site is shut down by at least two hours. Keith would like to determine if this is the case.

SOLUTION

Since the number of potential customers (the housing tracts) is only 4, this problem can be modeled as an M/M/1//4 queue. Because the mean time between work stoppages is 20 days, $\lambda = 1/20 = .05$ per day. Assuming Keith uses his current car, it takes him an average of two days to solve each problem. Thus his mean service rate, μ is $1/2 = .5$ per day. If the company purchases the Jaguar for Keith, the value of μ increases to $1/1.875 = .53333$.

The performance measures for both cases can be determined using the MM1 m worksheet on the queue.xls template shown in Figure 9.8. Parameter values corresponding to the situation of Keith using the new car are entered in cells C4 through C6. The performance measure outputs are reported in row 13. Note that rows 14 through 299 used in calculating intermediate terms used in determining P_0 are hidden.

Pacesetter Homes New Car queue.xls

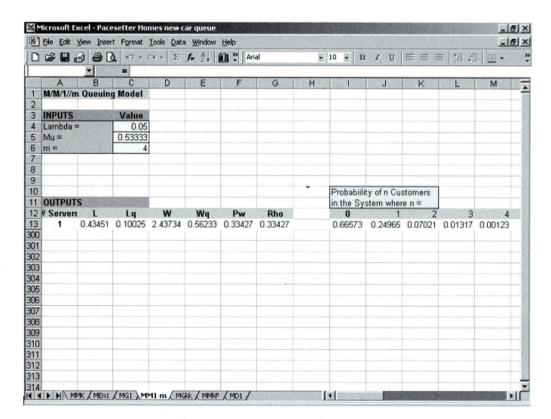

FIGURE 9.8   Excel Template Results for Pacesetter Homes

Table 9.3 summarizes the resulting performance measures for the situation when Keith uses his current car versus what would happen if he had the new car.

TABLE 9.3 Performance Measures for Pacesetter Homes

Performance Measure	Using Current Car	Using New Car
Average number of customers in the system (L)	.467	.435
Average number of customers in the queue (L_q)	.113	.100
Average number of days a customer is in the system (W)	2.641	2.437
Average number of days a customer is in the queue (W_q)	.641	.562
The probability that an arriving customer will wait (P_w)	.353	.334
Overall system effective utilization factor (ρ)	.353	.334
The probability that all servers are idle (P_o)	.647	.666

Giving Keith a new Jaguar will reduce the average time a job is stopped from 2.64 days to 2.44 days, a savings of .2 days or only 1.6 hours. Because the company president feels that this savings is not sufficient to justify the purchase of the new car, Keith must continue traveling between job sites using his existing vehicle.

9.9 Economic Analysis of Queuing Systems

Throughout this chapter, performance measure formulas have been developed for a number of different queuing models and have obtained results for specific cases using Excel. In this section, two analyses are presented that illustrate the use of such performance measures to determine a minimal cost queuing system.

Let us first see how we can use queuing models to determine an optimal staffing level for the Wilson Foods Talking Turkey Hot Line.

Wilson Foods queue.xls

WILSON FOODS TALKING TURKEY HOT LINE

Wilson Foods has an 800 phone number that consumers can call if they have questions about cooking a Wilson *Butterbaster* turkey. With the exception of busy holiday periods, such as Thanksgiving and Christmas, an estimated 225 customers per hour call the number. The average phone call is estimated to last 1.5 minutes.

Wilson has arranged sufficient phone lines with the telephone company so that if all customer service representatives are busy, a recorded message asks the caller to stay on the line until the next representative becomes available. Wilson believes that, as long as the average waiting time to speak to a representative is under three minutes, nearly all callers will stay on the line.

Wilson pays its customer service representatives $16 per hour in wages and benefits. The phone company charges Wilson $.18 for each minute a customer is either on hold or speaking to a customer service representative. Based on focus group studies, Wilson has concluded that there is a customer goodwill cost of approximately $.20 for each minute a caller is on hold. While a caller is speaking to a customer service representative, the goodwill cost drops to $.05 per minute.

Wilson would like to determine the number of customer service representatives it should use to minimize the hourly cost of operating the 800 phone line during nonholiday periods.

SOLUTION

In order to solve this problem, we need a model for total hourly costs. We will use the following notation:

k = number of customer service representatives
c_w = hourly compensation paid to each customer service representative
c_t = hourly telephone charge for each customer using the 800 line
g_w = goodwill cost per hour for a customer while waiting on hold
g_s = goodwill cost per hour for a customer while speaking to a customer service representative
$TC(k)$ = total average hourly cost of employing k customer service representatives

The average hourly cost consists of three basic components: wages, telephone charges, and goodwill costs. Thus,

$$TC(k) = (\text{wages of employees}) + (\text{telephone charges}) + (\text{goodwill costs})$$

We now analyze each of these hourly costs.

Wages

If there are k employees and each employee earns c_w per hour, then:

$$\text{Total hourly wages} = c_w k$$

Telephone Charges

The average number of customers on hold and being served is the average number of customers in the queuing system, L. Since the cost per hour for a single customer using this line is c_t, then:

$$\text{Total average hourly telephone charge} = c_t L$$

Goodwill Charges

There are two different goodwill charges in this scenario, depending on whether the caller is on hold or speaking to a customer service representative. Since the goodwill cost per hour for a customer on hold is g_w and the average number of customers on hold is L_q, the average hourly goodwill cost for customers on hold is $g_w L_q$.

Because L equals the average number of customers in the system and L_q is the average number of customers waiting on hold, the average number of customers speaking to customer service representatives must be $L - L_q$. Since the goodwill cost per hour for each of these customers is g_s, the average hourly goodwill cost of customers speaking to customer service representatives is $g_s(L - L_q)$, then:

$$\text{Total average customer goodwill cost per hour} = g_w L_q + g_s (L - L_q)$$

Total Average Cost Per Hour

Summing the three cost categories gives us the following equation for the total average hourly cost.[10]

$$TC(k) = c_w k + c_t L + g_w L_q + g_s(L - L_q) = c_w k + (c_t + g_w)L_q \\ + (c_t + g_s)(L - L_q) = c_w k + (c_t + g_s)L + (g_w - g_s)L_q$$

[10] Note that if $c_t = 0$, since $L - L_q = \lambda/\mu$, the total cost equation can be simplified as: $TC(k) = c_w k + g_w L_q(\lambda/\mu)$. Alternatively, if the goodwill cost for waiting in line is the same as the goodwill cost of being served ($g_w = g_s = g$), the expression becomes $TC(k) = c_w k + (c_t + g)L$.

For the Wilson Talking Turkey Hot Line, $c_w = \$16$, $c_t = \$.18 * 60 = \$10.80$, $g_w = \$.20 * 60 = \$12.00$, and $g_s = \$.05 * 60 = \$3.00$. The total average hourly cost is:

$$TC(k) = 16k + (10.8 + 3)L + (12 - 3)L_q = 16k + 13.8L + 9L_q$$

Assuming that callers to the 800 number follow a Poisson arrival process and that service times follow an exponential distribution, the system can be modeled as an M/M/k queuing system. Based on the information provided, $\lambda = 225$ per hour and $\mu = 60/1.5 = 40$ per hour. Since steady state is achieved only if $\lambda < k\mu$, the smallest value of k for which this condition holds is k = 6.

The MMk worksheet on the queue.xls template can be used to perform an economic analysis of an M/M/k queuing situation as shown in Figure 9.9. In addition to entering the arrival rate, λ, and service rate, μ, in cells B4 and B5, one enters the cost per time unit per server in cell H4, the goodwill cost per time unit incurred while the customer is waiting in line to begin service in cell H5, and the goodwill cost per time unit incurred while the customer is being served in cell H6. The resulting cost per time unit is given in column H beginning in row 11.

Wilson Foods queue.xls

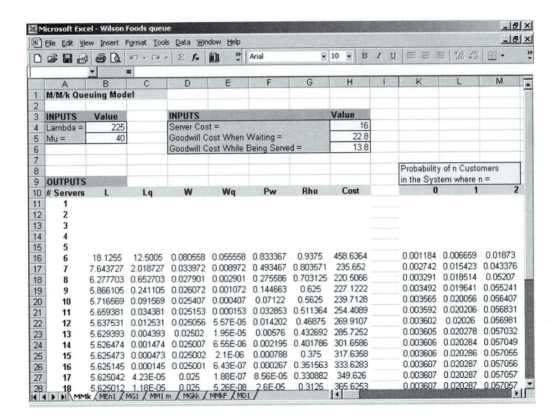

FIGURE 9.9 Excel Spreadsheet for Economic Analysis of Wilson Foods Problem

For the Wilson Foods Talking Turkey Hot Line problem, the arrival rate is $\lambda = 225$ per hour, the service rate is $\mu = 40$ per hour, and the cost of each server is $c_w = \$16$ per hour. The cost of a customer while waiting in line to begin service is $22.80 per hour. This is calculated by adding the cost of the hourly telephone charge, $c_t = \$10.80$ per hour plus the hourly goodwill cost of the customer while waiting in line, $g_w = \$12.00$. Similarly, the cost of a customer while being served is $13.80 per hour. This is calculated by adding the cost of the hourly telephone charge, $c_t = \$10.80$ per hour plus the hourly goodwill cost of the customer while being served, $g_s = \$3.00$.

Table 9.4 gives a summary of the Excel output contained in Figure 9.9 for between 6 and 10 servers. It is a fact that once total average costs begin increasing, they will continue to increase. Thus, according to this chart, Wilson should employ eight customer service representatives in order to minimize total average hourly costs. With eight representatives the average time a caller will spend on hold is .0029 hours, or 10.4 seconds.

TABLE 9.4   Service Measures and Costs for Wilson Foods Based on Number of Customer Service Representatives

k	L	L_Q	W_Q	TC(k)
6	18.1255	12.5000	.05556	$458.64
7	7.6437	2.0187	.00897	$235.65
8	6.2777	.6527	.00290	$220.51
9	5.8661	.2411	.00107	$227.12
10	5.7166	.0916	.00041	$239.71

Now consider the situation at the Hargrove Hospital maternity ward where a different queuing model is used to determine the optimal number of servers.

Hargrove Hospital queue.xls

HARGROVE HOSPITAL MATERNITY WARD

Hargrove Hospital is experiencing cutbacks in funding and revenues. One suggestion for saving money is to eliminate one of its two birthing stations. The hospital estimates that this cut will save $25,000 per year in direct expenses.

However, the hospital is also considering building additional birthing stations at an annual cost of $30,000 per station. This is because when all birthing stations are occupied women in labor are sent to one of the hospital's surgery rooms. The estimated cost per hour for the use of a surgery room for maternity purposes if $400 (due to the need to reschedule surgeries). Hence the expense of additional birthing stations may be more than offset by the savings from a decreased use of the hospital's surgery rooms.

Studies have indicated that an average of six women a day go into labor at the hospital and that the average time spent in a birthing station is two hours. Women who need a birthing station arrive at the hospital according to a Poisson process. The hospital wishes to determine the number of birthing stations that will minimize its costs.

Analysis of Current Situation

SOLUTION

Initially, Hargrove Hospital needs to know the daily cost savings associated with cutting back the number of birthing stations from two to one. The current situation can be modeled as an M/G/2/2 queuing system with $\lambda = 6$ per day and $\mu = 24/2 = 12$ per day.

The MGkk sheet on the Excel spreadsheet queue.xls on the accompanying CD-ROM can be used to analyze this problem. Figure 9.10 gives the spreadsheet for the M/G/2/2 queue with $\lambda = 6$ and $\mu = 12$. (Note that columns I and J, used to determine values for P_0, are hidden.)

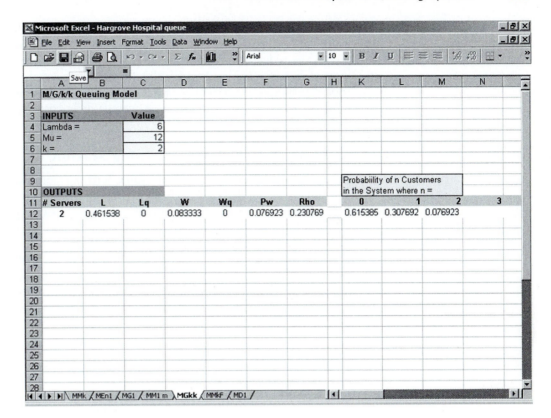

FIGURE 9.10 Excel Spreadsheet for Hargrove Hospital Problem

From Figure 9.10 it is seen that the system has the following performance measures.

- Average number of customers in the system (L) = .461538
- Average time a customer in the system (W) = .083333 day
- The probability that an arriving customer is blocked from service (P_w) = .076923
- Overall system effective utilization factor (ρ) = .230769
- The probability that all servers are idle (P_0) = .615385

The probability that a woman will need to use a birthing station and will not find one available is .076923. Hence, approximately 7.7% of all women who arrive to use a birthing station will be sent to a surgery room instead. Since an average of six women per day need to use a birthing center, the expected number of women who will give birth in a surgery room is 6(.076923) = .46154 per day.

The average time each woman spends in a birthing station is two hours; hence, the average number of hours the surgery rooms will be used for delivery each day is 2(.461538) = .923076 hours. At a cost per hour of $400, the average daily cost is .923076($400) = $369.23.

Analysis of Elimination of One Birthing Station

If the number of birthing stations is reduced to one, we have an M/G/1/1 queue with $\lambda = 6$ and $\mu = 12$. Using the worksheet MGkk, we would see that this results in a probability of .333 that a woman will need to use a surgery room to deliver. Hence an average of 6(.333) = 2 women a day will deliver in a surgery room, and the average time spent there is 2(2) = 4 hours per day. The average daily cost of using the surgery rooms therefore increases to 4($400) = $1600.

While reducing the number of birthing stations by one results in a daily savings of $25,000/365 = $68.49, the expense associated with using the surgery rooms increases by $1600 − $369.23 = $1230.77. Thus, rather than saving money, this policy actually increases average daily costs by $1230.77 − $68.49 = $1162.28, and annual costs by $424,232!

Analysis of Adding One Birthing Station

Let us now consider the option of adding birthing stations. If k stations are available, the average daily cost of women using a surgery room to give birth is $(P_k)(\lambda)(24/\mu)(c_h)$, where c_h is the hourly cost to use a surgery room.

For this problem, $\lambda = 6$, $\mu = 12$, and $c_h = \$400$. Hence the average daily cost is 4800 P_k. In addition, we must account for the daily cost of the additional birthing stations, which amounts to $30,000/365 = $82.19 per station. Based on these data, Table 9.5 details the costs of having between one and four birthing stations. This table shows that the total average daily cost is minimized when the maternity ward has three birthing stations. As a result, in this case a surgery room would be used for approximately 1.3% of all births.

TABLE 9.5 Hargrove Hospital Average Daily Cost Based on Number of Birthing Stations

k	P_k	$4800 P_k	Additional Daily Cost of Stations	Total Net Average Daily Cost
1	.333333	$1600	$(68.49)	$1531.51
2	.076923	$ 369.23	$ 0	$ 369.23
3	.012658	$ 60.76	$ 82.19	$ 142.95
4	.001580	$ 7.58	$164.38	$ 171.96

9.10 Tandem Queuing Systems

Thus far, only queuing models in which a customer leaves the system immediately after obtaining service have been considered. In many situations, however, a customer must visit several different servers before service is completed. Such systems are called *tandem queuing systems*.

An example of a tandem queue is a customer at a "soup and salad" cafeteria-style restaurant who may wait in one line for soup, move to a second line to select a salad, then proceed to a third line for a beverage, before waiting in a fourth line to pay a cashier. A second example is a business phone system in which a secretary answers all incoming phone calls, determines the purpose of the call, and then transfers the call to the appropriate party. Callers may have to wait to speak to both the secretary and the desired party.

Tandem queuing models can also be used to model a production setting in which an item is worked on at several different stations before completion. This topic, known as assembly-line balancing, is discussed in Appendix 9.8 on the accompanying CD-ROM.

Although tandem queues can be difficult to solve, for cases in which customers arrive according to a Poisson process and customer service times at each station follow exponential distributions, the total average time a customer spends in the system can be calculated by simply summing the average times a customer spends at each of the individual stations. This is possible because if customers arrive at station i according to a Poisson process at an average rate of λ_i per hour, with $\lambda_i <$ $k\mu_i$, the departure process from station i will also have Poisson distribution with average rate λ_i.

If all customers from this station proceed to the next station, arrivals at the next station also follow a Poisson distribution with an average rate of λ_i per hour. If, however, a certain proportion of those from the previous station fail to move on to the next station, the arrival process to the next station is still Poisson, but the rate is reduced proportionately.

To illustrate a tandem queuing situation, consider the operations of Big Boys Sound, Inc.

Big Boys Sound1 queue.xls
Big Boys Sound2 queue.xls
Big Boys Sound3 queue.xls

BIG BOYS SOUND, INC.

Big Boys Sound, Inc. is a chain of discount audio stores whose sales personnel wait on customers and take orders. After an order has been written up, the customer goes to a cashier to pay for the merchandise. Once payment has been made, the customer is sent to the merchandise pickup desk to obtain the goods.

On Saturday, the store is staffed with eight sales clerks, three cashiers, and two workers assigned to the merchandise pickup desk. Studies have shown that the average time a salesperson waits on a customer is ten minutes (regardless of whether or not the customer makes a purchase); the average time required to pay for merchandise is three minutes; and the average time it takes the merchandise pickup staff to get an item is two minutes. The service times for each of these three operations is distributed approximately exponentially.

Customers arrive according to a Poisson distribution, and an average of 40 customers an hour visit the store each Saturday, 75% of whom make a purchase. Management would like to know the average amount of time a customer who makes a purchase spends in the store.

SOLUTION

This problem can be modeled as a three-station tandem queuing system. Operations at the first station, where a customer works with a sales clerk to select merchandise, can be modeled by an M/M/8 queue with $\lambda_1 = 40$ per hour and $\mu_1 = 60/10 = 6$ per hour. The queue.xls template can be used to determine that the average time a customer spends waiting for and being served by a sales clerk, W_1, is .233252 hour or 14.00 minutes.

Because the steady-state condition holds $(40 < 8(6))$, the departure process from the sales clerks will follow a Poisson distribution with an average rate of $\lambda_1 = 40$ per hour. Since only 75% of customers actually purchase merchandise, however, the arrival process of customers to the cashiers (the second station) is a Poisson distribution with an average arrival rate of $\lambda_2 = (.75)(40) = 30$ per hour. Because the service distribution at this station is also exponential, the second phase in this tandem system is an M/M/3 system with $\lambda_2 = 30$ per hour and $\mu_2 = 60/3 = 20$ per hour. From the queue.xls template, the average waiting and service time at the cashiers is $W_2 = .057895$ hour, or 3.47 minutes.

At the merchandise pickup desk (the third station), customers arrive according to a Poisson distribution with a rate of $\lambda_3 = 30$ per hour. This station is an M/M/2 system with an average service rate of $\mu_3 = 60/2 = 30$ per hour. From the queue.xls template, the average customer waiting and service time at the pickup desk is $W_3 = .044444$ hour, or 2.67 minutes. Thus the average time customers who make purchases spend in the store is:

$$W = W_1 + W_2 + W_3 = 14.00 + 3.47 + 2.67 = 20.14 \text{ minutes}$$

9.11 Summary

The proper design of a queuing system has an important impact on the service provided by an enterprise. Steady-state measures can be obtained when the overall service rate exceeds the arrival rate. Measures such as the average time a customer spends in the system and queue, the average number of customers in the system and queue, the system utilization rate, and the probability of a given number of customers being present in the system can provide useful information in assessing service and developing optimal queuing systems.

If the arrival process is random and possesses the properties of orderliness, stationarity, and independence, it can be modeled by a Poisson process. In this case, formulas exist for the service measures of a wide range of queuing models.

If there is only one server and queue length is unlimited, steady-state solutions for models with a Poisson arrival process can be derived for any service distribution. Such solutions can also be derived in the case of multiple servers all working at the same rate if no waiting line is permitted.

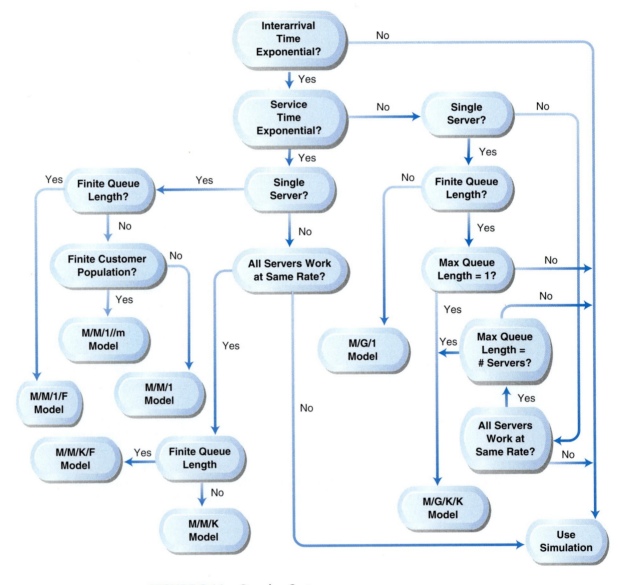

FIGURE 9.11   Queuing Systems

When the arrival process can be modeled by a Poisson distribution, the service time by an exponential distribution, and all servers work at the same rate, steady-state results can be derived for models in which the potential queue length is either finite or unlimited. Steady-state results can also be obtained for other models, including those characterized by a single server and a finite customer population and in which both the interarrival times of customers and the service times follow an exponential distribution. Figure 9.11 is a flow chart that can be used as a guide to select the appropriate modeling technique.

Tandem queuing systems, in which the arrival process at each station is Poisson, the servers at each station work at the same rate, and the service time follows an exponential distribution, can be analyzed by focusing on the individual stations. One type of tandem queue frequently found in a manufacturing setting is an assembly line.

Because of space limitation, only a limited set of queuing models and performance measures have been discussed in this chapter. Table 9.6 gives performance measures formulas for each of these models. Results for other systems exist and are found in advanced texts on queuing analyses. When performance measures cannot be obtained analytically, simulation can be used to approximate these values. Such analyses are discussed in the next chapter.

TABLE 9.6 Performance Measure Formulas for Queuing Models

Performance Measure	Queue	
	M/M/1	M/M/k
P_0	$1 - (\lambda/\mu)$	$\dfrac{1}{\left[\displaystyle\sum_{n=0}^{n=k-1} \dfrac{1}{n!}\left(\dfrac{\lambda}{\mu}\right)^n\right] + \dfrac{1}{k!}\left(\dfrac{\lambda}{\mu}\right)^k \dfrac{k\mu}{k\mu - \lambda}}$
P_n	$(1 - (\lambda/\mu))(\lambda/\mu)^n$	$P_n = \dfrac{(\lambda/\mu)^n}{n!}P_0 \quad$ for $n \le k$ $P_n = \dfrac{(\lambda/\mu)^n}{k!k^{(n-k)}}P_0 \quad$ for $n > k$
L	$\lambda/(\mu - \lambda)$	$\dfrac{(\lambda/\mu)^k \lambda\mu}{(k-1)!(k\mu - \lambda)^2}P_0 = \dfrac{\lambda}{\mu}$
L_q	$\lambda^2/(\mu(\mu - \lambda))$	$\dfrac{(\lambda/\mu)^k \lambda\mu}{(k-1)!(k\mu - \lambda)^2}P_0$
W	$1/(\mu - \lambda)$	$\dfrac{(\lambda/\mu)^k \mu}{(k-1)!(k\mu - \lambda)^2}P_0 + \dfrac{1}{\mu}$
W_q	$\lambda/(\mu(\mu - \lambda))$	$\dfrac{(\lambda/\mu)^k \mu}{(k-1)!(k\mu - \lambda)^2}P_0$
P_w	λ/μ	$\dfrac{1}{k!}\left(\dfrac{\lambda}{\mu}\right)^k \left(\dfrac{k\mu}{k\mu - \lambda}\right)P_0$
ρ	λ/μ	$\lambda/k\mu$

TABLE 9.6 Performance Measure Formulas for Queuing Models (continued)

Performance Measure	Queue		
	M/G/1	M/D/1	M/E$_n$/1
P_0	$1 - \lambda/\mu$	$1 - \lambda/\mu$	$1 - \lambda/\mu$
P_n			
L	$\dfrac{(\lambda\sigma)^2 + (\lambda/\mu)^2}{2(1 - \lambda/\mu)} + \dfrac{\lambda}{\mu}$	$\dfrac{(\lambda/\mu)^2}{2(1 - \lambda/\mu)} + \dfrac{\lambda}{\mu}$	$\left(\dfrac{n+1}{2n}\right)\dfrac{\lambda^2}{\mu(\mu - \lambda)} + \dfrac{\lambda}{\mu}$
L_q	$\dfrac{(\lambda\sigma)^2 + (\lambda/\mu)^2}{2(1 - \lambda/\mu)}$	$\dfrac{(\lambda/\mu)^2}{2(1 - \lambda/\mu)}$	$\left(\dfrac{n+1}{2n}\right)\dfrac{\lambda^2}{\mu(\mu - \lambda)}$
W	$\dfrac{\lambda\sigma^2 + \lambda/\mu^2}{2(1 - \lambda/\mu)} + \dfrac{1}{\mu}$	$\dfrac{\lambda/\mu^2}{2(1 - \lambda/\mu)} + \dfrac{1}{\mu}$	$\left(\dfrac{n+1}{2n}\right)\dfrac{\lambda}{\mu(\mu - \lambda)} + \dfrac{1}{\mu}$
W_q	$\dfrac{\lambda\sigma^2 + \lambda/\mu^2}{2(1 - \lambda/\mu)}$	$\dfrac{\lambda/\mu^2}{2(1 - \lambda/\mu)}$	$\left(\dfrac{n+1}{2n}\right)\dfrac{\lambda}{\mu(\mu - \lambda)}$
P_w	λ/μ	λ/μ	λ/μ
ρ	λ/μ	λ/μ	λ/μ

Performance Measure	Queue
	M/M/k/F
P_0	$\dfrac{1}{\left[1 + \displaystyle\sum_{n=1}^{k} \dfrac{(\lambda/\mu)^n}{n!} + \dfrac{(\lambda/\mu)^k}{k!} \displaystyle\sum_{n=k+1}^{F} \left(\dfrac{\lambda}{k\mu}\right)^{n-k}\right]}$
P_n	$\dfrac{(\lambda/\mu)^n}{n!} P_0 \qquad n = 1, 2, 3, \ldots, k$ $\dfrac{(\lambda/\mu)^n}{k! k^{n-k}} P_0 \qquad n = k+1, k+2, k+3, \ldots, F$
L	$\dfrac{P_0(\lambda/\mu)^k(\lambda/k\mu)[1 - (\lambda/k\mu)^{F-k} - (F - k)(\lambda/k\mu)^{F-k}(1 - (\lambda/k\mu))]}{k!\,(1 - (\lambda/k\mu))^2}$ $+ \displaystyle\sum_{n=0}^{k-1} n P_n + k\left(1 - \displaystyle\sum_{n=0}^{k-1} P_n\right)$
L_q	$L - \left(\displaystyle\sum_{n=0}^{k-1} n P_n + k\left(1 - \displaystyle\sum_{n=0}^{k-1} P_n\right)\right)$
W	$\dfrac{L}{\lambda \displaystyle\sum_{n=0}^{F-1} P_n}$
W_q	$\dfrac{L_q}{\lambda \displaystyle\sum_{n=0}^{F-1} P_n}$
P_w	$1 - \displaystyle\sum_{n=0}^{k-1} P_n$
ρ	$\dfrac{\lambda \displaystyle\sum_{n=0}^{F-1} P_n}{k\mu}$

TABLE 9.6 Performance Measure Formulas for Queuing Models (continued)

Performance Measure	Queue	
	M/M/1/F $\lambda \neq \mu$	M/M/1/F $\lambda = \mu$
P_0	$\dfrac{1 - (\lambda/\mu)}{1 - (\lambda/\mu)^{F+1}}$	$\dfrac{1}{F + 1}$
P_n	$P_0(\lambda/\mu)^n \quad n = 1, 2, 3, \ldots, F$	$\dfrac{1}{F + 1} \quad n = 1, 2, 3, \ldots, F$
L	$\dfrac{(\lambda/\mu)}{1 - (\lambda/\mu)} - \dfrac{(F + 1)(\lambda/\mu)^{F+1}}{1 - (\lambda/\mu)^{F+1}}$	$F/2$
L_q	$L - (1 - P_0)$	$L - (1 - P_0)$
W	$\dfrac{L}{\lambda(1 - P_F)}$	$\dfrac{L}{\lambda(1 - P_F)}$
W_q	$\dfrac{L_q}{\lambda(1 - P_F)}$	$\dfrac{L_q}{\lambda(1 - P_F)}$
P_w	$1 - P_0$	$1 - P_0$
ρ	$1 - P_0$	$1 - P_0$

Performance Measure	Queue	
	M/G/k/k	M/M/1//m
P_0	$\dfrac{1}{\displaystyle\sum_{n=0}^{k} \dfrac{(\lambda/\mu)^n}{n!}}$	$\dfrac{1}{\left[\displaystyle\sum_{n=0}^{m} \dfrac{m!}{(m - n)!}\left(\dfrac{\lambda}{\mu}\right)^n\right]}$
P_n	$\dfrac{(\lambda/\mu)^n}{n!} P_0 \quad n = 1, 2, 3, \ldots, k$	$\dfrac{m!}{(m - n)!}\left(\dfrac{\lambda}{\mu}\right)^n P_0$
L	$\dfrac{\lambda}{\mu}(1 - P_k)$	$m - \left(\dfrac{\mu}{\lambda}\right)(1 - P_0)$
L_q	0	$m - \left(\dfrac{\lambda + \mu}{\lambda}\right)(1 - P_0)$
W	$\dfrac{1}{\mu}$	$\dfrac{L}{\lambda(m - L)}$
W_q	0	$\dfrac{L_q}{\lambda(m - L)}$
P_w	$P_k{}^*$	$1 - P_0$
ρ	$\dfrac{\lambda}{k\mu}(1 - P_k)$	$1 - P_0$

* This is the probability an arriving customer is blocked.

ON THE **CD-ROM**

● Excel spreadsheet to calculate probabilities and graph for a poisson distribution	**Poisson distribution.xls**
● Excel spreadsheet to calculate density Function, graph and probabilities for an exponential distribution	**exponential distribution.xls**
● Excel spreadsheet for an M/M/1 system	**Mary's Shoes.xls**
● Excel spreadsheets for an M/M/k system	**Littletown Post Office queue.xls** **Wilson Foods queue.xls** **Big Boys Sound1 queue.xls** **Big Boys Sound2 queue.xls** **Big Boys Sound3 queue.xls**
● Excel spreadsheets for an M/G/1 system	**Ted's TV Repair Shop queue.xls** **Ted's TV Repair Shop New queue.xls**
● Excel spreadsheet for an M/M/k/F system	**Ryan Roofing queue.xls**
● Excel spreadsheets for an M/M/1//m system	**Pacesetter Homes queue.xls** **Pacesetter Homes New Car queue.xls**
● Excel spreadsheet for an M/G/k/k system	**Hargrove Hospital queue.xls**
● Excel template for solving queuing problems	**queue.xls**
● Goodness of Fit Testing to Determine the Appropriate Probability Distribution for the Arrival and Service Processes	**Appendix 9.2**
● The Erlangian Distribution	**Appendix 9.3**
● Derivation of Performance Measures for M/M/1 Queues Using Balance Equations	**Appendix 9.4**
● Derivation of Performance Measures for M/M/k Queues Using Balance Equations	**Appendix 9.5**
● Performance Measures for an M/M/k/F Queuing System	**Appendix 9.6**
● Performance Measures for an M/M/1//m Queuing System	**Appendix 9.7**
● Assembly-Line Balancing	**Appendix 9.8**
● Problem Motivations	**Problem Motivations**
● Problems 41–50	**Additional Problems/Cases**

APPENDIX 9.1

Using the Queue.xls Template

The template **queue.xls** included on the accompanying CD-ROM can be used to solve all of the queuing models discussed in this chapter. The template contains seven worksheets:

- **MMk**
- **MG1**
- **MGkk**
- **MD1**
- **MEn1**
- **MM1 m**
- **MMkF**

M/M/k QUEUING SYSTEMS

The **MMk** worksheet analyzes queuing system performance for up to 30 servers. Performance measures and probabilities are only presented for the number of servers, k, such that the steady-state condition, $k\mu > \lambda$, is satisfied. Probabilities for having between 0 and 30 customers present in the system are calculated for each server value. If cost data are entered, the template will calculate the per unit cost for each server value.

In this worksheet, parameters are entered in cells B4 (arrival rate) and B5 (service rate). Cost data is entered in cells H4 (cost per server per time unit), H5 (goodwill cost per customer per time unit while waiting in line to begin service), and H6 (goodwill cost per customer per time unit while being served). Outputs begin in row 11 with the performance measures shown in columns B through H and the customer probabilities shown in columns K through AO. Figures 9.6 and 9.9 are examples of the **MMk** worksheet.

M/En/1 QUEUING SYSTEMS

The worksheet **MEn1** is used to analyze an M/G/1 system in which the service time follows an Erlangian distribution. Figure A9.1 shows this worksheet.

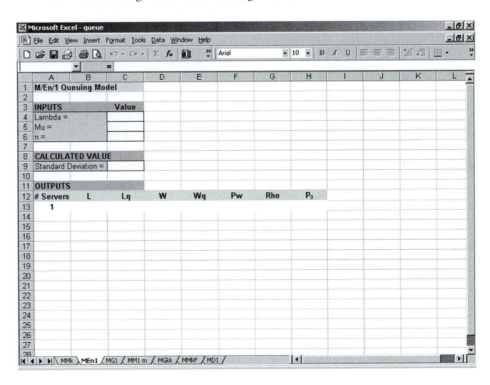

FIGURE A9.1 MEn1 Worksheet for Analyzing an M/En/1 Queuing System

In this worksheet, the arrival rate is entered in cell B4, the service rate is entered in cell B5, and the parameter n (see Appendix 9.3 on the accompanying CD-ROM) is entered in cell B6. The spreadsheet calculates the resulting standard deviation in cell B9 and the service measures in cells B13 through H13.

M/G/1 QUEUING SYSTEMS

The worksheet **MG1** can be used to analyze M/G/1 queuing systems. Figure A9.2 shows this worksheet.

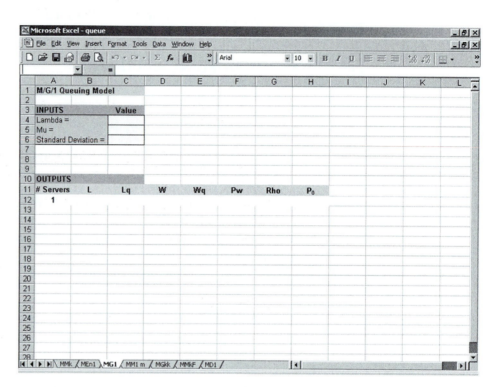

FIGURE A9.2 MG1 Worksheet for Analyzing an M/G/1 Queuing System

The arrival rate is entered in cell B4, the service rate is entered in cell B5, and the standard deviation of the service time is entered in cell B6. The performance measures for the system are calculated in cells B12 through H12. Note that since the M/En/1 and M/D/1 systems are special cases of the M/G/1 model, this worksheet can also be used to analyze these systems.

M/M/1//m QUEUING SYSTEMS

The worksheet **MM1 m** can be used to analyze M/M/1//m queuing systems. Figure 9.8 in Section 9.8 shows this worksheet.

The arrival rate is entered in cell B4, the service rate is entered in cell B5, and the customer population is entered in cell B6. The performance measures are shown in cells B13 through G13, and the probability of n customers (up to n = 30) being present in the system is shown in cells I13 through AM13. Rows 14 through 299 are used in calculating intermediate terms for P_0 and are hidden.

M/G/k/k QUEUING SYSTEMS

The worksheet **MGkk** can be used to analyze M/G/k/k queuing systems. Figure 9.10 in Section 9.9 shows this worksheet. In this worksheet the arrival rate is entered in cell B4, the service rate is entered in cell B5, and the number of servers present in the system is entered in cell B6. Service measures and customer probabilities are given in row 12 for the value of k specified in cell B6. Note that customer probabilities for values beyond k (the number of servers) are equal to 0 since the model assumes that there is no waiting line.

M/M/k/F QUEUING SYSTEMS

The worksheet **MMkF** can be used to analyze M/M/k/F queuing systems. Figure 9.7 in Section 9.7 shows this worksheet. For this worksheet to give correct values, it is necessary that F be strictly greater than k. If F equals k, the **MGkk** worksheet should be used to do the analysis. Data is entered in cells C4 through C7 and I4 through I6. Service measures and probabilities are calculated in row 12 based on the number of servers specified in cell C6.

M/D/1 QUEUING SYSTEMS

The worksheet **MD1** can be used to analyze M/D/1 queuing systems. Figure A9.3 shows this worksheet.

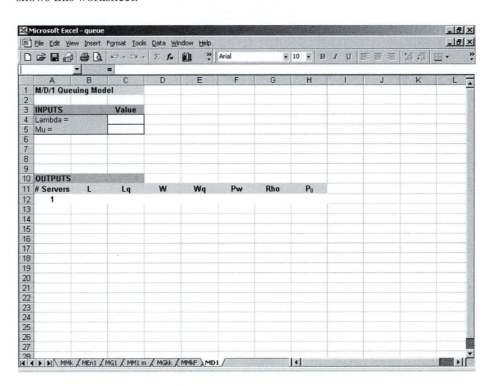

FIGURE A9.3 MD1 Worksheet for Analyzing an M/D/1 Queuing System

In this worksheet the arrival rate is entered in cell B4, and the service rate is entered in cell B5. The service measures are calculated in cells B12 through H12.

Problems

1. Students arrive at the Vermont University library reference desk according to a Poisson distribution at a mean rate of 12 per hour. The librarian spends an average of 4 minutes with each student, and service times follow an exponential distribution. What is the average number of students who will be present at the reference desk?

2. Customers arrive at Homestake Bank between the hours of 10 A.M. and 11 A.M. according to a Poisson distribution at a mean rate of 40 per hour. During the period from 10 A.M. to 11 A.M. the bank has 3 tellers working. The average time a teller spends with a customer is 3 minutes, and service time follows an exponential distribution. What is the average time a

customer will spend waiting in line before seeing a teller?

3. Cars arrive for servicing at Al's Repair Shop according to a Poisson distribution at a mean rate of 4 per day. The average time Al takes to work on a car is 2 hours, and the standard deviation is 15 minutes. Al is the only employee, and he works 10 hours a day. Determine the average number of cars that will be waiting for Al to begin working on them?

4. On Saturdays customers arrive at Patterson's Custom Jewels according to a Poisson distribution at a mean rate of 7 per hour. The store has 4 clerks working on Saturday, and the time a clerk spends with a customer follows an exponential distribution with a mean of 20 minutes. For security reasons, the entrance to the store is locked, and a maximum of 8 customers can be present in the store at any one time. It is assumed that customers who are not granted admittance to the store will leave and shop elsewhere. Determine the percentage of customers who will not be granted admittance to the store.

5. Randy Powell is responsible for maintaining the 60 personal computers at the Upbid.com corporate office. On the average a computer needs servicing by Randy once every 40 days, and Randy spends an average of 2 hours servicing a computer. If Randy works 8 hours a day and the time between when a computer needs servicing and the service time follow an exponential distribution, determine the average time (in days) it will take for a computer to finish being serviced.

6. Between the hours of 1 P.M. and 5 P.M. customers arrive at the downtown New York ticket office of United Airlines at the rate of 50 per hour. The average time a ticket agent spends with a customer is 6 minutes. Ticket agents earn $20 per hour in wages and benefits, and United Airlines estimates the goodwill cost of a customer waiting to begin service is $25 per hour while the goodwill cost of a customer being served is $5 per hour. Assuming customers arrive according to a Poisson distribution and service time follows an exponential distribution, determine the optimal number of ticket agents that United Airlines should have working in the New York ticket office between 1 P.M. and 5 P.M.

7. On Saturday morning customers arrive at the Armstrong Nursery at the average rate of 25 per hour. There are 8 employees who assist customers in selecting their plants. Each employee spends an average of 15 minutes with a customer. Following plant selection, customers then go to pay for their merchandise. There are two cashiers, and each can check out an average of 20 customers an hour. Once the merchandise has been paid for, customers either carry out their purchase or it is delivered to their car. Twenty percent of customers carry out their purchase. There are 3 workers who do the delivery, and each delivery requires an average of 5 minutes. Determine the average time a customer spends at Armstrong Nursery on a Saturday morning if the customer has the purchase delivered to his car. Assume that customers arrive according to a Poisson distribution

and that the service times follow an exponential distribution.

8. Customers arrive at Pete's Coffee Shop on the average of one every 5 minutes, according to a Poisson distribution. The average time Pete spends serving a customer is 3 minutes, and the service times are believed to follow an exponential distribution. The shop is run entirely by Pete, and customers are served on a first-come, first-served basis.
   a. What is the probability that exactly 2 customers will arrive at Pete's in a 15-minute period?
   b. What is the probability that more than 3 customers will arrive in a 30-minute period?
   c. What is the probability that the service time for a customer is under 2 minutes?
   d. On the average, how long does a customer spend waiting for service at Pete's?
   e. What is the probability that a customer spends less than 5 minutes at Pete's?
   f. What is the average number of customers present at Pete's?
   g. What percentage of Pete's time is spent serving customers?

9. At Dolly Foods, customers spend an average of 25 minutes selecting their groceries and checking out by entering a single-line queue served by two cashiers. The service times required for the cashiers to check out customers follow an exponential distribution and average 4 minutes. Customers arrive at the cashier counter according to a Poisson distribution at the average rate of 8 customers per hour.
   a. Determine: (i) the average time a customer spends in the store; (ii) the average number of customers waiting in line prior to being checked out; (iii) the proportion of customers who will have to wait in line.
   b. What assumptions did you make in part (a)?

10. Consider the information given in problem 9 for Dolly Foods. For the same amount that Dolly is paying the two cashiers, she can lay off one cashier and use the savings to lease an optical scanning system. The resulting checkout times will then follow a distribution, with a mean service time of 3 minutes and a standard deviation of 1 minute.
    a. If Dolly opts for the optical scanning system, determine: (i) the average time a customer would spend in the store; (ii) the average number of customers waiting in line prior to being checked out; (iii) the proportion of customers who would have to wait in line.
    b. Compare the results from part a of problems 9 and 10. Would you recommend that Dolly Foods lease the optical scanning system? Justify your answer.

11. INFOSERVE, Inc. is a 900 line telephone service that supplies various kinds of obscure information. The company is expanding its service to Monmouth County, New Jersey, and has allocated $60,000 to purchase the computer systems necessary to handle customer calls. INFOSERVE has received bids from two computer suppliers: Infotechnologies and Compufact. The system from Infotechnologies sells for $20,000 and can handle

an average customer inquiry in 3 minutes. Compufact's database system sells for $30,000 and can handle an average customer inquiry in 2 minutes. INFOSERVE can therefore purchase three of the Infotechnologies systems or two of the Compufact systems.

INFOSERVE estimates that an average of 40 customers per hour will call its service and that customer phone calls will arrive according to a Poisson process. If no computer system is available, callers remain on hold until a system is free. Service times are believed to follow an exponential distribution. If INFOSERVE's objective is to minimize the average time a caller must wait on hold to get information, which supplier should it select?

12. Customers arrive at random at the Lickety Dip Ice Cream store between the hours of 8 P.M. and 11 P.M. according to a Poisson distribution with an average rate of 18 per hour. Service times follow an exponential distribution, with the average service time depending on the server hired. The store has three potential workers it can hire to work that shift. If the company places a value of $4 for each hour a customer spends waiting in line or being served, which of the following applicants should be hired as the night server?

Server	Salary	Average Service Time
Ann	$ 6/hr.	3 min.
Bill	$10/hr.	2 min.
Charlie	$14/hr.	1.5 min.

13. Muncie State University runs its registration line by dividing the student population into three equal groups based on student ID numbers. A student will enter the appropriate line to register, and jockeying among lines *is not* permitted. The arrival rate of students for each line follows a Poisson process, with a mean rate of 30 students per hour. Service of a student follows an exponential distribution, and the average time it takes to serve a student is 90 seconds.
  a. Determine the average time required for a student to wait in line and register.
  b. Determine the total average number of students waiting to be served in the three lines.
  c. Muncie State University is contemplating eliminating the three-line system and replacing it by a single line staffed by two clerks supported by a microcomputer system. This would reduce the average service time to 72 seconds and save $2.60 per hour in labor costs. Muncie State estimates that the goodwill cost of a student's being in the system is $4 per hour. Assuming service times continue to follow an exponential distribution and students arrive according to a Poisson process at a mean rate of 90 per hour, should the university switch to the single-line system?

14. The Atlas Health Club has one tanning booth for its customers. Users of the tanning booth spend *exactly* 5 minutes in the facility. Customers arrive at the booth according to a Poisson process at the mean rate of 8 per hour.
  a. What is the average time a customer must wait in line to use the tanning booth?

  b. What is the average number of customers waiting to use the tanning booth?
  c. What is the probability that there is no waiting line at the tanning booth?
  d. What assumptions did you make in parts (a)–(c)?

15. Customers randomly arrive at the Northpointe wholesale flower market according to a Poisson distribution at an average rate of 100 per hour. Service times follow an exponential distribution with an average time of 5 minutes. How many servers should be hired so that the average time a customer waits for service is less than 30 seconds?

16. Jobs arrive randomly at Mike's Custom Framing at an average rate of 5 per hour. The store is considering purchasing one of two machines for automating the framing process. One machine results in a mean service time of 8 minutes and a standard deviation of .3 minute while the other machine results in a mean service time of 7.5 minutes with a standard deviation of 6 minutes. Which of the two machines seems preferable for Mike to purchase?

17. Harry's Variety Store has two checkstand locations—one at the front entrance to the store, the other at the rear. The checkstand locations are so far apart it is reasonable to expect that customers will *not* jockey between them. The checkstand in the front has two cashiers, while the checkstand in the rear has four. The service times for each cashier follow an exponential distribution, with a mean time of 2.5 minutes.

Customers arrive at the checkstand locations according to a Poisson process. Because there is more parking at the rear of the store, the arrival rate of customers at that checkstand averages 66 customers per hour, while the arrival rate at the front entrance checkstand averages 20 customers per hour.
  a. What is the average time a customer spends waiting in line prior to beginning service at each of the two checkstand locations?
  b. What is the average number of customers both waiting in line and being served at each of the two checkstand locations?
  c. What is the probability that there are exactly 2 people waiting in line at the rear entrance checkstand?
  d. What is the probability that there are 3 or fewer people waiting in line at the front entrance checkstand?
  e. As a customer, would you prefer to check out at the front or the rear of the store? Justify your answer.

18. Consider the situation at Harry's Variety Store (problem 17). Harry is considering consolidating the two checkstands into one centralized location in the middle of the store. He estimates that the combined average of 86 customers per hour would arrive at the centralized location. Cashiers will continue to check customers out in an average of two and a half minutes and earn $16 per hour in salary and benefits. Harry feels that the goodwill cost of having a customer waiting in line is $20 per hour, while the goodwill cost during a customer's service is $10 per hour. Determine the optimal number of cashiers Harry should use at the centralized location.

19. Pat Smith and Chris Brown are two applicants for the position of telephone receptionist at Taylar Industries. Both applicants can handle a phone call in an average of one minute. The standard deviation of Pat's service time is 10 seconds, while the standard deviation of Chris's service time is 20 seconds. The interarrival time of customer calls is expected to follow an exponential distribution, with a mean of 90 seconds. On the average, how much longer will a caller wait on hold to speak to a receptionist if Chris were hired than if Pat were hired?

20. Mr. Chips manufactures automated vending machines that can prepare a single order of french fries in exactly 45 seconds. The company has placed one of its machines in the student union building of a local community college, where it believes customers will arrive according to a Poisson process at the mean rate of 40 per hour. Determine the average amount of time an arriving customer will have to wait before ordering french fries from the vending machine.

21. Tie One On, an exclusive men's clothing store specializing in ties, is planning to develop a store in a new shopping mall. Customers are expected to arrive at the store location at random at an average rate of 40 per hour. The store will be open 10 hours per day. Service times are assumed to follow an exponential distribution. Excluding fixed costs such as wages and rent, the average sale nets $22. Clerks are paid $20/hr. including all benefits, and the cost of having a waiting customer is estimated to be $10 per customer per hour. One possibility is to have a small store staffed by 2 clerks serving at an average rate of 10 customers per hour each. This store, however, will only have room for a maximum of 3 customers to be present. Another possibility is to have a larger store with 6 clerks, each serving at a rate of 10 customers per hour. The larger store can accommodate up to a total of 15 customers. It is believed that customers who arrive when the store is full will shop elsewhere. If the small store leases for $200 per day and the large store leases for $2000 per day, which configuration should be used?

22. Steve Jackson is responsible for maintaining a fleet of 8 school buses. On the average, a bus will need repair work every 20 days. The average time required to perform this work is one day. Both the time between needed repairs and the time to perform repairs are expected to follow exponential distributions.
    a. What is the average amount of time a bus will be out of service for a needed repair?
    b. On the average, how many buses will be waiting for repair at any given time?
    c. What proportion of the time will all buses be operational?

23. The telephone system at WAVY Radio has 6 incoming phone lines and 2 operators to take listener requests for music. If both operators are busy, a customer is normally placed on hold. If all 6 phone lines are busy, however, callers will get a busy signal and probably not call back. Customer calls to WAVY can be modeled by a Poisson process, with a mean rate of 50 per hour. The service times follow an exponential distribution, with a mean of 90 seconds.
    a. What is the probability that a caller will be placed on hold?
    b. On the average, how many callers are on hold?
    c. If a caller does not get a busy signal, what is the average total time spent waiting on hold and speaking to an operator?
    d. What is the probability that there is exactly one caller on hold?

24. Bronco Burger has a drive-thru window for take-out orders. Because of space limitation, the restaurant has been designed to allow a maximum of 5 cars in the drive-thru window line (including the car being served). If the line is full, cars will not stop at Bronco Burger but will instead drive to a competing restaurant.

    Cars attempt to arrive to Bronco Burger's drive-thru window at an average of one every 80 seconds. Interarrival times are assumed to follow an exponential distribution. Service times also follow an exponential distribution, with a mean service time of one minute.
    a. What is the average number of cars waiting in line for service?
    b. What is the average time a car spends in line, including the service?
    c. What is the probability that there are no cars at the drive-thru window?
    d. Comment on the appropriateness of modeling the service time at Bronco Burger by an exponential distribution.

25. Soup Herman is a restaurant that serves soup and salad. Customers first line up in a cash register line to pay for their meals. After paying, they proceed to one of four salad bars. While all customers purchase salad, only 60% of customers go on to take the soup from one of the two soup stations.

    During the hours between 6:15 and 8:00 P.M., an average of 140 customers arrive at the restaurant. Assume that the arrival process can be modeled by a Poisson distribution. The time it takes to pay the cashier, get salad, and get soup each follows an exponential probability distribution. If the cashier takes an average of 40 seconds to collect money from a customer, and the customer averages two minutes to get a salad and one minute to get soup, determine the average time a customer spends paying for and getting food if; (i) the customer is getting salad only; and (ii) the customer is getting both soup and salad.

26. Circle J convenience store has two check-out counters. Customers arrive according to a Poisson process at an average rate of one every 90 seconds. On the average, each of the 2 checkers serves 50 customers per hour, and service times follow an exponential distribution.

    Circle J is considering eliminating one of the 2 check-out counters and having the 2 employees work together, one ringing up the merchandise, the other bagging it. How fast would their combined average service time have to be if the average time a customer spends in the store is to remain unchanged?

27. Larry Pembroke is a repair person for Copyco, a firm that has copying machines located at libraries, supermarkets,

and court houses. Larry is responsible for maintaining the copiers assigned to him. On the average, each copier needs service once every 25 working days. Including travel time to the location, Larry spends an average of half a day repairing a copier machine. Copyco's management wishes to determine how many copiers should be assigned to Larry so that, on the average, a copier is out of commission for no more than one day.

28. Customers arrive at Dave & Steve's bookstore according to a Poisson process at a mean rate of 48 per hour. The store pays its sales clerks $7.50 per hour in wages and benefits. Dave & Steve's estimates the goodwill cost of a customer waiting to be served at $6 per hour and the goodwill cost of a customer being served at only $1.00 per hour. Customer service times follow an exponential distribution and average 2 minutes.
    a. Determine the number of sales clerks Dave & Steve's should employ to minimize the store's total average hourly costs.
    b. If the customer arrival rate increases by 50% and the goodwill cost of a customer waiting to be served and being served were doubled, determine how many sales clerks Dave & Steve's should employ to minimize the store's total average hourly costs.

29. Ernest D. Johnson is a discount stock brokerage firm located in Sun Valley, Idaho. Johnson is the only employee, and he works out of his house, where he receives all customer orders by telephone. Johnson receives an average of 10 client calls per hour, and he spends an average of 4 minutes speaking to each client. If a client calls while Johnson is talking to another client, the caller is placed on hold. The call-waiting system Johnson has leased from the telephone company allows him to keep an unlimited number of callers on hold, and he believes that no customer placed on hold will hang up before talking to him. If customer calls arrive according to a Poisson distribution and the time required to provide service to a customer follows an exponential distribution, determine:
    a. The probability that Johnson will receive exactly 4 calls in a half hour.
    b. The probability that Johnson will receive 3 or fewer calls in a half hour.
    c. The probability that a telephone conversation will last less than 3 minutes (from the time Johnson begins speaking with the client).
    d. The average number of callers waiting on hold.
    e. The average time a caller will spend on the phone when calling Johnson.
    f. The percentage of time Johnson is on the phone.
    g. The probability that a customer will spend more than six minutes on the phone when calling Johnson.

30. Jack's Joke Shop of Boston sells novelty items (joy buzzers, rubber chickens, whoopy cushions, and so on). Customers arrive according to a Poisson process on the average of once every 5 minutes. Jack prides himself on the personal service he offers his customers. The time Jack spends with customers follows an Erlangian distribution with a mean of 4 minutes and a standard deviation of 2 minutes.

    a. What is the average number of customers in Jack's store at a given time?
    b. On the average, how long does a customer spend in the store?

31. An analysis of 31 customers at Pat's Pet Shop indicated the following 30 interarrival times (in seconds): 96, 84, 29, 61, 27, 231, 256, 243, 43, 117, 320, 267, 177, 605, 105, 653, 35, 18, 451, 34, 486, 2, 442, 46, 424, 562, 244, 1, 6, 103. The mean of this data set is 205.6 seconds, and the standard deviation is 200.08 seconds.
    Construct a histogram of collected data. Verify that the exponential distribution is a reasonable distribution to use to model the interarrival time of customers. (Use the goodness of fit approach described in Appendix 9.2.)

32. Mark Trading Company employs two workers in its order processing department. Each worker processes orders according to an exponential distribution with a mean of 5 minutes. Customer arrivals follow a Poisson process with a mean of 18 customers per hour.
    a. What is the probability that both workers are busy?
    b. What is the probability that both workers are idle?
    c. On the average, how long must an order wait before processing begins?
    d. On the average, how many orders are being processed or are waiting to be processed?
    e. What is the probability that exactly 3 customers will be in line waiting to be served at any given time?

33. Sue Patterson recorded the length (in seconds) of 50 messages left on her telephone answering machine. These data are as follows:

Conversation Number	Time	Conversation Number	Time
1	142	26	13
2	77	27	17
3	65	28	147
4	31	29	39
5	173	30	35
6	50	31	127
7	10	32	173
8	31	33	5
9	136	34	190
10	11	35	31
11	186	36	202
12	121	37	26
13	53	38	85
14	38	39	47
15	130	40	173
16	81	41	110
17	67	42	64
18	45	43	20
19	369	44	26
20	6	45	48
21	280	46	193
22	139	47	152
23	5	48	57
24	45	49	156
25	88	50	121

The mean is 92.72 seconds with a standard deviation of 77.15 seconds.
a. Draw a histogram of this data set.
b. Do a goodness of fit test to determine whether the data follow an exponential distribution with a mean of 90 seconds (see Appendix 9.2 on the CD-ROM).

34. Cars travel down Euclid Avenue at the mean rate of 12,000 per hour. The probability that a car will stop at the drive-thru window of Dinkie Donuts is .003. Hence, the arrival process of cars can be modeled using the Poisson distribution with average arrival rate $\lambda = 36$ per hour. The average time it takes to serve a customer is 75 seconds. If service times follow an exponential distribution, determine:
    a. The average number of cars in the drive-thru line (including cars receiving service).
    b. The average number of minutes a car must wait in line before being served.
    c. The probability that an arriving car can be served immediately.
    d. The probability that there are two or fewer cars waiting in line to be served.

35. Consider the situation faced by Dinkie Donuts (problem 34). Management feels that if the average number of cars waiting in line (excluding cars being served) were reduced to one or less, the probability that a car traveling down Euclid Avenue would stop at Dinkie Donuts would increase to .004. If Dinkie continues to operate a single drive-thru window, what would the average service time have to be to meet this objective?

36. The California Highway Patrol conducts random truck inspections on certain California highways. On a particular day, three Highway Patrol units have set up an inspection station for checking truck brakes. Whenever one of the three units become available, the next trucker to pass the inspection point is pulled over for inspection. When all three units are busy, no other trucks are stopped until a unit becomes free.

    Trucks travel down the highway according to a Poisson process. On the average, one truck approaches the inspection station every 50 seconds. The time required to inspect brakes averages five minutes and has a standard deviation of 1.5 minutes.
    a. What proportion of trucks on the highway will be inspected?
    b. What is the probability that all three Highway Patrol units are idle?
    c. On the average, how many trucks will be having their brakes inspected?

37. Daily Fax Incorporated (DFI) is an automated information system that operates as follows: Customers call an 800 phone number and input their fax number and information request (sports scores, stock market information, topical cartoons, jokes) using a touch-tone telephone. The computer then faxes a one-page sheet of paper containing the requested information as well as approximately a quarter page of advertising. The company earns its profits from the advertising revenue as well as from a directory of fax numbers that it publishes monthly (based on the fax numbers it receives from callers).

    The Daily Fax computer system is set up so that there are sufficient telephone lines to answer all incoming phone calls. However, there is only one outgoing fax transmission line. The total time to process each incoming fax request is exactly 25 seconds. Calls come into Daily Fax according to a Poisson process at an average rate of 2 per minute. DFI would like to be able to inform potential advertisers of the average time a customer must wait for a fax to arrive.
    a. What assumptions would you make to model this problem?
    b. Given these assumptions, what is your estimate of average time (in minutes) a customer must wait for a fax?

38. Zoro's Bistros is a chain of upscale, limited-item self-service restaurants. During the dinner hours, the restaurant serves a $7.95 fixed-price dinner consisting of a choice of soup, main dish, dessert, and beverage. Since there are four food categories, management believes that customer service time can best be modeled using an Erlangian distribution with n = 4.

    Studies have indicated that the arrival process during dinner hours at Zoro's uptown location can be approximated by a Poisson distribution with $\lambda = 40$ customers per hour. The average time required to serve a customer is 1.2 minutes. There is a single waiting line, and customers are served on a first-come, first-served basis.
    a. On the average, how many customers are waiting in line to begin being served at dinner time?
    b. What is the average length of time a customer waits in line before being served at dinner time?

39. Customers arrive at Burger Barn on the average of once every 72 seconds. The average time to serve a customer is 1.5 minutes. Employees earn $12 per hour in wages and benefits, and the goodwill cost of a customer being in the system is estimated to be $25 per hour. For the next two weeks Burger Barn is planning a special promotion that it believes will double the customer arrival rate. Management wishes to determine the optimal number of employees to have working in the store during this two-week time period.

40. Gameland is a combination miniature golf course and video arcade. One of the most popular games in the arcade is Thunderblaster, a virtual reality space trip. The playing time for Thunderblaster is exactly 2 minutes. An additional 30 seconds is required for a player to put on the virtual reality helmet. Customers arrive to play the game according to a Poisson process at an average rate of once every 3 minutes.
    a. What is the average time a player waits in line to play Thunderblaster?
    b. On the average, how many people are playing or waiting to play Thunderblaster?

PROBLEMS 41–50 ARE ON THE CD

CASE STUDIES

CASE 1: Saveway Supermarkets

Saveway Supermarkets is a major food retailer in upstate New York. The chain has over 60 stores that receive merchandise from their Rochester, New York, warehouse. The warehouse receives shipments of merchandise throughout the day from the various vendors and manufacturers with whom Saveway does business.

The Rochester warehouse has eight loading docks available for delivery of goods. Trucks arrive at the warehouse approximately once every six minutes according to a Poisson process. If all the loading docks are occupied, an arriving truck waits in a queue until a dock becomes available.

Currently, each dock is staffed by a single worker, who unloads a truck in an average of 30 minutes. Saveway management has been getting complaints from some of its suppliers that their truckers are spending too much time unloading merchandise at the Rochester warehouse. Hence Saveway has come up with a number of possible strategies to address this problem: (1) hire a second worker for each loading dock, reducing the average time to unload a truck to 18 minutes (workers earn $16 per hour in salary and benefits); (2) equip each loading dock with an electric forklift that can be leased for $5 per hour and reduce the time required to unload a truck to an average of 24 minutes; or (3) build up to two more loading docks (accounting for capital costs, each dock will cost Saveway $6 per hour to build).

While strategies 1 and 2 are mutually exclusive, the firm may decide to implement strategy 3 either alone or in combination with 1 or 2. Saveway estimates the goodwill cost of a delivery truck being in the system at $60 per hour.

Prepare a business report recommending a course of action to Saveway management assuming the objective is to minimize total system costs. Assume that service times for each option follow exponential distributions. Include in your report a comparison of the system parameters of your recommendation to those of current operations.

CASE 2: Boone Travel Agency

Having run a successful travel agency in Denver, Colorado, Jan Hall has decided to open a branch in Boone, Colorado. She must decide where to locate her office and which and how many employees to hire.

Jan has narrowed her choice of office to two locations. The one on Main Street is a large office with space for virtually any number of employees and customers. Jan estimates that the agency can attract an average of 12 customers per day at this location. Rent for this office is $1300 per month. Utilities, insurance, and other expenses should average an additional $500 per month.

The second choice for an office is on Frontier Street, approximately two blocks off Main Street. This is a much smaller office that can effectively hold only one worker and at most four customers (including the one being served). It rents for $400 per month. Utilities, insurance, and other expenses should average an additional $200 per month. This out-of-the-way location would reduce the number of potential customers by 20%, and any arriving customer finding the office full will presumably take his or her business to the other travel agency in town.

Jan has decided that if she opens the Main Street office, she will hire one or more local employees to staff the office. If she opens the Frontier Street office, however, she will hire either Wendy Brown, an experienced travel agent from the Denver area, or a local employee to staff the office. Jan would have to pay Wendy a monthly salary (including benefits) of $2100, whereas she could hire local employees for $1200 per month (including benefits). Because of her experience, Wendy's average customer service time is approximately 20 minutes, compared to 48 minutes for local employees.

Jan estimates that each customer served by the Boone Travel Agency will result in an average commission of $35. She also estimates a goodwill cost to the firm of $15 per hour for the time a customer spends waiting in the office for service to being. In addition, goodwill costs of $50 are associated with any customers who find the Frontier Street location full and leave to go to another travel agency.

The travel agency will be open an average of 20 days per month, eight hours each day. Customers arrive according to a Poisson process, and customer service times follow an exponential distribution.

Prepare a business report for Jan Hall detailing her various options and your recommendation as to her best course of action. Include in your report the financial information on which you base your recommendation.

CASE 3:   Shelley's Supermarket

Shelley's Supermarket is located in Virginia Beach, Virginia. It operates 16 hours a day, from 7:00 A.M. to 11:00 P.M. and has a maximum of four check-out stands. During the summer, volume at the supermarket increases dramatically due to the tourist traffic. The summer season runs approximately three months, from June 15 to September 15, although immediately prior to and immediately after this season, there is slightly more business than during the winter months. To simplify the analysis, however, Shelley's management assumes two seasons: peak (summer) and off-peak.

During the off-peak season, customers arrive according to a Poisson process at an average rate of 14 per hour, compared to an arrival rate of 46 customers per hour during the peak season. Shelley's estimates that its average gross profit per customer is $6 during the off-peak season and $4 during the peak season. However, Shelley's attaches the following costs *per customer in the check-out line* based on goodwill, and so on:

	Off-peak Season	*Peak Season*
While waiting to be served	$10/hour	$8/hour
While being served	$ 6/hour	$4/hour

Shelley's hires only union personnel as check-out clerks. Their pay, including benefits, averages $16 per hour. According to the union contract, these employees must be hired as permanent, year-round employees.

The union contract allows Shelley's management to hire part-time support personnel (baggers, stock clerks) to help deal with the store's increased traffic during the peak season, but there can never be more temporary employees than permanent employees working. These nonunion, temporary employees are paid $5 per hour.

Customers spend an average of 40 minutes selecting their groceries. Customer service time for each permanent check-out clerk follows an exponential distribution, with an average time of four minutes during the off-peak season. During the summer months, the average customer service time for each checker (in minutes) will equal x, where:

$$x = 4 - \frac{(1.5)(\text{number of temporary employees})}{(\text{number of permanent employees})}$$

For example, if Shelley's has three permanent employees and two temporary employees during the summer months, the average service time for each of the three checkers is $4 - (1.5)(2)/3 = 3$ minutes.

Prepare a business report detailing Shelley's various hiring options for staffing its store throughout the year and your recommendation as to the optimal strategy. Assume that the peak season lasts 90 days and that the off-peak season lasts 260 days (Shelley's is closed five days a year). Include in your report the financial information on which you base your recommendation.

Simulation Models

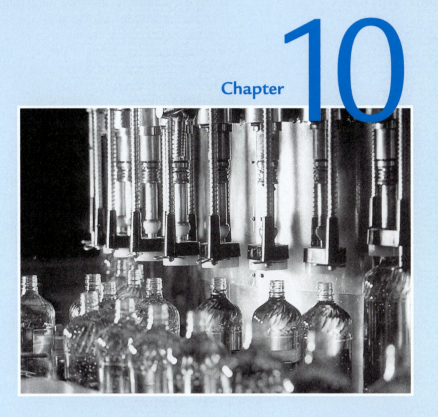

HUNT WESSON (http://www.hunt-wesson. com) IS one of the world's largest food processing companies. One of its principal product lines is Wesson Oil, which is made from a variety of vegetable oils and packaged in various-sized bottles. Management is particularly concerned about the operation of the production line used to bottle the oil.

The bottling process begins by using a decaser to remove empty plastic bottles from their shipping cases and place them on the bottling line. The bottles are then air cleaned and moved onto a conveyer belt for transport to the filling station. After filling, they are sealed and capped and proceed to a labeler. A caser places the filled bottles in cases. Finally, the cases are sealed using a case sealer and loaded on pallets by a palletizer.

Management conducted a simulation study to develop procedures for ensuring that the bottling line operates at a sufficient capacity to meet sales projections. They gathered data on the frequency, length, and repair cost of breakdowns for each workstation on the bottling line and determined the cost and effects of modifications to the existing equipment. They also investigated different line speeds as well as the placement of buffer areas (accumulation tables) between workstations.

As a result of the simulation analysis, management was able to redesign the bottling process to meet the firm's production requirements and to develop procedures for dealing with future breakdowns which will minimize the variation in production rates.

10.1   Overview of Simulation

In the preceding chapters, we have studied many analytical models. Often, however, the underlying assumptions necessary for these models to provide good results are not met. For example, in a single-server queuing system if service time does not follow an exponential distribution or if customers do not arrive according to a Poisson process we cannot expect the M/M/1 queuing formulas to accurately describe steady-state results. Inventory systems for which demand varies greatly from period to period cannot be adequately analyzed using the EOQ formula. In cases such as these, we may use a simulation approach to perform the desired analysis.

A **simulation** develops a model to evaluate a system numerically over some time period of interest. Its purpose is to estimate characteristics for the system, which can then be used to select the best policy from a set of alternatives under consideration. Unlike many analytical techniques, a simulation does not rely on an algorithm to solve for the optimal solution; instead, a computer program known as a **simulator** is used to evaluate each option.

It is important for the simulator to be as accurate as possible in capturing the important aspects of the operation of the system. A challenging aspect of developing a simulation, therefore, is to identify the relevant factors affecting system performance. For example, if we are interested in determining a customer's average waiting time in a queuing system, the arrival process, the service time, the number of servers, and the priority rule for selecting the next customer are all important attributes. By contrast, the hair color of an arriving customer does not affect waiting time and is ignored.

Other attributes, such as the gender of a customer, may or may not be a factor. If we are modeling a queuing system for a bank, for example, a customer's gender is probably not a factor. But if we are modeling the waiting line at a campground rest room, a customer's gender probably is an important factor, since the time men and women spend in a rest room generally differs.

Simulation is used for many purposes in business and industry. Airlines use flight simulators to train prospective pilots; the weather service uses simulation analysis to predict future weather patterns; and process engineers use simulation to determine the operating characteristics of projects, such as a proposed oil refinery. These are all examples of **continuous simulation systems**, in which the state of the system changes continuously over time. For example, a plane rises continuously as a pilot moves the throttle; weather changes from instant to instant; and oil flows continuously through the refining process. Since in many cases, continuous simulation systems require the use of differential equations to model changes in system parameters, these systems are beyond the scope of this text.

Other simulation models, such as those involving queuing or inventory systems, monitor changes that occur at discrete points in time. These are known as **discrete simulation systems**. Still other simulation models are hybrids of continuous and discrete simulation systems. For example, in simulating jet fuel inventory at an airport, customers (airplanes) arrive on a discrete basis, while the fuel going into each airplane is a continuous flow. In this chapter a number of discrete simulation systems, typical of those found in business and industry are considered.

Although simple simulation models may be solved by hand, simulation of most practical problems requires the use of a computer program. Computer simulations can be written in any computer language or performed by using a spreadsheet program such as Excel.

One advantage of using Excel to develop a simulation model is that specific Excel add-ins have been developed to allow the analyst to easily run multiple simulations so that confidence intervals and probabilities can be calculated for the various policies considered. Two of the most popular of these add-ins are @Risk and

Crystal Ball. A student version of Crystal Ball is included on the accompanying CD-ROM.

While many simulations have been written in general-purpose programming languages, such as FORTRAN, PL/1, Pascal, and BASIC, specialized computer simulation languages have been developed to assist in writing the computer code. Among the more popular simulation languages are GPSS, SIMSCRIPT, SIMAN, and SLAM. The principal advantage of using a specialized language is that compared to a general-purpose language, fewer lines of computer code are required, allowing the program to be written and debugged more quickly and easily. In addition, many specialized languages include an animation ability, enabling the user to view the effects of the simulation as the program is running. This can be especially valuable in identifying potential bottlenecks in the system or critical areas requiring further modeling. Even though these specialized languages share many similarities, they also have certain differences that make one language more appropriate than another for a particular application.

An alternative to using Excel or a programming or simulation language is to develop the simulation using a **simulator program**. These programs typically contain objects that can be dragged and dropped to allow easy creation of the simulation model. The resulting models usually include the ability to observe an animation of the process and contain the ability to provide the simulation results in a tabular or graphical format. Some of the more popular simulators currently used in business and industry are Alpha/Sim, SIMPROCESS, ProModel, and Extend. A student version of Extend is included on the accompanying CD-ROM. Appendix 10.1, also on the accompanying CD-ROM, covers the basic concepts of developing simulations using Extend by illustrating the simulation of a discrete system.

Deciding whether to learn a particular simulation language or simulator program depends on how frequently it will be necessary to develop simulation models. For the infrequent modeler, using Excel to develop simulation models may be the easiest and most accessible solution.

Approaches to Solving a Simulation Problem

- Excel—Including the Use of Add-In Programs such as Crystal Ball
- Using a General-Purpose Computer Language such as BASIC
- Using a Simulation Language such as SIMSCRIPT
- Using a Simulator Program such as Extend

THE SIMULATION PROCESS

The approach to simulation analysis is quite similar to that of a general management science process. The key steps in the analysis are:

- Defining the Problem
- Developing the Simulation Model
- Running the Simulation Model and Obtaining Results
- Communicating the Results

It is worthwhile commenting on the second step of the simulation process—developing the simulation model. Often in simulation studies, the first step in developing a model is to create a flow chart representation of the system being simulated. The modeler must then select an appropriate methodology for constructing the simulation model (i.e., a general-purpose computer language, a specialized simulation language, a simulator program, and Excel). The methodology selected depends on the type of problem being simulated.

Besides determining the approach to be used to develop the simulation, the analyst must also collect the data needed to construct the model. This involves estimating probability distributions for parts of the process being simulated. Once the methodology for model development has been determined and the data collected, the model can be constructed (programmed) and run.

As with any management science procedure, enhancements to the model can be made after the initial run. In this approach one starts with a relatively simple model that is easy to construct (program) and then, after analyzing the results of the model, adds desired enhancements. This iterative procedure is continued until the analyst is satisfied that the model is giving valuable insights into the problem being studied.

While the concept of simulation is quite intuitive, great care must be taken not only in modeling the system, but also in conducting the simulation. As discussed in this chapter, simulation requires both good modeling and good programming skills. Knowledge of statistics is also important for determining the overall design of the simulation and other critical factors, such as the required length of individual simulation runs and the number of runs that should make up the simulation study.

10.2 Monte Carlo Simulation

If the system being simulated includes data inputs that are random variables, the simulation model should reflect them as accurately as possible. One way of doing so is to use a technique known as **Monte Carlo simulation**, in which the simulator is designed so that the **simulated events** both occur randomly and reflect the theoretical frequencies being modeled.

Monte Carlo simulation uses *random numbers*, which can either be generated by a computer program (Excel has several ways to generate random numbers) or taken from a random number table (see Appendix C), to generate simulated events. The process for matching random numbers to simulated events is called **random number mapping**. To illustrate how random number mappings are developed and how random numbers are used in a Monte Carlo simulation consider the situation faced by Bill Jewel, owner of the Jewel Vending Company.

Jewel Vending.xls
JVCb.xls

JEWEL VENDING COMPANY

Bill Jewel is the owner of the Jewel Vending Company (JVC), which installs and stocks gum and novelty vending machines in supermarkets, discount stores, and restaurants. Bill is considering installing a Super Sucker jaw breaker dispenser at the new Saveway Supermarket on Lincoln Avenue. The vending machine holds 80 jaw breakers. Ideally, Bill would like to fill the machine whenever it becomes half empty. (Bill does not want the machine to appear too empty, because he fears that potential customers will believe the jaw breakers are not fresh and so will elect not to make a purchase.)

Based on performance of similar vending machine placements, Bill has estimated the following distribution for daily jaw breaker demand:

$$P(\text{daily demand} = 0 \text{ jaw breakers}) = .10$$
$$P(\text{daily demand} = 1 \text{ jaw breaker}) = .15$$
$$P(\text{daily demand} = 2 \text{ jaw breakers}) = .20$$
$$P(\text{daily demand} = 3 \text{ jaw breakers}) = .30$$
$$P(\text{daily demand} = 4 \text{ jaw breakers}) = .20$$
$$P(\text{daily demand} = 5 \text{ jaw breakers}) = .05$$

Bill would like to estimate the expected number of days it takes for a filled machine to become half empty (i.e., the average number of days it takes to sell 40 jaw breakers). This information will help him to determine how often to refill the machine.

SOLUTION

Bill might consider estimating the expected time between refills by calculating the average (expected) daily demand based on the assumed probability distribution and dividing this value into 40.

$$\frac{\text{Expected time}}{\text{between refills}} = \frac{40}{.10(0) + .15(1) + .20(2) + .30(3) + .20(4) + .05(5)}$$

$$= \frac{40}{2.5} = 16 \text{ days}$$

Bill is not certain that this method yields the true average number of days required to sell 40 or more jaw breakers, but he feels it probably yields a good approximation. To test it, Bill has decided to employ a simulation approach.

SIMULATION OF THE DAILY DEMAND FOR JAW BREAKERS

To properly simulate the JVC system, let us define the random variable:

$$X = \text{daily demand for jaw beakers at the Saveway store}$$

Based on Bill's estimates, the probability distribution function for X is as shown in Table 10.1.

TABLE 10.1 Probability Distribution for Daily Jaw Breaker Demand

x	P(X = x)
0	.10
1	.15
2	.20
3	.30
4	.20
5	.05

The theory behind generating a *random event*, such as daily demand, is that the event outcomes should not occur in any particular pattern, but, in the long run, they should occur with relative frequencies equal to the probability distribution being modeled. In particular, the probability distribution for each day's demand should follow the same distribution as that given above for X, regardless of the results of the simulated demand generated for any other day.

For example, if 1000 days of demand at JVC were simulated, one would expect demand to be zero on approximately 100 days (since $P(X = 0) = .10$), one on approximately 150 days (since $P(X = 1) = .15$) and so on. However, there should be no pattern, such as demand is zero on days 1, 11, 21, etc.

Random Number Mappings

One way to simulate random events that follow the desired probability distribution would be to generate numbers between 00 and 99 so that each number has an equal likelihood of being selected (e.g., follows a discrete uniform distribution). We could then assign 10 of these numbers to correspond to the event "daily demand = 0," 15 of the numbers to correspond to the event "daily demand = 1," and so on. Since each number between 00 and 99 has an equal likelihood of being selected, the probability of any one number being selected is 1/100. Hence, if 10 of the numbers are assigned to the event "daily demand = 0," this event will occur with a probability of .10.

The easiest way to do this assignment is to let the first 10 numbers correspond to the event "daily demand = 0," the next 15 numbers correspond to the event "daily demand = 1," and so on. This process is called a *random number mapping* because it "maps" a random number (the number corresponding to the ball selected) to the outcome of a simulated event (the daily demand for jaw breakers). Table 10.2 shows the random number mapping for JVC.[1]

TABLE 10.2   Random Number Mapping for JVC

Daily Demand (X)	Corresponding Random Numbers
0	00–09
1	10–24
2	25–44
3	45–74
4	75–94
5	95–99

The Cumulative Distribution Approach for a Random Number Mapping

Although this approach works well for discrete random variables, a more comprehensive approach is required for continuous distributions. One approach that can be used for both discrete and continuous distributions involves the use of the cumulative distribution function for the random variable, X. A cumulative distribution, $F(x)$, gives the probability that X is less than or equal to some value, x; that is, $F(x) = P(X \leq x)$. Table 10.3 provides the cumulative distribution function for customer arrivals in the JVC problem. This is illustrated graphically in Figure 10.1.

TABLE 10.3   Cumulative Distribution for Customer Arrivals

x	$F(x) = P(X \leq x)$
0	.10
1	.25
2	.45
3	.75
4	.95
5	1.00

[1] Two-digit numbers are used because the probability distribution for X is accurate to two decimal places. If the probabilities were accurate to three decimal places, three-digit numbers would be used, that is, 000–999. Similarly, if the probabilities were accurate to only one decimal place, one-digit numbers, 0–9 would be used.

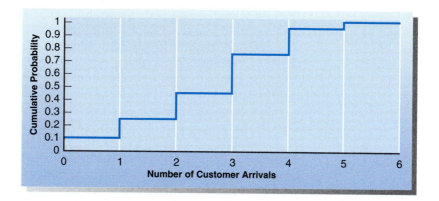

FIGURE 10.1
Cumulative Distribution for Customer Arrivals

Now if a random number Y (between 0 and 1) is chosen, we can determine the value for the event by finding the smallest value for x such that $F(x) \geq Y$. For example, suppose the number 34 is chosen. Since we are using only two-digit probabilities, the number 34 is converted to the two-digit decimal .34. Referring to the cumulative distribution function in Figure 10.1, you will note the smallest value of x such that $F(x) \geq .34$ is 2. This is the same value for demand we obtained using the random number mapping in Table 10.2. As we shall illustrate in this chapter, the VLOOKUP function in Excel can be used to easily determine the random variable value corresponding to a selected random number.

Generating Random Numbers

One way to generate numbers between 00 and 99 would be to mark each of one hundred balls, each with a different two-digit number and put them in a box. A random number could then be generated by selecting one ball at random from the box, looking at the number and then replacing the ball.

Of course, in practice, balls are not selected out of a box. Instead, this process is mimicked as closely as possible on a computer by using a **random number generator**. A random number generator actually generates what are called *pseudo-random numbers* ("pseudo" means false) because the numbers are not *truly* random but are obtained using a mathematical formula.

A random number generator begins with a starting value, known as a *seed* (which the user can supply), and produces a sequence of numbers that meets the following statistical properties for randomness:

1. Each number has an equally likely chance of occurring.
2. There is no apparent correlation between the numbers generated by the mathematical formula.

Appendix 10.2 on the accompanying CD-ROM describes a commonly used technique for generating pseudo-random numbers, known as the *linear congruential method*.

In Excel, pseudo-random numbers can be generated by using the RAND() function or the Random Number Generation option found in Data Analysis under Tools on the menu bar. The RAND() function returns a uniformly distributed random number greater than or equal to 0 and less than 1. A new random number is returned every time the worksheet is calculated. The values in Appendix C in the back of the book were generated by using the RAND() function in Excel.

If one wishes to generate uniformly distributed integer valued random numbers between two specified values, the RANDBETWEEN function can be used. For example, to generate a random valued integer between 7 and 10, one would type the formula =RANDBETWEEN(7,10).

Using Random Number Generation in Data Analysis allows one to generate numbers from a variety of different distributions. For example, in addition to the continuous uniform distribution, numbers can be generated that follow normal, Bernoulli, binomial, Poisson, or generalized discrete distributions. Information for using the Random Number Generation option in Excel can be found in Excel's Help commands.

One advantage that the Random Number Generation option has over the RAND() function is that one can specify a seed value when using Random Number Generation. The advantage of using a specific seed value is that the same set of random numbers will be generated each time the same seed is used. Using the same set of random numbers to evaluate different policies results in certain statistical efficiencies. As a result, typically fewer simulation runs are necessary to get the same level of statistical precision than when different random numbers are used to evaluate different policies.

SIMULATION OF THE JVC PROBLEM

We shall use the set of pseudo-random numbers in Appendix C to illustrate how to conduct a fixed time simulation for the JVC problem. The approach is as follows:

Beginning with day 1, a random number is selected to determine the demand for jaw breakers on that day. The demand value will be used to update the total demand to date. The simulation is repeated for a second day, then a third day, etc.; it stops once total demand to date reaches 40 or more. The number of "simulated" days required for the total demand to reach 40 or more is then recorded.

Since only two-digit random numbers are needed to generate jaw breaker demands, the simulation begins by using the first two digits in the top row of column 1 in Appendix C. For each subsequent day, a new demand is determined using the two-digit number in the next row down in column 1.

As you can see, the first number in column 1 is 6506. The first two digits of this number are 65. According to the random number mapping in Table 10.2, the random number 65 corresponds to a demand of three jaw breakers. For day 2, we use the first two digits of the random number in the second row of column 1 (77). This corresponds to a demand of 4 for day 2. Continuing down column 1 in this fashion generates the results shown in Table 10.4.

TABLE 10.4   A Typical Simulation for JVC

Day	Random Number	Demand	Total Demand to Date
1	65	3	3
2	77	4	7
3	61	3	10
4	88	4	14
5	42	2	16
6	74	3	19
7	11	1	20
8	40	2	22
9	03	0	22
10	62	3	25
11	54	3	28
12	10	1	29
13	16	1	30
14	69	3	33
15	16	1	34
16	02	0	34
17	31	2	36
18	79	4	40

TABLE 10.5   A Second Simulation for JVC

Day	Random Number	Demand	Total Demand to Date
1	42	2	2
2	74	3	5
3	93	4	9
4	84	4	13
5	89	4	17
6	89	4	23
7	12	1	24
8	64	3	25
9	64	3	28
10	38	2	30
11	61	3	33
12	53	3	36
13	12	1	37
14	76	4	41

In this simulation, we see that it took 18 days to sell 40 jaw breakers, two days more than the 16 days Bill had originally estimated. It is difficult, however, to draw any firm conclusions based on only one simulation run. To get a better estimate, additional simulation runs should be conducted and the results averaged.

Let us now perform a second simulation run by using the random numbers in column 15 in Appendix C. Table 10.5 shows these results. This time it took 14 days to sell 40 or more jaw breakers. Note, also, that by day 14 the total demand was 41 jaw breakers rather than 40.

Programmers often use flow charts to guide the development of a computer program for problem solving. Figure 10.2 shows a possible flow chart that could be used to perform the above JVC jaw breaker simulation.

Using Simulation Results to Conduct Hypothesis Tests

The purpose of performing the simulation runs is to determine whether the average number of days required to sell 40 jaw breakers is, in fact, 16. Neither run gave a value of 16; however, the *average* of the times of the two runs, 18 and 14, is 16. As additional simulation runs are done, the laws of probability suggest that the calculated average should become closer and closer to the true average. Thus, for the JVC problem, to test whether or not $\mu = 16$, the following two-tailed hypothesis test is performed:

$$H_O: \mu = 16$$
$$H_A: \mu \neq 16$$

If it is assumed that the distribution of the number of days to sell 40 jaw breakers, x, is approximately normal, then since the population variance is unknown, a t-test would be performed. If n is the number of simulation runs the test would have n − 1 degrees of freedom (df). To conduct this test, a level of significance, α, which is the probability of concluding that the alternate hypothesis, H_A, is true when it in fact is *not* must be selected. Then for a two-tailed test, the interval $-t_{\alpha/2,d.f.}$ to $+t_{\alpha/2,d.f.}$ is constructed. If the test statistic t lies outside this interval, the conclusion is that the alternate hypothesis is true (and the null hypothesis is false). If the test statistic lies within this interval, there is *not* enough evidence to conclude that the alternate hypothesis is true.

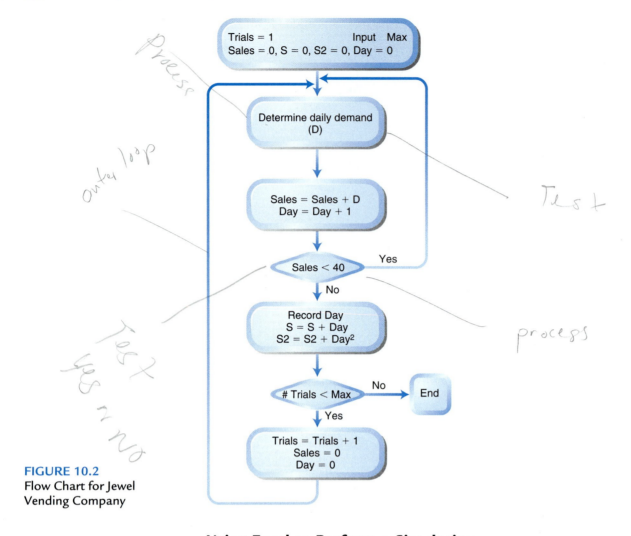

FIGURE 10.2
Flow Chart for Jewel
Vending Company

Using Excel to Perform a Simulation

Figure 10.3 shows the worksheet and formulas used to simulate the JVC problem using Excel. This simulation was set up as follows:

- Using IF statements, the day is printed in column A if 40 or fewer jaw breakers have been sold by that day.
- Daily demand is generated in column B using random variables and the VLOOKUP command shown on Figure 10.3. The lookup table, given in columns K and L, is based on the cumulative demand probabilities.
- The cumulative demand is generated in column C by summing the daily demand and the previous day's cumulative demand.
- Assuming it will never take more than 100 days to sell 40 jaw breakers, the formulas in cells A6:C6 are dragged 100 rows to cells A105:C105.
- The maximum number in column A is the number of simulated days it will take to sell 40 or more jaw breakers. This value is given in cell F1.
- Replication of this simulation can be made in Excel by pressing the **F9 function key** on the keyboard.

To test the hypothesis that the average number of days to sell 40 or more jaw breakers differs from 16, 10 such replications were performed. The results of these 10 replications are given in columns A and B of Figure 10.4.

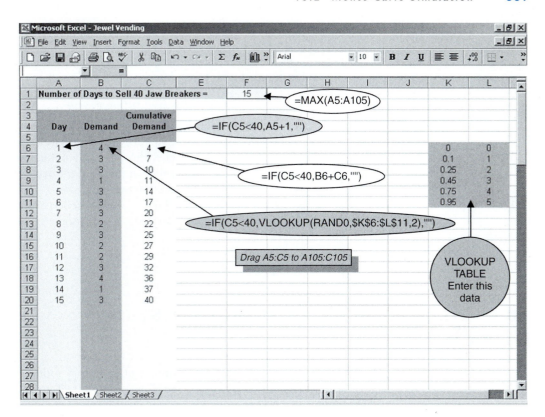

FIGURE 10.3   Excel Output—Simulation Run for JVC

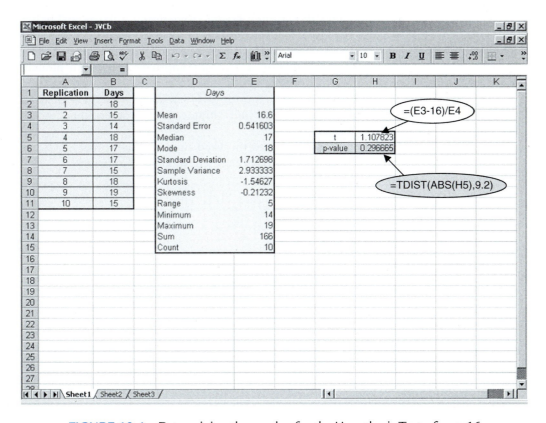

FIGURE 10.4   Determining the p-value for the Hypothesis Test of $\mu = 16$

To perform the two-tailed test, the t statistic must first be calculated. An easy way to do this is to generate the mean and standard error of the data in column B using Tools/Data Analysis/Descriptive Statistics. (Make sure Summary Statistics is checked in the dialogue box.) These values are given in column E of Figure 10.4. Then t = (Mean − 16)/(Standard Error). Once the t value is found, the p-value for the test is generated by the formula =TDIST(ABS (t-value), degrees of freedom, 2), in this case =TDIST(ABS(H5),9,2).

As can be seen from Figure 10.4, the p-value is quite high (.2967) compared to any reasonable significance level such as α = .05. Thus, *based on this data*, we cannot conclude that the mean number of days differs from 16. Collecting additional sample evidence could lead to a different conclusion.

This analysis was performed using only basic Excel spreadsheet commands. In Section 10.7 a more thorough analysis of this model using the Crystal Ball Excel add-in program is presented.

10.3 Simulation of an Inventory System Using a Fixed Time Approach

In Chapter 8 we presented a number of inventory models for which analytical solutions exist. Each was based on a particular set of assumptions. When these assumptions are not met, those models may not provide reasonable solutions. In such cases, simulation can predict the outcome of inventory policies.

By supplying the simulation with the values of parameters, such as the order and holding cost as well as the lead time and demand distributions, an average total inventory cost for a particular inventory policy can be estimated. While simulation cannot be used to determine an optimal policy, it can be used to identify which policy appears to yield the best results from the set of policies being considered.

Frequently, a *fixed time* approach is used for modeling an inventory system. In this approach, the system is monitored and updated at fixed time intervals (daily, weekly, monthly). During each time period, activities associated with demands, orders, and shipments are determined, and the system is updated accordingly.

To illustrate the fixed time simulation approach, we consider the inventory situation faced by the Allen Appliance Company.

AAC inventory.xls
allen(r,q).xls

ALLEN APPLIANCE COMPANY

Allen Appliance Company (AAC) is a small appliance wholesaler that stocks the KitchenChef electric mixer. Each unit costs Allen $200. Allen, in turn, sells them for $260 each. Allen uses an annual holding cost rate for the mixers of 26%. Orders are placed at the end of the week, and order costs seem to average about $45. Lead time for the receipt of orders from Kitchen Chef has been fairly consistent, averaging two weeks.

Management believes that if the company runs out of the mixers, all customers will backorder. Allen estimates that it will suffer a weekly goodwill cost due to future lost sales of $5 per backordered unit. The company also incurs a fixed administrative cost of $2 for each unit backordered, regardless of the length of time it is backordered.

Allen believes that the number of customers who arrive weekly can be approximated by the following distribution:

Number of Arrivals Per Week	Probability
0	.10
1	.30
2	.25
3	.20
4	.15

The number of machines each customer wishes to purchase can be approximated by the following distribution.

Demand Per Customer	Probability
1	.10
2	.15
3	.40
4	.35

Mixers arrive at the beginning of a week. That is, an order placed at the end of week 2 will arrive at the beginning of week 5. Allen wishes to determine an optimal inventory policy for the KitchenChef mixer.

SOLUTION

One approach is to apply the planned shortage model discussed in Chapter 8. While values for the order cost, C_o = $45, the weekly per unit backorder cost, C_s = $5, the administrative backorder cost, C_b = $2, and the lead time, L = 2 are given, estimates are needed for the average weekly demand, D, and the per unit weekly holding cost, C_h.

To estimate the average weekly demand, note that the average number of retailers who arrive each week is:

$$.10(0) + .30(1) + .25(2) + .20(3) + .15(4) = 2$$

The average demand for each retailer who purchases mixers is:

$$.10(1) + .15(2) + .40(3) + .35(4) = 3 \text{ units}$$

The average demand is found by multiplying the average number of retailers who arrive (2) by the average retailer demand (3). This gives an average weekly demand, D = 2*3 = 6 units.

The unit weekly holding cost, C_h, is:

$$C_h = \frac{(\text{annual holding cost rate})*(\text{wholesale cost per unit})}{52 \text{ weeks per year}}$$
$$= (.26*\$200/52) = \$1 \text{ per unit per week}$$

If this problem is solved using the planned shortage worksheet on the inventory.xls template by assuming demand is a constant 6 units per week, the results are those shown in Figure 10.5.

AAC inventory.xls

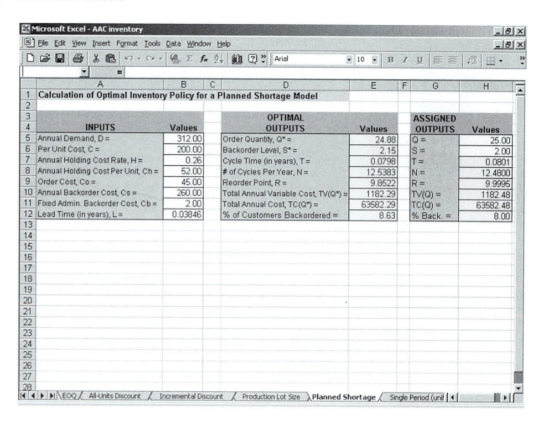

FIGURE 10.5 Excel Spreadsheet for Solving Allen Appliance Problem as a Planned Shortage Model

This output indicates an optimal inventory policy is to order 24.88 units, which should arrive when the backorder level reaches 2.15. Rounding these values gives an inventory policy of ordering 25 mixers when the inventory on hand reaches 10 units. Because the weekly demand is a random quantity, however, Allen has some concern that the solution generated by the planned shortage model may not be the optimal policy.

Selecting the Inventory System

Allen is considering implementing a continuous review system to monitor its inventory position. As discussed in Chapter 8, two types of continuous review systems are (1) the order point, order up to level (R,M) inventory system, and (2) the order point, order quantity (R,Q) inventory system.

Under both systems, orders are placed when the inventory level reaches R units or less. In an (R,M) system, the firm orders enough inventory to bring the inventory level back up to a projected level of M when the order arrives. In an (R,Q) system, the firm simply orders Q units each time an order is placed.

Based on the planned shortage results, Allen is considering using an (R,Q) system of ordering 25 mixers when inventory on hand reaches 10 units or less for controlling this inventory. To analyze the cost of using the policy, Allen has decided to develop a simulation model.

Using the specified probability distributions for the number of customer arrivals and customer demands, the random number mappings are shown in Tables 10.6 and 10.7.

TABLE 10.6   Random Number Mapping for Customer Arrivals

Number of Customer Arrivals	Random Number Mapping
0	00–09
1	10–39
2	40–64
3	65–84
4	85–99

TABLE 10.7   Random Number Mapping for Customer Demand

Demand Per Customer	Random Number Mapping
1	00–09
2	10–24
3	25–64
4	65–99

We will assume that holding and shortage costs are based on the inventory at the end of the week. While this may not be totally correct, it should produce fairly accurate results in terms of identifying the best policy.

To perform any simulation, the modeler must first decide what quantities to keep track of. Usually, if one thinks "chronologically," these quantities become apparent. For the Allen Appliance problem,

- Determine the **beginning inventory** for the week. This will equal the ending inventory of the previous week plus any order that has arrived.
- Then determine the **number of retailers** who will order.
- For each retailer that places an order, determine the **number of mixers demanded**.
- The sum of these demands gives the **total weekly demand**.
- The **ending inventory** of mixers for the week equals the inventory on hand at the beginning of the week less this weekly demand. Note that a negative quantity implies a backorder situation.
- Then determine if an **order is placed**. This will occur if the inventory on hand at the end of the week is at or below the reorder point and *no orders are outstanding*.
- Adjust the **lead time** until the delivery of an order, if applicable.
- Calculate the simulated weekly costs by adding the week's holding, ordering, and backordering costs.

Table 10.8 reflects a 10-week simulation for Allen Appliance using column 1 of Appendix C to generate the number of customers who arrive during the week and column 2 of Appendix C to generate the demand for each customer. The simulation begins in week 1 assuming a beginning inventory of 25 units.

The weekly order costs are calculated by (Order Cost) + $1(Stock on Hand) + $2(New Backorders) + $5(Total Backorders). The total cost over the 10-week period is calculated by summing the amounts in the weekly cost column. This gives a total cost of $422 or an average of $42.20 per week.

TABLE 10.8 10-Week Simulation for Allen Appliance Company

Week	Beginning Inventory	Random # (Col. 1)	# of Customers	Random # (Col. 2)	Customer Demand	Weekly Demand	Ending Inventory	Order Placed?	Lead Time	Weekly Cost
1	25	65	3	33	3					
				98	4					
				26	3	10	15	No	—	$15
2	15	77	3	91	4					
				96	4					
				48	3	11	4	Yes	2	$49
3	4	61	2	82	4					
				27	3	7	−3	No	1	$21
4	−3	88	4	96	4					
				46	3					
				20	2					
				44	3	12	−15	No	0	$99
5	10	42	2	84	4					
				94	4	8	2	Yes	2	$47
6	2	74	3	66	4					
				63	3					
				75	4	11	−9	No	1	$63
7	−9	11	1	05	1	1	−10	No	0	$52
8	15	40	2	10	2					
				18	2	4	11	No	—	$11
9	11	03	0				11	No	—	$11
10	11	62	2	03	1					
				07	1		9	Yes	2	$54

To get a better sense of the average cost, the simulation should be performed over many more than 10 weeks. To do this, we can construct an Excel spreadsheet to perform the simulation. Figure 10.6 gives a copy of the spreadsheet used to perform this simulation. The average weekly cost is based on simulating 1000 weeks of operation. As we can see from this simulation run, the average cost over the 1000 weeks is $32.72 per week as compared to the $42.20 calculated for doing the 10-week simulation.

The spreadsheet calculates the Total Cost in column I by summing the holding cost, ordering cost, and backorder costs. These costs are in columns F, G, and H, which are hidden in Figure 10.6. Also hidden in the figure are columns containing random numbers that are used to determine the number of customer arrivals and the total demand during each week. To see the formulas used in this spreadsheet, the interested reader may wish to examine file allen(r,q).xls on the accompanying CD-ROM.

Appendix 10.3 on the accompanying CD-ROM discusses a number of statistical techniques that can be used to analyze the results of simulation runs and compare different policies.

allen(r,q).xls

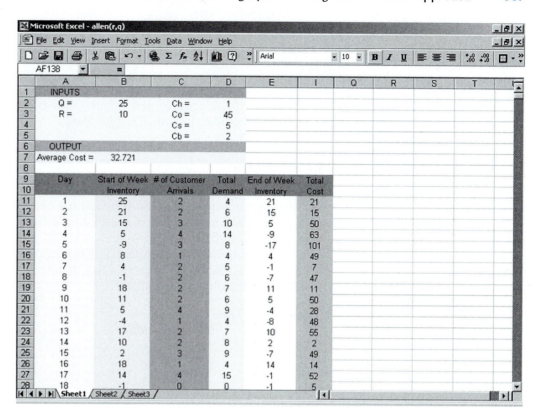

FIGURE 10.6 Excel Spreadsheet for Simulating the Allen Appliance Problem

10.4 Simulation of a Queuing System Using a Next-Event Approach

Management scientists frequently use simulation to analyze queues. While closed-form solutions for operating characteristics of several queuing situations were presented in Chapter 9, these models were based on a number of simplifying assumptions. For example, it was assumed that if a system has multiple servers, all servers work at the same rate. In many businesses (such as supermarkets that operate express check-out lines), this assumption simply is not valid. The queuing models in Chapter 9 also assumed that the interarrival times of customers follow an exponential distribution. Since in many queuing situations one or both of these assumptions may not be true, the models presented in Chapter 9 would not be valid.

NEXT-EVENT SIMULATION

When the underlying assumptions necessary to obtain closed-form solutions are not met, simulation can be used to estimate the steady-state values. In this section we present a **next-event simulation** model for a queuing process. In a next-event simulation, the simulated data are updated when a particular event occurs (such as the arrival or departure of a customer) rather than after a specific period of time (as is the case in a fixed time simulation).

Next-event simulations can be modeled using a **process-interaction approach** in which each iteration traces all relevant processes incurred by an item in the system under study. For example, in a queuing system the simulation considers everything that happens to a particular customer as he or she moves through the system. This includes arrival time, waiting time, selection of server(s), and service time(s). The next-event approach is preferred to a fixed time approach for simulating most queuing systems in part because if a fixed time approach were used, there would be many time periods in which no activity occurred and hence the simulation would be quite inefficient.

To illustrate the concept of developing a next-event simulation model for a queuing system, consider the case of Capital Bank.

Capital Bank.xls

CAPITAL BANK

Capital Bank serves the community of Valley Glen. The bank is open weekdays from 9 A.M. to 4 P.M. (6 P.M. on Fridays) and has five teller positions. To better serve its customers, management is considering opening the bank on Saturday morning from 9 A.M. to noon.

During the Saturday morning period, management believes that the interarrival time of customers will be between a half minute and two minutes, according to the following probability distribution:

Interarrival Time (minutes)	Probability
.5	.65
1	.15
1.5	.15
2	.05

Management is considering staffing the bank with Ann Doss, the head teller and two associate tellers, Bill Lee, and Carla Dominguez. Because of Ann's experience, on the average, she serves customers faster than the two associate tellers. In particular, her service time will be between half a minute and three and a half minutes, with the following probability distribution:

Ann's Service Time (minutes)	Probability
.5	.05
1	.10
1.5	.20
2	.30
2.5	.20
3	.10
3.5	.05

It is estimated that the time it takes either of the two associate tellers to serve a customer is between one minute and four and a half minutes, with the following probability distribution:

Bill and Carla's Service Time (minutes)	Probability
1	.05
1.5	.15
2	.20
2.5	.30
3	.10
3.5	.10
4	.05
4.5	.05

The bank uses a first-come, first-served priority rule for serving customers. Management would like to use simulation to determine the anticipated average customer waiting time on Saturday morning.

SOLUTION

Before developing the simulation model, let us determine if the requirement for steady-state will be satisfied. Here,

$$E(\text{Interarrival Time}) = \frac{1}{\lambda} = .5(.65) + 1(.15) + 1.5(.15) + 2(.05) = .80 \text{ minute}$$

This is equivalent to $\lambda = 1/.80 = 1.25$ customers per minute or $60*1.25 = 75$ customers per hour.

$$E(\text{Service Time} - \text{Ann}) = .5(.05) + 1(.10) + 1.5(.20) + 2(.30) + 2.5(.2) + 3(.10) + 3.5(.05) = 2 \text{ minutes}$$

$$E(\text{Service Time} - \text{Bill or Carla}) = 1(.05) + 1.5(.15) + 2(.20) + 2.5(.3) + 3(.10) + 3.5(.10) + 4(.05) + 4.5(.05) = 2.5 \text{ min.}$$

Hence Ann can serve $60/2 = 30$ customers per hour, and Bill and Carla can each serve $60/2.5 = 24$ customers per hour. Thus the average number of customers who can be served per hour is $30 + 2*24 = 78$. Since this is greater than the arrival rate of 75, steady-state will be reached.

The first step in developing the simulation is to determine the random number mappings. Based on the given probabilities, the random number mappings shown in Tables 10.9a, b and c were developed.

Table 10.10 shows the results of a 20-customer simulation using random numbers from column 4 of Appendix C to determine the customer interarrival times and numbers from column 5 to determine the customer service times.

TABLE 10.9a   Customer Interarrival Time

Time	Random #'s
.5 minute	00–64
1 minute	65–79
1.5 minutes	80–94
2 minutes	95–99

TABLE 10.9b   Ann's Service Time

Time	Random #'s
.5 minute	00–04
1 minute	05–14
1.5 minutes	15–34
2 minutes	35–64
2.5 minutes	65–84
3 minutes	85–94
3.5 minutes	95–99

TABLE 10.9c   Bill and Carla's Service Time

Time	Random #'s
1 minute	00–04
1.5 minutes	05–19
2 minutes	20–39
2.5 minutes	40–69
3 minutes	70–79
3.5 minutes	80–89
4 minutes	90–94
4.5 minutes	95–99

TABLE 10.10   Capital Bank Simulation for 20 Customer Arrivals

Customer	Random Number	Arrival Time	Random Number	Ann Start	Ann Finish	Bill Start	Bill Finish	Carla Start	Carla Finish	Waiting Time
1	89	1.5	63	1.5	3.5					0
2	88	3	46			3	5.5			0
3	90	4.5	86	4.5	7.5					0
4	26	5	00					5	6	0
5	79	6	56			6	8.5			0
6	55	6.5	67					6.5	9	0
7	26	7	59	7.5	9.5					0.5
8	16	7.5	28			8.5	10.5			1
9	40	8	79					9	12	1
10	65	9	64	9.5	11.5					0.5
11	61	9.5	33			10.5	12.5			1
12	68	10.5	81	11.5	14					1
13	75	11.5	17					12	13.5	0.5
14	65	12.5	63			12.5	15			0
15	08	13	66					13.5	16	0.5
16	31	13.5	27	14	15.5					0.5
17	20	14	04			15	16			1
18	40	14.5	34	15.5	17					1
19	99	16.5	07			16.5	18			0
20	09	17	69	17	19.5					0

The simulation prceeds as follows:

- A customer will go to Ann if she is free.
- If Ann is not free, the customer will go to Bill if he is free.
- If both Bill and Ann are busy, the customer will go to Carla if she is free.
- If all tellers are busy, the customer waits in line and then goes to the first teller who becomes available.
- The waiting time for a customer represents the time a customer spends in line prior to beginning service. This is calculated by taking the difference between the time the customer begins service and the time the customer arrives.

Let us examine a few of the customer arrivals to understand how the simulation is carried out. For customer 1 the random number used to determine the interarrival time is 89 (the first number in column 4 of Appendix C). Using the random number mapping in Table 10.9a this corresponds to an interarrival time of 1.5 minutes. Hence the arrival time of customer 1 is time 1.5. Since all three servers are free, customer 1 is served by Ann. The random number for customer 1's service time is 63 (the first number in column 5 of Appendix C). Using Table 10.9b for the random number mapping for Ann, this corresponds to a service time of 2 minutes. Hence for customer 1 service begins at time 1.5 (the time the customer arrives) and is completed at time 3.5 (arrival time 1.5 plus service time of 2). Thus Ann is busy serving customer 1 until time 3.5.

The interarrival time for customer 2 is determined by the random number 88 (the second number in column 4). From Table 10.9a this also corresponds to an interarrival time of 1.5 minutes. Since customer 1 arrived at time 1.5, this means that customer 2 arrives at time 3. Since Ann is busy at time 3, customer 2 is served by Bill. The random number for customer 2's service time is 46 (the second number in column 5). Using Table 10.9c the random number mapping for the associate tellers, the random number of 46 corresponds to a service time of 2.5 minutes. Hence customer 2 will complete service at time 5.5 (the arrival time of 3 plus the service time of 2.5) and Bill will be busy serving customer 2 during this time.

This process is repeated for all customers. Since both the first and second customers were served immediately, their waiting times are 0. To illustrate a customer for whom the waiting time is not 0, consider customer 7 who arrives at time 7. At this time all three servers are busy. The first server who becomes free is Ann at time 7.5. Hence service for customer 7 begins at time 7.5, and the waiting time for customer 7 is .5, the difference between the time service begins (7.5) and the time the customer arrives (7).

To estimate the average customer waiting time, you might think that we should simply add the values in the Waiting Time column and divide by the number of customers in the simulation (20). This would give an average waiting time of 8.5/20 = .425 minute. But as with most queuing simulations that start empty, there is a certain start up bias associated with the first several customers before the system reaches steady state. Hence a number of the initial waiting time values should be excluded from the calculation of the average waiting time.

If the first 10 customers are excluded then the average waiting time of the last 10 customers can be used to give the estimated average waiting time of 5.5/10 = .55 minute. This is probably a more valid estimate of the average customer waiting time. Of course, the true average customer waiting time may in fact be very different from .425 or .55 minute. A different set of simulation numbers would most likely generate a different value for the average waiting time. Doing a 20-customer simulation does not give enough waiting time values to yield a very accurate estimate.

However, one would not want to have to do a simulation of 10,000, 1000, or even 100 customers by hand. Fortunately, Excel spreadsheets can be constructed to do this simulation. Figure 10.7 shows such a portion of the spreadsheet Capital Bank.xls, given on the accompanying CD-ROM, that simulates 1000 customer arrivals. Note that both the time a customer spends in line and the time a customer spends in the system are calculated on this spreadsheet. With this

Capital Bank.xls

Average Waiting Time in Line = 1.432
Average Waiting Time in System = 3.732

Customer	Random Number	Arrival Time	Random Number	Ann Start	Ann Finish	Bill Start	Bill Finish	Carla Start	Carla Finish	Waiting Time Line	Waiting Time System
1	0.42	0.5	0.01	0.5	1					0	0.5
2	0.19	1.0	0.02	1	1.5					0	0.5
3	0.52	1.5	0.28	1.5	3					0	1.5
4	0.61	2.0	0.27			2	4			0	2.0
5	0.45	2.5	0.80					2.5	5.5	0	3.0
6	0.38	3.0	0.39	3	5					0	2.0
7	0.29	3.5	0.74			4	7			0.5	3.5
8	0.47	4.0	0.63	5	7					1	3.0
9	0.46	4.5	0.81					5.5	9	1	4.5
10	0.78	5.5	0.57	7	9					1.5	3.5
11	0.58	6.0	0.61			7	9.5			1	3.5
12	0.21	6.5	0.49	9	11					2.5	4.5
13	0.33	7.0	0.40					9	11.5	2	4.5
14	0.94	8.5	0.33			9.5	11.5			1	3.0
15	0.09	9.0	0.44	11	13					2	4.0
16	0.84	10.5	0.83			11.5	15			1	4.5
17	0.78	11.5	0.41					11.5	14	0	2.5
18	0.07	12.0	0.73	13	15.5					1	3.5
19	0.84	13.5	0.48					14	16.5	0.5	3.0
20	0.80	14.5	0.83			15	18.5			0.5	4.0
21	0.38	15.0	0.65	15.5	18					0.5	3.0

Interarrival Time

0	0.5
0.65	1
0.8	1.5
0.95	2

Ann	Service Time
0	0.5
0.05	1
0.15	1.5
0.35	2
0.65	2.5
0.85	3
0.95	3.5

Bill/Carla	Service Time
0	1
0.05	1.5
0.2	2
0.4	2.5
0.7	3
0.8	3.5
0.9	4
0.95	4.5

FIGURE 10.7
Excel Spreadsheet for Performing Capital Bank Simulation

many customers in the system, the start-up bias should have little effect and has been ignored.

The formulas for the spreadsheet shown in Figure 10.7 are discussed in Appendix 10.4 on the accompanying CD-ROM. It can be seen, however, that the simulation calculates the average waiting time in line in cell E1 and the average waiting time in the system in cell E2. Little's formulas can be used to determine the average number of customers in line and in the system. Specifically, the average number of customers in line and in the system are found by multiplying the average arrival rate by the simulated results for the average waiting time in line and in the system respectively.

Since for this problem, the expected interarrival time is .80 minute, the arrival rate, λ, is $1/.80 = 1.25$ customers per minute. Hence we have the following values from this simulation.

Average Customer Waiting Time in Line (W_q) = 1.432 minutes
Average Customer Waiting Time in the System (W) = 3.732 minutes
Average Number of Customers Waiting in Line (L_q) = 1.25*1.432 = 1.790
Average Number of Customers in the System (L) = 1.25*3.732 = 4.665

Using a Fixed Time versus a Next-Event Approach

Although it is generally easier to understand a fixed time simulation process, the majority of discrete simulations are carried out using the next-event approach. The reason for this is that simulations generally deal with events that do not occur in regular time intervals, and therefore the fixed time approach would not be very efficient.

For example, we could have conceivably developed the simulation model for the Capital Bank problem using a fixed time approach. However, we would have had to standardize the time unit at .5 minute (the largest time unit that divides into all possible interarrival and service times). Hence, if the fixed time approach were used there would be a great many periods in which there were no arrivals or completions of service. For example, in Table 10.10 it can be seen that after 20 customers the simulated time has reached 17 minutes. If a fixed time simulation with a time interval of .5 had been used, 20 time periods would have only simulated a time of 10 minutes.

10.5 Random Number Mappings for Continuous Random Variables

In Section 10.2 two methods for generating random variables corresponding to discrete probability distributions were illustrated. One used the probability distribution itself, and the other used the cumulative distribution function, F(x). In this section, techniques for simulating continuous random variables are discussed.

THE EXPLICIT INVERSE DISTRIBUTION METHOD

In the **explicit inverse distribution method** the cumulative distribution function, F(x), is used to determine a value for the random variable. In particular, an equation, known as the *inverse distribution function*, which expresses x in terms of F(x) is developed. A pseudo-random number, Y, which corresponds to a uniformly distributed random variable between 0 and 1 is then generated, and the inverse distribution function is used to find the value of x that corresponds to Y = F(x). For example, if the random number Y = .37268, is generated, the simulated event has a value x, such that F(x) = .37268.

To illustrate this technique, consider the M/M/k queuing system discussed in Chapter 9. In this model, an exponential distribution describes customer interarrival times. A different exponential distribution describes customer service times.

The probability density function for the exponential distribution of the service time is:

$$f(x) = \mu e^{-ux} \qquad \text{for } x \geq 0 \tag{10.1}$$

and its cumulative distribution is:

$$F(x) = 1 - e^{-\mu x} \tag{10.2}$$

In these expressions, μ is the server's mean service *rate*, and $1/\mu$ is the server's mean service *time*.

If Y is a random number generated from a uniform distribution over the interval from 0 to 1, a simulated service time, x, is generated by finding the value of x such that

$$Y = 1 - e^{-\mu x} \tag{10.3}$$

Rearranging these terms gives:

$$e^{-\mu x} = 1 - Y \tag{10.4}$$

Taking logarithms of both sides of Equation 10.4 to solve for x gives:

$$-\mu x = \ln(1 - Y) \tag{10.5}$$

or

$$x = \frac{-\ln(1 - Y)}{\mu} \tag{10.6}$$

In Equation 10.6, the time units for x are the same as those for μ. Thus, if μ is expressed in terms of customers per minute, x is in terms of minutes.

To illustrate the use of Equation 10.6, consider a queuing process that has an exponential service time distribution with an average service time of $1/\mu = .5$ minute. The service rate, therefore, is $\mu = 1/.5 = 2$ per minute. Using the *second* column of Appendix C to simulate service times we see that the first value is .3338. Hence, using Equation 10.6 gives the following service time, x:

$$x = \frac{-\ln(1 - .3338)}{2} = .203 \text{ minute}$$

Excel can be used to generate exponential service times using its RAND() and LN functions as shown in Figure 10.8.

Notice that in this simulation, although the mean value for the service time is .5 minute, the 10 values we generated using Excel range from a low of .0088 minute to a high of 2.0442 minutes.

explicit inverse.xls

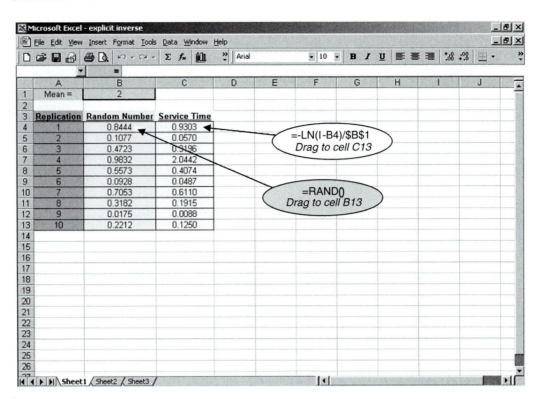

FIGURE 10.8   Excel Simulation of Service Times Using the Explicit Inverse Distribution Method

THE INTERPOLATION METHOD

Although it is easy to map pseudo-random numbers in the case of the exponential distribution, such mapping is not always so simple because it may not be possible to obtain a closed-form solution for x in terms of F(x). In such cases, the *interpolation method* can be used instead of the explicit inverse method. This method is described in Appendix 10.5 on the accompanying CD-ROM.

RANDOM NUMBERS AND EXCEL

When using Excel, a number of continuously distributed random variables can be generated. For example, if one wishes to generate a normally distributed random variable with mean μ and standard deviation σ, one could use the function =NORMINV (Rand(),μ,σ). To illustrate, suppose that a traffic engineer believes that the speed at which cars travel down a certain road is normally distributed with a mean of 35 mph and a standard deviation of 3 mph and she wishes to develop a simulation to investigate the impact of a stoplight on this street. Using the NORMINV[2] function to generate the speeds of 20 cars gives the spreadsheet shown in Figure 10.9.

For this set of numbers, the mean value is 34.72 and the standard deviation is 3.80. These values are very close to the true mean and standard deviation of the distribution.

In addition to generating normally distributed random variables, Excel can generate random variables from a Beta distribution (use the function BETAINV), a Chi Square distribution (use the function CHIINV), an F distribution (use the

[2] The function NORMSINV generates normally distributed random variables from a standard normal distribution (mean of 0 and standard deviation of 1).

traffic.xls

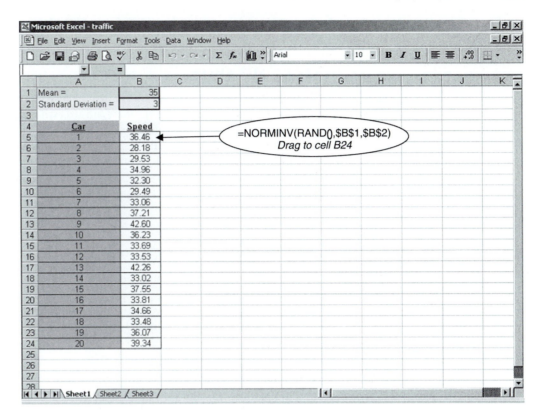

FIGURE 10.9 Twenty Normally Distributed Values Generated by Excel

function FINV), a Gamma distribution (use the function GAMMAINV), and a lognormal distribution (use the function LOGINV).

As mentioned earlier in the chapter, Excel can also generate random numbers following some specific distributions using Random Number Generation found under Data Analysis. One drawback of this technique, however, is that a series of numbers following the desired distribution is placed into cells rather than the formulas that generate the random numbers. This can present certain shortcomings when one wishes to use Excel add-ins to do multiple simulation runs.

10.6 Simulation of an M/M/1 Queue

In Section 10.4 it was illustrated how one could simulate a queuing system with three servers in which the arrival process did not meet the conditions for a Poisson process and did not have identical service distributions for each server. In this section, a simulation for an M/M/1 system is presented. Although an M/M/1 system would never actually be simulated (because the closed-form steady-state results for this model are known), the simulation is done to illustrate the accuracy of the next-event queuing simulation process.

As in Section 10.4, a process-interaction approach is followed. That is, the arrival time of each customer is determined by adding a random interarrival time to the time of the previous customer's arrival. If an arriving customer finds no other customers in the system, service begins immediately; otherwise it begins when the previous customer has completed service. The time at which a customer completes service equals the time service begins plus a random service time. The average waiting time in the queue or system is estimated by keeping track of the time each simulated customer spends in the system.

To illustrate, consider the following situation faced by the Lanford Sub Shop.

LANFORD SUB SHOP

Lanford Sub Shop.xls

The Lanford Sub Shop is a small sandwich shop serving downtown Dayton, Ohio. The sole employee is the owner, Frank Lanford, who makes a customer's sandwich in an average time of one minute.

During the lunch hour period (11:30 A.M. to 1:30 P.M.), an average of 30 customers an hour arrive at the Sub Shop. Frank believes that the customer arrival process is Poisson and that his service time follows an exponential distribution. He is interested in using simulation to determine the average time a customer must wait for service.

SOLUTION

The Lanford Sub Shop can be modeled as an M/M/1 queue (see Chapter 9) with an arrival rate $\lambda = 30$ customers per hour (.5 per minute) and a service rate $\mu = 60$ customers per hour (1 per minute). A hand simulation for this operation can be performed by generating and recording the following data:

1. The number of the arriving customer (C#).
2. The random number used to determine the interarrival time (R#1).
3. The interarrival time (IAT).
4. The arrival time for the customer (AT).
5. The time at which service begins for the customer (TSB).
6. The waiting time a customer spends in line (WT).
7. The random number used to determine the service time (R#2).
8. The service time (ST).
9. The time at which service ends for the customer (TSE).

The simulation "clock" begins at time t = 0, which corresponds to 11:30 A.M. The explicit inverse method will be used to generate the interarrival times (IAT) and service times (ST). The AT, TSB, and TSE columns are times measured from time t = 0 on the simulation clock.

While separate columns could be used to select random numbers for arrival times and service times, in Table 10.11 random numbers from column 1 are used to generate both R#1 for the interarrival times and R#2 for Frank's service times for the first 10 customers. (Times given are in minutes.)

TABLE 10.11   Lanford Sub Shop Simulation for First 10 Customers

C#	R#1	IAT	AT	TSB	WT	R#2	ST	TSE
1	.6506	2.10	2.10	2.10	0	.7761	1.50	3.60
2	.6170	1.92	4.02	4.02	0	.8800	2.12	6.14
3	.4211	1.09	5.11	6.14	1.03	.7452	1.37	7.51
4	.1182	.25	5.36	7.51	2.15	.4012	.51	8.02
5	.0335	.07	5.43	8.02	2.59	.6299	.99	9.01
6	.5482	1.59	7.02	9.01	1.99	.1085	.11	9.12
7	.1698	.37	7.39	9.12	1.73	.6969	1.19	10.31
8	.1696	.37	7.76	10.31	2.55	.0267	.03	10.34
9	.3175	.76	8.52	10.34	1.82	.7959	1.59	11.93
10	.4958	1.37	9.89	11.93	2.04	.4281	.56	12.49

To illustrate how the entries for this table were obtained, consider customer 3. At this point four random numbers (two for the interarrival times and two for the service times of customers 1 and 2) would have already been used. Thus the fifth random number from column 1, (.4211) is selected to determine the interarrival time for customer 3. Using the explicit inverse method generates an interarrival time of x = $-\ln(1 - .4211)/30$ = .0182 hour = 1.09 minutes. Hence customer 3 arrives 1.09 minutes after customer 2. Since the arrival time for customer 2 occurred at a simulated clock time of 4.02 minutes, the arrival time for customer 3 would be 4.02 + 1.09 = 5.11 minutes.

Customer 2 did not complete service until 6.14 minutes. Since customer 3 cannot begin service until customer 2 leaves, the customer must wait in line 6.14 − 5.11 = 1.03 minutes.

The sixth random number from column 1 (.7452) is then selected to determine the service time for customer 3. Using the explicit inverse method .7452 generates a service time of x = $-\ln(1 - .7452)/60$ = .0228 hour = 1.37 minutes. Hence, since customer 3's service begins at clock time 6.14 and lasts 1.37 minutes, his service ends at time 6.14 + 1.37 = 7.51 minutes.

From this limited simulation run, without correcting for start-up bias, the average waiting time for a customer in the queue can be estimated by averaging the 10 customers' waiting times:

(Average waiting time for this 10 customer simulation) =
$$[0 + 0 + 1.03 + 2.15 + 2.59 + 1.99 + 1.73 + 2.55 + 1.82 + 2.04]/10 = 1.59 \text{ minutes}$$

The true steady-state value for the average customer waiting time at the Lanford Sub Shop derived from the formula for W_q in Chapter 9 is:

$$W_q = \frac{\lambda}{\mu(\mu - \lambda)} = \frac{30}{60(60 - 30)} = \frac{1}{60} \text{ hours} = 1 \text{ minute}$$

It should be no surprise that the value calculated for W_q based on a single simulation run of only 10 customers is quite different from the steady-state value. However, as the number of customers used to calculate the average waiting time increases, we would expect the calculated value for W_q to become closer to the steady-state value.

Figure 10.10 shows the simulation of the same M/M/1 queue based on 1000 customer arrivals, using Excel.

The formulas used in this spreadsheet are as follows:

Cell	Value	Formula
E4	W_q	=AVERAGE(E8:E1007)
Row 8		
A8	Customer Number	=A7+1
B8	Customer Interarrival Time	=-LN(1-RAND())/($D$1/60)
C8	Arrival Time	=B8+C7
D8	Time Service Begins	=MAX(C8,G7)
E8	Waiting Time	=D8-C8
F8	Service Time	=-LN(1-RAND())/($D$2/60)
G8	Time Service Ends	=D8+F8

The formulas in row 8 are then dragged into rows 9 through 1007.

Note that for the simulation shown in Figure 10.10, the simulated average waiting time, 1.134243, differs approximately 13% from the steady-state value for W_q. This should not be unexpected since the simulation results are based on the set of random numbers selected. As additional simulations are run, the average waiting time taken over all simulation runs should become even closer to the steady-state value for W_q.

Lanford Sub Shop.xls

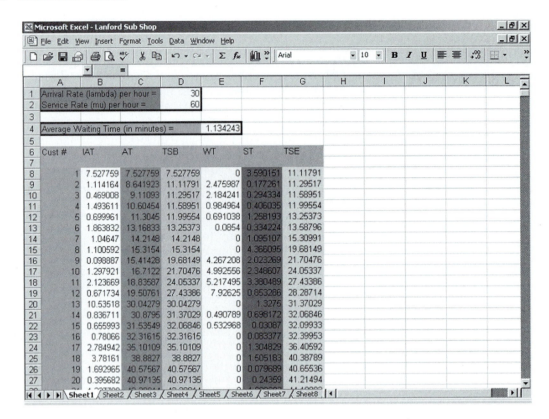

FIGURE 10.10 Simulation of an M/M/1 Queue Using Excel

10.7 Conducting Simulations Using Crystal Ball

OVERVIEW OF CRYSTAL BALL

As seen in the previous sections, running a simulation only once can lead to a value that may be far from the true mean value. To get a result that is close to the true mean value, the simulation should be run multiple times and the results of these multiple runs averaged. A number of Excel add-on modules have been developed to perform such multiple simulations. These programs also generate relevant statistics dealing with the simulation outcomes. One of the most popular software packages for doing such analyses is Crystal Ball, developed by Decisioneering, Inc. On the accompanying CD-ROM you will find a student version of Crystal Ball that can be used in performing Excel simulations. Although this version has a limited set of options as compared to the professional version, it is powerful enough to do many of the analyses one would wish to perform as part of a simulation study.

The Crystal Ball Toolbar

After loading Crystal Ball, three new menu items and a new toolbar become part of the Excel screen. The new menu items are *Cell*, *Run*, and *CBTools*, which are to the immediate left of the Help command on the toolbar. The options contained under the Cell, Run, and CBTools menus are shown in Figures 10.11*a*, 10.11*b*, and 10.11*c*.

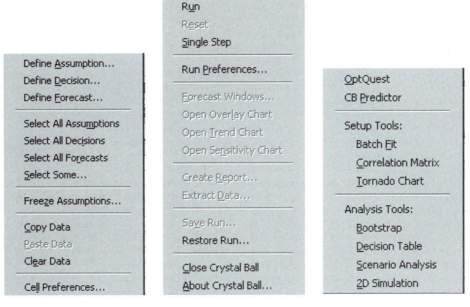

FIGURE 10.11a Cell Menu in Crystal Ball

FIGURE 10.11b Run Menu in Crystal Ball

FIGURE 10.11c CBTools Menu in Crystal Ball

Figure 10.12 shows the toolbar added by Crystal Ball:

FIGURE 10.12 Crystal Ball Toolbar

Of particular importance are the following selections:

Click on this icon to define an **assumption** (i.e., give a probability distribution) for the cell. However, in order to do this, the cell for which you wish to define an assumption must have a numeric value (e.g., it cannot be blank, contain a formula, or contain text). Typically, you would want the cell value to be equal to the mean of the desired probability distribution. Illustrations of assumptions will be given below.

Click on this icon to define a cell as a **decision variable**. Making a cell a decision variable gives the analyst the opportunity to vary the cell value during a simulation run.

Click on this icon to select the cells you wish to have the **simulation** forecast. Specifically, the forecast cells are the ones for which Crystal Ball collects relevant statistics as well as graphs of values.

Click on this icon to set up the simulation **preferences**. Of particular importance is the specification of the number of simulation runs you wish to perform and the random number seed value you wish to specify.

Click on this icon to **run** the simulation.

Click on this icon to **stop** the simulation while it is running.

Click on this icon to **reset** the simulation and clear the forecast values.

Click on this icon to **open up** the forecast.

Click on this icon to **open up an overlay chart**. Such a chart is useful in comparing different forecasts.

Hypothesis Testing Using Crystal Ball

To illustrate how one uses Crystal Ball, consider the Jewel Vending Company problem discussed in Section 10.2. Recall that Bill Jewel wishes to determine the average number of days it will take for the vending machine to sell 40 or more jaw breakers. Specifically, Bill wishes to determine whether the average number of days is 16.

File JVC.xls on the accompanying CD-ROM contains a simulation for one filling of the vending machine. Opening this file in Crystal Ball gives the screen shown in Figure 10.13. Note that columns G and H are hidden in this spreadsheet. These columns contain the lookup table used for the VLOOKUP function.

JVC.xls

Microsoft Excel - JVC
File Edit View Insert Format Tools Data Window Cell Run Help
Arial
Number of Days to Sell 40 Jaw Breakers =
16
Day
Demand
Cumulative Demand
1 5 5
2 0 5
3 3 8
4 3 11
5 4 15
6 4 19
7 1 20
8 3 23
9 3 26
10 3 29
11 1 30
12 4 34
13 0 34
14 0 34
15 3 37
16 4 41

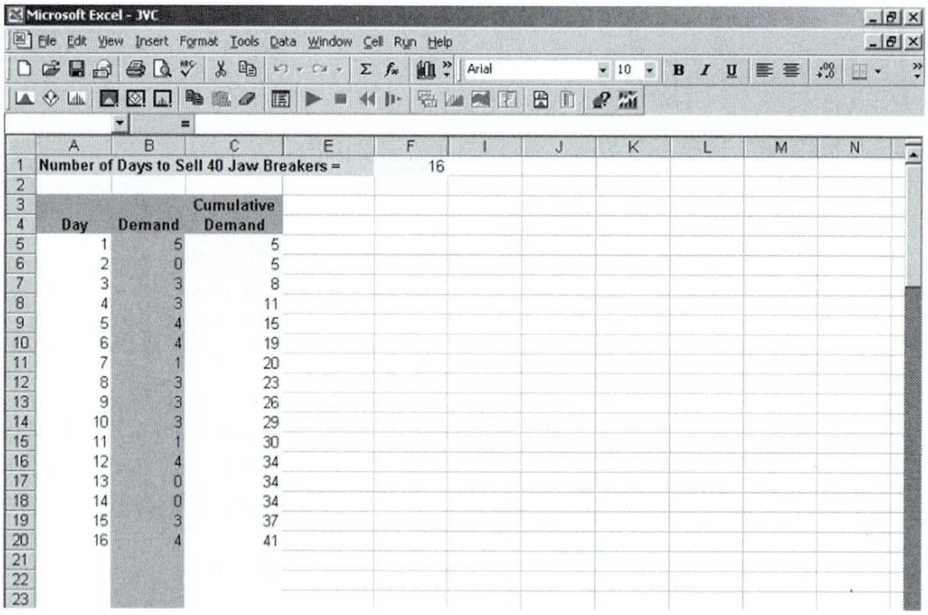

FIGURE 10.13
Crystal Ball Screen for the Jewel Vending Company Model

The following sequence of three steps is used to perform the simulation with Crystal Ball.

1. The item we wish to forecast (the number of days to sell 40 jaw breakers) is in cell F1. Highlight this cell and click on the forecast icon— . This brings the dialogue box up shown in Figure 10.14. Change the Forecast Name from F1 to Time to Sell 40 Jaw Breakers and make the Units equal to Days. Then click on OK.
2. Click the set-up preferences icon— to indicate the desired number of simulation runs (trials). This gives the dialogue box shown in Figure 10.15. Note that initially the maximum number of trials has been set to 500. Click on OK to run the simulation.

FIGURE 10.14 Crystal Ball Dialogue Box for Naming a Forecast Cell

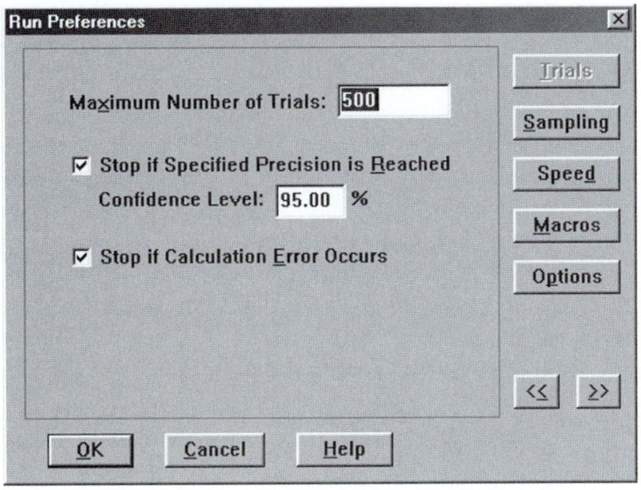

FIGURE 10.15 Crystal Ball Dialogue Box for Setting Run Preferences

3. The result is the frequency chart shown in Figure 10.16. (Your results will be somewhat different due to a different selection of random numbers by your computer.)

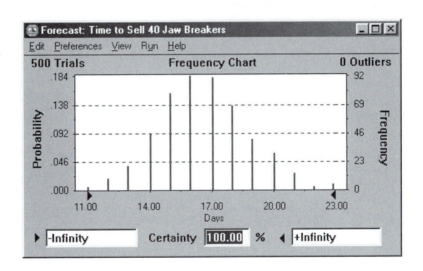

FIGURE 10.16
Crystal Ball Frequency Chart

Note: If you do not see this chart after running the simulation, you can view the chart by either clicking on the open forecast icon— 🖼 *or by selecting Forecast Window in the Run menu. This gives the dialogue box shown in Figure 10.17. Clicking on the Open All Forecasts box should give the Forecast.*

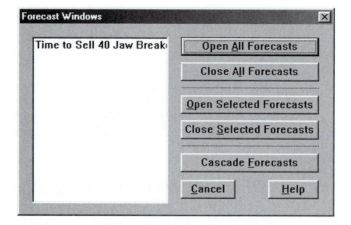

FIGURE 10.17
Crystal Ball Dialogue Box for
Opening or Closing Forecasts

Click on the View/Statistics in the menu bar to see the statistics associated with this chart. The output for the simulation is given in Figure 10.18.

Forecast: Time to Sell 40 Jaw Breakers

Edit Preferences View Run Help

Cell F1   **Statistics**

Statistic	Value
Trials	500
Mean	16.62
Median	17.00
Mode	16.00
Standard Deviation	2.19
Variance	4.80
Skewness	0.23
Kurtosis	3.04
Coeff. of Variability	0.13
Range Minimum	11.00
Range Maximum	23.00
Range Width	12.00
Mean Std. Error	0.10

FIGURE 10.18
Crystal Ball Statistical Output

ANALYSIS OF OUTPUT

Hypothesis Testing

Recall from Section 10.2 that Bill Jewel wished to do the following hypothesis test:

$$\text{Null:} \qquad H_0: \mu = 16$$
$$\text{Alternative:} \quad H_A: \mu \neq 16$$

From the frequency chart in Figure 10.16 the time to sell 40 jaw breakers appears to follow a normal distribution. (Crystal Ball actually has an option that allows one to do a goodness of fit test to check this assumption.) Assuming a normal distribution, the t distribution can be used to determine the outcome of this hypothesis test. Specifically, the t statistic is calculated by subtracting $\mu_0 = 16$ from the sample mean and dividing this amount by the mean standard error (the value in the last row of the output). From Figure 10.18 therefore the t statistic is:

$$t = \frac{mean - 16}{standard\ error} = \frac{16.62 - 16}{.10} = 6.2$$

A t statistic of 6.2 is clearly significant. Thus it can be concluded that the average number of days to sell 40 or more jaw breakers is not equal to 16.

Confidence Intervals

This same information can be used to generate a 95% confidence interval for the average number of days to sell 40 or more jaw breakers. However, for illustrative purposes let us rerun Crystal Ball, but this time with 5000 runs. To do this first reset the simulation (click on the ◄◄ icon) and then change the run preferences (click on the 🗐 icon) to make the Maximum Number of Trials equal to 5000. As you run the simulation with the view set to statistics, you will observe that the mean standard error keeps decreasing. For our simulation run, the output shown in Figure 10.19 was obtained.

Forecast: Time to Sell 40 Jaw Breakers

Edit Preferences View Run Help

Cell F1   **Statistics**

Statistic	Value
Trials	5,000
Mean	16.44
Median	16.00
Mode	16.00
Standard Deviation	2.22
Variance	4.94
Skewness	0.42
Kurtosis	3.17
Coeff. of Variability	0.14
Range Minimum	10.00
Range Maximum	25.00
Range Width	15.00
Mean Std. Error	0.03

FIGURE 10.19
Crystal Ball Statistical Output

From this output a 95% confidence interval for the mean time to sell 40 or more jaw breakers will be:

$$\left(\bar{x} - t_{.025}\frac{s}{\sqrt{n}}, \bar{x} + t_{.025}\frac{s}{\sqrt{n}} \right) = (16.44 - 1.96*.03, 16.44 + 1.96*.03)$$
$$= (16.38, 16.50)$$

Note that since n = 5000, $z_{.025}$ was used to approximate $t_{.025}$. Hence, Bill is 95% confident that the true average time to sell 40 or more jaw breakers is somewhere between 16.38 and 16.50 days. Increasing the number of runs done by Crystal Ball for this problem beyond 5000 would give an even smaller confidence interval.

USING CRYSTAL BALL TO DETERMINE AN INVENTORY POLICY

One of the important features of Crystal Ball is that it allows a comparison of policies. In Section 10.3 a simulation for the Allen Appliance Company based on an order point–order quantity or (R,Q) system we presented. One might be interested in whether an order point–order up to level or (R,M) system would be less expensive. To analyze this, the Excel simulation developed for the (R,Q) system (file allen(r,q).xls on the accompanying CD-ROM) was modified to represent a simulation of an (R,M) system. The corresponding simulation is contained in spreadsheet allen(r,m).xls on the accompanying CD-ROM.

In Chapter 8 it was asserted that on the average, an (R,M) policy is generally less expensive than an (R,Q) policy. To determine whether this is true for the situation faced by Allen Appliance, 500 simulation runs of each of the two policies using Crystal Ball were made.

The results of the simulation run for the (R,Q) policy are given in Figures 10.20 and 10.21, while those for the (R,M) policy are shown in Figures 10.22 and 10.23.

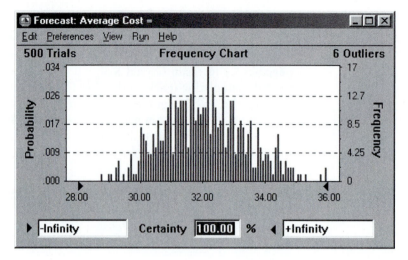

FIGURE 10.20   Crystal Ball Frequency Chart Output for (R,Q) Policy

Forecast: Average Cost =

Edit Preferences View Run Help

Cell B7   **Statistics**

Statistic	Value
Trials	500
Mean	32.14
Median	32.05
Mode	32.89
Standard Deviation	1.40
Variance	1.97
Skewness	0.50
Kurtosis	3.55
Coeff. of Variability	0.04
Range Minimum	28.74
Range Maximum	37.67
Range Width	8.93
Mean Std. Error	0.06

FIGURE 10.21   Crystal Ball Statistical Output for (R,Q) Policy

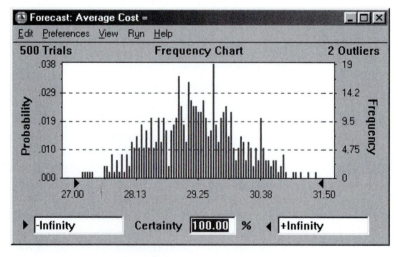

FIGURE 10.22   Crystal Ball Frequency Chart Output for (R,M) Policy

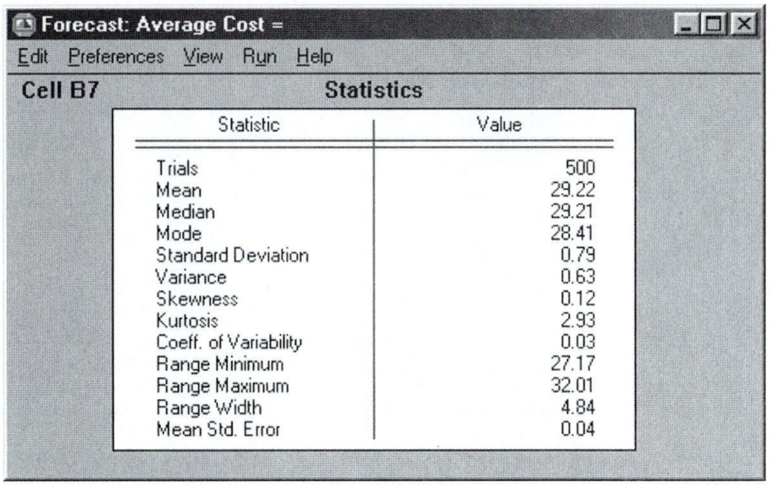

FIGURE 10.23 Crystal Ball Statistical Output for (R,M) Policy

To determine whether the (R,M) policy is less expensive on average than the (R,Q) policy, the following one-tailed hypothesis test is performed.

$$\text{Null:} \qquad H_0: \mu_1 - \mu_2 = 0$$
$$\text{Alternative:} \quad H_A: \mu_1 - \mu_2 > 0$$

Here population 1 refers to the (R,Q) policy and population 2 refers to the (R,M) policy. Since Figures 10.20 and 10.22 show that the average weekly cost for the two inventory policies approximately follows a normal distribution and large sample sizes have been taken from both populations, a z statistic can be used to approximate t to carry out this test. As the hypothesized mean difference is 0, the relevant z statistic is given by the formula:

$$z = \frac{(\bar{x}_1 - \bar{x}_2) - 0}{\sqrt{\frac{s_1^2}{n_1} + \frac{s_2^2}{n_2}}} = \frac{32.14 - 29.22}{\sqrt{\frac{1.40}{500} + \frac{.63}{500}}} = \frac{2.92}{.0637} = 45.83$$

Because this is an upper tail test, $z = 45.83$ is a clear indication that in this case the (R,M) policy is cheaper, on the average, than the (R,Q) policy.

Finding the Best (R,M) Policy

In light of the above result, one may be interested in finding the best (R,M) policy to use for Allen Appliance. Crystal Ball is ideal for analyzing different policies through the use of a **decision table**. For example, consider evaluating order quantities between 23 and 32 and reorder points between 8 and 17.

To have Crystal Ball perform the appropriate decision table analysis, the following steps are used:

1. Reset the simulation by pressing the [icon] icon.
2. Define the average cost (cell B7) as the forecast value by highlighting cell B7 and clicking on the [icon] icon.
3. Define the order quantity Q (cell B2) as a decision variable by highlighting cell B2 and clicking on the [icon] icon. This opens up the dialogue box shown in Figure 10.24. For this analysis, since Q will be evaluated for values between 23 and 32 the Lower bound is changed from 22.5 to 23 and the Upper bound from 27.5 to 32. We also wish the decision variable to be discrete and the step to be 1. Since decision names cannot contain an "=" sign, change the name of the decision variable from "Q =" to simply "Q."

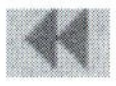

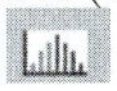

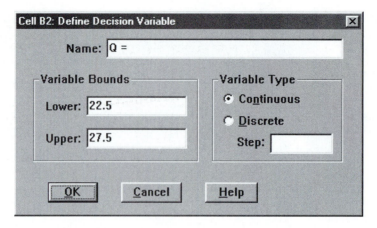

FIGURE 10.24   Crystal Ball Dialogue Box for Defining the Bounds for a Decision Variable

4. Define the reorder point R (cell B3) also as a decision variable by highlighting cell B3 and again clicking on the 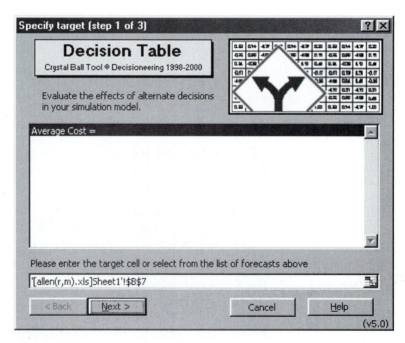 icon. For the reorder point the lower bound will be 8 and the upper bound 17. Again make the variable type discrete and the step equal to 1. Also change the name of the decision variable from "R =" to "R."

5. To set up the decision table, select Decision Table under CBTools in the menu bar. This brings up the dialogue box shown in Figure 10.25. Since Average Cost = is already highlighted, click on the Next button. This gives the dialogue box shown in Figure 10.26.

FIGURE 10.25   Initial Crystal Ball Dialogue Box for Setting Up a Decision Table

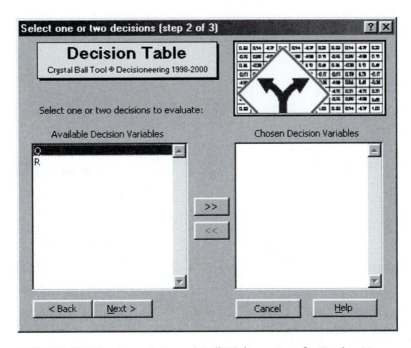

FIGURE 10.26   Second Crystal Ball Dialogue Box for Setting Up a Decision Table

6. As the values of both Q and R vary, we highlight both quantities are highlighted in the left hand (Available Decision Variables) box. Then click the >> box to move each to the Chosen Decision Variables column on the right side of the dialogue box. Then click on Next. This gives the dialogue box shown in Figure 10.27.

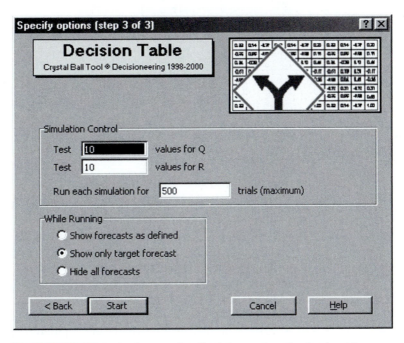

FIGURE 10.27   Third Crystal Ball Dialogue Box for Setting Up a Decision Table

7. As can be seen from this dialogue box, 10 different values for Q and 10 different values for R will be evaluated. Since this results in 100 different simulations, one may wish to reduce the number of simulation trials to less than 500, say 100. (After all, you do not want to tie up your computer for too long.) Change "Run each simulation for" to 100 and click on Start.

Analyzing the Simulation Results

The simulation results are shown in Figure 10.28.

	Trend / Overlay	Q (23)	Q (24)	Q (25)	Q (26)	Q (27)	Q (28)	Q (29)	Q (30)	Q (31)	Q (32)	
2	R (8)	32.49628	32.0207	31.50864	31.2252	30.78742	30.57182	30.12943	30.11337	29.97291	29.80672	1
3	R (9)	31.18105	30.61218	30.34156	29.893	29.6994	29.46378	29.14451	29.2245	29.01147	28.99288	2
4	R (10)	29.98043	29.51874	29.19553	28.90977	28.74925	28.58188	28.48685	28.4306	28.23725	28.31075	3
5	R (11)	28.99812	28.58733	28.34429	28.14743	27.92502	27.89588	27.87937	27.6989	27.77291	27.7307	4
6	R (12)	28.25184	27.88557	27.62985	27.41844	27.42022	27.33165	27.32303	27.28231	27.43939	27.37879	5
7	R (13)	27.4851	27.30369	27.17235	26.94866	27.05684	27.02325	27.08892	27.0442	27.09872	27.26346	6
8	R (14)	27.05469	26.89896	26.76435	26.78153	26.75517	26.75468	26.85777	26.97326	26.9967	27.16476	7
9	R (15)	26.82684	26.67352	26.57487	26.66804	26.69624	26.70844	26.76642	26.97769	27.04016	27.18736	8
10	R (16)	26.72675	26.69879	26.60806	26.60756	26.74371	26.83556	26.97054	27.0455	27.21496	27.44263	9
11	R (17)	26.72559	26.68186	26.69509	26.83311	26.93133	27.04635	27.26293	27.33327	27.53253	27.73008	10
12		1	2	3	4	5	6	7	8	9	10	

FIGURE 10.28
Decision Table Output for Allen Appliance Model

As can be seen from this figure, for this set of simulation runs the lowest average cost is 26.57487, which occurs when Q = 25 and R = 15. Of course, since many of the other values are close to this amount, additional simulation runs of greater duration may be done to further refine the analysis. In particular, if the analysis is redone based on 500 simulation runs but restricting attention to values of Q between 23 and 27 and values of R between 13 and 17 the output shown in Figure 10.29 is obtained.

	A	Q (24)	Q (25)	Q (26)	Q (27)		H
1	Trend Chart / Overlay Chart / Forecast Charts						
2	R (13)	27.357762	27.145664	27.074616	26.966922	1	
3	R (14)	26.886306	26.79954	26.742982	26.76362	2	
4	R (15)	26.668446	26.610806	26.598364	26.693134	3	
5	R (16)	26.657282	26.641588	26.653122	26.72946	4	
6	R (17)	26.737086	26.736996	26.813514	26.879124	5	
7		2	3	4	5		

FIGURE 10.29
Decision Table Output for Allen Appliance Model

Based on this simulation, it appears that the least expensive policy occurs when Q = 26 and R = 15. Of course, the difference in the average weekly cost between this policy and one where Q = 25 and R = 15 is approximately $.01, and that difference may be due to chance. While additional simulation runs could be undertaken to choose between the two policies, it does not appear that the difference in the average weekly costs would be significant enough to warrant further analysis. An order quantity, order up to policy based on Q equaling 26 and R equaling 15 is the recommended policy.

Based on this analysis, the following memorandum was prepared dealing with the situation faced by Allen Appliance Company. In this memorandum the effect of the weekly goodwill cost estimate on the optimal solution is considered by analyzing the effect of increasing this cost to $10 and decreasing it to $1.

·SCG·

STUDENT CONSULTING GROUP

MEMORANDUM

To: James P. Allen, President—Allen Appliance Company
From: Student Consulting Group, Inc.
Subj: Inventory Policy for Kitchen Chef Mixers

At your request, we conducted an analysis of the inventory policy for Kitchen Chef electric mixers at Allen Appliance Company. Based on historical data, we observed that both customer arrival and demand patterns possess a high degree of variability. We concluded that the problem could best be analyzed using a simulation approach.

We have held meetings with personnel in the accounting and marketing departments to gain information about relevant costs and demands for the product. On the basis of these meetings, we utilized the following data and assumptions in developing the simulation model:

1. Kitchen Chef mixers cost Allen $200 per unit.

2. A 26% annual holding cost rate is used for this product.

3. The cost of placing an order with Kitchen Chef is $45.

4. If Allen runs short of mixers due to a higher-than-expected lead time demand, all potential customers place backorders for the item, incurring an administrative cost of $2 per unit.

5. The company suffers a goodwill cost of $5 per unit per week for each week that a unit is on backorder.

6. Orders are placed at the end of a week, while delivery occurs at the beginning of a week.

Based on the data we collected, we developed probability distributions for:

1. Customer arrivals

2. Customer demands

Using only average values for these quantities, a simplified model indicates that Allen should implement an inventory policy of ordering 25 mixers when the supply reaches 10 or less. Using this policy as a starting point, we tested different inventory policies using simulation. Based on repeated runs simulating thousands of weeks (equivalent to approximately 200 years of operation), we recommend the following policy:

> 1. Reorder when the supply of Kitchen Chef mixers at the end of a week reaches 15 units or less.
>
> 2. Order an amount equal to 41 less the stock on hand at the end of the week in which the order is placed.

Under this policy, Allen can expect to incur an average total weekly inventory cost of approximately $26.60 for the Kitchen Chef mixers. This total includes all holding, backorder, and ordering costs but does not include the cost of the machines themselves. The analysis also reveals that small changes from the recommended inventory policy do not greatly affect the average weekly inventory cost. For example, inventory policies for which the reorder point is increased by one unit or the order up to level quantity varies by one unit increase the average total weekly inventory cost by less than 1%. Figure I shows the range in these weekly costs.

Since management is somewhat unsure of the assumed $5 goodwill cost per unit per week, we performed a sensitivity analysis to examine the effect that changing this cost to $1 and to $10 will have on the optimal inventory policy.

For a goodwill cost of $1 per week, we recommend a policy of ordering 35 units minus the stock on hand when supply reaches seven units or less. We estimate the average weekly cost of this policy at $21.93. In contrast, using the recommended policy of ordering 41 units less the stock on hand when supply reaches 15 or less results, in this case, in an average weekly cost of $23.84.

If the goodwill cost is $10 per week, we recommend ordering 43 units less the stock on hand when supply reaches 19 units or less. We estimate the average weekly cost of this policy at $28.90. In contrast, using the recommended policy of ordering 41 units less the stock on hand when supply reaches 15 or less results, in this case, in an average weekly cost of $30.13.

Hence, if the goodwill cost is actually $1/unit/week, the original recommended policy yields average weekly costs that are more than 8.7% greater than the optimal policy. If, however, the goodwill cost is actually $10/unit/week, the recommended policy yields an average weekly cost within 4.3% of the optimal policy. Because a significantly different policy results if the goodwill cost per unit per week is substantially less than the estimated $5 amount, we recommend that management undertake a focus group analysis to obtain firm estimates for the goodwill cost. We would be happy to assist you in this endeavor.

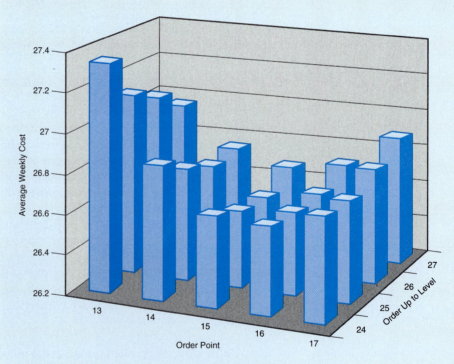

FIGURE I Range in Average Weekly Inventory Costs

OTHER APPLICATIONS OF CRYSTAL BALL

Crystal Ball can be used to analyze many different simulation models. Appendix 10.6 on the accompanying CD-ROM gives illustrations of the use of Crystal Ball in simulating queuing models, profit analysis models, and project management models.

10.8 Advantages and Disadvantages of Simulation

Simulation as an analysis tool has several important advantages and disadvantages. The following are some of the principal advantages:

Advantages of Simulation Analysis

1. Simulation provides insight into the problem solution when other management science methods fail.
2. Simulation enables the performance of an existing system under a proposed set of modifications to be analyzed without disrupting current system performance. Such performance may be analyzed over any time horizon.
3. Simulation models assist in the design of proposed systems by providing a convenient experimental laboratory for conducting "what-if" analyses.

These advantages do not come without a price, however. Some of the principal disadvantages of simulation are summarized as follows.

Disadvantages of Simulation

1. Simulation models are generally time consuming and expensive to develop.
2. Simulation models provide only an estimate of a model's true parameter values.
3. There is no guarantee that the policy shown to be optimal by the simulation is in fact, optimal.

The last disadvantage listed is an important one. It has been illustrated that simulation works by evaluating the results from different policies. Performance measures are calculated for each policy, and the "best" policy from this set is selected on the basis of such measures. If the true optimal policy is not one of the policies evaluated, however, or if a nonrepresentative set of random numbers occurs in the simulation, the optimal policy will not be found by the simulation.

For example, when simulation was used to study the Allen inventory problem in Sections 10.3 and 10.7, attention was restricted to a limited set of possible alternatives in order to make the analysis manageable. The EOQ model was initially used to get a rough idea of what the order quantity and reorder point should be, and then policy alternatives close to these values were considered. A policy such as ordering 40 units when the inventory level reaches 20 units was not considered. If this policy were indeed optimal, the simulation analysis would not have been able to detect it.

10.9 Summary

Simulation can be used to model many complex business models, including problems in queuing and inventory. In Monte Carlo simulation, a random number mapping is developed to ensure that random variable inputs to the simulation correspond to the desired probability distribution.

Fixed time simulations are used when the simulation is set up so that each iteration corresponds to a set time period. When events do not correspond to exact time periods, a next event approach is used in developing the simulation model.

Simulations may be developed by hand, using general-purpose programming languages, specialized simulation programming languages, simulator programs such as Extend (see Appendix 10.1), or Excel and add-ins such as Crystal Ball. Use of Crystal Ball greatly enhances Excel's ability to perform simulations and provides valuable information to the analyst. Because not all of the features of Crystal Ball were discussed within the limited space of this book, the reader interested in learning more details about this program should consult the Crystal Ball user manual. It is available from Decisioneering, Inc.

One purpose of developing a simulation is to identify a recommended policy. When standard analytical models cannot be used to determine an optimal policy, a simulation model can identify a best course of action from the set considered. The simulation model also frequently provides a convenient laboratory for performing "what-if" analyses.

Although the concepts behind simulation analysis are relatively straightforward, the execution can be fairly complex. Not only must one develop appropriate models for the system being simulated, but one must also write and debug computer code to carry out the analysis. Because the costs involved in developing simulation models are typically high, they are generally used only in cases in which the payoff from the analysis is considerable.

ON THE CD-ROM

• Fixed time simulation for Jewel Vending	**Jewel Vending.xls** **JVCb.xls** **JVC.xls**
• Fixed time simulation for Allen Appliance	**AAC inventory.xls** **allen(r,q).xls** **allen(r,m).xls**
• Next-event simulation for Capital Bank	**Capital Bank.xls**
• Simulation of exponentially distributed service times	**explicit inverse.xls**
• Simulation of normally distributed random variables	**traffic.xls**
• Simulation of an M/M/1 queue	**Lanford Sub Shop.xls**
• Simulation of a real estate investment using Crystal Ball	**Don Clark.xls**
• Simulation of a project schedule using Crystal Ball	**Gordon.xls**
• Simulation of Capital Bank using extend	**capitalbank.mox**
• Appendix 10.1—Conducting a Next-Event Simulation Using Extend	
• Appendix 10.2—Generating Pseudo-Random Numbers Using the Linear Congruential Method	
• Appendix 10.3—Statistical Tests for Comparing Simulation Results	
• Appendix 10.4—Simulation of Capital Bank Model Using Excel	

Problems

Note: The Excel file corresponding to Appendix C is included on the accompanying CD-ROM. If you are using Excel to solve these problems, you may wish to import these values into your spreadsheet.

1. Price changes of shares of the Saveway Stores, Inc. have been recorded over the past 50 days. The frequency distribution is as follows:

Price Change	Frequency
−1/2	3 days
−3/8	4 days
−1/4	5 days
−1/8	6 days
0	10 days
+1/8	12 days
+1/4	4 days
+3/8	3 days
+1/2	3 days

   a. Develop a relative frequency distribution for the price change of Saveway stock.
   b. Using the relative frequency distribution developed in part (a), determine the mean daily change in the price of shares of Saveway Stores, Inc. If the current stock price is 32, what would be the expected stock price 30 days from now?
   c. If the current price of Saveway stock is 32, use the first two numbers in column 1 of Appendix C to simulate the price of the stock over the next 30 trading days.
   d. Compare the answer in part (c) with the expected stock price after 30 days calculated in part (b). Comment on the difference between the two values.

2. It has been estimated that customers arrive at the Quick Stop Convenience store during the evening according to a Poisson process at a mean rate of 40 per hour. Each customer buys between zero and five lottery tickets according to the following probability distribution:

Number of Lottery Tickets Purchased	Probability
0	.45
1	.30
2	.15
3	.03
4	.02
5	.05

   If Quick Stop has 30 lottery tickets available at 6 P.M., use simulation to determine the time at which the store will sell out of the lottery tickets. Use column 1 of Appendix C to determine the interarrival times of customers and column 2 to determine the number of lottery tickets each customer will purchase.

3. Consider the following PERT project describing the planning of regional sales meetings by Craig Computer Corporation:

   The immediate predecessor jobs and expected completion time for each job are as follows:

Job	Immediate Predecessor Jobs	Expected Completion Time in Weeks
A	—	6
B	A	4
C	—	9
D	—	7
E	D	8
F	B	3
G	C	5

   a. Determine the critical path(s) and the expected completion time for the project.
   b. Suppose each job has a 25% chance of being completed two weeks early, a 25% chance of being completed on time, and a 50% chance of being completed two weeks late. Using the first two digits in column 4 of Appendix C to determine the job times, calculate the project completion time for five different sets of job times. On the basis of these five simulations, determine the probability that each job is on the critical path.
   c. Calculate a 95% confidence interval for the expected project completion time.

4. Taks Home Furnishing is currently having its year-end appliance clearance sale. The store has twelve 18-cubic-foot Whirlpool refrigerators on sale; 5 are white, 4 are almond, and 3 are harvest gold. Each day, the company expects between 0 and 4 customers interested in buying a refrigerator to arrive at the store according to the following probability distribution:

$$P(0 \text{ arrivals}) = .15$$
$$P(1 \text{ arrival}) = .25$$
$$P(2 \text{ arrivals}) = .30$$
$$P(3 \text{ arrivals}) = .20$$
$$P(4 \text{ arrivals}) = .10$$

For each of these customers, there is a 60% chance that the person will want to purchase one of the sale-priced Whirlpools.

Taks knows that 40% of customers desire a white refrigerator, 25% desire an almond refrigerator, and 35% desire a harvest gold refrigerator. If the store is sold out of a particular color choice, the customer will leave without making a purchase.

Use random numbers from column 1 of Appendix C to determine the number of customer arrivals, column 2 to determine whether an arriving customer will wish to purchase an 18-cubic-foot Whirlpool refrigerator, and column 3 to determine the choice of color. How many days will it take for Taks to sell all 12 refrigerators?

5. Dizzy Izzy is a discount appliance store specializing in home entertainment equipment. The firm carries two brands of satellite antenna systems: Panasony and ChannelMaster. Due to the high cost of ordering these systems and the rapid changes in the technology, Dizzy Izzy's policy is to not reorder additional systems until the store is completely sold out of both brands.

Presently, the store has six Panasony and four ChannelMaster systems in stock. The number of customers who arrive each day intending to buy a satellite system follows a Poisson distribution with a mean of 2. Forty percent of customers want to purchase a Panasony system, 50% want to purchase a ChannelMaster system, and 10% want to purchase a brand that Dizzy Izzy does not carry and therefore leave without making a purchase.

If a customer wants to purchase a Panasony system but Izzy is sold out, there is a 25% chance that the customer will buy the ChannelMaster system instead, a 35% chance of placing a backorder for the Panasony system, and a 40% chance that the sale will be lost.

If a customer wants to purchase a ChannelMaster system but Izzy is sold out, there is a 45% chance that the customer will buy a Panasony system instead, a 40% chance of placing a backorder, and a 15% chance that the sale will be lost.

Using simulation, determine how many days it will take for Dizzy Izzy to completely sell out of the existing inventory of satellite antennae systems. Determine the number of backordered systems and lost sales as of that date. Use column 3 of Appendix C to determine the number of customers who arrive each day to purchase satellite systems, column 4 to determine the choice of system, and column 5 to determine what will happen if the customer's selection is sold out.

6. At Steve's Super Scooper, two employees serve customers during the lunch hour. One employee gets the customer's ice cream selection, while the other receives payment. Customers arrive at Steve's according to a Poisson process, having a mean interarrival time of 1.5 minutes. The time it takes to get an ice cream selection follows an exponential distribution with a mean of one minute. The service time for payment follows a uniform distribution of between 30 and 80 seconds.

Using simulation, determine the average time a customer spends waiting in line to get and pay for ice cream. Base your results on a simulation of 20 customer arrivals using column 1 of Appendix C to determine the customer interarrival time, column 2 to determine the time a customer spends with the employee getting ice cream, and column 3 to determine the time a customer spends with the cashier.

7. Albright's Hardware sells Security brand dead-bolt locks in single packages and two-packs (one key fits both locks). Single packages sell for $12 each, while two-packs sell for $30. Albright's cost is one-half the retail selling price.

Albright's is open seven days a week and receives a delivery from Security once a week. If Albright runs out of single packages but still has two-packs available, the store will break open a two-pack and sell each of the two at the single-package price. If the store is out of stock of the type of dead-bolt set the customer wants to purchase, Albright management believes that it will suffer a goodwill loss of $10.

Each day, between zero and three customers arrive to purchase dead-bolt locks with the following distribution:

$$P(0 \text{ arrivals}) = .30$$
$$P(1 \text{ arrival}) = .35$$
$$P(2 \text{ arrivals}) = .20$$
$$P(3 \text{ arrivals}) = .15$$

Sixty percent of purchasers want a single set, while 40% want a two-pack. The store's policy is to order a sufficient number of dead bolts to bring the beginning-of-the-week inventory up to five single sets and five two-packs.

Neglecting holding and ordering costs, determine a 95% confidence interval for Albright's mean weekly profit based on a four week simulation. Use column 1 of Appendix C to determine the daily number of arriving customers and column 2 to determine whether a customer wants to purchase a single set or a two-pack.

8. Consider the data given in problem 7 for Albright's Hardware. The company is considering changing its

inventory policy so that it begins each week with six single sets and only four two-packs. Conduct a four-week simulation using the same random numbers as in problem 7 to determine whether there is any difference in the mean weekly profit. Test at a 5% significance level.

9. Attendees at the annual Orange County Small Business Administration Conference register by standing in line to pay their registration fee and then proceeding to a designated line based on their business interest to collect their materials. The conference addresses four types of small businesses: manufacturing, retailing, import/export, and financial services.

   The registration period lasts from 8:30 A.M. to 9:30 A.M. During this period, the conference organizers estimate that the interarrival time of attendees approximately follows an exponential distribution with a mean time of one minute. The time to register an attendee is anticipated to be 30 seconds if the attendee pays by cash or check, or 90 seconds if the attendee pays by a credit card. The organizers estimate that 60% of attendees will use a credit card.

   Based on similar conferences, the organizers estimate that 40% of attendees will be interested in manufacturing, 30% in retailing, 10% in import/export, and 20% in financial services. The time required to obtain materials for the manufacturing and retailing lines is estimated to be exactly two minutes, while the time to obtain materials for the import/export and financial services lines is estimated to be exactly three minutes.

   Simulate the arrival of the first 20 customers at the conference using appropriate random number selections from Appendix C. For this simulation, determine:
   a. The time it takes for the twentieth customer to complete registration.
   b. The average waiting time in each of the five lines (registration, manufacturing, retailing, import/export, and financial services).

10. The Treasure Trove Casino in Las Vegas has a free telephone booth that allows customers to make a one-minute telephone call anywhere in the United States at no charge. Customers arrive to make their free calls according to a Poisson process at a mean rate of $\lambda = 40$ per hour. The time each customer is allowed to be in the phone booth is a constant 72 seconds. Management is interested in using simulation to determine the average waiting time for a customer at the free telephone booth.

   Conduct the simulation for 20 customer arrivals assuming that there is no one initially present at the phone booth. Use column 5 of Appendix C to determine the customer interarrival times. Based on these 20 arrivals, calculate the average time a customer spends waiting in line to use the phone. Compare this result to that obtained for W_q using the formula for the M/G/1 queue.

11. The distribution for weekly demand of Cobra auto alarm systems at Big Al's Stereo is as follows:

Demand	Probability
0	.15
1	.10
2	.25
3	.20
4	.15
5	.10
6	.05

The alarm systems cost Big Al's $100 and sell for $200. The annual holding cost rate for these systems is 26%, and there is a $65 cost to place an order. Lead time can vary between one and three weeks according to the following probability distribution.

Lead Time	Probability
1 week	.10
2 weeks	.75
3 weeks	.15

Assume that orders are placed at the end of the week. For example, if the lead time is one week an order placed in week 2 will arrive at the start of week 4. If the firm runs out of stock of the alarm systems, a customer will leave without making any purchase.

   Simulate the inventory for the Cobra alarm system at Big Al's over a 15-week period and determine its profit during this period if Big Al's uses an inventory policy in which it orders 26 alarms whenever the stock on hand reaches 6 units. Assume the holding cost is calculated based on the end of the week inventory level. Use column 1 to determine the number of customer arrivals and column 2 to determine the lead time when an order is placed.

12. Ricon, Inc. uses an assembly line to produce its office copiers. The final step in the assembly process is quality control inspection. Copiers arrive at the quality inspection area exactly every 90 seconds. The time it takes to perform a quality control inspection follows an exponential distribution, with a mean of 72 seconds. Ricon management is interested in using simulation to determine the average time it takes a copier to complete its quality control inspection.

   Conduct a simulation for 20 copier arrivals assuming that the system starts empty. Use column 6 of Appendix C to determine the inspection times. Calculate the average time a copier spends in the system based on these 20 arrivals.

13. Shari Winslow has gone to Atlantic City to play roulette. Her strategy is to place $10 bets on red. She has $30 and will quit either when she loses all her money or wins $20.

   If the roulette wheel is operating properly, the chance of landing on red is 18/38, the chance of landing on black is 18/38, and the chance of landing on green is 2/38. Hence Shari's chance of winning her bet is 18/38 (approximately .4737) and of losing her bet, 20/38 (approximately .5263).

Data for Problem 14

Santa Ana		Orange		Costa Mesa		Riverside		Garden Grove	
Time	Probability	Time	Probability	Time	Probability	Time	Probability	Time	Probability
8	.30	6	.25	7	.35	5	.20	3	.20
9	.25	7	.35	8	.20	6	.30	4	.10
10	.30	8	.20	9	.10	7	.25	5	.20
11	.10	9	.20	10	.25	8	.10	6	.50
12	.05			11	.10	9	.15		

Use simulation to determine the number of spins it will take before Shari will stop playing roulette. Conduct four simulation runs and determine a 95% confidence interval for the average number of plays based on these four simulations.

14. Terry Moore has three alternative routes to travel from his home in Tustin to his office in Anaheim. He can take the Santa Ana Freeway to the Orange Freeway; the Costa Mesa Freeway to the Riverside Freeway; or the Garden Grove Freeway to the Orange Freeway.

The travel time (in minutes) on each of the five freeways follows the accompanying probability distributions. For each of the three routes, conduct 10 simulation runs and calculate the average commuting time. Which route appears to take the least travel time?

15. During the dinner hour, the distribution of the interarrival time of customers at Burger Barn is estimated to be as follows:

Interarrival Time	Probability
30 seconds	.45
60 seconds	.25
90 seconds	.15
120 seconds	.10
150 seconds	.05

Sixty percent of customers pay with cash, while 40% pay with credit cards. The service times of the cash and credit card customers are estimated to be as follows:

Cash		Credit Card	
Service Time	Probability	Service Time	Probability
20 seconds	.35	30 seconds	.20
40 seconds	.30	60 seconds	.45
60 seconds	.25	90 seconds	.25
80 seconds	.10	120 seconds	.10

Simulate this system for 20 customer arrivals and determine the average time a cash and credit card customer must wait in line before paying the cashier. Use column 5 of Appendix C to determine the customer interarrival time, column 6 to determine whether the customer pays with cash or credit, and column 7 to determine the service time.

16. Consider the situation faced by Burger Barn discussed in problem 15. The restaurant has hired a second cashier. One cashier will handle cash purchases only while the other cashier will only handle credit card customers.

Using Excel, develop a simulation that determines the average time a customer spends in the system. Base the simulation on 1000 customer arrivals and calculate the average customer waiting time assuming the first 100 customer arrivals are ignored.

17. Consider the situation faced by Burger Barn described in problems 15 and 16. Use Crystal Ball to develop a simulation for the model where each cashier handles both cash and credit card purchases. Run the simulation 500 times, each for 10 hours (36,000 seconds) and determine 95% confidence interval for the average time a customer must wait for service.

18. Harvest Supermarket has one loading dock for receiving deliveries. During any half-hour interval, either 0, 1, 2, or 3 delivery trucks arrive with the following probabilities:

P(0 arrivals) = .60
P(1 arrival) = .25
P(2 arrivals) = .10
P(3 arrivals) = .05

Eighty percent of the delivery trucks can be unloaded in a half hour, while 20% of the trucks take a full hour to unload. Using fixed-time simulation, determine the average number of trucks waiting to unload during a 10-hour period. Assume that the simulation starts with the loading dock empty. Use column 6 of Appendix C to determine the number of trucks that arrive in a half-hour period and column 7 to determine how long it will take to unload a truck.

19. Customers arrive at the Blinkies Donut shop between 6:30 A.M. and 8:30 A.M. according to a Poisson process with a mean rate of one every minute. Seventy percent of the arriving customers purchase one or two donuts, while 30% purchase the Blinkies Dozen pack. For customers purchasing one or two donuts, the service time is uniformly distributed between 30 and 50 seconds. For customers purchasing the Blinkies Dozen pack, the service time is exponentially distributed with a mean of 90 seconds.

Blinkies employs a single clerk to help customers. Simulate the arrival of the first 20 customers into the store during the 6:30 A.M. to 8:30 A.M. time period. Determine the maximum number of customers who will wait in line to begin service during this period. Use appropriate random number selections from Appendix C.

20. The Quick Stop Convenience Store has two gas pump islands, one for full service and one for self service. Cars arrive at the gas pumps according to a Poisson process at a mean rate of 20 per hour. Sixty percent of the cars want self serve, while 40% want full serve. The service time for the self-serve pump follows an exponential distribution with a mean of four minutes. The service time for the full-serve pump follows an exponential distribution with a mean of five minutes.

    If more than two cars are in line waiting for self serve, but no one is using the full-serve pump, an arriving car wanting self serve will join the self-serve queue with probability .3, balk (immediately leave without service) with probability .5, or go to the full-serve pump with probability .2. If more than two cars are in line waiting for self serve and the full-serve pump is occupied, an arriving car wanting self serve will join the self-serve pump queue with probability .4 and balk with probability .6.

    Simulate this system for 20 car arrivals. Use column 1 of Appendix C to determine the interarrival time of cars, column 2 to determine whether the car will want self serve or full serve, column 3 to determine the service time for obtaining the gasoline, and column 4 to determine whether an arriving car wanting self serve will join the queue, balk, or switch to full serve. What observations can you make based on this simulation?

21. Ontario, California, is a suburb of Los Angeles. Its airport serves primarily domestic air traffic; however, occasionally an international flight is diverted to Ontario if Los Angeles International Airport is fogged in. If an international flight arrives at Ontario, two customs inspectors set up operations to process the passengers.

    Passengers must line up to have their passports and visas checked by the first customs inspector. Inspection times follow a uniform distribution ranging between 20 and 70 seconds. Passengers then claim their baggage. The time it takes to retrieve baggage follows an exponential distribution with a mean of three minutes. Finally, the passengers join a line to have their baggage inspected by the second customs inspector. Forty percent of the passengers are waived through without inspection, 50% experience a cursory inspection of one minute duration, and 10% experience a full inspection of three minutes duration.

    Use simulation to determine how long it takes a plane load of 20 passengers to get through customs. Use column 1 of Appendix C to determine the time required to check a passenger's passport and visa, column 2 to determine the time required to obtain baggage, and column 3 to determine the type of baggage inspection a passenger experiences (none, cursory, or full).

22. Family Appliance specializes in selling major appliances for use in kitchen remodeling. One of its more popular items is the SubZero refrigerator. Over the past 40 weeks, the store has collected data regarding the weekly demand for this refrigerator. On the basis of these data, the following demand distribution has been estimated:

Weekly Demand	Probability
0	.25
1	.15
2	.15
3	.25
4	.10
5	.10

The store's policy is to reorder up to 15 refrigerators whenever the inventory on hand reaches five or fewer at the end of a week. The holding cost for each refrigerator is $2 per week, and the cost of reordering is $50. If a customer wants a SubZero refrigerator and Family is out of stock the customer will go elsewhere and the sale is lost. The company estimates that it suffers a goodwill cost of $40 for each lost sale. Currently, Family Appliance has an inventory of seven refrigerators.

Lead time for delivery can be described by the following distribution:

Lead Time	Probability
1 week	.30
2 weeks	.50
3 weeks	.20

a. Conduct a 10-week simulation of Family's inventory situation regarding the SubZero refrigerator to determine the total cost for this period. Use column 3 of Appendix C to determine the weekly demand and column 4 to determine the lead time.

b. SubZero is offering Family a new policy of automatically delivering five refrigerators every two weeks. The administrative cost of this policy is $5 per week, and the first delivery will be in two weeks. Conduct a 10-week simulation of Family's inventory situation under this plan and determine the total cost for the 10-week period.

c. On the basis of your answers to parts (a) and (b), what would you recommend to Family management regarding the supplier's offer?

23. Marv Portney is a salesman for Craftco Comfort Beds. Marv gets his leads when customers call the Craftco 800 number to arrange an in-house demonstration. (Customers receive a free clock-radio for agreeing to this demonstration.) Of the customers with whom Marv makes appointments, 10% turn out to be not at home. Of the others, 10% are single women, 30% are single men, and 60% are married couples.

    Craftco offers four sizes of beds: king, queen, double, and twin. The list price of the king is $4000, the queen $3000, the double $2500, and the twin $2000. Marv can discount each bed up to 50% in order to make a sale, however. Therefore, he estimates that his commission is uniformly distributed within the following ranges:

Bed Size	Commission Uniformly Distributed Between
King	$400 and $1000
Queen	$300 and $800
Double	$200 and $600
Twin	$250 and $500

Marv has found that, among the single women he calls upon, he makes a sale 70% of the time. Of those, 40% want to buy a twin bed, 50% want a double, 5% want a queen, and 5% want a king. Marv makes a sale to 65% of the single men he calls on. Of these, 30% want a twin bed, 40% want a double, 25% want a queen, and 5% want a king. Among the married couples, Marv makes a sale 55% of the time. Ten percent of these couples want to buy a single twin bed, 20% want two twin beds, 15% want a double, 40% want a queen, and 15% want a king.

Marv makes one, two, or three sales calls per day with the following probabilities:

Number of Sales Calls per Day	Probability
1	.50
2	.40
3	.10

a. Simulate Marv's activity over a 10-day period using an appropriate random number selection from Appendix C.

b. Calculate Marv's earnings over this 10-day period.

24. The speed at which cars travel down Main Street in Irvine, California, follows a normal distribution with a mean of 42 miles an hour and a standard deviation of 5 miles per hour. The Irvine Police Department is contemplating setting up a speed trap at the corner of Main and Alton streets to try to enforce the 45 mile per hour speed limit on Main Street. The speed trap is set up for a half hour each day. The interarrival time of cars passing the corner of Main and Alton follows an exponential distribution with a mean time of 45 seconds. If a police car does detect someone driving over the speed limit, the police officer will ticket the driver. The distribution of the time to write up a ticket is as follows:

Time to Write Up a Ticket	Probability
3 minutes	.15
3.5 minutes	.20
4 minutes	.25
4.5 minutes	.30
5 minutes	.10

While a police officer is writing up a ticket, he is unavailable to catch other speeders. Simulate a half hour of operations for this model to determine how many cars the police officer will catch speeding. Use column 3 to determine the interarrival time of a car, column 4 to determine the car's speed, and column 5 to determine the length of time the police officer spends writing up a ticket.

25. Among the products sold by Dominion Hardware is the Simoniz brand pressure washer. These are delivered to the store by a rack jobber who works under contract for Simoniz. The rack jobber comes to the store on Monday of each week, but in any week there is a 30% chance that he gets delayed and does not make it to the store. The store estimates that the holding cost per unit is $6 per week (based on the number of units that are in inventory at the end of the week). If the store runs short of pressure washers, it estimates that it suffers a goodwill cost of $7 for each unsatisfied customer and the sale is lost.

Dominion estimates the weekly washer demand has the following probability distribution.

Demand	Probability
0	.15
1	.20
2	.30
3	.15
4	.10
5	.05
6	.05

Not including inventory costs, the company calculates it earns $15 on each unit sold.

a. Do a 10-week simulation of operations and estimate the average weekly profit if the firm decides to have the rack jobber bring the inventory level up to 5 units when he arrives.

b. Develop an Excel simulation for this problem covering 100 weeks of operation. Then use Crystal Ball to determine the optimal stocking level for the firm. Base your results on doing 500 simulation runs of each policy considered.

26. During its first hour of operation customers arrive at the Wednesday Afternoon Store according to a Poisson process with a mean rate of 40 per hour. It takes the cashier an average of 90 seconds to check out a customer.

a. Simulate the arrival of 15 customers and determine the average time these customers spend waiting in line. Use column 3 of Appendix C to generate the interarrival times and column 4 to generate the service times.

b. Develop an Excel or Extend simulation for this problem and run it 10 times, each over a 60-minute interval. On the basis of these 10 simulation runs, determine a 95% confidence interval for the average time a customer must wait in line to begin service.

27. Daily demand for Webcor barbeques at Sharper Idea has the following probability distribution:

Demand	Probability
0	.08
1	.37
2	.33
3	.17
4	.05

Orders are placed at the end of the day, and lead time (in days) has the following probability distribution.

Lead Time	Probability
1	.05
2	.55
3	.30
4	.10

For example, an order placed on day 4 with a lead time of 2 days will be delivered at the beginning of day 7. Sharper Idea currently has an inventory of 10 Webcor barbeques. Order costs are approximately $50 per order, and inventory holding costs are estimated to be $2 per barbeque per day. The company suffers a goodwill cost of $30 for each barbeque demanded when it is out of stock and the sale is lost.

Sharper Idea's current policy is to reorder 10 barbeques when supply reaches 6 or less at the end of a day. Bob Hanson, one of the company's vice presidents, has recommended a new policy of reordering 12 barbeques when supply reaches 3 or less.

a. Develop a simulation in Excel for this model.

b. Using Crystal Ball, do 500 simulations of 1000 days each and determine whether Sharper Idea should switch to Bob Hanson's recommended policy.

28. MVC Computers is considering using e-commerce to sell its computers directly over the Internet. It is planning to staff the website 24 hours a day with a supervisor and a trainee. An incoming order that arrives when both the supervisor and trainee are busy is put in a "pending file" (a queue) for processing when one of the two servers becomes available. Operations data is estimated to be as follows.

Time Between Orders (minutes)	Probability	Supervisor's Service Time (minutes)	Probability	Trainee's Service Time (minutes)	Probability
2	.35	4	.30	6	.10
3	.30	5	.25	7	.10
4	.20	6	.25	8	.60
5	.15	7	.20	9	.20

Management is interested in the average amount of time incoming orders will spend in the "pending file."

a. Develop a simulation in Excel to model this problem. Run the simulation for 1000 orders and eliminate the first 100 orders when calculating the average time spent in the pending file.

b. Using Crystal Ball, run the simulation 500 times and determine a 95% confidence interval for the average time an order spends in the pending file.

29. Kokanee Springs Golf Resort in British Columbia has a season that typically begins on April 15 and lasts until October 10. Unusually cold weather, however, can delay the start of the season or hasten the season closing date. Hence management believes that the length of the golfing season can be modeled as a uniform distribution with a minimum time of 169 days and a maximum time of 178 days.

The golf course offers season passes for $800 and charges day golfers (those without a season pass) between $29 and $68 to play a day of golf. Management estimates that the number of season passes that it will sell can be modeled by a triangular distribution with a minimum of 250, a maximum of 360, and a likeliest value of 320. The distribution of revenue for the day golfers is as follows:

Revenue	Probability
$29	.10
$48	.85
$68	.05

On sunny days, management believes the number of day golfers will follow a normal distribution with a mean of 290 and a standard deviation of 17; on non-sunny days management believes the number of day golfers will follow a normal distribution with a mean of 81 and a standard deviation of 9. Approximately 75% of the days are sunny.

Fixed operating costs for the golf course are estimated to follow a normal distribution with a mean of $1,500,000 and a standard deviation of $100,000. The golf course has a $600,000 loan that is due at the end of this year. Using Crystal Ball, determine the probability that the golf course will earn more than $600,000 during the golf season. Base your result on doing 2000 simulation runs.

30. Customers arrive at Ted's TV Repair Shop according to a Poisson process at an average of once every 2.5 hours. By using existing equipment, the service time to repair a television set is 2.25 hours with a standard deviation of 45 minutes. Suppose Ted decides to hire a second repair person and this person also takes an average of 2.25 hours to fix a television with a standard deviation of 45 minutes.

a. Assuming that the service time of both Ted and his assistant follows a normal distribution, develop an Excel simulation for this system.

b. Run the simulation for 1000 customers and determine the average time a television set spends at the shop by excluding the first 100 customers.

31. Consider the Ted's TV Repair Shop simulation developed in problem 30. Using Crystal Ball, run 1000 simulations. Based on the results of your simulation, determine:

a. a 95% confidence interval for the average time a set spends in the system

b. the probability the average time a set waits before being served is less than 30 minutes

32. Among the items sold at Hal's Bakery are loaves of sourdough bread. The daily number of customers who arrive at Hal's approximately follows a normal distribution with a mean of 240 and a standard deviation of 15.49. There is a .25 probability that a customer wishes to buy one loaf of sourdough bread, a .05 probability that a customer wishes to buy two loaves, and a .70 probability that a customer does not purchase the bread.

The bread is baked once a day at 6 A.M. and sold beginning at 9 A.M. Each loaf of bread costs $.60 to produce and sells for $2.40. Unsold loaves of bread are donated to a soup kitchen and net the store a tax credit of $.20. If the store runs out of loaves of sourdough bread, it estimates that it suffers a goodwill loss of $3.00 for each loaf demanded when it is out of stock. Using Crystal Ball, determine how many loaves of sourdough bread the bakery should produce. Base your results on 500 simulations for each production quantity considered.

33. Bank Drug Store has two servers. One can serve a customer according to an exponential distribution with a mean speed of 1.5 minutes, and the other can serve a

customer according to an exponential distribution with a mean speed of 2 minutes. Customers arrive according to a Poisson process at a mean rate of 60 per hour. Develop an Excel simulation and determine the average time a customer spends waiting in line. Assume the simulation begins recording the waiting time of the 101st customer and runs for 1000 customers.

34. Consider the situation faced by Bank Drug Store in problem 33. Using Extend, develop a simulation for this model and run the simulation over 10,000 minutes to determine the average time a customer spends in line before being served.

35. Steve Wilson, a budding college impresario, is considering booking the rock band Soggy Crackers to play a college concert. There are two possible locations that Steve can book for the concert: the college's amphitheater and its sports arena. The amphitheater will cost Steve $1000 plus 5% of ticket revenues. The sports arens will cost Steve $800 plus 7% of ticket revenues. The amphitheater can seat 1300 people. The sports arena is currently undergoing remodeling, and Steve believes that when the remodeling is completed the number of people it will be able to seat will follow a discrete uniform distribution of between 1501 and 1550 people.

   Steve will sell tickets through student clubs. He estimates that the ticket demand will follow a normal distribution, with a mean of 1200 tickets and a standard deviation of 250 tickets. Steve estimates that the revenue he will earn per ticket is $11.

   Besides the location rental fee, Steve believes that the other fixed costs (e.g., advertising, paying the band, security, etc.) will follow a uniform distribution of between $10,000 and $11,500.

   Using Crystal Ball, determine which location Steve should book and give a 95% confidence interval for his expected profit from booking the band. Base your analysis on 1,000 simulation runs.

36. Joe Marino is contemplating signing on to work as a fisherman on a four-person Alaska fishing boat this season. As a crew member, Joe will receive 10% of the revenue that the ship generates.

   The fishing season lasts anywhere from 125 to 144 days, depending on when the waters start to freeze up. Joe believes that the length of the fishing season can be modeled as a discrete uniform distribution. On any day during the fishing season, there is a 15% chance of stormy weather that would prevent the ship from fishing. The daily catch on the days that the boat does fish can be modeled as a normal distribution with a mean of 2400 pounds and a standard deviation of 500 pounds. The revenue the ship receives per pound each day is uniformly distributed between $.85 and $1.05 per pound.

   Using Crystal Ball, develop a simulation for Joe Marino to estimate the likelihood he will earn more than $26,000 during the fishing season. Base your results on 1000 simulation runs.

37. Campus Bookstore is trying to decide on how many management science textbooks to purchase to serve students taking a summer course. The class anticipates having 25 students enrolled. For each student in the class, the following probability distribution is believed to hold.

Student	Probability
Wants to purchase new textbook	.55
Wants to purchase used textbook	.35
Does not want to purchase textbook	.10

The bookstore earns $20 on each new textbook it sells and $15 on each used textbook it sells. If it orders too few new books but has used books available, there is a 70% chance a student will purchase a used book. If it orders too few used books but has new books available, there is a 55% chance the student will purchase a new book. For every unsold new textbook the bookstore has it loses $5, whereas for every unsold used textbook the bookstore has it loses $10.

   Do a simulation by hand to estimate the expected profit the bookstore will earn if it orders 13 new textbooks and 10 used textbooks.

38. Consider the situation faced by the campus bookstore in problem 37. Develop an Excel spreadsheet that will determine the bookstore's profit for various order quantities of new and used textbooks. Using Crystal Ball, determine the optimal order quantity for new and used textbooks, basing each ordering policy on 100 simulation runs.

39. Chris Block is a student who works on Saturdays selling ice cream in Central Park. The ice cream cart Chris uses holds 200 ice cream bars. Chris earns $.20 on each bar she sells. The distribution of the interarrival time of customers is estimated to be as follows.

Interarrival Time	Probability
1 minute	.50
2 minutes	.30
3 minutes	.15
4 minutes	.05

Each customer purchases between one and five ice cream bars according to the following distribution.

Number of Bars Purchased	Probability
1	.60
2	.20
3	.10
4	.05
5	.05

Chris will work in the park for up to three hours. Develop an Excel spreadsheet that can be used to determine the expected amount of money Chris will earn during that time. Do 10 simulation runs and on the basis of these 10 runs determine a 95% confidence interval for the average profit Chris will earn per day.

40. Consider the situation faced by Chris Block in problem 39. Using Crystal Ball, conduct 1000 simulation runs and determine the probability Chris earns at least $30.

PROBLEMS 41–50 ARE ON THE CD

CASE STUDIES

CASE 1: Office Central

Office Central is a nationwide mail-order firm specializing in selling office supplies. One of the items the company carries is the Ricon 436 copier. The copiers cost the firm $1825 each, and Office Central sells them for $2499 each. The firm uses a 20% annual holding cost rate so that the daily holding cost per unit is approximately $1. The cost of placing an order with Ricon is $150, and orders have a lead time between three and six working days (the store is open six days a week). The following distribution holds for the lead time:

$$P(\text{lead time} = 3 \text{ days}) = .2$$
$$P(\text{lead time} = 4 \text{ days}) = .4$$
$$P(\text{lead time} = 5 \text{ days}) = .3$$
$$P(\text{lead time} = 6 \text{ days}) = .1$$

If Office Central is out of Ricon copiers, it offers customers a $150 discount off the price and agrees to airfreight the copier to the customer as soon as it arrives. Airfreight costs Office Central an additional $95. Eighty percent of customers agree to place a backorder, while 20% go elsewhere to buy their copier. The company has been considering eliminating the out-of-stock discount and estimates that the percentage of customers who will place a backorder will decline from 80% to 50%.

Daily demand for the copiers follows a Poisson distribution with a mean of three units. Office Central has decided to use an order point, order up to level policy for the copiers and wishes to determine an optimal policy.

Conduct a simulation analysis of this problem. From the output of this model, prepare a business report to Joe Dixon, Operations Manager of Office Central, with your recommendation regarding the inventory policy for the Ricon 436 copier under the current discount policy. Include in your report a recommendation regarding eliminating the discount as well as a discussion regarding the effect a 10% decrease in the holding cost would have on your inventory policy recommendations. Each simulation run should cover at least 5000 days of operations.

CASE 2: Four Wheel Tire Shop

Four Wheel Tire Shop is a single bay tire store located in Ames, Iowa. The interarrival time of cars in need of tires follows a uniform distribution with times between 10 and 50 minutes. Twenty percent of arriving customers want a single tire replaced, 40% want two tires replaced, 5% want three tires replaced, and 35% want all four tires replaced. Customer service time approximately follows a uniform distribution that varies with the number of tires that need to be replaced. The following statistics hold:

Number of Tires Needing Replacement	Service Time Is Uniformly Distributed Between
1	10 minutes and 20 minutes
2	15 minutes and 35 minutes
3	20 minutes and 40 minutes
4	25 minutes and 50 minutes

The owner of the store, Ben Stern, is considering leasing a new computerized tire balancing machine, which will reduce the average service time, resulting in the following uniform service distributions:

Number of Tires Needing Replacement	Service Time Is Uniformly Distributed Between
1	8 minutes and 18 minutes
2	12 minutes and 32 minutes
3	15 minutes and 35 minutes
4	20 minutes and 40 minutes

The machine lease cost averages $1.50 per hour. Mr. Stern estimates that the goodwill cost of a customer's being in the tire shop (either being served or waiting to be served) is $4.00.

Use Excel to perform the simulation analysis and prepare a business report for Mr. Stern recommending whether or not he should lease the machine. Include in your report relevant service statistics, such as the average time a customer spends waiting to begin service as well as time in the system using both the existing tire balancing machine and the proposed computerized balancing machine. Each simulation run should cover at least 1000 cars.

| CASE 3:   Scandia House

Scandia House sells Scandinavian-style furnishings. One of its more popular items is a five-shelf teak veneer bookcase that costs $58.40 and sells for $99. Scandia House uses a 25% annual inventory holding cost rate; thus the holding cost is $0.04 per bookcase per day. The cost of placing an order with the firm's supplier is $30, and lead time is between 8 and 12 days with the following probability distribution:

$$P(\text{lead time} = 8 \text{ days}) = .10$$
$$P(\text{lead time} = 9 \text{ days}) = .15$$
$$P(\text{lead time} = 10 \text{ days}) = .20$$
$$P(\text{lead time} = 11 \text{ days}) = .25$$
$$P(\text{lead time} = 12 \text{ days}) = .30$$

The number of customers who arrive at Scandia House to purchase the teak bookcases each day can be approximated by a Poisson distribution with a mean of 1.5. Each customer who arrives to purchase bookcases buys between one and four units, with the following probability distribution:

Number of Bookcases Demanded	Probability
1	.50
2	.30
3	.15
4	.05

CASE STUDY 4 ON THE CD

If a customer wants to purchase bookcases but the store does not have enough stock to satisfy the order, the store offers customers either a more expensive substitute bookcase or a discount of $20 per bookcase for each bookcase that is backordered. Scandia House management believes that 30% of customers will accept the substitute bookcase, while 50% of customers will take the discount and backorder. The other 20% of customers will go elsewhere for the bookcases, and their sales will be lost. The substitute bookcases cost the firm $80 each and are always available. (Note that if a customer elects to backorder and Scandia House has sufficient inventory to satisfy part of the order, the store will sell the customer as many bookcases as are available.)

Develop a simulation model to analyze this problem using Excel. Try numerous combinations of order quantity and reorder point values. Simulate at least 1000 days of demand. From the results of this model, prepare a business report to Gudrun Kroner, president of Scandia House, regarding a recommended inventory policy for the teak bookcases.

Statistical Tables

Standard Normal Distribution P(0 < Z < z)

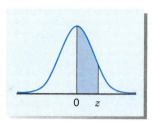

z	0.00	0.01	0.02	0.03	0.04	0.05	0.06	0.07	0.08	0.09
0.00	.0000	.0040	.0080	.0120	.0160	.0199	.0239	.0279	.0319	.0359
0.10	.0398	.0438	.0478	.0517	.0557	.0596	.0636	.0675	.0714	.0753
0.20	.0793	.0832	.0871	.0910	.0948	.0987	.1026	.1064	.1103	.1141
0.30	.1179	.1217	.1255	.1293	.1331	.1368	.1406	.1443	.1480	.1517
0.40	.1554	.1591	.1628	.1664	.1700	.1736	.1772	.1808	.1844	.1879
0.50	.1915	.1950	.1985	.2019	.2054	.2088	.2123	.2157	.2190	.2224
0.60	.2257	.2291	.2324	.2357	.2389	.2422	.2454	.2486	.2517	.2549
0.70	.2580	.2611	.2642	.2673	.2704	.2734	.2764	.2794	.2823	.2852
0.80	.2881	.2910	.2939	.2967	.2995	.3023	.3051	.3078	.3106	.3133
0.90	.3159	.3186	.3212	.3238	.3264	.3289	.3315	.3340	.3365	.3389
1.00	.3413	.3438	.3461	.3485	.3508	.3531	.3554	.3577	.3599	.3621
1.10	.3643	.3665	.3686	.3708	.3729	.3749	.3770	.3790	.3810	.3830
1.20	.3849	.3869	.3888	.3907	.3925	.3944	.3962	.3980	.3997	.4015
1.30	.4032	.4049	.4066	.4082	.4099	.4115	.4131	.4147	.4162	.4177
1.40	.4192	.4207	.4222	.4236	.4251	.4265	.4279	.4292	.4306	.4319
1.50	.4332	.4345	.4357	.4370	.4382	.4394	.4406	.4418	.4429	.4441
1.60	.4452	.4463	.4474	.4484	.4495	.4505	.4515	.4525	.4535	.4545
1.70	.4554	.4564	.4573	.4582	.4591	.4599	.4608	.4616	.4625	.4633
1.80	.4641	.4649	.4656	.4664	.4671	.4678	.4686	.4693	.4699	.4706
1.90	.4713	.4719	.4726	.4732	.4738	.4744	.4750	.4756	.4761	.4767
2.00	.4772	.4778	.4783	.4788	.4793	.4798	.4803	.4808	.4812	.4817
2.10	.4821	.4826	.4830	.4834	.4838	.4842	.4846	.4850	.4854	.4857
2.20	.4861	.4864	.4868	.4871	.4875	.4878	.4881	.4884	.4887	.4890
2.30	.4893	.4896	.4898	.4901	.4904	.4906	.4909	.4911	.4913	.4916
2.40	.4918	.4920	.4922	.4925	.4927	.4929	.4931	.4932	.4934	.4936
2.50	.4938	.4940	.4941	.4943	.4945	.4946	.4948	.4949	.4951	.4952
2.60	.4953	.4955	.4956	.4957	.4959	.4960	.4961	.4962	.4963	.4964
2.70	.4965	.4966	.4967	.4968	.4969	.4970	.4971	.4972	.4973	.4974
2.80	.4974	.4975	.4976	.4977	.4977	.4978	.4979	.4979	.4980	.4981
2.90	.4981	.4982	.4982	.4983	.4984	.4984	.4985	.4985	.4986	.4986
3.00	.4987	.4987	.4987	.4988	.4988	.4989	.4989	.4989	.4990	.4990
3.10	.4990	.4991	.4991	.4991	.4992	.4992	.4992	.4992	.4993	.4993
3.20	.4993	.4993	.4994	.4994	.4994	.4994	.4994	.4995	.4995	.4995
3.30	.4995	.4995	.4995	.4996	.4996	.4996	.4996	.4996	.4996	.4997
3.40	.4997	.4997	.4997	.4997	.4997	.4997	.4997	.4997	.4997	.4998
3.50	.4998	.4998	.4998	.4998	.4998	.4998	.4998	.4998	.4998	.4998

Generated from Excel using the z-row as row 1 and the z-column as column A. The entries in cell (i,j) are:
=NORMSDIST($Aj+i$1) − .5.

Partial Expectations of the Standard Normal Distribution L(Z)

z	.00	.01	.02	.03	.04	.05	.06	.07	.08	0.09
−2.90	2.9005	2.9105	2.9205	2.9305	2.9405	2.9505	2.9604	2.9704	2.9804	2.9904
−2.80	2.8008	2.8107	2.8207	2.8307	2.8407	2.8506	2.8606	2.8706	2.8806	2.8906
−2.70	2.7011	2.7110	2.7210	2.7310	2.7409	2.7509	2.7609	2.7708	2.7808	2.7908
−2.60	2.6015	2.6114	2.6214	2.6313	2.6413	2.6512	2.6612	2.6712	2.6811	2.6911
−2.50	2.5020	2.5119	2.5219	2.5318	2.5418	2.5517	2.5617	2.5716	2.5816	2.5915
−2.40	2.4027	2.4126	2.4226	2.4325	2.4424	2.4523	2.4623	2.4722	2.4821	2.4921
−2.30	2.3037	2.3136	2.3235	2.3334	2.3433	2.3532	2.3631	2.3730	2.3829	2.3928
−2.20	2.2049	2.2147	2.2246	2.2345	2.2444	2.2542	2.2641	2.2740	2.2839	2.2938
−2.10	2.1065	2.1163	2.1261	2.1360	2.1458	2.1556	2.1655	2.1753	2.1852	2.1950
−2.00	2.0085	2.0183	2.0280	2.0378	2.0476	2.0574	2.0672	2.0770	2.0868	2.0966
−1.90	1.9111	1.9208	1.9305	1.9402	1.9500	1.9597	1.9694	1.9792	1.9890	1.9987
−1.80	1.8143	1.8239	1.8336	1.8432	1.8529	1.8626	1.8723	1.8819	1.8916	1.9013
−1.70	1.7183	1.7278	1.7374	1.7470	1.7566	1.7662	1.7758	1.7854	1.7950	1.8046
−1.60	1.6232	1.6327	1.6422	1.6516	1.6611	1.6706	1.6801	1.6897	1.6992	1.7087
−1.50	1.5293	1.5386	1.5480	1.5574	1.5667	1.5761	1.5855	1.5949	1.6044	1.6138
−1.40	1.4367	1.4459	1.4551	1.4643	1.4736	1.4828	1.4921	1.5014	1.5107	1.5200
−1.30	1.3455	1.3546	1.3636	1.3727	1.3818	1.3909	1.4000	1.4092	1.4183	1.4275
−1.20	1.2561	1.2650	1.2738	1.2827	1.2917	1.3006	1.3095	1.3185	1.3275	1.3365
−1.10	1.1686	1.1773	1.1859	1.1946	1.2034	1.2121	1.2209	1.2296	1.2384	1.2473
−1.00	1.0833	1.0917	1.1002	1.1087	1.1172	1.1257	1.1342	1.1428	1.1514	1.1600
−0.90	1.0004	1.0086	1.0168	1.0250	1.0333	1.0416	1.0499	1.0582	1.0665	1.0749
−0.80	.9202	.9281	.9360	.9440	.9520	.9600	.9680	.9761	.9842	.9923
−0.70	.8429	.8505	.8581	.8658	.8734	.8812	.8889	.8967	.9045	.9123
−0.60	.7687	.7759	.7833	.7906	.7980	.8054	.8128	.8203	.8278	.8353
−0.50	.6978	.7047	.7117	.7187	.7257	.7328	.7399	.7471	.7542	.7614
−0.40	.6304	.6370	.6436	.6503	.6569	.6637	.6704	.6772	.6840	.6909
−0.30	.5668	.5730	.5792	.5855	.5918	.5981	.6045	.6109	.6174	.6239
−0.20	.5069	.5127	.5186	.5244	.5304	.5363	.5424	.5484	.5545	.5606
−0.10	.4509	.4564	.4618	.4673	.4728	.4784	.4840	.4897	.4954	.5011
−0.00	—	.4040	.4090	.4141	.4193	.4244	.4297	.4349	.4402	.4456

Generated from Excel using row 1 for the z-row and column A for the z-column. The cell entries are:
$$=EXP(-((\$Aj-i\$1)*(\$Aj-i\$1))/2)/((2*PI())^{0.5})-(\$A-i\$1)*(1-NORMSDIST(\$Aj-i\$1)))$$

z	.00	.01	.02	.03	.04	.05	.06	.07	.08	0.09
0.00	.3989	.3940	.3890	.3841	.3793	.3744	.3697	.3649	.3602	.3556
0.10	.3509	.3464	.3418	.3373	.3328	.3284	.3240	.3197	.3154	.3111
0.20	.3069	.3027	.2986	.2944	.2904	.2863	.2824	.2784	.2745	.2706
0.30	.2668	.2630	.2592	.2555	.2518	.2481	.2445	.2409	.2374	.2339
0.40	.2304	.2270	.2236	.2203	.2169	.2137	.2104	.2072	.2040	.2009
0.50	.1978	.1947	.1917	.1887	.1857	.1828	.1799	.1771	.1742	.1714
0.60	.1687	.1659	.1633	.1606	.1580	.1554	.1528	.1503	.1478	.1453
0.70	.1429	.1405	.1381	.1358	.1334	.1312	.1289	.1267	.1245	.1223
0.80	.1202	.1181	.1160	.1140	.1120	.1100	.1080	.1061	.1042	.1023
0.90	.1004	.0986	.0968	.0950	.0933	.0916	.0899	.0882	.0865	.0849
1.00	.0833	.0817	.0802	.0787	.0772	.0757	.0742	.0728	.0714	.0700
1.10	.0686	.0673	.0659	.0646	.0634	.0621	.0609	.0596	.0584	.0573
1.20	.0561	.0550	.0538	.0527	.0517	.0506	.0495	.0485	.0475	.0465
1.30	.0455	.0446	.0436	.0427	.0418	.0409	.0400	.0392	.0383	.0375
1.40	.0367	.0359	.0351	.0343	.0336	.0328	.0321	.0314	.0307	.0300
1.50	.0293	.0286	.0280	.0274	.0267	.0261	.0255	.0249	.0244	.0238
1.60	.0232	.0227	.0222	.0216	.0211	.0206	.0201	.0197	.0192	.0187
1.70	.0183	.0178	.0174	.0170	.0166	.0162	.0158	.0154	.0150	.0146
1.80	.0143	.0139	.0136	.0132	.0129	.0126	.0123	.0119	.0116	.0113
1.90	.0111	.0108	.0105	.0102	.0100	.0097	.0094	.0092	.0090	.0087
2.00	.0085	.0083	.0080	.0078	.0076	.0074	.0072	.0070	.0068	.0066
2.10	.0065	.0063	.0061	.0060	.0058	.0056	.0055	.0053	.0052	.0050
2.20	.0049	.0047	.0046	.0045	.0044	.0042	.0041	.0040	.0039	.0038
2.30	.0037	.0036	.0035	.0034	.0033	.0032	.0031	.0030	.0029	.0028
2.40	.0027	.0026	.0026	.0025	.0024	.0023	.0023	.0022	.0021	.0021
2.50	.0020	.0019	.0019	.0018	.0018	.0017	.0017	.0016	.0016	.0015
2.60	.0015	.0014	.0014	.0013	.0013	.0012	.0012	.0012	.0011	.0011
2.70	.0011	.0010	.0010	.0010	.0009	.0009	.0009	.0008	.0008	.0008
2.80	.0008	.0007	.0007	.0007	.0007	.0006	.0006	.0006	.0006	.0006
2.90	.0005	.0005	.0005	.0005	.0005	.0005	.0004	.0004	.0004	.0004

Generated from Excel using row 1 for the z-row and column A for the z-column. The cell entries are:
$$=EXP(-((\$Aj+i\$1)*(\$Aj+i\$1))/2)/((2*PI())^{0.5})-(\$Aj+i\$1)*(1-NORMSDIST(\$Aj+i\$1)))$$

Table of Pseudo-Random Numbers

	1	2	3	4	5	6	7	8	9	10	11	12	13	14	15
1	6506	3338	2197	8927	6320	1094	1995	5971	5147	3620	0582	2982	8731	6037	4231
2	7761	9874	9834	8848	4630	7371	7971	6600	1296	5299	1374	9517	8177	2403	7443
3	6170	2631	6268	9089	8657	2809	3554	4814	7401	9983	8613	3199	6005	1879	9339
4	8800	9139	8305	2605	0030	5148	6300	1762	2499	5417	2607	7111	9892	3703	8408
5	4211	9651	0051	7982	5624	9115	5495	2710	2888	9620	5078	6541	5066	9082	8981
6	7452	4883	5619	5541	6728	1469	5165	1908	9619	2043	9221	6405	6559	6343	8920
7	1182	8260	3367	2624	5925	6480	9339	5104	7435	4121	9234	9031	3506	6230	1202
8	4012	2781	6140	1603	2829	2447	6997	4947	3343	3125	1070	2998	1236	9821	6438
9	0335	9636	1645	4063	7939	7031	1443	7610	9665	3357	6415	4994	3780	8437	6475
10	6299	4696	8036	6519	6476	8442	3574	4978	7911	0759	7991	2677	4401	9996	3878
11	5482	2016	7017	6106	3319	7387	0150	7166	7336	2121	1006	4066	5675	8784	6141
12	1085	4426	4988	6807	8134	1788	0933	7209	3054	0107	0033	2795	9978	4542	5388
13	1698	8464	8208	7589	1712	4891	7082	3021	4519	2000	7987	4122	8150	3058	1281
14	6969	9424	1524	6590	6317	1149	5025	8181	0013	1805	7521	6735	1511	4255	7643
15	1696	6693	9525	0882	6605	8822	4081	0772	8234	9257	3985	5061	2021	9265	9641
16	0267	6317	1051	3193	2734	9451	4100	1471	3270	1065	6001	4366	7642	2800	5026
17	3175	7529	1759	2084	0432	2990	7190	4648	8760	9085	4591	3874	7636	3983	7406
18	7959	0515	8149	4053	3441	8314	6822	0714	7731	6648	3007	5625	8682	8699	3711
19	4958	1069	0318	9941	0726	7176	5053	5177	6950	9598	0640	0297	7153	5376	3610
20	4281	1877	8785	0967	6969	2766	8284	2528	0194	2496	4152	9645	3200	8762	1574
21	2231	0382	7782	7890	3434	5391	2022	6820	9294	8609	6437	3848	0668	2868	7085
22	0002	0786	2889	1522	0059	1313	9858	1336	4964	3223	3010	9118	6072	6432	1895
23	8434	7236	3686	8333	0617	1821	4297	9250	5737	2599	3785	4356	6943	1461	6921
24	8959	5886	9020	7247	5586	7136	0595	2432	0685	1058	6967	0202	8565	1423	6268
25	8975	6480	9478	5140	0996	6483	0881	4444	5587	4517	5402	4436	1516	8855	1132
26	1288	8758	5711	0916	1114	2046	2564	4713	5154	7742	1653	2428	8366	7530	8709
27	6412	0141	9310	7329	6063	4279	8996	6782	5013	1565	8090	8400	6118	5830	6202
28	6463	0315	2277	3642	4400	5030	9321	6107	8498	7838	8209	4891	8378	8816	2156
29	3856	1780	5371	1981	8971	2679	7859	1416	8795	4004	1302	2802	1445	8578	0356
30	6117	4088	7219	2557	6612	3386	2724	8737	6412	5548	5214	6804	4716	2134	6811
31	5396	2510	3168	9061	5963	2243	6824	6614	1074	6839	5576	8077	9191	2406	8859
32	1281	1710	4009	5721	5830	1755	1225	6382	4148	1870	3651	5876	9282	4682	6765
33	7644	0296	2395	7493	8626	4617	9388	2845	1363	4705	6759	2983	7857	8906	1027
34	8608	3656	0659	6827	2183	9893	4989	1855	9358	1041	4488	3197	1723	4120	6987
35	9359	0331	6735	1301	7891	5985	1119	8374	1817	4825	8017	2728	7241	6119	0439
36	4233	0282	0397	0646	0527	9247	2280	6931	3963	3227	9732	9148	6735	5047	0981
37	3871	1294	9059	7680	5964	5402	6068	1781	6103	3768	1999	2403	3006	3742	2539

A similar table can be generated in Excel by entering for each cell: =INT(RAND()*10000).

APPENDIX D

t Distribution: Values of t That Puts α in the Upper Tail

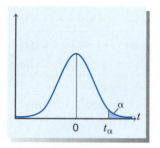

Degrees of Freedom	Values of α							
	.10	0.05	0.025	0.01	0.005	0.0025	0.001	0.0005
1	3.0777	6.3137	12.7062	31.8210	63.6559	127.3211	318.2888	636.5776
2	1.8856	2.9200	4.3027	6.9645	9.9250	14.0892	22.3285	31.5998
3	1.6377	2.3534	3.1824	4.5407	5.8408	7.4532	10.2143	12.9244
4	1.5332	2.1318	2.7765	3.7469	4.6041	5.5975	7.1729	8.6101
5	1.4759	2.0150	2.5706	3.3649	4.0321	4.7733	5.8935	6.8685
6	1.4398	1.9432	2.4469	3.1427	3.7074	4.3168	5.2075	5.9587
7	1.4149	1.8946	2.3646	2.9979	3.4995	4.0294	4.7853	5.4081
8	1.3968	1.8595	2.3060	2.8965	3.3554	3.8325	4.5008	5.0414
9	1.3830	1.8331	2.2622	2.8214	3.2498	3.6896	4.2969	4.7809
10	1.3722	1.8125	2.2281	2.7638	3.1693	3.5814	4.1437	4.5868
11	1.3634	1.7959	2.2010	2.7181	3.1058	3.4966	4.0248	4.4369
12	1.3562	1.7823	2.1788	2.6810	3.0545	3.4284	3.9296	4.3178
13	1.3502	1.7709	2.1604	2.6503	3.0123	3.3725	3.8520	4.2209
14	1.3450	1.7613	2.1448	2.6245	2.9768	3.3257	3.7874	4.1403
15	1.3406	1.7531	2.1315	2.6025	2.9467	3.2860	3.7329	4.0728
16	1.3368	1.7459	2.1199	2.5835	2.9208	3.2520	3.6861	4.0149
17	1.3334	1.7396	2.1098	2.5669	2.8982	3.2224	3.6458	3.9651
18	1.3304	1.7341	2.1009	2.5524	2.8784	3.1966	3.6105	3.9217
19	1.3277	1.7291	2.0930	2.5395	2.8609	3.1737	3.5793	3.8833
20	1.3253	1.7247	2.0860	2.5280	2.8453	3.1534	3.5518	3.8496
21	1.3232	1.7207	2.0796	2.5176	2.8314	3.1352	3.5271	3.8193
22	1.3212	1.7171	2.0739	2.5083	2.8188	3.1188	3.5050	3.7922
23	1.3195	1.7139	2.0687	2.4999	2.8073	3.1040	3.4850	3.7676
24	1.3178	1.7109	2.0639	2.4922	2.7970	3.0905	3.4668	3.7454
25	1.3163	1.7081	2.0595	2.4851	2.7874	3.0782	3.4502	3.7251
26	1.3150	1.7056	2.0555	2.4786	2.7787	3.0669	3.4350	3.7067
27	1.3137	1.7033	2.0518	2.4727	2.7707	3.0565	3.4210	3.6895
28	1.3125	1.7011	2.0484	2.4671	2.7633	3.0470	3.4082	3.6739
29	1.3114	1.6991	2.0452	2.4620	2.7564	3.0380	3.3963	3.6595
30	1.3104	1.6973	2.0423	2.4573	2.7500	3.0298	3.3852	3.6460
99	1.2902	1.6604	1.9842	2.3646	2.6264	2.8713	3.1746	3.3915
199	1.2858	1.6525	1.9720	2.3452	2.6008	2.8387	3.1317	3.3401
499	1.2833	1.6479	1.9647	2.3338	2.5857	2.8196	3.1067	3.3101

Generated from Excel using row 2 for the values of α and column A for the degrees of freedom. The entries in cell (i,j) are: =TINV(2*j$2,$Ai).

χ^2 Distribution:
Values of χ^2 That Puts α in the Upper Tail

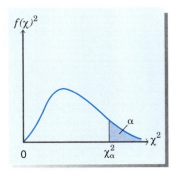

Degrees of Freedom	Values of α							
	.10	0.05	0.025	0.01	0.005	0.0025	0.001	0.0005
1	2.7055	3.8415	5.0239	6.6349	7.8794	9.1404	10.8274	12.1153
2	4.6052	5.9915	7.3778	9.2104	10.5965	11.9827	13.8150	15.2014
3	6.2514	7.8147	9.3484	11.3449	12.8381	14.3202	16.2660	17.7311
4	7.7794	9.4877	11.1433	13.2767	14.8602	16.4238	18.4662	19.9977
5	9.2363	11.0705	12.8325	15.0863	16.7496	18.3854	20.5147	22.1057
6	10.6446	12.5916	14.4494	16.8119	18.5475	20.2491	22.4575	24.1016
7	12.0170	14.0671	16.0128	18.4753	20.2777	22.0402	24.3213	26.0179
8	13.3616	15.5073	17.5345	20.0902	21.9549	23.7742	26.1239	27.8674
9	14.6837	16.9190	19.0228	21.6660	23.5893	25.4625	27.8767	29.6669
10	15.9872	18.3070	20.4832	23.2093	25.1881	27.1119	29.5879	31.4195
11	17.2750	19.6752	21.9200	24.7250	26.7569	28.7291	31.2635	33.1382
12	18.5493	21.0261	23.3367	26.2170	28.2997	30.3182	32.9092	34.8211
13	19.8119	22.3620	24.7356	27.6882	29.8193	31.8830	34.5274	36.4768
14	21.0641	23.6848	26.1189	29.1412	31.3194	33.4262	36.1239	38.1085
15	22.3071	24.9958	27.4884	30.5780	32.8015	34.9494	37.6978	39.7173
16	23.5418	26.2962	28.8453	31.9999	34.2671	36.4555	39.2518	41.3077
17	24.7690	27.5871	30.1910	33.4087	35.7184	37.9462	40.7911	42.8808
18	25.9894	28.8693	31.5264	34.8052	37.1564	39.4220	42.3119	44.4337
19	27.2036	30.1435	32.8523	36.1908	38.5821	40.8847	43.8194	45.9738
20	28.4120	31.4104	34.1696	37.5663	39.9969	42.3358	45.3142	47.4977
21	29.6151	32.6706	35.4789	38.9322	41.4009	43.7749	46.7963	49.0096
22	30.8133	33.9245	36.7807	40.2894	42.7957	45.2041	48.2676	50.5105
23	32.0069	35.1725	38.0756	41.6383	44.1814	46.6231	49.7276	51.9995
24	33.1962	36.4150	39.3641	42.9798	45.5584	48.0336	51.1790	53.4776
25	34.3816	37.6525	40.6465	44.3140	46.9280	49.4351	52.6187	54.9475
26	35.5632	38.8851	41.9231	45.6416	48.2898	50.8291	54.0511	56.4068
27	36.7412	40.1133	43.1945	46.9628	49.6450	52.2152	55.4751	57.8556
28	37.9159	41.3372	44.4608	48.2782	50.9936	53.5939	56.8918	59.2990
29	39.0875	42.5569	45.7223	49.5878	52.3355	54.9662	58.3006	60.7342
30	40.2560	43.7730	46.9792	50.8922	53.6719	56.3325	59.7022	62.1600
99	117.4069	123.2252	128.4219	134.6415	138.9869	143.0945	148.2297	151.9312
199	224.9568	232.9118	239.9598	248.3284	254.1350	259.5940	266.3860	271.2568
499	539.8898	552.0747	562.7896	575.4189	584.1246	592.2692	602.3506	609.5466

Generated from Excel using row 2 for the values of α and column A for the degrees of freedom. The entries in cell (i,j) are: =CHIINV(j$2,$Ai).

APPENDIX F (.01)

F Distribution:
Values of F That Puts .01 in the Upper Tail

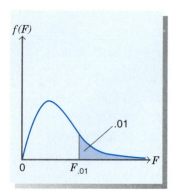

Denominator Degrees of Freedom	Numerator Degrees of Freedom												
	1	2	3	4	5	6	7	8	9	10	11	12	13
1	4052	4999	5404	5624	5764	5859	5928	5981	6022	6056	6083	6107	6126
2	98.50	99.00	99.16	99.25	99.30	99.33	99.36	99.38	99.39	99.40	99.41	99.42	99.42
3	34.12	30.82	29.46	28.71	28.24	27.91	27.67	27.49	27.34	27.23	27.13	27.05	26.98
4	21.20	18.00	16.69	15.98	15.52	15.21	14.98	14.80	14.66	14.55	14.45	14.37	14.31
5	16.26	13.27	12.06	11.39	10.97	10.67	10.46	10.29	10.16	10.05	9.96	9.89	9.82
6	13.75	10.92	9.78	9.15	8.75	8.47	8.26	8.10	7.98	7.87	7.79	7.72	7.66
7	12.25	9.55	8.45	7.85	7.46	7.19	6.99	6.84	6.72	6.62	6.54	6.47	6.41
8	11.26	8.65	7.59	7.01	6.63	6.37	6.18	6.03	5.91	5.81	5.73	5.67	5.61
9	10.56	8.02	6.99	6.42	6.06	5.80	5.61	5.47	5.35	5.26	5.18	5.11	5.05
10	10.04	7.56	6.55	5.99	5.64	5.39	5.20	5.06	4.94	4.85	4.77	4.71	4.65
11	9.65	7.21	6.22	5.67	5.32	5.07	4.89	4.74	4.63	4.54	4.46	4.40	4.34
12	9.33	6.93	5.95	5.41	5.06	4.82	4.64	4.50	4.39	4.30	4.22	4.16	4.10
13	9.07	6.70	5.74	5.21	4.86	4.62	4.44	4.30	4.19	4.10	4.02	3.96	3.91
14	8.86	6.51	5.56	5.04	4.69	4.46	4.28	4.14	4.03	3.94	3.86	3.80	3.75
15	8.68	6.36	5.42	4.89	4.56	4.32	4.14	4.00	3.89	3.80	3.73	3.67	3.61
16	8.53	6.23	5.29	4.77	4.44	4.20	4.03	3.89	3.78	3.69	3.62	3.55	3.50
17	8.40	6.11	5.19	4.67	4.34	4.10	3.93	3.79	3.68	3.59	3.52	3.46	3.40
18	8.29	6.01	5.09	4.58	4.25	4.01	3.84	3.71	3.60	3.51	3.43	3.37	3.32
19	8.18	5.93	5.01	4.50	4.17	3.94	3.77	3.63	3.52	3.43	3.36	3.30	3.24
20	8.10	5.85	4.94	4.43	4.10	3.87	3.70	3.56	3.46	3.37	3.29	3.23	3.18
21	8.02	5.78	4.87	4.37	4.04	3.81	3.64	3.51	3.40	3.31	3.24	3.17	3.12
22	7.95	5.72	4.82	4.31	3.99	3.76	3.59	3.45	3.35	3.26	3.18	3.12	3.07
23	7.88	5.66	4.76	4.26	3.94	3.71	3.54	3.41	3.30	3.21	3.14	3.07	3.02
24	7.82	5.61	4.72	4.22	3.90	3.67	3.50	3.36	3.26	3.17	3.09	3.03	2.98
25	7.77	5.57	4.68	4.18	3.85	3.63	3.46	3.32	3.22	3.13	3.06	2.99	2.94
26	7.72	5.53	4.64	4.14	3.82	3.59	3.42	3.29	3.18	3.09	3.02	2.96	2.90
27	7.68	5.49	4.60	4.11	3.78	3.56	3.39	3.26	3.15	3.06	2.99	2.93	2.87
28	7.64	5.45	4.57	4.07	3.75	3.53	3.36	3.23	3.12	3.03	2.96	2.90	2.84
29	7.60	5.42	4.54	4.04	3.73	3.50	3.33	3.20	3.09	3.00	2.93	2.87	2.81
30	7.56	5.39	4.51	4.02	3.70	3.47	3.30	3.17	3.07	2.98	2.91	2.84	2.79
31	7.53	5.36	4.48	3.99	3.67	3.45	3.28	3.15	3.04	2.96	2.88	2.82	2.77
32	7.50	5.34	4.46	3.97	3.65	3.43	3.26	3.13	3.02	2.93	2.86	2.80	2.74
33	7.47	5.31	4.44	3.95	3.63	3.41	3.24	3.11	3.00	2.91	2.84	2.78	2.72
34	7.44	5.29	4.42	3.93	3.61	3.39	3.22	3.09	2.98	2.89	2.82	2.76	2.70
35	7.42	5.27	4.40	3.91	3.59	3.37	3.20	3.07	2.96	2.88	2.80	2.74	2.69
36	7.40	5.25	4.38	3.89	3.57	3.35	3.18	3.05	2.95	2.86	2.79	2.72	2.67
37	7.37	5.23	4.36	3.87	3.56	3.33	3.17	3.04	2.93	2.84	2.77	2.71	2.65
38	7.35	5.21	4.34	3.86	3.54	3.32	3.15	3.02	2.92	2.83	2.75	2.69	2.64
39	7.33	5.19	4.33	3.84	3.53	3.30	3.14	3.01	2.90	2.81	2.74	2.68	2.62
49	7.18	5.07	4.21	3.73	3.42	3.19	3.03	2.90	2.79	2.71	2.63	2.57	2.52
59	7.08	4.98	4.13	3.65	3.34	3.12	2.96	2.83	2.72	2.64	2.56	2.50	2.45
69	7.02	4.93	4.08	3.60	3.29	3.08	2.91	2.78	2.68	2.59	2.52	2.45	2.40
79	6.97	4.88	4.04	3.57	3.26	3.04	2.87	2.75	2.64	2.55	2.48	2.42	2.36
89	6.93	4.85	4.01	3.54	3.23	3.01	2.85	2.72	2.61	2.53	2.45	2.39	2.34
99	6.90	4.83	3.99	3.51	3.21	2.99	2.83	2.70	2.59	2.51	2.43	2.37	2.32
199	6.76	4.71	3.88	3.41	3.11	2.89	2.73	2.60	2.50	2.41	2.34	2.28	2.22
499	6.69	4.65	3.82	3.36	3.05	2.84	2.68	2.55	2.44	2.36	2.28	2.22	2.17

Generated from Excel using row 2 for the numerator degrees of freedom and column A for the denominator degrees of freedom. The entries in cell (i,j) are: =FINV(0.01,j$2,$Ai).

F Distribution
Value of F That Puts .01 in the Upper Tail (cont.)

Denominator Degrees of Freedom	Numerator Degrees of Freedom												
	14	15	19	24	29	39	49	59	69	79	89	99	199
1	6143	6157	6201	6234	6257	6285	6301	6313	6320	6326	6330	6334	6350
2	99.43	99.43	99.45	99.46	99.46	99.47	99.48	99.48	99.48	99.48	99.49	99.49	99.49
3	26.92	26.87	26.72	26.60	26.52	26.42	26.36	26.32	26.29	26.27	26.25	26.24	26.18
4	14.25	14.20	14.05	13.93	13.85	13.75	13.69	13.66	13.63	13.61	13.59	13.58	13.52
5	9.77	9.72	9.58	9.47	9.39	9.30	9.24	9.20	9.18	9.16	9.14	9.13	9.08
6	7.60	7.56	7.42	7.31	7.24	7.15	7.10	7.06	7.03	7.01	7.00	6.99	6.93
7	6.36	6.31	6.18	6.07	6.00	5.91	5.86	5.83	5.80	5.78	5.77	5.76	5.70
8	5.56	5.52	5.38	5.28	5.21	5.12	5.07	5.03	5.01	4.99	4.98	4.96	4.91
9	5.01	4.96	4.83	4.73	4.66	4.57	4.52	4.49	4.46	4.44	4.43	4.42	4.36
10	4.60	4.56	4.43	4.33	4.26	4.17	4.12	4.08	4.06	4.04	4.03	4.01	3.96
11	4.29	4.25	4.12	4.02	3.95	3.87	3.81	3.78	3.75	3.74	3.72	3.71	3.66
12	4.05	4.01	3.88	3.78	3.71	3.63	3.57	3.54	3.51	3.49	3.48	3.47	3.41
13	3.86	3.82	3.69	3.59	3.52	3.43	3.38	3.34	3.32	3.30	3.29	3.27	3.22
14	3.70	3.66	3.53	3.43	3.36	3.27	3.22	3.18	3.16	3.14	3.12	3.11	3.06
15	3.56	3.52	3.40	3.29	3.23	3.14	3.09	3.05	3.02	3.01	2.99	2.98	2.92
16	3.45	3.41	3.28	3.18	3.11	3.02	2.97	2.94	2.91	2.89	2.88	2.86	2.81
17	3.35	3.31	3.19	3.08	3.01	2.93	2.87	2.84	2.81	2.79	2.78	2.77	2.71
18	3.27	3.23	3.10	3.00	2.93	2.84	2.79	2.75	2.73	2.71	2.69	2.68	2.62
19	3.19	3.15	3.03	2.92	2.86	2.77	2.71	2.68	2.65	2.63	2.62	2.60	2.55
20	3.13	3.09	2.96	2.86	2.79	2.70	2.65	2.61	2.58	2.56	2.55	2.54	2.48
21	3.07	3.03	2.90	2.80	2.73	2.64	2.59	2.55	2.52	2.50	2.49	2.48	2.42
22	3.02	2.98	2.85	2.75	2.68	2.59	2.54	2.50	2.47	2.45	2.44	2.42	2.36
23	2.97	2.93	2.80	2.70	2.63	2.54	2.49	2.45	2.42	2.40	2.39	2.37	2.32
24	2.93	2.89	2.76	2.66	2.59	2.50	2.44	2.41	2.38	2.36	2.34	2.33	2.27
25	2.89	2.85	2.72	2.62	2.55	2.46	2.40	2.37	2.34	2.32	2.30	2.29	2.23
26	2.86	2.81	2.69	2.58	2.51	2.42	2.37	2.33	2.30	2.28	2.27	2.25	2.19
27	2.82	2.78	2.66	2.55	2.48	2.39	2.33	2.30	2.27	2.25	2.23	2.22	2.16
28	2.79	2.75	2.63	2.52	2.45	2.36	2.30	2.27	2.24	2.22	2.20	2.19	2.13
29	2.77	2.73	2.60	2.49	2.42	2.33	2.28	2.24	2.21	2.19	2.17	2.16	2.10
30	2.74	2.70	2.57	2.47	2.40	2.31	2.25	2.21	2.18	2.16	2.15	2.13	2.07
31	2.72	2.68	2.55	2.45	2.37	2.28	2.23	2.19	2.16	2.14	2.12	2.11	2.04
32	2.70	2.65	2.53	2.42	2.35	2.26	2.20	2.16	2.14	2.11	2.10	2.08	2.02
33	2.68	2.63	2.51	2.40	2.33	2.24	2.18	2.14	2.11	2.09	2.08	2.06	2.00
34	2.66	2.61	2.49	2.38	2.31	2.22	2.16	2.12	2.09	2.07	2.05	2.04	1.98
35	2.64	2.60	2.47	2.36	2.29	2.20	2.14	2.10	2.07	2.05	2.04	2.02	1.96
36	2.62	2.58	2.45	2.35	2.28	2.18	2.12	2.08	2.06	2.03	2.02	2.00	1.94
37	2.61	2.56	2.44	2.33	2.26	2.17	2.11	2.07	2.04	2.02	2.00	1.99	1.92
38	2.59	2.55	2.42	2.32	2.24	2.15	2.09	2.05	2.02	2.00	1.98	1.97	1.90
39	2.58	2.54	2.41	2.30	2.23	2.14	2.08	2.04	2.01	1.99	1.97	1.95	1.89
49	2.47	2.43	2.30	2.19	2.12	2.02	1.96	1.92	1.89	1.87	1.85	1.84	1.77
59	2.40	2.36	2.23	2.12	2.05	1.95	1.89	1.85	1.81	1.79	1.77	1.76	1.69
69	2.35	2.31	2.18	2.07	2.00	1.90	1.84	1.79	1.76	1.74	1.72	1.70	1.63
79	2.32	2.27	2.14	2.03	1.96	1.86	1.80	1.75	1.72	1.70	1.68	1.66	1.58
89	2.29	2.25	2.12	2.01	1.93	1.83	1.77	1.72	1.69	1.66	1.64	1.63	1.55
99	2.27	2.22	2.09	1.98	1.91	1.81	1.74	1.70	1.66	1.64	1.62	1.60	1.52
199	2.17	2.13	2.00	1.89	1.81	1.70	1.64	1.59	1.55	1.52	1.50	1.48	1.39
499	2.12	2.07	1.94	1.83	1.75	1.64	1.57	1.52	1.48	1.45	1.43	1.41	1.31

Generated from Excel using row 2 for the numerator degrees of freedom and column A for the denominator degrees of freedom. The entries in cell (i,j) are: =FINV(0.01,j$2,$Ai).

F Distribution
Value of F That Puts .05 in the Upper Tail

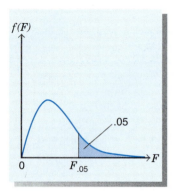

Denominator Degrees of Freedom	Numerator Degrees of Freedom												
	1	2	3	4	5	6	7	8	9	10	11	12	13
1	161.4	199.5	215.7	224.6	230.2	234.0	236.8	238.9	240.5	241.9	243.0	243.9	244.7
2	18.51	19.00	19.61	19.25	19.30	19.33	19.35	19.37	19.38	19.40	19.40	19.41	19.42
3	10.13	9.55	9.28	9.12	9.01	8.94	8.89	8.85	8.81	8.79	8.76	8.74	8.73
4	7.71	6.94	6.59	6.39	6.26	6.16	6.09	6.04	6.00	5.96	5.94	5.91	5.89
5	6.61	5.79	5.41	5.19	5.05	4.95	4.88	4.82	4.77	4.74	4.70	4.68	4.66
6	5.99	5.14	4.76	4.53	4.39	4.28	4.21	4.15	4.10	4.06	4.03	4.00	3.98
7	5.59	4.74	4.35	4.12	3.97	3.87	3.79	3.73	3.68	3.64	3.60	3.57	3.55
8	5.32	4.46	4.07	3.84	3.69	3.58	3.50	3.44	3.39	3.35	3.31	3.28	3.26
9	5.12	4.26	3.86	3.63	3.48	3.37	3.29	3.23	3.18	3.14	3.10	3.07	3.05
10	4.96	4.10	3.71	3.48	3.33	3.22	3.14	3.07	3.02	2.98	2.94	2.91	2.89
11	4.84	3.98	3.59	3.36	3.20	3.09	3.01	2.95	2.90	2.85	2.82	2.79	2.76
12	4.75	3.89	3.49	3.26	3.11	3.00	2.91	2.85	2.80	2.75	2.72	2.69	2.66
13	4.67	3.81	3.41	3.18	3.03	2.92	2.83	2.77	2.71	2.67	2.63	2.60	2.58
14	4.60	3.74	3.34	3.11	2.96	2.85	2.76	2.70	2.65	2.60	2.57	2.53	2.51
15	4.54	3.68	3.29	3.06	2.90	2.79	2.71	2.64	2.59	2.54	2.51	2.48	2.45
16	4.49	3.63	3.24	3.01	2.85	2.74	2.66	2.59	2.54	2.49	2.46	2.42	2.40
17	4.45	3.59	3.20	2.96	2.81	2.70	2.61	2.55	2.49	2.45	2.41	2.38	2.35
18	4.41	3.55	3.16	2.93	2.77	2.66	2.58	2.51	2.46	2.41	2.37	2.34	2.31
19	4.38	3.52	3.13	2.90	2.74	2.63	2.54	2.48	2.42	2.38	2.34	2.31	2.28
20	4.35	3.49	3.10	2.87	2.71	2.60	2.51	2.45	2.39	2.35	2.31	2.28	2.25
21	4.32	3.47	3.07	2.84	2.68	2.57	2.49	2.42	2.37	2.32	2.28	2.25	2.22
22	4.30	3.44	3.05	2.82	2.66	2.55	2.46	2.40	2.34	2.30	2.26	2.23	2.20
23	4.28	3.42	3.03	2.80	2.64	2.53	2.44	2.37	2.32	2.27	2.24	2.20	2.18
24	4.26	3.40	3.01	2.78	2.62	2.51	2.42	2.36	2.30	2.25	2.22	2.18	2.15
25	4.24	3.39	2.99	2.76	2.60	2.49	2.40	2.34	2.28	2.24	2.20	2.16	2.14
26	4.23	3.37	2.98	2.74	2.59	2.47	2.39	2.32	2.27	2.22	2.18	2.15	2.12
27	4.21	3.35	2.96	2.73	2.57	2.46	2.37	2.31	2.25	2.20	2.17	2.13	2.10
28	4.20	3.34	2.95	2.71	2.56	2.45	2.36	2.29	2.24	2.19	2.15	2.12	2.09
29	4.18	3.33	2.93	2.70	2.55	2.43	2.35	2.28	2.22	2.18	2.14	2.10	2.08
30	4.17	3.32	2.92	2.69	2.53	2.42	2.33	2.27	2.21	2.16	2.13	2.09	2.06
31	4.16	3.30	2.91	2.68	2.52	2.41	2.32	2.25	2.20	2.15	2.11	2.08	2.05
32	4.15	3.29	2.90	2.67	2.51	2.40	2.31	2.24	2.19	2.14	2.10	2.07	2.04
33	4.14	3.28	2.89	2.66	2.50	2.39	2.30	2.23	2.18	2.13	2.09	2.06	2.03
34	4.13	3.28	2.88	2.65	2.49	2.38	2.29	2.23	2.17	2.12	2.08	2.05	2.02
35	4.12	3.27	2.87	2.64	2.49	2.37	2.29	2.22	2.16	2.11	2.07	2.04	2.01
36	4.11	3.26	2.87	2.63	2.48	2.36	2.28	2.21	2.15	2.11	2.07	2.03	2.00
37	4.11	3.25	2.86	2.63	2.47	2.36	2.27	2.20	2.14	2.10	2.06	2.02	2.00
38	4.10	3.24	2.85	2.62	2.46	2.35	2.26	2.19	2.14	2.09	2.05	2.02	1.99
39	4.09	3.24	2.85	2.61	2.46	2.34	2.26	2.19	2.13	2.08	2.04	2.01	1.98
49	4.04	3.19	2.79	2.56	2.40	2.29	2.20	2.13	2.08	2.03	1.99	1.96	1.93
59	4.00	3.15	2.76	2.53	2.37	2.26	2.17	2.10	2.04	2.00	1.96	1.92	1.89
69	3.98	3.13	2.74	2.50	2.35	2.23	2.15	2.08	2.02	1.97	1.93	1.90	1.86
79	3.96	3.11	2.72	2.49	2.33	2.22	2.13	2.06	2.00	1.95	1.91	1.88	1.85
89	3.95	3.10	2.71	2.47	2.32	2.20	2.11	2.04	1.99	1.94	1.90	1.86	1.83
99	3.94	3.09	2.70	2.46	2.31	2.19	2.10	2.03	1.98	1.93	1.89	1.85	1.82
199	3.89	3.04	2.65	2.42	2.26	2.14	2.06	1.99	1.93	1.88	1.84	1.80	1.77
499	3.86	3.01	2.62	2.39	2.23	2.12	2.03	1.96	1.90	1.85	1.81	1.77	1.74

Generated from Excel using row 2 for the numerator degrees of freedom and column A for the denominator degrees of freedom. The entries in cell (i,j) are: =FINV(0.05,j$2,$Ai).

F Distribution
Value of F That Puts .05 in the Upper Tail (cont.)

Denominator Degrees of Freedom	Numerator Degrees of Freedom												
	14	15	19	24	29	39	49	59	69	79	89	99	199
1	245.4	245.9	247.7	249.1	250.0	251.1	251.7	252.2	252.5	252.7	252.9	253.0	253.7
2	19.42	19.43	19.44	19.45	19.46	19.47	19.48	19.48	19.48	19.48	19.48	19.49	19.49
3	8.71	8.70	8.67	8.64	8.62	8.60	8.58	8.57	8.57	8.56	8.56	8.55	8.54
4	5.87	5.86	5.81	5.77	5.75	5.72	5.70	5.69	5.68	5.67	5.67	5.66	5.65
5	4.64	4.62	4.57	4.53	4.50	4.47	4.45	4.43	4.42	4.42	4.41	4.41	4.39
6	3.96	3.94	3.88	3.84	3.81	3.78	3.76	3.74	3.73	3.72	3.72	3.71	3.69
7	3.53	3.51	3.46	3.41	3.38	3.34	3.32	3.31	3.29	3.29	3.28	3.28	3.25
8	3.24	3.22	3.16	3.12	3.08	3.05	3.02	3.01	3.00	2.99	2.98	2.98	2.95
9	3.03	3.01	2.95	2.90	2.87	2.83	2.80	2.79	2.78	2.77	2.76	2.76	2.73
10	2.86	2.85	2.79	2.74	2.70	2.66	2.64	2.62	2.61	2.60	2.59	2.59	2.56
11	2.74	2.72	2.66	2.61	2.58	2.53	2.51	2.49	2.48	2.47	2.46	2.46	2.43
12	2.64	2.62	2.56	2.51	2.47	2.43	2.40	2.39	2.37	2.36	2.36	2.35	2.32
13	2.55	2.53	2.47	2.42	2.39	2.34	2.32	2.30	2.29	2.28	2.27	2.26	2.23
14	2.48	2.46	2.40	2.35	2.31	2.27	2.24	2.22	2.21	2.20	2.19	2.19	2.16
15	2.42	2.40	2.34	2.29	2.25	2.21	2.18	2.16	2.15	2.14	2.13	2.12	2.10
16	2.37	2.35	2.29	2.24	2.20	2.15	2.13	2.11	2.09	2.08	2.08	2.07	2.04
17	2.33	2.31	2.24	2.19	2.15	2.11	2.08	2.06	2.05	2.04	2.03	2.02	1.99
18	2.29	2.27	2.20	2.15	2.11	2.07	2.04	2.02	2.00	1.99	1.99	1.98	1.95
19	2.26	2.23	2.17	2.11	2.08	2.03	2.00	1.98	1.97	1.96	1.95	1.94	1.91
20	2.22	2.20	2.14	2.08	2.05	2.00	1.97	1.95	1.93	1.92	1.91	1.91	1.88
21	2.20	2.18	2.11	2.05	2.02	1.97	1.94	1.92	1.90	1.89	1.88	1.88	1.84
22	2.17	2.15	2.08	2.03	1.99	1.94	1.91	1.89	1.88	1.87	1.86	1.85	1.82
23	2.15	2.13	2.06	2.01	1.97	1.92	1.89	1.87	1.85	1.84	1.83	1.82	1.79
24	2.13	2.11	2.04	1.98	1.95	1.90	1.86	1.84	1.83	1.82	1.81	1.80	1.77
25	2.11	2.09	2.02	1.96	1.93	1.88	1.84	1.82	1.81	1.80	1.79	1.78	1.75
26	2.09	2.07	2.00	1.95	1.91	1.86	1.83	1.80	1.79	1.78	1.77	1.76	1.73
27	2.08	2.06	1.99	1.93	1.89	1.84	1.81	1.79	1.77	1.76	1.75	1.74	1.71
28	2.06	2.04	1.97	1.91	1.88	1.82	1.79	1.77	1.75	1.74	1.73	1.73	1.69
29	2.05	2.03	1.96	1.90	1.86	1.81	1.78	1.76	1.74	1.73	1.72	1.71	1.67
30	2.04	2.01	1.95	1.89	1.85	1.80	1.76	1.74	1.73	1.71	1.70	1.70	1.66
31	2.03	2.00	1.93	1.88	1.83	1.78	1.75	1.73	1.71	1.70	1.69	1.68	1.65
32	2.01	1.99	1.92	1.86	1.82	1.77	1.74	1.72	1.70	1.69	1.68	1.67	1.63
33	2.00	1.98	1.91	1.85	1.81	1.76	1.73	1.70	1.69	1.68	1.67	1.66	1.62
34	1.99	1.97	1.90	1.84	1.80	1.75	1.72	1.69	1.68	1.66	1.65	1.65	1.61
35	1.99	1.96	1.89	1.83	1.79	1.74	1.71	1.68	1.67	1.65	1.64	1.64	1.60
36	1.98	1.95	1.88	1.82	1.78	1.73	1.70	1.67	1.66	1.64	1.63	1.63	1.59
37	1.97	1.95	1.88	1.82	1.77	1.72	1.69	1.66	1.65	1.63	1.62	1.62	1.58
38	1.96	1.94	1.87	1.81	1.77	1.71	1.68	1.66	1.64	1.63	1.62	1.61	1.57
39	1.95	1.93	1.86	1.80	1.76	1.70	1.67	1.65	1.63	1.62	1.61	1.60	1.56
49	1.90	1.88	1.80	1.74	1.70	1.64	1.61	1.58	1.56	1.55	1.54	1.53	1.49
59	1.86	1.84	1.77	1.70	1.66	1.60	1.57	1.54	1.52	1.51	1.50	1.49	1.44
69	1.84	1.81	1.74	1.68	1.63	1.57	1.54	1.51	1.49	1.48	1.46	1.45	1.41
79	1.82	1.79	1.72	1.66	1.61	1.55	1.51	1.49	1.47	1.45	1.44	1.43	1.38
89	1.80	1.78	1.70	1.64	1.59	1.53	1.50	1.47	1.45	1.43	1.42	1.41	1.36
99	1.79	1.77	1.69	1.63	1.58	1.52	1.48	1.45	1.43	1.42	1.40	1.39	1.34
199	1.74	1.72	1.64	1.57	1.52	1.46	1.42	1.39	1.37	1.35	1.33	1.32	1.26
499	1.71	1.69	1.61	1.54	1.49	1.42	1.38	1.35	1.32	1.31	1.29	1.28	1.21

Generated from Excel using row 2 for the numerator degrees of freedom and column A for the denominator degrees of freedom. The entries in cell (i,j) are: = FINV(0.5,j2,$Ai).

F Distribution
Value of F That Puts .10 in the Upper Tail

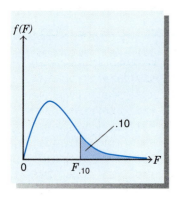

Denominator Degrees of Freedom	Numerator Degrees of Freedom												
	1	2	3	4	5	6	7	8	9	10	11	12	13
1	39.86	49.50	53.59	55.83	57.24	58.20	58.91	59.44	59.86	60.19	60.47	60.71	60.90
2	8.53	9.00	9.16	9.24	9.29	9.33	9.35	9.37	9.38	9.39	9.40	9.41	9.41
3	5.54	5.46	5.39	5.34	5.31	5.28	5.27	5.25	5.24	5.23	5.22	5.22	5.21
4	4.54	4.32	4.19	4.11	4.05	4.01	3.98	3.95	3.94	3.92	3.91	3.90	3.89
5	4.06	3.78	3.62	3.52	3.45	3.40	3.37	3.34	3.32	3.30	3.28	3.27	3.26
6	3.78	3.46	3.29	3.18	3.11	3.05	3.01	2.98	2.96	2.94	2.92	2.90	2.89
7	3.59	3.26	3.07	2.96	2.88	2.83	2.78	2.75	2.72	2.70	2.68	2.67	2.65
8	3.46	3.11	2.92	2.81	2.73	2.67	2.62	2.59	2.56	2.54	2.52	2.50	2.49
9	3.36	3.01	2.81	2.69	2.61	2.55	2.51	2.47	2.44	2.42	2.40	2.38	2.36
10	3.29	2.92	2.73	2.61	2.52	2.46	2.41	2.38	2.35	2.32	2.30	2.28	2.27
11	3.23	2.86	2.66	2.54	2.45	2.39	2.34	2.30	2.27	2.25	2.23	2.21	2.19
12	3.18	2.81	2.61	2.48	2.39	2.33	2.28	2.24	2.21	2.19	2.17	2.15	2.13
13	3.14	2.76	2.56	2.43	2.35	2.28	2.23	2.20	2.16	2.14	2.12	2.10	2.08
14	3.10	2.73	2.52	2.39	2.31	2.24	2.19	2.15	2.12	2.10	2.07	2.05	2.04
15	3.07	2.70	2.49	2.36	2.27	2.21	2.16	2.12	2.09	2.06	2.04	2.02	2.00
16	3.05	2.67	2.46	2.33	2.24	2.18	2.13	2.09	2.06	2.03	2.01	1.99	1.97
17	3.03	2.64	2.44	2.31	2.22	2.15	2.10	2.06	2.03	2.00	1.98	1.96	1.94
18	3.01	2.62	2.42	2.29	2.20	2.13	2.08	2.04	2.00	1.98	1.95	1.93	1.92
19	2.99	2.61	2.40	2.27	2.18	2.11	2.06	2.02	1.98	1.96	1.93	1.91	1.89
20	2.97	2.59	2.38	2.25	2.16	2.09	2.04	2.00	1.96	1.94	1.91	1.89	1.87
21	2.96	2.57	2.36	2.23	2.14	2.08	2.02	1.98	1.95	1.92	1.90	1.87	1.86
22	2.95	2.56	2.35	2.22	2.13	2.06	2.01	1.97	1.93	1.90	1.88	1.86	1.84
23	2.94	2.55	2.34	2.21	2.11	2.05	1.99	1.95	1.92	1.89	1.87	1.84	1.83
24	2.93	2.54	2.33	2.19	2.10	2.04	1.98	1.94	1.91	1.88	1.85	1.83	1.81
25	2.92	2.53	2.32	2.18	2.09	2.02	1.97	1.93	1.89	1.87	1.84	1.82	1.80
26	2.91	2.52	2.31	2.17	2.08	2.01	1.96	1.92	1.88	1.86	1.83	1.81	1.79
27	2.90	2.51	2.30	2.17	2.07	2.00	1.95	1.91	1.87	1.85	1.82	1.80	1.78
28	2.89	2.50	2.29	2.16	2.06	2.00	1.94	1.90	1.87	1.84	1.81	1.79	1.77
29	2.89	2.50	2.28	2.15	2.06	1.99	1.93	1.89	1.86	1.83	1.80	1.78	1.76
30	2.88	2.49	2.28	2.14	2.05	1.98	1.93	1.88	1.85	1.82	1.79	1.77	1.75
31	2.87	2.48	2.27	2.14	2.04	1.97	1.92	1.88	1.84	1.81	1.79	1.77	1.75
32	2.87	2.48	2.26	2.13	2.04	1.97	1.91	1.87	1.83	1.81	1.78	1.76	1.74
33	2.86	2.47	2.26	2.12	2.03	1.96	1.91	1.86	1.83	1.80	1.77	1.75	1.73
34	2.86	2.47	2.25	2.12	2.02	1.96	1.90	1.86	1.82	1.79	1.77	1.75	1.73
35	2.85	2.46	2.25	2.11	2.02	1.95	1.90	1.85	1.82	1.79	1.76	1.74	1.72
36	2.85	2.46	2.24	2.11	2.01	1.94	1.89	1.85	1.81	1.78	1.76	1.73	1.71
37	2.85	2.45	2.24	2.10	2.01	1.94	1.89	1.84	1.81	1.78	1.75	1.73	1.71
38	2.84	2.45	2.23	2.10	2.01	1.94	1.88	1.84	1.80	1.77	1.75	1.72	1.70
39	2.84	2.44	2.23	2.09	2.00	1.93	1.88	1.83	1.80	1.77	1.74	1.72	1.70
49	2.81	2.41	2.20	2.06	1.97	1.90	1.84	1.80	1.76	1.73	1.71	1.68	1.66
59	2.79	2.39	2.18	2.04	1.95	1.88	1.82	1.78	1.74	1.71	1.68	1.66	1.64
69	2.78	2.38	2.16	2.03	1.93	1.86	1.81	1.76	1.72	1.69	1.67	1.64	1.62
79	2.77	2.37	2.15	2.02	1.92	1.85	1.79	1.75	1.71	1.68	1.65	1.63	1.61
89	2.76	2.36	2.15	2.01	1.91	1.84	1.79	1.74	1.70	1.67	1.64	1.62	1.60
99	2.76	2.36	2.14	2.00	1.91	1.83	1.78	1.73	1.70	1.66	1.64	1.61	1.59
199	2.73	2.33	2.11	1.97	1.88	1.80	1.75	1.70	1.66	1.63	1.60	1.58	1.56
499	2.72	2.31	2.09	1.96	1.86	1.79	1.73	1.68	1.64	1.61	1.58	1.56	1.54

Generated from Excel using row 2 for the numerator degrees of freedom and column A for the denominator degrees of freedom. The entries in cell (i,j) are: =FINV(0.10,j$2,$Ai).

F Distribution
Value of F That Puts .10 in the Upper Tail (cont.)

Denominator Degrees of Freedom	Numerator Degrees of Freedom												
	14	15	19	24	29	39	49	59	69	79	89	99	199
1	61.07	61.22	61.66	62.00	62.23	62.51	62.68	62.79	62.86	62.92	62.97	63.00	63.17
2	9.42	9.42	9.44	9.45	9.46	9.47	9.47	9.47	9.48	9.48	9.48	9.48	9.49
3	5.20	5.20	5.19	5.18	5.17	5.16	5.16	5.15	5.15	5.15	5.15	5.14	5.14
4	3.88	3.87	3.85	3.83	3.82	3.80	3.80	3.79	3.79	3.78	3.78	3.78	3.77
5	3.25	3.24	3.21	3.19	3.18	3.16	3.15	3.14	3.14	3.13	3.13	3.13	3.12
6	2.88	2.87	2.84	2.82	2.80	2.78	2.77	2.76	2.76	2.75	2.75	2.75	2.73
7	2.64	2.63	2.60	2.58	2.56	2.54	2.52	2.51	2.51	2.50	2.50	2.50	2.48
8	2.48	2.46	2.43	2.40	2.39	2.36	2.35	2.34	2.33	2.33	2.32	2.32	2.31
9	2.35	2.34	2.30	2.28	2.26	2.23	2.22	2.21	2.20	2.20	2.19	2.19	2.17
10	2.26	2.24	2.21	2.18	2.16	2.13	2.12	2.11	2.10	2.10	2.09	2.09	2.07
11	2.18	2.17	2.13	2.10	2.08	2.05	2.04	2.03	2.02	2.01	2.01	2.01	1.99
12	2.12	2.10	2.07	2.04	2.01	1.99	1.97	1.96	1.95	1.95	1.94	1.94	1.92
13	2.07	2.05	2.01	1.98	1.96	1.93	1.92	1.91	1.90	1.89	1.89	1.88	1.86
14	2.02	2.01	1.97	1.94	1.92	1.89	1.87	1.86	1.85	1.84	1.84	1.83	1.82
15	1.99	1.97	1.93	1.90	1.88	1.85	1.83	1.82	1.81	1.80	1.80	1.79	1.77
16	1.95	1.94	1.90	1.87	1.84	1.81	1.79	1.78	1.77	1.77	1.76	1.76	1.74
17	1.93	1.91	1.87	1.84	1.81	1.78	1.76	1.75	1.74	1.74	1.73	1.73	1.71
18	1.90	1.89	1.84	1.81	1.79	1.76	1.74	1.72	1.71	1.71	1.70	1.70	1.68
19	1.88	1.86	1.82	1.79	1.76	1.73	1.71	1.70	1.69	1.68	1.68	1.67	1.65
20	1.86	1.84	1.80	1.77	1.74	1.71	1.69	1.68	1.67	1.66	1.66	1.65	1.63
21	1.84	1.83	1.78	1.75	1.72	1.69	1.67	1.66	1.65	1.64	1.63	1.63	1.61
22	1.83	1.81	1.77	1.73	1.71	1.67	1.65	1.64	1.63	1.62	1.62	1.61	1.59
23	1.81	1.80	1.75	1.72	1.69	1.66	1.64	1.62	1.61	1.61	1.60	1.59	1.57
24	1.80	1.78	1.74	1.70	1.68	1.64	1.62	1.61	1.60	1.59	1.58	1.58	1.56
25	1.79	1.77	1.73	1.69	1.66	1.63	1.61	1.59	1.58	1.58	1.57	1.56	1.54
26	1.77	1.76	1.71	1.68	1.65	1.62	1.60	1.58	1.57	1.56	1.56	1.55	1.53
27	1.76	1.75	1.70	1.67	1.64	1.61	1.58	1.57	1.56	1.55	1.54	1.54	1.52
28	1.75	1.74	1.69	1.66	1.63	1.60	1.57	1.56	1.55	1.54	1.53	1.53	1.50
29	1.75	1.73	1.68	1.65	1.62	1.59	1.56	1.55	1.54	1.53	1.52	1.52	1.49
30	1.74	1.72	1.68	1.64	1.61	1.58	1.55	1.54	1.53	1.52	1.51	1.51	1.48
31	1.73	1.71	1.67	1.63	1.60	1.57	1.55	1.53	1.52	1.51	1.50	1.50	1.47
32	1.72	1.71	1.66	1.62	1.59	1.56	1.54	1.52	1.51	1.50	1.49	1.49	1.46
33	1.72	1.70	1.65	1.61	1.59	1.55	1.53	1.51	1.50	1.49	1.49	1.48	1.46
34	1.71	1.69	1.65	1.61	1.58	1.54	1.52	1.51	1.49	1.49	1.48	1.47	1.45
35	1.70	1.69	1.64	1.60	1.57	1.54	1.51	1.50	1.49	1.48	1.47	1.47	1.44
36	1.70	1.68	1.64	1.60	1.57	1.53	1.51	1.49	1.48	1.47	1.46	1.46	1.43
37	1.69	1.68	1.63	1.59	1.56	1.52	1.50	1.49	1.47	1.47	1.46	1.45	1.43
38	1.69	1.67	1.62	1.58	1.56	1.52	1.50	1.48	1.47	1.46	1.45	1.45	1.42
39	1.68	1.67	1.62	1.58	1.55	1.51	1.49	1.47	1.46	1.45	1.45	1.44	1.41
49	1.65	1.63	1.58	1.54	1.51	1.47	1.45	1.43	1.42	1.41	1.40	1.39	1.36
59	1.62	1.61	1.56	1.51	1.48	1.44	1.42	1.40	1.39	1.38	1.37	1.36	1.33
69	1.60	1.59	1.54	1.49	1.46	1.42	1.40	1.38	1.36	1.35	1.34	1.34	1.30
79	1.59	1.58	1.52	1.48	1.45	1.41	1.38	1.36	1.35	1.34	1.33	1.32	1.29
89	1.58	1.57	1.51	1.47	1.44	1.40	1.37	1.35	1.33	1.32	1.31	1.31	1.27
99	1.57	1.56	1.51	1.46	1.43	1.39	1.36	1.34	1.32	1.31	1.30	1.30	1.26
199	1.54	1.52	1.47	1.42	1.39	1.34	1.31	1.29	1.27	1.26	1.25	1.24	1.20
499	1.52	1.50	1.45	1.40	1.36	1.32	1.28	1.26	1.24	1.23	1.22	1.21	1.16

Generated from Excel using row 2 for the numerator degrees of freedom and column A for the denominator degrees of freedom. The entries in cell (i,j) are: =FINV(0.10,j$2,$Ai).

Constants for Quality Control Charts

Number of Observations per Group, n	d_2	d_3	D_3	D_4
2	1.128	.853	.000	3.267
3	1.693	.888	.000	2.574
4	2.059	.880	.000	2.282
5	2.326	.864	.000	2.114
6	2.534	.848	.000	2.004
7	2.704	.833	.076	1.924
8	2.847	.820	.136	1.864
9	2.970	.808	.184	1.816
10	3.078	.797	.223	1.777
11	3.173	.787	.256	1.744
12	3.258	.778	.283	1.717
13	3.336	.770	.307	1.693
14	3.407	.762	.328	1.672
15	3.472	.755	.347	1.653
16	3.532	.749	.363	1.637
17	3.588	.743	.378	1.622
18	3.640	.738	.391	1.608
19	3.689	.733	.403	1.597
20	3.735	.729	.415	1.585
21	3.778	.724	.425	1.575
22	3.819	.720	.434	1.566
23	3.858	.716	.443	1.557
24	3.895	.712	.451	1.548
25	3.931	.709	.459	1.541

Source: ASTM *Manual on the Presentation of Data Collection and Control Analysis* (Philadelphia, Pa: American Society for Testing Materials, 1976), pp. 134–136.

Critical Values of Spearman's Rank Correlation Coefficient

The α values in this table correspond to a one-tailed test; they must be doubled for two-tailed tests.

n	α					
	.001	.005	.010	.025	.050	.100
4	—	—	—	—	.8000	.8000
5	—	—	.9000	.9000	.8000	.7000
6	—	.9429	.8857	.8286	.7714	.6000
7	.9643	.8929	.8571	.7450	.6786	.5357
8	.9286	.8571	.8095	.7143	.6190	.5000
9	.9000	.8167	.7667	.6833	.5833	.4667
10	.8667	.7818	.7333	.6364	.5515	.4424
11	.8364	.7545	.7000	.6091	.5273	.4182
12	.8182	.7273	.6713	.5804	.4965	.3986
13	.7912	.6978	.6429	.5549	.4780	.3791
14	.7670	.6747	.6220	.5341	.4593	.3626
15	.7464	.6536	.6000	.5179	.4429	.3500
16	.7265	.6324	.5824	.5000	.4265	.3382
17	.7083	.6152	.5637	.4853	.4118	.3260
18	.6904	.5975	.5480	.4716	.3994	.3148
19	.6737	.5825	.5333	.4579	.3895	.3070
20	.6586	.5684	.5203	.4451	.3789	.2977
21	.6455	.5545	.5078	.4351	.3688	.2909
22	.6318	.5426	.4963	.4241	.3597	.2829
23	.6186	.5306	.4852	.4150	.3518	.2767
24	.6070	.5200	.4748	.4061	.3435	.2704
25	.5962	.5100	.4654	.3977	.3362	.2646
26	.5856	.5002	.4564	.3894	.3299	.2588
27	.5757	.4915	.4481	.3822	.3236	.2540
28	.5660	.4828	.4401	.3749	.3175	.2490
29	.5567	.4744	.4320	.3685	.3113	.2443
30	.5479	.4665	.4251	.3620	.3059	.2400

Source: G. J. Glasser and R. F. Winter (1961), "Values of Rank Correlation for Testing the Hypothesis of Independence," *Biometrika* 48 (1961): 444–448, including corrections of W. J. Conover, *Practical Nonparametric Statistics* (New York: Wiley, 1971).

Glossary

absorbing state a state that is never left after it is entered (12)

activities the tasks of a project (5)

additivity assumption an assumption in linear programming that implies that the total value of some function can be found simply by adding the linear terms (2)

adjustable cells cells that store the values of decision variables in an Excel spreadsheet (2)

algorithm a structured series of steps involving simple, repetitious mathematical operations (1)

all units schedule a quantity discount schedule in which the price the buyer pays for all the units purchased is based on the total purchase volume (8)

all-inter linear programming model (AILP) an integer linear programming model in which all the decision variables must be integer valued (3)

analysis of variance (ANOVA) a statistical procedure that uses the variances of the data samples to test for equality of population means (10)

arc a connector between two nodes in a network over which network "flow" can occur (4)

assignment model a network model designed to find the minimum cost assignment of objects to tasks (4)

autocorrelation the measure of how the value at one time period affects the value at some subsequent time period (7)

autoregressive-integrated-moving average (ARIMA) forecasting model a forecasting model based on historic time series values and n period differences between time series values (7)

backordering the phenomenon of waiting for merchandise to be delivered (8)

balking a phenomenon that occurs when customers perceive that a waiting line is too long and decide to leave the system before being served (9)

Bayesian statistics a mathematical approach that argues that it is unnecessary to practice decision making under uncertainty since there is always at least *some* probabilistic information that can be used to assess the likelihoods of the states of nature (6)

Bellman's principle of optimality the underlying principle of dynamic programming that states that from a given state at a given stage, the optimal solution for the remainder of the process is independent of any previous decisions made to that point (13)

Beta distribution a statistical distribution useful in approximating distributions with limited data and fixed end points (5)

bill of materials the details of how a finished good is to be assembled (SUPPCD6)

binary integer linear program (BILP) a model in which all decision variables must assume values of 0 or 1 (3, SUPPCD4)

binary variables variables in a mathematical model that can only assume values of 0 or 1 (3, SUPPCD4)

binary integer linear programming model (BILP) an integer linear programming model in which all variables must assume values of only 0 or 1 (3)

binding constraint a constraint that is satisfied with equality at the optimal point (2)

binomial distribution function a distribution that can be used to determine the probability that k out of n sample items is defective (11)

Box-Jenkins method a forecasting technique that assists in selecting the appropriate underlying forecasting model by basing its forecasts on a combined autoregressive and moving average model (7)

branch and bound algorithm a mathematical approach for solving integer, mixed integer, and binary linear programs (2, SUPPCD4)

breakpoint the quantity at which the price changes under a quantity discount schedule (8)

canonical form a system of equations in which for each equation there exists a variable that appears only in that equation and its coefficient in that equation is +1 (SUPPCD3)

capacitated transshipment model a transshipment model problem in which an upper limit is placed on the amount of flow along one or more arcs in the network; also called a *general network model* (4)

carrying costs the costs incurred by a firm to maintain its inventory position; also called *holding costs* (8)

certainty assumption an assumption in linear programming that asserts that all parameters of the problem are fixed, known constants (2)

classical decomposition a forecasting technique in which the trend, cyclical, and seasonal components are isolated and forecast separately (7)

complementary slackness a linear programming property that states that, at the optimal solution, either the variable is 0 or the reduced cost for the variable is 0 and that either the slack and surplus on a constraint is 0 or its shadow price is 0 (2)

constant returns to scale (proportionality) assumption an assumption in linear programming that prohibits a "learning curve" or different unit values for lesser quantities (2)

constrained mathematical model a mathematical model with an objective and one or more constraints (1)

constraint   a restrictive condition that may affect the optimal value for an objective function (1)

continuous review system   an inventory system in which the inventory is constantly monitored and a new order placed when the inventory level reaches a certain critical point (8)

continuous simulation system   a simulation in which the state of the system changes continuously over time (10)

continuity assumption   an assumption in linear programming that implies that decision variables can take on any value within the limits of the functional constraints (2)

control chart   a graphical display that provides a view of the production process over time by plotting data based on samples selected from the process (11)

controllable input   a factor over which the decision maker has control; also called a *decision variable* (1)

convex programming problems   a class of non-linear programming models whose objective is to maximize a concave function or minimize a convex function and whose constraints form a convex set (13)

cost overrun   the amount that the actual expenditures of a project exceed the value of the work (5)

cost underrun   the amount that the value of the work of a project exceeds the actual expenditures (5)

critical activity   an activity that has no slack time and must be rigidly scheduled to start and finish at its earliest start and finish times, respectively, to ensure that the project completion time is not delayed (5)

critical path   the longest path in the directed network made up of critical activities (5)

critical path method (CPM)   a deterministic approach to cost analysis in project planning which assumes that an activity's completion time can be determined with certainty based on the amount spent on the activity (5)

Crystal Ball   an Excel Add-In for doing simulation analysis developed by *Decisioneering, Inc.* (10)

customer satisfaction costs   the measure of the degree to which a customer is satisfied with the firm's inventory policy and the impact this has on long-term profitability (8)

cutting plane approach   a mixed integer linear programming approach in which integer restrictions are initially ignored and the problem solved as a linear program; if the optimal solution fails to provide integer values, a new constraint is added to make the solution infeasible without eliminating any feasible point that provides integer values for these variables (2)

cycle   a circuitous path that starts at some node and returns to the same node without using any arc twice (6)

cycle time   the time that elapses between orders (8)

data envelopment analysis (DEA)   a linear programming modeling approach to determine if operations are performing efficiently (3)

damping factor   the amount $(1-\alpha)$ that multiplies the immediately prior time series value in an exponential smoothing approach to time series forecasting (7)

decision analysis   a process that allows an individual or organization to select from a set of possible alternatives when uncertainties regarding the future exist, with the goal of optimizing the resulting payoff in terms of some decision criterion (6)

decision making under certainty   a decision-making situation in which the decision maker knows for sure which state of nature will occur (6)

decision making under risk   a decision-making situation in which the decision maker has at least some knowledge of the probabilities of the states of nature occurring (6)

decision making under uncertainty   a decision-making situation in which the decision maker has no knowledge of the probabilities of the states of nature occurring (6)

decision tree   a chronological network representation of the decision process that utilizes decision nodes and state of nature nodes (6)

decision variable   a factor over which the decision maker has control; also called a *controllable input* (1)

Delphi technique   a method of coalescing different expert opinions into a consensus (7)

deterministic model   a mathematical model in which the profit, cost, and resource data are assumed to be known with certainty (1)

diet problem   a linear programming model with a minimization objective function and "≥" constraints (2)

Dijkstra algorithm   an algorithm used to find the shortest path from a start node to a terminal node in a network (4, SUPPCD5)

directed arc   a linkage that indicates that flow occurs in only one direction in a network model (4)

directed graph (digraph)   a graphic representation of a network made up entirely of directed arcs (4)

discrete simulation system   a simulation in which changes that occur at discrete points in time (10)

dual simplex method   an approach that can be used for solving linear programs by generating a new optimal solution when a change in a right-hand side coefficient extends beyond its range of feasibility or when a new constraint is added to a problem after an optimal solution has been found (SUPPCD3)

duality   a condition that exists when a linear programming problem called the primal has an associated linear programming problem called the dual (SUPPCD2)

dynamic programming (DP) model   a multistage problem in which a set of decisions is made "in sequence" (13)

economic order quantity (EOQ) model   a model for inventory optimization which involves analyzing stock keeping units, assuming that all parameters remain constant forever (over an infinite time horizon) (8)

efficiency   a measure of the relative value of sample information (6)

80/20 rule   a rule of thumb which states a client settles for 80% of the optimal solution at 20% of the cost to obtain it (1)

Erlangian distribution   a probability distribution which can be viewed as arising from the sum of n independent exponentially distributed random variables; often used to describe a service time distribution (9)

expected regret criterion   a decision-making criterion that determines the optimal decision by selecting the one with the minimum expected regret (6)

expected return using the expected value criterion (EREV) the expected return obtained using the expected value criterion (6)

expected return with perfect information (ERPI) the expected return one would obtain if one had perfect information regarding which state of nature would occur in the future (6)

expected utility criterion a decision-making criterion that determines the optimal decision by selecting the one with the highest expected utility (6)

expected value criterion a decision-making criterion that determines the optimal decision by selecting the one that has the best expected payoff (6)

expected value of perfect information (EVPI) the expected gain in return from knowing for sure which state of nature will occur (6)

expected value of sample information (EVSI) the expected gain from making decisions based on sample or indicator information (6)

explicit inverse distribution method a technique used in simulation that utilizes the cumulative distribution function to determine a value for the random variable (10)

exponential probability distribution a probability distribution with the density function being of the form $f(t) = \mu e^{-\mu t}$ (9)

exponential smoothing method a forecasting technique that creates the next period's forecast using a weighted average of the current period's actual value and the current period's forecasted value (7)

exposure unit a measure of the per unit effectiveness of an advertising medium (3)

Extend a simulator developed by *Imagine That, Inc.* (10)

extreme point a feasible point at the intersection of two lines in a two-dimensional feasible region or the intersection of three planes in a three-dimensional feasible region, etc. that would be the last point touched in a feasible region by some linear objective function (2)

facility location problem a linear programming model that determines which of several possible locations to operate in order to maximize or minimize some objective function (3)

feasible points possible solutions that satisfies all the constraints of a mathematical programming model (2)

feasible region the set of points that satisfy all the constraints of a linear programming model (2)

fishbone diagram a cause-and-effect diagram that graphically relates the factors that affect quality to their results (11)

fixed-charge problem a linear programming model that includes in the objective function the fixed costs of operating a facility if the facility is, in fact, operating (3)

fixed time simulation a simulation in which each iteration represents a fixed time period (e.g., one day of operation) (10)

flexible manufacturing system (FMS) a production system in which machines do several different operations, and goods to be manufactured are placed on pallets with

their movements about the factory controlled by a computer (SUPPCD6)

flow the amount of a resource that is delivered on an arc(s) between two nodes in a network (4)

flow models network models in which a flow is possible along the arcs (6)

forecast error the difference between the actual time series value for a period and the forecasted value (7)

forecasting the process of predicting the future (7)

functional constraint "≤," "≥," or "=" restrictions that involve expressions with one or more variables (1)

game theory an approach that uses competitive play to determine the optimal decision in the face of other decision-making players (6)

Gantt chart a bar cart used to display activities of a project and monitor their progress (5)

general network model a transshipment problem in which an upper limit can be placed on the amount of flow along one or more arcs in the network; also called a *capacitated transshipment model* (4)

general nonlinear programming (NLP) model a nonlinear model in which the objective function and constraints (if any) may be nonlinear relationships (18)

goal programming model a linear programming model that involves prioritized objectives (3, 13)

goodwill cost the future reduction in the firm's profitability associated with not having an item readily available for purchase (8)

Greedy algorithm an algorithm which sequentially selects the best course of action; used to solve a minimal spanning tree model (4, SUPPCD5)

heuristic a "rule of thumb," or common-sense procedure (1, 5, SUPPCD6)

holding costs the costs incurred by a firm to maintain its inventory position; also called *carrying costs* (8)

Holt's linear exponential smoothing technique smoothing technique that forecasts the time series' level and its trend, both of which are adjusted at each time period (7)

Hungarian algorithm an algorithm used to solve the assignment problem for a least cost assignment (SUPPCD5)

included costs the resource costs that are included in the calculation of objective function coefficients of a linear programming model (2)

incremental discount schedule a quantity discount schedule in which the price discount applies only to the additional units ordered beyond each breakpoint (8)

infeasible linear program a linear programming model that has no feasible solutions (2)

infeasible models mathematical models that have no possible solutions (2)

infeasible point a point lying outside the feasible region of a mathematical programming model (2)

integer linear programming a model for which some or all of the decision variables are restricted to integer values (5)

interior point a feasible solution to a mathematical programming model that satisfies none of the constraints with equality (2)

interior point method a linear programming solution procedure that ultimately approaches the optimal extreme point by starting from an interior point of the feasible region (2)

inventory policy a policy that consists of an order quantity and an inventory reorder point (8)

inventory position the stock on hand plus the size of any outstanding orders not yet delivered (8)

inventory records file information about the inventory status of each component for each period of time, the component vendors, required lead time for delivery, and specified lot sizes (SUPPCD6)

jockeying a phenomenon that occurs when customers switch between lines when they perceive that another line is moving faster (9)

just-in-time (JIT) an inventory/production control technique that reduces raw material and work-in-process inventories to the lowest possible level by keeping production lot sizes small (SUPPCD6)

kanban system a ticket-based inventory system that keeps track of the flow of components through the factory (SUPPCD6)

Kendall's notation the notation used to identify queuing models (9)

knapsack problem a resource allocation problem that is equivalent to the problem faced by a hiker carrying a knapsack with limited space for items, each with a weight or volume and a value; the objective is to fill the knapsack so that it contains the highest possible value of goods (13)

Kun-Tucker (K-T) conditions a set of necessary conditions for optimality in nonlinear programming models (13)

largest absolute deviation (LAD) a performance measure for evaluating forecasting models calculated by finding the largest absolute difference between the forecasted and actual values (7)

last period technique a forecasting technique in which the forecast of the value for the next period of a stationary time series is the last observed value (7)

latest finish time the latest time an activity in a PERT/CPM network can finish that allows the entire project be completed in minimum time (5)

latest start time the latest time an activity in a PERT/CPM network can be started that allows the entire project be completed in minimum time (5)

lead time the time that elapses between when an order is placed and when it arrives (8)

limiting transition matrix a matrix that gives the eventual likelihood that a Markov process will move from a transient state to an absorbing state (12)

linear assumption of CPM the assumption that if any amount between the normal cost and crash cost is spent to complete an activity, the percentage decrease in the activity's completion time from its normal time to its crash time equals the percentage increase in cost from its normal cost to its crash cost (5)

linear programming model a mathematical model that seeks to maximize or minimize a linear objective function subject to a set of linear constraints (2)

linearity assumption the assumption that an output value for a term is directly proportional to an input value for a variable (5)

Little's formulas relationships that exist between the average number of customers in a system and the average customer waiting time in the system as well as between the average number of customers waiting for service and the average time a customer spends waiting for service (9)

lower control limit (LCL) the value on a control chart that equals the centerline minus three standard deviations (11)

management information systems (MIS) a quantitative approach used to evaluate and transform raw data into useful, relevant, and organized information (1)

management science the scientific approach to executive decision making, which consists of the art of mathematical modeling of complex situations; the science of the development of solution techniques used to solve these models; and the ability to effectively communicate the results of the analysis to the decision maker (1)

Mann–Whitney text a statistical procedure used to determine whether two data sets are drawn from the same population (10)

Markov processes (chain) a process consisting of a countable sequence of stages that can be judged at each stage to fall into a future state, independent of how the process arrived at the previous state (12)

master production schedule a forecast of the finished goods demand over a particular planning horizon (SUPPCD6)

material requirements planning (MRP) a computer-based technique used for controlling inventory for a manufacturer that produces many different finished goods (SUPPCD6)

mathematical modeling a process that translates observed or desired phenomena into mathematical expressions (1)

mathematical programming a branch of management science that deals with solving optimization problems, in which the objective is to maximize or minimize a function, usually in a constrained environment (2)

matrix reduction the process of adding or subtracting a number from all numbers in a row or column of an assignment cost matrix (SUPPCD5)

max flow/min cut theorem a network theorem that asserts that the value of the maximum flow equals the sum of the capacities of the minimum cut, and all arcs on the minimum cut are saturated by the maximum flow (4)

maximal flow algorithm an algorithm used to find the maximum volume of flow from a source node to a terminal sink node in a capacitated network (SUPPCD5)

maximal flow model   a network model used to find the maximum total flow possible from a source node to a sink node without violating arc capacities (4)

maximax criterion   a decision-making criterion in which the optimal decision is determined by selecting the one that has the maximum payoff (6)

maximin criterion   a decision-making criterion in which the optimal decision is determined by selecting the one that maximizes the minimum payoff (6)

M/D/1 queuing system   a single-server queuing model in which customers arrive according to a Poisson process and are served at a constant (deterministic) rate (9)

mean absolute deviation (MAD)   a performance measure for evaluating forecasting models calculated by averaging the absolute values of the differences of the forecasted values from the actual values (7)

mean absolute percent error (MAPE)   a performance measure for evaluating forecasting models calculated by averaging the absolute values of the percentage differences of the forecasted values from the actual values (7)

mean recurrence time   the average time required for a Markov process to return to a given state (12)

mean squared error (MSE)   a performance measure for evaluating forecasting models calculated by averaging the squared differences of the forecasted values from the actual values (7)

M/G/1 queuing system   a single-server queuing model in which customers arrive according to a Poisson process and for which the mean and standard deviation of the service time distribution is known (9)

M/G/k/k queuing system   a k-server queuing model in which customers arrive according to a Poisson process, the mean and standard deviation of the service time distribution are known and no waiting line is permitted to form (9)

minimal spanning tree problem   a network model used to find the minimum total distance that connects all nodes in a network (4)

minimax criterion   a decision-making criterion in which the optimal decision is determined by selecting the one that minimizes the maximum costs (6)

minimax regret criterion   a decision-making criterion in which the optimal decision is determined by selecting the one that minimizes the maximum "lost opportunity" as measured by the regret values for each payoff (6)

minimin criterion   a decision-making criterion in which the optimal decision is determined by selecting the one that has the minimum cost (6)

mixed integer linear programming (MILP)   a model in which some, but not all, of the decision variables are restricted to integers (3, SUPPCD4)

M/M/1 queuing system   a single-server queuing model in which customers arrive according to a Poisson process and service time follows an exponential distribution (9)

M/M/1/F queuing system   a single-server queuing model in which customers arrive according to a Poisson process, service time follows an exponential distribution, and there is a limit of F customers who can be waiting for service (9)

M/M/1//m queuing system   a single-server queuing model in which there is a finite population of m customers and the interarrival time of customers as well as customer service times follows an exponential distribution (9)

M/M/k queuing system   a k-server queuing model in which customers arrive according to a Poisson process and the service time the same for all k servers follows exponential distribution (9)

M/M/k/F queuing system   a multiple-server queuing model in which customers arrive according to a Poisson process, service time follows an exponential distribution, and there is a limit of F customers who can be waiting for service (9)

M/M/k/k queuing system   a k-server queuing model in which customers arrive according to a Poisson process, service time follows an exponential distribution, and no waiting line is permitted to form (9)

modified distribution approach (MODI)   a method used to determine the reduced costs of nonbasic variables in a transportation model (SUPPCD5)

Monte Carlo simulation   a simulator designed so that data values occur randomly and reflect the theoretical frequencies being modeled (10)

moving average method   a forecasting technique in which the forecast for any time period is the average of the values for the immediately preceding k periods (7)

multicriteria decision problem   a problem comprised of two or more conflicting objectives (1, 13)

net marginal profit   the difference between the objective function coefficient and the total marginal cost of the value of the resources using the current values of the shadow prices (SUPPCD3)

network model   a model that consists of a set of nodes, a set of arcs, and functions defined on the nodes and arcs (4)

newsboy problem   an inventory model that deals with SKU's having a limited shelf life of one period; also called a *single-period inventory model* (8)

next-event simulation   a simulation that updates simulated data when a particular event occurs (10)

nodes   the beginning and end points for arcs on a network (4)

nonbinding constraint   a functional constraint that is not satisfied with equality at the optimal point of a mathematical programming model (4)

nonlinear programming (NLP) model   a mathematical model in which at least one term in the objective function or constraints does not satisfy the linearity assumption (2, 13)

non-linear term   any term other than one of the form A or AX, where A is a constant and X is a variable raised to the first power (2, 13)

nonpreemptive goal programming   an approach that involves determining the relative weights that act as a per unit penalty for failure to meet a stated goal, with the objective of minimizing the total weighted deviations from the goal (13)

objective function   an expression of the quantity the decision maker wishes to optimize (1)

opportunity costs return possible from investments that could have been made with available capital had the firm not used the funds to finance its inventory (8)

optimal service level the long-run percentage of periods in which inventory is sufficient to satisfy all customer demands (11)

optimization model a mathematical model that seeks to maximize or minimize a quantity that may be restricted by a set of constraints (1)

order costs costs incurred when a firm purchases goods from a supplier (8)

out-of-kilter algorithm a streamlined form of the simplex method applied to a general network problem with sources, destinations, intermediate nodes, unit shipping costs, and maximum capacities between nodes (SUPP-CD5)

p chart a process control chart used in attribute sampling to determine whether or not a process is in control (11)

parameter a factor over which the decision maker has no direct influence; also called an *uncontrollable input* (1)

payoff table the simplest way of presenting a decision problem in which the decision maker faces a finite set of discrete decision alternatives and states of nature and whose payoffs depend on the decision made and the state of nature that occurs (6)

periodic review system an inventory system in which the inventory position is investigated on a regular basis and orders are placed only at these times (8)

periodicity a phenomenon that occurs when a Markov process exhibits a regular pattern moving between states from one stage to the next (12)

PERT/COST an accounting information system that aids management in determining whether a project is coming in on time and within budget (5)

PERT/CPM an analysis used to determine the minimal possible completion time for a project and a range of start and finish times for each activity so that the project is completed within that time frame (5)

PERT/CPM network a network representation that reflects activity precedence relations, in which nodes designate activities and arcs describe the precedence relations between activities (5)

planned shortage model an inventory model that assumes that there is a cost associated with an out-of-stock situation but that all customers will backorder (8)

Poisson distribution a probability distribution used for describing customer arrival processes in which the conditions of orderliness, stationarity, and independence are satisfied (9)

post-optimality analysis a quantitative analysis that provides information about the effects of changes to the solution of a problem as certain parameters change; also called *sensitivity analysis* (1, 2)

precedence relations chart a chart used to identify the separate activities of a project that details which ones must precede others (5)

prediction model a mathematical model that describes or predicts events, given certain conditions (1)

preemptive goal programming an approach that involves arranging goals into different priority levels (13)

principle of insufficient reason decision criterion in which each state of nature is assumed to be equally likely (6)

probabilistic model a mathematical model in which one or more of the input parameters' values are determined by probability distributions; also called a *stochastic model* (1)

process flow diagram a flow chart diagram that details the chronology of the process used to produce a good or provide a service (11)

process-interaction approach a simulation in which each iteration traces all relevant processes incurred by an item in the system under study (10)

procurement costs the cost of obtaining items for inventory (8)

product mix problem a linear programming model with a maximization objective function and "$\leq$" functional constraints (2)

product tree a pictorial representation of the bill of materials that make up a product (SUPPCD6)

production lot size model a model that determines the optimal inventory policy for an item in which the demand for the item occurs at a constant rate, the production line for the enterprise is not continuously used to manufacture the same product, and the production facility operates at a rate greater than the demand rate for the item (8)

project a collection of tasks that must be completed in minimum time or at minimal cost (5)

project scheduling a means of planning and controlling a project efficiently (5)

pull system an inventory system in which a subcomponent is produced only on request from the work center that utilizes it in assembly (SUPPCD6)

push system an inventory system in which decisions are made regarding the production schedule for the subcomponents based on the forecast demand for the finished good, "pushing" completed subcomponents up to the next level of assembly (SUPPCD6)

quadratic loss function a quadratic function based on the assumption that there is an ideal measurement for product conformance and that any deviation from this ideal results in a potential loss to society (11)

quadratic programming model a nonlinear programming model in which the objective function is a concave quadratic function and whose constraints are linear (13)

quality the ability of a product or service to conform to its design specifications (11)

quantity discount schedule a list of the discounted cost per unit corresponding to different purchase volumes (8)

queuing theory the study of waiting lines, or queues (9)

R chart a planning control chart that records the range of each sample item to monitor the variability of the production process (11)

random number generator a computer program that generates pseudo-random numbers by a mathematical formula (10)

random number mapping   a process for matching random numbers to simulated events (10)

range of feasibility   the set of right-hand side values of a resource over which the shadow prices do not change (2)

range of optimality   the range of values of the objective function coefficients within which the current optimal solution remains unchanged (2)

ranked position weight technique   a method of assigning tasks to work situations by ranking the jobs in descending order based on the sum of the job time and the time for all jobs for which that job is a predecessor (9)

reduced cost   the amount the profit coefficient of a variable will have to increase before the variable can be positive in the optimal solution (2)

redundant constraint   a constraint that can be eliminated from a linear programming model without affecting the feasible region (2)

relaxed problem   a linear model that ignores integer constraints (3, SUPPCD4)

reorder point   the inventory level at which an order is placed (8)

resource leveling   a method of controlling daily resource requirements and smoothing out their use over the course of a project (5)

R_m control chart   a planning control chart that plots a moving range to estimate the common cause or uncontrollable variation in the production process (11)

safety stock   inventory that acts as a buffer to handle a firm's higher-than-average demand during lead time (8)

scenario writing   a decision-making technique that begins with a well-defined set of assumptions and builds several scenarios of the future based on these assumptions; the decision maker selects the scenario that corresponds to the set of assumptions believed most likely to occur (7)

sensitivity analysis   a quantitative analysis that provides information about the effects of changes to the solution of a problem as certain parameters change; also called *post-optimality analysis* (1, 2)

setup costs   the expense associated with beginning production of an item (8)

shadow price   the change to the optimal value of the objective function resulting from a one-unit increase in the right-hand side of a constraint (2)

shortest path model   a network model used to find the path of minimum total distance that connects a starting point to a destination (4)

shrinkage   losses due to breakage of inventory and theft (8)

Silver-Meal heuristic   a procedure for determining a close-to-optimal inventory policy for situations in which orders are placed once per period and demand may vary greatly from period to period (SUPPCD6)

simplex   the figure created in n dimensions by an extreme point and the n other extreme points adjacent to it (SUPPCD3)

simplex algorithm (method)   the algebraic technique commonly used to solve linear programs which requires that all functional constraints be written as equalities so that elementary row operations can be performed without

changing the set of feasible solutions to the problem (SUPPCD3)

simplex tableau   a matrix used to keep track of the equations and other relevant information utilized in the simplex method (SUPPCD3)

simulated events   random events in a simulation that occur with the probability distribution of the true events being modeled (10)

simulation   the development of a model to evaluate a system numerically over some time period of interest (10)

simulator   a computer program used to evaluate policy options in order to select the best action from a set of alternatives (10)

single-period inventory model   an inventory model that assumes that demand occurs according to a specified probability distribution and deals with a stock-keeping unit with a limited shelf life of one period; also called the *newsboy problem* (8)

slack   the amount of a resource that is left over when the value of the left-hand side of the constraint is subtracted from the constant on the right-hand side (2)

slack time   the amount of time an activity can be delayed from its earliest start time without delaying the project's estimated completion time (5)

smoothing constant   the weight given to the current period's actual value in the exponential smoothing method (7)

spanning tree   a tree that connects all the nodes in a network (4)

standard form   a linear program in which all the functional constraints are written as equations and all the variables are nonnegative (SUPPCD3)

state of nature   a possible future event that may affect a decision (6)

state probability   the probability that a process is in a particular state at a given stage (12)

state vector   the collection of state probabilities at a given stage (12)

stationary forecasting model   a time series forecasting model in which the mean value of the item being examined is assumed to be constant (7)

steady state   a condition in which the probabilities for the states of the process stabilize over time and assume their long-run values (9, 12)

steady-state probabilities   probabilities describing the long-run behavior of a Markov process (12)

stochastic model   a mathematical model in which one or more of the input parameters' values are determined by probability distributions; also called a *probabilistic model* (1)

stock-keeping units (SKU)   a collection of individual items in a firm's inventory (8)

summation constraint   a constraint that expresses one decision variable as the sum of two or more other decision variables (3)

summation variable   a decision variable that is set equal to the sum of two or more other decision variables (3)

sunk costs   the cost of the resources that is not included in the calculation of objective function coefficients of a mathematical programming model (2)

surplus   the amount by which some minimum restriction is exceeded at a given point when the constant on the right-hand side is subtracted from the value of the left-hand side (2)

tandem queuing system   a queuing model in which a customer must visit several different servers before service is completed (9)

time series   a past history of data values occurring at discrete time points used to prepare a forecast (7)

transient period   initial queuing system behavior not representative of long-run performance (9)

transition probability   the probability of a Markov process moving from state i at one state to state j at the next stage (12)

transshipment model   a network model in which goods may first be transported through one or more transshipment nodes before reaching their final destination (4)

transportation algorithm   a streamlined version of the simplex method used to find the minimum total shipping cost of a particular item from m sources, each with a different supply, to n destinations, each with a particular demand (SUPPCD5)

transportation model   a network model used to find the total minimum cost of shipping goods from supply points to destination points (4)

traveling salesman model   a network model used to determine the minimum cost of visiting all nodes of a network and returning to a starting node without repeating any node (4)

tree   a series of connected arcs containing no cycles (4)

unbounded feasible region   a feasible region that extends "forever" in some particular direction (2)

unbounded solution   a condition in which feasible solutions exist for a linear program but there is no bound for the value of the objective function (2)

uncontrollable input   a factor over which the decision maker has no direct influence; also called a *parameter* (1)

undirected arc   a linkage that indicates that flow is permissible in either direction in a network model (4)

upper control limit (UCL)   the value on a control chart that equals the centerline plus three standard deviations (11)

utility theory   the study of decision analysis taking into account the decision maker's preference for risk (6)

utility value   the relative value of a payoff when compared to achieving the best and worst payoffs possible (6)

variable constraint   a constraint in a mathematical model that involves only one of the decision variables (1)

Wagner-Whitin algorithm   a dynamic programming technique to determine an optimal inventory policy, for situations in which orders are placed once per period and demand may vary greatly from period to period (SUPP-CD6)

weighted moving average technique   a forecasting technique in which the sum of the weights used must equal one and the weights given to observation values are nonincreasing with their age (7)

work package   a set of related activities within a project that share common costs or are under the control of one contractor, department, or individual (5)

X-bar control chart   a planning control chart that records the mean value for each sample item in order to monitor the mean performance of the production process against a predetermined target value (11)

X control chart   a planning control chart that plots individual data values to determine if the production process is in control (11)

ANSWERS TO SELECTED PROBLEMS

CHAPTER 1

1. Problem definition, model building, model solution, communication of results

2. In solving for the optimal policies at Ford, even small improvements (a fraction of 1%) can affect the bottom line by millions of dollars—this more than justifies the cost of the management science employees. At Villa Park Ford, such a percentage savings would not justify the cost of a full-time management science employee.

4. a. $X_1 + X_2 = 1$
   $X_1 \geq 0$
   $X_1 \leq 1$
   $X_2 \geq 0$
   $X_2 \leq 1$
   X_1, X_2 integers

   b. MAX $-2500X_1 + 35000X_2$
   Optimal: $X_1 = 0$, $X_2 = 1$—hold tournament indoors.

5. a. MAX $4X_1 + 6X_2 + 10X_3$

   b. $40X_1 + 55X_2 + 70X_3 \leq 25000$

6. a. MAX $B - (30D)X_1 - (56E)X_2 - F$
   $X_1 \geq 2 + .001T$
   $X_2 \geq N$
   X_1 and $X_2 \geq 0$ and integers

   b. The negotiated price (B) and the fixed costs (F) are constants. Thus if the objective function is set to MIN $(30D)X_1 + (56E)X_2$ this is equivalent to MAX $-(30D)X_1 - (56E)X_2$.

   c. MAX $10,000 - 450X_1 - 672X_2 - 1,000$
   s.t. $X_1 \geq 4$
   $X_2 \geq 2$
   X_1 and $X_2 \geq 0$ and integers

   d. Change the right side of the first constraint to 4.4; 4.4 guards would make no sense but if you restricted the variables to be integers this would be the correct formulation.

7. a. MAX $X_1 + X_2$

   b. MAX $.02X_1 + .01X_2$

   c. MAX $4X_1 + 3X_2$

11. =SUM(B6:F6) *Result: 96*

13. =B6+B7+B8+B9+B10 *Result: 91*

14. Yes *Results: 118, 69, 90, 83*

17. =SUMPRODUCT(B4:F4, B6:F6) *Result: $269.45*

19. =MAX(B6:B10) *Result: 34*

23. =0.12*B6^2+0.02*C6^3+3.5*SQRT(D6)+0.05*E6*F6 *Result: $862.03*

24. =IF(C15>H6,"NEW","OLD") *Result: NEW*

28. =NORMDIST(50,47,5.5,TRUE)-NORMDIST(40,47,5.5,TRUE)
    Result: .605722

32. 1.2 to 11.2

37. Grade = 30.05319 + 6.797872(Study Hours)

39. In cell A3 the formula is: =A2+B2. Drag down to (A4:A6)
    Results for cells A2:A6:   0, .45, .65, .80, .92

41. A parameter is a quantity that cannot be controlled by the decision maker, whereas a decision variable is a controllable input whose values are determined by the decision maker.

47. a. MAX $.1905X_1 + .2000X_2 + .1719X_3 + .0500X_4$

s.t.

$$
\begin{array}{llllll}
X_1 + & X_2 + & X_3 + & X_4 & = 4000 \\
& X_2 & & & \geq 800 \\
& & & X_4 & \geq 1000 \\
X_1 & & & & \leq 2000 \\
& & X_3 & & \leq 2000
\end{array}
$$

All X's ≥ 0

b. MAX $\quad 8Y_1 + 6Y_2 + 11Y_3 + .05X_4$

s.t.

$$
\begin{array}{llll}
42Y_1 + 30Y_2 + 64Y_3 + & X_4 & = 4000 \\
30Y_2 & & \geq 800 \\
& X_4 & \geq 1000 \\
42Y_1 & & \leq 2000 \\
64Y_3 & & \leq 2000
\end{array}
$$

All Y's and $X_4 \geq 0$

c. Should get the same answer if shares were converted to dollars by $X_1 = 42Y_1$, $X_2 = 30Y_2$, and $X_3 = 64Y_3$ unless the shares (Y_1, Y_2, and Y_3) were also restricted to be integers.

50. a. $54X - 2X^2$

b. MAX $-2X^2 + 76X - 594$

s.t. $\quad X \geq 11$

$X \leq 21$

c. Price = \$19,000; # sold = 16; monthly profit = \$128,000

CHAPTER 2

1. 560 diagonal kites, 920 box kites; weekly profit = \$6280

3. b. 80 GE45's, 53.3333 GE60's   **c.** 106.6667 GE45's, 35.5556 GE60's

6. a. MAX $30000X_1 + 80000X_2$

s.t.

$$
\begin{array}{llll}
X_1 & & \leq & 26 \\
& X_2 & \leq & 5 \\
2000X_1 + 8000X_2 & \leq & 40000 \\
X_1 & & \geq & 8 \\
& X_2 & \geq & 2
\end{array}
$$

Solution: Place 12 daily ads and 2 Sunday ads—Exposure = 520,000
Much of the same population is probably reading both the daily and Sunday newspapers—may not get this increase in exposure on Sunday.

b. Given the budget, there can be a maximum of 20 daily ads or 5 Sunday ads.

c. Place 20 daily ads and no Sunday ads—Exposure = 600,000

8. a. MIN $\quad 100X_1 + 140X_2$

s.t.

$$
\begin{array}{ll}
20X_1 + 40X_2 & \geq 800 \\
20X_1 + 25X_2 & \geq 600 \\
20X_1 + 10X_2 & \geq 500 \\
X_1, X_2 \geq 0
\end{array}
$$

Purchase 2000 pounds of La Paz ore and 1000 pounds of Sucre ore

b. La Paz—(\$70, \$280), Sucre—(\$50, \$200); within these limits the optimal solution remains unchanged.

c. Outside the range of optimality; reduced cost = \$50

d. \$3 for copper in the range (700, 2000); \$0 for zinc in the range ($-\infty$, 6500); \$2 for iron in the range (400, 800). Within these ranges the cost per extra pound of requirements will remain unchanged.

e. Infeasible

10. a. \$1.50 per cow   **b.** Would cost \$1.60 per cow

c. 50 oz. Cow Chow per cow, 25 oz. Moo Town per cow—total savings \$25/day

12. Participate in the program and plant 125 acres of wheat and 125 acres of corn; profit = \$43,750; if he did not participate the optimal profit would be \$43,050.

14. a. 1680 phone hours, 4570 door to door hours; 132,660 voters reached

    b. 1260 phone hours, 4990 door to door hours; 217,440 voters reached

15. 4 magazine ads, 2 Internet ads

17. MIN $X_1 + X_2$

    s.t. $.06X_1 + .10X_2 \geq 4000$

           $.06X_1 + .03X_2 \geq 2000$

           $X_1 + X_2 \leq 60000$

              $X_1, X_2 \geq 0$

    Invest $19,047.62 in the C/D and $28,571.43 in the venture capital project. He can keep $12,380.95 for personal use.

19. a. 187.5 acres of garlic; 0 acres of onions; 12.5 acres of unfarmed land

    b. $412.50   **c.** 150 acres of garlic; 50 acres of onions   **d.** $0

21. a. MIN $3000X_1 + 1000X_2$

    s.t. $X_2 \leq 5$

         $2000X_1 + 800X_2 \geq 10000$

              $X_1, X_2 \geq 0$

    Optimal: Lease 3 and Purchase 5; monthly payments = $14,000

    b. The solution is unbounded

    c. The number of machines leased and purchased must be integers

22. a. 120 8-sq. ft. crates; 60 4-sq. ft. crates; profit = $13,200

    No slack on hours or space; 20 slack in the max number of 8-sq. ft. crates shipped and 60 slack in the maximum number of 4-sq. ft. crates shipped—these will not be shipped

    b. $8.33 in the range (720–1320); crates must be integers—the optimal solution with one extra sq. ft. of loading space is not integer valued.

    c. The shadow price reduces to $6.33; extra hours are still worth $18.33.

23. MAX $.10X_1 + .12X_2$

    s.t. $X_1 + X_2 = 100000$

     $.000002X_1 + .000004X_2 \geq .25$

     $.000003X_1 + .000008X_2 \leq .50$

              $X_1, X_2 \geq 0$

    Invest $60,000 in Tater, Inc. and $40,000 in Lakeside

26. a. MAX $15X_1 + 25X_2$

    s.t. $12X_1 + 10X_2 \leq 150$

            $50X_1 + 40X_2 \leq 500$

            $5X_1 + 10X_2 \leq 90$

               $15X_2 \leq 120$

         $X_1, X_2 \geq 0$

    Bake 4 2/3 dozen (=56) custard pies and 6 2/3 dozen (=80) fruit pies

    b. No, $15 extra is within the Allowable Increase

    c. No   **d.** No change   **e.** Yes $2.67 > $2.25

27. a. No   **b.** Yes   **c.** Same optimal solution; $28.50

28. Produce 300 KCU's and 600 KCP's; Profit = $180,000. Klone will use 1200 floppy drives (600 unused), 600 hard drives (100 unused) and 900 cases (100 unused). All 480 production hours are used.

32. Use 6 Nautilus machines and spend 21 minutes on the treadmill; 81 points

33. a. MAX $24000X_1 + 30000X_2$

    s.t. $X_1 \leq 3$

              $X_2 \leq 2$

       $50X_1 + 60X_2 \leq 160$

         $X_1, X_2 \geq 0$ and integer

    Sell 2 compactors and 1 drill press; profit = $78,000

    b. Linear solution is (.8,2)—rounding up (or off) to (1,2) is infeasible; rounding down to (0,2) produces a feasible solution that is not optimal.

    c. Fractional values would be work in progress.

34. a. MIN $3500X_1 + 800X_2$
s.t. $150X_1 + 35X_2 \geq 750$
$X_1 \geq 1$
$X_2 \leq 20$
$X_1, X_2 \geq 0$ and integer

b. Rounded solution is 1 60-inch and 18 27-in. sets; cost = $17,900

c. 2 60-inch and 13 27-in. sets; No; $17,400

48. 22 using process 1 and 28 using process 2

50. a. MIN $60000X_1 + 40000X_2$
s.t. $X_1 + X_2 \geq 6$
$3000X_1 + 1000X_2 \geq 9000$
$2X_1 + X_2 \geq 18$
$X_1, X_2 \geq 0$ and integer

(i) 1.5 Safeco trucks, 4.5 Kluge trucks (ii) 2 Safeco trucks, 4 Kluge trucks

b. (i) $270,000 (ii) $280,000

c. The integer problem has more constraints (the integer constraints)

CHAPTER 3

1. 150 20-in. girls, 100 20-in. boys, 100 26-in. girls, 100 26-in. boys; profit = $16,150

2. a. 266.67 stoves, 448.72 washers, 133.33 refrigerators; work in progress

b. 266.67 stoves, 227.15 washers, 63.58 electric dryers, 163.58 gas dryers, 133.33 refrigerators

3. a. 22.94 standard Z345's, 22.94 standard W250's, 45.87 industrial W250's; work in progress

b. 75%; if the limit were loosened or eliminated, the profit would increase

c. (i) Yes   (ii) No   (iii) Yes

4. a. $7500 in EAL, $2500 in TAT, $30,000 in long term bonds, $10,000 in the TDA

b. 10.5%; 11%—the maximum increase for the shadow price for funds is $+\infty$

c. EAL, BRU, long term bonds

d. $0.11 increase for each extra dollar invested, $0.15 decrease per extra dollar required in tax deferred annuities, $0.16 decrease for each extra dollar invested in TAT above 25%, $0.10 increase for each extra dollar allowed in low-yield funds

6. 12.69 oz. of steak; 16.67 oz. of milk; no apples or cheese

9. Conduct 500 telephone and 500 personal interviews with large William and Ryde investors, 600 telephone interviews with small William and Ryde investors, 200 personal telephone interviews with large investors from other firms and 200 interviews with small investors from other firms

12. a. 101.80 plates, 150 mugs, 87.54 steins; total profit = $1083.42

b. 128 plates, 298.67 mugs, 0 steins; total profit = $1290.67; increase of $207.25

15. a. 142.86 ac. Wheat, 142.86 ac. Corn, 14.29 ac. Soybeans; profit = $197,200

b. $486.21; $3.92   c. Yes; $4400   d. Yes; $22,698.20 in additional profit

18. Invest $2,075.14 in Bonanza Gold, $47,924.53 in Cascade Telephone, $20,000 in the money market account, and $30,000 in treasury bonds. Expected return = $8,424.53 (8.42453%)

23. a. This could violate the additivity assumption of linear programming.

b. Spend $300,000 on TV, $100,000 on radio, and $300,000 on newspaper ads

c. No effect; it is not binding

26. 7550 2-oz. Go bars, 2500 2-oz. Power bars, 5050 2-oz. Energy bars, 437.5 8-oz. Energy bars; total daily profit $7,273.375.

27. a. $550,000 in ketchup only, $450,000 in spaghetti sauce only, $750,000 in taco sauce only, $250,000 in joint advertising; $2,251,500; 12.575% return

28. Part-time: 7AM-11AM—7, 11AM-3PM—13, 3PM-7PM—12, 7PM-11PM—14
Full-time: 7AM-3PM—3, 11AM-7PM—6, 3PM-11PM—2; Total Cost = $1,661

29. 3 patrols only. Two possible solutions: (1) Sectors 3, 7, 11; (2) Sectors 1, 4, 14

34. a. Develop applications 1, 2, 3, 4; projected net worth $12,600,000

    b. Develop applications 1, 2, 6; projected net worth $11,800,000

35. Hire 2 CPA's and 19 experienced accountants; total payroll = $19,500

38. Purchase 12 shares of TCS and invest $1,044.44 in MFI; total investment = $1,704.44

39. 1581 Fords, 8 Chevrolets, 1411 Macks, 576 Nissans, 1424 Toyotas; outlay = $17,021,000

41. a. 52 turkey, 100 beef, 76 ham, 40 club, 32 all meat; $67,200

    b. Shadow price = $0.33; range of feasibility (336,448); in this range, each extra ounce of cheese will add $0.33 to the optimal profit

    c. Beef

47. a. Make 60,000 Jeeptrykes only; profit = $160,000

    b. Make 60,000 Herotrykes only; profit = $117,500

CHAPTER 4

1. Garberville-Eureka 1600, Grant's Pass-Eureka 200, Grant's Pass-Crescent City 1400, Willard-Eureka 100, Willard-Coos Bay 1500; Total Cost = $180,000

3. (in truckloads)

    a. Cal-I1 8, Cal-I2 1, Mex-I2 3, Mex-I3 5; I1-P1 3, I1-P2 5, I2-P3 4, I3-P4 5; $24,200

    b. Cal-I1 3. Cal-I2 3, Cal-I3 3, Mex-I1 2, Mex-I2 3, Mex-I3 3; I1-P1 3, I1-P2 2, I2-P2 3, I2-P3 1, I2-P4 2, I3-P3 3, I3-P4 3; $28,900

    c. Inspection will eliminate some bad tomatoes

5. Kansas City-St. Louis-Davenport-Lincoln-Tulsa-Kansas City; $810

7. 14N-Lakeview 400, 14N-Casual 500, Lakeview-Lakeside 100, Lakeview-Golf 300, Golf-Lakeside 200, Golf-Town Center 100, Casual-Ocean Breeze 300, Town Center-Ocean Breeze 300, Lakeview-14S 300, Ocean Breeze-14S 600; total capacity = 900

9. a. Tony (News), Jim (Sports), Connie (Development), Linda (Features), Ann (Marketing); total years = 47

    b. Jim (Sports), Connie (Features/Development), Linda (News), Ann (Marketing); total years = 46

11. a. Ann (Phoenix), Bill (Fresno), Ko (Austin), Dave (Miami); total cost = $10,350

    b. Ann's-Phoenix 20, Ann's-Austin 5, Bill's-Fresno 7, Bill's-Miami 11, Ko's-Fresno 8, Ko's-Austin 17, Dave's-Miami 25; total cost = $250,110

13. Attach 3 to 2, 2 to 1, 1 to 5, 5 to 4, 4 to 6; total distance = 39 millimeters

14. 396 meters

15. Amy (Information Systems), Bob (Personal Tax), Sue (Financial Analysis), Maya (Corporate Tax), Koo (Auditing), Lyn (General Accounting); total = 543

18. Budapest-Cieszyn-Lodz-Torun-Gdansk; 980 kilometers

25. Produce 1250 in quarter 1 (all in regular time)—all for quarter 1; 1875 in quarter 2 (1500 in regular time, 375 in overtime)—625 for quarter 2 and 1250 for quarter 3, 2500 in quarter 3 (1500 in regular time, 1000 in overtime)—all for quarter 3, and 2500 in quarter 4 (1500 in regular time, 1000 in overtime)—all for quarter 4; total cost $520,500

26. Build superstreets—cost is $20,000,000 vs. $21,000,000 for freeway extension

29. a. There should be links from the Server to Room 320; from Room 320 to Room 318 and the Dean's Office, from the Dean's Office to Room 317 and Room 322, from Room 322 to Support Lab 1, and from Support Lab 1 to Support Lab 2

    b. $1720

35. a. 19,000 in each plant

    b. From Tallahassee to Allentown 6, to Gary 8, to Houston 5
From Tucson to Houston 4, to Riverside 15; total cost $84,200

38. a. Alice (Stove), Chuck (Washer), Darren (Refrigerator), Ellen (Toilet), Francisco (Air Conditioner), George (Dishwasher); total cost $470

b. Washer $45.50, Dishwasher $32.50, Air Conditioner $234, Toilet $65, Refrigerator $130, Stove $104; total profit = $141

39. a. Smith (Moscow), Jones (Standby), Heinz (Vacation), Chang (Paris), Wells (London), Blinn (Hawaii), Klein (Tokyo)

b. The two most senior pilots got their lowest selections

41. (*In 1000's of gallons*) From Steel Plant to Station-1 25 to Station-2 20;
From Station-1 to Station-3 5, to Station-4 20;
From Station-2 to Station-3 10, to Station-5 10
From Station-3 to Station-5 15; from Station-4 to Station-5 10 to Treatment 10
From Station-5 to Treatment 35; Max Flow = 45

43. $2850

49. a. MIN $200X_{11} + 100X_{12} + 175X_{13} + 250X_{21} + 200X_{22} + 125X_{23}$

$$
\begin{aligned}
\text{s.t.} \quad & X_{11} + X_{12} + X_{13} & & & & \leq 20 \\
& & X_{21} + X_{22} + X_{23} & & & \leq 50 \\
& X_{11} & + X_{21} & & & = 15 \\
& X_{12} & + X_{22} & & & = 15 \\
& X_{13} & & + X_{23} & & = 15
\end{aligned}
$$

All X's ≥ 0

b. Atlanta-Jackson 5, Atlanta-Birmingham 15, Miami-Jackson 10, Miami-Orlando 15; total cost = $6875

c. Yes, there is a fixed cost per car; the prices are all effective at the same time.

50. a. 20 cars are purchased in Atlanta, painted in Columbus, fixed in Montgomery, and sent to Birmingham; 50 cars are purchased in Miami and painted and fixed in Jacksonville—then 15 are sent to Jackson, 5 to Birmingham and 30 to Orlando; total cost = $15,300

b. $337

c. From Atlanta to Orlando 195, to Birmingham 195, to Jackson 255
From Miami to Orlando 185, to Birmingham 255, to Jackson 305

d. From Atlanta to Birmingham 20
From Miami to Jackson 15, to Birmingham 5, to Orlando 30; total cost = $15,300

CHAPTER 5

3. 12 weeks; B-C-E-F; a delay in any one of these activities will delay the expected completion time of the project beyond 12 weeks.

7. .409561

8. a. 28 weeks

b. Crash A 4 weeks, B 3 weeks, E 2 weeks, F 5 weeks, G 4 weeks; $29,950

11. b. One worker works only jobs on the critical path—their times are fixed. The other worker works the other activities scheduled in such a way that the activities begin before their earliest start times. One possible schedule is: B(10:00–11:00), E(11:20–12:20), D(12:20–2:00), G(2:00–2:20), H(2:20–3:00), I(3:00–4:00), K(4:00–4:20)

12. a. 104 months b. (i) 5 months (ii) 3 months

c. (i) .000173 (ii) .012674 (iii) .185547 (iv) .672640

13. b. $10,000,000; one crashing solution—crash B by 1, D by .5, E by 3, G by 3.5

14. b. 21 weeks; crash E by 2 weeks

17. a. McDonnell-Douglas b. Boeing

20. a. 89 days; C-D-F-G-I-K b. 924136 c. Yes; Expected Cost(Yes) = $6150.55, Expected Cost(No) = $9103.67

22. It is $9,950 under budget but is running 3.4 weeks late. The remaining critical path is F-H-I. Spend some of the $9,950 on speeding up the completion of F, H, and/or I.

23. a. $476,500 Schedule A (0–12), B (12–23), C (23–31), D (31–40), E (40–58), F (58–74), G (60–74), H (74–95), I (106–116), J (95–116), K(116–125), L (125–140)

    b. It is impossible to complete the project in 18 weeks even with crashing

24. 135.5833 days

25. c. 8 weeks

26. a. 16.83333; A-C-E-F;   b. Market Analysis, Marketing Blitz   c. .003171

30. a. A-C-E-G; $\mu = 30$, $\sigma = 4.33$ b. (i) 5 (ii) 0 (iii) 4 (iv) 4 (v) 4 (vi) 9

31. Slightly over 40 days—41 days = July 6

33. Yes; expected cost if $3000 is spent = $9613.20; expected cost if $3000 is not spent = $12,428.20

37. b. B-I; 36 weeks   c. Use own landscaping crew; total extra cost $14,500

42. a. 117 days; A-B-C-D-E-J-L-N-R   b. .295670

    c. Yes; Expected Cost(Yes) = $6715.23, Expected Cost(No) = $7043.30

    d. $1328.07

43. It is currently $900 under budget and due to be completed 3 days early

CHAPTER 6

1. a. 400   b. 320   c. 360

4. a. 2 commercials   b. $170,000

6. a. 12 leases   b. 9 leases

9. a.

		Number of Adoptions						
		0	1	2	3	4	5	6
	Plan 1	2000	2000	2000	2000	2000	2000	2000
Plan	Plan 2	1000	1300	1600	1900	2200	2500	2800
	Plan 3	0	700	1400	2100	2800	3500	4200

    b. Plan 2   c. Plan 1

12. a. (i) custom (ii) unfurnished (iii) unfurnished

    b. $937.50 per lot.   c. 58%   d. GNP is not a good indicator. Other indicators that would specifically focus on the Atlanta housing market or economy (such as average per capita income) would be better.

14. a. 1 car   b. 2 cars   c. 3 cars

15. a. P(outstanding) = .15; King should order 3 cars   b. $3950

17. a.

		Demand		
		10000	50000	100000
	0	0	0	0
Order	40000	−130000	130000	80000
Quantity	80000	−250000	110000	360000
	120000	−370000	−10000	440000

    b. Order 80,000   c. Order 80,000   d. $58,899

19. .996

23. a. order 2 sets   b. EVPI = $587.50

24. a. If survey shows that at least one customer is likely to buy order 2, otherwise order 1.

    b. $82.50.   c. 14%   d. record number of survey customers who are likely to purchase.

28. a. introduce candy   b. introduce candy   c. EVSI = $1800; efficiency = 8%

29. a.

		Demand				
		0	1	2	3	4
	1	−300000	−75000	−105000	−135000	−165000
Number	2	−400000	−175000	50000	20000	−10000
Built	3	−300000	−75000	150000	375000	345000
	4	−400000	−175000	50000	275000	500000

    b. Building 3 computers and building 4 computers are undominated strategies.

    c. P(0) = .2401 P(1) = .4116 P(2) = .2646 P(3) = .0756 P(4) = .0081; − build 3 computers.

31. Select Plan II

34. a. $580 b. .9952 c. Approximately $1000

36. a. Bid $.02 b. Bid $.04

38 a. Spot + $.01 b. $116 c. Risk loving d. Spot + $.01

40. Import scooters and advertise only if tariff is not imposed.

43. Midge should wait two months before buying her ticket.

45. John should bid $1.2 million without having the survey done

47. a. Concave utility function—risk averse b. Hire consultant. If consultant predicts approval purchase the option. If the consultant predicts denial do nothing.

CHAPTER 7

1. a. Yes b. $t = −.412, p = .689$ c. January–19, for upcoming year–228 d. 20.4
    e. Four month simple moving average

3. b. $t = 37.1238, p = 0$
    c. 25-660.98 26-671.16 27-681.33 28-691.51 29-701.68 30-711.86 31-722.03
    32-732.21 33-742.38 34-752.56 35-762.73 36-772.91

5.

	Sunday	Monday	Tuesday	Wednesday	Thursday	Friday	Saturday
Week 5	318.90	371.72	353.72	397.54	404.22	362.08	366.49
Week 6	326.62	380.70	362.24	407.08	413.89	370.71	375.20

7. 367,274 bottles of shampoo

9. b. No, $t = −.428, p = .674$ c. 719 d. 736

11.

Period	6	7	8
Forecast	134,189	139,288	144,387

13.

Period	Year 5 Forecast
Fall	850
Spring	784
Summer	193

15. b. Since $t = 1.916$ and $p = .071$ a stationary model is appropriate.
    c. $63,819 d. Yes, futures are worthwhile.

17. a. 8.12
    b. −2.96. The model may be inappropriate since 2035 is too far into the future from the last obtained time period. If the model is deemed appropriate, Kerf will have to do something different in the future if it wishes to remain solvent.

20.

Period	Jan	Feb	March	April	May	June	July	Aug.	Sept.	Oct.	Nov.	Dec.
Forecast	1538	1525	1512	1498	1485	1472	1459	1446	1432	1419	1406	1393

22. a. 16,059   b. 16,515   c. $\alpha = .10$, MSE $= 964,750$ d. $\alpha = .10$, MAD $= 851.55$
e. $\alpha = .10$, MAPE $= 5.15$ f. $\alpha = .10$, LAD $= 1890$

24. b. Yes, t $= .402$, p $= .698$ c. 4.9%   d. .27

28. a. MA forecast $= 38.5$ for all weeks, AV8 forecast $= 38.4$ for all weeks.
b. AV8 has the lower MAD (MAD $= 5.25$).

31. a. 473   b. 461
c. $\alpha = .4$, MSE, MAD, MAPE, and LAD are all lower than when $\alpha = .2$ is used.

34. a.

Season	Forecast Next Year	Forecast Two Years
Summer	154	170
Fall	193	209
Winter	251	267
Spring	203	219

b. Forecast next year $= 801$, year after next $= 865$
c. $r_4 = .5007$. A seasonal model is warranted.

35.

1st Quarter	2nd Quarter	3rd Quarter	4th Quarter
6,573	11,201	10,816	9,850

37. $110,449

39. a.

Period	49	50	51	52	53	54	55	56	57	58	59	60
Forecast	2877	2878	2818	2691	2700	2828	2865	2900	2891	2909	2956	2950

b. MAD $= 16.152$ c. Classical decomposition has the lower MAD value.

41.

Period	61	62	63	64	65	66	67	68	69	70
Forecast	50.38	50.41	50.44	50.46	50.49	50.51	50.54	50.57	50.59	50.62

45. a. 1.178 for all three weeks
b. week 12–1.788, week 13–1.870, week 14–1.953

CHAPTER 8

1. $Q^* = 340$, R $= 25$

3. $Q^* = 2000$, there will be 3 production runs during the year

5. Order 145 dozen golf balls

7. a. $Q^* = 3448$ b. R $= 420$

10. Order 1,000,000 board feet when the inventory level reaches 53,600 board feet.

12. a. $Q^* = 277$ b. $1178

13. a. $Q^* = 894$, R $= 50$ b. 128
c. total inventory cost $= \$2189.37$, annual net profit $= \$1671.58$. It is assumed that annual demand occurs at a constant rate and will continue at this rate forever.

16. a. $Q^* = 2400$ b. $1.26

18. $Q^* = 135$

20. a. $Q^* = 400, R = 63$ b. 117 days   c. \$21,143.69

22. a. $Q^* = 485,917$, Production run lasts 68.3 hours   b. \$38,895.54

    c. 8.43 calendar days

    d. $Q^* = 532,295$, Production run lasts 74.8 hours

24. a. $Q^* = 1000, R = 77$ b. 100 days

    c. Total annual inventory cost = \$1,519,849.03, annual profit = \$508,119.79

26. a. 1817 (note goodwill cost = −\$40)   b. Profit = \$96,364

    c. Assume company pays a royalty on plates even if they are destroyed.

28. a. $Q^* = 677$ b. $R = 107$

30. Produce 750 pounds of French Roast and 200 pounds of Amaretto Cream

32. a. $Q^* = 111, R = 39$ b. 1.48   c. .4%   d. \$304,937

36. a. $Q^* = 46, R = 2$, Profit = \$22,332   b. $Q^* = 46, R = 17$, Profit = \$22,484

    c. Yes, allowing for backorders appears to be worthwhile as annual profits increase.

38. a. $Q^* = 37,427$ b. \$1,703,823

42. Recommend Machine I, annual profit is \$160,750 versus \$142,927 for Machine II.

45. $Q^* = 40$

CHAPTER 9

1. $L = 4$ (3.2 students waiting in line and .8 students being served)

3. $L_q = 4.1$

5. $W = .39$ days

7. $W = 29.6$ minutes

8. a. .224   b. .85   c. .49   d. 4.5 minutes   e. .49   f. 1.5   g. 60%

10. a. (i) $W = 29.11$ minutes (ii) $L_q = .15$ (iii) $P_w = .40$

    b. Yes, the average customer service time is less and the store saves the space of the additional checkstand.

13. a. $W = 6$ minutes   b. $L_q = 2.25$ in each line for a total of 6.75

    c. The existing system will cost 3*\$12 = \$36 per hour; the proposed system will cost \$35.29 per hour—switch to new system as it is less expensive.

17. a. Front − $W_q = .528$ minutes, Rear − $W_q = .816$ minutes

    b. Front − $L = 1.008$, Rear − $L = 3.651$

    c. .06   d. .99   e. Front, average checkout time is less.

20. $W_q = .375$ minutes

23. a. 0.4558*.9712 = .4427   b. $L_q = .52$ c. $W = 2.14$ minutes   d. $P(3) = .12$

26. The service rate would need to be 82 per hour.

28. a. Employ 3 clerks   b. Employ 4 clerks

30. a. $L = 2.8$ b. $W = 14$ minutes

32. a. $P_w = .6429$ b. $P(0) = .1429$ c. $W_q = 6.43$ minutes   d. $L = 3.429$

    e. Probability three customers waiting in line = probability 5 customers are in the system, $P(5) = .0678$

35. .77 minutes

37. a. Assumed an unlimited customer population, customers will not balk, and an unlimited queue size is possible

    b. $W = 1.458$ minutes

42. 6.28 minutes

44. a. With 4 instructors the profit/hr. = \$10.77, daily profit = \$107.70

    b. With 5 instructors the profit/hr. = \$8.46, hence it is not worthwhile to hire the fifth instructor.

45. Build 10 restrooms for women.

48. a. 4.48   b. .1669   c. $W = 13.09$ hours

CHAPTER 10

Note: The answers in this chapter correspond to the approach illustrated in the Instructor's Solutions Manual. Your answers will probably differ due to a different probability ordering or random number selection; your results should approximate these values, however.

1. b. .0025, price in 30 days would be 32.075   c. 31.125

  d. We would expect the simulation to give an answer close to the expected value, but not necessarily the same as the expected value.

3. a. D–E, expected completion time = 15 weeks

  b. $P(A) = .2, P(B) = .2, P(C) = .2, P(D) = .6, P(E) = .6, P(F) = .2, P(G) = .2$

  c. (16.244, 19.756)

5. It will take 8 days. There will be 4 backorders of ChannelMaster systems and 2 lost sales.

7. ($32.09, $109.91)

10. W_q from simulation is .994 minutes, W_q from steady state results is 2.4 minutes. One reason for the difference between the two values is the start up bias of the simulation.

12. The average waiting time, W, is .96 minutes.

14. The Garden Grove-Orange Freeway combination appears to give the lowest average time (12.9 minutes).

18. L_q = .35

20. The average waiting time appears to be much greater for full serve than for self serve (15.4 minutes versus 3.7 minutes).

22. c. Based on the two simulations, Family should take the supplier's offer; for the 10 weeks the total simulated cost under the current policy is $401.33 versus only $155 under the supplier's offer.

24. Officer will give out 6 tickets.

26. a. 1.938   b. (4.622, 10.978)

28. b. (31.99, 34.99)

31. a. (2.585, 2.593)   b. .505

32. 102 loaves

36. 44%

39. (33.47, 37.69)

41. (397.820, 532,065)

45. b. ($212.94, $214.78)

48. b. Yes, profit over the 10 days increases from $284 to $287 if the new machine is added.

CHAPTER 11

1. Brightness, ease of installation/removal, amount of heat produced, energy consumed.

3. Speed of service, temperature of food, freshness of food, taste of food, cleanliness of table, cleanliness of restrooms.

6. On-time performance, width of seats, leg room, quality of food served, cleanliness of restrooms, length of time you must wait on hold to speak to reservation agent.

13. Test 1—Periods 6 and 37; Test 2—Periods 9 through 12; Test 3—Periods 6 and 28; Test 4—Period 22; Test 5—Periods 6, 35 and 36; Test 6—Periods 5 through 10 and Periods 36 through 40; Test 8—Period 25.

15. Based on the R chart, the process was out of control in period 9 (test 2) and in periods 10 through 12 (test 1). Based on the $\overline{X}$ bar chart the process was out of control in period 9 (test 2) and period 12 (test 1).

17. a. 16.3132   b. LCL = 0, UCL = 80.214   c. LCL = 37.675, UCL = 81.448

  d. The R chart shows out of control behavior in periods 19 through 21 (test 2). The $\overline{X}$ chart shows out of control behavior in period 26 (test 8).

19. b. The process appears to be in control during this period.   c. 4%

21. a. $2.44   b. .0036 will fail to meet design specifications
    c. No, the expected loss is reduced by only $1.67
23. a. No, the mean weight is above 32 ounces, but 9.2% of the items weighed below 32 ounces.
    b. The $\overline{X}$ bar chart exhibits out of control behavior in period 14 (test 6) and periods 16 through 20 (test 2).
25. a. No, the p chart exhibits out of control behavior in period 37 (test 2).
    b. The process is in control over this period.
    c. The standardized p chart gives a better way of viewing the process since it only deals with the surveys returned.
27. The process is out of control in period 27 (test 2)
29. a. $.496   b. Yes, the cost savings is approximately $.42 per window.
31. The process appears to be in control over this period.
34. Approximately .14% of items will fail to meet design specifications.

CHAPTER 12

1. a.

	Coke	Pepsi	Other
Coke	.7	.2	.1
Pepsi	.25	.6	.14
Other	.3	.45	.25

   b. Next stage- .7, two stages- .57, three stages- .513, probability that all three purchases will be Coke is .343
   c. Next stage- .6, two stages- .478, three stages- .429, probability that all three purchases will be Pepsi is .216
   d. Coke—46.73%, Pepsi—39.20%, Other—14.07%
   e. 2.55
3. a. .314   b. .70   c. 3.73   d. .60
5. b. E(cost) = $5.20   c. E(cost) = $4.71
7. a.

		Channel	
Day	2	4	7
1	0.75	0.1	0.05
2	0.595	0.18	0.1025
3	0.499625	0.229625	0.148125
4	0.440313	0.25695	0.184838
5	0.402656	0.270798	0.213266
6	0.378143	0.277259	0.234817

   b. E(Profit) = −$368.14   c. 3.587
9. a. .0679   b. .031   c. .8653
   d. (i) 17.73; (ii) 17.27; (iii) 16.62
   e. 5.04%
11. a. .45   b. .333   c. .386   d. 3.89 years   e. 4.56 years
14. a. BR—20.14%, HD—26.04%, BJ—28.70%, DQ—25.12%
    b. Store should introduce frozen yogurt
16. b. .502   c. 16.42 plays
18. a. Exxon   b. Shell—37.17%, Exxon—29.20%, Arco—33.63%   c. $2,344.31

20. a. .503   b. .158   c. .2815   d. 18.41 weeks
24. a. .6369   b. $18.04   c. No, expected profit declines to $6.32
29. .44

CHAPTER 13

1. 4 barrels of medium oil, 1 barrel of heavy oil; profit = $26
2. 1 convoy to Chismayu, 1 convoy to Mogadishu, 3 convoys to Hargeisa—1360 lives
5. Keep 20 for June, hire 1 for July, fire 1 in August, fire 1 in September; cost = $24,000
7. a. Produce 4 in April, 3 in May, and 3 in June; total cost = $221,800
   b. Same answer as part a.
11. Keep all 20 sales representatives; spend $20,000 on the World Wide Web
12. b. Invest $78,571.43 in the income fund and $21,428.57 in the aggressive growth fund
16. 60 sec.: Commercial Day 15, Commercial Evening 5, Cable Evening 23, Late Night 7
   30 sec.: Commercial Day 9, Commercial Evening 5, Cable Evening 5, Late Night 31
18. a. $P = 1200 - .1X$ b. $f(X) = -.1X^2 + 1000X - 1,000,000$ c. $700   d. $10
19. a. 7000; $500   b. 5000; $700   c. 6000; $600   d. 2500; $950
24. a. $R = 60,000P - 3,000P^2$ b. $10   c. 30,000   d. $300,000
27. a. $S = -3.125X^2 + 37.5X + 65.625$ b. (i) 128.125 (ii) $2,000 (iii) $3,125
   c. (i) No change (ii) Sales = 114.84375 per week; profit = $3,093.75
28. a. Sales for AT20 = $-25X_2^2 + 300X_2 + 125$
   b. Sales for AT50 = $-5X_3^2 + 50X_3 + 2500$
   c. AT40: Production = 128.125   Advertising = $2000   Profit = $ 3,093.75
      AT20: Production = 1000   Advertising = $5000   Profit = $15,000.00
      AT50: Production = 100   Advertising = $3000   Profit = $ 2,000.00
      Optimal weekly profit = $20,093.75
   d. AT40: Production = 86.03   Advertising = $ 571   Profit = $ 350.96
      AT20: Production = 978.95   Advertising = $4643   Profit = $23,339.29
      AT50: Production = 83.16   Advertising = $2286   Profit = $ 3,423.57
      Optimal weekly profit = $27,113.82

PHOTO CREDITS

Chapter 1
Opener: Courtesy United Airlines

Chapter 2
Opener: Courtesy San Miguel Corporation

Chapter 3
Opener: 1995–2001 FedEx. All rights reserved

Chapter 4
Opener: Walter Hodges/Stone

Chapter 5
Opener: Courtesy Taco Bell Corporation

Chapter 6
Opener: Photo courtesy of Lindal Cedar Homes, Inc., Seattle, Washington

Chapter 7
Opener: Courtesy Franklin Covey Company

Chapter 8
Opener: Courtesy Ralph's Grocery Company

Chapter 9
Opener: Courtesy Carl Karcher Enterprises, Inc.

Chapter 10
Opener: Juan Silva/The Image Bank

Index